:: The Legal and Regulatory Environment of **BUSINESS**

Fifteenth Edition

O. Lee **REED**
Robert W. Scherer Chair in Public Affairs and Professor of Legal Studies

Peter J. **SHEDD**
University Professor of Legal Studies, University of Georgia

Marisa Anne **PAGNATTARO**
Associate Professor of Legal Studies, University of Georgia

Jere W. **MOREHEAD**
Professor of Legal Studies, University of Georgia

McGraw-Hill Irwin

Boston   Burr Ridge, IL   Dubuque, IA   New York   San Francisco   St. Louis
Bangkok   Bogotá   Caracas   Kuala Lumpur   Lisbon   London   Madrid   Mexico City
Milan   Montreal   New Delhi   Santiago   Seoul   Singapore   Sydney   Taipei   Toronto

McGraw-Hill
Irwin

THE LEGAL & REGULATORY ENVIRONMENT OF BUSINESS
Published by McGraw-Hill/Irwin, a business unit of The McGraw-Hill Companies, Inc., 1221 Avenue of the Americas, New York, NY, 10020. Copyright © 2010, 2008, 2005, 2002, 1999, 1996, 1993, 1990, 1987, 1984, 1981, 1977, 1973, 1968, 1963 by The McGraw-Hill Companies, Inc. All rights reserved. No part of this publication may be reproduced or distributed in any form or by any means, or stored in a database or retrieval system, without the prior written consent of The McGraw-Hill Companies, Inc., including, but not limited to, in any network or other electronic storage or transmission, or broadcast for distance learning.

Some ancillaries, including electronic and print components, may not be available to customers outside the United States.

This book is printed on acid-free paper.

1 2 3 4 5 6 7 8 9 0 DOW/DOW 0 9

ISBN: 978-0-07-337766-7
MHID: 0-07-337766-X

Vice president and editor-in-chief: *Brent Gordon*
Publisher: *Paul Ducham*
Sponsoring editor: *Dana L. Woo*
Developmental editor: *Megan Richter*
Editorial coordinator: *Sara Knox Hunter*
Senior marketing manager: *Sarah Schuessler*
Lead project manager: *Pat Frederickson*
Full service project manager: *Michelle Gardner, Pine Tree Composition, Inc.*
Senior production supervisor: *Debra R. Sylvester*
Interior designer: *Cara Hawthorne*
Senior photo research coordinator: *Lori Kramer*
Photo researcher: *PoYee Oster*
Media project manager: *Shannon Gattens*
Cover design: *JoAnne Schopler*
Typeface: *10.5/12 Sabon Roman*
Compositor: *Laserwords Private Limited*
Printer: *R.R. Donnelley*

Library of Congress Cataloging-in-Publication Data
The legal and regulatory environment of business / O. Lee Reed . . . [et al.]. — 15th ed.
    p. cm.
  Includes index.
  ISBN-13: 978-0-07-337766-7 (alk. paper)
  ISBN-10: 0-07-337766-X (alk. paper)
  1. Trade regulation—United States. 2. Business law—United States. 3. Industrial laws and legislation—United States. I. Reed, O. Lee (Omer Lee)

KF1600.C6 2010
346.7307—dc22   2008054521

www.mhhe.com

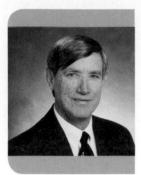

O. Lee **REED**

Lee Reed is Robert W. Scherer Chair in Public Affairs and Josiah Meigs Distinguished Teaching Professor of Legal Studies* in the Terry College of Business at the University of Georgia. He received his Doctor of Law degree at the University of Chicago and a B.A. degree at Birmingham-Southern College. Professor Reed holds a J.D. degree from the University of Chicago and a B.A. degree from Birmingham-Southern College. A former president of the Academy in Legal Studies in Business, he has received five national research awards for his scholarly articles and is former editor in chief of the *American Business Law Journal*. He has also testified before the Federal Trade Commission and has twice written invited introductions for *The Advertising Law Anthology*. Professor Reed is a frequent speaker to trade and scholarly groups on the fundamental importance of the rule of law and property to the private market system.*

Peter J. **SHEDD**

Peter Shedd is the University Professor of Legal Studies in the Terry College of Business at the University of Georgia where he received his B.B.A. and J.D. degrees. Professor Shedd has extensive experience as a teacher, researcher, administrator, and author of business-related texts. His teaching of undergraduate and MBA courses has earned Professor Shedd numerous teaching awards including being named a Josiah Meigs Distinguished Teaching Professor. Professor Shedd is an active member of the Academy of Legal Studies in Business and its Southeastern Regional. He served as national president during 1999–2000. Professor Shedd is a member of the State Bar of Georgia and is an experienced arbitrator and mediator.

Note that three of the four authors of this textbook hold the Meigs title, which is not granted lightly by the University of Georgia. Of the 115 faculty in UGA's Terry College of Business, only six hold Meigs professorships.

Marisa Anne **PAGNATTARO**

Marisa Anne Pagnattaro is an Associate Professor of Legal Studies in the Terry College of Business at the University of Georgia, where she received her Ph.D. degree in English. She received her J.D. from New York Law School and her B.A. from Colgate University. Prior to joining the Georgia faculty, Dr. Pagnattaro was a litigation attorney with Kilpatrick & Cody (now known as Kilpatrick Stockton LLP) in Atlanta. Dr. Pagnattaro is the recipient of several teaching awards and is the author of a number of scholarly articles on national and international employment law issues. She is an active member of the Academy of Legal Studies in Business and the American Bar Association. She is a member of the State Bar of Georgia, and is the former editor in chief of the *Georgia Bar Journal*.

Jere W. **MOREHEAD**

Jere Morehead is Josiah Meigs Distinguished Teaching Professor of Legal Studies in the Terry College of Business at the University of Georgia where he received his J.D. degree. Prior to joining the faculty, Professor Morehead served as an Assistant United States Attorney in the Department of Justice where he specialized in the prosecution of white-collar crime. Professor Morehead has extensive experience as a teacher, researcher, and academic administrator. His teaching of undergraduate courses has earned him numerous teaching awards including the Josiah Meigs Excellence in Teaching Award and the Richard B. Russell Undergraduate Teaching Award. He has been a visiting faculty member at the University of Michigan. Professor Morehead is the past president of the International Law Section of the Academy of Legal Studies in Business, and he has served as editor in chief of the *American Business Law Journal*. Professor Morehead is a member of the State Bar of Georgia and also serves as vice president for instruction at the University of Georgia.

This fifteenth edition continues in the long, rich tradition of this text. This edition expands on our efforts to make past editions the standard for superior, up-to-date coverage of essential topics that make up the legal and regulatory environment of business. We welcome your examination of this edition. In this preface, we attempt to highlight the themes, the additions, and the pedagogical devices in this edition.

:: Themes of Fifteenth Edition

With each edition of this text, we seek to maintain the reputation as the most up-to-date legal and regulatory environment text in the marketplace. As we prepare each edition, we consider the events that impact our environment. Sometimes themes emerge and sometimes a theme dominates our world. At this time, economic conditions that businesses and individuals face provide an overarching theme. We believe the legal and regulatory implications of the United States and global economy deserves special attention. We attempt to provide this attention while maintaining the traditional themes of past editions.

The fundamental message we wish our readers to grasp is that law is at the core of the private market because it determines who owns what and protects owners so they can make decisions about how to make what they own most productive. Law defines property, enforces property right, resolves disputes about where the boundaries of property right lie, and recognizes that compensation is appropriate when one person infringes across the boundary of what is proper to another.

When nations apply property right under the rule of law, they establish the maximum condition for creating prosperous, diversified economies. No nation with an adequate property system under the rule of law is poor. No nation without such a legal system is prosperous, except for a few, small, oil-fortunate ones that sell to others with strong property-based economies. It is important that our readers—mostly business students—appreciate the role of law in the economy.

Another important goal of this fifteenth edition is its accurate depiction of current events in the business world. Each chapter strives to include the most relevant examples and case opinions. Sidebars within each chapter provide students and instructors opportunities to learn about topics that illustrate the principles discussed within the text. Margin comments help the students know key themes and points of emphasis.

:: New Additions in Fifteenth Edition

This edition includes 21 chapters, an expansion of three chapters over the last few editions. This increase allows us to place special emphasis on legal and regulatory aspects of current economic conditions. We increase the coverage of property and contracts—each to two chapters. Chapter 7 focuses on the fundamental of property while Chapter 11 continues the focus on intellectual property. In Chapters 8 and 9, we expand coverage of contracts providing focus on formation and performance of promised obligations. The third new chapter (17) highlights consumer and financial protections. These new chapters emphasize the current impact of our economic condition.

As in the previous one, the fifteenth edition consists of five parts. The fifteenth edition begins with an Introduction which includes two chapters—on law as a business foundation and on ethical practices (or lack thereof) within business and management. Part Two covers methods used to resolve disputes. Chapters 3–5 focus on how courts resolve disputes, on the litigation process, and on ADR systems, such as arbitration and mediation. Part Three presents eight chapters on the foundations of business. Chapters 6–13 include an overview of constitutional provisions and protections, property, contract formation, contract performance, torts, intellectual property, criminal law, and international law. For over 40 years, this text has brought to the classroom an emphasis on government regulation of business activities; this topic is the focus of Part Four. Within this part, Chapters 14–18 discuss ways businesses are organized, Sarbanes-Oxley and securities regulations, antitrust laws, consumer and financial protections and environmental laws. Finally, Part Five (Chapters 19–21) discusses employment relations, including agency, employment discrimination, and labor laws.

:: Authorship Team

One of the strengths of this text is its stable team of authors. Lee Reed joined this team in 1977 on the fourth edition. He celebrates over 30 years as an author of 12 editions. Peter Shedd's name first appears as a co-author on the eighth edition in 1990. Jere Morehead became a part of this team in 1996 on the tenth edition. Together, these three co-authors have a combined total of more than 65 years associated with this text. Marisa Pagnattaro joined this team on the fourteenth edition. In this edition, she takes on greater responsibility. We are grateful she is becoming a significant part of our team. This edition also represents Bob Corley's official retirement following his 45 years association with this text. He created this text in 1963 and has been an active author throughout the first 14 editions. Once again, we express our individual and collective gratitude to Bob.

:: Pedagogy

This fifteenth edition continues the reputation of our prior editions for having many valuable teaching elements. The following list highlights the various pedagogical tools in this edition:

- **Learning Objectives**—each chapter begins with a list that guides the students reading, studying, and learning.
- **Marginalia**—in the margins, each chapter includes notes, points of emphasis, definitions, quotes, and recommendations about what to do and what to avoid. These notations emphasize key points throughout each chapter.

- **Sidebars**—examples or further descriptions are separated from the text into boxes labeled sidebars. As in the courtroom setting, when a judge calls for a conversation with the lawyers away from the jury, these boxes are sidebars to the overall discussion. Through these sidebars, we believe you will find the text is explained in more detail or is brought to life with a business-related example.
- **Cases**—except for the first two chapters, chapters include edited portions of actual court decisions. These cases illustrate the parties' arguments and the judge's decision of the issues. We have deleted most of the procedural aspects, citations, and footnotes. An alternative to these edited cases appear in some sidebars; there a case may be explained in our own language.
- **Case Questions**—at the end of each edited case, a series of questions about that case can be found. These questions help the students understand key points within the case.
- **Concept Summaries**—at appropriate points in each chapter, a summary of the preceding material appears. Through these summaries, complex and lengthy presentations are easily reviewable by the reader.
- **Key Terms**—a list of critical words or phrases is found at the end of each chapter. These terms are boldfaced in the text, and definitions are repeated in the glossary.
- **Review Questions and Problems**—following the text of each chapter is a series of questions and problems. These are tied to the various sections of each chapter and serve as an overview of the material covered.
- **Business Discussions**—the last item in each chapter is a factual situation designed to stimulate conversation among students causing them to review the material within the chapter.

:: ACKNOWLEDGMENTS

We take this space to thank a number of people who contributed to the fifteenth edition. Once again Mary Evans provided valuable typing assistance in the preparation of the manuscript. Like with previous editions, Mary continues the tradition of assisting us. We are grateful for her work with our drafts.

We are indebted to Dana Woo, our editor. This is Dana's first edition working on this text. Her dedication and words of encouragement kept us focused and on schedule. Megan Richter is our developmental editor, Sarah Schuessler is our marketing manager, Pat Frederickson is our project manager, and Sara Hunter is our editorial coordinator. Each of these outstanding individuals worked with us during the preparation of the manuscript and directed the production through every phase. The fifteenth edition would not be here without them. We express our gratitude for the contribution of this excellent editorial team.

The following colleagues gave of their time and provided insight during the review process. For their expert comments and suggestions, we are most grateful.

Robert L. Cherry Jr.
Appalachian State University

Richard Coffinberger
George Mason University

Dean A. Frantsvog
Minot State University

Wendy Gelman
Florida International University

Jack E. Karns
East Carolina University

Donna McCurley
Gadsden State Community College

Thomas Rhoads
California State University-Long Beach

LeVon E. Wilson
Georgia Southern University

Finally, we thank all of the professors and students who have used or are using our text. Your feedback continues to be important. Please feel free to share your thoughts with us. You many contact any of us through the Terry College of Business at the University of Georgia. Your feedback also may be sent to The McGraw-Hill Companies.

O. LEE REED
PETER J. SHEDD
MARISA ANNE PAGNATTARO
JERE W. MOREHEAD

This 15th edition continues the reputation of our prior editions for having many valuable teaching elements. In an effort to provide even more guidance and relevance for students, this edition introduces margin notes and comments and sidebars.

learning *objectives* ::

New to this edition are Learning Objectives at the beginning of each chapter. These objectives will act as a helpful road map of each chapter, narrowing the focus of each topic for both instructor and students. You will also find these Learning Objectives tagged for every test bank question to ensure that key points from each chapter are covered in every quiz and exam.

2

The Ethical Basis of Law and Business Management

Learning Objectives ::

In this chapter you will learn:

1. To appreciate the connection between law and ethical principles.
2. To grasp why ethical consequentialism and not ethical formalism has been the chief source of values for business ethics.
3. To develop an individual framework for ethical values in business.
4. To analyze the obstacles and rewards of ethical business practice in our property-based legal system.

CHAPTER 11 Intellectual Property in the Property System   319

Overall, individuals will work harder to benefit themselves, their families, and, perhaps, their close communities than they will to benefit strangers, their nation, or the people of the world. Yet, curiously, if allowed to produce and trade for their private benefit, individuals or groups of owners as businesses will usually benefit the "common good," defined here as producing for consumption the maximum quantities of what people need and want.

Abraham Lincoln said that intellectual property couples "the fuel of interest with the fire of genius." He was referring to how an exclusive right to what you acquire and produce gives incentive to create new things, new ways of doing things, and new invention generally. The framers of the U.S. Constitution, especially Thomas Jefferson, made sure that Congress could protect intellectual property. Article 1, Section 8, of the Constitution grants Congress the power "[t]o promote the Progress of Science and Useful Arts, by securing for limited Times to Authors and Inventors the exclusive Right to their respective Writings and Discoveries."

Note that the justification for "securing" an "exclusive Right" is "[t]o promote the Progress of Science [new things and new ways of doing things] and the useful Arts [business and trade]." The Constitution recognizes that exclusive property boundaries promote, or give incentive to, the business production of what people need and want. However, the Constitution also ensures that after "limited Times" defined by Congress the resources of new expression and invention, which were formerly exclusive to "Authors and Inventors," will be freely available to everyone.

Intellectual Property and Competition What would happen if there were no intellectual property in new invention? Most likely the pace of creative research and development (R&D) in business would slow dramatically. R&D is expensive. If businesses have to finance R&D and then compete against others who quickly copy new invention, the businesses paying for R&D will be at a competitive disadvantage. The prices they charge for their products will have to include (a) the cost of R&D, (b) the cost of production and distribution, and (c) a profit. The businesses who quickly copy the new invention of others will have to include only (b) and (c) in their prices. Competition is the lifeblood of the private market, and no business will deliberately place themselves at a competitive disadvantage.

Some people see the desire for private gain as "greed." Others see it as the driving force behind new products and new technologies that produces more of what people need and want at lower prices. However you characterize it, our unwillingness to work selflessly for a world of strangers is something natural to most of us, possibly the result of humans living for thousands of years in small bands and groups. Certainly, we are also capable of compassionate sharing and generosity to others, and society should constantly encourage these qualities. But at the same time, the exclusivity of property generally and intellectual property specifically will likely continue to be necessary to create the potential for the greatest wealth of nations.

Even the poor in a nation with strong, equally enforced property laws are wealthy by the per capita income standards of the poor in nations without such laws (see Sidebar 11.2). It is the capacity of intellectual property to help create the maximum likelihood for the production of what people need and want that ultimately justifies it.

Do remember that property serves the common good because property relationships produce what people need and want in greater quantities than other relationships for dealing with limited resources.

Don't forget that the poor in a nation with a strong property system under the rule of law are often wealthy by the average per person standards of the poor in nations without such laws.

26

marginalia ::

In the margins, each chapter includes notes, points of emphasis, definitions, quotes, and recommendations about what to do and what to avoid.

sidebars ::

Examples or further descriptions are separated from the text into boxes labeled Sidebars. As in the courtroom setting, when a judge calls for a conversation with the lawyers away from the jury, these boxes are sidebars to the overall discussion. Through these sidebars, the text is explained in more detail or is brought to life with a business-related example.

Can you explain the three different types of bailments?

Think about the examples mentioned above. Do you understand that storing your car in a friend's garage while you are on vacation is a bailment for the sole benefit of the bailor and that the furniture and equipment rentals are mutual benefit bailments? The loan of your mower to your neighbor to mow the grass is a bailment for the sole benefit of the bailee. Consider the following situation: you go to a business meeting at a hotel, removing your expensive leather coat, and hanging it on a hanger in a small room provided by the hotel. The coat turns up missing. Is the hotel responsible as a bailee? Would the situation have been different if the hotel had someone taking care of coats? The answers depend on whether or not the hotel has taken *intentional* possession of the coat, and it is likely that merely by providing a coat hanger, the hotel is not taking intentional possession of the coat. But if a hotel employee hangs up the coat for you, the hotel becomes a bailee.

In the business world, most bailments are of mutual benefit to both parties. Although the bailee has an absolute duty to return the object to the bailor (or to dispose out of it as the bailor directs), and becomes liable to the bailor for failing to do so correctly, an issue often arises when something happens to the object while it is in the bailee's possession and control. What if someone steals it? What if a natural disaster, called "an act of God," destroys it, or it is damaged in an accident? To understand the potential liability from these events, you have to understand the legal duty the bailee is under. In a mutual benefit bailment, such as a rental arrangement, the bailee is under a duty to use "reasonable care" in taking care of the object in possession, but if an Act of God destroys or damages the object, the bailee is not likely liable to the bailor. However, see Sidebar 7.5.

:: sidebar 7.5

Follow Instructions or Else

Roger, a graduate student, leases a car from Acme Car Dealership in Texas. The lease contract contains a clause that limits Roger's driving to the United States. However, Roger drives the car over the border down to Mexico City where an earthquake causes a building to collapse on the car after Roger parks it on the street. Although in mutual benefit bailments such as this one, the bailee is not often responsible to the bailor for acts of God, in this instance by using on a car in a way specifically prohibited by the bailor, Roger becomes liable to the car dealership in spite of the fact his fault did not cause the damage to the car. When a bailee uses an object in a way not authorized or prohibited by the bailor, the bailee becomes absolutely liable as an "insurer" for anything that happens to it.

Another example of this liability arises when a bailee returns an object improperly. In one instance a wealthy woman bought expensive jewelry on approval from Tiffany's, promising the manager to return the jewelry to him personally if she did not wish to keep it. Several days later there was a knock on her door and a man dressed in a Tiffany's uniform asked if she wished to return the jewelry, which she did, and she returned the jewelry to this man who turned out to be a thief in a stolen uniform. Tiffany's sued for the jewelry's price and won because the bailee became absolutely liable for loss when she returned the jewelry improperly.

In a bailment for the sole benefit of a bailor, the bailee owes only a slight duty of care while the object is in the bailee's possession, but in a bailment for the sole benefit of the bailee, such as where the bailee has borrowed the object, the bailee owes a very high duty of care, one that is greater than merely

---

concept *summary* ::

At appropriate points in each chapter, a summary of the preceding material appears. Through these summaries, complex and lengthy presentations are easily reviewable by the reader.

---

to local laws and customs, which makes international agreements complex and tricky to negotiate.

North American Free Trade Agreement The passage of the **North American Free Trade Agreement (NAFTA)** in 1993 set in motion increased trade and foreign investment and opportunities for economic growth in the United States, Mexico, and Canada. Free trade is at the core of NAFTA, through the reduction and eventual elimination of tariffs and other barriers to business between these three countries. NAFTA also provides for a dispute settlement mechanism that makes it easier to resolve trade disputes between the three countries. Based upon concerns that cheap labor and poor environmental controls might cause U.S. firms to relocate to Mexico, side agreements also were reached to improve labor rights and environmental protection in Mexico. Since its enactment, NAFTA has expanded shipments of U.S. goods to Mexico and Canada, as well as Mexican and Canadian exports to the United States.

Jimmy Carter supported the passage of CAFTA-DR as a "chance to reinforce democracies in the region."

Central America-Dominican Republic Free Trade Agreement Similar to NAFTA, the passage of the **Central America-Dominican Republic Free Trade Agreement (CAFTA-DR)** in 2005 opened up many opportunities for business in Central America. CAFTA-DR is a comprehensive trade agreement between Costa Rica, El Salvador, Guatemala, Honduras, Nicaragua, the Dominican Republic, and the United States. This agreement is designed to eliminate the barriers on products trades between the member countries. Prior to CAFTA-DR, many exports of American goods to Central America faced high tariffs. This trade agreement is a step to create a fairer playing field for American exports.

Pending Free Trade Agreements The United States is continually seeking opportunities to open global trade. Currently, there are free trade agreements pending in three key markets: Colombia, Panama, and South Korea. The agreements are fully negotiated and are pending Congressional approval. According to the U.S. Trade Representative's office, there are five major reasons to approve the U.S.-Colombia Free Trade Agreement: (1) To open a significant new export market; (2) to level the playing field for American business,

concept :: *summary*

International Law and Organizations

1. International law is classified as either public or private.
2. The International Court of Justice is the traditional place for determining public international law.
3. The World Trade Organization regulates world trade for member nations.
4. The Convention on the International Sale of Goods governs international practices for the sale of goods.
5. The European Union has evolved into the most important economic force in Europe.
6. The North American Free Trade Agreement has substantially expanded trade with Mexico and Canada.

cases ::

Except for the first two chapters, chapters include edited portions of actual court decisions. These cases illustrate the parties' arguments and the judge's decision of the issues. We have deleted most of the procedural aspects, citations, and footnotes. An alternative to these edited cases appears in some sidebars; there a case may be explained in our own language.

---

ence of standing is determined by the nature and source of the plain-tiff's allegations. Standing is determined at the outset of the litigation, not by the outcome. Case 4.1 illustrates the critical nature of standing in winning a lawsuit. The case reinforces the rule that the courts are careful to avoid overstepping their constitutional role and will only rule on actual cases or controversies.

case 4.1

HEIN V. FREEDOM FROM RELIGION FOUNDATION
127 S.Ct. 2553 (2007)

The president, by executive orders, created a White House office and several centers within federal agencies to ensure that faith-based community groups are eligible to compete for federal financial support. No congressional legislation specifically authorized these entities, which were created entirely within the executive branch, nor has Congress enacted any law appropriating money to their activities, which are funded through general executive branch appropriations. Respondents, an organization opposed to government endorsement of religion and three of its members, brought this suit alleging that petitioners, the directors of the federal offices, violated the Establishment Clause by organizing conferences that were designed to promote, and had the effect of promoting, religious community groups over secular ones. The only asserted basis for standing was that the individual respondents are federal taxpayers opposed to executive branch use of congressional appropriations for these conferences. The district court dismissed the claims for lack of standing. Because petitioners acted on the president's behalf and were not charged with administering a congressional program, the court held that the challenged activities did not authorize taxpayer standing. The Seventh Circuit reversed granting federal taxpayers standing to challenge executive branch programs on Establishment Clause grounds so long as the activities are financed by a congressional appropriation, even where there is no statutory program and the funds are from appropriations for general administrative expenses.

ALITO, J.: This is a lawsuit in which it was claimed that conferences held as part of the President's Faith-Based and Community initiatives program violated the Establishment Clause of the First Amendment because, among other things, President Bush and former Secretary of Education Paige gave speeches that used "religious; and praised the efficacy of faith-based programs in delivering social services. The plaintiffs contend that they meet the standing requirements of Article III of the Constitution because they pay federal taxes.

It has long been established, however, that the payment of taxes is generally not enough to establish standing to challenge an action taken by the Federal Government. In light of the size of the federal budget, it is a complete fiction to argue that an unconstitutional federal expenditure causes an individual federal taxpayer any measurable economic harm. And if every taxpayer could sue to challenge any Government expenditure, the federal courts would cease to function as courts of law and would be cast in the role of general complaint bureaus.

In 2001, the President issued an executive order creating the White House Office of Faith-Based and Community Initiatives within the Executive Office of the President. The office was specifically charged with the task of eliminating unnecessary bureaucratic, legislative, and regulatory barriers that could impede such organizations' effectiveness and ability to compete for federal assistance.

By separate executive orders, the President also created Executive Department Centers for Faith-Based and Community Initiatives within several federal agencies and departments. The centers were given the job of ensuring that faith-based community groups would be eligible to compete for federal financial support without impairing their independence or autonomy, as long as they did "not use direct Federal financial assistance to support any inherently religious activities, such as worship, religious instruction, or proselytization." Petitioners, who have been sued in their official capacities, are the directors of the White House Office and various Executive Department Centers.

The respondents are Freedom From Religion Foundation, Inc., a nonstick corporation "opposed to government endorsement of religion," and three of its members. Respondents brought suit in the United States District Court for the Western District of Wisconsin, alleging that petitioners violated the Establishment Clause by organizing conferences at which faith-based organizations allegedly "are singled out as being particularly worthy of federal funding, and the belief in God is extolled as distinguishing the claimed effectiveness of faith-based social services." Respondents further alleged that the content of these conferences sent a message to religious believers "that they are insiders and favored members of the political community" and that the conferences sent the message to nonbelievers "that they are outsiders" and "not full members of the political community." In short, respondents alleged that the conferences were designed to promote, and had the effect of promoting, religious community groups over secular ones.

The only asserted basis for standing was that the individual respondents are federal taxpayers who are "opposed to the use of Congressional taxpayer appropriations to advance and promote religion."

Article III of the Constitution limits the judicial power of the United States to the resolution of "Cases" and "Controversies," and "Article III standing . . . enforces the Constitution's case-or-controversy requirement."

[O]ne of the controlling elements in the definition of a case or controversy under Article III is standing. The requisite elements of Article III standing are well established. A plaintiff must allege personal injury fairly traceable to the defendant's allegedly unlawful conduct and likely to be redressed by the requested relief.

The constitutionally mandated standing inquiry is especially important in a case like this one, in which taxpayers seek to challenge laws of general application where their own injury is not distinct from that suffered in general by other taxpayers or citizens. This is because [t]he judicial power of the United States defined by Art. III is not an unconditional authority to determine the constitutionality of legislative or executive acts. The federal courts are not empowered to seek out and strike down any governmental act that they deem to be repugnant to the Constitution. Rather, federal courts sit "solely, to decide on the rights of individuals."

As a general matter, the interest of a federal taxpayer in seeing that Treasury funds are spent in accordance with the Constitution does not give rise to the kind of redressable "personal injury" required for Article III standing. Of course, a taxpayer has standing to challenge the *collection* of a specific tax assessment as unconstitutional; being forced to pay such a tax causes a real and immediate economic injury to the individual taxpayer. But that is not the interest on which respondents assert standing here. Rather, their claim is that, having paid lawfully collected taxes into the Federal Treasury at some point, they have a continuing, legally cognizable interest in ensuring that those funds are not *used* by the Government in a way that violates the Constitution.

We have consistently held that this type of interest is too generalized and attenuated to support Article III standing. . . . Respondents do not challenge any specific congressional action or appropriation; nor do they ask the Court to invalidate any congressional enactment or legislatively created program as unconstitutional. These appropriations did not expressly authorize, direct, or even mention the expenditures of which respondents complain. Those expenditures resulted from executive discretion, not congressional action.

We have never found taxpayer standing under such circumstances. Respondents set out a parade of horribles that they claim could occur if [standing] is not extended to discretionary Executive Branch expenditures. For example, they say, a federal agency could use its discretionary funds to build a house of worship or to hire clergy of one denomination and send them out to spread their faith. Or an agency could use its funds to make bulk purchases of Stars of David, crucifixes, or depictions of the star and crescent for use in its offices or for distribution to the employees or the general public. Of course, none of these things has happened. In the unlikely event that any of these executive actions did take place, Congress could quickly step in. And respondents make no effort to show that these improbable abuses could not be challenged in federal court by plaintiffs who would possess standing based on grounds other than taxpayer standing.

For these reasons, the judgment of the Court of Appeals is reversed.

It is so ordered.

:: CASE QUESTIONS

1. Why did the president create the Office of Faith-Based and Community Initiatives?
2. What must a plaintiff show in order to establish standing to sue?
3. Why was standing lacking in this case?

---

case *questions* ::

At the end of each edited case, a series of questions about that case can be found. These questions help the students understand key points within the case.

Some laws encourage the parties to be creative in utilizing ADR systems. For example, the Magnuson-Moss Warranty Act provides that if a business adopts an informal dispute resolution system to handle complaints about its product warranties, then a customer cannot sue the manufacturer or seller for breach of warranty without first going through the informal procedures. This law does not deny consumers the right to sue, nor does it compel a compromise solution. It simply allows a manufacturer to require mediation, for instance, before the complaining consumer can litigate.

:: Key Terms

Arbitration 131	Mandatory arbitration 132	Predispute arbitration
Arbitrator 131	Med-Arb 149	clause 140
Award 132	Mediation 146	Principled, interest-based
Caucus 148	Mediator 146	negotiations 127
Conflict 124	Negotiation 125	Submission 132
De novo judicial review 143	Positional bargaining 126	Voluntary arbitration 132
Dispute 124	Postdispute arbitration	
Focus groups 130	clause 140	

:: Review Questions and Problems

Conflicts and Negotiation

1. *Conflicts and Disputes*

   What are the distinguishing characteristics of a conflict versus a dispute? Think about a recent conflict that did and did not become a dispute. Think about a recent dispute and describe how you handled it.

2. *Styles and Methods of Negotiation*

   List the five instinctive responses used in negotiation and describe how each of these applies to you.

3. *Positional Negotiation*

   In business disputes, what two items are most likely to dominate a position-based negotiation?

4. *Principled Negotiation*

   (a) Summarize the seven elements of principled, interest-based negotiations.

   (b) How does focusing on these elements assist the negotiation process?

Alternative Dispute Resolution (ADR) Systems

5. *Range of Options*

   What are the various items along the spectrum of ADR systems between litigation and negotiated settlements?

6. *Settlements*

   Why do businesses have incentives to settle disputes rather than relying on jury verdicts and the litigation process?

---

review *questions &*
problems ::

Following the text of each chapter is a series of questions and problems. These are tied to the sections of each chapter and serve as an overview of the material covered.

---

6. *Federal Courts*

   XYZ makes and markets a product that it believes will help control weight by blocking the human body's digestion of starch. The Food and Drug Administration (FDA) has classified the product as a drug and orders it removed from the market until it can evaluate its use through testing. XYZ disputes the FDA's action and seeks to bring suit in the federal courts. Will the federal courts have jurisdiction to hear the case? Why or why not?

7. *Decisions by the U.S. Supreme Court*

   Susan files a petition for certiorari in the U.S. Supreme Court following an adverse decision in the Illinois Supreme Court on a claim arising under a breach of contract. What chance does Susan have of the Supreme Court granting the petition? What special circumstances would she need to show?

The Power of Judicial Review

8. *Judicial Restraint*

   Define the power of judicial review. How do advocates of judicial restraint exercise that power?

9. *Judicial Activism*

   Define judicial activism. Compare and contrast judicial restraint and judicial activism.

10. Why are dissenting opinions important?

11. *Nature of the Judicial Process*

    What are the forces that Justice Cardozo says shape the judicial process? How is the law made? In light of the liberal versus conservative divisions in the courts, are Cardozo's observations still relevant?

business :: *discussions*

1. You have spent the past four weeks away from work serving as a juror in a case deciding whether a pharmaceutical company should be held liable for the heart attack of a woman who took its painkiller, Oxxy-1. The lengthy case has taken a toll on your professional career, and you have many unanswered questions as jury deliberations begin.

1. Where does your duty lie in serving on a jury?

2. Are you protected against adverse employment action by your firm for missing work to serve on a jury?

3. How do you reconcile the woman's prior heart palpitations from years ago with her recent attack? Was her heart already compromised before she began taking the painkiller Oxxy-1?

4. Why didn't the pharmaceutical company withdraw the painkiller from the market at the first sign of a problem?

2. You are the president of a large corporation which is in the business of manufacturing, among other things, chemical products used to eradicate termites. You have just reviewed a confidential report, prepared by one of your top scientists, questioning the effectiveness of the product and the claims your business has been making to homeowners, pesticide treatment firms, and the general public. You have heard rumors that a lawsuit will be filed shortly against your corporation claiming that this product is ineffective.

Who should you turn to for advice?

Should you destroy the report?

In which court can a lawsuit be filed?

If you lose the lawsuit at trial, can you appeal?

---

expanded *business*
discussions ::

The last item in each chapter are scenarios designed to stimulate conversation among students allowing them to review and apply the material within the chapter.

Instructor's Resource CD

The Instructor's Resource CD includes the Instructor's Manual, the computerized Test Bank, and the PowerPoint presentation all on one CD so you can format your lectures. Below is a description of each of these elements.

Instructor's Resource Manual

This manual consists of the teaching outline section, transparency masters, a case brief supplement, and video guide. The teaching outline section makes up the bulk of this Instructor's Manual, which is organized by text chapter. This section corresponds with the headings in the text, and typically includes suggestions on points of emphasis, answers to the case questions that appear within each chapter of the text, cases for discussion, and additional matters for discussion. Each chapter of this manual also includes a list of references that might be useful secondary sources of information; and suggested answers to all case questions and responses to the end-of-chapter review questions. The Case Brief section of the Instructor's Manual contains a brief of each edited case found in the text. For ease of use, the briefs are numbered by chapter in the order they appear in the text. There is a reference to the page in the text where the edited case appears. The tear-out format of this supplement allows instructors to remove any material and incorporate it into their lecture notes.

Test Bank

The Test Bank was written by Michael Katz of Delaware State University. Instructors can test students' mastery of concepts as the instructors create exams with the use of this Test Bank. Organized by chapter, the Test Bank contains at least 40 multiple-choice questions, 20 true/false questions, and 10 essay questions per chapter. Many of the questions have been modified to correspond with the text's revision. Answers immediately follow each question, along with page references and corresponding Learning Objectives.

EZ Test

McGraw-Hill's flexible and easy-to-use electronic testing program allows instructors to create tests from book-specific items. It accommodates a wide range of question types, and instructors may add their own questions. Multiple versions of the test can be created, and any test can be exported for use with online course management systems. EZ Test Online allows you to administer EZ Test-created exams and quizzes online. The test bank includes approximately 100 test questions per chapter, including true-false, multiple choice, and essay, with answers, page references, and level coding.

PowerPoint Presentation

The PowerPoint Presentation, which is also available with narrated scripts for student use, was prepared by Rick Jones of Lebanon Valley College. With approximately 700 slides, this instructional tool provides detailed lecture outlines for discussing key points and figures from the book.

Online Learning Center
www.mhhe.com/reed15e

The Online Learning Center (OLC) is a website that follows the text chapter by chapter. OLC content is designed to reinforce and build on the text content. As students read the book, they can go online to take self-grading quizzes and read chapter review material. Students can also download the online quizzes directly to their iPod, for convenient, on-the-go use.

You Be the Judge Online

This interactive product features case videos that showcase courtroom arguments of business law cases. These case videos give students the opportunity to watch profile interviews of the plaintiff and defendant, read background information, hear each case, review the evidence, make their decisions, and then access an actual, unscripted judge's decision and reasoning. There are also instructor's notes available with each video to help prepare you for classroom discussion.

brief table of *contents* ::

table of *contents* ::

2 The Ethical Basis of Law and Business Management   26

Part**TWO** :: Dispute Resolution 61

3 The Court System 62

9   Contractual Issues—Form, Interpretation, Performance, and Discharge   260

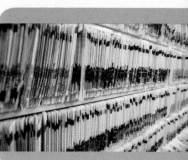

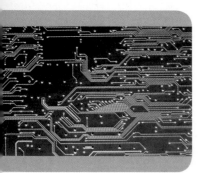

21 Labor-Management Relationship 624

Part
ONE

:: Introduction to Law

President John Adams said that the United States is a nation "of law." Certainly, law is all around us. The news media are full of stories about law, and many of our most popular television programs concern lawyers, courts, and law enforcement. Law surrounds how we buy and sell things, when we can drive a car and vote, and who we can see for many licensed services. Law taxes and punishes us as well as grants rights and privileges. Marriage and divorce apply rules of law, and even birth and death have legal significance. The conduct of modern business is hardly possible without the support of law, and everything you own is yours because of law. Part One of this book helps you make sense of this blooming, buzzing confusion of law and laws.

Chapter 1 explains that there are understandable organizing principles to the legal system, and it asserts that these principles—law, the rule of law, and property—provide a necessary foundation for successful modern business and set maximum conditions for generating what Adam Smith called the "wealth of nations." Chapter 1 also covers the concepts of jurisprudence, explains the sources of law, sets out various classifications of law, identifies legal sanctions, and introduces the concept of corporate governance. A good part of what you do in this course is to learn a legal vocabulary. Even more important, you must then learn to apply it. Chapter 1 gets this important process under way.

Chapter 2 emphasizes that the social basis of legal rules in a democracy are the traditional values, morals, and ethics of society. In a democracy, law is a very significant expression of society's moral beliefs and concerns. Law often prohibits behavior that we consider morally wrong and permits or tolerates customary behaviors. In business, ethical issues frequently concern property relationships between employees and employers, between management and business owners, and between businesses and society. Respect for what properly belongs to others and restraint in using what we own so as not to injure what belongs to others make up much of what we consider ethical behavior.

Chapter 2 looks at two ethical systems: formalism and consequentialism. It then examines various sources of values for business ethics, including legal regulation, professional and organizational codes of ethics, and individual values. It also suggests an approach to individual ethics in business organizations. After considering various difficulties of achieving an ethical business organization, Chapter 2 concludes with a section discussing the moral pros and cons of private property, the central concept of our legal system. •

1

Law as the Foundation of Business

 Learning Objectives ::

In this chapter you will learn:

1. To understand why the legal systems of nations contribute to making the economies of some nations much stronger than the economies of other nations.

2. To grasp that "property" in the law refers not to something that is owned but to the right of ownership itself, which gives maximum incentive for wealth creation.

3. To appreciate what legal sources lawyers turn to in answering legal questions from their clients, and the hierarchy of those sources.

4. To be able to explain why *stare decisis* is different in common law nations than in civil law nations.

:: Introduction

To understand the legal and regulatory environment of business, you must appreciate the role of law as the foundation for business practice in the private market system. The purpose of this book is to explain the legal system and its rules and regulations that provide the foundation for the private market. Note that Chapter 1 maintains, however, that not just any kind of law creates a basis for modern business practice. Only a property-based legal system does this. To appreciate law as the foundation of business and the private market, we first examine some possible causes of national wealth.

1. WHY NATIONS ARE ECONOMICALLY WEAK OR STRONG

Why some nations are economically weak and others economically strong is of great importance in the world today. According to the United Nations, 30,000 children worldwide die every day from malnourishment and largely preventable diseases. Most of these children are located in economically weak countries. In economic poverty lies the roots of much hunger, disease, discontent, despair, revolution, and terrorism.

According to Nobel economist Douglass North, 500 years ago all nations of the world were poor. Today, however, some are much wealthier than others. A recent World Bank study shows that 22 nations have average national incomes per person above $20,000 a year, with the figure in the United States being $41,400. In contrast 21 countries have average per person incomes of a dollar a day or less, under $365 annually. The economically stronger nations tend to be in Europe, North America, and along the Pacific Rim, with the economically weaker nations being found in the rest of the world. But sometimes they are side by side. For instance, although the United States and Mexico share a common border, the former has seven times the national income per person of the latter. Also sharing a common border are Singapore and Indonesia, with the former nation enjoying per person almost 20 times the income of the latter.

Several explanations attempt to show why national economies are weak or strong.

Wealthy Singapore has almost no natural resources or fertile land. Its wealth comes from shipping and financial services.

- Dependency theory. This theory argues that economically strong nations exploit the resources and labor of weaker nations through trade. It asserts that some nations grow and flourish at the expense of keeping others economically poor. Yet nations with stronger economies invest and trade much more with each other than they do with nations having weaker economies, and international trade usually accounts for only a small fraction of national income in even the poorest countries. Lack of conditions encouraging internal economic activity rather than overdependence on international trade causes weak national economies.

- Natural resources. Whether or not a nation has abundant natural resources has been offered to explain economic prosperity. Yet economically wealthy Japan has relatively few natural resources and little fertile land while economically weak Russia has an abundance of both. Many economically poor regions of South America and Africa possess much fertile land, various minerals, and considerable other natural resources. Even those small nations that are comparatively well-off because they have a large amount of a single natural resource like oil are wealthy only because they are able to sell to other nations with strong, diverse economies.

In economically weaker countries like Egypt, many college graduates can get jobs only with the government because there are few jobs available in private business that require education.

- Education and technology. Economically strong nations usually have more schools and implement technology more quickly than economically weak nations. Technology and education are certainly important to the continuing economic strength of wealthy nations, but in some parts of the world, well-educated people have few job opportunities, and powerful technologies are easily transferred between countries. Widespread education and rapid technology implementation in nations seem to be more a result rather than the primary cause of strong economies.

- Climate. Some geographers have thought that climate helps explain whether nations are economically strong or weak. They believe that when temperatures average too hot, people are less able to work, especially outdoors. However, strong economies can exist in hot climates. Singapore lies near the equator and has one of the world's most prosperous economies and highest national per person incomes.

- Private market. According to many economists, the presence or absence of a modern private market is the single most significant reason why some economies are strong and others are weak. Yet the mere existence of a private market may not be enough to create an economically prosperous economy. After the former Soviet Union collapsed, Russia ended much state planning, leaving individuals free to carry on business privately. Many economists expected the Russian economy to take off. Instead, it declined 41 percent over the next seven years.

- Law and the legal system. An adequately enforced system of equally applied law is increasingly recognized as a necessary foundation for strong, productive economies. A certain framework of law is necessary for maximum incentive to entrepreneurs, investors, and inventors. The law of property, contract, tort, and various government regulations provides a foundation for institutions such as corporations, banks, and securities exchanges. Law secures the elements of trust and certainty that are vital to economic transactions among strangers. No nations with weak economies have adequate legal systems, and all nations that have these systems are economically strong in comparison.

Abundant natural resources, education and technology, a temperate climate, and the institutions of the private market all contribute to strong national economies. However, a certain type of legal system is most fundamental to national wealth creation.

:: Law, the Rule of Law, and Property

Three concepts establish a necessary framework for the most effectively functioning market in the modern nation: law, the rule of law, and property. Note how they connect to each other.

2. LAW

In the last 10,000 years, human society has moved from roving bands of hunter-gatherers to large modern nations with populations in the hundreds of millions. The social forces that hold together societies range from custom and religion to law and economic ties. In the modern nation, however, the most significant of the social forces is **law** because law can glue together diverse peoples of different backgrounds into very large, organized groups. Law is known by everyone as being intended to tell members of society what they can or cannot do. Strangers to a society may not understand or appreciate complex and subtle customs of behavior, but they can observe the formal laws governing what kinds of activities are permitted and prohibited in

"Privatization without necessary institutional infrastructure [such as law] in the transition countries led to asset stripping rather than wealth creation."

–Joseph E. Stiglitz, economist

"One of the things that I see, the more I travel and the longer I live, is that intelligence and hard work are evenly distributed throughout the world. But opportunity and investment and organization are not. The systems often don't exist for clever, hardworking, inventive poor people to be rewarded for their endeavors."

–William Jefferson Clinton, 41st U.S. president

society. Lawyers, judges, and other trained interpreters of the rules can help them in this process.

A simple definition of law follows:

- Law is made up of rules.
- These rules are laid down by the state and backed up by enforcement.

Law is a formal social force, meaning that laws come from the state and are usually written down and accessible so those who need to understand and obey them can. To maintain order in society, adequate enforcement institutions such as courts and the police are a necessary part of the legal system. As the countries of the former Soviet Union are finding out, written laws mean little unless they can be promptly and fairly enforced. Without adequate enforcement, resources can be taken from those who have them, and agreements can be disregarded. The certainty and trust necessary to make complex, long-term business arrangements are absent. People must spend much of their time guarding their resources rather than developing them.

3. THE RULE OF LAW

In a modern nation, law is important to implement either the commands of a dictator or the will of the people in a democracy. However, only in democracies is there true concern for the rule of law, which goes beyond merely thinking of law as governmental commands backed up by force. Under the **rule of law,** laws that are made are *generally* and *equally* applicable. They apply to all or most members of society and they apply to various groups in the same way.

Under the rule of law, law applies to lawmakers as well as to the rest of society. Thus, lawmakers have an incentive to make laws that benefit everyone. Rule-of-law nations adopt laws supporting the private market because it is in everyone's interest, including the lawmakers'.

In today's international business environment, more and more voices are calling for the rule of law. The secretary-general of the United Nations says that "without confidence based on the rule of law; without trust and transparency—there could be no well-functioning markets." The managing director of the International Monetary Fund asserts that "high quality" economic growth depends "in particular on the rule of law" which is a "lodestar for all countries." Observes the managing director of J. P. Morgan and Co.: "An environment in which courts cannot be relied upon to adhere to the rule of law is an environment in which businesses will be reluctant to invest and in which development will be stunted." He calls the rule of law "a cornerstone of free trade."

Unfortunately, the rule of law is an ideal rather than a complete fact in even the most democratic nation. Special interest groups attempt to persuade lawmakers to benefit these groups at the expense of others. And it is not always clear what it means to apply laws generally and equally. Still, in a democracy well-educated voters who understand the importance of the rule of law can hold to account lawmakers who excessively favor special interests. Judges also play a vital role in maintaining the rule of law. (See Sidebar 1.1.)

Almost all wealthy countries embrace the rule of law; for example, most European countries. Article 6 of the Treaty on European Union, called the Maastricht Treaty, says the EU is "founded" on "the rule of law."

The first known written set of laws was the Code of Hammurabi, named after the Babylonian king of the 18th century BC.

"Without the rule of law, major economic institutions such as corporations, banks, and labor unions would not function, and the government's many involvements in the economy—regulatory mechanisms, tax systems, customs structure, monetary policy, and the like—would be unfair, inefficient, and opaque."

–Thomas Carothers, Director, Democracy and Rule of Law Project, Carnegie Endowment for International Peace

---

"While economic growth can occur in the short run with autocratic regimes, long-run economic growth entails the development of the rule of law."

–Douglas C. North, acceptance speech for the Nobel Prize in Economics, 1993

:: *sidebar* 1.1

The Chief Justice and the Rule of Law

Before someone can become a justice of the U.S. Supreme Court, the president must nominate and the U.S. Senate must confirm that person. The Senate must also confirm the president's choice to be chief justice. During the confirmation, the senators always ask questions about the rule of law. Here is how Chief Justice John Roberts responded to a confirmation question about the rule of law.

> Somebody asked me. . ., "Are you going to be on the side of the little guy," he said. And you obviously want to give an immediate answer, but, as you reflect on it, if the Constitution says that the

little guy should win, the little guy's going to win in court before me. But if the Constitution says that the big guy should win, well, then the big guy's going to win, because my obligation is to the Constitution.

Compare Chief Justice Roberts's statement to what Justice Anthony Kennedy wrote in *Texas v. Johnson,* 491 U.S. 397 (1989), a case about how the First Amendment protects flag burning: "The hard fact is that sometimes we must make decisions we do not like. We make them because they are right, right in the sense that the law and the Constitution, as we see them, compel the result."

4. PROPERTY

The third concept necessary for a successful private market in the modern nation is property. **Property** is the legal right to exclude or keep others from interfering with what you own, with your resources. "The legal right to exclude" means that you can turn to public authorities like the police or the courts to help you keep others from interfering with what you own. Three ways of applying the exclusionary right of property are

- Public property, which applies to public resources owned by the government (or "state") like roads, public buildings, public lands, and monuments.
- Private property, which applies to resources that you own as an individual.
- Common property, which applies to resources like land that more than one individual owns jointly.

So important is the right of private property that in this book we often just refer to private property as "property." We will specifically say "public property" or "common property" if we mean those applications of exclusionary right.

It is through the law of property that individuals and business organizations can possess, use, and transfer their private resources. Without law that guarantees property in resources, there is little incentive for anyone to develop resources since they may be seized by the state or by others who want them. Where there is inadequate property law, individuals either have few resources or must guard their resources by force, and the conduct of modern business is almost impossible due to lack of trust.

Even attorneys sometimes confuse the right of property with the resources, especially the physical resources, that property guarantees. We think of "my land" as being the same thing as "my property," but in a legal sense it is not. Consider the following example: *Tree* is a general word that can describe all sorts of specific things like *oak, pine, elm,* or *maple.* You may even see a new leafy thing and ask, "What kind of tree is that?" However, *property* is not a

Property is a legal right that allows you to exclude others from your resources. It makes what is yours "yours."

Don't think of property as the things owned. In law property means "ownership."

general word meaning *land, car, widget,* or *banana,* and you do not see a new thing for the first time, for example, a new automobile, and ask, "What kind of property is that?"

To understand property, think of the word as meaning *ownership.* If you own a piece of land you enjoy the right of property to it. The legal significance of property is that an owner of land (one who has property in it) can exclude or keep others from interfering with the land. Owners can exercise their right of property by having the police or courts keep others from interfering with what they own. You may also understand property as a type of fence, not an actual fence but rather a legal fence that keeps others out by announcing private ownership and enforcing it. The enforcement of the property fence is enormously important to the growth of national economies. Many nations claim they have private property systems, but they still remain poor because they cannot or do not adequately enforce the legal fence with police and institutions like courts to settle disputes.

The enforcement of the property right under the rule of law gives people incentive to develop the resources they own. Something deeply natural to human beings encourages them to exert the greatest productive effort only when they can prevent others from taking the resources they produce. Only when people control what they produce will they give production their maximum effort. It is a property-based legal system that enables such control by allowing people to exclude others from interfering with what their efforts produce. Importantly, such a system protects and assists the poor as well as the wealthy. (See Sidebar 1.2.)

Do remember that the property right gives a major incentive to develop resources.

Property right helps the poor as much as the wealthy. Why?

:: *sidebar* 1.2

How Property Protects the Poor

Many people have difficulty grasping how property protects the poor. After all, do the poor even have "property"? Legally, the answer is "yes," because property is an exclusive right to keep others from interfering with one's resources, not the resources themselves, and under the rule of law, this right protects the resources of the poor as well as those of the wealthy.

In many parts of the world that have no adequate property systems, poor "squatters" lack formally recognized ownership of the land they live on. They spend much of their time defending their possession and cannot use their houses and land to secure loans that would allow them to start small businesses. Peru, however, has begun recognizing and registering the legal ownership of these squatters in their homes.

Princeton graduate student Erica Field compared areas of Peru where legal property has been formally secured with areas where it is yet to be recognized. She found the granting of the right of property to the "average squatter family" was associated with a 17 percent total household work increase, a 47 percent increase in the probability of working outside the home, and a 28 percent decline in the likelihood of child labor in the family. Her 2002 study concluded that formal ownership means the families no longer have to spend as much time protecting their homes and can engage in more productive work, which makes them less poor.

The ownership program in Peru was initiated following the ideas of economist Hernando de Soto. De Soto's ideas and work have spread to other countries, and he has gained support from many world leaders, including Presidents George W. Bush and Bill Clinton. De Soto believes that Western and Pacific Rim nations are the world's most wealthy because they have had the rule of law and the law of property the longest. He maintains that law is the "hidden architecture" of the modern private market.

State-controlled production does not come close to matching the national levels of goods and services produced under private property systems (capitalism). This illustrates that the incentive to maximum effort comes from the property right. The countries that have enjoyed strong property systems for the past several centuries uniformly have the highest national incomes, and those countries that do not protect private productive efforts under a strong property system are the world's poorest. The exclusionary right of property provides a basis for the private market and modern business. Scholars have traced the economic flourishing of Western civilization during the last several hundred years to the increasing recognition of the right of property in the nations of the West.

Consider the following. If a nation with a property-based legal system averages only 2 percent a year greater productivity than a nation without such a system, in 34.5 years the first nation has twice the annual total income (called Gross National Income or GNI) of the second nation. In 206 years, the first nation has 64 times the annual GNI of the second nation. Note that abundant goods and services, educational excellence, rapidly developing technology, food availability, and sufficient medical service are usually related to the economic wealth of GNI.

5. PROPERTY IN ITS BROADEST SENSE

Property can be thought of as the central concept underlying Western legal systems. (See Figure 1.1.) Most of the topics discussed in this book relate to the exclusionary right of property. Contract law enables an owner to exchange resources (Chapters 8 and 9), especially at a future date. Tort law compensates owners whose resources are wrongfully harmed by the actions of others (Chapter 10). Criminal law punishes those who harm an owner's resources in particular ways, for example, by theft (Chapter 12). The law of business organizations identifies how individuals can own and use private resources in groups (Chapter 14).

*Property is the central concept of Western legal systems.

Regulatory law both protects ownership and sets limits on private resource use (Chapter 14). Antitrust law forbids owners from monopolizing classes of resources and sets rules for how businesses can compete to acquire ownership in new resources (Chapter 16). Securities laws regulate the transfer of ownership in certain profit-making opportunities (Chapter 15). Environmental law controls how owners can use their resources when creating pollution (Chapter 18). Even labor laws and antidiscrimination laws involve property in the sense they protect the employees' right to exclude employers from interfering with certain self-ownership interests of the employees (Chapters 20 and 21). Finally, a theme of the entire book, corporate governance, specifically concerns the law protecting the owners of a business organization from the managers who run it for them. Generally speaking, corporate governance also refers to any law regulating and limiting private owners' productive resources and their use.

To say that you have a "right" means that legally you can keep others from interfering with that right. To be able to exclude others is the essence of property.

In its broadest sense, property includes an ownership of individual constitutional and human rights in ourselves that excludes the state from interfering with these rights. Today, we usually call our relationship to these rights "liberty," but liberty and property in this sense have almost identical meanings. John Locke, the seventeenth-century English philosopher who greatly influenced the framers of the Constitution, asserted that private property begins

Without any opposition to their statements by the others, 4 of the 55 members of the U.S. Constitutional Convention were quoted by James Madison, the secretary of the convention, as saying that the reason that government is formed is to protect what is privately proper to people, that is, private property fences.

Figure 1.1
The wheel of property

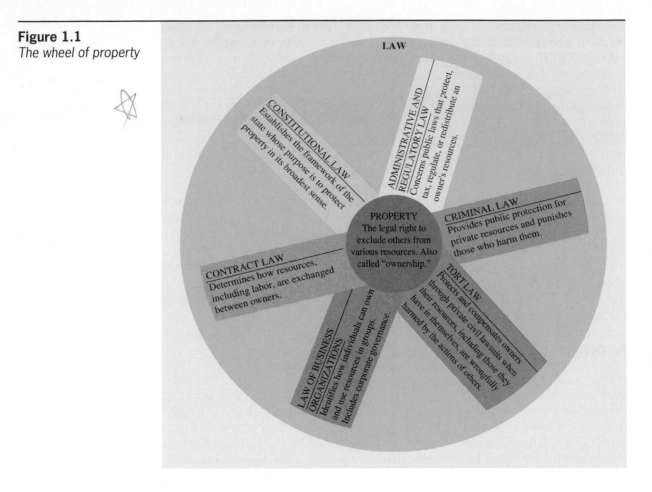

with the right we have in ourselves and in our efforts and actions. He said that an individual is the "proprietor [owner] of his own person, and the actions or labour of it" and that this is "the great foundation of property." Later, James Madison wrote that property "in its larger and juster meaning . . . embraces everything to which a man may attach value and have a right. . . . [A] man has property in his opinions and free communication of them. . . . In a word, as a man is said to have a right to his property, he may be equally said to have a property in his rights." For Madison and other constitutional framers, property protected not only physical resources like land but also human rights like freedom of speech, freedom of religion, and freedom from unreasonable intrusion by the government. The individual's very relationship to society was defined by the word *property*. Scholars have pointed out that the modern understanding of human rights began with the concept of property.

Nearly two million students study business in the United States; one hundred thousand of them are from other countries. As necessary as it is for them to grasp business subjects involving computers, debits and credits, balance sheets, financial statements, employee and consumer behavior, and stakeholder theory, it is equally vital for them to appreciate how law and the legal concept of property establish conditions for the private market in society. The secret to economic prosperity and the wealth of nations lies in the foundation of property law and the legal system to implement it under the rule of law. Modern private markets within nations simply do not work well without generally and equally applied property law.

:: *sidebar* 1.3

Russia's Property Problems

When the former Soviet Union collapsed, many observers thought that the new private market would promptly improve Russia's economy. However, that economy went into a serious decline from which it has been slow to recover. Why? Most now consider that Russia's lack of the rule of law and the law of property accounts for its poor economy.

The government still controls over half of the resources in Russia. Much of what private control of resources exists in Russia has been gotten through force, fraud, and corruption. One study in Moscow found that small business owners must pay over $30,000 a year in bribes to corrupt officials and extortionists. Developing property law in Russia often does not allow a single individual to control all the ways that land can be used. When disputes over agreements arise, businesses cannot depend on the courts to resolve issues justly and impartially. Recently, the Russian economy has been strengthened by the sale of oil to wealthy countries, but per person income in Russia remains low. In comparison, per person income in the United States is still approximately 10 times that in Russia.

Generally and equally applied property rights, their transfer by contract, and the support of adequate enforcement institutions like courts will provide a necessary basis to move the Russian economy toward prosperity. But the Russian people will have to be educated about the legal foundation of the wealth of nations.

6. JURISPRUDENCE

Over the centuries, several philosophies have developed that explain the origin, justification, meaning, and essence of law. We call these philosophies of law **jurisprudence.** Briefly, the main types or "schools" of jurisprudence include the following:

- Natural law. Going back to Aristotle and other ancient philosophers, natural law theory asserts that law contains universal moral principles. These principles are observable in nature, and we can determine them through human reason. John Locke, the British philosopher whose writing influenced the framers of the U.S. Constitution, thought that "property" was part of natural law. Merely human laws that contradict the principles of natural law are improper. Compare natural law to "formalism," discussed in Chapter 2.

- Positive law. Positive law jurisprudence believes that law is simply the commands of the state backed up by force and punishments. It is contrary to the philosophy of natural law. Eighteenth-century philosopher Jeremy Bentham ridiculed the idea of natural law as "nonsense upon stilts." Compare positive law to "consequentialism," discussed in Chapter 2 .

- Historical school. The historical school of jurisprudence emphasizes that contemporary law should focus on legal principles that have withstood the test of time in a nation. The historical school believes that law reflects the cultural traditions of a people and recognizes that different nations may have different traditions and, consequently, different laws. Friedrich Savigny, a prominent German legal philosopher, helped develop this jurisprudence.

Jurisprudence is the philosophy of law.

"True law is right reason in agreement with nature; it is of universal application, unchanging and everlasting. . . ."

–Cicero, Roman historian

The definition of law at the beginning of this chapter is taken from positive law jurisprudence.

- Sociological jurisprudence. Sociological jurisprudence supports the idea that law can and should change to meet new developments in society. From this point of view, the Second Amendment to the U.S. Constitution, which asserts the right to "bear arms," or weapons, should not be interpreted today to allow citizens to own and carry lightweight fully automatic rifles that can fire hundreds of rounds a minute. When the Second Amendment was written, a highly trained person carrying a 25-pound rifle could fire only about two rounds a minute.

- Legal realism. Legal realism tries to go beyond just the words of law to examine what police, administrators, prosecutors, and judges are actually doing as they enforce, interpret, and apply laws. When Supreme Court Justice Oliver Wendell Holmes, Jr., said that "law is what officials do about it," he reflected the jurisprudence of legal realism. For instance, the posted speed limit around the Atlanta perimeter highway, Interstate 285, is 55 mph. However, almost no one drives within the posted speed limit and traffic police rarely ticket drivers until they go faster than 75 mph. In terms of legal realism, what is the actual speed limit on Atlanta's perimeter highway?

Several of these types of jurisprudence overlap. For instance, sociological jurisprudence and legal realism are types of legal positivism. Jurisprudence may also certainly influence the actual rules of law, but jurisprudence is a philosophy about law rather than the law itself. However, complicating matters is that the word *jurisprudence* also refers to the general body of law interpretations by judges as different from legislation passed by legislators.

:: Classifications of Law

Even when you understand jurisprudence and grasp the significance of our property-based legal system to the private marketplace, you still have much left to know about the legal and regulatory environment of business. In large part, learning about law demands an extensive vocabulary of legal terms and concepts. It will be useful in organizing this vocabulary to examine several major classifications of law.

7. COMMON LAW AND CIVIL LAW

The world has two major legal systems: common law and civil law. The United Kingdom, the United States, Canada, Jamaica, India, Nigeria, New Zealand, and a few other countries—all colonized by England—follow the common law. The **common law** legal system emphasizes the role of judges in determining the meaning of laws and how they apply. It arose beginning in the eleventh and twelfth centuries as the English monarch appointed royal judges to ride circuits around the English countryside and to resolve disputes in the name of the king (or queen). As there was little formal law to apply to many disputes, the decisions handed down by the judges literally made the law.

Common law
emphasizes the role of judges in determining the meaning of laws.

By the time the English legislature (Parliament) emerged, a huge body of written judicial decisions was "common" to all of England. The role of judges in making and interpreting law was in place. English colonists then brought the common law to what became the United States and various other countries. The common law continues its development even today, and so significant is the role of judges in the United States that they determine the meaning of the Constitution and can declare void the legislation of Congress and the acts of the president.

The world's nations not colonized by England generally observe civil law legal systems. The **civil law** relies more on legislation than judicial decisions to determine what the law is. Like common law courts, courts in civil law nations decide the facts in a disputed case (for example, who did what, who committed a crime or breached a contract), but civil law courts do not make law nor do their judges think themselves obligated to follow prior judicial decisions, called *precedents,* as they do in common law nations, although they do refer to "settled" cases. Essentially, judges play a much more important role in determining law and its meaning in common law nations than in civil law nations. Only Louisiana among the U.S. states, follows a partial civil law system. This is due to Louisiana's historical ties with France, a civil law nation.

Civil law relies more on legislation than judicial decisions for law.

8. PUBLIC AND PRIVATE LAW

Another way of classifying the law is to divide it into matters of public law and matters of private law. **Public law** includes those matters that involve the regulation of society as opposed to individuals interacting. In each of these matters, a government official represents society, or "the people," and the official is responsible for seeking justice to achieve the ends of society. The main types of public law include:

Public law includes constitutional law, administrative law, and criminal law.

- **Constitutional law,** which involves the interpretation and application of either the federal or state constitutions.
- **Administrative law,** which covers the legal principles that apply to government agencies, bureaus, boards, or commissions.
- **Criminal law,** which specifies various offenses against the proper order of the state.

Special areas of property concern land, goods, copyrights, patents, and trademarks.

Private law covers those legal problems and issues that concern your private resource relationships with other people. Private law traditionally includes:

- **Property law,** which involves the recognition of exclusive right in both tangible (physically touchable) and intangible resources. Special areas of property law concern land, goods, copyrights, trademarks, patents, and trade secrets.
- **Contract law,** which covers the rules of how owners transfer resources by exchanging them. Contracts often involve enforceable promises to exchange resources in the future.
- **Tort law,** which establishes rules for compensation when an owner's legal boundaries are wrongfully crossed by another. Tort law often but not always requires actual injury to the owner's resources.

We live in a time of the rapid generation and distribution of new information through computers and technology. This development raises many issues of property, contract, and tort law. The text contains chapters on each of these areas of the private law. For examples of new questions of public and private law see Sidebar 1.4.

:: *sidebar* 1.4

Internet Law Connection

New developments in society raise fresh issues of law because law is the principal social force ordering society. Consider the following questions of public and private law raised by computers, the Internet, and the Information Age.

- Do the creators of software have a property interest in the "look and feel" of the software? A property interest in what it does (i.e., in its functionality)?
- How do we create legally binding agreements over the Internet?
- Is it unconstitutional for the FBI to monitor e-mail transmissions without a search warrant through software that can detect possible evidence of criminal communication?
- Do the purchasers of copyrighted music and video have a legal right to give copies of that expression to others?

- Do employers violate federal labor law by monitoring employee e-mail and disciplining employees for criticizing the employers?
- Can Congress constitutionally regulate sexually explicit materials transmitted over the Internet?
- Can states prohibit in-state delivery of untaxed alcoholic beverages ordered from out-of-state sellers over the Internet?
- Are Internet providers like America Online ever liable for what users say over their services?

The chapters of this textbook discuss these and other questions of law. Answers to these questions will come through a series of court cases that interpret and apply existing public and private law, prior case precedents, and new legislation and regulations. This emphasis on the courts is key to understanding our common law legal system.

9. CIVIL LAW AND CRIMINAL LAW

Don't confuse our reference to *civil* (or noncriminal) lawsuits with a *civil* law legal system, which is one emphasizing the importance of the legislature in determining the meaning of laws.

Another means of classifying the law is to divide it into civil law and criminal law. For administrative purposes, courts usually separate criminal actions from all other lawsuits. *Civil* cases may include suits for breach of contract or tort cases, such as suits for personal injuries. Typically, they involve a request for damages or other appropriate relief that does not involve punishment of the wrongdoer. *Criminal* cases involve a representative of government attempting to prove the wrong committed against society and seeking to have the wrongdoer punished by the court system.

10. SUBSTANTIVE LAW AND PROCEDURAL LAW

That a plaintiff must prove the defendant failed to use reasonable care in order to establish the tort of negligence is an example of substantive law.

Another important classification or distinction in law is between substance and procedure. **Substantive law** defines the legal relationship of people with other people or between them and the state. Thus, the rules of law governing the creation or enforcement of a contractual promise are substantive in nature. **Procedural law** deals with the method and means by which substantive law is made and administered. The time allowed for one party to sue another and the rules of law governing the process of the lawsuit are examples of procedural laws. Thus, substantive rules of law define rights and duties, while procedural rules of law provide the machinery for enforcing those rights and duties.

Judicial procedures involve the conduct of lawsuits and appeals and the enforcement of judgments. The rules for conducting civil trials are different from those for criminal trials. For example, each party may call the other party to the witness stand for cross-examination in a civil trial, but the defendant may not be required to testify in a criminal case. Procedural problems some-times arise concerning papers filed in lawsuits, the admission of evidence, and various other techniques involved in trying the case. They are the rules of the game. In Chapter 4 , you will study these procedural aspects of law in greater depth.

:: Sources of Law

For Sections 11–14 consider that you have a dry cleaning business and have gone to a lawyer to ask what the law says about your emitting certain chemi-cal cleaning pollutants into the air. What sources of law will the lawyer have to be familiar with in order to answer your questions? The following sources form a hierarchy of law, which means that if a lower source of law conflicts with a higher source of law, it is legally void; that is, the higher source trumps, or prevails over, the lower.

11. CONSTITUTIONS

The U.S. Constitution is the supreme law of the nation. Your lawyer, in answering your legal question, knows that as a source of law the U.S. Con-stitution overrides all other sources of law. The Constitution establishes the federal government, and its amendments guarantee basic rights and liberties to the people of the nation. States also have constitutions but their author-ity as a source of law applies only to the particular states that have adopted them. If state constitutional provisions conflict with the U.S. Constitution or with federal walls at all, the provisions are void as a source of law, meaning that they do not apply to your question about pollutants.

In consulting constitutional sources of law, your attorney will look closely to determine if regulations or legislation that affects you violates your con-stitutional rights. If your rights are violated, the laws violating them are void (i.e., these laws have no legal effect on you). Chapter 6 examines more closely how the U.S. Constitution in particular applies to business practice.

12. LEGISLATION

After the constitutions, your attorney will consult formal written laws known as **legislation** as the most significant source of law. Our elected representa-tives serving in the legislative branch of government create and adopt leg-islation. Legislative bodies exist at all levels of government, including not only the federal Congress but also state general assemblies, city councils, and many other local government bodies that adopt or enact laws. Legislation in its broad sense also includes treaties entered into by the executive branch of government and ratified by the Senate.

Legislation adopted by Congress or a state legislature is usually referred to as a **statute** or **act.** Laws passed by local governments are frequently called **ordinances.** Compilations of legislation at all levels of government are called **codes.** For example, we have local traffic codes covering such matters as speed limits, and state laws, such as the Uniform Commercial Code, that cover all aspects of commercial transactions. The statutes of our federal gov-ernment are compiled in the United States Code.

"The American Constitution is the most wonderful work ever struck off at a given time by the brain and purpose of man."

–William Gladstone, four-time prime minister of Great Britain in the 1800s

An ordinance of Athens, Georgia, prohibits the carrying of alcoholic beverages in open containers on public sidewalks and other public areas.

Uniformity of Legislation

Because Congress, 50 state legislatures, and countless local governments enact statutes and ordinances, there is concern about the lack of uniformity in the law. If the law lacks uniformity from town to town and state to state across the nation, it decreases the certainty necessary for the conduct of interstate business and the general ordering of society. How do businesses, or citizens for that matter, follow all laws which may vary from place to place?

Legislators can achieve uniformity in the law through two methods. First, Congress can enact a single law that preempts (overrides) varying state laws. Second, the state legislatures can all adopt a single uniform law in a particular area. The latter method has been attempted by a legislative drafting group known as the National Conference of Commissioners on Uniform State Laws. These commissioners endeavor to promote uniformity by drafting model acts. When approved by the National Conference, proposed uniform acts are recommended to the state legislatures for adoption.

Uniform Commercial Code

"Goods" are tangible (touchable) things like clothing, food, electronic items, and jewelry.

The most significant uniform law for business is the **Uniform Commercial Code (UCC)**. It collects in one body the law that "deals with all the phases which may ordinarily arise in the handling of commercial transactions from start to finish." It covers the law relating to the sale of goods, the use of checks and other forms of "commercial paper," and the giving of security to ensure the buyer will pay the purchase price of goods.

The UCC applies only to purchases and sales of personal property like goods. It does not apply to contracts to sell land or contracts for personal services. Chapter 8 on contracts discusses the UCC further.

Interpretation of Legislation

Statutory construction concerns how courts interpret and apply the meaning of legislation.

Legislation often is written in general terms. The precise meaning of the law often is unclear. In our legal system, it is up to the judiciary to determine the meaning of general language in a legislative enactment and apply it to the limited facts of a case. The court's purpose in interpreting a statute or an ordinance is to determine the intent of the legislature when the statute was enacted. Such a process is called **statutory construction**. Considering the legislative history of statutes, applying rules for interpreting specific types of legislation, and using rules for interpreting various kinds of statutory words are all a part of statutory construction.

13. ADMINISTRATIVE REGULATION

Whatever legal problem your business has, your attorney must consider administrative regulation as a major source of law. As previously stated, legislatures often enact statutes in broad, general terms. Legislative bodies, recognizing the need for greater specificity, often authorize the creation of administrative agencies to provide clarity and enforcement of a legal area. Examples of such actions include the establishment of the Environmental Protection Agency (EPA), the Securities and Exchange Commission (SEC), and the Occupational Safety and Health Administration (OSHA).

Each of these agencies and hundreds more regulate business activities through the adoption of rules and regulations. Many administrative agencies also investigate businesses to determine if they have violated rules and regulations. The agencies hold their own hearings to determine if civil violations have occurred. Other agencies criminally prosecute illegal violations of some administrative rules and regulations.

Chapter 14 provides additional details on the creation, operation, and impact of administrative agencies. For now, it is enough to say that federal, state, or local agencies regulate to some degree almost every business activity.

14. JUDICIAL DECISIONS OR CASE LAW

Finally, your attorney must consult the decisions of judges as a source of law. Even after considering constitutional language, reading legislation, and referring to administrative regulation, your attorney must still know the judicial decisions, called *case law*, that apply to your legal problem. These decisions interpret the relevant constitutional, legislative, and regulatory laws. As previously discussed, judges also make and interpret the common law.

When judges, especially judges who decide appeals from trial courts, make decisions on legal issues, they write their decisions, or **opinions,** setting out reasons. These case opinions are collected and published in book volumes known as "reporters," and these opinions now become **precedents** for future cases involving similar facts and legal issues. To locate prior precedents, it is helpful to know the **citation** for the case where a precedent is found. For example, a case opinion cited as 313 N.W.2d 601 (1982) can be located on page 601 of volume 313 of the *Northwestern Reporter,* second edition, a case decided in 1982. Knowing a case citation, you can easily locate the case in a library or through computer databases.

The extensive reliance of our legal system on judicial case law has both advantages and disadvantages. It is useful to summarize these.

Advantages **Stare decisis** is the doctrine of prior precedents. The Latin meaning of these words is "let the prior decision stand." Under *stare decisis,* judges in current cases follow whenever possible the interpretation of law determined by judges in prior cases. This doctrine arose from the desire for certainty and predictability in the law. One important advantage of *stare decisis* was people became secure in their right of property. They then became willing to invest resources in fixed locations for factories and other immovable valuables because they were certain the state would not seize these resources for its own use. Case law helps specify in great detail the boundaries of our property-based legal system, and it protects what is "proper" to people from the interference of others.

Disadvantages Several disadvantages of case law are also important to know. Keep in mind, however, that we do not believe these disadvantages destroy the benefits of certainty, predictability, and stability provided by case law and *stare decisis.* Disadvantages of case law include:

- Volume of cases. Even with computers, searching through hundreds of thousands of cases and then identifying and reading the significant ones is often a very great task. At the very least, it is both time consuming for the attorney and expensive for the client.
- Conflicting precedents. Sometimes in searching prior cases, attorneys find cases in which judicial decisions conflict with each other. Conflicting precedents do not create confidence in the certainty of law.

Don't forget that there are court systems in all 50 states plus a federal system. According to the U.S. Department of State, more than 31,000 judges nationwide make numerous decisions every year, adding to the volume of case law.

"*Stare decisis* is the viaduct over which the law travels in transporting the precious cargo of justice."

–Bosely v. Andrews,
393 Pa. 161 (1958)

A baseball fan is hurt by a foul ball and sues the baseball team's owner. The court writes, "Whether a fan is injured by a foul ball or an accidentally thrown bat, the result is the same. The fan cannot recover damages against the team because the fan assumes the risk." The comment about "thrown bat" is dicta because the case involved only a foul ball. Bats are heavier and more dangerous than balls, and a judge in a future case may not feel obligated to follow the dicta in this case concerning bats.

Originalism is the opposite of constitutional relativity. It stands for the idea that courts should interpret the Constitution *only* according to the intentions of those who wrote it.

- Dicta. Increasing the difficulty of determining how to follow prior precedent is the distinction between the **holding** in a prior case and mere **dicta.** The holdings in prior cases are precisely what was necessary to the decision reached. Dicta are whatever else the court said. Judges in future cases are not so likely to follow the dicta in prior cases as they are the holdings.
- Rejection of precedent. Because of *stare decisis,* courts usually hesitate to reject the precedents of prior cases, but sometimes they do. They may think that prior cases were wrongly decided, or they may think that times have changed. In constitutional law the idea that courts should understand the meaning of the Constitution relative to the times in which they interpret it is known as **constitutional relativity.**

If the contract specifies no particular state's law, a court interpreting the contract will usually apply the law of the state where the contract was made.

- Conflicts of law. A buyer in Georgia orders equipment by telephone from a seller's representative in Illinois. The buyer directs the seller to ship the equipment to New York. When the equipment breaks down while being used in Pennsylvania, the buyer sues the seller in Ohio where the seller is incorporated. What state's law applies? Courts resolve such problems by applying **conflicts of law** rules, but even these rules may vary from state to state. A better solution is for the buyer and seller to specify in the contract which state's law will apply in case of a dispute. In a tort case, the usual conflicts of law rule applies the law of the state where the injury occurred, no matter where the injury occurred.

15. SOURCES OF LAW HIERARCHY IN REVIEW

So your lawyer has to know many sources of law and how they interact in order to answer your question about the pollutants from your cleaning business. It is mistaken to think that lawyers know all of the law that applies to every legal question that you may ask them. However, they should know how to go about answering your questions, including the fact that some questions may not have answers that can be known in advance and that require formal dispute resolution, that is, they require that a judge, or perhaps an arbitrator, decide them.

The hierarchy of the sources of law, however, is well understood. That hierarchy is as follows. Remember that each higher source of law voids, or prevails, over every lower source of law in the hierarchy, except that in many instances there will be no conflict between higher and lower sources of law and in other instances it may not be clear whether or not a higher source of law (such as a constitutional right of speech) conflicts with a lower source of law (such as a law regulating advertising expression).

Hierarchy of sources of law from highest to lowest:

- U.S. Constitution and Amendments.
- Statutes (also called "acts" or "legislation") of Congress.
- Federal administration regulation.
- State constitutions (apply only in individual states).
- State statutes (apply only in individual states).
- State administrative regulation (applies only in individual states).
- Local ordinances (apply only in cities, towns, and other such areas).
- Case law (court cases, as they interpret all of the other sources, may or may not void sources lower than the source being interpreted).

:: Legal Sanctions

The enforcement of the law is vital to the rule of law and a "proper" legal system. Law enforcement officials and the courts use several methods to encourage or to force compliance with the obedience to the law. These methods, often called **sanctions,** may be used against a person who has failed to comply with the law. The sanctions are in effect a form of punishment for violating the law. Sanctions also have a preventive function. The threat of sanctions usually results in compliance with the requirements of law.

Because punishment is used to secure obedience to the law, the Fourteenth Amendment to the Constitution of the United States provides in part: "No State shall . . . deprive any person of life, liberty or property without due process of law." This provision recognizes that the law is enforced by taking a person's life, freedom, or the resources that he or she owns. The taking of an owner's resources may be (1) for the benefit of society generally, as when land is taken through eminent domain; (2) to punish someone, as with a traffic fine; or (3) for the benefit of another person, as an award of damages. The right of an individual to take another person's resources (especially money) because that person has failed to meet the requirements of the law (e.g., the breach of a contract) is known as a **remedy.** As you study the following sections, identify the remedies available to those seeking through the courts what belongs to another, and keep in mind how important that adequately and fairly enforced sanctions are to a property-based legal system and how nations lacking adequate enforcement sanctions tend to be poor even when they claim to believe in private property.

16. FOR CRIMINAL CONDUCT

A *crime* is a public wrong against society. Criminal cases are brought by the government on behalf of the people. The people are represented by a state's attorney or U.S. attorney or other public official. When a person is convicted of a crime, one of the following punishments may be imposed:

> **Do** remember that the law divides crimes into misdemeanors and felonies.

- Death.
- Imprisonment.
- Fine.
- Removal from office.
- Disqualification from holding any office and from voting.

Among the purposes of such punishments are to protect the public and to deter persons from wrongful conduct.

17. FOR BREACH OF CONTRACT

Legally enforceable agreements, called *contracts* (see Chapter 8), are vitally important to business because they allow buyers and sellers to exchange resources and shape their agreements any legal way they wish. When one party to a contract fails to do what he or she agreed to do, a **breach of contract** occurs. The usual remedy for a breach is a suit for dollar damages. These damages, called **compensatory damages,** are awarded to make the victim of the breach "whole" in the economic sense. Such damages compensate the

> **Compensatory damages** awarded for breach of contract attempt to make a plaintiff "whole," as though in an economic sense the defendant had not breached the contract.

party for all losses that are the direct and foreseeable result of the breach of contract. The objective is that the party be in as good a position as he or she would have been in had the contract been performed. Damages do not make most parties totally "whole," however, because they do not as a general rule include attorney's fees. Unless the contract or some special law provides to the contrary, parties to the contract litigation pay their own attorneys.

In addition to compensatory damages, breach-of-contract cases may award consequential damages when the breaching party knew or had reason to know that special circumstances existed that would cause the other party to suffer additional losses if the contract were breached.

There are other remedies available for a breach of contract. If a breach by one party is serious enough, the other party may be permitted to rescind or cancel the contract. In some circumstances, the remedy of an injured party may be a decree of **specific performance**—an order by the court commanding the other party actually to perform a bargain as agreed. The single largest number of lawsuits today, especially in the federal courts, involves one business suing another business for breach of contract.

> **Do** make sure to include a provision for the payment of attorney's fees in any contract loaning money or extending credit to someone.

18. FOR TORTIOUS CONDUCT

> Tort law helps protect property boundaries by providing *compensation* when someone wrongfully crosses such boundaries.

A **tort** is a civil wrong other than a breach of contract. Torts involve improper crossing of property boundaries, usually causing injury to our person or other things we own. The boundaries may be physical as when someone trespasses across the boundaries of another's land. Boundaries may also be behavioral as when someone acts unreasonably and injures another.

The law divides torts into the following three categories:

- **Intentional torts.** These torts all require the plaintiff (the person who initiates a lawsuit) to prove the defendant intended to cross the boundaries protecting the plaintiff. Intentional torts include assault (intentionally placing someone in apprehension of his physical safety), battery (intentionally making offensive, unconsented to physical contact with someone), conversion (intentionally depriving someone of goods owned), and trespass (intentionally crossing someone else's land boundaries without permission).
- **Negligence.** This tort requires the plaintiff to show that the defendant injured what was proper to the plaintiff through unreasonable behavior.
- **Strict liability.** Strict liability torts usually require the plaintiff to prove only that the defendant has injured something proper to the plaintiff. Injury caused by an ultrahazardous activity like blasting is an example.

> **Punitive damages** are a civil punishment for intentional or extremely negligent wrongdoing. Their purpose is to deter others from such conduct in the future.

In law, the sanction (or remedy) for tortious conduct is money damages. The damages compensate injured plaintiffs for medical expenses, lost wages or earning power, pain and suffering, and damages to other owned goods and land. **Punitive damages**—also called **exemplary damages**—are also appropriate when the tort is intentional or the unreasonable conduct is extremely severe.

19. FOR VIOLATING STATUTES AND REGULATIONS

Statutes at both the federal and state levels of government impose a variety of sanctions for violating the statutes or regulations of administrative agencies adopted to accomplish statutory purposes. These sanctions are often similar to those imposed for criminal conduct, breach of contract, or tortious conduct. Many statutes, for example, impose a fine for a violation and authorized damages to injured parties as well. Although common law did not make a defendant pay a plaintiff's attorney fees, many statutes do require so in various circumstances.

You should keep in mind that the sanctions imposed for violating statutes or administrative agency regulations are an important part of enforcing the property-based legal system. These laws help define boundaries and protect us from the boundary infringements of others. Regulations often set boundaries of what it is proper for businesses to do in producing and selling goods and competing with other producers in the market. Many of the chapters in this book examine the boundaries set by various business regulations.

concept :: *summary*

1. Persons and businesses convicted of criminal conduct may be fined, imprisoned, or both.
2. A party who breaches a contract may be required to pay as compensatory damages to the other party the sum of money required to make the victim whole. In addition, special circumstances may justify consequential damages.
3. A tort victim is entitled to collect as damages the amount of money necessary to compensate the injured party for the total harm caused by the intentional or negligent conduct of the wrongdoer.
4. Punitive damages may be awarded in the case of intentional torts.
5. Statutes and regulations issued by government agencies often authorize sanctions similar to those used in the criminal law, contracts, and torts. They usually go further by using a multiplier for damages and award attorney's fees as well.

:: A Property-Based Legal System and Corporate Governance

Under the rule of law in a property-based legal system, all persons have an equal right to their resources. Property problems arise when one person harms another's resources or takes them without permission or authorization. When a stranger takes your car without permission, we call this "theft," and it is easy to appreciate how it violates your right of property under the rule of law. However, more complex property problems can arise.

Much, if not most, business in the United States is transacted through large corporate business organizations. A **corporation** is a business chartered by the state to do business as a legal person in a certain form of organization. Chapter 11 will explain to you the details of corporate legal ownership but, briefly, a corporation is owned by *shareholders* who have *stock* in the business. They vote to elect the *board of directors* who legally run the business but who often hire *managers* to be in charge of day-to-day business operations. In large corporations, few shareholders sit on the board of directors or are managers of these businesses, and thus ownership is usually separate from resource control.

Corporations are businesses chartered by the state to do business as legal persons.

20. THE SPECIFIC SENSE OF CORPORATE GOVERNANCE

Because of the separation of ownership and control, corporate governance is very important. **Corporate governance** refers to the legal rules that structure, empower, and regulate the *agents* (primarily the board of directors and managers) of corporations and define their relationship to the owners (shareholders). Specifically, *corporate governance rules protect the property interest that the owners have in corporations.*

Because of the complexity of modern corporations, there are sometimes breakdowns in corporate governance. Managers like the president, vice presidents, or chief financial officer of a corporation can abuse their control of its resources to benefit themselves in ways that impair or even destroy the corporation's value to the shareholders. For example, often these top managers have salaries, bonuses, or stock options that are tied to the corporation's profitability or stock price. If they manipulate the corporation's profit by puffing up assets or concealing debts, they may be able to raise their incomes by millions of dollars even as they mislead the owners about the true value of the corporation and risk corporate collapse when the true situation is disclosed. Other examples of corporate misgovernance include managers' engaging in insider trading of stock, running up stock prices in order to exercise stock options, and taking advantage of business opportunities that rightfully belong to the corporation and its shareholders.

All of these corporate governance failures adversely affect the owners of the corporation, especially when the misgovernance becomes publicly known. Only a relatively few business leaders may engage in such illegal conduct, but in recent years some spectacular failures of corporate governance have occurred. Managers at companies like Enron, Qwest, Global Crossing, Tyco, HealthSouth, Kmart, WorldCom, Adelphia, and ImClone have been criminally prosecuted and/or civilly sued. Tens of billions of dollars in shareholder value have been destroyed. At Enron alone, thousands of workers whose retirements were based on stock ownership of that mismanaged corporation have lost their entire pensions.

21. THE GENERAL SENSE OF CORPORATE GOVERNANCE

In a general sense, corporate governance also applies to the legal relationships that businesses have with each other, with their customers, and with society. For instance, in 2008 the collapse of many financial institutions led to a major economic recession. In part, the recession may have been caused by the government's encouragement of mortgage loans to expand housing. However, a major factor in the collapse was the risky lending practices of banks and other financial institutions that repackaged, sold, and resold hundreds of billions of dollars of housing loans that were inadequately secured. As long as housing prices were rising, many people made great deal of money, but when the housing bubble burst and prices began to decline, economic collapse occurred, affecting not only the financial institutions but also the entire economy because credit was too expensive or unavailable. It has been suggested that lack of adequate corporate governance has allowed the risky lending practices that ultimately have led to the biggest recession since the Great Depression of the 1930s. A number of the chapters that follow discuss the general corporate governance that has followed this recession.

:: Key Terms

:: Review Questions and Problems

Introduction

1. *Why Nations Are Economically Weak or Strong*

   (a) Identify several reasons put forth to explain why nations are prosperous or poor.

   (b) What does this section say is the foundation of the private market and prosperity?

Law, the Rule of Law, and Property

2. *Law*

   (a) Define law. Compare and contrast law and custom.

   (b) What role do the courts and police play in the legal system?

3. *The Rule of Law*

   (a) Define the rule of law. How does the rule of law differ from law as the commands of the state?

   (b) Explain why the rule of law is "an ideal rather than a complete fact."

4. *Property*

   (a) What is property? How does property differ from "resources"?

   (b) Why is property important to society? To private enterprise?

5. *Property in Its Broadest Sense*

   (a) Explain why property can be thought of as the central concept underlying Western legal systems.

   (b) What does James Madison mean when he says we have property in our opinions "and free communication of them."

6. *Jurisprudence*

   (a) Define jurisprudence and name four schools of jurisprudence.

   (b) Describe the main difference between the jurisprudences of natural law and sociological jurisprudence.

Classifications of Law

7. *Common Law and Civil Law*

   (a) What is "common law"? Why is the United States a "common law country"?

   (b) What is the primary distinction between common law and civil law legal systems?

8. *Public and Private Law*

    (a) What is public law? Give three examples of public law.

    (b) Explain private law. Give three examples.

9. *Civil Law and Criminal Law*

    (a) What is the difference between civil law and criminal law?

    (b) Explain the two ways that the words *civil law* are used in this chapter.

10. *Substantive Law and Procedural Law*

    (a) Define substantive law and procedural law.

    (b) Is contract law substantive law or procedural law? How about a rule specifying that a defendant has 30 days to respond to a complaint?

Sources of Law

11. *Constitutions*

    (a) Explain what it means to say that constitutions are the "highest laws of the nation"?

    (b) Explain the important distinctions between state and federal constitutions.

12. *Legislation*

    (a) Give two additional terms for *legislation*.

    (b) Why is uniformity of law important to business? How can legislators achieve uniformity of the laws affecting business? What is the most significant uniform law affecting business?

    (c) What is statutory construction?

13. *Administrative Regulation*

    (a) Where do administrative agencies come from?

    (b) For what purposes do administrative agencies exist?

14. *Judicial Decisions or Case Law*

    (a) Define *stare decisis*. What are its advantages? Disadvantages?

    (b) What is the distinction between a precedent and dicta in judicial decisions, and how does this distinction relate to *stare decisis*?

    (c) Alex was on a coast-to-coast trip by automobile. While passing through Ohio, Alex had a flat tire. It was fixed by Sam's Turnpike Service Station, and later, while Alex was driving in Indiana, the tire came off and Alex was injured. Alex was hospitalized in Indiana, so he sued Sam in Indiana for the injuries. What rules of substantive law will the Indiana court use to determine if Sam is at fault? Explain.

15. *Sources of Law Hierarchy in Review*

    (a) Explain the relationship of case law to the other sources of law.

Legal Sanctions

16. *For Criminal Conduct*

    (a) What is a sanction? A remedy?

    (b) What are the criminal sanctions?

17. *For Breach of Contract*

    (a) What is the purpose of compensatory damages?

    (b) What is specific performance of a contract?

18. *For Tortious Conduct*

    (a) What are the two premises of tort liability?

    (b) When are punitive damages appropriate in a tort case?

19. *For Violating Statutes and Regulations*

    (a) What types of sanctions are used for the violation of statutes and regulations?

    (b) What is an injunction?

A Property-Based Legal System and Corporate Governance

20. *The Specific Sense of Corporate Governance*
    (a) What is the "specific" sense of corporate governance?
    (b) Why might some managers try to artificially raise or "puff up" the market price of their stocks? Describe several ways they could do this.

21. *The General Sense of Corporate Governance*
    (a) What is the "general" sense of corporate governance?
    (b) Discuss how effective corporate governance contributes to the creation of economic wealth.

business :: *discussions*

1. As the vice president of finance for a company producing and selling electronic switchboards, you are considering foreign investment to build a plant to assemble electronic components. A source in Russia advises you that a town near Moscow may be an excellent location for a new plant. Russians are well educated and willing to work for reasonable wages. Projected construction costs are acceptable. Both rail lines and airports are nearby, and the current Russian government seems politically stable. The town even has a technical college that will be an excellent source for skilled employees. The plant will ship most of the finished electronic components back to the United States.

Do you know everything you need to make an investment decision?

If not, what else do you need to know about investment in foreign countries?

What does it mean to say that law is the foundation of the private enterprise system?

2. Three years ago the Darden Corporation bought a thousand acres of land that borders the Potowac River in Washam County. While waiting on development opportunities, Darden cut timber to help repay the mortgage loan it took out to buy the land. On March 2, the Washam County Commission proposed an ordinance to establish a 250-foot-wide greenway along the south side of the Potowac that will effectively ban both development and timbering on nearly 80 acres of Darden's land. The same day in an unrelated accident a Darden truck ran over a hunter who was hunting without permission on the company's land. Darden immediately contacted an attorney in Washam City.

- What is law?
- What does it mean to say that Darden has "property" in the land? That the hunter has "property" in himself?
- What sources of law will the attorney have to understand in order to advise Darden about the proposed greenway? The company's potential responsibility to the hunter?

2

The Ethical Basis of Law and Business Management

Learning Objectives ::

In this chapter you will learn:

1. To appreciate the connection between law and ethical principles.

2. To grasp why ethical consequentialism and not ethical formalism has been the chief source of values for business ethics.

3. To develop an individual framework for ethical values in business.

4. To analyze the obstacles and rewards of ethical business practice in our property-based legal system.

Historian Barbara Tuchman was asked, "What's happened to the world of Washington, Adams, and Jefferson?" She replied that we suffer today from "a loss of moral sense, of knowing the difference between right and wrong, and being governed by it." In recent years the emphasis on business ethics shows concern about regaining this moral sense. The close connection between ethics and law makes a discussion of moral sense especially significant to a book on the legal environment.

Justice Oliver Wendell Holmes wrote, "The law is the witness and external deposit of our moral life. Its history is the history of the moral development of the race." Ethical (or moral) values underlie much law, including the law of how business operates and is regulated, making it important for business students to know about the nature of ethics, sources of ethics, and problems of achieving an ethical business organization. This chapter introduces the study of business ethics by examining the current concern over business ethics. It explores the relationship of morality and ethics and then of ethics and law. Two principal approaches to ethics are presented: formalism and consequentialism.

Next, the chapter looks at ethical values for business decision making. It examines trends and looks at four sources of ethical values:

- Legal regulation.
- Professional codes of ethics.
- Codes of ethics from business organizations.
- Individual values.

The chapter also considers the problems faced in achieving an ethical business organization. When in groups, people often decide and act differently from the way they act as individuals. This fact has special significance for ethics in business corporations. The chapter examines how the profit motive and business bureaucracy put pressure on ethical decision making and how ethical reform must begin with the top leadership of business organizations. The importance of open communication to the ethical life of a business organization is emphasized, and several strategies for implementing corporate ethics are presented.

Finally, the chapter examines the morality of property, the legal right to exclude others from the resources one has or acquires. The concept of property has moral implications because it recognizes an exclusive private sphere of effort and resources on which the community and the state have no legal claim. It also permits individuals to acquire unequal amounts of the resources that others may need or want. In the broad sense, property reflects moral values concerning the allocation of resources among people.

:: Contemporary Business Ethics

U.S. customs agents caught the president of Ann Taylor, a large chain store, trying to avoid paying duty on $125,000 worth of wristwatches for his personal collection. A substantial civil penalty was proposed. At an Ann Taylor board of directors meeting, one director told the president: "This calls into question your integrity." The president resigned from the company.

More than ever before, business ethics are of concern to the business community and to society. In the 1980s few corporations hired people as ethics officers. Today over 20 percent of big companies have ethics officers whose job is to develop ethics policies, listen to complaints of ethics violations, and investigate ethics abuses. Yet large numbers of employees continue to report ethical misconduct according to the National Business Ethics Survey. In 2007, 56 percent of the employees surveyed reported observing misconduct such as conflicts of interest, abusive or intimidating behavior, and lying to employees.

According to the 2007 National Business Ethics Survey, an increasing percentage of employees believe their fellow employees are *not* committed to ethics. The figure rose from 25 percent of employees in 2003 who believed this, to 34 percent in 2005, and 39 percent in 2007.

1. ETHICS AND SOCIETY

Ours is a diverse society, formed from many ethnic backgrounds, races, and religions. As a result, we have few shared ethical values to guide behavior. When a business decision maker does not share common values with society in general, any decision made has a greater likelihood of arousing ethical concern than if there is a common code of behavior and universally accepted values. Diversity fosters concern over values, and in recent years American society has become more openly pluralistic. Several trends illustrate society's concern over the possible fragmentation of ethical values at home, at school, and in business.

Public Education and Family Structure The rising concern over business ethics responds to a decline in public education and the family structure as sources for ethical teaching. Increasingly sensitive to challenges of bias, school systems have reduced their involvement in promoting shared ethical values and increased their emphasis on the teaching of "value-free" facts. At the same time, the rising divorce rate and numbers of single parents, as well as the tendency of both spouses to work outside the home, have decreased the time families spend together and their power in sharing and shaping ethical values.

Economic Interdependence Increasing economic interdependence promotes concerns about business ethics. Not even farm families are self-sustaining. Each of us depends on business and industry for our every necessity—food, clothing, shelter, and energy. The marketplace dominates all aspects of life, and how the marketplace is conducted concerns us. The decisions people in business make have a significant impact on us. When there is a labor-management dispute in the coal industry, our source of electricity is threatened. When manufacturers conspire to raise prices, the cost of our goods goes up. The sale of dangerous pesticides or impure drugs threatens our health. A management decision to close a plant may threaten our jobs.

News Media and the Internet Extensive coverage of business decisions and their impact on society makes us more aware than ever of failures of business ethics. The news media and the Internet make it increasingly difficult to hide the questionable behavior of large organizations. From the coverage of stock market manipulations to accounts of Enron's and Arthur Andersen's collapse, the news media and Internet heighten public attention and concern. What used to be considered private is now considered public. The ethical issues that surround nearly every significant business decision are easier to see than they once were.

Refer now to Sidebar 2.1. These trends are of particular concern, since by the time they are in high school, students have often formed values that are not appropriate for ethical business practice.

2. ETHICS AND GOVERNMENT

These changes in society have been accompanied by changes in the role of government. When business fails to make ethical decisions, when it fails to

When asked "which of the following statements about ethics was most often transmitted by those of your professors who discussed ethical or moral issues?" 73 percent of college students chose "what is right and wrong depends on differences in individual values and cultural diversity."
Source: National Association of Scholars

Numerous blogs criticize the ethical missteps of business and government.

:: sidebar 2.1

Ethics and High School Students

In 2006 the nonpartisan Josephson Institute of Ethics surveyed 25,000 high school students. They found that 92 percent of the students claim they are "satisfied with my own ethics and character." Yet, consider what these same students believe and admit to doing:

- 59 percent say that "In the real world, successful people do what they have to do to win even if others consider it cheating."
- 42 percent think that "A person has to lie or cheat sometimes in order to succeed."
- 82 percent admit that they lied to their parents within the past 12 months "about something significant."

- 62 percent admit they lied to a teacher within the past 12 months "about something significant."
- 60 percent cheated during a test at school within the past 12 months.
- 23 percent stole something from a parent or other relative within the past 12 months.
- 19 percent stole something from a friend within the past 12 months.
- 28 percent stole something from a store within the past 12 months.

live up to society's expectations for ethical behavior, government may step in. As the chapters in this book demonstrate, in the last century, government has been increasingly active in regulating business.

In response, business leaders have become increasingly concerned with business ethics precisely because they want to limit further governmental regulation. They recognize that by encouraging ethical conduct and self-regulation within business organizations, they will prevent outside standards from being imposed on them through public law. As a consequence, both business and industry have, in recent decades, developed codes of ethics. Such efforts by professions and businesses to set standards of behavior are evidence of the increasing tendency toward self-regulation.

Federal law also encourages self-regulation. Federal sentencing guidelines reduce criminal fines for legal violations in companies that have taken specific steps to self-police ethical/legal conduct. See Chapter 12.

Don't forget that federal law reduces criminal punishment for companies that take certain steps to control their ethical/legal conduct.

:: The Nature of Ethics

In 1759 Adam Smith wrote, "However selfish man believes himself to be, there is no doubt that there are some elements in his nature which lead him to concern himself about the fortune of others, in such a way that their happiness is necessary for him, although he obtains nothing from it except the pleasure of seeing it." With this statement the author of *The Wealth of Nations,* perhaps the most famous book on economic theory ever written, recognized a moral element in human nature that goes beyond self-interest.

What is it that makes us care about the fortunes of others? The next sections examine the nature of ethics. What is morality? What are ethics? How are morality and ethics similar? How do ethics relate to law? What are the major ethical systems? How do these systems apply to business decision making? When you have finished reading these sections, come back to these questions and see if you can answer them.

3. ETHICS AND MORALITY

Since earliest childhood we have been told about "right and wrong," "good and bad." It is right (good) to tell the truth. It is right to help others. It is right to obey your parents. It is wrong (bad) to lie. It is wrong to cheat and steal. It is wrong to hurt others. Through such teaching we develop values about right and wrong. These values that guide our behavior constitute our **morality.**

In society at large the sharing of moral values promotes social cooperation and is a significant means of social control. Shared moral values lead us to accept and trust others. Shared values allow us to recognize when there is proper behavior in others and where limits to behavior rightfully belong. Shared moral values create social harmony.

The sharing of values in business life is as important as it is in other aspects of our lives. Today many businesses try to foster shared moral values in employees. It is right to strive for quality in products and service. It is wrong to discriminate against or harass a person because of race, gender, or religion. One of the successes of many Japanese companies has been to instill shared moral values in their employees.

Internationally, businesses often face problems when they do business with nations with different moral values. What is wrong in the United States may be right somewhere else and vice versa. Is it right to bribe customs officials so that your company's goods can enter a country? Is it wrong for a woman to appear in public without her face covered? Is it right to eat meat and consume alcohol? Is it wrong to talk business on Sunday? On Saturday? On Friday evening? To succeed in international operations, businesses must be sensitive to differences in moral values.

If morals involve what is right and wrong, **ethics** is a systematic statement of right and wrong together with a philosophical system that both justifies and necessitates rules of conduct. In the Judeo-Christian tradition, for example, private ownership of land and goods is highly valued. It is wrong to take something that does not belong to you—hence the rule "Thou shalt not steal."

Ethics involves a rational method for examining our moral lives, not only for recognizing what is right and wrong but also for understanding why we think something is right or wrong. "The unexamined life is not worth living," said the Greek philosopher Socrates. In other words, ethical self-examination is necessary for a meaningful human life.

The end result of ethical examination is what philosophers call **the good.** The concept of the good is central to the study of morality. *The good* may be defined as those moral goals and objectives we choose to pursue. It serves to define who we are. Thus, *leading a good life* means more than *having the good life.* It means more than material possessions and luxury. It means pursuing intangibles, being concerned, as Adam Smith put it, about the fortunes

Morality is the collection of values that guides our behavior.

Ethics is a systematic statement of our *morality.* Sometimes the two terms are used interchangeably.

of others. That many in contemporary society do not achieve the good is evident. Mortimer Adler has observed: "Go on a hiking trip with a typical American and listen to what he talks about. . . . He'll talk about food, the weather, football, money, sex. He may seem to be having a good time, but he lacks much that is needed for the good life." Too often, we confuse a good time with a good life.

In summary, morality involves what we mean by our values of right and wrong. Ethics is a formal system for deciding what is right and wrong and for justifying moral decisions. In everyday language, the terms *morality* and *ethics* are often used interchangeably. This chapter will also sometimes use the two words to mean the same thing.

4. ETHICS AND LAW

Ethics and law have similar or complementary purposes. Both consist of rules to guide conduct and foster social cooperation. Both deal with what is right and wrong. Society's ethical values may become law through legislation or court decisions, and obedience to law is often viewed as being ethically correct. That society's ethical values often become law is the subject of Sidebar 2.2.

:: *sidebar* 2.2

Price Gouging after Hurricane Katrina

In 2005, Hurricane Katrina crippled many oil rigs in the Gulf of Mexico and temporarily put out of commission several oil refineries along the coast. The devastation caused a shortage of gasoline.

Responding to reduced supply and constant or increased demand, the price of gasoline shot up, doubling or in some instances tripling in price. Economists urge that retail price increases help ensure that those drivers who need and want gasoline the most will be able to get it during times of shortage. Price increases reduce unimportant driving and promote conservation.

However, many people see soaring prices during times of emergency as unethical. Almost half the states have passed laws prohibiting too rapid rises of retail prices during times of declared emergency. Throughout the South, there were numerous fines imposed for illegal "price gouging" after Katrina. And when following the hurricane the oil companies reported record profits, there was an outpouring of public criticism. Do you think it should be illegal to profit during times of public emergency?

However, there are also differences between ethics and law. Unlike ethical systems, the legal system is an institution of the state. The state enforces legal rules through civil and criminal sanctions, like monetary damage awards, fines, and imprisonment. Many ethical values (regarding the treatment of animals, for example) are not enforced by the state, and many laws (regarding traffic violations, for example) do not address ethical concerns.

Another difference between ethics and law concerns motivation. Although values found in ethics may be imposed on an individual (by the family, the company, or the law), the motivation to observe moral rules comes from within. On the other hand, even though the values found in law may also be personal ethical values of an individual, the motivation to observe the law comes from outside the individual in the form of state sanctions. As Justice Oliver Wendell Holmes explained:

> You can see very plainly that a bad man has as much reason as a good one for wishing to avoid an encounter with the public force, and therefore you can see the practical importance of the distinction between morality and law. A man who cares nothing for an ethical rule which is believed and practiced by his neighbors is likely nevertheless to care a good deal to avoid being made to pay money, and will want to keep out of jail if he can.

Ethical systems also involve a broader-based commitment to proper behavior than does the law. Law sets only the minimum standards acceptable to a society. As a former chief executive officer of Procter & Gamble points out: "Ethical behavior is based on more than meeting minimum legal requirements. It invariably involves a higher, moral standard."

Ultimately, the commitment to ethical values is superior to mere observance of the law in ensuring responsible business behavior. Legal rules can never be specific enough to regulate all business actions that may have socially undesirable or even dangerous consequences. And lawmakers often do not have the information to know whether specific conduct threatens employees, consumers, or the public generally. They may also lack the consensus to act quickly, or to act at all, in the face of potentially harmful business actions. However, a commitment to acceptable business ethics will usually ensure responsible business behavior.

*Ethical values are ultimately superior to law in ensuring responsible business behavior.

:: Two Systems of Ethics

Two principal systems of ethics dominate thinking about morality in Western civilization. They are formalism and consequentialism. Although these two systems are not mutually exclusive in the outcomes of their moral analyses, they begin from different assumptions. Most people adopt elements of both systems in making ethical choices. *It is very important to appreciate how these systems have influenced your own values and moral beliefs even though until now you may have been unaware of it.*

5. FORMALISM

Formalism is an approach to ethics that affirms an absolute morality. A particular act is in itself right or wrong, always and in every situation. For example, lying is wrong. There are no justifications for it, and its wrongness does not depend on the situation in which the lie is told. Formalism is primarily a duty-based view of ethics. To be ethical, you have a **duty,** or moral obligation, not to lie. You have a duty to keep promises. You have a duty not to divulge confidences.

For the formalist (one who expresses the ethics of formalism), the ethical focus is on the worth of the individual. Individuals have rights, and these rights should not be infringed, even at the expense of society as a whole, because they have an intrinsic moral value to them. The Bill of Rights illustrates this view of the rights of individuals. When the First Amendment states "Congress shall make no law . . . abridging the freedom of speech," it takes the formalist approach.

Do remember that formalism says certain behaviors are *always* wrong.

Adam Smith meant that the right of ownership was an absolute value when he referred to "sacred property."

Categorical imperative
(Kant) says that you have a moral duty to act in the way you believe everyone should act.

Kant and Formalism   For the formalist thinker Immanuel Kant (1724–1804), to be ethical requires that you act with a good intent. To have a good intent, you have to act in ways that are ethically consistent. This emphasis on consistency Kant called the **categorical imperative.** You have a moral duty to act in the way you believe everyone should act. You should never act in a certain way unless you are willing to have everyone else act in the same way. You cannot make an exception for your own action. You cannot say, "I can lie (cheat) (steal) (cause injury), but others should not do this to me (to my family) (to my friends)." Kant said that to make an exception for your own behavior is immoral and unethical. Note the similarities between Kant's categorical imperative and the Golden Rule: "Do to others as you would have others do to you."

Formalist thinking raises many questions for business ethics. Are you treating your employees with respect for their rights as individuals, or are you treating them only as units of production to make a profit? If you are willing to lie about your ability to meet a production schedule in order to get a new customer, are you willing to have the customer lie to you about his or her ability to pay? If you pass on information that was told to you in confidence, are you willing to have your confidences passed on? Can business function with widespread lying, cheating, and stealing and without respect for the rights of individuals?

In his novel *The Turquoise Lament,* John D. MacDonald puts words into the mouth of his Travis McGee character that illustrate well a formalist approach:

> Integrity is not a conditional word. It doesn't blow in the wind or change in the weather. It is your inner image of yourself, and if you look in there and see a man who won't cheat, then you know he never will. Integrity is not a search for the rewards for integrity.

Table 2.1 illustrates other examples of a formalist approach to ethics.

The Social Contract   The social contract theory of Harvard philosopher John Rawls furnishes an important recent example of how formalism has influenced thinking about business and personal ethics. This theory is based not on duty but on contract (agreement).

table 2.1 :: Examples of Ethical Formalism

:: Statement	:: Source
"We hold these truths to be self-evident."	Declaration of Independence
"Thou shalt not steal."	The Ten Commandments
"A sale made because of deception is wrong. . . . The end doesn't justify the means."	Caterpillar Code of Ethics
"There are fundamental values that cross cultures, and companies must uphold them."	Thomas Donaldson, business ethics scholar
"Openness in communications is deemed fundamental."	Business Roundtable
The moral sense is "the sense of what is inherently right and wrong. . . ."	Barbara Tuchman, historian

Social contract theory concerns itself with how to construct a just society given the many inequalities of wealth, knowledge, and social status. Rawls suggests a simple first step in determining the ethical values on which a just society can be built. We should assume that we do not know our age, gender, race, intelligence, strength, wealth, or social status. This step is vital because it keeps us from being self-interested in the ethical values we consider. For example, not knowing our sex or race, will we agree that it is ethical to discriminate in employment compensation based on sex or race? Not knowing our wealth, will we agree that owning property is a fair prerequisite to being able to vote? Not knowing our age or work status, will we agree that it is just for a company to have mandatory retirement of its officers at age 65? Freeing ourselves of self-knowledge, Rawls argues, improves our ability to evaluate the terms of a fair agreement (contract) under which we enter society or join an organization like a corporation.

Placing himself behind a veil of self-ignorance, Rawls proposes two ethical principles. First, everyone is entitled to certain equal basic rights, including liberty, freedom of association, and personal security. Second, although there may be social and economic inequalities, these inequalities must be based on what a person does, not on who a person is, and everyone must have an equal opportunity for achievement. Since there are natural differences of intelligence and strength and persistent social differences of wealth, class, and status, defining "equal opportunity" is crucial to this second ethical principle. Rawls insists that individuals in a just society have the right to an equal place at the starting line. This is as true within a corporation as it is within a country.

Because of its emphasis on individual rights and self-worth, social contract theory has its origin in formalism. It provides a powerful process for ethical business decision making. Social contract theory is especially valuable in international business. In this arena, in the absence of much law, businesses from various cultures must agree as to the terms under which international business is to take place.

*Rawls's "veil of ignorance" means to think ethically you must lose the assumption that what you personally need or want is necessarily morally correct.

6. CONSEQUENTIALISM

The second principal system of ethics is consequentialism. **Consequentialism** concerns itself with the moral consequences of actions rather than with the morality of the actions themselves. For the consequentialist, lying itself is not unethical. It is the consequences, or end results of lying, that must be evaluated for their ethical implications. It is the loss of trust or harm done by lying that is unethical.

If formalism focuses on individual rights, consequentialism focuses on the common good. The ethics of actions are measured by how they promote the common good. If actions increase the common good, they are ethical. If actions cause overall harm to society, they are unethical.

The dominant form of consequentialism is **utilitarianism.** Utilitarianism judges actions by *usefulness,* by whether they serve to increase the common good. For utilitarians, the end justifies the means. But to judge the utility of a particular action, it is necessary to consider alternative courses of action. Only after you consider all reasonable courses of action can you know whether a particular one has the greatest utility.

The International Franchising Association (IFA) adopted a new code of ethics. Officers of the association indicated that an important reason for adopting the new code was to head off government regulation of franchising

Modern economic theory reflects utilitarianism.

through self-policing. The code states that when a franchiser is going to make a decision about adding a new franchise outlet into an area where a franchisee already owns an existing outlet, it should weigh "the positive or negative effect of the new outlet on the existing outlet." Another factor to be considered is "the benefit or detriment to the franchise system as a whole in operating the new outlet." The motivation of the IFA in adopting the new ethics code and the quoted language of the code suggest a consequentialist ethical view. Table 2.2 gives other examples of consequentialism.

Although business ethics reflect elements of both formalism and consequentialism, they focus more heavily on the latter. Business leaders feel a need to justify what they do in terms of whether or not it produces dividends for their shareholders. Their primary goal or end is to produce a profit. This orientation reflects consequentialism.

The many statements of business leaders that ethics are "good for business" illustrate this point. These statements imply that certain values are important because their end result is useful in increasing productivity and profit rather than because the values are intrinsically good. The way business managers evaluate alternative courses of action through cost-benefit analysis is a form of consequentialism.

One approach to business ethics, called "values-based management," also illustrates consequentialism. The emphasis of this approach teaches ethical values to employees that enhance the profitability of the company. Examples include why it is wrong to use company computers for personal entertainment during work hours and why it is unethical to use company long-distance phone service to contact friends and relatives. Sidebar 2.3 explores one of these examples.

The Protestant Ethic   In part, the current focus on consequentialism in business ethics is due to the decline in business life of what has been described as the **Protestant ethic.** With the Protestant Reformation of the sixteenth century came a new emphasis on the importance of the individual. Instead of relying on the intercession of a church hierarchy to achieve grace, each person, Protestants asserted, had the means to address God personally. Thus religion provided the impetus to hard work and achievement. Human desire and indulgence, said

> In the book *Moral Intelligence: Enhancing Business Performance & Leadership Success* (2004), Doug Lennick and Fred Kiel use research to show that the best performing companies are led by those who can effectively promote moral principles throughout their organizations.

table 2.2 :: Examples of Ethical Consequentialism	
:: Statement	**:: Source**
"There is no doubt that ethics pays off at the bottom line."	CEO, Procter & Gamble
"Loss of confidence in an organization is the single greatest cost of unethical behavior."	CEO, KPMG
"The strongest argument for raising the ethics bar boils down to self-interest."	CEO, KPMG
"Cost-benefit analysis (used by various governmental agencies and in business and finance)."	Economic theory, finance theory, and policy studies
"The greatest happiness of the greatest number is the foundation of morals and legislation."	Jeremy Bentham (1748–1832), English social philosopher

---

:: *sidebar* 2.3

Virtual Morality

Computers and the ease with which employees can use them for personal as well as employment reasons raise many ethical issues, which some have begun terming *virtual morality.* Is it wrong to use the Internet from work for holiday shopping? To help one's children with schoolwork? To send personal e-mail to a friend on the other side of the country? To hunt for a new job? Some businesses prohibit all personal use of company computers. Others, such as Boeing Company, permit personal use of computers during working hours, but limit such use to "reasonable duration and frequency." Even then such use should not cause "embarrassment to the company."

From the perspective of values-based management, it is easy to see that keeping employees from wrongful computer use may improve the profitability of the employer. On the other hand, improper use of what another owns raises individual moral issues as well. Similarly, if an employer has purchased the time and effort of an employee, is it morally right for the employee to use those resources for personal reasons?

Increasingly, employers are monitoring how employees use their computers. Currently over a third of large U.S. companies use software to monitor employee e-mails and website visits.

Protestants, should be bent to God's will through self-denial, rational planning, and productivity. The Protestant ethic was rooted in a formalist approach: honesty and keeping promises were intrinsically good.

The Protestant ethic was a boon to capitalism. The quest for economic independence fueled commercial growth, which fueled industrial growth, which created our modern consumer society. Along the way, however, the religious basis of the Protestant ethic was eroded by rising wealth and the encouragement of mass consumption. The part of the ethic that supported hard work, success, and rational planning continued, but without the original absolute moral values. The Protestant ethic became transformed into an organizational ethic that supports the modern bureaucratic managerial system. The sociologist Robert Jackall identifies this system as having "administrative hierarchies, standardized work procedures, regularized timetables, uniform policies, and centralized control." The goal of this system is to produce profit. Business actions are justified by their usefulness in accomplishing the goal. The religious formalism of the Protestant ethic has become a type of utilitarian consequentialism.

> The absolute moral values of the Protestant ethic declined. Hard work and planning become justified by the consequentialist results they produce.

7. COMPARING THE TWO ETHICAL SYSTEMS

Formalists and consequentialists can arrive at the same conclusion for an ethical course of action, but they use a different evaluation process. Figure 2.1 illustrates how this might happen. Take as an example a company's decision whether or not to secretly monitor its employees' use of the e-mail system. The company suspects that some employees are using the system for personal business and to spread damaging rumors about the company and its executives. How would formalists and consequentialists approach this decision?

Formalists might say that secret monitoring treats employees only as a means to the end of increasing organizational efficiency and does not respect their self-worth as individuals. The monitoring also does not respect their dignity and their privacy. Formalists might conclude that secret monitoring

Figure 2.1
A common result

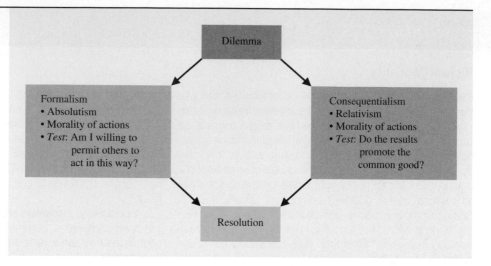

In 2005 someone discovered that Sony BMG had secretly inserted a spyware program in several million CDs. The spyware installed itself when buyers ran the CDs on their computers. What are the ethics of this business decision?

is unethical. Explaining the problem to the employees and asking for their consent to monitor would be a more ethical action to take.

For a consequentialist, the act of secret monitoring itself is ethically neither right nor wrong. It is the end result that is ethically important. Secret monitoring and the punishment of wrongdoers are useful in improving productivity, which is an appropriate company goal and beneficial to society at large. To that extent, secret monitoring is ethically acceptable. But the punishment of wrongdoers will likely reveal to all employees that their e-mail has been secretly monitored. This breach of trust can lower employee morale and lessen employee loyalty to the company. Overall productivity may fall. In the examination of alternative solutions to the problem, a more beneficial overall solution, and thus a more ethical one, might be to explain the problem to the employees and ask for their consent to monitor all e-mail messages.

This example of the thinking processes of formalists and consequentialists does not exhaust all of the possible approaches that these groups might take to the e-mail problem. It does emphasize the fact that both formalist and consequentialist thinking can lead to the same business decision.

One of the most complex problems of contemporary business ethics concerns the promotion and sale of tobacco products. Cigarette smoking alone kills hundreds of thousands of people every year in the United States. Bring to bear your new knowledge about ethics by evaluating the tobacco facts presented in Sidebar 2.4. No one ever said that ethical evaluation would be easy.

:: Sources of Values for Business Ethics

There are at least four sources of values for business ethics. The sections that follow identify them as:

- Legal regulation.
- Professional codes of ethics.
- Organizational codes of ethics.
- Individual values.

:: *sidebar* 2.4

Tobacco Facts

Consider the ethical significance of the following facts:

Tobacco products have been consumed in the United States since at least the early 1600s.

Hundreds of thousands of people are involved in the growing, manufacturing, distributing, and selling of tobacco products.

In the first 20 years of tobacco litigation, juries did not award plaintiffs a single penny against tobacco companies.

Scientists and doctors accept that tobacco consumption is an important contributing factor in cancer and heart disease. Excess consumption of fatty foods and lack of exercise are also contributing factors to these diseases.

Some 435,000 people in the United States, or 1 percent of all cigarette smokers, die prematurely every year due to tobacco consumption.

Health-related tobacco disease costs more than $75 billion annually in spending for medical care.

The average age of beginning tobacco consumption is around 16.

Almost no one begins tobacco consumption past age 21. Three thousand new teenagers begin tobacco consumption every day.

Tobacco companies spend approximately $13 billion annually in advertising and marketing tobacco sales. A main strategy of tobacco promotion is to associate glamour, excitement, sex, and desirable life images with tobacco consumption. Another strategy is to get young people to sample cigarettes and other tobacco products.

The law requires that health warnings accompany the advertising and sale of tobacco products.

The nicotine in tobacco is considered addictive. However, millions have stopped tobacco consumption.

*Primary sources: Federal Trade Commission Cigarette Report (2007), Centers for Disease Control, *The New York Times*

8. LEGAL REGULATION

Insider trading, bribery, fraudulent practices, and conflicts of interest are often cited as examples of ethical failures. But these practices are illegal as well. That the unethical may be illegal and vice versa is often confusing to students.

The way to understand the ethical-legal relationship is to realize that in our society ethical values frequently become law and that legal regulation can reflect society's ethical values. For example, society's ethical commitment to equal opportunity became law in the Civil Rights Act of 1964, which prohibits employment discrimination based on "race, sex, color, religion, and national origin."

At the same time, the very existence of legal regulation can influence society's view of what is ethical. In 1964, when the Civil Rights Act was passed, few people were concerned about sex discrimination in employment. Opponents of the bill inserted the prohibition against sex discrimination in hopes of preventing its passage. Obviously, these legislators believed that sex discrimination in employment was acceptable and that many others agreed with them. Despite their efforts, however, the Civil Rights Act passed, and over the years, as legal battles involving sex discrimination in employment were fought, Americans' moral sense of the importance of equal employment opportunity regardless of sex caught up with the law. Today a great

Don't forget that respect for law itself can help change moral values. Anti-discrimination laws have helped convince many people that discrimination based on race, gender, and religion is morally wrong.

majority of Americans believe women should not be discriminated against in employment simply because they are women and that such discrimination is wrong. To a significant extent, the law itself contributed to the change in values.

Legal regulation is, then, a significant source of values for business ethics. In fact, many business and professional organizations look to the law when drawing up their codes of ethical conduct. At least five major ethical rules can be drawn from the law. These include:

- Respect for the liberty and rights of others.
- The importance of acting in good faith.
- The importance of exercising due care.
- The importance of honoring confidentiality.
- Avoidance of conflicts of interest.

The following sections elaborate these concepts. These values derived from legal regulation are appropriate for use in ethical business decision making even when decisions do not involve legal issues.

Liberty and Rights   First, the law requires respect for the liberty and rights of others. We see this requirement in legislation protecting the right of privacy, promoting equal employment opportunity, and guaranteeing freedom of expression and due process of law. In one form or another, these legal rights often appear in ethical codes. Do you think that the concern for individual rights represents formalism or consequentialism?

*As legal principles, both liberty and property involve keeping others from interfering with what is *yours*.

Remember from Chapter 1 that respect for individual rights is historically connected to the legal concept of private property. To have exclusive legal rights over what you say (freedom of speech), for example, is quite similar to having exclusive rights to an area of land or a piece of machinery. The philosopher John Locke, who influenced the framers of the U.S. Constitution, even referred to "lives, liberties, and estates which I call by the general name *property.* "

Good Faith   The law requires that good faith be demonstrated in various economic and other transactions. An example comes from the Uniform Commercial Code, adopted in 49 of the 50 states. It requires that all sales of goods must be carried out in *good faith*, which means "honesty in intent" and "honesty in fact."

The reverse of good faith is *bad faith*, which can be understood as dishonesty in intent. In cases involving a bad faith withholding of amounts due under insurance policies, some courts and juries have severely punished defendant insurance companies with large punitive damage awards. Acting with an honest intent is the key to understanding good faith. Is looking at the intent of parties to a business contract evidence of formalism or consequentialism?

Constitutional law also involves many balancing tests. Do these tests illustrate formalism or consequentialism?

Due Care   Another ethical value reflecting legal rules requires the exercise of *due care* in our behavior. This value comes from the law of torts, which Justice Oliver Wendell Holmes said "abounds in moral phraseology." Due care derives from society's expectations about how fair and reasonable actions are. Due care promotes the common good. In negligence law, failure to exercise due (or reasonable) care is the principal element that triggers liability against the defendant. Courts have examined due care in negligence cases in terms of a balancing test. The likelihood that the defendant's conduct will cause harmful consequences, taken with the seriousness of the harmful consequences, is balanced against the effort required to avoid the harmful consequences. The balancing test is central to the concept of due care.

Consider the following problem of due care. Bridgestone/Firestone became aware that certain of its tires were showing defects at much higher rates than what might be thought of as normal. Still, the tires operated perfectly on hundreds of thousands of vehicles. Was the company ethically required to warn the public about the tires? To recall the tires? A very small fraction of all tires showed defects. What level of defect is acceptable without warning those who use a product? Ford Explorer sport utility vehicles used the Firestone tire, and Ford decided to recall and replace the tires in Saudi Arabia. But Ford did not notify U.S. safety authorities or the public about what it was doing overseas, even though the same tires were on Ford Explorers in the United States. Was Ford acting ethically? What would you need to know in order to decide?

Another form of the requirement to exercise due care comes from the Federal Guidelines for Sentencing for Criminal Convictions, which focus specifically on corporate white-collar crime. In determining what punishment a company should receive for the illegal business acts of its employees, the guidelines look at whether the company has "an effective program to prevent and detect violations of the law." An effective program is measured by whether "the organization exercised due diligence in seeking to prevent and detect criminal conduct by its employees and other agents." *Due diligence* is another way of saying "due care."

Chapter 12 further discusses the Federal Sentencing Guidelines.

As with the determination of due care in negligence law, the determination of due diligence in sentencing guidelines requires use of a balancing test. Considering the significance of the balancing test to the exercise of due care (or due diligence), do you think that formalist or consequentialist values are reflected?

Confidentiality   Honoring confidentiality is the fourth major ethical value emerging from the law and legal regulation. The legal requirement of honoring confidentiality appears in agency law generally and in the professional-client relationship in particular. For a CPA to share with unauthorized third parties what has been learned during a client's audit is professional malpractice. Likewise, it is malpractice for an attorney, physician, real estate broker, or any professional agent to tell others what a client (principal) has related in confidence.

In addition to not telling others of a confidence, an agent must in many instances not act on the confidence related by a principal. The securities laws make it a crime for agents like the officers and managers of a corporation to buy and sell corporate stock on information only they know. (See Chapter 15.) Many "insider trading" scandals have occurred because corporate agents illegally traded on confidential information they learned from their positions in the corporation.

The legal requirement of honoring confidences contains both formalist and consequentialist ethical values. Can you identify these values?

Conflicts of Interest   Often embodied in business codes of ethics, avoiding conflicts of interest is a final ethical value flowing from the law, especially from agency law. A conflict of interest occurs when one attempts to "serve two masters," and no agent or employee of one principal can secretly

Many people consider it a type of conflict of interest for accounting firms to both advise their clients on general financial matters and to audit them when audits may uncover financial wrongdoing.

work for another whose interest competes with that of the first principal. That is why a real estate agent may not represent both the seller and the buyer in a real estate transaction without permission from both parties.

Sometimes when corporations "go public" or otherwise sell new stock issues, they will give employees of their customers or suppliers the option of buying a number of the new stock shares at a special fixed price. If the market value of the stock rises, exercise of the stock options can be quite valuable to these employees as they resell the stock at market price. Is it a conflict of interest for employees of other companies to accept these stock options? Does it impair their objective judgment about continuing to do business with the corporation that has given them such a gift? Compaq Computer Corporation, Cisco Systems, and AT&T specifically forbid employees from accepting stock options from their suppliers or customers.

Conflicts of interest also arise in public service. For instance, it is a conflict of interest for a judge or administrative regulator to make a decision involving a company in which he or she owns stock. Note that in this instance the conflict of interest does not involve "serving two masters." The conflict arises because of the ownership interests that will make it difficult for the judge or regulator to make an unbiased decision. In terms of formalism and consequentialism, how do you evaluate the prohibition against conflicts of interest?

Twenty-three percent of 3,000 employees surveyed for the 2007 National Business Ethics Survey reported observing conflicts of interest at work.

concept :: *summary*

Ethical Values from Legal Regulation

- Respect the liberty and rights of others.
- Act in good faith.
- Exercise due care.
- Honor confidentiality.
- Avoid conflicts of interest.

9. PROFESSIONAL CODES OF ETHICS

Another important source of business ethics comes from the historic tradition of the professional codes of ethics. Professions such as law and medicine have long traditions of codes of ethical conduct. Other professions, and more recently business and industry in general, have developed and adopted codes of ethical conduct. Here we use portions of professional codes to demonstrate sources of ethical values that come from the development of group standards for ethical conduct.

We begin with selected excerpts from codes of conduct for two professions: marketing and accounting. These codes are the Ethical Norms and Values for Marketers from the American Marketing Association, shown in Sidebar 2.5, and the American Institute of Certified Public Accountants Code of Professional Conduct, which appears in Sidebar 2.6. Understand that what follows are only excerpts from these codes, which in full may run several pages.

Another set of group standards is the ethical code of certified public accountants. So important are ethics to the conduct of accounting that when

:: *sidebar* 2.5

Ethical Norms and Values for Marketers

PREAMBLE

The American Marketing Association commits itself to promoting the highest standard of professional ethical norms and values for its members. Norms are established standards of conduct that are expected and maintained by society and/or professional organizations. Values represent the collective conception of what people find desirable, important and morally proper. Values serve as the criteria for evaluating the actions of others. . . .

ETHICAL VALUES

Honesty—to be truthful and forthright in our dealings with customers and stakeholders.

- We will tell the truth in all situations and at all times.
- We will offer products of value that do what we claim in our communications.
- We will stand behind our products if they fail to deliver their claimed benefits.
- We will honor our explicit and implicit commitments and promises.

Responsibility—to accept the consequences of our marketing decisions and strategies.

- We will make strenuous efforts to serve the needs of our customers.
- We will avoid using coercion with all stakeholders.
- We will acknowledge the social obligations to stakeholders that come with increased marketing and economic power.
- We will recognize our special commitments to economically vulnerable segments of the market such as children, the elderly and others who may be substantially disadvantaged.

Fairness—to try to balance justly the needs of the buyer with the interests of the seller.

- We will represent our products in a clear way in selling, advertising and other forms of communication; this includes the avoidance of false, misleading and deceptive promotion.
- We will reject manipulations and sales tactics that harm customer trust.
- We will not engage in price fixing, predatory pricing, price gouging or "bait-and-switch" tactics.

- We will not knowingly participate in material conflicts of interest.

Respect—to acknowledge the basic human dignity of all stakeholders.

- We will value individual differences even as we avoid stereotyping customers or depicting demographic groups (e.g., gender, race, sexual orientation) in a negative or dehumanizing way in our promotions.
- We will listen to the needs of our customers and make all reasonable efforts to monitor and improve their satisfaction on an ongoing basis.
- We will make a special effort to understand suppliers, intermediaries and distributors from other cultures.
- We will appropriately acknowledge the contributions of others, such as consultants, employees and coworkers, to our marketing endeavors.

Openness—to create transparency in our marketing operations.

- We will strive to communicate clearly with all our constituencies.
- We will accept constructive criticism from our customers and other stakeholders.
- We will explain significant product or service risks, component substitutions or other foreseeable eventualities that could affect customers or their perception of the purchase decision.
- We will fully disclose list prices and terms of financing as well as available price deals and adjustments.

Citizenship—to fulfill the economic, legal, philanthropic and societal responsibilities that serve stakeholders in a strategic manner.

- We will strive to protect the natural environment in the execution of marketing campaigns.
- We will give back to the community through volunteerism and charitable donations.
- We will work to contribute to the overall betterment of marketing and its reputation.
- We will encourage supply chain members to ensure that trade is fair for all participants, including producers in developing countries.

:: *sidebar* 2.6

American Institute of Certified Public Accountants Code of Professional Conduct

These Principles of the Code of Professional Conduct of the American Institute of Certified Public Accountants express the profession's recognition of its responsibilities to the public, to clients, and to colleagues. They guide members in the performance of their professional responsibilities and express the basic tenets of ethical and professional conduct. The Principles call for an unswerving commitment to honorable behavior, even at the sacrifice of personal advantage.

In carrying out their responsibilities as professionals, members should exercise sensitive professional and moral judgments in all their activities.

As professionals, certified public accountants perform an essential role in society. Consistent with that role, members of the American Institute of Certified Public Accountants have responsibilities to all those who use their professional services. Members also have a continuing responsibility to cooperate with each other to improve the art of accounting, maintain the public's confidence, and carry out the profession's special responsibilities for self-governance. The collective efforts of all members are required to maintain and enhance the traditions of the profession.

Members should accept the obligation to act in a way that will serve the public interest, honor the public interest, and demonstrate commitment to professionalism.

A distinguishing mark of a profession is acceptance of its responsibility to the public. The accounting profession's public consists of clients, credit grantors, governments, employers, investors, the business and financial community, and others who rely on the objectivity and integrity of certified public accountants to maintain the orderly functioning of commerce. This reliance imposes a public interest responsibility on certified public accountants. The public interest is defined as the collective well-being of the community of people and institutions the profession serves.

In discharging their professional responsibilities, members may encounter conflicting pressures from among each of those groups. In resolving those conflicts, members should act with integrity, guided by the precept that when members fulfill their responsibility to the public, clients' and employers' interests are best served.

Arthur Andersen, once one of the world's oldest and largest accounting firms, was implicated in a cover-up of why the energy firm Enron collapsed, the entire accounting firm went out of business. Enron had contributed only a small percentage of the worldwide business of Arthur Andersen.

From these excerpts, the ethical values expressed in the codes of ethics for marketers and accountants may seem overly general in nature. But each code has pages of rules that apply to specific situations arising in the marketer-client and accountant-client relationship. As the state does not enforce these codes, it is not proper to call them law. Yet the professional organizations that have adopted these codes employ specific sanctions to back them up. Because the state will likely regulate these professions if they do not do so themselves, it is appropriate to term their ethical codes **self-regulation.**

10. ORGANIZATIONAL CODES OF ETHICS

There are few industrywide codes of ethics, so many businesses have adopted ethical codes at the individual organization level. Nearly all large corporations now have their own codes of business ethics, often called codes of conduct. These codes are obviously an important source of business ethics.

The Business Roundtable, a national group of senior business leaders, has identified a general list of topics that organizational codes of business ethics should cover. These include:

- Fundamental honesty and adherence to the law.
- Product safety and quality.
- Health and safety in the workplace.
- Conflicts of interest.
- Fairness in selling/marketing practices.
- Financial reporting.
- Supplier relationships.
- Pricing, billing, and contracting.
- Trading in securities/using inside information.
- Payments to obtain business/Foreign Corrupt Practices Act.
- Acquiring and using information about others.
- Security.
- Political activities.
- Protection of the environment.
- Intellectual property/proprietary information.

Different Approaches to Ethical Codes

Individual companies take different approaches to ethical codes. The Hertz Corporation has a one-page statement of general ethical principles. In part that statement reads: "We will conduct business ethically and honestly in dealing with our customers, suppliers and employees. We will treat our employees in the same fashion as we expect them to treat our customers—with dignity and respect."

*Some companies provide only general ethics guidelines to employees. Other companies provide very specific and detailed ethics rules.

Hertz's statement provides only general guidelines to ethical conduct rather than detailed definitions of what kind of ethical behavior the company expects in specific instances.

Boeing Corporation also has a short code of conduct (see Sidebar 2.7).

Other companies spell out their expectations for employees' behavior in considerable detail. For instance, the Martin Marietta Corporation Code of Ethics and Standard of Conduct is 17 pages long and covers a wide variety of company activities and practices.

Many codes of business ethics contain both general statements of shared ethical values and more specific applied examples of these values. General statements of shared values remind employees what their companies stand for and at the same time serve to encourage ethical behavior in situations not covered by specific ethical guides. The applied examples address specific types of business conduct like those listed above by the Business Roundtable.

A majority of organizational codes of business ethics provide sanctions for their violation, up to and including employee termination. As with professional codes of conduct, it is appropriate to call these organizational codes self-regulation. Whether companies pursue ethical self-regulation with enthusiasm and commitment or the codes are mere window dressing to satisfy the government and the general public is an important issue in determining the value of these codes.

:: *sidebar* 2.7

Boeing Code of Conduct

The Boeing Code of Conduct outlines expected behaviors for all Boeing employees. Boeing will conduct its business fairly, impartially, in an ethical and proper manner, and in full compliance with all applicable laws and regulations. In conducting its business, integrity must underlie all company relationships, including those with customers, suppliers, communities and among employees. The highest standards of ethical business conduct are required of Boeing employees in the performance of their company responsibilities. Employees will not engage in conduct or activity that may raise questions as to the company's honesty, impartiality, reputation or otherwise cause embarrassment to the company.

Employees will ensure that:

- They do not engage in any activity that might create a conflict of interest for the company or for themselves individually.
- They do not take advantage of their Boeing position to seek personal gain through the inappropriate use of Boeing or non-public information or abuse of their position. This includes not engaging in insider trading.

- They will follow all restrictions on use and disclosure of information. This includes following all requirements for protecting Boeing information and ensuring that non-Boeing proprietary information is used and disclosed only as authorized by the owner of the information or as otherwise permitted by law.
- They observe that fair dealing is the foundation for all of our transactions and interactions.
- They will protect all company, customer and supplier assets and use them only for appropriate company approved activities.
- Without exception, they will comply with all applicable laws, rules and regulations.
- They will promptly report any illegal or unethical conduct to management or other appropriate authorities (i.e., Ethics, Law, Security, EEO).

Every employee has the responsibility to ask questions, seek guidance and report suspected violations of this Code of Conduct. Retaliation against employees who come forward to raise genuine concerns will not be tolerated.

Although many businesses have codes of ethics, fewer actually implement them effectively. According to the 2007 National Business Ethics Survey, businesses implementing ethics programs have risen from 25 percent in 2005 to 38 percent in 2007. Moreover, in companies that have such programs only 29 percent of employees failed to report ethical misconduct, whereas in companies that do not have such programs, 61 percent fail to report ethical misconduct. However, only 11 percent of the employees surveyed believed their companies had "strong" ethics programs. And the survey concludes, "High numbers of (ethical) misconduct reports . . . suggests that ethics programs are not being instituted successfully, or at all."

11. INDIVIDUAL VALUES

The ultimate source of ethical values for business decision making comes from the individual. Others can tell you what is right or wrong. They can sanction you for failing to live up to their expectations. But only you can make your behavior ethical. Only you can intend your actions to be honest and fair or to serve the common good.

How to act ethically in every business situation is beyond the scope of this chapter, or that of any book, for that matter. Business life is just too complex. There is no way to create enough rules to cover all possible ethically significant situations, even if they could be identified in advance. However, there are five questions that you can ask yourself that will help you explore your ethical values before making personal or business decisions about what to do.

1. **Have I thought about whether the action I may take is right or wrong?** John Smale, former CEO of Procter & Gamble, has said that "there is an ethical dimension to most complex business problems." If this is so, then you should consider whether any decision you propose to make to solve such a problem is ethical or not. The philosopher Hannah Arendt explained that evil often comes from a kind of thoughtlessness. Plato wrote that immoral behavior often flows from ignorance. A major goal of this chapter is to encourage you to think about the ethical implications of what you decide and what you do. It is the first step in leading a good life.

   Do remember that a "good life" means more than having material possessions and a good time. It means being concerned about others.

2. **Will I be proud to tell of my action to my family? To my employer? To the news media?** An excellent way to uncover whether there are ethical difficulties with a possible decision is to consider how proud you would be to share it with others. Before reaching an important business decision, consider how you would feel about telling your decision to your family, your employer, and the public through the news media. The less proud you are to share your decision with others, the more likely your decision is to be unethical. As Stephen Butler, former CEO of KPMG, said, "An essential part of an ethics process is identifying issues that would mortify a chief executive if he were to read about them on the front page of the newspaper."

3. **Am I willing for everyone to act as I am thinking of acting?** With this question you encompass a major principle of ethical formalism. If you consider suggesting to a co-worker that it would be advantageous for him or her to develop a sexual relationship with you, are you willing to have your superior suggest this relationship to you? Or to your friends or a member of your family? Trying to convince yourself that it is acceptable for you to do something but not acceptable for others in your situation to do it is virtually always immoral.

4. **Will my decision cause harm to others or to the environment?** Asking this question exposes a significant principle of ethical consequentialism: promotion of the common good. Promoting the common good within your business organization is important, but it is even more important to consider whether your decision is good for society.

   Numerous commentators have asserted that "harm" to the interests of others is the major limitation on both liberty and the use of an owner's resources.

   You can approach this issue of the common good by asking whether your decision will cause harm. If the decision will cause no harm and will advance your business interests, it will also usually advance the good of society by increasing productivity, efficiency, or innovation.

   Many business decisions, however, do cause harm to others or to the environment. It is difficult to construct an interstate highway without workers being injured and trees being cut. The point of asking yourself the question about potential harm is so you can weigh the harm against the increase in the common good and so you can evaluate whether an alternative course of action might bring about the same increase in the common good with less harm.

Note also that if the harm caused would be avoidable, legal problems can arise from a decision to accept the costs of the harm. An internal memorandum at General Motors that estimated the cost at $2.40 per car of settling fire-related claims due to the gas tank design in GM cars has plagued that company in lawsuits for years. Plaintiffs' lawyers have claimed that GM was not willing to spend this average amount per car in order to avoid having to change a defective gas tank design. Juries have assessed huge punitive damage awards against GM.

Recall that ethical formalists maintain that harm to some individual rights is never justified by an increase in organizational or common good. But as ethical decision making in business often involves a mixed approach, including both formalism and consequentialism, it is appropriate for you to evaluate potential business decisions by weighing harms against benefits to the common good.

5. **Will my actions violate the law?** Both formalists and consequentialists believe that you have an ethical duty to obey the law except in very limited instances. The law provides only minimum standards for behavior, but they are standards that should be observed. Thus, to be ethical, you should always consider whether any business decision you make will require illegal actions.

Sometimes it is not clear whether proposed actions will violate the law. Then you should consult with legal counsel. Many regulatory agencies will also give legal advice about whether actions you are considering are legal or not.

*To be ethical and violate a law, you should be willing to accept the consequences for it.

When you are convinced that a law itself is morally wrong, you may be justified in disobeying it. Even then, to be ethical, you should be willing to make public your disobedience and to accept the consequences for it. Both Mohandas Gandhi and Martin Luther King, Jr., deliberately disobeyed laws they thought were morally wrong, and they changed society by doing so. Ultimately they changed both laws and ethics. But they made their disobedience to these laws public, and they willingly accepted punishment for violating them. Dr. King wrote: "I submit that an individual who breaks a law that conscience tells him is unjust, and who willingly accepts the penalty of imprisonment in order to arouse the conscience of the community over its injustice, is in reality expressing the highest respect for the law."

Leading an ethical business life may be difficult at times. You will make mistakes. You will be tempted. It is unlikely that you will be perfect. But if you want to be ethical and will work hard toward achieving your goal, you will be rewarded. As with achieving other challenging business objectives, there will be satisfaction in ethical business decision making.

In business as well as in personal life, the key to ethical decision making is wanting to be ethical and having the will to be ethical. If you do not want to be ethical, no code of conduct can make you ethical. Potential harm you may cause to individuals and to society will best be deterred by the threat of legal punishment and the sanctions of professional and corporate codes. You may never get caught, lose your job, or go to jail. But, as Mortimer Adler observed, you will lack "much that is needed for the good life."

concept :: *summary*

Self-Examination for Self-Regulation

- Have I thought about whether the action I may take is right or wrong?
- Will I be proud to tell of my action to my family? To my employer? To the news media?

- Am I willing for everyone to act as I am thinking of acting?
- Will my decision cause harm to others or to the environment?
- Will my actions violate the law?

:: Achieving an Ethical Business Corporation

The dominant form of organization in modern business is the corporation. Currently, the top 100 manufacturing corporations produce more than two-thirds of the nation's entire manufacturing output. In 1840 the largest manufacturing firm in the United States, the Springfield Armory, employed only 250 workers. Today, many corporations have tens of thousands of employees. Some have hundreds of thousands. In substantial part, the development of the corporate form of business organization made possible this growth in business size.

Ethical problems, however, arise in corporate life that are not present in one's individual experience. In a study published of Harvard MBAs during their first five years following graduation, 29 of 30 reported that business pressures had forced them to violate their own ethical standards. The next sections focus on the ethical problems of an individual in the corporation and suggest several ways of dealing with them.

> The primary reason that corporations dominate the business landscape is that their ownership is divisible into small shares that make them easily sellable.

12. THE OBSTACLES

Some may contend that the corporation by its very nature, with its dependence on a competitive edge and on profit and its limited liability, is so constituted as to make ethical behavior unlikely. That is not true, but there are certain obstacles to ethical corporate behavior that deserve serious consideration.

The Emphasis on Profit The primary goal of the modern business corporation is to produce profit. Management demands it, the board of directors demands it, and shareholders demand it. Making profit motivates our entire economic system, and it promotes the common good by providing incentive for job creation and the efficient fulfillment of social needs for goods and services.

Unfortunately, with the decline of the Protestant ethic, emphasis on corporate profit alone sometimes conflicts with ethical responsibility. How a profit is made becomes less important than that it is made. Various business scandals illustrate this point.

In many corporations the responsibility for profit making is decentralized. The home office expects a plant in another state to meet certain profit goals, but the home office does not know much about the particular operations of that plant. Meeting profit goals places enormous pressure on the local plant

> "The cult of short-term stockholder value has been corrupting."
>
> **–John S. Reed, former chair of the New York Stock Exchange**

manager. The manager's career advancement depends on the plant's profitability, yet the home office does not appreciate the difficulties under which the plant is operating. In such a situation the overemphasis on profit can easily lead to the manager's taking ethical and legal shortcuts to ensure profit.

An example of such shortcuts involved Columbia/HCA Healthcare Corporation, one of the major national hospital chains. Following a government investigation, many units of the company were accused of enhancing profits by improperly billing Medicare for laboratory tests and home health care services. It was also alleged that managers were "upcoding," or exaggerating patient illness, in order to get greater reimbursements from the Medicare system. Several managers were criminally indicted and convicted. The company's CEO resigned. To settle charges, the company agreed to pay the federal government $745 million to resolve fraud allegations. As part of its response, the company also stationed ethics and compliance officers in nearly every hospital, in part to prevent managers from "looking good" by producing profits through improper billings.

Does the emphasis on profit in a property-based private market mean that *only* profit must be considered in business decision making? For an example of a nation where not only profit is important in business, see Sidebar 2.8.

:: *sidebar* 2.8

The Swedish Example of *Lagom*

The Swedes have a strong property-based private market, but the business emphasis in Sweden is not solely on profit making. Instead, the Swedes have a strong ethic of *lagom*, which means "not too much, not too little, but just enough."

As a result, the pay of corporate chief executive officers (CEOs) is only a small fraction of what it is in the United States and the average take-home pay of employees (excluding CEOs) varies from highest to lowest by a ratio of only 3 to 1. Sweden provides universal health care, public nursing homes, and subsidized child care and parental leave-taking during a child's first year. When Swedish companies go overseas, they treat employees there with much of the same ethic as In Sweden.

Lagom means that there are few wealthy Swedes, and Sweden's social welfare system of "just enough" depends on a tax rate of approximately twice that in the United States. Note also that Sweden is a small, homogenous country whose citizens share a common ethical culture that is often not found in larger nations.

*Source: Susan Wennemyer, "Sweden: The Kindness Economy," *Business Ethics*, Fall 2003.

Don't forget that a nation is just a large group. This means that "culture matters" in the implementation (or not) of moral values.

The Effect of the Group   The social critic Ambrose Bierce once remarked that the corporation is "an ingenious device for obtaining individual profit without individual responsibility." He was referring to the fact that individuals in large groups such as the corporation feel less responsibility for what happens in the group than they do for what happens in their individual lives. They may also act differently, and to some extent less ethically, in a group.

That individuals will do unethical things as part of a mob which they would never do alone is widely recognized, and the same pattern can be observed in corporate behavior. Within corporations it becomes easy for a researcher not to pass on lately discovered concerns about the possible (yet not certain) side effects of a new skin lotion that upper management is so enthusiastic about. In corporate life it is not difficult to overlook the unethical behavior of a superior when many fellow employees are also overlooking it. And of course, "I did it because everyone else did it" is a common rationalization in groups of all kinds. "Just following orders" is a similar rationalization.

That individuals in groups may feel a diminished sense of responsibility for decisions made and actions taken invites ethical compromise. Coupled with an overemphasis on profit, the group effect increases the difficulty of achieving an ethical business corporation.

The Control of Resources by Nonowners In the modern corporation, the owners (or *shareholders*) are often not in possession and control of corporate resources. Top management of many corporations effectively possess and control vast resources that they do not own. This produces the problems of corporate governance mentioned in Chapter 1. Managerial agents like the president and vice presidents of a large corporation have ethical and legal duties to manage the corporate resources for the benefit of their owners. But because they control corporate resources, it may be easy to manipulate the resources in their own interest and difficult for others to find out that they have done so. In other words, managers may be in an ideal position to infringe on the property interest of the corporate owners.

Sometimes, managers embezzle corporate money or abuse expense accounts. At other times they misrepresent the financial condition of the corporation in order to exercise stock options, obtain huge bonuses, or prop up loans they have secured with company stock. Because the very nature of corporate structure gives managers the opportunity to abuse and misappropriate corporate resources owned ultimately by the shareholders, ethical business practice is made more important yet more difficult. Consider Sidebar 2.9.

> Corporate misgovernance is an ethical as well as a legal problem.

:: *sidebar* 2.9

Failure and Collapse

In the financial collapse and recession of 2008, many financial institutions were paying executives enormous sums of money. Lehman Brothers Holdings Inc., an investment bank, paid its CEO, Richard Fuld, a reported $480 million in salary and bonuses between 2000 and 2008. During this period, Lehman Brothers had leveraged its assets more than 30 to 1, meaning that it had debts of over 30 times the value of its assets, and it bought and sold extremely high-risk, mortgage-based securities. However, when the housing market declined and these securities turned out to have little value, Lehman Brothers fell, helping to start a series of worldwide financial collapses. Consider the ethical implications, both to shareholders and society, of business agents like Richard Fuld taking risks with money they do not own in return for the possibility of enormous personal returns.

Consider also that the executives of Lehman Brothers were telling investors, right up until the time of their collapse, that the company was in good financial shape. Are such statements unethical, illegal? In 2002, Bernard J. Ebbers, the chief executive officer of WorldCom, characterized investors's concerns as mostly "unfounded nonsense" and said that "bankruptcy or a credit default is not a concern" and that "it has been 10 years since WorldCom has been so well positioned from an operating perspective." Immediately following these statements, the company's stock rose in market value. However, five months later WorldCom filed for bankruptcy. Mr. Ebbers was arrested and in 2005 a court sentenced him to 25 years in prison.

13. THE STEPS

Despite the obstacles that sometimes stand in the way of ethical corporate behavior, certain steps can be taken to promote business ethics in corporate life.

Involvement of Top Management   To encourage corporate ethics, it is not enough merely to adopt a code of conduct. For the code to change behavior, corporate employees must believe that the values expressed by the code represent the values of the corporation's top management. Top management must act as a role model for values it wishes corporate employees to share.

The sociologist Robert Jackall attributes the importance of a corporation's top management in encouraging business ethics to the bureaucratic system for career advancement. Each employee owes loyalty to his or her immediate corporate superior. As a practical matter, career advancement for the employee is generally tied to career advancement for the superior. In turn, that supervisor has a corporate superior to whom loyalty is owed, and so on up the corporate bureaucratic hierarchy.

Beyond a certain level in corporate bureaucracy, argues Jackall, social indicators about how well an employee "fits in" to the company management are as important as merit performance in securing further career advancement. For this reason, corporate employees tend to be very sensitive to the values of top corporate management and take these values as their own. Due to the interlocking system of loyalties that run between employment levels of the corporate hierarchy, top management's values filter down quite effectively to lower-level employees.

The values adopted by lower-level employees, however, will be top management's *real* values. So if the corporation has a code of conduct that expresses excellent ethical values, but top management shows that it expects profit at any cost, then the values adopted by lower-level employees will likely relate to profit at any cost rather than to values appearing in the code of conduct.

Top management must really believe in the ethical values expressed in codes of conduct for these values to take hold throughout the corporation. But if they do believe them and will communicate this belief through the corporation, there is an excellent chance that these values will be adopted within the corporate group. As Stephen Butler, former CEO of KPMG, says, "I really believe that corporate ethics are essential for a successful business today, and the CEOs of corporate America are the only ones who can institutionalize them."

Openness in Communication   For ethical corporate values to make their most significant impact on decision making, corporate employees must be willing to talk with each other about ethical issues. "Openness in communication is deemed fundamental," states the Business Roundtable. Openness promotes trust, and without trust even the best-drafted code of ethics will likely fall short of achieving an ethical business corporation.

Beyond helping establish trust, openness in communication is necessary for ethical corporate decision making because of the complexity of information required to evaluate the implications of many business decisions. Without open discussion of these implications among employees and between employees and their superiors, ethical decision making is severely hindered. Information crucial to making an ethical decision may be lacking.

For example, consider the complexity of a firm's decision to sell in other countries a pesticide that is banned for sale in the United States. Evaluating the ethical

> "Ethics . . . is a responsibility given to every employee in the company, but it must be led by top leadership.
>
> **–Ira A. Lipman, chairman, Guardsmark LLC**

*The complexity of information required to evaluate the implications of many business decisions requires openness in communication.

implications of the sale (assuming there are no legal ones) will demand considerable information. To make a fully informed decision the firm must know:

- What the effects of the pesticide on humans and the environment are.
- Why the pesticide was banned in the United States.
- Why the pesticide is useful in other countries.
- Whether in spite of its ban for use in the United States there may be good reasons to use the pesticide in other countries.
- Whether there are alternatives to its use in other countries.

The sharing of information about the implications of this pesticide sale will greatly assist the making of an ethical decision about its use. Openness in communication among employees on these implications will be vital in reaching an ethically informed corporate decision about this complex matter.

How is openness in communication on ethical issues promoted within the corporation? There is no single answer. For top management to provide a good role model of concern for speaking out on ethical issues is certainly a right beginning. Another possibility is for employees to meet periodically in small groups to consider either real or hypothetical ethical problems. In general, a shared corporate commitment to the ideal of ethical decision making is important to openness in communication.

Consideration of All Stakeholders Large corporations affect the interests of many different groups in society, which are called "stakeholders" because they have something at risk when the company acts and thus have a "stake" in it. Investor-owners, employees, the board of directors, and managers typically have a stake in the actions of large corporations, but so do customers, suppliers, financial creditors like banks, and the community in which a company is located. If a company pollutes as a by-product of production, society itself may have a stake in what actions a corporation takes.

The consequentialist ethics known as **stakeholder theory** maintains that ethical corporate behavior depends on managers who recognize and take into account the various stakeholders whose interests the corporation impacts. Stakeholder theory includes but goes beyond the responsibilities of corporate governance, which focuses on the *legal* responsibilities of managers to society and to the investor-owners of the corporation. Stakeholder theory suggests that through its managers, an ethical corporation

Stakeholder theory holds that ethical corporate behavior requires that directors and managers take into account everyone whose interests the corporation impacts, called "stakeholders."

- Considers the concerns of all proper stakeholders and weighs their interests when making decisions.
- Allows stakeholders to communicate with decision makers and informs them about risks to their interests that may arise from corporate action.
- Adopts communication methods that are appropriate to the sophistication levels of various stakeholders.
- Realizes the interdependence of all stakeholders and demonstrates fairness toward both voluntary stakeholders (e.g., employees) and involuntary stakeholders (e.g., the community).
- Works actively and cooperatively to reduce the risk of corporate harm to all stakeholders and to compensate them when harm occurs.
- Avoids risks to stakeholders which, if explained, would be clearly unacceptable.

Stakeholder theory is part of the ethics sometimes also called "corporate social responsibility."

- Acknowledges the potential conflict between managerial self-interest and the ethical responsibility of managers to other stakeholders, and promotes open procedures that allow managers to monitor their own ethical performance.

For an example of what can happen to a large business when ethical values collapse at the top, see Sidebar 2.10.

:: sidebar 2.10

The Demise of Arthur Andersen

For much of the last century, the firm of Arthur Andersen was one of the largest and most influential accounting firms in the world. Yet in 2002 it collapsed following the firm's criminal prosecution for obstruction of justice in shredding the documents of Enron, one of its clients known for massive corporate governance problems. In the end, three of the five largest bankruptcies ever recorded involved Arthur Andersen clients with financial accounting problems.

In her book *Final Accounting: Ambition, Greed and the Fall of Arthur Andersen,* business ethicist and former Harvard professor Barbara Ley Toffler recounts what led to the demise of the accounting firm. Although the firm employed thousands of honest accountants, its top management cut ethical and legal corners in the auditing of some of its biggest clients,

clients from whom the firm also collected millions of dollars in financial consulting fees. Within a business culture that encouraged loyalty, conformity, and obedience to the leadership of its senior partners, the conflicts of interest between impartial accounting and partisan consulting set the stage for the final corruption leading to the fall of the firm.

Companies attract investors (and lenders) who depend on the reputation of the accountants who audit the companies' books for accurate financial information about the companies. When almost all their clients abandoned them after their prosecution, Arthur Andersen fell. The firm's demise illustrates Robert Jackall's emphasis on the importance of top management on the ethical values within business organizations.

---

14. THE REWARDS

Wal-Mart also has over one million employees.

Of the world's 100 largest economies, 49 of them are countries and 51 are companies. General Motors has greater annual sales than the gross national products of Denmark, Thailand, Turkey, South Africa, or Saudi Arabia. Wal-Mart's economy is larger than that of Poland, Ukraine, Portugal, Israel, or Greece. Because of the size and influence of modern corporations, business ethics take on special significance. Although there are unique problems with promoting ethical corporate decision making, the rewards for making the attempt are important both to business and society.

The Spanish journal *Boletín Círculo* makes four observations about business ethics. A paraphrase of these observations provides a good way to highlight a chapter on ethics and self-regulation:

1. Profits and business ethics are not contradictory. Some of the most profitable businesses have also historically been the most ethical.
2. An ethical organizational life is a basic business asset that should be accepted and encouraged. The reverse is also true. Unethical behavior is a business liability.
3. Ethics are of continuing concern to the business community. They require ongoing reevaluation. Businesses must always be ethically sensitive to changes in society.

4. Business ethics reflect business leadership. Top firms can and should exercise leadership in business ethics.

Business plays a vital role in serving society, and we cannot isolate the impact of important business decisions from their social consequences. For businesses merely to observe the law is not sufficiently responsible. Legal regulation lacks flexibility and is inadequately informed to be the only social guide for business decision making. Ethics belong in business decision making. A business that does not act ethically severs itself from society, from the good, and ultimately from its own source of support.

In reading the next chapters on the regulatory environment, consider how passage of much of the regulation was preceded by breaches of business ethics. If ethical self-regulation does not guide business behavior, legal regulation often follows quickly.

15. THE MORALITY OF PROPERTY

This chapter has approached business ethics in a way to illustrate the moral problems and ethical approaches of individuals in the corporate world. It might have taken a different approach and discussed the morality of business from the perspective of "stakeholders" such as stock owners, but also including employees and others in the community whom business decisions affect. It could have considered techniques of values-based management, a how-to implementation of business ethics for managers. But with its emphasis on the basics, this chapter has examined the moral dilemmas of individual ethical choice in business organizations.

One important issue of business ethics remains. It goes to the heart of whether it is ethical to engage in modern private enterprise. It concerns the fundamental morality of the law of property that is the foundation of private enterprise, which we call "business."

Criticism of Property   Throughout history some people have criticized the law of private property and what it stands for (see Sidebar 2.11). They have challenged the morality of property, which is the legally enforced exclusive right to possess, use, and transfer resources. The primary criticism involves the moral issue of how some can possess more resources than they need while others go hungry and homeless. How can the wealthy ignore the plight of the poor and how can society endure a system that permits it? Property critics seem to long for a time when the abundant resources of nature were common to everyone, sufficient to satisfy the needs of all, and free for the taking.

Of concern also to the critics is the power over others conveyed by the possession of great capital resources. Karl Marx saw capitalists as oppressing workers and exploiting their labor resources. "[T]he theory of the Communists," wrote Marx, "may be summed up in a single sentence: Abolition of private property." Religious critics often associate greed with property and argue that property discourages sharing and deprives us of a spiritual focus to life. They argue the Bible says that "the love of money is the root of all evil" and that it is easier to thread "a camel through the eye of a needle than for a rich man to enter the kingdom of heaven." Finally, critics observe that humans are social creatures who live in community. The culture of values, education,

*Legal regulation lacks flexibility and is inadequately informed to be the only social guide for business decision making.

Don't forget that the United Nations says 30,000 children die worldwide every day from a lack of food and easily preventable diseases.

"Capitalists" are those owners who control large productive resources and employ others.

:: *sidebar* 2.11

Moral Criticism of Property

"I do nothing but go about persuading you all . . . not to take thought for your persons or your properties, but first and chiefly to care about the greatest improvement of the soul."–Socrates (circa 400 B.C.)

"Private property is the fruit of inequity."–Clement of Alexandria (circa second century)

"Property hath no rights. The earth is the Lord's, and we are his offspring. The pagans hold the earth as property. They do blaspheme God."–St. Ambrose (fourth century)

"Property is theft."–Judah ibn Tibbon (twelfth century)

"This 'I and mine' causes the whole misery. With the sense of possession comes selfishness and selfishness brings on misery."–Vivekanda (nineteenth century)

"In actual history it is notorious that conquest, enslavement, robbery, murder—briefly, force—play the great part [in the original accumulation of property]."–Karl Marx (1867)

"It is the preoccupation with possession, more than anything else, that prevents men from living freely and nobly."–Bertrand A. Russell (twentieth century) "Property is not theft, but a good deal of theft becomes property."–Richard H. Tawney (1926)

"Private property does not constitute for anyone an absolute and unconditional right. No one is justified in keeping for his exclusive use what he does not need when others lack necessities."–Pope Paul VI (1967)

and information that surrounds us and influences us in every way is not the creation of any individual but of all of us. What then is the moral basis for an individual's exclusive property in resources that the community may need?

Support of Property Supporters of property (see Sidebar 2.12) counter its criticism with a strong moral defense that begins with the acknowledgment that we cannot go back to some time in nature, possibly imaginary, when there were no resource allocation problems. Given limited resources, considerable evidence exists that the more resources that can be put under the legal system of property the less wastefully those resources will be treated. People are more careful with their own resources than with resources that are common to all. For example, the destruction of the world's rainforests is not caused by a system of property, but because property in these important resources largely does not exist, prompting a free-for-all clear-cutting of the forests.

Further, adequate property in resources maximizes total wealth in society. It provides incentives for individuals and groups to develop both physical and human resources to produce the goods that society values. Since property is not limited to legal rights in physical resources, but also includes one's creative, scientific, and technological innovations, societies that recognize property flourish more than societies that do not in almost all areas. Over the years the economic and social disparity between property-strong and property-weak societies grows ever wider.

Property supporters maintain that enforcing legally exclusive rights to resources is also a just system. It protects the resources of the poor as much as those of the rich. And the poor may actually benefit from an adequately enforced property system more than the rich since the rich are often able to guard their resources better than the poor and are less likely to have their resources coerced from them. Property also supports personal freedoms and individual autonomy, a fact recognized by the framers of the U.S. Constitution

*The legal right of ownership, called *property,* is justified ethically because it gives maximum incentive for production of what people need and want.

Do remember that the right of property may be more important in protecting the possessions of the poor than in protecting the possessions of the rich.

:: *sidebar* 2.12

Moral Support for Property

"The end of government being the good of mankind points out its great duties: it is above all things to provide for the security, the quiet, the happy enjoyment of life, liberty, and property."–James Otis (1764)

It is an "essential, unalterable right in nature . . . that what a man has honestly acquired is absolutely his own, which he may freely give, but cannot be taken from him without his consent."–Samuel Adams (1768)

"The rights of man in society are liberty, equality, security, and property."–Declaration of the Rights and Duties of Man and the Citizen (1795)

"The natural tendency of every society in which property enjoys tolerable security is to increase in wealth."–Thomas B. Macaulay (1835)

"Property is desirable, is a positive good in the world. Let not him who is houseless pull down the house of another, but let him work diligently and build one for himself, thus by example assuring that his own shall be safe from violence when built."–Abraham Lincoln (1864)

"Private property was the original source of freedom. It still is its main bulwark."–Walter Lippmann (1937)

"The system of private property is the most important guarantee of freedom, not only for those who own property, but scarcely less for those who do not."–Friedrich A. Hayek (1944)

"Private property is a natural fruit of labor, a product of intense activity of man, acquired through his energetic determination to ensure and develop with his own strength his own existence and that of his family, and to create for himself and his own an existence of just freedom, not only economic, but also political, cultural, and religious."–Pope Pius XII (1944)

"A fundamental interdependence exists between the personal right to liberty and the right to property. Neither could have meaning without the other."–Justice Potter Stewart (1972)

who believed that personal rights to speech, religion, and privacy were possessed by individuals as a type of property. Wrote John Adams, the second president of the United States: "The moment the idea is admitted into society that property is not as sacred as the laws of God, and there is not a force of law and public justice to protect it, anarchy and tyranny commence."

Acquisitiveness and territoriality appear to be very important parts of human nature. They are also seen in many other species and are a tendency connected to personal survival and mating. Capable of cooperative effort and the reciprocal sharing of resources within fairly small groups, we tend to resist strangers who take what is "ours," although we will trade with strangers for mutual benefit when we feel secure that our resources will not be tricked or coerced from us. In modern society the legal recognition of our natural acquisitiveness and territoriality is called "property."

With the worldwide decline of socialism and communism, those who support the morality of property are strengthened in the argument that the law of property provides the most moral social foundation known for encouraging prosperity and personal freedom. However, both critics and supporters of property recognize that moral controversy concerning the distribution of resources continues. Moral questions about property concern the legitimacy of the original acquisition of resources, how voluntary an exchange of resources is, whether one's use of resources interferes with another's resources, the limits to taxation, and society's responsibility to its weak, old, young, and sick members. Ultimately, business ethics and the morality of property embrace many of the most important issues of society.

:: **Property as a System of Personal Ethics**

Once you understand property as a "right" rather than a "thing," you appreciate how property can be the basis for a system of personal ethics. Property is a system of law enforced by the state but the values underlying this system are moral ones.

*Once you understand that property identifies what is legally "proper" or right as to who controls what resources, you understand property's connection to ethics.

Property provides an ordering of relations between people. It acknowledges that each person has an exclusive sphere for private resources that all other persons must observe. If in the broad sense we apply property not only to the external resources that a person has lawfully acquired, but also—as James Madison did—to a person's internal resources, we must acknowledge that to harm others' safety and health, freedom of choice, or liberty of movement is to infringe their right of property. It is to deprive others of what is "proper" to them.

Property applies both to what is mine and to what is yours. As a part of the system of property, you must recognize what is mine but I also must recognize what is yours. Morally, as well as legally, each must respect the equal right of others to what is proper to them. It is as unethical for an employer to fail to warn employees of safety risks in the workplace as it is for the employee to embezzle money from the employer.

The property system does not explain which resources belong in the first instance within the exclusive sphere of property's protection. Some property critics are uncomfortable with this result, yet long tradition, custom, and law place almost all resources that are originally possessed (e.g., your liberty) or are acquired without force, fraud, or theft within this personal exclusive sphere. Once within this sphere, these resources become proper to private persons. By law and morality, each must not interfere with or harm (common law said "trespass" on) the resources of others, and this value applies as much in as out of the workplace.

The rule of law and property are fundamental not only to the structure but also to the values of the private market and of ethical behavior in the business community. The next three chapters concern when the values that underlie law are not enough to resolve disputes and legal enforcement becomes necessary.

:: **Key Terms**

Categorical imperative 34	Formalism 33	Social contract theory 35
Consequentialism 35	Morality 31	Stakeholder theory 53
Duty 33	Protestant ethic 36	The good 31
Ethics 31	Self-regulation 44	Utilitarianism 35

:: **Review Questions and Problems**

Contemporary Business Ethics

1. *Ethics and Society*

   Describe the reasons for the rising concern over business ethics.

2. *Ethics and Government*

   How has government action in recent years encouraged increased business attention to ethical matters?

The Nature of Ethics

3. *Ethics and Morality*

   Compare and contrast ethics and morality. What do philosophers call the end result of ethical examination?

4. *Ethics and Law*

   A marketing consultant to your firm comments that being ethical in business means nothing more than obeying the law. Discuss.

Two Systems of Ethics

5. *Formalism*

   As amended in 1988, the Foreign Corrupt Practices Act prohibits bribery as a practice for U.S. companies to use in obtaining business in other countries. In passing the act, Congress expressed the concern that bribery was inherently wrong. Which major system of ethical thought does this concern suggest? Explain.

6. *Consequentialism*

   A headline from *The Wall Street Journal* read "U.S. Companies Pay Increasing Attention to Destroying Files." The article discussed how many companies are routinely shredding files in the ordinary course of business to prevent future plaintiffs from obtaining the files and finding incriminating evidence. Is this practice unethical? Evaluate.

7. *Comparing the Two Ethical Systems*

   (a) Is it ethical to advertise tobacco products in association with a desirable, exciting, or sophisticated lifestyle?

   (b) Is it ethical to advertise these products in association with a cartoon character that is appealing to young people?

Sources of Values for Business Ethics

8. *Legal Regulation*

   Explain how in our society, ethical values frequently become law, and how legal regulation can promote change in ethical values. Describe several common ethical values that are found in law.

9. *Professional Codes of Ethics*

   Discuss why lawyers are sometimes viewed as being unethical. Is the average lawyer more or less ethical than the average business manager?

10. *Organizational Codes of Ethics*

    A study of one major company's code of ethics by the Business Roundtable found that the lower the level of employees on the corporate ladder, the greater their hostility and cynicism toward codes of business ethics.

    (a) Why might this be true?

    (b) What can top business management do to change this view?

11. *Individual Values*

    In addition to the five questions listed in the text, can you think of questions to ask yourself to help explore your ethical values before making a business (or personal) decision?

Achieving an Ethical Business Corporation

12. *The Obstacles*

    A *Newsweek* article on business ethics concludes, "Even in today's complex world, knowing what's right is comparatively easy. It's doing what's right that's hard." Explain why this statement may be true in modern corporate decision making.

13. *The Steps*

    Another article from *The Wall Street Journal* carries the headline "Tipsters Telephoning Ethics Hot Lines Can End Up Sabotaging Their Own Jobs." Discuss why whistle-blowing is unpopular within the corporation. Apply to your discussion what sociologist Robert Jackall said about a subordinate's loyalty to supervisors within the corporation. Is whistle-blowing an appropriate subject for corporate ethics codes?

14. *The Rewards*

Why are formal legal rules alone not an adequate ethical system for business?

15. *The Morality of Property*

The law of property describes what is "proper" and "right" between people regarding the things people need and want. Explain how property is related to ethics.

business :: *discussions*

1. As the chief executive officer of a Silicon Valley software company, you become aware that your chief competitor is working on a new computer program that will revolutionize interactive voice-based applications. You know that if you can find out about several key functions relating to your competitor's program, your own programmers can duplicate the function of the program without actually copying its code.

Is it ethical for you to hire away from your competitor a secretary who may have overheard something that will be useful to you?

Is it ethical for you to send an attractive employee to a bar where your competitor's programmers hang out in the hope of getting the information you want?

Is it ethical for you to have someone hunt up and read everything published by your competitor's programmers in case they may have let slip something that will help you?

2. The research director of PharmCo, a midsize pharmaceutical company, tells top management of an important new discovery. After years of effort, one of the company's research teams has discovered a drug that will reverse pattern baldness, the leading cause of male hair loss. The potential for profit from such a drug is enormous, but the director cautions that two of the eight principal researchers on the team believe that the drug may also increase the possibility of potentially fatal cerebral aneurysms in a very tiny percentage of users.

- If follow-up animal studies of the new drug do not show significant side effects, would it be ethical for the company to tell the two researchers to keep quiet about their concerns?
- Is it ethical to put animals at risk in order to test the drug's safety?

Many poor men in the world will be unable to afford the new drug if PharmCo sets the price too high.

- Is it morally right for PharmCo to maximize its profit even if it means that many men will have to remain bald?
- Does your answer change if the drug cures rheumatoid arthritis? AIDS?

Part
TWO

:: Dispute Resolution

In a legal system based on the right of private property, there will be many disputes. Disputes often take place over exactly who owns what. These disputes concern the boundaries of the property right and often involve not physical boundaries but boundaries to the use of what is owned. Can you file-share music and movies created by others? Can you record your professor's lectures and share them with absent classmates? Can you sell them to the public? Disputes also arise because people sometimes act in ways that interfere with or wrongfully harm what belongs to others. Disputes over traffic accidents in tort law illustrate such harm to others in our property-based legal system.

Having fair and impartial ways to settle disputes promptly is absolutely vital to a property-based legal system. It provides the certainty of private ownership that encourages you to use and exchange resources in the private market, minimizing the concern that others will take what belongs to you and assuring that if others harm what is yours you can get compensation. Very importantly for business, dispute resolution also means that, most of the time, even strangers will live up to their contractual promises to exchange resources with you. And if they fail to live up to their promises, you can get compensation.

The next three chapters cover dispute resolution in our property-based legal system. Courts are at the center of dispute resolution, and Chapter 3 explains the court system. It identifies the key players in the courts—judges, jurors, and lawyers—and makes clear their roles. It explains the organization of the court system into state and federal trial and appellate courts. At the very top of the court system, which is shaped like a pyramid, are supreme courts at the state and federal levels. Chapter 3 discusses the most significant power of the courts: the power of judicial review, which is the power to declare unconstitutional the acts of the legislative and the executive branches of government. This chapter concludes with a guided reading of the book's first court opinion.

Chapter 4 focuses on how actual cases go through the court system, a process known as *litigation*. Litigation begins when the complaining party or plaintiff files a complaint in court against the defendant. Chapter 4 discusses various issues of the complaint, like standing to sue and jurisdiction, and explains how the plaintiff and defendant define their dispute through the "pleadings." Chapter 4 covers discovery and pretrial motions, the stages of the actual trial, and the possible appeal of the trial court's judgment. It also discusses the enforcement of court judgments.

Chapter 5 illustrates that there are alternative ways to resolve disputes other than litigation in the courts. In fact, people negotiate most of their disputes instead of litigating them, and Chapter 5 discusses how to negotiate disputes. It then considers mediation and arbitration, both of which use a neutral third person to assist in resolving a dispute. The decision of a mediator merely advises the parties to a dispute, but the decision of an arbitrator can be legally enforced. Chapter 5 concludes with a look at other alternatives to resolving disputes by litigation. •

3

The Court System

⬜ Learning Objectives ::

In this chapter you will learn:

1. To gain an understanding of the key personnel associated with the court system, including the role of judges, jurors, and lawyers.

2. How the state and federal court systems are organized and how they function.

3. About the power of judicial review and the conflicting philosophies of judicial restraint and judicial activism.

4. To appreciate the background and judicial alignment of the current members of the U.S. Supreme Court.

5. To be exposed to a sample case from the U.S. Supreme Court, including the majority and dissenting opinions.

UNDER·LAW

Corporate governance, in a property-based legal environment, requires a viable court system. This chapter deals with the court system and the court's authority to decide disputes between parties. First, it examines the personnel who operate our courts, including the role of judges, jurors, and lawyers in a case. It next explores the organizational structure of both the state and federal courts and the differences between trial courts and appellate courts. Finally, the chapter examines the U.S. Supreme Court and the concept of judicial review and the role of courts in interpreting the Constitution, state and federal legislation, and the making of common law in the process of deciding cases (*stare decisis*).

By the time you have completed this chapter, you should have an understanding of the court system and a greater sensitivity for how the courts apply the law. You will understand the importance of every citizen willingly serving on

Managers often are involved in the litigation process as either parties or witnesses in a case.

a jury and receiving the cooperation of employers and the protection of the government for doing so. You will appreciate the difficult questions jurors must answer and the complex cases juries must decide. Finally, you will appreciate the difficulty that arises in resolving legal disputes.

:: *sidebar* 3.1

Corporate Governance and the Soaring Cost of Legal Representation

How much does it cost to defend a company and its executives when a lawsuit is filed? In some cases, the mere investigation may run into the tens of millions. Massive legal expenses are a major concern for corporate executives and shareholders alike. Legal fees can bankrupt a small business. In an accounting fraud investigation, Qwest Communications International spent $75 million on legal fees in one year. Tyco International spent about $50 million to defend and investigate its practices. Problems with corporate governance and rising legal fees go hand in hand.

:: Personnel

Before we look at the court system, you should have some background and understanding of the individuals who operate our court system. Judges apply the law to the facts, jurors find or determine the facts from conflicting evidence, and the facts as found by the jury are given great deference. In the process of representing clients, lawyers present evidence to the jury and argue the law to the court. Collectively, these persons conduct the search for truth. The court system is the way we enforce our laws in a property-based legal system. Without the courts, our legal system could not operate.

1. JUDGES AND JUSTICES

"Facts are stubborn things; and whatever may be our wishes, our inclinations, or the dictates of our passion, they cannot alter the state of facts and evidence."

–John Adams

The individuals who operate our courts are called judges or magistrates. In some appellate courts, such as the U.S. Supreme Court, members of the court are called justices. In this discussion, we will refer to trial court persons as judges and reviewing court persons as justices.

In all cases, the function of the trial judge is to determine the applicable rules of law to be used to decide the case. Such rules may be procedural or substantive. In cases tried without a jury, the judge is also responsible for finding the facts. In cases tried before a jury, the function of the jury is to decide questions of fact. The judge still is responsible for deciding questions of law.

Trial judges are the main link between the law and the citizens it serves. The trial judge renders decisions that deal directly with people in conflict. These judges have the primary duty to observe and to apply constitutional limitations and guarantees. They bear the burden of upholding the dignity of the courts and maintaining respect for the law.

Most cases are resolved before trial and even fewer cases lead to an appeal.

Justices do more than simply decide an appeal—they often give reasons for their decisions. These reasoned decisions become precedent and a part of our body of law that may affect society as a whole, as well as the litigants. So in deciding cases, justices must consider not only the result between the parties but also the total effect of the decision on the law. In this sense, their role is similar to that of legislators. When reviewing appeals, justices are essentially concerned with issues of *law;* issues of *fact* normally are resolved at the trial court level.

For these reasons, the personal characteristics required for a justice or appellate judge are somewhat different from those for a trial judge. The manner of performing duties and the methods used also vary between trial and reviewing courts. A trial judge who has observed the witnesses is able to use knowledge gained from participation as an essential ingredient in his or her decisions. A justice must spend most of the time studying the briefs, the record of proceedings, and the law in reaching decisions.

The judiciary, because of the power of judicial review, has perhaps the most extensive power of any branch of government. This issue will be extensively examined later in the chapter. Lower court judges' decisions may be reviewed by a reviewing court, but they have personal immunity from legal actions against them based on their judicial acts.

*Judges and justices often sacrifice considerable financial opportunities by giving up the practice of law in the prime of their careers.

2. JURORS

It is important to understand the role of the jury as a fact-finding body. Since litigation may involve both questions of law and questions of fact, the deference given to the decisions of a jury is very important. Trial by jury is a cherished right guaranteed by the Bill of Rights. The Sixth and Seventh Amendments to the Constitution guarantee the right of trial by jury in both criminal and civil cases. The **petit jury** is the trial jury that returns a verdict in both situations.

Although juries are used in only a very small percentage of all cases, they remain critical to the administration of justice. In civil cases the right to trial by a jury is preserved in suits at common law when the amount in controversy exceeds $20. State constitutions have similar provisions guaranteeing the right of trial by jury in state courts.

Historically, a jury consisted of 12 persons. Today many states and some federal courts have rules of procedure that provide for smaller juries in both criminal and civil cases. Such provisions are acceptable since the federal law does not specify the *number* of jurors—only the *types* of cases that may be brought to trial before a jury at common law. Several studies have found no discernible difference between results reached by a 6-person jury and those reached by a 12-person jury. As a result, many cases are tried before six-person juries today.

In most states, a jury's decision must be unanimous because many believe that the truth is more nearly to be found and justice rendered if the jury acts only on one common conscience. However, there is growing evidence that the requirement of unanimity is taking its toll on the administration of justice in the United States. Holdout jurors contribute to mistrials and many cases are routinely deadlocked by margins of 11–1 or 10–2. Many states have eliminated the requirement of unanimity in their courts in civil cases and two states have done so in criminal cases. Several legal commentators have argued that unanimous jury verdicts are not constitutionally mandated and should be eliminated to help restore public confidence in our jury system.

Thanks to a series of sensationalized trials, the jury system has been subject to much criticism. Many argue that jurors are not qualified to distinguish

Rule 48 of the Federal Rules of Civil Procedure states that the "court shall seat a jury of not fewer than six and not more than twelve members." Local rules allow district courts to set the number of jurors consistent with this rule.

*The quality of a jury depends upon the ability to get competent and dedicated citizens to serve.

fact from fiction, that they vote their prejudices, and that their emotions are too easily swayed by skilled trial lawyers. However, most members of the bench and bar feel the right to be tried by a jury of one's peers in criminal cases is the most effective method of discovering the truth and giving the accused his or her "day in court."

:: *sidebar* 3.2

Jury System Reforms

Several reforms in the jury system have been launched in recent years. Many states now permit jurors to have a more active role. In several jurisdictions, jurors are permitted to take notes during trials. Some states allow jurors to submit questions directly to the judges who, using their discretion, may require witnesses to answer during their testimony. A few jurisdictions even permit jurors during the trial to discuss the evidence as the case progresses rather than waiting until the end of the proceeding to begin deliberations. Most of these recent reforms are based upon the belief that active and engaged jurors (much like students in a classroom), who do more than merely listen, pay closer attention to the evidence during the course of the trial and make better decisions at the end of the trial.

"I do not assert that the jury trial is an infallible mode of ascertaining truth. Like everything human, it has its imperfection. I only say, that it is the best protection for innocence and the surest mode of punishing guilt that has yet been discovered. It has borne the test of longer experience, and borne it better than any other legal institution that ever existed among men."

–Jeremiah Black, defense attorney in the case of *Ex Parte Milligan*, 71 U.S. 2 (1886).

Jurors normally do not give reasons for their decisions, although some special verdicts may require juries to answer a series of questions. Actually, it would be almost impossible for the jury to agree on the reasons for its verdict. A jury may agree as to the result but disagree on some of the facts, and different jurors may have different ideas or understandings of the testimony.

Many individuals attempt to avoid jury duty. Some lose money because of time away from a job or profession. Others feel great stress in having to help make important decisions affecting the lives of many people. Because so many potential jurors seek relief from jury duty, many trials often end up with more jurors who are unemployed or retired than should be the case. Today, there is a strong trend toward requiring jury duty of all citizens, irrespective of any hardship that such service may entail. Courts often refuse to accept excuses because jury duty is a responsibility of all citizens in a free society.

One of the most difficult issues facing the judicial system is the right to a trial by jury in very complex and complicated cases that frequently take a long time to try. For example, many antitrust cases involve economic issues that baffle economists, and such cases may last for several months or even years. The average juror may not comprehend the meaning of much of the evidence, let alone remember it when it is time to make a decision. As a practical matter, many persons cannot serve on a jury for several weeks or months. How does a free and democratic society deliver a trial by jury of one's peers, if busy people are excused from jury service? For these and other reasons, some experts recommend that the right to a trial by jury be abolished in very complex and time-consuming cases.

Complex cases can result in huge verdicts as juries send important messages to the business community. In 2006 the nation's 10 largest jury verdicts included three over $500 million (Table 3.1). Only 10 years earlier the largest award by a jury was $75 million, which would not even make a top 20 list today. Of course, most of the verdicts are appealed or settled for lesser amounts.

table 3.1 :: Ten Largest Jury Verdicts of 2006		
MAN, AG v. Freightliner, LLC	Fraud	$850 million
Gulsby Engineering v. Gulf Liquids New River Project	Contracts	$699.54 million
Cook v. Rockwell International Corp.	Torts	$553.90 million
Citgo Petroleum Corp. v. Babcock & Wilcox	Property damage	$455.79 million
Hynix Semiconductor Inc. v. Rambus Inc.	Intellectual property	$306.90 million
Navarro v. Austin	Medical malpractice	$216.85 million
Celebrity Cruises Inc. v. Essef Corp.	Products liability	$193.08 million
City of Modesto v. Dow Chemical	Products liability	$178.25 million
Estate of Mendoza v. Summit Care Corp.	Nursing home	$160.05 million
Hexion Specialty Chemicals, Inc. v. Formosa Plastics Corp.	Intellectual property	$152.70 million

*Source: www.verdictsearch.com

Many of the largest jury verdicts involve medical malpractice, products liability, fraud, or breach of contract. Juries have been increasingly generous to plaintiffs who suffer death or serious physical injury. Many plaintiffs' lawyers now contend that million dollar awards—once the standard for measuring a successful case—are no longer indicative of a major victory.

3. LAWYERS

Our court system is an adversarial one. Although private parties may represent themselves without a lawyer, as a practical matter, lawyers are required in most cases. Since knowledge of court procedures and substantive law is required as a bare minimum in most cases, lawyers serve as the representative advocates in our court system. They present the evidence, the points of law, and the arguments that are weighed by juries and judges in making their decisions.

Lawyers can be sanctioned for unethical conduct and some have gone to jail for illegal conduct.

A lawyer's first duty is to the administration of justice. As an officer of the court, he or she should see that proceedings are conducted in a dignified and orderly manner and that issues are tried on their merits only. The practice of law should not be a game or a battle of wits, but a means to promote justice. The lawyer's duties to each client require the highest degree of fidelity, loyalty, and integrity.

A lawyer serves in three capacities: counselor, advocate, and public servant. As a counselor, a lawyer by the very nature of the profession knows his or her client's most important secrets and affairs. A lawyer is often actively involved in the personal decisions of clients, ranging from their business affairs and family matters such as divorce to their alleged violations of the criminal law. These relationships dictate that a lawyer meet the highest standards of professional and ethical conduct.

*Lawyers may have many clients and often handle complex and complicated cases. The American Bar Association reported over 1 million licensed lawyers in the United States in 2005.

The tension between the business community and the legal profession has been growing in recent years. This conflict has been fueled by the increasing number of lawsuits filed by lawyers on behalf of their clients, by resistance from organized lawyer advocacy groups like the American Bar Association to reforms, and by the high costs of attorney fees that businesses must absorb.

table 3.2 :: 2007 Law Firm Gross Revenues

:: Firm	:: Headquarters	:: Gross Revenue
Skadden	New York, NY	$2.17 billion
Latham & Watkins	Los Angeles, CA	$2.01 billion
Baker & McKenzie	Chicago, IL	$1.83 billion
Jones Day	Cleveland, OH	$1.44 billion
Sidley Austin	Chicago, IL	$1.39 billion
White & Case	New York, NY	$1.37 billion
Kirkland & Ellis	Chicago, IL	$1.31 billion
Greenberg Traurig	Miami, FL	$1.20 billion
Mayer Brown	Chicago, IL	$1.18 billion
Weil Gotshal	New York, NY	$1.17 billion

*Source: www.americanlawyer.com

As the size and revenue generated by law firms grows every year, many of the nation's largest law firms take on the look of a large business enterprise. Table 3.2 provides you with a sense of the size and scope of larger law firms today. Two law firms each topped the $2 billion barrier in total revenues in 2007. According to the *American Lawyer*, it took 51 years to climb above the $1 billion gross mark, but only eight more years to hit $2 billion. The big law firm surge has been fueled by the demand for high-end legal services needed by corporations and other large businesses. Many firms have as many as 2,000 lawyers.

Obviously, if a lawyer is to give competent advice, he or she must know to the fullest extent possible all the facts involved in any legal problem presented by the client. To encourage full disclosure by a client, the rules of evidence provide that confidential communications to a lawyer are privileged. The law does not permit a lawyer to reveal such facts and testify against a client, even if called to do so at a trial. This is the attorney-client privilege, and it may extend to communications made to the lawyer's employees in certain cases. This is especially important today because law firms frequently use paralegals (legal assistants) to gather facts and assist attorneys.

concept :: *summary*

Personnel

1. Trial judges determine the applicable law and, in cases without a jury, they also are responsible for finding the facts.

2. Appellate courts act as reviewing courts and generally are concerned with issues of law.

3. The petit jury is the trial jury that returns a verdict.

4. The nation's top 10 jury verdicts include 3 over $500 million.

5. Lawyers serve three roles: counselor, advocate, and public servant.

:: Organization of the Court System

There are two major court systems in the United States: the federal courts and the 50 state courts. The federal court system and those in most states contain three levels—trial courts, courts of appeals, and supreme courts. Lawsuits begin at the **trial court** level, and the results may be reviewed at one or more of the other two **appellate court** levels. Critical to every lawsuit is the question of subject matter jurisdiction.

Courts are the foundation of a property-based legal system.

4. SUBJECT MATTER JURISDICTION

Jurisdiction refers to the power of a court, at the state or federal level, to hear a case. For any court to hear and decide a case at any level, it must have **subject matter jurisdiction,** which is the power over the issues involved in the case. Some state trial courts have what is called general jurisdiction, or the power to hear any type of case. Other state courts have only limited jurisdiction, or the power to hear only certain types of cases. Jurisdiction may be limited as to subject matter, amount in controversy, or area in which the parties live.

Courts, especially those of limited jurisdiction, may be named according to the subject matter with which they deal. Probate courts deal with wills and the estates of deceased persons, juvenile courts with juvenile crime and dependent children, criminal and police courts with violators of state laws and municipal ordinances, and traffic courts with traffic violations.

Courts of different scope and subject matter jurisdiction help create order and efficiency.

Even trial courts (courts of general jurisdiction) cannot attempt to resolve every dispute or controversy that may arise. Some issues are simply nonjusticiable. For example, courts would not attempt to referee a football or basketball game. They would not hear a case to decide how English or math should be taught in the public schools. Moreover, courts do not accept cases involving trivial matters.

5. STATE COURTS

State court systems are created, and their operations are governed, from three sources. First, state constitutions provide the general framework for the court system. Second, the state legislature, pursuant to constitutional authority, enacts statutes that add body to the framework. This legislation provides for various courts, establishes their jurisdiction, and regulates the tenure, selection, and duties of judges. Other legislation may establish the general rules of procedure to be used by these courts. Each court sets forth its own rules of procedure within the statutory bounds. These rules are detailed and may specify, for example, the times when various documents must be filed with the court clerk.

Currently, 39 states elect judges at some level.

Trial Courts Depending upon the particular state, a general trial court can take on any number of names: the *superior court,* the *circuit court,* or the *district court.* In the trial courts, parties file their lawsuits or complaints seeking to protect their property rights or redress a wrongdoing. The complaint describes the parties (John Doe versus Sally Smith), the facts and law giving rise to a cause of action, the authority of the court to decide the case, and the relief requested from the court. (See Chapter 4 for a more complete explanation of

Figure 3.1
Typical state court system

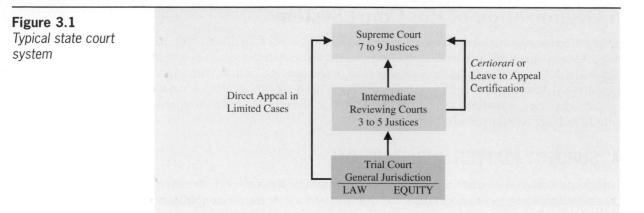

the litigation process including a sample complaint.) The trial court is responsible for determining both the facts and the law in the case.

95 to 98 percent of all complaints are settled or fully resolved at the trial court level. Very few cases, by comparison, are appealed.

Appellate Courts   The parties to litigation are entitled as a matter of right to a review of their case by a higher court, or an **appeal,** if the requirements of procedural law are followed in seeking the review. In some states there is only one appellate court, which is usually called the supreme court of the state. In more populous states, there often are two levels of reviewing courts—an intermediate level and a court of final resort. In states with two levels of review, the intermediate courts are usually called the **courts of appeal,** and the highest court is again called the **supreme court.** In states with two levels of reviewing courts, most appeals are taken to the lower of the two courts, and the highest court of the state will review only very important cases. Intermediate courts of review typically consist of three to five judges. A state supreme court typically has seven to nine judges.

Reviewing courts review are essentially concerned with questions of law. Although a party is entitled to one trial and one appeal, he or she may obtain a second review if the higher reviewing court, in the exercise of its discretion,

:: *sidebar* 3.3

Small-Claims Courts

One court of limited jurisdiction, falling below the trial court, is especially important to the business community. This court, usually known as **small-claims court,** handles much of the litigation between business and its customers. Small-claims courts are used by businesses to collect accounts and by customers to settle disputes with the business community that are relatively minor from a financial perspective. Such suits are often quite important from the standpoint of principle. Landlord-tenant disputes are an example of controversies decided in these courts. Small-claims courts have low court costs and simplified procedures. The informality of the proceedings speeds up the flow of cases. The services of a lawyer are not usually required, and some states do not allow lawyers to participate in these proceedings. Lawsuits filed in small-claims courts usually are subject to a dollar limitation, such as a maximum of $25,000, often ranging from $500 to $5,000.

agrees to such a review. The procedure for requesting a second review is called in some states a *petition for leave to appeal* and in others a petition for a **writ of certiorari.** The process for requesting a review is explained more fully in Section 7 in this chapter. Deciding such requests is a major function of the highest court in each state. As a practical matter, less than 5 percent of all such requests are granted.

6. FEDERAL COURTS

Article III of the Constitution (see Appendix) provides that judicial power be vested in the Supreme Court and such lower courts as Congress may create. Figure 3.2 shows you the hierarchy of the federal court system. The judicial power of the federal courts has been limited by Congress. Essentially, it extends to matters involving (1) questions of federal law (federal question cases), (2) the United States as a party, (3) controversies among the states, and (4) certain suits between citizens of different states (diversity of citizenship). Federal question cases and diversity of citizenship cases require further discussion as presented in the following paragraphs.

Federal question cases may be based on issues arising out of the U.S. Constitution or out of federal statutes. Any amount of money may be involved

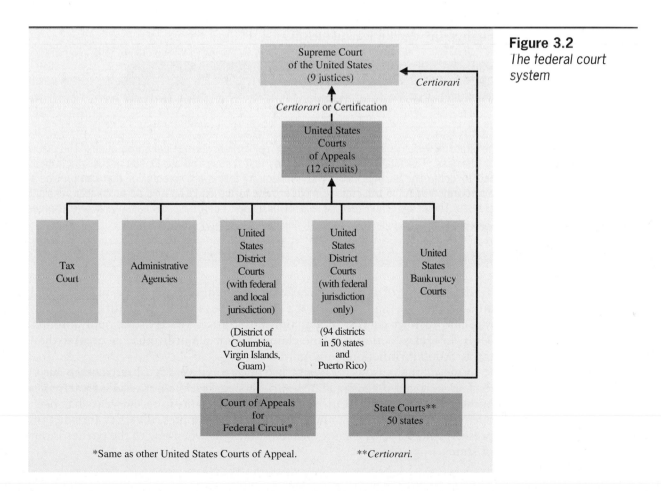

Figure 3.2
The federal court system

*Federal courts have subject matter jurisdiction over federal question cases and diversity of citizenship cases.

in such a case, and it need not be a suit for damages. For example, a suit to enjoin a violation of a constitutional right can be filed in a federal court as a federal question case. These civil actions may involve matters based on federal laws such as those dealing with patents, copyrights, trademarks, taxes, or employment discrimination. The rights guaranteed by the Bill of Rights of the Constitution also may be the basis for a federal question case.

Diversity of citizenship requires that all plaintiffs be citizens of different states from all defendants. If a case involves a party on one side that is a citizen of the same state as a party on the other, there will then be no diversity of citizenship and thus no federal jurisdiction. Courts have held that it is the citizenship of the party in the case that determines whether diversity of citizenship exists. For example, diversity jurisdiction is based on the citizenship of all members of a partnership.

The fact that business corporations, which are considered persons before the law, are frequently incorporated in one state and have their principal place of business in another state also causes problems in determining when diversity of citizenship exists. For purposes of diversity jurisdiction, a corporation is a citizen of the state of incorporation and also a citizen of the state in which it has its principal place of business. Thus, a Delaware corporation with its principal place of business in Illinois is a citizen of both Delaware and Illinois for purposes of diversity. If any party on the other side of a lawsuit with such a corporation is a citizen of either Illinois or Delaware, there is then no diversity and no federal jurisdiction.

:: *sidebar* 3.4

Total Activity Test

Questions arise regarding the state in which a corporation has its principal place of business. The total activity of the corporation is examined to determine its principal place of business. This test incorporates both the *place of activities* and the *nerve center* tests. The nerve center test places general emphasis on the locus of the managerial and policy-making functions of the corporations. The place of activities test focuses on production or sales activities. The *total activity* test is not an equation that can provide a simple answer to the question of a corporation's principal place of business. Each case necessarily involves somewhat subjective analysis.

In diversity of citizenship cases, the federal courts have a jurisdictional amount of more than $75,000. If a case involves multiple plaintiffs with separate and distinct claims, *each* claim must satisfy the jurisdictional amount. Thus, in a class-action suit, the claim of each plaintiff must be greater than the $75,000 jurisdictional amount.

One of the reasons Congress provides for diversity of citizenship jurisdiction is to guard against state court bias against the nonresident party in a lawsuit. Since the biggest increase in federal lawsuits in recent years has been over businesses suing one another in contract disputes, diversity jurisdiction preserves the sense of fairness in such situations when one of the parties is out of state.

District Courts The federal district courts are the trial courts of the federal judicial system. There is at least one such court in every state and the District of Columbia. These courts have subject matter jurisdiction over all the cases mentioned above. These courts have the authority to review lawsuits, receive evidence, evaluate testimony, impanel juries, and resolve disputes. Most significant federal litigation begins in this court. The **Federal Rules of Civil Procedure** provide the details concerning procedures to be followed in federal court litigation. These rules are strictly enforced by the courts and must be followed by the parties in every lawsuit.

An adverse decision from a federal district court in Atlanta may be appealed to the Eleventh Circuit Court of Appeals.

Appellate Courts Under its constitutional authorization, Congress has created 12 U.S. Courts of Appeal plus a special Court of Appeals for the Federal Circuit as intermediate appellate courts in the federal system. This special reviewing court, located in Washington, D.C., hears appeals from special courts such as the U.S. Claims Court and Contract Appeals as well as from administrative decisions such as those made by the Patent and Trademark Office. Other courts, such as the Court of Appeals for Armed Forces, have been created to handle special subject matter. Figure 3.3 illustrates the location of the Courts of Appeals.

7. DECISIONS BY THE U.S. SUPREME COURT

In addition to the court of appeals, the federal court system provides for a Supreme Court. Because the litigants are entitled to only one review, or appeal, a subsequent review by the U.S. Supreme Court must be obtained through a petition for a *writ of certiorari* to the Supreme Court.

A petition for a *writ of certiorari* is a request by the losing party in the court of appeals for permission to file an appeal with the U.S. Supreme Court. In such situations, the Supreme Court has discretion as to whether or not it will grant the petition and allow another review. This review is not a matter of right. *Writs of certiorari* are granted only in cases of substantial federal importance or where there is an obvious conflict between decisions of two or more U.S. Circuit Courts of Appeal in an important area of the law that needs clarification. The Supreme Court's decision becomes the law of the land and reconciles the division of opinion between the lower courts.

*Four U.S. Supreme Court justices must vote yes to grant a petition for a *writ of certiorari*.

When the U.S. Supreme Court reviews petitions for a *writ of certiorari*, the writ is granted if four of the nine justices vote to take the case. The Supreme Court spends a great deal of time and effort in deciding which cases it will hear. It is able to pick and choose those issues with which it will be involved and to control its caseload. The Supreme Court normally resolves cases involving major constitutional issues or interpretation of federal law. In recent years, the Court has been very reluctant to review many lower court decisions. In the 2006–2007 term of the U.S. Supreme Court, only 75 cases were heard. (See Sidebar 3.5.)

The Supreme Court is far more likely to review and reverse a decision rendered by the Ninth Circuit Court of Appeals—treating it, as one commentator noted, like a wayward child. Many commentators attribute the difference to the judicial activism of the Ninth Circuit, which often is at odds with the philosophy of judicial restraint found in the Supreme Court in recent years. In contrast, decisions rendered by the Fourth Circuit Court of Appeals

*Supreme Court case reviews have been steadily declining in recent years.

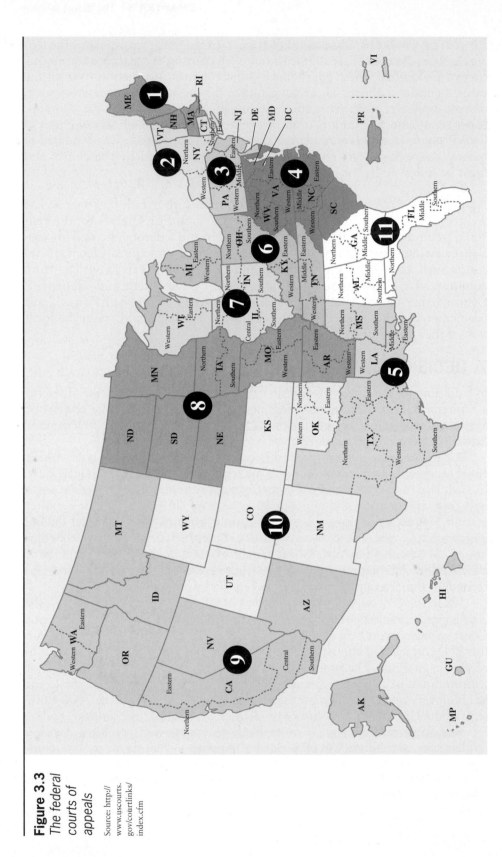

Figure 3.3
The federal courts of appeals

Source: http://
www.uscourts.
gov/courtlinks/
index.cfm

:: *sidebar* 3.5

The Very Slim Odds

Every year between seven and eight thousand petitions are filed in the U.S. Supreme Court from parties seeking review of adverse decisions issued by federal circuit courts of appeal or state supreme courts. Parties pay a $300 filing fee and thousands of dollars to appellate lawyers to prepare their petitions. However, the odds heavily favor the decisions issued by the lower courts. In the 2001–2002 term of court, the Supreme Court agreed to hear only 88 cases. In the 2004–2005 term of court, that number fell to just 80 cases or about 1 percent of the petitions filed. For the 2006–2007 term of court, the number of cases fell even further to 75.

tend to be far more conservative or consistent with the philosophy of judicial restraint. A more thorough discussion of these two philosophies will follow in Sections 8 and 9 of this chapter.

The federal district courts and the courts of appeal cannot review, retry, or correct judicial errors charged against a state court. Final judgments or decrees rendered by the highest court of a state are reviewed only by the Supreme Court of the United States. State cases reviewed by the U.S. Supreme Court must concern a federal question involving the validity of state action on the grounds that the statute under review is repugnant to the Constitution, treaties, or laws of the United States. If the case does not involve a federal question, the decision of the highest state court is not subject to review by the Supreme Court of the United States.

:: *sidebar* 3.6

The Role of the Reviewing Court

Since reviewing courts create case law or precedent in the process of deciding cases, most final decisions of reviewing courts are published in order to make the precedent of each case available for inclusion into the total body of law. The opinions usually include the procedures which have been followed, the facts of the case, the law applicable to the facts, the decision of the court, and the reasons for the decision. Opinions may be written in the name of the author of the opinion or they may be written *per curiam*—by the court without identifying the author.

It is not surprising that the decisions of a reviewing court often are not unanimous. Some Supreme Court decisions are closely divided and 5–4 or 6–3 decisions in cases involving highly controversial issues are quite common. The *Roe v. Wade* decision legalizing abortions, and the cases involving abortions which followed, often have been decided 5–4 or 6–3. Presidential appointments to the Supreme Court are evaluated, in part, on their potential effect on the court alignment as perceived in the close decisions of the past.

The written opinions in the cases in this textbook reflect the majority opinion of the reviewing court and as such they reflect the current status of the law. Dissenting opinions of the court also make a contribution to our jurisprudence and to the public debate on important social and public policy issues. Dissents often provide the foundation for changes in public policy and they often provide guidance to legislative bodies on issues under consideration.

concept :: *summary*

Organization of the Court System

1. The court system—both at the federal and state level—operates on three levels: the trial court, the court of appeals, and the supreme court.
2. Trial courts focus on the law and facts while reviewing courts focus only on the law.
3. The parties to litigation are entitled as a matter of right to one review of their case by a higher court.
4. Subject matter jurisdiction must exist for a court to hear a case.

5. Federal courts typically obtain jurisdiction upon diversity of citizenship or federal questions.
6. The highest legal authority in the United States is the U.S. Supreme Court.
7. Parties seek permission to bring their case to the Supreme Court through a petition for a *writ of certiorari.*

:: The Power of Judicial Review

*Judicial review is the ultimate power to invalidate actions by the president or the Congress.

In the United States the most significant power of the courts, or "judiciary," is **judicial review,** which is the power to review laws passed by the legislative body and to declare them to be unconstitutional and void. It also allows the courts to review actions taken by the executive branch and to declare them unconstitutional. Although the Constitution does not expressly provide that the judiciary shall be the overseer of the government, the net effect of this power is to make it so. Chief Justice John Marshall in *Marbury v. Madison,* 5 U.S. 137 (1803), announced the power of judicial review using in part the following language and reasoning:

> It is a proposition too plain to be contested, that the constitution controls any legislative act repugnant to it; or, that the legislature may not alter the constitution by an ordinary act. . . .
>
> It is emphatically the province and duty of the judicial department to say what the law is. Those who apply the rule to particular cases, must of necessity expound and interpret that rule. If two laws conflict with each other, the courts must decide on the operation of each. So, if a law be in opposition to the constitution; if both the law and the constitution apply to a particular case, so that the court must either decide that case, conformably to the law, disregarding the constitution; or conformably to the constitution, disregarding the law; the court must determine which of these conflicting rules governs the case: this is of the very essence of judicial duty. If then, the courts are to regard the constitution, and the constitution is superior to any ordinary act of the legislature, the constitution, and not such ordinary act, must govern the case to which they both apply.

In practice, the U.S. Supreme Court rarely exercises its extraordinary powers and has developed carefully crafted rules as self-imposed limits on its authority as individual jurists.

The terms judicial restraint and judicial activism are not exclusive to particular judges. Many judges may share aspects of both in their judicial philosophy.

As individual jurists exercise the power of judicial review, they do so with varying political attitudes and philosophies. Some judges believe that judicial power should be used very sparingly, although others are willing to use it more often. Those who believe that the power should not be used except in unusual cases are said to believe in **judicial restraint.** Those who think that the power should be used whenever the needs of society justify its use believe in **judicial activism.** All members of the judiciary believe in judicial restraint and all are activists to some extent. Often a jurist may be an activist in one area of the law and a firm believer in judicial restraint in another. Both judicial restraint and judicial activism describe attitudes or tendencies by matters of degree. Both terms are also used to describe general attitudes toward the exercise of the power of judicial review.

In recent years, judicial restraint has been associated with conservative judges often appointed by Republican presidents. Judicial activism primarily is linked to liberal judges generally appointed by Democratic presidents. The tension between these philosophies has become more pronounced in the past several years often leading to bitterly divided confirmation hearings before the U.S. Senate where less attention often is paid to a nominee's qualifications than to his or her political views. Sidebar 3.7 describes the process of becoming a Supreme Court justice.

:: *sidebar* 3.7

Choosing a Supreme Court Justice

In the federal system, the U.S. Constitution gives the president the power to appoint federal judges, including Supreme Court justices, subject to the advice and consent of the U.S. Senate. In practical terms, this means a majority of the U.S. Senate must vote to confirm the president's nominee. Typically, after the president announces his nominee, interest groups on both sides search out information, including past decisions, about the candidate. The nominee is questioned by the Senate Judiciary Committee, which also hears testimony from others about the nominee's qualifications and judicial philosophy. If the Judiciary Committee approves the nominee, the nomination is forwarded to the entire Senate for debate before a vote is taken. The confirmation process can take months and is often subject to bitter conflict between Republican and Democratic senators and the White House.

8. JUDICIAL RESTRAINT

The philosophy of judicial restraint developed naturally from the recognition that, in exercising the power of judicial review, the courts are overseeing coequal branches of government. When the power of judicial review is used to set aside decisions by the other branches of government, the courts are wielding great power. A commitment to the constitutional system dictates that this almost unlimited power be exercised with great restraint.

Those who believe in judicial restraint think that many constitutional issues are too important to be decided by courts unless absolutely necessary and are to be avoided if there is another legal basis for a decision. They believe the proper use of judicial power demands that courts refrain from determining the constitutionality of an act of Congress unless it is absolutely necessary to a decision of a case. This modest view of the role of the judiciary is based on the belief that litigation is not the appropriate technique for bringing about social, political, and economic change.

The philosophy of judicial restraint is sometimes referred to as *strict constructionism,* or *judicial abstention.* Strict constructionists believe that

Most recently, Chief Justice Roberts and Justice Alito were selected based upon the expectation that they favored judicial restraint.

˄Followers of judicial restraint favor a very limited role for the courts in our system of government.

the Constitution should be interpreted in light of what the Founding Fathers intended. They place great weight on the debates of the Constitutional Convention and the language of the Constitution. Those who promote judicial abstention hold that courts should decide only those matters they must to resolve actual cases and controversies before them. Courts should abstain from deciding issues whenever possible, and doubts about the constitutionality of legislation should be resolved in favor of the statute. Cases should be decided on the facts if possible and on the narrowest possible grounds.

Those who believe in judicial restraint believe that social, political, and economic change in society should result from the political process rather than from court action. Justice John Harlan, in *Republic v. Sims*, 84 S.Ct. 1362 (1964), epitomized the philosophy of judicial restraint in a famous dissenting opinion contained in Sidebar 3.8.

:: *sidebar* 3.8

Understanding Judicial Restraint

The vitality of our political system, on which in the last analysis all else depends, is weakend by reliance on the judiciary for political reform. . . . These decisions give support to a current mistaken view of the Constitution and the constitutional function of this Court. This view, in a nutshell, is that every major social ill in the country can find its cure in some constitutional "principle," and that this Court should "take the lead" in promoting reform when other branches of government fail to act. The Constitution is not a panacea for every blot upon the public welfare, nor should this Court, ordained as a judicial body, be thought of as a general haven for reform movements. The Constitution is an instrument of government, fundamental to which is the premise that in a diffusion of governmental authority lies the greatest promise that this nation will realize liberty for all its citizens. This Court, limited in function in accordance with that premise, does not serve its high purpose when it exceeds its authority, even to satisfy justified impatience with the slow working of the political process.

Since Roberts and Alito joined the Supreme Court, their rulings and writings have rested primarily with the conservative wing of the Court.

Judges who identify with judicial restraint give great deference to the political process. They believe that the courts, especially the federal courts, ought to defer to the actions of the states and of the coordinate branches of government unless these actions are clearly unconstitutional. They allow the states and the federal legislative and executive branches wide latitude in finding solutions to the nation's problems.

Judicial restraint jurists have a deep commitment to precedent. They overrule cases only when the prior decision is clearly wrong. They try to refrain from writing their personal convictions into the law. They do not view the role of the lawyer and the practice of law as that of social reform. To them, reform is the function of the political process.

Followers of judicial restraint often take a pragmatic approach to litigation. Whenever possible, decisions are based on the facts rather than a principle of law. Reviewing courts exercising judicial restraint tend to accept the trial court decisions unless they are clearly wrong on the facts or the law. If there is any reasonable basis for the lower court decision, it will not be reversed. Such courts often engage in a balancing approach to their decisions.

They weigh competing interests. For example, justices who adhere to judicial restraint often weigh the rights of the person accused of crime with the interests of the victim and of society in determining the extent of the rights of the accused in criminal cases.

Throughout most of our history, judicial restraint has been the dominant philosophy. Today, a majority of the justices of the U.S. Supreme Court usually follow this philosophy, but all courts to some degree also are activist. Sidebar 3.9 illustrates some typical judicial restraint decisions. The Court allowed these decisions by other branches of government and the political process to stand.

:: *sidebar* 3.9

Typical Judicial Restraint Decisions

1. Male-only draft is not a denial of equal protection of the law.
2. States can regulate nuclear power.
3. States can tax the foreign income of multinational corporations.
4. Prayer in the legislature does not violate the First Amendment.
5. Unanimous verdicts are not required, and juries may consist of fewer than 12 persons.
6. A federal law cannot require state law enforcement officers to conduct background checks on gun purchasers.
7. Class-action suits require actual notice to members of the class.
8. Congress cannot create religious freedoms pursuant to Section 5 of the Fourteenth Amendment.
9. Seniority has preference over affirmative action layoffs.
10. State and local employees are subject to the Federal Fair Labor Standards Act.

---

9. JUDICIAL ACTIVISM

Those who believe in the philosophy of judicial activism believe that courts have a major role to play in correcting wrongs in our society. To them, courts must provide leadership in bringing about social, political, and economic change because the political system is often too slow or unable to bring about those changes necessary to improve society. Activists tend to be innovative and less dependent on precedent for their decisions. They are value oriented and policy directed. Activist jurists believe that constitutional issues must be decided within the context of contemporary society and that the meaning of the Constitution is relative to the times in which it is being interpreted. Activists believe that the courts, and especially the Supreme Court, sit as a continuing constitutional convention to meet the needs of today.

During the 1950s and 1960s, there was an activist majority on the Supreme Court. This activist majority brought about substantial changes in the law, especially in such areas as civil rights, reapportionment, and the criminal law. For example, the activist court of this period ordered desegregation of public schools and gave us the one-man, one-vote concept in the distributing of legislative bodies. Earl Warren, chief justice during that period, used

*Followers of judicial activism favor a more expansive role for the courts in our system of government.

to request that lawyers appearing before the Court address themselves to the effect of their clients' positions on society. "Tell me why your position is 'right' and that of your opponent is 'wrong' from the standpoint of society" was a common request to lawyers arguing cases before him.

Activist courts tend to be more result conscious and to place less reliance on precedent. Activists are often referred to as liberals, but that description is too narrow to explain their belief in the role of the judiciary as an instrument of change. Activists also believe that justices must examine for themselves the great issues facing society and then decide these issues in light of contemporary standards. Otherwise, they believe we are governed by the dead or by people who are not aware of all of the complexities of today's problems.

Sidebar 3.10 illustrates typical judicial activist decisions. These examples are of decisions in which that judiciary has imposed its will on society.

> Although dissenting opinions are not usually included in this textbook, they remain an important part of the judicial process and may become the law of the land in the future as the composition of the Supreme Court changes over time. See Justice Scalia's dissent in the sample case.

:: *sidebar* 3.10

Typical Judicial Activist Decisions

1. Welfare recipients have a right to travel among states and be treated like others in their new states.
2. The Pledge of Allegiance is an unconstitutional endorsement of religion when recited in public schools because of the reference to "under God."
3. No prayer is permitted in school.
4. The *Miranda* warning shall be given to all criminal suspects prior to interrogation.
5. Statutes outlawing abortion are unconstitutional.
6. Female pensions must be the same as male pensions, even though, on average, females live longer.
7. There shall be equal pay for comparable worth.
8. Residency requirements for public assistance violates equal protection.
9. State laws that require teaching "creation science" as well as evolution are unconstitutional.
10. Certain public employees, such as public defenders, cannot be fired because of political affiliation.

Chief Justice John Roberts began presiding over the Supreme Court in 2005. The Court's decisions are often split along 5–4 lines with Justice Anthony Kennedy usually deciding whether the consistently conservative foursome of Roberts, Antonin Scalia, Clarence Thomas, and Samuel Alito, or the more activist foursome of John Paul Stevens, David Souter, Ruth Bader Ginsburg, and Stephen Breyer prevail. In many cases, Justice Kennedy joins to create a conservative majority favoring judicial restraint as illustrated in Sidebar 3.11.

Mirroring societal trends, the Supreme Court's divided decisions are often peppered with angry words about each other. Justices use phrases like "scanty and equivocal evidence" and "analytical confusion" and words such as "unrealistic" and "indefensible" in response. The importance of the issues and the close division of the Court contributes to the tension found in many divided opinions. Sidebar 3.12 offers another perspective on the differences found on the Supreme Court.

> In the 2007–2008 term, there were fewer 5–4 decisions than usual with Justice Stevens, the anchor of the Court's activist wing, siding with his more conservative colleagues in several high-profile cases. In several other cases, the court's normal division was not as apparent as in previous years.

:: *sidebar* 3.11

Typical Alignment of Justices

:: Judicial Activism	:: Moderate	:: Judicial Restraint
Stevens		Roberts
Souter		Scalia
Ginsburg		Thomas
Breyer		Alito
	Kennedy	

:: *sidebar* 3.12

Labeling Judges As Liberal or Conservative

Some legal scholars do not think it is fair to label judges as liberal or conservative. Peter G. Verniero, a former justice of the New Jersey Supreme Court, made the following argument against this traditional approach: "In particular, labeling judges as 'conservative' or 'liberal' can result in false impressions of the judiciary. Those labels wrongly suggest that judges should resolve disputes on the basis of partisan ideology. . . . Jurists are not robots. When the law is unclear, judges must do their best to determine the intent of the lawmakers. That process of judicial decision-making is not activism—it's judging. In an earlier, less partisan era, terms like 'conservative' or 'liberal' might have communicated something useful about the philosophies of sitting or potential jurists. Indeed, there's nothing inherently bad about being known by either label. Still, in today's climate, use of those terms can have a polarizing effect and erode confidence in judges by casting them in a purely political way. That weakens the judiciary, to everyone's detriment."

Source: Atlanta Constitution, April 22, 2008.

10. A SAMPLE CASE

We present the following case at the outset of this edition as an example of how the Supreme Court influences critically important areas of the law. While not a case involving a business dispute, the law is an interconnected web so that the principles that apply to one case can have application in the next. The case demonstrates the tense and controversial nature of the Court clashing with the president during a time of war. The case arose out of a series of conflicts with the Bush Administration over the handling of detainees held at the Guantanamo Bay Naval Base in Cuba. In the case, the Court declared unconstitutional a provision in the Military Commissions Act of 2006 that withdrew federal court jurisdiction to hear habeas corpus petitions from detainees held at Guantanamo Bay who had been classified as enemy combatants as a result of their alleged involvement with terrorism.

In a bitterly divided 5–4 ruling, Justice Kennedy wrote the majority opinion, and he was joined in the decision by Justices Breyer, Ginsburg, Souter, and

Habeas corpus is a legal doctrine that gives prisoners the right to challenge their confinement and requires the government to offer valid reasons for imprisonment.

:: *sidebar* 3.13

Supreme Court Justices

John Roberts, Chief Justice of the United States (born 1955). He received his B.A. from Harvard College and his J.D. from Harvard Law School. President George W. Bush nominated him as chief justice, and he took office in 2005.

John Paul Stevens, Associate Justice (born 1920). He received an A.B. from the University of Chicago, and a J.D. from Northwestern University School of Law. President Ford nominated him as an associate justice of the Supreme Court, and he took office in 1975.

Antonin Scalia, Associate Justice (born 1936). He received his A.B. from Georgetown University and the University of Fribourg, Switzerland, and his LL.B. from Harvard Law School. President Reagan nominated him as an associate justice of the Supreme Court, and he took office in 1986.

Anthony Kennedy, Associate Justice (born 1936). He received his B.A. from Stanford University and the London School of Economics, and his LL.B. from Harvard Law School. President Reagan nominated him as an associate justice of the Supreme Court, and he took office in 1983.

David Souter, Associate Justice (born 1939). He received his A.B. from Harvard College, was a Rhodes Scholar at Oxford University where he received another A.B. and an M.A. He received his LL.B. from Harvard Law School. President

George H. W. Bush nominated him as an associate justice of the Supreme Court, and he took office in 1990.

Clarence Thomas, Associate Justice (born 1948). He attended Conception Seminary and received an A.B., cum laude, from Holy Cross College, and a J.D. from Yale Law School. President George H. W. Bush nominated him as an associate justice of the Supreme Court, and he took office in 1991.

Ruth Bader Ginsburg, Associate Justice (born 1933). She received her B.A. from Cornell University, attended Harvard Law School, and received her LL.B. from Columbia Law School. President Clinton nominated her as an associate justice of the Supreme Court, and she took office in 1993.

Stephen Breyer, Associate Justice (born 1938). He received an A.B. from Stanford University, a B.A. from Magdalen College, Oxford, and an LL.B. from Harvard Law School. President Clinton nominated him as an associate justice of the Supreme Court, and he took office in 1994.

Samuel Alito, Associate Justice (born 1950). He received his A.B. from Princeton University and his J.D. from Yale Law School. President George W. Bush nominated him as associate justice and he took office in 2006.

Stevens. The majority decreed that "[t]he laws and Constitution are designed to survive, and remain in force, in extraordinary times." Justice Scalia, in a dissent joined by Chief Justice Roberts, Justices Thomas, and Alito, predicted devastating consequences from the decision and concluded that "[i]t will almost certainly cause more Americans to be killed." He accused the majority of having an "inflated notion of judicial supremacy."

The case shows controversial issues before the Supreme Court can be decided by a single vote. The appointment of only one justice can have significant consequences on the future course of the law. Although other case examples throughout the text are limited to the majority opinion, the following sample case includes language from a dissenting opinion to show you how various justices can express far different points of view on the state of the law.

BOUMEDIENE v. BUSH
128 S. Ct. 2229 (2008)

Petitioners are aliens detained at Guantanamo after being captured in Afghanistan or elsewhere abroad and designated enemy combatants. Denying membership in the al Qaeda terrorist network that carried out the September 11 attacks and the Taliban regime that supported al Qaeda, each petitioner sought a writ of habeas corpus.

Congress passed the Detainee Treatment Act of 2005 (DTA) to provide that "no court, justice, or judge shall have jurisdiction to consider an application for habeas corpus filed by or on behalf of an alien detained at Guantanamo," and gave the D.C. Circuit "exclusive" jurisdiction to review Combatant Status Review Tribunal (CSRT) decisions. In Hamdan v. Rumsfeld, 548 U.S. 557, the court held this provision inapplicable to cases (like petitioners') pending when the DTA was enacted. Congress responded with the Military Commissions Act of 2006 (MCA), to deny jurisdiction with respect to habeas corpus actions by detained aliens determined to be enemy combatants, while also denying jurisdiction as to "any other action against the United States . . . relating to any aspect of the detention, transfer, treatment, trial, or conditions of confinement" of a detained alien determined to be an enemy combatant.

The D.C. Circuit Court of Appeals concluded that the MCA must be read to strip from it, and all federal courts, jurisdiction to consider petitioners' habeas applications; that petitioners are not entitled to habeas or the protections of the Suspension Clause, U.S. Const., Art. I, § 9, cl. 2, which provides that "[t]he Privilege of the Writ of Habeas Corpus shall not be suspended, unless when in Cases of Rebellion or Invasion the public Safety may require it."

KENNEDY, J.: . . . Petitioners are aliens designated as enemy combatants and detained at the United States Naval Station at Guantanamo Bay, Cuba. There are others detained there, also aliens, who are not parties to this suit.

Petitioners present a question not resolved by our earlier cases relating to the detention of aliens at Guantanamo: whether they have the constitutional privilege of habeas corpus, a privilege not to be withdrawn except in conformance with the Suspension Clause, Art. I, §9, cl. 2. We hold these petitioners do have the habeas corpus privilege. Congress has enacted a statute, the Detainee Treatment Act of 2005 (DTA) that provides certain procedures for review of the detainees' status. We hold that those procedures are not an adequate and effective substitute for habeas corpus. Therefore the Military Commissions Act of 2006 (MCA) operates as an unconstitutional suspension of the writ [of habeas corpus]. . . .

As a threshold matter, we must decide whether MCA denies the federal courts jurisdiction to hear habeas corpus actions pending at the time of its enactment. We hold the statute does deny that jurisdiction, so that, if the statute is valid, petitioners' cases must be dismissed. . . .

In deciding the constitutional questions now presented we must determine whether petitioners are barred from seeking the writ or invoking the protections of the Suspension Clause either because of their status, *i.e.*, petitioners' designation by the Executive Branch as enemy combatants, or their physical location, *i.e.*, their presence at Guantanamo Bay. The Government contends that non-citizens designated as enemy combatants and detained in territory located outside our Nation's borders have no constitutional rights and no privilege of habeas corpus. Petitioners contend they do have cognizable constitutional rights and that Congress, in seeking to eliminate recourse to habeas corpus as a means to assert those rights, acted in violation of the Suspension Clause.

[The] protection for the privilege of habeas corpus was one of the few safeguards of liberty specified in a Constitution that, at the outset, had no Bill of Rights. In the system conceived by the Framers the writ had a centrality that must inform proper interpretation of the Suspension Clause. . . .

The Framers viewed freedom from unlawful restraint as a fundamental precept of liberty, and they understood the writ of habeas corpus as a vital instrument to secure that freedom. Experience taught, however, that the common law writ all too often had been insufficient to guard against the abuse of monarchial power. That history counseled the necessity for specific language in the Constitution to secure the writ and ensure its place in our legal system. . . .

The Framers' inherent distrust of governmental power was the driving force behind the constitutional plan that allocated powers among three independent branches. This design serves not only to make Government accountable but also to secure individual liberty. . . .

That the Framers considered the writ a vital instrument for the protection of individual liberty is evident from the care taken to specify the limited grounds for its suspension: "The Privilege of the Writ of Habeas Corpus shall not be suspended, unless when in Cases of Rebellion or Invasion of public Safety may require it." Art. I, §9, cl. 2. . . . Surviving accounts of the ratification debates provide additional evidence that the Framers deemed the writ to be an essential mechanism in the separation-of-powers scheme. . . . Alexander Hamilton explained that by providing the detainee a judicial forum to challenge detention, the writ preserves limited government. . . .

In our system the Suspension Clause is designed to protect against these cyclical abuses. The Clause protects the rights of the detained by a means consistent with the essential design of the Constitution. It ensures that, except during periods of formal suspension, the Judiciary will have a time-tested device, the writ, to maintain the "delicate balance of governance" that is itself the surest safeguard of liberty. . . .

Drawing from its position that at common law the writ ran only to territories over which the Crown was sovereign, the Government says the Suspension Clause affords petitioners no rights because the United States does not claim sovereignty over the place of detention. Guantanamo Bay is not formally part of the United States.

Our cases do not hold it is improper for us to inquire into the objective degree of control the Nation asserts over foreign territory. The Court has discussed the issue of the Constitution's extraterritorial application on many occasions. The Framers foresaw that the United States would expand and acquire new territories. . . . The United States has maintained complete and uninterrupted control of the bay for over 100 years. . . .

We recognize that there are costs to holding the Suspension Clause applicable in a case of military detention abroad. Habeas corpus proceedings may require expenditure of funds by the Government and may divert the attention of military personnel from other pressing tasks. While we are sensitive to these concerns, we do not find them dispositive. Compliance with any judicial process requires some incremental expenditure of resources. Yet civilian courts and the Armed Forces have functioned along side each other at various points in our history. . . .

The United States Naval Station at Guantanamo Bay consists of 45 square miles of land and water. The base has been used, at various points, to house migrants and refugees temporarily. At present, however, other than the detainees themselves, the only long-term residents are American military personnel, their families, and a small number of workers. The detainees have been deemed enemies of the United States. At present, dangerous as they may be if released, they are contained in a secure prison facility located on an isolated and heavily fortified military base.

No Cuban court has jurisdiction over American military personnel at Guantanamo or the enemy combatants detained there. While obligated to abide by the terms of the lease, the United States is, for all practical purposes, answerable to no other sovereign for its acts on the base.

It is true that before today the Court has never held that noncitizens detained by our Government in territory over which another country maintains *de jure* sovereignty have any rights under our Constitution. But the cases before us lack any precise historical parallel. They involve individuals detained by executive order for the duration of a conflict that, if measured from September 11, 2001, to the present, is already among the longest wars in American history. The detainees, moreover, are held in a territory that, while technically not part of the United States, is under the complete and total control of our Government. Under these circumstances the lack of a precedent on point is no barrier to our holding.

We hold that Art. I, §9, cl. 2, of the Constitution has full effect at Guantanamo Bay. If the privilege of habeas corpus is to be denied to the detainees now before us, Congress must act in accordance with the requirements of the Suspension Clause. . . .

In light of this holding the question becomes whether the statute stripping jurisdiction to issue the writ avoids the Suspension Clause mandate because Congress has provided adequate substitute procedures for habeas corpus. . . .

Although we do not hold that an adequate substitute must duplicate [habeas corpus] in all respects, it suffices that the Government has not established that the detainees' access to the statutory review provisions at issue is an adequate substitute for the writ of habeas corpus. The MCA thus effects an unconstitutional suspension of the writ.

The real risks, the real threats, of terrorist attaches are constant and not likely soon to abate. The ways to disrupt our life and laws are so many and unforeseen that the Court should not attempt even some general catalogue of crises that might occur. Certain principles are apparent, however. Practical considerations and exigent circumstances inform the definition and reach of the law's writs, including habeas corpus. The cases and our tradition reflect this precept. . . .

Our opinion does not undermine the Executive's powers as Commander in Chief. On the contrary, the exercise of those powers is vindicated, not eroded, when confirmed by the Judicial Branch. Within the Constitution's separation-of-powers structure, few exercises of judicial power are as legitimate or as necessary as the responsibility to hear challenges to the authority of the Executive to imprison a person. Some of these petitioners have been in custody for six years with no definitive judicial determination as to the legality of their detention. Their access to the writ is a necessity to determine the lawfulness of their status, even if, in the end, they do not obtain the relief they seek.

The determination by the Court of Appeals that the Suspension Clause and its protections are inapplicable to petitioners was in error. The judgment of the Court of Appeals is reversed.

It is so ordered.

DISSENT: SCALIA, J.: Today, for the first time in our Nation's history, the Court confers a constitutional right to habeas corpus on alien enemies detained abroad by our military forces in the course of an ongoing war. The procedures prescribed by Congress provide the essential protections that habeas corpus guarantees; there has thus been no suspension of the writ, and no basis exists for judicial intervention beyond what the Act allows. My problem with today's opinion is more fundamental still: The writ of habeas corpus does not, and never has, run in favor of aliens abroad; the Suspension Clause thus has no application, and the Court's intervention in this military matter is entirely *ultra vires*.

America is at war with radical Islamists. The enemy began by killing Americans and American allies abroad: 241 at the Marine barracks in Lebanon, 19 at the Khobar Towers in Dhahran, 224 at our embassies in Dar es Salaam and Nairobi, and 17 on the USS Cole in Yemen. On September 11, 2001, the enemy brought the battle to American soil, killing 2,749 at the Twin Towers in New York City, 184 at the Pentagon in Washington, D.C., and 40 in Pennsylvania. It has threatened further attacks against our homeland; one need only walk about buttressed and barricaded Washington, or board a plane anywhere in the country, to know that the threat is a serious one. Our Armed Forces are now in the field against the enemy, in Afghanistan and Iraq.

The game of bait-and-switch that today's opinion plays upon the Nation's Commander in Chief will make the war harder on us. It will almost certainly cause more Americans to be killed. . . . Astoundingly, the Court today raises the bar, requiring military officials to appear before civilian courts and defend their decisions under procedural and evidentiary rules that go beyond what Congress has specified. . . . Even when the Military has evidence that it can bring forward, it is often foolhardy to release that evidence to the attorneys representing our enemies. And one escalation of procedures that the Court *is* clear about is affording the detainees increased access to witnesses (perhaps troops serving in Afghanistan?) and to classified information. . . .

It is clear that Congress and the Executive—*both* political branches—have determined that limiting the role of civilian courts in adjudicating whether prisoners captured abroad are properly detained is important to success in the war that some 190,000 of our men and women are now fighting. As the Solicitor General argued, the Military Commissions Act and the Detainee Treatment Act . . . represent an effort by the political branches to strike an appropriate balance between the need to preserve liberty and the need to accommodate the weighty and sensitive governmental interests in ensuring that those who have in fact fought with the enemy during a war do not return to battle against the United States.

What competence does the Court have to second-guess the judgment of Congress and the President on such a point? None whatever. But the Court blunders in nonetheless. Henceforth, as today's opinion makes unnervingly clear, how to handle enemy prisoners in this war will ultimately lie with the branch that knows least about the national security concerns that the subject entails. . . .

What drives today's decision is neither the meaning of the Suspension Clause, nor the principles of our precedents, but rather an inflated notion of judicial supremacy. . . .

Today the Court warps our Constitution in a way that goes beyond the narrow issue of the reach of the Suspension Clause, invoking judicially brainstormed separation-of-powers principles to establish a manipulable "functional" test for the extraterritorial reach of habeas corpus (and, no doubt, for the extraterritorial reach of other constitutional protections as well). It blatantly misdescribes important precedents. It breaks a chain of precedent as old as the common law that prohibits juridical inquiry into detentions of aliens abroad absent statutory authorization. And, most tragically, it sets our military commanders the impossible task of proving to a civilian court, under whatever standards this Court devises in the future, that evidence supports the confinement of each and every enemy prisoner.

The Nation will live to regret what the Court has done today. I dissent.

:: CASE QUESTIONS

1. What is the procedural background of this lawsuit resulting in this Supreme Court decision?
2. What question did the Supreme Court take the case to answer and what was its answer?
3. Who ultimately is responsible for the decisions about the limits of habeas corpus?
4. What major differences are there between the majority's decision and the dissent?
5. From what you have learned about judicial restraint and judicial activism, which do you think the majority was exercising in this opinion?
6. Why does Justice Scalia dissent?

11. THE NATURE OF THE JUDICIAL PROCESS

In deciding cases and in examining the powers discussed in the prior sections, courts are often faced with several alternatives. They may decide the case by use of existing statutes and precedents and demonstrate a deep commitment to the common law system. They may also refuse to apply existing case law or declare a statute to be void as unconstitutional. If there is no statute or case law, the court may decide the case and create law in the process. However, case law as a basis for deciding controversies often provides only the point of departure from which the difficult labor of the court begins. The court must examine and compare cases cited as authority to it so it can determine not only which is correct, but also whether the principles should continue to be followed. In reaching its decision, the court must consider whether the ruling will provide justice in the particular case and whether it will establish sound precedent for future cases.

The foregoing alternatives raise several questions: Why do courts reach one conclusion rather than another in any given case? What formula, if any, is used in deciding cases and in determining the direction of the law? What forces tend to influence judicial decisions when the public interest is involved?

There is no simple answer to these questions. Many people assume that logic is the basic tool of the judicial decision. But Justice Oliver Wendell Holmes stated, "the life of the law has not been logic; it has been experience."[1] Others argue that courts merely reflect the attitudes of the times and simply follow the more popular course in decisions where the public is involved.

Justice Benjamin Cardozo, in a series of lectures on the judicial process,[2] discussed the sources of information judges utilize in deciding cases. He stated that if the answer were not clearly established by statute or by unquestioned precedent, the problem was twofold: "He [the judge] must first extract from the precedents the underlying principle, the *ratio decidendi*; he must then determine the path or direction along which the principle is to work and develop, if it is not to wither or die." The first part of the problem is separating legal principles from dicta so that the actual precedent is clear.

In Cardozo's judgment, the rule of analogy also was entitled to certain presumptions and should be followed if possible. He believed that the judge who molds the law by the method of philosophy is satisfying humanity's deep-seated desire for certainty. History, in indicating the direction of precedent, often illuminates the path of logic and plays an important part in decisions in areas such as real property. Custom or trade practice has supplied much of the direction of the law in the area of business. All judicial decisions are at least in part directed by the judge's viewpoint on the welfare of society. The end served by law must dictate the administration of justice, and ethical considerations, if ignored, will ultimately overturn a principle of law.

Noting the psychological aspects of judges' decisions, Cardozo observed that it is the subconscious forces that keep judges consistent with one another.

[1]*Holmes*, The Common Law 1 *(1938).*

[2]*Cardozo*, The Nature of the Judicial Process *(1921). Excerpts are used by permission from the Yale University Press.*

He recognized that all persons, including judges, have a philosophy that gives coherence and direction to their thought and actions whether they admit it or not.

> All their lives, forces which they do not recognize and cannot name, have been tugging at them—inherited instincts, traditional beliefs, acquired conviction; and the resultant is an outlook on life, a conception of social needs, . . . which when reasons are nicely balanced, must determine where choice shall fall. In this mental background every problem finds its setting. We may try to see things as objectively as we please. None the less, we can never see them with any eyes except our own. To that test they are all brought—a form of pleading or an act of parliament, the wrongs of paupers or the rights of princes, a village ordinance or a nation's charter.

In the following comments, Cardozo summarized his view of the judicial process.

case 3.2 ::

THE NATURE OF THE JUDICIAL PROCESS
Benjamin N. Cardozo

. . . My analysis of the judicial process comes then to this, and little more: logic, and history, and custom, and utility, and the accepted standards of right conduct are the forces which singly or in combination shape the progress of the law. Which of these forces shall dominate in any case must depend largely upon the comparative importance or value of the social interests that will be thereby promoted or impaired. One of the most fundamental social interests is that law shall be uniform and impartial. There must be nothing in its action that savors of prejudice or favor or even arbitrary whim for fitfulness. Therefore in the main there shall be adherence to precedent. There shall be symmetrical development, consistently with history or custom when history or custom has been the motive force, or the chief one, in giving shape to existing rules, and with logic or philosophy when the motive power has been theirs. But symmetrical development may be bought at too high a price. Uniformity ceases to be a good when it becomes uniformity of oppression. The social interest served by symmetry or certainty must then be balanced against the social interest served by equity and fairness or other elements of social welfare. These may enjoin upon the judge the duty of drawing the line at another angle, of staking the path along new courses, of marking a new point of departure from which others who come after him will set out upon their journey.

If you ask how he is to know when one interest outweighs another, I can only answer that he must get his knowledge just as the legislator gets it, from experience and study and reflection; in brief, from life itself. Here, indeed, is the point of contact between the legislator's work and his. The choice of methods, the appraisement of values, must in the end be guided by like considerations for the one as for the other. Each indeed is legislating within the limits of his competence. No doubt the limits for the judge are narrower. He legislates only between gaps. He fills the open spaces in the law. How far he can go without traveling beyond the walls of the interstices cannot be staked out for him upon a chart. He must learn it for himself as he gains the sense of fitness and proportion that comes with years of habitude in the practice of an art. Even within the gaps, restrictions not easy to define, but felt, however impalpable they may be, by every judge and lawyer, hedge and circumscribe his action. They are established by the traditions of the centuries, by the example of other judges, his predecessors and his colleagues, by the collective judgment of the profession, and by the duty of adherence to the pervading spirit of the law. . . . Nonetheless, within the confines of these open spaces and those of precedent and tradition, choice moves with a freedom which stamps its action as creative. The law which is the resulting product is not found, but made. The process, being legislative, demands the legislator's wisdom. . . .

concept :: *summary*

Judicial Review

1. Judicial review allows the courts to review actions taken by legislative and executive branches of government.
2. The philosophy of judicial restraint is sometimes referred to as strict constructionism or a conservative approach.
3. Supporters of judicial activism believe the courts are the appropriate body to bring about social, political, and economic change.
4. The Supreme Court is deeply divided between these two competing views of judicial decision making.

:: Key Terms

Appeal   70
Appellate court   69
Courts of appeal   70
Diversity of citizenship   72
Federal question cases   71
Federal Rules of Civil
    Procedure   73

Judicial activism   77
Judicial restraint   76
Judicial review   76
Petit jury   65
Small-claims court   70

Subject matter
    jurisdiction   69
Supreme court   70
Trial court   69
Writ of certiorari   71

:: Review Questions and Problems

Personnel

1. *Judges and Justices*

   What are the essential responsibilities of a trial judge?

2. *Jurors*

   Why have several states eliminated the requirement of unanimity in jury trials?

3. *Lawyers*

   Name the three critical roles a lawyer serves in society. Why have many lawyers and their business clients had such conflict in recent years?

Organization of the Court System

4. *Subject Matter Jurisdiction*

   Mark, a citizen of Georgia, was crossing a street in Atlanta when he was struck by a car driven by David, a citizen of New York visiting Atlanta. The car was owned by David's employer, a Delaware corporation that has its principal place of business in Atlanta, Georgia. Mark sues both David and the corporation in federal district court in Atlanta alleging damages in the amount of $500,000. Does the court have subject matter jurisdiction? Why or why not?

5. *State Courts*

   What role do reviewing or appellate courts play in the judicial process? How do they differ from trial courts?

6. *Federal Courts*

XYZ makes and markets a product that it believes will help control weight by blocking the human body's digestion of starch. The Food and Drug Administration (FDA) has classified the product as a drug and orders it removed from the market until it can evaluate its use through testing. XYZ disputes the FDA's action and seeks to bring suit in the federal courts. Will the federal courts have jurisdiction to hear the case? Why or why not?

7. *Decisions by the U.S. Supreme Court*

Susan files a petition for certiorari in the U.S. Supreme Court following an adverse decision in the Illinois Supreme Court on a claim arising under a breach of contract. What chance does Susan have of the Supreme Court granting the petition? What special circumstances would she need to show?

The Power of Judicial Review

8. *Judicial Restraint*

Define the power of judicial review. How do advocates of judicial restraint exercise that power?

9. *Judicial Activism*

Define judicial activism. Compare and contrast judicial restraint and judicial activism.

10. Why are dissenting opinions important?

11. *Nature of the Judicial Process*

What are the forces that Justice Cardozo says shape the judicial process? How is the law made? In light of the liberal versus conservative divisions in the courts, are Cardozo's observations still relevant?

business :: *discussions*

1. You have spent the past four weeks away from work serving as a juror in a case deciding whether a pharmaceutical company should be held liable for the heart attack of a woman who took its painkiller, Oxxy-1. The lengthy case has taken a toll on your professional career, and you have many unanswered questions as jury deliberations begin.

1. Where does your duty lie in serving on a jury?
2. Are you protected against adverse employment action by your firm for missing work to serve on a jury?
3. How do you reconcile the woman's prior heart palpitations from years ago with her recent attack? Was her heart already compromised before she began taking the painkiller Oxxy-1?
4. Why didn't the pharmaceutical company withdraw the painkiller from the market at the first sign of a problem?

2. You are the president of a large corporation which is in the business of manufacturing, among other things, chemical products used to eradicate termites. You have just reviewed a confidential report, prepared by one of your top scientists, questioning the effectiveness of the product and the claims your business has been making to homeowners, pesticide treatment firms, and the general public. You have heard rumors that a lawsuit will be filed shortly against your corporation claiming that this product is ineffective.

Who should you turn to for advice?

Should you destroy the report?

In which court can a lawsuit be filed?

If you lose the lawsuit at trial, can you appeal?

4

Litigation

Learning Objectives ::

In this chapter you will learn:

1. To understand the litigation process and the parties to a case.

2. How issues such as standing to sue, personal jurisdiction, and class-action can impact litigation.

3. To understand the steps and costs associated with discovery.

4. About the pretrial and trial procedures in litigation.

5. To appreciate how cases are decided and the process for appeal and enforcement of judgments.

The court system and the litigation process help the business community resolve actual disputes under the rule of law. An impartial enforcement and dispute resolution process is essential to any system that preserves private property interests. In order to conduct business and enforce rights, we need a process to resolve disputes. Effective business leaders should develop an appreciation and understanding of the litigation process. Lawsuits and the threat of lawsuits impact every business regardless of size. By the time you have completed this chapter, you should have acquired a knowledge base regarding litigation and greater sensitivity to how a lawsuit is an immense drain of time, money, and energy on everyone involved in the case.

In this chapter, you will study the parties to litigation and the barriers presented to the resolution of a case in court. You will study a lawsuit itself—from pretrial procedures to the trial. Finally, you will learn about the process for resolving appeals and, ultimately, the enforcement of a final judgment.

The complaint formally starts the lawsuit. However, parties often have already attempted to informally or formally resolve their dispute through negotiation and alternative dispute resolution, which you will learn about in Chapter 5.

A sample complaint, is contained in Appendix II. The complaint sets out the parties, jurisdiction, venue, facts, and legal causes and remedies just like a real case. You should study it carefully before reading this chapter and refer back to it often to help you understand this chapter better.

:: Litigation—An Overview

To fully understand the litigation process, you need to be familiar with the terminology used to describe the parties who are adversaries in lawsuits. The next section reviews a variety of relevant terms. Following that, the legal concepts of when a party has the right to file a lawsuit, when a court has power over the parties, and when one person might sue on behalf of a much larger number of other persons are discussed.

The first of these issues is generally described as *standing to sue.* It is discussed in Section 2. If a plaintiff has standing to sue, the court next must determine if it has *personal jurisdiction* over the defendant. This issue is discussed in Section 3. The third problem area relates to *class-action suits,* which involve one or more individuals suing on behalf of all who may have the same grounds for suit. These suits are discussed more fully in Section 4.

1. PARTIES

*The sample complaint keeps things very simple. However, in many complex cases there may be several plaintiffs and defendants and multiple claims.

The party who files a civil action is called the **plaintiff.** The party sued is known as the **defendant.** The term *defendant* also is used to describe the person against whom a criminal charge is filed by the prosecuting state or federal government. When a defendant wants to sue the plaintiff, the defendant files a **counterclaim.** Most jurisdictions use the terms **counterplaintiff** and **counterdefendant** to describe the parties to the counterclaim. Thus, the defendant becomes a counterplaintiff and the plaintiff becomes a counterdefendant when a counterclaim is filed.

:: *sidebar* 4.1

Understanding the Sample Complaint

The sample complaint sets out the parties (plaintiff and defendant) and also explains how the court has subject-matter jurisdiction over the case (discussed in Chapter 3, Section 4). The sample complaint also explains how the parties can be served. In criminal cases, by contrast, the government files the case as the prosecutor and the defendant is the party charged with a crime. See Appendix II.

In most state jurisdictions and in federal courts, the law allows all persons to join in one lawsuit as plaintiffs if the causes of action arise out of the same transaction or series of transactions and involve common questions of law or fact. In addition, plaintiffs may join as defendants all persons who are necessary to a complete determination or resolution of the questions involved.

In addition, if a defendant alleges that there cannot be a complete determination of a controversy without the presence of other parties, he or she may bring in new third parties as **third-party defendants.** This procedure usually is followed when there is someone who may have liability to a defendant if the defendant has liability to the plaintiff. For example, assume Never-Fail, Inc., supplies brake shoes to the Ready-to-Go Mechanics Corporation. Ready-to-Go worked on your brakes, and thereafter you were injured when your car failed to stop at an intersection. After you filed a lawsuit against Ready-to-Go, it could bring Never-Fail, Inc., into the case as a third-party defendant. In essence, Ready-to-Go is arguing that if it is liable to you, then Never-Fail is liable to Ready-to-Go since the cause of the accident easily could be faulty brake shoes.

2. STANDING TO SUE

A court's power to resolve a controversy is limited by the subject matter involved in the case. The plaintiff must show the court that it has subject matter jurisdiction to hear the case. Moreover, a plaintiff must establish that he or she is entitled to have the court decide the dispute, that is, he or she has **standing to sue.**

To establish the required standing, a plaintiff must allege two things. First, the plaintiff must allege that the litigation involves a case or controversy. Courts are not free to litigate matters that have no connection to the law. For example, one business cannot maintain a suit against another business just because the two are competitors. There must be some allegation of a wrong that would create a dispute between plaintiff and defendant.

Second, the plaintiff must allege a personal stake in the resolution of the controversy. This element of standing prevents any individual from asserting the rights of the general public or of a group of which he or she is not a member. For instance, only a shareholder of one of the two companies involved in a merger could sue to stop the combination of these companies, despite the fact that such a merger may have a substantial adverse impact on competition in general.

In essence, through the standing-to-sue requirements, courts are able to insist that there be an adversarial relationship between plaintiff and defendant. This adversarial relationship helps present the issues to be litigated in sharper focus. To establish standing, plaintiffs must assert their personal legal positions and not those of third parties. Without the requirements of standing, courts would

In the sample complaint, the plaintiff satisfies standing by alleging facts demonstrating that the defendant has committed two legal wrongs causing a serious property loss to the plaintiff.

*In environmental harm cases, standing often is satisfied by showing the plaintiff uses the affected area and its aesthetic and recreational value has been lessened by the pollution.

:: *sidebar* 4.2

Identity Theft and Standing to Sue

The issue of identity is one of increasing concern to everyone personally both in the business arena and in the legal field. The Federal Trade Commission, the federal agency charged with handling these cases, has estimated the total costs because of identity theft are around $50 billion per year and that one out of eight Americans is a victim of some form of identity theft. The most common form is credit card theft, followed by making an unauthorized purchase on an existing account. Another source of theft is when there is a leak at a credit reporting agency. Those companies collect credit information about consumers and then release the information to legitimate users such as potential employers, potential lenders, or potential landlords.

When there is a break or leak at the credit reporting agency, thousands and sometimes millions of consumers' personal information is stolen. But, the consumer may not have a remedy. The credit reporting agency has a business relationship with the people to whom it provides the data. They have a duty to ensure the information is accurate. However, the credit reporting agency does not have a business relationship directly with the consumer. The courts up to this point have not been willing to allow defrauded consumers to bring suits against reporting agencies. Because of the lack of business relationship, the defrauded consumers lack a personal stake in the controversy, and thus lack standing to sue.

be faced with abstract legal questions of potentially wide public significance, questions generally best left to legislative bodies or administrative agencies.

It is very important to note that standing to sue does not depend upon the merits of the plaintiff's contention that particular conduct is illegal. The presence of standing is determined by the nature and source of the plaintiff's allegations. Standing is determined at the outset of the litigation, not by the outcome. Case 4.1 illustrates the critical nature of standing in winning a lawsuit. The case reinforces the rule that the courts are careful to avoid overstepping their constitutional role and will only rule on actual cases or controversies.

case **4.1**

HEIN v. FREEDOM FROM RELIGION FOUNDATION
127 S.Ct. 2553 (2007)

The president, by executive orders, created a White House office and several centers within federal agencies to ensure that faith-based community groups are eligible to compete for federal financial support. No congressional legislation specifically authorized these entities, which were created entirely within the executive branch, nor has Congress enacted any law appropriating money to their activities, which are funded through general executive branch appropriations. Respondents, an organization opposed to government endorsement of religion and three of its members, brought this suit alleging that petitioners, the directors of the federal offices, violated the Establishment Clause by organizing conferences that were designed to promote, and had the effect of promoting, religious community groups over secular ones. The only asserted basis for standing was that the individual respondents are federal taxpayers opposed to executive branch use of congressional appropriations for these conferences. The district court dismissed the claims for lack of standing. Because petitioners acted on the president's behalf and were not charged with administering a congressional program, the court held that the challenged activities did not authorize taxpayer standing. The Seventh Circuit reversed granting federal taxpayers standing to challenge executive branch programs on Establishment Clause grounds so long as the activities are financed by a congressional appropriation, even where there is no statutory program and the funds are from appropriations for general administrative expenses.

ALITO, J.: This is a lawsuit in which it was claimed that conferences held as part of the President's Faith-Based and Community initiatives program violated the Establishment Clause of the First Amendment because, among other things, President Bush and former Secretary

of Education Paige gave speeches that used "religious imagery" and praised the efficacy of faith-based programs in delivering social services. The plaintiffs contend that they meet the standing requirements of Article III of the Constitution because they pay federal taxes.

It has long been established, however, that the payment of taxes is generally not enough to establish standing to challenge an action taken by the Federal Government. In light of the size of the federal budget, it is a complete fiction to argue that an unconstitutional federal expenditure causes an individual federal taxpayer any measurable economic harm. And if every taxpayer could sue to challenge any Government expenditure, the federal courts would cease to function as courts of law and would be cast in the role of general complaint bureaus.

In 2001, the President issued an executive order creating the White House Office of Faith-Based and Community Initiatives within the Executive Office of the President. The office was specifically charged with the task of eliminating unnecessary bureaucratic, legislative, and regulatory barriers that could impede such organizations' effectiveness and ability to compete for federal assistance.

By separate executive orders, the President also created Executive Department Centers for Faith-Based and Community Initiatives within several federal agencies and departments. The centers were given the job of ensuring that faith-based community groups would be eligible to compete for federal financial support without impairing their independence or autonomy, as long as they did "not use direct Federal financial assistance to support any inherently religious activities, such as worship, religious instruction, or proselytization." Petitioners, who have been sued in their official capacities, are the directors of the White House Office and various Executive Department Centers.

The respondents are Freedom From Religion Foundation, Inc., a nonstick corporation "opposed to government endorsement of religion," and three of its members. Respondents brought suit in the United States District Court for the Western District of Wisconsin, alleging that petitioners violated the Establishment Clause by organizing conferences at which faith-based organizations allegedly "are singled out as being particularly worthy of federal funding, and the belief in God is extolled as distinguishing the claimed effectiveness of faith-based social services." Respondents further alleged that the content of these conferences sent a message to religious believers "that they are insiders and favored members of the political community" and that the conferences sent the message to nonbelievers "that they are outsiders" and "not full members of the political community." In short, respondents alleged that the conferences were designed to promote, and had the effect of promoting, religious community groups over secular ones.

The only asserted basis for standing was that the individual respondents are federal taxpayers who are "opposed to the use of Congressional taxpayer appropriations to advance and promote religion."

Article III of the Constitution limits the judicial power of the United States to the resolution of "Cases" and "Controversies," and "Article III standing . . . enforces the Constitution's case-or-controversy requirement."

[O]ne of the controlling elements in the definition of a case or controversy under Article III is standing. The requisite elements of Article III standing are well established. A plaintiff must allege personal injury fairly traceable to the defendant's allegedly unlawful conduct and likely to be redressed by the requested relief.

The constitutionally mandated standing inquiry is especially important in a case like this one, in which taxpayers seek to challenge laws of general application where their own injury is not distinct from that suffered in general by other taxpayers or citizens. This is because [t]he judicial power of the United States defined by Art. III is not an unconditioned authority to determine the constitutionality of legislative or executive acts. The federal courts are not empowered to seek out and strike down any governmental act that they deem to be repugnant to the Constitution. Rather, federal courts sit "solely, to decide on the rights of individuals."

As a general matter, the interest of a federal taxpayer in seeing that Treasury funds are spent in accordance with the Constitution does not give rise to the kind of redressable "personal injury" required for Article III standing. Of course, a taxpayer has standing to challenge the *collection* of a specific tax assessment as unconstitutional; being forced to pay such a tax causes a real and immediate economic injury to the individual taxpayer. But that is not the interest on which respondents assert standing here. Rather, their claim is that, having paid lawfully collected taxes into the Federal Treasury at some point, they have a continuing, legally cognizable interest in ensuring that those funds are not *used* by the Government in a way that violates the Constitution.

We have consistently held that this type of interest is too generalized and attenuated to support Article III standing. . . . Respondents do not challenge any specific congressional action or appropriation; nor do they ask the Court to invalidate any congressional enactment or legislatively created program as unconstitutional. These appropriations did not expressly authorize, direct, or even mention the expenditures of which respondents complain. Those expenditures resulted from executive discretion, not congressional action.

We have never found taxpayer standing under such circumstances. Respondents set out a parade of horribles that they claim could occur if [standing] is not extended to discretionary Executive Branch expenditures. For example, they say, a federal agency could use its discretionary funds to build a house of worship or to hire clergy of one denomination and send them out to spread their faith. Or an agency could use its funds to make bulk purchases of Stars of David, crucifixes, or depictions of the star and crescent for use in its offices or for distribution to the employees or the general public. Of course, none of these things has happened. In the unlikely event that any of these executive actions did take place, Congress could quickly step in. And respondents make no effort to show that these improbable abuses could not be challenged in federal court by plaintiffs who would possess standing based on grounds other than taxpayer standing.

For these reasons, the judgment of the Court of Appeals is reversed.

It is so ordered.

:: CASE QUESTIONS

1. Why did the president create the Office of Faith-Based and Community Initiatives?
2. What must a plaintiff show in order to establish standing to sue?
3. Why was standing lacking in this case?

The Pledge of Allegiance and Standing to Sue

In *Elk Grove Unified School District v. Newdow*, 542 U.S. 1 (2004), the Supreme Court denied standing to an atheist who objected to his daughter participating in the Pledge of Allegiance at her elementary school in California. The father objected to the Pledge because it contained the words "under God," which he viewed as religious indoctrination of his child. The Court found that the divorced mother actually had legal custody of her daughter under California law and that the father lacked standing to assert legal claims for his daughter. The mother also alleged that the daughter believed in God and had no objection to the Pledge.

3. PERSONAL JURISDICTION

Power to hear a case means a court must have authority not only over the subject matter of the case but also over the parties to the case. This latter authority is called **personal jurisdiction.** Personal jurisdiction over the plaintiff is obtained when the plaintiff files the suit. Such action indicates voluntary submission to the court's power.

Personal jurisdiction over the defendant usually is obtained by the service of a **summons,** or notice to appear in court, although in some cases it is obtained by the publication of notice and mailing a summons to the last known address. This delivery of notice is referred to as *service of process.* Service of a summons on the defendant usually is valid if it is served upon any member of the household above a specified age and if another copy addressed to the defendant is mailed to the home.

*No case can proceed forward without the existence of both subject matter and personal jurisdiction.

For many years, a summons could not be properly served beyond the borders of the state in which it was issued. However, states now have what are called **long-arm statutes,** which provide for the service of process beyond their boundaries. Such statutes are valid and constitutional if they provide a defendant with due process of law. Under the Fifth Amendment to the Constitution, no person shall "be deprived of life, liberty, or property without due process of law." The Fourteenth Amendment provides that states must also guarantee due process protection. Due process requires that if a defendant is not present within the state where the lawsuit is filed, he or she must have certain minimum contacts with the state so that maintenance of the suit does not offend "traditional notions of fair play and substantial justice."

The typical long-arm statute allows a court to obtain jurisdiction over a defendant even though the process is served beyond its borders if the defendant:

1. Has committed a tort within the state.
2. Owns property within the state that is the subject matter of the lawsuit.
3. Has entered into a contract within the state or transacted the business that is the subject matter of the lawsuit within the state.

Long-arm statutes do not authorize out-of-state service of process in all cases. Personal jurisdiction is obtained under long-arm statutes only when requiring an out-of-state defendant to appear and defend does not violate due process.

:: *sidebar* 4.4

The Car Crash

The *World-Wide Volkswagen* case is the leading case on the constitutional limits associated with personal jurisdiction on out-of-state defendants. In this case, the plaintiff filed a products liability lawsuit in Oklahoma to recover for personal injuries sustained in an automobile accident in that state. The defendants were the German manufacturer of the automobile, the importer of the car, the wholesale distributor, and the retail dealership. The wholesaler and retailer were located in New York State, and they challenged personal jurisdiction because they did not do business in Oklahoma and had no ties or contacts to the state. The court held in favor of the defendants, under the due process clause of the Fourteenth Amendment to the U.S. Constitution, because these defendants had not "purposefully availed" themselves of the privilege of conducting business in Oklahoma. The plaintiff should have sued these defendants in New York State. The manufacturer and importer were proper defendants in Oklahoma since they envisioned that the cars they made and imported had contacts with all states, including Oklahoma.

*Source: *World-Wide Volkswagen v. Woodson*, 100 S.Ct. 559 (1980).

In criminal suits, the crime must have been committed within the state for the court to have jurisdiction over the case. Jurisdiction over the person of the defendant is obtained by arrest. In the event of arrest in a state other than that in which the crime was committed, the prisoner must be transported back to the state where the crime occurred. This is done by the governor of the state of arrest voluntarily turning the prisoner over to the governor of the requesting state. The process of requesting and transporting the prisoner from one state to another is called **extradition.**

Regardless of the type of case, a defendant may decide not to object to a court's exercise of personal jurisdiction. In other words, a defendant may agree to submit to a court's authority even though personal jurisdiction may not be obtained under the rules discussed in this section. A defendant may waive or forgo any objection to a court's exercise of personal jurisdiction.

In the context of the Internet, courts have held that there are sufficient minimum contacts with the state when the website is targeted to the state or knowingly conducts business within the state.

:: *sidebar* 4.5

Virtual World and Personal Jurisdiction

In the case of *Bragg v. Linden Research,* a federal district court ruled that it had personal jurisdiction over the defendant in a case involving a virtual world based on representations by the defendant in national advertisements and attendance at virtual town meetings. The parties became involved in a dispute over the purchase of a parcel of virtual land that the defendant had confiscated. The plaintiff brought suit in Pennsylvania, a place where neither the defendant was headquartered nor incorporated. The court held that a national advertising campaign can provide the basis for jurisdiction, if the advertisement induces an individual to interact and establish direct contact with the company. The court found that the defendant had orchestrated the national campaign with the purpose of inducing individuals to purchase virtual property.

*Source: 487 F. Supp. 2d 593 (2007).

4. CLASS-ACTION SUITS

A **class-action suit** is one in which one or more plaintiffs file suit on their own behalf and on behalf of all other persons who may have a similar claim. For example, all sellers of real estate through brokers were certified as a class in an antitrust suit against the brokers. All persons suing a drug company, alleging injuries from a product, constituted a class for a tort action. Class-action suits may also be filed on behalf of all shareholders of a named corporation. The number of people constituting a class is frequently quite large. Class-action suits are popular because they often involve matters in which no one member of the class would have a sufficient financial interest to warrant litigation. However, the combined interest of all members of the class not only makes litigation feasible, it quite often makes it very profitable for the lawyer who brings the suit. In addition, such litigation avoids a multiplicity of suits involving the same issue, especially when the issues are complex and the cost of preparation and defense is very substantial.

*The Supreme Court discourages class-action suits.

At the federal level, the Supreme Court discourages class-action suits. Federal cases require that members of the class be given notice of the lawsuit; actual notice and not merely notice by newspaper publication is usually required. This notice must be given to all members of the class whose names and addresses can be found through reasonable efforts. In addition, those plaintiffs seeking to bring the class-action suit must pay all court costs of the action, including the cost of compiling the names and addresses of those in the class. If the trial court denies the plaintiff a right to represent the class, that decision cannot be appealed until there is a final decision in the lawsuit itself. Denial of class-action status making it impractical to continue the litigation does not give grounds for an immediate appeal.

One legal commentator has described the class-action suit as the law's version of a nuclear weapon—it is so destructive no side wants to set it off. A plaintiff's threat to aggregate thousands of individual claims is so powerful that it can destroy a defendant business. However, if the class action fails, the plaintiff wins nothing and loses the investment in the litigation. Simple cost-benefit analysis leads the litigants to settle a class-action suit.

If a class-action suit is in federal court because of diversity of citizenship, only one member of the class must meet the jurisdictional amount of $75,000. Sidebar 4.6 explains the Supreme Court's rationale for this rule.

:: *sidebar* 4.6

Class-Actions in Federal Court

In the case of *Exxon Mobil Corp. v. Allapattah Service,* 125 S. Ct. 2611 (2005), the Court considered a class-action case filed by Exxon dealers against Exxon Corporation. The Court found that it could consider the claims of class members who had not met the $75,000 minimum amount in controversy requirement in diversity cases. "Once a court has original jurisdiction over some claims in the action, it may exercise supplemental jurisdiction over additional claims that are part of the same case or controversy. . . . [The law] confers supplemental jurisdiction over all claims, including those that do not independently satisfy the amount-in-controversy requirement."

In the past, the federal courts routinely approved class-action settlements provided there was some benefit to the class and a release of all class members' claims. Typically, large attorneys' fees were included in the settlements. However, in recent years, the federal courts have begun carefully examining class-action settlements and have developed a much higher standard for approving settlements. A tougher standard is especially important where settlements have been proposed because of the risk that the class representatives and their lawyers could sacrifice the interests of the class in order to financially benefit themselves. Class-action suits in federal courts may be settled on a classwide basis only if the settlement's terms are fair and equitable and only if all the class certification requirements for trial have also been met. Sidebar 4.7 offers some recent examples of class-action lawsuits.

Don't assume that class-action suits can be easily settled.

:: *sidebar* 4.7

Examples of Recent Class-Action Lawsuits

- $295 million settlement to pay consumers against the world's largest diamond company, DeBeers, over alleged price fixing of gems.
- $107 million settlement by TJX Companies after a security breach of customer data involving at least 45 million credit and debit cards.
- $135 million settlement of State Farm adjusters' overtime claims.

- $30 million settlement by RC2 Corporation, alleging that toys were contaminated with lead paint.
- $700 million settlement with the State of Texas over Medicaid reimbursement rates
- $58 million settlement by drugmaker Merck over claims that its ads deceptively played down health risks of taking Vioxx.

Some attorneys have found a way around the costs of litigation and continue to file class-action lawsuits. The practice of consumers' and plaintiffs' lawyers of combining a single grievance into a lawsuit on behalf of every possible litigant is quite common in state courts. Numerous state class-action statutes allow consumers and others to file suit in state courts on behalf of all citizens of that state. So although the Supreme Court has attempted to reduce class-action cases, it is apparent that public companies are still subject to this type of claim.

"Justice is the great interest of man on earth. It is the ligament which holds civilized beings and civilized nations together."

–Daniel Webster

:: *sidebar* 4.8

Class-Actions and Kickbacks

In 2008, the Milberg law firm agreed to pay $75 million to settle a federal kickback case involving class-action lawsuits filed against many major U.S. corporations such as AT&T, Lucent, WorldCom, and Microsoft. The law firm, which once dominated the field of class-action lawsuits, was accused of making as much as $250 million over two decades by filing class-action suits using professional plaintiffs. The plaintiffs then received kickbacks for being the named parties in the cases. A lengthy Justice Department investigation also resulted in guilty pleas by three former partners in the law firm.

concept :: *summary*

Litigation—An Overview

1. The party who files a civil action is called the plaintiff and the party sued is known as the defendant.
2. To establish standing to sue, a plaintiff must establish that a case or controversy exists and that he or she has a personal stake in the resolution of the case.
3. Long-arm statutes are constrained or limited by the requirement the defendant has sufficient minimum contacts with the state.
4. Many requirements must be met to bring a class-action suit, particularly in a federal court.

:: Pretrial Procedures

How does a lawsuit begin, and how are issues presented to a court? How does a court decide whether it is the proper place for the lawsuit to be tried? To what extent do the parties in a civil lawsuit learn of the opposing party's legal arguments and factual presentations? How can one party test the validity of the other party's claims prior to trial? And what are the protections against one party harassing another by filing improper or unwarranted lawsuits? The following sections provide the answers to these questions. See Figure 4.1 for a graphic representation.

5. PLEADINGS

Do review the sample complaint in Appendix II.

The legal documents that are filed with a court to begin the litigation process are called **pleadings.** Through the contents of the pleadings, the issues to be resolved are brought into sharper focus. Lawsuits begin by a plaintiff filing a pleading, called a **complaint,** with the court clerk. The complaint contains allegations by the plaintiff and a statement or request of the relief sought. The clerk issues the summons, and a court official (usually a sheriff or marshal) delivers the summons and a copy of the complaint to the defendant.

*The complaint and the answer provide the framework for the lawsuit.

The summons provides the date by which the defendant must respond to the complaint. This response usually takes the form of a written pleading, called an **answer.** The defendant's answer will either admit or deny each allegation of the plaintiff's complaint and may contain affirmative defenses that will defeat the plaintiff's claim. The answer may also contain causes of action the defendant has against the plaintiff. These statements are called *counterclaims.* If the defendant does not respond in any way, the court may enter an order of **default** and grant the plaintiff the relief sought by the complaint.

After receiving an answer that contains one or more counterclaims, the plaintiff files a reply that specifically admits or denies each allegation of the defendant's counterclaims. The factual issues of a lawsuit are thus formed by one party making an allegation and the other party either admitting it or denying it. In this way, pleadings give notice of each party's contentions and serve to set the boundary lines of the litigation.

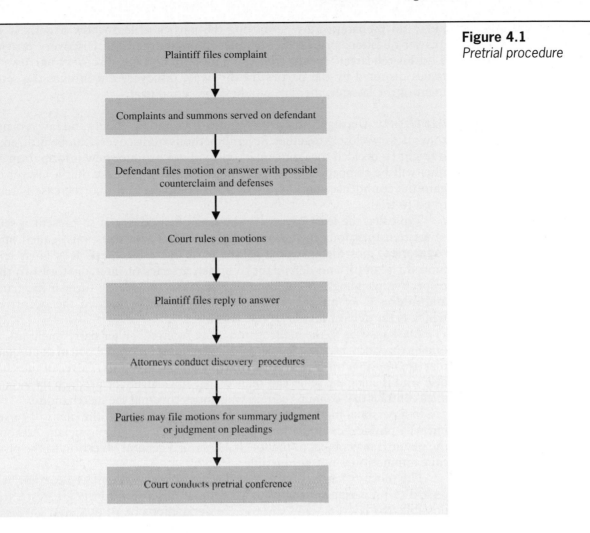

Figure 4.1
Pretrial procedure

6. STEPS IN DISCOVERY

Lawsuits are often high drama in the movies and on television. Inevitably, in these dramatized courtroom scenes, some element of surprise is the turning point, thereby ensuring a favorable outcome for the popular client or lawyer. In reality, civil litigation seldom concludes with a surprise witness or new piece of evidence. The reason the surprises do not occur is the process of **discovery**.

Purpose Discovery procedures are designed to take the "sporting aspect" out of litigation and ensure that the results of lawsuits are based on the merits of the controversy and not on the ability, skill, or cunning of counsel. Historically, an attorney who had a weak case on the facts or law could win a lawsuit through a surprise witness at the trial. Today, the law is such that verdicts should not be based on the skill of counsel but on the relative merits of the controversy.

Discovery practice is designed to ensure that each side is fully aware of all the facts involved in the case and of the intentions of the parties. Discovery

Do take advantage of the discovery process to learn as much as you can about the strengths and weaknesses of the case.

aids trial preparation by permitting the parties to learn how a witness will answer questions prior to actual questioning at the trial. Discovery provides a "dress rehearsal" for the trial. Even more important, discovery narrows the issues disputed by the parties. In this way, discovery encourages the settlement of the lawsuit, thereby avoiding the actual trial.

Methods   During the discovery phase of litigation, clients and lawyers need to work very closely together. Several methods of discovery can be utilized, or it might be decided that some methods will not produce new information and thus will be skipped. It is only through the aid of a client that a lawyer can gain the confidence that the discovery is complete and that the case is ready to go to trial.

> The plaintiff's lawyer often will want to have a trial without delay as opposed to the defendant's lawyer who will have a greater incentive to extend the case through discovery and other pretrial procedures.

Typically, the least expensive method of discovery is to present a series of written questions to the opposing parties. These questions, called **interrogatories,** must be answered by the party receiving them. It is fairly common for plaintiff and defendant to attach a series of interrogatories to their respective pleadings. A common interrogatory is "Please furnish the names and addresses of all persons known to you that witnessed the occurrence which is the subject matter of this lawsuit."

After answers to the interrogatories are received, either party might ask the other to produce specific documents, called **request for production of documents,** that are important to the lawsuit's outcome. For example, a buyer of merchandise who is suing the seller can request that this defendant produce the original sales contract that contains certain warranties covering the merchandise.

In a personal injury action, the defendant can require the plaintiff to submit to a physical examination by the defendant's expert physician. Although the plaintiff may object to the specific doctor, a general objection to the physical examination is not permissible.

> *Depositions of all potential witnesses can be very expensive and burdensome. Lawyers advise their witnesses to answer truthfully but not volunteer information in a deposition.

The most expensive method of discovery is also the most revealing with regard to preparing for the trial. To conduct discovery to the greatest extent possible, the lawyers will want to take **depositions** of all potential witnesses. In a deposition, the lawyer orally asks questions of the possible witness and an oral response is given. All the spoken words are recorded by a court reporter, and a written transcript is prepared. In this way, a permanent record of the anticipated testimony is created. With depositions, lawyers seldom need to ask a question during a trial to which they do not already know the answer.

Finally, after some or all of these methods of discovery are used, either party may request the other to admit that certain issues presented in the pleadings are no longer in dispute. The **request for an admission** narrows some issues and makes settlement more likely.

7. SCOPE OF DISCOVERY

The discovery procedures are intended to be used freely by the parties to litigation without the court's direct supervision. At times, a question about the scope of what is discoverable arises, and the party objecting to discovery seeks the judge's opinion. In this setting, a ruling must be given. Generally, judges provide a very broad or liberal interpretation of the degree of discoverable information. The usual rule is that as long as the information sought in discovery will lead to evidence admissible during the trial, the information is discoverable and an objection is overruled. See Sidebar 4.9 for a discussion about the costs of discovery.

Costs of Discovery

Although the use of discovery is essential to our system of litigation, it also carries significant costs. In a recent survey of 1,000 judges, abusive discovery was rated highest among the reasons for the high cost of litigation. Discovery imposes several costs on the litigant. These burdens include the time spent searching for and compiling relevant documents; the time, expense, and aggravation of preparing for and attending depositions; the costs of copying and shipping documents; and the attorneys' fees generated in interpreting discovery requests, drafting responses to

interrogatories and coordinating responses to production requests, advising the client as to which documents should be disclosed and which ones withheld, and determining whether certain information is privileged. The party seeking discovery also bears costs, including attorneys' fees generated in drafting discovery requests and reviewing the opponent's objections and responses. Both parties incur costs related to the delay discovery imposes on reaching the merits of the case. Many companies want to be very aggressive in discovery.

Discovery imposes a tremendous burden on the judicial system because judges must be diverted from other important matters, such as hearing criminal cases or conducting trials, to resolve heated discovery disputes. Rule 37 of the Federal Rules of Civil Procedure provides that "a party, upon reasonable notice to the other parties and all persons affected thereby, may apply for an order compelling disclosure or discovery." Sidebar 4.10 illustrates the perils for a business when a judge fails to properly monitor abuses in the discovery process.

Don't try to impede the discovery process. Such efforts often backfire.

Consequences of Discovery Abuse

In a products liability dispute between the planitiff, the owner of a Mazda MPV minvan, and Mazda Motor Corporation, the Eleventh Circuit Court of Appeals had to settle a protracted discovery dispute. The court noted that what began as a relatively common discovery dispute quickly deteriorated into unbridled legal warfare thanks, in large part, to lack of oversight by the district court. The court noted that discovery requests by the plaintiffs "were models of vague and overly broad discovery requests." The defendant responded by objecting on almost every imaginable ground, requesting dismissal of some counts in the

complaint as vague and overbroad, and even withheld information that it later conceded was properly discoverable. The Court of Appeals criticized the district court for failing to take proper control of the case by ruling promptly on the motion to dismiss and for imposing extreme discovery sanctions on Mazda that constituted a clear abuse of discretion. The court sent the case back for further proceedings and directed that the case be reassigned to a different judge.

*Source: *Chudasma v. Mazda Motor Corp.*, 123 F. 3d 1353 (11th Cir. 1997).

Parties can become very aggressive during the discovery process causing significant damage to the litigation process. The key for both sides is to act in a reasonable and prudent manner. The plaintiff should only ask for things needed to prepare for trial, and the defendant should be open and responsive to reasonable requests for discoverable information. In the end, the plaintiff and the defendant can do themselves great harm by acting otherwise. One of the faults with the litigation process is the tendency for both sides to stake out extreme positions and engage in a strategy of open warfare leading up to trial. Since many cases are settled without a trial, the best chance of that taking place quickly, and thereby avoiding greater lawyer expense, is for the parties to act in a moderate and reasonable manner during the discovery process.

:: *sidebar* 4.11

Destruction of Evidence

The Eleventh Circuit Court of Appeals considered a products liability case in which the plaintiff had failed to preserve the allegedly defective product—a Dodge Ram pickup truck. The court found fault with the plaintiff for failing to preserve an allegedly defective vehicle after the automobile accident. "The vehicle was the most crucial and reliable evidence available to the parties at the time plaintiff secured representation and notified defendant of the accident. By the time plaintiff filed suit, years after the accident had taken place, plaintiff had allowed the vehicle to be sold for salvage despite a request from defendant for the vehicle's location. For these reasons, we believe the resulting prejudice to the defendant incurable, and dismissal necessary."

*Source: *Flury v. Daimler Chrysler Corp.*, 427 F.3d 939 (11th Cir. 2005).

8. MOTIONS

During the pretrial phase of litigation, either plaintiff or defendant or both may attempt to convince the court that there are no questions about the factual setting of the dispute. An argument is presented that there are only questions of law for the judge to resolve. For example, the parties may be in complete agreement that the plaintiff has not been paid by the defendant for the merchandise that was delivered by the plaintiff and received by the defendant. The dispute between these parties is simply whether, under the stated facts, the defendant must pay the plaintiff. This dispute presents only an issue of law, not of fact.

*Motion practice is a critical part of the litigation process.

When a question of law is at issue, the parties can seek a pretrial determination of their rights by filing a **motion** with the court. These motions can be made at any point in the litigation process. First, the defendant may, instead of filing an answer, file a *motion to dismiss for failure to state a cause of action*. By this pleading the defendant, in effect, says to the court, "Even if everything the plaintiff says in his complaint is true, he is not entitled to the relief he seeks." For example, the defendant in the case involving the nonpayment for merchandise can argue the plaintiff failed to allege that the defendant ordered the goods. By federal law, merchandise sent unsolicited does not have to be paid for even when it is kept. In essence, the defendant, in the motion to dismiss, argues that the plaintiff failed to plead an essential element of a valid claim.

In addition, a defendant may move to dismiss a suit for reasons that as a matter of law prevent the plaintiff from winning his or her suit. Such matters as a lack of jurisdiction of the court to hear the suit, or expiration of the time limit during which the defendant is subject to suit, may be raised by such a motion. This argument is usually referred to as the **statute of limitations.** Each state has prescribed a time limit after which a suit cannot be filed. For example, if the plaintiff fails to sue within the stated period, the defendant is not liable for the nonpayment of the merchandise.

The rules of procedure in the federal court system and in most of the state systems provide for motions for a **judgment on the pleadings** or for **summary judgment.** In the former motion, a party is asking the judge to decide the case based solely on the complaint and the answer. If in the example involving the nonpayment for the merchandise the complaint does contain all the elements needed to state a claim and if the defendant offers no explanation or excuse for nonpayment in the answer, the judge can enter a judgment that the defendant must pay the plaintiff a specified amount. Through this motion, a time-consuming but unnecessary trial can be avoided.

A motion for summary judgment seeks a similar conclusion to the litigation prior to trial. However, the party filing this motion is asking the judge to base a decision not only on the pleadings but also on other evidence. Such evidence usually is presented in the form of sworn statements called **affidavits.** The judge also may conduct a hearing and allow the lawyers to argue the merits of the motion for summary judgment. If there are no material disputed issues of fact, the judge will decide the legal issues raised by the case and enter a judgment in favor of one party over the other. Even if the motion for summary judgment is not granted in full, its use often narrows the issues for trial. Figure 4.2 presents typical motions.

*Many cases settle after a ruling on the motion for summary judgment.

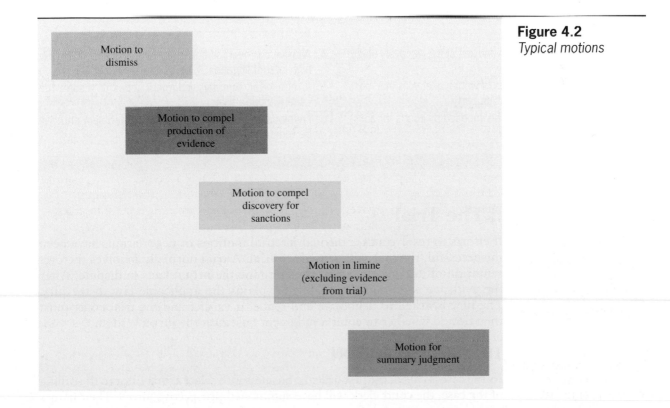

Figure 4.2
Typical motions

9. FRIVOLOUS CASES

A recent study by the Federal Judicial Center found that the overwhelming majority of federal judges do not believe that frivolous litigation is a major problem in the federal court system.

Frivolous lawsuits are misunderstood by many individuals and corporations. Judges have the tools to address such matters if they operate their courts with care and efficiency.

Either on a motion by a party or on their own initiative, judges may terminate the litigation process if there is a finding that the lawsuit is frivolous, that is, totally lacking in merit. The difficulty is in the determination of what is frivolous. What initially may appear to be a frivolous complaint may upon the presentation of evidence become a legitimate case.

During the past decade, courts within the federal judiciary and most state court systems have increased the frequency of assessing fines against lawyers who file frivolous cases. For example, Rule 11 of the Federal Rules of Civil Procedure authorizes the imposition of fines for filing frivolous papers. These fines are justified because Rule 11 states:

> The signature of an attorney or party constitutes a certificate by the signer that the signer has read the pleading, motion, or other paper; that to the best of the signer's knowledge, information, and belief formed after reasonable inquiry it is well grounded in fact and is warranted by existing law, and that it is not interposed for any improper purpose, such as to harass or to cause unnecessary delay or needless increase in the cost of litigation.

Most states have a rule similar to Federal Rule 11. The courts have upheld fines against lawyers and clients who sign frivolous documents. These holdings make it essential that businesspeople have thorough discussions with their lawyers about litigation strategies.

concept :: *summary*

Pretrial Procedures

1. Lawsuits typically are won and lost at the discovery stage of litigation.
2. Interrogatories are a series of written questions that must be answered by the opposing party.
3. Substantial penalties can be imposed by courts for abusing the discovery process.
4. Abusive discovery is one of the primary reasons for the high cost of litigation.
5. A motion for summary judgment seeks to resolve the case without a trial.
6. Frivolous cases are not a significant problem and can be redressed.

"I consider trial by jury as the only anchor yet devised by man, by which a government can be held to the principles of its constitution."

–Thomas Jefferson

:: The Trial

If efforts to resolve a case through pretrial motions or negotiations have been unsuccessful, the case will proceed to trial. A trial normally involves the presentation of evidence to a jury to determine the actual facts in dispute. After the evidence is presented, the judge explains the applicable law to the jury. The jury is asked to deliberate and render a verdict and the trial court must then decide whether to enter a judgment based on the jury's verdict.

10. JURY SELECTION

Do remember that most civil cases are settled or resolved prior to trial.

As the case is called, the first order of business is to select a jury. Prior to the calling of the case, the court clerk will have summoned prospective jurors. Their names

are drawn at random from lists of eligible citizens, and the number of jurors required is selected or called into the jury box to conduct the *voir dire* examination. **Voir dire** literally means to speak the truth. This examination allows the court and often the attorneys for each party to examine each potential juror as to his or her qualifications and ability to be fair and impartial. A party to a lawsuit is entitled to fair and impartial jurors in both civil and criminal cases. Prospective jurors are sworn to give truthful answers to the questions on *voir dire*.

:: *sidebar* 4.12

Corporate Governance and the Jury Selection Process

A judge in Corpus Christi, Texas, asked a district attorney to investigate Bayer, a giant drug company based in Germany, after the firm sent thousands of letters to residents in the community before jury selection in a lawsuit involving its anticholesterol drug, Baycol. Bayer sent the letters describing its position in the case and noting that it employs nearly 2,000 individuals at several Texas operations. The letter asked recipients to "keep an open mind" about the drug company. Bayer claimed the letter was "a miscommunication" intended only for members of the local chamber of commerce. Was Bayer's explanation reasonable? Did the court properly respond or overreact?

Either party in the lawsuit may challenge or excuse a prospective juror for a specific reason or cause. For example, if a prospective juror is related to one of the parties or to a witness or the juror admits bias favoring one side, that person may be excused as a juror because of the specific reason. In addition to the excuses for cause, the plaintiff and defendant are given a certain number of challenges, known as **peremptory challenges,** for which no cause or reason need be given to excuse a prospective juror. The number of peremptory challenges varies from court system to court system and on the type of case being tried. The number also may vary between the parties. For instance, in a criminal case, the defendant may have twelve peremptory challenges, and the government may have only six. The process of *voir dire* examination continues until all the peremptory challenges are exhausted and a full jury panel is selected.

On the basis of a series of U.S. Supreme Court decisions, beginning with *Batson v. Kentucky,* 476 U.S. 79 (1986), outlawing racial discrimination in jury selection, the jury has become increasingly more representative of the racial diversity in the United States. *Batson* represented a major development in Supreme Court jurisprudence allowing lawyer misconduct in a single case to establish discriminatory motive in making peremptory strikes. The Court banned gender discrimination in jury selection in the case of *J.E.B. v. Alabama Ex Rel. T.B.,* 511 U.S. 127 (1994) (see Sidebar 4.13).

The peremptory challenge, the method by which attorneys have traditionally been able to disqualify prospective jurors without having to state any reason, occupies an increasingly uneasy position in the law today as more questions are raised by each passing decision. In the case on page 108, the Supreme Court seemed to take another step in weakening the use of peremptory challenges by shifting the burden of an ambiguous record from the opponent of the peremptory strike to the proponent of the strike. The Court, in Case 4.2, also decided to review the written record without apparently giving any deference to the trial court's ability to judge the demeanor of the prospective juror.

Peremptory challenge means no cause or reason needs to be given to excuse a prospective juror. It can be traced at least as far back as 14th century England.

:: *sidebar* 4.13

The Jury and Constitutional Limits on Peremptory Challenges

J.E.B. v. Alabama Ex Rel T.B., 511 U.S. 127 (1994), was the Supreme Court's initial expansion of the protections of the Fourteenth Amendment in the jury selection context. In a paternity suit, the state used nine of its ten preemptory challenges to remove males from the jury. As a result, the trial court empanelled in all-female jury. After the jury found the defendant to be the father of the child in question and the court ordered him to pay child support, the defendant appealed on the basis of the Equal Protection Clause of the Fourteenth Amendment.

The Supreme Court held that the Equal Protection Clause prohibits discrimination on the basis of gender in the jury selection process. The state maintained its reason for the gender-based peremptory challenges was stereotypes of the genders that indicated men were more sympathetic to the man in a paternity action. The Court held this reason was based on actions that the Fourteenth Amendment was aimed at eliminating. By relying on those stereotypes when it made the peremptory challenges, the state ratified and reinforced prejudicial views of the abilities of men and women. The Supreme Court reversed the trial court's determination and remanded for a new trial with a new jury.

---

case **4.2**

SNYDER v. LOUISIANA
128 S.Ct. 1203 (2008)

During voir dire *in petitioner's capital murder case, the prosecutor used peremptory strikes to eliminate black prospective jurors who had survived challenges for cause. The jury convicted petitioner and sentenced him to death. Both on direct appeal and on remand, the Louisiana Supreme Court rejected petitioner's claim that the prosecution's peremptory strikes of certain prospective jurors were based on race.*

ALITO, J.: Petitioner Allen Snyder was convicted of first-degree murder in a Louisiana court and was sentenced to death. He asks us to review a decision of the Louisiana Supreme Court rejecting his claim that the prosecution exercised some of its peremptory jury challenges based on race, in violation of *Batson v. Kentucky,* 476 U.S. 79 (1986). We hold that the trial court committed clear error in its ruling on a *Batson* objection, and we therefore reverse.

Eighty-five prospective jurors were questioned as members of a panel. Thirty-six of these survived challenges for cause; 5 of the 36 were black (as is petitioner); and all 5 of the prospective black jurors were eliminated by the prosecution through the use of peremptory strikes. The jury found petitioner guilty of first-degree murder and determined that he should receive the death penalty.

Petitioner centers his *Batson* claim on the prosecution's strikes of two black jurors, Jeffrey Brooks and Elaine Scott. Because we find that the trial court committed clear error in overruling petitioner's *Batson* objection with respect to Mr. Brooks, we have no need to consider petitioner's claim regarding Ms. Scott.

When defense counsel made a *Batson* objection concerning the strike of Mr. Brooks, a college senior who was attempting to fulfill his student-teaching obligation, the prosecution offered two race-neutral reasons for the strike. The prosecutor explained:

> "I thought about it last night. Number 1, the main reason is that he looked very nervous to me throughout the questioning. Number 2, he's one of the fellows that came up at the beginning [of *voir dire*] and said he was going to miss class. He's a student teacher. My main concern is for that reason, that being that he might, to go home quickly, come back with guilty of a lesser verdict so there wouldn't be a penalty phase. Those are my two reasons."

Defense counsel disputed both explanations, and the trial judge ruled as follows: "All right. I'm going to allow the challenge. I'm going to allow the challenge." We discuss the prosecution's two proffered grounds for striking Mr. Brooks in turn.

With respect to the first reason, the Louisiana Supreme Court was correct that nervousness cannot be shown from a cold transcript, which is why the [trial] judge's evaluation must be given much deference. Here, however, the record does not show that the trial judge actually made a determination concerning Mr. Brooks' demeanor. The trial judge was given two explanations for the strike. Rather than making a specific finding on the record concerning Mr. Brooks' demeanor, the trial judge simply allowed the challenge without explanation.

The second reason proffered for the strike of Mr. Brooks—his student-teaching obligation—fails even under the highly deferential standard of review that is applicable here. At the beginning of *voir dire*, when the trial court asked the members of the venire whether jury service or sequestration would pose an extreme hardship, Mr. Brooks was 1 of more than 50 members of the venire who expressed concern that jury service would interfere with work, school, family, or other obligations.

The prosecutor claimed to be apprehensive that Mr. Brooks, in order to minimize the student-teaching hours missed during jury service, might have been motivated to find petitioner guilty, not of first-degree murder, but of a lesser included offense because this would obviate the need for a penalty phase proceeding. But this scenario was highly speculative. Even if Mr. Brooks had favored a quick resolution, that would not have necessarily led him to reject a finding of first-degree murder. If the majority of jurors had initially favored a finding of first-degree murder, Mr. Brooks' purported inclination might have led him to agree in order to speed the deliberations. Perhaps most telling, the brevity of petitioner's trial—something that the prosecutor anticipated on the record during *voir dire*—meant that serving on the jury would not have seriously interfered with Mr. Brooks' ability to complete his required student teaching.

With many weeks remaining in the term, Mr. Brooks would have needed to make up no more than an hour or two per week in order to compensate for the time that he would have lost due to jury service. When all of these considerations are taken into account, the prosecutor's second proffered justification for striking Mr. Brooks is suspicious.

The implausibility of this explanation is reinforced by the prosecutor's acceptance of white jurors who disclosed conflicting obligations that appear to have been at least as serious as Mr. Brooks'. . . . A comparison between Mr. Brooks and Roland Laws, a white juror, is particularly striking. During the initial stage of *voir dire*, Mr. Law approached the court and offered strong reasons why serving on the sequestered jury would cause him hardship. Mr. Laws stated that he was a self-employed general contractor, with two houses that are nearing completion, one with the occupants moving in this weekend.

Although these obligations seemed substantially more pressing than Mr. Brooks', the prosecution questioned Mr. Laws and attempted to elicit assurances that he would be able to serve despite his work and family obligations. If the prosecution had been sincerely concerned that Mr. Brooks would favor a lesser verdict than first-degree murder in order to shorten the trial, it is hard to see why the prosecution would not have had at least as much concern regarding Mr. Laws.

We have held that, once it is shown that a discriminatory intent was a substantial or motivating factor in an action taken by a state actor, the burden shifts to the party defending the action to show that this factor was not determinative. For present purposes, it is enough to recognize that a peremptory strike shown to have been motivated in substantial part by discriminatory intent could not be sustained based on any lesser showing by the prosecution. And in light of the circumstances here—including absence of anything in the record showing that the trial judge credited the claim that Mr. Brooks was nervous, the prosecution's description of both of its proffered explanations as main concern[s], and the adverse inference noted above—the record does not show that the prosecution would have pre-emptively challenged Mr. Brooks based on his nervousness alone.

We therefore reverse the judgment of the Louisiana Supreme Court and remand the case for further proceedings not inconsistent with this opinion.

It is so ordered.

:: CASE QUESTIONS

1. What is the basis of the defendant's claim that a *Batson* violation took place?
2. Why does the court extend *Batson* to the facts of this case?
3. Why does the court doubt the explanation offered by the prosecution?

:: *sidebar* 4.14

Religion and Peremptory Challenges

The next big question in jury selection is whether peremptory strikes based on religion violate the Equal Protection Clause. Lower courts are divided on this issue. One distinguishing factor between religion as opposed to race and gender is that religion is not visible from a juror's appearance. The Supreme Court of Minnesota, in *State v. Davis,* 504 N.W.2d 767 (Min. 1993), held that *Batson* protection does not extend to religious affiliation. It reasoned that such protection of religion was not necessary because "the use of the peremptory strike to discriminate purposefully on the basis of religion does not appear to be common and flagrant . . . there is no indication that irrational religious bias so pervades the peremptory challenge as to determine the integrity of the jury system." The Second Circuit, however, in *United States v. Brown,* 352 7.3d 654 (2nd Cir. 2003), held that a peremptory strike based on a person's religious affiliation was a *Batson* violation.

Given all of the criticism raised about juries today, particularly their ability to decide celebrity criminal cases or complex civil cases, we are likely to see further court decisions clarifying the use of peremptory challenges. Several legal commentators have suggested following the example of England and eliminating the use of peremptory challenges altogether. These commentators argue that there would be fewer problems and more just results if the first 12 prospective jurors who walked through the courtroom door were seated. By taking this action, the cost spent on hiring jury selection experts or litigating the use of peremptory challenges would be eliminated.

11. OTHER STEPS DURING A TRIAL

After selecting jurors to hear the case, the attorneys make their opening statements. An opening statement is not evidence; it familiarizes the jury with the essential facts that each side expects to prove. So that the jury may understand the overall picture of the case and the relevancy of each bit of evidence as presented, the lawyers inform the jury of the facts they expect to prove and of the witnesses they expect to call to make such proof.

After the opening statements, the trial continues with the plaintiff introducing evidence to establish the truth of the allegations made in the complaint. Evidence is normally presented in open court by the examination of witnesses and production of documents and other exhibits. After the plaintiff has presented his or her evidence, the defendant may make a motion for a **directed verdict.** The court can only direct a verdict for one party if the evidence, taken in the light most favorable to the other party, establishes as a matter of law that the party making the motion is entitled to a verdict. Just as a plaintiff must *allege* certain facts or have the complaint dismissed by motion to dismiss, he or she must have some *proof* of each essential allegation or lose the case on a motion for a directed verdict.

After the parties have completed the presentation of all the evidence, the lawyers have an opportunity to summarize the evidence. Unlike the opening

*Defendants typically make a motion for a directed verdict after the plaintiff has presented his or her case.

:: *sidebar* 4.15

Technology in the Courtroom

As a result of several initiatives by federal and state judges, courtrooms across the nation are being updated with computer technology—laptops, flat-screen monitors, PowerPoint presentations, and video clips—which have invaded the courtroom. One commentator noted that "we are a TV generation now," and jurors expect to see information presented to them in a way that seems up-to-date and accessible.

Improved technology also makes it easier for jurors to sift through what has become increasingly greater amounts of evidence presented in recent years. The lawyer's previous tools, ballpoint pens and Magic Markers, are a thing of the past. Of course, one commentator observed that "[t]he goal is justice at all times, not technology."

statements, which involved simply a preview of what was to come, the lawyers in closing argument try to convince the jury (or judge if no jury is used) of what the case's outcome should be.

Following the closing arguments, the judge acquaints the jury with the law applicable to the case. These are the **jury instructions**. As the function of the jury is to find the facts and the function of the court is to determine the applicable law, the purpose of jury instructions is to bring the facts and the law together in an orderly manner that will result in a decision. A typical jury instruction might be:

> The plaintiff in his complaint has alleged that he was injured as the proximate cause of the negligence of the defendant. If you find from the evidence that the defendant was guilty of negligence, which proximately caused plaintiff's injuries, then your verdict should be for the plaintiff.

In this instruction, the court is in effect saying that the plaintiff must prove that the defendant was at fault. Thus, the jury is instructed as to the result to be returned if the jurors have found certain facts to be true. At the conclusion of the jury instructions, the judge informs the jurors to begin their deliberations and to return to the courtroom when they have reached a decision. See Figure 4.3 for a list of the steps in a trial.

Don't underestimate the importance of jury instructions given at the close of the case.

12. BURDEN OF PROOF

The term **burden of proof** has two meanings depending on the context in which it is used. It may describe the burden or responsibility that a person has to come forward with evidence on a particular issue. The party alleging the existence of certain facts usually has the burden of coming forward with evidence to establish those facts.

Burden of proof may also describe the responsibility a person has to be persuasive as to a specific fact. This is known as the *burden of persuasion*. The party with this burden must convince the trier of fact on the issue involved. If a party with the burden of persuasion fails to meet this burden, that party loses the lawsuit. Thus, the burden of persuasion is a legal device used to help determine the rights of the litigating parties.

The burden of proof used in a case often can determine the outcome for one side or the other.

Figure 4.3
Trial steps

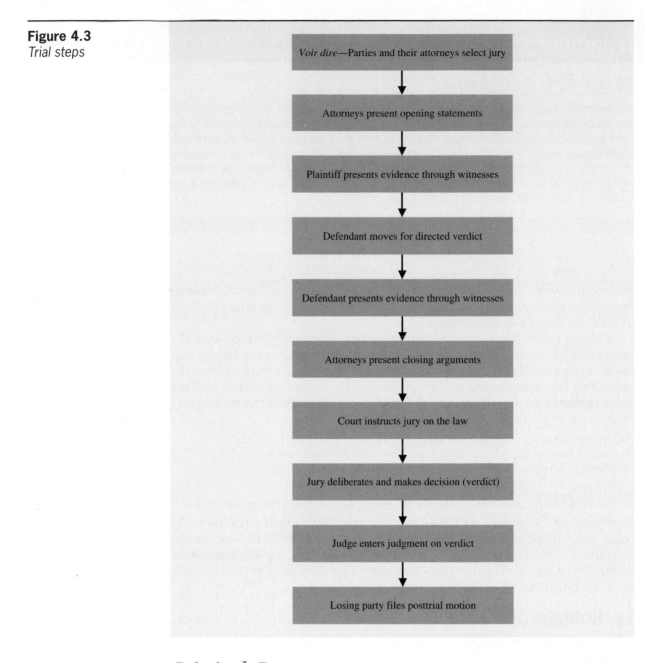

Voir dire—Parties and their attorneys select jury

Attorneys present opening statements

Plaintiff presents evidence through witnesses

Defendant moves for directed verdict

Defendant presents evidence through witnesses

Attorneys present closing arguments

Court instructs jury on the law

Jury deliberates and makes decision (verdict)

Judge enters judgment on verdict

Losing party files posttrial motion

Criminal Cases   The extent of proof required to satisfy the burden of persuasion varies, depending upon the issue and the type of case. There are three distinct levels of proof recognized by the law. For criminal cases, the burden of proof is described as **beyond a reasonable doubt.** This means that the prosecution in a criminal case has the burden of convincing the trier of fact, usually a jury, that the defendant is guilty of the crime charged and that the jury has no reasonable doubt about the defendant's guilt. This burden of proof does not require evidence beyond any doubt, only beyond a reasonable doubt. A reasonable doubt is one that a reasonable person viewing the evidence might reasonably entertain. This standard is not used in civil cases.

Civil Cases In civil cases, the party with the burden of proof is subject to one of two standards: the **preponderance of evidence** standard or the **clear and convincing proof** standard. The preponderance of evidence standard is used most frequently. It requires that a party convince the jury by a preponderance of evidence that the facts are as he or she contends. Preponderance of evidence is achieved when there is greater weight of evidence in support of the proposition than there is against it. The scales of justice, in other words, tilt more one way than the other. The clear and convincing proof standard is used in situations where the law requires more than a simple preponderance of the evidence but less than proof beyond a reasonable doubt. The scales of justice must tilt heavily one way. Unless the evidence clearly establishes the proposition, the party with the burden of proof fails to sustain it and loses the lawsuit.

Preponderance of the evidence standard is typically used in contract and tort cases.

:: *sidebar* 4.16

Televising Jury Deliberations

A raging debate has developed in recent years over televising jury deliberations. Some legal scholars believe that jurors are oblivious to the cameras and that the televised proceedings better inform the public in the modern age of mass communication. They argue that the American jury system is excellent and that we should not be ashamed to see how it works. Other scholars think that televising the jury deliberation process is a terrible idea because it will turn a civic duty into a public performance. They fear it could adversely impact the jury deliberations by turning them into a form of reality television. What do you think?

13. DECIDING THE CASE

The principal job of the jury is to determine what the facts are and to apply the law, as instructed by the judge, to these facts. The jury's decision is called a **verdict,** and it is announced in the courtroom when the jury's deliberations are completed. An example of a verdict might be "We, the jury, find in favor of the plaintiff and award $1,000,000 to be paid by the defendant" or "We, the jury, find the defendant is not liable to the plaintiff and should pay nothing." The judge must decide whether to accept the verdict. If the judge agrees with the verdict, a **judgment** is entered in favor of the party that won the jury's verdict.

The party who is dissatisfied with the jury's verdict may file a posttrial motion with the judge seeking either a **judgment notwithstanding the verdict,** (state court) or motion for judgment as a matter of law (federal court). The judge may enter a judgment opposite to that of the jury's verdict if the judge finds that the verdict is erroneous as a matter of law. The test used by the judge is the same one used to decide a motion for a directed verdict. To grant a motion for a judgment notwithstanding the verdict, the judge must find that reasonable persons viewing the evidence would not reach the verdict the jury returned. Because jurors are presumed to be reasonable, this motion is not frequently granted.

*Judges do not like to admit to making mistakes during the trial.

The party who receives the adverse judgment may file a motion for a new trial. This motion may be granted if the judge is convinced that a legal mistake was made during the trial. Because a judge is not usually inclined to acknowledge that mistakes have been made, a motion for a new trial is usually denied. It is from the ruling on this motion that the losing party appeals.

---

concept :: *summary*

The Trial

1. Peremptory challenges may not be based upon race or gender discrimination.
2. A direct verdict may be granted when the evidence establishes, as a matter of law, that the moving party is entitled to a verdict.
3. Jury instructions are used to acquaint the jury with the law applicable to the case.
4. In most civil cases, the preponderance standard is used to evaluate the case.
5. A judgment notwithstanding the verdict may be entered if the verdict is erroneous as a matter of law.

:: Posttrial Issues

Even after the trial, a number of issues may still exist. First among these is this one: How can a disappointed litigant obtain a review of the trial judge's legal rulings? If the trial court's judgment is final, what can the victorious party do to collect the dollar damages awarded? Finally, can the same subject matter be relitigated? These questions are the subject of the final three sections of this chapter.

When the result at the trial court level is appealed, the party appealing is usually referred to as the **appellant,** and the successful party in the trial court is called the **appellee.** Most jurisdictions, in publishing decisions of reviewing

table 4.1 :: Litigating Parties

:: Action Filed	:: Party Filing the Action	:: Party against Whom the Action Is Filed
Civil case	Plaintiff	Defendant
Criminal case	State or federal government as represented by a prosecutor	Defendant
Appeal	Appellant	Appellee
Petition for a writ of certiorari	Petitioner	Respondent

:: *sidebar* 4.17

Qualcomm and Posttrial Sanctions

The 2008 Qualcomm versus Broadcom case should send shock waves far outside of the state of California. Following the completion of a trial, the trial court referred six attorneys to the State Bar of California for investigation of possible ethical lapses. The lawyers for Qualcomm called a witness to testify. During cross-examination by Broadcom's lawyers, the witness revealed receiving multiple e-mails that had not been produced during discovery. The case ended, and the jury found for Broadcom. However, the court retained jurisdiction to address the discovery misconduct. Several months after the adverse verdict, lawyers for Qualcomm advised the court that Qualcomm had located thousands of other unproduced e-mails that appeared to be inconsistent with certain arguments made on Qualcomm's behalf during the case. The documents were located by searching the e-mail archives of less than two dozen key Qualcomm employees, searches that had not earlier been undertaken.

The court found that Qualcomm's failure to conduct basic searches at any time prior to trial amounted to an intentional withholding of documents. The court rejected Qualcomm's assertion that its legal counsel should have given more guidance on the scope of searches that should have been performed. Qualcomm was responsible for its own failings and for the failings of its chosen counsel.

The case likely would not have been brought, or would have been quickly dismissed, if Qualcomm had produced the documents that made Broadcom's defense effective. So the court imposed a discovery sanction of over $8.5 million—the full amount of Broadcom's legal fees. The court rejected the possibility that Qualcomm had hoodwinked its lawyers. The lawyers should have seen through Qualcomm's failures to conduct basic searches, whether that failure was intentional or negligent. The court noted that the lawyers ignored obvious signs that Qualcomm's production was incomplete.

*Source: Jerold S. Solovy and Robert L. Byman, *The National Law Journal*.

courts, list the appellant first and the appellee second, even though the appellant may have been the defendant in the trial court. As a result, the names used in a case are somewhat misleading. When a petition for certiorari is filed to the Supreme Court, the party initiating the petition is the **petitioner** and the other party is known as the **respondent.**

*Losing parties have the right to appeal the case to a higher court.

14. APPEALS

Each state prescribes its own appellate procedure and determines the jurisdiction of its various reviewing courts. Although having knowledge of the procedure used in an appeal is essentially a responsibility for the lawyer, understanding certain aspects of this procedure may assist you in understanding our judicial system.

Appellate Procedures Courts of appeal deal with the record of the proceedings in lower court. All the pleadings, testimony, and motions are reduced to a written record, which is filed with the court of review. The court of appeal studies the issues, testimony, and proceedings to determine whether prejudicial errors occurred or whether the lower court reached an erroneous result. In addition to the record from the trial, each party files a **brief.** The briefs contain a short description of the case; a factual summary; legal points and authorities; and arguments for reversing or affirming the lower court decision.

*Courts of appeal are looking to see if harmful errors were made by the trial court.

Figure 4.4
Appellate review

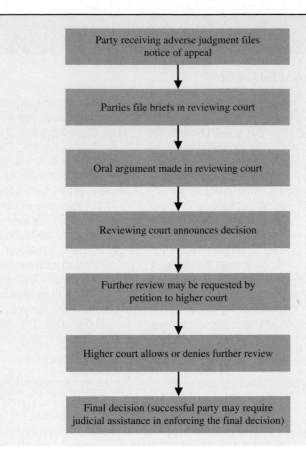

In addition to the brief, the reviewing court is often given the benefit of **oral argument** in deciding the case. The attorneys are given a specified amount of time to explain orally to the court their position in the case. This also gives the court of review an opportunity to question the attorneys about various aspects of the case.

After oral argument, an initial vote of the judges' or justices' impressions is usually taken. The case is assigned to one judge or justice to prepare an opinion. Each judge or justice has a staff of clerks assisting in the preparation of opinions. After the opinion is prepared, it is circulated among the other members of the court. If a majority approve the opinion, it is adopted. Those who disagree may prepare a dissenting opinion. If the review is conducted by an intermediate appellate court, the losing party may petition the highest court in the system for a *writ of certiorari.*

Deference to Trial Courts   Courts of appeal are essentially concerned with questions of law. However, a reviewing court may be asked to grant a new trial on the ground that the decision in the lower court is contrary to the manifest weight of the evidence found in the record. In the federal courts and in many states, appellate courts are not allowed to disturb factual findings unless they are clearly erroneous. This limitation recognizes the unique opportunity afforded the trial judge in evaluating the credibility of witnesses and weighing the evidence. Determining the weight

Oral argument is used less frequently today with courts often relying on written briefs.

Great deference is given to the trial court in reviewing appeals.

and credibility of the evidence is the special function of the trial court. An appellate court cannot substitute its interpretation of the evidence for that of the trial court simply because it construes the facts or resolves the ambiguities differently.

:: *sidebar* 4.18

Appealing an Evidentiary Ruling

Judges are required to make split-second rulings on the admissibility of evidence during trial. Lawyers, in order to preserve an argument for appeal, must show the following:

1. An objection is made
2. In a timely manner
3. Challenging the evidence on specific grounds
4. The lower court's ruling was wrong and
5. The error harmed your client.

---

15. ENFORCEMENT OF JUDGMENTS AND DECREES

After a judgment in a court has become final, either because of the decision on appeal or because the losing party has failed to appeal within the proper time, it may become necessary for the successful party to obtain judicial assistance in enforcing the court decision. For example, the loser (judgment debtor) may not have voluntarily paid the amount of the judgment to the winner (judgment creditor).

The primary enforcement mechanism is for the judgment creditor to request the court's assistance to have the **execution** of the judgment or decree. An execution of a judgment occurs when a court official, such as a sheriff or marshal, seizes some property of the debtor, sells it at public auction, and applies the proceeds to the creditor's claim.

Another form of execution is **garnishment.** This method of enforcement involves having a portion of the debtor's wages paid to the court, which in turn pays the creditor.

> An adverse judgment can lead to the partial loss of wages to satisfy the creditor.

:: *sidebar* 4.19

How Do You Prevent a Lawsuit in Your Firm?

- Make sure supervisors and managers have access to legal counsel and use it before small issues explode into major disputes.
- Encourage teambuilding and development of cooperative relationships in the workplace.
- Develop internal mechanisms for resolving disputes.
- Perform regular audits to ensure compliance with legal rules and best practices.
- Require legal analysis of major decisions under consideration.

16. *RES JUDICATA*

> "A judgment is held to be conclusive upon those who were parties to the action in which the judgment was rendered."
>
> *–Cummings v. Dresher*, 218 N.E. 2d 688 (N.Y. 1966)

Once a decision of the court has become final, it is said to be ***res judicata*** (the thing has been decided), meaning that a final decision is conclusive on all issues between the parties, whether raised in the litigation or not. *Res judicata* means either that the case has been finally decided on appeal or that the time for appeal has expired and a cause of action finally determined by a competent court cannot be litigated by the parties in a new proceeding by the same court or in any other court. *Res judicata* prevents successive suits involving the same factual setting between the same parties and brings disputes to a conclusion. A matter once litigated and legally determined is conclusive between the parties in all subsequent proceedings.

:: Key Terms

Affidavits   105
Answer   100
Appellant   114
Appellee   114
Beyond a reasonable
   doubt   112
Brief   115
Burden of proof   111
Class-action suit   98
Clear and convincing
   proof   113
Complaint   100
Counterclaim   92
Counterdefendant   92
Counterplaintiff   92
Default   100
Defendant   92
Depositions   102

Directed verdict   110
Discovery   101
Execution   117
Extradition   97
Garnishment   117
Interrogatories   102
Judgment   113
Judgment notwithstanding the
   verdict   113
Judgment on the
   pleadings   105
Jury instructions   111
Long-arm statutes   96
Motion   104
Oral argument   116
Peremptory challenges   107
Personal jurisdiction   96

Petitioner   115
Plaintiff   92
Pleadings   100
Preponderance of
   evidence   113
Request for an admission   102
Request for production of
   documents   102
Res judicata   118
Respondent   115
Standing to sue   93
Statute of limitations   105
Summary judgment   105
Summons   96
Third-party defendants   92
Verdict   113
Voir dire   107

:: Review Questions and Problems

Litigation—An Overview

1. *Parties*

   A building contractor is sued by homeowners alleging that their homes were poorly constructed resulting in several defects. The contractor adds to the lawsuit a building supplier that it claims provided faulty support beams. How can the contractor add the building supplier as a party to the lawsuit? What is this procedure called and how does it work?

2. *Standing to Sue*

   A group of environmentalists filed a lawsuit challenging commercial fishing in Glacier Bay National Park and sued the secretary of the interior and the National Park Service in order to prevent more commercial fishing.

(a) What must the environmentalists show in order to satisfy the requirement of standing to sue in this case?

(b) At what point should the issue of standing be decided by the court during the course of litigation?

3. *Personal Jurisdiction*

Smith, a resident of Michigan, was in Florida for a business meeting where he was served with a divorce petition filed by his wife, who had moved to Florida recently. Smith objected to the Florida court's exercise of personal jurisdiction. What is the basis of Smith's objection? Should he prevail? Why or why not?

4. *Class-Action Suits*

How have the federal courts discouraged class-action lawsuits? What are the key requirements for federal courts to permit class-action suits?

Pretrial Proceedings

5. *Pleadings*

Describe the purpose of a complaint and an answer in civil litigation. What is the function of the pleading stage in a lawsuit?

6. *Steps in Discovery*

(a) Why do surprises rarely occur at trial?

(b) What are some of the key devices a litigant can use in discovery?

7. *Scope of Discovery*

How do abusive discovery practices raise the cost of litigation?

8. *Motions*

Under what circumstances may a court grant a motion for summary judgment?

9. *Frivolous Cases*

Federal Rule 11 sanctions are available against both lawyers and their clients to curb frivolous litigation. Under what circumstances may sanctions be imposed?

The Trial

10. *Jury Selection*

In light of recent court decisions restricting the use of peremptory challenges, should they be eliminated from litigation altogether? Would the elimination of peremptory challenges improve the efficiency of the trial process?

11. *Other Steps during a Trial*

What is the purpose of jury instructions?

12. *Burden of Proof*

There are three distinct levels of proof required by law depending upon the kind of case involved. Describe them and when they are used.

13. *Deciding the Case*

Under what circumstances should a judge enter a judgment notwithstanding the verdict?

Posttrial Issues

14. *Appeals*

What normally is contained in an appellate brief? An oral argument?

15. *Enforcement of Judgments and Decrees*

How does the court enforce judgments?

16. *Res Judicata*

Why is the notion of *res judicata* critical in civil litigation?

1. You are the manager of a used car firm known as Reliant Motor Company. Your lawyer has called to tell you that John Doe, a customer you have been dealing with for several months, has filed a lawsuit against the firm. The customer claims the vehicle he purchased is a lemon and no longer even operates. You knew the vehicle was not in the best of condition at the time of sale, but you believe the buyer caused most of the problems by taking the vehicle "off road" several times. You are not looking forward to discovery or trial in this case. You have several questions.

How does discovery work?

Can you be required to testify twice in a deposition and at trial?

Should you shred all documents you have about this case? You know that some of the documents will not put the firm in the best light.

You wonder what will happen at trial. Will it be like what you have seen on TV or in the movies?

2. You are the owner of a small firm that manufactures lawn mowers. While using one of your products, a person suffers severe injury and now is suing, claiming that your product was negligently designed because it did not adequately protect the user. You have no experience with the legal system. You learn that lawyers charge as much as $250 per hour and must be paid whether they win or lose their cases. You are surprised at what must happen before a trial can occur to determine who is at fault. First, your lawyer may move to dismiss the case on jurisdictional grounds. If that fails, both sides will take costly depositions of likely witnesses. You will have to turn over reams of internal documents related to the design of your mower. Each side also will have to pay several hundred dollars per hour for experts as the lawyers prepare the case. These experts will have to be paid again when they testify at trial. As the time for the trial approaches, each side will spend money trying to discern the most sympathetic type of jury. Years after the lawsuit was first filed, the parties will be sitting in the courtroom waiting for jury selection to begin. More money will have been spent defending this case than the plaintiff was seeking when the lawsuit was first filed. Many questions come to mind:

- Should you have settled the case at the beginning?
- Has your attorney been getting rich at your expense?
- Is discovery more of a burden than a help?

5

Negotiation and Alternative Dispute Resolution Systems

Learning Objectives ::

In this chapter you will learn:

1. To understand why disputing parties seek alternatives to the litigation process as methods to revolve their differences.

2. To appreciate the importance of effective negotiation and to recognize the basic methods of negotiation.

3. To evaluate the various forms of ADR systems so that efficient choices can be made as to the means of resolving disputes.

4. To be able to explain the differences between arbitration and mediation and to know when each is the most appropriate method of ADR.

5. To comprehend why courts have a very limited role in reviewing the actions of arbitrators and mediators.

From the preceding chapter, you should appreciate that the litigation process within the court system imposes tremendous costs in terms of time, money, emotional stress, and harmony in relationships. This fact is a major reason why you probably have very little personal experience with litigation. It also is the reason most businesses try to avoid litigation and use it as a means of last resort to resolve disputes.

One way to confirm how seldom we litigate is to examine some data. Ask yourself, have I ever had a conflict with someone? Maybe a better question is, does a day go by without my experiencing one or more conflicts? We constantly and consistently deal with conflicts, and even disputes, without filing a lawsuit to resolve our problems.

However, sometimes lawsuits are necessary. Even after beginning the litigation process, most parties reach some type of resolution before the case is presented to a jury for a verdict and judgment. The general rule, usually cited, is 95 percent or more of the lawsuits filed settle prior to the completion of the litigation process.

The litigation process provides individuals and businesses with a formal method to enforce agreements. It can be said that business cannot be conducted without the existence of the court system to protect property interests. A more accurate statement probably is we transact business, personally and professionally, in a way that hopefully avoids the need to use litigation as our dispute resolution system.

In this chapter, you will study a variety of alternatives to litigation. Prior to reviewing more formal alternative dispute resolution (ADR) systems, we take a look at the distinction between conflicts and disputes and how negotiation can serve us all the time.

:: Conflicts and Negotiation

In answer to one of the earlier questions, a day doesn't go by without our encountering conflicts at home, on the road, and at work. Only a day of total isolation might be the exception. Even then the lonely person likely experiences internal conflicts over how best to utilize this time alone.

In the following sections, the distinction between a conflict and a dispute helps emphasize the importance of how people negotiate.

1. CONFLICTS AND DISPUTES

Conflict is ubiquitous and can be productive.

Conflict exists whenever there are two or more points of view. Even in productive relationships, involving amicable co-workers or happily married couples, conflict is always present. Conflicts are not negative; indeed, conflict can stimulate significant thoughts and produce great discoveries. So, why do we shy away from conflict? Why do most of us perceive conflict as bad and try to avoid it?

Conflict + Claim that is rejected = Dispute

The answer likely lies in the fact that conflict leads to disputes. A **dispute** arises when one party makes a claim that another party denies. For example, two co-workers may have a conflict because they both think they need to use a copy machine right now. This conflict escalates when one person asks the other to move aside and the request is refused. These parties now are in dispute as to who gets to use the copier first. In essence, the process of both workers claiming a right to the machine likely causes the dispute to become more emotional and thus uncomfortable for both involved.

Does this example prove disputes are bad and conflicts should be left alone? Not necessarily. Suppose one worker simply stood in line and waited for the other to finish. The worker doing the copying may not know about the frustration and angst that exists inside the co-worker. On the other hand, the worker waiting may be expressing impatience through comments or sighs without ever asking or claiming to go ahead. The worker making the copies may feel this pressure and become upset by what is perceived as rudeness or a lack of respect. Leaving the conflict unresolved may cause larger problems among those co-workers later. Thus, it may be more beneficial to everyone involved to have the conflict become a dispute so the parties can more easily express their emotions. Such expressions may lead to an earlier resolution between these co-workers.

2. STYLES AND METHODS OF NEGOTIATION

All of us instinctively engage in some form of negotiation. Even as evidence of a conflict is exhibited (through comments or sighs or groans), the parties are negotiating. **Negotiation** is the process used to persuade or coerce someone to do what you want them to do. All of us negotiate all the time with ourselves, our family members, our co-workers, and even with strangers.

The issue to focus on is not *when* do I negotiate but *how* do I negotiate. Think again about the co-workers and the copy machine. The actual request (or claim) to make copies first is the beginning of a negotiation. How the other worker responds to this request likely will set a tone for the negotiation process. An examination of how this tone is set can be viewed through the illustration in Sidebar 5.1.

> "When do we negotiate? Always!"
>
> **–Dialogue from the movie *The Devil's Advocate***

:: *sidebar* 5.1

Negotiation Styles

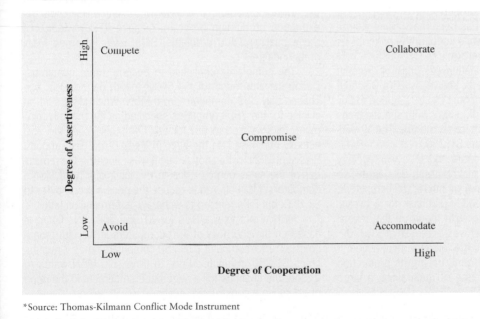

*Source: Thomas-Kilmann Conflict Mode Instrument

Can you imagine the conversation between these two co-workers that illustrates each style listed? Avoiding could be seen through the person at the copier ignoring the request by pretending not to hear. Accommodating occurs if the request to go first is granted. Competing comes into play if the worker at the copier turns around and tells the co-worker who requested priority to stand in line and be patient. Collaborating might exist if the worker making the copies agrees to use another copier or explains to the co-worker how another machine is available to use. Compromising is the hardest to demonstrate even though it is a common response in a negotiation. Perhaps a compromise occurs in this example if these two co-workers get into a discussion/argument and a third worker takes over the use of the copier such that neither of the disputing parties gets the work done.

Understanding the styles used in negotiations is not enough. Analyses of negotiation processes also need to focus on the methods used by the negotiators. The next two sections examine two of the most studied methods of negotiations. To help illustrate these methods, consider the factual situation in Sidebar 5.2.

:: sidebar 5.2

A Business Dispute

Mickey Shears and Naomi Hamilton operate a business that manufactures personal computers. The business name is M&N PCs, Inc. The principal market for M&N computers has been buyers for home use. M&N's reputation is based on assembling a high-quality computer for a relatively low price. M&N's biggest problem has been maintaining a large enough, qualified sales force while keeping the price for its computer below the market average.

William Dalton operates a nationwide chain of discount department stores. This chain is known as Bill's Discount Centers. One year ago, Bill's Discount Centers agreed to buy from M&N a minimum of 250 computers (with specifications stated in the contract) per month for six months. The agreed-upon price of each computer was $1,250.

The relationship between M&N and Bill's worked very well. In the fifth month of this initial contract, Bill's agreed to increase its minimum purchase per month to 750 computers, and Bill's committed to this monthly purchase for a twelve-month period to begin after the sixth month of the original contract. The price per computer was to remain at $1,250.

M&N was delighted with the arrangement since it allowed M&N to concentrate on increasing its production capacity while reducing the costs of maintaining a large active sales force.

Unlike the success of its initial relationship with M&N, Bill's began receiving complaints from its customers about the lack of quality of M&N's computers. These complaints were traced by Bill's customer service representatives to the newer computers that M&N was assembling under its expanded production program. Despite its knowledge of these quality-related problems, Bill's never informed M&N of its findings.

The complaints continued to become more numerous. During the fifth month of the twelve-month period, Bill's purchased only 350 computers from M&N. When M&N sent an invoice for the 750 computers specified as the monthly minimum, Bill's refused to pay for any computers over the 350 actually purchased. In the second week of the sixth month, Bill's sent M&N written notice that it was canceling the remainder of the sales contract due to declining quality of M&N's computers. M&N offered to reduce the price per computer to $1,050, but Bill's refused to withdraw its termination letter.

M&N wants to sue Bill's for $7,062,500. This figure is based on the shortfalls of 400 computers in the fifth month times $1,250/computer plus 750 computers times 7 months times $1,250/computer. Prior to filing suit, M&N wants to explore the chances for a negotiated settlement in the hope of salvaging a constructive relationship with Bill's.

---

3. POSITIONAL NEGOTIATION

Most people instinctively use a negotiation method called **positional bargaining.** Typically, these parties begin in a competitive style by stating their respective expectations. For example, in a sales transaction, the seller starts with as high an asking price as is considered reasonable. Likewise, the buyer begins with the lowest reasonable price. The gap between these two opening prices provides room for give and take. If the negotiation remains focused on the sales price, all the parties do is change their respective positions on the acceptable price. This process of exchange moves the parties toward the middle of the gap.

In the factual situation in Sidebar 5.2 , Bill's is saying that it owes nothing to M&N. On the other side, M&N is demanding payment of more than $7 million. The difference between these two positions is so wide that it may be difficult to bring these parties into agreement.

Even if Bill's was willing to buy some computers at a revised price and even if M&N agreed to a reduced quantity or selling price, the issue of quality is not being addressed. Does Bill's gain any market advantage in selling an inferior product, albeit at a lower price, to its customers? Clearly not.

If the positions on quantity and price are the only items open for negotiation, Bill's and M&N are unlikely to reach a satisfactory compromise. Hence, the chances of a negotiated settlement through positional bargaining are minimal. This result occurs because positional bargaining does not focus on the underlying conflicts.

There is another method of negotiation that might help these parties. This alternative is discussed in the next section.

Positional Bargaining

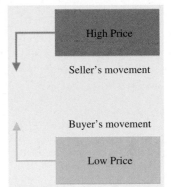

4. PRINCIPLED NEGOTIATION

A better approach to negotiating among disputing parties has been described as **principled, interest-based negotiations** in the book *Getting to Yes* by Roger Fisher, William Ury, and Bruce Patton.[1] These authors present seven elements that should become the focus of negotiators. The elements will vary in importance depending on the factual situation in dispute and on the parties' individual perspectives. However, concentrating on these elements can help remove some of the barriers created by positional negotiation. A quick focus on these elements illustrates how M&N and Bill's can be more productive in their negotiation efforts.

The Seven Elements of Interest-Based Negotiation:
Communication
Relationship
Interests
Options
Legitimacy
Alternatives
Commitment

Communication   First, as expressed in the factual situation above, Bill's has not openly explained to M&N the nature of its dissatisfaction. Sharing customer complaints, either in general or with specificity, might help M&N locate a production operations problem. Likewise, M&N does not appear to be informing Bill's of any difficulties it faced as it expanded production capacities. Clear communication between these parties may assist them in becoming joint problem solvers. Without this exchange of information, these parties are likely to continue blaming each another. To change from a "game" of blaming, effective negotiators put significant energy into listening to the other party. Communication involves a balance of talking and listening.

"If negotiation is half talking and half listening, the more important half is listening."

–Roger Fisher

---

[1]*Penquin Books, 2d ed., 1991.*

Relationship   Second, these parties would likely benefit by discussing how each could benefit by continuing their relationship of customer and supplier. Can they solve the current problem and maintain, if not enhance, their future business opportunities together? Maintaining, or even enhancing, the relationship may be possible if these parties focus on effective communications.

Interests   Third, have M&N and Bill's communicated their real interests to each other? Perhaps these interests are not mutually exclusive. For example, Bill's might want to expand its offerings in computing technology to customers. M&N might want to dissolve its sales force and concentrate on production of a variety of computers. These interests, once communicated, may help the parties realize that a continuing relationship is in their mutual best interests.

Options   Fourth, M&N and Bill's should brainstorm possible options or solutions to their dispute. This exploration process is best done with the parties agreeing that an option mentioned is not necessarily a proposal for compromise. One attractive option might be for Bill's to agree to buy all the computers M&N can produce and for Bill's to market these computers under its own name. Rather than severing their business relationship, M&N could become the exclusive supplier of store-brand computers. The renaming of these products also can help overcome the "quality problems" customers associate with M&N's computers.

Legitimacy   Fifth, legitimacy involves the application of accepted standards to the topic negotiated—rather than having the parties state unsupported propositions. Bill's probably will not be impressed by M&N stating it will improve the quality of its computers. Instead the parties should focus on how quality can be improved and how customers will accept the improvements. Production engineers may help address the former issue while specific test marketing plans may assist in legitimizing the latter.

Alternatives   Sixth, alternatives are outcomes that are possible without the agreement of the other party. In essence, alternatives are the thing that parties to a negotiation can do away from the bargaining table. If the parties understand their alternatives to negotiating a settlement and understand the unattractive nature of these alternatives, the desire to negotiate, instead of litigating, is enhanced. M&N, for example, may perceive that bankruptcy is a very likely result if this dispute is not resolved. Bill's, on the other hand, may believe that another supplier is readily available. The desirable result of any negotiation is to agree on an outcome that is better than both parties' alternatives.

Commitment   Seventh, any successful negotiation must conclude with the parties making realistic commitments that can be put into practice. Perhaps an initial commitment that assists the overall process of negotiation is to have the parties agree that they will continue to meet and focus on these seven elements. Hopefully, the conclusion of the negotiation will be an agreement between the parties that avoids the expense (dollars, time, and emotions) of litigation. If that commitment is not a settlement, then it might be an agreement to utilize one of the following ADR systems.

---

concept :: *summary*

Conflicts, Disputes, and Negotiation

1. Conflicts are everywhere; each personal interaction can cause conflicts or be impacted by them.

2. Conflicts may be insignificant and easily avoided, or they may produce significant anxiety if ignored.

3. A dispute arises from a conflict when one party makes a claim that another denies or refuses to honor.

4. Conflicts and disputes can be managed and perhaps resolved through negotiations.

5. Styles of negotiation include avoiding, accommodating, competing, compromising, and collaborating.

6. Two methods of negotiation include positional bargaining and principled (interest-based) bargaining.

:: Alternative Dispute Resolution (ADR) Systems

Negotiations occur in everything we do. Thus, even as we present the following material on formal and informal ADR systems, remember the negotiation processes still govern the success or failure of such ADR systems.

It is important to remember several things at the outset of this discussion. First, litigation does not preclude the use of ADR techniques. Indeed, it is very common for disputes to be arbitrated, mediated, or settled through negotiations during the pretrial process discussed in the preceding chapter.

Second, disputing parties do not have to begin a lawsuit to use any form of ADR. In the rest of this chapter, you will study how ADR systems relate to formal litigation and how they are utilized independently from the litigation process.

Third, ADR systems used by disputing parties may be part of a contractual relationship between these parties. For example, even before any problem arises, it is an effective dispute resolution tool to have the parties' contract specify a preferred ADR system. Disputing parties also may agree to use an ADR technique after the dispute arises even if they did not foresee the possibility of needing to use a dispute resolution system at the time of their original agreement.

Fourth, effective use of ADR systems can save disputing parties many of the costs associated with litigation. Especially important is the preservation of an ongoing business relationship. The ability to keep doing business often is destroyed through litigation. ADR systems, when used appropriately, help ensure the productive relationships needed for successful business transactions.

5. RANGE OF OPTIONS

Figure 5.1 illustrates an array of ADR systems. These are arranged along a spectrum of high cost (in dollars, time, emotions, and relationships) to lowest cost. Although any given factual situation may cause the items on this spectrum to shift places, this figure presents a generally accepted view of dispute resolution systems.

Figure 5.1
Scale of dispute resolution systems

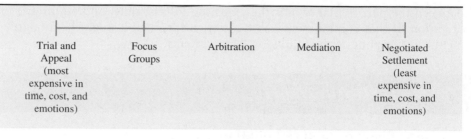

The next two sections briefly address why settlement is attractive and how lawyers utilize focus groups. Arbitration and mediation are discussed in more detail since they are the most popular ADR systems used by businesses and people attempting to resolve disputes.

6. SETTLEMENTS

It is universally acknowledged that both parties to litigation are losers. The winning party in a lawsuit is a loser to the extent of the attorney's fees—which are often substantial. The fact that the loser usually also has to pay court costs is an added incentive to settlement without litigation.

There are also personal reasons to settle controversies. The desire to resolve differences is instinctive for many Americans. Most of us dislike trouble, and many fear going to court. The opinions of others are often a motivating force in encouraging amicable settlements.

Businesses tend to settle disputes with customers for two additional reasons. First, it is simply not good business from a goodwill and public relations standpoint to sue a customer. Second, juries are frequently sympathetic to individuals who have suits against large corporations or defendants who are covered by insurance. Juries often decide close questions of liability, as well as size of the verdict, against business organizations because of their presumed ability to pay. As a result, businesses settle many disputes even though they might possibly prevail in litigation.

Table 5.1 provides a summary of cases settled during 2008. The size of these settlements represents evidence that companies want to avoid the litigation process even when the settlement costs are high.

The Department of Justice reports 98 percent of tort cases filed in the U.S. District Courts settled prior to either a bench or jury trial. www.ojp.usdoj.gov/bjs/civil.htm

7. FOCUS GROUPS

Recognizing that a jury's function is to determine the facts, attorneys frequently use **focus groups** in significant cases. The attorneys assemble a group of citizens and present their evidence. This group then deliberates and makes findings. This dress rehearsal gives attorneys insight into possible jury reaction to the evidence and points up weaknesses in the case. Sometimes issues are tested without introducing evidence. Lawyers argue the case on the basis of assumed facts to the mock jury for a few hours, and this jury returns a verdict.

The verdicts often cause plaintiffs to take a more realistic view of the damages to which they think they are entitled. This "reality test" helps disputing parties to engage in more meaningful negotiations. Through such negotiations, these parties often settle their dispute without having to go through the formal process of either a trial or an arbitration.

table 5.1 :: Examples of Major Settlements in 2008		
:: **Company**	:: **Product or Action**	:: **Settlement**
Merck	Vioxx linked to heart attacks and strokes	$4.85 billion to 47,000 possible claimants
Citicorp	Conspiring with Enron executives to misstate Enron's financial condition	$1.66 billion to Enron Creditors Recovery Corporation
Eli Lilly	Failure to disclose information about side-effects of Zyprexa	$1.2 billion to 31,000 possible claimants
		$15 million with State of Alaska
Xerox	Securities litigation with shareholders	$670 million to shareholders
Royal Dutch Shell	Overstatement of energy reserves	$400 million to European shareholders
		$118 with U.S. shareholders

*Source: Various articles in *The Wall Street Journal*.

:: Arbitration

To avoid the various expenses of litigation, disputing parties sometimes agree to have a third party decide the merits of the dispute. This formal ADR system is called **arbitration.** The decision maker, who should be disinterested in any financial impact of the decision and neutral regarding the issues presented in the dispute, is known as an **arbitrator.** The distinctive characteristic of this form of ADR is the arbitrator's decision on the merits. In essence, the arbitrator takes the place of the jury and judge in the litigation process.

Over the past 80 years, arbitration has played an increasingly important role in resolving business disputes. Historically, arbitration has been the most commonly used ADR system. The primary reason for the use of arbitration is the laudable goal of providing a relatively quick and inexpensive resolution of disputes. Arbitration not only helps the parties avoid the expense of litigation but also provides a means of avoiding the formalities of the courtroom. Formal pleadings, for example, and other procedural steps such as discovery and the rules of evidence are usually not used in an arbitration hearing.

Arbitration also serves to help ease congested court dockets. A primary function of arbitration is to serve as a substitute for and not a prelude to litigation. It is a private proceeding with no public record available to the press and others. Thus, by keeping their dispute private, adversaries may be more likely to preserve their business relationship.

Arbitration also has the advantage of submitting many disputes to experts for solutions. For example, if the issue involves whether a building has been properly constructed, the matter could be submitted to an architect for resolution. If it involves a technical accounting problem, it could be submitted to a certified public accountant. The Securities and Exchange Commission (SEC) has approved an arrangement whereby investors with complaints against securities

Arbitrators are authorized to make decisions that are binding on the parties, thereby resolving the dispute.

"Studies show that employment arbitrations are resolved twice as quickly on average as lawsuits."

–Nathan Koppel,
The Wall Street Journal,
December 18, 2007.

dealers must submit them for arbitration to arbitrators assigned by the various stock exchanges and the Financial Industry Regulatory Authority. These arbitrators are selected because they possess the special knowledge required to determine if a customer of a brokerage house has a legitimate complaint.

Arbitration is of special importance in labor relations, where it provides the grievance procedures under collective bargaining contracts. Arbitration is a means for industrial self-government, a system of private law for all problems that may arise in the workplace.

Sidebar 5.3 illustrates the growing importance and widespread use of arbitration as an alternative dispute resolution system.

:: *sidebar* 5.3

Examples of Contracts with Arbitration Clauses

Stockbroker and client

Commodities broker and customer

Brokerage firm and employee

Attorney* and client

Union-management collective bargaining agreements

Owner-contractor and contractor-subcontractor

Insurance company and insured

Public carrier and shipper of goods

*Most bar associations require lawyers to arbitrate disputes with clients.

The parties authorize an arbitrator to make a decision that binds these parties and resolves their dispute. The act of referring a matter to arbitration is called **submission**. Submission to arbitration often occurs when the disputing parties agree to use this form of ADR. Such an agreement by the parties is a submission to **voluntary arbitration**. Generally, an agreement to submit an issue to arbitration is irrevocable, and a party that thinks the process is not going well cannot withdraw from the arbitration and resort to litigation. Another form of a submission occurs when a statute or court requires parties to arbitrate. This type of submission results in a **mandatory arbitration**.

After the submission, a hearing is conducted by the arbitrator or arbitrators. Both parties are allowed to present evidence and to argue their own points of view. Then a decision, known as an **award,** is handed down. In most states the arbitrator's award must be in writing. The award is valid as long as it settles the entire controversy and states which party is to pay the other a sum of money.

Sidebar 5.4 discusses recent trends in the use and popularity of arbitration. It will be interesting, throughout your business careers, to see how arbitration is utilized when compared to other ADR systems.

8. SUBMISSIONS

Submission is the process of beginning an arbitration proceeding.

Submission by contract occurs if the parties enter into an agreement to arbitrate an existing dispute. The arbitration agreement is the submission in this case. In addition, the parties may contractually agree to submit to arbitration all issues that may arise in the future. Submission in these circumstances occurs when a demand to arbitrate is served on the other party.

:: *sidebar* 5.4

Recent Trends in Arbitration

Throughout the second half of the twentieth century, businesses increasingly included arbitration clauses in various types of contracts. Most common among these examples have been business-to-business contracts (e.g., customer-supplier), employment contracts, and securities broker-investor contracts. Beginning in 2007, pressures mounted to provide employees and investors with options to either pursue arbitration or to litigate. To achieve this system of choice, the Arbitration Fairness Act of 2007 was proposed in both the U.S. House and Senate; however, no final legislative enactment has occurred. Advocates for litigation cite studies showing that arbitration in securities brokerage cases tends to favor the brokerage firm. "In 2006, investors in NASD arbitrations won 42% of the cases decided by arbitrators, down from a recent high of 54% in 2001."[1] This argument is countered with statistics and polls about efficiency. "A poll released this week finds that most Americans do not want their day in court. Rather they prefer cheaper and faster methods of settling arguments. When asked how they'd like to settle a dispute with a company, 82% chose arbitration, which avoids the time and expense of going to court. Only 15% opted for litigation. Americans are not confident that a lawsuit will produce a fair result, but a sold majority looks favorably on mediation and arbitration."[2] The truth of the situation is summarized by the following: "Take your argument that there is not empirical study to show that investors would do better in court. Of course this is true, since there can be no case litigated both before a jury and then relitigated before a securities arbitration panel."[3] In the years ahead, the trend may be toward mediation clauses, rather than arbitration clauses, in contracts. In mediation, parties maintain control over the outcome of dispute and decide whether to settle or continue litigation. This choice may be preferable over the arbitration process.

[1]Jamie Levy Pessin, *The Wall Street Journal*, March 29, 2007.
[2]Editorial, *The Wall Street Journal*, April 5, 2008.
[3]Ted Eppenstein, *The Wall Street Journal*, August 8, 2007.

Most state statutes authorizing voluntary arbitration require the agreement to arbitrate to be in writing. Since the goal of arbitration is to obtain a quick resolution of disputes, most statutes require submission within a stated time period, usually six months, after the dispute arises.

In the absence of a statute, the rights and duties of the parties to a submission are described and limited by their agreement. Parties that have contracted to arbitrate are not required to arbitrate any matters other than those they contractually agree to arbitrate. Sidebar 5.5 contains an example of an agreement to arbitrate.

:: *sidebar* 5.5

Sample Arbitration Clause

All disputes, claims, or controversies arising from or relating to this contract shall be resolved by binding arbitration by one arbitrator selected by the parties from an American Arbitration Association list of qualified arbitrators. This arbitration contract is made pursuant to a transaction in interstate commerce, and it shall be governed by the Federal Arbitration Act. The parties voluntarily and knowingly waive any right they have to a jury trial. The parties agree and understand the arbitrator shall have all powers provided by the law and this contract. These powers shall include all legal and equitable remedies, including, but not limited to, money damages, declaratory relief, and injunctive relief.

The issues submitted to arbitration, as framed in the submission, may be questions of fact, questions of law, or mixed questions of fact and law. They may include the interpretation of the arbitration agreement. Sometimes a dispute arises as to whether the parties have agreed to submit an issue to arbitration. In such a case, one party refuses to arbitrate and the other files suit to compel arbitration. The court hearing the case decides the issue of arbitrability but does not decide the basic issue between the parties. The U.S. Supreme Court explained these distinct roles of the court and the arbitrator in a case summarized in Sidebar 5.6.

:: *sidebar* 5.6

To Arbitrate or Litigate

The communication workers union, as the bargaining agent of employees working for AT&T Tech., Inc., negotiated a contract that contained an arbitration clause covering disputes that might arise. Another provision of the contract allowed management to make decisions regarding hiring, placement, and termination of employees. Exercising its authority, management laid off 79 employees due to a lack of work. The union challenged this action by claiming there was no lack of work justifying the layoffs. The union sought to have this dispute arbitrated; however, management refused to arbitrate claiming its authority to terminate employees was clear. The union filed suit and asked the court to compel arbitration.

Does a judge or an arbitrator decide what issues should be submitted to arbitration?

The question of whether the parties agreed to arbitrate is decided by a judge, not an arbitrator. However, in deciding what issues can be arbitrated, a judge is not to rule on the merits of the underlying claim. Judges should presume arbitration is appropriate; thus, any doubt should be resolved in favor of arbitration over litigation.

Source: AT&T Tech., Inc. v. Communications Workers, 106 S. Ct. 1414 (1986).

---

9. ARBITRATORS

For information about available arbitrators and their expertise, examine the following websites:

- *American Arbitration Association* www.adr.org
- *JAMS* www.jamsadr .com/neutrals/ neutrals.asp
- *National Arbitration Forum* www.arb-forum .com/arbitrators/ index.asp
- *Arbitrator.com* (listing by states) www.arbitrator.com

Arbitrators generally are chosen by the disputing parties. A provision in the agreement to arbitrate or in the statute that requires the arbitration describes how the arbitrator is selected. Of concern in the selection process are the expertise of the arbitrator and the number of arbitrators to be chosen.

Expertise   One reason arbitration is frequently preferable to litigation is the use of an expert to resolve the dispute. Appraisers can be used to decide disputes about the value of real estate, medical doctors can be used to decide health care disputes, and academicians can be used to decide issues within their area of expertise.

This use of experts is especially important in labor-management relations. Arbitration is the technique used in collective-bargaining contracts to settle grievances of employees against their employers. Arbitration is able to resolve disputes arising out of labor contracts without resorting to judicial intervention. It is quick and efficient and minimizes disruption in the workplace. Labor arbitration has attracted a large number of experts—both lawyers and academicians.

Arbitration provides for decision making by experts with experience in the particular industry and with knowledge of the customs and practices of the particular work site. Parties expect the arbitrator to look beyond strictly legal criteria to other factors that bear on the proper resolution of a dispute. These factors may include the impact of a particular result on productivity, its consequences to morale, and whether tensions will be heightened or diminished. The ablest judge usually does not bring the same experience and competence to bear upon the determination of a grievance, because the judge cannot be as informed as the expert arbitrator.

Number Chosen   Another issue relates to the number of arbitrators to hear a dispute. It is common to use one arbitrator who is considered objective and impartial. Any person the disputing parties agree upon can be an arbitrator. There are no licensing requirements an arbitrator must satisfy. However, an arbitrator often is chosen from a list of qualified arbitrators provided by the arbitration service. The disputing parties are not limited to the list unless they have agreed to make their selection from this list.

It is also common to have a panel of three arbitrators. In such cases, each party selects an arbitrator and the two so selected choose a third. It is not surprising that when this procedure is used, allegations of bias are often made by the losing party. Courts generally do not allow such allegations to form a basis for overturning a panel's award unless there is evidence of overt corruption or misconduct in the arbitration proceedings. Since such evidence usually is difficult to obtain, allegations of bias normally do not impact the results of arbitration.

> The number of arbitrators is based on the agreement of the parties.

Authority over Certain Matters   What arbitrators have authority to decide has been a topic of controversy and litigation. The following case attempts to clarify whose responsibility it is to decide preliminary matters prior to the actual arbitration. You should read this case as a clarification of the *AT&T* case discussed in Sidebar 5.6.

---

case **5.1** ::

HOWSAM v. DEAN WITTER REYNOLDS, INC.
123 S. Ct. 588 (2002)

Karen Howsam was an investment client of Dean Witter Reynolds, Inc. Between 1986 and 1994, Howsam bought interests in four limited partnerships. She claims that Dean Witter misrepresented the attributes of these investments. Howsam's claim is subject to the arbitration clause of the Client Service Agreement. To pursue her claim, Howsam chose to use the National Association of Securities Dealers (NASD) arbitration process. The NASD's Uniform Submission Agreement states that no dispute over six years old may be arbitrated. Prior to the arbitration, Dean Witter filed a lawsuit asking the District Court to declare the dispute is more than six

years old and thus not eligible for arbitration. The District Judge declined to enjoin the arbitration concluding the arbitrator is authorized to determine the applicable statute of limitations. Dean Witter appealed, and the Tenth Circuit Court of Appeals reversed. Howsam petitioned for a writ of certiorari, and it was granted.

BREYER, J.: . . . This Court has determined that arbitration is a matter of contract and a party cannot be required to submit to arbitration any dispute which he has not agreed so to submit. Although the Court has also long recognized and enforced a liberal federal policy favoring arbitration agreements, it has made clear that there is an exception to this policy: The question whether the parties have submitted a particular dispute to arbitration, i.e., the "question of arbitrability," is an issue for judicial determination unless the parties clearly and unmistakably provide otherwise. We must decide here whether application of the NASD time limit provision falls into the scope of this last-mentioned interpretive rule.

Linguistically speaking, one might call any potentially dispositive gateway question a "question of arbitrability," for its answer will determine whether the underlying controversy will proceed to arbitration on the merits. The Court's case law, however, makes clear that, for purposes of applying the interpretive rule, the phrase "question of arbitrability" has a far more limited scope. The Court has found the phrase applicable in the kind of narrow circumstance where contracting parties would likely have expected a court to have decided the gateway matter, where they are not likely to have thought that they had agreed that an arbitrator would do so, and, consequently, where reference of the gateway dispute to the court avoids the risk of forcing parties to arbitrate a matter that they may well not have agreed to arbitrate.

Thus, a gateway dispute about whether the parties are bound by a given arbitration clause raises a "question of arbitrability" for a court to decide. Similarly, a disagreement about whether an arbitration clause in a concededly binding contract applies to a particular type of controversy is for the Court.

At the same time the Court has found the phrase "question of arbitrability" not applicable in other kinds of general circumstance where parties would likely expect that an arbitrator would decide the gateway matter. Thus procedural questions which grow out of the dispute and bear on its final disposition are presumptively not for the judge, but for an arbitrator, to decide. So, too, the presumption is that the arbitrator should decide allegations of waiver, delay, or a like defense to arbitrability. . . .

[W]e find that the applicability of the NASD time limit rule is a matter presumptively for the arbitrator, not for the judge. The time limit rule closely resembles the gateway questions that this Court has found not to be "questions of arbitrability.". . .

Moreover, the NASD arbitrators, comparatively more expert about the meaning of their own rule, are comparatively better able to interpret and to apply it. In the absence of any statement to the contrary in the arbitration agreement, it is reasonable to infer that the parties intended the agreement to reflect that understanding. . . .

We consequently conclude that the NASD's time limit rule falls within the class of gateway procedural disputes that do not present what our cases have called "questions of arbitrability." . . .

For these reasons, the judgment of the Tenth Circuit is **Reversed.**

:: CASE QUESTIONS

1. When considering the roles of the judge and the arbitrator, who decides "questions of arbitrability"? Why?
2. How is a "question of arbitrability" distinct from "matters of gateway procedural disputes"?
3. In the Court's opinion, who makes the final decision on the statute of limitations that applies in an arbitration case?

10. AWARDS

An **award** is the decision by an arbitrator.

Generally an arbitrator's award does not need to set forth findings of fact, conclusions of law, or the reasons for the award. However, a disclosure of findings and the reasons must be given if the applicable statute, arbitration agreement, or submission so requires. When the arbitrator does provide the basis for decision in the form of an opinion or letter, that document becomes a part of the award.

Because the parties themselves, by virtue of the submission, frame the issues to be resolved and define the scope of the arbitrator's powers, the parties are generally bound by the resulting award. A court will make every reasonable presumption in favor of the arbitration award and the arbitrator's acts and proceedings. The U.S. Supreme Court favors a broad scope of the arbitrators' authority. Restrictions on this authority will be allowed only when the disputing parties clearly state such limits.

An arbitrator's award is final on all issues submitted, and it will be enforced by the courts as if it were a judgment of the court. As is discussed in Section 14, awards are not subject to judicial review on the merits of the decision. Only when fraud or other clearly inappropriate action by the arbitrator can be shown is a court willing to reverse the award granted in a voluntary arbitration proceeding.

After the award is made by the arbitrator, it is usually filed with the clerk of an appropriate court. If no objections are filed within a statutory period, it becomes final and enforceable, like a judgment.

11. THE FEDERAL ARBITRATION ACT

The important role and positive perception of arbitration among businesses today probably would not exist without the Federal Arbitration Act (FAA). Prior to the enactment of the FAA, our common law system preferred litigation over arbitration as a means of resolving disputes. In 1925, congressional enactment of the FAA began to change this presumed way of dispute resolution. However, it was not until after the revision and reenactment of the FAA in 1947 that courts began to encourage disputing parties to use arbitration instead of litigation. Clearly, the FAA changed public policy perceptions of arbitration and how states can regulate its use. These two impacts of the FAA are discussed now.

> The Federal Arbitration Act encourages disputing businesses to utilize arbitration.

Impact on Policy The FAA covers any arbitration clause in a contract that involves interstate commerce. Under it, courts are "rigorously" to enforce arbitration agreements. A court assumes arbitration was intended unless it can say with positive assurance that the arbitration clause was not intended to include the particular dispute. The federal policy clearly favors arbitration of commercial disputes. The FAA provides that arbitration agreements "shall be valid, irrevocable, and enforceable, save upon such grounds as exist at law or in equity for the revocation of any contract."

The U.S. Supreme Court, through its decisions, gives strong support to the use of arbitration. However, this deference is not absolute. For example, the Supreme Court does not allow a collective-bargaining agreement's arbitration clause to prevent an individual worker from using the court to pursue a Title VII claim of discrimination.

The Supreme Court continues to search for the proper balance between encouraging arbitration and allowing access to the court system. When legislation clearly grants the disputing parties the right to litigate claims, arbitration clauses signed by these parties do not prevent access to the courts. Sidebar 5.7 describes a case in which the Supreme Court concludes other federal laws provide the EEOC the right to litigate even though an employee signed an arbitration clause.

Impact on State Laws The federal policy favoring arbitration frequently conflicts with state laws favoring litigation as the means to resolve a dispute. Sometimes a state law specifically provides that designated matters are not to be submitted to arbitration. Are these state laws constitutional

> State laws cannot prevent arbitration of disputes if the parties are engaged in or impact interstate commerce.

:: *sidebar* 5.7

Do Agreements to Arbitrate Limit the EEOC's Remedies?

The Equal Employment Opportunity Commission (EEOC) has authority to bring enforcement actions against employers whenever the EEOC believes illegal discrimination has occurred. An employee of Waffle House was discharged from employment because he had a seizure at work. This employee did not pursue the contractual remedy of arbitration; however, he did file a complaint with the EEOC. His complaint alleged Waffle House fired him because of his disability. After investigating the factual situation, the EEOC filed a lawsuit against Waffle House in federal district court. Waffle House sought to have the suit dismissed since the remedy provided by the employment contract was arbitration, and the employee did not seek arbitration. Waffle House argues that the EEOC takes the place of the employee and therefore cannot avoid the requirement of arbitration.

The Supreme Court reviews the legislative history of the EEOC by examining the Civil Rights Act of 1964, the Equal Employment Opportunity Act of 1972, and the Civil Rights Act of 1991. The Court finds that the EEOC can be a plaintiff in its own right and not simply a representative of an aggrieved employee. Due to the authority given to the EEOC, it can pursue court-ordered victim-specific relief, such as backpay, reinstatement, and damages for violations involving discrimination without first resorting to arbitration.

*Source: *Equal Employment Opportunity Commission v. Waffle House, Inc.*, 122 S. Ct. 754 (2002).

when applied to businesses engaged in interstate commerce? The Commerce Clause and the Supremacy Clause of the U.S. Constitution are often used to set aside such state laws that deny arbitration of certain disputes.

Sidebar 5.8 summarizes two recent cases in which the Supreme Court reiterates the deference to arbitration and the authority of the arbitrator.

:: *sidebar* 5.8

Who Decides? Judge, Agency, or Arbitrator?

As a customer of Buckeye Check Cashing, Inc., John Cardegna signed a contract that included a standard arbitration clause covering "any claim, dispute, or controversy arising from or related to this Agreement." This customer filed a lawsuit alleging Buckeye Check Cashing's charge of an excessive interest rate rendered the contract illegal, void, and unenforceable. Buckeye Check Cashing asked the trial judge to order the parties to arbitrate the issue of an illegal interest rate.

The U.S. Supreme Court agreed to hear this case and ruled "regardless of whether the challenge is brought in federal or state court, a challenge to the validity of the contract as a whole, and not specifically to the arbitration clause, must go to the arbitrator." This case provides further support for the general proposition that judges must defer to arbitrators when an arbitration clause has been signed by the parties.

More recently, the Supreme Court decided who has authority—the arbitrator or an administrative agency. This issue arose between Alex Ferrer, known as Judge Alex on FOX television, and Arnold Preston. Preston seeks money for services rendered to Judge Alex under a contract that includes an arbitration clause. Preston seeks arbitration and Judge Alex asks the California Labor Commissioner to declare that Preston is not properly licensed as a talent agent and thus is not eligible to collect his fees.

The Supreme Court, after reviewing a number of decisions, decides that the Federal Arbitration Act overrides a state law that attempts to vest authority in an administrative agency to make an initial decision. Thus, Judge Alex is subject to the arbitration process pursuant to the clause he signed. Arbitrators, not administrators, have the authority to make initial determinations in cases covered by the Federal Arbitration Act.

*Sources: *Buckeye Check Cashing, Inc. v. Cardegna*, 126 S. Ct. 1204 (2006) and *Preston v. Ferrer*, 128 S. Ct. 978 (2008).

12. STATUTORILY MANDATED ARBITRATION

Another reason why arbitration has become more widespread during the last few decades is that legislation may require disputing parties to submit to arbitration. A growing number of states have adopted statutes that require mandatory arbitration for certain types of disputes. Those whose disputes fall within the boundaries of the mandatory arbitration statute must submit the dispute to arbitration prior to being allowed to litigate. On the basis of studies showing that a dispute requiring three days for resolution before a 12-person jury takes only two to four hours for resolution by an arbitrator, the mandatory arbitration statute is clearly a viable alternative for controlling court congestion.

The arbitrators in the mandatory arbitration process are retired judges and practicing lawyers, usually experienced trial attorneys. A list of eligible arbitrators is maintained by court officials in charge of the mandatory process. Although the parties may agree on using only one arbitrator, mandatory arbitration cases are usually presented to a panel of three. Arbitrators are paid a per-diem fee. The parties involved in the arbitration are responsible for paying these costs.

Types of Cases Mandatory arbitration statutes cover only a few types of cases. A typical statute might apply the procedure to claims exclusively for money of a small amount, such as those for less than $15,000, not including interest and costs. Some statutes require arbitration of specific subject matter, like issues arising out of divorces. In addition, arbitration is required only in those cases in which a party has demanded a jury trial, as it can be assumed that a judge hearing a case is basically as efficient as an arbitrator.

Do check with your state and local courts to determine which cases are subject to mandatory arbitration.

Procedures Mandatory arbitration, while requiring substantially less time than litigation, does not necessarily provide speedy justice. The usual procedure for a claim filed in court that is covered by the mandatory arbitration law is to place the claim in the arbitration track at time of filing. At this time the date and time of hearing are assigned, typically eight months from the date of filing.

Discovery procedures may be used prior to the hearing on arbitration. Since no discovery is permitted after the hearing without permission of the court, an early and thorough degree of preparation is necessary to achieve a full hearing on the merits of the controversy. This preparation also prevents the hearing from being used as an opportunity to discover the adversary's case en route to an eventual trial. Most discovery is by interrogatories rather than by deposition.

The arbitrators have the power to determine the admissibility of evidence and to decide the law and the facts of the case. Rulings on objections to evidence or on other issues that arise during the hearing are made by the arbitrators. States have different rules relating to the admissibility of evidence. In most states the established rules of evidence must be followed by the arbitrators. Several jurisdictions, however, do not require hearings to be conducted according to the established rules of evidence. New Jersey law, for example, provides: "The arbitrator shall admit all relevant evidence and shall not be bound by the rules of evidence." Other states leave to the discretion of the arbitrator the extent to which the rules of evidence apply.

13. VOLUNTARY/CONTRACT-BASED ARBITRATION

Although the statutes that mandate arbitration of certain types of disputes clearly have increased the use of this ADR method, the larger growth in the number of arbitration cases comes from disputing parties agreeing to arbitrate, not litigate.

These agreements to voluntarily arbitrate come in two basic forms. One is known as the **predispute arbitration clause.** Such clauses commonly appear in business contracts. In essence, the contracting parties show good judgment in understanding conflicts exist, conflicts give rise to disputes, and disputes are better resolved through arbitration rather than by litigating.

People often view a contract as the beginning of a productive business relationship. They do not want to lessen the forthcoming opportunities with any expectation that problems might occur. And they view including an arbitration clause in the contract as an indication that bad things will happen. These people may need to utilize a **postdispute arbitration agreement.** Such agreements arise when parties already in dispute decide that arbitration is better than litigation.

On the basis of your study of this chapter, we trust you understand why a predispute arbitration is the wiser and ultimately more efficient approach to ADR than the postdispute agreement. An obvious disadvantage to relying on the latter approach is that disputing parties may not be able to find the common ground to agree to arbitrate.

To encourage businesspeople to use voluntary arbitration, the goal of an efficient and affordable alternative to litigation must be achieved. When arbitration is as expensive and time-consuming as litigation, the attractiveness of the ADR system declines. Often, an arbitration clause does not specify the cost of the process. Case 5.2 describes a situation wherein the courts are asked to decide the impact of not specifying the costs of arbitration.

Don't rely on getting a party to sign a postdispute arbitration agreement; relying on a predispute arbitration clause is smarter.

case 5.2 ::

GREEN TREE FINANCIAL CORP. v. RANDOLPH
121 S. Ct. 513 (2000)

Larketta Randolph purchased a mobile home and financed it through the Green Tree Financial Corporation. One condition of this financing arrangement was Randolph's having to purchase insurance to protect Green Tree from the expense of repossession should that become necessary. The contract between Green Tree and Randolph provided that any disputes arising from the relationship would be referred to arbitration. Randolph filed a lawsuit in federal district court alleging Truth-in-Lending Act (TILA) and Equal Credit Opportunity Act violations. Green Tree successfully sought to dismiss this suit and to have the court order arbitration. Randolph appealed, and the Eleventh Circuit Court of Appeals found "the arbitration agreement was silent with respect to payment of filing fees, arbitrators' costs, and other arbitration expenses." The Court of Appeals ruled that the arbitration clause was unenforceable since it posed a risk that Randolph would not be able to afford to protect her interests through arbitration. Green Tree petitioned for a writ of certiorari, and it was granted.

REHNQUIST, C. J.: . . . We . . . turn to the question whether Randolph's agreement to arbitrate is unenforceable because it says nothing about the costs of arbitration, and thus fails to provide her protection from potentially substantial costs of pursuing her federal statutory claims in the arbitral forum. . . . In considering whether respondent's agreement to arbitrate is unenforceable, we are mindful of the FAA's purpose to reverse the longstanding judicial hostility to arbitration agreements and to place arbitration agreements upon the same footing as other contracts.

In light of that purpose, we have recognized that federal statutory claims can be appropriately resolved through arbitration, and we have enforced agreements to arbitrate that involve such claims. We have likewise rejected generalized attacks on arbitration that rest on suspicion of arbitration as a method of weakening the protections afforded in the substantive law to would-be complainants. These cases demonstrate that even claims arising under a statute designed to further important social policies may be arbitrated because so long as the prospective litigant effectively may vindicate his or her statutory cause of action in the arbitral forum, the statute serves its functions.

In determining whether statutory claims may be arbitrated, we first ask whether the parties agreed to submit their claims to arbitration, and then ask whether Congress has evinced an intention to preclude a waiver of judicial remedies for the statutory rights at issue. In this case, it is undisputed that the parties agreed to arbitrate all claims relating to their contract, including claims involving statutory rights. Nor does Randolph contend that the TILA evinces an intention to preclude a waiver of judicial remedies. She contends instead that the arbitration agreement's silence with respect to costs and fees creates a "risk" that she will be required to bear prohibitive arbitration costs if she pursues her claims in an arbitral forum, and thereby forces her to forgo any claims she may have against petitioners. Therefore, she argues, she is unable to vindicate her statutory rights in arbitration.

It may well be that the existence of large arbitration costs could preclude a litigant such as Randolph from effectively vindicating her federal statutory rights in the arbitral forum. But the record does not show that Randolph will bear such costs if she goes to arbitration. Indeed, it contains hardly any information on the matter. As the Court of Appeals recognized, we lack information about how claimants fare under Green Tree's arbitration clause. The record reveals only the arbitration agreement's silence on the subject, and that fact alone is plainly insufficient to render it unenforceable. The "risk" that Randolph will be saddled with prohibitive costs is too speculative to justify the invalidation of an arbitration agreement.

To invalidate the agreement on that basis would undermine the liberal federal policy favoring arbitration agreements. It would also conflict with our prior holdings that the party resisting arbitration bears the burden of proving that the claims at issue are unsuitable for arbitration. We have held that the party seeking to avoid arbitration bears the burden of establishing that Congress intended to preclude arbitration of the statutory claims at issue. Similarly, we believe that where, as here, a party seeks to invalidate an arbitration agreement on the ground that arbitration would be prohibitively expensive, that party bears the burden of showing the likelihood of incurring such costs. Randolph did not meet that burden. How detailed the showing of prohibitive expense must be before the party seeking arbitration must come forward with contrary evidence is a matter we need not discuss; for in this case neither during discovery nor when the case was presented on the merits was there any timely showing at all on the point. The Court of Appeals therefore erred in deciding that the arbitration agreement's silence with respect to costs and fees rendered it unenforceable.

Reversed.

:: CASE QUESTIONS

1. Why did Randolph file a lawsuit against Green Tree rather than pursue her claim through arbitration?
2. What is the basis of the Court of Appeals' ruling that the arbitration clause in the Randolph–Green Tree contract is unenforceable?
3. What is the ruling of the Supreme Court with respect to the Court of Appeals' decision? Why did the Court rule that way?

14. JUDICIAL REVIEW

The arbitration process is less time consuming and less costly than litigation only if the parties are limited in seeking judicial review of the arbitrators' awards. From this perspective, voluntary arbitration is a more effective alternative to litigation than mandatory arbitration. The following subsections discuss the extent of judicial review of awards depending on the type of arbitration.

Review of Voluntary/Contract-Based Arbitration Awards

Generally, the award resulting from the voluntary arbitration procedure is judged as final. The arbitrator's findings on questions of both fact and law are conclusive. The judicial review of an arbitrator's award is quite restricted and is more limited than the appellate review of a trial court's decision.

Arbitration clauses are liberally interpreted when the issue contested is the scope of the clause. If the scope of an arbitration clause is debatable or reasonably in doubt, the clause is construed in favor of arbitration.

The fact that the arbitrator made erroneous rulings during the hearing, or reached erroneous findings of fact from the evidence, is no ground for setting aside the award because the parties have agreed that he or she should be the judge of the facts. An erroneous view of the law no matter how egregious is binding because the parties have agreed to accept the arbitrator's view of the law. Error of law renders the award void only when it would require the parties to commit a crime or otherwise to violate a positive mandate of the law. Courts do not interfere with an award by examining the merits of the controversy, the sufficiency of the evidence supporting the award, or the reasoning supporting the decision. Were it otherwise, arbitration would fail in its chief purpose: to preclude the need for litigation. Instead of being a substitute for litigation, arbitration would merely be the beginning of litigation. Broad judicial review on the merits would render arbitration wasteful and superfluous.

Judicial review can correct fraudulent or arbitrary actions by an arbitrator. Further, courts of review are sometimes called upon to set aside an award when the decision is allegedly against public policy. In such cases, the reviewing court must establish that an arbitration award is contrary to the public policy which arises from laws and legal precedents. A reviewing court cannot reject an award simply because that court bases public policy on general considerations of presumed public interests. In essence, the scope of review by courts of an arbitrator's award in a voluntary/contract-based arbitration is extremely limited, as discussed in Sidebar 5.9.

Review of Statutorily Mandated Arbitration

Although a party may voluntarily consent to almost any restriction upon or deprivation of a right, a similar restriction or deprivation, when compelled by government, must be in accord with procedural and substantive due process of law. Therefore, a higher level of judicial review of an arbitration award is warranted where the arbitration is statutorily mandated.

Laws providing for mandatory arbitration are subject to numerous constitutional challenges. Many courts have generally held that mandatory arbitration statutes that effectively close the courts to the litigants by compelling

Don't count on courts to correct your perceptions of an arbitrator's mistake. Especially in voluntary arbitrations, courts defer to the arbitrator's judgment.

:: *sidebar* 5.9

Judicial Review of Arbitrator's Award

Can a judge reject an arbitrator's factual findings and award and substitute a decision by that judge? This is the issue that the Supreme Court resolved in a case involving major league baseball. Steve Garvey sought damages of $3,000,000 after his contract with the San Diego Padres was not extended because of the team's alleged collusion with other teams. This collusion was supposedly in violation of the Major League Baseball Players Association collective bargaining agreement with the various Major League baseball clubs.

Garvey's claim was submitted to arbitration, and the arbitrator denied the claim stating that Garvey had failed to establish proof of the fact that his contract was not extended because of collusion. Garvey sought review at the district court level, and that judge denied Garvey's motion to set aside the arbitrator's award. Garvey appealed to the Ninth Circuit Court of Appeals. This court of appeals reversed the district court's decision, vacated the arbitrator's award, and decided the case on the basis of record established by the arbitrator.

The Supreme Court reversed the decision of the court of appeals. It held when a court finds that the arbitrator made a mistake, that court should vacate the award and remand the matter to the arbitrator for further arbitration proceedings. The court should not resolve the merits of the parties' dispute.

Source: Major League Baseball Players Association v. Garvey, 121 S. Ct. 1724 (2001).

---

them to resort to arbitrators for a final and binding determination are void as against public policy and are unconstitutional in that they:

1. Deprive one of property and liberty of contract without due process of law.
2. Violate the litigant's Seventh Amendment right to a jury trial and/or the state's constitutional access to courts' provisions.
3. Result in the unconstitutional delegation of legislative or judicial power in violation of state constitutional separation-of-powers provisions.

Mandatory arbitration may be constitutional, however, if fair procedures are provided by the legislature and ultimate judicial review is available. Courts throughout the United States have uniformly upheld mandatory arbitration statutory schemes as against the constitutional challenges previously mentioned where a dissatisfied party can reject the arbitrator's award and seek a **de novo judicial review** of that award. *De novo* review means that the court tries the issues anew as if no arbitration occurred.

De novo hearings may be possible following a mandatory arbitration.

In mandatory arbitrations, a record of proceedings is required. Also, findings of fact and conclusions of law are essential if there is to be enough judicial review to satisfy due process. Judicial review of mandatory arbitration requires a *de novo* review of the interpretation and application of the law by the arbitrators.

The right to reject the award and to proceed to trial is the sole remedy of a party dissatisfied with the award. In a sense, the award is an intermediate step in resolving the dispute if the trial itself is desired. The right to reject the award exists without regard to the basis for the rejection. Many jurisdictions authorize fee and cost sanctions to be imposed on parties who fail to improve their positions at the trial as compared to the arbitration. It is hoped that the quality of the arbitrators, the integrity of the proceedings, and the fairness of the awards will keep the number of rejections to a minimum.

The failure of a party to be present, either in person or by counsel, at an arbitration constitutes a waiver of the right to reject the award and seek *de novo* judicial review. In essence, a party's lack of participation operates as a consent to the entry by the court of a judgment on the award. Since the procedure of mandatory-court-annexed arbitration is an integral part of the judicial process of dispute resolution, its process must be utilized either to resolve the dispute or as the obligatory step prior to resolution by trial. To allow any party to ignore the arbitration would permit a mockery of this deliberate attempt to achieve an expeditious and less costly resolution of private controversies.

Review under the Federal Arbitration Act

If the arbitration is conducted pursuant to state statute, that statute must be consulted to determine what, if any, grounds are available to challenge an award in court. In cases that involve interstate commerce issues, the provisions of the Federal Arbitration Act control.

Section 10 of the Federal Arbitration Act provides that an arbitration award may be vacated or set aside on any one of four grounds:

(a) Where the award was procured by corruption, fraud, or other undue means.

(b) Where the arbitrators were obviously partial or corrupt.

(c) Where the arbitrators were guilty of misconduct in refusing to postpone the hearing, upon sufficient cause shown, or in refusing to hear evidence pertinent and material to the controversy or by engaging in any other misbehavior by which the rights of any party have been prejudiced.

(d) Where the arbitrators exceeded their powers or so imperfectly executed them that a mutual, final, and definite award upon the subject matter submitted was not made.

As set forth in subsection (a), the Federal Arbitration Act provides that an award can be vacated if it can be proved that it was procured by "corruption, fraud, or other undue means." "Undue means" goes beyond the merely inappropriate or inadequate nature of the evidence and refers to some aspect of the arbitrator's decision or decision-making process obtained in some manner that was unfair and beyond the normal process contemplated by the arbitration act. The courts tend to interpret "undue means" in conjunction with the terms "corruption" and "fraud" which precede it, and thus, "undue means" requires some type of bad faith in the procurement of the award.

When the disputing parties each choose an arbitrator and these arbitrators choose a third to make up a three-person panel, the disputing parties may be inclined to charge that the arbitrator chosen by the parties is partial or corrupt. Under subsection (b), the use of "partial or corrupt" in the FAA is interpreted to mean that an arbitrator lacks the ability to consider evidence and to reach a fair conclusion.

Subsection (c) covers arbitral misconduct. The concept of arbitral "misconduct" does not lend itself to a precise definition. Among the actions that

The grounds for overturning an arbitrator's award are very limited; being disappointed with an award is not a basis for changing the award.

have been found to constitute such misconduct on the part of an arbitrator as would warrant vacating an arbitration award are the following:

1. Participation in communications with a party or a witness without the knowledge or consent of the other party.
2. Receipt of evidence as to a material fact without notice to a party.
3. Holding hearings or conducting deliberations in the absence of a member of an arbitration panel or rendering an award without consulting a panel member.
4. Undertaking an independent investigation into a material matter after the close of hearings and without notice to the parties.
5. Accepting gifts or other hospitality from a party during the proceedings.

An award may likewise be set aside on the basis of procedural error if an arbitrator denies a reasonable request for postponement of a hearing or commits an egregious evidentiary error, such as refusing to hear material evidence or precluding a party's efforts to develop a full record.

Finally, subsection (d), involving the question of whether the arbitrators exceeded their power, relates to the arbitrability of the underlying dispute. An arbitrator exceeds powers and authority when attempting to solve an issue that is not arbitrable because it is outside the scope of the arbitration agreement. Conversely, if the issues presented to the arbitrators are within the scope of the arbitration agreement, subsection (d) does not require the court to review the merits of every construction of the contract.

Sidebar 5.10 describes how parties to an arbitration cannot grant courts greater authority to review an arbitrator's award than described in the Federal Arbitration Act.

:: *sidebar* 5.10

Standard of Review of Arbitrator's Decision—Can Parties Expand the Statute?

A complicated factual situation involving whether Mattel, Inc., as a tenant is liable to its landlord, Hall Street Associates, for the cost of an environmental cleanup forms the issue of whether parties can expand the scope of the Federal Arbitration Act. To resolve the lawsuit filed in federal district court over whether Mattel has to pay for the cost of cleaning up a manufacturing site, these parties agreed to arbitrate this dispute. These parties' agreement to arbitrate gave the U.S. District Court for the District of Oregon the authority to "vacate, modify or correct any award; (i) where the arbitrator's findings of fact are not supported by substantial evidence, or (ii) where the arbitrator's conclusions of law are erroneous."

Following arbitration resulting in a finding favoring Mattel (finding it was not liable to pay for the environmental cleanup), Hall Street Associates asked the district court judge to vacate or modify the arbitrator's findings and conclusions. The judge did vacate the arbitrator's award. The Ninth Circuit reversed the judge's order, and the Supreme Court granted certiorari. The Supreme Court states, "Under the terms of section 9, a court must confirm an arbitration award unless it is vacated, modified, or corrected as prescribed in sections 10 and 11. Section 10 lists grounds for vacating an award, while section 11 names those for modifying or correcting one."

The Justices decide that parties, even under the jurisdiction of a district court, cannot expand this quoted language. The parties cannot set a standard of review of an arbitrator's award that is different from the Federal Arbitration Act. The arbitrator's decision favoring Mattel must be reviewed in such a way as to confirm to the limits of the statute.

*Source: Hall Street Associates, LLC v. Mattel, Inc., 128 S. Ct. 1396 (2008).

concept :: *summary*

Voluntary versus Mandatory Arbitration

	:: Voluntary	:: Mandatory Arbitration
Submission	Based on parties' agreement after dispute arises or on contract clause before dispute arises.	Required by statute.
Procedures	Since process is not tied to a court, it is quick, informal, often with no discovery, and not bound by rules of evidence.	The procedure is associated with a court's supervision; discovery usually is done, and many states require arbitrators to follow the formal rules of evidence.
Review of award	The award is final with no judicial review, unless a party can prove that the arbitrator engaged in fraudulent, arbitrary, or other inappropriate actions.	The court will conduct a *de novo* hearing as if the arbitration process had not occurred.

:: Mediation

As the preceding sections document, arbitration has played a significant role in ADR, particularly throughout the last half of the twentieth century. More recently, individuals and businesses have been utilizing the process of mediation as a preferred means of ADR. **Mediation** is the process by which a third person, called a **mediator,** attempts to assist disputing parties in resolving their differences. A mediator cannot impose a binding solution on the parties. However, as an unbiased and disinterested third party, a mediator is often able to help the parties bring about an understanding of a dispute and thus avoid litigation of it. Typically, mediators utilize the principles of interest-based negotiations, discussed in Section 4.

Parties in a mediation are the decision makers; mediators provide a procedure of facilitated negotiation; and the parties are responsible for finding a solution to the dispute.

The process of mediation may be utilized by the disputing parties as a result of their agreement to mediate. This agreement may have been made as a part of a contract before a dispute arose. On the other hand, parties to a dispute may agree that mediation should be attempted as an alternative to litigating their controversy.

A trial judge can require the disputing parties to submit to the mediation process before a complaint can be litigated formally. There is a growing movement in this court-annexed mediation as one means of controlling the heavy caseload faced by courts. Rules related to court-annexed mediation are local in nature; thus, there are wide variations as to the type of cases that courts require to be mediated. Generally, cases involving domestic-relations issues (such as divorce and child custody) and cases involving a dollar amount in dispute below a stated threshold level are examples of those that are subject to court-annexed mediation.

The number of mediations have increased for three primary reasons. First, and perhaps most important, the disputing parties retain control over when to settle and when to continue disputing. This fact allows an effective mediation procedure to help parties address the conflicts that cause the dispute to erupt. An arbitrator's award may benefit one party while punishing another; however, the award likely does not assist the parties in developing a constructive, ongoing business relationship. Since mediation typically focuses on getting the parties to negotiate through an interest-based method, existing and potential conflicts can be handled productively. Sidebar 5.11 attempts to capture this point.

Mediation often allows disputing parties to preserve or reestablish relationships.

:: *sidebar* 5.11

Bill's and M&N Revisited

At the end of Section 2 of this chapter, you were introduced to the business transactions and resulting disputes between Bill's Discount Centers and M&N PC, Inc. Let's suppose these parties litigated or arbitrated the dispute involving the quality of M&N's computers and the reduced purchases, over time, by Bill's. What would be the likely result? The court's judgment or arbitrator's award probably would take the form of a dollar amount in favor of one party or the other. Would such a judgment or award address the underlying concerns of the parties, thereby helping them continue to do business? Probably not!

To achieve some creative result, like the one suggested in Section 4, above, the parties will have to negotiate. The mediation form of ADR is the process that focuses on the parties negotiating.

The second reason mediation is growing in popularity relates to the cost savings compared to litigation and even arbitration. Since there is no presentation of evidence in a mediation, the active role of lawyers is reduced. The resulting savings in time and money can be quite substantial. In mediations, parties are actively engaged in negotiation, which allows these parties to be more efficient with their time.

A third reason businesses are relying more and more on mediation is found in the reduction of the legal system governing the process. As Section 17 of this chapter concludes, the role of courts in mediation is minimal.

15. PROCEDURES

Despite the fact that mediations are informal and controlled by the disputing parties, the odds for a successful mediation occurring increase greatly when the mediator follows some basic procedures. Sidebar 5.12 summarizes the typical steps of the mediation process, and a more complete description follows.

First, the mediator usually makes an opening statement. During this statement, mediators should explain the procedures to which they are asking the parties to agree. In essence, the mediator explains much of what you are reading in this section. Also, any "rules"—such as the common courtesy of not interrupting the party speaking—are specified.

Second, all parties are allowed to make a statement about their views of this dispute. These statements are made in the presence of each other and the mediator. A party's attorney may be the spokesperson; however, it often is more enlightening when the parties speak for themselves.

:: *sidebar* 5.12

Steps in the Mediation Process

1. Mediator's introduction and explanation of mediation.
2. Parties' opening statements.
3. Parties' exchange (or dialogue or negotiation).
4. Brainstorming possible options (or solutions).
5. The agreement (written and signed).
6. Private sessions or caucuses. (These are optional at the mediator's discretion.)

"Mediators must have the facility to listen to what the negotiators are saying and to hear priorities and demands that may not be articulated explicitly. When they start making progress, more tradeoffs follow pretty quickly, once you can break the ice."

–Jerome Lefkowitz, a labor lawyer, on the end of the New York City Transit strike in December 2005 (Source: Sewell Chan and Steven Greenhouse, "From Back-Channel Contacts, Blueprint for a Deal," *The New York Times*, **December 23, 2005)**

A **caucus** in mediation occurs when the mediator meets privately with one party without the other party.

Third, the mediator attempts to get the parties talking to one another in what some refer to as the dialogue or exchange phase of mediation. Through an exchange based on open communication, the parties "clear the air" and hopefully begin to shift their focus from "the wrongs done in the past" to "how can business be conducted in the future."

Fourth, once the parties concentrate on how to work together or how best to end a relationship, the mutual generation of possible solutions should occur. Brainstorming options that resolve the dispute becomes the purpose of this stage of the mediation process. Skillful mediators assist parties in evaluating the possible solutions. Through productive questioning (some call this reality testing) by the mediator, parties should be able to make informed choices as to the best solution. At this point, the parties hopefully are ready to make a realistic commitment to resolve their dispute and conflict.

Sometimes, the mediator may decide that the process will be more productive if the parties and their attorneys meet with the mediator outside the presence of the other disputant. This private meeting is called a **caucus**. After each side caucuses with the mediator, the mediator may call the parties back together for continued discussions, or the mediator may begin to act as a shuttle diplomat, moving back and forth between the parties who are in separate rooms. Especially during these caucuses, the mediator must win the trust and confidence of each party to the dispute.

Through the good judgment and experience of the mediator, the differences between the parties hopefully will be resolved and a common agreement can be produced. The final step to a successful mediation is the writing of the agreement and the signing of the agreement by the parties.

16. ADVANTAGES/DISADVANTAGES

The basic advantage of mediation over litigation and arbitration is that the disputing parties retain full control over the resolution (or lack thereof) of their controversy. Through retaining this control, the parties can decide how much time and effort to put into the mediation process. The fact that mediation is party driven and does not involve even an informal presentation of evidence makes the process much more efficient than other ADR systems. If parties are making progress toward a settlement, the mediation can be continued and perhaps expanded to involve a possible agreement on other potential disputes. When the mediation is not aiding the parties, any of them can stop the process by simply stating that they will not participate further.

This same aspect of the parties controlling the mediation process may be viewed as a disadvantage rather than as an advantage when compared to other ADR systems. Even in the court-annexed mediations, a party usually satisfies the court's order to mediate by simply showing up. Generally, there is no enforcement mechanism that ensures the parties will mediate in good faith.

An additional disadvantage relates to the selection of the neutral mediator. The parties must be able to agree at least on who will be their mediator. The parties can avoid the need to agree on a mediator by allowing the person or organization that administers the mediation program to select the mediator. If the disputing parties cannot "get together" to select a mediator, the mediation process cannot begin.

Finally, the requirements for training as a mediator are not universally defined. Furthermore, licensing requirements are nonexistent at present. Therefore, anyone can serve as a mediator. The disputing party should be aware of the experience (or lack thereof) of the party chosen as their mediator. The Federal Mediation and Conciliation Service, the American Arbitration Association, and other similar organizations are valuable sources of credible mediators.

> **Do** weigh the benefits and detriments of the mediation process. Remember, some disputes can involve issues that need to be litigated for society's gain.

17. LACK OF JUDICIAL INVOLVEMENT

There is no need for judicial review of the mediation process. If mediation is successful, it is the parties' agreement that resolves the dispute. If the parties are not pleased with the mediation, they are free to end their voluntary involvement. A court-mandated mediation either will result in the parties settling their differences and dismissing the lawsuit or will result in no agreement being reached, which likely means the litigation process continues.

In essence, mediations do not involve the legal issues found in the arbitration process. Typically, the conduct of the mediator is not subject to judicial review. Furthermore, mediators usually have the disputing parties sign a consent to mediate that states the mediator cannot be subpoenaed or otherwise be made to testify in any judicial hearing.

18. COMBINATION OF ADR SYSTEMS

The benefit of flexibility related to mediation allows parties to utilize this process in conjunction with other dispute resolution systems. For example, in the middle of heated litigation, parties can agree to mediate just one issue. The resolution of one issue may help the litigation of the remaining issues proceed in a more efficient manner.

One of the more popular variations has given rise to what some people are calling an additional ADR technique. This variation involves the mediation of a dispute. The parties resolve all the matters of contention that they can and they agree to arbitrate the unresolved matters. This variation has become known as **Med-Arb.** The opportunities to use mediation in beneficial ways are limited only by the creativity of the parties involved.

Some laws encourage the parties to be creative in utilizing ADR systems. For example, the Magnuson-Moss Warranty Act provides that if a business adopts an informal dispute resolution system to handle complaints about its product warranties, then a customer cannot sue the manufacturer or seller for breach of warranty without first going through the informal procedures. This law does not deny consumers the right to sue, nor does it compel a compromise solution. It simply allows a manufacturer to require mediation, for instance, before the complaining consumer can litigate.

:: Key Terms

Arbitration   131
Arbitrator   131
Award   132
Caucus   148
Conflict   124
De novo judicial review   143
Dispute   124
Focus groups   130

Mandatory arbitration   132
Med-Arb   149
Mediation   146
Mediator   146
Negotiation   125
Positional bargaining   126
Postdispute arbitration
   agreement   140

Predispute arbitration
   clause   140
Principled, interest-based
   negotiations   127
Submission   132
Voluntary arbitration   132

:: Review Questions and Problems

Conflicts and Negotiation

1. *Conflicts and Disputes*

   What are the distinguishing characteristics of a conflict versus a dispute? Think about a recent conflict that did and did not become a dispute. Think about a recent dispute and describe how you handled it.

2. *Styles and Methods of Negotiation*

   List the five instinctive responses used in negotiation and describe how each of these applies to you.

3. *Positional Negotiation*

   In business disputes, what two items are most likely to dominate a position-based negotiation?

4. *Principled Negotiation*

   (a) Summarize the seven elements of principled, interest-based negotiations.

   (b) How does focusing on these elements assist the negotiation process?

Alternative Dispute Resolution (ADR) Systems

5. *Range of Options*

   What are the various items along the spectrum of ADR systems between litigation and negotiated settlements?

6. *Settlements*

   Why do businesses have incentives to settle disputes rather than relying on jury verdicts in the litigation process?

7. *Focus Groups*

What is the benefit to lawyers and parties of conducting a focus group?

Arbitration

8. *Submissions*

   (a) What is the purpose of a submission in an arbitration?

   (b) What is the proper role of the courts in determining whether a submission to arbitrate is valid?

9. *Arbitrators*

   While conducting an arbitration hearing, an arbitrator allowed laypersons to testify about the cause of injuries to the claimant. The arbitrator awarded dollar damages to be paid to this claimant. May the losing party have this award set aside on the basis that nonexpert testimony was allowed? Why or why not?

10. *Awards*

    Generally, what does an arbitrator have to include in the award to make it valid?

11. *The Federal Arbitration Act*

    (a) A dispute arose between partners. The partnership agreement provided that if the parties were unable to agree on any matter, it would be submitted to arbitration. One partner filed suit asking a court to appoint a receiver for the business. The other insisted on arbitration. How will the dispute be resolved? Why?

    (b) What impact does the FAA have on state laws that prefer the litigation process to arbitration?

12. *Statutorily Mandated Arbitration*

    (a) What is meant by the phrase *statutorily mandated arbitration?*

    (b) Is arbitration required in all cases? Why or why not?

13. *Voluntary/Contract-Based Arbitration*

    How is voluntary/contract-based arbitration distinguished from statutorily mandated arbitration?

14. *Judicial Review*

    (a) Explain why there are different standards of review of arbitration awards depending on whether the arbitration is voluntary or statutorily mandated.

    (b) Barbara and Cole, Inc., disputed the amount of money due as "minimum royalties" under a mineral lease. They submitted the dispute to arbitration, and the arbitrators awarded Barbara $37,214.67. The court held that there was no substantial evidence in the record to support an award of less than the minimum royalty of $75,000 and directed entry of a judgment for that amount. Was it proper for the court to increase the award? Why or why not?

Mediation

15. *Procedures*

    What steps usually are followed to provide an effective and efficient mediation? Explain.

16. *Advantages/Disadvantages*

    (a) How is mediation fundamentally different from an arbitration?

    (b) What are some of the advantages and disadvantages of the mediation process?

17. *Lack of Judicial Involvement*

    What is the nature of mediation that reduces the degree of judicial supervision?

18. *Combination of ADR Systems*

    Describe how mediation can be used in conjunction with arbitration.

1. Your employer, Let's-Get-It-Done, has a history of multiple employee disputes. These disputes range from claims of illegal discrimination to general complaints of worker dissatisfaction with supervisors. You have been assigned the task of changing the organization's culture. Since litigation is the typical method of resolving company disputes, you are considering alternatives to litigation.

What are possible alternative dispute resolution systems (ADRs)?

Should employees be required to sign a contract that an ADR method will be used before any lawsuit is filed against the organization?

2. As the vice president for sales of a company that manufactures and sells commercial carpet, you notice an alarming increase in the number of customers filing complaints with your company service representatives. Of particular importance is the number of complaints that involve claims in excess of $10,000. Because these large dollar amounts can lead to lawsuits being filed, you want to investigate what is causing the increase in complaints and how your company can be processing these complaints to avoid burdensome litigation.

What steps should you take to discover, in the most accurate and efficient manner, the reasons customers are filing complaints?

What is the distinction between mediation and arbitration?

Should your company's sales contracts include a clause that requires the parties to attempt resolution of dispute by mediation? By arbitration? By some other mechanisms?

If your company's sales contracts did include a dispute resolution (other than litigation) clause, when can the courts still be used?

3. After working as a consultant for the "We Can Help You" firm for seven years, you recently received a promotion to manager. In this new role, you report to a partner and are responsible for various consulting teams. You now create these teams in collaboration with the partner. These teams typically consist of four to seven consultants with a senior consultant serving as the team leader. Teams are organized or adjusted as the client demands dictate. As a new manager, you are becoming increasingly aware of conflicts among team members and disputes between the teams and clients.

What is the difference between a conflict and a dispute?

What steps should you take to discover, in an accurate and efficient manner, the reasons conflicts and disputes exist?

Should your consulting firm's contracts with employees contain a dispute resolution clause? What about the firm's consulting agreement with clients? If so, what system of dispute resolution should be included?

Part THREE

:: Legal Foundations of Business

A complex, modern economy cannot function well without the private market, often called the *free market*. The private market refers to millions of individual and corporate owners using what they own and producing, selling, and buying tens of thousands of goods and services. This market, which is guided by the "invisible hand" of competition, requires the rules of a property-based legal system to achieve the maximum conditions for production and distribution. Part Three introduces the principal areas of law that set the rules for the private market.

Chapter 6 discusses the U.S. Constitution, the basic framework for the property-based legal system. Chapter 6 focuses on the structure of the national government and what legal powers the government has to regulate business under the Commerce Clause of the Constitution. Regulation sets and enforces boundaries for how business owners can use their resources in competing against one another. It also protects from harm the personal and material resources of those who buy goods and services from business owners.

In the Bill of Rights, the Constitution guarantees from government interference certain personal rights of self-ownership, such as freedom of religion and freedom of speech. Chapter 6 discusses these rights, and it covers the rights of due process and equal protection, which are at the heart of the rule of law. You may never have thought of personal rights as similar to ownership but you can exclude the government from interfering with your speech and religious expression just as you exclude others from interfering with your land or car. And there are legal boundaries preventing you from harming others through your speech and religious practice just as there are boundaries preventing you from harming others through how you use your land or car.

Chapter 7 on the property-based legal system introduces you to the rules of ownership, how ownership is acquired, and different common applications of ownership. It broadly defines "property" to include the ownership of security interests. Chapter 7 concludes by asserting that the private property fence promotes the common good.

Contracts are the agreements under which owners buy and sell goods and services in a property-based legal system. Chapter 8 examines the rules of contract formation and the interpretation of contracts. Chapter 9 covers the performance of contracts.

Torts are legal wrongs other than breaches of contract. In business, the law of torts sets boundaries for how business owners and managers can use what they own in the private market by defining when that use wrongfully injures what belongs to others. Tort law also sets liability rules of "damages," or compensation for wrongful injuries. Chapter 10 discusses these torts and also examines tort reform and alternatives to the tort system, such as workers' compensation acts.

Tort law and criminal law have much in common and torts are also often (but not always) crimes. But tort law mostly concerns private enforcement of compensation for behavior that injures what belongs to others, whereas criminal law involves the government's punishment of wrongful acts through fines and/or imprisonment.

Chapter 11 examines the important application of the exclusive right of property in the areas of trade secrets, copyrights, patents, and trademarks. The nations that lead the world in producing new products and services all have strong protection of intellectual property. Chapter 11 emphasizes that growth and wealth in an economy increasingly based on information depends importantly on the rules of intellectual property.

Chapter 12 examines constitutional issues of criminal law like search and seizure, the protection against self-incrimination, prohibition against double jeopardy, and the famous "Miranda rights." It focuses on various specific business-related crimes like endangering workers, obstruction of justice, Internet crime, and, particularly, fraud, which concerns lying to get what belongs to others. The chapter concludes with valuable advice about the sentencing of business criminals and other trends in criminal law.

Chapter 13 considers business at an international level. It looks at the sources of international law, the various methods of transacting business internationally, different types of risks involved in international trade, and how businesses resolve disputes at the international level. Note that the concept of property and the rule-based exchange of privately owned resources is almost as important internationally as it is nationally. •

6

The Constitution and Regulation of Business

The U.S. Constitution provides the legal framework of our federal government and the authority it has to regulate business activities. You should take time to read the Constitution and its amendments found in Appendix III. You may react, like many people do, by being surprised how short the Constitution is. The original document was drafted in 1787 as an alternative to the Articles of Confederation. Today, the U.S. Constitution is upheld as a cherished document of democracy. However, the Constitution was an experiment in government since the states, under the Articles of Confederation, were not acting as a nation.

In some ways, the genius of the Constitution is in its simplicity. In other ways, the Constitution is hailed for the way it balances the complexity of government. There are seven articles in the original Constitution. The first three articles establish the legislative, executive, and judicial branches, respectively.

The Constitution creates the Congress, the presidency and vice presidency, and the Supreme Court.

Article IV ensures one nation versus individual states will provide the framework for citizenship and commercial activities. This article contains the full faith and credit clause and the privileges and immunities clause.

Article V provides the process governing the amendment of the Constitution. Article VI describes how this Constitution will be the supreme law of the land. This article also clarifies that federal laws take priority when there is a conflicting state or local law. Some of these constitutional clauses impacting business make up Sections 2–3, and 10–13 of this chapter.

Finally, Article VII states the Constitution will become effective upon ratification of the states. This ratification occurred in 1789. Two years later, in 1791, the first ten amendments also were ratified. These amendments, known as the Bill of Rights, provide clear statements of individuals' freedoms and protections from government action. Some of the key provisions of the Bill of Rights related directly to business are discussed in Sections 4–7 of this chapter. Other provisions from these amendments are found in Chapter 12 on criminal law.

There have been a total of 27 amendments to the Constitution; thus, only 17 amendments have been approved since 1791. Twelve of these 17 amendments relate to how the federal government operates or who has the right to vote.

The 12 amendments include the eleventh, twelfth, fifteenth, seventeenth, nineteenth, twentieth, twenty-second, twenty-third, twenty-forth, twenty-fifth, twenty-sixth, and twenty-seventh.

This leaves five amendments, beyond the Bill of Rights, that substantially impact the government and the rights of individuals. Of these five, one amendment operates to cancel out or repeal another. The Eighteenth Amendment made the manufacture and sale of alcohol illegal. This is known as the Prohibition amendment. The Twenty-first Amendment repealed Prohibition and the Eighteenth Amendment.

It can be argued that only three amendments influence social policy. The Thirteenth Amendment abolished slavery. The Fourteenth Amendment provides protection to citizens against the actions of the states. This amendment contains three important clauses—privileges and immunities, due process, and equal protection. The latter two clauses make up Sections 8 and 9 of this chapter. The Sixteenth Amendment authorizes the federal income tax.

Do understand that an amendment must be ratified by 38 states through legislative action or by a constitutional convention. The U.S. has never held a convention for the purposes of amending the Constitution.

This analysis of the amendments hopefully helps explain why calls for amendments on abortion, public prayer, displays of religious symbols, gun control, and other social issues usually do not result in action. Amending the Constitution is not the typical way social policy is adopted and implemented.

:: Basic Concepts

The Constitution contains many concepts that frame how the federal government operates and interacts with state and local governments. Three of these are of great significance to the creation of a strong centralized, federal government. They are the separation of powers concept, the supremacy clause, and the contract clause. Each is discussed in the following sections.

1. SEPARATION OF POWERS

Historians describe the success of "the constitutional experiment" as founded in the division of powers. The concept of checks and balances among the three branches of the federal government is well known. A lesser emphasized separation of powers is that between the federal government and governments at the state and local levels.

This **separation of powers** between levels of government is known as **federalism.** This concept recognizes that each level of government has a separate and distinct role to play. The federal government recognizes that it was created by the states and that states have some sovereignty. The Tenth Amendment reserves some powers to the states and to the people. Congress may not impair the ability of state government to function in the federal system. Likewise, state government may not limit the federal government's exercise of powers. Federalism, the separation of powers between the federal and state/local governments, is an important topic facing the Supreme Court every year.

Section 12 of this chapter discusses federalism.

2. SUPREMACY CLAUSE

In allocating power between federal and state levels of government, the Constitution, in Article VI, makes it clear that the Constitution is supreme under all laws and that federal law is supreme over a state law or local ordinance. Under the **supremacy clause,** courts may be called upon to decide if a state law is invalid because it conflicts with a federal law. They must construe or interpret the two laws to see if they are in conflict. A conflict exists if the state statute would prevent or interfere with the accomplishment and execution of the full purposes and objectives of Congress.

When various laws are not consistent, the order of priority is (1) U.S. Constitution, (2) U.S. laws, (3) state and local laws.

It is immaterial that a state did not intend to frustrate the federal law if the state law in fact does so. For example, an Arizona statute provided for the suspension of licenses of drivers who could not satisfy judgments arising out of auto accidents, even if the driver was bankrupt. The statute was declared unconstitutional since it was in conflict with the federal law on bankruptcy. The purpose of the Bankruptcy Act is to give debtors new opportunity unhampered by the pressure and discouragement of preexisting debt. The challenged state statute hampers the accomplishment and execution of the full purposes and objectives of the Bankruptcy Act enacted by Congress.

Preemption   Sometimes a federal law is said to preempt an area of law. If a federal law preempts a subject, then any state law that attempts to regulate the same activity is unconstitutional under the supremacy clause. The concept of **preemption** applies not only to federal statutes but also to the rules and regulations of federal administrative agencies. Sidebar 6.1 lists several examples of business-related cases in which the courts have found federal preemption of areas involving business regulations. The federal laws in this list are covered throughout this book. When you study these laws, remember the constitutional issues related to preemption. This concept helps explain the vast authority of the federal government.

The U.S. Supreme Court recently ruled that the state of Michigan cannot regulate the mortgage lending subsidiary of a major national bank.[1] This ruling reaffirms that the federal Office of the Comptroller of the Currency (OCC) has greater authority than a state to regulate banks and associated activities.

---

[1] *Watters v. Wachovia Bank NA,* 127 S.Ct. 1559 (2007).

:: *sidebar* 6.1

Examples of State Laws Preempted by Federal Law

:: State or Local Law Preempted by	:: Federal Law
A city conditions renewal of taxicab franchise on settlement of a labor dispute.	National Labor Relations Act
Municipal zoning ordinance governs size, location, and appearance of satellite dish antennas.	Federal Communications Commission Regulation
A state statute permits indirect purchasers to collect damages for overcharges resulting from price-fixing conspiracies.	Sherman Antitrust Act
A state law authorizes a tort claim by workers that a union has breached its duty to ensure a safe workplace.	Labor-Management Relations Act (Landrum-Griffin)
A state law prohibits repeat violators of labor laws from doing business with the state.	National Labor Relations Act
A state nuisance law purports to cover out-of-state sources of water pollution.	Clean Water Act
State criminal prosecution for aggravated battery is filed against corporate officials because of unsafe workplace conditions.	Occupational Safety and Health Act
State statute prohibits use of the direct molding process to duplicate unpatented boat hulls or knowing sale of hulls so duplicated.	Patent Law

3. CONTRACT CLAUSE

Article I, Section 10, of the Constitution says, "No State shall . . . pass any . . . Law impairing the Obligation of contracts." This is the **contract clause.** It does not apply to the federal government, which does in fact frequently enact laws and adopt regulations that affect existing contracts. For example, the Department of Agriculture from time to time embargoes grain sales to foreign countries, usually as a result of problems in foreign affairs. Prohibitions of sales of electronic equipment to certain nations are upheld if the federal government prohibits such sales.

> The contract clause regulates state and local government; it does not restrict the federal govenrnment's power to impact contractual relationships.

Under the contract clause, states cannot enact laws that impact rights and duties under existing contracts. Suppose your company has a contract to provide natural gas to customers for stated minimum costs. A state or local government cannot impose new lower minimum prices on these existing contracts. The new minimum prices would be applicable only to newly created contracts.

The limitation on state action impairing contracts has not been given a literal application. As a result of judicial interpretation, some state laws that affect existing contracts have been approved, especially when the law is passed to deal with a specific emergency situation. On the other hand, this constitutional provision does generally limit alternatives available to state government and prevents the enactment of legislation that changes existing contract rights.

:: Amendments and Basic Protections

The original seven constitutional articles created basic, fundamental concepts or principles of a centralized government. However, the language of the original Constitution was criticized for not restricting the newly formed federal government in some important ways. The first ten amendments, known as the Bill of Rights, establish a variety of important protections. Oftentimes we do not think of the protections in a business context. Instead, we think of them as the personal rights of individuals living in a free society. Indeed, many of the basic protections are referred to as freedoms. As you read the next four sections of this chapter keep in mind how constitutional protections relate to economic opportunity and business activities.

As you study the impact of these basic protections keep four important aspects in mind. First, basic constitutional rights are not absolute. Second, the extent of any limitation on a basic constitutional guarantee depends upon the nature of the competing public policy. Cases involving the Bill of Rights almost always require courts to strike a balance either between some goal or policy of society and the constitutional protection involved or between competing constitutional guarantees. For example, such cases may involve conflict between the goal of protecting an individual's or business's reputation and the right of another to speak freely about the reputation. The courts are continually weighing the extent of constitutional protections.

Third, constitutional guarantees exist in order to remove certain issues from the political process and the ballot box. They exist to protect the minority from the majority. Freedom of expression (press and speech) protects the unpopular idea or viewpoint. Freedom of assembly allows groups with ideologies foreign to most of us to meet and express their philosophy.

Finally, constitutional rights vary from time to time and may be narrowly interpreted during emergencies such as war or civil strife. Even during peace time, constitutional principles are constantly reapplied and reexamined.

The next four sections cover topics arising from the Bill of Rights. Then Sections 8 and 9 examine provisions of the Fourteenth Amendment that extend constitutional protections by restricting the authority of state and local governments.

4. FREEDOM OF RELIGION

The First Amendment states that Congress shall make no law "respecting an establishment of religion" (the **establishment clause**) "or prohibiting the free exercise thereof" (the **free exercise clause**). These clauses guarantee freedom of religion through the separation of church and state.

Most business-related freedom of religion cases involve the free exercise clause. The Supreme Court has held that the denial of unemployment benefits to a worker who refused a position because the job would have required him to work on Sunday violated the free exercise clause of the First Amendment. The constitution requires that the owner of the business either allow the person to have Sunday off or allow the state to pay unemployment compensation and increase the business's taxes. Most businesses are likely to face this constitutional issue in employment discrimination claims. These issues appear in detail in Chapter 20.

Freedom of religion has been used to challenge legislation requiring the closing of business establishments on Sunday. Although the motive for such legislation may be, in part, religious, there are also economic reasons for such legislation. As a result, if a law is based on economic considerations, it may be upheld if its classifications are reasonable and in the public interest.

The First Amendment to the Constitution of the United States establishes the following basic freedoms:
Freedom of religion
Freedom of the press
Freedom of speech
Freedom of assembly
The right to petition the government for a redress of grievances

However, many such laws have been held invalid as a violation of the First Amendment.

Other examples of freedom of religion cases that concern business appear in Sidebar 6.2.

:: *sidebar* 6.2

Examples of Freedom of Religion Issues Affecting Business

	:: Case Decisions	
	Yes	No
Is it constitutional to apply the Fair Labor Standards Act (minimum-wage law) to a nonprofit religious organization?	X	
Is it constitutional to apply the labor laws relating to union elections to parochial school teachers?		X
Is a state law constitutional when it provides Sabbath observers with an absolute and unqualified right not to work on their Sabbath?		X
Is religious belief justification for refusing to participate in the Social Security system?		X
Does the 1964 Civil Rights Act, which obligates employers to make reasonable accommodations of employees' religious beliefs, violate the First Amendment's establishment clause?		X
May a state impose a 6 percent sales tax on religious merchandise sold in the state by religious organizations?	X	
May a state exempt religious periodicals from a sales tax that applies to all other periodicals?		X

---

5. FREEDOM OF THE PRESS

Do realize that the concept of prohibiting prior restraints means a community must allow a performance to occur; the community can charge the actors with violating a local ordinance if the performance is inappropriate.

The publishing business is the only organized private business given explicit constitutional protection. The First Amendment states that "Congress shall make no law . . . abridging the freedom of . . . the press." This guarantee essentially authorizes a private business to provide organized scrutiny of government.

Freedom of the press is not absolute. The press is not free to print anything it wants without liability. Rather, freedom of the press is usually construed to prohibit **prior restraints** on publications. If the press publishes that which is illegal or libelous, it has liability for doing so. This liability may be either criminal or civil for damages.

There are many examples of limitations on freedom of the press. For example, courts have allowed the Federal Communications Commission to censor "filthy" words and indecent exposure on television. The power of the commission extends to upholding the public's interest in responsible broadcasting.

Don't forget to determine whether a person is a public or private figure when deciding if defamation exists.

A major area of litigation involving freedom of the press involves **defamation**. The tort theory known as **libel** is used to recover damages as a result of printed defamation of character. Libel cases compensate individuals for harm inflicted by defamatory printed falsehoods. Since the threat of a libel suit could have a chilling effect on freedom of the press and on the public's rights to information, the law has a different standard for imposing liability when the printed matter concerns an issue of public interest and concern. If the person involved is a public official or figure, a plaintiff seeking damages for emotional distress caused by offensive publications must prove actual **malice** in order to recover. *Actual malice* includes knowledge that the printed statements are false or circumstances showing a reckless disregard for whether they are true or not. If the plaintiff is not a public figure or public official, there is liability for libelous statements without proof of malice.

6. FREEDOM OF SPEECH

Freedom of speech, sometimes referred to as freedom of expression, covers both verbal and written communications. This protection relates to governmental action that restricts our ability to express ourselves. The first Amendment protection does not apply to private action. For example, a private employer may legally impose a policy that certain topics, such as salaries, are not to be discussed in the workplace. Whether a restriction is imposed by the government or a private company is critical to understand.

Free speech also covers conduct or actions considered **symbolic speech.** Although freedom of speech is not absolute, it is as close to being absolute as any constitutional guarantee. It exists to protect the minority from the majority. It means freedom to express ideas antagonistic to those of the majority. Freedom of speech exists for thoughts many of us hate and for ideas that may be foreign to us. It means freedom to express the unorthodox, and it recognizes that there is no such thing as a false idea.

The issue of freedom of speech arises in many business situations. Sidebar 6.3 discusses several situations that arise when considering the protection of picketing and the limitation of free speech.

:: *sidebar* 6.3

Picketing as Free Speech

Cases involving picketing, for example, especially with unions, often are concerned with the issue of free speech. The right to picket peacefully for a lawful purpose is well recognized. A state or local law that prohibits all picketing would be unconstitutional since the act of picketing, itself, is a valuable form of communication. However, a state law that limits picketing or other First Amendment freedoms may be constitutional if:

- The regulation is within the constitutional power of government.
- It furthers an important or substantial governmental interest.
- It is unrelated to suppression of free expression.
- The incidental restriction on First Amendment freedoms is no greater than is essential to further the government's interest.

Under these principles, laws that prevent pickets from obstructing traffic and those designed to prevent violence would be constitutional. For example, a Texas statute that prohibits "mass picketing," defined as picketing by more than two persons within 50 feet of any entrance or of one another, does not violate the First Amendment. The Supreme Court has held that a city ordinance prohibiting picketing in front of an individual residence was constitutional. The law was enacted to prevent picketing of the homes of doctors who perform abortions.

Courts may limit the number of pickets to preserve order and promote safety, but they will not deny pickets the right to express opinions in a picket line. For example, a court order preventing a client from picketing her lawyer was held to be a violation of the First Amendment. Freedom of speech even extends to boycotts of a business for a valid public purpose such as the elimination of discrimination.

In some free-speech cases, an individual whose own speech or conduct may not be prohibited is nevertheless permitted to challenge a statute limiting speech because it also threatens other people not before the court. The person is allowed to challenge the statute because others who may desire to engage in legally protected expression may refrain from doing so. They may fear the risk of prosecution, or they may not want to risk having a law declared to be only partially invalid. This is known as the **overbreadth doctrine**. It means that the legislators have gone too far in seeking to achieve a goal.

For example, an airport authority resolution declared the central terminal area "not open for First Amendment activities." The resolution was unconstitutional under the First Amendment overbreadth doctrine. The resolution reached the "universe of expressive activity" and in effect created a "First-Amendment-Free Zone" at the airport. Nearly every person who entered the airport would violate the resolution, since it bars all First Amendment activities, including talking and reading.

As you can see, the freedom of speech is cherished as a fundamental right of citizenship. While this right's importance provides significant protection, it sometimes can contradict other critical interests, such as the right of privacy. Sidebar 6.4 highlights the balance that courts often seek to find.

> The overbreadth doctrine was used by the courts to declare certain versions of child pornography laws unconstitutional. Governmental restrictions on expression must be narrowly drafted.

:: *sidebar* 6.4

Free Speech versus an Individual's Right of Privacy

Through wiretapping and electronic surveillance statutes, the federal government and most states make it illegal to intercept and record oral, wire, and electronic conversations. A more complicated issue arises when an illegally obtained conversation involving public issues is broadcast or published by someone who is not involved in the illegal activity. For example, does the free speech clause protect a radio commentator who broadcasts a cell phone conversation when that conversation is illegally recorded but when the commentator is not the party who illegally taped the conversation?

The U.S. Supreme Court holds it would be most unusual to hold "speech by a law-abiding possessor of information can be suppressed in order to deter conduct by a non-law-abiding third party." When the recorded conversation involves public issues (such as the pay of public school teachers), the publication of this public information is protected compared to the interest of individuals to have their conversation remain private.

*Source: *Bartnicki v. Vopper*, 121 S. Ct. 1753 (2001).

Commercial Speech   Historically, **commercial speech** was not protected by the First Amendment. However, in the 1970s the Supreme Court began to recognize that free commercial speech was essential to the public's right to know. Therefore, today, freedom of speech protects corporations as well as individuals. The public interests served by freedom of expression protect the listener as well as the speaker. Freedom of expression includes freedom of information or the rights of the public to be informed. Since corporations may add to the public's knowledge and information, they also have the right to free speech. Freedom of speech for corporations may not be as extensive as the right of an individual. However, a government cannot limit commercial speech without a compelling state interest expressed to justify the restriction. State regulatory commissions often seek to limit the activities of public utilities. Such attempts usually run afoul of the First Amendment. Sidebar 6.5 explains why and to what extent commercial speech is protected.

:: *sidebar* 6.5

Balancing the Protection of Commercial Speech

The Food and Drug Administration Modernization Act (FDAMA) of 1997 allows drug compounding and the advertisement of such services. However, this law prohibits the advertising or any other promotional announcement that a specific compounded drug is available. Pharmacists, fearing their promotional materials related to drug compounds might be found to violate the FDAMA, sought a declaratory judgment that this law's prohibition on advertising specific compounded drugs was unconstitutional.

The Supreme Court reviews the four tests used to protect commercial speech. The compounding of drugs, as practiced by the pharmacists involved in this case, is a lawful activity. The government's interests in limiting the availability of compound drugs, which are not thoroughly tested by the FDA, are significant and substantial. The ban on advertisement of specific compound drugs does directly relate to the government's interest stated above. However, the Court discusses numerous examples of how the FDA could restrict the compounding drugs without resorting to a restriction on commercial advertisement. Since the FDA did not show why these less-restrictive examples were not feasible, the Court affirms the lower courts' decisions that the FDAMA violates the First Amendment's free speech clause.

Source: Secretary of Health and Human Services v. Western Medical Center, 122 S. Ct. 1497 (2002).

7. RIGHT TO POSSESS GUNS

Unlike the extensive litigation that defines the meaning of the First Amendment, there have been very few Supreme Court opinions involving the Second Amendment. The language of this amendment is as follows: "A well regulated Militia, being necessary to the security for a free State, the right of the people to keep and bear Arms, shall not be infringed."

Only recently, in 2008, has the U.S. Supreme Court addressed the meaning of the Second Amendment as it applies to the maintenance of a militia versus an individual's right to possess and use guns in their homes.[2] By a 5–4 margin, the Court ruled that the Second Amendment is not limited by its introductory phrase. The Court struck down, as unconstitutional, the District of Columbia's ban on handguns and its requirement that other guns, such as rifles, be kept unloaded or disassembled, or subject to a trigger-locking mechanism. The Court's majority concluded individuals in the District of Columbia can possess handguns in their homes and can have their guns loaded and ready for use in self-defense.

Even as this opinion was announced, commentators speculate that this decision will lead to increases in litigation under the Second Amendment. Regulation of guns by states and cities will be challenged since this Supreme Court opinion is very narrow even as it strikes down, as unconstitutional, a very broad restriction. The Supreme Court's majority opinion simply affirms the right to possess guns, including handguns, in one's home and to have them ready for use in self-defense. Left unanswered are many questions. For example, can individuals carry guns, especially concealed handguns, in public places like restaurants, parks, transit systems, and even airports? These and

Guns are big business. According to industry reports, the U.S. firearms industry consists of 200 companies with annual revenue of $2 billion.

---

[2]*District of Columbia v. Heller,* 128 S. Ct. 2783 (2008).

other issues related to the language of the Second Amendment should become a significant part of future constitutional cases.

8. DUE PROCESS OF LAW

The Fourteenth Amendment to the Constitution states, "No state shall make or enforce any law which shall abridge the privileges or immunities of citizens of the United States; nor shall any state deprive any person of life, liberty or property, without due process of law, nor deny to any person within its jurisdiction the equal protection of the laws." Two of this amendment's provisions are of very special importance to businesspeople—the **due process clause** and the **equal protection clause**.

> The Fourteenth Amendment restricts actions by state and local governments.

Prior to reading about these clauses, look again at the language quoted in the preceding paragraph. It is critical to understand that the first ten amendments describe individual protections against action by the federal government. The Fourteenth Amendment explicitly clarifies that certain restrictions also apply to state (and local) governments.

The term *due process of law* as used in the Fourteenth Amendment probably arises in more litigation than any other constitutional phrase. It cannot be narrowly defined. The term describes fundamental principles of liberty and justice. Simply stated, due process means "fundamental fairness and decency." It means that *government* may not act in a manner that is arbitrary, capricious, or unreasonable. The clause does not prevent private individuals or corporations, including public utilities, from acting in an arbitrary or unreasonable manner. The due process clause applies only to governmental bodies; it does not apply to the actions of individuals or businesses.

Procedural due process cases involve whether proper notice has been given and a proper hearing has been conducted. Such cases frequently involve procedures established by statute. However, many cases involve procedures that are not created by statute. For example, the due process clause has been used to challenge the procedure used in the dismissal of a student from a public university.

In essence, the due process clause can be invoked anytime procedures of government are questioned in litigation. For example, in recent years, the Supreme Court has used the due process clause as its justification for defining the limits for a jury awarding punitive damages to a plaintiff in a civil lawsuit. Sidebar 6.6 illustrates this use of the due process clause.

Incorporation Doctrine The due process clause has played a unique role in constitutional development—one that was probably not anticipated at the time of its ratification. This significant role has been to make most of the provisions of the Bill of Rights applicable to the states. The first phrase of the First Amendment begins: "Congress shall make no law." How then are state and local governments prohibited from making such a law? Jurists have used the due process clause of the Fourteenth Amendment to "incorporate" or "carry over" the Bill of Rights and make these constitutional provisions applicable to the states. Starting in 1925, the Supreme Court began applying various portions of the first eight amendments to the states using the due process clause of the Fourteenth Amendment as the reason for this incorporation and application.

The role of the due process doctrine goes well beyond incorporation. For example, the Fifth Amendment contains a due process clause applicable to the

:: *sidebar* 6.6

Punitive Damages and the Supreme Court

In a series of decisions over the past several years, the U.S. Supreme Court describes how the due process clause limits the authority of trial juries and judges to award punitive damages, the type of awards intended to punish a wrongdoer.

The Campbells had their car insured with State Farm. The Campbells were involved in a car accident and were sued. A State Farm representative told the Campbells that their insurance would protect them and that they did not need their own lawyer. The Campbells were found liable for an amount greater than their insurance coverage. The Campbells then sued State Farm claiming the company's bad faith misrepresentations resulted in the Campbells' damages. Using evidence that State Farm had been involved in similar claims throughout the United States, the Campbells won a jury verdict of $2.6 million in compensatory damages and $145 million in punitive damages. The trial judge reduced the compensatory damages to $1 million and the punitive damages to $25 million. Following appeals, the Utah Supreme Court reinstated the $145 million in punitive damages. State Farm asked the U.S. Supreme Court to declare that these punitive damages violated the due process clause of the Fourteenth Amendment.

The Court expresses concern that the degree of reprehensibility of State Farm's bad faith is unreasonably increased by the evidence from cases outside of Utah. In addressing a proper ratio of punitive damages to compensatory damages, the Court seems to want to limit such ratio to a single digit. In light of Utah's civil sanction for State Farm's bad faith being limited to $10,000, the Court finds the $145 million in punitive damages is unreasonable, arbitrary, and unconstitutional under the Fourteenth Amendment's due process clause.

In 2007, a jury awarded the estate of a deceased smoker $21,000 in economic damages, $800,000 in noneconomic damages, and $79.5 million in punitive damages. These awards arose out of a lawsuit against Philip Morris, the manufacturer of Marlboros, the preferred cigarette of the deceased. This lawsuit was not a class-action; it involved only one plaintiff.

The U.S. Supreme Court vacated the punitive damages award on the basis that the jury cannot punish a defendant for its action involving people (other smokers) who are not parties to the litigation. The Court does not issue a ruling that the nearly 100:1 ratio of punitive to nonpunitive damages is grossly excessive. Before deciding that issue, the Supreme Court wants the lower court to decide whether the jury considered other smokers, who are not involved in the lawsuit, when deciding on the amount of the punitive damages. If so, the punitive damages award would be unconstitutional since it would be a taking of Philip Morris's property without due process.

In 2008, the U.S. Supreme Court addressed the punitive damages awarded to commercial fishermen and native Alaskans against the Exxon Shipping Company for the harm created by the oil spill from the *Exxon Valdez* running aground. A jury awarded $5 billion in punitive damages, and this amount was reduced to $2.5 billion by the Ninth Circuit Court of Appeals. These awards were in addition to $507 million in compensatory damages.

In applying federal maritime law, instead of constitutional principles, the Supreme Court concluded that no more than a 1:1 ratio of punitive damages to compensatory damages was reasonable. Thus, the justices reduced the $2.5 billion punitive damages award to approximately $500 million, a five-fold reduction.

*Sources: *State Farm Mutual Automobile Insurance Company v. Campbell*, 123 S. Ct. 1513 (2003); *Philip Morris USA v. Williams*, 127 S. Ct. 1057 (2007); *Exxon Shipping Company v. Baker*, 128 S. Ct. 2605 (2008).

federal government. The Fourteenth Amendment contains a due process clause, applicable to state and local governments. Due process essentially means the same thing under both amendments. Through the due process clause, all of the constitutionally guaranteed freedoms we discuss in this chapter and in Chapter 12 have been incorporated into the Fourteenth Amendment and are applicable to the state government's regulation of our personal and professional lives.

> The concept of incorporation through the due process clause has made the protections of the Bill of Rights applicable to individuals subject to state and local regulations.

9. EQUAL PROTECTION

The Fourteenth Amendment's equal protection language is also involved in a great deal of constitutional litigation. No law treats all persons equally; laws draw lines and treat people differently. Therefore, almost any state or local law imaginable can be challenged under the equal protection clause. It is obvious that the equal protection clause does not always deny states the power to treat different persons in different ways. Yet the equal protection clause embodies the ethical idea that law should not treat people differently without a satisfactory reason. In deciding cases using that clause to challenge state and local laws, courts use three distinct approaches. One is the traditional, or **minimum rationality,** approach, and a second is called the **strict scrutiny** approach. Some cases are analyzed as falling in between these approaches. Courts in these cases use the **quasi-strict scrutiny** approach.

> **Do** understand the role of each test under the equal protection clause.

As a practical matter, if the traditional (minimum rationality) approach is used, the challenged law and its classifications are usually found *not* to be a violation of equal protection. On the other hand, if the strict scrutiny test is used, the classifications are usually found to be unconstitutional under the equal protection clause.

Minimum Rationality   Under the minimum rationality approach, a law creating different classifications will survive an equal protection challenge if it has a *rational* connection to a *permissible* state end. A permissible state end is one not prohibited by another provision of the Constitution. It qualifies as a legitimate goal of government. The classification must have a reasonable basis (not wholly arbitrary), and the courts will assume any statement of facts that can be used to justify the classification. These laws often involve economic issues or social legislation such as welfare laws.

Such laws are presumed to be constitutional because courts recognize that the legislature must draw lines creating distinctions and that such tasks cannot be avoided. Only when no rational basis for the classification exists is it unconstitutional under the equal protection clause. For example, a state law restricting advertising to company-owned trucks was held valid when the rational-basis test was applied to it because it is reasonable to assume less advertising on trucks provides for safer roads. Therefore, under this state law, a trucking company could not use the sides of its trucks to carry other companies' ads. Sidebar 6.7 provides an additional case example of the rational-basis test.

:: *sidebar* 6.7

Economic Regulations and the Rational-Basis Test

The state of Iowa taxes revenues from slot machines on riverboats at a maximum rate of 20 percent. Iowa provides a maximum tax rate of 36 percent on revenues from slot machines at racetracks. A group of racetracks and an association of dog owners filed a lawsuit to have these different tax rates declared unconstitutional under the equal protection clause.

The U.S. Supreme Court wrote that these tax rates are subject to the rational-basis test under the equal protection analysis, stating:

> The Equal Protection Clause is satisfied so long as there is a plausible policy reason for the classification, the legislative facts on

which the classification is apparently based rationally may have been considered to be true by the governmental decisionmaker, and the relationship of the classification to its goal is not so attenuated as to render the distinction arbitrary or irrational.

The Court finds that the Iowa legislators could rationally support riverboats by providing a lower tax on slot machines. This action does not unconstitutionally harm the racetracks since this case simply involves an economic decision of the legislature.

Source: Fitzgerald v. Racing Association of Central Iowa, 123 S. Ct. 2156 (2003).

Strict Scrutiny Under the strict scrutiny test, a classification will be a denial of equal protection unless the classification is necessary to achieve a *compelling* state purpose. It is not enough that a classification be permissible to achieve any state interest; it must be a compelling state objective. To withstand constitutional challenge when this test is used, the law must serve important governmental objectives and the classification must be substantially related to achieving these objectives.

The strict scrutiny test is used if the classification involves either a suspect class or a fundamental constitutional right. A suspect class is one that has such disabilities, has been subjected to such a history of purposeful unequal treatment, or has been placed in such a position of political powerlessness that it commands extraordinary protection from the political process of the majority. For example, classifications directed at race, national origin, and legitimacy of birth are clearly suspect. As a result, the judiciary strictly scrutinizes laws directed at them. Unless the state can prove that its statutory classifications have a compelling state interest as a basis, the classifications will be considered a denial of equal protection. Classifications that are subject to strict judicial scrutiny are presumed to be unconstitutional. The state must convince the court that the classification is fair, reasonable, and necessary to accomplish the objective of legislation that is compelling to a state interest.

Case 6.1 focuses on the application of racial consideration in the award of government contracts.

---

case **6.1**

ADARAND CONSTRUCTORS, INC. v. PENA
115 S. Ct. 2097 (1995)

O'CONNOR, J.: In 1989, the Central Federal Lands Highway Division (CFLHD), which is part of the United States Department of Transportation (DOT), awarded the prime contract for a highway construction project in Colorado to Mountain Gravel & Construction Company. Mountain Gravel then solicited bids from subcontractors for the guardrail portion of the contract. Adarand, a Colorado-based highway construction company specializing in guardrail work, submitted the low bid. Gonzales Construction Company also submitted a bid.

The prime contract's terms provide that Mountain Gravel would receive additional compensation if it hired subcontractors certified as small businesses controlled by "socially and economically disadvantaged individuals." Gonzales is certified as such a business; Adarand is not. Mountain Gravel awarded the subcontract to Gonzales, despite Adarand's low bid. Federal law requires that a subcontracting clause similar to the one used here must appear in most federal agency contracts, and it also requires the clause to state that "the contractor shall presume that socially and economically disadvantaged individuals include Black Americans, Hispanic Americans, Native Americans, Asian Pacific Americans, and other minorities, or any other individual found to be disadvantaged by the [Small Business] Administration pursuant to section 8(a) of the Small Business Act." Adarand claims that the presumption set forth in that statute discriminates on the basis of race in violation of the Federal Government's Fifth Amendment obligation not to deny anyone equal protection of the laws. . . .

The contract giving rise to the dispute in this case came about as a result of the Surface Transportation and Uniform Relocation Assistance Act of 1987, a DOT appropriations measure. Section 106(c)(1) of STURAA provides that "not less than 10 percent" of the appropriated funds "shall be expended with small business concerns owned and controlled by socially and economically disadvantaged individuals."

STURAA adopts the Small Business Act's definition of "socially and economically disadvantaged individual," including the applicable race-based presumptions, and adds that "women shall be presumed to be socially and economically disadvantaged individuals for purposes of this subsection.". . .

After losing the guardrail subcontract to Gonzales, Adarand filed suit against various federal officials in the United States District Court for the District of Colorado, claiming that the race-based presumptions involved in the use of subcontracting compensation clauses violate Adarand's right to equal protection. The District Court granted the Government's motion for summary judgment. The Court of Appeals for the Tenth Circuit affirmed. It understood our decision in *Fullilove v. Klutznick,* 100 S. Ct. 2758 (1980), to have adopted "a lenient standard, resembling intermediate scrutiny, in assessing" the constitutionality of federal race-based action. Applying that "lenient standard," as further developed in *Metro Broadcasting, Inc. v. FCC,* 110 S. Ct. 2997 (1990), the Court of Appeals upheld the use of subcontractor compensation clauses. We granted certiorari. . . .

In 1978, the Court confronted the question whether race-based governmental action designed to benefit such groups should also be subject to "the most rigid scrutiny." *Regents of Univ. of California v. Bakke,* 98 S. Ct. 2733, involved an equal protection challenge to a state-run medical schools' practice of reserving a number of spaces in its entering class for minority students. The petitioners argued that "strict scrutiny" should apply only to "classifications that disadvantage 'discrete and insular minorities.'" *Bakke* did not produce an opinion for the Court, but Justice Powell's opinion announcing the Court's judgment rejected the argument. In a passage joined by Justice White, Justice Powell wrote that "the guarantee of equal protection cannot mean one thing when applied to one individual and something else when applied to a person of another color." He concluded that "racial and ethnic distinctions of any sort are inherently suspect and thus call for the most exacting judicial examination.". . .

Two years after *Bakke,* the Court faced another challenge to remedial race-based action, this time involving action undertaken by the Federal Government. In *Fullilove v. Klutznick,* the Court upheld Congress' inclusion of a 10% set-aside for minority-owned businesses in the Public Works Employment Act of 1977. As in *Bakke,* there was no opinion for the Court. Chief Justice Burger, in an opinion joined by Justices White and Powell, observed that "any preference based on racial or ethnic criteria must necessarily receive a most searching examination to make sure that it does not conflict with constitutional

guarantees." That opinion, however, "did not adopt, either expressly or implicitly, the formulas of analysis articulated in such cases as [*Bakke*]." It employed instead a two-part test which asked, first, "whether the objectives of the legislation are within the power of Congress," and second, "whether the limited use of racial and ethnic criteria, in the context presented, is a constitutionally permissible means for achieving the congressional objectives." It then upheld the program under that test. . . .

In *Wygant v. Jackson Board of Ed.,* 106 S. Ct. 1842 (1986), the Court considered a Fourteenth Amendment challenge to another form of remedial racial classification. The issue in *Wygant* was whether a school board could adopt race-based preferences in determining which teachers to lay off. Justice Powell's plurality opinion observed that "the level of scrutiny does not change merely because the challenged classification operates against a group that historically has not been subject to governmental discrimination," and stated the two-part inquiry as "whether the layoff provision is supported by a compelling state purpose and whether the means chosen to accomplish that purpose are narrowly tailored." In other words, "racial classifications of any sort must be subjected to 'strict scrutiny.'" The plurality then concluded that the school board's interest in "providing minority role models for its minority students, as an attempt to alleviate the effects of societal discrimination," was not a compelling interest that could justify the use of a racial classification. It added that "societal discrimination, without more, is too amorphous a basis for imposing a racially classified remedy," and insisted instead that "a public employer . . . must ensure that, before it embarks on an affirmative-action program, it has convincing evidence that remedial action is warranted. That is, it must have sufficient evidence to justify the conclusion that there has been prior discrimination.". . .

The Court's failure to produce a majority opinion in *Bakke, Fullilove,* and *Wygant* left unresolved the proper analysis for remedial race-based governmental action.

The Court resolved the issue, at least in part, in 1989. *Richmond v. J. A. Croson Co.,* 109 S. Ct. 706 (1989), concerned a city's determination that 30% of its contracting work should go to minority-owned businesses. A majority of the Court in *Croson* held that "the standard of review under the Equal Protection Clause is not dependent on the race of those burdened or benefited by a particular classification," and that the single standard of review for racial classifications should be "strict scrutiny." As to the classification before the Court, the plurality agreed that "a state or local subdivision . . . has the authority to eradicate the effects of private discrimination within its own legislative jurisdiction," but the Court thought that the city had not acted with "a 'strong basis in evidence for its conclusion that remedial action was necessary.' " The Court also thought it "obvious that [the] program is not narrowly tailored to remedy the effects of prior discrimination."

With *Croson*, the Court finally agreed that the Fourteenth Amendment requires strict scrutiny of all race-based action by state and local governments. But *Croson* of course had no occasion to declare what standard of review the Fifth Amendment requires for such action taken by the Federal Government. . . .

A year later, however, the Court took a surprising turn. *Metro Broadcasting, Inc. v. FCC* involved a Fifth Amendment challenge to two race-based policies of the Federal Communications Commission. In *Metro Broadcasting*, the Court repudiated the long-held notion that "it would be unthinkable that the same Constitution would impose a lesser duty on the Federal Government" than it does on a State to afford equal protection of the laws. It did so by holding that "benign" federal racial classifications need only satisfy intermediate scrutiny, even though *Croson* had recently concluded that such classifications enacted by a State must satisfy strict scrutiny. "Benign" federal racial classifications, the Court said, "—even if those measures are not *remedial* in the sense of being designed to compensate victims of past governmental or societal discrimination—are constitutionally permissible to the extent that they serve important governmental objectives within the power of Congress and are substantially related to achievement of those objectives.". . .

By adopting intermediate scrutiny as the standard of review for congressionally mandated "benign" racial classifications, *Metro Broadcasting* departed from prior cases in two significant respects. First, it turned its back on *Croson*'s explanation of why strict scrutiny of all governmental racial classifications is essential. . . .

Second, *Metro Broadcasting* squarely rejected one of the three propositions established by the Court's earlier equal protection cases, namely, congruence between the standards applicable to federal and state racial classifications, and in so doing also undermined the other two—skepticism of all racial classifications and consistency of treatment irrespective of the race of the burdened or benefited group. Under *Metro Broadcasting*, certain racial classifications ("benign" ones enacted by the Federal Government) should be treated less skeptically than others; and the race of the benefited group is critical to the determination of which standard of review to apply. *Metro Broadcasting* was thus a significant departure from much of what had come before it.

The three propositions undermined by *Metro Broadcasting* all derive from the basic principle that the Fifth and Fourteenth Amendments to the Constitution protect persons, not groups. It follows from that principle that all governmental action based on race . . . should be subjected to detailed judicial inquiry to ensure that the personal right to equal protection of the laws has not been infringed. These ideas have long been central to this Court's understanding of equal protection, and holding "benign" state and federal racial classifications to different standards does not square with them. . . . Accordingly, we hold today that all racial classifications, imposed by whatever federal, state, or local governmental actor, must be analyzed by a reviewing court under strict scrutiny. In other words, such classifications are constitutional only if they are narrowly tailored measures that further compelling governmental interests. To the extent that *Metro Broadcasting* is inconsistent with that holding, it is overruled. . . .

Because our decision today alters the playing field in some important respects, we think it best to remand the case to the lower courts for further consideration in light of the principles we have announced. The Court of Appeals, following *Metro Broadcasting* and *Fullilove*, analyzed the case in terms of intermediate scrutiny. It upheld the challenged statutes and regulations because it found them to be "narrowly tailored to achieve [their] significant governmental purpose of providing subcontracting opportunities for small disadvantaged business enterprises." The Court of Appeals did not decide the question whether the interests served by the use of sub-contractor compensation clauses are properly described as "compelling." It also did not address the question of narrow tailoring in terms of our strict scrutiny cases, by asking, for example, whether there was "any consideration of the use of race-neutral means to increase minority business participation" in government contracting, or whether the program was appropriately limited such that it "will not last longer than the discriminatory effects it is designed to eliminate.". . .

The question whether any of the ways in which the Government uses subcontractor compensation clauses can survive strict scrutiny, and any relevance distinctions such as these may have to that question, should be addressed in the first instance by the lower courts.

Accordingly, the judgment of the Court of Appeals is vacated, and the case is remanded for further proceedings consistent with this opinion.

Vacated and remanded.

:: CASE QUESTIONS

1. Why was Adarand Constructors, as low bidder on the guardrail subcontract, not awarded the job?
2. What were the holdings of *Bakke*, *Fullilove*, and *Wygant*? Why did these decisions not resolve the standard of review question?
3. What is the conflict between the opinions in *Croson* and *Metro Broadcasting*?
4. Why is the holding in this case so important? Does this opinion stand for the proposition that affirmative action programs are unconstitutional?
5. Why did the Supreme Court decide not to resolve the issue of which party should be awarded the guardrail subcontract?

Strict judicial scrutiny is applied to a second group of cases involving classifications directed at fundamental rights. If a classification unduly burdens or penalizes the exercise of a constitutional right, it will be stricken unless it is found to be necessary to support a compelling state interest. Among such rights are the right to vote, the right to travel, and the right to appeal. Doubts about such laws result in their being stricken by the courts as a denial of equal protection.

Quasi-Strict Scrutiny Some cases actually fall between the minimum rationality and strict scrutiny approaches. These cases use what is sometimes called quasi-strict scrutiny tests because the classifications are only partially suspect or the rights involved are not quite fundamental. For example, classifications directed at gender are partially suspect. In cases involving classifications based on gender, the courts have taken this position between the two tests or at least have modified the strict scrutiny approach. Such classifications are unconstitutional unless they are *substantially* related to an *important* government objective. This modified version of strict scrutiny has resulted in holdings that find laws to be valid as well as unconstitutional.

One reason gender has not been moved to the strict scrutiny analysis is cases involving gender discrimination are so infrequent; states understand that unequal protection on the basis of gender is unacceptable.

Equal protection cases run the whole spectrum of legislative attempts to solve society's problems. For example, courts have used the equal protection clause to require the integration of public schools. In addition, the meaning and application of the equal protection clause have been central issues in cases involving:

- Apportionment of legislative bodies.
- Racial segregation in the sale and rental of real estate.
- Laws distinguishing between the rights of legitimates and illegitimates.
- The makeup of juries.
- Voting requirements.
- Welfare residency requirements.
- Rights of aliens.

Sidebar 6.8 summarizes the legal approaches courts use when analyzing equal protection cases.

:: *sidebar* 6.8

Analysis of Equal Protection

	:: Minimum Rationality	:: Quasi-Strict Scrutiny	:: Strict Scrutiny
Classifications Must Be	Rationally connected to a permissible or legitimate government objective	Substantially related to an important government interest	Necessary to a compelling state interest
	Presumed Valid	*Quasi-Suspect Classes*	*Suspect Classes*
Examples	Height	Gender	Race
	Weight		National origin
	Age		Legitimacy
	Testing		*Fundamental Rights*
	School desegregation		To vote
	Veteran's preference		To travel
	Marriage		To appeal

The equal protection clause is the means to the end, or goal, of equality of opportunity. As such, it may be utilized by anyone claiming unequal treatment in any case. At the same time the clause will not prevent states from remedying the effect of past discrimination. As you will study in Chapter 20, courts have upheld laws that provide for preferential treatment of minorities if this remedy is narrowly tailored to serve a compelling governmental interest in eradicating past discrimination against the minority group.

:: The Commerce Clause—Government's Authority to Regulate Business

The power of the federal government to regulate business activity is found in the **commerce clause** of the Constitution. Article I, Section 8, states, "Congress shall have Power . . . to regulate Commerce with foreign Nations, and among the several States, and with the Indian Tribes."

This simple-sounding clause has been interpreted as creating at least four important areas involving various aspects of the government regulating business. These areas can be summarized by the following headings:

- Regulation of foreign commerce.
- Regulation of interstate commerce.
- Limitation on state police power.
- Limitation on state taxation.

The next four sections focus on the impact of the commerce clause on businesses and businesspeople.

10. REGULATION OF FOREIGN COMMERCE

The first part of the commerce clause grants the federal government power to regulate foreign commerce. The power to regulate foreign commerce is vested exclusively in the federal government, and it extends to all aspects of foreign trade. In other words, the power to regulate foreign commerce is total. The federal government can prohibit foreign commerce entirely. In recent years, for example, the federal government has imposed trade embargoes on countries such as Iraq, Iran, and Haiti. It can also allow commerce with restrictions.

That the federal power to regulate foreign commerce is exclusive means state and local governments may not regulate such commerce. State and local governments sometimes attempt directly or indirectly to regulate imports or exports to some degree. Such attempts generally are unconstitutional. However, a state may regulate activities that relate to foreign commerce if such activities are conducted entirely within the state's boundaries. For example, the U.S. Supreme Court has upheld a state tax on the leases of cargo containers used in international trade. This decision was based on the tax being fairly apportioned to the use of the cargo containers within the state. Hence, the Court concluded that the state tax did not violate the foreign commerce clause.[3]

11. REGULATION OF INTERSTATE COMMERCE

Do appreciate the significant grant of power given to the federal government through the commerce clause.

Among the constitutional clauses that lead to extensive litigation is the phrase in the commerce clause granting the federal government the power to regulate commerce "among the several States." At first this phrase was interpreted to mean only interstate commerce as contrasted with intrastate commerce. Later, in a long series of judicial decisions, the power of the federal government was expanded through interpretation to include not only persons *engaged* in interstate commerce but also activities *affecting* interstate commerce.

The power of Congress over commerce is very broad; it extends to all commerce, be it great or small. Labeling an activity a "local" or "intrastate" activity does not prevent Congress from regulating it under the commerce clause. The power of Congress to regulate commerce "among the several states" extends to those intrastate activities that affect interstate commerce as to make regulation of them appropriate. Regulation is appropriate if it aids interstate commerce. Even activity that is purely intrastate in character may be regulated by Congress, when the activity, combined with like conduct by others similarly situated, substantially affects commerce among states. As a result of various Supreme Court decisions, it is hard to imagine a factual situation involving business transactions that the federal government cannot regulate.

12. LIMITATION ON STATE POLICE POWER

To avoid needless repetition, the phrase *state government* is used to refer to both state and local governments.

Whereas the authority of the federal government to regulate business activity comes from the express language of the commerce clause, state and local government authority arises from a concept known as **police powers**. These powers can be summarized as requiring state legislation and regulation to

---

[3]*Itel Containers In't Corp. v. Huddleston,* 113 S. Ct. 1095 (1993).

protect the public's health, safety, morals, and general welfare. These words, particularly the last phrase, give state government expansive power to regulate business activities.

These powers are not limitless. For example, state regulations must not be arbitrary, capricious, or unreasonable. Furthermore, the state regulation must not violate the commerce clause. These limitations imposed by the U.S. Constitution are referred to as the **dormant commerce clause concept.**

Three distinct subject areas of government regulation of commerce emerge from Supreme Court decisions. Some areas are exclusively federal, some are said to be exclusively state, and still others are such that regulation of them may be dual.

Exclusively Federal   The subject area that is exclusively federal concerns those internal matters where uniformity on a nationwide basis is essential. Any state regulation of such subjects is void whether Congress has expressly regulated the area or not.

A classic example of a regulatory area that needs to be limited to the federal government is the opening and closing of airports. Because airlines need access to airports consistent with their routes, havoc could ensue if local authorities were allowed to set the hours that their airports operate. The regulation of the operating hours of airports is best left to the Federal Aviation Administration so that a coordinated effort is present.

Exclusively State   In theory, those matters that are exclusively within the states' power are intrastate activities that do not have a substantial effect on interstate commerce. This topic of what is solely within the domain of the states' regulatory authority creates both interesting history and current-day controversy. Prior to 1937, Supreme Court opinions frequently upheld the authority of states to regulate business activities. Court decisions declaring federal legislation to be unconstitutional as interfering with state regulation caused Franklin Roosevelt to propose increasing the number of Supreme Court justices. Although his efforts to "pack the Court" failed, Roosevelt may have convinced the sitting justices and subsequent ones that society was looking to the federal government to get the economy growing to overcome the negative impact of the Great Depression.

Beginning in 1937, the one consistent outcome of Supreme Court cases considering the commerce clause has been that the federal authority is unlimited and there is nothing reserved exclusively for the states. Throughout the past several years, the justices seem to signal that the federal authority under the commerce clause must have limitations. Sidebar 6.9 summarizes an important case along this line of analysis.

Commentators on the *Gonzales* decision speculate that it is a signal that the Supreme Court will not approve every federal action as being justified by the commerce clause. Other cases, including ones involving drug- and gun-free school zones and violence against women, have resulted in the Court limiting federal regulation in favor of state legislation. However, *Gonzales v. Oregon* is closer to a decision directly impacting businesses and professionals. This case may be a trendsetter. What is even more interesting about this particular case is its illustration of the complexities of labeling justices philosophically. Two of the three dissenters (Scalia and Thomas) traditionally

Don't rely on one historical perspective to predict the outcome of future cases.

:: *sidebar* 6.9

Federalism and State Rights under the Commerce Clause

The state of Oregon, in 1994, legalized doctor-assisted suicide when voters approved a ballot issue enacting the Oregon Death with Dignity Act (ODWDA). This act allows an Oregon resident to request a prescription under the ODWDA to hasten death. The law specifies the following requirements:

- The resident's attending physician must determine this patient has an incurable and irreversible disease that will cause death within six months.
- The physician must decide the patient's request is voluntary.
- The physician must determine the patient is informed.
- The physician must refer the patient to counseling.
- A second physician must examine the patient, the medical records, and confirm the attending physician's decision.
- Any prescription that a physician provides must be administered by the patient and not by the physician.

In 2001, U.S. Attorney General John Ashcroft interpreted the federal Controlled Substances Act (CSA) as prohibiting any physician the legal right to prescribe controlled substances for the purpose of assisting suicide. Under this interpretation, the attorney general concludes that it is not a legitimate medical practice to assist any patient with hastening death. In essence, this interpretation subjected any Oregon physician complying with ODWDA to punishment for violating the federal CSA.

The U.S. Supreme Court, in a 6–3 opinion, finds Congress, through the CSA, did not grant the attorney general authority to interpret this federal law in a way to override a state's standards of acceptable medical practice. The Court rejects the attorney general's decision to criminalize doctor-assisted suicide. In doing so, the Court states "the CSA's prescription requirement does not authorize the Attorney General to ban dispensing controlled substances for assisted suicide in the face of a state medical regime permitting such conduct."

*Source: Gonzales v. Oregon, 126 S. Ct. 904 (2006).

Do look back at Chapter 3 for discussion of judicial philosophies.

advocate states' rights over federal regulation. In this case they seem to value preservations of life over state rights. Interestingly, Chief Justice Roberts also dissented in one of his first major decisions. Time will help us put the new chief justice's philosophy into a clearer picture.

Dual Regulation   Between the two extremes, joint regulation is permissible. This area can be divided into the following three subparts:

- Federal preemption.
- Federal regulation but no preemption.
- No federal regulation.

Federal Preemption   The first subpart concerns those subjects over which the federal government has preempted the field. By express language or by comprehensive regulation, Congress has shown that it intends to exercise exclusive control over the subject matter. When a federal statute preempts a particular area of regulation, any state or local law pertaining to the same subject matter is unconstitutional under the commerce clause and the supremacy clause, and the state regulation is void. The net effect of a law that preempts an area of regulation is to make that subject matter of the law exclusively federal. In essence, the commerce clause combines with the supremacy clause to prohibit any state regulation.

No Preemption   The second subpart includes situations in which the federal regulation of a subject matter is not comprehensive enough to preempt the field. Here state regulation is permitted. However, when state law is inconsistent or conflicts irreconcilably with the federal statute, it is unconstitutional

and void. **Irreconcilable conflicts** exist when it is not possible for a business to comply with both statutes. If compliance with both is not possible, the state law must fall under the supremacy clause and the commerce clause. If compliance with both is reasonably possible, dual compliance is required. This usually has the effect of forcing business to meet the requirements of the law with the greatest burden. For example, if the state minimum wage is $8.00 per hour and the federal is $7.75, employers would be required to pay $8.00 since the conflict can be reconciled.

The commerce clause also invalidates state laws imposing an **undue burden** on interstate commerce. The commerce clause does not prohibit the imposing of burdens on interstate commerce—only the imposition of *undue* burdens. The states have the authority under the police power to regulate matters of legitimate local concern, even though interstate commerce may be affected. Furthermore, as Sidebar 6.10 illustrates, states can regulate intrastate commerce.

:: *sidebar* 6.10

$100 Fee: Regulating Interstate Commerce

Under the Michigan Motor Carrier Act, any motor carrier operating vehicles in intrastate commerce within Michigan must pay an annual fee of $100 for each vehicle that undertakes point-to-point hauls within the state. The U.S. Supreme Court concludes that this fee is applicable only to carriers doing business locally and is not applicable to carriers engaged only in interstate commerce. The fee taxes only purely local activity; it does not tax a truck carrying goods through Michigan; nor does it tax activities spanning multiple states. The Court finds the Michigan fee does not burden or discriminate against interstate commerce. Thus, there is no violation of the commerce clause.

Source: American Trucking Associations, Inc. v. Michigan Public Service Commission, 125 S. Ct. 2419 (2005).

State statutes fall into two categories: those that burden interstate commerce only incidentally and those that affirmatively discriminate against such transactions. For cases in the first category, courts weigh the burdens against the benefits and find undue burdens only if they clearly exceed the local benefits. Cases in the second category are subject to more demanding scrutiny. If a state law either in substance or in practical effect discriminates against interstate commerce, the state must prove not only that the law has a legitimate purpose but also that the purpose cannot be achieved by nondiscriminatory means. If a state law is pure economic protectionism, the courts apply a virtual per se or automatic rule of invalidity.

No Federal Regulation   The third area of possible joint regulation exists where there is no federal law at all. When there is no federal regulation of a subject, state regulation of interstate commerce is permissible, providing, of course, that it does not impose an undue burden on interstate commerce and does not discriminate against interstate commerce in favor of local business.

The commerce clause also has been construed as **prohibiting discrimination** against interstate commerce in favor of intrastate commerce. State and local governments frequently attempt by legislation to aid local business in its competition with interstate business. The commerce clause requires that all regulations be the same for local businesses as for businesses engaged in interstate

Key analysis of state regulation relates to the undue burden on or discrimination against interstate commerce activities.

commerce. A state may not place itself in a position of economic isolation from other states. Case 6.2 illustrates the interpretation of the commerce clause as it impacts the discriminatory nature of state regulations.

case **6.2** ::

GRANHOLM v. HEALD
125 S. Ct. 1885 (2005)

This case involves challenges against laws in Michigan and New York restricting out-of-state wineries from selling wine to in-state consumers. Michigan's law permits in-state wineries to sell and ship directly to Michigan consumers. However, out-of-state wineries must utilize a three-tier system of distribution. These wineries must distribute their wines through Michigan wholesalers who sell to retailers who sell to Michigan consumers.

The New York law is similar with one exception. A winery's product may be sold directly to New York consumers if the wine is made from grapes at least 75 percent of which are grown in New York. This percentage requirement applies to both in-state and out-of-state wineries. Furthermore, to sell directly to consumers, the out-of-state winery must have a branch factory, office, or storeroom in New York.

In the Michigan case, residents of that state and a California winery filed suit contending that the Michigan law discriminates against interstate commerce in violation of the commerce clause. The district judge upheld the Michigan law, but the Sixth Circuit Court of Appeals reversed, holding the Michigan law is unconstitutional.

In the New York case, similar arguments were made by New York residents who filed suit. That district judge found in favor of the plaintiffs; however, the Second Circuit Court of Appeals reversed, finding the New York law to be constitutional.

KENNEDY, J.: . . . We consolidated these cases and granted certiorari on the following question: "Does a State's regulatory scheme that permits in-state wineries directly to ship alcohol to consumers but restricts the ability of out-of-state wineries to do so violate the dormant Commerce Clause in light of § 2 of the Twenty-first Amendment?"

For ease of exposition, we refer to the respondents from the Michigan challenge and the petitioners in the New York challenge collectively as the wineries. We refer to their opposing parties—Michigan, New York, and the wholesalers and retailers—simply as the States.

Time and again this Court has held that, in all but the narrowest circumstances, state laws violate the Commerce Clause if they mandate differential treatment of in-state and out-of-state economic interests that benefits the former and burdens the latter. This rule is essential to the foundations of the Union. The mere fact of nonresidence should not foreclose a producer in one State from access to markets in other States. States may not enact laws that burden out-of-state producers or shippers simply to give a competitive advantage to in-state businesses. This mandate reflects a central concern of the Framers that was an immediate reason for calling the Constitutional Convention: the conviction that in order to succeed, the new Union would have to avoid the tendencies toward economic balkanization that had plagued relations among the Colonies and later among the States under the Articles of Confederation.

Laws of the type at issue in the instant cases contradict these principles. They deprive citizens of their right to have access to the markets of other States on equal terms. The perceived necessity for reciprocal sale privileges risks generating the trade rivalries and animosities, the alliances and exclusivity, that the Constitution and, in particular, the Commerce Clause were designed to avoid. . . .

The discriminatory character of the Michigan system is obvious. Michigan allows in-state wineries to ship directly to consumers, subject only to a licensing requirement. Out-of-state wineries, whether licensed or not, face a complete ban on direct shipment. The differential treatment requires all out-of-state wine, but not all in-state wine, to pass through an in-state wholesaler and retailer before reaching consumers. These two extra layers of overhead increase the cost of out-of-state wines to Michigan consumers. The cost differential, and in some cases the inability to secure a wholesaler for small shipments, can effectively bar small wineries from the Michigan market.

The New York regulatory scheme differs from Michigan's in that it does not ban direct shipments altogether. Out-of-state wineries are instead required to establish a distribution operation in New York in order to gain the privilege of direct shipment. This, though, is just an indirect way of subjecting out-of-state wineries, but not local ones, to the three-tier system. . . .

The New York scheme grants in-state wineries access to the State's consumers on preferential terms. The suggestion of a limited exception for direct shipment from out-of-state wineries does nothing to eliminate the discriminatory nature of New York's regulations. In-state producers, with the applicable licenses, can ship directly to consumers from their wineries. Out-of-state wineries must open a branch office and warehouse in New York, additional steps that drive up the cost of their wine. For most wineries, the expense of establishing a bricks-and-mortar distribution operation in one State, let alone all fifty, is prohibitive. It comes as no surprise that not a single out-of-state winery has availed itself of New York's direct-shipping privilege. We have viewed with particular suspicion state statutes requiring business operations to be performed in the home State that could more efficiently be performed elsewhere. New York's in-state presence requirement runs contrary to our admonition that States cannot require an out-of-state firm to become a resident in order to compete on equal terms. . . .

We have no difficulty concluding that New York, like Michigan, discriminates against interstate commerce through its direct-shipping laws.

State laws that discriminate against interstate commerce face a virtually per se rule of invalidity. The Michigan and New York laws by their own terms violate this proscription. The two States, however, contend their statutes are saved by § 2 of the Twenty-first Amendment, which provides:

> The transportation or importation into any State, Territory, or possession of the United States for delivery or use therein of intoxicating liquors, in violation of the laws thereof, is hereby prohibited.

The States' position is inconsistent with our precedents and with the Twenty-first Amendment's history. Section 2 does not allow States to regulate the direct shipment of wine on terms that discriminate in favor of in-state producers. . . .

The aim of the Twenty-first Amendment was to allow States to maintain an effective and uniform system for controlling liquor by regulating its transportation, importation, and use. The Amendment did not give States the authority to pass nonuniform laws in order to discriminate against out-of-state goods, a privilege they had not enjoyed at any earlier time. . . .

The modern § 2 cases fall into three categories.

First, the Court has held that state laws that violate other provisions of the Constitution are not saved by the Twenty-first Amendment. The Court has applied this rule in the context of the First Amendment, the Establishment Clause, the Equal Protection Clause, the Due Process Clause, and the Import-Export Clause.

Second, the Court has held that § 2 does not abrogate Congress' Commerce Clause powers with regard to liquor. The argument that the Twenty-first Amendment has somehow operated to repeal the Commerce Clause for alcoholic beverages has been rejected. . . .

Finally, and most relevant to the issue at hand, the Court has held that state regulation of alcohol is limited by the nondiscrimination principle of the Commerce Clause. When a state statute directly regulates or discriminates against interstate commerce, or when its effect is to favor in-state economic interests over out-of-state interests, we have generally struck down the statute without further inquiry. . . .

Our determination that the Michigan and New York direct shipment laws are not authorized by the Twenty-first Amendment does not end the inquiry. We still must consider whether either State regime advances a legitimate local purpose that cannot be adequately served by reasonable nondiscriminatory alternatives. The States offer two primary justifications for restricting direct shipments from out-of-state wineries: keeping alcohol out of the hands of minors and facilitating tax collection. We consider each in turn.

The States . . . claim that allowing direct shipment from out-of-state wineries undermines their ability to police underage drinking. Minors, the States argue, have easy access to credit cards and the Internet and are likely to take advantage of direct wine shipments as a means of obtaining alcohol illegally.

The States provide little evidence that the purchase of wine over the Internet by minors is a problem. Indeed, there is some evidence to the contrary. A recent study by the staff of the FTC found that the 26 States currently allowing direct shipments report no problems with minors' increased access to wine. This is not surprising for several reasons. First, minors are less likely to consume wine, as opposed to beer, wine coolers, and hard liquor. Second, minors who decide to disobey the law have more direct means of doing so. Third, direct shipping is an imperfect avenue of obtaining alcohol for minors who, in the words of the past president of the National Conference of State Liquor Administrators, "want instant gratification." Without concrete evidence that direct shipping of wine is likely to increase alcohol consumption by minors, we are left with the States' unsupported assertions. Under our precedents, which require the clearest showing to justify discriminatory state regulation, this is not enough.

[continued]

Even were we to credit the States' largely unsupported claim that direct shipping of wine increases the risk of underage drinking, this would not justify regulations limiting only out-of-state direct shipments. As the wineries point out, minors are just as likely to order wine from in-state producers as from out-of-state ones. Michigan, for example, already allows its licensed retailers (over 7,000 of them) to deliver alcohol directly to consumers. Michigan counters that it has greater regulatory control over in-state producers than over out-of-state wineries. This does not justify Michigan's discriminatory ban on direct shipping. Out-of-state wineries face the loss of state and federal licenses if they fail to comply with state law. This provides strong incentives not to sell alcohol to minors. In addition, the States can take less restrictive steps to minimize the risk that minors will order wine by mail. For example, the Model Direct Shipping Bill developed by the National Conference of State Legislatures requires an adult signature on delivery and a label so instructing on each package.

The States' tax-collection justification is also insufficient. Increased direct shipping, whether originating in state or out of state, brings with it the potential for tax evasion. With regard to Michigan, however, the tax-collection argument is a diversion. That is because Michigan, unlike many other States, does not rely on wholesalers to collect taxes on wines imported from out of state. Instead, Michigan collects taxes directly from out-of-state wineries on all wine shipped to in-state wholesalers. If licensing and self-reporting provide adequate safeguards for wine distributed through the three-tier system, there is no reason to believe they will not suffice for direct shipments.

New York and its supporting parties also advance a tax-collection justification for the State's direct-shipment laws. While their concerns are not wholly illusory, their regulatory objectives can be achieved without discriminating against interstate commerce. In particular, New York could protect itself against lost tax revenue by requiring a permit as a condition of direct shipping. This is the approach taken by New York for in-state wineries. The State offers no reason to believe the system would prove ineffective for out-of-state wineries. Licensees could be required to submit regular sales reports and to remit taxes. Indeed, various States use this approach for taxing direct interstate wine shipments and report no problems with tax collection. . . . The States have not shown that tax evasion from out-of-state wineries poses such a unique threat that it justifies their discriminatory regimes.

Michigan and New York offer a handful of other rationales, such as facilitating orderly market conditions, protecting public health and safety, and ensuring regulatory accountability. These objectives can also be achieved through the alternative of an evenhanded licensing requirement. Finally, it should be noted that improvements in technology have eased the burden of monitoring out-of-state wineries. Background checks can be done electronically. Financial records and sales data can be mailed, faxed, or submitted via e-mail.

In summary, the States provide little concrete evidence for the sweeping assertion that they cannot police direct shipments by out-of-state wineries. Our Commerce Clause cases demand more than mere speculation to support discrimination against out-of-state goods. . . . The Court has upheld state regulations that discriminate against interstate commerce only after finding, based on concrete record evidence, that a State's nondiscriminatory alternatives will prove unworkable. Michigan and New York have not satisfied this exacting standard.

States have broad power to regulate liquor under § 2 of the Twenty-first Amendment. This power, however, does not allow States to ban, or severely limit, the direct shipment of out-of-state wine while simultaneously authorizing direct shipment by in-state producers. If a State chooses to allow direct shipment of wine, it must do so on evenhanded terms. Without demonstrating the need for discrimination, New York and Michigan have enacted regulations that disadvantage out-of-state wine producers. Under our Commerce Clause jurisprudence, these regulations cannot stand.

We affirm the judgment of the Court of Appeals for the Sixth Circuit; and we reverse the judgment of the Court of Appeals for the Second Circuit and remand the case for further proceedings consistent with our opinion.

It is so ordered.

:: CASE QUESTIONS

1. What is the procedural background of the courts' holdings in these Michigan and New York cases?
2. Why does the Supreme Court conclude the states' laws are discriminatory against out-of-state wineries?
3. What is the Court's conclusion regarding the states' authority to regulate alcohol sales under Section 2 of the Twenty-first Amendment to the U.S. Constitution?
4. Why does the Court reject Michigan's and New York's arguments that the discriminatory laws are justified?

The Supreme Court's recent decisions clarify that this ban on discrimination under the commerce clause does not apply to functions traditionally conducted by the government for the public's benefit within a specific state. A New York law that favored government-sponsored trash disposal over private companies in New York and other states does not violate the commerce clause's prohibition of discrimination.[4] Likewise, Kentucky has a law that exempts taxes on interest paid on Kentucky-issued bonds while not exempting taxes on the interest paid on bonds issued by other states. The Supreme Court ruled this state-sponsored activity is not subject to analysis under the commerce clause.[5]

concept :: *summary*

Possible Subjects for Government Regulation

:: EXCLUSIVELY FEDERAL SUBJECTS

- Any state regulatory law is unconstitutional under the supremacy and commerce clauses.

:: EXCLUSIVELY LOCAL SUBJECTS

- The impact on state and local government of laws based on the commerce clause is very limited; very few subjects are exclusively local.

:: POSSIBLE DUAL REGULATION SUBJECTS

- Federal law preempts the field. The subject matter is considered exclusively federal.

- Federal law does not preempt the field. A state law is unconstitutional if it:
  1. Is in irreconcilable conflict with federal law.
  2. Constitutes an undue burden on interstate commerce.
  3. Discriminates against interstate commerce in favor of intrastate commerce.

- No federal law. A state law is unconstitutional if it:
  1. Constitutes an undue burden on interstate commerce.
  2. Discriminates against interstate commerce in favor of intrastate commerce.

13. LIMITATION ON STATE TAXATION

Taxation is a primary form of regulation. Therefore, taxes imposed by state and local governments are subject to the limitations imposed by the commerce clause. The commerce clause limits property taxes, income taxes, and sales or use taxes levied by state and local governments on interstate commerce. Since taxation distributes the cost of government among those who receive its benefits, interstate commerce is not exempt from state and local taxes. The purpose of the commerce clause is to ensure that a taxpayer engaged in interstate commerce pays only its fair share of state taxes.

To prevent multiple taxation of the same property or income of interstate businesses, taxes are apportioned. **Apportionment** formulas allocate the tax burden of an interstate business among the states entitled to tax it. The commerce clause requires states to use reasonable formulas when more than one state is taxing the same thing.

> Apportionment and nexus are fundamental to determining the validity of any state tax on businesses engaged in interstate commerce.

---

[4]*United Haulers Association, Inc. v. Oneida-Herkimer Solid Waste Management Authority*, 127 S.Ct. 1786 (2007).

[5]*Department of Revenue of Kentucky v. Davis*, 128 S. Ct. 1801 (2008).

Professional ballplayers may be taxed by the state of the home team on the portion of their salaries earned in each game.

To justify the tax, there must be sufficient contact, connection, tie, or link between the business and the taxing state. There must be sufficient local activities to justify the tax in a constitutional sense. This connection is called the **nexus.** A business operating in a state directly benefits from its police and fire protection, the use of its roads, and the like. Indirectly, it will be able to recruit employees more easily if they have easy access to good schools, parks, and civic centers. If the state gives anything for which it can reasonably expect payment, then the tax has a sufficient nexus. In cases involving property taxes, the term *taxable situs* is used in place of nexus, but each is concerned with the adequacy of local activities to support the tax.

Case 6.3 is an important decision since it clarifies how these constitutional principles must be applied when more than one state is taxing a business activity. At issue is the meaning of the phrases *unitary business* and *operational function.*

case **6.3** ::

MEADWESTVACO CORPORATION v. ILLINOIS DEPARTMENT OF REVENUE
128 S. Ct. 1498 (2008)

Mead Corporation is a domestic corporation of Ohio and has its headquarters there. Throughout its long history, Mead's business has revolved around paper, packaging, and office and school supplies. During the 1970s and 1980s, Mead developed an information retrieval system that became known as Lexis/Nexis (Lexis). The headquarters of Lexis is in Illinois.

In 1994, Mead sold Lexis for $1.5 billion realizing a capital gain of a little more than $1 billion. Mead considered this gain as nonbusiness income and reported all of it on its Ohio tax return. The State of Illinois assessed Mead with $4 million in taxes and penalties for not reporting an apportioned share of the Lexis sale and gain. Mead paid Illinois under protest and filed a lawsuit seeking a refund.

Although it found Lexis and Mead were not a unitary business, the trial judge ruled in favor of Illinois concluding that Lexis served an "operational purpose in Mead's business." The Illinois Appellate Court affirmed, and the Illinois Supreme Court denied review. Mead's petition for a writ of certiorari was granted.

ALITO, J.: The *Due Process* and *Commerce Clauses* forbid the States to tax extraterritorial values. A State may, however, tax an apportioned share of the value generated by the intrastate and extrastate activities of a multistate enterprise if those activities form part of a "unitary business." We have been asked in this case to decide whether the State of Illinois constitutionally taxed an apportioned share of the capital gain realized by an out-of-state corporation on the sale of one of its business divisions. The Appellate Court of Illinois upheld the tax and affirmed a judgment in the State's favor. Because we conclude that the state courts misapprehended the principles that we have developed for determining whether a multistate business is unitary, we vacate the decision of the Appellate Court of Illinois. . . .

Petitioner contends that the trial court properly found that Lexis and Mead were not unitary and that the Appellate Court of Illinois erred in concluding that Lexis served an operational function in Mead's business. According to petitioner, the exception for apportionment of income from nonunitary businesses serving an operational function is a narrow one that does not reach a purely passive investment such as Lexis. We perceive a more fundamental error in the state courts' reasoning. In our view, the state courts erred in considering whether Lexis served an "operational purpose" in Mead's business after determining that Lexis and Mead were not unitary.

The *Commerce Clause* and the *Due Process Clause* impose distinct but parallel limitations on a State's power to tax out-of-state activities. The *Due Process Clause* demands that there exist "some definite link, some minimum connection, between a state and the person, property or transaction it seeks to tax," as well as a rational relationship between the tax and the "values connected with the taxing State." The *Commerce Clause* forbids the States to levy taxes that discriminate against interstate commerce or that burden it by subjecting activities to multiple or unfairly apportioned taxation. The broad inquiry subsumed in both constitutional requirements is whether the taxing power exerted by the state bears fiscal relation to protection, opportunities and benefits given by the state—that is, whether the state has given anything for which it can ask return.

Where, as here, there is no dispute that the taxpayer has done some business in the taxing State, the inquiry shifts from whether the State may tax to what it may tax. To answer that question, we have developed the unitary business principle. Under that principle, a State need not "isolate the intrastate income-producing activities from the rest of the business" but "may tax an apportioned sum of the corporation's multistate business if the business is unitary." The court must determine whether instrastate and extrastate activities formed part of a single unitary business, or whether the out-of-state values that the State seeks to tax derived from "unrelated business activity" which constitutes a "discrete business enterprise.". . .

With the coming of the Industrial Revolution in the 19th century, the United States witnessed the emergence of its first truly multistate business enterprises. These railroad, telegraph, and express companies presented state taxing authorities with a novel problem: A State often cannot tax its fair share of the value of a multistate business by simply taxing the capital within its borders. The whole of the enterprise is generally more valuable than the sum of its parts; were it not, its owners would simply liquidate it and sell it off in pieces. . . .

The unitary business principle addressed this problem by shifting the constitutional inquiry from the niceties of geographic accounting to the determination of the taxpayer's business unit. If the value the State wished to tax derived from a "unitary business" operated within and without the State, the State could tax an apportioned share of the value of that business instead of isolating the value attributable to the operation of the business within the State. Conversely, if the value the State wished to tax derived from a "discrete business enterprise," then the State could not tax even an apportioned share of that value.

We recognized as early as 1876 that the *Due Process Clause* did not require the States to assess trackage in each county where it lies according to its value there. We went so far as to opine that "[i]t may well be doubted whether any better mode of determining the value of that portion of the track within any one county has been devised than to ascertain the value of the whole road, and apportion the value within the county by its relative length to the whole." We . . . held that apportionment could permissibly be applied to a multistate business lacking the physical unity of wires or rails but exhibiting the same unity in the use of the entire property for the specific purpose, with the same elements of value arising from such use. We extended the reach of the unitary business principle further still in later cases, when we relied on it to justify the taxation by apportionment of net income, dividends, capital gain, and other intangibles.

As the unitary business principle has evolved in step with American enterprise, courts have sometimes found it difficult to identify exactly when a business is unitary. . . .

We concluded that the unitary business principle is not so inflexible that as new methods of finance and new forms of business evolve it cannot be modified and supplemented where appropriate. We explained that situations could occur in which apportionment might be constitutional even though the payee and the payor were not engaged in the same unitary business. It was in that context that we observed that an asset could form part of a taxpayer's unitary business if it served an "operational rather than an investment function" in that business. Hence, for example, a State may include within the apportionable income of a nondomiciliary corporation the interest earned on short-term deposits in a bank located in another State if that income forms part of the working capital of the corporation's unitary business, notwithstanding the absence of a unitary relationship between the corporation and the bank. . . .

[O]ur references to "operational function" . . . were not intended to modify the unitary business principle by adding a new ground for apportionment. The concept of operational function simply recognizes that an asset can be a part of a taxpayer's unitary business even if what we may term a "unitary relationship" does not exist between the "payor and payee."

Where, as here, the asset in question is another business, we have described the hallmarks of a unitary relationship as functional integration, centralized management, and economies of scale. The trial court found each of these hallmarks lacking and concluded that Lexis was not a unitary part of Mead's business. The appellate court, however, made no such determination. Relying on its operational function test, it reserved judgment on whether Mead and Lexis formed a unitary business. The appellate court may take up that question on remand, and we express no opinion on it now. . . .

The State . . . argues that vacatur is not required because the judgment of the Appellate Court of Illinois may be affirmed on an alternative ground. They contend that the record amply demonstrates that Lexis did substantial business in Illinois and that Lexis' own contacts with the State suffice to justify the apportionment of Mead's capital gain. The State . . . invites us to recognize a new ground for the constitutional apportionment of intangibles based on the taxing State's contacts with the capital asset rather than the taxpayer.

We decline this invitation because the question that the State . . . calls upon us to answer was neither raised nor passed upon in the state courts. It also was not addressed in the State's brief in opposition to the petition. We typically will not address a question under these circumstances even if the answer would afford an alternative ground for affirmance. . . .

The judgment of the Appellate Court of Illinois is vacated, and this case is remanded for further proceedings not inconsistent with this opinion.

Vacated and remanded.

:: CASE QUESTIONS

1. What is the history of Mead's development and operation of Lexis?
2. After Mead successfully sold Lexis, what claim was made by the State of Illinois?
3. What was the ruling of the Illinois Appellate Court and the decision of the Illinois Supreme Court?
4. What does the U. S. Supreme Court find regarding the phrases "unitary business" and "discrete business enterprise"?
5. Why does the Supreme Court refuse to find for Illinois even through Lexis operates within that state?

:: Regulatory Process—Administrative Agencies

The authority of the federal, state, and local governments to regulate our professional and personal lives is founded in the constitutional principles of the commerce clause and police powers. Typically, the actual regulatory activity is performed by administrative agencies. The term **administrative agencies** describes the boards, bureaus, commissions, and organizations that make up the governmental bureaucracy. Sidebar 6.11 lists several federal agencies and briefly describes their functions.

These agencies have either one or both types of regulatory authority. The first type is called **quasi-legislative** in that an agency can issue rules (regulations) that have the impact of laws. The second type is **quasi-judicial** in that agencies can make decisions like a court.

The direct day-to-day legal impact on business of the rules and regulations adopted and enforced by these agencies is probably greater than the impact of the courts or other branches of government. Administrative agencies create and enforce the majority of all laws constituting the legal environment of business. The administrative process at either the state or federal level regulates almost every business activity.

Although we focus on federal agencies in this chapter, keep in mind that state and local governments also have many agencies. For example, state workers' compensation boards hear cases involving industrial accidents and injuries to employees, and most local governments have zoning boards that make recommendations that impact business activities. State governments usually license and regulate intrastate transportation, and state boards usually set rates for local utilities supplying gas and electricity.

The regulatory process involves agencies at all levels of government.

What relief is available to a person, business, or industry group that is unhappy with a rule adopted by an agency or with its decisions? What are

:: *sidebar* 6.11

Major Federal Agencies

:: Name	:: Functions
Consumer Product Safety Commission (CPSC)	Protects the public against unreasonable risks of injury associated with consumer products.
Environmental Protection Agency (EPA)	Administers all laws relating to the environment, including laws on water pollution, air pollution, solid wastes, pesticides, toxic substances, etc.
Federal Aviation Administration (FAA) (part of the Department of Transportation)	Regulates civil aviation to provide safe and efficient use of airspace.
Federal Communications Commission (FCC)	Regulates interstate and foreign communications by means of radio, television, wire, cable, and satellite.
Federal Energy Regulatory Commission (FERC)	Promotes dependable, affordable energy through sustained competitive markets.
Federal Reserve Board (FRB)	Regulates the availability and cost of money and credit; the nation's central bank.
Federal Trade Commission (FTC)	Protects the public from anticompetitive behavior and unfair and deceptive business practices.
Food and Drug Administration (FDA)	Administers laws to prohibit distribution of adulterated, misbranded, or unsafe food and drugs.
Equal Employment Opportunity Commission (EEOC)	Seeks to prevent discrimination in employment based on race, color, religion, sex, or national origin and other unlawful employment practices.
National Labor Relations Board (NLRB)	Conducts union certification elections and holds hearings on unfair labor practice complaints.
Nuclear Regulatory Commission (NRC) Occupational Safety and Health Administration (OSHA) Securities and Exchange Commission (SEC)	Ensures all workers a safe and healthy work environment. Enforces the federal securities laws that regulate sale of securities to the investing public.

the powers of courts to review conclusions of administrative agencies? What chance does a party upset with an agency's decision have in obtaining a reversal of the decision? How much deference is given to an agency's decisions? Answers to these questions must be clearly understood to appreciate the role of administrative agencies in our system.

The following section discusses a requirement that must be satisfied by the parties challenging an agency's rule-making or adjudicating function. Then, in Sections 15 through 17, you will see that the issues before a court reviewing an agency's decision vary depending on whether a quasi-legislative or quasi-judicial decision is being reviewed.

14. STANDING TO SUE

Any party seeking the judicial review of any administrative agency's decision must be able to prove *standing to sue*. To establish standing, the challenging party must address two issues.

Reviewability   First, is the action or decision of the agency subject to judicial review? Not all administrative decisions are reviewable. The Federal Administrative Procedure Act provides for judicial review except where "(1) statutes preclude judicial review or (2) agency action is committed to agency discretion by law." Few statutes actually preclude judicial review, and preclusion of judicial review by inference is rare. It is most likely to occur when an agency decides not to undertake action to enforce a statute. For example, prison inmates asked the Food and Drug Administration (FDA) to ban the use of lethal injections to carry out the death penalty. It refused to do so. The Supreme Court held that this decision of the FDA was not subject to judicial review.

Aggrieved Party   Second, is the plaintiff "an aggrieved party"? Generally the plaintiff must have been harmed by an administrative action or decision to have standing. This aspect of standing was discussed in Chapter 4. It is clear that persons who may suffer economic loss due to an agency's action have standing to sue. Recent decisions have expanded the group of persons with standing to sue to include those who have noneconomic interests, such as First Amendment rights.

Sidebar 6.12 summarizes the U.S. Supreme Court's explanation of why broad meaning should be given to the concept of standing to sue.

:: *sidebar* 6.12

Standing to Sue or Who May Challenge an Administrative Policy

The Administrative Procedures Act states:

> A person suffering legal wrong because of agency action, or adversely affected or aggrieved by agency action within the meaning of a relevant statute, is entitled to judicial review thereof.

Through United States Supreme Court cases, we know that a plaintiff must show a claim within the "zone of interest" protected by the statute under consideration. The plaintiff does not need to prove that the legislative body envisioned protecting this particular plaintiff.

An example of this broad nature of standing to sue is found in the decision of the Supreme Court allowing banks to challenge whether credit unions must limit membership to persons who have a common bond, such as employment with the same company.

Source: National Credit Union Administration v. First National Bank & Trust Co., 118 S. Ct. 927 (1998).

15. REVIEW OF RULE MAKING

The rule-making function in the administrative process is essentially legislative in character. Legislatures usually create administrative agencies or quasi-legislative power to the agency. An administrative agency must propose rules and regulations within the confines of its grant of power from the legislature, or a court will find the proposal void.

Do remember to ask two critical questions: Is the delegation valid? Has authority been exceeded?

However, once courts decide that an act of the legislature is constitutional or a rule of an agency is authorized, the courts will not inquire into its wisdom or effectiveness. An unwise or ineffectual law may be corrected by political action at the polls; an unwise rule or regulation adopted by an agency may be corrected by the legislature that gave the agency power to make the rule in the first place.

There are two basic issues in litigation challenging the validity of a rule made by an administrative agency. First, is the delegation valid? Second, has the agency exceeded its authority?

Is Delegation Valid?

Delegation of quasi-legislative authority to administrative agencies is subject to two constitutional limitations:

- It must be definite.
- It must be limited.

First, delegation of authority must be definite or it will violate due process. Definiteness means that the delegation must be set forth with sufficient clarity so that all concerned, and especially reviewing courts, will be able to determine the extent of the agency's authority. Broad language has been held sufficiently definite to meet this test. For example, the term *unfair methods of competition* is sufficiently definite to meet the requirements of due process and validate the delegation of this authority to the Federal Trade Commission (FTC).

Second, the delegation of authority to an agency from the legislative or executive branch must have limitations. This delegation of authority must provide that the agency's power to act is limited to areas that are certain, even if these areas are not specifically defined. For example, the FTC regulates unfair methods of competition *in or affecting commerce*. Regulations or enforcement activities by the FTC that focus solely on intrastate business are void as being beyond the "limited" authority delegated to that agency. Also, procedural safeguards must exist to control arbitrary administrative action and any administrative abuse of discretionary power.

Just as broad language has been approved as being sufficiently definite for a delegation to be valid under the due process clause since the 1930s, broad standards meet the limited-power test. Today, it is generally agreed that delegations of authority to make rules may involve very broad language. For example, the delegation of authority to make such rules as the "public interest, convenience, and necessity may require" is a valid standard.

The general language used in delegating quasi-legislative authority usually involves grants of substantial discretion to an agency. It must be kept in mind that this delegation of discretion is to the agency and not to the judiciary. Therefore, courts cannot interfere with the discretion given to the agency and cannot substitute their judgment for that of the agency. In essence, there is a policy of deference by the judges to the decision of the administrators. This practice of deference further emphasizes why a businessperson's influence on the rule-making process is greater in the administrative process than through appellate procedures.

While the delegation of administrative authority may be quite broad it must be focused or limited. As stated earlier, unlimited administrative authority cannot be passed from Congress to an agency or official of the executive branch. Sidebar 6.13 describes the Congressional action contained in the 2008 legislation passed to aid the financial crisis.

Authority Exceeded?

Although it is highly unlikely that a court would hold a delegation invalid because of indefiniteness or lack of standards, from time to time courts do find that agencies exceed their authority. Courts will hold that an agency exceeds its authority if an analysis of legislative intent confirms the view that the agency has gone beyond that intent, however noble its purpose may be.

> State and local agencies may regulate areas of business that are not subject to federal regulation.

:: *sidebar* 6.13

FINANCIAL STABILITY OVERSIGHT BOARD

The Emergency Economic Stabilization Act of 2008 provides an interesting example of how Congress utilizes administrative agencies to ensure expertise and control over the government's authority. In response to the economic crisis of late 2008, Treasury Secretary Henry Paulson presented to Congress draft legislation seeking authority to purchase up to $700 billion in troubled assets. The language of Secretary Paulson's proposal included the following:

> "Decisions by the Secretary pursuant to the authority of this Act are non-reviewable and committed to agency discretion, and may not be reviewed by any court of law or any administrative agency."

Among the controversial aspects of the "bailout" plan, this unfettered authority granted to the Treasury Secretary was at the top of the list. Congress not only objected to this proposal; the leadership of the House and Senate realized such a delegation of authority was unprecedented and likely unconstitutional.

After two weeks of negotiation, the Emergency Economic Stabilization Act of 2008 created the Financial Stability Oversight Board. This Board has authority to ensure that all policies implemented by the Treasury Department are consistent with the Act, in the economic interests of the United States, and consistent with protecting taxpayers. The Board consists of the following five persons:

- The Chairman of the Federal Reserve
- The Treasury Secretary
- The Director of the Federal Home Finance Agency
- The Chairman of the Securities and Exchange Commission
- The Secretary of Housing and Urban Development

This Oversight Board certainly is an example of how Congress both grants and limits authority within the administrative process.

Case 6.4 presents a case that impacts all of us. Regardless of your personal views on smoking, the Supreme Court's analysis of the agency's authority to regulate cigarettes is quite interesting. Notice how the Court struggles with the dilemma present in this case and how the rules of administrative law assist in reaching a decision.

case **6.4** ::

FOOD AND DRUG ADMINISTRATION v. BROWN & WILLIAMSON TOBACCO CORPORATION
120 S. Ct. 1291 (2000)

O'CONNOR, J.: This case involves one of the most troubling public health problems facing our Nation today: the thousands of premature deaths that occur each year because of tobacco use. In 1996, the Food and Drug Administration (FDA), after having expressly disavowed any such authority since its inception, asserted jurisdiction to regulate tobacco products. The FDA concluded that nicotine is a "drug" within the meaning of the Food, Drug, and Cosmetic Act (FDCA or Act), and that cigarettes and smokeless tobacco are "combination products" that deliver nicotine to the body. Pursuant to this authority, it promulgated regulations intended to reduce tobacco consumption among children and adolescents. The agency believed that, because most tobacco consumers begin their use before reaching the age of 18, curbing tobacco use by minors could substantially reduce the prevalence of addiction in future generations and thus the incidence of tobacco-related death and disease.

Regardless of how serious the problem an administrative agency seeks to address, however, it may not exercise its authority in a manner that is inconsistent with the administrative structure that Congress enacted into law. And although agencies are generally entitled to deference in the interpretation of statutes that they administer, a reviewing court, as well as the agency, must give effect to the unambiguously expressed intent of Congress. In this case, we believe that Congress has clearly precluded the FDA from asserting jurisdiction to regulate tobacco products. Such authority is inconsistent with the intent that Congress has expressed in the FDCA's overall regulatory scheme and in the tobacco specific legislation that it has enacted subsequent to the FDCA. In light of this clear intent, the FDA's assertion of jurisdiction is impermissible.

The FDCA grants the FDA . . . the authority to regulate, among other items, "drugs" and "devices." The Act defines "drug" to include "articles (other than food) intended to affect the structure or any function of the body." It defines "device," in part, as "an instrument, apparatus, implement, machine, contrivance, . . . or other similar or related article, including any component, part, or accessory, which is . . . intended to affect the structure or any function of the body." The Act also grants the FDA the authority to regulate so-called "combination products," which "constitute a combination of a drug, device, or biologic product." The FDA has construed this provision as giving it the discretion to regulate combination products as drugs, as devices, or as both.

On August 11, 1995, the FDA published a proposed rule concerning the sale of cigarettes and smokeless tobacco to children and adolescents. The rule, which included several restrictions on the sale, distribution, and advertisement of tobacco products, was designed to reduce the availability and attractiveness of tobacco products to young people. A public comment period followed, during which the FDA received over 700,000 submissions, more than "at any other time in its history on any other subject."

On August 28, 1996, the FDA issued a final rule entitled "Regulations Restricting the Sale and Distribution of Cigarettes and Smokeless Tobacco to Protect Children and Adolescents." The FDA determined that nicotine is a "drug" and that cigarettes and smokeless tobacco are "drug delivery devices," and therefore it had jurisdiction under the FDCA to regulate tobacco products. . . .

Based on these findings, the FDA promulgated regulations concerning tobacco products' promotion, labeling, and accessibility to children and adolescents. The access regulations prohibit the sale of cigarettes or smokeless tobacco to persons younger than 18; require retailers to verify through photo identification the age of all purchasers younger than 27; prohibit the sale of cigarettes in quantities smaller than 20; prohibit the distribution of free samples; and prohibit sales through self-service displays and vending machines except in adult-only locations. The promotion regulations require that any print advertising appear in a black-and-white, text-only format unless the publication in which it appears is read almost exclusively by adults; prohibit outdoor advertising within 1,000 feet of any public playground or school; prohibit the distribution of any promotional items, such as T-shirts or hats, bearing the manufacturer's brand name; and prohibit a manufacturer from sponsoring any athletic, musical, artistic, or other social or cultural event using its brand name. . . .

Respondents, a group of tobacco manufacturers, retailers, and advertisers, filed suit . . . challenging the regulations. They moved for summary judgment on the grounds that the FDA lacked jurisdiction to regulate tobacco products as customarily marketed, the regulations exceeded the FDA's authority, and the advertising restrictions violated the First Amendment. The court held that the FDCA authorizes the FDA to regulate tobacco products as customarily marketed and that the FDA's access and labeling regulations are permissible, but it also found that the agency's advertising and promotion restrictions exceed its authority. . . .

The Court of Appeals for the Fourth Circuit reversed, holding that Congress has not granted the FDA jurisdiction to regulate tobacco products. . . .

We granted the Government's petition for certiorari to determine whether the FDA has authority under the FDCA to regulate tobacco products. . . .

A threshold issue is the appropriate framework for analyzing the FDA's assertion of authority to regulate tobacco products. Because this case involves an administrative agency's construction of a statute that it administers, our analysis is governed by *Chevron U.S.A. Inc. v. Natural Resources Defense Council, Inc.,* 104 S. Ct. 2778 (1984). Under *Chevron,* a reviewing court must first ask "whether Congress has directly spoken to the precise question at issue." If Congress has done so, the inquiry is at an end; the court "must give effect to the unambiguously expressed intent of Congress." But if Congress has not specifically addressed the question, a reviewing court must respect the agency's construction of the statute so long as it is permissible. Such deference is justified because the responsibilities for assessing the wisdom of such policy choices and resolving the struggle between competing views of the public interest are not judicial ones, and because of the agency's greater familiarity with the ever-changing facts and circumstances surrounding the subjects regulated.

In determining whether Congress has specifically addressed the question at issue, a reviewing court should not confine itself to examining a particular statutory provision in isolation. The meaning—or ambiguity—of certain words or phrases may only become evident when placed in context. . . .

Viewing the FDCA as a whole, it is evident that one of the Act's core objectives is to ensure that any product regulated by the FDA is "safe" and "effective" for its intended use. This essential purpose pervades the FDCA. . . .

In its rulemaking proceeding, the FDA quite exhaustively documented that "tobacco products are unsafe," "dangerous," and "cause great pain and suffering from illness." It found that the consumption of tobacco products "presents extraordinary health risks," and that "tobacco use is the single leading cause of preventable death in the United States." It stated that "more than 400,000 people die each year from tobacco-related illnesses, such as cancer, respiratory illnesses, and heart disease, often suffering long and painful deaths," and that "tobacco alone kills more people each year in the United States than acquired immunodeficiency syndrome (AIDS), car accidents, alcohol, homicides, illegal drugs, suicides, and fires, combined." Indeed, the FDA characterized smoking as "a pediatric disease," because "one out of every three young people who become regular smokers . . . will die prematurely as a result."

These findings logically imply that, if tobacco products were "devices" under the FDCA, the FDA would be required to remove them from the market. . . .

Congress, however, has foreclosed the removal of tobacco products from the market. A provision of the United States Code currently in force states that "the marketing of tobacco constitutes one of the greatest basic industries of the United States with ramifying activities which directly affect interstate and foreign commerce at every point, and stable conditions therein are necessary to the general welfare:" 7 U.S.C. § 1311(a). More importantly, Congress has directly addressed the problem of tobacco and health through legislation on six occasions since 1965. . . . Congress stopped well short of ordering a ban. Instead, it has generally regulated the labeling and advertisement of tobacco products, expressly providing that it is the policy of Congress that "commerce and the national economy may be . . . protected to the maximum extent consistent with" consumers "being adequately informed about any adverse health effects." 15 U.S.C. § 1331. Congress' decisions to regulate labeling and advertising and to adopt the express policy of protecting "commerce and the national economy . . . to the maximum extent"

reveal its intent that tobacco products remain on the market. Indeed the collective premise of these statutes is that cigarettes and smokeless tobacco will continue to be sold in the United States. A ban of tobacco products by the FDA would therefore plainly contradict congressional policy. . . .

[O]ur inquiry into whether Congress has directly spoken to the precise question at issue is shaped, at least in some measure, by the nature of the question presented. Deference under *Chevron* to an agency's construction of a statute that it administers is premised on the theory that a statute's ambiguity constitutes an implicit delegation from Congress to the agency to fill in the statutory gaps. In extraordinary cases, however, there may be reason to hesitate before concluding that Congress has intended such an implicit delegation.

This is hardly an ordinary case. Contrary to its representations to Congress since 1914, the FDA has now asserted jurisdiction to regulate an industry constituting a significant portion of the American economy. In fact, the FDA contends that, were it to determine that tobacco products provide no "reasonable assurance of safety," it would have the authority to ban cigarettes and smokeless tobacco entirely. Owing to its unique place in American history and society, tobacco has its own unique political history. Congress, for better or for worse, has created a distinct regulatory scheme for tobacco products, squarely rejected proposals to give the FDA jurisdiction over tobacco, and repeatedly acted to preclude any agency from exercising significant policymaking authority in the area. Given this history and the breadth of the authority that the FDA has asserted, we are obliged to defer not to the agency's expansive construction of the statute, but to Congress' consistent judgment to deny the FDA this power. . . .

By no means do we question the seriousness of the problem that the FDA has sought to address. The agency has amply demonstrated that tobacco use, particularly among children and adolescents, poses perhaps the single most significant threat to public health in the United States. Nonetheless, no matter how important, conspicuous, and controversial the issue, and regardless of how likely the public is to hold the Executive Branch politically accountable, an administrative agency's power to regulate in the public interest must always be grounded in a valid grant of authority from Congress. . . . Reading the FDCA as a whole, as well as in conjunction with Congress' subsequent tobacco-specific legislation, it is plain that Congress has not given the FDA the authority that it seeks to exercise here. For these reasons, the judgment of the Court of Appeals for the Fourth Circuit is

Affirmed.

:: CASE QUESTIONS

1. What regulations adopted by the Food and Drug Administration are challenged in this case?
2. Describe the dilemma that the Court discusses regarding its role of determining an agency's authority and deferring to the finding of that agency.
3. What does the Court conclude in this case? Why?
4. If regulation of tobacco is to occur, what has to happen first?

16. REVIEW OF ADJUDICATIONS: PROCEDURAL ASPECTS

Judicial review of agencies' adjudications by its very nature is quite limited. Legislatures have delegated authority to agencies because of their expertise and knowledge, and courts usually exercise restraint and resolve doubtful issues in favor of an agency. For example, courts reviewing administrative interpretations of law do not always decide questions of law for themselves. It is not unusual for a court to accept an administrative interpretation of law as final if it is warranted in the record and has a rational basis in law. Administrative agencies are frequently called upon to interpret the statute governing an agency, and an agency's construction is persuasive to courts.

Administrative agencies develop their own rules of procedure unless mandated otherwise by an act of the legislature. These procedures are far less formal than judicial procedures, because one of the functions of the administrative process is to decide issues expeditiously. To proceed expeditiously usually means, for example, that administrative agencies are not restricted by the strict rules of evidence used by courts. Such agencies cannot ignore all rules, but they can use some leeway. They cannot, for example, refuse to permit any cross-examination or unduly limit it. Because an agency "is frequently the accuser, the prosecutor, the judge and the jury," it must remain alert to observe accepted standards of fairness. Reviewing courts are, therefore, alert to ensure that the true substance of a fair hearing is not denied to a party to an administrative hearing.

The principle that federal administrative agencies should be free to fashion their own rules of procedure and pursue methods of inquiry permitting them to discharge their duties grows out of the view that administrative agencies and administrators will be familiar with the industries they regulate. Thus, they will be in a better position than courts or legislative bodies to design procedural rules adapted to the peculiarities of the industry and the tasks of the agency involved.

In reviewing the procedures of administrative agencies, courts lack the authority to substitute their judgment or their own procedures for those of the agency. Judicial responsibility is limited to ensuring consistency with statutes and compliance with the demands of the Constitution for a fair hearing. The latter responsibility arises from the due process clause. Due process usually requires a hearing by an agency, but on occasion sanctions may be imposed prior to the hearing.

Two doctrines guide courts in the judicial review of agency adjudications:

- Exhaustion of remedies
- Primary jurisdiction

Don't ignore what may appear to be a biased administrative hearing. Relying on courts to reverse the agency's decision is a bad plan.

Your school likely has an administrative process for handling students' grade appeals. You must follow this administrative procedure.

Exhaustion of Remedies   The doctrine of **exhaustion of remedies** is a court-created rule that limits when courts can review administrative decisions. Courts refuse to review administrative actions until a complaining party has exhausted all of the administrative remedies and procedures available to him or her for redress. Judicial review is available only for final actions by an agency. Preliminary orders such as a decision to file a complaint are not reviewable. Otherwise, the administrative system would be denied important opportunities to make a factual record, to exercise its discretion, or to apply its expertise in its decision making. Also, exhaustion allows an agency to discover and correct its own errors, and thus it helps to dispense with any reason for judicial review. Exhaustion clearly should be required in those cases involving an area of the agency's expertise or specialization; it should require no unusual expense. It should also be required when the administrative remedy is just as likely as the judicial one to provide appropriate relief. The doctrine of exhaustion of remedies avoids the premature interruption of the administrative process.

This doctrine is not an absolute principle. Courts do allow parties to litigate prior to exhausting administrative remedies. Sidebar 6.14 provides explanation for exceptions to this administrative requirement.

:: *sidebar* 6.14

Exceptions to Requirement of Exhaustion

When there is nothing to be gained from the exhaustion of administrative remedies and when the harm from the continued existence of the administrative ruling is great, the courts have not been reluctant to discard this doctrine. This is especially true when very fundamental constitutional guarantees such as freedom of speech or press are involved or when the administrative remedy is likely to be inadequate.

Also, probably no court would insist upon exhaustion when the agency is clearly acting beyond its jurisdiction (because its action is not authorized by statute or the statute authorizing it is unconstitutional) or where it would result in irreparable injury (such as great expense) to the petitioner. Finally, an exception to the doctrine is fraud. If an agency is acting fraudulently, immediate access to the court is appropriate.

A judge hearing a case involving a dispute over licensing requirements for a nuclear power plant likely would refer this case to the Nuclear Regulatory Commission (NRC).

Primary Jurisdiction   A doctrine similar to exhaustion of remedies is known as **primary jurisdiction.** *Exhaustion* applies when a claim must go in the first instance to an administrative agency alone. *Primary jurisdiction* applies when a claim is originally filed in the courts. It comes into play whenever enforcement of the claim requires the resolution of issues that, under a regulatory scheme, have been placed within the special competence of an administrative body. In such a case, the judicial process is suspended pending referral of such issues to the administrative body for its views. Primary jurisdiction ensures uniformity and consistency in dealing with matters entrusted to an administrative body. The doctrine is invoked when referral to the agency is preferable because of its specialized knowledge or expertise in dealing with the matter in controversy. Statutes such as those guaranteeing equal employment opportunity that create a private remedy for dollar damages sometimes require the parties to resort to an administrative agency as a condition precedent to filing suit. Some of these are federal statutes that require referral to state agencies. In these cases, referral must occur, but the right to sue is not limited by the results of the administrative decision.

17. REVIEW OF FACTUAL DETERMINATIONS

When it reviews the findings of fact made by an administrative body, a court presumes them to be correct. A court of review examines the evidence by analyzing the record of the agency's proceedings. It upholds the agency's findings and conclusions on questions of fact if they are supported by substantial evidence in the record. In other words, the record must contain material evidence from which a reasonable person might reach the same conclusion as did the agency. If substantial evidence in support of the decision is present, the court will not disturb the agency's findings, even though the court itself might have reached a different conclusion on the basis of other conflicting evidence also in the record. For example, the determination of credibility of the witnesses who testify in quasi-judicial proceedings is for the agency to determine and not the courts.

Courts do not (1) reweigh the evidence, (2) make independent determinations of fact, or (3) substitute their view of the evidence for that of the agency. However, courts do determine if there is substantial evidence to support the action taken. But in their examination of the evidence, all that is required is evidence sufficient to convince a reasonable mind to a fair degree of certainty. Thus, substantial evidence is that which a reasonable mind might accept as adequate to support the conclusion.

For the courts to exercise their function of limited review, an agency must provide a record that sets forth the reasons and basis for its decision. If this record shows that the agency did not examine all relevant data and that it ignored issues before it, a court may set aside the agency's decision because such a decision is arbitrary and capricious. Agencies cannot assume their decisions. They must be based on evidence, and the record must support the decision.

After reading this section and the preceding ones, do you understand why it is important for businesses to take seriously the procedures within the administrative agency?

concept :: *summary*

Judicial Review of Agency Decisions

1. Regardless of whether a party is challenging an agency's rule making or adjudication, that party must have standing to sue.
2. To establish standing to sue, the challenger must show the reviewing court that the agency's decision is subject to review and that the challenger is personally affected by the agency's decision.
3. When the decision challenged involves the agency's rule-making function, the court must determine if the agency's authority was validly delegated.
4. If the delegation of authority is definite and limited, the court will decide if the agency has exceeded its authority. If the answer is no, the agency's rule will be upheld.
5. When the decision challenged involves the agency's adjudicatory function, the law requires the challenger to exhaust the available administrative remedies and the court to determine whether an agency should have primary jurisdiction.
6. The factual findings of an agency are presumed to be correct.
7. Courts are not permitted to substitute their personal views for the agency's findings and conclusions if a reasonable person could reach the same result as the agency.
8. An agency's expertise is entitled to great deference and will not be reversed unless it is clearly erroneous.

18. CONCLUSION

Perhaps from the time the U.S. Constitution was debated and adopted, people have complained "There is too much government." This feeling probably exists today anytime a governmental action interferes with a property interest we have.

How did we get to this situation? you might ask. The answer is rather complicated and subject to some controversy. What is clear is all levels of governments are larger and more complex in this first decade of the twenty-first century than even 25 years ago. Indeed, each generation of Americans has seen an increase in the government's influence.

Sidebar 6.15 presents a historical overview of the growth of the regulatory process and some corresponding administrative agencies.

The topics presented in Sidebar 6.15 are not exhaustive of important administrative agencies. In fact, a complete list of agencies would take up too much space. One federal government website lists 136 federal agencies. And there are countless state and local administrative agencies.

:: *sidebar* 6.15

Trends in Regulations: Growth of Government in the Twentieth Century

As the 1800s ended and the 1900s began, a major concern of the federal government was the concentration of economic power into the hands of America's wealthiest. This concern led to the creation of antitrust laws. Although it was not the first federal administrative agency, the Federal Trade Commission (FTC), created in 1914 to prevent unfair methods of competition, started the growth of administrative agencies in the twentieth century. (*Note:* This topic is the subject matter of Chapter 16.)

The financial crash of the country's capital markets and the ensuing depression caused Congress to pass several laws attempting to restore economic order. Among some of the most important laws were the securities acts. These laws, passed in the 1930s, and subsequent laws intended to address the business scandals of the 1980s, 1990s, and early twenty-first century, make up the subject matter of Chapter 15. This chapter emphasizes the role of the Securities and Exchange Commission (SEC).

Throughout the first half of the twentieth century, Congress attempted to balance the bargaining power of business management and organized labor. These various laws and others impacting the employment relationship are the topics of Chapter 21. A key administrative agency studied in that chapter is the National Labor Relations Board (NLRB).

The second half of the twentieth century saw a focus on discriminatory practices and their negative impact on society and business. At the heart of regulating and preventing discrimination is the Equal Employment Opportunity Commission (EEOC). This agency and the related laws are described in Chapter 20.

Also, in the latter portion of the last century we saw a growing concern for protecting the environment. In the 1970s, Congress passed clean air and clean water legislation. To ensure businesses and individuals remain aware of their environmental impact, Congress created the Environmental Protection Agency (EPA). Chapter 18 discusses this area of the law.

Do review the agencies found at www.whitehouse.gov/government/independent-agencies.html.

Some additional data provides further insight as to the growth of government. In colonial times, more than 90 percent of the people were engaged in some agricultural activity. The westward expansion continued this trend. In 1840, four out of every five adults were self-employed. Ask yourself: How much government protection/influence/interference did this society need? Today, over 90 percent of adults are employees. This shift in our economy has resulted in a larger role for government regulation.

:: Key Terms

:: Review Questions and Problems

Basic Concepts

1. *Separation of Powers*

   Describe the two concepts that (a) balance power within the federal government and
   (b) provide distinctions in the role of the federal, state, and local governments.

2. *Supremacy Clause*

   In 1916, the federal government passed a law that allows national banks to sell insurance in
   towns with a population of less than 5,000. In 1974, Florida passed a law prohibiting insurance
   agents from associating with financial institutions that are owned by or affiliated with a bank
   holding company. A bank located in a small Florida town is affiliated with a national bank. This
   bank wants to sell insurance through licensed insurance agents. Can the bank successfully challenge the Florida prohibition as being preempted by the federal law? Explain your reasoning.

3. *Contract Clause*

   (a) Does this provision of the Constitution apply to the federal government, state government,
       or both? Explain.

   (b) Does this provision of the Constitution apply to present contractual relationships, future
       ones, or both? Explain.

Amendments and Basic Protections

4. *Freedom of Religion*

   Explain the purposes of and distinction between the establishment clause and the free exercise
   clause.

5. *Freedom of the Press*

   (a) A promoter of theatrical productions applied to a municipal board (charged with managing a
       city-leased theater) for a license to stage the play *Hair*. Relying on outside reports that because
       of nudity the production would not be in the best interests of the community, the board
       rejected the application. The promoter sought a court order permitting it to use the audito-
       rium. Why should the court allow the production to proceed?

   (b) What are the distinctions in how the law treats public persons versus private persons with
       respect to defamation?

6. *Freedom of Speech*

   Silvia, an attorney in Florida, also was a licensed certified public accountant (CPA) and a
   certified financial planner (CFP). Silvia placed an ad in the yellow pages listing her credentials,
   including the CPA and CFP designations. The Florida Board of Accountancy reprimanded Silvia
   for using both the CPA and CFP credentials in an ad essentially emphasizing her legal work.

Silvia challenged the board's right to issue this reprimand. What is the legal basis for Silvia's challenge? Explain.

7. *Right to Possess Guns*

   The Supreme Court recently interpreted the Second Amendment for the first time in decades. Based on that decision, can individuals have guns in their homes for self-defense or is the right to possess guns limited only to members of a governmental-approved militia unit?

8. *Due Process of Law*

   Explain what is meant by the Incorporation Doctrine and how it was used to expand the impact of the due process clause.

9. *Equal Protection*

   There are three levels of judicial scrutiny under this clause. Describe what these levels are and when they are applicable.

The Commerce Clause—Government's Authority to Regulate Business

10. *Regulation of Foreign Commerce*

    Why is it important that regulation of international business transactions is reserved exclusively to the federal government?

11. *Regulation of Interstate Commerce*

    What is the legal analysis used by the courts to grant the federal government almost limitless authority to regulate business activity?

12. *Limitation on State Police Powers*

    (a) Describe the five factual situations wherein the commerce clause might be used to restrict a state or local governmental action. What analysis is used in each situation?

    (b) A Maine statute imposed a tax on trucks. The tax required owners and operators of foreign-based (out-of-state) trucks using Maine highways to purchase either an annual highway use permit or a one-trip permit. Trucks based in-state were exempt. An out-of-state trucker challenged the constitutionality of the statute. Is this Maine statute constitutional? Why or why not?

13. *Limitation on State Taxation*

    (a) Define the terms *apportionment* and *nexus*.

    (b) How are these concepts applied to restrict state government taxation of businesses engaged in interstate commerce?

Regulatory Process—Administrative Agencies

14. *Standing to Sue*

    What are the two issues that must be considered by courts to determine whether a person has standing to challenge an agency's decision?

15. *Review of Rule Making*

    (a) Again, there are two issues that must be addressed by courts when they review the rule-making (quasi-legislative) functions of agencies. What are these two issues? Explain each.

    (b) A national bank sought permission from the comptroller of the currency to sell annuities. This permission was granted as "incidental to the business of banking." The Variable Annuity Life Insurance Company filed suit claiming the comptroller should not have granted this permission. What standard of review of this administrative decision should courts apply?

16. *Review of Adjudications: Procedural Aspects*

    Plaintiffs purchased state lottery tickets and were winners along with 76 others. The state had advertised that $1,750,000 would be the prize, but it distributed only $744,471. Plaintiff sued the lottery director, alleging fraud in the conduct of the lottery. The state lottery law provides for administrative hearings upon complaints charging violations of the lottery law or of regulations thereunder. It also allows any party adversely affected by a final order of the administrative agency to seek judicial review. Must the plaintiffs exhaust their administrative remedies? Why or why not?

17. *Review of Factual Determinations*

What standard of review do courts use to decide whether to uphold the factual determinations made by an administrative agency?

18. *Conclusion*

Why has the complaint against excessive government been consistent throughout the years?

business :: *discussions*

1. Other retail businesses in the mall in which your sports shoes shop is located have decided to open on Sundays from 12 noon to 6 p.m. You decide to follow suit, but two of your employees refuse to go along, saying it is against their religious beliefs to work on the Sabbath. You terminate their employment. They apply for unemployment compensation, and contend their unemployed status is your fault. If the state grants them benefits, you will be penalized since your unemployment compensation taxes will go up.

Should you contest their claim?

What would be the result if the employees refuse to work on Sunday because of their desire to play golf on that day?

2. In both your personal and professional lives, you realize how much government at the federal, state, and local levels influences what you can and cannot do. For example, since your business employs more than 15 people, there are numerous federal statutes dictating the physical condition of the workplace, the amount you must pay your employees, the taxes you owe, and the paperwork you must file with regulatory agencies. At the state level, you know you have to obtain certain licenses to conduct business or to engage in recreational activities, such as fishing. And your local government regulates how you can use the land you own.

In light of this multitude of regulatory activity, you ask yourself the following questions:

By what authority do governmental entities impose various regulations?

Is there any limit to the extent such regulations impact our lives?

How can an individual or a business organization challenge the application of regulatory authorities?

3. Suppose it has been two years since your graduation. During the time you have worked for a large energy company. In your work, you have been exposed to the numerous ways your employer is investing in energy. These sources include oil, coal, natural gas, solar, wind, nuclear, and electrical plants.

Just last month, you were told you were being transferred to the CEO's office. Your first assignment is to work with the general counsel's staff to determine how your company is regulated and how all divisions are complying with the various, relevant laws and regulations. As you ponder this assignment, you ask yourself the following questions:

Is this company regulated only by the federal government, or are state and local regulations relevant?

How does the company and its divisions keep track of laws and regulations?

If an administrative agency begins an investigation of your company, should your company cooperate with or fight the agency's action?

7

The Property-Based Legal System

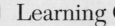 Learning Objectives ::

In this chapter you will learn:

1. To analyze the connection between a property-based legal system and prosperity.

2. To understand property as an exclusive legal fence and to identify narrow applications of property even when they are not traditionally called "property."

3. To grasp and apply the rules of security interests.

4. To evaluate the statement that private property promotes the common good and be able to furnish examples.

At the Constitutional Convention in 1789, no fewer than 5 of the 55 delegates asserted without any opposition that the state (or government) comes into being to protect property, meaning what is privately proper to people. Likely, all or almost all of the delegates held this opinion, which was not controversial in the late 1700s. As you read this chapter and study many of the specific rules applying the legal fence that is property, keep in mind that property is something very basic and important to our nation.

As explained in Chapter 1, the legal concept of property is vital to understanding how law provides a foundation for the private market. Property also establishes a central focus, or hub, for grasping the subjects of this book, including contracts, tort laws, and much public law regulation of business. Contracts involve the exchange of what people own (Chapters 8–9). Tort law permits compensation when one person harms or infringes what belongs to another (Chapter 10). Public law regulation of business helps define and protect the equal right of all to what they own. For instance, antitrust law protects what company A owns from certain competitive harms by company B (Chapter 16), and securities law protects what investors own from misappropriation by corporate agents like managers (Chapter 15).

What is property? In everyday conversation we use *property* interchangeably with things like land or other resources, but it is clear that "property" has some additional meaning. Property indicates legal ownership, that something is recognized by law as being "mine" or "yours." Further, property indicates exclusiveness. You can legally exclude others from things that are yours (i.e., things you own). For example, if you can exclude others from a car that you own, you can do many things with it. You can possess and drive it; you can sell it or give it away; you can rent it out or start a taxi company with it; or you can use it as security for a loan or add it to your car collection. All of these uses of the car, however, are possible because you can legally exclude others from interfering with these uses. As the Supreme Court stated, "The hallmark of a protected property interest is the right to exclude others." [527 U.S. 666, 673 (1999)]

> Property is not an object or resource. It is the legal right to exclude others from interfering with an object or resource.

> Think of property not as a physical fence but as a legal fence that protects resources inside the fence from the acquisitiveness of others.

Here is a definition of property that regards it as a legal right rather than a thing or a bunch of things: **Property** *is the legal right to exclude others from resources that are originally possessed or are acquired without force, theft, or fraud.* A "resource" includes anything that someone may need or want. Land, widgets, shares of corporate stock, and the uses of these things are all resources. In a sense, someone's labor or efforts are also resources. "Originally possessed" resources like your capacity for work and health are protected by the property right in that you can legally exclude others from interfering with them or sue others if they harm these resources. Property acts like a legal fence, protecting the resources inside the fence from the acquisitiveness of others. But since the fence protects everyone's resources, property means that everyone is so protected. A property system requires limitations on how you can use what you own because it affects what others own. In other words, property is not just for the benefit of a solitary person, but for the benefit of everyone. Property is an absolute right, but it does not extend infinitely: the property fence has limits. Property fences also change slowly over time as they are defined, redefined, and interpreted. For another way of regarding property, see Sidebar 7.1.

The state through its legislatures and courts establishes how property applies to various resources. Sometimes the state does not permit you property in particular resources. You cannot sell human kidneys, although you can give away one of yours. The state recognizes that you have the right to exclude others from your kidney for some purposes but not to sell it to them. Although a great many legal rules limit the right of property as applied to resources and their uses (which can also be considered resources), prosperous nations in general apply the property right widely to the things that people need or want.

:: *sidebar* 7.1

Property as a Bundle of Rights

Many scholars describe property as "a bundle of sticklike rights" that apply to things. Thus, if you have property in land, you have the rights to *possess* it, *control* it, *use* it in various ways, *transfer* it, *gain income* from it, and so forth. Sometimes it is desirable to think of property in this way when deciding whether or not the state has "taken" one's property through regulation under the Fifth Amendment to the Constitution. The Supreme Court has ruled that the state does not have to compensate owners when it has taken only some but not all of the bundle of property rights through regulatory limitations.

For example, regulations in Athens, Georgia, prohibit more than two unrelated people from living in residences zoned for single families. This upsets University of Georgia students who like to rent houses and live in them with three or more unrelated people to the house. It also deprives owners of houses of the right to use their realty to rent to groups of students. But since the owners may still sell their houses and rent them to single families, the city of Athens has not deprived the owners of the entire bundle of property rights and thus need not compensate them.

Rather than regarding property as a bundle of rights, we regard it as a single right, the right to exclude. If you can legally exclude others from something, whether it be physical or various uses of something physical, you have "property." If you cannot exclude others from something, including the uses of something physical, to that extent you lack property. In this example your authors would say that owners of single-family residences in Athens lack the property of using their houses to rent to three or more unrelated people. The city has defined property boundaries protecting other single-family residence owners from being "harmed" in their ownership by excessive numbers of renters. Do you agree with this conclusion?

Property law does not function well when it is not adequately enforced. Honest police are needed to deter robbery and theft. Impartial courts are required to settle disputes over who owns what and whether X has wrongfully injured Y's resources. Property becomes not just an exclusionary right but also an entire system, and it is upon this property system of law that business depends.

This chapter explores the benefits of the property system and many of the rules that apply the property fence to different kinds of resources. It concludes with an examination of how various principles of property protect the common good. As you read the chapter, you should note that the various rules you study are not themselves "property," which is the principle of the legally exclusive private fence. The rules you study simply describe different ways of applying the fence. You should finish this chapter with a deeper knowledge of the central significance of property law to business. Quite simply, property is the necessary foundation for private enterprise and the market in the modern nation.

:: The Property System

Arguably, the most significant issue for any society is how it orders the relationships among people concerning limited and valued resources, resources needed to survive and flourish. As long as people need or want more resources than they have available to them, society will order how people relate to each other in acquiring and possessing these resources. Such resources include land, food, raw materials, manufactured products, and even some types of information. Importantly, limited resources also include useful applications of the physical world and the human effort necessary for these applications. In other words, limited resources include the uses of physical raw materials and of yourself.

1. THE PROBLEM OF LIMITED RESOURCES

In Western political theory, the state comes into being in response to the problem of limited resources. Through law, the state establishes a framework for handling the problem. At least two basic legal frameworks exist. In one framework the state itself, represented by a ruler or legislature, makes the major decisions about the production and distribution of resources. The state takes ownership of resources or acquires them through taxation. It also may direct people in how, when, and where to work, thus assuming rights over the resources people have in themselves, their efforts, and talents. Distribution of resources occurs through state planning.

Communism is one system providing such a framework. The state requires that its citizens produce according to their abilities and share according to the needs of everyone else. The communist state expects people to want to do this, but it legally coerces them when necessary.

A second legal framework that orders how people relate to each other concerning scarce resources is private property. Private property, which we will just call "property," is a system of law under which the state recognizes and enforces an individual's rights to acquire, possess, use, and transfer scarce resources. (As for property other than private property, see Sidebar 7.2). In the property system, the state does not plan what people should have nor does it acquire and redistribute resources to them. Rather, the people themselves determine how resources are distributed through voluntary exchange, usually for money that they use to acquire other resources they need or want. The role of the state is to recognize legally when people have exclusive property

---

:: *sidebar* 7.2

The Three Faces of Property

Legal scholars divide the word "property" into three main usages: private, public, and common. *Private property* protects private persons and allows them to exclude others, including in most instances the state, from interfering with resources that are acquired without force, theft, or fraud. *Public property* refers to the state's right under various circumstances to exclude people from state monuments, buildings, equipment, land, and other public resources.

Common property has two meanings. First, it refers to the right we all have to common resources like the air,

rivers, or oceans. However, this meaning is appropriate only to the extent we can legally exclude others from interfering with our usage of these resources, for example, as when anyone who uses a river can sue to prevent or stop its illegal pollution. Second, "common property" sometimes refers to the private ownership by two or more people of a specific resource such as a piece of land.

For studying the legal and regulatory environment of business, private property is most important. It provides the foundation for the conduct of the modern market, and it is often just called "property."

rights in scarce resources and to allow them to enforce their rights through legal institutions like courts.

All nations recognize some applications of private property. Even the most communist society may allow individuals some right as to how they use their productive efforts, and it usually allows them exclusive control over limited personal possessions and food consumption. On the other hand, societies founded on private property law always have legal limitations on how owners can use their resources, prohibiting harm to others and recognizing both some state taxation and regulation over property. The difference in the two frameworks is a matter of degree, and most societies have mixed frameworks for dealing with the reality of limited resources.

However, if the goal of society is to produce more of what people need and want (i.e., to increase the total amount of limited resources), one of the legal frameworks is superior to the other. The available evidence suggests that a property system produces more for a society than a state planning system. And if "freedom" is measured as individual autonomy and the absence of state coercion, then a property system also makes people more free.

For the property system to function most effectively in promoting prosperity, it should be applied according to the rule of law, which means it should be applied generally and equally to everyone. All members of society must have an equal guarantee of exclusive rights to their resources. The following section discusses more specifically how property promotes prosperity.

> What does it mean to say that all nations recognize private property?

2. PROPERTY AND PROSPERITY

Property is central to the legal environment of business. It is also central to society's achievement of prosperity. In fact, property creates some of the maximum conditions known for producing and sustaining prosperity. Since property refers to a particular system of laws, rather than to useful resources, it is fair to conclude that certain laws are a major contributing factor to prosperity. Let us examine how property helps generate prosperity.

First, property powerfully promotes *incentive.* By allowing people to keep and benefit from what they produce, property motivates effort in a way that Chapter 1 suggested is very natural to human beings. Whether the activity is growing crops, manufacturing cars, or starting a new business, people will generally expend more effort when they have a protected property in what they produce than when they do not. Likewise, they are willing to produce more when they do not have to spend much of their time defending their homes or other acquisitions from those who may desire to take them. Under conditions where others are likely to take through force, theft, fraud, or even government mandate what people have or produce, there comes a point at which people will simply not work as hard, take as many risks, nor innovate as much. We may debate where that point is (e.g., how much people can be taxed before they slow their efforts), but the fact that property and incentive bear a direct relationship seems beyond debate.

> Private property establishes maximum conditions for wealth creation through promoting incentive.

Next, property helps generate prosperity by establishing the conditions necessary for *capital formation,* which refers to that quality of resources that produces new or different resources. For example, property enables people to borrow money at reasonable cost. In the United States most entrepreneurs start businesses by capitalizing the resource they have in their houses. They borrow money, and in a **mortgage** agreement put up their houses to secure the loans. (See Section 13.)

Lenders are willing to loan money at affordable rates primarily because property law guarantees (1) that a borrower's house is on an identifiable piece of land recognized by the state, (2) that the state recognizes a borrower's claim to the house, and (3) that the state permits lenders to enforce the mortgage agreement through the courts and sell a borrower's house to satisfy the loan if the borrower fails to repay it. The law of property enables entrepreneurs to change the form of their resources from houses to money, so they can start a business. This type of capital formation may seem curiously obvious to business students in the United States. However, as Sidebar 7.3 discusses, it is virtually unavailable in the poorer nations of the world due to the absence of adequate property law.

:: *sidebar* 7.3

The Mystery of Capital

In the book *The Mystery of Capital,* Peruvian economist Hernando de Soto asserts that the reason "why capitalism triumphs in the West but fails everywhere else" is because of the secure system of property law that exists in Western nations. Not new technology, hard work, a superior culture, better management techniques, nor "exploitation" account principally for prosperity in the West, but rather the willingness of lenders in an adequate property system to risk their money to entrepreneurs with business ideas. De Soto's research team estimates that in less-developed countries there exists $9 trillion of "dead capital"—resources that people possess which they cannot capitalize because the laws in their countries do not adequately guarantee property in these resources, and affordable collateral-secured loans are unavailable. Without the legal recognition of property, many resources may also be difficult to sell since a buyer cannot be sure that the state will recognize and protect a seller's right to transfer the resources. This problem is especially acute with the sale of land and buildings. The lack of an adequate property law system may not account totally for poverty in less-developed countries, but it is arguably the most important contributing factor.

Of course, the relationship of capital formation to property law means more than just mortgages or other collateral-secured loans. Large-scale businesses are capitalized by investors who buy ownership shares. For instance, corporations capitalize by selling stock shares, which are legally recognized property interests in a corporation. This method of capitalization is feasible only because the law recognizes stockholders' property interests in corporations (see Chapter 14). Likewise, securities markets (i.e., markets for stocks, bonds, and other ownership interests in businesses) are not possible without law enforcing the property interests in what these markets sell. Securities markets are vital to capital formation and prosperity in modern nations. Both corporate stock shares and securities markets enable businesses to change a property interest in future profit potential into the money necessary for business operation.

A final contribution property makes to prosperity is to make resources easily divisible. *Divisibility* also relates to capital formation and refers to how property permits resources to be broken into parts and used in many ways while the owner still retains a property interest in each part. Under property law, an owner of a single piece of land can sell part of it outright (change it into money), sell another part of it on credit and hold a mortgage to ensure payment, lease part of it to tenants who pay rent, incorporate part of it and sell shares to investors, and secure a loan against part of it in order to start an Internet business. In each of these transactions regarding the single piece of land, the owner retains identifiable and protected property interests. Each transaction is made practically possible because the law of property enables resources to be subdivided as an owner may find advantageous.

This feature of property facilitates the development of resources, which creates new wealth and causes prosperity. The next section further elaborates the divisibility of property.

3. TWO BASIC DIVISIONS OF PROPERTY

The preceding section asserted that the easy divisibility of property contributes to prosperity, and it gave several examples of how property can be divided. This section introduces the two basic legal divisions of property: real property and personal property. **Real property** law applies ownership to land and interests in land such as mining rights or leases. All other types of resources are protected under the law of **personal property.**

> **Real property** law applies to land and interests in land. All other resources are protected by **personal property** law.

Because of the historical importance of land, real property rules are very formal. As Chapter 8 on contracts discusses, agreements transferring interests in land ownership should be written, and many special rules apply to the registration and taxation of land ownership. Land ownership is also known as *real estate* or *realty.*

A particular kind of interest in land is the fixture. A **fixture** is an object of personal property that has become an object of real property (1) by physical annexation (attachment) to the land or its buildings, or (2) whose use has become closely associated with the use to which the land is put. Unless sellers and buyers agree differently when they sell land, the fixtures go with the land to the buyers. Manufacturing equipment is a fixture when it is sold along with a manufacturing plant. Carpeting is a fixture if it is nailed down or glued to the floor. Not being attached to the land, rugs are usually not fixtures. To prevent misunderstandings in land sales, sellers and buyers should identify which things are fixtures and stay with the buyers and which things remain protected under personal property and go with the sellers.

Personal property applies to movable resources, those things that people do not annex to the land. The law divides personal property into rules applying to tangible and intangible resources. *Tangible property* applies to things one can touch, that is, to physical things. Computers, cars, and carrots are such touchable things. The sale of tangible things, also known as "goods," is controlled by the Uniform Commercial Code, a type of contract law explained in the next chapter. Chapter 15 discusses the sale of corporate stock, which is an intangible thing. Real property rules and personal property rules are often different as are rules applying personal property to tangible or intangible things.

:: Acquiring Resources in a Property System

How do you come to own resources in a property system? In other words, how does the right of property to something attach to a specific person? Although you can acquire resources in many ways, including by force (called "robbery"), theft (various forms of stealing), and fraud (intentionally lying and harming others to get what belongs to them), there are only five basic legal ways to become an owner of something in a property system. As you read what follows, consider that **ownership** means the same thing as "property." Both terms refer to the legal right that makes resources exclusive, that makes resources "mine," instead of "yours," or "no one's."

4. ACQUIRING RESOURCES THROUGH EXCHANGE

The most common way of coming to have a property in something is through exchanging resources. For example, when you buy a car, or buy a company, you exchange one form of resources you own (money) for another form of resources (car or company). You are now the legal owner of the car or company. Resources have been switched but property (or ownership) remains. Likewise, when you exchange your services for a paycheck, you become the owner of the paycheck and the money it represents. The employer becomes the owner of your services and what they produce.

Contract rules control the way owners make agreements to exchange resources in the property-based legal system.

The rules under which people exchange resources in a property system are called the rules of **contract.** Contract rules are the subject of Chapters 8 and 9, but you should understand now that contract rules make agreements to exchange resources between owners legally binding and enforceable. In particular, the rules of contract make it possible for owners to commit legally to future exchange of resources. These rules also make it possible for one owner to sue another if agreements to exchange resources in the future are broken by one of the owners. Further, contract rules allow lawsuits against those who have not adequately performed their agreements. If owner A agrees to sell goods to owner B in 30 days and then does not deliver them, owner B may sue owner A for damages. Likewise, owner B may sue owner A if owner A does deliver the goods, but they turn out to be defective. In addition to damages, contract rules may specify other remedies for contract breach.

It is difficult to overemphasize the importance of contract rules in the property system. Professor Philip Nichols of the Wharton School asserts that observing legally enforceable contracts is the single most significant indicator that a country's economy is ready for international trade. If the right of property is the foundation for the modern private market, the rules of contract are perhaps the keystone of that foundation.

5. ACQUIRING RESOURCES THROUGH POSSESSION

The rule of first possession is that the first person to reduce previously unowned things to possession becomes their owner.

Sometimes you can become an owner of something merely through possession, that is, by physically holding and controlling it. The **rule of first possession** is that the first person to reduce previously unowned things to possession becomes their owner. In Sylacauga, Alabama, a meteorite crashed through the roof of a rented house in 1954 and struck the tenant on the leg, the only recorded instance in history when a meteorite has struck a person. Initially, both the owner of the house and the tenant (owner of the lease) claimed the meteorite, but because the tenant was the first person to reduce it to possession, she acquired the right of property to it.

Similar to the rule of first possession, is the rule that when someone has *abandoned* what they own, the first person to reduce it to possession owns it. The law determines whether or not someone has abandoned what they previously owned by measuring *intent,* whether the previous owner intended to abandon something. The law measures intent by the circumstances of the situation. If it looks like someone meant to abandon something, we say they intended to do it. When it is not clear who is the first person to reduce previously unowned or abandoned resources to possession, lawsuits may follow. See Sidebar 7.4.

:: *sidebar* 7.4

Barry Bonds Home-Run Ball

When Barry Bonds blasted his record-setting 73rd home run ball into the stands of PacBell Park on October 7, 2001, ownership of the ball was abandoned. Unlike in football, where a ball that goes into the stands must be returned, Major League baseball—the association of team owners—deliberately abandons the balls and allows fans to keep them. But who had the right of property in the record-setting ball, Alex Popov who initially appeared to catch it before a wild crowd of fans knocked him to the ground, or Patrick Hayashi who shortly afterward saw the ball rolling free, grabbed it, and stuck it in his pocket?

Popov sued Hayashi, arguing that he was the owner because he had caught and first possessed the ball, which had an estimated value of $1 million. After trial, Judge Kevin McCarthy recognized that the principle of first possession applied to the ball, but did Popov or Hayashi first possess it?

The facts were not clear as to whether Popov caught or dropped the ball. The judge stated, "An award of the ball to Mr. Popov would be unfair to Mr. Hayashi. It would be premised on the assumption that Mr. Popov would have caught the ball. That assumption is not supported by the facts. An award of the ball to Mr. Hayashi would unfairly penalize Mr. Popov. It would be based on the assumption that Mr. Popov would have dropped the ball. That conclusion is also unsupported by the facts."

With the facts unclear, Judge McCarthy ruled that it was fairest to divide the ownership of the ball. "The court therefore declares that both plaintiff and defendant have an equal and undivided interest in the ball. . . . In order to effectuate this ruling, the ball must be sold and the proceeds divided equally between the parties." Rather than appeal, Popov and Hayashi agreed they would sell the ball and divide the proceeds.

Lost Items Things that are *lost* also can acquire a new owner through possession. The finder of a lost item becomes its owner by reducing it to possession and following a statutory procedure, which may require the finder to turn the item over to the police and to advertise it in a local paper for a period of time to allow the original owner to claim it. But at the end of the specified statutory period the finder becomes the new owner.

The law distinguishes things that have been lost from things that have simply been mislaid. Things that have been lost go to the first person who subsequently reduces them to possession, but things that have been *mislaid* go to the person who owns the premises where the item was mislaid. A $100 bill on the table in the library has been mislaid, but if it is on the floor it

Can you distinguish between things that are lost and things that are merely mislaid?

has been lost. The difference in the way the law treats these two situations is based on an assumption that the original owner will know where to come back and reclaim mislaid things. Consider the following instance: A man who had a box in a bank vault was examining the contents of his box at a table in the vault room when he found $25,000 in a pile under the table. A lawsuit arose over whether the money was lost or mislaid and whether it went to the bank or to the finder. The court held that since the money was under the table the money had been lost and belonged to the finder. Question: Why didn't the person who "lost" the money come forward and claim it? Was it because the money had been acquired illegally, or because tax had not been paid on it?

Adverse Possession   Another form of ownership through possession arises through **adverse possession.** Adverse possession gives you ownership of land (and it only applies to land) under state statute when the possession is:

- Open and notorious. The possessor must occupy the land in such a way as to put the true owner of the land on notice.
- Actual and exclusive. The possessor must physically occupy the land. However, the building of a fence around the land or construction of a building on it constitutes physical occupation.
- Continuous. Possession must not be interrupted.
- Wrongful. The possessor must not have the owner's permission to be on the land, for example, under a lease.
- For a prescribed period of time. Most states specify an adverse possession of between 10 and 20 years before the possessor becomes the new owner.

You should appreciate that there may be more than one solution to a property problem.

In one instance, the author was teaching about adverse possession when a student suddenly jumped up and ran out of class. Later the student reported that he had called his parents because about the time the student had been born, their neighbor had built a fence for half a mile about five or ten feet onto land belonging to the student's parents. To maintain good relations, the parents had simply said nothing to their neighbor about the wrongful location of the fence. The student had wanted to notify his parents about the rule of adverse possession. The author asked the class what the student's parents might do in this situation, assuming wrongful possession. Some students said to confront the neighbor and tear down the fence if the 20-year time required by the statute had not expired. But what about the good relations with the neighbor? Eventually, the students concluded that the parents could either sell the strip of land to the neighbor, or give the neighbor permission to have the fence on the land, meaning that the occupation of the land would no longer be "wrongful." Even if the 20-year period for adverse possession had expired, the neighbor might have been willing to deed back the land to the student's parents.

The Homestead Act of 1862 illustrates ownership through possession. This act allowed those who lived on certain public land to obtain legal ownership of it by possessing it for five years and making certain improvements. Upward of a half million settlers possessed and then gained title to the 160-acre homesteads under the act.

In parts of the world today, governments are granting ownership of land to "squatters" who possess it without legal right. Studies show that this is one of the best ways to distribute land in poor nations. Squatters become owners and can then capitalize land by selling it or borrowing money and putting up the land as collateral.

Some have criticized the "squatter-to-owner" process because many of the new owners sell their land. However, the process enables poor squatters to raise money for the first time. It is also less violent than a situation where squatting alone occurs, and squatters may have to defend their possession by force. Further, it is more efficient than for the government to specify that the land cannot change ownership. In U.S. history there were numerous instances in which legal title was given to settlers who at first possessed land by squatting. Many of them, too, sold their land after receiving legal title to it.

Peruvian economist Hernando de Soto believes that nations can strengthen their economies through the "squatter-to-owner" process.

6. ACQUIRING RESOURCES THROUGH CONFUSION

Ownership through **confusion** arises when *fungible* goods (i.e., goods that are identical) are mixed together. The common example involves grain in a silo when two or more batches of separately owned grain are mixed together. If the confusion occurs by honest mistake or agreement, the owners of the originally separate goods now own a proportional share of the confused goods. Careful records of who owned what grain must be kept since lacking evidence, a court in the case of dispute will assume that everyone claiming the confused mass owns an equal share. If a court determines that the confusion was intentionally wrongful, perhaps done by someone willfully attempting to defraud another, the court will grant ownership of the entire confused mass to the innocent party.

The doctrine of confusion also illustrates the importance of *boundaries* to the concept of property, and it explains one determination of ownership when resource boundaries are not certain. Problems of where boundaries lie are common, however, to various types of resources. Boundaries to the ownership of the water in a creek that crosses your land may be measured by a certain volume of water per minute. Landowners upstream may legally not be able to divert that flow.

Be aware that disputes arise concerning not only boundary problems involving physical location but they concern also boundaries of permissible uses of things.

7. ACQUIRING RESOURCES THROUGH ACCESSION

When the owner of an old airplane engine has it restored and has an airplane built around it, the owner of the engine now owns the entire airplane through the doctrine of **accession,** which refers to something "added." Normally, this is not a problem, but suppose a thief steals the engine, repairs it, and builds it into an airplane. A court will likely grant ownership of the entire airplane to the engine's owner.

However, if the builder *accidentally* picked up someone else's engine and builds it into an airplane, a court will probably give ownership of the airplane to the builder, requiring only that the builder adequately compensate the engine's original owner. An exception gives ownership of the entire airplane to the engine's owner if the engine is substantially more valuable than the additions to it. The court may even require the engine's owner to pay for the valuable additions.

The law of accession also explains that when you apply your efforts or ingenuity to any raw materials you own and change their nature into finished products, you own the finished products. Generally, because you own your efforts, you own what they produce, whether it is an airplane, a paycheck (through exchange), or a work of art. Much of the property foundation of the modern private market arises from the right to exclude others legally from what you own and what you add to that.

The philosopher John Locke, whose ideas were very important to the framers of the U.S. Constitution, said that the principle of property was justified when someone contributed labor to a previously unowned natural resource. In other words, if people own themselves and their work efforts and transform something previously unowned into something new by their work, they also own the new thing. This view and the rule of accession have strong similarities.

> Can you explain how Locke used the concept of **accession** to justify how people come to own previously unowned things?

8. ACQUIRING RESOURCES THROUGH GIFT

Receiving a **gift** is also a way of acquiring ownership. In the making of a gift, no mutual exchange of resources occurs. Instead, a *donor* who owns something gives it to a *donee*, who becomes the new owner. The rules of gift specify that the gift does not generally take place until the donor (1) *intends* to make the gift, and (2) *delivers* the gift by physical transfer to the donee. Note that in some instances, a *constructive delivery*, like turning over the keys to a car or the deed to land, constitutes an adequate delivery.

A particular kind of gift is a *testamentary gift*, or one that is made through a will. The rules of such a gift pass ownership not by delivery but upon the death of the donor (called a "testator") and the proving of a valid will that specifies the gift. Some people believe that the purpose of a property system is to stimulate efforts to generate further wealth which benefits society. They argue that permitting people to pass property to vast fortunes through testamentary gifts does not give incentive to those who receive such gifts. What do you think? How would the behavior of owners change during their lifetimes if they could not make testamentary gifts?

> In your opinion, what justifies people being able to pass large wealth on to their children through testamentary gifts?

9. TYPES OF OWNERSHIP

The law allows division of resource ownership into various types, or degrees. This division is another indication of how sensitive property law is in allowing owners to do exactly what they need and want with their resources: Not all states still use the common law terms that follow, but all states recognize the various aspects of ownership that the terms represent. *These terms usually apply to land ownership, but ownership of movable and intangible things can be held practically in the same way.*

1. Fee simple. The bundle of rights and powers of land ownership are called an **estate**. **Fee simple** represents the maximum estate allowed under law, the owner having the fullest legal rights and powers to possess, use, and transfer the land. The fee simple *absolute* estate has no limitations or conditions attached. The fee simple *defeasible* may have a condition attached to its conveyance (transfer). For example, a seller may convey land to a buyer "as long as it is used for agricultural purposes." If the new

owner (buyer) develops the land for other than agricultural purposes, the ownership goes back to the original owner (seller).

2. Life estate. A **life estate** grants an ownership in land for the lifetime of a specified person. "To Brodie Davis for her life" grants such an estate. Upon Brodie Davis's death the land reverts to the original grantor who is said to keep a *reversion* interest in the land. If the land goes to someone other than the grantor upon Brodie Davis's death, that person has a *remainder* interest. Reversion and remainder property interests are also called *future* interests as opposed to the life estate, which is a *present* interest. Subject to any attached conditions, all of these estates can be capitalized or transferred. For example, it is possible to borrow upon or sell a future interest.

Having a **life estate** means that the property fence only protects your interest in something for your lifetime.

3. Leasehold estate. A **leasehold estate** is simply the property right granted to tenants by a landlord. Although it is not common to think of tenants as "owners," they do in a meaningful way have an estate or property. Tenants have a qualified possession, use, and transfer of the land, qualified in that they cannot *waste* the land, which means do something that substantially reduces the value of the land. For an apartment tenant to rip up carpeting and knock holes in the walls would be a waste of the interest in the land. The landlord could terminate the lease and sue the tenant.

When you lease an apartment for a year, what is it that you own?

Unless prohibited by the lease, the rights owned by tenants can be capitalized by transfer to someone else. Thus, unless prohibited, a tenant who is paying $3,000 per month under a two-year lease of an office can sell the balance of time remaining on the lease at $5,000 per month. Many leases, however, do require that a tenant obtain approval from a landlord, or even of the other tenants, before transferring lease rights.

A landlord may lease land for a *definite duration* of time like two years, or for an *indefinite duration* with rent payable at periodic intervals like monthly, or simply *at will*, which means "for as long as both shall agree." State law generally specifies that the landlord and tenant must give each other written notice of 30 or 60 days in order to terminate a lease that does not run for a definite duration.

4. Concurrent ownership. Both personal and real property interests can have concurrent owners. That is, more than one person can own the same thing. The ownership is undivided, meaning that no concurrent owner owns a specific piece of the resources that are owned. The shareholders of a corporation are concurrent owners as are the partners of a partnership. In fact, concurrent ownership greatly facilitates almost all forms of modern private enterprise.

Other forms of concurrent ownership include the **joint tenancy** and the **tenancy in common.** In both of these forms of ownership, the property interest is undivided, but the tenants in common can own different shares of the resource (e.g., two-thirds and one-third), whereas the joint tenants must have equal ownership shares (e.g., one-half and one-half). On the other hand, joint tenants, but not tenants in common, can have the *right of survivorship*. This right means that if one of the joint tenants dies, the remaining tenant becomes the sole owner of the entire resource. To create a joint tenancy requires special words, such as "convey to X and Y as

The surviving tenant in a joint tenancy with right of survivorship becomes the sole owner of the entire resource, usually interests in land.

joint tenants, and not as tenants in common, together with the right of survivorship."

The owners themselves, or the creditors, of a joint tenancy or tenancy in common can usually force the separation of these concurrent ownerships under the doctrine of *partition*.

10. TITLE AND PROPERTY REGISTRATION

Land, automobiles, and in many states, boats, require a registration of ownership called title.

Ownership is frequently referred to by the term **title.** Thus, someone who owns something has title to it. When an owner transfers ownership, the owner is said to "pass title." For specific types of resources the law requires that the title be represented by a physical document registered with the state. The title to an automobile is one example of such an ownership document that must be registered with the state. Many states also require the registration of boat titles.

A **deed** is the document of title that transfers ownership of land. The deed contains a precise legal description of the land that specifies the exact location and boundaries according to a mapping or surveying system. Without this description, few buyers or lenders would be willing to risk their money on the land. That exact, accepted boundaries identify land ownership provides the basis for much capital formation.

What does it mean to say that a quitclaim deed does not convey ownership?

Even knowing the precise location of the land does not always ensure that there are no problems with the ownership. A lender may have a mortgage claim against the land, or the grantor of a deed may have conveyed the land to more than one person. There are two protections against these problems. First, the kind of deed the buyer receives from the seller can protect the buyer. A *warranty deed* promises the grantee (usually, the buyer) that the grantor (seller) has good ownership and the full power to convey it. The buyer can sue the seller if someone else claims the land. A *special warranty deed* specifies that certain legal claims against the land, like mortgages, exist but guarantees that no other claims exist. A *quitclaim deed* makes no guarantees other than that the grantor surrenders all claim against the land. Several other types of deeds may apply in certain states.

Second, buyers and lenders are protected by registration statutes. The law enables buyers to register their deeds to land and lenders to register their mortgage claims against land. Potential buyers or other lenders are thus put on notice regarding the land, and the legal owner or claimant is legally and publicly identified. By going to the county courthouse or other place of record, you can often trace the ownership history of a piece of land for 200 years or more.

:: Specialty Applications of Property

The following sections discuss specialty applications of property. Generally, the private legal fence of property allows an owner to exclude others from interfering with (1) the possession of an object or resource, (2) the transfer of the object or interest by gift or through exchange with other owners, and (3) all uses of the object that do not harm other owners in what belongs to them. However, a number of specialty applications are quite narrow and one or more of the three general property characteristics may be lacking. In fact, many scholars do not recognize some of the specialty applications discussed here to apply to property at all. However, we note that all of these specialty applications involve some object or interest that is legally exclusive in some important fashion, leading us to believe these applications deserve the name "property."

11. EASEMENTS

An **easement** places a particular use of land behind the exclusive legal fence. Usually, this use involves the right of passage across the land, for example, when a timbering company has purchased the right to bring its harvest of trees out across an owner's land. Once the easement has been acquired, the timbering company can exclude others, especially the titleholder of the land, from interfering with passage of its trucks across the land. An easement can also be reserved in a deed, for example, when Martina sells a piece of her land to George and the deed reserves an easement for George to cross over Martina's remaining land. Easements can also involve such uses as the laying of water pipes or the stringing of power wires across land.

An easement can be acquired in various ways. For instance, it can be bought directly from a titleholder, or reserved in a deed as part of the purchase and sale of land. At common law owners of land also had a *natural easement* (also called easement by necessity) to get from their land to the nearest public road. A *negative easement* means that an adjoining landowner cannot do anything that would cause your land to cave in or collapse, such as digging a ditch that would cause the land on your side to collapse. Finally, an *easement by prescription* arises when one person has used another's land, such as by crossing it openly, wrongfully, and continuously for a period of years (frequently 20), and once an easement by prescription arises, a titleholder of the land can no longer prevent a person from continuing to use the land by crossing it. The titleholder cannot now use the land in such a way to prevent the easement holder from crossing it, and the easement holder can legally exclude a titleholder from trying to prevent passage.

Statutes in many states set standards for easements and their acquisition. The easements mentioned here merely give you a general idea about these specialty applications of property.

12. BAILMENTS

In many common situations, an owner puts an object protected by personal property into the intentional possession of another person with the understanding that the other person must return the object at some point or otherwise dispose of it. This property arrangement is known as a **bailment,** with the owner known as the **bailor** and the possessor of the object known as the **bailee.** Bailments arise when you store something in a warehouse, rent furniture from the rental store, lease a piece of equipment, loan your lawnmower to a neighbor, or store your car in a friend's garage while you are on vacation. Can you figure out in each instance who is the bailor and who is the bailee? Bailments fall into three categories:

- For the sole benefit of the bailor.
- For the sole benefit of the bailee.
- For the mutual benefit of both parties.

An **easement** is often a right to cross over land.

Can you explain the three different types of bailments?

Think about the examples mentioned above. Do you understand that storing your car in a friend's garage while you are on vacation is a bailment for the sole benefit of the bailor and that the furniture and equipment rentals are mutual benefit bailments? The loan of your mower to your neighbor to mow the grass is a bailment for the sole benefit of the bailee. Consider the following situation: you go to a business meeting at a hotel, removing your expensive leather coat, and hanging it on a hanger in a small room provided by the hotel. The coat turns up missing. Is the hotel responsible as a bailee? Would the situation have been different if the hotel had someone taking care of coats? The answers depend on whether or not the hotel has taken *intentional* possession of the coat, and it is likely that merely by providing a coat hanger, the hotel is not taking intentional possession of the coat. But if a hotel employee hangs up the coat for you, the hotel becomes a bailee.

In the business world, most bailments are of mutual benefit to both parties. Although the bailee has an absolute duty to return the object to the bailor (or to dispose out of it as the bailor directs), and becomes liable to the bailor for failing to do so correctly, an issue often arises when something happens to the object while it is in the bailee's possession and control. What if someone steals it? What if a natural disaster, called "an act of God," destroys it, or it is damaged in an accident? To understand the potential liability from these events, you have to understand the legal duty the bailee is under. In a mutual benefit bailment, such as a rental arrangement, the bailee is under a duty to use "reasonable care" in taking care of the object in possession, but if an Act of God destroys or damages the object, the bailee is not likely liable to the bailor. However, see Sidebar 7.5.

:: *sidebar* 7.5

Follow Instructions or Else

Roger, a graduate student, leases a car from Acme Car Dealership in Texas. The lease contract contains a clause that limits Roger's driving to the United States. However, Roger drives the car over the border down to Mexico City where an earthquake causes a building to collapse on the car after Roger parks it on the street. Although in mutual benefit bailments such as this one, the bailee is not often responsible to the bailor for acts of God, in this instance by using an an a car in a way specifically prohibited by the bailor, Roger becomes liable to the car dealership in spite of the fact his fault did not cause the damage to the car. When a bailee uses an object in a way not authorized or prohibited by the bailor, the bailee becomes absolutely liable as an "insurer" for anything that happens to it.

Another example of this liability arises when a bailee returns an object improperly. In one instance a wealthy woman bought expensive jewelry on approval from Tiffany's, promising the manager to return the jewelry to him personally if she did not wish to keep it. Several days later there was a knock on her door and a man dressed in a Tiffany's uniform asked if she wished to return the jewelry, which she did, and she returned the jewelry to the man, who turned out to be a thief in a stolen uniform. Tiffany's sued for the jewelry's price and won because the bailee became absolutely liable for loss when she returned the jewelry improperly.

In a bailment for the sole benefit of a bailor, the bailee owes only a slight duty of care while the object is in the bailee's possession, but in a bailment for the sole benefit of the bailee, such as where the bailee has borrowed the object, the bailee owes a very high duty of care, one that is greater than merely what is "reasonable." These duties of care become important when the parties are negotiating a settlement, or when a judge is instructing a jury about the bailee's responsibility to the bailor. Many times it may be difficult for a bailor who sues a bailee to prove why the object in the bailee's possession has been damaged and how the bailee has breached the duty of care. Therefore, the law presumes that the bailee has breached the duty of care when the bailee cannot return the object to the bailor in proper condition, placing the burden of proof on the bailee to prove that she has met the duty of care.

> When your roommate borrows your car and returns it with a dent in it, the law makes your roommate liable unless she can prove she has met the duty of extremely high care.

The bailor also has duties to the bailee. In a mutual benefit bailment, the bailor must pay the bailee for storing or otherwise keeping possession of something, such as when the bailee is a warehouse. According to the type of bailment, the bailor also warrants or guarantees that she has no knowledge of defects in the objects bailed or no knowledge of defects that could have been discovered through reasonable inspection. In a number of states, courts have made merchants in mutual benefit bailments liable for any defect in a bailed object that causes personal injury.

Many states have laws that apply to particular kinds of bailments, such as those involving common carriers, warehouses, and innkeepers (hotels). In particular, these bailees are often able to limit their potential liability to bailors for damage to the bailed objects, for example, by inserting contractual terms that limit compensation to a certain value. Common carriers, which include airlines, railroads, and public trucking companies, carry packages for the public. Common carriers are also not responsible for acts of God or of public enemies, the acts of the bailor in failing to package properly, defects in the packaged object itself, or acts of the public authority (such as the stopping of a truck carrying produce at a state border because of concern about plant disease).

> You should read the terms of a bailment contract very carefully.

In legal terms, a bailor is usually not considered to have "property" regarding the bailed object. However, the bailor has both possession and control over the object and can exclude the rest of the world, including the bailor in some instances, from interfering with this possession and control. For this reason, we are treating bailments as a specialty application of property, although they are often a very narrow one.

:: Property and Security Interests

In a property-based legal system resources can be highly divisible. Importantly, they are divisible both in specific type and by time. Sellers can transfer resources to buyers now and depend upon getting paid for these resources later. That is a subject of contract law, which begins in the next chapter. The following sections, however, deal with how sellers can increase their confidence in the risky business of transferring goods, rendering services, and making loans by securing particular types of property interests in something usually possessed by the buyer. These property interests are usually conditional and end when a buyer-debtor fulfills some condition, frequently repayment of what is owed. The two principal types of **security interests** are mortgages and secured transactions under Article 9 of the Uniform Commercial Code.

Many scholars do not appreciate that these security interests are in fact property applications because these interests are not physical objects. But they involve a legal fence that protects the holder of the security interest from the general claims of all other persons, and if the buyer-debtor (from here on,

> How is a security interest a property arrangement?

just *debtor*), fails to comply with the condition, the seller-creditor (from here on, just *creditor* or *secured party*) can usually seize (and/or sell) the object of the security interest to help satisfy the obligation of repayment. Identifying security interests as applications of property helps explain why we say that property, the concept of the private fence, is the central concept of capitalism and private markets.

13. SECURITY INTERESTS IN LAND

The major way that small business owners raise money to begin their businesses is through mortgaging their homes.

Security interests in land and the structures on the land include mortgages, deeds of trust, and land sales contracts. As observed at the beginning of this chapter, the major way that small business owners raise money to begin their businesses is through mortgaging their homes. They borrow money from a bank or financial institution and in return give that creditor a security interest called a *mortgage* on their homes and the land associated with their homes. In recent years it has also become quite common for homeowners in their capacity as consumers to take out a mortgage on their homes in order to access the value of their homes for purchases they wish to make.

Similar to mortgages are **deeds of trust.** Under the deed of trust, a borrower signs a *note,* which shows the borrower's debt to the lender, and then signs a deed of trust, which grants the lender a security interest in the building and land put up to secure the loan. The deed is held by a third party called a *trustee* who holds full legal ownership to the land. Under this arrangement the debtor will obtain legal ownership, or *title,* only when the deed has been repaid.

Unimproved land and farmland are often sold through land sales contracts. Under a **land sales contract,** the owner of land sells it by contract subject to the condition that the seller retains title to the land until the buyer pays the purchase price. Until that time, the buyer has the legal right to possess and use the land and is responsible for paying taxes and insurance.

Recording Statutes   Generally, mortgages and deeds of trust must be registered in a recording office in the county where the land is located. Recording gives notice of the security interest to potential buyers of the land and to potential lenders who will then consider that fact in determining whether or not to buy the land or to loan money. That potential buyers or lenders become aware of the mortgage is important since the land is subject to satisfy the mortgagee's debt whether or not the land is sold or a subsequent mortgage is taken out on the land.

If mortgagees failed to record mortgages, new buyers of the lands who are unaware of mortgages will take the lands free and clear of the mortgages.

If **mortgagees** (the creditors) fail to record mortgages, new buyers of the lands who are unaware of mortgages will take the lands free and clear of the mortgages, although the debts will still be owed by the **mortgagors** (debtors). Likewise, a creditor who registers a subsequent mortgage on land, being unfamiliar with the unrecorded first mortgage, will have priority over the first mortgage.

Foreclosure, Deficiency, and Redemption   Almost all states regulate how mortgagees can exercise their property interest when the obligation owed to them is not satisfied. **Foreclosure** is the term used for the exercise of the secured property interest, and foreclosure usually means that the creditor must go through the court system to ensure that procedures are properly followed before debtors lose their homes and land. Foreclosure as it relates to land sales contracts is generally simpler and less expensive to exercise than foreclosure of mortgages and deeds of trust. Foreclosure means that the court will order the land sold to satisfy the debt owed, usually by auction to the highest bidder, with any excess after payment of what is owed to the secured creditor going to the debtor.

You should appreciate that the property represented by these types of security interests is separate from the loan obligation owed by the debtor-mortgagor. In many states, if foreclosure and auction does not produce enough money to satisfy the debt owed by the mortgagor, the creditor-mortgagee can still sue the debtor for the balance owed, called a **deficiency.** Some states, however, have passed statutes, called *antideficiency judgment statutes,* that prevent mortgagees from obtaining anything else from mortgagors once the land has been foreclosed and auctioned. These statutes generally only apply to protect homeowners.

Before the actual foreclosure, most states permit a **right of redemption,** which allows the mortgagor to get back the land upon payment of the full amount of the debt, including all interest and costs. Even after foreclosure some states have a statutory period of redemption, usually six months or one year after foreclosure, in which the mortgagor can redeem the land from a new buyer. If a first mortgagor fails to redeem, most states permit second mortgage holders to redeem the land.

In 2008 a huge scandal broke out regarding the so-called subprime mortgages. The scandal had little to do with the mortgage rules discussed here, but related to the eagerness of borrowers to obtain homes that they could not afford to buy if interest rates went up under their mortgages, which were adjustable according to the rate of inflation, and the eagerness of financial institutions to make money by loaning to these borrowers, obtaining secured debts, then turning around and reselling the debts in complex financial packages as investments. The collapse of the subprime market has severely injured many financial institutions, caused many hundreds of thousands of homeowners to lose their homes, and has led to new regulation of how financial institutions may loan money to mortgagors.

> The **right of redemption** allows a mortgagor, before foreclosure, to get back land upon payment of the full amount of the debt. Statutory redemption allows a mortgagor to regain ownership of the land upon payment of all interest and costs for a period of time after foreclosure.

14. SECURED TRANSACTIONS

Article 9 of the Uniform Commercial Code is the principal set of laws controlling security interests in objects of personal property. Article 9 contains the law of **secured transactions.** This law is highly complicated and technical, and what follows merely introduces you to some of the concepts found in Article 9. A secured transaction involves a creditor who has sold something on credit or made a loan to a debtor who agrees to give the creditor a security interest in a valuable object, called **collateral.**

Secured transaction law applies to a variety of things, including consumer goods (which are not bought for business purposes), farm products, inventory, equipment, stocks, bonds, negotiable instruments (orders or promises to pay in a certain form, such as checks), valuable documents such as those transferring goods, accounts receivable (money owed, but not in a certain form like negotiable instruments), and "general intangibles" like interests in patents, trademarks, and copyrights. A security interest in any of these things

> Article 9 of the Uniform Commercial Code covers the law of secured transactions.

> Explain to yourself how **attachment** takes place.

arises when it attaches. **Attachment** takes place when (1) a secured party has given value, (2) the debtor owns the collateral, and (3) a security agreement is given. This agreement must be in writing, signed by the debtor, and contain a reasonable description of the collateral. The collateral may include not only things currently owned by the debtor but collateral known as *after-acquired property* that the debtor acquires in the future. Proceeds realized from the sale of the collateral can also be covered by the security interest.

Perfection As soon as the security interest attaches it is effective against the debtor, but to be effective against third parties, such as other creditors and people to whom the collateral may be sold or transferred, the secured party must *perfect* the security interest. **Perfection** arises when a security interest has attached and the creditor has taken all proper steps required by Article 9. A creditor perfects a security interest differently according to the type of collateral.

Be able to discuss all the different ways that **perfection** can take place.

The general way of perfecting a security interest under Article 9 is to file a **financing statement.** The form of the financing statement differs from state to state, but the statement should contain the names and addresses of the creditor and debtor, a reasonable description of the collateral, and the signature of the debtor. Financing statements expire five years after the date of filing unless a maturity date is stated and are usually filed in the county where the collateral is located or with an office of the state government, depending on the state and the type of collateral. Financing statements are appropriate to perfect any type of collateral except negotiable ones, which can always be transferred free of a secured creditor's claim unless they are kept in the creditor's possession.

A PMSI secures the purchase price of goods bought for personal or household use.

Some types of security interests are perfected by attachment alone, for example, a **purchase money security interest (PMSI)** in consumer goods, meaning a security interest that secures the purchase price of goods bought for personal or household use. Such security interests perfect as soon as they properly attach. Similarly, there is a temporary 21-day perfection in negotiable instruments or documents as soon as they attach, which allows the creditor time to take possession of these valuables. An automatic 10-day perfection in proceeds realized from the sale of collateral also exists even if the perfected security interest in the original collateral did not mention proceeds.

15. PRIORITY PROBLEMS AND EXAMPLES

Consider the following problems and examples that illustrate the complexity of determining the outcomes of several different situations involving secured creditors. Are you sure you want to be a business attorney?

1. A secured creditor with an attached security interest has priority over a creditor without a security interest. However, a secured creditor does not have priority over a purchaser who gives value for collateral and takes it before a security interest is perfected.

2. John loans Carl $5,000 and attaches a security interest in Carl's printing machinery. John's security interest takes priority against a judgment creditor who tries to seize the machinery to satisfy a damage award.

An attached security interest wins over an unattached creditor's claim, but if neither a creditor's claim nor a security interest has attached, the first to attach has priority.

3. A perfected security interest has priority over one that is not perfected but merely attached. If John loans Carl $5,000 on April 5 and attaches a security interest in the printing machinery on that day, John will lose priority to the bank that has filed a financing statement perfecting a security interest in the same machinery on April 15.

4. In the same situation, if John perfects his security interest on April 18, he still loses to the bank. Generally, when two creditors each have a perfected security interest, the creditor to perfect first has priority over the other, and the times the security interests attached are not important.

5. However, an exception to the rule in (3) occurs in that a PMSI in non-inventory collateral, such as a printing machine for a print shop, which is received on August 1, takes priority over a bank's perfected financing statement in "all equipment presently owned or after acquired" that is perfected in the printing shop's equipment on July 9, *but only if the August 1 creditor perfects within a statutory period defined by state law, frequently 20 days.*

6. Likewise, if a publishing company sells books to a retail bookstore on credit, and has a purchase money security interest in the books sold, which will go into the inventory of the bookstore, the publishing company will have priority over a secured creditor like a bank that has previously filed a financing statement on the bookstore's "present inventory and after-acquired inventory," but *only if the publishing company has perfected its interest in the inventory at the time the bookstore receives the books.* Also, the publisher must check financing statements covering the bookstore's inventory, which are a matter of public record, and inform previously perfected security interests of the publisher's PMSI, and must describe the new inventory to them.

7. Print shop B that buys a piece of printing machinery from print shop A in another town will find that the machinery is still subject to the security interest held by a bank that has filed a proper financing statement on the machinery prior to B's purchase. However, a **buyer in the ordinary course of business** will have priority over a perfected security interest, meaning that if the seller of the printing machinery is a manufacturer of that machinery and is selling *in the ordinary course of business,* a buyer would take the machinery free and clear of a bank's previously perfected security interest. Note that in this latter instance the bank does continue to have a security interest for a period of time in the proceeds realized from the sale of the machinery that will have priority over a judgment creditor or a trustee in bankruptcy.

8. Susan sells her computer to Greg for his personal use and a computer store holding a PMSI in the computer attempts to repossess it from Greg. The rule is that if Greg had no knowledge of the security interest he takes the computer free and clear of the computer store's perfected interest.

9. Artisan's liens and mechanic's liens usually have priority over even perfected Article 9 security interests. See Sidebar 7.6.

Generally, a creditor with an attached security interest has priority over a creditor without a security interest, a creditor with a perfected security interest has priority over one whose security interest has not been perfected, and when two creditors have perfected security interests the one whose interest was perfected first has priority.

A **buyer in the ordinary course of business** has priority over a perfected security interest.

:: *sidebar* 7.6

Artisan's Liens and Mechanic's Liens

You take your car to the garage for a new transmission but when the work is complete, the credit card company refuses to extend additional credit, asserting that your limit has been reached. You are unable to pay the garage for its materials and labor. The garage can legally refuse to release your car until you have paid it. This is because the garage has an **artisan's lien** on your car, a narrow property interest that arises when someone who contributes parts and/or services to an object of personal property is not paid. This lien has priority over even an Article 9 perfected security interest held by the bank that loaned you the money to buy the car. This result is so because the garage has added value to the car by its parts and labor, and if the garage has to sell the car, it can only realize the value of the parts and labor it added. An artisan's lien is *possessory*, meaning that generally the lien has

priority only as long as the creditor keeps possession of the collateral.

A **mechanic's lien** arises when someone contributes materials and/or services to real estate, usually a building, and is not paid. Unlike the artisan's lien, this lien is not possessory and has priority only if it is perfected by the filing of a written notice, usually in the county where the real estate is found. This lien also has priority over an Article 9 perfected security interest when a fixture, an object of personal property like a carpet, is incorporated into real estate by becoming a physical part of it. The carpet can be subject to a perfected security interest that will follow the carpet's incorporation into the real estate if the owner of the real estate receives the required notice. However, a mechanic's lien that adds value to the real estate has priority over a perfected security interest in a fixture.

A secured creditor can repossess collateral only if the repossession is peaceful.

After a debtor has defaulted, which usually means it has failed to repay the credit that the secured creditor extended, the secured creditor may peacefully repossess the collateral without going to court unless the debtor orally protests the repossession, in which case the secured party will have to obtain a court order to repossess. Following repossession, the secured creditor can dispose of the collateral in any "commercially reasonable" fashion, such as sale or lease, and must return to the debtor any excess money realized over the amount owed. The secured party can also propose to keep the collateral in complete satisfaction of the debt.

:: Limitations on Property and the Common Good

Some people consider private property to be an unacceptably selfish social principle. Karl Marx said in the *Communist Manifesto* that the first thing communists should do when coming to power is to abolish "private property." Yet this chapter argues that the tremendous national wealth created by a fairly enforced private property system justifies the institution of private property. In other words, private property serves the common good or general welfare of the nation. Importantly, private property has limits, and these limits tell us that an individual private property right is always subject at some point to the right of others. Further, individual private property gives way to the common good of society both through eminent domain and taxation, which are recognized by the U.S. Constitution. Read the sections that follow and develop your own view of private property and the common good.

16. PROPERTY, THE USE OF RESOURCES, AND THE EQUAL RIGHT OF OTHERS

In law, property is not a *thing*. It is an owner's *right* to exclude others from resources. One of the most important resources is the use owners can make of another resource, for example, a piece of land. Owners can build a house, a shopping mall, or a skyscraper on their land. Or farm it. Or leave it unoccupied. They can take their money and open a computer store with it, or save it for retirement, or invest it in the stock market. All of these ways of using resources come within the legal guarantee of property. Implied in the exclusive rights to private resources is the legal protection to use them in many ways. This quality helps make the marketplace dynamic and responsive to needs and wants.

In an important and meaningful sense, owners also have a property in using their efforts. They have an exclusive right to direct their resource in themselves any way they wish. They can use it to pursue any line of employment, or they can leave the job market and do volunteer work for Meals on Wheels. Or go back to school for an MBA. Or retire on their savings and garden, travel, or watch football.

Having a property right to direct the resources of one's efforts and to be able to exclude others from the further resources one acquires with these efforts is closely related to other concepts like "freedom" and "liberty." The American colonists and the framers of the Constitution certainly thought so. John Dickinson, who helped draft the Constitution, observed that Americans "cannot be happy, without freedom; nor free, without security of property; nor so secure, unless the sole power to dispose of it be lodged within themselves." Revolutionary War diplomat Arthur Lee wrote, "The right of property is the guardian of every other right, and to deprive people of this, is in fact to deprive them of their liberty." In 1768 a colonial American observed, "Liberty and Property are not only join'd in common discourse, but are in their own natures so nearly ally'd [allied], that we cannot be said to possess the one without the other." The early Americans firmly believed they had a property not only in their material possessions but also in liberty, speech, and other rights. In summary, they had an exclusive right to use freely their resource in themselves and the resources produced by their efforts.

Generally speaking, owners are prohibited from using their resources in ways that harm or injure the resources of other owners. As James Madison explained, the concept of property "leaves to everyone else a like advantage." Under the rule of law, a property system protects the equal right of all to their resources, including the resources they have in themselves. Tort law (Chapter 10), criminal law (Chapter 12), and much of the regulatory law discussed throughout this book attempt to prevent owners from using their resources to injure the resources that belong to others. See also Sidebar 7.7.

Two limits on land use that protect the equal right of all landowners is especially relevant to this chapter. They involve the law of nuisance and zoning.

> Explain what it means to say that you have a property in your efforts. How is such a property related to *liberty?*

17. NUISANCE AND ZONING

The law limits certain uses of one's land through the doctrine of nuisance. What constitutes a nuisance is somewhat vague, but in most jurisdictions the common law cases have been put in statutory form. Several common elements

:: *sidebar* 7.7

The Property System and Corporate Governance

Chapter 1 explained why the issues of corporate governance are property issues. The explanation bears reemphasizing.

The property system allows us to enjoy exclusive resources. It protects our resources from the harm of others, but at the same time it limits us from harming the resources of others. Corporate governance illustrates how this property system functions.

In the *specific* sense, corporate governance laws protect the investment resources of corporate owners, or shareholders. These laws define the authority and responsibility of the board of directors, who are elected by the shareholders. The laws also regulate the managers appointed by the board.

In the *broad* sense, corporate governance also includes those laws that protect the resources of others from harm by the corporation. Such laws include antitrust laws, employment discrimination and employee protection laws, environmental protection laws, and a great many antifraud laws.

Sometimes the law does not protect the boundary between what is *mine* and what is *yours*. Sometimes there is disagreement about where proper boundaries lie. Sometimes we have failures of corporate governance. But under a system that permits private resource ownership, corporate governance issues are property issues.

exist in the law of nuisance in most states. To begin with, there are two types of nuisance: public and private.

A **public nuisance** is one arising from some use of land that causes inconvenience or damage to the public. For example, discharging industrial waste from one's land that kills the fish in a river constitutes a public nuisance since fishing rights are publicly held. Public nuisance claims may be brought only by a public official, not private individuals, unless the latter have suffered some special damage to their property as a result of the public nuisance. Note that many public nuisances can also violate various regulatory laws, such as environmental laws (see Chapter 18).

Any unreasonable use of one's property so as to cause substantial interference with the enjoyment or use of another's land establishes a common law **private nuisance.** The unreasonableness of the interference is measured by a balancing process in which the character, extent, and duration of harm to the plaintiff is weighed against the social utility of the defendant's activity and its appropriateness to its location. Since society needs industrial activity as well as natural tranquility, people must put up with a certain amount of smoke, dust, noise, and polluted water if they live in concentrated areas of industry. But what may be an appropriate industrial use of land in a congested urban area may be a private nuisance if it occurs in a rural or residential location.

Once the plaintiff establishes a substantial and unreasonable interference with the use or enjoyment of his or her property, the court must decide what remedy the plaintiff is entitled to. The court may award damages if the plaintiff has suffered economic loss, but when damages are inadequate the court may also order the defendant to do something, like correct the problem, or else cease the nuisance-creating activity. In determining whether to issue an injunction, the court will take into consideration (1) the relative economic hardship that will be placed upon the parties if such relief is granted, and (2) the public interest in the continuation of the defendant's

A **private nuisance** is an *unreasonable* use of one's property so as to cause substantial interference with the enjoyment or use of another's land.

activity. This balancing of interests required by nuisance law can bring about some unusual remedies.

Can you see how nuisance law attempts to balance the equal right of all in the property system? It does so by preventing landowners from *unreasonably* interfering with other publicly and privately owned resources. Determining what is unreasonable is an ongoing and controversial process in a property-based legal system. Consider Case 7.1.

 case **7.1** ::

SPUR INDUSTRIES, INC. v. DEL E. WEBB DEVELOPMENT CO.
494 P. 2d 700 (1972)

Near Phoenix, Arizona, Spur Industries owned a large cattle feedlot, and at the same time the Del Webb Development Co. was developing a residential area known as Sun City. The lots being sold on the tract of land that Del Webb owned were moving closer and closer to the feedlot. Finally, Del Webb sued Spur, arguing that Spur's feeding operation was a public nuisance because of the flies and odor which were being blown into the residential areas. Del Webb sought a permanent injunction ordering Spur to shut down and/or move. The case finally reached the Arizona Supreme Court.

CAMERON: . . . In the so-called "coming to the nuisance" cases, the courts have held that the residential landowner may not have relief if he knowingly came into a neighborhood reserved for industrial or agricultural endeavors and has been damaged thereby. . . . [e.g., a Kansas court stated]:

> Plaintiffs chose to live in an area uncontrolled by zoning laws or restrictive covenants. In such an area plaintiffs cannot complain that legitimate agricultural pursuits are being carried on in the vicinity, nor can plaintiffs having chosen to build in an agricultural area, complain that the agricultural pursuits carried on in the area depreciate the value of their homes. The area being primarily agricultural, any opinion reflecting the value of such property must take this factor into account. The standards affecting the value of residence property in an urban setting, subject to zoning controls and controlled planning techniques, cannot be the standards by which agricultural properties are judge.
>
> People employed in a city who build their homes in suburban areas of the county beyond the limits of a city and zoning regulations do so for a reason. Some do so to avoid the high taxation rate imposed by cities, or to avoid special assessments for street, sewer and water projects. They usually build on improved or hard surface highways, which have been built either at state or county expense and thereby avoid special assessments for these improvements. It may be that they desire to get away from the congestion of traffic, smoke, noise, foul air and the many other annoyances of city life. But with all these advantages in going beyond the area which is zoned and restricted to protect them in their homes, they must be prepared to take the disadvantages. . . .

Were Webb the only party injured, we would feel justified in holding that the doctrine of "coming to the nuisance" would have been a bar to the relief asked by Webb, and, on the other hand, had Spur located the feedlot near the outskirts of a city and had the city grown toward the feedlot, Spur would have to suffer the cost of abating the nuisance as to those people locating within the growth pattern of the expanding city. . . .

There was no indication in the instant case at the time Spur and its predecessors located in western Maricopa County that a new city would spring up, full-blown, alongside the feeding operation and that the developer of that city would ask the court to order Spur to move because of the new city. Spur is required to move not because of any wrongdoing on the part of Spur, but because of a proper and legitimate regard of the courts for the rights and interests of the public.

Del Webb, on the other hand, is entitled to the relief prayed for (a permanent injunction), not because Webb is blameless, but because of the damage to the people who have been encouraged to purchase homes in Sun City. It does not equitably or legally follow, however, that Webb, being entitled to the injunction, is then free of any liability to Spur if Webb has in fact been the cause of the damage Spur has sustained. It does not seem harsh to require a developer, who has taken advantage of the lesser land values in a rural area as well as the availability of large tracts of land on which to build and develop a new town or city in the area, to indemnify those who are forced to leave as a result.

Having brought people to the nuisance to the foreseeable detriment of Spur, Webb must indemnify Spur for a reasonable amount of the cost of moving or shutting down. It should be noted that this relief to Spur is limited to a case wherein a developer has with foreseeability, brought into a previously agricultural or industrial area the population which makes necessary the granting of an injunction against a lawful business and for which the business has no adequate relief.

It is therefore the decision of this court that the matter be remanded to the trial court for a hearing upon the damages sustained by the defendant Spur as a reasonable and direct result of the granting of the permanent injunction. Since the result of the appeal may appear novel and both sides have obtained a measure of relief, it is ordered that each side will bear its own costs.

Affirmed in part, reversed in part, and remanded for further proceedings consistent with this opinion.

:: CASE QUESTIONS

1. Describe the businesses of Spur and Del Webb and explain what you think happened leading up to this lawsuit.
2. When Del Webb asserted that the feedlot constituted both a public and a private nuisance, how did Spur respond?
3. What did the court order Spur to do?
4. Why did the court order Del Webb to compensate Spur, which was maintaining a nuisance?

Do you agree with the principle of **zoning ordinances** or not?

Through their exercise of the police powers, states and local governments protect the public health, safety, morals, and general welfare (see Chapter 6). It is under the police powers that a major governmental regulation of land use takes place: zoning. **Zoning ordinances** are generally laws that divide counties or municipalities into use districts designated residential, commercial, or industrial. Zoning limits the use to which land can be put to that specified. For instance, industrial facilities cannot be built in residential districts. Zoning may also specify the height, size, number, and location of buildings that can be built on land. Restricting buildings in a commercial district to no more than eight stories in height is an example. Zoning may additionally impose aesthetic requirements concerning color and exterior design. Zoning boards (or commissions), which are generally agencies of local governments, enforce the zoning ordinances. Owners should always check to determine how zoning limits land use.

An owner can ask a zoning board for a *variance* to allow use of land in a way not permitted under a zoning ordinance. The board is likely to grant a variance only when the owner can prove that the ordinance prevents a reasonable economic return on the land as zoned. Zoning ordinances allow uses of land that existed prior to passage of the ordinances. Such uses are called "nonconforming" uses.

Like nuisance law, zoning regulations are highly controversial because they involve limits on how owners can use their land. The purpose of zoning laws may be to protect the right of all to their lands, but not everyone is going to agree with the limits that zoning laws establish.

18. PROPERTY LIMITATIONS AND THE COMMON GOOD

Even limitations on property illustrate that this exclusive right serves the common good. Several property-related concepts illustrate that when society believes that property no longer promotes the general public welfare, owners lose the resources protected by property:

- Duration limitations
- Eminent domain
- Taxation

Duration Limitations on Property Do not believe for a minute that when you own something you own it forever. For instance the Constitution grants patents and copyrights—only for "limited Times." The reasoning behind the limitation is to ensure that inventions and creative expressions enter the public domain so to serve the common good as quickly as possible after allowing for the profit necessary to encourage people to create new things in the first place.

Patents and copyrights, however, are not the only property concept that limits the duration of an owner's exercise of exclusive right over resources. The **rule against perpetuities** limits all exercise of property over resources to a duration of "lives in being plus twenty-one years." The rule prevents an owner from controlling resources through many future generations by setting up *trust* arrangements, under which trustees are legally required to carry out the wishes of the owner for extended duration. As it is, a trust may not extend the control of an owner beyond twenty-one years of the death of someone who is alive at the time of the owner's death.

*The **rule against perpetuities** serves the common good by preventing dead owners from indefinitely limiting the new productive ways that resources can be used.

19. EMINENT DOMAIN

Zoning and many regulatory limitations on property protect some owners from being harmed by other owners. Eminent domain, however, is quite different. This important concept specifically exists to limit the exclusive right of property in order to serve the common good by allowing the government to take away property-protected resources from owners.

Eminent Domain and the Common Good Jeremy Bentham, a philosopher who lived a century after John Locke, thought that Locke's ideas about property being a natural right from God were "nonsense upon stilts." He called the right of property the "noblest triumph" but believed that property served only the common good, which he defined as the "greatest happiness for the greatest number." This definition is similar to the one expressed earlier that the common good reflects the maximum conditions for providing what people need and want. It assumes only that satisfying what people need and want makes them happy.

Eminent domain means the government can take private property for public use upon paying just compensation.

The takings clause of the Fifth Amendment to the Constitution favors Bentham's view that property serves the common good. It allows the government to take specific resources (usually but not always land) away from private owners for "public use" upon the payment of "just compensation." The clause recognizes the existence and importance of private ownership, but allows the government to "condemn" and take specific private resources for money under the power called **eminent domain.**

Three significant questions of interpretation arise:

- What constitutes a "taking"?
- What is a "public use"?
- What is "just compensation"?

As to the first question, it is clear that when the government builds a public road through private land, it has *taken* the land and must pay compensation. But what if the government merely limits specific uses of the land, perhaps for environmental purposes? Does it have to pay compensation? The cases have been unclear, but they seem to say that as long as some economic use has been left to the landowner, no taking has occurred. One way to determine whether regulation is a taking is to see if it is necessary to protect an established property right of others that concerns safety, health, or other general welfare. The courts do not consider such regulation a taking. It is merely determining the location of boundaries, often boundaries of use.

Over the years *public use* has come to mean *public purpose.*

Public Use   The easiest way to define *public use* is to say it is a use *by* the public. A public road, a public park, a public building, a public sewage treatment plant or landfill—taking a private owner's land for any of these uses is a public use. What about the government's taking a right to string power wires across your land, then selling it to a private electric company that charges you for electricity? Is that a public use?

Courts have certainly allowed the government to take private property right for use by electric and other private utility companies. These companies benefit the public greatly. Over the years public use has come to mean *public purpose,* that is, any *purpose* that benefits the public, whether the public uses the resource or not.

What about the government's taking of land in order to sell it for private development in order to stimulate employment and increase the public tax base? Is employment stimulation and increased tax revenue a public use, or at least a public purpose? Consider Case 7.2.

*A number of states have passed laws preventing the units of government (cities and counties) from taking private land for private development purposes.

A national uproar arose after *Kelo* over whether private property interest should *ever* be taken and turned over for private development. Note that state and local governments have been taking private land and turning it over in this way for many years. The *Kelo* case merely represents the first time the Supreme Court has squarely decided the issue. The Supreme Court did not require that state governments take anyone's land for private development. It merely decided that it was a constitutional public use to do so under the given circumstances. Under pressure from voters, a number of states have passed laws preventing the units of government from taking private land for private development purposes.

KELO v. CITY OF NEW LONDON, CONNECTICUT
125 S.Ct. 2655 (2005)

In 2000, the city of New London, Connecticut, approved a development plan that was projected to create in excess of 1,000 jobs, increase tax and other revenues, and revitalize an economically distressed community. In assembling the land needed for this project, the city's development agency, the New London Development Corporation (NLDC), purchased property from willing sellers and initiated condemnation proceedings against the plaintiffs for the remainder of the land. The plaintiffs are nine landowners of property within the area where the new development was planned.

The trial court prohibited NLDC from taking part of the land but on appeal the Supreme Court of Connecticut reversed, allowing the NLDC to take all of the land. The U. S. Supreme Court granted Ms. Kelo's petition for a writ of certiorari to decide the question of whether a city's decision to take property for the purpose of economic development satisfies the "public use" requirement of the Fifth Amendment.

STEVENS, J: . . . Two polar propositions are perfectly clear. On the one hand, it has long been accepted that the sovereign may not take the property of *A* for the sole purpose of transferring it to another private property *B*, even though *A* is paid just compensation. On the other hand, it is equally clear that a State may transfer property from one private party to another if future "use by the public" is the purpose of the taking; the condemnation of land for a railroad with common-carrier duties is a familiar example. Neither of these propositions, however, determines the disposition of this case.

The disposition of this case therefore turns on the question whether the City's development plan serves a "public purpose." Without exception, our cases have defined that concept broadly, reflecting our longstanding policy of deference to legislative judgments in this field.

In *Berman v. Parker*, 348 U.S. 26 (1954), this Court upheld a redevelopment plan targeting a blighted area of Washington, D.C., in which most of the housing for the area's 5,000 inhabitants was beyond repair. Under the plan, the area would be condemned and part of it utilized for the construction of streets, schools, and other public facilities. The remainder of the land would be leased or sold to private parties for the purpose of redevelopment, including the construction of low-cost housing.

The owner of a department store located in the area challenged the condemnation, pointing out that his store was not itself blighted and arguing that the creation of a "better balanced, more attractive community" was not a valid public use. Writing for a unanimous Court, Justice Douglas refused to evaluate this claim in isolation, deferring instead to the legislative and agency judgment that the area "must be planned as a whole" for the plan to be successful. The Court explained that "community redevelopment programs need not, by force of the Constitution, be on a piecemeal basis—lot by lot, building by building." The public use underlying the taking was unequivocally affirmed:

> We do not sit to determine whether a particular housing project is or is not desirable. The concept of the public welfare is broad and inclusive. . . . The values it represents are spiritual as well as physical, aesthetic as well as monetary. It is within the power of the legislature to determine that the community should be beautiful as well as healthy, spacious as well as clean, well-balanced as well as carefully patrolled.

Viewed as a whole, our jurisprudence has recognized that the needs of society have varied between different parts of the Nation, just as they have evolved over time in response to changed circumstances. . . . For more than a century, our public use jurisprudence has wisely eschewed rigid formulas and intrusive scrutiny in favor of affording legislatures broad latitude in determining what public needs justify the use of the takings power. . . .

The City has carefully formulated an economic development plan that it believes will provide appreciable benefits to the community, including but by no means limited to new jobs and increased tax revenue. . . . To effectuate this plan, the City has invoked a state statute that specifically authorizes the use of eminent domain to promote economic development. . . . Because that plan unquestionably serves a public purpose, the takings challenged here satisfy the public use requirement of the Fifth Amendment.

To avoid this result, petitioners urge us to adopt a new bright-line rule that economic development does not qualify as a public use. Putting aside the unpersuasive suggestion that the City's plan will provide only purely economic benefits, neither precedent nor logic supports petitioners' proposal. Promoting economic development is a traditional and long accepted function of government. There is, moreover, no principled way of distinguishing economic development from the other public purposes that we have recognized. . . . It would be incongruous to hold that the City's interest in the economic benefits to be derived from the development has less of a public character than any of those other interests. Clearly, there is no basis for exempting economic development from our traditionally broad understanding of public purpose.

Petitioners contend that using eminent domain for economic development impermissibly blurs the boundary between public and private takings. Again, our cases foreclose this objection. Quite simply, the government's pursuit of a public purpose will often benefit individual private parties. . . . The owner of the department store in *Berman* objected to "taking from one businessman for the benefit of another businessman," referring to the fact that under the redevelopment plan land would be leased or sold to private developers for redevelopment. Our rejection of that contention has particular relevance to the instant case: The public end may be as well or better served through an agency of private enterprise than through a department of government—or so the Congress might conclude. We cannot say that public ownership is the sole method of promoting the public purposes of community redevelopment projects. . . .

It is further argued that without a bright-line rule nothing would stop a city from transferring citizen *A*'s property to citizen *B* for the sole reason that citizen *B* will put the property to a more productive use and thus pay more taxes. Such a one-to-one transfer of property, executed outside the confines of an integrated development plan, is not presented in this case. While such an unusual exercise of government power would certainly raise a suspicion that a private purpose was afoot, the hypothetical cases posted by petitioners can be confronted if and when they arise. They do not warrant the crafting of an artificial restriction on the concept of public use. . . .

Just as we decline to second-guess the City's considered judgments about the efficacy of its development plan, we also decline to second-guess the City's determinations as to what lands it needs to acquire in order to effectuate the project. It is not for the courts to oversee the choice of the boundary line nor to sit in review on the size of a particular project area. Once the question of the public purpose has been decided, the amount and character of land to be taken for the project and the need for a particular tract to complete the integrated plan rests in the discretion of the legislative branch. . . .

The judgment of the Supreme Court of Connecticut is affirmed.

It is so ordered.

DISSENT: THOMAS, J.: Long ago, William Blackstone wrote that "the law of the land . . . postpone[s] even public necessity to the sacred and inviolable rights of private property." The Framers embodied that principle in the Constitution, allowing the government to take property not for "public necessity," but instead for "public use." Defying this understanding, the Court replaces the Public Use Clause with a " '[P]ublic [P]urpose' " Clause, a restriction that is satisfied, the Court instructs, so long as the purpose is "legitimate" and the means "not irrational." This deferential shift in phraseology enables the Court to hold, against all common sense, that a costly urban-renewal project whose stated purpose is a value promise of new jobs and increased tax revenue, but which is also suspiciously agreeable to the Pfizer Corporation, is for a "public use."

I cannot agree. If such "economic development" takings are for a "public use," any taking is, and the Court has erased the Public Use Clause from our Constitution. I do not believe that this Court can eliminate liberties expressly enumerated in the Constitution. Regrettably, however, the Court's error runs deeper than this. Today's decision is simply the latest in a string of our cases construing the Public Use Clause to be a virtual nullity, without the slightest nod to its original meaning. In my view, the Public Use Clause, originally understood, is a meaningful limit on the government's eminent domain power. Our cases have strayed from the Clause's original meaning, and I would reconsider them.

The Fifth Amendment provides: "No person shall. . . . be deprived of life, liberty, or property, without due process of law; *nor shall private property be taken for public use without just compensation.*" (Emphasis added.)

In my view, it is "imperative that the Court maintain absolute fidelity to" the Clause's express limit on the power of the government over the individual, no less than with every other liberty expressly enumerated in the Fifth Amendment or the Bill of Rights more generally. . . .

The most natural reading of the Clause is that it allows the government to take property only if the government owns, or the public has a legal right to use, the property, as opposed to taking it for any public purpose or necessity whatsoever. . . .

More fundamentally, *Berman* erred by equating the eminent domain power with the police power of States. . . . The question whether the State can take property using the power of eminent domain is therefore distinct from the question whether it can regulate property pursuant to the police power. . . .

The consequences of today's decision are not difficult to predict, and promise to be harmful. So-called "urban renewal" programs provide some compensation for the properties they take, but no compensation is possible for the subjective value of these lands to the individuals displaced and the indignity inflicted by uprooting them from their homes. Allowing the government to take property solely for public purposes is bad enough, but extending the concept of public purpose to encompass any economically beneficial goal guarantees that these losses will fall disproportionately on poor communities. Those communities are not only systematically less likely to put their lands to the highest and best social use, but are also the least politically powerful. . . .

I would reverse the judgment of the Connecticut Supreme Court.

:: CASE QUESTIONS

1. What constitutional issue did the Supreme Court take the case to answer, and what was its answer?
2. How does the majority opinion address the point that if NLDC can take this land, the state can take any private land and pass it along to any private person?
3. In his dissent, Justice Thomas says, "Allowing the government to take property solely for public purposes is bad enough. . . ." What do you think he means by this statement? Do you agree?
4. Does private property exist under our legal system for the common good? Discuss in light of the *Kelo* case opinions.

Just Compensation   The government can only take what belongs to private owners upon payment of "just compensation." The courts have generally defined just compensation in terms of market value. In most instances the government offers compensation to an owner, a negotiation follows, and an amount is agreed upon as a just compensation. However, courts have ruled that due process requires that an owner can go to court and have a jury determine a just compensation if the owner cannot agree with the government's offer.

Do you understand now how eminent domain illustrates that property right is limited by the common good? *Public use* means basically the same thing as *common good*. When the state decides to take an owner's resources, it is determining that the right of property in these resources no longer serves the common good and that the greater common good requires that the resources be taken. Even so, the owner who has lost a property interest through eminent domain must receive just compensation.

* Public use means basically the same thing as common good. These terms are also similar to general welfare.

20. TAXATION

The justification for property may be the common good. And the common good may consist primarily of setting conditions for the maximum private production of what people need and want. However, the government provides other resources that people need and want, including public roads, public education, law enforcement, a judicial system, defense of the nation, and public assistance for the poor. These services are also a part of the general welfare (or common good) of the nation, and they are expensive. Some people believe that in the common good the government should provide even more public services such as more public health care. The taxes to support these services limit the right of private property and suggest that property's claim to promoting the common good is not absolute.

Federal taxation is a specified power of Congress, contained in Article 1, Section 8 of the Constitution: "The Congress shall have the Power to lay and collect Taxes . . . to . . . provide for the common Defense and general Welfare of the United States. . . ." Because the Supreme Court ruled that Article 1, Section 8, did not authorize indirect taxes, like the progressive income tax, the Constitution was amended in 1913 by the Sixteenth Amendment, which permits such taxes.

According to the Congressional Budget Office, the top 1 percent of federal income taxpayers pay more dollars of tax than the bottom 60 percent of taxpayers do. On the other hand, poorer taxpayers pay a higher percentage of their incomes in state and local sales taxes than do wealthier taxpayers. The fairness of the tax system and the adequacy of public services are frequent issues around election time. One thing is certain, however: These issues intertwine with perceptions of the common good, which in turn connects with the exclusive right called property. They illustrate that property, which promotes the common good, is also limited by it.

The wealth produced by the property system must actually reach people in order to produce the greatest happiness for the greatest number. Exclusive right is not an ethical or moral end in itself. Although there can be much debate about its extent, taxation of wealth generated by the incentives of the property system is part of what contributes to the common good.

> The CBO also reports that the top 20 percent of taxpayers pay 60 percent of all federal income tax.

> Can property exist both as an individual right and for the common good? Discuss.

21. PROPERTY: A CONCLUSION AND COMMENT

This chapter has introduced the law of property as it orders society's limited resources. Although many chapter sections have explained the rules making up property law, the chapter has also focused on the general importance of the legal property system to private enterprise and society. The key to the most rapid increase of total wealth—the greatest expansion of limited resources—is a property system that applies generally and equally to everyone's resources.

In the modern nation, property law founds the marketplace by establishing an essential framework for the voluntary and certain exchange of identifiable private resources. There is strong reason to think that a prime determinant of wealth in the world today is the presence or absence of an adequate property system under the rule of law. Thus, it is significant that business students appreciate the fundamental role of law in business and the necessity for a strong legal system even when they oppose the wisdom of specific rules or regulations.

Although effective property law may be the foundation for society's material flourishing and the liberty of the individual, it also has another side to it. Property law permits the accumulation of unequal exclusive resources, and as James Madison wrote in *The Federalist:* "The most common and durable source of factions has been the various and unequal distribution of property." A property system functions best when there is a large middle class with adequate resources, or at least a well-educated populace that understands the benefits of property. Otherwise, in a democracy the temptation is great to

> Why does a property system function best when there is a large middle class with adequate resources?

redistribute resources through taxation, and at some point the motivation to produce additional limited resources diminishes.

The major issues of poverty and prosperity in the new millennium involve the understanding of property law's effects on society. To deal knowledgeably with the legal environment of business, students must grasp how law founds the private marketplace for the common good.

:: Key Terms

:: Review Questions and Problems

The Property System

1. *The Problem of Limited Resources*

   The Soviet Constitution guaranteed the citizens' private property. Why then was the former Soviet Union so poor?

2. *Property and Prosperity*

   (a) How does property help generate prosperity? Discuss.

   (b) Explain the importance of the visibility of resources to the wealth of nations.

3. *Two Basic Divisions of Property*

   (a) Explain the two basic divisions of property.

   (b) Martin sold his house to Cheryl. Later, when he tried to take the beautiful chandelier in the dining room, which had belonged to his grandparents, with him, Cheryl objected. What is the issue here? Legally, who is likely to win this dispute? Discuss.

Acquiring Resources in a Property System

4. *Acquiring Resources through Exchange*

   (a) How does the law of contracts fit into our property-based legal system?

   (b) Explain why more resources are exchanged by contracts than by any other method.

5. *Acquiring Resources through Possession*

   (a) Along a winding dirt road, Lee finds an old, rusty car with no license plates. Looking through the car, which is unlocked, he finds a valuable diamond ring. Later, the original buyer of the ring comes forward and admits that he has dumped the old car along the road, but wants his ring back. Who is legally entitled to the ring? Explain.

   (b) The owner of Downtown Condos discovers that Schuyler Skyscraper actually extends 6 inches on to land belonging to Downtown. Discuss the legal ramifications.

6. *Acquiring Resources through Confusion*

   (a) What are fungible goods? Give an example.

   (b) Discuss why boundaries of use are sometimes difficult to determine.

7. *Acquiring Resources through Accession*

   (a) Explain what it means to acquire ownership by accession.

   (b) Discuss why to John Locke a doctrine similar to accession justifies who owns what.

8. *Acquiring Resources through Gift*

   (a) In terms of a gift, explain *delivery* and constructive *delivery.*

   (b) What is a testamentary gift?

9. *Types of Ownership*

   (a) What does it mean to have a fee simple defeasible estate?

   (b) What is the difference between a remainder interest and a reversion?

   (c) Arla and Jack own a house as joint tenants with right of survivorship. What is the legal significance of this?

10. *Title and Property Registration*

    (a) Name three kinds of deeds to land and explain what they mean.

    (b) Why is it important to register a deed? Discuss.

Specialty Applications of Property

11. *Easements*

    (a) In what way is an easement protected by a property fence?

    (b) Explain an easement by prescription.

12. *Bailments*

    (a) Is a lease of a mowing tractor a bailment? Explain.

    (b) A warehouse contract requires that your equipment be stored in "warehouse 314." For its own convenience the warehouseman moves your equipment to warehouse 212, and your equipment is destroyed by a tornado that sweeps through town. Is the warehouse liable to you for the value of the equipment? What if the equipment had been destroyed in warehouse 314? Would your answer be different? Because of these types of problems, what sort of arrangements do bailors and bailees often make regarding bailed goods?

    (c) How are common carriers different from other sorts of bailees?

Property and Security Interests

13. *Security Interests in Land*

    (a) Name three types of security interests in land and explain them.

    (b) Discuss why recording mortgages and deeds of trust is so important. Why is recording less important in the case of the land sales contract?

14. *Secured Transactions*

    (a) Describe the requirements for attachment of a security interest under UCC, Article 9.

    (b) Describe four different instances that demonstrate perfection of a security interest.

15. *Priority Problems*

   Roger sells his expensive mowing tractor to his neighbor Zan. Shortly after Zan takes possession, someone representing the lawn equipment company tells Zan that the store holds a purchase money security interest in the tractor. Does the store have priority regarding the mower, meaning does the security interest continue on the mower following Zan's purchase of it?

Limitations on Property and the Common Good

16. *Property, the Use of Resources, and the Equal Right of Others*

   Discuss why it is important to have a property in the uses of things.

17. *Nuisance and Zoning*

   (a) Distinguish a public nuisance from a private nuisance. What does nuisance have to do with the common good? Discuss.

   (b) What is the "coming to the nuisance" doctrine?

18. *Property Limitations and the Common Good*

   What is the rule against perpetuities? What does it have to do with the common good?

19. *Eminent Domain*

   Several people unhappy with the majority decision in *Kelo* tried to have the city council in Justice Souter's hometown condemn his house under eminent domain, take it, and turn it over to a private bed and breakfast business. Discuss whether or not this taking would have been constitutional.

20. *Taxation*

   Why is taxation of private property legal?

21. *Property: A Conclusion and Comment*

   What does James Madison think is the problem with a private property system, a system he nevertheless supported?

business :: *discussions*

1. While you are attending a business conference in South America, someone approaches you and says, "A private property system might work well in your country, but it will never work in mine. There are only a few wealthy families in my country who own almost everything. Our only hope for the people is for the government to confiscate their lands and administer our resources through socialism."

   What do you say to this person in light of what you have read in this chapter? What strategy might you suggest regarding getting more private land into the hands of the poor in that country?

2. Richard Epstein, a University of Chicago law professor, said in his book *Takings* that the principles of nuisance illustrate more clearly than any other doctrine how our property-based legal system functions.

   What did he mean by this statement? Discuss.

   Explain what it means to say that property is the central concept in our legal system.

8

Introduction to Contracts— Classifications, Terminology, and Formation

☐ Learning Objectives ::

In this chapter you will learn:

1. The fundamental concepts of contracts.
2. How contracts are classified and the terminology used to describe contracts.
3. The requirements needed to create a contractually enforced commitment.
4. How the required elements of a contract are used by courts to decide whether or not a contract exists.
5. How contracts can benefit parties other than the original parties to an agreement.

Think about the simplest of childhood business activities—setting up a lemonade stand. There are many questions that could arise. For example:

- Does the seller (child) have to pay the supplier (parent) for the cups, ice, and actual lemonade?

- If a buyer (neighbor) says, "I'd like a cup," is a contract to purchase created?

- Is the seller obligated to give the buyer a cup of lemonade?

- Is the buyer obligated to pay for the cup before, when, or after the cup is handed over?

Contracts involve promises made as commitments.

These and many other questions about contracts are fundamental to the environment in which people conduct business. Here, at the beginning of this chapter, understanding the basic definition of contracts is essential. Simply stated, a contract involves a **promise** or an exchange of promises. Although the details of contract classifications, terminology, formation, and performance make up the bulk of this and the next chapter, remember at the heart of this topic is a promise or commitment to do or not to do something.

The preceding chapters and those that follow emphasize the importance of property as the foundation of our free-enterprise system. The enforcement of contracts is essential in the operation of this property-oriented system. Without contracts and the court systems to enforce contracts, buyers and sellers would not have confidence in exchanging valuable property interests.

Every day millions of contracts—legally enforceable promises—are created and performed. Businesspeople and consumers make contractual agreements. No other area of the law has been as important as the law of contracts in supporting private enterprise. As you read and study this and the next chapter, keep in mind the role that property and contracts have in making business possible. Indeed, we believe these aspects of the law are the fundamental elements of today's modern business world.

There are also nonlegal business considerations in every contract. If your company tries to get out of the deal the customer believes exists, you risk losing that customer's future business. Although your company may settle a dispute through negotiation rather than litigation, your bargaining power is enhanced when you know the rules of contract law.

In this chapter, you will study such topics as:

- Laws governing contracts.
- What happens when a contractual promise is broken.
- When communications become a contract.
- What parties have to do when changes to a contract occur.
- Who has the capacity to create contracts.
- How third parties benefit from contracts.

The next chapter continues our examination of contracts by examining the format and performance of contracts.

:: Basic Concepts

When was the last time you entered into a contract? Was it last month when you signed an apartment or dorm lease? If so, you must be very hungry. This is because one enters a contract when buying a meal or a snack from a vending machine. Actually, most people contract daily for a great variety of goods and services that they purchase or lease. The rules of contract law underlie the private enterprise system at every turn.

1. CONTRACT LAW IN PRIVATE ENTERPRISE

A contract need not be a formal, written document, and those who make a contract do not have to use the word *contract* or recognize that they have made a legally enforceable promise. Still, the rules of contract law apply. If the expectations of the parties to a contract are not met, these rules affect legal negotiations and may result in a lawsuit. For instance, contract law says that a restaurant "promises" that its food is fit to eat. Should the restaurant serve a meal that gives the buyer food poisoning, it could be liable for the injury caused by breaking its promise.

Contract law enables private agreements to be legally enforceable. Enforceability of agreements is desirable because it gives people the certainty they need to rely on promises contained in agreements. For instance, a shirt manufacturer in Los Angeles must know that it can rely on the promise of a store in Boston to pay for a thousand specially manufactured shirts. The manufacturer is more likely to agree to sew the shirts if it can enforce payment from the buyer, if necessary, under the law of contracts. In an important sense, then, the law of contracts is vital for our private enterprise economy. It helps make buyers and sellers willing to do business together.

Contract law provides enormous flexibility and precision in business dealings. It provides flexibility in that you can agree (or require agreement) to literally anything that is not illegal or against public policy. It gives precision in that with careful thinking you can make another agree to exactly the requirements that accomplish even a very complex business purpose. Sidebar 8.1 provides an example of the precise use of contractual language to accomplish a business purpose. Failure to follow this language can result in an outcome very different from the intended one.

:: *sidebar* 8.1

The Confidentiality Agreement

Many companies require employees to sign contractual confidentiality agreements. In these agreements employees promise not to disclose certain things they learn during their employment. Confidentiality agreements are very useful in keeping employees or ex-employees from telling a company's research discoveries, marketing plans, customer lists, and other sensitive information.

Confidentiality agreements are especially important in the tobacco industry. Most medical opinion holds that tobacco is an addictive product that can cause heart and lung disease. What do tobacco industry executives think about these issues? Publicly, the tobacco industry downplays that tobacco is addictive and minimizes tobacco health risks. Discussion within the industry, however, may show concern about the effects of tobacco. Precisely worded confidentiality agreements prohibit tobacco industry employees from revealing documents or discussions at work concerning the risks of tobacco consumption, or even how cigarettes and other tobacco products are made. The tobacco industry can enforce these agreements through court injunctions or damage clauses. Over the years confidentiality agreements have been very useful in keeping industry information out of the hands of those who wish to sue or regulate the industry.

A paralegal who worked for a law firm representing a major tobacco company copied and then released many internal company documents that indicated concern within the tobacco industry over the risks of tobacco consumption. *The New York Times, Washington Post,* and other publications carried stories on the contents of these documents. Not long afterward, the tobacco industry began negotiating for a comprehensive settlement to the legal claims arising from tobacco consumption and to the government's regulation of the tobacco industry.

---

2. SOURCES OF CONTRACT LAW

Most of the contract law outlined in this chapter is common law. Hopefully, you remember from Chapter 1 that common law comes from judges' decisions. The courts have developed principles controlling contract formation, performance, breach, and remedies in countless cases. This judge-made law affects many types of contracts, including real property, service, employment, and general business contracts.

Do remember there are special rules applicable to the sale of goods.

Another source of contract law is legislation. Various states have enacted the common law as a part of the state statutes. A particularly important example of state-based legislation impacting contract law is the Uniform Commercial Code (UCC). Article 2 of the UCC covers the sale of **goods.** Goods are tangible, movable items of personal property. Every state has adopted this portion of the UCC, thereby making state contract law uniform in the area of contracts

Figure 8.1 *Remedies for breach of contract*

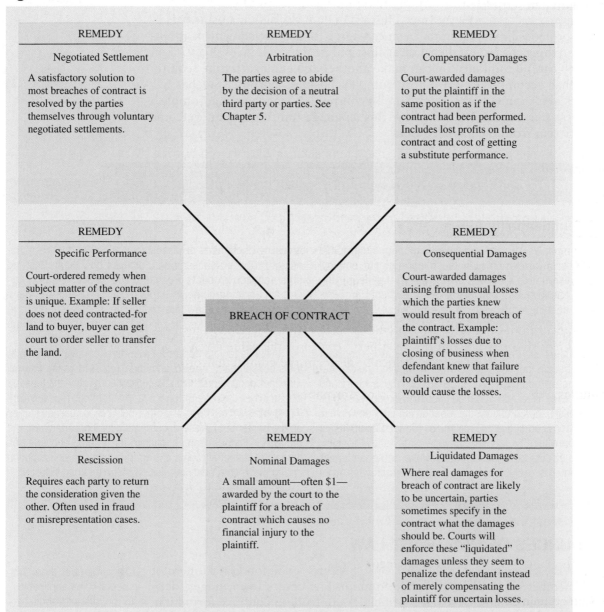

REMEDY

Negotiated Settlement

A satisfactory solution to most breaches of contract is resolved by the parties themselves through voluntary negotiated settlements.

REMEDY

Arbitration

The parties agree to abide by the decision of a neutral third party or parties. See Chapter 5.

REMEDY

Compensatory Damages

Court-awarded damages to put the plaintiff in the same position as if the contract had been performed. Includes lost profits on the contract and cost of getting a substitute performance.

REMEDY

Specific Performance

Court-ordered remedy when subject matter of the contract is unique. Example: If seller does not deed contracted-for land to buyer, buyer can get court to order seller to transfer the land.

BREACH OF CONTRACT

REMEDY

Consequential Damages

Court-awarded damages arising from unusual losses which the parties knew would result from breach of the contract. Example: plaintiff's losses due to closing of business when defendant knew that failure to deliver ordered equipment would cause the losses.

REMEDY

Rescission

Requires each party to return the consideration given the other. Often used in fraud or misrepresentation cases.

REMEDY

Nominal Damages

A small amount—often $1— awarded by the court to the plaintiff for a breach of contract which causes no financial injury to the plaintiff.

REMEDY

Liquidated Damages

Where real damages for breach of contract are likely to be uncertain, parties sometimes specify in the contract what the damages should be. Courts will enforce these "liquidated" damages unless they seem to penalize the defendant instead of merely compensating the plaintiff for uncertain losses.

involving goods. Throughout this chapter and the next, you will study both the common law principles of contracts and the UCC. Remember this distinction between these two primary sources of contract law. The UCC relates to contracts involving goods, and the common law governs other contracts.

3. BREACH OF CONTRACT

A party that does not live up to the obligation of contractual performance is said to breach the contract. There are several remedies or solutions available for a breach of contract. These include the following:

- Negotiated settlement.
- Arbitration.
- Various awards, including compensatory, consequential, liquidated, and nominal damages.
- Specific performance.
- Rescission.

You contract with *P* to paint your house for $2,000. *P* does not complete the job, and you hire *R* and pay $3,000. You are entitled to $1,000 from *P* as compensatory damages.

Figure 8.1 provides a summary of these remedies for breach of contract.

Awarding money damages is the more common way courts provide remedies to nonbreaching parties. The theory behind such awards rests in putting the damaged person in the same financial position as if the contract was fully performed. Usually compensatory damages suffice to achieve this objective of making a party whole. Occasionally courts will add consequential damages to create a fair remedy. Liquidated, or agreed-upon, damages can simplify disputes when a breach occurs.

The victim of a contract breach must **mitigate** damages when possible. To mitigate damages requires the victim to take reasonable steps to reduce them. For example, when a tenant breaches a house lease by moving away before the lease expires, the landlord must mitigate damages by renting the house to another willing and suitable tenant if such a person is available.

Mitigation is the purposeful reduction of damages; it usually is the responsibility of the nonbreaching party.

At times, money damages are not what a party wants as a remedy. Instead, the nonbreaching party might desire either a return of the value given or an order that the breaching party specifically perform the contractual promise made. The former situation involves the equitable remedy of **rescission** or **restitution.** The latter describes **specific performance.**

Sidebar 8.2 provides a summary of a case illustrating when restitution helps restore the parties to their precontractual positions.

:: Contractual Classifications and Terminology

We use a number of terms to help classify different types of contracts. Learning these terms will greatly help you understand contract law. This section introduces the following contractual terminology:

- Bilateral and unilateral contracts.
- Express and implied-in-fact contracts.
- Implied-in-law or quasi-contracts.
- Enforcement terminology.
- Performance terminology.

:: *sidebar* 8.2

Restitution Puts Parties in Precontractual Position

Mobil and other oil companies received the right to explore and develop oil found off the coast of North Carolina. The companies paid the United States $158 million for such rights in the form of 10-year renewal leases. Under the laws in existence at the time of these leases, the Interior Department was required to respond within 30 days of an exploration plan being filed by a lessee oil company. In August 1990 (two days before the final exploration plan was filed), a new law called the Outer Banks Protection Act became effective. This law required the Interior Department to wait at least 13 months before approving an exploration plan so that an Environmental Sciences Review Panel could study and comment on any exploration plan.

The oil companies sued to have their lease payments returned since the U.S. government could not perform the contract as originally written. The Supreme Court ordered the return of the $158 million lease payments. Due to the change in laws, the United States in fact delayed in responding to the exploration plan for four years. This delay essentially acted as a repudiation of the original commitment to respond within 30 days of a plan being presented. The appropriate remedy for this repudiation of its obligation is to pay restitution by returning to the oil companies the $158 million in lease payments.

*Source: *Mobil Oil Exploration and Producing Southeast, Inc. v. United States,* 120 S. Ct. 2423 (2000).

4. BILATERAL AND UNILATERAL CONTRACTS

Bilateral contracts involve a promise-for-promise exchange.

Contracts involve either an exchange of promises by the parties or a promise conditioned on the performance of an act. A **bilateral contract** is an agreement containing mutual promises. For example, suppose Paul promises to sell his laptop computer to Pearl if she promises to pay $1,000 for the equipment. When Pearl makes her promise in response to Paul's, a bilateral contract is formed. This relationship is depicted in Figure 8.2. Notice that a bilateral contract involves two promises, two rights, and two duties.

Unilateral contracts exist when a promise is made to motivate an action.

While a bilateral contract involves a promise for a promise, a **unilateral contract** is an agreement with only one promise. The maker of such a promise seeks an action rather than a promise in return. Suppose Pat tells Alex, "I am tired of your idle commitments; when you install my new stereo equipment, I will pay you $200." Here Pat no longer wants Alex's promise to perform. Pat seeks the actual performance. In Figure 8.3, notice that there is only one promise, one duty, and one right.

Figure 8.2
Bilateral contract

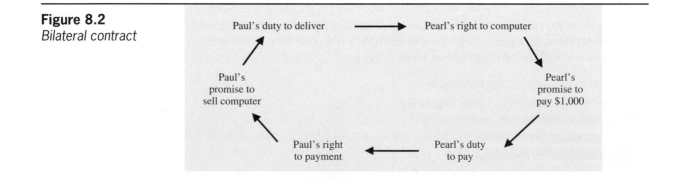

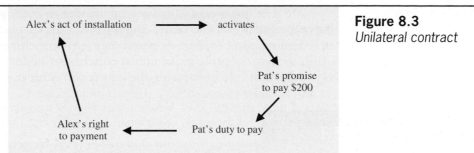

Figure 8.3
Unilateral contract

Most business contracts take the bilateral form. Indeed, courts presume a bilateral nature of an agreement whenever there is doubt about the form. Nevertheless, the party making a promise can control the application of many concepts of contract law by understanding the distinction between bilateral and unilateral contracts.

5. EXPRESS AND IMPLIED-IN-FACT CONTRACTS

Many contracts arise from discussions in which parties actually discuss the promised terms of their agreement. These are called **express contracts**. A negotiated purchase of land for construction of a manufacturing plant is an example of an express contract. There are also **implied-in-fact contracts,** which arise from the conduct of the parties rather than from words. For instance, asking a person such as an accountant for professional advice *implies* a promise to pay the going rate for this advice even though you do not make an *express* promise to pay for it.

In most business contracts, many conflicts and disputes can be avoided if the parties take time to express clearly the terms of the agreement. However, businesspeople can get in a hurry to complete the contract arrangements so they can begin doing business. For example in a typical customer-supplier relationship, a written contract may omit specific terms of delivery. These terms will be implied by the courts to ensure the contractual relationship is ongoing. Details about delivery terms, as an aspect of performing contractual promises, are presented in the next chapter. For now, you should understand courts will try to fill in the gaps the parties fail to expressly state.

> A typical rule of thumb— parties expressing the detail of contractual commitments is better than leaving terms unstated.

6. IMPLIED-IN-LAW OR QUASI-CONTRACTS

When one party is unjustly enriched at the expense of another, the law may imply a duty on the first party to pay the second even though there is no contract between the two parties. The doctrine that requires this result is based on an **implied-in-law contract.** Since there really is no actual contractual agreement, the phrase **quasi-contract** often is used.

If a debtor overpays a creditor $5,000, the debtor can force the creditor to return that amount by suing under quasi-contract. It would be an unjust enrichment to allow the creditor to keep the $5,000. Likewise, when John has paid taxes on land, thinking that he owns it, and Mary comes along with a superior title (ownership) to the land and has John evicted, the remedy of quasi-contract requires that Mary reimburse John for the taxes paid.

> **Quasi-contracts** are a judicial remedy to prevent one party from receiving unjust enrichment.

Note that quasi-contract is not an answer to every situation in which no contract exists. Over the years, courts have come to apply quasi-contract in a fairly limited number of cases based on unjust enrichment. However, as Case 8.1 illustrates, the principle of unjust enrichment under quasi-contract plays a very important role in ensuring the courts can achieve justice.

case **8.1**

NORTHEAST FENCE & IRON WORKS, INC. v. MURPHY QUIGLEY CO., INC.
933 A.2d 664 (Pa. Super.2007)

Murphy Quigley Co., Inc., is a general contractor for fencing and security upgrade projects at the Bucks County (Pennsylvania) Correctional Facility. The fencing contract required the installation of perimeter fencing and the creation of seven fence-enclosed recreational yards. Murphy Quigley contracted with Eagle Fence, as a subcontractor, to do the actual fencing work. Eagle Fence began this work. After completing only 10 to 15 percent of the required work, it quit the job due to disputes with Murphy Quigley over nonpayment.

In somewhat of an emergency situation, Murphy Quigley granted a contract to Northeast Fence & Iron Works, Inc., to complete the unfinished fencing. Both Murphy Quigley and Northeast Fence & Iron Works agree the cost to finish the perimeter fence was $26,500. However, these parties never agreed on the specific contract price and the actual cost of the fencing of the recreational yards. Murphy Quigley thought the work would be done at the rate of $3,500 per day with a cap of $122,500. Officials at Northeast Fence & Iron Works agree with the daily rate; however, they dispute the existence of a cap. Despite the lack of a contractual agreement, Northeast Fence & Iron Works did the work. Believing it had an agreement, Murphy Quigley did not object to this work being done or try to stop it.

Having completed the fencing work, Northeast Fence & Iron Works submits invoices totaling $134,428.30. Murphy Quigley disputes this total and refused to pay. Northeast Fence & Iron Works sues Murphy Quigley. The trial judge decided these parties did not have a contract for the fencing of the recreational yards. The judge did find Northeast Fence & Iron Works was entitled to recover $114,246.06 in damages on a quasi-contract theory to avoid the unjust enrichment of Murphy Quigley. These damages were calculated by taking 15 percent (the work done by Eagle Fence) from the amount of the submitted invoices.

Murphy Quigley appeals the trial court's judgment.

BOWES, J.: . . . Appellant first suggests that the concept of unjust enrichment is not applicable in this case because the relationship between the parties was founded on a contract. A cause of action for unjust enrichment arises only when a transaction is not subject to a written or express contract. In this case, there was no written contract, and there also was a conflict over the contractual price during the verbal exchange. Both parties agreed on the price of the perimeter fencing and that the recreational yard work would be performed at a per diem rate of $3,500. However, Appellant claimed that there was a contractual maximum cost while Appellee denied this claim.

Thus, the evidence established the existence of a dispute over the contract price, an essential term of a contact, and supported the trial court's refusal to find the existence of an express contract. If no express contract exists between the parties due to the absence of an agreed-upon contract price, a plaintiff may recover under a quasi-contract theory of unjust enrichment. Moreover, the plaintiff can recover under this quasi-contractual theory even when the plaintiff has been partially paid if the benefit conferred on the defendant is greater than the value paid to the plaintiff. Indeed, we recently held that a subcontractor can recover based upon unjust enrichment when it performed work outside the coverage of the parties' contractual provisions.

. . . Appellant recruited Appellee to install the fencing. After the original subcontractor responsible for the work performed by Appellee left the worksite, Appellee was engaged to perform that work on an emergency basis in the face of impending contractual deadlines. . . . Appellant was the general contractor for the construction project at issue herein. Appellee submitted evidence that it performed approximately $134,000 worth of work for which it had not been paid by Appellant. This work clearly benefited

Appellant because it satisfied Appellant's contractual obligations to a third party. Appellant thereafter accepted and retained Appellee's work.

. . . The benefit to Appellant was the performance of work at Appellant's request in order to satisfy Appellant's contractual obligation to the prison. Once a benefit is conferred and retained under circumstances where it would be unjust to deny payment, the evidence is sufficient to sustain a verdict based upon this cause of action. . . .

Appellant also alleges that Appellee never proved the value of the fencing because it only submitted invoices. . . . Our review of . . . cases establishes that they do not stand for the proposition that a subcontractor cannot establish the value of a benefit conferred on a contractor through the submission of unpaid invoices. . . .

Appellant also maintains that the trial court should have accepted its unrebutted evidence that the value of the fencing installed by Appellee was about $40,000.

Specifically, Appellant contends that it presented unrebutted evidence that it paid "$75,818.82 to Northeast Fence . . . and that it incurred $26,220.14 in damages to repair Northeast Fence's defective work," and in light of this evidence, the damage award of the court cannot be upheld.

The trial court, sitting as factfinder, was free to reject Appellant's evidence of value conferred as not credible. The trial court herein specifically concluded that Appellant's evidence that it had expended money to repair Appellee's work was not worthy of belief. Furthermore, Appellant's evidence of value was indeed rebutted by Appellee, who submitted evidence that the value conferred far exceeded the amount paid. The invoices submitted by Appellee demonstrated that the amount owed, after credit for the amount paid by Appellant, was approximately $134,000. Thus, there was sufficient evidentiary support for the $114,000 damage award rendered by the trial court.

Judgment affirmed.

:: CASE QUESTIONS

1. What is the relationship between the parties in this case?
2. What caused these parties to fail to enter into a binding, express contract?
3. Why does the court conclude that a quasi-contract exists?

7. CONTRACTUAL ENFORCEMENT TERMINOLOGY

Terms used in contract law related to the enforceability of agreements include *enforceable, unenforceable, valid, void,* and *voidable.*

The ultimate purpose of a contract is the creation of an agreement which courts will order parties to perform or to pay consequences for the failure of performance. When courts uphold the validity of such promises, the resulting agreement is an **enforceable contract.** If a nonperforming party has a justifiable reason for noncompliance with a promise, the result is an **unenforceable contract.** In essence, in this latter situation, a defense exists that denies the legal enforcement of an agreement.

When an agreement is enforceable because all the essential requirements (discussed in Sections 9–13) are present, courts refer to a **valid contract.** At the other end of the spectrum, a **void contract** is one that appears to be an agreement but lacks an essential requirement for validity and enforceability. The most typical example of a void contract is an apparent agreement that has an illegal purpose. For example, a business contract that involves the shipment of contraband is void and unenforceable. As described in Section 13 in more detail, courts usually refuse to hear arguments of parties to a void contract. Courts simply leave these parties where they are regardless of whether

> Valid contracts are enforceable; void contracts are unenforceable; voidable contracts are enforceable until a party with the right to do so elects to void the agreement.

the illegal agreement has been partially or fully performed. Thus, in states where gambling is illegal, a bet on a football game is void. Courts will not enforce the betting agreement and do not care if the losing party has or has not paid off the bet.

A **voidable contract** is an agreement when one party has the right to withdraw from the promise made without incurring any legal liability. One party has the power to end the enforcement of a voidable contract. An interesting aspect of voidable contracts involves the fact that these agreements are enforceable in court until a party with the legal right to do so decides to void the contract, thereby making the agreement unenforceable. Typically this middleground situation arises when a party to the contract lacks capacity or is disadvantaged by specific situations. This existence of voidable contracts is discussed in detail in Section 12 on page 251.

8. CONTRACTUAL PERFORMANCE TERMINOLOGY

In addition to issues related to enforcing contracts in court, the topic of parties performing their commitments is vital to contract law. The key terms related to performance are *executed* and *executory*. An **executed contract** is one in which the parties have performed their promises. When the parties have not yet performed their agreement, it is called an **executory contract.**

Since most business contracts are bilateral in nature involving an exchange of promises by the parties, most contracts are executory at some time. For example, if you promise your new employer to begin working next month and that employer promises to pay you at the end of the first month's work, this employment contract is executory from both parties' perspective.

Contracts cover a multitude of situations and these performance terms may be more or less relevant. Suppose you take a grocery item to the cashier and pay for it. The resulting contract is executed at the time of its creation. In fact, there probably was no exchange of spoken promises. The exchange of money for the item results in the performance being the proof of the contract.

In more complicated business transactions, the performance or lack thereof by one party becomes very important in determining the rights and duties under the contracts. A supplier of raw materials may ship its product and await the buyer's payment. The seller's performance is executed while the buyer's performance remains executory. How these terms impact enforceability issues is a part of the discussion in the next chapter.

:: Contract Formation

The five essential elements of forming a valid contract:
- Offer
- Acceptance
- Consideration
- Capacity
- Lawful purpose

How a contract is formed is one of the most important issues to understand about contract law. Many agreements are void, and thus unenforceable, because they lack some essential element of contract formation.

The following sections (9–13) focus on the essential elements and how they come together to form contracts. Before an agreement can become a legally binding contract, someone must make a specific promise to another and also a specific demand of that person. This is the offer. The other person must accept the terms of the offer in the proper way. Both parties must give consideration to the other. Consideration is the promise to give, or the actual giving, of a requested benefit or the incurring of a legal detriment (i.e., doing something one does not have to). Both parties must be of legal age and sound mind, and the purpose of the agreement cannot be illegal or against public policy.

9. OFFER TO CONTRACT

An **offer** contains a specific promise and a specific demand. "I will pay $15,000 for the electrical transformer" promises $15,000 and demands a specific product in return. An *offeror* (person making the offer) must intend to make the offer by making a commitment to the offeree (the person to whom the offer is made). Many issues about an offer can and do arise. For example, is the language of the offer clear enough to conclude that a valid contract can result? What if a person makes a statement ("I'll give you $100 for a ride to the mall"), intending it as a joke. Is this an offer? Courts answer this question by measuring intent from a reasonable person's perspective. This standard is known as the objective, rather than the subjective, intent of the offeror.

Sidebar 8.3 uses an interesting case to emphasize some key principles to determine whether or not an offer exists.

:: *sidebar* 8.3

Does an Offer Exist?

Pepsi ran an advertising campaign encouraging customers to drink its products and earn points to buy "Pepsi Stuff." The company produced a catalog specifying the number of points needed to "buy" sunglasses, shirts, caps, coolers, and similar items. In the catalog, Pepsi provides that a point can be purchased for 10 cents.

Pepsi produced a television advertisement that promoted this campaign. In the ad, a young man lands a Harrier jet in front of a high school building and proclaims, "It sure beats the bus." A subtitle on this scene reads 7,000,000 Pepsi points. John Leonard purchased Pepsi products and sent in a check for nearly $700,000 to buy enough additional points to acquire the Harrier jet. Pepsi denied Mr. Leonard's request for the jet and returned his check.

In litigation, the judge ruled in favor of Pepsi by concluding the advertisement for the Harrier jet was a joke. Reasonable people would not conclude Pepsi was selling this type of product in its campaign. Furthermore, the advertisement was not an offer subject to Mr. Leonard's acceptance. Thus, Mr. Leonard's attempt to purchase the jet was an offer that was not accepted by Pepsi.

*Source: Leonard v. Pepsico, Inc., 88 F. Supp. 2d 116 (S.D.N.Y. 1999).

When does the language used in negotiation become an offer? Suppose a seller asks a potential buyer, "Would you be willing to pay $1,500 for this?" Is this an offer or an invitation to continue negotiating? The answers to these questions relate to the specificity of the language used to state a commitment or willingness to be bound. An offer is much more likely to exist when a seller says, "I am ready to sell this to you for $1,500."

Definition of Terms Under the common law of contracts, contractual terms must be definite and specific. An offer to purchase a house at a "reasonable price" cannot be the basis for a contract because of **indefiniteness.** Most advertisements and catalog price quotes are considered too indefinite to form the basis for a contract unless they are specific about the quality of goods being offered.

Do be very thoughtful in the choice of spoken words; decide whether you are ready to make an offer or want to continue discussions about possible arrangements.

However, under the UCC, contracts for the sale of goods can leave open nonquantity terms to be decided at a future time (§ 2-305). For example, an agreement for the sale of 500 cameras will bind the parties even though they leave open the price to be decided on delivery in six months. Note that this rule applies only to sales of goods. It does not apply to sales of real estate or services.

Termination of Offer Offers create a legal power in the offeree to bind the offeror in a contract. However, that legal power does not last forever. When an offer *terminates,* the offeree's legal power to bind the offeror ends. Review carefully Sidebar 8.4 describing various instances when an offer terminates.

:: *sidebar* 8.4

When an Offer Terminates

By provision in the offer: "This offer terminates at noon Friday."

By lapse of a reasonable period of time if the offer fails to specify a time: What is "reasonable" depends on the circumstances.

By rejection of the offer: "Thank you, but I do not want the flooring you are offering." A **counteroffer** is also a rejection: "Your offer of $10,000 for the land is too low. I will sell it to you for $12,500."

By revocation of the offer: "I regret to inform you that I am withdrawing my offer."

By destruction of the subject matter: The carpet is destroyed by fire before the offer of their sale has been accepted.

By the offeror's death or insanity: Offeror dies before the offer has been accepted.

By the contractual performance becoming illegal: Congress declares that sales of certain computers to Iran are illegal. This terminates an offer to sell the computers to an Iranian trading company.

---

10. ACCEPTANCE OF OFFER

Don't change the terms of the offer if you are trying to accept these terms.

Acceptance of an offer is necessary to create a valid, enforceable contract. An offer to enter into a bilateral contract is accepted by the offeree's making the required promise. When Toni offers Aaron certain vinyl flooring for $2,500 to be delivered by November 30 on 90-day credit terms, and Aaron accepts, Aaron is promising to pay $2,500 on 90-day credit terms.

Unilateral contracts are accepted by performing a requested act, not by making a promise. A company's offer of a $2,500 reward for information leading to the conviction of anyone vandalizing company property is not accepted by promising to provide the information. Only the act of providing information accepts such an offer.

The language of the offer determines whether acceptance should be a promise resulting in a bilateral contract or an act resulting in a unilateral contract. The rights and duties of the contracting party can turn on the form of the acceptance.

Other issues relating to the importance of acceptance in the formation of a valid contract are discussed under the following headings.

Mirror Image Rule For an acceptance to create a binding contract, standard contract law requires that the acceptance must "mirror" the offer, that is, must match it exactly. This is the **mirror image rule.** If the acceptance changes the terms of the offer or adds new terms, it is not really an acceptance. It is a *counteroffer,* and negotiations continue. Sidebar 8.5 highlights how in sales of goods contracts the UCC changes this common law principle. To fully understand these UCC provisions, you need to know that special rules apply to merchants. **Merchants** are people who deal in the business of goods.

Between merchants means both parties to a contract do business in the goods being bought and sold.

:: *sidebar* 8.5

UCC's Battle of the Forms

Suppose your company receives a purchase order from a buyer offering to purchase an executive desk and chair for $3,500. This order states the buyer will accept delivery at its company's offices. Your company responds by sending a confirmation form agreeing to the purchase price. However, your form states delivery will be made in two weeks.

Is there a contractual agreement? If so, which terms are used to determine the rights and obligations of the parties?

The UCC changes the mirror image rule. An expression of acceptance or a written confirmation is treated as an acceptance even if such communication adds or changes terms to those stated in the offer. Under the UCC, it appears there is a contract governing the purchase and sale of the desk and chair. The issue now focuses on the different term describing the timing of delivery.

In general, contracts involving the sale of goods treat additional terms as proposals for addition to the contract. When the contract is between merchants, the additional terms become a part of the contract unless one of the following takes place:

1. The offer expressly limits acceptance to the original terms.
2. The proposed terms materially (importantly) alter the contract.
3. The offeror rejects the proposed terms.

Therefore, in the example of the desk and chair, if the buyer does not respond to the confirmation form, a contract exists and the desk and chair should arrive at the buyer's office within two weeks. Do you see how the UCC attempts to facilitate the business transactions? Of course, sometimes parties may not want these gap-filling provisions to complete or govern their contracts. In such situations, clear, specific, and definite language should be used in contract negotiations.

*Source: UCC § 2-207.

Silence Not Acceptance In general, an offeree's failure to reject an offer does not imply acceptance. Another way to say this is that silence alone is not acceptance. The offeree has no usual duty to reply to the offer even if the offer states that the offeror will treat silence as acceptance.

There are major exceptions to this rule. For instance, parties may have a contract that specifies that future shipments of goods be made automatically unless the offeree expressly rejects them. Many book- and record-club contracts operate in this manner.

A related doctrine looks at the parties' prior *course of dealing*—the way they have done business in the past. Silence may well imply acceptance if

Don't rely on the other party's silence as evidence of acceptance. It can mislead you concerning the existence of a contract.

the parties previously dealt with each other by having the buyer take shipments from the seller unless the buyer notified the seller in advance not to ship.

Finally, the UCC says that a contract may arise from the *conduct* of a buyer and seller of goods. Emphasis is placed on how the parties act rather than on a formal offer and acceptance of terms.

Deposited Acceptance Rule   When does the acceptance become legally binding on the offeror? Unless the offeror specifies a particular time, the acceptance usually binds the parties when the offeree dispatches it. Since the offeree frequently mails the acceptance, the acceptance becomes binding when it is "deposited" with the postal service—hence the **deposited acceptance rule,** also called the **mailbox rule.**

The importance of the deposited acceptance rule is that the offeror cannot revoke the offer once the offeree has accepted it. An added significance is that an offeror's revocation is not effective until the offeree actually receives it. Thus, a deposited acceptance creates a binding contract even though a revocation is also in the mail.

Sidebar 8.6 highlights the significant impact the mailbox rule can have on deciding whether a contract does or does not exist.

:: *sidebar* 8.6

Impact of Mailings

Emergency Medicine provides doctors to emergency rooms at hospitals. It contracted with Rapier to have MBS (a subsidiary of Rapier) perform coding, billing, collection, and accounts receivable services. The contract between Emergency Medicine and MBS was to renew on an annual basis unless either party gave a four-month notice of nonrenewal. The contract, which was to expire on September 30, required notice of nonrenewal on or before May 31. On May 30, Emergency Medicine mailed letters of nonrenewal to the offices of Rapier and MBS. The letter to Rapier was returned as not deliverable. The letter to MBS was delivered on June 2. MBS argued that the contract was renewed for

another year since the May 31 deadline was not satisfied. The appeals court ruled the mailing on May 30 satisfies the requirement that notice of nonrenewal be delivered on or before May 31. The contract between Emergency Medicine and MBS specifically stated that a nonrenewal notice had to be mailed. The mailbox (or deposited acceptance) rule permits the effective date of delivery to be the date of mailing. The May 30 mailing came before the May 31 deadline. Thus, the contract was not automatically renewed.

Source: University Emergency Medicine Foundation v. Rapier Investments, Ltd. and Medical Business Systems, Inc., 197 F. 3d 18 (1st Cir. 1999).

As this section and the prior one illustrate, the application of finding the parties' mutual assent to a contract can become complex. Despite the variety of rules associated with offers and acceptances, the purpose of these essential contractual elements remains simple. Case 8.2, involving a very common factual situation, illustrates the basics.

11. CONSIDERATION

All promises are not enforceable through legal action. There must be some incentive or inducement for a person's promise or it is not binding. The legal mechanism for evaluating the existence of this incentive is **consideration,** the

DOUGLAS v. TALK AMERICA INC.
495 F.3d 1062 (9th Cir. 2007)

PER CURIAM: We consider whether a service provider may change the terms of its service contract by merely posting a revised contract on its website.

Joe Douglas contracted for long distance telephone service with America Online. Talk America subsequently acquired this business from AOL and continued to provide telephone service to AOL's former customers. Talk America then added four provisions to the service contract: (1) additional service charges; (2) a class-action waiver; (3) an arbitration clause; and (4) a choice-of-law provision pointing to New York law. Talk America posted the revised contract on its website but, according to Douglas, it never notified him that the contract had changed. Unaware of the new terms, Douglas continued using Talk America's services for four years.

After becoming aware of the additional charges, Douglas filed a class-action lawsuit in district court, charging Talk America with violations of the Federal Communications Act, breach of contract and violations of various California consumer protection statutes. Talk America moved to compel arbitration based on the modified contract and the district court granted the motion. . . .

Douglas alleges that Talk America changed his service contract without notifying him. He could only have become aware of the new terms if he had visited Talk America's website and examined the contract for possible changes. The district court seems to have assumed Douglas had visited the website when it noted that the contract was available on "the web site on which Plaintiff paid his bills." However, Douglas claims that he authorized AOL to charge his credit card automatically and Talk America continued this practice, so he had no occasion to visit Talk America's website to pay his bills. Even if Douglas had visited the website, he would have had no reason to look at the contract posted there. Parties to a contract have no obligation to check the terms on a periodic basis to learn whether they have been changed by the other side. Indeed, a party can't unilaterally change the terms of a contract; it must obtain the other party's consent before doing so. This is because a revised contract is merely an offer and does not bind the parties until it is accepted. And generally an offeree cannot actually assent to an offer unless he knows of its existence. Even if Douglas's continued use of Talk America's service could be considered assent, such assent can only be inferred after he received proper notice of the proposed changes. Douglas claims that no such notice was given. . . .

The district court's order compelling arbitration is vacated.

:: CASE QUESTIONS

1. What caused the long distance telephone service provided to Joe Douglas to shift from AOL to Talk America?
2. How did Talk America attempt to modify the contracts it received from AOL?
3. How did Talk America notify its customers of these changes to their service contracts?
4. Why did the court rule in favor of Joe Douglas?

receipt of a legal benefit or the suffering of a legal detriment. Courts will not enforce contractual promises unless they are supported by consideration.

Before Robert can enforce a promise made by Peter, Robert must have given consideration that induced Peter to make the promise. In a bilateral

> To be valid, a contract must involve the exchange of consideration between the parties.

contract, each party promises something to the other. The binding promises are the consideration. In a unilateral contract, the consideration of one party is a promise; the consideration of the other party is performance of an act. When it is not clear whether there is consideration to support a promise, a court will often examine a transaction as a whole.

Must Be Bargained For

Must Be Bargained For   An important part of consideration is that it must be *bargained for.* Sometimes the parties to an agreement specify an insignificant consideration in return for a great one. For example, a promise of $1 might be made in return for a promise to convey 40 acres of land. In such situations a court must decide whether the party promising to convey the land really bargained for the $1 or merely promised to make a gift. Promises to make gifts are not binding, because no bargained-for consideration supports the promise.

Similarly, *prior consideration* is no consideration. For instance, after many years of working at Acme Co., Bigman retires as vice president for financial planning. The company's board of directors votes him a new car every year "for services rendered." One year later the board rescinds this vote. If Bigman sues for breach of contract, he will lose. He gave no consideration to support the board's promise. The past years of service were not "bargained for" by the company's board when it took its vote. The board merely promised to give an unenforceable gift to Bigman.

Agreement Not to Sue

The phrase "paid in full" placed on a check offered in settlement of a disputed amount acts as an accord and satisfaction if the check is cashed or deposited.

Agreement Not to Sue   When reasonable grounds for a lawsuit exist, an agreement not to sue is consideration to support a promise. If First Bank agrees not to sue Maria, who has failed to repay a student loan, in return for the promise of Maria's parents to repay the loan, First Bank has given consideration. It has promised to surrender its legal right to sue Maria.

Likewise, suppose that a consulting firm bills a client $5,000 for 50 hours of work at $100 per hour. The client disputes the bill and contends that the consulting firm worked only 25 hours and should get only $2,500. If the two parties compromise the bill at $3,500 for 35 hours, this agreement binds them both. Each has surrendered the right to have a court determine exactly what amount is owed. Such an agreement and the payment of the $3,500 to resolve a dispute over the amount owed is an **accord and satisfaction.**

Preexisting Obligation

Many contractual modifications are not enforceable because there is a lack of consideration. If Gerald agrees to paint your house for $2,000 and halfway through the job insists on receiving another $1,000, what consideration would you receive if you agree to pay the additional amount?

Preexisting Obligation   A party to an agreement does not give consideration by promising to do something that he or she is already obligated to do. For example, suppose a warehouse owner contracts to have certain repairs done for $20,000. In the middle of construction, the building contractor demands an additional $5,000 to complete the work. The owner agrees, but when the work is finished, he gives the contractor only $20,000. If the contractor sues, he will lose. The owner's promise to pay an extra $5,000 is not supported by consideration. The contractor is under a *preexisting obligation* to do the work for which the owner promises an additional $5,000. If the contractor promises to do something he was not already obligated to do, there would be consideration to support the promise of the additional $5,000. Promising to modify the repair plans illustrates such new consideration.

Sidebar 8.7 discusses how the UCC changes the legal requirement of consideration.

Consideration Not Necessary

The preexisting obligation rule does not apply to a sale-of-goods contract. The UCC states that parties to a sale-of-goods contract may make binding modifications to it without both parties giving new consideration. If a buyer of more than $500 of supplies agrees to pay your company an additional $500 over and above the amount already promised, this buyer is bound, although your company gives only the consideration (supplies) that it is already obligated to give (§2-209(1)).

Under the UCC, the rules of consideration also do not apply to a **firm offer.** A firm offer exists when a merchant offering goods promises in writing that the offer will not be revoked for a period not to exceed three months. This promise binds the merchant, although the offeree buyer gives no consideration to support it (§2-205).

In contracts that are not between merchants selling goods, a promise to keep an offer open for a certain time period must be supported by the offeree's consideration. Such agreement to not revoke an offer is called an **option.** A typical use of options is found in real estate transactions. A seller of land may promise to let a prospective buyer have two weeks to study the deal and accept the offer at a specific price. The buyer must provide some consideration (usually a small sum of money) to the seller, or the seller's offer is not an enforceable option because it can be revoked.

An important exception to the rule requiring consideration to support a promise is the doctrine of **promissory estoppel.** This doctrine arises when a promisee justifiably relies on a promisor's promise to his or her economic injury. The promisor must know that the promisee is likely to rely on the promise. Promissory estoppel is increasingly used when the facts of a business relationship do not amount to an express or implied contract.

> Promissory estoppel often is used to prevent a party who has made a unilateral offer from withdrawing the offer after the requested work has begun.

An example arises in situations when an employer promises its employees that they will not be terminated without finding a justifiable cause. Often these types of promises are found in employee handbooks. Courts have ruled that employers cannot withdraw the pledge in a handbook and reinstate the employee-at-will status without their employees receiving some form of consideration.[1] To achieve this change, the employer must explicitly give employees more pay, greater benefits, or some type of inducement.

12. CAPACITY OF PARTIES TO CONTRACT

Capacity refers to a person's ability to be bound by a contract. Courts have traditionally held three classes of persons to lack capacity to be bound by contractual promises:

- Minors (also called "infants").
- Intoxicated persons.
- Mentally incompetent persons.

---

[1] *Ross v. May Company d/b/a Marshall Fields*, 800 N.E.2d 210 (Ill. App. 2007).

Minors   In most states, a *minor* is anyone under age 18. Minors usually cannot be legally bound to contractual promises unless those promises involve *necessaries of life* such as food, clothing, shelter, medical care, and—in some states—education. Even for necessaries, minors often cannot be sued for the contract price, only for a "reasonable" value. In a number of states, courts will hold a minor who has misrepresented his or her age to contractual promises.

A contract into which a minor has entered is voidable at the election of the minor. The minor can *disaffirm* the contract and legally recover any consideration that has been given an adult, even if the minor cannot return the adult's consideration. On the other hand, the adult is bound by the contract unless the minor elects to disaffirm it.

The minor may disaffirm a contract anytime before reaching the age of majority (usually 18) and for a reasonable time after reaching majority. If the minor fails to disaffirm within a reasonable time after reaching majority, the minor is said to *ratify* the contract. Upon ratification, the minor loses the right to disaffirm.

Intoxicated and Mentally Incompetent Persons   Except when a court has judged an adult to be mentally incompetent, that adult does not lose capacity to contract simply because of intoxication or mental impairment. In most cases involving adult capacity to contract, courts measure capacity by whether the adult was capable of understanding the nature and purpose of the contract. Obviously, the more complex a contractual transaction gets, the more likely a court is to decide that an intoxicated or mentally impaired person lacks capacity to contract and has the right to disaffirm the contract. In such factual situations, the contracts are voidable by the intoxicated or mentally impaired person.

Traditionally, the descriptive phrase *mentally impaired* applies to adults with a history of medically documented disabilities. With the aging of the population, the number of cases involving elderly citizens claiming contractual incapacity grows. These cases will develop additional nuances in the law of capacity to contract. Practical business advice is to be aware when contracting with an elderly person. It may be best to insist that a friend or family member assist (if not cosign with) an older contracting party. Take steps to ensure you will not be accused of taking advantage of the elderly.

Other Situations Involving Voidable Contracts   Contracts based on fraud or misrepresentation are two important examples of voidable contracts. **Fraud** involves an intentional misstatement of a material (important) fact that induces one to rely justifiably to his or her injury. Intentionally calling a zircon a diamond and persuading someone to purchase it on that basis is a fraud. Sometimes failures to disclose a material fact can also be a fraud, as when a landowner sells a buyer land knowing that the buyer wishes to build a home on it and does not disclose that the land is underwater during the rainy season. The defrauded party can withdraw from the contract. **Misrepresentation** is simply a misstatement without intent to mislead. However, a contract entered into through misrepresentation is still voidable by the innocent party.

Other examples of voidable contracts are those induced by duress or undue influence. **Duress** means force or threat of force. The force may be physical or, in some instances, economic. **Undue influence** occurs when one is taken advantage of unfairly through a contract by a party who misuses a position of relationship or legal confidence. Contracts voidable because of undue influence often arise when persons weakened by age or illness are persuaded to enter into a disadvantageous contract.

What happens when each party misunderstands something very basic and material about a contract? Such a situation goes right to the heart of whether there has been a "voluntary" consent to a contract. When there is a **mutual mistake** as to a material fact inducing a contract, rescission is appropriate. The test of materiality is whether the parties would have contracted had they been aware of the mistake. If they would not have contracted, the mistaken fact is material.

There is a difference between a mutual, or bilateral, mistake and a unilateral mistake. A **unilateral mistake** arises when only one of the parties to a contract is wrong about a material fact. Suppose that Royal Carpet Co. bids $8.70 per yard for certain carpet material instead of $7.80 per yard as it had intended. If the seller accepts Royal Carpet's bid, a contract results even though there was a unilateral mistake.

13. LAWFUL PURPOSE

A basic requirement of a valid contract is *legality of purpose*. A "contract" to murder someone is hardly enforceable in a court of law. Contracts that require commission of a crime or tort or violate accepted standards of behavior (*public policy*) are void. Courts will generally take no action on a void contract, and they will leave the parties to a contract where they have put themselves. Sidebar 8.8 gives common examples of illegal contracts.

> A party disadvantaged by a mutual mistake can void the contract; a party who makes a unilateral mistake suffers the burden of that mistake.

> A person finds a pretty rock while hiking through a field. This person sells the rock to a jeweler for $50. The jeweler honestly did not know what the rock was worth. If this rock turns out to be an uncut gem worth more than $10,000, does the seller have any recourse against the jeweler?

:: *sidebar* 8.8

Examples of Illegal Contracts

Gambling agreements (except where permitted).

Contracts for usurious interest (greater interest than allowed by law).

Professional contracts made by unlicensed persons in which a regulatory statute requires licensing.

Contracts that unreasonably restrain trade (see Chapter 16).

Many contracts that attempt to limit negligence liability of a seller of goods or services to the public (called **exculpatory contracts**).

Unconscionable contracts involving a sale of goods under the UCC (usually applied when a difference in bargaining power or education leads a merchant to take unreasonable advantage of a consumer) (§2-302).

Other contracts prohibited by statute or against public policy.

There are several exceptions to the general rule that courts will take no action on an illegal contract. A contract may have both legal and illegal provisions to it. In such a case, courts will often enforce the legal provisions and refuse to enforce the illegal ones. For instance, a contract providing services or leasing goods sometimes contains a provision excusing the service provider or lessor from liability for negligently caused injury. Courts usually will not enforce this provision but will enforce the rest of the contract.

Often, courts will allow an innocent party to recover payment made to a party who knows (or should know) that a contract is illegal. For example, courts will allow recovery of a payment for professional services made by an innocent person to a person who is unlicensed to provide such services.

In some cases courts may allow a person to recover compensation under quasi-contract for services performed on an illegal contract. Recovery may be allowed when an otherwise qualified professional lets his or her license expire and provides services to a client before renewing the license.

Contracts That Restrain Trade   Contracts that restrain trade often are illegal and void. They include contracts to monopolize, to fix prices between competitors, and to divide up markets. Chapter 16 on antitrust law discusses these contracts and their illegality.

> Any agreement not to compete that you sign must be reasonable in its restrictions on the type of business being prohibited and the time and geography covered.

Other contracts that restrain trade are important to the efficient operation of business. **Covenants not to compete** are important in protecting employers from having the employees they train leave them and compete against them. They also protect the buyer of a business from having the seller set up a competing business.

However, some covenants not to compete are illegal. Courts will declare such agreements illegal unless they have a valid business purpose, such as to protect the goodwill a business buyer purchases from the seller of the business. Covenants not to compete must also be "reasonable as to time and space." If they restrain competition for too long or in an area too large, the courts will declare them unreasonable and void them as being illegal. Four or five years is generally as long a time as the courts are willing to find reasonable, and even then the length of time must be justified. As to space, the courts will void covenants not to compete any time the area restrained exceeds the area in which the restraining business operates.

:: Third Parties' Rights

Parties usually negotiate and enter into contracts for personal or organizational reasons. The purpose of the contractual agreement is to gain a direct benefit. Despite this common practice, sometimes third parties become involved in the performance of the contract. This occurrence could be anticipated by the original contracting parties, or it could arise due to the occurrence of unforeseen circumstances. Regardless of the factual situations, third parties and contract rights provide the focus of the concluding part of this chapter. The next two sections discuss third-party beneficiaries and assignments. The final section examines how a novation impacts the liability of the original contracting parties.

14. BENEFICIARIES

One or more of the original parties to a contract may intend for their agreement to benefit a third party. Such parties are called **third-party beneficiaries.** In general, persons who are not parties to a contract have no rights to sue to enforce the contract or to get damages for breach of contract.

However, a third-party beneficiary can sue if the parties to the contract *intended* to benefit that person.

Intended third-party beneficiaries fall into two distinct categories; however, any intended beneficiary has rights to enforce the contract to gain the intended benefit. The first category involves a *creditor beneficiary.* Suppose Carl owes Terry $10,000 for work Terry already has performed. Also assume Carl does work for Chris and contracts to have Chris pay Terry. Terry is a creditor beneficiary of the Carl–Chris contract and can sue Chris for the payment owed.

When the performance under a contract is meant as a gift to a third party, that person is a *donee beneficiary.* Donee beneficiaries can sue the party who owes them a performance under a breached contract, but they cannot sue the party who contracted to make them a gift. The beneficiary of a life insurance policy is usually a donee beneficiary.

An *incidental beneficiary* is a third party who unintentionally benefits from a contract. The incidental beneficiary has no rights under a contract. If merchant A contracts to have security service patrol her property—a contract that will likely also protect the other merchants on the block—and if one evening when the service fails to show up merchant B on the block is burglarized, B cannot sue the security service for breach of contract. B is only an incidental beneficiary of the contract between A and the service.

> You are a donee beneficiary if a parent buys a car for you. If the seller does not deliver the car, you can sue.

15. ASSIGNMENT OF CONTRACTS

Contracts often are thought as involving only two parties—the offeror and the offeree. In business, such a view is overly simplistic. Contracts may involve many original parties and sometimes third parties who are not a part of the negotiation resulting in the original contract. This section discusses how these third parties become involved in the contract's performance through the process of assignment.

Electronics, Inc., sells 250 radios on credit at $20 apiece to Radio Land Retail. Electronics then sells its rights under the contract to Manufacturers' Credit Co. When payment is due, can Manufacturers' Credit legally collect the $5,000 owed to Electronics by Radio Land? This transaction is controlled by the law of **assignment,** which is a transfer (generally a sale) of rights under a contract. Figure 8.4 shows the transaction and introduces important terminology.

As Figure 8.4 illustrates, in an assignment one of the original contracting parties becomes an **assignor** and assigns rights or duties or both to a third party, known as the **assignee.** If the assignment is properly structured, the assignee can enforce the original contract. When an assignor assigns rights, an implied warranty is made that the rights are valid and enforceable. If the assignee is unable to enforce the rights against the obligor because of illegality, incapacity, or breach of contract, the assignee can sue the assignor for breach of the implied warranty. However, if the obligor simply refuses to perform for the assignee, the assignee's legal claim is against the obligor, not the assignor.

Notice of Assignment   When an assignment is made, an assignee should notify the obligor immediately. Otherwise, the obligor may perform

Figure 8.4
Assignment

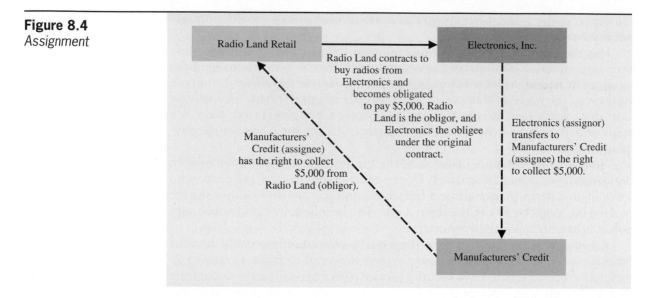

for the obligee-assignor. If Radio Land pays Electronics before being notified by Manufacturers' Credit of the assignment, Radio Land cannot be held liable to Manufacturers' Credit.

A dishonest or careless assignor may assign the same contract rights to two different assignees. Notification of the obligor is especially important in this situation. In most states, the law says that the first assignee to notify the obligor has priority no matter which assignee receives the first assignment of rights.

The order of multiple assignments is not as important as when an assignee gives notice that an assignment occurred.

Contracts That Cannot Be Assigned Although most contracts can be assigned, certain ones cannot. An assignment that increases the burden of performance to the obligor cannot be assigned. For instance, a right to have goods shipped to the buyer's place of business cannot be assigned by an Atlanta buyer to a Miami buyer if a New York seller has to ship the goods to Miami instead of Atlanta. Similarly, a *requirements contract* to supply a retail buyer with all the radios needed cannot be assigned because it depends upon the buyer's personal situation.

Most states regulate the assignment of wages. They limit the amount of wages a wage earner can assign to protect wage earners and their families.

A party to a contract cannot assign (delegate) performance of duties under a contract when performance depends on the character, skill, or training of that party. Otherwise, duties under a contract can be assigned as well as rights.

16. NOVATIONS

Typically, an assignor who delegates duties under a contract is not automatically relieved of future liability. In your current role as a student, suppose you find someone to take your place on your lease of an apartment or house. Assume you have six months left under the original term of the lease when you assign rights and delegate duties to the friend substituting for you. If the friend moves out and stops paying rent after only two months, you are still liable to the landlord for the last four months of rent. How can you avoid this lingering responsibility? The answer lies in understanding the impact of a novation. A **novation** is a three (or more) party contract wherein the original contracting parties agree to relieve the obligor from liability by substituting an assignee in the place of this party. For example, in your landlord-tenant-friend situation, when you have your friend take your place, you could seek an agreement with the landlord to remove you from the lease and to make your friend liable for the remainder of the lease period. This arrangement is a novation.

Such agreements usually are found in business contracts when an organization is acquired through purchase or merger transactions. In Case 8.2, earlier in this chapter, AOL would likely seek novations associated with as many contracts for which Talk America assumes responsibility.

:: Key Terms

Acceptance 246	Express contract 241	Promise 236
Accord and satisfaction 250	Firm offer 251	Promissory estoppel 251
Assignee 255	Fraud 252	Quasi-contract 241
Assignment 255	Goods 238	Rescission 239
Assignor 255	Implied-in-fact contract 241	Restitution 239
Bilateral contract 240	Implied-in-law contract 241	Specific performance 239
Capacity 251	Indefiniteness 245	Third-party beneficiary 254
Consideration 248	Mailbox rule 248	Undue influence 253
Counteroffer 246	Merchant 247	Unenforceable contract 243
Covenant not to compete 254	Mirror image rule 247	Unilateral contract 240
Deposited acceptance rule 248	Misrepresentation 252	Unilateral mistake 253
Duress 252	Mitigate 239	Valid contract 243
Enforceable contract 243	Mutual mistake 253	Void contract 243
Exculpatory contract 253	Novation 257	Voidable contract 244
Executed contract 244	Offer 245	
Executory contract 244	Option 251	

:: Review Questions and Problems

Basic Concepts

1. *Contract Law in Private Enterprise*

   Discuss the importance of contract law to the private market system. How does contract law provide flexibility and precision in business dealings?

2. *Sources of Contract Law*

   (a) What is meant by the common law of contracts?

   (b) What is the UCC?

3. *Breach of Contract*

Gustavson contracts with Sanders to buy 51 percent of the stock of Gilmet Corporation. When Sanders breaches the contract, Gustavson sues for specific performance. Is specific performance an appropriate remedy under these circumstances? Explain.

Contractual Classifications and Terminology

4. *Bilateral and Unilateral Contracts*

   (a) What is the distinction between a bilateral and a unilateral contract?

   (b) Which type is more common in business?

5. *Express and Implied-in-Fact Contracts*

   (a) Using the lemonade stand example at the beginning of the chapter, describe an example of an express contract that might arise between the supplier and the seller.

   (b) When would an implied-in-fact contract arise between the seller and a buyer?

6. *Implied-in-Law or Quasi-Contracts*

   Why are courts willing to apply contractual principles when the parties fail to create contractual relationships?

7. *Contractual Enforcement Terminology*

   How can someone reasonably say that a voidable contract is both enforceable and unenforceable?

8. *Contractual Performance Terminology*

   Pat hires a tailor to make a suit. The tailor completes all the sewing and now waits for Pat to pick up the suit and pay for it. Is this contractual agreement executed or executory? Explain.

Contract Formation

9. *Offer to Contract*

   Condor Equipment Company offers to sell a dough cutting machine to Snappy Jack Biscuits, Inc. The offer states: "This offer expires Friday noon." On Thursday morning, the sales manager for Condor calls the president of Snappy Jack and explains that the machine has been sold to another purchaser. Discuss whether Condor has legally revoked its offer to Snappy Jack.

10. *Acceptance of Offer*

    Fielding Bros. offers to ship six furnaces to Central City Heating and Cooling Co. for $4,500 cash. Central City accepts on the condition that Fielding give 120 days' credit. Has a contract resulted? Explain.

11. *Consideration*

    Jefferson and Goldberg enter a contract for the sale of five acres of land at $10,000 per acre. Later, Goldberg, the buyer, asks if Jefferson will agree to modify the contract to $9,000 per acre.

    (a) Jefferson agrees. Is Jefferson's promise binding on him?

    (b) Would your answer be different if five used cars were being sold instead of five acres of land?

12. *Capacity of Parties to Contract*

    Describe the circumstances under which an adult lacks the capacity to contract.

13. *Lawful Purpose*

    Hunt signs an equipment lease contract with Edwards Rental. The contract contains a clause stating: "Lessor disclaims all liability arising from injuries caused by use of this equipment." Because the equipment has been improperly serviced by Edwards Rental, Hunt is injured while using it. If Hunt sues, will the disclaimer clause likely be enforced? Explain.

Third Parties' Rights

14. *Beneficiaries*

   What is the distinction between an intended and an incidental beneficiary?

15. *Assignment of Contracts*

   Franchetti Rifle Distributors assigns a $20,000 claim against Top Gun, Inc., to the Zenith Collection Agency. When Zenith sues Top Gun, Top Gun asserts that it rejected a shipment of rifles from Franchetti out of which the claim arose because they had defective trigger guards. Explain whether Top Gun can properly assert its defense against plaintiff Zenith.

16. *Novations*

   Explain the purpose of a novation and who must be party to it.

business :: *discussion*

You are the Marketing Manager for We-Can-Furnish-It Office Supply Company. In your role, you work with your company's sales staff. This staff is divided between personnel who travel to make face-to-face calls and those who answer the phones and accept orders during these conversations. In addition to the sales staff, you also are responsible for the technicians that ensure online orders can be placed and filled.

The transactions with customers range from supplying an entire office building with furniture and everything that allows an office to function to delivering small amounts of basic office supplies. As you study the documentation, including purchase order forms and confirmation statements, of these various transactions, you wonder about the answers to the following questions:

When does the negotiation end and a binding contract exist?

If there is conflicting language in the buyer's purchase order and the seller's confirmation, which language controls?

How can you determine when a contract has been performed fully?

9

Contractual Issues— Form, Interpretation, Performance, and Discharge

Learning Objectives ::

In this chapter you will learn:

1. To appreciate that valid, enforceable contacts can take many forms.

2. To understand concepts of how contract performance analysis occurs.

3. To appreciate that contractual agreements are discharged through performance.

4. That nonperformance of contracts results in a breach unless performance is excused.

In the preceding chapter, you studied the basics of contract terminology and classifications. You learned about the essential elements required to create a valid, enforceable contract. Finally, you read about how contracts impact third parties.

In this chapter, your study of contracts continues as you learn about the formalities and performance of contracts. These topics are of critical importance to businesspeople. After studying this chapter, you should have answers to the following questions:

- Are orally stated contracts as enforceable as (as good as) the contracts written and signed?
- Are there rules that businesspeople should know about deciding what contract language means?

- How do parties (and courts) decide if promises in a contract have been fully performed?
- What do I need to know if a contract is not fully performed?

:: Form and Interpretation

Knowing what elements must exist to form a valid contract is only the beginning of understanding concepts of how contracts help with business transactions. Among the other important topics is whether contracts have to be in writing and signed by the parties. The following sections examine the formality of contracts and how contractual language should be interpreted.

1. WRITTEN VERSUS ORAL CONTRACTS

Because of the importance of contracts in our personal and professional lives, people believe a contract has to be written and signed to be valid. Typically, this impression is wrong. Oral contracts generally are as enforceable as written ones. Think about the agreements you made recently.

- Have you driven through or eaten in a fast-food restaurant?
- Have you been in a store and bought anything?
- Have you purchased something from a vending machine?
- Have you agreed to help someone get some work done in return for that person helping you or giving you something (money or a ride)?

Most of our transactions involve informal contracts. This does not mean we should ignore reasons for greater formality. When contracts are of significant importance or the dollars involved are larger than typical day-to-day transactions or it is important to have a record of the precise agreement, writing and signing a contract is best.

In certain situations, the law requires contracts to be in a written, signed format. The next two sections discuss this requirement and explain the types of agreements that must be in writing. Section 4 then examines the impact of oral changes to written contracts.

> Oral contracts generally are valid and enforceable. Certain types of contracts must be evidenced by a writing that is signed by the party to be bound.

2. STATUTE OF FRAUDS

The law requiring that certain contracts be in writing is the **statute of frauds.** Designed to prevent potential frauds from oral contracts, the original English statute was adopted in 1677. Today, every state has its own statute of frauds. The role of these statutes requiring written contracts is to minimize confusion (potential fraud and deceit) in court whenever a party claims a contract is breached. If courts have to decide the validity of an oral agreement, parties can make allegations that contradict one another. One party says to the judge, "We have a contract." The other party says, "We never finalized a contract; none exists." Judges can have difficulty knowing whom to believe.

To remove the potential for confusion, fraud, and deceit, written contracts are required. If the required writing is not met, the judges do not have to determine which party is telling the truth. The case is dismissed from the court, and the parties are left with an unenforceable contract. The statute of frauds require certain types of business-related contracts to be in writing. Sidebar 9.1 provides a list of these agreements.

:: *sidebar* 9.1

Types of Contracts Required to be Evidenced by a Signed Writing

- Contracts involving an interest in land.
- Collateral contracts to pay the debt of another person.
- Contracts that cannot be performed within one year from the date of the agreement.
- Contracts for the sale goods of $500 or more.

In some states, the statute of frauds requires that the actual contract between the parties must be in writing. However, most states merely require that the contract be *evidenced* by writing and be signed by the party against whom enforcement is being sought. This requirement means that the party being sued must have signed a note, memorandum, or another written form short of a formal contract that describes with reasonable certainty the terms of the oral agreement. In sales of goods between merchants, the writing may not need to be signed by the party being sued. Despite these rules, the best practice is to have contracts carefully written and signed. Written documentation will save time and expense if a dispute arises. Section 5 provides more detail about how written contracts get interpreted.

Exchange of e-mail messages may satisfy the requirement of a writing.

Sale of an Interest in Land Sales of interests in land are common contracts covered by the statute of frauds. Although "sales of interests in land" covers a contract to sell land, it includes much more. Interests in land include contracts for mortgages, mining rights, easements (rights to use another's land, such as the right to cross it with electric power wires), and leases of longer than one year. However, a contract to insure land or to erect a building is not an interest in land.

Collateral Promise to Pay Another's Debt A collateral promise is a secondary or conditional promise. Such a commitment arises when one person, a business shareholder for example, promises to repay the loan of the corporation if and only when that organization does not make payments. This collateral promise usually arises at a time different from the original obligation. Suppose the corporation borrows money from a bank and later finds it is having trouble making payments on time. To avoid the bank's calling the entire loan in default, the shareholder may promise to pay if the corporation does not. This promise by the shareholder is of a collateral nature and must be in writing to be enforced by the bank.

To avoid this situation of a collateral promise, banks often require a small business organization to have someone guarantee the performance of its contracts. If a shareholder makes an original promise to be responsible for the corporation's performance, this commitment is not collateral and does not have to be in writing. In essence, in such situations the corporation and the shareholder are considered equally obligated to perform the contract. There is no conditional promise by the shareholder. Although such original promises often are in writing, the law does not require a written agreement.

Remember the difference between guaranteeing a person's performance and agreeing to become liable if a person fails to perform.

If it is possible, even if unlikely, to perform a contract within one year, an oral contract involving that performance is enforceable.

Cannot Be Performed within One Year   The statute of frauds applies to a contract the parties cannot perform within one year after its making. Courts usually interpret the one-year requirement to mean that the contract must specify a period of performance longer than one year. Thus, an oral contract for services that last 20 months is not enforceable. But an oral contract for services to be completed "by" a date 20 months away is enforceable. The difference is that the latter contract can be performed within one year, even if it actually takes longer than that to perform it.

As interpreted by the courts, the statute of frauds applies only to executory contracts that the parties' cannot perform within a year. Once one of the parties has completed his or her performance for the other, that party can enforce an oral multiyear contract.

Sale of Goods of $500 or More   Under the UCC, the statute of frauds covers sales of goods of $500 or more. Modifications to such concluded are also included and must be in writing. While this provision appears arbitrary with respect to the $500 amount, its purpose is clear. Contracts involving the sale and purchase of goods that are less than $500 usually are performed quickly. There is very little room for disputes about terms or performance that arise. As the dollar amount increases, the need for a written agreement also increases. This is particularly true if the contract will remain executory (not performed) for an extended period of time.

As you think about this requirement in sale of goods transactions, ponder a typical transaction. Assume you go into a computer store and buy a new laptop computer for $1,500. Do you and the seller sign a written contract before completing the purchase? Probably not! The reason is there is no need for a written contract. The agreement to buy and the actual sale occur almost simultaneously—at least in very quick order.

Suppose, instead of going to the store, you go online to order a laptop. The online transaction contains information telling you the laptop will be assembled and shipped within three weeks. The paperwork generated through the website likely will include a contract for you to sign electronically. This writing is needed to satisfy the statute of frauds. The written agreement governs the parties' relationship until the contract is performed—you pay and the manufacturer delivers the laptop.

Others   In addition to the basic contracts covered by the statute of frauds, other contracts must be in writing in various states. Most states require insurance policies to be written. Several states require written estimates in contracts for automobile repair.

3. EXCEPTIONS TO THE WRITING REQUIREMENT

In addition to understanding that the statute of frauds requires certain types of contracts to be in writing, it is important to know there are exceptions to the writing requirement. If an agreement is orally stated, parties may be able to convince a judge that a contract does exist. If such proof can be established in a way that convinces the judge the contract was agreed upon, there is little chance of fraud. Under certain circumstances, oral contracts are enforceable.

Such exceptions fall into the following categories:

- Part Performance
- Rules Involving Goods
- Judicial Admissions

Part Performance   The doctrine of **part performance** creates an exception to the requirement that sales of interests in land must be in writing. When a buyer of land has made valuable improvements in it, or when the buyer is in possession of it and has paid part of the purchase price, even an oral contract to sell is enforceable. The courts will enforce an oral agreement involving land title if the part performance clearly establishes the intent of the parties as buyer and seller. If a court can envision the parties in some other relationship, such as landlord and tenant, the part performance is not sufficient to substitute for a written agreement.

> The part performance exception sometimes is called *promissory estoppel.*

Rules Involving Goods   The UCC creates a number of situations that allow the enforcement of oral agreements involving the sale of goods. In essence, the law strives to facilitate transactions involving goods as long as the parties cannot deceive the judge who is asked to determine a contract's validity. Sidebar 9.2 lists exceptions to the writing requirement for transactions involving the sale of goods.

:: *sidebar* 9.2

Exceptions to Statute-of-Frauds Requirement That Sale-of-Goods Contracts Be in Writing

- Contract for goods specially manufactured for the buyer on which the seller had begun performance.
- Contract for goods for which payment has been made and accepted or that have been received and accepted.
- Contract for goods in which the party being sued admits in court or pleadings that the contract has been made.

- Contract for goods between merchants in which the merchant sued has received a written notice from the other merchant confirming the contract and in which merchant sued does not object to the confirmation within 10 days.

*Source: UCC § 2–201.

The first exception is known as the *specifically manufactured goods rule.* If a buyer places an oral order for more than $500 worth of goods that are made especially for this buyer, the seller who has started production on this special order can enforce this agreement to avoid undue hardship. Since the seller would not be able to resell this special goods to other buyers, courts enforce the oral contact.

A *written confirmation between merchants* is another example of how the law facilitates business transactions. A merchant can avoid the impact of this provision by simply noting its objection to any written confirmation within 10 days of receiving it.

Judicial Admissions   If one party sues another party for failing to perform promises that are made orally, the defendant might argue the contract cannot be enforced since it must be in writing under the statute of frauds. This defense asks the judge to dismiss the lawsuit. Based on the historical background of the statute of frauds, a judge does not want the burden of deciding which party is telling the truth about the existence or nonexistence of an oral contract. However, if the defendant admits in court or in documents filed in court that an oral contract does exist, the judge does not have to guess about the contract's existence.

This **judicial admissions** exception is most important when the acknowledged oral contract is for the sale of goods. The UCC explicitly recognizes this exception [2-201(3)(b)]. Does this exception apply when the oral contract involves the sale of an interest in land, a collateral promise to pay another's debt, or performances that cannot be completed in one year? The answer is mixed among the states. Courts in a number of states permit the plaintiff to ask the defendant to admit the oral contract exists. If there is a judicial admission, the statute of fraud-based defense disappears. The judge proceeds to decide whether the oral contract is valid and enforceable.

4. THE PAROL EVIDENCE RULE

> The parol evidence rule prohibits testimony about the oral negotiation that results in a written contract; thus, read the contract before signing.

Like the statute of frauds, the **parol evidence rule** influences the form of contracts. This rule states that parties to a complete and final written contract cannot introduce oral evidence in court that changes the intended meaning of the written terms.

The parol evidence rule applies only to evidence of oral agreements made at the time of or prior to the written contract. It does not apply to oral modifications coming after the parties have made the written contract (although the statute of frauds may apply).

Suppose that Chris Consumer wants to testify in court that a merchant of an Ultima washing machine gave him an oral six-month warranty on the machine, even though the $450 written contract specified "no warranties." If the warranty was made after Chris signed the contract, he may testify about its existence. Otherwise, the parol evidence rule prevents him from testifying about an oral agreement that changes the terms of the written contract.

An exception to the parol evidence rule allows evidence of oral agreement that merely explains the meaning of written terms without changing the terms. Also, oral evidence that changes the meaning of written terms can be given if necessary to prevent fraud.

5. INTERPRETATION OF CONTRACTS

> In the interpretation of contract terms, handwriting is the best evidence of intention.

If each party is satisfied with the other's performance under a contract, there is no problem with interpreting the contract's terms. But when disagreement about contractual performance exists, interpretation of the terms often becomes necessary. Courts have devised several rules to assist in interpreting contracts.

Common words are given their usual meaning. "A rose is a rose is a rose," said the poet, and a court will interpret this common word to refer to a flower.

However, if the word has a particular *trade usage,* courts will give it that meaning. In a contract in the wine trade, the term *rose* would not refer to a flower at all but to a type of wine.

Many businesses today use printed form contracts. Sometimes the parties to one of these printed contracts type or handwrite additional terms. What happens when the typed or handwritten terms contradict the printed terms? What if the printed terms of a contract state "no warranties," but the parties have written in a 90-day warranty? In such a case, courts interpret handwritten terms to control typed terms and typed terms to control printed ones. The written warranty will be enforced since the writing is the best evidence of the parties' true intention.

Another rule is that when only one of the parties drafts (writes) a contract, courts will interpret ambiguous or vague terms against the party that drafts them. Courts often apply this rule to insurance contracts and interpret the policy to give the policyholder the benefit of the doubt when deciding the meaning of a confusing term or phrase.

Case 9.1 illustrates how important a court's interpretation of contractual language is in determining the rights of the parties.

> *HANDWRITTEN* terms
>
> *control*
>
> TYPED terms
>
> *control*
>
> PRINTED terms/forms

case 9.1 ::

NORFOLK SOUTHERN RAILWAY COMPANY v. KIRBY, PTY. LTD., DBA KIRBY ENGINEERING
125 S. Ct. 385 (2004)

James N. Kirby, Pty. Ltd. is a manufacturing company in Australia. It contracted with a freight-forwarding company, International Cargo Control (ICC), to ship 10 containers of machinery to a General Motors plant in Huntsville, Alabama. These containers were to travel by ship from Sydney to Savannah, Georgia. From Savannah's port, the containers were to be placed on a train for delivery in Huntsville. The terms of this transportation contract were described in a bill of lading limiting liability to $500 per container while at sea. A similar clause limited the liability for damage on land to $17,373 for all containers. The bill of lading also included a Himalaya clause. This clause extends the liability limitation to all agents and independent carriers involved in the transportation of Kirby's containers.

As a freight forwarder, ICC contracted with Hamburg Sud, a German shipping company, to transport these containers from Sydney, through Savannah, to Huntsville. Hamburg Sud issued a bill of lading to

ICC that contained similar liability limitation and Himalaya clauses. The only distinction in this bill of lading and the one issued by ICC to Kirby was the $500 per container limit applied to both sea and land transportation.

The 10 containers arrived in Savannah in good shape. Hamburg Sud contracted with Norfolk Southern Railroad to take the containers to Huntsville. While on the train, the containers were damaged when a derailment occurred. The total damage suffered by Kirby was $1,500,000. Kirby and its insurance company sued Norfolk Southern for its losses. The district court granted Norfolk Southern's motion for summary judgment on the grounds that its liability was limited to $500 per container. Upon Kirby's appeal, the 11th Circuit Court of Appeals reversed. The appellate court found that Norfolk Southern was not protected by the liability limitation clauses since it had only an indirect relationship with Kirby and ICC. Norfolk Southern petitioned for a writ of certiorari, which was granted.

O'CONNOR, J.: . . . Turning to the merits, we begin with the ICC bill of lading, the first of the contracts at issue. Kirby and ICC made a contracts for the carriage of machinery from Sydney to Huntsville, and agreed to limit the liability of ICC and other parties who would participate in transporting the machinery. The bill's Himalaya Clause states: "These conditions [for limitations on liability] apply whenever claims relating to the performance of the contract evidenced by this [bill of lading] are made against any servant, agent or other person (including any independent contractor) whose services have been used in order to perform the contract."

The question presented is whether the liability limitation in Kirby's and ICC's contract extends to Norfolk, which is ICC's sub-subcontractor. . . .

The Court of Appeals' ruling is not true to the contract language or to the intent of the parties. The plain language of the Himalaya Clause indicates an intent to extend the liability limitation broadly—to "any servant, agent or other person (including any independent contractor)" whose services contribute to performing the contract . . . There is no reason to contravene the clause's obvious meaning. The expansive contract language corresponds to the fact that various modes of transportation would be involved in performing the contract. Kirby and ICC contracted for the transportation of machinery from Australia to Huntsville, Alabama, and, as the crow flies, Huntsville is some 366 miles inland from the port of discharge. Thus, the parties must have anticipated that a land carrier's services would be necessary for the contract's performance. It is clear to us that a railroad like Norfolk was an intended beneficiary of the ICC bill's broadly written Himalaya Clause. Accordingly, Norfolk's liability is limited by the terms of that clause.

The question arising from the Hamburg Sud bill of lading is more difficult. It requires us to set an efficient default rule for certain shipping contracts, a task that has been a challenge for courts for centuries. ICC and Hamburg Sud agreed that Hamburg Sud would transport the machinery from Sydney to Huntsville, and agreed to the "package limitation" on the liability of Hamburg Sud, its agents, and its independent contractors. The second question presented is whether that liability limitation, which ICC negotiated, prevents Kirby from suing Norfolk (Hamburg Sud's independent contractor) for more. As we have explained, the liability limitation in the ICC bill, the first contract, sets liability for a land accident higher than this bill does. Because Norfolk's liability will be lower if it is protected by the Hamburg Sud bill too, we must reach this second question in order to give Norfolk the full relief for which it petitioned.

To interpret the Hamburg Sud bill, we turn to a rule drawn from our precedent about common carriage: When an intermediary contracts with a carrier to transport goods, the cargo owner's recovery against the carrier is limited by the liability limitation to which the intermediary and carrier agreed. The intermediary is certainly not automatically empowered to be the cargo owner's agent in every sense. That would be unsustainable. But when it comes to liability limitations for negligence resulting in damage, an intermediary can negotiate reliable and enforceable agreements with the carriers it engages.

. . . In holding that an intermediary binds a cargo owner to the liability limitations it negotiates with downstream carriers, we do not infringe on traditional agency principles. We merely ensure the reliability of downstream contracts for liability limitations. . . .

Respondents also contend that any decision binding Kirby to the Hamburg Sud bill's liability limitation will be disastrous for the international shipping industry. Various participants in the industry have weighed in as *amici* on both sides in this case, and we must make a close call. It would be idle to pretend that the industry can easily be characterized, or that efficient default rules can easily be discerned. In the final balance, however, we disagree with respondents for three reasons.

First, we believe that a limited agency rule tracks industry practices. In intercontinental ocean shipping, carriers may not know if they are dealing with an intermediary, rather than with a cargo owner. Even if knowingly dealing with an intermediary, they may not know how many other intermediaries came before, or what obligations may be outstanding among them. If the Eleventh Circuit's rule were the law, carriers would have to seek out more information before contracting, so as to assure themselves that their contractual liability limitations provide true protection. That task of information gathering might be very costly or even impossible, given that goods often change hands many times in the course of intermodal transportation.

Second, if liability limitations negotiated with cargo owners were reliable while limitations negotiated with intermediaries were not, carriers would likely want to charge the latter higher rates. A rule prompting downstream carriers to distinguish between cargo owners and intermediary shippers might interfere with statutory and decisional law promoting nondiscrimination in common carriage. . . .

Finally, . . . our decision produces an equitable result. Kirby retains the option to sue ICC, the carrier, for any loss that exceeds the liability limitation to which they agreed. And indeed, Kirby has sued ICC in an Australian court for damages arising from the Norfolk derailment. It seems logical that ICC—the only party that definitely knew about and was party to both of the bills of lading at issue here—should bear responsibility for any gap between the liability limitations in the bills. Meanwhile, Norfolk enjoys the benefit of the Hamburg Sud bill's liability limitation.

We hold that Norfolk is entitled to the protection of the liability limitations in the two bills of lading.

Having undertaken this analysis, we recognize that our decision does no more than provide a legal backdrop against which future bills of lading will be negotiated. It is not, of course, this Court's task to structure the international shipping industry. Future parties remain free to adapt their contracts to the rules set forth here, only now with the benefit of greater predictability concerning the rules for which their contracts might compensate.

Reversed and remanded.

:: CASE QUESTIONS

1. Why were there two bills of lading in this case?
2. What different clauses did these contracts contain?
3. What were the holdings of the district court, appellate court, and Supreme Court?
4. What three reasons does the Supreme Court provide for concluding that its ruling will not adversely impact the international shipping industry?

:: Performance

The fundamental reason any of us enter into a contract is to assure the performance of the promise made or to secure the performance of the action desired. What we want is the other party's **duty of performance.** In turn, they want this same duty to be performed by us. An extremely high percentage of contracts are performed in such a way that makes the contracting parties happy. Thus, the most simple (and realistic) statement concerning performance of contracts is that it typically happens. When the parties perform, the obligations of the contract are discharged. A party to a contract is **discharged** when that party is relieved from all further responsibility of performance.

Not all contractual obligations are fully performed. When less than full performance occurs, a number of legal issues arise. For example, a complete lack of performance results in a breach of the contract. The possible legal and equitable remedies arising from a breached contract are discussed in Chapter 8. Figure 9.1 reviews these remedies and much more about contractual performance.

As summarized in Figure 9.1, less than full performance results in issues about the level of performance and excuses for nonperformance. As you study this figure and read the next sections, keep in mind that contracting parties ultimately arrive at one of two conclusions: (1) they are discharged from the obligation to perform further or (2) they are liable for breaching the contract.

Figure 9.1 *Analysis of contractual performance*

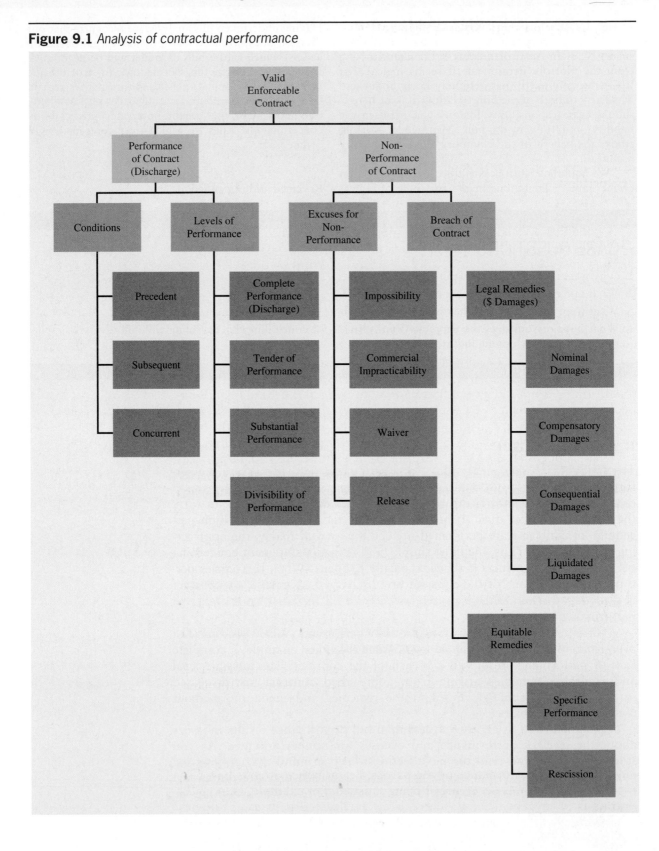

6. CONDITIONS OF PERFORMANCE

Parties typically put conditions in their contracts to clarify when performance is due. While conditions reflect the creativity of the contracting parties, classifications of conditions usually take three forms.

If something must take place in future, before a party has a duty to perform, it is a **condition precedent.** For example, a building developer may contract to buy certain land "when the city annexes it." The annexation is a condition precedent to the developer's duty to purchase the land. Parties should think through their business environment and state clearly the conditions governing their performance. For example, in a supplier-customer contract, the parties should state whether payment by the customer is a condition precedent for the seller to deliver or is delivery by the seller a condition precedent for payment.

A **condition subsequent** excuses contractual performance if some future event takes place. A marine insurance policy might terminate coverage for any shipping losses "if war is declared." This is a condition subsequent. Another typical example of this type of condition is the requirement that an insured motorist or homeowner must notify the insurance company of a claim (from a car accident or homeowner's loss) within a short time period (five days perhaps) of the claim arising from the accident of the loss. Failure to provide this notice relieves the insurance company of its duty to provide coverage.

The distinction between conditions precedent and conditions subsequent can appear quite subtle. The key difference is found in the timing of the duty to perform. A contracting party has no duty to perform prior to a condition precedent being satisfied. Once the condition precedent is met, the duty to perform is owed. The failure to meet a condition subsequent relieves the other contracting party from having to perform the duties previously promised.

What happens if the parties do not have **express conditions** governing performance specified in their contract? Courts may be asked whether **implied conditions** can be read into the parties' obligations to perform. When courts decide the conditions of performance, a common decision can be the parties have a simultaneous duty to perform. In essence, there is a **concurrent condition** of performance. In a contract for the transfer of title to land, the buyer and seller usually expect to meet at a closing event and perform their obligations concurrently. The buyer provides the necessary funds to cover the purchase price while, at the same time, the seller signs and delivers the legal documents transferring ownership.

Most of our everyday purchases involve implied concurrent conditions of performance. While shopping you take items to a cashier and expect to pay and take the items with you. Your contractual duty to pay and the store's contractual duty to deliver are exchanged simultaneously. As business contracts often involve more complicated transactions, issues related to performance require further examination.

7. PAYMENT, DELIVERY, SERVICES TENDERED

The preceding sections' content on conditions allows us to examine more fully the order of performance by the parties. Performance often is based on one or more conditions occurring or being satisfied. For example, in a typical contract involving the delivery of goods by a seller and payment of money by a buyer, what is the required order of performance? In essence, who goes

---

As an employee, you usually have a responsibility to work for a certain amount of time (equivalent to a pay period) before your employer is obligated to pay you. You are entitled to be paid before working the next period. The performance of work is a condition to be paid, and receiving your pay is a condition for you to continue working. Do you see how contractual conditions govern performance?

Employers required to notify their insurance companies of claims by employees should provide this notice when an employee files a claim of discrimination with the EEOC.

first? The best way to answer these questions is to have the contracting parties provide specific guidance in the contract. When the parties fail to provide this level of detail, the law states the buyer's payment is a condition that must be satisfied before the seller has the duty to deliver (§ 2-511(1)).

Delivery is a legal term referring to the transfer of possession from the seller to the buyer. The buyer and seller may presume to know implicitly how and when the goods will be delivered. Sidebar 9.3 illustrates how the UCC serves as a gap-filler, thereby not leaving the terms of delivery of goods to the parties' uncertain presumptions.

:: *sidebar* 9.3

Terms of Delivery in the UCC

Suppose your company sells office equipment to a buyer. Further suppose that the contract carefully describes the equipment and the purchase price. However, the contract provides no specific guidance as to when or where the equipment is to be delivered.

The UCC permits and encourages the enforceability of this contract by providing a series of gap-filling provisions. In essence, if the parties fail to write clear instructions on delivery of the equipment, the UCC controls.

The seller's obligation is to tender delivery of the goods, and the buyer's duty is to accept and pay for them (§2-301). The phrase *tender of delivery* means the seller must make the goods available to the buyer. If, as in our example, the contract makes no statement about delivery, the presumption is the buyer must make arrangements to pick up the goods at the location the seller designates (§2-503(1)).

Many buyers may not want to assume the burden of picking up the goods at the seller's location. Thus, it is common for the buyer and seller to agree the goods will be shipped to the buyer. If the contract does not provide additional details, how does the seller satisfy its obligation to ship the goods? The UCC states the seller satisfies its obligation to ship goods once they are transferred to the shipper for transportation (§2-504). If the goods are damaged in transit, the liability rests on the buyer, not the seller.

To avoid the assumption of risk, experienced buyers may insist on what is called a destination contract. This contract requires the seller to get the goods shipped and delivered to a specific place of business designated by the buyer. The risk of loss for damage to the goods remains with the seller until the goods safely arrive at the buyer's destination (2-310(1)(b)).

Do you now see why negotiation over the terms of performance, such as shipment and delivery, should be so important to your company?

Performance of contractual obligations presents parties and courts with legal issues. The resolution of these issues often requires analysis of principles relating to formation as well as performance of contracts. Case 9.2 involves a typical business transaction. Notice how the court examines the questions of which party made the offer and which one accepted it. The conclusion of this formation issue impacts which party has failed to perform.

The UCC provides valuable guidance to performance issues in contracts for the sales of goods. However, when a contract involves the performance of services, the parties to the contract should take time to provide specific conditions. If their agreement lacks specificity, reasonableness needs to govern the relationship and performance. For example, let's assume your manufacturing company hires software consultants to oversee the installation and implementation of new programs that hopefully will enhance your overall efficiency. The contract specifies the date for the completion of this work by the consultants; however, the contract does not provide a beginning date.

VENTURE MEDIA LIMITED PARTNERSHIP v. COLTS PLASTICS COMPANY, INCORPORATED
168 F. 3d 484 (4th Cir. 1999)

PER CURIAM: . . . Venture sells cosmetic products through direct-response marketing. Colt manufactures and sells plastic containers for cosmetic products.

In 1994, Venture approached Colt seeking to purchase plastic containers for its line of cosmetic products. Meetings were held between representatives of both Colt and Venture. . . . When all of these issues were settled, Venture began placing orders with Colt.

In its business, Colt uses a number of forms including a Quotation/Proposal Form (Proposal Form) and an Invoice Form (Invoice). . . .

Between 1994 and September 1995, Venture ordered from Colt, and Colt manufactured and shipped, plastic containers for Venture's cosmetic products. . . . Venture placed orders with Colt using a purchase order. After manufacturing and shipping the plastic containers requested in the various purchase orders, Colt sent an Invoice to Venture requesting payment. The Invoice stated that payment was "due 30 days from the Invoice date," and "amounts 30 days past due [were] subject" to twelve percent annual interest. This period of time passed with the two companies transacting without incident.

However, in August and early September 1995, Venture felt as if there were problems. The deliveries were arriving late, and Colt refused to increase Venture's line of credit. To resolve these issues, Venture requested a meeting with Colt. At this meeting, Colt assured Venture it would resolve the concerns raised by Venture.

Based on these assurances, on September 21, 1995, Venture sent a purchase order to Colt for plastic containers totaling $339,996.25. The purchase order specified exact quantities, exact prices for each quantity, and the total price. In addition, the purchase order explicitly specified the location where the products should be shipped and stated: "Please notify us immediately if this order cannot be shipped complete on or before 11/03/95." Colt never sent an acknowledgment to Venture but began to manufacture the plastic containers requested in the purchase order.

Between late February and early March 1996, Colt shipped plastic containers aggregating $47,922.18 to Venture in a series of shipments. Colt also sent Invoices for each shipment to Venture. Venture never paid Colt for these deliveries and did not give notice to Colt of any defects in the delivered goods within the

thirty-day period required by the Proposal Form. Colt continued to manufacture plastic containers totaling $122,799.59 after the deadline date for delivery specified in Venture's purchase order. Because of the outstanding balance owed by Venture, Colt never shipped these plastic containers to Venture. Colt sold what it could of these products to third parties, but because these plastic containers were specially manufactured for Venture, they were difficult to sell on the open market. Consequently, Colt continues to hold in its inventory $108,793.84 in plastic containers manufactured for Venture.

On December 30, 1996, Venture filed this suit against Colt in the Circuit Court of Maryland for Baltimore County alleging breach of contract. . . . Colt removed the case to the United States District Court for the District of Maryland based on diversity jurisdiction. Colt filed a counterclaim alleging breach of contract and seeking $47,922.18 plus interest for the plastic containers sent to Venture and $108,793.84 for the plastic containers specially manufactured for, but not sent to Venture.

Both parties moved for summary judgment with respect to all claims. The district court granted Colt's motion for summary judgment, and therefore, entered judgment in favor of Colt on Venture's claims and on Colt's counterclaim. . . . On appeal, Venture contends the district court erred when it granted summary judgment in favor of Colt. . . .

The parties agree that a contract existed for the sale of plastic containers amounting to $339,996.25, but vigorously dispute which terms control the sale. According to Venture, a $339,996.25 contract for plastic containers was formed when it sent its purchase order to Colt and Colt began to manufacture the plastic containers. Venture further maintains that Colt breached the contract by: (1) delivering defective plastic containers; (2) delivering damaged plastic containers; (3) failing to deliver the plastic containers by the agreed upon dates; (4) failing to extend Venture a volume purchase discount; and (5) failing to extend Venture's line of credit. In response, Colt contends that a $339,996.25 contract for plastic containers was formed when Colt sent its Proposal Form to Venture and Venture sent its purchase order to Colt. According to Colt, Venture breached the contract when it failed to make payment for the plastic containers that were manufactured and delivered to Venture. Colt further maintains that it never breached its contract with Venture because the plain language of the Proposal Form disposes of Venture's breach of contract allegations.

The district court granted summary judgment in favor of Colt on Venture's breach of contract claim, concluding that a contract was formed when Colt sent the Proposal Form to Venture and Venture sent the purchase order for $339,996.25 of plastic containers to Colt. Further, the district court concluded that Venture breached the contract when it failed to make payment for the plastic containers that Colt manufactured and delivered to Venture. Finally, the district court concluded that Colt did not breach its contract with Venture because the plain language of the Proposal Form was dispositive of Venture's breach of contract allegations. . . .

Under Maryland common law, an offer is "a expression by the offeror . . . that something over which he at least assumes to have control shall be done or happen or shall not be done or happen if the conditions stated in the offer are complied with." An offer must be definite and certain. Further, the intention of the parties is one of the primary factors when deciding whether an offer was made. Therefore, the facts and circumstances of each particular case are crucial.

In this case, Colt's Proposal Form was an offer. From 1994 through September 1995, Venture placed purchase orders with Colt for various plastic containers. Throughout this period, Colt sent numerous Proposal Forms to Venture. The Proposal Form explicitly sought acceptance by means of a purchase order. In conformity with this condition, Venture placed all of its orders by means of purchase order. Venture always abided by Colt's terms and never objected to them. Accordingly, we agree with the district court that Colt's Proposal Form was an offer made to Venture.

The Code states that once a certain and definite offer is made, acceptance may be made in any manner that is reasonable. However, an offeror may be particular about the appropriate means of acceptance. Here, Colt's Proposal Form was explicit: the proposal "may be accepted only by written purchase order." Venture abided by this requirement when it submitted its purchase order on September 21, 1995, accepting Colt's offer, thus creating a binding contract between the two companies under the terms of Colt's Proposal Form.

Having determined that Colt's Proposal Form constituted a valid offer and Venture's purchase order constituted a valid acceptance, thereby creating an enforceable contract, we agree with the district court that the contract's terms are dispositive of Venture's breach of contract claim. Accordingly, for the reasons stated above, the district court appropriately granted summary judgment in favor of Colt on Venture's breach of contract claim.

Turning to Colt's counterclaim for breach of contract, the district court awarded Colt $47,922.18 plus $7,524.50 in interest for the plastic containers Colt manufactured and shipped to Venture. Because Venture accepted the shipment, did not object to the quality, and did not make payment, Colt was entitled to summary judgment on its counterclaim for these damages. Further, because the explicit terms of the Invoices sent to Venture by Colt allow interest at a twelve percent annual rate beginning sixty days after the date the Invoice was due, the district court correctly awarded the sales price and interest to Colt in the total amount of $55,446.68.

Colt is also entitled to damages for the plastic containers that it manufactured specifically for Venture. The aggregate contract price for these plastic containers is $122,799.59. Colt has sold some of these containers on the open market but still has $108,793.84 of the plastic containers manufactured for Venture in its inventory. The district court correctly awarded this amount to Colt.

We conclude that the district court properly granted summary judgment in favor of Colt on Colt's counterclaim for breach of contract. The district court properly awarded Colt: (1) $55,446.68 (sales price and interest) for the plastic containers delivered to Venture; and (2) $108,793.84 for the plastic containers that Colt specially manufactured for Venture and has been unable to sell on the open market. . . .

For the reasons stated herein, the judgment of the district court is

Affirmed.

:: CASE QUESTIONS

1. In what businesses are Venture and Colt involved?
2. According to the court, who is the offeror and the offeree in this case?
3. What are the actual offer and acceptance in this factual situation?
4. How does the answer to the preceding question impact the conclusion of which party is entitled to a finding in its favor?
5. Which party is liable to the other?

Reasonable standards should govern your company and these consultants. Hopefully, effective negotiation will overcome the lack of direction in the contract. The concept of tendering performance may help. To **tender performance** means to offer to perform. When the consultants offer to send a team to your plant next week, they are tendering performance. A reasonable response is to permit this work to begin by allowing the consultants access to your facility. Once work begins, the contract's provisions on when payment is owed will govern your performance.

One party's tender of performance may satisfy a required condition leading to the other party's duty to perform.

8. SUBSTANTIAL PERFORMANCE

Beyond the order of performance as determined through conditions, the degree or amount of performance can become an issue. A party to a contract may not always perfectly perform the duties owed. The more complex a contract is, the more difficult it is for a party to complete every aspect of performance. Courts generally recognize three levels of performance. These levels are summarized in Sidebar 9.4.

:: *sidebar* 9.4

Levels of Performance

1. *Complete Performance* recognizes that a contracting party has fulfilled every duty required by the contract. Payment of money, for example, is a contractual duty of performance that a party can perform completely. A party that performs completely is entitled to a complete performance by the other party and may sue to enforce this right.

2. *Material Breach* is a level of performance below what is reasonably acceptable. A party that has materially breached a contract cannot sue the other party for performance and is liable for damages arising from the breach.

3. *Substantial Performance* represents a less-than-complete performance. However, the work done is sufficient to avoid the claim of a breach. A party who substantially performs may be entitled to a partial recovery under the contract.

Substantial performance is a middle ground between full performance and a breach due to nonperformance. Substantial performance is much more than some performance. It is even greater than significant performance. A very typical example when substantial performance is applicable occurs in service-oriented contracts. The consultants in the software installation/implementation contract should recover for work performed even if the entire contract is not completed on time.

Substantial performance is close to, but less than, full performance. Some or even significant performance may not satisfy the requirement of substantial performance.

Likewise, a construction contractor who gets a home built but has not finished all the landscaping and finishing details by the due date is not denied a financial recovery. This builder can recover under the contract but remains liable for any damages to the homeowner for delays. It would be unfair, from the legal perspective, to allow the homeowner to refuse to pay the builder because a deadline is missed.

9. DIVISIBILITY OF PERFORMANCE

Up to this point, we have assumed a contract specified aspects of performance by one party followed by the next party's performance. Alternatively, a contract may call for both parties to perform concurrently. It is possible, and indeed quite common, for a contract to be divided into segments or installments. An employment contract is a good example. One party (the employee) performs services for a period of time followed by the other party (the employer) paying the wages that are due. This pattern of recurring conditions precedent allows the employment contract to be divided into parts. This contract is considered to be divisible, typically into segments timed as pay periods.

> The divisibility or entirety of a contract helps determine when performance of duties should occur.

Contracts that at first glance may appear divisible actually are not. While our consulting contract example may look to be divided into monthly or quarterly periods, the manufacturer would have a good argument that it wants the installation and implementation of the software complete. A portion of the work is not what is desired. The contract calls for all the work to be done. Thus, this contract is not divisible. Similarly most construction contracts are viewed as a whole and not as divisible into installments. The fact that the contract may call for payment to be forthcoming following certain benchmarks are met does not make the contract divisible.

With respect to performance, the benefit of divisibility is to view the duty to perform as a series of smaller contracts. This may reduce the amount of disputes (numbers of them and the dollar figures involved) that arise due to nonperformance of the contract.

:: Excuses for Nonperformance

Generally speaking, in contracts the party who refuses to perform a promise can expect to be sued for breaching the agreement. Even beyond the special situations related to performance presented in the previous sections, the law may provide for nonperforming with a valid excuse. If such an excuse for nonperformance exists, there can be no legitimate claim of a breach. The next sections of this chapter present material relevant to most business contracts.

> Remember, a discharge relieves a party from the obligation to perform contractual promises.

Prior to studying these topics, it is important to revisit the fact there are many ways to discharge a party's obligation under a contract. The most common ways to achieve a discharge follow:

1. Complete performance of the contract.
2. Tendering performance if that tender is rejected.
3. Substantial performance.
4. Performance of part of a divisible contract.

In addition, a legitimate excuse for nonperformance can result in a party being discharged from contractual performance.

10. IMPOSSIBILITY OF PERFORMANCE

A party's nonperformance is excused because of **impossibility of performance**. This may occur because of the death of an essential party, the destruction of essential materials, or the subject matter of the contract becomes illegal.

If the subject matter of the contract is destroyed, the contract becomes impossible to perform. When a contract exists for the sale of a building, and the building burns, the seller is discharged from performance. Likewise, when there is a contract for personal services, and the party promising the services becomes ill or dies, the party receives discharge from performances.

The party that promises performance that becomes illegal is also discharged because of impossibility of performance. Mere increased difficulty or reduced profitability, however, does not constitute impossibility of performance.

Impossibility of performance is less likely to occur compared to impracticability.

11. COMMERCIAL IMPRACTICABILITY

Under the UCC a party to a sale-of-goods contract receives discharge from performance because of **commercial impracticability** (§2–615). The *impracticability* standard is not as difficult to meet as the *impossibility* standard. What constitutes impracticability of performance depends upon the circumstances of the situation. For instance, a manufacturer may be discharged from an obligation to make goods for a buyer when the manufacturer's major source of raw materials is unexpectedly interrupted. But if the raw materials are reasonably available from another supplier, the manufacturer may not receive discharge because of impracticability.

12. WAIVER OR RELEASE

A party may be excused from not performing contractual obligations by the other party to the agreement. When a party intentionally relinquishes a right to enforce the contract, a **waiver** occurs. When a party announces the other party does not have to perform as promised, a **release** exists. The distinction between a waiver and a release is not important when examining the resulting discharge of the contract. Nonperformance of the contract is forgiven and there is no liability for a breach of contract.

To gain some clarity regarding these closely related terms, focus on the timing of the nonperformance. Waivers generally occur after a contracting party fails to perform. In this situation, nonperformance by one party may cause the other party to waiver its right to enforce the contract. The waiver typically is unilateral. The nonbreaching party grants the waiver. A landlord may waive the right to collect a late payment fee when the rent is only two days overdue.

Releases usually occur before a contracting party fails to perform. A release often takes the form of a negotiated contract. The release is bargained for and is supported by consideration. A borrower may seek the lender's release to avoid having to make an interim payment. This borrower may have to agree to pay the entire debt before its original due date to get the lender's release from the interim payment.

:: Additional Thought On Contracts

Before concluding your study of contracts, the point made at the beginning of Chapter 8 should be reemphasized. Understanding contracts is critical because they are the key to transacting business. Having an appreciation for contract law may make you a more effective negotiator in some instances. However, as your career advances and you get involved in more complicated business transactions, you will work closely with lawyers to create contractual documentation. Sidebar 9.5 offers some concluding guidance on how to maintain a balanced relationship with your lawyer. Remember, your goal should always be to create contracts that enhance your business activities.

:: *sidebar* 9.5

Suggestions for Businessperson/Lawyer Relationship on the Drafting of Contracts

- Contracts are business documents.
- Don't let lawyer create a legal document.
- Use plain English.
- Tell story of relationship; provide timeline of obligations.
- Avoid legalese (where as; party of the first part, etc.); be careful with "and," "or," "before," "on," "after," "each," "every," etc.

- There should be a flow from section to section.
- Create clear definitions, if necessary.
- Proofread carefully.
- Use hard copy, not computer screen.
- Let document be alive.
- Consistently redraft to update.

:: Key Terms

Commercial
  impracticability 277
Concurrent condition 271
Condition precedent 271
Condition subsequent 271
Delivery 272
Discharge 269

Duty of performance 269
Express conditions 271
Implied conditions 271
Impossibility of
  performance 276
Judicial admissions 266
Parol evidence rule 266

Part performance 265
Release 277
Statute of frauds 262
Substantial performance 275
Tender performance 275
Waiver 277

:: Review Questions and Problems

Form and Interpretation

1. *Written versus Oral Contracts*

    (a) In general, are oral contracts as valid and enforceable as written ones?

    (b) Why should contracting parties consider reducing their agreement to writing?

2. *Statute of Frauds*

    (a) Explain the purpose of requiring certain types of contracts to be in writing.

    (b) List four types of contracts covered by the traditional statute of frauds.

3. *Exceptions to the Writing Requirement*

    Elegante Haberdashery telephones an order to Nordic Mills for 500 men's shirts at $15 each. Each shirt will carry the Elegante label and have the Elegante trademark over the pocket. After the shirts are manufactured, Elegante refuses to accept delivery of them and raises the statute of frauds as a defense. Discuss whether this defense applies to these facts.

4. *The Parol Evidence Rule*

    Caryn negotiates to buy 50 washers and 50 dryers from the "We-Clean-It Company." These machines are going into laundermats that Caryn operates with her family. Because these machines will be heavily used, Caryn got the company to agree to a one-year warranty instead of the standard 90-day warranty. Following the negotiation, Caryn signs a written contract. Only later, Caryn realizes there is no warranty provision in the written contract. What should Caryn do to be able to enforce the original extended warranty agreement?

5. *Interpretation of Contracts*

Gus contracts to buy a used car from Cars Galore, Inc. The printed contract specifies "no warranties." But Gus and the sales manager of Cars handwrite into the contract a 90-day guarantee on the transmission. If the transmission fails after 60 days, is there a warranty protecting Gus? Explain.

Performance

6. *Conditions of Performance*

(a) Why are conditions important in understanding how and when contracts are performed?

(b) List the three types of conditions that are most common in contractual performance.

7. *Payment, Delivery, Services Tendered*

(a) Explain the role of tender of performance.

(b) What is the impact of one party tendering its performance?

8. *Substantial Performance*

Ace Contracting constructs an office building for Realty Enterprises. Realty's tenants quickly find a number of minor problems with the plumbing and insulation of the new building. When Realty contacts Ace about bringing its work up to standard, Ace promises to correct the problems, but never does.

(a) Can Realty rescind the contract?

(b) What are Realty's legal remedies?

9. *Divisibility of Performance*

Why is an employment contract usually viewed as being divisible while a construction contract is not considered divisible?

Excuses for Nonperformance

10. *Impossibility of Performance*

To be a legitimate excuse for nonperformance, impossibility must be real and absolute. What are three examples of factual situations involving real impossibility of performance?

11. *Commercial Impracticability*

A tripling of prices by an illegal cartel of uranium producers caused Westinghouse Electric Corp. to default on uranium delivery contracts to a number of utility companies. The companies sued and Westinghouse settled. If the case had gone to trial, what defense might Westinghouse have raised to excuse its nonperformance under the contracts?

12. *Waiver or Release*

What do waivers and releases have in common?

business :: *discussion*

As a new sales representative for Misco Equipment Corporation, you take a customer out to dinner. Before dinner is over, you have shaken hands on a deal to sell the customer nearly a half-million dollars' worth of industrial equipment. In writing up the formal contract the next morning, you discover that you misfigured the equipment's price. Your error could cost Misco $60,000. You telephone your customer and explain the situation.

Is the "deal" you made an enforceable contract?

Does the mistake you made permit you to get out of an enforceable contract?

What do you think will happen in this situation?

10

Torts in the Business Environment

▢ Learning Objectives ::

In this chapter you will learn:

1. To appreciate how tort law is related to property.

2. To understand the three divisions of torts and to develop a theory of why torts are so divided.

3. To explain the elements of negligence and to relate these elements to the development of negligence law.

4. To grasp why tort litigation is so controversial in society today.

5. To explain why some torts are also crimes.

The word **tort** means "wrong." Legally, a tort is a civil wrong other than a breach of contract. If property is the central legal concept of private enterprise and much of Western civilization, contract concerns transfer of an owner's resources, and tort involves defining when others injure an owner's resources, including the resources of the person. Tort law sets limits on how people can act and use their resources so they do not violate the right others have to their resources. If you think of property as a type of legal fence surrounding resources, then tort law defines when someone has crossed that fence wrongfully so that compensation is due to the owner.

Legal wrongs inflicted on the resources of others may be crimes as well as torts (see Chapter 12), but the law of tort itself is civil rather than criminal. The usual remedy for a tort is dollar damages. Behavior that constitutes a tort is called *tortious* behavior. One who commits a tort is a *tortfeasor*.

*Torts are divided into intentional torts, negligence, and strict liability.

This chapter divides torts into three main categories: intentional torts, negligence torts, and strict liability torts. Intentional torts involve deliberate actions that cause injury. Negligence torts involve injury following a failure to use reasonable care. Strict liability torts impose legal responsibility for injury even though a liable party neither intentionally nor negligently causes the injury.

Important to torts are the concepts of duty and causation. One is not liable for another's injury unless he or she has a *duty* toward the person injured. And, of course, there is usually no liability for injury unless one has *caused* the injury. We explain these concepts under the discussion of negligence, where they are most relevant.

This chapter also covers the topic of damages. The topic concerns the business community because huge damage awards, frequently against businesses, have become common in recent years. Finally, the chapter explores some alternatives to the current tort system, including workers' compensation.

:: **Intentional Torts**

Intent is the desire to bring about certain results.

An important element in the following torts is *intent,* as we are dealing with intentional torts. **Intent** is usually defined as the desire to bring about certain results. But in some circumstances the meaning is even broader, including not only desired results but also results that are "substantially likely" to result from an action. Recently, employers who knowingly exposed employees to toxic substances without warning them of the dangers have been sued for committing the intentional tort of battery. The employers did not desire their employees' injuries, but these injuries were "substantially likely" to result from the failure to warn.

The following sections explain the basic types of intentional torts. Sidebar 10.1 lists these torts.

:: *sidebar* 10.1

Types of Intentional Torts

- Assault and battery
- Intentional infliction of mental distress
- Invasion of privacy
- False imprisonment and malicious prosecution
- Trespass

- Conversion
- Defamation
- Fraud
- Common law business torts

1. ASSAULT AND BATTERY

An **assault** is the placing of another in immediate apprehension for his or her physical safety. "Apprehension" has a broader meaning than "fear." It includes the expectation that one is about to be physically injured. The person who intentionally creates such apprehension in another is guilty of the tort of assault. Many times a battery follows an assault. A **battery** is an illegal touching of another. As used here, "illegal" means that the touching is done without justification and without the consent of the person touched. The touching need not cause injury.

A store manager who threatens an unpleasant customer with a wrench, for example, is guilty of assault. Actually hitting the customer with the wrench would constitute battery.

2. INTENTIONAL INFLICTION OF MENTAL DISTRESS

Intentional **infliction of mental distress** is a battery to the emotions. It arises from outrageous, intentional conduct that carries a strong probability of causing mental distress to the person at whom it is directed. Usually, one who sues on the basis of an intentional infliction of mental distress must prove that the defendant's outrageous behavior caused not only mental distress but also physical symptoms, such as headaches or sleeplessness.

The most common cases of intentional infliction of mental distress (also called *emotional distress*) have concerned employees who have been discriminated against or fired. Many such cases, however, do not involve the type of outrageous conduct necessary for the mental distress tort. In Case 10.1, the court decides whether or not an employer's conduct is outrageous. Pay special attention to the precedent cases the court discusses in its opinion.

> This tort usually requires the plaintiff to prove not only mental distress but also physical symptoms.

case 10.1 ::

VAN STAN v. FANCY COLOURS & COMPANY
125 F. 3d 563 (7th Cir. 1997)

WOOD, JR., J.: . . . After Fancy Colours & Company ("Fancy Colours") terminated his employment, Michael D. Van Stan ("Van Stan") sued Fancy Colours contending that Fancy Colours' conduct in firing him amounted to intentional infliction of emotional distress. A jury awarded Van Stan damages of $150,000 for intentional infliction of emotional distress. We reverse the entry of judgment against Fancy Colours on the intentional infliction of emotional distress claim.

Under Illinois law, which the parties both agree applies, a plaintiff may recover damages for intentional infliction of emotional distress only if he establishes that (1) the defendant's conduct was extreme and outrageous, (2) the defendant intended to inflict severe emotional distress or knew that there was at least a high probability that his conduct would inflict severe

emotional distress, and (3) the defendant's conduct did cause severe emotional distress. Conduct is extreme and outrageous only if "the conduct has been so outrageous in character and so extreme in degree, as to go beyond all possible bounds of decency. . . ." "Mere insults, indignities, threats, annoyances, petty oppressions, or other trivialities" do not amount to extreme and outrageous conduct, nor does conduct "characterized by malice or a degree of aggravation which would entitle the plaintiff to punitive damages for another tort." Moreover, we judge whether conduct is extreme and outrageous on an objective standard based on all the facts and circumstances of a particular case. Thus, to serve as a basis for recovery, the defendant's conduct must be such that the "recitation of facts to an average member of the community would arouse his resentment against the actor, and lead him to exclaim 'Outrageous!'"

In the employment context, Illinois courts have recognized that personality conflicts and questioning of job performance are "unavoidable aspects of employment" and that "frequently, they produce concern and distress." The courts have reasoned, however, that if such incidents were actionable, nearly all employees would have a cause of action for intentional infliction of emotional distress. Thus, Illinois courts have limited recovery to cases in which the employer's conduct has been truly egregious. See, e.g., *Pavilon v. Kaferly* . . . (the employer, knowing that the plaintiff was susceptible to emotional distress, offered her money for sexual favors, fired her after she refused, and after he fired her, threatened to kill her, to rape her, and to file a legal action challenging her rights to custody of her child and attempted to disrupt her new employment relationship); *Milton v. Illinois Bell Tel. Co.* . . . (the employer engaged in an extensive course of disciplinary and harassing conduct to coerce the plaintiff to falsify work reports).

In contrast, Illinois courts have denied recovery for distress resulting from recognizably reprehensible conduct which has been linked to an employer's legitimate interest. In *Harris v. First Fed. Sav. & Loan Ass'n of Chicago* an Illinois appellate court held that a plaintiff who alleged that her employer criticized, demoted, and discharged her after she reported allegedly criminal activity to her supervisor did not state a claim because she did not allege that her employer engaged in this course of conduct to coerce her into engaging in illegal activity. While the court characterized the employer's conduct as "reprehensible," the court held that it did not rise to the level of extreme and outrageous conduct because the employer merely acted out of displeasure with the plaintiff's exercise of judgment regarding another employee's conduct.

Recognizing this high threshold, this Court and other federal courts applying Illinois law have denied recovery to plaintiffs who alleged that their employers subjected them to a continuous series of intentionally discriminatory acts. For example, in *Harriston* we held that the plaintiff failed to allege conduct that rose to the level of extreme and outrageous conduct even though she contended that among other things her employer refused to allow her to supervise white subordinates, reprimanded her for no reason, refused to allow her to participate in a management incentive fund, forced her out of her management position, promised her a promotion she never received, took away from her major accounts and gave her less lucrative accounts in return, excluded her from office activities, monitored her telephone calls with an eavesdropping device and ignored concerns of her health and safety after her personal property was damaged on company property. See also *Briggs v. North Shore Sanitary Dist*. (Allegations that the plaintiff's employer and fellow employees hung a pickaninny doll in her office, subjected her to racial slurs, excluded her from office social activities, placed her on probation, and refused to train her properly did not rise to the level of extreme and outrageous conduct, but allegations that co-workers exposed her to toxic fumes for more than eight hours did).

In this case, Van Stan maintains that viewing the evidence in the light most favorable to him, a reasonable jury could have found that Walters [Van Stan's supervisor,] and other Fancy Colours supervisors knew that Van Stan suffered from a bipolar disorder, that Fancy Colours fired Van Stan because his disorder required him to work less hours, that Walters telephoned Van Stan at home while he was on vacation to inform him that he had been terminated and that after Van Stan requested an explanation, Walters falsely told Van Stan that he was being fired for low productivity. While we do not mean to condone such conduct, we do not believe that this course of conduct was akin to the type of egregious conduct present in *Pavilon* and *Milton,* nor do we believe that it exceeded all possible bounds of decency. Thus, as a matter of law Fancy Colours' conduct did not rise to the level of extreme and outrageous conduct, and Fancy Colours is entitled to a judgment in its favor.

Reversed.

:: CASE QUESTIONS

1. What was the conduct that plaintiff Van Stan claimed was "extreme and outrageous"?
2. What does the court say about what would happen if more "personality conflicts and questioning of job performance" amounted to intentional infliction of mental and emotional distress?
3. Why is the Illinois case in federal court?

In the business world, other examples of infliction of mental distress come about from the efforts of creditors to extract payment from their debtors. Frequent, abusive, threatening phone calls by creditors might provide the basis for a claim of intentional infliction of mental distress. As torts go, this one is of fairly recent origin. It is a judge-made tort, which furnishes a good example of how the courts are becoming increasingly sensitive to the range of injuries for which compensation is appropriate. In some states, courts have gone so far as to establish liability for carelessly inflicted mental distress, such as the distress of a mother who sees her child negligently run down by a delivery truck.

3. INVASION OF PRIVACY

The tort of **invasion of privacy** is one that is still in the early stages of legal development. As the statutes and court cases recognize it, the tort at present comprises three principal invasions of personal interest. An invasion of any one of these areas of interest is sufficient to trigger liability.

Most commonly, liability will be imposed on a defendant who appropriates the plaintiff's name or likeness for his or her own use. Many advertisers and marketers have been required to pay damages to individuals when pictures of them have been used without authorization to promote products, or when their names and identities have been used without permission for promotional purposes. Before using anyone's picture or name, an advertiser must obtain a proper release from that person to avoid possible liability. Appropriating another's name and identity in order to secure credit is an additional example of this invasion-of-privacy tort. See Sidebar 10.2.

That you can recover damages for misappropriation of likeness illustrates that you own your name and likeness in certain respects.

:: *sidebar* 10.2

The Man on the Coffee Jar

Russell Cristoff had been told he looked like the man on a coffee jar. When he passed the coffee aisle in a drugstore, he saw why. There was his picture as a satisfied coffee drinker on a jar of Nestlé's Taster's Choice. Although he had posed several years previously for a photographer, he had never given permission for his likeness to be used on anything. In 2005 a Los Angeles County Superior Court jury awarded $15.6 million to the 58-year-old kindergarten teacher for the misappropriation of his likeness. Nestlé appealed and the court reversed the decision on technical grounds relating to how long it had taken the plaintiff to bring the lawsuit and the difference between a single publication of his image and "republication" of it. To the business community, however, the lesson is clear: misappropriate someone's image and you will get sued.

A second invasion of privacy is the defendant's intrusion upon the plaintiff's physical solitude. Illegal searches or invasions of home or possessions, illegal wiretapping, and persistent and unwanted telephoning can provide the basis for this invasion-of-privacy tort. In one case, a woman even recovered damages against a photographer who entered her sickroom and snapped a picture of her. Employers who enter their employees' homes without permission have also been sued successfully for invasions of privacy. If the invasion of privacy continues, it may be enjoined by the court. Jacqueline Kennedy Onassis sought and obtained an injunction that forbade a certain photographer from getting too close to her and her children. Under this tort, the invasion of physical solitude must be highly objectionable to a reasonable person.

The third invasion of personal interest that gives rise to the invasion-of-privacy tort is the defendant's public disclosure of highly objectionable, private information about the plaintiff. A showing of such facts can be the basis for a cause of action, even if the information is true. Thus, publishing in a newspaper that the plaintiff does not pay his or her debts has been ruled to create liability for the defendant creditor. Communicating the same facts to a credit-reporting agency or the plaintiff's employer usually does not impose liability, however. In these cases, there has been no disclosure to the public in general. Also, the news media are protected under the First Amendment when they publish information about public officials and other public figures.

Don't forget that the First Amendment protects you when you publish even highly personal truthful information about public officials and public figures.

4. FALSE IMPRISONMENT AND MALICIOUS PROSECUTION

One false imprisonment lawsuit arose when a tow-truck operator towed a car with the driver still in it.

Shoplifting accounts for some $18 billion a year in business losses, almost 1 percent of retail sales. Claims of **false imprisonment** stem most frequently in business from instances of shoplifting. This tort is the intentional unjustified confinement of a nonconsenting person. Although most states have statutes that permit merchants or their employees to detain customers suspected of shoplifting, this detention must be a reasonable one. The unnecessary use of force, lack of reasonable suspicion of shoplifting, or an unreasonable length of confinement can cause the merchant to lose the statutory privilege. The improperly detained customer is then able to sue for false imprisonment. Allegations of battery are also usually made if the customer has been touched. Not all false imprisonment lawsuits arise because of shoplifting. In one instance a KPMG employee sued for false imprisonment alleging that his manager blocked a door with a chair during a performance review and caused the employee to have to remain in the room against his will.

The tort of **malicious prosecution** is often called *false arrest*. Malicious prosecution arises from causing someone to be arrested criminally without proper grounds. It occurs, for instance, when the arrest is accomplished simply to harass someone. In Albany, New York, a jury awarded a man $200,000 for malicious prosecution. His zipper had broken, leaving his fly open, and a store security guard had him arrested for indecent exposure even after he explained that he had not noticed the problem.

5. TRESPASS

To enter another's land without consent or to remain there after being asked to leave constitutes the tort of **trespass.** A variation on the trespass tort arises when something (such as particles of pollution) is placed on another's land without consent. Although the usual civil action for trespass asks for an injunction to restrain the trespasser, the action may also ask for damages.

Union pickets walking on company property (in most instances), customers refusing to leave a store after being asked to do so, and unauthorized persons entering restricted areas are all examples of trespass. Note that trespass is often a crime as well as a tort. Intentional wrongdoing is frequently criminal.

Trespass concerns the crossing of an owner's boundaries. Today, trespass usually refers to violating the physical boundaries of an owner's land, but in legal history trespass was the legal remedy for direct injuries caused by another to one's person as well. The famous British constitutional historian Frederick Maitland wrote, "Trespass is the fertile mother of actions." By this he meant that many of our modern day causes of action in tort—like battery—come from trespass. Now do you appreciate better the connection of tort law to property in our legal system? In an important sense, we own ourselves and various things we have acquired, and those who violate our boundaries become liable to compensate us.

The reason for emphasizing how tort relates to property is to show you how our legal system has historically centered on the concept of exclusive right, which applies to your person as well as to land and other physical resources.

6. CONVERSION

Conversion is the wrongful exercise of dominion (power) and control over the personal (nonland) resources that belong to another. Conversion deprives owners of their lawful right to exclude others from such resources. The deprivation may be either temporary or permanent, but it must constitute a serious invasion of the owner's legal right. Abraham Lincoln once convinced an Illinois court that a defendant's action in riding the plaintiff's horse for 15 miles was not sufficiently serious to be a conversion since the defendant had returned the horse in good condition. The plaintiff had left the horse with the defendant to be stabled and fed.

In one case a student drove a rental car into Mexico although the lease specifically prohibited cross-border driving. When an earthquake destroyed the car while it was parked in Mexico City, the rental company successfully sued the student for conversion.

Conversion often arises in business situations. Stealing something from an employer is conversion, as is purchasing—even innocently—something that has been stolen. Failing to return something properly acquired at the designated time, delivering something to the wrong party, and destruction or alteration of what belongs to another are all conversions when a deprivation of ownership is serious or long-lived. Even if you intend to return something, if you have converted it you are absolutely liable for any damage done to it. A warehouse operator who improperly transfers stored goods from a designated to a nondesignated warehouse is absolutely liable when a tornado destroys the goods or when a thief steals them.

7. DEFAMATION

Defamation is the publication of untrue statements about another that hold up that individual's character or reputation to contempt and ridicule. "Publication" means that the untruth must be made known to third parties. If defamation is oral, it is called **slander.** Written defamation, or defamation published over radio or television, is termed **libel.**

False accusations of dishonesty or inability to pay debts frequently bring on defamation suits in business relationships. Sometimes, such accusations arise during the course of a takeover attempt by one company of another through an offering to buy stock. In a recent instance, the chairman of one company called the chairman of a rival business "lying, deceitful, and treacherous" and charged that he "violated the standards by which decent men do business." If untrue, these remarks provide a good example of defamation of character. At one major university, a former business professor received a multimillion-dollar settlement following allegations made by university administrators that he had vandalized the new business school. The allegations

In 2008, publisher Judith Reagan and her employer News Corporation settled her $100 million lawsuit against News Corporation for defaming her by saying it had fired her because she had made anti-Semitic remarks.

cost him a deanship at another university. Punitive or punishment damages, as well as actual damages, may be assessed in defamation cases.

Individuals are not the only ones who can sue for defamation. A corporation can also sue for defamation if untrue remarks discredit the way the corporation conducts its business. Untruthfully implying that a company's entire management is dishonest or incompetent defames the corporation.

Nearly one-third of all defamation suits are currently brought by employees against present and former employers. Often these suits arise when employers give job references on former employees who have been discharged for dishonesty. As a result, many employers will now not give job references or will do no more than verify that former employees did work for them.

There are two basic defenses to a claim of defamation. One defense is that the statements made were true. *Truth* is an absolute defense. The second defense is that the statement arose from *privileged communications*. For example, statements made by legislators, judges, attorneys, and those involved in lawsuits are privileged under many circumstances.

Dick Grasso, former chairman of the New York Stock Exchange, filed a defamation claim against the Exchange and against John Reed, who succeeded Grasso as NYSE chairman.

Defamation and the First Amendment   Because of the First Amendment, special rules regarding defamation apply to the news media. These media are not liable for the defamatory untruths they print about public officials and public figures unless plaintiffs can prove that the untruths were published with "malice" (evil intent, that is, the deliberate intent to injure) or with "reckless disregard for the truth." Public figures are those who have consciously brought themselves to public attention. See Sidebar 10.3.

:: *sidebar* 10.3

Football Coaches as Public Figures

The U.S. Supreme Court issued the "public official" standard requiring defamation plaintiffs to prove "malice" or "reckless disregard for the truth" in *New York Times v. Sullivan,* 376 U.S. 254 (1964), a case involving criticism of an Alabama police commissioner. The Court extended essentially the same standard to defamation cases against "public figures" in *Curtis Publishing Co. v. Butts,* 388 U.S. 130 (1967). The facts of this case are interesting.

The *Saturday Evening Post,* one of the nation's leading feature story magazines for many years, published a story about the University of Georgia's athletic director and former football coach Wallace ("Wally") Butts and the University of Alabama's football coach Paul ("Bear") Bryant. The *Post* alleged that in a telephone conversation overheard accidentally by an Atlanta insurance salesman, Butts told Bryant how to beat Georgia in an upcoming game. "Before the University of Georgia played the University of Alabama . . ., Wally Butts . . . gave to Bear Bryant Georgia's plays, defensive

patterns, all the significant secrets Georgia's football team possessed." The article continued, "The Georgia players, their moves analyzed and forecast like those of rats in a maze, took a frightful physical beating." Georgia lost the game, and Alabama went on to win the national championship.

Although the conversation between the two coaches may really have involved only a routine request to exchange game films, Butts ended up being forced to resign as athletic director. Both he and Bryant sued the *Post* for defamation. The coaches won their lawsuit, which was appealed to the Supreme Court.

The Court determined that the two coaches were "public figures" and that the First Amendment protected comment about them in much the same way it protected comment about public officials. However, the Court also concluded that the coaches had met their heavy burden of proof. It affirmed the judgment against the *Post.* Within a short time, the *Saturday Evening Post* went out of business.

Plaintiffs' verdicts in media defamation cases are often overturned by trial or appellate judges. In one instance a Houston investment firm, now defunct, sued *The Wall Street Journal*, claiming that a story published by the newspaper caused the firm to go out of business. Following a huge jury verdict, the trial judge threw out $200 million in damages, ruling that the firm had not proved the newspaper published certain statements with knowledge of their falsity or with reckless disregard for the truth.

Plaintiffs' verdicts in defamation cases are often overturned by appellate courts. Because of the constitutional protection given to speech and the media, appellate judges reexamine trial evidence very closely to determine whether the necessary elements of defamation had been proven.

8. FRAUD

Business managers must be alert to the intentional tort of **fraud.** A fraud is an intentional misrepresentation of a material fact that is justifiably relied upon by someone to his or her injury. An intentional misrepresentation means a lie. The lie must be of a material fact—an important one. The victim of the fraud must justifiably rely on the misrepresentation and must suffer some injury, usually a loss of money or other resource one owns.

Fraud applies in many different situations. Business frauds often involve the intentional misrepresentation of property or financial status. Lying about assets or liabilities in order to get credit or a loan is a fraud. Likewise, intentionally misrepresenting that land is free from hazardous waste when the seller knows that toxic chemicals are buried on the land constitutes fraud.

You can also prove fraud by giving evidence that another has harmed you by failing to disclose a material (important) hidden fact. The fraud of failure to disclose arises when the defendant is under a legal duty to disclose a fact, such as when a defendant seller knows that the foundations of a house are weakened by termites and must disclose this to the buyer. Likewise, a defendant who has intentionally concealed an important fact and has induced reliance on it to the plaintiff's injury is liable for fraud.

In Case 10.2, the Supreme Court of Arizona discusses the difference between fraud for failure to disclose and fraud in the concealment.

According to a survey by the Association of Certified Fraud Examiners, U.S. companies lose an average of 6 percent of their profit to fraud.

---

case 10.2 ::

WELLS FARGO BANK v. ARIZONA LABORERS, TEAMSTERS, AND CEMENT MASONS
38 P. 3d 12 (2002)

J. Fife Symington and his development firm requested funding for a mall construction from the Wells Fargo Bank in Phoenix, Arizona. The bank agreed to offer temporary financing if Symington could secure permanent financing from another source. Symington arranged a loan from various union funds ("the Funds"). Subsequently, Symington defaulted in repaying the Funds, and the Funds sued Wells Fargo, alleging that the bank knew of financial misrepresentations by Symington to the Funds and had actively concealed them from the

Funds. The trial court ruled that Wells Fargo had no duty to disclose Symington's true financial condition to the Funds, and the court of appeals affirmed.

JONES, C. J.: . . . Arizona recognizes the tort of fraudulent concealment:

> One party to a transaction who by concealment or other action intentionally prevents the other from acquiring material information is subject to the same liability to the other, for pecuniary loss as though he had stated the nonexistence of the matter that the other was thus prevented from discovering.

Where failure to disclose a material fact is calculated to induce a false belief, "the distinction between concealment and affirmative misrepresentation is tenuous." The court of appeals dismissed the Funds' claims for fraudulent concealment on the basis that the Bank's fiduciary and contractual duty was to Symington and not to the Funds. Both the court of appeals and the Bank mistakenly cite *Frazier v. Southwest Savings & Loan Association* for the proposition that concealment was not proven because there was no duty to speak.

In *Frazier,* the court explained that liability for concealment requires knowledge of the false information and action by the defendant that intentionally prevented the plaintiff from finding the truth. The *Frazier* court found concealment unproven, not because there was no duty to disclose, but because there was no evidence from which the jury could have found active concealment.

In Arizona, whether a duty to speak exists at all is determined by reference to all the circumstances of the case. On the issue of duty in a fraudulent concealment claim, we are persuaded by and affirm the reasoning articulated by the court of appeals decision in *King v. O'Rielly Motor Co.*

In *King,* a car buyer sued a car dealer for fraudulently representing that the car the buyer purchased was "as good as new" when in fact the car had been in an accident and, unbeknownst to the buyer, had been repaired by the dealer. The car dealer argued that the dealer could not be liable to the buyer because the dealer was under no duty to disclose. The court stated that, while "*it is often difficult to distinguish misleading representations and fraudulent concealment from mere nondisclosure* and the classification of the act or acts in question must, of course, depend on the facts of each case," it was nevertheless true that "the facts of this case . . ." would be supportive of a finding of misleading representation or fraudulent concealment. An Oregon court advanced similar reasoning in *Paul v. Kelley,* concluding that a duty to disclose is not necessary to prevail on a fraudulent concealment claim.

In *Paul,* the seller of real estate knew, before the closing, that he was required to install a storm sewer if a drainage ditch on the property were eliminated. Instead of installing the storm sewer, the sellers simply filled the ditch and sold the property. Buyers of the land sued the sellers when they learned they had to put in an expensive sewer system. The sellers defended on the grounds that they had no affirmative duty to disclose the ditch to the buyers. The court found this argument meritless, stating:

> Such a duty is not necessary. . . . An active concealment such as the filling in of the ditch alleged in this case is to be distinguished from a simple nondisclosure. . . . Plaintiff's complaint sets forth facts alleging an active concealment of the drainage ditch and is *sufficient without the assertion of a duty to speak.*

The common law clearly distinguishes between concealment and nondisclosure. The former is characterized by deceptive acts or contrivances intended to hide information, mislead, avoid suspicion, or prevent further inquiry into a material matter. The latter is characterized by mere silence. "Thus, fraudulent concealment—without any misrepresentation or duty to disclose—can constitute common law fraud."

The Funds in the instant case allege the Bank actively strategized to cover up the pending collapse of Symington's financial condition. This allegation fits the definition of concealment, not nondisclosure. Three evidentiary points are clear: the "unjustified and imprudent" loan extensions; the forbearance until one day after the date for the Mercado take-out obligation; and the failure to report Symington's false statements to federal banking authorities. The record reveals evidence of internal bank communications and communication between Symington aides and the Bank. Applying the law, we conclude that the Funds were not required to establish an affirmative duty to speak in order to prove fraudulent concealment. Actions by the Bank which intended to conceal material facts are, if proven, sufficient.

In the final analysis, we reach two conclusions as to the fraudulent concealment claim: there are reasonable inferences from which a jury could find (1) the Bank had knowledge of false information being given the Funds, and (2) the Bank took measures intended to prevent the Funds from learning the truth. These inferences are grounded in fact and are sufficient to take the concealment theory to the jury. The opinion of the court of appeals is vacated, the judgment of the trial court is reversed, and this case is remanded to the trial court for proceedings consistent with this opinion.

:: CASE QUESTIONS

1. What are three types of fraud?
2. Why was the bank under no duty to disclose Symington's financial condition to the Funds?
3. Give an example to illustrate the difference between knowing a material fact and failing to disclose it and "concealing" the fact.

In 2005 New York State filed a lawsuit based on fraud against Guidant Corporation. The complaint alleged that heart defibrillators manufactured by the company were defective and that the implanted devices had already failed in 28 patients. Further, the complaint asserted that Guidant had known of the defect for several years and concealed this information while continuing to sell the defibrillators. Said New York's former attorney general, "Concealment of negative facts that might influence a consumer to purchase another manufacturer's product is the essence of fraud."

Fraud is not only a tort but a crime as well. Do you understand the difference between torts and crimes? (See Sidebar 10.4.)

:: *sidebar* 10.4

Tort or Crime? Or Both?

Some torts are crimes and some are not. How do we make sense out of this? Crimes, which you will study in Chapter 12, generally require *intent* (also called *willfulness*). The prosecutor has to prove that the defendant intended to cross the proper boundaries (property) established by law. If the primary purpose of the state (government) is to protect people and their resources with the legal fence of property, as was thought by many framers of the Constitution, it becomes clear that most crimes, which are offenses against the proper order (property order) enforced by the government, involve the most serious and intentional crossings of the legal fences that protect people. These crossings injure or harm what belongs to people and the state punishes such harm. But people also deserve compensation because of the injury. That is where tort law comes in.

The most serious torts like assault, battery, conversion, and fraud, which are also frequently crimes, are all intentional. Accidental boundary crossings are usually not criminal unless they are extremely reckless, but when they injure what belongs to an owner, the owner can still get compensation through tort law, for example, through proof of unreasonable and careless boundary crossing called *negligence* (see Sections 11–13). Likewise, certain other accidental boundary crossings that cause injury, like the sale of a defective product, result in the person crossing the legal fence being held *strictly liable*, that is, liable even in the absence of unreasonable behavior in the crossing (see Sections 15–17). However, because these torts are unintentional, they are usually not crimes as well.

Since torts are civil and crimes are, well, criminal in nature, they have different burdens of proof, as explained in Chapter 4. The judge instructs the jury that the plaintiff must prove the tort by a preponderance of the evidence but instructs the jury in a criminal case that the prosecutor must prove the victim's intentional injury by the defendant beyond a reasonable doubt. The burdens of proof are different because to deprive criminal defendants of their freedom is considered much more serious than merely to deprive them civilly of their money. And burdens of proof exist in both civil and criminal cases because to punish a criminal defendant to protect the proper order of the state or to compensate a civil plaintiff for a wrongful boundary crossing involves the taking of something that was previously proper to defendants, whether it is their freedom, their money, or some other resource belonging to them.

Do you understand better now why the same trespass across a legal fence can be both a tort and a crime?

Additional Fraud Examples   Fraud also can be committed in the hiring process. For instance, courts have found employers liable for misrepresenting to employees about conditions at a business that later affect employment adversely. In one case, former professional football player Phil McConkey received a $10 million award because his employer misrepresented the status of merger talks with another company. McConkey lost his job the year after he was hired when the two companies merged.

Other instances of business fraud can include:

- Misrepresentation in employment. Screenwriter Benedict Fitzgerald sued actor–director Mel Gibson and his production company for defrauding him into taking a much smaller salary based on their representation that the movie budget was only $4 million–$7 million instead of the estimated $25 million–$50 million that had been actually budgeted.

- Misrepresentation about products. The tobacco industry is beginning to lose lawsuits when plaintiffs allege fraud based on the industry's claiming for years that no tobacco consumption harm had been scientifically proved when it knew that such harm had been established. In 2008, for instance, the Oregon Supreme Court affirmed a $79.5 million punitive damage award in the fraud case of deceased smoker Jesse Williams.

- Concealment about products. Farmers and growers have received over $1 billion from DuPont in settlements based on the damage the fungicide Benlate caused various plants. DuPont allegedly committed fraud by concealing that Benlate could cause crop damage even when the company was asked about the possibility.

- Nondisclosure to third parties about home sale prices. Fannie Mae, the nation's largest investor in home loans, told lenders in 2008 that it considered certain "practices that may distort or artificially inflate" house prices to be potentially fraudulent. Fannie Mae referenced situations where home developers or builders represented that they sold homes in an area for reported high prices but in reality gave back part of the purchase price to buyers. The concern is that such practices can defraud future home buyers in that development into paying higher prices than they actually should and also mislead banks that loan money for home mortgages in the area.

The previous chapter on contracts discussed fraud as voiding a contract. But fraud is also an intentional tort, and one who is a victim of fraud can sue for damages, including punitive or punishment damages. Fraud is both a common law intentional tort and a type of tort covered in many statutes that prohibit lying to a bank or in various documents that businesses must supply to the government. Note that frauds are sometimes also crimes. Chapter 12 discusses criminal frauds like mail fraud and wire fraud. Today many frauds, as well as other intentional torts, occur on the Internet. See Sidebar 10.5.

Fraud and Corporate Governance   Antifraud laws are a major weapon in the enforcement of good corporate governance. Much corporate misgovernance, especially by managers, arises because of misrepresentations of fact about corporate assets or liabilities. These misrepresentations usually induce investors to buy corporate stock shares at higher prices and

:: *sidebar* 10.5

Internet Torts

A variety of intentional torts take place on the Internet. Defamation occurs when e-mailers place messages on Listservs or public chatrooms that hold others up to "public contempt or ridicule." Intentional infliction of mental distress arises, for example, when threats are made via e-mail or websites. A jury in Oregon awarded plaintiffs over $100 million when it found that a website threatened abortion providers. When computer hackers break into company databases, trade secrets are easily misappropriated.

Perhaps the most common intentional cyber-related tort is fraud. The Federal Trade Commission has released a list of such frauds or scams that include a variety of pyramid schemes, fraudulent auctions, deceptive travel offers, sale of unmiraculous "miracle" products, health care rip-offs, phony credit card charges, and work-at-home frauds. There was even a "rebate" check sent to consumers that if cashed gave them new Internet service that could not be canceled. The FTC reports that its enforcement actions against Internet scams have risen steadily in recent years.

benefit corporate managers or others inside the corporation who sell their stock. Sometimes a misrepresentation that raises stock price obtains a bonus or other perk for managers or a loan for the corporation. Usually, a misrepresentation amounts to fraud because investors (who become owners) or lenders rely on it to their injury, that is, they lose some or all of their investment.

Many specific laws create civil and criminal liability for the fraud of corporate managers and other corporate agents. Chapter 15 covers the most important of these laws. As you think about fraud, remember that it violates the principle of property. One does not acquire proper ownership by defrauding others of their resources. Fraud does not respect the equal property right of others.

9. COMMON LAW BUSINESS TORTS

The label *business torts* embraces different kinds of torts that involve intentional interference with business relations.

Injurious Falsehood **Injurious falsehood,** sometimes called *trade disparagement,* is a common business tort. It consists of the publication of untrue statements that disparage the business owner's product or its quality. General disparagement of the plaintiff's business may also provide basis for liability. As a cause of action, injurious falsehood is similar to defamation of character. It differs, however, in that it usually applies to a product or business rather than character or reputation. The requirements of proof are also somewhat different. Defamatory remarks are presumed false unless the defendant can prove their truth. But in disparagement cases the plaintiff must establish the falsity of the defendant's statements. The plaintiff must also show actual damages arising from the untrue statements.

As an example of injurious falsehood, consider the potential harm to Procter & Gamble of the assertions that associated its former logo of moon and stars with satanism. The company threatened to sue a number of individuals.

Do remember that you can be sued for making statements about a competitor's product that the competitor considers false.

In another instance Warnaco sued Calvin Klein, alleging that Klein had made publicly disparaging remarks about how Warnaco made Calvin Klein clothing under license. The lawsuit alleged that Klein "falsely accused [Warnaco] of effectively 'counterfeiting' Calvin Klein apparel."

Intentional Interference with Contractual Relations   A second type of business tort is **intentional interference with contractual relations.** Probably the most common example of this tort involves one company raiding another for employees. If employees are under contract to an employer for a period of time, another employer cannot induce them to break their contracts. In a variation on this tort, the brokerage firm PaineWebber Group sued Morgan Stanley Dean Witter & Company over PaineWebber's merger agreement with J. C. Bradford & Company. PaineWebber claimed that Morgan Stanley pursued "a carefully planned, broadbased campaign to raid Bradford personnel and interfere with the merger agreement between PaineWebber and Bradford."

One of the most famous tort cases in history involved interference with a contract of merger. In that case a jury awarded Pennzoil over $10 billion against Texaco for persuading Getty Oil to breach an agreement of merger with Pennzoil. After Texaco filed for bankruptcy, Pennzoil accepted a settlement of around $3 billion.

Don't induce the employees of another company to come to work for you when they are under contract to work for a period of time.

:: Negligence

The second major area of tort liability involves unreasonable behavior that causes injury. This area of tort is called **negligence.** In the United States more lawsuits allege negligence than any other single cause of action.

Negligence takes place when one who has a duty to act reasonably acts carelessly and causes injury to another. Actually, five separate elements make up negligence, and the following sections discuss these elements. Sidebar 10.6

:: *sidebar* 10.6

Elements of Negligence

Existence of a duty of care owed by the defendant to the plaintiff.

Unreasonable behavior by the defendant that breaches the duty.

Causation in fact.

Proximate causation.

An actual injury.

---

also summarizes them. In business, negligence can occur when employees cause injury to customers or others; when those invited to a business are injured because the business fails to protect them; when products are not carefully manufactured; when services, such as accounting services, are not carefully provided; and in many other situations.

10. DUTY OF CARE

A critical element of the negligence tort is **duty.** Without a duty to another person, one does not owe that person reasonable care. Accidental injuries occur daily for which people other than the victim have no responsibility, legally or otherwise.

Duty usually arises out of a person's conduct or activity. A person doing something has a duty to use reasonable care and skill around others to avoid injuring them. Whether one is driving a car or manufacturing a product, she or he has a duty not to injure others by unreasonable conduct.

Usually, a person has no duty to avoid injuring others through *nonconduct.* There is no general duty requiring a sunbather at the beach to warn a would-be surfer that a great white shark is lurking offshore, even if the sunbather has seen the fin. There is moral responsibility but no legal duty present.

When there is a special relationship between persons, the situation changes. A person in a special relationship to another may have a duty to avoid unreasonable nonconduct. A business renting surfboards at the beach would probably be liable for renting a board to a customer who was attacked by a shark if it knew the shark was nearby and failed to warn the customer. The special business relationship between the two parties creates a duty to take action and makes the business liable for its unreasonable nonconduct.

In recent years, negligence cases against businesses for nonconduct have grown dramatically. Most of these cases have involved failure to protect customers from crimes. The National Crime Prevention Institute estimates that such cases have increased tenfold since the mid-1970s.

One famous case involved the Tailhook scandal. A group of male naval aviators was sexually groping female guests as they walked down the hallway at a Hilton hotel. (Remember that an unconsented-to touching is an intentional tort.) One of the females who was sexually touched sued the Hilton hotel for negligence in knowing of the aviators' behavior and failing to protect her. A jury awarded her a total of $6.7 million against Hilton.

The extent of a business's duty to protect customers is still evolving. Note that in Case 10.3 the New Hampshire Supreme Court says that the defendant

> *A person doing something has a legal duty to act reasonably to avoid injuring others.

---

case 10.3 ::

IANNELLI v. BURGER KING CORP.
200 N. H. Lexis 42 (N. H. Sup. Ct. 2000)

McHUGH, J.: The plaintiffs, Nicholas and Jodiann Iannelli, individually and on behalf of their three children, brought a negligence action against the defendant, Burger King Corporation, for injuries sustained as a result of an assault at the defendant's restaurant. During the late afternoon or early evening hours of December 26, 1995, the Iannelli family went to the defendant's restaurant for the first time. Upon entering the restaurant, the Iannellis became aware of a group of teenagers consisting of five males and two females, whom they alleged were rowdy, obnoxious, loud, abusive, and using foul language. Some in the group claimed they were "hammered." Initially this group was near the ordering counter talking to an employee whom they appeared to know. The Iannellis alleged that one of the group almost bumped into Nicholas. When that fact was pointed out, the teenager exclaimed, "I don't give an F. That's his F'ing problem."

Nicholas asked his wife and children to sit down in the dining area as he ordered the food. While waiting for the food to be prepared, Nicholas joined his family at their table. The teenagers also moved into the dining area to another table. The obnoxious behavior and foul language allegedly continued. One of the Iannelli children became nervous. Nicholas then walked over to the group intending to ask them to stop swearing. As Nicholas stood two or three feet from the closest of the group, he said, "Guys, hey listen, I have three kids." Whereupon, allegedly unprovoked, one or more of the group assaulted Nicholas by hitting him, knocking him to the ground and striking him in the head with a chair.

The plaintiffs argue that a commercial enterprise such as a restaurant has a general duty to exercise reasonable care toward its patrons, which may include a duty to safeguard against assault when circumstances provide warning signs that the safety of its patrons may be at risk. The most instructive case, given the issues presented, is *Walls v. Oxford Management Co.* In *Walls*, a tenant of an apartment complex alleged that the owner's negligent maintenance of its property allowed her to be subjected to a sexual assault in the parking lot. We held that as a general principle landlords have no duty to protect tenants from criminal attacks. In as much as landlords and tenants have a special relationship that does not exist between a commercial establishment and its guests, it follows that the same general principle of law extends to restaurants and their patrons. We recognized in *Walls*, however, that particular circumstances can give rise to such a duty. These circumstances include when the opportunity for criminal misconduct is brought about by the actions or inactions of the owner or where overriding foreseeability of such criminal activity exists.

Viewing the evidence in the light most favorable to the plaintiffs, we must decide whether the behavior of the rowdy youths could have created an unreasonable risk of injury to restaurant patrons that was foreseeable to the defendant. If the risk of injury was reasonably foreseeable, then a duty existed. We hold that the teenagers' unruly behavior could reasonably have been anticipated to escalate into acts that would expose patrons to an unreasonable risk of injury. The exact occurrence or precise injuries need not have been foreseen.

Viewed in a light most favorable to the plaintiffs, the evidence could support a finding that the teenagers' obnoxious behavior in the restaurant was open and notorious. Because the group was engaging in a conversation at times with a restaurant employee, it could be found that the defendant was aware of the teenagers' conduct. The near physical contact between one teenager and Nicholas Iannelli at the counter and the indifference expressed by the group member thereafter could be deemed sufficient warning to the restaurant manager of misconduct such that it was incumbent upon him to take affirmative action to reduce the risk of injury. The plaintiffs allege that at least one other restaurant patron expressed disgust with the group's actions prior to the assault. The manager could have warned the group about their behavior or summoned the police if his warnings were not heeded.

In summary, the trial court's ruling that as a matter of law the defendant owed no duty to the plaintiffs to protect them from the assault was error. While as a general principle no such duty exists, here it could be found that the teenagers' behavior in the restaurant created a foreseeable risk of harm that the defendant unreasonably failed to alleviate. Accordingly, we **reverse and remand.**

:: CASE QUESTIONS

1. Under the decision in this case, when does a duty arise for the defendant restaurant to protect its customers?
2. What does the court suggest that the restaurant manager should have done in this case that would have satisfied the duty?
3. What do you think is the difference in this case between a "special relationship" duty and the duty of the restaurant?

restaurant has no special relationship to the plaintiff, but still rules that it may have a duty to protect restaurant customers.

Note that the duty to act reasonably also applies to professional providers, like doctors, lawyers, CPAs, architects, engineers, and others. In most negligence cases, however, the standard of reasonableness is that of a *reasonable person*. In negligence cases involving professionals, the negligence standard applied is that of the *reasonable professional*. The negligence of professionals is called *malpractice*.

As Sidebar 10.7 suggests, professional negligence is a controversial area of tort law.

:: *sidebar* 10.7

Medical Malpractice Crisis

Few people would disagree that physicians are extremely unhappy about the rapidly growing insurance premiums they have to pay. Some physicians have gone on strike; others have left the practice of medicine. The exact causes of the situation, however, are difficult to determine. Consider the following and make your own evaluation,

- Studies suggest between 44,000 and 98,000 people die annually from medical errors.
- A study in the *New England Journal of Medicine* found that 9 out of 10 patients who suffer disability from medical errors go uncompensated.

- In 2004 total payments for medical malpractice claims fell 8.9 percent nationally.
- As of 2005, 27 states have capped malpractice awards.
- In 2004 malpractice insurance costs for various medical specialties rose between 6.9 and 24.9 percent.

*Sources: *BusinessWeek*, *The New York Times*, Department of Health and Human Services

---

11. UNREASONABLE BEHAVIOR—BREACH OF DUTY

At the core of negligence is the unreasonable behavior that breaches the duty of care that the defendant owes to the plaintiff. The problem is how do we separate reasonable behavior that causes accidental injury from unreasonable behavior that causes injury? Usually a jury determines this issue, but negligence is a mixed question of law and fact. Despite the trend for judges to let juries decide what the standard of reasonable care is, judges also continue to be involved in the definition of negligence. A well-known definition by Judge Learned Hand states that negligence is determined by "the likelihood that the defendant's conduct will injure others, taken with the seriousness of the injury if it happens, and balanced against the interest which he must sacrifice to avoid the risk."

A train rounds a bend but cannot stop in time to avoid running over an intoxicated person who has fallen asleep on the track. A jury is not likely to find the railroad's behavior "unreasonable."

Examples of Negligence Failure to exercise reasonable care can cost a company substantial sums. In one instance the licensed owner of a National

Car Rental agency in Indianapolis was ordered to pay $5.5 million to a man who slipped on the floor and broke his hip. To save overtime pay the rental agency had had its floors mopped during, instead of after, normal working hours. Unaware that someone was mopping the floors behind him, the plaintiff had stepped backwards, slipped, and fallen on the wet floor.

In another case arising from unreasonable behavior, Wal-Mart Stores agreed to pay two young girls a settlement of up to $16 million. A store employee had sold the girls' father a shotgun used to kill their mother in spite of the fact that a federal form filled out by the buyer indicated that he was under a restraining order. Federal law bars those under restraining orders from purchasing guns.

Even before the terrorist attacks of 9/11, New York's World Trade Center (WTC) had been bombed. In 2005 a Manhattan jury determined that the Port Authority of New York was negligent in the earlier attack, which involved a blast from a truck filled with explosives that terrorists had driven into the public parking lot under the WTC. Six people died and over a thousand were injured. Is it an example of litigation gone wild to hold the Port Authority liable for a terrorist act? Consider that before the bombing a report commissioned by the Port Authority, which controlled the WTC parking, had specifically warned against such a bombing and recommended: "Eliminate all public parking at the World Trade Center." Citing potential loss of revenue, the Port Authority had declined to follow the report's recommendation.

Willful and Wanton Negligence   A special type of aggravated negligence is **willful and wanton negligence.** Although this does not reveal intent, it does show an extreme lack of due care. Negligent injuries inflicted by drunk drivers show willful and wanton negligence. The significance of this type of negligence is that the injured plaintiff can recover punitive damages as well as actual damages. For example, following the *Exxon Valdez* oil spill in Alaska, commercial fishers sued Exxon for damage to their livelihoods. A jury awarded substantial actual and punitive damages when it found that Exxon was willful and wanton in allowing the ship captain to be in charge of the ship when they knew he was an alcoholic.

> *Willful and wanton negligence allows an injured plaintiff to recover punitive as well as actual damages.

In 2005 a New Jersey state court awarded a 2-year-old boy $105 million for an accident that left him permanently paralyzed from the neck down. A drunken Giants football fan had caused the accident. Before driving, the fan consumed at least 12 beers sold him by a Giants Stadium concessionaire. The award for willful and wanton negligence against the concessionaire is the largest ever for the careless sale of alcohol. The award included $30 million in compensatory and $75 million in punitive damages.

Because employers are also liable for the intentional torts of employees in advancing the interests of their employers (see Chapter 14), employers face punitive damage awards in those instances even when they are also liable for simple negligence, or have not acted negligently at all. (See Sidebar 10.8.)

12. CAUSATION IN FACT

Before a person is liable to another for negligent injury, the person's failure to use reasonable care must actually have "caused" the injury. This observation

:: *sidebar* 10.8

Strip Search Hoax Costs McDonald's $6.1 Million

The caller identified himself as a police officer and told the McDonald's assistant manager that Louise Ogburn had stolen the purse of a customer who had recently left the restaurant and should be searched. For more than an hour the assistant manager and other McDonald employees detained, searched, and even committed sexual battery against Ogburn at the instruction of the caller. However, the caller was not a police officer and the call was a hoax.

Ogburn sued McDonald's and the jury awarded her a million dollars in actual damages for pain and suffering and $5 million in punitive damages against the company. To understand why McDonald's is liable, you have to understand that numerous instances of such hoaxes were known to the company involving various fast-food restaurants, yet the jury found that the company had not reasonably trained its employees such calls might be hoaxes.

If McDonald's negligence were extreme, that is, willful and wanton, that would justify the $5 million punitive damage award, but McDonald's is also liable for the intentional torts of its employees that justify awarding punitive damages. In this case the employees committed such intentional torts as false imprisonment and battery in the course of Ogburn's detention. Such detention advanced the interests of McDonald's in dealing with dishonest employees and made the intentional acts accompanying Ogburn's treatment the company's responsibility when they turned out to be wrongful.

is not so obvious as it first appears. A motorist stops by the roadside to change a tire. Another motorist drives past carelessly and sideswipes the first as he changes the tire. What caused the accident? Was it the inattention of the second motorist or the fact that the first motorist had a flat tire? Did the argument the second motorist had with her boss before getting in the car cause the accident, or was it the decision of the first motorist to visit one more client that afternoon? In a real sense, all these things caused the accident. Chains of causation stretch out infinitely.

Still, in a negligence suit the plaintiff must prove that the defendant actually caused the injury. The courts term this **cause in fact**. In light of the many possible ways to attribute accident causation, how do courts determine if a plaintiff's lack of care, in fact, caused a certain injury? They do so very practically. Courts leave questions of cause in fact almost entirely to juries as long as the evidence reveals that a defendant's alleged carelessness could have been a substantial, material factor in bringing about an injury. Juries then make judgments about whether a defendant's behavior in fact caused the harm.

A particular problem of causation arises where the carelessness of two or more tortfeasors contributes to cause the plaintiff's injury, as when two persons are wrestling over control of the car which strikes the plaintiff. Tort law handles such cases by making each tortfeasor *jointly and severally* liable for the entire judgment. The plaintiff can recover only the amount of the judgment, but she or he may recover it wholly from either of the tortfeasors or get a portion of the judgment from each.

Approximately 40 states have limited joint and several liability in certain cases, for example, medical injury cases. In these states and types of cases, multiple defendants are each liable usually only for that portion of the damages juries believe they actually caused.

Many states are currently modifying the common law of torts regarding rules like that of joint and several liability.

13. PROXIMATE CAUSATION

It is not enough that a plaintiff suing for negligence prove that the defendant caused an injury in fact. The plaintiff also must establish proximate causation. **Proximate cause** is, perhaps, more accurately termed *legal cause*. It represents the proposition that those engaged in activity are legally liable only for the *foreseeable* risk that they cause.

Defining proximate causation in terms of foreseeable risk creates further problems about the meaning of the word *foreseeable*. In its application, foreseeability has come to mean that the plaintiff must have been one whom the defendant could reasonably expect to be injured by a negligent act. For example, it is reasonable to expect, thus foreseeable, that a collapsing hotel walkway should injure those on or under it. But many courts would rule as unforeseeable that someone a block away, startled upon hearing the loud crash of the walkway, should trip and stumble into the path of an oncoming car. The court would likely dismiss that person's complaint against the hotel as failing to show proximate causation.

Another application of proximate cause doctrine requires the injury to be caused *directly* by the defendant's negligence. Causes of injury that intervene between the defendant's negligence and the plaintiff's injury can destroy the necessary proximate causation. Some courts, for instance, would hold that it is not foreseeable that an owner's negligence in leaving keys in a parked car should result in an intoxicated thief who steals the car, crashing and injuring another motorist. These courts would dismiss for lack of proximate cause a case brought by the motorist against the car's owner. For one of the most famous tort cases in history, see Sidebar 10.9.

:: *sidebar* 10.9

Explosion on the Long Island Railroad

Helen Palsgraf stood on the loading platform on the Long Island Railroad. Thirty feet away, two station guards were pushing a man onto a departing train when one guard dislodged an unmarked package held by the man. The package, which contained fireworks, fell to the ground with a loud explosion.

The explosion caused a heavy scale to fall on Helen Palsgraf, injuring her. She sued the railroad for the negligence of its guard and won at trial and in the appellate court. Three justices of the Court of Appeals (New York's supreme court) agreed with the lower courts: "The act [of the guard] was negligent. For its proximate consequences the defendant is liable."

However, four justices of the Court of Appeals decided that proximate causation was "foreign to the case before us." The majority ruled that what the guard did could not be considered negligence at all in relation to the plaintiff Palsgraf. The guard owed no duty to someone 30 feet away not to push a passenger—even carelessly—onto a train. The Court of Appeals reversed the damage award to the plaintiff.

The famous *Palsgraf* case illustrates the complexity of legal analysis. Question: Was it negligent for the passenger to carry fireworks in a crowded railroad station? Why didn't the plaintiff just recover damages from the passenger?

*Source: *Palsgraf v. Long Island R.R.*, 162 N.E. 99 (1928).

14. DEFENSES TO NEGLIGENCE

There are two principal defenses to an allegation of negligence: contributory negligence and assumption of risk. Both these defenses are *affirmative defenses*, which means that the defendant must specifically raise these defenses to take advantage of them. When properly raised and proved, these defenses limit or bar the plaintiff's recovery against the defendant. The defenses are valid even though the defendant has actually been negligent.

Contributory Negligence As originally applied, the **contributory negligence** defense absolutely barred the plaintiff from recovery if the plaintiff's own fault contributed to the injury "in any degree, however slight." The trend today, however, in the great majority of states is to offset the harsh rule of contributory negligence with the doctrine of **comparative responsibility** (also called *comparative negligence* and *comparative fault*). Under comparative principles, the plaintiff's contributory negligence does not bar recovery. It merely compares the plaintiff's fault with the defendant's and reduces the damage award proportionally. For example, a jury determined damages at $3.1 million for an Atlanta plaintiff who was run over and dragged by a bus. But the jury then reduced the damage award by 20 percent ($620,000) on the basis that the plaintiff contributed to his own injury by failing reasonably to look out for his own safety in an area where buses come and go.

Adoption of the comparative negligence principle seems to lead to more frequent and larger awards for plaintiffs. This was the conclusion of a study by the Illinois Insurance Information Service for the year following that state's adoption of comparative negligence.

Assumption of Risk If contributory negligence involves failure to use proper care for one's own safety, the **assumption-of-the-risk** defense arises from the plaintiff's knowing and willing undertaking of an activity made dangerous by the negligence of another. When professional hockey first came to this country, many spectators injured by flying hockey pucks sued and recovered for negligence. But as time went on and spectators came to realize that attending a hockey game meant that one might occasionally be exposed to flying hockey pucks, courts began to allow the defendant owners of hockey teams to assert that injured spectators had assumed the risk of injury from a speeding puck. It is important to a successful assumption-of-the-risk defense that the assumption was voluntary. Entering a hockey arena while knowing the risk of flying pucks is a voluntary assumption of the risk. However, that the injured person has really understood the risk is also significant to the assumption-of-the-risk defense. In one 2007 case, a University softball coach smacked his player in the face with a bat while demonstrating a batting grip to her. She required surgery for multiple fractures of her face and sued the coach and his employer, the university. The court denied the assumption-of-the-risk defense, asserting that it was up to the jury to determine whether the coach had acted negligently in hitting his player. The court observed that the player did not appreciate the risk of being hit by her coach with the bat.

Contractual notices regarding assumption of the risk are more likely to be enforced if they prominently bring to attention the risk involved.

Courts have often ruled that people who imperil themselves while attempting to rescue their own or others' property from a risk created by the defendant have not assumed the risk voluntarily. A plaintiff who is injured while attempting to save his possessions from a fire negligently caused by the defendant is not subject to the assumption-of-the-risk defense.

Assumption of the risk may be implied from the circumstances, or it can arise from an express agreement. Many businesses attempt to relieve themselves of potential liability by having employees or customers agree contractually not to sue for negligence, that is, to assume the risk. Some of these contractual agreements are legally enforceable, but many will be struck down by the courts as being against public policy, especially where a business possesses a vastly more powerful bargaining position than does its employee or customer.

:: Strict Liability in Tort

Strict liability is a catchall phrase for the legal responsibility for injury-causing behavior that is neither intentional nor negligent. There are various types of strict liability torts, some of which are more "strict" than others. What ties them together is that they all impose legal liability, regardless of the intent or fault of the defendant. The next sections discuss these torts and tort doctrines.

15. STRICT PRODUCTS LIABILITY

Don't forget that strict products liability applies only against *commercial* sellers.

A major type of strict tort liability is **strict products liability,** for the commercial sale of defective products. In most states any retail, wholesale, or manufacturing seller who sells an unreasonably dangerous defective product that causes injury to a user of the product is strictly liable. For example, if a forklift you are using at work malfunctions because of defective brakes and you run off the edge of the loading dock and are injured, you can sue the retailer, wholesaler, and manufacturer of the product for strict liability. The fact that the retailer and wholesaler may have been perfectly careful in selling the product does not matter. They are strictly liable.

Strict products liability applies only to "commercial" sellers, those who normally sell products like the one causing injury, or who place them in the stream of commerce. Included as commercial sellers are the retailer, wholesaler, and manufacturer of a product, but also included are suppliers of defective parts and companies that assemble a defective product. Not included as a commercial seller is your next door neighbor who sells you her defective lawnmower. The neighbor may be negligent, for instance, if she knew of the defect that caused you injury and forgot to warn you about it, but she cannot be held strictly liable.

In one case, a jury found the defendant liable when its cleaning product warned users to "vent" rooms being cleaned but failed to say "vent to outside." Vapors from the product injured several people when it was used in a room with a closed circulation venting system.

An important concept in strict products liability is that of "defect." Strict liability only applies to the sale of unreasonably dangerous *defective* products. There are two kinds of defects. **Production defects** arise when products are not manufactured to a manufacturer's own standards. Defective brakes on a new car are a good example of a production defect. Another example involves the clam chowder in which a diner found a condom, which led in 2005 to a rapid settlement between the diner and a seafood restaurant chain. **Design defects** occur when a product is manufactured according to the manufacturer's standards, but the product injures a user due to its unsafe design. Lawsuits based on design defects are common but often very controversial. Recent such lawsuits have included one against Ford that claimed Ford should have designed its vans to have a heat-venting system so children accidentally locked in the vans would be safe. Lack of adequate warnings concerning inherently dangerous products can also be considered a design defect. American Home Products settled a wrongful death lawsuit for an estimated $10 million. The lawsuit alleged that the company had not adequately warned users of its diet drug about the risks of hypertension, which had been linked to diet-drug use.

In practice, strict products liability is useful in protecting those who suffer personal injury or property damage. It does not protect businesses that have economic losses due to defective products. For instance, a warehouse that loses profits because its defective forklift will not run cannot recover those lost profits under strict products liability. The warehouse would have to sue for breach of contract. However, if the forklift defect causes injury to a worker, the worker can successfully sue the forklift manufacturer for strict products liability.

Under strict products liability, contributory negligence is not a defense but assumption of the risk is. The assumption-of-the-risk defense helped protect tobacco manufacturers from health injury liability for many years. Misuse is another defense that defendants commonly raise in product liability cases. Removing safety guards from equipment is a common basis for the misuse defense. Defendants have also argued that if a product meets some federally required standard, it cannot be considered defective. Most courts, however, have ruled that federal standards only set a minimum requirement for safe design and that meeting federal standards does not automatically keep a manufacturer from being sued for strict products liability.

In recent years many states have changed or modified the rules of product liability. See Sidebar 10.10. These changes to the rules of products liability (and modifications to the rules of medical malpractice) are often known

:: *sidebar* 10.10

Tort Reform

The rapid growth of products litigation during the past two decades has brought forth many calls for "tort reform." Numerous states have changed their laws to modify the tort doctrines discussed in this section and chapter. At the federal level, comprehensive tort reform has been strongly advocated although it has not passed as of this writing. Some of the tort reforms proposed or passed by the states include:

- Permitting only negligence actions against retailers and wholesalers unless the product manufacturer is insolvent.
- Eliminating strict liability recovery for defective product design.
- Barring products liability claims against sellers if products have been altered or modified by a user.

- Providing for the presumption of reasonableness defense in product design cases in which the product meets the **state-of-the-art;** that is, the prevailing industry standards at the time of product manufacture.
- Creating a **statute of repose** that would specify a period (such as 25 years) following product sale after which plaintiffs would lose their rights to bring suits for product-related injuries.
- Reducing or eliminating punitive damage awards in most product liability cases.

Importantly, note that not all, or even most, of these reforms have been adopted by every state.

generally as "tort reform." The federal government has also enacted tort reform that applies to product liability. As of 2005, federal courts can decide any *class-action* lawsuit involving over $5 million and involving persons from different states. Federal plaintiffs in such class-action lawsuits need no longer claim the usual $75,000 jurisdictional amount.

16. ULTRAHAZARDOUS ACTIVITY

Some states have analyzed fireworks-related explosions that cause accidental injury by the standard of ultrahazardous activity.

In most states, the courts impose strict liability in tort for types of activities they call *ultrahazardous*. Transporting and using explosives and poisons fall under this category, as does keeping dangerous wild animals. Injuries caused from artificial storage of large quantities of liquid can also bring strict liability on the one who stores. For an example of the unusual dangers of ultrahazardous activity, see Sidebar 10.11.

:: *sidebar* 10.11

The Great Molasses Flood

The Purity Distilling Co. had filled the enormous steel tank on the Boston hillside with two million gallons of molasses to be turned into rum. Unusually warm weather caused the molasses to expand. On January 15, 1919, with sounds like gunfire as the restraining bolts sheared, the tank exploded. A wave of hot molasses 30-feet high raced down the street toward Boston Harbor, faster than people could run, engulfing entire buildings. Before it subsided, 150 people were injured and 21 drowned. "The dead," reported the *Boston Herald,* "were like candy statues."

It took months to clean up the harbor. It took six years to resolve the 125 lawsuits that followed. The artificial storage of large quantities of liquid can be a sticky matter indeed.

*Source: Anthony V. Riccio, *Portrait of an Italian-American Neighborhood* (1998).

17. OTHER STRICT LIABILITY TORTS

The majority of states impose strict liability upon tavern owners for injuries to third parties caused by their intoxicated patrons. The acts imposing this liability are called **dram shop acts.** Because of the public attention given in recent years to intoxicated drivers, there has been a tremendous increase in dram shop act cases.

Common carriers, transportation companies licensed to serve the public, are also strictly liable for damage to goods being transported by them. Common carriers, however, can limit their liability in certain instances through contractual agreement, and they are not liable for (1) acts of God, such as natural catastrophes; (2) action of an alien enemy; (3) order of public authority, such as authorities of one state barring potentially diseased fruit shipments from another state from entering their state; (4) the inherent nature of the goods, such as perishable vegetables; and (5) misconduct of the shipper, such as improper packaging.

:: **Damages**

One legal scholar concludes that "the crucial controversy in personal injury torts today" is in the area of damages. This is because the average personal injury award has been increasing at nearly double the rate of inflation. For dramatic examples of the size of recent awards, refer to Sidebar 10.12. Juries determine the size of damage awards in most cases, but judges also play a role in damages, especially in damage instructions to the jury and in deciding whether to approve substantial damage awards.

:: *sidebar* 10.12

Highest Jury Tort Awards of 2007

:: Event Causing Injury	:: Jury Award in Millions of Dollars
1. Medical malpractice causing massive memory loss.	$109
2. Negligent security in strip club parking lot leading to paralysis.	$102.7
3. Defective transmission causing man to be run over by his own truck.	$55.2
4. Crash injuring a flight instructor and student caused by defective airplane float carburetor.	$54.5
5. Nursing home negligence causing woman to bleed to death over several days.	$54[1]
6. Pickup truck driven by a drunk driver severely brain injuring young boy in crash.	$50
7. Defective water heater exploding and killing man.	$50
8. Heart attack that a jury believed was caused by the painkiller drug Vioxx.	$47.5[2]
9. Failure to warn that hormone replacement drug caused breast cancer.	$47
10. Truck driver's negligence killing nine-year-old and unborn child and severely injuring woman.	$45[3]

Note: The size of the largest jury verdicts has been steadily declining since 2002. The top 10 verdicts of 2002 were 41 times larger in amount than those in 2007. Further, punitive damages as a percentage of these verdicts has also declined substantially in recent years. However, there were very substantial settlements of cases in 2007, including a $4.85 billion class action settlement involving the drug Vioxx and a $200 million settlement with the Roman Catholic Diocese of San Diego.

[1]The size of this verdict represents punitive damages due to the nursing home company's pattern of similar negligence in other facilities.
[2]The size of this verdict involving a single plaintiff may have prompted the pharmaceutical company Merck to settle a class-action claim against it for nearly $5 billion a few weeks after the jury handed down this verdict.
[3]In this case, the negligent driver's employer was liable under *respondeat superior*, and the employer's insurance company rejected a $200,000 settlement offer by the plaintiff.

18. COMPENSATORY DAMAGES

Most damages awarded in tort cases compensate the plaintiff for injuries suffered. The purpose of damages is to make the plaintiff whole again, at least financially. There are three major types of loss that potentially follow tort injury and are called **compensatory damages.** They are:

- Past and future medical expenses.
- Past and future economic loss (including property damage and loss of earning power).
- Past and future pain and suffering.

Compensatory damages may also be awarded for loss of limb, loss of consortium (the marriage relationship), and mental distress.

Calculation of damage awards creates significant problems. Juries frequently use state-adopted life expectancy tables and present-value discount tables to help them determine the amount of damages to award. But uncertainty about the life expectancy of injured plaintiffs and the impact of inflation often makes these tables misleading. Also, awarding damages for pain and suffering is an art rather than a science. These awards measure jury sympathy as much as they calculate compensation for any financial loss. The recent dramatic increases in the size of damage awards helps underline the problems in their calculation. One result is that many individuals and businesses are underinsured for major tort liability.

Currently, compensatory damage awards for pain and suffering are very controversial. How do you compensate injured plaintiffs for something like pain which has no market value? Many plaintiffs suffer lifelong pain or the permanent loss of vision, hearing, or mobility. No amount of damages seems large enough to compensate them, yet no amount of damages, however high, will cause their pain and suffering to stop. In 2003, President Bush called for the limitation of tort damages for pain and suffering in a case to $250,000 per person. Do you agree or disagree?

19. PUNITIVE DAMAGES

Punitive or exemplary damages arise from intentional torts or extreme "willful and wanton" negligence.

Compensatory damages are not the only kind of damages. There are also **punitive damages.** By awarding punitive damages, courts or juries punish defendants for committing intentional torts and for negligent behavior considered "gross" or "willful and wanton." The key to the award of punitive damages is the defendant's motive. Usually the motive must be "malicious," "fraudulent," or "evil." Increasingly, punitive damages are also awarded for dangerously negligent conduct that shows a conscious disregard for the interests of others. These damages punish those who commit aggravated torts and act to deter future wrongdoing. Because they make an example out of the defendant, punitive damages are sometimes called *exemplary damages.*

Presently, there is much controversy about how appropriate it is to award punitive damages against corporations for their economic activities. Especially when companies fail to warn of known danger created by their activities, or when cost-benefit decisions are made at the risk of substantial human injury, courts are upholding substantial punitive damage awards against companies. Yet consider that these damages are a windfall to the injured plaintiff who has already received compensatory damages. And instead of punishing guilty management for wrongdoing, punitive damages may end up punishing innocent shareholders by reducing their dividends.

Many court decisions also overlook a very important consideration about punitive damages. Most companies carry liability insurance policies that reimburse them for "all sums which the insured might become legally obligated to pay." This includes reimbursement for punitive damages. Instead of punishing guilty companies, punitive damages may punish other companies, which have to pay increased insurance premiums, and may punish consumers, who ultimately pay higher prices. As a matter of public policy, several states prohibit insurance from covering punitive damages, but the great majority of states permit such coverage. This fact severely undermines arguments for awarding punitive damages against companies for their economic activities.

Consider also that an award of punitive damages greatly resembles a criminal fine. Yet the defendant who is subject to these criminal-type damages lacks the right to be indicted by a grand jury and cannot assert the right against self-incrimination. In addition, the defendant is subject to a lower standard of proof than in a criminal case. However, defendants in tort suits have challenged awards of punitive damages on a constitutional basis. See Sidebar 10.13.

> "If you were to talk to foreign businesses about what scares them the most about the U.S. judicial process, they would say class actions and punitive damages."
>
> **–Carter G. Phillips, Sidney Austin Brown & Wood (law firm)**

:: *sidebar* 10.13

Punitive Damage Guidelines

In 2003 the Supreme Court determined that $145 million in punitive damages in a case was unconstitutional. In *State Farm v. Campbell*, the Court decided that the large difference between punitive and compensatory damages violated due process. The Court suggested that a single-digit ratio of punitive to compensatory damages (9/1 or less) would be more constitutionally appropriate than a 145/1 ratio.

State Farm v. Campbell also reaffirmed general punitive damage guidelines from an earlier case. The Court stated, in evaluating the appropriateness of punitive damages, that courts should consider:

- "the responsibility of the defendant's conduct (how bad it was),
- the ratio of punitive to actual damages
- how the punitive damages compare with criminal or civil penalties for the same conduct."

Note that juries award punitive damages in only about 2 percent of litigated cases.

Finally, note that almost no other country in the world except the United States permits civil juries to award punitive damages. For instance, in 2007 Italian court refused to enforce a $1 million award against an Italian helmet maker whose defective helmet had caused the death of a 15-year-old motorcyclist in Alabama because the award contained punitive damages. However, a few courts in other countries have enforced U.S. punitive damage awards even though courts in their own countries cannot award them.

:: Alternatives to the Tort System

Of common law origin, the tort system has developed slowly over several centuries. Today, the tort system has come under much criticism because of aspects of its development. The **contingency fee,** which permits a plaintiff to sue without first having to pay an attorney, encourages litigation. Others see litigation as promoted by the fact that even if a plaintiff loses a tort action, the plaintiff does not have to reimburse the defendant's often substantial legal expenses. Apprehension about the easy availability of punitive damages and general concern over the role of the civil jury in handing down large damage awards are also directed at the tort system.

Only approximately half of every insurance dollar paid out in lawsuits goes to injured plaintiffs.

Perhaps the most important problem of the tort system, however, is that it is rarely a cost-effective way of compensating those who are injured by others. For example, the Rand Corporation estimates that only 40 to 60 percent of the insurance dollars paid out due to tort litigation go to injured plaintiffs. Litigation expenses, including legal fees, consume the rest.

There are many alternatives to tort litigation. Arbitration (discussed in Chapter 5) is an important one. No-fault insurance, like that found in many states' automobile liability plans, is another. Workers' compensation acts are a third alternative. Because of their importance to the business community, the next section focuses on this alternative. As you read about workers' compensation, consider if it would be possible to apply some variation of workers' compensation to tort situations that do not involve the employer-employee relationship.

20. WORKERS' COMPENSATION ACTS

Around the turn of the century, the tort system was largely replaced in the workplace by a series of workers' compensation acts. These statutes were enacted at both the state and federal level, and they imposed a type of strict liability on employers for accidental workplace injuries suffered by their employees. The clear purpose of these statues was to remove financial losses of injury from workers and redistribute them onto employers and ultimately onto society.

Workers' compensation laws are an alternative to litigation for employees from the risks of accidental injury, death, or disease that arise out of and in the course of employment.

History **Workers' compensation** laws are state statutes designed to protect employees and their families from the risks of accidental injury, death, or disease resulting from their employment. They were passed because the common law did not give adequate protection to employees from the hazards of their work. At common law, anyone was liable in tort for damages resulting from injuries caused to another as a proximate result of negligence. If an employer acted unreasonably and his or her carelessness was the proximate cause of physical injury suffered by an employee, the latter could sue and recover damages from the employer. However, the common law also provided the employer with the means of escaping this tort liability in most cases through three defenses:

- Assumption of the risk.
- Contributory negligence.
- The fellow-servant rule.

For example, assume that employer E knowingly instructed workers to operate dangerous machinery not equipped with any safety devices, even though it realized injury to them was likely. W, a worker, had his arm mangled when it was caught in the gears of one of these machines. Even though E was negligent in permitting this hazardous condition to persist, if W were aware of the dangers that existed, he would be unable to recover damages because he knowingly *assumed the risk* of his injury. In addition, if the injury were caused by *contributory negligence* of the employee as well as the negligence of the employer, the action was defeated. And if the injury occurred because of the negligence of another employee, the negligent employee, rather than the employer, was liable because of the *fellow-servant rule.*

The English Parliament passed a workers' compensation statute in 1897. Today all states have such legislation, modeled to a greater or lesser degree on the English act. These laws vary a great deal from state to state as to the industries subject to them, the employees they cover, the nature of the injuries or diseases that are compensable, the rates of compensation, and the means of administration. In spite of wide variances in the laws of the states in this area, certain general observations can be made about them.

The System   State workers' compensation statutes provide a system to pay workers or their families if the worker is accidentally killed or injured or incurs an occupational disease while employed. To be compensable, the death, illness, or injury must arise out of and in the course of the employment. Under these acts, the negligence or fault of the employer in causing an on-the-job injury is not an issue. Instead, these laws recognize the fact of life that a certain number of injuries, deaths, and diseases are bound to occur in a modern industrial society as a result of the attempts of businesses and their employees to provide the goods and services demanded by the consuming public.

This view leads to the conclusion that it is fairer for the consuming public to bear the cost of such mishaps rather than to impose it on injured workers. Workers' compensation laws create strict liability for employers of accidentally injured workers. Liability exists regardless of lack of negligence or fault, provided the necessary association between the injuries and the business of the employer is present. The three defenses the employer had at common law are eliminated. The employers, treating the costs of these injuries as part of the costs of production, pass them on to the consumers who created the demand for the product or service being furnished.

Workers' compensation acts give covered employees the right to certain cash payments for their loss of income due to accidental, on-the-job injuries. In the event of a married employee's death, benefits are provided for the surviving spouse and minor children. The amount of such awards usually is subject to a stated maximum and is calculated by using a percentage of the wages of the employee. If the employee suffers permanent, partial disability, most states provide compensation both for injuries that are scheduled in the statute and those that are nonscheduled. As an example of the former, a worker who loses a hand might be awarded 100 weeks of compensation at $95 per week. Besides scheduling specific compensation for certain specific injuries, most acts also provide compensation for nonscheduled ones based upon the earning power the employee lost due to his or her injury. In addition to the above payments, all statutes provide for medical benefits.

Even if an employee's contributory negligence or assumption of risk leads to an accidental injury, the employee still receives workers' compensation.

Do remember that workers' compensation is a form of insurance required by the states.

In some states, employers have a choice of covering their workers' compensation risk with insurance or of being self-insured (that is, paying all claims directly) if they can demonstrate their capability to do so. Approximately 20 percent of compensation benefits are paid by self-insurers. In other states, employers pay into a state fund used to compensate workers entitled to benefits. In these states, the amounts of the payments are based on the size of the payroll and the experience of the employer in having claims filed against the system by its employees.

Workers' compensation laws are usually administered exclusively by an administrative agency called the industrial commission or board, which has quasi-judicial powers. Of course, the ruling of such boards is subject to review by the courts of the jurisdiction in the same manner as the actions of other administrative agencies.

Tests for Determining Compensation
The tests for determining whether an employer must pay workers' compensation to an employee are simply:

1. Was the injury accidental?
2. Did the injury arise out of and in the course of employment?

Don't forget that the legal test for applying workers' compensation is whether an employment injury (1) is accidental and (2) arises out of and in the course of business.

Because workers' compensation laws benefit workers, courts interpret them liberally to favor workers.

In recent years, cases have tended to expand employers' liability. For instance, courts have held that heart attacks (as well as other common ailments in which the employee has had either a preexisting disease or a physical condition likely to lead to the disease) are compensable as "accidental injuries." One ruling approved an award to a purchasing agent who became mentally ill because she was exposed to unusual work, stresses, and strains. Her "nerve-racking" job involved a business whose sales grew over sixfold in 10 years. Factors contributing to her "accidental injury" included harsh criticism by her supervisor, long hours of work, and inability to take vacations because of the requirements of her position.

In Case 10.4, the South Carolina Supreme Court gives a broad meaning to the requirement "injury by accident."

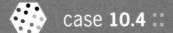

case 10.4 ::

PEE v. AUM, INC.
573 S. E. 2d 785 (2002)

MOORE, J.: . . . Respondent (Claimant) was awarded workers' compensation benefits for disability from carpal tunnel syndrome resulting from repetitive trauma to both wrists. Petitioners (Employer) appealed. The circuit court and the Court of Appeals affirmed. The only issue is whether a repetitive trauma injury is compensable under the South Carolina Workers' Compensation Act. We find it is and affirm.

Claimant worked for Employer in various capacities beginning in 1987. Each of her jobs involved the repetitive use of her hands. In the spring of 1995 she began experiencing tingling and numbness in both hands. On April 25, 1995, she was diagnosed with moderately severe carpal tunnel syndrome caused by compression of the median nerve as it passes through the carpal tunnel in the wrist. The evidence is uncontradicted that claimant's injury is work-related.

After surgery in June 1995, Claimant's left wrist improved temporarily but her symptoms returned within six months. Claimant's treating doctor removed her from work beginning April 20, 1996. By May 1996, she had severe carpal tunnel syndrome in her right wrist. Surgery was recommended for her right wrist in October 1996 with no guarantee of relief from her symptoms.

Meanwhile, on July 21, 1996, Claimant filed this action claiming benefits for an on-the-job injury. Claimant was awarded temporary total benefits continuing until she reaches maximum medical improvement.

The circuit court and the Court of Appeals held a repetitive trauma injury is compensable as an "injury by accident" as provided in the Workers' Compensation Act. Employer contends a repetitive trauma injury does not qualify as an "injury by accident" because the cause of the injury is not unexpected and the injury lacks definiteness of time.

1. *Unexpectedness*

Employer contends the repetitive event which causes a repetitive trauma injury is not unexpected but is part of the worker's normal work activity. Because the event causing the injury is not unexpected, Employer argues repetitive trauma injury cannot be compensable as an injury by accident.

Under the Act, a claimant is entitled to an "injury by accident arising out of and in the course of employment." In *Layton v. Hammond-Brown-Jennings Co.,* we interpreted for the first time the meaning of "injury by accident" under the newly enacted Workman's Compensation Act. We noted that two lines of cases had evolved in other jurisdictions: some jurisdictions, including North Carolina upon which our Act is modeled, held there must be some unusual or unlooked-for mishap resulting in injury to constitute an accident; other jurisdictions held no mishap was required for an accident as long as there was an unexpected injury occurring while the employee was performing his usual duties in his customary manner. We chose the latter definition, focusing on the unexpected nature of the injury rather than requiring that the event causing the injury be unexpected. This definition of accident as an unexpected injury has been reiterated in a long line of cases.

As we more recently stated, "in determining whether something constitutes an injury by accident the focus is not on some specific event, but rather on the injury itself." Further, an injury is unexpected if the worker did not intend it or expect it would result from what he was doing. Therefore, if an injury is unexpected from the worker's point of view, it qualifies as an injury by accident. Here, there is no evidence Claimant intended or expected to be injured as a result of her repetitive work activity.

Employer's contention that the cause of the injury must be unexpected is incorrect. Under South Carolina law, if the injury itself is unexpected, it is compensable as an injury by accident.

2. *Definiteness of Time*

Employer contends the injury resulting from repetitive trauma has no definite time of occurrence and therefore it is not compensable as an injury by accident.

Definiteness of time, while relevant to proving causation, is not required to prove an injury qualifies as an injury by accident. For instance, in *Sturkie v. Ballenger Corp.,* we found the claimant's emphysema, which developed gradually, was caused by repeated exposure to high humidity and dust on the job and was therefore compensable as an injury by accident. Similarly, in *Stokes v. First Nat'l Bank*, we found a psychological disorder which developed over a period of months compensable as an injury by accident.

Further, under the Worker's Compensation Act, a disease, which typically has a gradual onset, is compensable as an injury by accident "when it results naturally and unavoidably from the accident." This provision indicates the legislature intended an accident to be compensable under the Act, even where the effects of the accident develop gradually. The fact that a repetitive trauma injury is disease-like in its gradual onset does not preclude it from coverage as an injury by accident.

Here, is it uncontested that Claimant's carpal tunnel syndrome was caused by her work activities. The lack of a definite time of injury is therefore not dispositive.

Affirmed.

:: CASE QUESTIONS

1. Why does the employer contend that the injury was not accidental?
2. What is the court's test for whether an injury is accidental?
3. Did the injury arise "out of and in the course of employment"? Explain.

Likewise, the courts have been liberal in upholding awards that have been challenged on the grounds that the injury did not arise "out of and in the course of employment." Courts routinely support compensation awards for almost any accidental injury that employees suffer while traveling for their employers. A Minnesota Supreme Court decision upheld a lower court award of compensation to a bus driver. On a layover during a trip, the driver had been shot accidentally in a tavern parking lot following a night on the town.

Exclusive Remedy Rule   Recently, some courts have been liberal in their interpretations of the **exclusive remedy rule.** This rule, which is written into all compensation statutes, states that an employee's sole remedy against an employer for workplace injury or illness shall be workers' compensation. In the past few years, courts in several important jurisdictions have created exceptions to this rule. Note that these exceptions recognize in part that workers' compensation laws do not adequately compensate badly injured workers.

Since workers' compensation laws apply only to accidentally injured workers, the exclusive remedy rule does not protect employers who intentionally injure workers. But the issue arises as to how "intentional" such an injury has to be. What if an employer knowingly exposes employees to a chemical that may cause illness in some employees over a long term?

Should compensation for injuries arising from other accidents, such as automobile accidents, be included under a system like workers' compensation? Why or why not?

The Future of State Workers' Compensation   Currently, many problems confront the state workers' compensation system. Fifty separate nonuniform acts make up the system. Many acts exclude from coverage groups such as farmworkers, government employees, and employees of small businesses. Many state legislatures have enacted changes in their compensation laws. However, states that have broadened coverage and increased benefits have greatly boosted the cost of doing business within their borders. This discourages new businesses from locating within these states and encourages those already there to move out.

In the last decade, workers' compensation payments have tripled. Many workers exaggerate their injuries to get compensation. At the same time, compensation payments to seriously injured workers are often inadequate, and this has led to attempts to get around the exclusive remedy rule.

As our national economy moves from a manufacturing to a service emphasis, the nature of injuries suffered under workers' compensation programs begins to change. In particular, the number of mental stress claims rises. The National Council on Compensation Insurance states that these claims have increased fivefold in the past few years. Problems of proving (or disproving) mental stress claims bring new concerns for the workers' compensation system.

A major problem concerns slowly developing occupational diseases. Many toxic chemicals cause cancer and other diseases only after workers have been exposed to them over many years. Often it is difficult or impossible for workers or their survivors to recover workers' compensation for such diseases.

One solution to the problems confronting the workers' compensation system would be federal reform. Those advocating such reform have put forth several plans, but Congress has shown little inclination so far to adopt a uniform federal act.

:: Key Terms

:: Review Questions and Problems

Intentional Torts

1. *Assault and Battery*

   Under what theory can an employee sue her employer for merely touching her? Explain.

2. *Intentional Infliction of Mental Distress*

   In business the intentional infliction of mental distress tort has most often involved what type of situation?

3. *Invasion of Privacy*

   Explain the three principal invasions of personal interest that make up invasion of privacy.

4. *False Imprisonment and Malicious Prosecution*

   Explain the difference between false imprisonment and malicious prosecution. In what business situation does false imprisonment most frequently arise?

5. *Trespass*

   In recent months, homeowners downwind from International Cement Company have had clouds of cement dust settle on their property. Trees, shrubbery, and flowers have all been killed. The paint on houses has also been affected. Explain what tort cause of action these homeowners might pursue against International.

6. *Conversion*

   Bartley signs a storage contract with Universal Warehouses. The contract specifies that Bartley's household goods will be stored at Universal's midtown storage facility while he is out of the country on business. Later, without contacting Bartley, Universal transfers his goods to a suburban warehouse. Two days after the move, a freak flood wipes out the suburban warehouse and Bartley's goods. Is Universal liable to Bartley? Explain.

7. *Defamation*

   Acme Airlines attempts to get control of Free Fall Airways by making a public offer to buy its stock from shareholders. Free Fall's president, Joan, advises the shareholders in a letter that Acme's president, Richard, is "little better than a crook" and "can't even control his own company." Analyze the potential liability of Free Fall's president for these remarks.

8. *Fraud*

   Fraud can be used to void a contract and as a basis for intentional tort. What is the advantage to a plaintiff of suing for the tort of fraud as opposed to using fraud merely as a contractual defense?

9. *Common Law Business Torts*

You are concerned because several of your employees have recently broken their employment contracts and left town. Investigation reveals that Sly and Company, your competitor in a nearby city, has paid bonuses to your former employees to persuade them to break their contracts. Discuss what legal steps you can take against Sly.

Negligence

10. *Duty of Care*

(a) Do you have a duty of care to warn a stranger on the street of the potential danger of broken glass ahead?

(b) Do you have a duty to warn an employee of similar danger at a place of employment? Explain.

11. *Unreasonable Behavior—Breach of Duty*

In litigation who usually determines if the defendant's behavior is unreasonable?

12. *Causation in Fact*

(a) What does it mean to say that "chains of causation stretch out endlessly"?

(b) What is the standard used by the judge in instructing the jury about causation?

13. *Proximate Causation*

Explain the difference between proximate causation and causation in fact.

14. *Defenses to Negligence*

A jury finds Lee, the defendant, liable in a tort case. It determines that José, the plaintiff, has suffered $200,000 in damages. The jury also finds that José's own fault contributed 25 percent to his injuries. Under a comparative negligence instruction, what amount of damages will the jury award the plaintiff?

Strict Liability in Tort

15. *Strict Products Liability*

While driving under the influence of alcohol, Joe runs off the road and wrecks his car. As the car turns over, the protruding door latch hits the ground and the door flies open. Joe, who is not wearing his seat belt, is thrown from the car and badly hurt. Joe sues the car manufacturer, asserting that the door latch was defectively designed. Discuss the legal issues raised by these facts.

16. *Ultrahazardous Activity*

Through no one's fault, a sludge dam of the Phillips Phosphate Company breaks. Millions of gallons of sludge run off into a nearby river that empties into Pico Bay. The fishing industry in the bay area is ruined. Is Phillips Phosphate liable to the fishing industry? Explain.

17. *Other Strict Liability Torts*

Explain when common carriers are not strictly liable for damage to transported goods.

Damages

18. *Compensatory Damages*

Explain the three types of loss that give rise to compensatory damages.

19. *Punitive Damages*

During a business lunch, Bob eats salad dressing that contains almond extract. He is very allergic to nuts and suffers a severe allergic reaction. There are complications and Bob becomes almost totally paralyzed. Because Bob had instructed the restaurant waiter and the chef that he might die if he ate any nuts, he sues the restaurant for negligence. Discuss the types of damages Bob may recover.

Alternatives to the Tort System

20. *Workers' Compensation Acts*

If Corgel fails to wear a hard hat as required by Hammersmith, his employer, and is injured by a falling hammer, can he recover workers' compensation from Hammersmith? Your answer should explain the basis for recovering workers' compensation.

business :: *discussions*

1. You own University Heights Apartments, a business that rents primarily to students. One evening, your tenant Sharon is attacked by an intruder who forces the lock on the sliding glass door of her ground-floor apartment. Sharon's screams attract the attention of Darryl, your resident manager, who comes to Sharon's aid. Together, he and Sharon drive the intruder off, but not before they both are badly cut by the intruder.

Is the intruder liable for what he has done?

Do you have legal responsibilities to Sharon and Darryl?

What should you consider doing at your apartments?

2. You manufacture trunk locks and your major account is a large car company. When an important piece of your equipment unexpectedly breaks, you contact Mayfair, Inc., the only manufacturer of such equipment, and contract to replace it. The Mayfair sales representative assures you orally and in writing that the prepaid equipment will arrive by October 1, in time for you to complete your production for the car company. Instead, there is a union strike in the Mayfair trucking division, and the equipment does not arrive until December 1.

By December 1 the car company has made an agreement with another lock manufacturer. You threaten to sue Mayfair for their failure to deliver on time, but Mayfair reminds you of a contract term that relieves them of contractual liability because of "labor difficulties." Then you learn from a former secretary to the Mayfair sales representative that Mayfair knew that its trucking division was likely to strike. In fact the sales representative and the sales vice president had discussed whether or not to tell you of this fact and decided not to out of concern that you would not place your order.

Has Mayfair done anything legally wrong?

Is your legal remedy against Mayfair limited to breach of contract?

Will you be able to get damages from Mayfair other than a refund of your prepayment? Explain.

11

Intellectual Property in the Property System

 Learning Objectives ::

In this chapter you learn:

1. To grasp why intellectual property is so important to our economic system.
2. To identify the various types of intellectual property.
3. To apply the exclusive legal fence in trade secret law.
4. To appreciate why patent and trademark registration is so much more difficult and complicated than copyright registration.
5. To explain the importance of enforcement in intellectual property.
6. To grasp why the law limits the duration of patents and copyrights and arrive at a conclusion about how new discoveries should be shared with the world's poor.

In reading the previous chapters, you should have come to understand that the essence of "property" is a certain system of law. **Property** establishes a relationship of legal exclusion between an owner and other people regarding limited resources. It makes a particular resource like a new discovery legally "proper" to the owner rather than someone else.

Many rules describe how law makes various resources become legally proper to an owner. For example, to become an owner, you have to acquire resources in only certain ways, such as by contract, gift, accession (adding on to existing resources), and first possession (reducing something previously unowned to possession). You cannot become an owner by acquiring something by force or theft, and many criminal laws punish you for depriving proper owners of something in such manner. But criminal laws also protect you as an owner by punishing those who rob, steal, and defraud you of what you own.

317

Keep in mind that it is a mistake to think that you can always know the exact boundaries of what is legally proper to you. Your property includes the legal uses of what you own, and the full extent of these uses is frequently unclear. By using what you own, you will at some point collide with the equal right of others to what they own. It is the job of both common law and statutory tort law to determine when you cross the boundary separating your proper use from wrongful injury to what belongs legally to others. See Sidebar 11.1.

:: *sidebar* 11.1

Enforcement and Dispute Resolution in the Property System

As Chapters 3–5 illustrate, the adequate enforcement of property laws requires fair and honest ways of resolving disputes. A private property system needs accepted ways of settling disputes over who owns what, when boundary lines have been crossed, and when compensation is due for crossing boundaries and causing injury. On the other hand, the need for formal legal enforcement is less and fewer disputes arise when views on what is proper to whom are commonly shared in society.

Legal historian John Phillip Reid read every journal, letter, and diary available that gave first-hand accounts of the great periods of migration in the 1800s across the western territory. People traveled the Overland Trail to what is today the state of California by covered wagon, horseback, and on foot, often carrying their entire possessions with them. In his book *Law for the Elephant*, Professor Reid notes the hardships and perils the travelers faced, but observes that even though they were outside the jurisdiction of the then United States and there was no law enforcement, they had a strong sense of private property. There were relatively few instances of theft among the tens of thousands of travelers and almost no instances of robbery (taking by force). They negotiated and contracted for what they needed from others, even when the need was very great. Professor Reid attributes this to a common view of private property.

When property boundaries are unknown or difficult to determine and to enforce, much concern arises about the property system. We see this today with **intellectual property,** which includes the application of property in the areas of trade secrets, patents, trademarks, and copyrights. Intellectual property represents protection of some of the most valuable resources that businesses possess, yet it is relatively easy to deprive a business of its intellectual property merely by copying and selling or using a protected resource, which may be an invention, an expression, a design or mark, or a business secret like marketing plans or lists of customers.

This chapter begins by considering the justification for intellectual property. It then explores the importance of knowledge assets to businesses, followed by the major forms of intellectual property: trade secrets, patents, trademarks, and copyrights. It concludes by examining various property concepts that illustrate how property serves the common good.

1. THE JUSTIFICATION FOR INTELLECTUAL PROPERTY

The justification for intellectual property is the same as for the private property system generally. Property relationships are more productive of new resources than legal relationships that merely divide resources equally.

Overall, individuals will work harder to benefit themselves, their families, and, perhaps, their close communities than they will to benefit strangers, their nation, or the people of the world. Yet, curiously, if allowed to produce and trade for their private benefit, individuals or groups of owners as businesses will usually benefit the "common good," defined here as producing for consumption the maximum quantities of what people need and want.

Abraham Lincoln said that intellectual property couples "the fuel of interest with the fire of genius." He was referring to how an exclusive right to what you acquire and produce gives incentive to create new things, new ways of doing things, and new invention generally. The framers of the U.S. Constitution, especially Thomas Jefferson, made sure that Congress could protect intellectual property. Article 1, Section 8, of the Constitution grants Congress the power "[t]o promote the Progress of Science and Useful Arts, by securing for limited Times to Authors and Inventors the exclusive Right to their respective Writings and Discoveries."

Note that the justification for "securing" an "exclusive Right" is "[t]o promote the Progress of Science [new things and new ways of doing things] and the useful Arts [business and trade]." The Constitution recognizes that exclusive property boundaries promote, or give incentive to, the business production of what people need and want. However, the Constitution also ensures that after "limited Times" defined by Congress the resources of new expression and invention, which were formerly exclusive to "Authors and Inventors," will be freely available to everyone.

Intellectual Property and Competition

What would happen if there were no intellectual property in new invention? Most likely the pace of creative research and development (R&D) in business would slow dramatically. R&D is expensive. If businesses have to finance R&D and then compete against others who quickly copy new invention, the businesses paying for R&D will be at a competitive disadvantage. The prices they charge for their products will have to include (a) the cost of R&D, (b) the cost of production and distribution, and (c) a profit. The businesses who quickly copy the new invention of others will have to include only (b) and (c) in their prices. Competition is the lifeblood of the private market, and no business will deliberately place themselves at a competitive disadvantage.

Some people see the desire for private gain as "greed." Others see it as the driving force behind new products and new technologies that produces more of what people need and want at lower prices. However you characterize it, our unwillingness to work selflessly for a world of strangers is something natural to most of us, possibly the result of humans living for thousands of years in small bands and groups. Certainly, we are also capable of compassionate sharing and generosity to others, and society should constantly encourage these qualities. But at the same time, the exclusivity of property generally and intellectual property specifically will likely continue to be necessary to create the potential for the greatest wealth of nations.

Even the poor in a nation with strong, equally enforced property laws are wealthy by the per capita income standards of the poor in nations without such laws (see Sidebar 11.2). It is the capacity of intellectual property to help create the maximum likelihood for the production of what people need and want that ultimately justifies it.

Do remember that property serves the *common good* because property relationships produce what people need and want in greater quantities than other relationships for dealing with limited resources.

Don't forget that the poor in a nation with a strong property system under the rule of law are often wealthy by the average per person standards of the poor in nations without such laws.

:: *sidebar* 11.2

Relative Poverty and Property

According to the U.S. Department of Health and Human Services, the official level for financial poverty in the United States for an individual is $10,210. Contrast this poverty level with the estimated fact that today a billion people in the world live on less than a dollar a day, or $365 per year. Over a hundred nations of the world have average per individual annual incomes below the poverty level for individuals in the United States. For the two largest nations in the world, China and India, the estimated annual per individual incomes in 2007 averaged $5,292 and $2,659 respectively according to the International Monetary Fund, both substantially below the U.S. poverty level. In the United States, the average individual figure was approximately $43,000.

Studies strongly suggest that nations with well-defined and enforced private property legal systems are generally the financially wealthiest countries of the world and nations that lack adequate private property legal systems are universally the world's financially poorest. Some of the wealthy countries tax more and spend more on social welfare programs than others, but the poor in all wealthy countries are, relatively speaking, usually much better off than the poor in nonwealthy countries.

*Statistical Sources: U.S. Census Bureau, World Bank

2. THE KNOWLEDGE ASSETS OF MODERN BUSINESS

Knowledge assets are perhaps the most valuable resources of modern businesses. How to make things, how to do things, where to get things, how to sell things, how to buy things, and how to manage people are all vitally important to businesses. To some extent, knowledge assets can be protected by property, and property enables businesses to capture or realize the value of knowledge assets.

Law applies the exclusive right of property to both tangible and intangible resources. *Tangible* resources are physical like land and equipment. *Intangible* resources are not physical. According to one estimate, intangible knowledge resources represent 75 percent of the total value of 500 of the largest U.S. companies. This figure is double what it was 10 years ago. Increasingly, we live in a knowledge economy.

The different kinds of intangible, mostly knowledge-based assets that businesses may possess include the following:

- Employee skills and talents.
- Production designs, inventions, and technologies.
- Processes and methods of business operation.
- Reports, manuals, and databases.
- Relationships with customers and suppliers.
- Software.
- New product or service research.
- Marketing plans.

Sometimes you must assert the exclusive right of property in order to benefit from it, for example, with trade secrets.

The boundaries of property often do not apply automatically to protect ownership of these intangible resources. You must assert property in order to protect the time, effort, and money spent in developing knowledge and transforming it into valuable intangible assets.

The sections that follow explain important applications of property that protect knowledge-based intangible business resources. Remember that property, in these business resources, encourages (gives incentive to) the new production of what people need and want. This chapter concludes by examining the right of property and the common good.

:: Trade Secrets

One of the most common ways of asserting property in knowledge-based intangible business resources is through the trade secret. Trade secret law developed in the common law industrial revolutions of the 1800s. Before this time, the relationship of confidence and trust between skilled artisans (craftspersons) and their apprentices protected what the artisans knew from harmful competition by their former apprentices. But the 1800s brought large factories to the economy. The employees of these factories were not apprentices and at first were free to take their employers' knowledge, leave employment, and compete against their former employers. Trade secret law arose to protect the employers' valuable knowledge. It also facilitated economic development by making employers willing to hire employees who might come into contact with the employers' knowledge.

A **trade secret** is any form of knowledge or information (1) that the owner (usually a business owner) has taken reasonable measures to keep secret and (2) that has economic value from not being known to the public. The majority of states have adopted the Uniform Trade Secrets Act (UTSA), but common law also protects trade secrets in every state. The UTSA does not differ substantially from common law. Let us now examine the two elements of a trade secret.

> "More than ever before, information is what gives businesses their competitive edge, and they want to make sure that inside dope on products and services doesn't walk out the door."
>
> **–BusinessWeek, November 12, 2007, p. 76.**

3. TRADE SECRET: TAKING REASONABLE MEASURES TO KEEP THE SECRET

As listed in Section 2, businesses may possess many different forms of valuable knowledge. It may be financial, technical, scientific, economic, or engineering knowledge. When a business has spent time, effort, or money in training skills, preparing materials, making plans, or developing relationships with customers and suppliers, the business may wish that its competitors not have access to this knowledge. To protect it as a trade secret, however, the business must take *reasonable measures* to keep the knowledge secret.

A first step in keeping trade secrets is to identify knowledge-based resources. It is useful for all businesses to conduct a *trade secret audit,* which simply lists all the valuable forms of information possessed by the business, including formulas, plans, reports, manuals, research, and knowledge of customers and suppliers. Having identified potential trade secrets, a business must next assert its property by preserving secrecy.

Reasonable measures to preserve secrecy over valuable knowledge resources include locking away formulas, research results, blueprints, and various written plans. In the era of e-mail and the Internet, companies routinely protect computer-stored knowledge with protective "firewalls" to keep hackers from obtaining access. Some companies maintain two different computer systems in order to protect proprietary (owned) knowledge, one

Trade secret audits help you identify the valuable information that a business produces.

connected to the Internet and one networked only internally. Employees use the internal network to send messages about matters that are not for public consumption. To protect trade secrets from outsiders, companies often also carefully regulate who can visit the business and what areas of the business visitors can see. Visitors are sometimes required to sign agreements not to disclose to the public what they see and learn in a company they visit.

Business customers, suppliers, and repair technicians—in addition to visitors—may also have access to knowledge that a company values and protects. Like visitors, these parties may also be asked to sign nondisclosure agreements (contracts). As long as a company takes such reasonable measures to protect the public dissemination of trade secrets, it does not lose its property in knowledge-based resources merely because customers, suppliers, repair technicians, or even visitors come into contact with the secrets.

However, if the trade secret owner does not take reasonable steps to let a customer know that a trade secret must be kept confidential, the trade secret property protection may be lost, as Case 11.1 illustrates.

---

case 11.1

INCASE INC. v. TIMEX CORP.
488 F.3d 46 (1st Cir., 2007)

Incase designs and manufactures injection-molded plastic packaging products. The company discussed at length with Timex, a manufacturer of watches, about providing packaging for some of Timex's watches. Incase showed Timex two watch packages, but after extensive talks and negotiations, Timex got its packaging made by a Philippines manufacturer. Later, Incase noticed that the Timex watch packages incorporated one of the Incase designs and sued Timex for misappropriating trade secrets. Although the jury returned a verdict of damages for Incase, the trial judge overturned the jury's verdict and ruled as a matter of law that Incase had not taken reasonable steps to preserve the secrecy of the design. Incase appealed.

STAHL, J.: . . . To prevail on this type of claim of misappropriation of trade secrets, a plaintiff must show (1) the information is a trade secret; (2) the plaintiff took reasonable steps to preserve the secrecy of the information; and (3) the defendant used improper means, in breach of a confidential relationship, to acquire and use the trade secret.

The appeal on this claim turns on . . . whether Incase took reasonable steps to preserve the secrecy of the design. The district court noted that no documents were marked "confidential" or "secret"; there were no security precautions or confidentiality agreements; Incase had not told Timex the design was a secret; and

Incase's principal designer on the project, Bob Shelton, did not think the design was a secret. Timex adds that Frank Zanghi, Incase's vice president, did not tell anyone at Timex that the design was confidential.

Incase argues that the jury could have found evidence of steps to preserve secrecy in the fact that Incase showed the designs only to Timex, the trade practice of the watch industry, and the fact that Timex treated the designs as confidential in its dealing with the Philippine manufacturer. It also argues that Shelton's testimony should not have been given the weight it was by the court, since he was speaking for himself, not the company, when he said that he did not believe the design was secret. Incase also points to other testimony by Shelton where he said that he did not show the work to anyone other than Timex.

After a careful review of the record, we have not found any evidence to support Incase's argument that it took reasonable steps to preserve the secrecy of the design. Although Frank Zanghi testified, for example, that when Incase works on a project, it is treated as "confidential between Incase and the company," that the design is "proprietary" and "our property," and that he believed that the designs were secret, he admitted under cross-examination that this policy was never articulated to Timex. The fact that Incase kept its work for Timex private from the world is not sufficient; discretion is a normal feature of a business relationship. Instead, there must be affirmative steps to preserve the secrecy of the information as against the party against whom the misappropriation claim is made. Protecting a trade secret "calls for constant warnings to all persons to whom the trade secret has become known and obtaining from each an agreement, preferably in writing, acknowledging its secrecy and promising to respect it. To exclude the public from the manufacturing area is not enough." Here, there is no evidence that any such steps were taken. Therefore, **we affirm the district court's judgment** as a matter of law on the misappropriation of trade secrets claim.

:: CASE QUESTIONS

1. Why was this case tried in federal court, rather than state court?
2. Why did Incase think it had a trade secret?
3. What did the appellate court say on the issue of whether Incase had preserved its trade secret?
4. What should Incase have done to preserve exclusive private boundaries on its trade secret?

Employees and Reasonable Measures Businesses have to take reasonable measures to protect trade secrets even from employees. Employees may leave an employer and use the knowledge they have gained to compete against their former employer, or they may go to work for their former employer's competitors.

Increasingly, employers require employees to sign confidentiality contracts promising not to disclose what they learn in confidence in the workplace. This promise, however, applies only to knowledge that is unknown publicly and amounts to trade secrets. Because it may be difficult to define exactly what is or is not publicly known, employers frequently take the additional step of having employees agree not to compete against them if the employees leave their employment.

The law states that employers can enforce agreements (or contractual "covenants") not to compete only when there is a "valid business purpose" for the contract. Generally, this means that employers are protecting trade secrets, or, at least protecting their investment in the training of their employees, which itself can be a trade secret. The laws of unfair competition limit the extent to which employers can prevent employees from competing against them. The contracts and antitrust chapters discuss these limitations in greater detail. You should appreciate, however, how businesses use contracts to ensure recognition of property over intangible resources.

> **Do** remember the role of contractual confidentiality agreements and do not compete agreements in preserving trade secrets.

4. TRADE SECRET: THE ECONOMIC VALUE REQUIREMENT

Businesses can claim trade secret only if the knowledge protected has economic value. This requirement is easy for a business to meet since there is little reason for businesses to claim trade secret regarding knowledge that their competitors do not value. The economic value of the knowledge need not be great, but, again, businesses have little reason to go to the time and expense of asserting their right of trade secret protection unless the knowledge is quite valuable in the hands of competitors. The value must come specifically from the knowledge not being available to the public.

Interestingly, multiple business competitors may have trade secret property in substantially the same knowledge. For example, they may each have customer lists that overlap with many of the same names. As long as there are actual or potential competitors who are not aware of all the customer names, the knowledge still has economic value. It has not become general public knowledge just because multiple competitors likely have overlapping customer lists.

5. TRADE SECRET: CIVIL ENFORCEMENT

The worngful taking of any kind of intellectual property is called *misappropriation or infringement.*

The owner of a trade secret may go into court and get an injunction to prevent others—often former employees—from divulging or using a trade secret. An **injunction** is an order by a judge either to do something or to refrain from doing something. In the case of trade secrets, the injunction orders those who have *misappropriated* the trade secret to refrain from using it or telling others about it. In rare instances the injunction may also order that one delay in taking a new job. See Sidebar 11.3.

:: *sidebar* 11.3

Sport Drink Secrets

William Redmond was a general manager with PepsiCo. He had access to its competitive plans, financial goals, marketing plans, strategies for manufacturing, pricing strategies, and plans for new selling and delivery systems. Mr. Redmond specialized in PepsiCo's sport drink AllSport. Like other PepsiCo employees, he had signed a confidentiality contract with his employer, which stated in important part that he

> would not disclose at anytime, . . . or make use of, confidential information relating to the business of [PepsiCo]. . . obtained while in the employ of [PepsiCo], which shall not be generally known or available to the public or recognized as standard practices.

Mr. Redmond accepted a job with Quaker, a major competitor of PepsiCo, to be the vice president in charge of their sport drink Gatorade. Even though he signed a contract with Quaker agreeing not to disclose "any confidential information belonging to others," he and Quaker were sued by PepsiCo, which sought an injunction. The federal district court granted the injunction under Illinois law, and Mr. Redmond and Quaker appealed.

On appeal, the Seventh Circuit Court of Appeals affirmed the injunction, ordering Mr. Redmond not to take the new job with Quaker for six months until the trade secrets he knew were out of date. The court observed that "PepsiCo finds itself in the position of a coach, one of whose players has left, playbook in hand, to join the opposing team before the big game." The court asserted that

> when we couple the demonstrated inevitability that Redmond would rely on [PepsiCo's] trade secrets in his new job at Quaker with the district court's reluctance to believe that Redmond would refrain from disclosing these secrets in his new position (or that Quaker would ensure Redmond did not disclose them), we conclude that the district court correctly decided that PepsiCo demonstrated a likelihood of success on its claim of trade secret misappropriation.

Question: Why did PepsiCo not insist that Mr. Redmond sign both a confidentiality agreement *and* an agreement not to compete?

Source: PepsiCo v. Redmond, 54 F.3d 1262 (1995).

Trade secret owners can also obtain damages against those who misappropriate trade secrets. In 2005, a trial court assessed damages of $465.4 million against Toshiba Corporation. The court determined that Toshiba broke a contract to develop flash memory storage with Lexar Media, Inc., and then shared the technology with SanDisk Corp., Lexar's biggest competitor.

6. TRADE SECRET: CRIMINAL ENFORCEMENT

In addition to civil enforcement of trade secret boundaries, criminal prosecution can also result from misappropriation of trade secrets. Although various state laws make intentional trade secret misappropriation a crime, the primary criminal prosecutions today result under the Economic Espionage Act. The act makes it a crime to steal (intentionally misappropriate) trade secrets and provides for fines and up to 10 years' imprisonment for individuals and up to a $5 million fine for organizations.

According to the American Society for Industrial Security, U.S. business losses from misappropriation of intellectual property may total $250 billion a year.

Here are some examples of arrests that the FBI has made under the Economic Espionage Act:

- A 19-year-old University of Chicago student for posting confidential documents about DirecTV's latest generation of satellite television smart cards to three websites.
- A former employee of Jasmine Networks, Inc., a San Jose company, for downloading secret materials from Jasmine's computer system and trying to e-mail them as attachments to his personal e-mail account.
- A former Corning Incorporated employee for stealing certain flat-panel display technology and selling it to Picvue, a competitor.
- A former employee of Joy Mining Machinery for attempting to buy designs for certain of the company's proprietary equipment from a Joy employee.
- An employee of Wright Industries, a subcontractor of Gillette, for disclosing technical drawings to Gillette's competitors.
- Two Lucent scientists and their business partner for stealing source code and sharing it with Datang Telecom, a Chinese company.
- A scientist and her husband for stealing genetic information from a Harvard Medical School laboratory.

As business becomes increasingly global in nature, efforts to prevent international theft of trade secrets and other intellectual property (IP) have also grown (see Sidebar 11.4).

:: *sidebar* 11.4

ONCIX and Trade Secret Spies

In 2002, the Counterintelligence Enhancement Act created the Office of the National Counterintelligence Executive (ONCIX). ONCIX develops strategy to "protect critical U.S. technologies, trade secrets, and sensitive financial or proprietary information from foreign collectors."

According to Executive Michelle Van Cleave of ONCIX, "Globalization, while benefiting the United States economically, is making it challenging to isolate trade secrets from foreign managers and employees." In 2005 testimony to Congress, she stated that foreign access to IP "has undercut the competitiveness of U.S. industry by allowing foreign firms to acquire . . . technology that U.S. firms spent hundreds of millions of dollars developing. . . . Our general culture of openness has provided foreign entities easy access to sophisticated technologies."

The following sections discuss other types of intellectual property and the boundaries they establish.

:: Patent Law

Hundreds of years ago a patent was any legal monopoly openly issued by the government. The monarchs of Europe sold these patents for large sums of money by issuing "letters of patent," which gave private persons sole control over such things as the operation of toll roads, river ferries, and profitable trade routes. Patent sales helped reduce the need for government taxation.

> Ideas are not themselves patentable. Only invention that *applies* new ideas is patentable.

Today, a **patent** is a specific legal monopoly in the intangible resource of copying and marketing a new invention. The Constitution authorizes Congress to create patents, and Congress has passed numerous laws affecting exclusive patent right, which, of course, is property. Since colonial times, the United States has been a world leader in establishing patent law. Many of the constitutional framers were interested in technology and new invention, and during the Constitutional Convention in Philadelphia, the framers apparently took time off one afternoon to watch a newly invented steamboat cruising on the Delaware River.

In 1790, Thomas Jefferson helped draft the first federal patent law, and he personally invented numerous new devices and ways of doing things. Abraham Lincoln, however, was the first American president to patent an invention. In 1849 he applied for a patent on a system of air chambers to help boats float in shallow water. The application began:

> *To all whom it may concern:*
>
> Be it known that I, Abraham Lincoln, of Springfield, in the County of Sangamon, in the State of Illinois, have invented a new and improved manner of combining adjustable buoyant air chambers with a steamboat or other vessel for the purpose of enabling their draught of water [how deep the boat sinks in the water] to be readily lessened to enable them to pass over bars, or through shallow water, without discharging their cargoes. . . .

Many other famous Americans have held patents. For an example, see Sidebar 11.5.

:: *sidebar* 11.5

A Famous Writer's Love Affair with Patents

Mark Twain is best known as one of America's most famous writers. His single most profitable property right, however, came not from any of his books but from a 1873 patent issued on a self-pasting scrapbook. In part, his books were not so profitable because of inadequate enforcement of property law (copyright) to protect their copying and sale.

So fond was Mark Twain of patent law that he wrote about it in *A Connecticut Yankee in King Author's Court* (1889). In the book the main character, Hank Morgan, gets in a barroom brawl and is knocked out. When he wakes up, he is in the time of King Arthur. By predicting a solar eclipse, he gains the king's favor and is appointed the king's "perpetual minister and executive." He later explains:

> [T]he very first official thing I did in my administration—and it was on the very first day of it too—was to start a patent office; for I knew that a country without a patent office and good patent laws was just a crab, and couldn't travel any way but sideways or backways.

7. OBTAINING A PATENT

A patent is an exclusive right created by statute and recognized by the U.S. Patent and Trademark Office (PTO) for a limited period of time. This property applies to inventions, which are new applications of information. Patent law is very complex, as numerous lawsuits involving patents illustrate, and the settlements and judgment awards for violating patent right can be quite high. For instance:

> **Don't** forget that patents apply for only a limited period of time.

- Medtronic Inc., a medical device maker, agreed to pay $550 million to settle a patent lawsuit brought by inventor and spinal surgeon Dr. Gary K. Michelson.

- Immersion Corp. won an $82 million judgment against Sony Corp. for violating Immersion's patented technology that makes game controllers shake to increase realism.

- Genentech agreed to pay the University of California at San Francisco $200 million to settle a patent dispute. The university had sued Genentech alleging that it misappropriated patented technology to produce a growth hormone that is one of the company's largest selling products.

To obtain a patent, an inventor must pay a filing fee and file an application with the PTO. The application must in words and drawings (1) explain how to make and use the basic invention; (2) show why the invention is different from *prior art*, that is, from all previous and related inventions or state of knowledge; and (3) precisely describe what aspects of the invention (called *claims*) deserve the patent.

> In 2006, the Patent and Trademark Office received 443,652 patent applications, which more than doubled the number from 1996. The PTO issued patents on 183,187 of these applications.

The PTO assigns a *patent examiner* to consider the application, and there is usually a great deal of communication between the examiner and the applicant over the adequacy of the application's explanations, the scope of the proposed patent (exactly what the patent applies to), and whether the invention even qualifies at all for a patent. The applicant can amend the application. Since the PTO receives 1,200 or more patent applications a day, the application process can take several years from start to finish. Note that the patent issuance provides a presumption of a valid property rather than a final determination of one. As the next section discusses, only a court can finally determine patent validity.

8. PATENTABLE SUBJECT MATTER

After the PTO issues a patent, the patent owner may have to defend its property against *infringers*—those who make, use, or sell the invention without a license from the owner. When the patent owner files a lawsuit, it is common for the alleged infringer to respond by attacking the validity of the patent. If the court finds the patent invalid, the alleged infringer will win.

> A *process* is a way of doing something through a series of operations.

Attacking the "subject matter" of a patent is one common way of testing the validity of a patent. The Patent Statute of 1952 and its amendments identify patentable subject matter as the following:

- Processes.
- Machines.
- Compositions of matter.
- Improvements to processes, machines, or compositions of matter.

- Nonfunctional designs of a manufactured article.
- Certain plants.

Although not unlimited, the subject matter for a potential patent is quite broad. In *Diamond v. Chakrabarty,* 447 U.S. 303 (1980), the Supreme Court ruled that a scientist could patent a genetically modified bacterium which ate hydrocarbons found in oil spills. The Court said, "Congress is free to amend § 101 [the subject matter section of the general patent law] so as to exclude from patent protection organisms produced by genetic engineering. . . . Or it may choose to craft a statute specifically designed for such living things. But until Congress takes such action, the language of § 101 fairly embraces the respondent's invention."

In Case 11.2, the Supreme Court considers whether a modified hybrid plant is patentable subject matter when Congress had earlier passed laws establishing some plant patents, but not the type on appeal.

case **11.2**

J.E.M. AG SUPPLY, INC. v. PIONEER HI-BRED INTERNATIONAL, INC.
534 U.S. 124 (2001)

Respondent Pioneer Hi-Bred held patents on hybrid corn seeds. It licensed its corn seeds to petitioner Farm Advantage (the business name of J.E.M. Ag) for use in growing corn, and specifically not for creating new seeds or resale. When petitioner Farm Advantage resold the seed corn, Pioneer sued for patent violation. Farm Advantage argued that the patent was invalid because the hybrid corn was not patentable subject matter. It pointed out that the Plant Patent Act of 1930 (PPA) protected only sexually reproduced plants (those grown without seeds) and that the Plant Variety Protection Act of 1970 (PVPA) gave only limited property protection to seeds that reproduced plants. Because of these specific acts, Farm Advantage claimed that the corn hybrids were not patentable subject matter under § 101 of the general patent law.

When the federal district court and the court of appeals ruled for Pioneer, the Supreme Court agreed to hear the case.

THOMAS, J.: . . .The question before us is whether utility patents may be issued for plants pursuant to § 101. The text of § 101 provides:

"Whoever invents or discovers any new and useful process, machine, manufacture, or composition of matter, or any new and useful improvement thereof, may obtain a patent therefor, subject to the conditions and requirements of this title."

As this Court recognized over 20 years ago in *Chakrabarty* the language of § 101 is extremely broad. "In choosing such expansive terms as 'manufacture' and 'composition of matter,' modified by the comprehensive 'any,' Congress plainly contemplated that the patent laws would be given wide scope." This Court thus concluded in *Chakrabarty* that living things were patentable under § 101, and held that a manmade micro-organism fell within the scope of the statute. As Congress recognized, "the relevant distinction was not between living and inanimate things, but between produces of nature, whether living or not, and human-made inventions."

In *Chakrabarty,* the Court also rejected the argument that Congress must expressly authorize protection for new patentable subject matter:

"It is, of course, correct that Congress, not the courts, must define the limits of patentability; but it is equally true that once Congress has spoken it is 'the province and duty of the judicial department to say what the law is.' Congress has performed its constitutional role in defining patentable subject matter in § 101; we perform ours in construing the language Congress has employed. . . . The subject-matter provisions of the patent law have been cast in broad terms to fulfill the constitutional and statutory goal of promoting 'the Progress of Science and the useful Arts' with all that means for the social and economic benefits envisioned by Jefferson."

Petitioners do not allege that Pioneer's patents are invalid for failure to meet the requirements for a utility patent. Nor do they dispute that plants fall within the terms of § 101's broad language that includes "manufacture" or "composition of matter." Rather, petitioners argue that the PPA and PVPA provide the exclusive means of protecting new varieties of plants, and so awarding utility patents for plants upsets the scheme contemplated by Congress.

Petitioners essentially ask us to deny utility patent protection for sexually reproduced plants because it was unforeseen in 1930 that such plants could receive protection under § 101. Denying patent protection under § 101 simply because such coverage was thought technologically infeasible in 1930, however, would be inconsistent with the forward-looking perspective of the utility patent statute. As we noted in *Chakrabarty*, "Congress employed broad general language in drafting § 101 precisely because [new types of] inventions are often unforeseeable."

Second, petitioners maintain that the PPA's limitation to asexually reproduced plants would make no sense if Congress intended § 101 to authorize patents on plant varieties that were sexually reproduced. But this limitation once again merely reflects the reality of plant breeding in 1930. At that time, the primary means of reproducing bred plants true-to-type was through asexual reproduction. Congress thought that sexual reproduction through seeds was not a stable way to maintain desirable bred characteristics. Thus, it is hardly surprising that plant patents would protect only asexual reproduction, since this was the most reliable type of reproduction for preserving the desirable characteristics of breeding.

By passing the PVPA in 1970, Congress specifically authorized limited patent-like protection for certain sexually reproduced plants. Petitioners therefore argue that this legislation evidences Congress' intent to deny broader § 101 utility patent protection for such plants. Petitioners' argument, however, is unavailing for two reasons. First, nowhere does the PVPA purport to provide the exclusive statutory means of protecting sexually reproduced plants. Second, the PVPA and § 101 can easily be reconciled. Because it is harder to qualify for a utility patent than for a Plant Variety Protection (PVP) certificate, it only makes sense that utility patents would confer a greater scope of protection.

We also note that the PTO [Patent and Trademark Office] has assigned utility patents for plants for at least 16 years and there has been no indication from either Congress or agencies with expertise that such coverage is inconsistent with the PVPA or the PPA. The Board of Patent Appeals and Interferences, which has specific expertise in issues of patent law, relied heavily on this Court's decision in *Chakrabarty* when it interpreted the subject matter of § 101 to include plants. This highly visible decision has led to the issuance of some 1,800 utility patents for plants. Moreover, the PTO, which administers § 101 as well as the PPA, recognizes and regularly issues utility patents for plants. In addition, the Department of Agriculture's Plant Variety Protection Office acknowledges the existence of utility patents for plants.

For these reasons, we hold that newly developed plant breeds fall within the terms of § 101, and that neither the PPA nor the PVPA limits the scope of § 101's coverage. As in *Chakrabarty,* we decline to narrow the reach of § 101 where Congress has given us no indication that it intends this result. Accordingly, we **affirm the judgment of the Court of Appeals.**

:: CASE QUESTIONS

1. How does this case differ from *Chakrabarty?*
2. Why does Farm Advantage argue that § 101 does not protect Pioneer's corn?
3. Why does the Supreme Court rule that § 101 does protect Pioneer's corn?
4. Suppose that the Court had agreed with Farm Advantage. What could Pioneer have done in the future to protect its hybrid seed products?

Consider the following. GeneCure Laboratory develops genetically changed human genes that when injected into cancer patients will cure their form of disease. The laboratory can get a 20-year patent on this gene or on a gene that helps people lose weight or change the color of their eyes. But the gene must not be a "naturally" occurring "composition of matter." It must come into existence as an application of human knowledge that, in the words of the Constitution, promotes the "Progress of Science."

Currently, one of the most controversial areas of potentially patentable subject matter concerns "processes." What is a process? Is a computer program a process? Are ways of doing business a process? Mere ideas are not a patentable process. Nor are mathematical algorithms or formulas like $E = mc^2$ that express truths about the universe. Historically, business methods like double-entry bookkeeping were considered unpatentable, but they are after all processes, methods for doing things.

In *State Street Bank and Trust Co. v. Signature Financial Group, Inc.*, 149 F.3d 1360 (1998), a federal circuit court of appeals upheld the patent on a data processing system that allowed an administrator to monitor and record the financial information flow and make all calculations necessary for maintaining a mutual fund investment partnership. Following this case, thousands of patents have been filed on business-related processes. However, in 2007 a federal circuit court of appeals in *In re Comisky*, 499 F.3d 1365 decided that a process and method for conducting mandatory arbitration involving legal documents such as contracts was not patentable subject matter. The court asserted that a claim involving mental processes or algorithms is patentable subject matter only if it is tied to a machine or involves the transformation of a physical object. It seems likely that courts will increasingly invalidate patents that only involve mental processes. A Supreme Court case is expected.

9. NONOBVIOUSNESS, NOVELTY, AND USEFULNESS

Perhaps the most common way of challenging a patent's validity is to claim that the "invention" is obvious to someone with knowledge in the field.

To be patentable, it is not enough for something to be appropriate subject matter. An invention must also have certain characteristics. Namely, it must be nonobvious, novel, and useful. An alleged infringer can always defend against an infringement lawsuit by proving that the patent is invalid because the invention is obvious, previously known, or useless.

The characteristic of *nonobviousness* refers to the ability of an invention to produce surprising or unexpected results, that is, results not anticipated by *prior art* (the previous state of knowledge in the field). The nonobviousness standard is measured in relation to someone who has at least an ordinary understanding in the prior art. For instance, to be patentable a computer hardware invention would need to be nonobvious to an ordinary computer engineer.

Patent litigation over the obviousness of an invention is typically very subjective with each side to the lawsuit producing experts who disagree. Further complicating matters is that obviousness is usually measured from the date the litigation takes place, which can be many years after the application. Ultimately, it is up to the court to determine the state of knowledge existing when the inventor filed the application and whether the invention is nonobvious. See Sidebar 11.6.

:: *sidebar* 11.6

The Determination of Obviousness

A problem of the patent system is that a single manufactured item like an automobile may have hundreds of patents applying to various parts. Any time an improvement is made on a part by manufacturer X, there is always the possibility that a current patent holder Y will sue claiming infringement. X often responds that Y's patent claim is invalid because it was obvious. If Y's patent claim is obvious, then the fact that X based its new improvement on technology covered by Y's claim is not patent infringement because the patent is invalid.

The Supreme Court faced this situation in *KSR International Co. v. Teleflex, Inc.*, 127 S. Ct. 1727 (2007), a case involving Teleflex's accusation that KSR infringed its patent by adding a new electronic sensor to an adjustable automobile accelerator pedal. Teleflex believed it had a patent that covered the use of electronic sensors to automobile accelerator pedals. KSR responded by asserting that the patent claim was invalid because the underlying technology of attaching the electronic sensor was obvious. In its decision favoring KSR, the Supreme Court rejected a prior decision by the United States Court of Appeals for the Federal Circuit, which deals with patents. That prior case decided that a patent claim is only proved obvious when some specific reference like a journal article prior to the patent in question suggests that claim (in this case suggesting the attaching of the electronic sensor to an automobile accelerator pedal prior to the Teleflex patent).

Instead, the Supreme Court observed that a variety of factors could lead a court to conclude legally that a patent was invalid for obviousness. Importantly, the Court said, "We build and create by bringing to the tangible and palpable reality around us new works based on instinct, simple logic, ordinary inferences, extraordinary ideas, and sometimes even genius. These advances, once part of our shared knowledge, define a new threshold for which innovation starts once more. And as progress beginning from higher levels of achievement is expected in the normal course, the results of ordinary innovation are not the subject of exclusive rights under the patent laws. Were it otherwise patents might stifle, rather than promote, the progress of useful arts."

What the Supreme Court has done is to make it somewhat easier to challenge the validity of patents by arguing that patent claims are obvious and that new improvements in technology or designs do not violate patents in the old technology or designs.

To qualify for a patent, an invention must also possess the characteristic of novelty. *Novelty* indicates that something is new and different from the prior art. The test is met when no single prior element of art meets all of the invention's claims. However, under patent law even if an invention is otherwise new, it fails the novelty test if it has been previously described in a publication or put to public use more than one year before a patent application on it is filed (the *one-year rule*).

Except for patents issued on designs or plants, an invention to be valid must be useful, that is, it must do something. *Usefulness* is also defined as *utility,* and patents that are not plant or design patents are called utility patents. Suppose that Acme Laboratory scientists invent a new chemical compound. Until the compound has a use, say, ridding pets of fleas, Acme will be unable to get a utility patent on it. Usefulness was the issue in *Diamond v. Diehr,* 450 U.S. 175 (1981), the first Supreme Court decision to recognize a patent on computer software. The Court stated that the software involved controlled the timing for curing rubber and thus was useful. Since this case, the mathematical algorithms contained in computer software have been patentable if they do something in the real world.

Computer software code has long been copyrightable. See Sections 15–17 of this chapter. The importance of patenting software as opposed to just copyrighting is that the copyright protects *only* the actual programming code; what the code does, however, can be easily copied using different code. But if you patent the computer code you may have a legal monopoly over the way the computer *does* something, such as controlling rubber curing. Merely changing the code will not keep someone from infringing a patent.

Patent Duration and Enforcement   As the U.S. Constitution specifies, the property represented by patents runs for limited duration. Statute limits utility patents to 20 years, plant patents to 17 years, and design patents to 14 years. When a patent expires, the invention is in the *public domain*, and others may use it without limitation. Remember that when the patent expires, it is easy to use the invention since the patent application explains exactly how the invention works, including drawings of its construction. The explicit purpose of patent law is to make inventions public following the limited period of legal property right.

For the duration of a patent, the owner can sue those who infringe on it. If successful, the owner can get an injunction prohibiting future infringement, damages, including triple damages for intentional infringement, and an order requiring that any infringing items be destroyed. Intentional violation of patent law is also a crime.

> When a patent expires, the patent is in the *public domain,* and others may use it without limitation.

> In 2007, a federal jury ordered Microsoft to pay $1.52 billion in a patent dispute over the MP3 format.

10. CURRENT ISSUES IN PATENT LAW

What property protects is not always clear. As a patent is an application of property, what patents protect are not always clear. Even when what patents protect is quite certain, the question arises as to whether a property monopoly is appropriate. Consider the following issues.

Business Method Patents   Business method patents date only to the *State Street Bank* case (see page 330). Following that case, numerous Internet businesses patented business methods and sued imitators. Amazon.com patented the one-click method of ordering over the Internet and sued to keep Barnes&Noble.com from implementing a similar ordering system. Priceline. com sued Microsoft over the latter's use of a "reverse auction." Concerned that it might be issuing patents for business methods that were not novel or were obvious, the PTO has begun to look more carefully at past practices before issuing business method patents.

Business method litigation continues, however. One company, Data Treasury Corporation, has sued numerous banks and credit card processors over two patents it holds that describe the electronic storage and retrieval of transaction records. Several defendants have settled with the patent holder. Other defendants have resisted settlement, arguing that the patents are invalid because what they describe is not new. If the defendants can prove by "clear and convincing evidence" (a higher standard than "preponderance of the evidence") that the plaintiff's invention was in commercial use at least one year before the patent was taken out, the patent is invalid. The commercial use does not have to be public and may have taken place behind closed doors.

> Approximately 3,000 patent lawsuits are filed every year according to federal court records.

Increasingly, business method patent licensing and enforcement is done by *patent holding companies.* These companies threaten to sue other companies that fail to pay a patent royalty (license fee) on the patents held by the holding companies. A company owned by Ronald A. Katz held 52 patents on various technologies for direct dial telephone marketing. Before the patents expired in 2009, this one company collected over $2 billion in license fees. Individuals or companies that own patents but do not develop them, and merely sue others who violate the patents, are called *patent trolls.* One so-called patent troll sued Research in Motion, maker of the popular BlackBerry wireless messaging system. Research in Motion settled with the patent holder for $612.5 million.

Pharmaceutical Patents   Patents on medicines to cure human disease are some of the most controversial of property applications. Many senior citizens in the United States have difficulty affording the expensive drugs that keep them alive and healthy. Throughout the world, billions of people simply cannot afford expensive patented medicines at all. In Africa millions of people are dying of AIDS, but they could be kept alive except for the high cost of patented AIDS treatments.

The moral issues of millions dying when treatment is available must be balanced against the incentives to produce pharmaceutical invention in the first place. Drug companies spend billions of dollars annually on research, much of which does not produce effective new drugs. Even for potentially effective drugs, the testing and regulatory approval process is time-consuming and expensive. Even after approval, the potential demand for some effective drugs is relatively small because comparatively few people suffer from the disease the drug cures. As a result, the drug manufacturers often charge high prices. See Table 11.1.

Recognizing the moral issues of drug prices, some pharmaceutical manufacturers have granted free licenses to produce limited amounts of certain drugs, for example AIDS drugs. In the United States, some of the drug companies give to charities that buy drugs for needy patients. What else should be done? Some people advocate eliminating patents for pharmaceuticals or fixing drug prices by law, actions that almost certainly would affect the private willingness to conduct new drug research. Others urge

table 11.1 :: Expensive Patented Drugs

:: Drug	:: Disease	:: Average Cost Per Year
Avonex	Multiple sclerosis	$14,000
Cerezyme	Gaucher disease	$200,000
Gleevec	Chronic myeloid leukemia	$37,000
Rituxan	Non-Hodgkin's lymphoma	$12,500
Velcade	Multiple myeloma	$22,000 (for a 4-month treatment)

that the government itself purchase the drugs as part of a national health plan or for the world's poor.

Patenting Genes Another controversial issue surrounding patent law concerns the patenting of human genes. In part, the controversy arises because many people do not understand what a gene is or what it means to patent one. A gene is not a small thing one can see under a microscope but rather a sequence of DNA that occupies a specific location on a chromosome and determines a particular inherited characteristic.

To patent a human gene does not mean that the patent holder owns some part of you. Only when the gene has been isolated and purified in a way that can be put to use can someone patent it. What is really being patented is knowledge about how to isolate the gene, so it can be used for new-drug creation and disease treatment. Worldwide, patent offices have received over three million gene-related patent applications.

Still, many believe that one should not be able to patent basic knowledge about specific genes. They argue that there should be a common use of this knowledge and that its production does not depend on the same incentives that justify other types of patents. In any event, there is likely to be a great deal of patent litigation over who owns what genetic knowledge as commercial uses of genes grow.

> **Do** remember that to patent a gene really means that its owner has only an exclusive right to use certain information for 20 years.

:: Trademark Law

For thousands of years, people have used marks on what they produce to represent the origin of goods and services. In Roman times the sign of a boy being whipped identified the presence of a school. Today, we generally call such marks **trademarks** and when they indicate a specific producer, the law protects them against use by others.

Trademarks are a form of intellectual property. Like patents you can register them with the PTO, and also like patents, trademarks are some of the most valuable properties that businesses own. McDonald's golden arches, the Nike "swoosh," Coca-Cola, the Marlboro man, Amazon.com, the Colonel, Exxon, Kodak, Kleenex, the Olympic rings, Rolex, Levi—the list of famous trademarks is almost endless, but always recognizable.

> According to *BusinessWeek* magazine, the four most famous trademarks belong to Coca Cola, General Electric, IBM, and Microsoft.

Recognizability or *distinctiveness* is the function of trademarks. In a world cluttered with stimulation, information, and advertising, trademarks pierce through the clutter and let people know that the goods or service represented are "the real thing"—that they come from one source. They are an information property, exclusively distinguishing the reputation and goodwill of a particular business from that of all other businesses. Trademarks protect both businesses and consumers from confusion regarding who makes or provides what. As one recent Federal Court of Appeals case observed:

> Trademarks are designed to inform potential buyers who makes the goods on sale. Knowledge of origin may convey information about a product's attributes and quality, and consistent attribution of origin is vital when vendors reputations matter. Without a way to know who makes what reputations cannot be created and evaluated, and the process of competition will be less effective. *Top Tobacco, L.P. v. North Atlantic Operating Co.*, 509 F. 3d 380, 381 (2007)

Misappropriation of trademarks, which may involve intentional use of the owner's mark or an accidental design of one's own mark too similarly to another's, is a major business problem, especially in the Digital Age when often the only point of contact people have with a goods or service provider is a computer screen.

11. TYPES OF TRADEMARKS

Although common law protects trademarks, this chapter focuses on the federal protection given trademarks by the Lanham Act of 1946. The Lanham Act protects the following marks used to represent a product, service, or organization:

- Trademark—any mark, word, picture, or design that attaches to goods to indicate their source.
- Service mark—a mark associated with a service, for example, Monster.com.
- Certification mark—a mark used by someone other than the owner to certify the quality, point of origin, or other characteristics of goods or services, for example, the Good Housekeeping Seal of Approval.
- Collective mark—a mark representing membership in a certain organization or association, for example, the National Football League logo.

For convenience, all of these marks will be referred to as trademarks.

Trade Dress Similar to trademarks, and also protected by the Lanham Act, is trade dress. **Trade dress** refers to a colored design or shape associated with a product or service. The red color scheme of Coca-Cola when associated with the general design of Coca-Cola labeling constitutes trade dress. Trade dress protection prevents Coca-Cola competitors from designing a shape that resembles "Coca-Cola" and attaching the characteristic Coke red to the design in such a way as to confuse potential Coke customers about what they are getting. Trade dress also includes distinctive store decorating motifs (e.g., McDonald's) or package shapes and colors. In 2007, Wham-O Inc., the manufacturer of the popular toy Slip 'N Slide, received a $6 million jury verdict that found competitor ToyQuest infringed Wham-O's federally registered trademark for yellow slide toys.

The distinctive "wasp-shaped" Coca-Cola bottle is part of its trade dress.

An important trade dress case is *Two Pesos, Inc. v. Taco Cabana, Inc.*, 505 U.S. 763 (1992). In that case the Supreme Court defined trade dress as "the total image and overall appearance" of a business. The Court upheld a decision that Two Pesos had violated Taco Cabana's trade dress. The Court stated that "trade dress [in this case] may include the shape and general appearance of the exterior of the restaurant, the identifying sign, the interior kitchen floor plan, the décor, the menu, the equipment used to serve food, the servers' uniforms and other features reflecting on the total image of the restaurant." The law protects trade dress from being copied as long as it is distinctive. If it is distinctive and registered, the law protects it even when the public has not yet come to identify the trade dress with a specific source.

12. TRADEMARK REGISTRATION

Under the Lanham Act, a person must qualify a trademark for registration with the PTO by using it in interstate commerce. Posting the trademark on an Internet website meets this qualification. Alternatively, an intent-to-use application may be filed, followed by an amended application when actual use begins.

To be registerable, a trademark must be distinctive. The PTO will deny registration in the following circumstances:

- If the mark is the same or similar to a mark currently used on similar related goods, for example, a computer company's cherry mark that resembles the apple mark of Apple Inc.
- If the mark contains certain prohibited or reserved names or designs, including the U.S. flag, other governmental symbols, immoral names or symbols, the names or likenesses of living persons without their consent, and the names or likenesses of deceased American presidents without the permission of their spouses.
- If the mark merely describes a product or service, for example, "Fast Food" for a restaurant franchise.
- If the mark is generic and represents a product or service, for example, "Telephone" for a communication company.

Note that a mark that is descriptive or generic in one context may be unique and distinctive in another. "Fast Food" used to mark a restaurant franchise is not registerable, but an overnight textbook delivery service could register "Fast Food for the Mind" because the mark easily distinguishes this delivery service from other similar delivery services.

As part of the trademark application process, the PTO places a proposed mark in the *Official Gazette,* which gives existing mark owners notice and allows them to object that the proposed mark is similar to their own. If existing mark owners object to the proposed mark's registration, the PTO holds a hearing to resolve the objection and, possibly, to deny registration. Finally, if the PTO determines the mark acceptable, it registers the mark on the *Principal Register.* This registration provides notice of official trademark status.

Unlike a patent, which specifies a limited property duration, the trademark enjoys a potentially unlimited protection period. But after six years the trademark owner must notify the PTO that the trademark is still in use. Currently, every 10 years the owner must renew the trademark.

The attempt to trademark certain descriptive terms, or a person's name, presents a special problem. Generally, the PTO will not accept a person's name or a descriptive term for protection on the *Principal Register.* However, there is a process by which a name or descriptive term can achieve full trademark status and protection. If it is listed on the PTO's *Supplemental Register* for five years *and* acquires a secondary meaning, it can then be transferred to the *Principal Register* for full protection.

Secondary meaning refers to a public meaning that is different from its meaning as a person's name or as a descriptive term, a public meaning that makes the name or term distinctive. In the public mind, "Ford" now refers to an automobile rather than a person, "Levi" means jeans rather than a family, and "Disney" refers to a specific entertainment company rather than its founder.

13. TRADEMARK ENFORCEMENT

Trademark law protects the trademark's owner from having the mark used in an unauthorized way. Manufacturing, distributing, selling, or possessing products (or services) with an unauthorized mark violates the law. The law establishes both civil and criminal trademark violation.

Civil violation of a trademark (or a patent) is termed **infringement.** The violator infringes on the trademark's property right through an unintentional or a willful unauthorized use, misappropriating the goodwill and reputation that the trademark represents and confusing the public about the identity of the user. Remedies for civil infringement include a variety of damages, injunctions, prohibiting future infringement, and orders to destroy infringing products in anyone's possession.

Trademark owners must be vigilant in protecting their marks because if a trademark becomes **generic,** if it loses its distinctiveness, it also loses its status as a protected trademark. A trademark is most likely to become generic (1) when an owner does not defend against unauthorized use and (2) when the public becomes confused as to whether a term refers to a particular product/service or refers to a general class of products/services. Due to concern that its famous trademark not become generic, Coca-Cola seeks to prevent trademark infringement by employees at soda fountains who without comment give customers other colas when asked for a "Coke." Employers are warned to advise employees to specify that another cola will be substituted if Coke is not available.

The band Metallica has sued a variety of defendants for using its trademark: Guerlain for Metallica perfume, Pierre Cardin for a Metallica tuxedo, Victoria's Secret for its Metallica lip liner, and even the Metallika furniture store of Waco, Texas. It is not clear that all of these uses violated trademark precedent. Will there be public confusion between a heavy metal band and a furniture store if the latter sells metal furniture under the name "Metallika"? As Table 11.2 illustrates, a number of trademarks have been lost because the public came to think of them as generic terms.

> **Don't** forget what it means for a trademark to become **generic.**

table 11.2 :: Trademarks Lost Due to Generic Use	
The following generic terms were once trademarks:	
Aspirin	Monopoly (the game)
Cellophane	Refrigerator
Cola	Softsoap
Escalator	Thermos
Lite Beer	Zipper

To ensure that its well-known trademark not be lost to generic use, the Xerox Corporation spent millions of dollars advertising to the public that *xerox* is a registered trademark and that the term should not be used as a verb (to "xerox" a copy) or as a noun (a "xerox").

To win a trademark infringement lawsuit, a defendant will usually present one of three basic defenses: (1) the mark is not distinctive, (2) there is little chance of the public's being confused by use of a term trademarked by someone else, or (3) the use is a "fair use." In arguing the first defense, the defendant maintains that the mark is descriptive or generic and that the PTO should not have protected it in the first instance. Alternatively, the defendant argues that the mark has become generic since its trademarking and that it now stands for a class of items. Note that a court can declare a mark invalid even if the PTO accepted registration.

The second defense argues that there is little chance of public confusion over two uses of the same mark. For example, the public is not likely confused between the Ford automobile and the Ford Modeling Agency. But the confusion defense does not always work. In 1999 a federal district court jury awarded Trovan, an electronics manufacturer, $143 million against Pfizer for willful trademark infringement in using the trademark "Trovan" on its antibiotic product, which was eventually withdrawn from the market following the deaths of several people who used it.

The third defense raised in trademark infringement lawsuits is that of fair use. *Fair use* of a registered trademark is allowed by the Lanham Act and relates to a discussion, criticism, or parody of the trademark, the product, or its owner, for example, in the news media, on the Internet, or in a textbook. The courts have been explicit that the use of a rival's trademark in comparative advertising is also a fair use. You can legally advertise the results of a study that show your product to be superior to a competitor's, even if you mention the competitor's trademarked product by name.

Criminal trademark penalties apply to those who manufacture or traffic in *counterfeit* trademarked products, products such as imitation "Rolex" watches or "Levi" jeans. What makes counterfeiting criminal is the deliberate intent to pass off, or *palm off,* fake products as real by attaching an unauthorized trademark.

Trademarks and the Internet Cyber technology and the Internet produce a combination of old and new trademark issues. One new issue concerns the relationship between a website domain name registered with the Internet Corporation for Assigned Names and Numbers and a trademark registered with the Patent and Trademark Office. There have been numerous instances in which people attempt to register domain names containing well-known trademarks that did not belong to them. Generally, it is a violation of trademark law to use another's registered mark in your domain name. Further, the Anticyber-squatting Consumer Protection Act of 1999 provides a remedy of statutory damages and transfer of a *famous* trademark domain name to its owner if it was registered in "bad faith."

14. TRADEMARK DILUTION

In 1995, Congress passed the Federal Trademark Dilution Act. This law prohibits you from using a mark the same as or similar to another's "famous" trademark so as to dilute its significance, reputation, and goodwill. Even if an owner of a famous trademark cannot prove that the public is confused by another's use of a similar mark (called a "junior" mark), the owner of the "senior" famous trademark can still get an injunction prohibiting further use of the junior mark on the basis of **trademark dilution.** The court also has discretion to award the owner the infringer's profits, actual damages, and attorney's fees if the infringer "willfully intended to trade on the owner's reputation or to cause dilution of the famous mark."

In Case 11.3 the Supreme Court examines the kind of evidence needed to prove trademark dilution. Note that Justice Stevens says the lower courts have misinterpreted the federal act under which this case was brought with certain state antidilution laws.

case **11.3** ::

MOSELY v. V SECRET CATALOGUE, INC.
123 S. Ct. 1115 (2003)

Victor and Cathy Mosely (petitioners) owned and operated a retail store named "Victor's Secret" in Elizabethtown, Kentucky. The store sold a variety of "intimate lingerie" and "adult novelties." Following a tip, the respondent who owns the "Victoria's Secret" trademark demanded that the Moseleys change the store's name or cease operation, claiming that the name "Victor's Secret" for a store selling lingerie was likely to cause confusion with the trademark "Victoria's Secret" and also was likely to "dilute the distinctiveness" of that mark. The petitioners changed the name of their store to "Victor's Little Secret," but the respondent was not satisfied and sued the Moseleys. The federal district court ruled that "Victor's Little Secret" did not violate the respondent's trademark by confusing the public but that "Victor's Little Secret" did violate the Federal Trademark Dilution Act (FTDA) by diluting "Victoria's Secret." The Court of Appeals affirmed and the Supreme Court granted certiorari.

STEVENS, J.: . . . The VICTORIA'S SECRET mark is unquestionably valuable and petitioners have not challenged the conclusion that it qualifies as a "famous mark" within the meaning of the statute. Moreover, as we understand their submission, petitioners do not contend that the statutory protection is confined to identical uses of famous marks, or that the statute should be construed more narrowly in a case such as this. Even if the legislative history might lend some support to such a contention, it surely is not compelled by the statutory text.

The District Court's decision in this case rested on the conclusion that the name of petitioners' store "tarnished" the reputation of respondents' mark, and the Court of Appeals relied on both "tarnishment" and

"blurring" to support its affirmance. Petitioners have not disputed the relevance of tarnishment, presumably because that concept was prominent in litigation brought under state antidilution statutes and because it was mentioned in the legislative history. Whether it is actually embraced by the statutory text, however, is another matter. Indeed, the contrast between the state statutes, which expressly refer to both "injury to business reputation" and to "dilution of the distinctive quality of a trade name or trademark," and the federal statute which refers only to the latter, arguably supports a narrower reading of the FTDA.

The contrast between the state statutes and the federal statute, however, sheds light on the precise question that we must decide. For those statutes, like several provisions in the federal Lanham Act, repeatedly refer to a "likelihood" of harm, rather than to a completed harm. The relevant text of the FTDA provides that "the owner of a famous mark" is entitled to injunctive relief against another person's commercial use of a mark or trade name if that use *causes dilution of the distinctive quality"* of the famous mark. This text unambiguously requires a showing of actual dilution, rather than a likelihood of dilution.

This conclusion is fortified by the definition of the term "dilution" itself. That definition provides:

"The term 'dilution' means the lessening of the capacity of a famous mark to identify and distinguish goods or services, regardless of the presence or absence of—'(1) competition between the owner of the famous mark and other parties,' or '(2) likelihood of confusion, mistake, or deception.' "

The contrast between the initial reference to an actual "lessening of the capacity" of the mark, and the later reference to a "likelihood of confusions, mistake, or deception" in the second caveat confirms the conclusion that actual dilution must be established.

Of course, that does not mean that the consequences of dilution, such as an actual loss of sales or profits, must also be proved. To the extent that language in the Fourth Circuit's opinion in the *Ringling Bros.* case suggests otherwise, we disagree. We do agree, however, with that court's conclusion that, at least where the marks at issue are not identical, the mere fact that consumers mentally associate the junior user's mark with a famous mark is not sufficient to establish actionable dilution. As the facts of that case demonstrate, such mental association will not necessarily reduce the capacity of the famous mark to identify the goods of its owner, the statutory requirement for dilution under the FTDA. For even though Utah drivers may be reminded of the circus when they see a license plate referring to the "greatest *snow* on earth," it by no means follows that they will associate "the greatest show on earth" with skiing or snow sports, or associate it less strongly or exclusively with the circus. "Blurring" is not a necessary consequence of mental association. (Nor, for that matter, is "tarnishing.")

The record in this case establishes that an army officer who saw the advertisement of the opening of a store named "Victor's Secret" did make the mental association with "Victoria's Secret," but it also shows that he did not therefore form any different impression of the store that his wife and daughter had patronized. There is a complete absence of evidence of any lessening of the capacity of the VICTORIA'S SECRET mark to identify and distinguish goods or services sold in Victoria's Secret stores or advertised in its catalogs. The officer was offended by the ad, but it did not change his conception of Victoria's Secret. His offense was directed entirely at petitioners, not at respondents. Moreover, the expert retained by respondents had nothing to say about the impact of petitioners' name on the strength of respondents' mark.

Noting that consumer surveys and other means of demonstrating actual dilution are expensive and often unreliable, respondents argue that evidence of an actual "lessening of the capacity of a famous mark to identify and distinguish goods or services" may be difficult to obtain. It may well be, however, that direct evidence of dilution such as consumer surveys will not be necessary if actual dilution can reliably be proven through circumstantial evidence—the obvious case is one where the junior and senior marks are identical. Whatever difficulties of proof may be entailed, they are not an acceptable reason for dispensing with proof of an essential element of a statutory violation. The evidence in the present record is not sufficient to support the summary judgment on the dilution count. The judgment is therefore reversed, and the case is remanded for further proceedings consistent with this opinion. **It is so ordered.**

:: CASE QUESTIONS

1. What is the difference between traditional trademark violation and trademark dilution under the FTDA?
2. What does the Court say is the difference between trademark dilution under statutes and under the FTDA?
3. What resource does the respondent have now in light of the Court's decision?

:: Copyright Law

Like patent, **copyright** gives those who have this property a monopoly over copying and marketing for a limited period of time. Unlike patent, copyright deals with *expression* rather than invention. The importance of copyright began with the development of the printing press in the early 1400s, but the first copyright law was the Statute of Anne, enacted in England in 1710. In the United States copyright is authorized in the Constitution, and Congress has revised copyright several times. Until the late 1800s, however, the United States did not recognize foreign copyright laws as they protected the works of foreign authors. As a result, U.S. publishers felt free to publish the works of foreign authors without permission or the payment of fees called *royalties*.

Today the United States has joined most other countries in international agreements, such as the Berne Convention, in protecting the copyright of other nations, but once again copyright has come to a turning point in the road. Digital technology makes it ever easier to copy not only printed material, but music, movies, and software as well. No longer is a large business necessary to copy and distribute copyrighted materials illegally. Individuals can copy materials quickly and almost without cost and send them around the world in a blink of an eye. As you read the following sections on copyright law, keep in mind the new digital age you have entered.

Copyright law grants property in certain creative expressions that keeps others from reproducing it without the owner's permission. The copyright attaches not to an idea or to facts but to the original *expression* of an idea or facts. Three criteria are necessary for copyright protection to occur:

- A work must be original. It must be created, not copied.
- The work must be fixed in a tangible medium of expression like a book, canvas, compact disk, tape, or computer disk.
- The work must show some creativity. For example, the Supreme Court ruled in *Feist Publications, Inc. v. Rural Telephone Service Co.*, 499 U.S. 340 (1991), that the mere effort and alphabetic arrangement of names that went into a telephone directory's white pages was insufficiently creative to warrant a copyright.

Copyright laws protect authors rather than inventors. An author creates works of a literary, dramatic, musical, graphic, choreographic, audio, or visual nature. Ranging from printed material to photographs to records and motion pictures, these works receive automatic federal protection under the Copyright Act of 1976 from the moment the author creates them. The copyright allows the holder to control the reproduction, display, distribution, and performance of a protected work. The copyright runs for the author's lifetime, plus 70 additional years for all works published after 1977. Copyrights held by corporations and published after 1977 protect expression for 75 years. Congress has granted some extension of the copyright period for works published before 1977.

> Congress has extended the length of copyrights for works published before 1977. Many think that the purpose for doing this was to protect the Disney copyright in Mickey Mouse cartoons.

15. COPYRIGHT PROTECTION

Although common law copyright protection attaches at the moment a work is created, an action for federal copyright infringement cannot be begun unless the author has properly filed copies of the protected work with the Copyright Office. One who infringes on a copyright cannot be held liable for actual or statutory damages unless a copyright symbol or notice accompanies the protected work. When the author has observed the proper formalities, however, she or he may recover actual or statutory damages, attorney's fees, and any profits the infringer has made. Illegally reproduced copies may also be seized, and willful copyright violations are criminal offenses.

The Copyright Act specifies that a fair use of copyrighted materials is not an infringement of the owner's property. **Fair use** includes copying for "criticism, comment, news reporting, teaching (including multiple copies for classroom use), scholarship, or research." In determining whether a particular use is a fair one, a court will consider

> An important part of what copyright holders own is a limited resource in the market for their music or other expressions. That means the object of their property right is the market itself.

- The purpose and character of the use, including whether such use is for commercial or nonprofit educational purposes.
- The nature of the copyrighted work.
- The amount and substantiality of the portion used in relation to the copyrighted work as a whole.
- The effect of the use upon the potential market for the copyrighted work.

The determination of a fair use in light of these factors is made on a case-by-case basis. In Case 11.4, the Supreme Court considers whether one song makes a fair use of a previous song's copyrighted lyrics. The fair use being considered concerns *parody,* a form of expression that criticizes by poking fun at something through exaggeration.

case 11.4 ::

CAMPBELL v. ACUFF-ROSE MUSIC, INC.
510 U.S. 569 (1994)

The rap group 2 Live Crew recorded and sold a commercial parody of Roy Orbison's copyrighted song "Oh Pretty Woman." Acuff-Rose Music, Inc., the copyright holder, sued the 2 Live Crew members after nearly a quarter million copies of the recording had been sold. The case came before the Supreme Court after the court of appeals decided that 2 Live Crew's parody had taken too much of "Oh Pretty Woman" to be protected as a fair use.

SOUTER, J: It is uncontested here that 2 Live Crew's song would be an infringement of AcuffRose's rights in "Oh Pretty Woman," under the Copyright Act of 1976, but for a finding of fair use through parody. From the infancy of copyright protection, some opportunity for fair use of copyrighted materials has been thought necessary to fulfill copyright's very purpose, "to promote the Progress of Science and useful Arts. . . ." For as Justice Story explained, "in truth, in literature, in science and in art, there are, and can be, few, if any, things, which in an abstract sense, are strictly new and original throughout. Every book in literature, science and art, borrows, and must necessarily borrow, and use much which was well known and used before."

The first factor in a fair use enquiry is "the purpose and character of the use, including whether such use is of a commercial nature or is for nonprofit educational purposes." The enquiry here may be guided by looking to whether the use is for criticism, or comment, or news reporting, and the like. The central purpose of this investigation is to see, in Justice Story's

words, whether the new work merely "supersede[s] the objects" of the original creation, or instead adds something new, with a further purpose or different character, altering the first with new expression, meaning, or message; it asks, in other words, whether and to what extent the new work is "transformative." Although such transformative use is not absolutely necessary for a finding of fair use, the goal of copyright, to promote science and the arts, is generally furthered by the creation of transformative works. Such works thus lie at the heart of the fair use doctrine's guarantee of breathing space within the confines of copyright, and the more transformative the new work, the less will be the significance of other factors, like commercialism, that may weigh against a finding of fair use.

The second statutory factor, "the nature of the copyrighted work," calls for recognition that some works are closer to the core of intended copyright protection than others, with one consequence that fair use is more difficult to establish when the former works are copied. We agree with both the District Court and the Court of Appeals that the Orbison original's creative expression for public dissemination falls within the core of the copyright's protective purposes. This fact, however, is not much help in this case, or ever likely to help much in separating the fair use sheep from the infringing goats in a parody case, since parodies almost invariably copy publicly known, expressive works.

The third factor asks whether "the amount and substantiality of the portion used in relation to the copyrighted work as a whole" are reasonable in relation to the purpose of the copying. The District Court considered the song's parodic purpose in finding that 2 Live Crew had not helped themselves overmuch. The Court of Appeals disagreed, stating that "while it may not be inappropriate to find that no more was taken than necessary, the copying was qualitatively substantial. . . . We conclude that taking the heart of the original and making it the heart of a new work was to purloin a substantial portion of the essence of the original."

Suffice it to say here that, as to the lyrics, we fail to see how the copying can be excessive in relation to its parodic purpose, even if the portion taken is the original's "heart." As to the music, we express no opinion whether repetition of the bass riff is excessive copying, and we remand to permit evaluation of the amount taken, in light of the song's parodic purpose and character, its transformative elements, and considerations of the potential for market substitution sketched more fully below.

The fourth fair use factor is "the effect of the use upon the potential market for or value of the copyrighted work." It requires courts to consider not only the extent of market harm caused by the particular actions of the alleged infringer, but also "whether unrestricted and widespread conduct of the sort engaged in by the defendant . . . would result in a substantially adverse impact on the potential market" for the original. The enquiry "must take account not only of harm to the original but also of harm to the market for derivative works."

Although 2 Live Crew submitted uncontroverted affidavits on the question of market harm to the original, neither they, nor Acuff-Rose, introduced evidence or affidavits addressing the likely effect of 2 Live Crew's parodic rap song on the market for a nonparody, rap version of "Oh Pretty Woman." And while Acuff-Rose would have us find evidence of a rap market in the very facts that 2 Live Crew recorded a rap parody of "Oh Pretty Woman" and another rap group sought a license to record a rap derivative, there was no evidence that a potential rap market was harmed in any way by 2 Live Crew's parody, rap version.

It was error for the Court of Appeals to conclude that the commercial nature of 2 Live Crew's parody of "Pretty Woman" rendered it presumptively unfair. No such evidentiary presumption is available to address either the first factor, the character and purpose of the use, or the fourth, market harm, in determining whether a transformative use, such as parody, is a fair one. The court also erred in holding that 2 Live Crew had necessarily copied excessively from the Orbison original, considering the parodic purpose of the use. We therefore reverse the judgment of the Court of Appeals and remand the case for further proceedings consistent with this opinion.

Reversed and remanded.

16. COPYRIGHT IN THE DIGITAL AGE

Under copyright law it is illegal not only to make copies that violate the law but also to assist others in doing so. When copyright holders challenged certain programs that assisted file sharing of materials—mostly, copyrighted music—one case went to the Supreme Court. In *Metro-Goldwyn-Mayer Studios v. Grokster*, 125 S. Ct. 2764 (2005), the Court asserted: "We hold that one who distributes a device with the object of promoting its use to infringe copyright, as shown by clear expression or other affirmative steps taken to foster infringement, is liable for the resulting acts of infringement by third parties."

What if you distribute a program or other device without "clear expression" that its purpose is to promote copyright infringement? The Court referred to an earlier case that dealt with whether the manufacture and sale of videocassette recorders contributed illegally to copyright infringement. The Court observed:

> Copyright holders sued Sony as the manufacturer, claiming that is was contributorily liable for infringement that occurred when VCR owners taped copyrighted programs. . . . [T]he evidence showed that the principle use of the VCR was for "time

shifting," or taping a program for later viewing at a more convenient time, which the Court found to be a fair, not an infringing use. There was no evidence that Sony had expressed an object of bringing about taping in violation of copyright or had taken steps to increase its profits from unlawful taping.

Criminal prosecutions and civil lawsuits for "file sharing" copyrighted material over the Internet are growing. One FBI probe of a "warez" website devoted to sharing pirated computer software produced 17 arrests.

Note that the users of file-sharing programs who send or download copyrighted songs and videos are violating copyright law. A survey by Ipsos Reid showed 52 percent of 12- to 17-year-olds and 44 percent of 18- to 24-year-olds admitted to downloading music files from a file-sharing service, over half of them within the previous 30 days. Music companies have filed more than 26,000 lawsuits against alleged illegal uploaders of music since 2003. In the first such case to reach a jury verdict, a jury awarded a music company $220,000, more than $9,250 for each of the 24 pieces of music misappropriated.

Some say that intellectual property does not diminish the way that tangible property does when someone misappropriate it. But consider this: property is a legal right to exclude, not a physical thing, and the object of a property copyright includes the reproduction of music for commercial profit. The holder of a copyright owns the right to market what is copyrighted, and the market resource is diminished for the copyright owner when file sharers misappropriate music. In the early years of this century, the volume of sales for copyrighted music has declined significantly, largely due to misappropriation.

If you are a file sharer, do you consider yourself a thief? To explore your own feelings about this, think back to the ethics chapter (Chapter 2). Do you publicly proclaim your file sharing, or do it in secret? Are you proud to tell your families or potential employers about what you are doing?

> International piracy of copyrighted material is a major problem, but international enforcement efforts are slowly improving. The Federal Bureau of Investigation reported in 2007 that in one bust U.S. and Chinese authorities had arrested 25 people and seized more than $500 million worth of counterfeit computer software being made in China for worldwide sale.

17. DIGITAL MILLENNIUM COPYRIGHT ACT

Because copyrighted property is easily misappropriated over the Internet, Congress passed a new law in 1998 that prohibits certain activities leading to copyright violation. The *Digital Millennium Copyright Act* makes illegal the effort to get around devices used by copyright owners to keep their works from being infringed. In particular, the act will be used to prevent the production, marketing, or sales of a product or service designed to get around technological protections of computer software, videos, and compact disks.

The act also restricts the import, distribution, and sales of analog video recorders and camcorders that lack certain features making it difficult to copy copyrighted materials. It further exempts Internet service providers from liability (1) for illegal copies that pass temporarily through their systems and (2) for permanent illegal copies stored in their systems, for example, at a website, if the service provider removes the offending material upon request of a copyright owner. Finally, the act relieves service providers from liability for unintentionally linking to a website that contains infringing materials.

Violations of the act permit civil remedies, including injunction, actual damages, and statutory damages. A court can assess triple damages against a repeat offender. Willful violation for financial gain can also result in up to 10 years' imprisonment.

:: A Conclusion about Intellectual Property

Intellectual property, like property itself, serves the common good. The U.S. Constitution points this out in Article 1, Section 8, by asserting that the purpose for Congress granting "to authors and inventors the exclusive right to their respective writings and discoveries" is to promote the progress of science and business, which society believes promotes the common good. The framers of the Constitution believed, as do modern economists, that property, including intellectual property, gives incentive for private production of goods and services, which benefits not only the owners providing goods and services, but also to the overall wealth of society.

According to one analysis the value of U.S. intellectual property is valued at between $5 trillion and $5.5 trillion annually, which is more than the gross domestic product of every other nation. A large proportion of that, however, is lost to theft. According to a study conducted by the nonpartisan Institute for Policy Innovation, copyright losses alone due to file-sharing theft affect the recording industry to the tune of $58 billion annually, causing 373,000 job losses. The point is that a property system is only as effective as the mechanism for enforcing it. Without adequate enforcement, a property system cannot function for the common good, and enforcement relies upon more than laws and courts. It depends also on the attitudes of people toward legitimacy of the property. Without social recognition of the exclusive legal fences that are at the heart of the property system and without adequate enforcement of property, the system cannot provide the incentive necessary for private productive effort.

Increasingly, we live in a global society, and the information that is the resource of intellectual property moves easily across national borders. This means that the enforcement of intellectual property is something important to all nations that are part of the global trading system. Approximately half of the patents granted in the United States go to businesses from other nations, and these businesses depend upon the U.S. enforcement authorities and the attitudes of the American people to protect their property right to the market. Likewise, U.S. companies depend upon the international enforcement of intellectual property to prevent the violation of trade secrets, patents, copyrights, and trademarks. Although there is significant international cooperation in the enforcement of intellectual property, both in the United States and elsewhere, people's attitudes in some nations coupled with lax enforcement means that the realization of intellectual property right is far from total.

:: Key Terms

Copyright 340	Injunction 324	Trade dress 335
Fair use 341	Intellectual property 318	Trademark 334
Generic 337	Patent 326	Trademark dilution 339
Infringement 337	Property 317	Trade secret 321

:: Review Questions and Problems

1. *The Justification for Intellectual Property*
   (a) What is the purpose of patents and copyrights as identified in the Constitution?
   (b) Explain the claim that the pace of research and development of new products would slow if intellectual property right did not protect it.

2. *The Knowledge Assets of Modern Business*
   Explain the assertion that 75 percent of the total value of the largest 500 companies in the United States is knowledge-based.

Trade Secrets

3. *Trade Secret: Taking Reasonable Measures to Keep the Secret*
   (a) How do trade secrets differ from other applications of property?
   (b) Discuss several ways of preserving trade secrets.

4. *Trade Secret: The Economic Value Requirement*
   If multiple business competitors may legally have the same or overlapping trade secrets, what good are they as an exclusive right?

5. *Trade Secret: Civil Enforcement*
   What are the remedies available for the civil enforcement of trade secrets?

6. *Trade Secret: Criminal Enforcement*
   Why has criminal misappropriation of trade secrets become more common in recent years?

Patent Law

7. *Obtaining a Patent*
   Describe the process for obtaining a patent.

8. *Patentable Subject Matter*
   Through long, expensive research you determine that both a bowling ball and a feather fall at the rate of 32 feet per second in a vacuum. Can you patent this knowledge? Explain.

9. *Nonobviousness, Novelty, and Usefulness*
   (a) In 1995 several people applied for a patent for turmeric, a type of spice. The patent examiner rejected the application when it turned out that the spice has been used in parts of Asia for centuries. Explain.
   (b) Discuss the patent requirement of nonobviousness.

10. *Current Issues in Patent Law*

    (a) You discover a new type of basketball "dunk" that no one has ever thought of before. Can you patent it so that only you can use it? Analyze.
    (b) You discover a specific human gene that determines male pattern baldness. Explain what it means to say that you can patent this gene.

Trademark Law

11. *Types of Trademarks*
    Name four types of marks that are often called "trademarks."

12. *Trademark Registration*
    (a) Can you register the name "Fast Food" as a trademark? Explain.
    (b) Under what conditions can you *not* register a mark?

13. *Trademark Enforcement*

Do you ever "google" things on the Internet? Is the company Google in danger of losing its name as a trademark? Explain.

14. *Trademark Dilution*

Why should the Victoria's Secret company mind if a small adult novelty shop owned by Victor Mosley calls itself Victor's Secret? Explain.

Copyright Law

15. *Copyright Protection*

(a) If you spend the time and effort necessary to alphabetize the names of the students at your school and list their e-mail addresses, can you copyright a printed version? Explain.

(b) A legal studies of business professor copied movie clips and showed them to his class to illustrate various points of law. Is this a "fair use"? Suppose he copies the clips and sends them upon request to other faculty around the country who request them for their classrooms. Has he violated copyright law?

16. *Copyright in the Digital Age*

Is it illegal for you to loan your friend your CD burner so he can copy his favorite hits onto CDs and sell them to raise vacation cash? Discuss.

17. *Digital Millennium Copyright Act*

Discuss the prohibitions of the DMCA.

business :: *discussions*

1. Colonel Cars, Inc., plans to introduce a new speaker complex in the steering wheels of its automobiles. It believes the change will revolutionize the drivers' music-listening enjoyment. The company is also preparing an advertising campaign around the improved listening experience. Both the new steering-wheel speakers and the ad campaign are carefully kept secrets. But Colonel Cars's vice president for marketing is hired by European Motor Works (EMW) to be the president of its international division. Before Colonel Cars can begin its advertising, EMW comes out with an ad campaign centered on—you guessed it—speakers in the steering wheels of its new model cars.

What is "property"?

Can a company have property in its marketing plans the way you can have property in your car?

Can EMW use Colonel Car's marketing plans without permission?

2. You know by now that property is an exclusive legal fence and not the resource that is protected. With this in mind, what exactly is the resource protected by the exclusive legal fence in patent and copyright law? *Hint:* Consider the resource protected by the old "letters of patent" when the monarch gave someone a monopoly on a toll road, a ferry crossing, or the development of a colonized land.

12

Criminal Law and Business

Learning Objectives ::

In this chapter you will learn:

1. To recognize the kind of acts that constitute white-collar crimes.
2. To explain Fourth, Fifth, and Sixth Amendment rights.
3. To identify the elements of specific crimes.
4. To understand how the same acts can give rise to both civil and criminal liability.
5. To realize the far-reaching impact of criminal behavior on corporations and individuals.

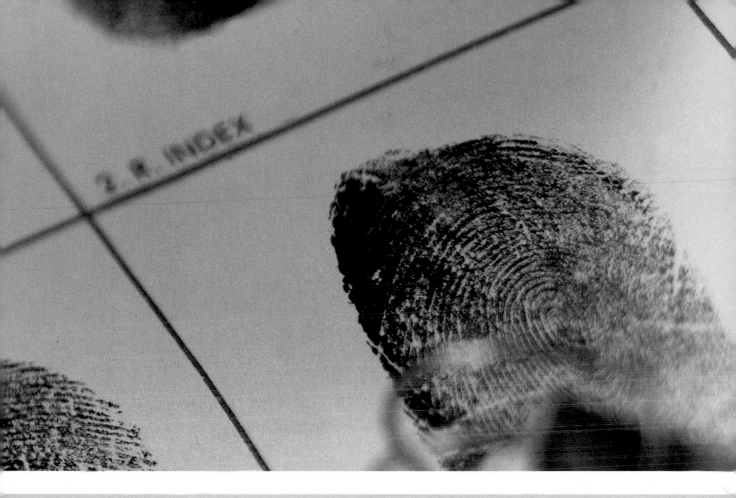

Just as civil law protects an individual's property, criminal law punishes wrongdoers who affect the ownership of property. Crimes are wrongs against society, and the government has the power to impose punishment and fines on individuals and corporations convicted of crimes. Federal and state penal codes define criminal acts and omissions.

Criminal conduct is extremely destructive for business. The fall of the accounting firm Arthur Andersen, the energy firm Enron, and the telecommunications company WorldCom, illustrate the devastating effects of criminal wrongdoing. Documentaries, such as *Enron: The Smartest Guys in the Room*, detail some of these effects and the impact on business, employees, and investors.

Civil law allows individuals to bring actions for damages and criminal law allows society, or "the people," to punish wrongdoers. Some crimes, such as rape or murder, are said to be *malum in se* or inherently wrong. They are universally recognized as wrongful conduct that society must punish even where the victim is a single person.

A legislative body can, however, decide that it is in the interest of society to criminalize conduct that is not inherently wrongful. By passing laws declaring certain conduct to be criminal, legislative bodies purport to act in the interest of all society. An example of such a crime is price fixing among competitors. In 1890, price fixing was made illegal by the Sherman Antitrust Act when it became apparent that such behavior was an impediment to fair competition.

Crimes can involve acts of violence, such as arson, burglary, and robbery. Businesses are often the target of these crimes, which are frequently perpetrated by persons who have no connection to the business. The terrorist attack on the World Trade Center is an example of a crime of violence against the resident businesses and their employees. That crime also immediately impacted many of the businesses in New York City, as well as many international businesses, ultimately affecting the economies of countries throughout the world.

Many crimes against businesses do not involve acts of violence. Sometimes, employees of a business will commit nonviolent crimes against their employer. Crimes by employees can have a significant negative impact on business. In addition, society is financially harmed by criminal conduct that injures business. In the 1930s, Edwin H. Sullivan coined the term **white-collar crime** to apply to criminals of high socioeconomic status, such as corporate executives who commit fraud. Today, *white-collar crime* usually means any illegal offense that occurs in a business or professional setting. Such crimes are generally committed for personal financial gain. These crimes are not dependent on the threat of physical force or violence. They are committed to obtain money, property, or services; to avoid the payment or loss of money, property or services; or to achieve a personal or business advantage. White-collar crime costs business over $100 billion annually. See Table 12.1 for examples of white-collar crimes.

Employees may commit white-collar crime for personal gain or to harm the business. Other times, the criminal activity benefits the business and there is no intention to harm others, such as competitors or customers. White-collar crime takes many forms. Common examples include embezzling money, making electronic advances to fictitious employees, accepting kickbacks from suppliers in exchange for orders, rigging bids, selling trade secrets, falsifying inventories to conceal theft, and paying false invoices. White-collar crime affects the targeted companies as well as consumers who must pay higher prices to make up for the losses.

> More than 1 in 100 America adults is in prison.
>
> **–Pew Center on the States.**

table 12.1 :: Examples of White-Collar Crimes

Accounting fraud	Forgery	Obstruction of justice
Bankruptcy fraud	Income tax evasion	Price fixing
Bribery	Insider trading	Racketeering
Conspiracy	Kickbacks	Securities fraud
Counterfeiting	Larceny	Wire fraud
Embezzlement	Mail fraud	
False statements	Money laundering	

Although a corporation cannot be put in jail or in a prison, it can be fined and face other criminal penalties. Ordering a company out of business is a type of "death sentence" for business. Individuals found guilty of a crime can be sent to jail or prison, ordered to pay fines, or excluded from certain types of work.

To raise awareness and combat the effects of criminal activity on business, most business schools include courses on business ethics. Most major corporations have ethical codes and extensive compliance programs. Despite these efforts, television and print media regularly depict executives in handcuffs, pictures that mark a surge in white-collar crime in recent years.

Many of the examples of criminal activity in this chapter are the result of greed replacing integrity. The purpose of this chapter is to help you understand what activity is criminal, the penalties that can result, and the effect on business. See Sidebar 12.1 for example of successful prosecutions.

:: *sidebar* 12.1

Handcuffs and Jail Time

:: SUCCESSFUL PROSECUTIONS: A SAMPLE OF CONVICTIONS AND GUILTY PLEAS

- Phillip R. Bennett, former Refco Inc. CEO, having pled guilty to fraud (in connection with hiding hundreds of millions of dollars from investors who bought stock) could be sentenced to up to 315 years in prison under federal sentencing guidelines.

- Conrad Black, Hollinger International CEO and chairman, convicted for obstruction of justice and mail fraud, sentenced to 6½ years in prison.

- Bernard Ebbers, former CEO of World-Com, convicted for securities fraud, conspiracy, and filing false statements with regulators, 25 years in prison.

- L. Dennis Kozlowski, former chief executive of Tyco International, convicted for grand larceny, conspiracy, falsifying business records, and securities fraud, $97 million in restitution, $70 million in fines, and 8⅓ to 25 years in prison.

- F. David Radler, COO of Hollinger International, guilty plea to a mail and wire fraud charge in exchange for 29 month prison sentence and a $250,000 fine.

- John J. Rigas, founder of Adelphia Communications, and his son, Timothy, convicted for looting the company of $2.3 billion in assets and misrepresenting the company's health to investors, respectively 15 and 20 years in prison. The Rigas family also agreed to forfeit 95 percent of their holdings (about $1.5 billion) to compensate investors.

- Jeffrey Skilling, former Enron CEO, convicted for fraud and conspiracy, over 24 years in prison.

- Actor Wesley Snipes, convicted for failing to file income tax returns, 3 years in prison. In a civil suit, the IRS is also seeking repayment of all of the taxes owed, plus interest.

:: Terms and Procedures

1. CLASSIFICATIONS OF CRIMINAL CONDUCT

There are several ways to classify criminal conduct. Some crimes are violations of federal law, some crimes violate state laws, and other crimes violate both federal and state laws. Although many crimes involve violence, nonviolent conduct may also be criminal.

Crimes are classified as **felonies** or **misdemeanors.** This classification is based on the punishment imposed if the person is convicted of the alleged crime. Felonies are punishable by fine or imprisonment in a penitentiary for a period of one year or more. Misdemeanors are punishable by a fine or jail sentence of less than one year.

Felony cases are commenced by a grand jury **indictment;** misdemeanor cases are usually commenced when the government files a charge called an **information.** Grand juries are different from petit juries. A grand jury determines if there is sufficient evidence to warrant a trial. A petit jury determines the guilt or innocence of the accused. The role of the grand jury is discussed in more detail later in this chapter.

2. BASIC CONCEPTS

Intent is an important element of many criminal laws. Many laws use either the term **willfully** or **knowingly** to define criminal intent. If an act is done willfully, it is committed voluntarily and purposefully with the specific intent to do something. A person does not act willfully if there is a good-faith misunderstanding of the requirements of the law. Similarly, if an act is done knowingly, it is voluntary and intentional, not because of mistake or accident.

Knowledge usually cannot be established by demonstrating that the accused was negligent, careless, or foolish; knowledge, however, can be inferred if the accused deliberately ignored the existence of a fact.

Some laws provide that reckless conduct is a crime even though the one doing the act does not intend to do harm. Reckless driving is an obvious example of such a crime. Reckless disregard for the truth is often the basis of white-collar criminal conduct.

Criminal cases are brought or prosecuted by public officials such as a U.S. attorney or a state's attorney (often called a *district attorney*) on behalf of the people. In the case of federal crimes, the United States brings an action against the individual defendant. Imagine your feelings if a case style read: "The United States v. you."

In a criminal case, the defendant has three possible pleas to enter: *guilty, not guilty,* or **nolo contendere.** The last plea, Latin for "no contest," allows sentencing just as if the defendant pleaded guilty or was found guilty. Pleading "nolo," as it is sometimes referred to, advantages the defendant by avoiding the cost of trial and avoiding the effect of a guilty plea or finding in a subsequent civil action. Criminal convictions may provide a basis for civil damage suits. This can be avoided by the nolo contendere plea. The high cost of white-collar crime is illustrated in Sidebar 12.2.

In 1973, Vice President Spiro Agnew made one of the most famous *nolo contendere* pleas (to tax evasion) on the condition that he resign from office.

3. THE GRAND JURY

The Fifth Amendment to the U.S. Constitution provides that before anyone can be tried for a capital or otherwise infamous crime, there must be a presentment or an indictment by a grand jury. This protection prevents political trials and unjustified prosecutions by placing a group of citizens between prosecutors and persons accused of major crimes.

A grand jury normally consists of 23 citizens who live within the jurisdiction of the court that would try one accused of a crime. At least 16 persons

It is a felony for prosecutors, court reporters, and grand jury members to leak testimony heard in grand jury proceedings.

:: *sidebar* 12.2

The Price of the $11 Billion Accounting Fraud at WorldCom

Bernard J. Ebbers, the former chief executive officer, president, and a director of WorldCom, Inc., was convicted of securities fraud, conspiracy, and filing false documents with regulators. The acts at the heart of the case were fraudulent adjustments to WorldCom's books and records; false statements and misleading omissions in WorldCom's SEC filings and public statements; and fraud in connection with the purchase and sale of securities.

Federal prosecutors argued that Ebbers was motivated to commit fraud during a time when there was tremendous pressure on the company's share price. Ebbers's personal fortune was largely based on WorldCom shares and he borrowed nearly $400 million using the shares as collateral.

Scott Sullivan, former WorldCom CFO, testified that Ebbers knew about the massive accounting fraud. Sullivan also testified that Ebbers intimidated him into committing fraud so that the company could meet Wall Street expectations.

Ebbers was sentenced to serve 25 years in prison. This $11 billion accounting scandal also resulted in nearly 17,000 employees losing their jobs.

Recommended Reading: Cynthia Cooper, *Extraordinary Circumstances: The Journey of a Corporate Whistleblower* (Wiley, 2008).

---

must be present for the grand jury to hear evidence and vote on cases. For an indictment to be returned, a majority of the grand jury must find that a crime has been committed and that the evidence is sufficient to warrant the accused's standing trial. This determination is **probable cause**.

The grand jury does not attempt to determine if the accused is guilty, only that probable cause exists to believe the accused committed the crime. Since probable cause is the standard for grand jury action, it is not difficult to obtain an indictment. Even an indicted person, however, is entitled to the **presumption of innocence**—to be presumed innocent until found guilty by a petit jury.

Grand juries also serve as an investigative body and occupy a unique role in our criminal justice system. Law enforcement officials such as agents for the Federal Bureau of Investigation, U.S. Customs Service, U.S. Postal Service, and Secret Service often act as arms of federal grand juries investigating possible criminal activities. Persons who are the targets or subjects of investigations may be called before grand juries and may be questioned under oath about possible illegal conduct. In such cases, the persons subpoenaed to testify before the grand jury are entitled to invoke their Fifth Amendment privilege against compulsory self-incrimination and refuse to answer questions. Although they are entitled to have the benefit of legal advice, defense counsel is not allowed to accompany a witness before a grand jury. However, counsel may be outside the grand jury room and thus available for consultation whenever a witness desires it.

Grand jurors may also subpoena business records. Witnesses may be called and questioned about documents and records delivered in response to a subpoena. However, grand juries are not authorized to engage in arbitrary fishing expeditions and may not select targets of criminal probes out of malice.

Proper functioning of the grand jury system depends upon the secrecy of the proceedings. This secrecy protects the innocent accused from disclosure

After testifying before the grand jury in the Valerie Plame case, *New York Times* reporter Judith Miller broke her silence and spoke with reporters on the courthouse steps.

of the accusations made against him or her before the grand jury. In judicial proceedings, however, transcripts of grand jury proceedings may be obtained if necessary to avoid possible injustice. For example, a defendant may use a grand jury transcript at a trial to impeach a witness, to refresh the witness's recollection, or to test his or her credibility. The disclosure of a grand jury transcript is appropriate only in those cases where the need for it outweighs the public interest in secrecy, and the burden of demonstrating this balance rests upon a private party seeking disclosure.

:: Constitutional Issues

Before covering the elements of some of the more important business-related crimes, it is essential to understand the protections all individuals have under the U.S. Constitution. These protections are in the Bill of Rights, the first ten amendments to the Constitution. The Bill of Rights was Congress's response to concerns that the Constitution gave too much power to a central government at the expense of the individual citizen. Often referred to as "civil liberties," these rights protect individuals from the power of government, including individuals accused of crimes. The Bill of Rights also protects businesses from excessive regulation. As you study the Fourth, Fifth, and Sixth Amendments to the Constitution, pay particular attention to their impact on the regulatory process.

4. THE FOURTH AMENDMENT: ILLEGAL SEARCH AND SEIZURE

The Fourth Amendment protects persons and corporations from unreasonable searches and seizures.

The Fourth Amendment protects individuals and corporations from **unreasonable searches and seizures** by the government. It primarily protects persons from unwarranted intrusions on their privacy by requiring the police to obtain a court order called a **search warrant.** As a general rule, the search warrant must be obtained by the police prior to a search of a person, any premises, or other property such as the trunk of an automobile. Before a court will issue a search warrant, the police must offer evidence that a crime has been committed and there is cause to believe that the intended search will assist in its investigation.

To protect police officers, courts have held that officers making an arrest do not need a search warrant to search that person and the immediate area around that person for weapons. Officers are given far more latitude in searching an automobile than in searching a person, a home, or a building. The right to search for evidence also extends to the premises of persons not suspected of criminal conduct. Such premises may include offices of newspapers and attorneys. Electronic surveillance may not violate the Fourth Amendment if used pursuant to a court-authorized order.

Fourth Amendment protection also extends to certain civil matters. For example, building inspectors do not have the right to inspect for building code violations without a warrant if the owner of the premises objects. The Securities and Exchange Commission (SEC) cannot use confidential reports obtained in the course of its routine operations to establish a violation of federal law. The Occupational Safety and Health Act (OSHA) inspectors must go to court and obtain a search warrant if an owner of a business objects to an inspection. To obtain this warrant, inspectors must show that the standards for conducting an inspection are satisfied; they do not need to show probable cause that a violation exists.

The protection of the Fourth Amendment provides an expectation of privacy. The Supreme Court has said that warrantless searches of junkyards are constitutional because operators of commercial premises in closely regulated industries have a reduced expectation of privacy. In pervasively regulated industries the privacy interests of the business are weakened and government interests in regulating particular businesses are heightened. Generally, a warrantless inspection of commercial premises may well be reasonable within the meaning of the Fourth Amendment, whereas a warrantless inspection of a private residence is unconstitutional.

Many business operations do not have an **expectation of privacy.** For example, nursing homes that receive Medicaid funds are presumed to have voluntarily consented to warrantless searches. Random surveys for compliance with federal standards should be expected by businesses required to conform to the standards.

Today's increased security at airports and at border crossings does not violate the Fourth Amendment. Neither a warrant, probable cause, nor any level of suspicion is required to search vehicles, persons, or goods arriving in the United States. Presenting oneself at an airport checkpoint is an irrevocable consent to a warrantless search.

Employees of some businesses also do not have Fourth Amendment protection because of public policy. For example, alcohol and drug testing of railroad employees and airline pilots cannot be successfully challenged using the Fourth Amendment.

The Fourth Amendment does not prohibit drug testing in most workplaces.

5. THE FIFTH AMENDMENT: PROTECTION AGAINST SELF-INCRIMINATION

The Fifth Amendment is best known for its protection against compulsory self-incrimination. When a person giving testimony pleads "the Fifth," he or she is exercising the right to this protection. The privilege against self-incrimination protects an accused from being compelled to testify against himself or herself. The Fifth Amendment does not protect the accused from being compelled to produce real or physical evidence. Fingerprints can be taken, as can voice samples and bodily fluids. In order to be testimonial and protected, an accused's communication must itself, explicitly or implicitly, relate to a factual assertion or disclosure information.

Issues concerning the Fifth Amendment protection as it relates to a business may arise when a businessperson is called to testify about a business matter or is served with a subpoena requiring the production of records. A businessperson may not be called upon to testify against himself or herself in any governmental hearing such as a congressional proceeding. But the protection against compulsory self-incrimination does not protect a businessperson from having to produce, in court, records prepared in the ordinary course of business. Since the production of records does not compel oral testimony, the Fifth Amendment does not prevent the use of written evidence, including documents in the hands either of the accused or of someone else such as an accountant. Of course, corporate officials, union officials, and

"The Fifth" protects the accused from being compelled to testify against himself or herself.

partners cannot be required to give oral testimony if such testimony may tend to incriminate them. However, these individuals must produce subpoenaed documents. Therefore, business records can be obtained even if they are incriminating.

Obviously a corporation or other collective entity cannot be called upon to testify; only individuals can do so. Therefore, the protection against compulsory self-incrimination does not apply to corporations, including professional corporations and partnerships. These collective entities have no Fifth Amendment right to refuse to submit their books and records in response to a subpoena. The only business protected by the Fifth Amendment privilege against compulsory self-incrimination is a sole proprietorship. A closely held corporation with only one shareholder is not protected.

6. THE FIFTH AMENDMENT: DOUBLE JEOPARDY

The same offense may give rise to both a criminal prosecution and a civil suit for damages.

The Fifth Amendment provides in part that no "person [shall] be subject for the same offense to be twice put in jeopardy of life or limb." This language is known as the **double jeopardy** clause. Courts do not allow individuals to be tried twice by the same governmental entity for the same crime based on the same factual situation. If an illegal activity violates both federal and state laws, double jeopardy does not prohibit two trials, one in federal court and the other in the state court system. Although federal and state governmental prosecutors may cooperate resulting in only one conviction, the double jeopardy clause does not prevent two prosecutions. In its essence, this clause keeps a U.S. district attorney from having a second trial on the same facts if a defendant is found innocent or has the charges dismissed. The same prohibition of a second trial holds true for state prosecutors also. Note that in civil law, the doctrine of *res judicata* bars subsequent civil actions involving the same parties, claims, demands, or causes of action.

Sometimes, interesting arguments are made under the double jeopardy clause. In Case 12.1, businesspersons attempted to use the double jeopardy clause to prevent criminal prosecution following the imposition of civil penalties for violating various federal laws.

case 12.1

HUDSON v. UNITED STATES
522 U.S. 93 (1997)

Petitioner John Hudson was the chairman and controlling shareholder of the First National Bank of Tipton (Tipton) and the First National Bank of Hammon (Hammon). Petitioner Jack Rackley was president of Tipton and a member of the board of directors of Hammon, and petitioner Larry Baresel was a member of the board of directors of both Tipton and Hammon.

The Office of the Comptroller of the Currency (OCC) concluded that petitioners used their bank positions to arrange a series of loans to third parties, in violation of various federal banking statutes and regulations. OCC issued a "Notice of Assessment of Civil Money Penalty." OCC assessed penalties of $100,000 against Hudson and $50,000 each against both Rackley *and Baresel. OCC also issued a "Notice of Intention to Prohibit Further Participation" against each petitioner.*

Petitioners resolved the OCC proceedings against them by each entering into a "Stipulation and Consent Order." These consent orders provided that Hudson, Baresel, and Rackley would pay assessments and each petitioner agreed not to "participate in any manner" in the affairs of any banking institution without the written authorization of the OCC and all other relevant regulatory agencies.

Petitioners subsequently were indicted in the Western District of Oklahoma in a 22-count indictment on charges of conspiracy, misapplication of bank funds, and making false bank entries. The violations charged in the indictment rested on the same lending transactions that formed the basis for the prior administrative actions brought by OCC. Petitioners moved to dismiss the indictment on double jeopardy grounds.

REHNQUIST, J.: We hold that the Double Jeopardy Clause of the Fifth Amendment is not a bar to the later criminal prosecution because the administrative proceedings were civil, not criminal. . . .

The Double Jeopardy Clause provides that no "person [shall] be subject for the same offense to be twice put in jeopardy of life or limb.". . .

Whether a particular punishment is criminal or civil is, at least initially, a matter of statutory construction. A court must first ask whether the legislature, in establishing the penalizing mechanism, indicated either expressly or impliedly a preference for one label or the other. Even in those cases where the legislature has indicated an intention to establish a civil penalty, we have inquired further whether the statutory scheme was so punitive either in purpose or effect as to "transform what was clearly intended as a civil remedy into a criminal penalty."

In making this latter determination, several factors provide useful guideposts, including: (1) whether the sanction involves an affirmative disability or restraint; (2) whether it has historically been regarded as a punishment; (3) whether it comes into play only on a finding of scienter; (4) whether its operation will promote the traditional aims of punishment—retribution and deterrence; (5) whether the behavior to which it applies is already a crime; (6) whether an alternative purpose to which it may rationally be connected is assignable for it; and (7) whether it appears excessive in relation to the alternative purpose assigned. . . .

Applying traditional double jeopardy principles to the facts of this case, it is clear that the criminal prosecution of these petitioners would not violate the Double Jeopardy Clause. It is evident that Congress intended the OCC money penalties and debarment sanctions to be civil in nature. As for the money penalties, which authorize the imposition of monetary penalties, they expressly provide that such penalties are civil. While the provision authorizing debarment contains no language explicitly denominating the sanction as civil, we think it significant that the authority to issue debarment orders is conferred upon the appropriate federal banking agencies. That such authority was conferred upon administrative agencies is prima facie evidence that Congress intended to provide for a civil sanction.

In sum, there simply is very little showing, to say nothing of the "clearest proof," that OCC money penalties and debarment sanctions are criminal. The Double Jeopardy Clause is therefore no obstacle to their trial on the pending indictments, and it may proceed.

The judgment of the Court of Appeals for the Tenth Circuit is accordingly affirmed.

:: CASE QUESTIONS

1. What protections against governmental overreaching are provided by the Double Jeopardy Clause?
2. Under which circumstances could a civil penalty be so punitive as to implicate the Double Jeopardy Clause?
3. Why were the money penalties and debarment sanctions insufficient to render the sanctions criminal in nature?

7. THE SIXTH AMENDMENT: RIGHTS IN A CRIMINAL CASE

The Sixth Amendment, like the Fifth, provides multiple protections in criminal cases. Its protections give you the right:

- To a speedy and public trial.
- To a trial by jury.

- To be informed of the charge against you.
- To confront your accuser.
- To subpoena witnesses in your favor.
- To have the assistance of an attorney.

The American concept of a jury trial contemplates a jury drawn from a fair cross-section of the community. The jury guards against the exercise of arbitrary power by using the common sense judgment of the community as a hedge against the overzealous or mistaken prosecutor. The jury's perspective on facts is used in preference to the professional, or perhaps biased, response of a judge.

Consider: What is a "jury of one's peers"?

Community participation in administering criminal law is consistent with our democratic heritage, and it is also critical to public confidence in the fairness of the criminal justice system. Therefore, a state may not restrict jury service only to special groups or exclude identifiable segments playing major roles in the community. Likewise, minorities may not be systematically excluded from jury duty. As discussed in Chapter 4, peremptory challenges during *voir dire* examination cannot be used to deny a defendant a jury of one's peers.

The right to a jury trial does not extend to state juvenile court delinquency proceedings because they are not criminal prosecutions. However, juveniles do have the right to counsel, to confront the witnesses against them, and to cross-examine them.

The right to an attorney exists in any cases where incarceration is a possible punishment. It exists at every stage of the proceeding, beginning with an investigation that centers on a person as the accused. See Sidebar 12.3. There are many technical aspects to the Sixth Amendment, and numerous cases still arise concerning it. For example, a criminal defendant's right to counsel of his or her choice may be limited in certain situations by the attorney's

:: *sidebar* 12.3

Know Your *Miranda* Rights

Despite challenges, the rights set forth in *Miranda v. Arizona* (1966) are still the law. If you are taken into custody, the law enforcement officer must read you your "Miranda Rights" and make sure that you understand them.

:: WARNING OF RIGHTS

1. You have the right to remain silent and refuse to answer questions. Do you understand?
2. Anything you do say may be used against you in a court of law. Do you understand?
3. You have the right to consult an attorney before speaking to the police and to have an attorney present

during questioning now or in the future. Do you understand?

4. If you cannot afford an attorney, one will be appointed for you before any questioning if you wish. Do you understand?
5. If you decide to answer questions now without an attorney present you will still have the right to stop answering at any time until you talk to an attorney. Do you understand?
6. Knowing and understanding your rights as I have explained them to you, are you willing to answer my questions without an attorney present?

prior representation of a corporation. By representing the corporation, an attorney may obtain potentially privileged information from employees who later become adverse witnesses against the corporation or individual officers in criminal prosecutions. These potential conflicts of interest also become very complicated when employees provide incriminating information to corporate counsel on the mistaken belief that he or she represents their interests as well as those of the corporation.

To further complicate the issue of representation, a 1994 U.S. Department of Justice rule allows government lawyers to contact workers who are not "high level" in a company without going through the company's legal department. Prosecutors may interview middle managers or line workers about company practices and try to persuade them to blow the whistle on upper management in criminal investigations. Normally, ethical rules would bar an attorney from directly contacting a person who is already represented by counsel. The Justice Department has rejected that rule in the context of corporate counsel primarily on the ground that it would frustrate the development of successful criminal investigations against corporations and corporate officials.

:: Specific Crimes

Specific crimes relevant to business are discussed below. Such crimes may be prosecuted at the federal level and many states also have laws prohibiting these acts. Federal crimes are set forth in the U.S. Code. As illustrated by numerous media examples over the last 10 years, these crimes are committed by individuals at all levels. Many crimes against business may also result in civil suits for money damages against a company. An individual convicted of a crime may face jail time and may also be required to pay money damages in a civil case.

8. FRAUD

As you learned earlier in the text, **fraud** can be a defense to a contract and can also form the basis of a civil tort action. The same fraudulent acts can also create criminal liability. The U.S. Code contains a number of provisions making it a crime to carry out a scheme to defraud. In general, whoever knowingly and willfully (1) falsifies, conceals, or covers up any trick, scheme, or device a material fact; (2) makes any materially false, fictitious, or fraudulent statement or representation; or (3) makes or uses any false writing or document knowing the same to contain any materially false, fictitious, or fraudulent statement or entry can face fines and/or imprisonment. There are many examples of fraud. After Hurricane Katrina, federal criminal investigations of fraud exceeded 1,000. The cases involved using debit cards meant for Katrina victims; claims submitted by individuals who did not live in affected areas; fraud by contractors submitting fake claims; and organized rings of criminals submitting multiple fake claims to maximize the amount of money they can fraudulently receive from the government.

Fraud is also actionable under state criminal codes. For example, in many states "theft by deception" is a crime. Theft by deception may occur when a person intentionally creates or reinforces an impression that is false; fails to correct an impression that is false and that the person does not believe to be true if there is a confidential or fiduciary relationship between the parties; preventing another from acquiring information that is relevant to a transaction; and failing to disclose a known lien or other legal impediment to property being transferred.

Federal law outlaws fraud in many specific contexts, including mail and wire transactions, securities transactions, health care, use of counterfeiting devices, and bankruptcy. A prosecutor must establish the presence of a **scheme to defraud**—a plan or program designed to take from a person the tangible right of honest services. In essence, a scheme involves a course of action to deceive others. See Sidebar 12.4 for examples of fraud schemes. Nearly all major white-collar criminal prosecutions involve some type of fraud.

:: *sidebar* 12.4

FBI Report: Common Fraud Schemes

Telemarketing Fraud. Use care when sending money to people you do not know personally and never give personal or financial information to unknown callers.

Advance Fee Scheme. This fraud occurs when the victim pays money to someone in anticipation of receiving something of greater value, then receives little or nothing in return.

Nigerian Letter or "419" Fraud. This fraud combines the threat of impersonation fraud with a variation of an advance fee scheme where the recipient has the "opportunity" to share a percentage of millions of dollars.

Impersonation/Identity Fraud. This fraud occurs when someone assumes your identity to perform a fraud or other criminal act.

Ponzi Schemes. These frauds are a kind of investment fraud where the operator promises high financial returns or dividends that are not available through traditional investments. Instead of investing the funds, the operator pays "dividends" to initial investors, then once he has a sufficient number of new investors, the operator flees with the remainder of the money.

Mail and Wire Fraud Various provisions of the U.S. Code make it illegal to use either the U.S. Postal Service or electronic means of interstate communication to carry out a scheme to defraud. These provisions provide significant criminal penalties for **mail** or **wire fraud.** The statutory penalties involve fines set by judges and up to 20 years in prison. If mail or wire fraud impacts a financial institution, the fine may be as high as $1 million and imprisonment may be up to 30 years. Each use of the mail or wire communication constitutes a separate violation. Thus, the criminal sanctions can be enormous.

"To mail" means a communication is sent or received through use of the U.S. Postal Service or any interstate carrier. A "wire transmission" includes the use of radio, television, telephone, Internet, or other wired form of communication. Prosecutors must prove the person accused of mail or wire fraud used the mail or wire communication. However, the government has substantial leeway in proving its case. Courts have held that the use of mail or wire communication can be proven by circumstantial evidence. For example, evidence of business custom and practice may establish that a mailing or wire communication occurred. The accused does not have to actually place a letter in the mail or send an e-mail message. Others may do so as long as the mailing is a part of the fraudulent scheme, the accused person does not have to be the party using the mail (see Case 12.2).

SCHMUCK v. UNITED STATES
489 U.S. 705 (1989)

BLACKMUN, J.: In August 1983, petitioner Wayne T. Schmuck, a used-car distributor, was indicted in the United States District Court for the Western District of Wisconsin on 12 counts of mail fraud, in violation of 18 U.S.C. § § 1341 and 1342.

The alleged fraud was a common and straightforward one. Schmuck purchased used cars, rolled back their odometers, and then sold the automobiles to Wisconsin retail dealers for prices artificially inflated because of the low-mileage readings. These unwitting car dealers, relying on the altered odometer figures, then resold the cars to customers, who in turn paid prices reflecting Schmuck's fraud. To complete the resale of each automobile, the dealer who purchased it from Schmuck would submit a title application form to the Wisconsin Department of Transportation on behalf of his retail customer. The receipt of a Wisconsin title was a prerequisite for completing the resale; without it, the dealer could not transfer title to the customer and the customer could not obtain Wisconsin tags. The submission of the title-application form supplied the mailing element of each of the alleged mail frauds.

Before trial, Schmuck moved to dismiss the indictment on the ground that the mailings at issue—the submissions of the title-application forms by the automobile dealers—were not in furtherance of the fraudulent scheme and, thus, did not satisfy the mailing element of the crime of mail fraud. . . . The District Court denied both motions. After trial, the jury returned guilty verdicts on all 12 counts. . . .

We granted certiorari to define further the scope of the mail fraud statute. . . .

The federal mail fraud statute does not purport to reach all frauds, but only those limited instances in which the use of the mails is a part of the execution of the fraud, leaving all other cases to be dealt with by appropriate state law. To be part of the execution of the fraud, however, the use of the mails need not be an essential element of the scheme. It is sufficient for the mailing to be incident to an essential part of the scheme or a step in the plot.

Schmuck. . . argues that mail fraud can be predicated only on a mailing that affirmatively assists the perpetrator in carrying out his fraudulent scheme. The mailing element of the offense, he contends, cannot be satisfied by a mailing, such as those at issue here, that is routine and innocent in and of itself, and that, far from furthering the execution of the fraud, occurs after the fraud has come to fruition, is merely tangentially related to the fraud, and is counterproductive in that it creates a paper trail from which the fraud may be discovered. We disagree both with this characterization of the mailings in the present case and with this description of the applicable law.

We begin by considering the scope of Schmuck's fraudulent scheme. Schmuck was charged with devising and executing a scheme to defraud Wisconsin retail automobile customers who based their decisions to purchase certain automobiles at least in part on the low-mileage readings provided by the tampered odometers. This was a fairly large-scale operation. Evidence at trial indicated that Schmuck had employed a man known only as "Fred" to turn back the odometers on about 150 different cars. Schmuck then marketed these cars to a number of dealers, several of whom he dealt with on a consistent basis over a period of about 15 years. . . . Schmuck's was not a "one-shot" operation in which he sold a single car to an isolated dealer. His was an ongoing fraudulent venture. A rational jury could have concluded that the success of Schmuck's venture depended upon his continued harmonious relations with, and good reputation among, retail dealers, which in turn required the smooth flow of cars from the dealers to their Wisconsin customers.

Under these circumstances, we believe that a rational jury could have found that the title-registration mailings were part of the execution of the fraudulent scheme, a scheme which did not reach fruition until the retail dealers resold the cars and effected transfers of title. Schmuck's scheme would have come to an abrupt halt if the dealers either had lost faith in Schmuck or had not been able to resell the cars obtained from him. These resales and Schmuck's relationships with the retail dealers naturally depended on the successful passage of title among the various parties. Thus, although the registration-form mailings may not have contributed directly to the duping of either the retail dealers or the customers, they were necessary to the passage of title, which in turn was essential to the perpetuation of Schmuck's scheme.

For these reasons, we agree with the Court of Appeals that the mailings in this case satisfy the mailing element of the mail fraud offenses.

Affirmed.

:: CASE QUESTIONS

1. What was the factual basis of the fraudulent scheme used by Schmuck in this case?
2. How was the mail associated with this factual situation?
3. Why does the Supreme Court conclude that mail fraud existed in this case?

Legal Aspects of Mail and Wire Fraud A statement or representation is *false* or *fraudulent* if it is known to be untrue or is made with reckless indifference as to its truth or falsity. A statement or representation may also be *false* or *fraudulent* if it constitutes a half-truth or effectively conceals a material fact with intent to defraud. A *material fact* is a fact that would be important to a reasonable person in deciding whether to engage or not to engage in a particular transaction.

Intent to defraud means to act knowingly and with the specific intent to deceive someone, ordinarily for the purpose of causing some financial loss to another or bringing about some financial gain to oneself. In many fraud cases the defendant asserts a good-faith defense to the allegations of the indictment. **Good faith** is a complete defense because good faith on the part of a defendant is inconsistent with intent to defraud or willfulness, purposes essential to the charges. A person who expresses an opinion honestly held or a belief honestly entertained does not have fraudulent intent even though the opinion is erroneous or the belief is mistaken. Evidence that establishes only that a person made a mistake in judgment or an error in management or was careless does not establish fraudulent intent.

The burden of proof is not on the defendant to prove good faith or honesty, because he or she has no burden to prove anything. The government must establish beyond a reasonable doubt that the defendant acted with specific intent to defraud. The government does not have to prove actual reliance upon the defendant's misrepresentations. Proof of damage has no application to criminal liability for mail and wire fraud. By prohibiting the "scheme to defraud" rather than the completed fraud, the elements of reliance and damage would clearly be inconsistent with the statutes Congress enacted.

A recent example of wire fraud involves former Wal-Mart Stores, Inc., Vice Chairman Thomas M. Coughlin. Mr. Coughlin pled guilty to wire fraud and tax evasion charges for using fraudulent expense reports. Wal-Mart alleged that he stole cash, gift cards, and equipment worth about $500,000. Coughlin is serving a home-confinement sentence of 27 months, plus 1,500 hours of community service. He also had to pay $400,000 in restitution. Coughlin was a company icon who worked closely with company founder Sam Walton.

Don't be pressured to "change the numbers" to meet unrealistic corporate goals.

Securities Fraud One of the most important federal laws defining criminal conduct is the Securities Exchange Act of 1934. This act and Rule 10(b)5 of the Securities and Exchange Commission cover fraud in the purchase or sale of a security. The details of this law are discussed in Chapter 15.

:: *sidebar* 12.5

Preventing Identity Theft

:: WHAT ARE THE MOST COMMON FORMS OF IDENTITY THEFT?

1. Dumpster Diving. Rummaging through trash looking for personal information.
2. Skimming. Stealing credit/debit card numbers using a special storage device when processing a card.
3. Phishing. Pretending to be financial institutions or companies to get individuals to reveal their personal information.
4. Changing Your Address. Diverting billing statements to other locations.
5. "Old-Fashioned" Stealing. Stealing wallets, purses, mail, credit cards, checks, tax information, and so forth.

:: WHAT CAN I DO TO DETER IDENTITY THIEVES?

1. Shred financial documents and paperwork before you discard them.
2. Protect your Social Security number.
3. Don't give out personal information over the phone, through the mail or Internet, unless you know the person.
4. Never click on links sent in unsolicited e-mails and protect your computer with firewalls, anti-spyware, and anti-virus software.
5. Keep all personal information in a secure location, away from roommates and others who may be in your home.

Source: www.ftc.gov/idtheft

Many of the prosecutions stem from accounting fraud based on false financial statements. The defendants are typically corporate officers responsible for the financial statements furnished to the investing public.

Health Care Fraud Another important area of criminal law enforcement against businesses is the health care industry. The Department of Justice has specialized investigative units concentrating on health care fraud. The prosecution usually involves false claims under the False Claims Act. Prosecuting false claims results in the recoupment of millions of dollars for the federal government.

Examples of health care fraud include:

- Billing for services not actually performed.
- Falsifying a patient's diagnosis to justify tests, surgery, or other procedures that are not medically necessary.
- "Uncoding" or billing for a more costly procedure than the one actually performed.
- "Unbundling" or billing each stage of a procedure as if it were a separate procedure.
- Accepting kickbacks for patient referrals.
- Billing a patient more than the copay amount for services that were paid in full by a benefit plan under the terms of a managed care contract.

Health care fraud investigations are aided by information revealed by "whistleblower" suits brought under the False Claims Act. This act allows a citizen "relator" who successfully brings a lawsuit that recovers fraudulently obtained federal funds to keep a portion of the recovery as a bounty.

Losses due to health care fraud are estimated to add $100 billion to the annual cost of health care in the United States.

Always review your medical bills. One expert estimates that "eight out of every ten" bills she reviews contain multiple errors.

Counterfeiting Federal law outlaws the use of counterfeit access devices, including bank cards, plates, codes, account numbers, or other means of account to initiate a transfer of funds. The use of an *unauthorized access device*, such as a lost, stolen, expired, revoked, canceled, or fraudulently obtained bank card, is also prohibited. The counterfeit or unauthorized access device used must result in at least $1,000 being fraudulently obtained within a one-year period.

The Criminal Investigation Unit of the IRS is actively involved in uncovering bankruptcy fraud. For examples of successful actions, see: www.irs.gov/compliance/.

Bankruptcy Fraud Bankruptcy proceedings are conducted in federal courts. To protect the interests of all parties to the proceedings, the U.S. Code makes certain conduct by the debtor and certain conduct by creditors and others a federal crime. These are **bankruptcy crimes.** First, it is a crime for the bankrupt debtor to falsify the information filed in the bankruptcy proceedings. Similarly, it is a crime for anyone to present a false claim in any bankruptcy proceeding.

Any person, including the debtor, in possession of property belonging to the estate of a debtor in bankruptcy is guilty of a felony if he or she conceals the property from the person charged with control of the property in the bankruptcy proceeding. The law requires that the act of concealment be fraudulent. An act is done fraudulently if done with intent to deceive or cheat any creditor, trustee, or bankruptcy judge. In this context, *conceal* means to secrete, falsify, mutilate, fraudulently transfer, withhold information or knowledge required by law to be made known, or take any action preventing discovery. Since the offense of **concealment** is a continuing one, the acts of concealment may have begun before as well as be committed after the bankruptcy proceeding began.

It is no defense that the concealment may have proved unsuccessful. Even though the property in question is recovered for the debtor's estate, the defendant may still be guilty of concealment. Similarly, it is no defense that there was no demand by any officer of the court or creditor for the property alleged to have been concealed.

9. CONSPIRACY

It is a separate criminal offense for anyone to conspire or agree with someone else to do something that, if carried out, would be a criminal offense. A **conspiracy** is an agreement or a "kind of partnership" for criminal purposes in which each member becomes the agent or partner of every other member. A formal agreement is not required, and all members of the conspiracy need not plan all of the details of the scheme.

To convict a person of a conspiracy, it is not necessary for the government to prove the conspirators actually succeeded in accomplishing their intended crime. The evidence must show beyond a reasonable doubt that:

- Two or more persons, in some way or manner, came to a mutual understanding to try to accomplish a common and unlawful plan.
- The defendant willfully became a member of such conspiracy.
- During the existence of the conspiracy, one of the conspirators knowingly committed at least one of the overt acts described in the indictment.
- Such overt act was knowingly committed in an effort to carry out or accomplish some object of the conspiracy.

A person may be convicted of conspiracy even if he or she did not know all the details of the unlawful scheme. If a defendant has an understanding of the unlawful nature of a plan and knowingly and willfully joins in that plan on one occasion, that is sufficient evidence for conviction.

:: *sidebar* 12.6

Anatomy of a Prosecution: The Fall of Enron

The fall of Enron Corp. is one of this country's largest corporate scandals. According to the prosecution, Enron's founder, Kenneth Lay, and former CEO, Jeffrey Skilling, instigated a massive fraud before the company collapsed. The prosecution alleged that Lay and Skilling committed crimes "through accounting tricks, fiction, hocus-pocus, trickery, misleading statements, half-truths, omissions and outright lies."

The prosecution scorecard includes: Convictions:

Kenneth Lay—Found guilty on all six counts relating to fraud, including conspiracy to commit wire fraud, perpetrating wire and bank fraud, making false and misleading statements to employees, banks, securities analysts and corporate credit-rating agencies. Lay died unexpectedly before sentencing and his conviction was vacated under legal precedent.

Jeffrey Skilling—Found guilty of 19 of the 28 counts accusing him of insider trading, securities fraud and conspiracy. Sentenced to prison for 24 years and 4 months.

Eighteen Guilty Pleas, including Enron Chief Financial Officer Andrew Fastow. Facing 98 counts, Fastow pleaded guilty to conspiracy to commit wire fraud and conspiracy to commit wire and securities fraud. Fastow's "cooperation" with prosecutors significantly contributed to the successful criminal case against Lay and Skilling. Sentence: six years in prison.

*Source: *www.chron.com/news/specials/enron/*. For additional information, see *Power Failure: The Inside Story of the Collapse of Enron* by Mimi Swartz with Enron whistleblower Sherron Watkins.

The essence of a conspiracy offense is the making of the agreement itself followed by the commission of any overt act. An **overt act** is any transaction or event knowingly committed by a conspirator in an effort to accomplish some object of the conspiracy. Standing alone, the act may be entirely innocent; the context of the conspiracy makes it criminal. For example, driving a car to a bank to pick up a bank robber would constitute an overt act by the driver.

The law on conspiracies is often used to "drag in" defendants who did not actually participate in the commission of an offense. A person may become a coconspirator through participation in routine business meetings if the meetings are followed by illegal conduct. If illegal plans or conduct are in the planning process, it is imperative that persons not wishing to participate in the conspiracy disassociate themselves from the process immediately upon discovery of the illegal scheme.

Circumstantial evidence may prove a conspiracy. A person can be charged with conspiracy even if the individual becomes involved after the conspiracy is stopped and the criminal conduct does not occur. The fact that law enforcement discovers a plot to commit a crime and thwarts it does not prevent prosecution for a conspiracy. The threat of a conspiracy is a public danger beyond the commission of the crime because it is likely that the conspirators will commit more crimes.

A party may be guilty even though one of the coconspirators is acquitted by a jury. In Case 12.3, note that the real culprit escaped punishment and his employer did not.

UNITED STATES OF AMERICA v. HUGHES AIRCRAFT CO., INC.
20 F. 3d 974 (9th Cir. 1994)

PER CURIAM: Hughes Aircraft Co., Inc. ("Hughes") appeals from its conviction and sentence for conspiring to defraud and make false statements to the federal government. . . .

Hughes contracted with the United States to manufacture microelectronic circuits, known as "hybrids," which are used as components in weapons defense systems. The contracts required Hughes to perform a series of tests on each hybrid. As the hybrids made their way through the testing process, they were accompanied by paperwork indicating what tests had been performed, the results of those tests, and the identity of the operator of the testing equipment.

Hughes's former employee, Donald LaRue ("LaRue"), was a supervisor responsible for ensuring the accuracy of the hybrid testing process. LaRue arranged for the paperwork to indicate falsely that all tests had been performed and that each hybrid had passed each test. When LaRue's subordinates called his actions to the attention of LaRue's supervisors, the supervisors did nothing about it. Instead, they responded that LaRue's decisions were his own and were not to be questioned by his subordinates.

Hughes and LaRue were charged with . . . conspiracy to defraud. . . . LaRue was acquitted. . . . Hughes was convicted. . . . Hughes appeals from both its conviction and fine of $3.5 million. . . .

Hughes first argues that it must be acquitted as a matter of law because the same jury that convicted Hughes acquitted its "indispensable coconspirator," LaRue, of the identical charges on identical evidence. . . .

Inconsistent verdicts can just as easily be the result of jury lenity as a determination of the facts. Thus, the acquittal of all conspirators but one does not necessarily indicate that the jury found no agreement to act. . . . Accordingly, the conviction of one co-conspirator is valid even when all the other co-conspirators are acquitted. . . .

Hughes next argues that it is entitled to a judgment of acquittal because the evidence against it and LaRue was identical, yet one was convicted while the other was acquitted. This argument is predicated on the assumption that LaRue was the sole employee for whose actions Hughes could be found vicariously guilty and that the evidence against each of the two defendants was necessarily identical. However, some of the evidence of conspiracy was offered against Hughes alone. Moreover, as this evidence indicates, the jury could have found Hughes guilty based on the actions or omissions of its supervisors and employees other than LaRue. As Hughes's assumption that the facts against both defendants were identical is erroneous, and no other facts support its argument, we reject this contention.

Hughes's third argument is that the plain language of 18 U.S.C. § 371, which states that if "two or more persons conspire . . . each" may be punished, prevents its conviction because it is legally impossible for a party to conspire with itself. Hughes argues that, because it is vicariously liable for each of its employees, a conspiracy between employees would necessitate a finding that Hughes conspired with itself. We reject this creative construction. The statutory language does not exclude criminal liability for a corporation simply because its employees are the actual conspirators. To rule otherwise would effectively insulate all corporations from liability for conspiracies involving only employees acting on behalf of that corporation. We hold that a corporation may be liable under § 371 for conspiracies entered into by its agents and employees. . . .

Hughes argues that a corporation could only violate 18 U.S.C. § 1001 through the efforts of at least two of its employees due to the supervisory and reporting structure of a corporation. Of course, that is not true: a corporation could be liable under § 1001 for false statements to the government by just one of its employees. A conspiracy arises when more than one of its employees agree to defraud the government.

Moreover, the consequences of government fraud certainly do not rest on the parties themselves rather than society. Government fraud has an adverse effect on the government treasury, the quality of government projects, and in cases such as this one, the safety of individuals utilizing the government goods purchased. This argument is rejected.

Affirmed.

:: CASE QUESTIONS

1. Why do you think that the jury returned a verdict of not guilty for LaRue?
2. What mistake did Hughes management make that resulted in the company being a party to the conspiracy?
3. Why are corporations liable for the conspiracies of its employees?

10. OBSTRUCTION OF JUSTICE

Obstruction of justice occurs when an individual commits an act with the intent to obstruct the legislative process or a judicial process. Obstruction of justice laws are designed to protect the integrity of legislative proceedings, judicial proceedings, and the proceedings before federal departments or agencies. The term *obstruction of justice* is interpreted broadly to encompass all steps and stages from the inception of an investigation to the conclusion of a trial.

Do be fully forthcoming with any investigation. Never be tempted into altering or destroying documents when an investigation or litigation is pending.

Section 1505 of Title 18 of the U.S. Code provides

> Whoever, with intent to avoid, evade, prevent, or obstruct compliance, in whole or in part, with any civil investigative demand duly and properly made under the Antitrust Civil Process Act, willfully withholds, misrepresents, removes from any place, conceals, covers up, destroys, mutilates, alters, or by other means falsifies any documentary material, answers to written interrogatories, or oral testimony, which is the subject of such demand; or attempts to do so or solicits another to do so; or
>
> Whoever corruptly, or by threats or force, or by any threatening letter or communication influences, obstructs, or impedes or endeavors to influence, obstruct, or impede the due and proper administration of the law under which any pending proceeding is being had before any department or agency of the United States, or the due and proper exercise of the power of inquiry under which any inquiry or investigation is being had by either House, or any committee of either House or any joint committee of the Congress—Shall be fined under this title or imprisoned not more than five years, or both.

As you can see, this law is worded very broadly and can encompass a range of acts. The law was drafted with the recognition that there is an unlimited variety of methods by which the proper administration of justice might be impeded or thwarted by those who are criminally inclined. Any act made with the intent to obstruct the legislative process or judicial process may be a crime. Sidebar 12.7 contains examples of obstruction of justice.

11. FALSE STATEMENT TO A BANK

Borrowers from banks are routinely required to furnish financial statements. These statements intend to supply information to the bank so it can make its decision on the loan request. Financial statements are relied upon by banks even though many of them are not certified as correct by a certified public accountant. It is a federal crime for anyone willfully to make a false statement to a federally insured financial institution. The purpose behind making such falsehoods a crime is to protect banks and attempt to ensure the accuracy of financial information. To prove the crime of a false statement to a bank, the prosecutor must prove beyond a reasonable doubt that the false statement or

There is no requirement that the institution was influenced or misled.

:: *sidebar* 12.7

Think Before You Act: Examples of Obstruction of Justice

E-mailing a message to "clean up the files."

Changing records of phone conversations.

Shredding documents when an investigation or litigation is pending.

Exploiting a special relationship with a judge to obtain a favorable decision.

Testifying falsely before Congress.

Hiring a law firm with close political ties to the chairman of a congressional committee to get the chairman to stop an investigation of a corporation.

:: EXAMPLES OF SUCCESSFUL PROSECUTIONS

- I. Lewis "Scooter" Libby, Vice President Dick Cheney's former Chief of Staff, convicted of perjury and obstruction of justice, 2½ years in prison.

- Frank P. Quattrone, Wall Street banker, convicted for obstruction of justice, 18 months in prison.
- Martha Stewart convicted for obstruction of justice and lying to investigators, 5 months in prison, 5 months home confinement, 2 years probation.
- Kenneth Branch, former Boeing Co. manager, pleaded guilty to obstruction of justice stemming from an investigation into the theft of sensitive documents from competitor Lockheed Martin Corp. (during a battle for $1.99 billion in U.S. government contracts), 6 months home detention and a fine.

report was made with the intent to influence the action of the insured financial institution upon an application, advance, commitment, loan, or any change or extension thereof. An *insured bank* is one whose deposits are insured by the Federal Deposit Insurance Corporation. An insured credit union is one whose deposits are insured by the National Credit Union Administration.

A statement or report is *false* when made if it relates to a material fact and is untrue and is then known to be untrue by the person making it. A fact is *material* if it is important to the decision to be made by the officers or employees of the institution involved and has the capacity of influencing them in making that decision. It is not necessary, however, to prove that the institution involved was, in fact, influenced or misled. The gist of the offense is an attempt to influence such an institution by willfully making the false statement or report concerning the matter. The maximum penalty for a violation is two years' imprisonment and a $5,000 fine.

12. FALSE STATEMENT TO A FEDERAL AGENCY

> "I truly hope people will learn from my mistakes."
>
> **–Olympic track star Marion Jones, sentenced to six months in prison for lying to investigators.**

The U.S. Code makes it a federal crime for anyone willfully and knowingly to make a false or fraudulent statement to a department or agency of the United States. The false statement must be related to a material matter, and the defendant must have acted willfully and with knowledge of the falsity. It is not necessary to show that the government agency was in fact deceived or misled. The issue of materiality is one of law for the courts. The maximum penalty is five years' imprisonment and a $10,000 fine.

A person may be guilty of a violation without proof that he or she had knowledge that the matter was within the jurisdiction of a federal agency. A businessperson may violate this law by making a false statement to another firm or person with knowledge that the information will be submitted to a government agency. Businesses must take care to avoid puffery or exaggerations in the context of any matter that may come within the jurisdiction of a federal agency.

Due to the sweeping nature of this statute, seven federal appellate courts recognized an **exculpatory no** exception for simple denials made in response to government questioning as part of a criminal investigation. This narrow exception protected an individual from prosecution for making a false statement when the person's statement simply denies criminal wrongdoing. The exculpatory no was permitted when a person, in response to governmental questioning, had to choose between three undesirable options: self-incrimination by telling the truth; remaining silent and raising greater suspicions; or denying guilt by making a false statement to the governmental official. Courts permitting this exception believed it balanced the need for protecting the basic functions of government agencies conducting investigations against the Fifth Amendment protection against self-incrimination.

In early 1998, the Supreme Court rejected the exculpatory no exception in the case of *Brogan v. United States,* 118 U.S. 805 (1998). The Court found the exception was not supported by the plain language of the statute and held that the Fifth Amendment does not confer a privilege to lie.

13. LARCENY

Larceny is the unlawful taking of personal property with the intent to deprive the rightful owner of it permanently. Larceny is commonly referred to as theft or stealing. Shoplifting by customers is a common form of larceny. Larceny by violence or threat such as with a gun is **robbery.** Breaking into a building with the intent to commit a felony is **burglary.** The most common felony in burglary cases is larceny.

Larceny by employees of a business is a common white-collar crime. If an employee appropriates funds of his employer to his or her own use, the employee is guilty of embezzlement. Embezzlement is often committed by highly trusted employees with access to cash or to the check-writing process. It is a crime easily committed when there is a lack of internal control over funds. Simple policies such as using cosigned checks, dividing check-writing duties from bank reconciliation duties, and requiring all employees to take vacations can often prevent embezzlement.

Larceny by employees takes many forms. Use of company property such as vehicles or computers without permission is a form of larceny. Padding expense accounts and falsifying time records are also a taking of property and they are a sophisticated form of theft.

Although larceny by rank-and-file employees is important, it pales to insignificance when compared to the larcenies committed by some corporate officers and directors. Larceny at the top-management level of some corporations in recent years has involved millions of dollars. In some cases, the stealing can only be described as looting the business just as if a mob broke into a store and stole its inventory.

Larceny by directors and officers usually has the appearance of being legal. The business may loan large sums to an officer at little or no interest. If there is no intent to repay the loan and no expectation of repayment, larceny as well as conspiracy to commit larceny has occurred. A company may purchase an airplane or yacht ostensibly for the business. If these are used only by the president for his personal enjoyment, larceny may have been committed. Likewise,

Embezzlement
occurs when a person entrusted with another's money or property fraudulently appropriates it.

Money laundering
is falsely reporting income that is obtained through criminal "dirty" activity as income obtained through a legitimate "clean" business enterprise.

if a company buys season tickets for the games of a local professional sports team and the tickets are used only by the officers, a form of larceny occurs. Technically, these examples could be stealing as well as tax fraud because the executive may not report receiving these benefits on his or her tax returns.

Company lawyers are not immune from prosecution for white-collar crimes. The general counsel for a company who helped cover up $600 million in looting of the corporation by company executives was given a $12 million bonus. He was indicted for grand larceny.

14. RACKETEER INFLUENCED AND CORRUPT ORGANIZATIONS ACT (RICO)

The most controversial of the federal criminal laws relating to business is the Racketeer Influenced and Corrupt Organizations Act, commonly known as **RICO**. This law imposes criminal and civil liability upon those businesspersons who engage in certain *prohibited activities* and who engage in interstate commerce. Specifically, liability extends to any person who:

- Uses or invests income from prohibited activities to acquire an interest in or to operate an enterprise.
- Acquires or maintains an interest in or control of an enterprise.
- Conducts or participates in the conduct of an enterprise while being employed by or associated with it.

Each prohibited activity is defined to include, as one necessary element, proof either of a **pattern of racketeering** *activity* or of *the collection of an unlawful debt*. **Racketeering** is defined in RICO to mean "any act or threat involving" specified state law crimes, any "act" indictable under various specified federal statutes, and certain federal "offenses." As to the term *pattern*, the statute says only that it "requires at least two acts of racketeering activity" within a 10-year period. It is not otherwise defined. See Table 12.2 for examples of racketeering activity.

---

table 12.2 :: RICO: What Is "Racketeering Activity"?

Racketeering activity encompasses many criminal acts, including:

- Acts or threats involving murder, kidnapping, gambling, arson, robbery, bribery, extortion, dealing in obscene matter, or controlled substances.
- Counterfeiting.

- Mail and wire fraud.
- Financial institution fraud.
- Obstruction of justice.
- Bribery, including sports bribery.
- Tampering with a witness, victim, or informant.
- Trafficking in counterfeit goods.

Successful Prosecution

Former powerhouse plaintiffs' lawyer, Melvyn I. Weiss, faced a multicount indictment, including RICO and money laundering charges. Weiss pled guilty to a conspiracy charge that he conspired to pay off plaintiffs in class-action lawsuits against major corporations. His sentence: 30 months in prison, forfeiture of $9.7 million in "ill-gotten gains," and a $250,000 fine. In Weiss's own words: "I deeply regret my conduct and apologize to all those who have been affected, including all of the wonderful and extremely talented lawyers and other employees of the firm, none of whom had any involvement in any wrongdoing."

The requirement of a pattern of racketeering activity is not the only issue created by the wording of the RICO statute. The law makes it unlawful for any person employed by or associated with any enterprise to conduct or participate in a violation. Thus, the law foresees two separate entities, a person and a distinct enterprise. An issue arises when a person incorporates and that person is the president and sole shareholder of the corporation. Courts have held in such cases that there are two separate entities and both may have RICO liability.

RICO allegations of fraud must be pled with particularity. A RICO plaintiff must describe the predicate acts of fraud with some specificity and state the time, place, and content of the alleged communications perpetrating the fraud. If there are multiple defendants, the allegations must put each defendant on notice of his alleged participation.

A plaintiff in a civil action is, in effect, a private attorney general. In filing a complaint, the plaintiff must also allege that the defendant participated in the operation or management of the enterprise and played a part in directing the affairs of the enterprise. Mere employment in an organization is not sufficient to hold someone liable under RICO.

RICO provides drastic remedies. Conviction for a violation of RICO carries severe criminal penalties and forfeitures of illegal proceeds. Upon filing a RICO indictment, the government may seek a temporary restraining order to preserve all forfeitable assets until the trial is completed and judgment entered. A person in a private civil action found to have violated RICO is liable for treble, or triple, damages as well as for costs and attorneys' fees.

Remember, RICO provides for both civil remedies and criminal penalties.

15. CYBER CRIME

One of the most significant trends in criminal law is a product of the rapid increase of the Internet. The Internet is a part of everyday business and, along with that fact, is the opportunity to use the Internet in connection with criminal activity. With billions of dollars flowing through cyberspace, it is not surprising that criminals are taking advantage of the system. Hackers commit crimes throughout the world that are very costly to business. Identity theft—when someone uses stolen information to create a new form of identity—is also a high-tech threat.

Federal law provides that a person who intentionally accesses a computer without authorization or exceeds authorized access to obtain classified, restricted, or protected data, or attempts to do so, is subject to criminal prosecution (See Sidebar 12.8). Protected data includes financial and credit records, information from any department or agency of the United States, and information from any protected computer if the conduct involves an interstate or foreign communication.

Electronic theft is not limited to money. Employees have been caught issuing corporate stock to themselves. Trade secrets, personnel records, and customer lists have been stolen by hackers. Company plans are sometimes stolen and sold to competitors.

Most experts agree that cyber crime is more difficult to detect than crimes that preceded the Internet. Proof based on digital evidence about anonymous persons seldom leads to convictions. There has been an increase in law enforcement agents assigned to combat cyberspace thieves, and the training

Are you the victim of an Internet crime? Complaints may be filed with the Internet Crime Complaint Center, www.ic3.gov/. The center operates in partnership with the FBI.

:: *sidebar* 12.8

Prosecution for Cyberbullying

A Missouri woman, Lori Drew, was indicted by a federal grand jury for allegedly perpetrating a hoax against her 13-year-old neighbor using MySpace. Posing as a 16-year-old boy, Drew allegedly used the account to flirt with the girl and later sent cruel messages, including one stating that the world would be better off without her.

After the girl committed suicide, Drew was charged with one count of conspiracy (18 U.S.C. § 371) and three counts of accessing protected computers without authorization (18 U.S.C. §1030) to get information used to inflict emotional distress on the girl. Both the girl and MySpace are named as victims in the case. This is the first time this federal law prohibiting fraud and related activity in connection with computers has been used in a social-networking case. Each of the four counts carries a maximum possible penalty of five years in prison.

For the latest news on computer crimes, *see* the Department of Justice website: www.cybercrime.gov.

and their education in this area have improved. There are several companies in the security intelligence business that are attempting to help the business community install systems to prevent hacking.

Certain aspects of cyberspace crime should be recognized by managers and shareholders. Electronic crimes are most often committed by employees. Access to confidential information should be limited and carefully controlled. Losses from such crimes are easily hidden in cost of goods sold or in bad debt write-offs. They are usually kept secret for fear of encouraging other criminal acts. Investors typically have little or no knowledge of losses resulting from cyber crime.

16. ENDANGERING WORKERS

Most of the crimes committed by business are white-collar crimes. It is possible for corporate officials to be charged with crimes, such as assault and battery, reckless **endangerment of workers** if a worker is injured, or even accidental homicide if a worker is killed on the job. *In most cases,* when a worker is injured on the job, the appropriate remedy is through the workers' compensation system, which is discussed in Chapter 10. If a company is involved in an extremely dangerous process, such as handling dangerous chemicals, or does not have adequate safety precautions, criminal liability *may be imposed* if a worker is injured or killed.

Some states have specific statutes requiring employers to warn employees of life-threatening hazards in the workplace. In California, any corporation or person who is a manager is required to report any serious concealed danger in the workplace. Serious concealed danger encompasses products and practices that create a substantial probability of death, great bodily harm, or serious exposure to an employee. Failure to do so is a crime.

The Occupational Safety and Health Administration (OSHA) can also bring actions against businesses for violation of health and safety standards. If a business exposes workers to dangerous situations, such as exposing workers to dangerous falls and hazardous chemicals, OSHA has the power to impose money penalties for each violation.

17. AIDING AND ABETTING

The law recognizes that businesspeople accused of criminal behavior likely did not act alone. Such persons can be assisted by co-workers, subordinates, or individuals outside the business organization. If a person acts under the direction of someone accused of criminal activities, this person might be held responsible for **aiding and abetting** in the commission of the crime. The charge of aiding and abetting is similar to the allegation of participating in a conspiracy. This individual accused of aiding and abetting did not necessarily commit the same criminal acts as others. For example, the accountant who assists the chief financial officer in embezzling funds likely is guilty of aiding and abetting in the actual theft. This accountant also may be guilty of conspiring to steal money.

Indictments often charge persons both with a conspiracy to commit a crime and with aiding and abetting others to do so. These allegations are used to indict persons only minimally involved with the actual substantive crime. To avoid going to trial, many will agree to testify against those more directly involved in return for lesser punishment or even immunity from prosecution. The value to the government of the conspiracy theory and the charge of aiding and abetting should not be underestimated. Corporate officials may be potentially liable for criminal acts committed without their direct involvement.

At the state level, a charge similar to the federal charge of aiding and abetting is that a person is an **accessory** to a crime. A person may be an accessory before the crime is committed. If the person is accused of being involved after the crime is committed, the charge is as an accessory after the fact. A person who assists a perpetrator of a crime in eluding the police would be such an accessory. *Accessories before the crime* assist in preparation for the crime, and they may be punished the same as the person who committed the crime. *Accessories after the fact* are usually subject to specific penalties for their actions as determined by the laws of the various states.

18. SENTENCING GUIDELINES

Historically, the fate of a person convicted of a crime depended heavily on the judge doing the sentencing. Because some judges were lenient and others were tough, the sentencing of criminals was sometimes referred to as "judicial roulette." To make the criminal system more just and to help ensure that similar crimes receive similar sentences, in the late 1980s a federal sentencing commission developed **sentencing guidelines** for federal crimes.

These guidelines were the subject of much study, debate, and controversy. Many federal judges resented the loss of control during the sentencing phase of a case. Judges also criticized the complexity of the guidelines, which are hard to follow. Initially, the guidelines were mandatory. In accordance with a U.S. Supreme Court decision, the guidelines are now advisory, requiring a court to consider the guideline ranges, but permitting it to tailor the sentence in light of other concerns. Federal judges are now free to decide for themselves if the defendants deserve sentences longer or shorter than the ranges in the guidelines. If, however, an appeals court finds the sentence to be "unreasonable" under the facts of the case, the sentencing decision can be reversed. The Supreme Court, however, ruled in 2007 that sentences falling

"No punishment has ever possessed enough power of deterrence to prevent the commission of crimes."

–Hannah Arendt, political theorist.

within the guidelines may be presumed "reasonable" by courts reviewing sentences on appeal.

Because corporations cannot be jailed, the sentencing commission has developed special guidelines for sentencing organizations convicted of federal crimes. The emphasis is on monetary penalties. It must be kept in mind, however, that in most criminal cases involving organizations, corporate officers can also be charged. As a result, the guidelines are designed so that the sanctions imposed upon organizations and their agents, taken together, will provide just punishment, adequate deterrence, and incentives for organizations to maintain internal mechanisms for preventing, detecting, and reporting criminal conduct. Punishment and deterrence are goals of the guidelines.

To illustrate how these guidelines would work, assume that a large corporation committed fraud in selling its product to the federal government. Perhaps the test results on the product were falsely reported. If a high official in the company and some middle managers knew that the test results were falsified and the company had a previous conviction of fraud within 10 years, the fine would be $20 to $40 million. However, if the company received good points for cooperation with investigators and had an aggressive internal audit program to detect and prevent fraud, the fine would be only $4 to $8 million. In either case, the court would also order *restitution*. The court may also put the business on probation, preventing it from selling stock and paying dividends, or the court may otherwise be involved in major corporate decisions. This probation provision serves to get and keep the attention of senior management. Management in a company on probation must prevent violations of federal laws by its employees.

19. TRENDS

One of the more significant trends is an increase in prosecution of white-collar criminals and legislative efforts to protect the public from fraud. To this end, the Sarbanes-Oxley Act (discussed in detail in Chapter 15) is causing companies to employ rigorous new accounting and compliance mechanisms. The goal is to renew investor confidence in the markets.

Another important trend is the government's effort to obtain proof of illegal activity by top corporate officials. Initiating an investigation that focuses on lower-mid-level managers, the government will obtain evidence the assists it in implicating higher-level executives. If wrongful conduct is found in the lower ranks, these employees are charged with conspiracy to violate a federal law. Prosecutors will then plea bargain with these defendants in exchange for testimony against persons higher on the organizational chart. This enables prosecutors to go after the real high-value target: top management. Although plea bargains typically require that prosecutors agree to drop or reduce charges, it is becoming increasingly more likely for prosecutors to insist on some jail time.

Prosecutors are also capitalizing on high-profile prosecutions. Where the stakes are high, prosecutors use the media to characterize white-collar criminals as "common street thugs." After an arrest, prosecutors may also seek millions of dollars in bail money and may object to the source of the funds if the money is the product of illegal activity. For example, a $5 million bond was required of Enron's chief financial officer. The size of the bond made it necessary for his parents to offer their home as security. Likewise, prosecutors may seek criminal penalties that include forfeiture of illegally obtained assets such as luxury homes, bank accounts, yachts, and automobiles. All of this is designed to deter similar conduct by other would-be corporate felons.

:: Key Terms

Accessory 373	Good faith 362	Presumption of innocence 353
Aiding and abetting 373	Indictment 352	Probable cause 353
Bankruptcy crime 364	Information 352	Racketeering 370
Burglary 369	Intent 352	RICO 370
Concealment 364	Intent to defraud 362	Robbery 369
Conspiracy 364	Knowingly 352	Scheme to defraud 360
Double jeopardy 356	Larceny 369	Search warrant 354
Endangerment of	Mail fraud 360	Sentencing guidelines 373
workers 372	Misdemeanor 352	Unreasonable search and
Exculpatory no 369	*Nolo contendere* 352	seizure 354
Expectation of privacy 355	Obstruction of justice 367	White-collar crime 350
Felony 352	Overt act 365	Willfully 352
Fraud 359	Pattern of racketeering 370	Wire fraud 360

:: Review Questions and Problems

Terms and Procedures

1. *Classifications of Criminal Conduct*
   (a) Why is it important for business persons to have an understanding of the basic principles of criminal law and white collar crime?
   (b) What is the difference between felonies and misdemeanors?

2. *Basic Concepts*
   Who are the parties to a criminal case?

3. *The Grand Jury*
   James was indicted by a federal grand jury. During the trial jury's deliberation one juror said, "I think James is guilty or else the grand jury would not have sent us the case." Another juror objected to this statement and said, "The action of the grand jury is irrelevant in our determination of guilt or innocence." Which juror is more accurate about the role of grand juries in our criminal justice system?

Constitutional Issues

4. *The Fourth Amendment: Illegal Search and Seizure*
   Burger's junkyard business consists of dismantling automobiles and selling their parts. A New York statute authorized warrantless inspections of automobile junkyards. Police officers entered his junkyard, conducted an inspection, and discovered stolen vehicles and parts. Burger, who was charged with possession of stolen property, moved to suppress the evidence obtained as a result of the inspection. He contends that the administrative inspection statute is unconstitutional when it authorizes warrantless searches. Is he correct? Why or why not?

5. *The Fifth Amendment: Protection against Self-Incrimination*

   Roberts was the president and sole shareholder of a corporation. A federal grand jury issued a subpoena to him in his capacity as president. The subpoena required Roberts to produce corporate records. Roberts moves to quash the subpoena on Fifth Amendment grounds.

   (a) Must Roberts deliver the records? Why or why not?

   (b) Could Roberts be required to testify about the documents? Why or why not?

   (c) If Roberts takes steps to dissolve the corporation, can he then avoid the subpoena? Why or why not?

6. *The Fifth Amendment: Double Jeopardy*

   Does the double jeopardy clause apply to civil penalties? Why or why not?

7. *The Sixth Amendment: Rights in a Criminal Case*

   What are the six constitutional rights provided in the Sixth Amendment?

Specific Crimes

8. *Fraud*

   Mary lost her billfold, which contained credit cards and an ATM access card. She had written her pin number on a piece of paper, which was also in the billfold. Al found the billfold. He used the credit cards and ATM card to obtain over $2,500 in goods, services, and cash. Is Al guilty of a federal offense?

9. *Conspiracy*

   Allen, Mary, and Jon agreed to participate in a program to manipulate the values of securities. Allen made several telephone calls to securities brokers in which he delivered false information about a number of companies. Before any further actions were taken, Mary and Jonathan decided to withdraw as active participants in the program. Did Mary and Jon commit any crime? Why?

10. *Obstruction of Justice*

    Quincy was a successful investment banker specializing in underwriting and merger advice. A federal grand jury was investigating the sales of initial public offerings, and Quincy knew that the grand jury had issued subpoenas seeking information about Quincy's deals. Quincy sent an e-mail to colleagues and encouraged them to "clean up" their files. What crimes, if any, did Quincy commit? If a colleague shredded files, what crimes may have been committed?

11. *False Statement to a Bank*

    Your business is in need of additional working capital. You contact your bank about a loan. A line of credit of $500,000 is tentatively approved pending you furnish audited financial statements. You meet with your auditor who is also a personal friend. Suppose you ask your auditor to add $250,000 as an account receivable. In fact, this asset does not exist. The auditor certifies the financial statements with this phantom asset. You mail the audited financial statements to the bank. What crimes have you committed? What crimes did the auditor commit? What should have been the auditor's response to your request?

12. *False Statement to a Federal Agency*

    Adam was hired by a defense contractor for a position that required a clearance for classified material. He failed to disclose a criminal conviction on a Department of Defense personnel security questionnaire, but admitted that he knew there was false information on the form which he signed.

    (a) Did Adam willfully violate any federal law?

    (b) If Adam didn't actually realize that the form would be submitted to a federal agency, is that a defense?

13. *Larceny*

    Joe, a purchasing agent of ABC Company, entered into a contract to purchase software on behalf of ABC from a software company represented by Harry. The contract stated a price of $10,000 but the actual cost was $8,000. Joe and Harry split the $2,000. What crimes were committed?

14. *Racketeer Influenced and Corrupt Organizations Act (RICO)*

Don, a promoter of prize fights, formed a corporation. Don was the sole shareholder, sole director, and president of the corporation. Don was charged with a violation of RICO. Is the requirement of both a person and an enterprise met?

15. *Cyber Crime*

Why is cyber crime difficult to detect and to prosecute successfully?

16. *Endangering Workers*

Beth was killed when a trench collapsed. An investigation revealed that the trench was 27 feet deep and without adequate shoring, in violation of safety standards. Bob, the president of the firm, is charged with negligent homicide. Is a finding of guilt possible? Why or why not?

17. *Aiding and Abetting*

Susan, a partner in a CPA firm, prepares a federal income tax return knowing that it contains false information. Because the client wants the return prepared in this manner, Susan obtains the taxpayer's signature on the return and files it with the IRS. Has Susan aided and abetted in the commission of a crime? Why?

18. *Sentencing Guidelines*

The U.S. sentencing guidelines apply a mathematical formula to sentencing. How do the guidelines operate?

19. *Trends*

Describe three trends in criminal law that impact business organizations and businesspeople.

business :: *discussion*

A drug company applied for the approval of the Food and Drug Administration (FDA) to market a miracle drug that the company believed could cure some cancers. During the period that the application was under consideration the company's stock rose to $65 per share. The president of the company learned that the FDA application was about to be denied. You are a personal friend of the president, and he told you that he believed that the stock will start trading downward. You sell 4,000 shares of stock which you purchased for $10 per share. Your decision appears to be a good one since you made a profit of about $200,000. When questioned about the sale by an investigator from the Securities and Exchange Commission, you state that the sale was because of a preexisting arrangement to sell the shares when the price fell below $60 per share. Following the announcement that the FDA application was denied, the stock went to $7 per share.

Did you commit a crime when you sold the stock?

Did you commit a crime in your answer to the federal agent?

Were you part of an illegal conspiracy?

13

International Law

 Learning Objectives ::

In this chapter you will learn:

1. To identify the basic sources of international law and major institutions.

2. To consider the importance of free trade agreements on the global economy.

3. To grasp the basic methods of transacting international business.

4. To understand the legal risk inherent in international transactions, including the requirements of the Foreign Corrupt Practices Act.

5. To realize the complexity of resolving international disputes.

The collapse of Lehman Brothers Holdings, Inc. during the fall of 2008, illustrates the interconnectedness of international business. Lehman's bankruptcy triggered a "cash crunch" around the world, precipitating losses and accelerating the demise of other businesses. The U.S. laws and regulations governing financial institutions immediately were subjected to international scrutiny.

Law is fundamental to business in the United States and throughout the globe. As American businesses become increasingly global in a very competitive international marketplace, some understanding of legal issues in this context is essential. Throughout this text, the importance of *the rule of law* is emphasized. This concept is particularly important for companies doing business abroad. Property rights and contracts must be enforced to minimize risk in international transactions.

The United States enters into treaties and trade agreements to govern competition and the way goods and technology are sold from one country to the next. Every country is interested in developing rules that make its products and services more competitive in the global market. Nation-states and corporations alike are protected by a mutual respect for property and contractual rights.

The goal of American trade policy is to open markets throughout the world. The idea is to create new opportunities for business and also higher living standards. The United States is a party to many trade agreements and is continually negotiating new ones to further open markets to free trade. National economies rely on their ability to export products and services abroad to create jobs and economic growth at home. Companies likewise are continually looking for productive ways to expand their international business. Overall, however, the United States has a huge trade deficit because it buys more than it sells abroad. At the end of 2007, the trade deficit was $711.61 billion. For a chart of the top trading partners with the United States, see Figure 13.1.

This chapter provides a basic understanding about international law as it affects business. International organizations and major agreements affecting trade are discussed to lay a foundation for global transactions. Methods of transacting international business are explained, as well as the risks involved in global trade. This chapter also addresses ways of resolving international disputes. In addition to international law and organizations regulating the conduct of global companies, many companies also have their own internal codes of conduct or policy statements defining their ethical standards (see Sidebar 13.1).

:: International Law and Organizations

What is "international law"? Inasmuch as there is no "world government" or "world legislature," international law is not created the same way as domestic law. International law is found in a variety of sources, including

> "Travel is fatal to prejudice, bigotry, and narrow-mindedness . . . Broad, wholesome, charitable views of men and things cannot be acquired by vegetating in one little corner of the earth all one's lifetime."
>
> – **Mark Twain, American humorist (1857)**

FIGURE 13.1
Top 10 Trading Partners with the United States

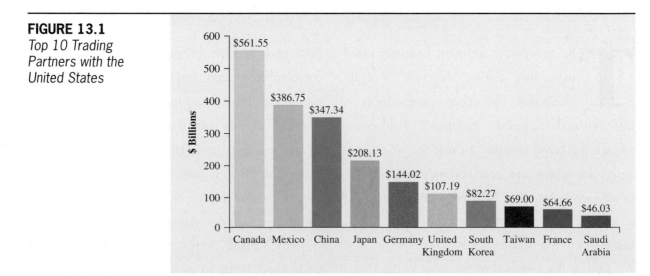

Source: *U.S. Census Bureau as of December 2007*

:: *sidebar* 13.1

What Are Corporate Codes of Conduct?

Corporate codes of conduct are policy statements adopted by companies to define ethical standards for their conduct. These are completely voluntary, often addressing topics such as:

- Forced labor.
- Child labor.
- Discrimination.
- Health and safety of workers.
- Freedom of association and collective bargaining.
- Hours of work, wages, benefits, and overtime compensation.
- Working conditions.
- Environmental issues.
- Monitoring and enforcement of the code of conduct.

Recognizing that there are different legal and cultural environments around the world, companies often develop a code of conduct to establish a foundation for their standards in international business. Seeking to promote global corporate citizenship, the United Nations developed the Global Compact, a voluntary code of conduct supported by companies and organizations around the world. For a list of participants, see www.globalcompact.org. Many major corporations engaging in global operations, including Microsoft, GAP, Inc., and Cisco Systems, Inc., also have supplier or vendor codes of conduct. These codes allow companies to set standards for their suppliers and vendors consistent with the companies' mission and values.

U.S. domestic law, national laws of other countries, international agreements, treaties, and even in what is called "customary international law." Customary international law involves principles that are widely practiced and acknowledged by many civilized nations to be law.

In the landmark case of *The Paquette Habana* (1900), the United States Supreme Court held that "[i]nternational law is part of our law, and must be ascertained and administered by the courts of justice of appropriate jurisdiction as often as questions of right depending upon it are duly presented for their determination."

International organizations, such as the United Nations, the World Trade Organization, and the European Union, directly impact international business transactions. Agreements entered into by the United States, including the Convention on the International Sale of Goods, the North American Free Trade Agreement, and the Dominican Republic-Central American Free Trade Agreement also affect the global sale of goods. These agreements facilitate trade and minimize risk for business.

1. SOURCES OF INTERNATIONAL LAW

What are the principles or rules of international law that apply to a particular contract or dispute? Generally, international law is classified as either **public international law** or **private international law**. Public international law examines relationships between nations and uses rules that are binding on all countries in the international community. Private international law examines relationships created by commercial transactions and utilizes international agreements, as well as the laws of nations to resolve business disputes. Business managers are primarily concerned with private international law issues.

The ICJ's hearings are open to the public, unless one of the parties asks for the proceedings to be *in camera* or the Court so decides. The hearings take place in the Great Hall of Justice in the Peace Palace, in The Hague.

Public International Law   Article 38 of the Statute of the **International Court of Justice (ICJ)** is the traditional place for ascertaining what is public international law. However, in contrast to what you learned in Chapter 1 regarding U.S. cases, the decisions made by the ICJ, the World Court, do not create binding rules of law or precedent in future cases.

The ICJ is the judicial branch of the United Nations and sits at The Hague in the Netherlands. It consists of 15 judges representing all of the world's major legal systems. The judges are elected by the U.N. General Assembly and the Security Council after having been nominated by national groups, not governments. No more than one judge may be a national of any country.

The ICJ has not been a major force in settling disputes since it began functioning in 1946. The ICJ renders, on average, only one contested decision per year and one advisory opinion every two years. There has been widespread reluctance to resort to the ICJ as a forum for resolving international disputes for several reasons. First, only countries have access to the Court. Private parties or corporations may not directly present claims before the Court. No device exists under U.S. law by which a firm or individual can compel the U.S. government to press a claim on its behalf before the ICJ. Furthermore, only countries that have submitted to the Court's jurisdiction may be parties, since there is no compulsory process for forcing a country to come before the Court. A country may choose to accept the Court's jurisdiction only when the use of the Court may suit its own interests. Moreover, the ICJ has no enforcement authority and must rely on diplomacy or economic sanctions against countries that breach international law. For these reasons, infractions of international law often are settled through diplomacy or arbitration, rather than by the presentation of formal charges to the ICJ.

Of course, deciding whether international law has been violated is often a very difficult question. Article 38 sets forth the following order of importance for determining what is international law in a given case:

> The Court, whose function is to decide in accordance with international law such disputes as are submitted to it, shall apply:
>
> a. *International Conventions*, whether general or particular, establishing rules expressly recognized by the contesting states;
> b. *International Custom*, as evidence of a general practice accepted as law;
> c. *The General Principles of Law* recognized by civilized nations;
> d. *Judicial Decisions and the Teachings of the Most Highly Qualified Publicists* of various nations, as subsidiary means for the determination of rules of law.

International Conventions are similar to legislation or statutes and represent formal agreements between nations. International Custom describes common legal practices followed by nations in working with each other over a long period of time. General Principles of Law may be found in national rules common to the countries in a dispute. Finally, Judicial Decisions and Teachings, although not binding, may be used for guidance in resolving a dispute. See Sidebar 13.2 for an example of an ICJ decision and the interplay with U.S. courts.

Private International Law   Private international law is represented by the laws of individual nations and the multilateral agreements developed between nations to provide mutual understanding and some degree

:: *sidebar* 13.2

Medellin v. Texas (2008): The U.S. Supreme Court and the International Court of Justice (ICJ)

What is the effect of an ICJ judgment in the United States? In a 6–3 ruling, the U.S. Supreme Court held that President Bush went too far when he decreed that the states must abide by a 2004 decision by the ICJ. The ICJ found that several dozen Mexican citizens sentenced to death in the United States had not been given the assistance of Mexican diplomats that they were entitled to under the Vienna Convention.

The case in question involved Jose Medellin, a onetime Houston gang member who took part in the rape and murder of two teenaged girls. After he was arrested, and read his Miranda Rights, Medellin confessed to the crimes, including revealing particularly egregious details. The conviction was challenged because law enforcement authorities failed to inform him of his right under the Vienna Convention.

In the majority opinion, Chief Justice Roberts states that neither the defendant nor his supporters "have identified a single nation that treats ICJ judgments as binding in domestic courts." In response, Mexico has asked the ICJ to declare that the United States "must provide review and reconsideration of the convictions and sentences" consistent with its 2004 decision.

---

of continuity to international business transactions. Even in purely domestic business deals, the law is rarely predictable or certain. When different national laws, languages, practices, and cultures are added to the transaction, the situation can become very unstable for international business.

International law can be complicated and a single business transaction can involve several companies in different nations. For example, a contract dispute between a Chinese manufacturer, an American wholesaler, and a Canadian retailer could potentially involve the law of all three countries. Which law controls? The answer could affect the outcome of the case. Determining which nation's court may hear the case can be difficult. For this reason, most international contracts contain choice of law and forum provisions to eliminate this uncertainty.

Do include choice of law and forum selection clauses in all international contracts.

2. INTERNATIONAL ORGANIZATIONS

Several international organizations play important roles in the development of political, economic, and legal rules for the conduct of international business. The two primary organizations are the United Nations and the World Trade Organization. Additionally, the European Union plays an important role in international trade.

United Nations Established after World War II, the **United Nations** has grown considerably from the 51 founding nations. Almost every country in the world is a member today. The Charter of the United Nations sets forth as its primary goal "to save succeeding generations from the scourge of war" and, to that end, authorizes "collective measures for the prevention and removal of threats to the peace, and for the suppression of acts of aggression or other breaches of the peace."

The General Assembly is composed of every nation represented in the United Nations and permits each country to cast one vote. The real power in the United Nations rests in the Security Council, which is composed of

Eight UN Millennium Development Goals:

1. Eradicate extreme poverty and hunger.
2. Achieve universal primary education.
3. Promote gender equality and empower women.
4. Reduce child mortality.
5. Improve maternal health.
6. Combat HIV/AIDS, malaria, and other diseases.
7. Ensure environmental sustainability.
8. Develop a global partnership for development.

15 member states. The Security Council has the power to authorize military action and to sever diplomatic relations with other nations. The five permanent members of the Council (United States, Russia, China, France, and United Kingdom) have veto power over any action proposed in the Council. France and Russia used the threat of a veto in 2003 to force the United States to go forward with the war in Iraq without clear United Nations' authority. Although the United States contended that its authority for war came from previously passed UN resolutions regarding Iraq, the U.S. government was disturbed by the veto threat. The failure of the United Nations to dictate the resolution of the U.S.-Iraq conflict created serious questions about the future authority and role of the United Nations in international conflicts.

A number of organizations affiliated with the United Nations have authority over activities that directly affect international business. The United Nations Commission on International Trade Law (UNCITRAL) was created in 1966 to develop standardized commercial practices and agreements. One of the documents drafted by UNCITRAL is the Convention on the International Sale of Goods, which is discussed in more detail later in this chapter. UNCITRAL has no authority to force any country to adopt any of the conventions or agreements that it proposes. The United Nations Conference on Trade and Development (UNCTAD) deals with international trade reform and the redistribution of income through trading with developing countries. UNCTAD drafted both the Transfer of Technology Code and the Restrictive Business Practices Code, which are largely ignored by most nations.

At the Bretton Woods Conference of 1944, two important institutions were also created under the auspices of the United Nations. The **International Monetary Fund (IMF)** encourages international trade by maintaining stable foreign exchange rates and works closely with commercial banks to promote orderly exchange policies with members. The **World Bank** promotes economic development in poor countries by making loans to finance necessary development projects and programs.

For more information about current projects at the World Bank and IMF, see www.worldbank.org/ and www.imf.org/.

> "The human spirit is indomitable. Each individual matters. The seeds of policies and innovations planted today can influence tomorrow. And free men and women can move the world."
>
> **–Robert B. Zoellick, president of the World Bank Group (2008)**

World Trade Organization Every nation has the right to establish its own trading policies and has its own national interests at stake when dealing with other nations. Ultimately, after years of economic conflict, many countries concluded that their own interests could be served best by liberalizing trade through reduced tariffs and free markets. The **General Agreement on Tariffs and Trade (GATT)** was originally signed by 23 countries after World War II and represented the determination of a war-weary world to open trade and end the protection of domestic industries. Since GATT was created in 1948, it has undergone eight major revisions, including the 1994 Uruguay Round, which culminated in the creation of the **World Trade Organization (WTO)** as an umbrella organization to regulate world trade. The 1994 agreement was signed by 125 countries.

The WTO is an international organization which, as its primary purpose, seeks to resolve trade disputes between member nations. The WTO administers the GATT but does not have the authority to regulate world trade in any manner it desires. The WTO expects nations to avoid unilateral trade wars and rely on GATT dispute settlement procedures to avert conflict. At the heart of the 1994 Uruguay Round are several enduring GATT principles:

1. Nondiscrimination (treating all member countries equally with respect to trade).
2. National treatment (countries not favoring their domestic products over imported products.
3. Elimination of trade barriers (reducing tariffs and other restrictions in foreign products).

Under the WTO, existing tariffs are reduced and the agreement extends GATT rules to new areas such as agricultural products and service industries. The WTO further restricts tariffs on textiles, apparel, and forest products. It also requires countries to upgrade their intellectual property laws to protect patents and copyrights and to guard against the piracy of items such as computer software and videotapes.

Another important aspect of the WTO is the **Agreement on Trade-Related Aspects of Intellectual Property Rights (TRIPS),** including trade in counterfeit goods. Recognizing that there are widely different standards for the protection of intellectual property, as well as a lack of a multilateral framework of rules for dealing with counterfeit goods, the WTO directly addressed this issue with TRIPS. This agreement discusses the applicability of GATT principles and those of relevant international property agreements in an effort to strengthen the protection of intellectual property in the international sphere.

The WTO has the power to hear disputes involving member states. The United States has been involved in a number of disputes. For example, the United States brought an action against the European Union claiming that the European-wide restrictions on genetically modified food violate WTO rules. Additionally, the United States brought a successful challenge against Mexico; the WTO held that Mexico's beverage tax on soft drinks made with imported sweeteners is discriminatory. Under the beverage tax, soft drinks made with cane sugar are tax exempt. Because the beverage tax discriminates against U.S. products, it is contrary to WTO rules.

If a nation does not comply with a WTO ruling, the organization has the power to impose sanctions. Like any international institution, compliance by the most powerful trading nations is necessary to give the WTO credibility.

The WTO faces opposition from antiglobalization protesters. There are many reasons to support the WTO and the important role it plays in trade. Concerns, however, are raised by opponents who are concerned about human rights, environmental, and labor issues. Tensions between developed and developing nations are hindering negotiations to cut tariffs. Overall, the future of the WTO is uncertain. The cooperation of member states is critical to its success in liberalizing trade.

The WTO is the only global international trade organization dealing with the rules of trade between nations.

The European Union The European Union is an economic and political partnership between 27 democratic European countries. In 1957, six European countries, Belgium, France, Germany, Luxembourg, and the Netherlands signed the Treaty of Rome, creating the European Community. Six successive enlargements created the **European Union (EU),** as it is known today. See Table 13.1 for a complete list of states, accession dates, and those countries using the euro as legal tender. Negotiations are ongoing with Croatia, the Republic of Macedonia, and Turkey about possible membership in the EU.

table 13.1 :: Twenty-Seven European Union Member States	
Original Members 1957	Belgium €
	France €
	Germany €
	Italy €
	Luxembourg €
	Netherlands €
Accession in 1973	Denmark
	Ireland €
	United Kingdom
Accession in 1981	Greece €
Accession in 1986	Portugal €
	Spain €
Accession in 1995	Austria €
	Finland €
	Sweden
Accession in 2004	Cyprus €
	Czech Republic
	Estonia
	Hungary
	Latvia
	Lithuania
	Malta €
	Poland
	Slovakia
	Slovenia €
Accession in 2007	Bulgaria
	Romania

€ *Notes member countries in which the euro is the legal tender.*

Europe's mission in the twenty-first century is to:

- Provide peace, prosperity, and stability for its peoples.
- Overcome the divisions on the continent.
- Ensure that its people live in safety.
- Promote balanced economic and social development.
- Meet the challenges of globalization and preserve the diversity of the peoples of Europe.
- Uphold the values that Europeans share, such as sustainable development and a sound environment, respect for human rights, and the social market economy.

For more detailed information about these goals, see the official website of the EU at http://europa.eu.

The major institutions of the EU are the Council of Ministers, the Commission, the Parliament, and the Court of Justice. The Council is composed of one representative from each member state. The Council coordinates the policies of the member states in a variety of areas from economics to foreign affairs. The Commission consists of individuals who represent the will and interests of the entire EU, rather than specific national concerns. Elected representatives from each member state compose the Parliament, which plays an active role in drafting legislation that has an impact on the daily lives of its citizens. The Parliament, for example, has addressed environmental protection, consumer rights, equal opportunities, transport, and the free movement of workers, capital, services, and goods. Parliament also has joint power with the Council over the annual budget of the European Union. Finally, the Court of Justice decides the nature and parameters of EU law. Justices are appointed by the Council, and each member state has a justice seated on the Court.

> The aims of the European Union are: "Peace, prosperity and freedom for its 495 million citizens — in a fairer, safer world."

3. MAJOR AGREEMENTS AFFECTING TRADE

In addition to the international institutions discussed in this chapter, a number of international agreements also facilitate trade.

> The U.S. Trade Representative is a Cabinet member who serves as the president's principal trade adviser, negotiator, and spokesperson on trade issues. See www.ustr.gov for current trade news.

Convention on the International Sale of Goods The **Convention on the International Sale of Goods (CISG)** outlines standard international practices for the sale of goods. It took several years to develop, and represents many compromises among nations that follow a variety of practices in the area of contracts. Effective in 1988, it has been adopted by the United States and most of the other countries that engage in large quantities of international trade. The CISG represents the cumulative work of over 60 nations and international groups and is widely accepted around the globe.

The CISG applies to contracts for the commercial sale of goods (consumer sales for personal, family, or household use are excluded) between parties whose businesses are located in different nations, provided that those nations have adopted the convention. If a commercial seller or buyer in the United States, for example, contracts for the sale of goods with a company located in another country that also has adopted the CISG, the convention and not the U.S. Uniform Commercial Code (UCC) applies to the transaction.

Under the CISG, a significant degree of freedom is provided for the individual parties in an international contract. The parties may negotiate contract terms as they deem fit for their business practices and may, if desired, even opt out of the CISG entirely. One of the most interesting provisions in the CISG includes a rule that contracts for the sale of goods need not be in writing. The CISG also provides that in contract negotiations an acceptance that contains new provisions that do not materially alter the terms of the offer becomes part of the contract, unless the offeror promptly objects to the change. The CISG sets forth the fundamental elements that will materially alter a contract such as price, payment, quality, and quantity of the goods, place and time of delivery of goods, provisions related to one party's liability to the other, and methods for settling disputes. Since international transactions typically involve sophisticated parties, the CISG also makes it easier to disclaim warranties on goods than under traditional U.S. law. The CISG does not resolve all areas of contract law; parties are still subject

> "We must continue to open markets if we want our exports to grow. . . . Open markets create higher paying jobs and help support the prosperity of American workers, farmers, and entrepreneurs."
>
> **–Susan C. Schwab, U.S. Trade Representative (2008)**

to local laws and customs, which makes international agreements complex and tricky to negotiate.

North American Free Trade Agreement   The passage of the **North American Free Trade Agreement (NAFTA)** in 1993 set in motion increased trade and foreign investment and opportunities for economic growth in the United States, Mexico, and Canada. Free trade is at the core of NAFTA, through the reduction and eventual elimination of tariffs and other barriers to business between these three countries. NAFTA also provides for a dispute settlement mechanism that makes it easier to resolve trade disputes between the three countries. Based upon concerns that cheap labor and poor environmental controls might cause U.S. firms to relocate to Mexico, side agreements also were reached to improve labor rights and environmental protection in Mexico. Since its enactment, NAFTA has expanded shipments of U.S. goods to Mexico and Canada, as well as Mexican and Canadian exports to the United States.

Jimmy Carter supported the passage of CAFTA-DR as a "chance to reinforce democracies in the region."

Central America-Dominican Republic Free Trade Agreement   Similar to NAFTA, the passage of the **Central America-Dominican Republic Free Trade Agreement (CAFTA-DR)** in 2005 opened up many opportunities for business in Central America. CAFTA-DR is a comprehensive trade agreement between Costa Rica, El Salvador, Guatemala, Honduras, Nicaragua, the Dominican Republic, and the United States. This agreement is designed to eliminate the barriers on products trades between the member countries. Prior to CAFTA-DR, many exports of American goods to Central America faced high tariffs. This trade agreement is a step to create a fairer playing field for American exports.

Pending Free Trade Agreements   The United States is continually seeking opportunities to open global trade. Currently, there are free trade agreements pending in three key markets: Colombia, Panama, and South Korea. The agreements are fully negotiated and are pending Congressional approval. According to the U.S. Trade Representative's office, there are five major reasons to approve the U.S.-Colombia Free Trade Agreement: (1) To open a significant new export market; (2) to level the playing field for American business,

concept :: *summary*

International Law and Organizations

1. International law is classified as either public or private.
2. The International Court of Justice is the traditional place for determining public international law.
3. The World Trade Organization regulates world trade for member nations.
4. The Convention on the International Sale of Goods governs international practices for the sale of goods.
5. The European Union has evolved into the most important economic force in Europe.
6. The North American Free Trade Agreement has substantially expanded trade with Mexico and Canada.

farmers, ranchers, and workers; (3) to strengthen peace, democracy, freedom, and reform; (4) to promote economic growth and poverty reduction; and (5) to anchor longstanding ties with a vital regional ally. Opponents to the Colombia agreement argue that the agreement does not contain adequate provisions to address labor concerns and human rights violations, including violence against union members.

:: Methods of Transacting International Business

A U.S. business that wants to engage in international trade is presented with an almost limitless array of possibilities. Choosing a method of doing business in foreign countries not only requires understanding the factors normally involved in selecting an organization and operating a business domestically but also demands an appreciation of the international trade perspective. Depending upon the country, type of export, and amount of export involved in a particular transaction, international trade may involve direct foreign sales, licensing agreements, franchise agreements, or direct foreign investment.

4. FOREIGN SALES

The most common approach for a manufacturer to use when trying to enter foreign markets is to sell goods directly to buyers located in other countries. However, with foreign sales, increased uncertainty over the ability to enforce the buyer's promise to pay for goods often requires that more complex arrangements for payment be made than with the usual domestic sale. International sales involve many risky legal issues. Commonly, an **irrevocable letter of credit** is used to ensure payment. Transactions using such a letter involve, in addition to a seller and buyer, an *issuing bank* in the buyer's country. The buyer obtains a commitment from the bank to advance (pay) a specified amount (i.e., the price of the goods) upon receipt, from the carrier, of a **bill of lading,** stating that the goods have been shipped. The issuing bank's commitment to pay is given, not to the seller directly, but to a *confirming bank* located in the United States from which the seller obtains payment. The confirming bank forwards the bill of lading to the issuing bank in order to obtain reimbursement of the funds that have been paid to the seller. The issuing bank releases the bill of lading to the buyer after it has been paid, and with the bill of lading the buyer is able to obtain the goods from the carrier. Use of a letter of credit in the transaction thus reduces the uncertainties involved. The buyer need not pay the seller for goods prior to shipment, and the seller can obtain payment for the goods immediately upon shipment.

There is no room in documentary transactions for substantial performance. All of the duties and responsibilities of parties must be evaluated based upon the documents tendered, and these documents must comply *strictly* with the letter of credit. The tradition and purpose of the letter of credit in international transactions is demonstrated in Case 13.1, where the issue of notice became the central issue for the court.

Do learn more about the traditions, culture, and etiquette of a host nation before you travel, including business card protocol.

VOEST-ALPINE TRADING USA v. BANK OF CHINA
288 F. 3d 262 (5th Cir. 2002)

Jiangyin Foreign Trade Corporation ("JFTC"), a Chinese company, agreed to purchase 1,000 metric tons of styrene monomer from Voest-Alpine Trading USA Corporation ("Voest-Alpine"), an American company. At Voest-Alpine's insistence, JFTC obtained a letter of credit from the Bank of China for the purchase price of $1.2 million. The letter of credit provided for payment to Voest-Alpine after it delivered the monomer and presented several designated documents to the Bank of China. By the time Voest-Alpine was ready to ship its product, the market price of styrene monomer had dropped significantly from the original contract price. JFTC asked for a price concession, but Voest-Alpine refused. After shipping the monomer to JFTC, Voest-Alpine presented the documents specified in the letter of credit to Texas Commerce Bank ("TCB"), which would forward the documents to the Bank of China. TCB noted several discrepancies between what Voest-Alpine presented and what the letter of credit required. Because it did not believe any of the discrepancies would warrant refusal to pay, Voest-Alpine instructed TCB to present the documents to the Bank of China "on approval," meaning that JFTC would be asked to waive the problems.

The Bank of China received the documents. The bank notified TCB that the documents contained several discrepancies and that it would contact JFTC about acceptance. On August 15, 1995, TCB, acting on behalf of Voest-Alpine, responded that the alleged discrepancies were not adequate grounds for dishonoring the letter of credit and demanded payment. On August 19, the Bank of China reiterated its position that the documents were insufficient and stated: "Now the discrepant documents may have us refuse to take up the documents according to article 14(B) of UCP 500." JFTC refused to waive the discrepancies, and the Bank of China returned the documents to TCB on September 18, 1995.

CLEMENT, J.: Voest-Alpine filed the instant action for payment on the letter of credit.

The Bank of China's primary contention on appeal is that the district court erroneously concluded that the bank failed to provide proper notice of refusal to Voest-Alpine. In order to reject payment on a letter of credit, an issuing bank must give notice of refusal to the beneficiary no later than the close of the seventh banking day following the day of receipt of the [presentation] documents. If the Bank of China did not provide timely notice, it must honor the letter of credit despite any questions as to Voest-Alpine's compliance.

The Bank of China received Voest-Alpine's documents on August 9. Since August 12 and 13 were Chinese banking holidays, the deadline for giving notice of dishonor was August 18. The Bank of China's only communication before the deadline was its telex of August 11. Accordingly, the issue is whether that telex provided notice of refusal. The bank's August 11 telex stated:

> Upon checking documents, we note the following discrepancy:
>
> 1. Late presentation.
> 2. Beneficiary's name is differ (*sic*) from L/C.
> 3. B/L should be presented in three originals (*sic*) i/o duplicate, triplicate.
> 4. Inv. P/L. and cert. Of origin not showing "original."
> 5. The date of surver (*sic*) report later than B/L date.
> 6. Wrong L/C no. in fax copy.
> 7. Wrong destination in cert. Of origin and beneficiary's cert.
>
> We are contacting the applicant for acceptance of the relative discrepancy. Holding documents at your risk and disposal.

The district court found that the telex failed to provide notice of refusal because (1) the bank did not explicitly state that it was rejecting the documents; (2) the bank's statement that it would contact JFTC about accepting the documents despite the discrepancies holds open the possibility of acceptance upon waiver and indicates that the Bank of China has not refused the documents; and (3) the Bank of China did not even mention refusal until its August 19 telex in which it wrote: "Now the discrepant documents may have us refuse to take up the documents according to article 14(B) of UCP 500." In light of these circumstances, the district court concluded that the August 11 telex was merely a status report, the bank would not reject the documents until after it consulted JFTC, and the bank did not raise the possibility of refusing payment on the letter of credit until August 19. Accordingly, the district court held that the Bank of China forfeited its right to refuse the documents and was obligated to pay Voest-Alpine.

We find ample evidence supporting the district court's decision. The court's determination that the August 11 telex did not reject the letter of credit is based primarily on the Bank of China's offer to obtain waiver from JFTC. The offer to solicit a waiver, the district court reasoned, suggests that the documents had not in fact been refused but might be accepted after consultation with JFTC. In reaching this conclusion, the district court relied heavily on the testimony of Voest-Alpine's expert witness on international standard banking practices. [The expert] testified that the bank's telex would have given adequate notice had it not contained the waiver clause. The waiver clause, he explained, deviated from the norm and introduced an ambiguity that converted what might otherwise have been a notice of refusal into nothing more than a status report. Faced with this evidence, the district court correctly decided that the Bank of China noted discrepancies in the documents, and, instead of rejecting the letter of credit outright, contacted JFTC for waiver.

Viewed in the context of standard international banking practices, the Bank of China's notice of refusal was clearly deficient. The bank failed to use the standard language for refusal, failed to comply with generally accepted trade usages, and created ambiguity by offering to contact JFTC about waiver, thus leaving open the possibility that the allegedly discrepant documents might have been accepted at a future date. Accordingly, the district court properly found that the August 11 telex was not an adequate notice of refusal. Since we agree with the district court that the bank failed to provide timely notice, we need not reach the question of whether the alleged discrepancies warranted refusal.

The Bank of China failed to provide Voest-Alpine with adequate notice that it was refusing payment on the letter of credit. Without a valid excuse for nonpayment, the bank is liable for the full amount of the letter of credit and for VoestAlpine's legal fees. Accordingly, we affirm the judgment of the district court.

Affirmed.

:: CASE QUESTIONS

1. Why is the issue of "timely notice" so important in the case?
2. What is the primary importance of a letter of credit?
3. Why did the court rule against Bank of China?

5. LICENSES OR FRANCHISES

In appropriate circumstances, a domestic firm may choose to grant a foreign firm the means to produce and sell its product. The typical method for controlling these transfers of information is the **license** or **franchise** contract. In this manner, intangible property rights, such as patents, copyrights, trademarks, or manufacturing processes, are transferred in exchange for royalties in the foreign country. A licensing arrangement allows the international business to enter a foreign market without any direct foreign investment. Licensing often is used as a transitional technique for firms expanding international operations since the risks are greater than with foreign sales but considerably less than with direct foreign investment. Licensing and franchise agreements also must follow the local laws where they operate.

Licensing technology or the sale of a product to a foreign firm is a way to expand the company's market without the need for substantial capital. The foreign firm may agree to this arrangement because it lacks sufficient research and development capability or the management skills or marketing strategies to promote the product alone. Of course, as with all international trade agreements, there is some level of risk. The licensor must take care to restrict the use of the product or technology to agreed-upon geographic areas

Do take steps to protect your intellectual property from infringement in the global marketplace.

McDonald's has franchises in 118 countries around the world, and more than 70 percent of its restaurants are owned and operated by independent men and women.

and must take adequate steps to protect the confidential information that is licensed to the foreign firm so that third parties cannot exploit it.

6. DIRECT FOREIGN INVESTMENT

As a business increases its level of international trade, it may find that creation of a **foreign subsidiary** is necessary. Most countries will permit a foreign firm to conduct business only if a national (individual or firm) of the host country is designated as its legal representative. Since this designation may create difficulties in control and result in unnecessary expense, the usual practice for multinational corporations is to create a foreign subsidiary in the host country. The form of subsidiary most closely resembling a U.S. corporation is known as a *société anonyme (S.A.)* or, in German-speaking countries, an *Aktiengesellschaft (AG)*. Other forms of subsidiaries may also exist that have characteristics of limited liability of the owners and fewer formalities in their creation and operation.

Creation of a foreign subsidiary may pose considerable risk to the domestic parent firm by subjecting it to foreign laws and the jurisdiction of foreign courts. An industrial accident in Bhopal, India, where hundreds of people were killed and thousands injured as a result of toxic gas leaks from a chemical plant, resulted in lawsuits against both the Indian subsidiary corporation and Union Carbide, the parent firm in the United States. Union Carbide agreed to pay more than $450 million to settle outstanding claims and compensate the victims of the disaster.

In many instances, however, the only legal or political means a firm has to invest directly in a foreign country is to engage in a **joint venture** with an entity from that host country. A host country's participant may be a private enterprise or, especially in developing countries, a government agency or government-owned corporation. Many foreign countries favor joint ventures because they allow local individuals and firms to participate in the benefits of economic growth and decrease the risk of foreign domination of local industry. Many of the developing countries require that the local partner have majority equity control of the venture and also insist on joint ventures with government participation.

:: Risks Involved in International Trade

Because international trade means dealing with different legal systems, cultures, and ways of doing business, there are a number of risks involved. For example, when a firm expends globally, a host of potential risks and concerns are raised, such as:

- Are property rights enforced?
- Will foreign courts uphold the validity of contracts?
- Is intellectual property protected or is it vulnerable to infringement?
- Are there export or import restrictions on the firm's products?
- Are there risks associated with political instability and/or war?
- What U.S. laws have an "extraterritorial" reach?
- What international trade agreements will affect the firm's expansion?
- What national laws (e.g., labor and environmental) affect the firm?
- How should language and cultural differences be bridged?

See Sidebar 13.3 as an example of problems that can arise with outsourcing manufacturing. This section addresses specific concerns about expropriation and nationalization, export controls, and pressures for bribes.

7. EXPROPRIATION AND NATIONALIZATION

If a domestic firm is involved in a foreign country to the extent of locating assets there (whether through branches, subsidiaries, joint ventures, or otherwise), it may be subject to the ultimate legal and political risk of international business activity—expropriation. **Expropriation,** as used in the context of international law, is the seizure of foreign-owned property by a government. When the owners are not fairly compensated, the expropriation is also considered to be a *confiscation* of property. Usually, the expropriating government also assumes ownership of the property, so the process includes **nationalization** as well. In the United States, the counterpart of expropriation is called the *power of eminent domain*.

This power of a government to take private property is regarded as inherent; yet it is subject to restraints upon its exercise. The U.S. Constitution (as well as the constitutions and laws of most nations) prohibits the government from seizing private property except for "public purposes" and upon the payment of "just compensation."

However, the extent of such protection varies widely. Treaties (or other agreements) between the United States and other countries provide additional protection against uncompensated takings of property. It is customary for international law to recognize the right of governments to expropriate the property of foreigners only when accompanied by "prompt, adequate, and effective compensation." This so-called modern traditional theory is accepted by most nations as the international standard and requires full compensation to the investor including fair market value as a going concern. See Sidebar 13.4 for an example of nationalization.

Creeping expropriation is a series of acts, such as taxes, regulation, or other changes in law that have an expropriatory effect, reducing or eliminating foreign investments.

:: *sidebar* 13.4

ExxonMobil Corp. v. Petróleos de Venezuela: Chavez and Nationalization of the Oil Industry

Venezuelan President Hugo Chavez nationalized the last privately run oil fields in the country in 2007. The government took over four oil projects run by some of the world's biggest petroleum companies, including ExxonMobil Corp. In his announcement of the takeover, Chavez told cheering workers that foreign oil companies damaged Venezuela's national interests and that reclaiming them represented an historic victory.

Exxon is not taking the loss without a fight. Exxon brought an action against state-owned Petróleos de Venezuela (PDVSA)

in the United States. In early 2008, Exxon won a $315 million freeze of PDVSA's assets, as well as a ruling blocking PDVSA's transactions with Britain and the Netherlands, affecting as much as $12 billion in assets. Ultimately, what compensation will Exxon receive for the loss of its assets in Venezuela? Will other foreign oil companies whose assets were nationalized in Venezuela be compensated? The matter is far from resolved and has far-reaching political implications.

Chavez is also taking steps to nationalize utilities, the telecommunications industry, and the Venezuelan subsidiary of Mexican cement company Cemex SEB.

8. EXPORT CONTROLS

Exports from the United States to countries such as Cuba, Iran, Libya, North Korea, Sudan, and Syria are restricted.

Query: Should the U.S. lift its trade embargo with Cuba? The EU agreed to lift its sanctions against Cuba in June 2008.

Another risk involved in doing business abroad is **export controls** placed on the sale of U.S. strategic products and technology abroad. Controlling the export of such items has been the cornerstone of Western policy since the conclusion of World War II. Most of the attention was focused on preventing the acquisition of technology by the former Soviet Union and its allies. However, since the end of the Cold War the policy rationale behind export controls has been drawn into question, with many Western countries contending they should be eliminated to increase trading opportunities with Russia, China, Eastern Europe, and the Middle East. Indeed, the Coordinating Committee for Multilateral Export Controls (COCOM), an organization created by the major Western nations (including the United States, Europe, and Japan) to control exports, came to an end in 1994.

Since that time, a new organization supported by 33 countries, known as the Wassanaar Arrangement, has come into existence to help control the spread of both military and dual-use technology to unstable areas of the world. Participating nations seek, through their national policies, to ensure that transfer of conventional arms and strategic goods and technologies do not destabilize regional and international security. The 2002 plenary meeting of the Wassanaar Arrangement, held in Vienna, resulted in several significant initiatives to combat terrorism. The member countries agreed on several measures aimed at intensifying cooperation to prevent terrorist groups and individuals from acquiring arms and strategic goods and technologies.

The U.S. export control system currently is regulated by the Department of State and the Department of Commerce under authority provided by the Export Administration Act and the Arms Export Control Act. The Department of Defense also plays a key role in determining the technology to be controlled as does the U.S. Customs Service in the enforcement of the controls. Significant criminal and administrative sanctions may be imposed upon corporations and individuals convicted of violating the law.

According to the U.S. Export Control and Related Border Security Assistance (EXBS) Program, exporters should be aware of the following "red flags":

- A *customer* is reluctant to provide end-use/user information; is willing to pay cash for high-value shipments; has little background in the relevant business; declines normal warranty/service/installation; or orders products incompatible with the business.

- A *shipment* involves a private intermediary in a major weapons sale; shipments are directed to entities with no connection to the buyer; requests for packing are inconsistent with the normal mode of shipping; or circuitous or illogical routing.

- *The end-user* requests equipment inconsistent with inventory; spare parts in excess of projected needs; the end-use is at variance with standard practices; a middleman from a third country places the order; or the end-user refuses to state whether the goods are for domestic use, export, or re-export.

In 2000, the U.S. government extended the Export Administration Act and raised the penalties for violators. The export control agenda for the twenty-first century remains focused on maintaining national security and reducing the proliferation of weapons, while also facilitating U.S. competitiveness in the global economy.

The successful prosecution of two leading American aerospace companies, Hughes Electronics and Boeing Satellite Systems, illustrates the government's commitment to vigorous export control to prevent harmful proliferation of weapons. The companies paid a record $32 million in penalties to settle charges in connection with 123 alleged violations of export control laws regarding the transfer of rocket and satellite data to China.

However, the future of the U.S. system remains in doubt with many proposals pending in Congress to reform and limit the current export control system. Over the past several years, these controls have become an extremely controversial topic in the international business community. Export controls make successful business deals more difficult because foreign buyers may be reluctant to trade with a U.S. firm due to the red tape involved in obtaining governmental approval as compared with Europe or Japan.

9. PRESSURES FOR BRIBES

Following widespread disclosure of scandalous payments by domestic firms to officials of foreign government, Congress enacted the **Foreign Corrupt Practices Act (FCPA)** in 1977. The law is designed to stop bribery of foreign officials and to prohibit U.S. citizens and companies from making payments to foreign officials whose duties are not "essentially ministerial or clerical" for the purpose of obtaining business.

This statute has two principal requirements:

1. Financial records and accounts must be kept "which, in reasonable detail, accurately and fairly reflect the transactions and dispositions of assets" of the business.

2. The business must "devise and maintain a system of internal accounting controls sufficient to provide reasonable assurances" that transactions are being carried out in accordance with management's authorization.

These provisions are intended to correct the previously widespread practice of accounting for bribes as commission payments, payments for services, or other normal business expenses and then illegally deducting the payments on income tax returns.

Many legal observers criticized the FCPA for creating a significantly chilling effect on U.S. companies seeking business in many developing countries where under-the-table payments to government officials are an accepted practice. Indeed, many civil servants in other nations are expected to supplement their salaries in this manner. The U.S. prohibition of such payments is perceived as an attempt to impose U.S. standards of morality in other parts of the world, and it has caused resentment and discrimination against U.S. businesses. Moreover, the FCPA arguably puts U.S. firms at a competitive disadvantage with businesses in other countries that are not operating under similar constraints.

As a result of intensive lobbying by the U.S. business community, Congress amended the FCPA in 1988 in an effort to eliminate ambiguity and uncertainty over what constitutes improper conduct. Although the law still prohibits bribery and corruption, the amendments establish clearer standards for firms to follow in overseas operations. The amendments limit criminal liability for violations of accounting standards to those who "knowingly" circumvent accounting controls or falsify records of corporate payments and transactions. The amendments also clarify the level of detail required in such record keeping and should improve compliance by businesses and enforcement by the government. Moreover, under the new law otherwise prohibited payments to foreign officials may be defended if they were legal under the written laws of the host country or if they cover "reasonable and bona fide" expenses associated with the promotion of the product and the completion of the contract (see Table 13.2).

The FCPA also prohibits corrupt payments through intermediaries. It is unlawful to make a payment to a third party, while knowing that all or a portion of the payment will go directly or indirectly to a foreign official. The term *knowing* includes conscious disregard and deliberate indifference. Additionally, the antibribery provisions of the FCPA apply to foreign firms and persons who take action in furtherance of a corrupt payment while in the United States.

Criminal penalties may be imposed for violations of the FCPA: corporations and other business entities are subject to a fine of up to $2,000,000; officers, directors, stockholders, employees, and agents are subject to a fine of up to $100,000 and imprisonment for up to five years. Fines imposed on individuals may *not* be paid by their employer or principal. The attorney general or the SEC, as appropriate, may also bring a civil action for fines against any

table 13.2 :: FCPA: Legal or Permissible Payments

The following payments are permissible under the FCPA:

"Facilitating," "expediting," or "grease" payments for "routine government action." Examples include obtaining permits, licenses, or other official documents; processing governmental papers (e.g., visas and work orders); providing police protection; loading and unloading cargo; and scheduling inspections associated with contract performance or transit of goods across country.

Any payments permitted under the written laws of the foreign country.

Travel expenses of a foreign official for the purpose of demonstrating a product or for performing a contractual obligation.

firm, as well as any officer, director, employee, or agent of a firm or stockholder acting on behalf of the firm who violates the antibribery provisions. The conduct that violates the antibribery provisions of the FCPA may also give rise to a private cause of action for treble damages under the Racketeer Influenced and Corrupt Organizations Act (RICO). For example, a RICO action could be brought by a competitor who alleges that the bribery caused the defendant to obtain a foreign contract. See Sidebar 13.5 for examples of successful FCPA prosecutions.

:: *sidebar* 13.5

FCPA Prosecutions: U.S. Government Success Stories

Baker Hughes Services International paid $44 million following accusations that the company used bribes to win an oil fields contract in Kazakhstan.

Wilbros Group Inc. paid $32.3 million in connection with improper payments made to Nigerian and Ecuadorian officials.

Statoil (now Statoill Iydro) paid $18 million in penalties (without admitting guilt) for allegedly paying bribes in Iran.

AGA Medical Corporation paid $2 million for causing improper payments to be made through its Chinese distributor to physicians employed by Chinese government owned or controlled hospitals and officials in the Chinese State Intellectual Property Office.

Faro Technologies Inc. paid $1.1 million as part of a nonprosecution agreement for FCPA violations arising from China operations.

Pending Investigation: German conglomerate **Siemens AG**, which allegedly doled out questionable payments totaling $1.9 billion worldwide to obtain business. The U.S. Department of Justice and the Securities Exchange Commission is investigating Siemens transactions in many countries, including China, Hungary, Indonesia, Israel, Italy, Norway, and Russia. In Germany, Siemens has already paid $290 million in fines. According to Joe Kaesar, finance chief of Siemens, the company's "control system was very fragmented . . . There were a number of red flags" which were not checked, including high payments to individuals. Siemens has already paid New York-based law firm Debevoise & Plimpton $500 million on its own internal investigation.

concept :: *summary*

Risks Involved in International Trade

1. Expropriation and nationalization are risks involved in international business.
2. Expert controls seek to balance national security interests against global trade.
3. The Foreign Corrupt Practices Act seeks to stop the bribery of foreign government officials.

:: Resolving International Disputes

International law can be complicated, and a single business transaction may involve several companies in different nations. For example, a contract dispute between a Chinese manufacturer, an American wholesaler, and a Canadian retailer could potentially involve the law of all three countries. Which law controls? What jurisdiction has the power to resolve the dispute? The answers to these questions could affect the outcome of the case. As such, most international contracts contain choice of law and forum provisions to eliminate this uncertainty. This section addresses the limitations on suing foreign governments in the United States, issues raised when suing foreign firms in the United States, and international arbitration options. See Sidebar 13.6 for an example of multiple levels of liability for a U.S. company.

:: *sidebar* 13.6

Chiquita Brands International: Payments to Death Squads for "Protection"

Chiquita Brands International pled guilty to doing business with the United Self-Defense Forces of Colombia (UAC), a right-wing paramilitary group in Colombia. Prosecutors said the banana company made $1.7 million in "protection payments" to this death squad, which is reportedly responsible for some of Colombia's worst massacres. In 2001, the U.S. State Department declared that UAC was an "international terrorist group," making it a violation of U.S. law to conduct business with the group. To settle the charges, Chiquita paid $25 million, arguing that it had no

choice but to pay protection money to prevent the UAC from turning death squads loose on its banana workers.

Families of over 350 people thought to have been killed by UAC are suing Chiquita in U.S. federal court seeking $7.86 billion in civil damages. The families claim that Chiquita aided and abetted terrorism, war crimes, and crimes against humanity because of its financial support of UAC.

Colombia's attorney general has also threatened to seek extradition of eight Chiquita executives to face criminal prosecution.

10. SUING FOREIGN GOVERNMENTS IN THE UNITED STATES

The doctrine of **sovereign immunity** provides that a foreign sovereign is immune from suit in the United States. Under the doctrine of sovereign immunity, the foreign sovereign claims to be immune from suit entirely based on its status as a state.

Until approximately 1952, this notion was absolute. From 1952 until 1976, U.S. courts adhered to a *restrictive theory* under which immunity existed with regard to sovereign or public acts but not with regard to private or commercial acts. In 1976, Congress enacted the **Foreign Sovereign Immunities Act (FSIA)**, which codifies this restrictive theory and rejects immunity for *commercial acts* carried on in the United States or having direct effects in this country.

The Supreme Court held that the doctrine should not be extended to foreign governments acting in a commercial capacity and "should not be extended to include the repudiation of a purely commercial obligation owed by a foreign sovereign or by one of its commercial instrumentalities." This interpretation recognizes that governments also may act in a private or commercial capacity and, when doing so, will be subjected to the same rules of law as are applicable to private individuals. A nationalization of assets, however, probably will be considered an act in the "public interest" and immune from suit under the FSIA. Case 13.2 demonstrates the limitations of the FSIA.

Sovereignty is defined as the supreme, absolute, and uncontrollable power by which any state is governed.

DOLE FOOD COMPANY v. DEAD SEA BROMINE CO. AND BROMINE COMPOUNDS, LTD.
538 U.S. 463 (2003)

The plaintiffs, a group of farm workers from Latin America, filed a state-court action against Dole Food Company and others alleging injury from chemical exposure. The Dole Company sued Dead Sea Bromine Co. and Bromine Compounds, Ltd. (collectively, the Dead Sea Companies) claiming that Dead Sea Companies would be liable if Dole lost the case. The Dole Company removed the action to federal court, arguing that the federal common law of foreign relations provided federal-question jurisdiction. Dead Sea Companies claimed they could not be sued because they were acting as an instrumentality of Israel.

KENNEDY, J.: Foreign states may invoke certain rights and immunities in litigation under the *Foreign Sovereign Immunities Act.* Some of the Act's provisions also may be invoked by a corporate entity that is an "instrumentality" of a foreign state as defined by the Act. The corporate entities in this action claim instrumentality status to invoke the Act's provisions allowing removal of state-court actions to federal court. As the action comes to us, it presents two questions. The first is whether a corporate subsidiary can claim instrumentality status where the foreign state does not own a majority of its shares but does own a majority of the shares of a corporate parent one or more tiers above the subsidiary. The second question is whether a corporation's instrumentality status is defined as of the time an alleged tort or other actionable wrong occurred or, on the other hand, at the time suit is filed.

The FSIA defines "foreign state" to include an "agency or instrumentality of a foreign state."

The lower court resolved the question of the FSIA's applicability by holding that a subsidiary of an instrumentality is not itself entitled to instrumentality status. Its holding was correct.

The State of Israel did not have direct ownership of shares in either of the Dead Sea Companies at any time pertinent to this suit. Rather, these companies were, at various times, separated from the State of Israel by one or more intermediate corporate tiers. For example, Israel wholly owned a company called Israeli Chemicals, Ltd.; which owned a majority of shares in another company called Dead Sea Works, Ltd.; which owned a majority of shares in Dead Sea Bromine Co., Ltd.; which owned a majority of shares in Bromine Compounds, Ltd.

The Dead Sea Companies, as indirect subsidiaries of the State of Israel, were not instrumentalities of Israel under the FSIA at any time. Those companies cannot come within the statutory language which grants status as an instrumentality of a foreign state to an entity a majority of whose shares or other ownership interest is owned by a foreign state or political subdivision thereof. We hold that only direct ownership of a majority of shares by the foreign state satisfies the statutory requirement.

A basic tenet of American corporate law is that the corporation and its shareholders are distinct entities. A corporate parent which owns the shares of a subsidiary does not, for that reason alone, own or have legal title to the assets of the subsidiary; and, it follows with even greater force, the parent does not own or have legal title to the subsidiaries of the subsidiary.

Applying these principles, it follows that Israel did not own a majority of shares in the Dead Sea Companies. The State of Israel owned a majority of shares, at various times, in companies one or more corporate tiers above the Dead Sea Companies, but at no time did Israel own a majority of shares in the Dead Sea Companies. Those companies were subsidiaries of other corporations.

Where Congress intends to refer to ownership in other than the formal sense, it knows how to do so. The absence of this language instructs us that Congress did not intend to disregard structural ownership rules.

The reason for the official immunities in those cases does not apply here. The immunities for government officers prevent the threat of suit from "crippling the proper and effective administration of public affairs." Foreign sovereign immunity, by contrast, is not meant to avoid chilling foreign states or their instrumentalities in the conduct of their business but to give foreign states and their instrumentalities some protection from the inconvenience of suit as a gesture of comity between the United States and other sovereigns.

Any relationship recognized under the FSIA between the Dead Sea Companies and Israel had been severed before suit was commenced. As a result, the Dead Sea Companies would not be entitled to instrumentality status even if their theory that instrumentality status could be conferred on a subsidiary were accepted.

[continued]

For these reasons, we hold first that a foreign state must itself own a majority of the shares of a corporation if the corporation is to be deemed an instrumentality of the state under the provisions of the FSIA; and we hold second that instrumentality status is determined at the time of the filing of the complaint.

It is so ordered.

:: CASE QUESTIONS

1. When may a corporate entity invoke the FSIA as a defense in court?
2. What is the policy rationale for exempting governments from the threat of lawsuits?
3. Why did the Court rule against the Dead Sea Companies?

11. SUING FOREIGN FIRMS IN THE UNITED STATES

As foreign products and technology are imported into the United States, disputes may arise over either the terms of contract or the performance of the goods. To sue a foreign firm in the United States, the Supreme Court held that the plaintiff must establish "minimum contacts" between the foreign defendant and the forum court. The plaintiff must demonstrate that exercise of personal jurisdiction over the defendant "does not offend traditional notions of fair play and substantial justice."

Once the plaintiff decides to sue in the United States, he or she also must comply with the terms of the Hague Service Convention when serving the foreign defendant notice of the lawsuit. The Hague Service Convention is a treaty that was formulated "to provide a simpler way to serve process abroad, to assure that defendants sued in foreign jurisdictions would receive actual and timely notice of suit, and to facilitate proof of service abroad." Many countries, including the United States, follow this convention. The primary requirement of the agreement is to require each nation to establish a central authority to process requests for service of documents from other countries. After the central authority receives the request in proper form, it must serve the documents by a method prescribed by the internal law of the receiving state or by a method designated by the requester and compatible with the law.

In Case 13.3, the court considers a lawsuit against a foreign firm over whether U.S. employment laws can be imposed on its domestic employees. Also, see Sidebar 13.7 for another example of the reach of U.S. law.

Although punitive damages may be awarded in U.S. courts against a foreign company doing business in the United States, it may be difficult or impossible to enforce the award in the company's home country. Outside of the United States, very few countries allow punitive damage awards, which are viewed as a "peculiarity of American law."

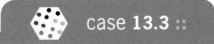 case **13.3** ::

MORELLI v. CEDEL
141 F. 3d 39 (2d Cir. 1998)

CUDAHY, J.: This appeal requires us to decide whether the domestic employees of certain foreign corporations are protected under the Age Discrimination and Employment Act of 1967 (the ADEA), and, if so, whether a foreign corporation's foreign employees are counted for the purpose of determining whether the corporation has enough employees to be subject to the ADEA. We answer both questions in the affirmative.

After the defendant fired the plaintiff, the plaintiff sued the defendant. The plaintiff's amended complaint asserted that the defendant violated the ADEA, the Employment Retirement Security Act (ERISA), and New York State's Human Rights Law. The district court dismissed the complaint on the grounds that the defendant was not subject to the ADEA.

As alleged in the complaint, the facts relevant to this appeal are as follows. The plaintiff, Ida Morelli, was born on April 11, 1939. The defendant is a Luxembourg bank. On or about June 29, 1984, the defendant hired the plaintiff to work in its New York office. On or about February 26, 1993, the plaintiff became an assistant to Dennis Sabourin, a manager in the defendant's New York office. Mr. Sabourin summoned the then 54-year-old plaintiff to his office on January 18, 1994, handed her a separation agreement, and insisted that she sign it.

Under the terms of the separation agreement, the plaintiff would resign, effective April 30, 1994. She would continue to receive her salary and benefits until the effective date of her resignation, but she would be relieved of her duties as an employee, effective immediately. Both the defendant and the employee would renounce all claims arising out of "their past working relationship." Mr. Sabourin told the plaintiff that she would receive the three months' severance pay, medical coverage for three months, and her pension only on the condition that she sign the agreement on the spot. The plaintiff had never seen the separation agreement before and had no warning that she was going to be asked to resign. But in the face of Mr. Sabourin's ultimatum, she did sign the agreement immediately and returned it to him. The defendant, however, never provided her with a pension distribution.

The ADEA was enacted to prevent arbitrary discrimination by employers on the basis of age. In order to determine whether the defendant is subject to the ADEA, we must first determine whether the ADEA generally protects the employees of a branch of a foreign employer located in the United States.

[T]he ADEA provides that the prohibitions of [the ADEA] shall not apply where the employer is a foreign person not controlled by an American employer. At a minimum, this provision means that the ADEA does not apply to the foreign operations of foreign employers—unless there is an American employer behind the scenes. An absolutely literal reading of [the statute] might suggest that the ADEA also does not apply to the domestic operations of foreign employers. But the plain language is not necessarily decisive if it is inconsistent with Congress' clearly expressed legislative purpose. Congress' purpose was not to exempt the domestic workplaces of foreign employers from the ADEA's prohibition of age discrimination. . . .

We have previously concluded that even when a foreign employer operating in the United States can invoke a Friendship, Commerce and Navigation treaty to justify employing its own nationals, this does not give the employer license to violate American laws prohibiting discrimination in employment. Although the Supreme Court vacated our judgment in that case on the grounds that the defendant could not invoke the treaty, the Court observed that "the highest level of protection afforded by commercial treaties" to foreign corporations operating in the United States is generally no more than "equal treatment with domestic corporations." Here equal treatment would require that antidiscrimination rules apply to foreign enterprises' U.S. branches, since defending personnel decisions is a fact of business life in contemporary America and is a burden that the domestic competitors of foreign enterprise have been required to shoulder. Also, U.S. subsidiaries of foreign corporations are generally subject to U.S. antidiscrimination laws, and, absent treaty protection—not an issue in this case—a U.S. branch of a foreign corporation is not entitled to an immunity not enjoyed by such subsidiaries.

Cedel will still not be subject to the ADEA by virtue of its U.S. operations unless Cedel is an "employer" under the ADEA. A business must have at least twenty "employees" to be an "employer." Cedel maintains that, in the case of foreign employers, only domestic employees should be counted. The district court agreed, and, since Cedel had fewer than 20 employees in its U.S. branch, the court granted Cedel's motion to dismiss for lack of subject matter jurisdiction without considering the number of Cedel's overseas employees.

The district court reasoned that the overseas employees of foreign employers should not be counted because they are not protected by the ADEA. But there is no requirement that an employee be protected by the ADEA to be counted; an enumeration, for the purpose of ADEA coverage of an employer, includes employees under age 40, who are also unprotected. The nose count of employees relates to the scale of the employer rather than to the extent of protection.

Cedel contends that because it has fewer than 20 employees in the United States, it is the equivalent of a small U.S. employer. This is implausible with respect to compliance and litigation costs; their impact on Cedel is better gauged by its worldwide employment. Cedel would not appear to be any more a boutique operation in the United States than would a business with ten employees each in offices in, say, Alaska and Florida, which would be subject to the ADEA. Further, a U.S. corporation with many foreign employees but fewer than 20 domestic ones would certainly be subject to the ADEA.

Accordingly, in determining whether Cedel satisfies the ADEA's 20-employee threshold, employees cannot be ignored merely because they work overseas. We therefore vacate the judgment on the plaintiff's ADEA count.

So ordered.

:: CASE QUESTIONS

1. What is the purpose behind the ADEA?
2. How did the court find that the ADEA covered a U.S. branch of a foreign employer?
3. Why did the court count foreign employees of the firm in determining whether the employer was subject to the ADEA?

:: *sidebar* 13.7

The Reach of U.S. Law: *Spector v. Norwegian Cruise Line, Ltd.* 545 U.S. 119 (2005)

Issue: Whether foreign-flagged cruise ships serving U.S. ports must comply with the public accommodations provisions in Title III of the Americans with Disabilities Act.

Key Facts: Disabled plaintiffs and their companions alleged that physical barriers on the Norwegian Cruise Line Ltd. (NCL) ships denied them access to various equipment, programs, and facilities on the ships. They sought injunctive relief requiring NCL to remove certain barriers that obstructed their access to the ships' facilities.

Procedural History: The district court found that foreign-flagged cruise ships *are* subject to the ADA. The Fifth Circuit Court of Appeals *reversed.*

Outcome: The U.S. Supreme Court reversed, holding that Title III of the ADA is applicable to foreign-flag cruise ships in U.S. waters.

The ATCA is viewed by some as a way to hold U.S. companies responsible for their participation in human rights abuses abroad.

Alien Tort Claims Act The **Alien Tort Claims Act (ATCA),** enacted in 1789, grants jurisdiction to U.S. federal district courts over "any civil action by an alien for a tort only, committed in violation of the law of nations or a treaty of the United States." For nearly 200 years, the law lapsed into obscurity. In the last 20 years, however, it has been revived in a number of human rights contexts, including claims brought against U.S. global companies. An essential aspect of a successful claim under the ATCA is to demonstrate that the acts committed violate the law of nations. This prompts many unanswered legal questions in the international labor context. What constitutes the "law of nations"? In general, the law of nations is embodied in international agreements, treaties, and conventions. ATCA actions have been alleged against many U.S. companies, including Bridgestone, Chevron, Del Monte, Drummond Company, Dyncorp, ExxonMobil, Gap, Inc., Texaco, Inc., Unocal Corp., Wal-Mart, and, most recently, Yahoo. Claims typically involve allegations of forced labor, but may also include other human rights abuses such as murder, rape, torture, unlawful detention, and kidnapping.

It is not unusual for these cases to also allege that acts were committed by paramilitaries hired by the company.

12. INTERNATIONAL ARBITRATION

International businesses now are focusing on the need for new methods of resolving international commercial disputes and, as a result, are frequently resorting to the use of arbitration. The advantages of arbitration in domestic transactions, previously discussed in Chapter 5, are more pronounced in international transactions where differences in languages and legal systems make litigation costs still more costly.

The United Nations Convention on the Recognition and Enforcement of Foreign Arbitral Awards of 1958 (New York Convention), adopted in more than 50 countries, encourages the use of arbitration in commercial agreements made by companies in the signatory countries. Under the New York Convention it is easier to compel arbitration, where previously agreed upon by the parties, and to enforce the arbitrator's award once a decision is reached.

Once the parties to an international transaction agree to arbitrate disputes between them, the U.S. courts are reluctant to disturb that agreement. In the case of *Mitsubishi Motors v. Soler Chrysler-Plymouth* (1985) the Supreme Court upheld an international agreement even where it required the parties to arbitrate all disputes, including federal antitrust claims. The Court decided that the international character of the undertaking required enforcement of the arbitration clause even as to the antitrust claims normally heard in a U.S. court.

There are many advantages to arbitrating international disputes. The arbitration process likely will be more streamlined and easier for the parties to understand than litigating the dispute in a foreign court. Moreover, the parties can avoid the unwanted publicity that often results in open court proceedings. Finally, the parties can agree, before the dispute even arises, on a neutral and objective third party to act as the arbitrator. Several organizations, such as the International Chamber of Commerce in Paris and the Court of International Arbitration in London, provide arbitration services for international disputes.

The World Intellectual Property Organization: Arbitration and Mediation Center The World Intellectual Property Organization (WIPO) Arbitration and Mediation Center hears cases involving domain name disputes and cybersquatting. The Uniform Domain Name Dispute Resolution Policy (UDRP) went into effect in 1999. Since that time, over 8,350 disputes involving 127 countries and some 16,000 domain names have been handled by the WIPO.

Many UDRP cases involve high-value, well-known brands. In fact, cases involving most of the 100 largest international brands by value have been heard by the WIPO. Well-known individuals, including Madonna, Julia Roberts, Eminem, Pamela Anderson, J K Rowling, Morgan Freeman, and Lance Armstrong have used the WIPO's services. For more information about WIPO cases, see www.wipo.int.

:: Key Terms

:: Review Questions and Problems

International Law and Organizations

1. *Sources of International Law*

    (a) What are the essential differences between the International Court of Justice and the U.S. Supreme Court?

    (b) How does the ICJ determine international law?

2. *International Organizations*

    (a) What are the three major principles of the World Trade Organization?

    (b) Has adherence to those principles improved international trade?

    (c) Describe the organization of the European Union.

    (d) How is it similar to the structure of the government of the United States?

3. *Major Agreements Affecting Trade*

    (a) How does the CISG facilitate international sales of goods?

    (b) How do free trade agreements, such as NAFTA and CAFTA-DR, benefit U.S. businesses?

Methods of Transacting International Business

4. *Foreign Sales*

    BMW, a German buyer, opens an irrevocable letter of credit in favor of Goodyear, an American seller, for the purchase of tires on BMW automobiles. BMW confirms the letter of credit with Goodyear's bank in New York, JPMorgan Chase. How will the seller obtain payment?

5. *Licenses or Franchises*

    (a) How should a licensor protect its investment in a foreign country?

    (b) Is licensing a less risky approach for the seller than direct foreign investment?

6. *Direct Foreign Investment*

    What are the advantages and disadvantages of a joint venture with a foreign firm?

Risks Involved in International Trade

7. *Expropriation and Nationalization*

    Explain the "modern traditional theory" of compensation related to the taking of private property by a foreign government.

8. *Export Controls*

    (a) Why is the future of export controls in doubt?

    (b) What are some of the dangers associated with having an inadequate export control regime as nations combat terrorism?

9. *Pressures for Bribes*

    XYZ Company, a U.S. firm, is seeking to obtain business in Indonesia. XYZ learns that one of its major competitors, a German firm, is offering a key Indonesian governmental official a trip around the world for choosing their firm in the transaction. Can XYZ report this bribe to the Department of Justice and have the German firm prosecuted under the Foreign Corrupt Practices Act?

Resolving International Disputes

10. *Suing Foreign Governments in the United States*

    Belgium arrests an American citizen, while he is visiting Brussels, on suspicion that he is an international drug smuggler. After a thorough investigation, Belgium realizes that it has arrested the wrong person. Can the American citizen successfully sue Belgium in the United States for false arrest?

11. *Suing Foreign Firms in the United States*

    What is the primary requirement of the Hague Service Convention and how does it help a plaintiff when filing a lawsuit?

12. *International Arbitration*

    Why are arbitration clauses in international agreements favored by the courts and likely to be enforced when conflicts arise between the contracting parties?

business :: *discussions*

1. XYZ Company is a U.S. firm that makes communication software used in a variety of consumer goods manufactured and sold in the United States. XYZ recently learned that one of the manufacturing firms it supplies, ABC Company, is exporting finished goods to a country where U.S. goods and component parts are prohibited because of numerous conflicts with the U.S. government.

Does XYZ have any moral or legal responsibility in this case?

How should XYZ protect itself under these circumstances?

Should American business practices be impacted by conflicts between governments?

2. Hello-Hello is a U.S. telecommunications company with global operations. Sophia is an assistant vice president of Hello-Hello. She is dispatched to China to handle two situations. First, a shipment of 500 cases of cell phones is stalled in customs. She is assigned the task of getting the goods out of customs and into retail stores. Sophia learns through the grapevine that customs officials expect $5 (U.S. per case) to help "speed things along." Second, she is instructed by her boss to do "whatever is necessary" to secure cell tower permits from local officials in two outlying areas. A local agent suggests that she give him $500,000 in cash so they can get to know the officials better. When Sophia asks him what the money will be used for, he tells her that he wants to take them out to dinner, maybe on a weekend outing in the city, and that he generally needs "flexibility."

Should Sophia call the home office to ask for advice?

If her boss says to pay the money, should she do it?

What potential legal problems are presented by the payments?

Part
FOUR

:: Formation and Regulation of Business

As you use resources, you bump up against others and their security and enjoyment of their resources. Tort law and much criminal law establishes limits or boundaries to what society considers as harm to what belongs to others. The following five chapters illustrate also that the government's regulation of business sets limits that define the boundaries of what you can do with what you own as it comes in contact with what belongs to others. Within your boundaries the government protects you, allowing you to exclude others. Outside your boundaries, the government protects others, enforcing their boundaries to exclude you. In business the defining and enforcing of boundaries protects, encourages, and limits what we call the *private market*.

Chapter 14 explains the laws that set boundaries within which private owners can join their resources into business organizations called *corporations, partnerships, limited liability companies,* and *limited liability partnerships*. These organizations are the driving force behind modern business production.

Laws in our property system not only protect existing owners (called *investors*) in business organizations but potential investors as well. These laws regulate the sale of securities like stocks and bonds in business organizations that sell them to the public. The sale of securities is a primary way large businesses raise money, so the laws regulating the way they raise money are very important.

Securities laws require the registration of investment opportunities offered to the public. The Securities and Exchange Commission (SEC) is the regulatory administrative agency that accepts registrations. The SEC also requires various reports on a regular basis from registered businesses.

Insiders, who are usually agents who are the officers and managers of corporations, cannot trade their company's stock in certain ways. These limitations protect noninsider owners from being taken advantage of because of information not available to the public. Chapter 15 discusses these securities laws and the Sarbanes-Oxley Act, which added new disclosures and requirements that attempt to prevent insiders from taking advantage of the investing public.

A principle purpose for private property is to set conditions for the maximum creation of new resources, for what people need and want. To achieve this goal, private owners compete against one another to ensure that society gets the best products and services at the lowest prices. The antitrust laws covered in Chapter 16 attempt to maintain productive competition in the market. To do so, antitrust laws set limits about how business owners can eliminate competition in the marketplace.

Chapter 17 examines various consumer laws and some of the financial protections of those laws. Consumer law protects people only in buying goods and services for personal and household use. If antitrust law regulates by establishing legal fences that protect businesses and their resources from economically harmful competition from other businesses, consumer law regulates by establishing legal fences that protect consumers and their resources from harmful trade practices. Chapter 17 focuses on the Federal Trade Commission's consumer protection authority, various laws protecting consumers in the extension of credit, limitations on debt collection, and the financial discharge of consumers in bankruptcy.

The right of property gives maximum incentive to produce. If society wants to produce more of something, the law should recognize a property right in whatever it is that society wants to produce more of. This fact is definitely true in environmental matters. If society wants to produce more widgets (which, let us pretend, you can produce only with much pollution), it should recognize an exclusive right to pollute to produce widgets. But if society wants to produce more clean air and water, it should recognize a property right in people to keep others from engaging in excessive pollution, for example, a right to sue to prevent others from engaging in such pollution.

When it is difficult or too costly for private individuals to enforce a property right in a clean environment, the government often steps in with laws limiting pollution of air, water, and land that protect possession of, especially, health. Chapter 18 examines environmental laws that protect human health, endangered species, and other aspects of the environment. •

14

Formation and Operation of Business Organizations

Have you ever thought about how businesses are organized? Why is one business a partnership and another a corporation? How do these businesses get transactions completed through someone other than the owner? There must be some legal principles at work because you know you do not have to deal with the owner of the clothing store when you make a purchase. A multinational company transacts business all over the world and its shareholders (owners) are not parties to its contracts.

Previous chapters discuss legal issues related to various business transactions. In this chapter, we focus on how these transactions are accomplished and the selection of which organizational form is best to complete such transactions. As you begin the study of this chapter, ask yourself, How

411

does a company enter into a contract? How does an organization become liable to its customers, shareholders, or other parties. The answers to these questions depend on how the business is organized. In addition, to understand the material in this chapter, the material on agency in Chapter 19 is important. When you study that topic, the foundation of this chapter will be helpful.

In the chapter, you will examine the factors that should be considered when deciding the most appropriate organizational form. You also will review the various choices of organizations used to conduct business. Prior to this examination and review, a quick introduction to the forms of organizations follows.

1. FORMS OF BUSINESS ORGANIZATIONS

People conduct business using a number of different organizational forms. The law recognizes three basic forms and several hybrid forms that contain attributes of two or more basic forms. These various forms are listed in Sidebar 14.1.

:: *sidebar* 14.1

Possible Forms of Business Organizations

The three basic forms include:

- Sole proprietorships
- Partnerships
- Corporations

The hybrid forms include:

- Limited partnerships
- S corporations
- Limited liability companies
- Limited liability partnerships

Two terms are important as they relate to the number of owners of a business organization. Some organizations are owned by only a few persons. Such organizations are said to be **closely held.** Family-owned and family-operated businesses are common examples of closely held organizations. Other businesses may be owned by hundreds, if not thousands, of persons. These organizations are **publicly held** ones. Examples of publicly held businesses include those whose stock is traded on a public exchange.

You should understand that the decision of selecting an appropriate organizational form usually is limited to those situations involving the few owners of a closely held business. When a business is publicly held by a large number of owners, the form of organization usually is a corporation. The reason for this corporate form being used is that shareholders can transfer their ownership without interfering with the organization's management.

The issue of which organizational form is best usually involves closely held businesses; publicly held businesses typically are corporations.

:: Factors to Consider When Selecting a Business's Organizational Form

Significant factors to consider in selecting the best organizational form for a particular business activity include:

- The cost of creating the organization.
- The continuity or stability of the organization.
- The control of decisions.
- The personal liability of the owners.
- The taxation of the organization's earnings and its distribution of profits to the owners.

In the following sections, each of these factors is defined so that you can more easily apply their meaning in Sections 7 through 12.

2. CREATION

The word *creation* means the legal steps necessary to form a particular business organization. At times, a businessperson may be concerned with how much it will cost to have each form established. Usually, the cost of creation is not a major factor in considering which form of business organization a person will choose to operate a business. The most significant creation-related issues are how long it will take to create a particular organization and how much paperwork is involved.

The issues when considering methods of creating business organizations usually are time and money.

3. CONTINUITY

Another factor to consider when selecting the best organizational form for a business activity is the continuity of the organization. How does an organization's existence relate to its owners? By this question the meaning of the word *continuity* becomes associated with the stability or durability of the organization.

The crucial issue with this continuity factor is the method by which a business organization can be dissolved. A **dissolution** is any change in the ownership of an organization that changes the legal existence of the organization. In essence, the questions become: Is the organization easily dissolved? What impact does a dissolution of the organizational form have on the business activity of that organization?

The death, retirement, or withdrawal of an owner creates issues of whether an organization and its business will continue.

4. MANAGERIAL CONTROL

The factor of control concerns who is managing the business organization. Often this issue is of vital importance to the owners. The egos of businesspeople can cause them to insist on equal voices in management. As you study this factor under each organizational form, keep in mind the difficulties that can arise when a few strong-willed business owners disagree with one another. Usually when people are excited about getting started in a business opportunity, no one takes time to discuss methods of resolving potential deadlocks.

Don't assume you and your co-owners have to be equal in all aspects; voice in management can be decided among you.

The failure to consider how to overcome disputes involving managerial control can cause business activities to suffer and the organization to fail. Therefore, consideration of potential conflict and mechanisms to resolve disputes are essential to consider when selecting a form for a business venture.

5. LIABILITY

Do always examine how liability passes from the organization to the owner.

When considering the liability factor, you should ask yourself: To what degree is the owner of a business personally liable for the debts of the business organization? Generally, businesspeople want to limit their personal liability. Although there are organizations that appear to accomplish this goal, you will see that such appearances might be misleading when actually conducting business transactions. For this reason, this liability factor is very important and deserves significant consideration as it relates to each of the organizational forms presented below.

6. TAXATION

Remember a single tax is not always better than a double tax.

This factor often is viewed as the most critical when selecting the form of business organization. At issue is: How is the income earned by the business taxed? How is the money distributed to the business owners taxed? Is it possible that owners may have to pay taxes on money that is attributed to them as income but which they have not actually received? The answers to these questions provide much needed guidance when deciding which form of organization is best suited for a business's operation.

People have stated that the double taxation of corporate income should be avoided by selecting a different form of organization. As you will see, there are specific advantages to creating the organizational forms that are "single taxed." However, advantages also exist when an organization is subject to the supposed "double tax."

:: Selecting the Best Organizational Form

The following six sections apply the various factors to consider when deciding which organizational form is best for a particular business activity. Following these sections is a brief discussion on how to make a good decision when selecting the best organizational form.

7. SOLE PROPRIETORSHIPS

DO IT! this phrase describes how a proprietorship is formed.

When considering the five factors introduced above, it has been said that the **sole proprietorship** has many virtues. However, the use of this business organization is very limited because multiple owners cannot create a proprietorship. Depending on the factual situation presented, greater continuity, less liability, and more flexible tax planning may be required than those afforded by the law of the sole proprietorship.

A sole proprietorship is the easiest and least expensive business organization to create. In essence, the proprietor obtains whatever business licenses are necessary and begins operations. Legally, no formal documentation is needed. The ease of (perhaps the lack of) the steps used to create a proprietorship makes it an attractive alternative when beginning a new business venture. However, as the other factors might dictate, a business might shift away from the proprietorship form as it becomes more successful.

A proprietorship's continuity is tied directly to the will of the proprietor. In essence, the proprietor may dissolve his or her organization at any time by simply changing the organization or terminating the business activity. The fact that the proprietorship's business activity may be more stable than the proprietor's willingness to remain actively involved in the business indicates that the sole proprietorship is a less desirable organizational form. Ownership of a sole proprietorship cannot be transferred.

The sole proprietor is in total control of his or her business's goals and operations. While the proprietor has complete responsibility for the business's success or failure, the owners of all other organizational forms usually share control to some degree. As long as this control issue is carefully thought out, there can be real value in having more than one voice in control of managing a business enterprise.

A sole proprietor is personally obligated for the debt of the proprietorship. Legally speaking, this owner has unlimited liability for the obligations of this type of business organization. The business organization's creditors can seek to hold the proprietor personally liable for 100 percent of the debts that the proprietorship cannot pay. The desire to avoid the potentially high risk of personal liability is an important reason why other organizational forms might be viewed as preferable to the proprietorship.

A sole proprietorship is not taxed as an organization. All the proprietorship's income subject to taxation is attributed to the proprietor. The initial appearance of this tax treatment may appear favorable because the business organization is not taxed. However, the individual proprietor must pay the applicable personal tax rate on the income earned by the proprietorship whether the proprietor actually receives any of the income from the organization or not. If the organization retains its profits for business expansion purposes instead of distributing this money to the proprietor, that owner still must pay taxes on the income made by the proprietorship.

> A sole proprietorship may appear to have many advantages; sharing responsibility and liability with others are not among them.

8. PARTNERSHIPS

Whenever two or more people wish to own a business together, a partnership is a possible organizational form. In general, a **partnership** is an agreement between two or more persons to share a common interest in a commercial endeavor and to share profits and losses. The word *persons* in the previous sentence should be interpreted broadly enough to allow business organizations, as well as individuals, to form a partnership. For example, two or more individuals, an individual and a corporation, a partnership and a corporation, or any combination of these entities may agree to create a business organization called a partnership.

Due to the potentially complex relationships established through a partnership, factors to consider when studying the appropriateness of this organizational form are presented under subheadings that correspond to the factors presented above.

Creation When compared to other forms of business organizations (other than the sole proprietorship), a partnership is easily formed. The cost of forming a partnership is relatively minimal. In addition, the creation of a partnership is made easier since it does not need to get permission from each state in which it does business.

The key to a partnership's existence is satisfying the elements of its definition:

1. Two or more persons.
2. A common interest in business.
3. Sharing profits and losses.

Don't operate a business with one or more co-owners without a carefully drafted partnership agreement; unresolved issues lead to major legal problems.

If the parties conduct their affairs in such a way as to meet these definitional elements, a partnership exists regardless of whether the persons involved call themselves partners or not. Sidebar 14.2 presents issues related to the existence and naming of a partnership.

:: *sidebar* 14.2

Formation and Naming of a Partnership

Since the existence of a partnership is based on the partners' agreement, it is possible that this agreement is implied from the conduct or actions of the parties. Partners should never rely on implied agreements. Rather, their agreement should be explicitly stated among the parties and drafted into a formal document. The formal agreement is called the **articles of partnership.**

Since a partnership is created by agreement, the partners select the name of the partnership. This right of selection is subject to two limitations in many states. First, a partnership may not use any word in the name, such as "company," that would imply the existence of a corporation. Second, if the name is other than that of the partners, the

partners must give notice as to their actual identity under the state's **assumed-name statute.** Failure to comply with this disclosure requirement may result in the partnership being denied access to courts, or it may result in criminal actions being brought against those operating under the assumed name.

An example of these naming concepts could arise in the creation of a partnership to conduct business as a consulting firm. If the firm's name is a listing of your surname and those of your partners, your identities are clear via your firm's name. However, if you called your partnership "We are the Best Consulting," you and your partners would need to comply with any applicable assumed-name statute.

Continuity   A general partnership is dissolved any time there is a change in the partners. For example, if a partner dies, retires, or otherwise withdraws from the organization, the partnership is dissolved. Likewise, if a person is added as a new partner, there is a technical dissolution of the organization. Therefore, it generally is said that the partnership organization is easily dissolved. Even if the partnership agreement provides that the partnership will continue for a stated number of years, any partner still retains the power to dissolve the organization. Although liability may be imposed on the former partner for wrongful dissolution in violation of the agreement, the partnership nevertheless is dissolved.

A dissolution does not necessarily destroy the business of a partnership. Dissolution is not the same thing as terminating an organization's business activity. Termination involves the winding up or liquidating of a business; dissolution simply means the legal form of organization no longer exists. Sidebar 14.3 addresses how parties might prevent dissolution from destroying a partnership's business success.

:: *sidebar* 14.3

Anticipating a Partnership's Dissolution—Buy and Sell Agreements

To prevent problems that may arise when a partner dies or withdraws from a partnership, the articles of partnership should include a **buy and sell agreement.** This agreement, which should be entered into when the business entity is created, provides for the amount and manner of compensation for the interest of the deceased or withdrawing owner.

Buy and sell agreements frequently use formulas to compute the value of the withdrawing partner's interest and provide for the time and method of payment. In the case of death, the liquidity needed is often provided by the cash proceeds from life insurance taken out on the life of the deceased and made payable to the business or to the surviving partners. Upon payment of the amount required by the buy and sell agreement to the estate of the deceased, the interest of the deceased ends, and all the surviving partners can continue the business, as members of a new partnership.

Managerial Control   In a general partnership, unless the agreement provides to the contrary, each partner has an equal voice in the firm's affairs. Partners may agree to divide control in such a way as to make controlling partners and minority partners. The decision of who has what voice in management is of crucial importance to the chances of the business's success and to the welfare of the partners' relationship with each other. The possibility of a deadlock among partners is very real, especially when there are only a few partners and there are an even number of them. Care should be taken to design mechanisms to avoid or at least handle the disputes that will arise when partners share managerial control. A written partnership agreement should provide specific language governing issues of managerial control.

DON'T rely on partners having an equal voice in managing the organization; negotiate how to share this managerial responsibility.

Liability   All partners in a general partnership have unlimited liability for their organization's debts. These partners' personal assets, which are not associated with the partnership, may be claimed by the partnership's creditors. From a creditor's perspective, this personal liability of each partner extends to the organization's entire debt, not just to a pro rata share. These partners are **jointly and severally liable** for the partnership's obligations. For example, assume that a general partnership has three partners and that it owes a creditor $300,000. If it is necessary to collect the debt, this creditor can sue all three partners jointly for the $300,000. As an alternative, the creditor can sue any one partner or any combination of two for the entire $300,000. Among the partners, anyone who has to pay the creditor more than her or his pro rata share of the liability usually can seek contribution from the remaining partners.

Taxation   Like proprietorships, partnerships are not a taxable entity. The fact that this type of organization pays no income tax does not mean that the profits of the partnership are free from income tax. A partnership files an information return that allocates to each partner his or her proportionate share of profits or losses from operations, dividend income, capital gains or losses, and other items that would affect the income tax owed by a partner. Partners then report their share of such items on their individual income tax returns, irrespective of whether they have actually received the items.

A partnership does not pay taxes; this may be a benefit or detriment to the partners depending on whether the organization makes or loses money and whether it distributes or retains any profits made.

This aspect of a partnership is an advantage to the partners if the organization suffers a net loss. The pro rata share of this loss is allocated to each partner, and it can be used to reduce these partners' personal taxable income. However, by this same reasoning, a partnership is a disadvantage if the organization retains any profits made by the organization for the purpose of expansion. Suppose a partnership with three equal partners has $30,000 in net income. If the partnership keeps this money, there still is a constructive distribution of $10,000 to each partner for tax purposes. Assuming that these partners are in a 28 percent personal income tax bracket, they each would have to pay $2,800 in taxes even though they actually received nothing from the partnership.

---

concept :: *summary*

Advantages and Disadvantages of Partnerships

The basic law relating to partnerships is found in the Uniform Partnership Act. According to this statute, the partnership form of organization generally has the following advantages:

1. A partnership is easily formed because it is based on a contract among persons.
2. Costs of formation are not significant.
3. Partnerships are not a tax-paying entity.
4. Each partner has an equal voice in management, unless there is a contrary agreement.
5. A partnership may operate in more than one state without obtaining a license to do business.
6. Partnerships generally are subject to less regulation and less governmental supervision than are corporations.

Offsetting these advantages, the following aspects of partnerships have been called disadvantages:

1. For practical reasons, only a limited number of people can be partners.
2. A partnership is dissolved anytime a partner ceases to be a partner, regardless of whether the reason is withdrawal or death.
3. Each partner's liability is unlimited, contrasted with the limited liability of a corporate shareholder.
4. Partners are taxed on their share of the partnership's profits, whether the profits are distributed or not. In other words, partners often are required to pay income tax on money they do not receive.

---

9. CORPORATIONS

The third basic organizational form which might be used to operate a business is the corporation. A **corporation** is an artificial, intangible entity created under the authority of a state's law. A corporation is known as a **domestic corporation** in the state in which it is incorporated. In all other states, this corporation is called a **foreign corporation.** As a creature of state legislative bodies, the corporation is much more complex to create and to operate than other forms of businesses. These legal complexities associated with the corporation are presented in a way that parallels the preceding section so that comparisons with partnerships can be easily made.

Creation   A corporation is created by a state issuing a **charter** upon the application of individuals known as **incorporators.** In comparison with partnerships, corporations are more costly to form. Among the costs of incorporation are filing fees, license fees, franchise taxes, attorneys' fees, and the cost of supplies, such as minute books, corporate seals, and stock certificates. In addition to these costs of creation, there also are annual costs in continuing a corporation's operation. These recurring expenses include annual reporting fees and taxes, the cost of annual shareholders' meetings, and ongoing legal-related expenses. Sidebar 14.4 describes the process of incorporation.

DO check the website of your state's authority responsible for issuing corporate charters. In most states, this authority is under the secretary of state.

:: *sidebar* 14.4

Steps in Creation of a Corporation

The formal application for a corporate charter is called the **articles of incorporation.** These articles must contain the proposed name of the corporation. So that persons dealing with a business will know that it is a corporation, the law requires that the corporate name include one of the following words or end with an abbreviation of them: "corporation," "company," "incorporated," or "limited." In addition, a corporate name must not be the same as, or deceptively similar to, the name of any domestic corporation or that of a foreign corporation authorized to do business in the state to which the application is made. The corporate name is an asset and an aspect of goodwill. As such, it is legally protected.

In addition to the proposed corporate name, the articles of incorporation usually will include the proposed corporation's period of duration, the purpose for which it is formed, the number of authorized shares, and information about the initial corporate officials.

Once drafted, these papers are sent to the appropriate state official (usually the secretary of state), who approves them and issues a corporate charter. Notice of this incorporation usually has to be advertised in the local newspaper in order to inform the public that a new corporation has been created. The initial board of directors then meets, adopts the corporate bylaws, and approves the sale of stock. At this point, the corporation becomes operational.

If a corporation wishes to conduct business in states other than the state of incorporation, that corporation must be licensed in these foreign states. The process of qualification usually requires payment of license fees and franchise taxes above and beyond those paid during the initial incorporation process. If a corporation fails to qualify in states where it is conducting business, the corporation may be denied access to the courts as a means of enforcing its contracts.

Continuity   In contrast to a partnership, a corporation usually is formed to have perpetual existence. The law treats a corporation's existence as distinct from its owners' status as shareholders. Thus, a shareholder's death or sale of her or his stock does not affect the organizational structure of a corporation. This ability to separate management from ownership is an often cited advantage of the corporation.

Although the sale of stock by a major shareholder or the shareholder's death has no legal impact on the organization's existence, this event may have a very real adverse impact on that corporation's ability to do business. The shareholder may have been the driving force behind the corporation's success. Without this shareholder, the corporation's business may fail.

The separation of the corporate organization's existence from its owners' willingness to remain associated with it is viewed as a major advantage to the corporation's stability.

Managerial Control   In the corporate form of organization, the issue of control is complicated by three groups. First, the **shareholders** elect the members of the board of directors. These **directors** set the objectives or goals of the corporation, and they appoint the officers. These **officers,** such as the president, vice president, secretary, and treasurer, are charged with managing the daily operations of the corporation in an attempt to achieve the stated organizational objectives or goals. Thus, which one of these three groups really controls the corporation?

To answer this question effectively, you must realize that the issue of who controls a corporation varies depending on the size of the ownership base of the organization. In essence, matters of managerial control require us to examine the publicly held corporation as distinct from the closely held corporation.

Publicly Held Corporations   In very large corporations, control by management (a combination of the directors and officers) is maintained with a very small percentage of stock ownership through the use of corporate records and funds to solicit proxies. Technically, a **proxy** is an agent appointed by a shareholder for the purpose of voting the shares. Management can, at corporate expense, solicit the right to vote the stock of shareholders unable to attend the meetings at which the directors of the company are elected. An outsider must either own sufficient stock to elect the directors or must solicit proxies at his or her own expense. The management of a large corporation usually can maintain control with only a small minority of actual stock ownership.

During the first years of this century, we have seen evidence of the negative aspects arising from a few shareholders, who also serve as officers and directors, controlling large, publicly held corporations. The lack of sufficient review and influence from those called "outside directors" contributed to corporate scandals that shocked the public confidence in business and the economy. Chapter 12 contains material on the criminal aspects of these scandals, and Chapter 15 describes the specific violations of securities law. At this point, we want you to appreciate that limiting the role of corporate governance to only a few people can lead to massive fraud. Sidebar 14.5 emphasizes the vital role corporate directors must fulfill to achieve proper

:: *sidebar* 14.5

Role of Corporate Boards

Directors are not ceremonial figureheads. They play a vital role in setting the vision and direction of a corporation. They also make sure that the executive officers carry out the vision/direction on a day-to-day basis. Directors should not micromanage; rather they should provide broad guidance and hold company executives accountable for the management of personnel, revenue, and expenses. In essence, directors serve as the shareholders' watchdog. Because of the corporate reforms imposed following the collapse of Enron and WorldCom and the scandals at Tyco, HealthSouth, and Adelphia, corporate directors are more independent from the organizations they govern.

These trends are discussed in more detail in Section 14 of this chapter.

governance. Despite legal requirements designed to increase the influence of corporate directors, all accounting records are not perfect.

Closely Held Corporations Unlike the situation with a large, publicly held corporation, one shareholder (or at least a small group of shareholders) may be able to control a closely held corporation. This can result because this individual (or the group) can own an actual majority of the issued shares. This majority can control the election of a board of directors. In fact, the shareholders with the largest amount of stock are often elected to this board of directors. The directors, in turn, elect officers, who again may be the shareholders with the largest interests. In a very real sense, those who own a majority of a closely held corporation can rule with near-absolute authority.

What are the rights of those who do not possess control in a closely held corporation—the so-called minority interest? To a large degree, the owners of the minority interest are subject to the decisions of the majority. The majority may pay themselves salaries that use up profits and may never declare a dividend. However, the minority interest is not without some rights, because the directors and officers stand in a fiduciary relation to the corporation and to the minority shareholders if the corporation is closely held. This relation imposes a duty on directors to act for the best interests of the corporation rather than for themselves individually.

If the majority is acting illegally or oppresses the rights of the minority shareholders, a lawsuit known as a **derivative suit** may be brought by a minority shareholder on behalf of the corporation. Such suits may seek to enjoin the unlawful activity or to collect damages for the corporation. For example, contracts made between the corporation and an interested director or officer may be challenged. If a suit is brought, the burden is on the director or officer (who may be the majority shareholder) to prove good faith and inherent fairness in such transactions.

The basic difficulty of owning a minority interest in a closely held corporation arises from the fact that there is no ready market for the stock should the shareholder desire to dispose of it. Of course, if there is a valid buy and sell agreement, then there is a market for the stock. Thus, as with partnerships, buy and sell agreements are absolutely essential in closely held corporations.

Do realize that any minority ownership interest in a corporation provides you with very little influence.

Liability The legal ability to separate a corporation's shareholders from its managers means that the owners are liable for the debts of the corporation only to the extent of those shareholders' investment in the cost of the stock. Thus, corporate shareholders are said to have **limited personal liability.**

The generalization that the investors in a corporation have limited liability but those in a partnership have unlimited liability is too broad and needs qualification. To be sure, someone investing in a company listed on the New York Stock Exchange will incur no risk greater than the investment, and the concept of limited liability certainly applies. However, if the company is a small, closely held corporation with limited assets and capital, it will be difficult for it to obtain credit on the strength of its own net worth. As a practical matter, shareholders will usually be required to add their own individual liability as security for borrowing. For example, if the XYZ Company seeks a loan at a local bank, the bank often will require the owners, X, Y, and Z, to personally guarantee repayment of the loan.

Your status as a shareholder in a closely held corporation probably limits your liability for torts; you likely forgo your limited liability for contracts by cosigning your corporation's contracts.

The phrases *limited liability* and *unlimited liability* are overly simplistic; an understanding of a business owner's liability goes beyond these simple terms.

This is not to say that shareholders in closely held corporations do not have some degree of limited liability. Shareholders have limited liability for contractlike obligations that are imposed as a matter of law (such as taxes). Liability also is limited when the corporate obligation results from torts committed by company employees while doing company business.

Even in these situations, the mere fact of corporate existence does not mean the shareholders will have liability limited to their investment. When courts find that the corporate organization is being misused, the corporate entity can be disregarded. This has been called **piercing the corporate veil.** When this veil of protection has been pierced, the shareholders are treated like partners who have unlimited liability for their organization's debts.

The **alter-ego theory,** by which the corporate veil can be pierced, may also be used to impose personal liability upon corporate officers, directors, and stockholders. If the corporate entity is disregarded by these officials themselves, so that there is such a unity of ownership and interest that separateness of the corporation has ceased to exist, the alter-ego theory will be followed and the corporate veil will be pierced.

Simply alleging that a person is the sole owner of a corporation engaged in wrongful activity will not result in a piercing of the corporate veil. This conclusion is appropriate when the owner has respect for the existence of the organization. In Case 14.1, notice the Supreme Court's effort to protect the corporate owner, especially since the statute being interpreted seems to limit the liability to the corporate organization.

case 14.1 ::

MEYER v. HOLLEY
123 S. Ct. 824 (2003)

Emma Mary Ellen Holley and David Holley, an interracial couple, tried to purchase a house. Grove Crank, a real estate salesperson, working for Triad, Inc., discriminated against the Holleys and prevented them from buying a home. The Holleys filed two lawsuits. First, the Holleys sued Triad, Inc., and Mr. Crank. Later, the Holleys filed a suit against David Meyer in his capacity as real estate broker, president, and sole owner of Triad, Inc. The Holleys argued that Mr. Meyer was vicariously liable for the discrimination of his salesperson. The District Court combined these suits and dismissed all claims since it held the statute of limitations prevented the claims. The Court further held that Mr. Meyer could not be vicariously responsible for the acts of his salesperson under the Fair Housing Act. The Holleys appealed to the Ninth Circuit Court of Appeals. That court reversed the dismissal. Further, the appellate court held that the Fair Housing Act did permit liability to pass through to a person who had

authority to control the salesperson. The court found that Mr. Meyer had such authority, and thus he was vicariously liable.

Mr. Meyer petitioned for a writ of certiorari, which was granted by the Supreme Court

BREYER, J.: . . .The Fair Housing Act itself focuses on prohibited acts. In relevant part the Act forbids any person or other entity whose business includes engaging in residential real estate–related transactions to discriminate, for example, because of race. It adds that "person" includes, for example, individuals, corporations, partnerships, associations, labor unions, and other organizations. It says nothing about vicarious liability.

Nonetheless, it is well established that the Act provides for vicarious liability. This Court has noted that an action brought for compensation by a victim of housing discrimination is, in effect, a tort action. And the Court has assumed that, when Congress creates a tort action, it legislates against a legal background of ordinary tort-related vicarious liability rules and consequently intends its legislation to incorporate those rules.

It is well established that traditional vicarious liability rules ordinarily make principals or employers vicariously liable for acts of their agents or employees in the scope of their authority or employment. And in the absence of special circumstances it is the corporation, not its owner or officer, who is the principal or employer, and thus subject to vicarious liability for torts committed by its employees or agents. . . .

The Ninth Circuit held that the Fair Housing Act imposed more extensive vicarious liability— that the Act went well beyond traditional principles. The Court of Appeals held that the Act made corporate owners and officers liable for the unlawful acts of a corporate employee simply on the basis that the owner or officer controlled (or had the right to control) the actions of that employee. We do not agree with the Ninth Circuit that the Act extended traditional vicarious liability rules in this way.

For one thing, Congress said nothing in the statute or in the legislative history about extending vicarious liability in this manner. And Congress' silence, while permitting an inference that Congress intended to apply ordinary background tort principles, cannot show that it intended to apply an unusual modification of those rules. . . .

For another thing, the Department of Housing and Urban Development (HUD), the federal agency primarily charged with the implementation and administration of the statute, has specified that ordinary vicarious liability rules apply in this area. And we

ordinarily defer to an administering agency's reasonable interpretation of a statute.

A HUD regulation applicable during the relevant time periods for this suit provided that analogous administrative complaints alleging Fair Housing Act violations may be filed

> against any person who directs or controls, or has the right to direct or control, the conduct of another person with respect to any aspect of the sale . . . of dwellings . . . if that other person, acting within the scope of his or her authority as employee or agent of the directing or controlling person . . . has engaged . . . in a discriminatory housing practice.

. . . Respondents, conceding that traditional vicarious liability rules apply, argue that those principles themselves warrant liability here. For one thing, they say, California law itself creates what amounts, under ordinary common-law principles, to an employer/employee or principal/agent relationship between (a) a corporate officer designated as the broker under a real estate license issued to the corporation, and (b) a corporate employee/salesperson. Insofar as this argument rests solely upon the corporate broker/officer's right to control the employee/salesperson, the Ninth Circuit considered and accepted it. But we must reject it given our determination. . . that the "right to control" is insufficient by itself, under traditional agency principles, to establish a principal/agent or employer/employee relationship. . . .

The judgment of the Court of Appeals is vacated, and the case is remanded for further proceedings consistent with this opinion.

Vacated and remanded.

:: CASE QUESTIONS

1. What is the relationship of David Meyer to the parties in the various lawsuits filed?
2. On what basis did the District Court and the Ninth Circuit Court of Appeals reach different legal conclusions regarding Meyer's liability for the acts of his salesperson?
3. Did the Supreme Court conclude that vicarious liability could be imposed under the language of the Fair Housing Act?
4. Did the Supreme Court conclude that Meyer could not be held personally liable for his saleperson's discriminatory actions? Why?

Taxation   Corporations must pay income taxes on their earnings. Sidebar 14.6 on the next page sets forth these tax rates. The fact that there is a separate corporate income tax may work as an advantage. For example, if the corporation makes a profit that is to be retained by the corporation to support growth, no income is allocated to the shareholders. These shareholders will not have their personal taxable income increased, as would a partner in a similar situation. In addition, the corporate rate may be lower than the individual rates.

:: *sidebar* 14.6

Corporate Tax Rates*

:: Income	:: Tax Rate
$0–$50,000	15%
$50,000–$75,000	25%
$75,000–$10,000,000	34%
over $10,000,000	35%

In addition to these rates, there are excess taxes when corporate taxable income exceeds $100,000. These taxes increase again if corporate taxable income exceeds $15,000,000.

*Source: 26 U.S.C. § 11.

But corporations also have tax disadvantages. Suppose a corporation suffers a loss during a given tax year. The existence of the corporate tax works as a disadvantage, since this loss cannot be distributed to the shareholders in order to reduce their personal tax liability. Indeed, a net operating loss to a corporation can be used only to offset corporate income earned in other years. And the allocation of such a loss can be carried back only for 3 years and carried forward for 15 years. (*Note:* There are many different rules concerning specialized carryover situations. The Internal Revenue Code should be examined prior to relying on the general rule just stated.)

Perhaps a greater disadvantage of the corporate tax occurs when a profit is made and the corporation wishes to pay a dividend to its shareholders. The money used to pay this dividend will have been taxed at the corporate level. It is then taxed again because the shareholder must take the amount of the dividend into his or her own personal income. Although the rate of this second tax is reduced to 15 percent, as a part of a 2003 tax reduction, the existence of the second tax is potentially significant in selecting the best organizational form for a business. This situation has been called the **double tax** on corporate income. A similar situation of double taxation occurs when a corporation is dissolved and its assets are distributed to shareholders as capital gains. Yet, as the discussion next indicates, the double tax may not be as big a disadvantage as it appears at first.

Avoiding Double Taxation Corporations have employed a variety of techniques for avoiding the double taxation of corporate income. First, reasonable salaries paid to corporate officials may be deducted in computing the taxable income of the business. Thus, in a closely held corporation in which all or most shareholders are officers or employees, this technique may avoid double taxation of substantial portions of income. As might be expected, the Internal Revenue Code disallows a deduction for excessive or unreasonable compensation and treats such payments as dividends. Therefore, the determination of the reasonableness of corporate salaries is often a tax problem in that form of organization.

Second, corporations provide expense accounts for many employees, including shareholder employees. These are used to purchase travel, food, and entertainment. When so used, the employee, to some extent, has compensation that is not taxed. In an attempt to close this tax loophole, the law limits deductions for business meals and entertainment to 50 percent of the cost. Meal expenses and entertainment are deductible only if the expenses are directly related to or associated with the active conduct of a trade or business. For a deduction, business must be discussed directly before, during, or directly after the meal. Additionally, meal expenses are not deductible to the extent the meal is lavish or extravagant. Thus, the use of the expense account to avoid taxation of corporate income is subject to numerous technical rules and limitations.

Third, the capital structure of the corporation may include both common stock and interest-bearing loans from shareholders. For example, assume that a company needs $100,000 cash to go into business. If $100,000 of stock is issued, no expense will be deducted. However, assume that $50,000 worth of stock is purchased by the owners and $50,000 is lent to the company by them at 10 percent interest. In this case, $5,000 interest each year is deductible as an expense of the company and thus subject to only one tax as interest income to the owners. Just as in the case of salaries, the Internal Revenue Code has a counteracting rule relating to corporations that are undercapitalized. If the corporation is undercapitalized, interest payments will be treated as dividends and disallowed as deductible expenses.

The fourth technique for avoiding double taxation, at least in part, is simply not to pay dividends and to accumulate the earnings. The Internal Revenue Service seeks to compel corporations to distribute those profits not needed for a business purpose, such as growth. When a corporation retains earnings in excess of $250,000, there is a presumption that these earnings are being accumulated to avoid a second tax on dividends. If the corporations cannot rebut this presumption, an additional tax of 39.6 percent is imposed.

Fifth, a corporation may elect to file under Subchapter S of the Internal Revenue Code. This election eliminates the corporate tax; this subject is discussed further in Section 11 of this chapter.

10. LIMITED PARTNERSHIPS

A limited partnership basically has all the attributes of a partnership except that one or more of the partners are designated as **limited partners.** This type of partner is not personally responsible for the debts of the business organization. However, these limited partners are not permitted to be involved in the control or operations of the limited partnership. The management is left in the hands of one or more **general partners** who remain personally liable for the organization's debts.

> Ways corporate shareholders might avoid paying two taxes on the business's income and dividend payments:
> Reasonable salaries.
> Reasonable expense accounts.
> Reasonable loans from shareholders.
> Reasonable accumulation of earnings.
> Subchapter S election.

concept :: *summary*

Advantages and Disadvantages of Corporations

The usual advantages of the corporate form of organization include the following:

1. This form is the best practical means of bringing together a large number of investors.
2. Control may be held by those with a minority of the investment.
3. Ownership may be divided into many unequal shares.
4. Shareholders' liabilities are limited to their investments.
5. The organization can have perpetual existence.
6. In addition to being owners, shareholders may be employees entitled to benefits such as workers' compensation.

Among the frequently cited disadvantages of the corporate organization are the following:

1. The cost of forming and maintaining a corporation, with its formal procedural requirements, is significant.
2. License fees and franchise taxes often are assessed against corporations but not partnerships.
3. A corporation must be qualified in all states where it is conducting local or intrastate business.
4. Generally, corporations are subject to more governmental regulation at all levels than are other forms of business.
5. Corporate income may be subject to double taxation.

The attributes of a general partnership and a corporation that combine to make the limited partnership an attractive alternative form of business organization are discussed under the subheadings that follow.

Creation   Like a general partnership, a limited partnership is created by agreement. However, as in the case of a corporation, state law requires that the contents of a certificate must be recorded in a public office so that everyone may be fully advised as to the details of the organization. This certificate contains, among other matters, the following information: the name of the partnership, the character of the business, its location, the name and place of residence of each member, those who are to be the general partners and those who are to be the limited partners, the length of time the partnership is to exist, the amount of cash or the agreed value of property to be contributed by each partner, and the share of profit or compensation each limited partner shall receive.

The limited partnership certificate is required to be recorded in the county where the partnership has its principal place of business. An additional copy has to be filed in every community where the partnership conducts business or has an office. Whenever there is a change in the information contained in the filed certificate, a new certificate must be prepared and recorded. If an accurate certificate is not on record and the limited partnership continues its operation, the limited partners become liable as general partners. Substantial compliance with all the technical requirements of the limited partnership law is essential if the limited partners are to be assured of their limited liability.

The terms of the limited partnership agreement control the governance of the organization. These terms should be read carefully and understood by all general and limited partners before the agreement is signed. Failure of the

Limited partnerships are complex organizations that have been used to raise money for real estate investments and management of complex entities, such as professional sports teams.

parties to state their agreement clearly may result in a court's interpreting the limited partnership agreement.

Continuity The principles guiding partnerships also apply to limited partnerships if there is a change in the general partners. A limited partner may assign his or her interest to another without dissolving the limited partnership.

Managerial Control In a limited partnership, the general partners are in control. Limited partners have no right to participate in management. The impact of this relationship on the operations of a limited partnership is discussed in detail in the next subsection.

Liability The true nature of the limited partnership being a hybrid is in the area of owners' liability. Traditionally, the general partners in a limited partnership have unlimited liability. However, the limited partners are not personally liable for the partnership's debts. These limited partners' liability typically will not exceed the amount of their investments.

Under the Revised Uniform Limited Partnership Act (RULPA), a limited partner's surname may not be used in the partnership's name unless there is a general partner with the same name. If a limited partner's name is used in the firm's name, that partner will become personally liable to unsuspecting creditors.

Limited partners also may not participate in the management of the limited partnership. Under the RULPA, a limited partner who participates in the organization's management becomes liable as a general partner if a third party had knowledge of the limited partner's activities. Sidebar 14.7 lists actions by a limited partner that are not considered participation in management.

:: *sidebar* 14.7

Actions by Limited Partner

Limited partners do not lose the benefit of limited personal liability when performing the following:

- Acting as an agent or employee of the partnership.
- Consulting with or advising a general partner.
- Acting as a guarantor of the partnership's obligations.
- Inspecting and copying any of the partnership's financial records.
- Demanding true and full information about the partnership whenever circumstances render it just and reasonable.

- Receiving a share of the profits or other compensation by way of income.
- Approving or disapproving an amendment to the partnership's certificate.
- Voting on matters of fundamental importance such as dissolution, sale of assets, or change of the partnership's name.
- Having contribution returned upon dissolution.

11. S CORPORATIONS

Beginning in 1958, the federal government permitted shareholders of certain corporations to unanimously elect to have their organization treated like a partnership for income tax purposes. This election is made possible through the language of subchapter S of the Internal Revenue Code. Today, organizations that are subject to this election often are referred to simply as **S corporations.**

The S corporation has all the legal characteristics of the corporation previously discussed in this chapter. The one exception to this similar treatment is that shareholders in the S corporation are responsible for accounting on their individual income tax returns for their respective shares of their organization's profits or losses. In essence, these shareholders can elect to have their business organization treated, for tax purposes, as if it were a partnership. Through this election, the shareholders avoid having a tax assessed on the corporate income itself. Even though the S corporation does not pay any taxes, like a partnership, it must file an information return with the Internal Revenue Service. Sidebar 14.8 summarizes the U.S. Supreme Court case deciding whether it is the corporate or shareholder's personal return on which the statute of limitations for challenges is based.

:: *sidebar* 14.8

Applicable Tax Return—Personal versus Organizational

Bufferd was the treasurer and a shareholder of Compo Financial Services, Inc. Compo did business as an S corporation. In 1979, Compo had a loss which was passed through to Bufferd. Compo's informational return was filed on February 1, 1980. Bufferd filed his personal return on April 15, 1980. The Internal Revenue Code authorizes the IRS to assess tax deficiencies within three years of a return being filed. In March 1983, the IRS indicated to Bufferd that the amount of the "pass-through" was questionable. When the IRS assessed a tax deficiency against Bufferd, he argued that the assessment was beyond the three-year period based on when Compo filed its return.

Which return—the S Corporation's or the shareholder's—is used to determine the running of an applicable statute of limitations? The shareholder's personal return is the appropriate one to use. The IRS sought to assess taxes which Bufferd owed since his return contained an erroneous loss. The S Corporation's return, even with errors in it, does not affect the tax liability of that corporation. The IRS can only assess a deficiency against the shareholder-taxpayer whose return contains the erroneous information.

*Source: Bufferd v. Commissioner, 113 S. Ct. 927 (1993)

Do remember the limitation on the number of shareholders in an S corporation reduces it as an option for many business ventures.

S corporations cannot have more than 75 shareholders, each of whom must elect to have the corporate income allocated to the shareholders annually in computing their income for tax purposes, whether actually paid out or not. Only individuals are eligible to elect under subchapter S. Therefore, other forms of business organization, such as partnerships, limited partnerships, or corporations, cannot be shareholders in an S corporation.

In addition to the limitations just stated, there are many technical rules of tax law involved in S corporations. However, as a rule of thumb, this method of organization has distinct advantages for a business operating at a loss because the loss is shared and immediately deductible on the returns of the shareholders. It is also advantageous for businesses capable of paying out net profits as earned. In the latter case, the corporate tax is avoided. If net profits must be retained in the business, subchapter S tax treatment is disadvantageous because income tax is paid on earnings not received, and there is a danger of double taxation to the individual because undistributed earnings that have been taxed once are taxed again in the event of the death of a shareholder. Thus, the theoretical advantage of using an S corporation to avoid double taxation of corporate income must be carefully qualified.

12. LIMITED LIABILITY ORGANIZATIONS

The **limited liability company** is a relatively new organizational alternative. In 1977, Wyoming was the first state to pass a law permitting the creation of this type of business organization.

In 1988, the Internal Revenue Service ruled that limited liability companies (LLCs) would be treated as nontaxable entities, much like partnerships, for federal income tax purposes. Following this ruling, states rushed to pass legislation authorizing businesspeople to operate their businesses as LLCs. In essence, its owners have more flexibility than with the S corporation while not having to struggle with the complexities of the limited partnership.

A variation of the LLC is known as the **limited liability partnership.** This organization often is used by professionals, such as doctors, lawyers, and accountants. In the true sense of a hybrid, an LLC and an LLP have characteristics of both a partnership and a corporation.

The growing popularity of these forms of business organizations requires a careful examination of the various factors to consider. The focus of the following subheadings is on the LLC.

Creation An LLC is created through filings much like those used when creating a corporation. **Articles of organization** are filed with a state official, usually the secretary of state. Instead of "incorporators," the term **organizers** is used. The name of any LLC must acknowledge the special nature of this organizational form by including the phrase "limited liability company," or "limited company," or some abbreviation, such as "LLC" or "LC." An LLC created in a state other than the one in which it is conducting business is called a foreign LLC. Like a foreign corporation, this LLC must apply to the state to be authorized to transact business legally. An LLC also must file annual reports with the states in which it operates.

Continuity The owners of LLCs are called **members** rather than shareholders or partners. Membership in LLCs is not limited to individuals. Unlike in the S corporation, a business organization can be an owner in any LLC. The transferability of a member's interest is restricted in the fashion of a partner as opposed to the free transferability of a corporate shareholder. Anytime a member dies or withdraws from the LLC, there is a dissolution of the business organization. However, the business of a dissolved LLC is not necessarily adversely impacted if the remaining members decide to continue business. Either as provided in the articles of organization or by agreement of the remaining members within 90 days of the withdrawing member's disassociation, the business of the LLC may be continued rather than wound up.

Over the last two decades, the growth of LLPs and LLCs has made these organizational forms very popular for closely held businesses.

Managerial Control The managerial control of an LLC is vested in its members, unless the articles of organization provide for one or more **managers.** Regardless of whether members or managers control the LLC, a majority of these decision makers decide the direction of the organization. In a few situations enumerated in the state law authorizing LLCs, unanimous consent of the members is required for the organization to make a binding decision. Similarly to partners in a partnership, members of LLCs make contributions of capital. They have equal rights to share in the LLC's profits and losses, unless these members have agreed otherwise. When a member is in the minority with respect to decisions being made on behalf of the LLC, that dissenting member has rights very much like a dissenting shareholder in a corporation. These rights include bringing a derivative lawsuit against the controlling members of the LLC. Ultimately, a dissenting member has the right to sell the membership interest to the other members of the LLC.

Liability For liability purposes, members do act as agents of their LLC. However, they are not personally liable to third parties. Thus, these members have attributes of both partners and shareholders with respect to liability.

Taxation Finally, state laws and the IRS recognize LLCs as nontaxable entities. Although the LLC appears to have many advantages, do not forget that careful analysis is needed in every situation to determine whether this type of tax treatment is in the members' best interests.

:: Operating the Organization

With an understanding of the various organizational forms and the factors businesspeople need to consider when deciding how to do business, we are ready to focus on making the decision as to which form of organization is most appropriate for conducting business. Following the next section, this chapter concludes with some thoughts on trends in operating business organizations.

13. MAKING THE DECISION

Don't assume there is an easy answer to which organizational form is best; careful analysis and consultation with experts help businesspeople make wise decisions in the selection process.

There usually is no absolutely right answer to the question, Which organizational form is best for a particular business's operation? Hopefully the preceding sections have presented you with some helpful background material to consider when this important decision is made.

The criteria used to select a form of organization needs to be reviewed periodically. This review should be done in consultation with close advisers such as attorneys, accountants, bankers, and insurers. These people weigh the factors and costs involved and then select the most suitable organizational form for the business's needs at that time. Because this selection process balances advantages against disadvantages, the decision often is to choose the least objectionable form of organization.

Today, the growth in limited liability partnerships and limited liability companies could lead you to think these are the best options for your business activities. While one of these forms may be best, a careful analysis will consider the various factors discussed in this chapter.

It is not unusual for the growth in a business to be reflected in changes in organizational forms as a part of a life cycle. For example, business activity could begin through the efforts of a sole proprietor. As the business grows and investors join the business, the organizational form could shift to a partnership or limited partnership (depending on the active or passive nature of the investor). An alternative to the partnership or limited partnership could be a limited liability organization. As the business matures and prepares to conduct a public offering of its stock, the corporate form becomes the most feasible organization.

14. TRENDS IN MANAGING THE ORGANIZATION

Throughout the early years of this twenty-first century, a lot of public attention and legal response have focused on management of publicly held corporations. In the next chapter, you will study the Sarbanes-Oxley Act of 2002 and read about its impact on corporate governance. Since control of business organizations is a major factor in this chapter, this section addresses three important trends.

First, leaders of organizations can create dire consequences by making bad decisions. The Enron debacle is wide-reaching because so many poor business decisions were made. One of the sad stories was the failure of Arthur Andersen as one of the premier accounting firms. Through the acts of its partners and employees, Arthur Andersen lost the trust of the public. Case 14.2 describes the background and legal processes from which Arthur Andersen, as a major accounting firm, could not recover. The actions of individuals caused the public to lose trust in the organization.

> "In 2006, 31.9 percent of CEOs who stepped down worldwide did so due to conflict with the board, up from 12.4 percent in 1995."
>
> **–Booz Allen study, cited in The Wall Street Journal, January 14, 2008.**

case **14.2** ::

ARTHUR ANDERSEN LLP v. UNITED STATES
125 S. Ct. 2129 (2005)

Arthur Andersen LLP served as Enron Corporation's auditor. In Fall 2001, as Enron faced a series of accounting scandals, Arthur Andersen formed an "Enron Crisis Response Team." During October, on several occasions, Arthur Andersen emphasized to its employees that its documentation and retention policy should be followed. In late October, the Enron Crisis Response Team received specific instructions to comply with the firm's documentation and retention policy. These instructions caused team members to shred Enron-related documents. This shredding involved thousands of documents and continued for days. Even on October 30, when the SEC opened a formal investigation and asked Enron for accounting documents, the shredding at Arthur Andersen did not

stop. On November 8, the SEC served both Enron and Arthur Andersen with subpoenas for accounting records. Finally, the next day, Arthur Andersen officials stopped the document-shredding process.

In March 2002, Arthur Andersen was indicted for "knowingly, intentionally, and corruptly persuading" its employees to destroy documents to obstruct a criminal investigation. A the end of the trial, the judge instructed the jury that Arthur Andersen could be found guilty if the jury found the firm intended to "subvert, undermine, or impede" a governmental investigation. The jury deliberated for ten days before finding Arthur Andersen guilty. The 5th Circuit of Appeals affirmed the conviction and Arthur Andersen was granted this review by the Supreme Court to determine the degree of conscious wrongdoing needed to support a conviction.

REHNQUIST, C.J.: . . .Chapter 73 of Title 18 of the United States Code provides criminal sanctions for those who obstruct justice. Sections 1512(b)(2)(A) and (B), part of the witness tampering provisions, provide in relevant part:

> Whoever knowingly uses intimidation or physical force, threatens, or corruptly persuades another person, or attempts to do so, or engages in misleading conduct toward another person, with intent to . . . cause or induce any person to . . . withhold testimony, or withhold a record, document, or other object, from an official proceeding [or] alter, destroy, mutilate, or conceal an object with intent to impair the object's integrity or availability for use in an official proceeding . . . shall be fined under this title or imprisoned not more than ten years, or both.

In this case, our attention is focused on what it means to "knowingly . . . corruptly persuade" another person "with intent to . . . cause" that person to "withhold" documents from, or "alter" documents for use in, an "official proceeding."

We have traditionally exercised restraint in assessing the reach of a federal criminal statute, both out of deference to the prerogatives of Congress and out of concern that a fair warning should be given to the world in language that the common world will understand, of what the law intends to do if a certain line is passed.

Such restraint is particularly appropriate here, where the act underlying the conviction—"persuasion"—is by itself innocuous. Indeed, "persuading" a person "with intent to . . . cause" that person to "withhold" testimony or documents from a Government proceeding or Government official is not inherently malign. Consider, for instance, a mother who suggests to her son that he invoke his right against compelled self-incrimination, or a wife who persuades her husband not to disclose marital confidences.

Nor is it necessarily corrupt for an attorney to "persuade" a client "with intent to . . . cause" that client to "withhold" documents from the Government. In *Upjohn Co. v. United States*, 101 S. Ct. 677 (1981), for example, we held that Upjohn was justified in withholding documents that were covered by the attorney-client privilege from the Internal Revenue Service (IRS). No one would suggest that an attorney who "persuaded" Upjohn to take that step acted wrongfully, even though he surely intended that his client keep those documents out of the IRS' hands.

Document retention policies, which are created in part to keep certain information from getting into the hands of others, including the Government, are common in business. It is, of course, not wrongful for a manager to instruct his employees to comply with a valid document retention policy under ordinary circumstances.

Acknowledging this point, the parties have largely focused their attention on the word "corruptly" as the key to what may or may not lawfully be done in the situation presented here. Section 1512(b) punishes not just "corruptly persuading" another, but "knowingly . . . corruptly persuading" another. The Government suggests that "knowingly" does not modify "corruptly persuades," but that is not how the statute most naturally reads. It provides the *mens rea*—"knowingly"—and then a list of acts—"uses intimidation or physical force, threatens, or corruptly persuades." We have recognized with regard to similar statutory language that the *mens rea* at least applies to the acts that immediately follow, if not to other elements down the statutory chain. . . .

The parties have not pointed us to another interpretation of "knowingly . . . corruptly" to guide us here. In any event, the natural meaning of these terms provides a clear answer. "Knowledge" and knowingly" are normally associated with awareness, understanding, or consciousness. "Corrupt" and "corruptly" are normally associated with wrongful, immoral, depraved, or evil. Joining these meanings together here makes sense both linguistically and in the statutory scheme. Only persons conscious of wrong-doing can be said to "knowingly . . . corruptly persuade." And limiting criminality to persuaders conscious of their wrongdoing sensibly allows § 1512(b) to reach only those with the level of culpability . . . we usually require in order to impose criminal liability.

The outer limits of this element need not be explored here because the jury instructions at issue simply failed to convey the requisite consciousness of wrongdoing. Indeed, it is striking how little culpability the instructions required. For example, the jury was told that, "even if [petitioner] honestly and sincerely believed that its conduct was lawful, you may find [petitioner] guilty." The instructions also diluted the meaning of "corruptly" so that it covered innocent conduct.

The parties vigorously disputed how the jury would be instructed on "corruptly." The District Court based its instruction on the definition of that term found in the Fifth Circuit Pattern Jury Instruction. . . . This pattern instruction defined "corruptly" as "knowingly and dishonestly, with the specific intent to subvert or undermine the integrity" ' of a proceeding. The Government, however, insisted on excluding "dishonestly" and adding the term "impede" to the phrase "subvert or undermine." The District Court agreed over petitioner's objections, and the jury was told to convict if it found petitioner intended to "subvert, undermine, or impede" governmental fact-finding by suggesting to its employees that they enforce the document retention policy.

These changes were significant. No longer was any type of "dishonesty" necessary to a finding of guilt, and it was enough for petitioner to have simply "impeded" the Government's factfinding ability. As the Government conceded at oral argument, "impede" has broader connotations than "subvert" or even "undermine," and many of these connotations do not incorporate any "corruptness" at all. The dictionary defines "impede" as "to interfere with or get in the way of the progress of" or "hold up" or "detract from." By definition, anyone who innocently persuades another to withhold information from the Government gets in the way of the progress of the Government. With regard to such innocent conduct, the "corruptly" instructions did no limiting work whatsoever.

The instructions also were infirm for another reason. They led the jury to believe that it did not have to find any nexus between the "persuasion" to destroy documents and any particular proceeding. In resisting any type of nexus element, the Government relies heavily on § 1512(e)(1), which states that an official proceeding "need not be pending or about to be instituted at the time of the offense." It is, however, one thing to say that a proceeding "need not be pending or about to be instituted at the time of the offense," and quite another to say a proceeding need not even be foreseen. A "knowingly . . . corrupt persuader" cannot be someone who persuades others to shred documents under a document retention policy when he does not have in contemplation any particular official proceeding in which those documents might be material. . . .

For these reasons, the jury instructions here were flawed in important respects. The judgment of the Court of Appeals is reversed, and the case is remanded for further proceedings consistent with this opinion.

Reversed and remanded.

:: CASE QUESTIONS

1. With respect to the intent of Arthur Andersen, what was the trial judge's instruction to the jury?
2. What are the conclusions of the trial court, court of appeals, and Supreme Court?
3. Why is the concept of conscious wrongdoing important to the Supreme Court?

Even though Arthur Andersen succeeded in getting its criminal conviction reversed, the misdeeds of its partners and employees caused the organization's demise as a public accounting firm. Once the public trust is lost, it is almost impossible to restore it. As a result, the decisions of some Arthur Andersen partners led to a major restructuring among large accounting firms.

The second trend can be seen through examples of boards of directors increasing their oversight of management. As discussed in Sidebar 14.5, the post-Enron/WorldCom era involves corporate directors becoming more active and not idly approving proposals from corporate officers. An additional reason for more action on the part of directors arises from their potential financial exposure. Sidebar 14.9 summarizes what were groundbreaking developments at the time of these settlements.

A third significant trend in corporate governance relates to shareholders becoming increasingly active. For example, shareholders have asked for more say in the level of executive compensation. AFLAC is the first company to adopt a policy that shareholders will annually review and vote on the compensation of its top five executives. Even though this shareholders' vote is nonbinding on the AFLAC Board of Directors, serious consideration should be given to the shareholders. Verizon and several other companies

"In the past, boards were content to act as overseers, approving management's plans and rarely taking an active role in developing these plans. Today, boards are more likely to want their input sought throughout the process."

–Chuck Lucier, The Wall Street Journal, January 14, 2008.

:: *sidebar* 14.9

Director's Personal Liability

Historically corporate directors relied on insurance, furnished by their corporations, to cover any liability arising out of their decisions. In 2005, former directors of WorldCom and Enron reached agreements with creditors and shareholders. In both cases, the directors agreed to contribute money out of their personal funds to the settlement. Ten former WorldCom directors agreed to pay $18 million, and ten former Enron directors agreed to contribute $13 million in settlement payments.

*Sources: Gretchen Morgenson, "10 Directors from WorldCom to Pay Millions," *The New York Times*, January 6, 2005; and Kurt Eichenwald, "Ex-Directors at Enron to Chip In on Settlement," *The New York Times*, January 8, 2005.

> "The real value of say-on-pay is not to slash executive salaries as a matter of principle, but to force corporate boards and their compensation committees to better explain their decisions."
>
> **– The New York Times, May 25, 2007.**

have adopted what is known as **say-on-pay** proposals. Congress also is considering making shareholders voting on pay required, even though such votes would be advisory and nonbinding.

We encourage you to use what you learn in this chapter to stay current in this area of operating and managing business organizations.

:: Key Terms

Alter-ego theory 422	Domestic corporation 418	Member 429
Articles of incorporation 419	Double tax 424	Officer 420
Articles of organization 429	Foreign corporation 418	Organizer 429
Articles of partnership 416	General partner 425	Partnership 415
Assumed-name statute 416	Incorporator 419	Piercing the corporate veil 422
Buy and sell agreement 417	Jointly and severally liable 417	Proxy 420
Charter 419	Limited liability company 429	Publicly held 412
Closely held 412	Limited liability	S corporation 428
Corporation 418	partnership 429	Say-on-pay 434
Derivative suit 421	Limited partner 425	Shareholder 420
Director 420	Limited personal liability 421	Sole proprietorship 414
Dissolution 413	Manager 430	

:: Review Questions and Problems

1. *Forms of Business Organizations*

    (a) What are the three traditional business organizations and the four hybrid forms?

Factors to Consider When Selecting a Business's Organizational Form

2. *Creation*

   Relative to other factors discussed in this chapter, how important is the factor of creation?

3. *Continuity*

   Why does dissolution of a business organization not necessarily impact that organization's business activities?

4. *Managerial Control*

   Why should business owners take time to discuss the control each will exert over the organization's activities?

5. *Liability*

   What is meant by the phrase liability of a business organization as compared to the liability of the owners?

6. *Taxation*

   Why is taxation an important element to consider when selecting the appropriate organization for your business activities?

Selecting the Best Organizational Form

7. *Sole Proprietorships*

   What are the limitations of the sole proprietorship?

8. *Partnerships*

   Terry is the senior partner in an accounting firm. One of Terry's partners performs an audit. The audited firm sues Terry, as the senior partner, for alleged errors in the audit. If Terry is found liable, can Terry sue to collect a pro rata share of this liability from the other partners? Why or why not?

9. *Corporations*

   (a) Who controls the closely held corporation? Explain.

   (b) Describe five techniques that a corporation might use to avoid the double taxation of corporate profits.

10. *Limited Partnerships*

    Laura and Gary have formed a limited partnership, with Gary agreeing to be the general partner. This partnership has purchased supplies from Sam. Sam has received a promissory note signed on behalf of the partnership as payment. If the partnership is unable to pay this note, can Sam hold Gary personally liable? Explain.

11. *S Corporations*

    (a) Although it is technically a corporation, the S corporation has the attributes of which business organization when considering the taxation factor?

    (b) What is the implication of this treatment if the S corporation has a profitable year but does not distribute dividends to its shareholders?

12. *Limited Liability Organizations*

    What is the advantage of this organizational form compared to the S corporation?

Operating the Organization

13. *Making the Decision*

    Albert and Barbara wish to enter into the business of manufacturing fine furniture. Which form of business organization would you recommend in each of the following situations? Explain each of your answers.

    (a) Barbara is a furniture expert, but she has no funds. Albert knows nothing about such production, but he is willing to contribute all the money needed to start the business.

(b) The furniture-manufacturing process requires more capital than Albert or Barbara can raise together. However, they wish to maintain control of the business.

(c) The production process can be very dangerous, and a large tort judgment against the business is foreseeable.

(d) Sales will be nationwide.

(e) A loss is expected for the first several years.

14. *Trends in Managing the Organization*

Explain three trends and the reasons for boards of directors and shareholders becoming more active in the operations of publicly held corporations.

business :: *discussions*

1. You and two of your college roommates have discussed plans to open a restaurant. You intend to attract college-age students who are health- and fitness-minded to your restaurant. You and your co-owners agree that each will invest equally in terms of time and money. However, in addition to contributions made by each of you, another $700,000 is essential for the restaurant to succeed.

What type of organization is best suited for this business activity?

Who will manage the restaurant during times that you and your co-owners are not present?

What liabilities do you and your co-owners face?

2. Three years following your graduation with a business degree, you and three classmates began operating a consulting business. Your firm specializes in offering support related to payroll-and account-management computer applications. So far, your firm has relied on the four of you as its only consultants. A potential major client requests that your firm make a proposal for a year-long project. This project would result in your firm hiring several additional consultants and support staff. Because of the length of time and financial commitment this project may take, you and your co-owners take time to address the following questions:

How would your firm conduct business on such a large scale?

How could you limit potential liability for and by various consultants?

Which form of business organization is best suited to meet the needs of your growing firm?

15

Sarbanes-Oxley and Securities Regulations

The previous chapter examines how business activity can be organized. That chapter focuses on how the concept of corporate governance relates to the creation and management of business organizations. One way to view this chapter is as a continuation of those topics. The phrase corporate governance as used in this chapter relates to government regulation of the ownership of business organizations. Indeed, of all the topics covered in this text, enforcement and revisions of securities regulations are the principal means used by the federal and state government to create and restore investor confidence following scandals involving Enron, WorldCom, Tyco, Adelphia, HealthSouth, and other major corporations.

Your reading and study of this chapter will expose you to numerous examples as to how businesspeople are required to manage their organizations. This chapter also acquaints you, as a potential investor, with the laws protecting you and your fellow investors.

As you study this chapter, remember that the regulation of securities began as part of the program to help the United States overcome the great depression of the early 1930s. You should also realize that these securities laws are designed to give potential investors sufficient information so that they can make intelligent investment decisions based on factual information rather than on other less certain criteria. Although federal securities laws are now more than 70 years old, their application is at the heart of corporate governance during the first years of the twenty-first century. These laws are substantially modified by the Sarbines-Oxley Act of 2002. Table 15.1 provides a chronological summary of various securities laws covered in this chapter.

table 15.1 :: Laws Regulating Securities Transactions

:: Statute	:: Summary of Major Provisions
Securities Act of 1933	• Disclosure law governing initial sale of securities to public.
	• Defines the term *security.*
	• Creates liability for false or misleading registration statement (Section 11).
	• Creates liability for failure to file a registration statement (Section 12[1]).
	• Creates liability for false or misleading prospectus (Section 12[2]).
	• Creates liability for fraudulent communications used in the offer of sales of securities (Section 17[a]).
Securities Exchange Act of 1934	• Created Securities and Exchange Commission.
	• Governs exchanges of securities beyond the initial sale.
	• Creates liability for fraudulent manipulation of securities'value (Section 10[b]).
	• Creates liability for short-swing profits made by insiders (Section 16).
	• Creates liability for false or misleading filings with the SEC (Section 18).
	• Creates liability for fraudulent transactions related to tender offers (Section 14[e]).
Insider Trading and Securities Fraud Enforcement Act of 1988	• Provides for recovery of triple damages in civil actions against user of nonpublic information.
	• Increases criminal sanctions for use of nonpublic information.
Private Securities Litigation Reform Act of 1995	• Clarifies that individuals and organizations can sue primary parties, but not secondary parties, for securities violations.
	• Requires pleading of specific allegations of wrongdoing.
	• Attempts to reduce nuisance filings.

Securities Enforcement Remedies Act of 1990	• Increases civil fines for violations of securities laws.
	• Prohibits an individual's service as an officer or director.
Sarbanes-Oxley Act of 2002	• Increases budgetary support to Securities and Exchange Commission.
	• Creates Public Company Accounting Oversight Board.
	• Changes membership requirements of corporate audit committees.
	• Requires CEOs to certify financial statements.
	• Increases criminal penalties for fraud and false statements.
State blue sky laws	• Impose another level of securities regulations beyond federal laws.
	• Govern intrastate securities transactions not regulated by federal laws.

Before we examine any of the laws in depth, the next two sections present introductory materials on the meaning of the term *security* and the role of the federal Securities and Exchange Commission.

1. WHAT IS A SECURITY?

Because the objective of securities laws is to protect uninformed people from investing their money without sufficient information, the term **security** has a very broad definition. Indeed, the federal securities laws provide the following definition:

> "Security" means any note, stock, treasury stock, bond, debenture, evidence of indebtedness, certificate of interest or participation in any profit-sharing agreement, collateral-trust certificate, preorganization certificate or subscription, transferable share, investment contract, voting-trust certificate, certificate of deposit for a security, fractional undivided interest in oil, gas, or other mineral rights, or in general, any interest or instrument commonly known as a "security," or any certificate of interest or participation in, temporary or interim certificate for receipt for, guarantee of, or warrant or right to subscribe to or purchase, any of the foregoing.[1]

As this definition indicates, the word *security* includes much more than corporation stock. Historically, the Supreme Court has held that a security exists when one person invests money and looks to others to manage the money for profit. On the basis of this statement, courts seek positive answers to the following three questions when determining whether a person has purchased a security:

1. Is the investment in a common business activity?
2. Is the investment based on a reasonable expectation of profits?
3. Will these profits be earned through the efforts of someone other than the investor?

---

[1]*15 U.S.C.A. § 77b(1). This definition is a part of the 1933 Securities Act. It is virtually identical to the definition of security found in the 1934 Securities Exchange Act.*

If the answer to all three questions is yes, then a security is involved regardless of the form it takes. Case 15.1 is a recent one that illustrates the broad application of securities laws.

case 15.1 ::

SECURITIES AND EXCHANGE COMMISSION v. EDWARDS
124 S. Ct. 892 (2004)

Charles Edwards, the CEO and sole shareholder of ETS Payphones, Inc., offered the public investment opportunities in payphones. The basic arrangement involves an investor paying $7,000 to own a payphone. Each investor was offered $82 per month under a lease-back and management arrangement with ETS. The investor also was to receive their $7,000 investment at the end of five years. ETS did not generate enough revenue to pay its investors and it filed for bankruptcy. The SEC sued ETS for civil damages arising from alleged violations of federal securities laws. The SEC won at the trial level when the district judge ruled that payphone leaseback and management agreements were investment contracts covered by federal securities laws. The Eleventh Circuit Court of Appeals reversed this judgment and ruled in favor of ETS. That court concluded the guaranteed fixed payments and the return of the investment at the end of the leaseback and management agreement remove these investments from federal securities laws. The SEC was granted certiorari to have the Supreme Court review the definition and application of the term security.

O'CONNOR, J.: "Opportunity doesn't always knock . . . sometimes it rings." (ETS Payphones promotional brochure). And sometimes it hangs up. So it did for the 10,000 people who invested a total of $300 million in the payphone sale-and-leaseback arrangements touted by respondent under that slogan. The Securities and Exchange Commission (SEC) argues that the arrangements were investment contracts, and thus were subject to regulation under the federal securities laws. In this case, we must decide whether a moneymaking scheme is excluded from the term *investment contract* simply because the scheme offered a contractual entitlement to a fixed, rather than a variable, return. . . .

Congress's purpose in enacting the securities laws was to regulate investments, in whatever form they are made and by whatever name they are called. To that end, it enacted a broad definition of *security* , sufficient to encompass virtually any instrument that might

be sold as an investment. *Investment contract* is not itself defined.

The test for whether a particular scheme is an investment contract was established in our decision in *SEC v. W. J. Howey Co.* , 66 S. Ct. 1100 (1946). We look to whether the scheme involves an investment of money in a common enterprise with profits to come solely from the efforts of others. This definition embodies a flexible rather than a static principle, one that is capable of adaptation to meet the countless and variable schemes devised by those who seek the use of the money of others on the promise of profits . . .

There is no reason to distinguish between promises of fixed returns and promises of variable returns for purposes of the test. . . In both cases, the investing public is attracted by representations of investment income, as purchasers were in this case by ETS's invitation to watch the profits add up. Moreover, investments pitched as low-risk (such as those offering a "guaranteed" fixed return) are particularly attractive to individuals more vulnerable to investment fraud, including older and less sophisticated investors. Under the reading respondent advances, unscrupulous marketers of investments could evade the securities laws by picking a rate of return to promise. We will not read into the securities laws a limitation not compelled by the language that would so undermine the laws' purposes.

Respondent protests that including investment schemes promising a fixed return among investment contracts conflicts with our precedent. We disagree. . . .

Given that respondent's position is supported neither by the purposes of the securities laws nor by our precedents, it is no surprise that the SEC has consistently taken the opposite position, and maintained that a promise of a fixed return does not preclude a scheme from being an investment contract. It has done so in formal adjudications and in enforcement actions.

The Eleventh Circuit's perfunctory alternative holding, that respondent's scheme falls outside the definition because purchasers had a contractual entitlement to a return, is incorrect and inconsistent with our precedent. We are considering investment contracts. The fact that investors have bargained for a return on their investment does not mean that the return is not also expected to come solely from the efforts of others. Any other conclusion would conflict with our holding that an investment contract was offered in *Howey* itself.

We hold that an investment scheme promising a fixed rate of return can be an *investment contract* and thus a *security* subject to the federal securities laws. The judgment of the United States Court of Appeals for the Eleventh Circuit is reversed, and the case is remanded for further proceedings consistent with this opinion.

Reversed and remanded.

:: CASE QUESTIONS

1. What was the nature of the investment made with ETS?
2. Why does ETS argue it is not selling a security and therefore is not subject to the federal securities laws?
3. What is the Supreme Court's definition of a security and how does it apply to ETS payphones?

This three-prong analysis permits courts to find the sale of oil-well interests, the syndication of racehorses, and shares of limited partnerships are securities. The *Howey* case mentioned in the case above involved the sale of orange trees in a Florida orchard. The Howey in the-Hills Services Company offered buyers of trees a management service contract whereby Howey provided care for the trees and harvesting of the fruit. When the investors did not receive the return they expected, Howey was held liable for failing to comply with securities laws.

2. SECURITIES AND EXCHANGE COMMISSION

The **Securities and Exchange Commission (SEC)** is an administrative agency created in 1934 that is responsible for administering the federal securities laws. The SEC consists of five commissioners appointed by the president for five-year terms. In addition to these commissioners, the SEC employs staff personnel such as lawyers, accountants, security analysts, security examiners, and others.

The SEC has both quasi-legislative and quasi-judicial powers. Under its quasi-legislative power, it has adopted rules and regulations relating to financial and other information that must be furnished to the Commission. Other rules prescribe information that must be given to potential investors. The SEC also regulates the various stock exchanges, utility holding companies, investment trusts, and investment advisers. Under its quasi-judicial power, the SEC also is involved in a variety of investigations. Sidebar 15.1 highlights recent actions by the SEC.

:: Sarbanes-Oxley Act of 2002

When the collapse of Enron was followed by the even larger accounting fraud and bankruptcy of WorldCom, congressional response was passage of the **Sarbanes-Oxley Act of 2002.** This law is named for its sponsors—Senator Paul Sarbanes, a Democrat from Maryland, and Representative Michael Oxley, an Ohio Republican. The Sarbanes-Oxley Act receives mixed reviews; however,

> Sarbanes-Oxley is "the most significant change to securities law since they were put into effect in the mid-1930s"
>
> **–Dennis M. Nalley Chairman of Pricewaterhouse Coopers**

:: *sidebar* 15.1

The Securities and Exchange Commission in the Headlines

The SEC's involvement in addressing the massive corporate fraud revealed through accounting and auditing irregularities has resulted in some staggering fines. For example, in 2003, WorldCom, while under the protection of the bankruptcy court, settled all claims with the SEC by agreeing to pay a fine of $500 million. Also in 2003, the SEC settled claims with the 10 largest securities brokerage firms for a combined total of approximately $1.4 billion. These firms agreed to resolve allegations they participated in inappropriate dealings during the 1990s stock market mania. These 10 firms paid $487.5 million in fines. They created a pool of $387.5 million from which their customers can make claims. Finally, these firms agreed to pay $432.5 million to support financial research that will be available free of charge to their customers, and $80 million to support investor education programs.

Various sections in this chapter discuss other enforcement actions by the SEC.

most businesspeople agree it has overwhelming positive impacts on the way business is conducted and audited.

3. REVITALIZATION OF SEC

> "Our goal is to effectively balance the goal of providing shareholders with timely disclosure of accurate and complete compensation information with the need to prevent strategic company information from being revealed to competitors and damaging a company."
>
> **–John J. Castellani**
> **President of Business**
> **Roundtable**

Through the Sarbanes-Oxley Act of 2002 and in response to the corporate scandals of the first few years of this century, Congress increased the authority it delegated to the SEC. A primary way of accomplishing this reinvigoration of a 70-year-old agency was to increase its budget. Because the budget is not controlled solely by Congress, there initially was some controversy with the Bush Administration as to the amount of the increase. The proposed increase of more than 75 percent of the SEC budget was not accomplished in one year; however, the SEC's current budget does allow for more investigative and enforcement staff. The increased budget has led to a more active SEC.

Sarbanes-Oxley (SOX) increases the SEC's power over many of the governance issues discussed in Section 5 of this chapter. The following are among the new or proposed rules issued by the SEC in the past several years:

- The need for public companies to have a majority of independent directors on their boards.
- The focus on the agency's effort to collect civil damages against executives and their company so long as the shareholder's value will not be harmed.
- The increase in emphasis on how the Internet can assist shareholders in expressing their views through voting and other communications.
- The disclosure of executive compensation, including severance packages and other perks such as stock options, travel benefits, club memberships, and retirement plans. These disclosures cover the CEO, CFO, and the three other highest paid executives.

4. ACCOUNTING REFORMS

Sarbanes-Oxley creates the Public Company Accounting Oversight Board (PCAOB). This Board consists of five members appointed by the SEC commissioners. The PCAOB reports to the commissioners. Congress viewed accounting firms as a major contributor to the corporate scandals involving Enron, WorldCom, HealthSouth, Tyco, and others. This view is based, in part, on the role that the Arthur Andersen accounting firm played with Enron and WorldCom. Review, from Chapter 14, the *Arthur Andersen* case that documents the mistakes the firm made.

The PCAOB is given oversight of accounting firms that audit public companies. One of the first steps required of accounting firms was the separation of the auditing and consulting functions. The belief is that firms tainted their independence in the auditing function because they made so much more money consulting with these same corporate clients. This separation of the auditing and consulting functions is the reason why Arthur Andersen consultants formed a separate organization, which is now called Accenture. The management consulting services of PricewaterhouseCoopers (PWC) were sold to IBM, so that PWC can concentrate on its tax and audit practices.

The PCAOB requires that auditing firms refrain from conducting a variety of nonauditing services. These services include bookkeeping, system designs and implementation, appraisals and valuations, actuarial services, human resources functions, and investment banking.

The effectiveness of the role of PCAOB is still being determined. Some critics question the Sarbanes-Oxley Act for not making this Board truly an independent agency. Others believe that having the Board report within the SEC strengthens the new and existing administrative structure. In the years ahead, it will be interesting to observe the PCAOB's role in governing the effectiveness of public accounting firms.

5. CORPORATE GOVERNANCE

Over time, this area of regulation may be the major contribution of the Sarbanes-Oxley Act. Although other parts of the law get more attention because of the financial impact (see the next section of this chapter), restructuring how corporations govern themselves and the governance requirements required by the SEC and the PCAOB are of critical importance. Under this heading, several items relate to the audit of public companies.

Sarbanes-Oxley focuses on increasing the independence of the auditors. Congress seeks to ensure that auditors maintain the trust of the public and the corporate shareholders and not the loyalty of the corporate officers and directors. This effort principally is oriented to the public company's audit committee. Each member of this committee must be independent from the control of the company. No longer may a public company place its finance officer or other employee on the audit committee.

Further, at least one member of the audit committee has to be a financial expert. To qualify as a financial expert, it must be shown that through experience or education this person has an understanding of generally accepted accounting practices (GAAP), financial statements, audits of public companies, internal audit controls, and the functions of an audit committee.

Sarbanes-Oxley requires that the auditor report to this independent audit committee. The auditor should not have a close working relationship with the company's CFO, accounting staff, and other company officials. In addition,

These legal requirements allow the audit firm to do what it historically did—review the company's finances and ensure accuracy.

the audit partner of the auditing firm must rotate off the engagement every five years. Auditors also must preserve audit records for seven years.

6. FINANCIAL STATEMENTS AND CONTROLS

These requirements of the Sarbanes-Oxley Act have been the most controversial. One of the major reasons for the controversy is the cost associated with complying with these provisions. Section 302 of the law requires CEOs and CFOs to certify the accuracy of the quarterly and annual financial statements filed with the SEC. These officials also must certify the existence of internal financial controls. These controls are subject to an independent auditor's review, in the same manner that the financial statements must be audited. The certification of internal financial controls is mandated by Section 404 of Sarbanes-Oxley.

The Big Four accounting firms commissioned a study of the cost of implementing Section 404 certification of internal financial controls. This study divided companies into large ones with over $700 million in market capitalization and into smaller ones with between $75 million and $700 million in market capitalization. Table 15.2 shows this study's first-year cost of compliance.

Because the compliance costs issue creates political debate, the SEC extended the beginning date of compliance for smaller companies to 2008. The SEC also offered guidelines to reduce the burden on larger companies in certifying internal reporting controls. These actions and the repetitive nature of complying with Section 404 seem to bring down the compliance costs. Each year since 2004, larger companies find efficiencies related to Section 404 certification.

Other evidence that Sarbanes-Oxley is having a positive impact is found in the number of restatements of financial reports. During 2007, there were fewer restatements than in 2006. This was the first year to show a decline since Sarbanes-Oxley was enacted. Other good news was that the amount or severity of the average restatement also declined. These trends indicate that the impact of Sarbanes-Oxley is positive.

An additional provision of Sarbanes-Oxley emphasizes the importance of accurate financial records. Despite the fact that corporate scandals caused shareholders to lose billions of dollars, corporate executives received millions in bonuses and incentive payments. Sarbanes-Oxley provides that whenever there is a restatement of the company's financial condition, executives must return any bonuses paid as a result of the incorrect financial statements. The law also prohibits personal loans from the company to its executives.

> The requirements of Section 404 "offered us an opportunity to look at our processes and in many cases improve them. We found our people really benefited from understanding the processes. It has made Staples a better company."
>
> **–John J. Mahoney CFO of Staples**

> "Nearly 70% of the executives said auditors had reduced the number of 'key controls' they examined last year. Auditors were more likely to take a risk-based approach, to rely on the work of others and to use their own judgment in evaluating the effectiveness of the company's controls"
>
> **–Judith Burns, "Sarbanes-Oxley Costs For Compliance Declines," The Wall Street Journal, April 29, 2008.**

table 15.2 :: Cost of Section 404 Compliance in First Year	:: Smaller Companies	:: Larger Companies
Average cost of Section 404 compliance	$1.5 million	$7.3 million
Average company revenues	$324 million	$7.9 billion
Cost as % of revenues	0.46%	0.09%

Source: CRA International Study, December 2005, commissioned by Deloitte & Touche LLP, Ernst & Young LLP, KPMG LLP, and PricewaterhouseCoopers LLP.

concept :: *summary*

Sarbanes-Oxley Act of 2002

:: INCREASED AUTHORITY TO SEC

- Mandates budgetary increases for SEC.
- Increases power of SEC over many of governance matters.
- Since 2002, SEC enforcement much more active.

:: ACCOUNTING REFORMS

- Creates Public Company Accounting Oversight Board.
- Oversight of auditing of public companies.
- Requires separation of auditing and consulting functions within accounting firms.

:: CORPORATE GOVERNANCE

- Increases independence of auditors.
- Requires audit committees to be independent with at least one member being a financial expert.
- Audit partner must rotate off engagement after five years.
- Auditors must preserve audit records for seven years.

:: FINANCIAL STATEMENTS AND CONTROLS

- CEO and CFO must certify accuracy of financial statements.
- Also must certify existence of internal financial controls.
- Internal financial controls are subject to audit, just like financial statements.
- When restatement is made, executives must return any bonuses paid on incorrect financial statements.

:: SECURITIES FRAUD

- Creates crime of conspiring to commit securities fraud.
- Increases criminal sentences in securities fraud cases to 20 years.
- Lengthens statute of limitation in civil cases.
- Protects whistle-blowers.

7. SECURITIES FRAUD

Through Sarbanes-Oxley, Congress strengthened the punishment for committing securities fraud. In Section 16 of this chapter, you will see the serious sanctions imposed on those guilty of fraud. In those sections we will revisit how Sarbanes-Oxley increases these potential sentences. In Section 15, you will see how Sarbanes-Oxley increases the statute of limitations in civil cases.

Other provisions of this law create the crime of conspiring to commit securities fraud. As discussed in Chapter 12, the proof needed to establish a conspiracy often is less than the proof required to prove the underlying crime.

Finally, Sarbanes-Oxley provides protections for whistle-blowers so that individuals are more willing to report the corruption that can lead to major scandals. Audit committees are required to adopt procedures ensuring that whistle-blowers' reports are taken seriously. Whistle-blowers that suffer retaliation are able to recover civil damages and can be reinstated if terminated improperly.

> "About 1,000 whistle-blowing claims have been filed under Sarbox. Only 17 were determined after federal investigation to have merit and only six of this group have kept their wins after full evidentiary hearings before administrative law judges."
>
> **–Michael Delikat, "Blowing the Whistle on Sarbox," The Wall Street Journal, August 22, 2007.**

:: The Securities Act of 1933: Going Public

The **Securities Act of 1933** is a disclosure law with respect to the initial sale of securities to the public. This law makes it illegal to use the mails or any other means of interstate communication or transportation to sell securities without disclosing certain financial information to potential investors. The following sections discuss several aspects of the act in detail, including who is regulated, what documents are required, when criminal and civil liability exist, and what defenses are available. As you read, remember that this law applies only to the initial sale of the security. Subsequent transfers of securities are governed by the Securities Exchange Act of 1934, discussed in Sections 12 through 16 of this chapter.

In essence, the 1933 Securities Act requires the disclosure of information to the potential investor or other interested party. The information given must not be untrue or even misleading. If this information is not accurate, liability is imposed upon those responsible.

The act recognizes three sanctions for violations:

- Criminal punishment.
- Civil liability, which may be imposed in favor of injured parties in certain cases.
- Equitable remedy of an injunction.

Proof of an intentional violation usually is required before criminal or civil sanctions are imposed. Proof of negligence will, however, support an injunction.

8. PARTIES REGULATED

Parties subject to the 1933 act include issuers, underwriters, controlling persons, and sellers.

The Securities Act of 1933 regulates anyone who is involved with or who promotes the initial sale of securities. Typically, these parties who must comply with the disclosure requirements of the 1933 Act fall into one or more of four roles.

An **issuer** is the individual or business organization offering a security for sale to the public. An **underwriter** is anyone who participates in the original distribution of securities by selling such securities for the issuer or by guaranteeing their sale. Often securities brokerage firms or investment bankers act as underwriters with respect to a particular transaction. A **controlling person** is one who controls or is controlled by the issuer, such as a major stockholder of a corporation. Finally, a **seller** is anyone who contracts with a purchaser or who is a motivating influence that causes the purchase transaction to occur.

Whenever you operate a business, you and your co-owners must understand the requirements of the 1933 Securities Act. Your organization clearly is an issuer. You and your co-owner clearly are controlling persons. Whether you also are an underwriter or seller or both will depend on the factual situation and relationships you create with other individuals or firms to promote and sell stock in your organization. Regardless of whether you occupy one or more of these roles, you must comply with the 1993 Act or face significant liability.

9. DOCUMENTS INVOLVED

In regulating the initial sales of securities, the Securities Act of 1933 is viewed as a disclosure law. In essence, this law requires that securities subject to its provisions be registered prior to any sale and that a prospectus be furnished to any potential investor prior to any sale being consummated. Thus, an issuer of securities who complies with the federal law must prepare:

- A registration statement
- A prospectus

Registration Statement In an attempt to accomplish its purpose of disclosure, the Securities Act of 1933 contains detailed provisions relating to the registration of securities. These provisions require that a **registration statement** be filed with the SEC. The statement includes a detailed disclosure of financial information about the issuer and the controlling individuals involved in the offering of securities for sale to the public.

With respect to the filing of the registration statement, the law describes selling activities permitted at the various stages of the registration process. This procedure and its time frame are a primary reason why you and your co-owner described in the Business Decision cannot begin business immediately.

During the **prefiling period,** it is legal for the issuer of a security to engage in preliminary negotiations and agreements with underwriters. It is illegal to sell a covered security during this period. Offers to sell and offers to buy securities also are prohibited during this prefiling period.

After the registration statement is filed, a **waiting period** commences. This period typically lasts 20 days. During this time, the SEC staff investigates the accuracy of the registration statement to determine whether the sale of the securities should be permitted. During the waiting period, it is still illegal to sell a security subject to the act. However, it is not illegal to solicit a buyer or receive offers to buy. Since contracts to sell are still illegal, offers cannot be accepted during the waiting period. However, during these waiting periods, sellers may solicit offers for later acceptance.

Many solicitations during the waiting period are made in advertisements called **tombstone ads.** These ads are brief announcements identifying the security and stating its price, by whom orders will be executed, and from whom a prospectus may be obtained. Solicitations may also be made during the waiting period by use of a statistical summary, a summary prospectus, or a preliminary prospectus. These techniques allow dissemination of the facts that are to be ultimately disclosed in the formal prospectus.

A registration becomes effective at the expiration of the waiting period, 20 days after it is filed, unless the SEC gives notice that it is not in proper form or unless the SEC accelerates the effective date. Any amendment filed without the commission's consent starts the 20-day period running again. The end of the waiting period is the beginning of the **posteffective period.** During this period, contracts to buy and sell securities are finalized.

Prospectus During the posteffective period, securities may be sold. A **prospectus** must be furnished to any interested investor, and it must conform to the statutory requirements. Like the registration statement, the prospectus contains financial information related to the issuer and controlling persons. Indeed, the prospectus contains the same essential information contained in the registration statement. The prospectus supplies the investor with sufficient facts (including financial information) so that he or she can make an

Three time periods involved in the registration process are the prefiling period, the waiting period, and the posteffective period.

intelligent investment decision. The SEC has adopted rules relating to the detailed requirements of the prospectus. The major requirements are detailed facts about the issuer and financial statements, including balance sheets and statements of operations of the issuer.

Theoretically, any security may be sold under the act, provided the issuser and others follow the law and the rules and regulations enacted under it are followed. The law does not prohibit the sale of worthless securities. An investor may "foolishly" invest his or her money, and a person may legally sell the blue sky if the statutory requirements are met. In fact, the prospectus must contain the following in capital letters and boldface type:

> **THESE SECURITIES HAVE NOT BEEN APPROVED OR DISAPPROVED BY THE SECURITIES AND EXCHANGE COMMISSION NOR HAS THE COMMISSION PASSED UPON THE ACCURACY OR ADEQUACY OF THIS PROSPECTUS. ANY REPRESENTATION TO THE CONTRARY IS A CRIMINAL OFFENSE.**

The SEC has alternative processes to this formal registration process for companies that sell securities to institutional investors. Rule 144A is an example of an SEC-approved regulation allowing sale of securities to investors such as pension funds. Under this Rule, the securities are labeled as restricted. All other provisions of the securities law, such as those related to any fraudulent transactions, remain applicable to transactions involving these restricted securities.

10. LIABILITY

Under the federal Securities Act of 1933, both criminal and civil liability may be imposed for violations. Criminal liability results from a willful violation of the act or fraud in *any* offer or sale of securities. Fraud occurs when any material fact is omitted, causing a statement to be misleading. The penalty is a fine of up to $10,000 or five years in prison or both.

Civil liability under the 1933 Act usually involves a buyer of securities suing for a refund of the investment. This liability on the issuser, controlling person, underwriter, and seller is significant because the investors' money typically is lost at the time of these civil claims.

Three sections of the Securities Act of 1933 directly apply to civil liability of parties involved in issuing securities:

- Section 11 deals with registration statements.
- Section 12 relates to prospectuses and oral and written communication.
- Section 17 concerns fraudulent interstate transactions.

Section 11: Registration Statement   The civil liability provision dealing with registration statements imposes liability on the following persons in favor of purchasers of securities:

1. Every person who signed the registration statement.
2. Every director of the corporation or partner in the partnership issuing the security.
3. Every person who, with his or her consent, is named in the registration statement as about to become a director or partner.
4. Every accountant, engineer, or appraiser who assists in the preparation of the registration statement or its certification.
5. Every underwriter.

Don't rely on the prospectus as assurance the investment will make money.

"In 2006, for example, for the first time, more equity financing was raised in private transactions under the SEC's Rule 144A ($162 billion) than was raised in IPOs on the NYSE, Nasdaq, and the Amex combined ($154 billion)."

–Peter J. Wallison, "Capital Complaints," The Wall Street Journal, March 20, 2007.

These persons are liable if the registration statement:

- Contains untrue statements of material facts.
- Omits material facts required by statute or regulation.
- Omits information that if not given makes the facts stated misleading.

This last situation describes the factual situation of a statement containing a half-truth, which has the net effect of being misleading. The test of accuracy and materiality is as of the date the registration statement becomes effective.

A plaintiff-purchaser need not prove reliance on the registration statement in order to recover the amount of an investment. All the plaintiff has to show is omitted or misleading information in the registration statement. A defendant can defend the suit by proving actual knowledge of the falsity by the purchaser. Knowledge of the falsity by a defendant need not be proved. However, a defendant's reliance on an expert such as an accountant is a defense. For example, a director may defend a suit on the basis of a false financial statement by showing reliance on a certified public accountant. This reliance exception logically does not apply to the issuer. Because the issuer provides information to the expert, the issuer should not be allowed to rely on the expert's use of the inaccurate information.

> The issuer and experts assisting must make sure the registration materials are truthful and not misleading.

Section 12: Prospectus and Other Communications This section of the 1933 act is divided into two parts. The first subsection of Section 12 imposes liability on those who offer or sell securities that are not registered with the SEC. This liability exists regardless of the intent or conduct of those who fail to comply with the registration requirements. Thus, liability traditionally has been imposed against violators even though they lacked any wrongful intent. The Supreme Court has held that a defendant is free from liability if the plaintiff is equally responsible for the failure to file the registration statement.

The second subsection of Section 12 imposes liability on sellers who use a prospectus or make communications (by mail, telephone, or other instrumentalities of interstate commerce) that contain an untrue statement of material facts required to be stated or necessary to make statements not misleading. As under Section 11, the plaintiff does not have to prove reliance on the false or misleading prospectus or communication. Nor does the plaintiff have to establish that the defendant intended the deception.

> Plaintiffs can recover for harm done by false or misleading information in a prospectus even if the prospectus is not read or reviewed.

Purchasers of such securities may sue for their actual damages. If the purchaser still owns the securities and he or she can prove a direct contractual relationship with the seller, the remedy of rescission and a refund of the purchase price is also available.

Section 17: Fraudulent Transactions This provision concerning fraudulent interstate transactions prohibits the use of any instrument of interstate communication in the offer or sale of any securities when the result is:

1. To defraud.
2. To obtain money or property by means of an untrue or misleading statement.
3. To engage in a business transaction or practice that may operate to defraud or deceive a purchaser.

The requirement that a defendant-seller must act with the intent (**scienter**) to deceive or mislead in order to prove a Section 17 violation has caused much controversy over the years. The Supreme Court has resolved this issue by holding that a plaintiff must prove the defendant's intent to violate 1. However, no proof of the defendant's intent is required to find a violation of 2 or 3. The Court's decision is limited to when the plaintiff is seeking an injunction, because Section 17 does not explicitly provide for the private remedy of monetary damages.

11. DEFENSES

The Securities Act of 1933 recognized several defenses that may be used to avoid civil liability. Among the most important defenses are:

- Materiality.
- The statute of limitations.
- Due diligence.

Materiality   A defendant in a case involving the 1933 act might argue that the false or misleading information is not *material* and thus should not have had an impact on the purchaser's decision-making process. Determining whether or not a particular fact is material depends on the facts and the parties involved.

The SEC and the courts have attempted to define materiality. The term *material* describes the kinds of information that an average prudent investor would want to have so that he or she can make an intelligent, informed decision whether or not to buy the security. A material fact is one that if correctly stated or disclosed would have deterred or tended to deter the average prudent investor from purchasing the securities in question. The term does not cover minor inaccuracies or errors in matters of no interest to investors. Facts that tend to deter a person from purchasing a security are those that have an important bearing upon the nature or condition of the issuing corporation or its business.

Statute of Limitations   The statute of limitations is a defense for both civil and criminal liability. The basic period is one year. The one year does not start to run until the discovery of the untrue statement or omission. Or it does not start to run until the time such discovery would have been made with reasonable diligence. In no event may a suit be brought more than three years after the sale.

> Sarbanes-Oxley does not increase the statute of limitations under the 1933 act.

A defense similar to the statute of limitations is also provided. The 1933 act provides that if the person acquiring the security does so after the issuer has made generally available an earnings statement covering at least 12 months after the effective date of the registration statement, then this person must prove actual reliance on the registration statement.

Due Diligence   A very important defense for experts such as accountants is the **due diligence defense.**

To establish this defense, the expert must prove that a reasonable investigation of the financial statements of the issuer and controlling persons was conducted. As the result of this investigation, an expert exercising due diligence must prove that there was no reason to believe any of the information in the registration statement or prospectus was false or misleading.

In determining whether or not an expert, such as an accountant, has made a reasonable investigation, the law provides that the standard of *reasonableness* is that required of a prudent person in the management of his or her own property. The burden of proof of this defense is on the expert, and the test is as of the time the registration statement became effective. The due diligence defense, in effect, requires proof that a party was not guilty of fraud or negligence.

concept :: *summary*

Liability under the Securities Act of 1933

:: SECTION 11

Purpose: Creates liability for false or misleading registration statements.

Plaintiff's case: Not required to prove defendant's intent to deceive or plaintiff's reliance on documents.

Defendant's defenses: Proof of no false or misleading information; proof that plaintiff knew of false or misleading nature of information; except for issuers, proof of reliance on an expert (attorney or accountant).

:: SECTION 12

Purpose: (1) Creates liability for failing to file a required registration statement; (2) creates liability for false or misleading prospectus.

Plaintiff's case: Not required to prove defendant's intent to deceive or plaintiff's reliance on documents.

Defendant's defenses: For (1), plaintiff equally at fault for failing to file a registration statement; for (2), same as Section 11 defenses.

:: SECTION 17

Purpose: In an interstate transaction, it is unlawful to
(1) employ any device, scheme, or artifice of fraud;
(2) obtain money or property by untrue statement or omission of material fact;
(3) engage in events that operate or would operate as fraud or deceit.

Plaintiff's case: For (1), required to prove defendant's intent to deceive; for (2) and (3), not required to prove intent to deceive.

Defendant's defenses: For (1), proof of no intent to deceive and proof of good faith; for (2), proof of no material misstatement or omission; for (3), proof of no involvement in unlawful activities.

:: CRIMINAL LIABILITY

$10,000 fine or 5 years in prison or both.

:: Securities Exchange Act of 1934: Being Public

Whereas the Securities Act of 1933 deals with original offerings of securities, the **Securities Exchange Act of 1934** regulates transfers of securities after the initial sale. The 1934 act, which created the Securities and Exchange Commission, also deals with regulation of securities exchanges, brokers, and dealers in securities.

The Securities Exchange Act makes it illegal to sell a security on a national exchange unless a registration is effective for the security. Registration under the 1934 act differs from registration under the 1933 act. Registration under the 1934 act requires filing prescribed forms with the applicable stock exchange and the SEC.

Provisions relating to stockbrokers and dealers prohibit the use of the mails or any other instrumentality of interstate commerce to sell securities unless the broker or the dealer is registered. The language is sufficiently broad to cover attempted sales as well as actual sales. Brokers and dealers must keep detailed records of their activities and file annual reports with the SEC.

The SEC requires that issuers of registered securities file periodic reports as well as report significant developments that would affect the value of the security. For example, the SEC requires companies to disclose foreign pay-offs or bribes to obtain or retain foreign business operations. Businesses must disclose their minority hiring practices and other social data that may be of public concern. Business has been forced by the SEC to submit certain share-holder proposals to all shareholders as a part of proxy solicitation. When a new pension law was enacted, the SEC required that financial reports disclose the law's impact on the reporting business. The SEC requires more complete disclosure of executive compensation packages.

> Sarbanes-Oxley, through the PCAOB and SEC regulations, impacts the accounting and audit practices.

The SEC's activity concerning information corporations must furnish to the investing public is almost limitless. With the actions of the PCAOB, SEC regulations are of paramount significance to all persons concerned with the financial aspects of business. This area of regulation directly affects the accounting profession. Since the SEC regulates financial statements, it frequently decides issues of proper accounting and auditing theory and practices.

The following sections examine how the Securities Exchange Act of 1934 affects the businessperson, the accountant, the lawyer, the broker, and the investor. These sections cover some fundamental concepts of this law, such as civil liability in general and insider transactions in particular, as well as criminal violations and penalties under the 1934 act.

12. SECTION 10(b) AND RULE 10b-5

Most of the litigation under the Securities and Exchange Act of 1934 is brought under Section 10(b) of the act and Rule 10b-5 promulgated by the SEC pursuant to the act. Section 10(b) and Rule 10b-5 declare that it is unlawful to use the mails or any instrumentality of interstate commerce or any national securities exchange to defraud *any person* in connection with the *purchase or sale* of any security. Sidebar 15.2 contains the actual language of this section and rule.

Common issues regarding litigation under Section 10(b) and Rule 10b-5 include the following:

- Who is liable?
- What can be recovered by the plaintiff, and does the defendant have the right to seek contribution from third parties?
- When is information material to the transaction?

Liability   Recently, the Supreme Court used Case 15.2 as a means to emphasize there is a limited answer to the question who is liable. While many cases clarify that parties directly connected to the sale of securities are liable, the following case focuses on the liability of third parties.

:: *sidebar* 15.2

Language of Section 10(b) of the 1934 Act and SEC's Rule 10b-5

Section 10(b) states:

It shall be unlawful for any person, directly or indirectly, by the use of any means or instrumentality of interstate commerce or of the mails, or of any facility of any national securities exchange—

(b) To use or employ, in connection with the purchase or sale of any security registered on a national securities exchange or any security not so registered, any manipulative or deceptive device or contrivance in contravention of such rules and regulations as the [SEC] may prescribe.

Rule 10b-5, adopted by the SEC in 1942, states:

It shall be unlawful for any person, directly or indirectly, by the use of any means or instrumentality of interstate commerce, or of the mails or of any facility of any national securities exchange,

(a) To employ any device, scheme, or artifice to defraud,

(b) To make any untrue statement of a material fact or to omit to state a material fact necessary in order to make the statements made, in the light of the circumstances under which they were made, not misleading, or

(c) To engage in any act, practice, or course of business which operates or would operate as a fraud or deceit upon any person, in connection with the purchase or sale of any security.

---

case 15.2

STONERIDGE INVESTMENT PARTNERS, LLC, PETITIONER v. SCIENTIFIC-ATLANTA, INC., ET AL.
128 S. Ct. 761 **(2008)**

Charter Communications operates cable companies throughout the United States. Both Scientific-Atlanta and Motorola supply Charter with digital cable converter boxes that Charter provides to its customers. In 2000, Charter became concerned that it would not meet cash flow projections causing it to miss the financial estimates Wall Street established. To remedy this shortfall, Charter arranged to overpay Scientific-Atlanta and Motorola by the amount of $20 for each converter box. This deal was conditioned on these companies purchasing advertising from Charter in the amount equal to the overpayment. While these transactions had no economic impact, Charter recorded the advertisement purchases as revenue and capitalized the purchases of the converter boxes. This scheme allowed Charter to fool its auditor and to create financial statements that appeared to meet expectations by increasing its cash flow by about $17 million.

Purchasers of Charter stock, upon discovering this fraud, sued Charter, Scientific-Atlanta, and Motorola

under the 1934 Securities Exchange Act. The latter two companies asked the District Judge to dismiss these claims since the companies were not parties to any securities fraud and are not subject to a private cause of action under the securities laws. The District Court and the Eighth Circuit Court of Appeals ruled in favor of Scientific-Atlanta and Motorola finding there was not a private right of action against these third parties since they did not make a public misstatement and did not fail to disclose required information. The Supreme Court granted certiorari to address the conflict among the appellate courts concerning when third parties are liable under the 1934 Securities Exchange Act.

KENNEDY, J.: . . . Though the text of the Securities Exchange Act does not provide for a private cause of action for § *10(b)* violations, the Court has found a right of action implied in the words of the statute and its implementing regulation. In a typical § *10(b)* private action a plaintiff must prove (1) a material misrepresentation or omission by the defendant; (2) scienter; (3) a connection between the misrepresentation or omission and the purchase or sale of a security; (4) reliance upon the misrepresentation or omission; (5) economic loss; and (6) loss causation. .

. . . [I]n § 104 of the Private Securities Litigation Reform Act of 1995 (PSLRA), [Congress] directed prosecution of aiders and abettors by the SEC.

The § *10(b)* implied private right of action does not extend to aiders and abettors. The conduct of a secondary actor must satisfy each of the elements or preconditions for liability; and we consider whether the allegations here are sufficient to do so.

The Court of Appeals concluded petitioner had not alleged that respondents engaged in a deceptive act within the reach of the § *10(b)* private right of action, noting that only misstatements, omissions by one who has a duty to disclose, and manipulative trading practices . . . are deceptive within the meaning of the rule. . . . Conduct itself can be deceptive, as respondents concede. In this case, moreover, respondents' course of conduct included both oral and written statements, such as the backdated contracts agreed to by Charter and respondents.

A different interpretation of the holding from the Court of Appeals opinion is that the court was stating only that any deceptive statement or act respondents made was not actionable because it did not have the requisite proximate relation to the investors' harm. That conclusion is consistent with our own determination that respondents' acts or statements were not relied upon by the investors and that, as a result, liability cannot be imposed upon respondents.

Reliance by the plaintiff upon the defendant's deceptive acts is an essential element of the § *10(b)* private cause of action. It ensures that, for liability to arise, the requisite causal connection between a defendant's misrepresentation and a plaintiff's injury exists. . . . We have found a rebuttable presumption of reliance in two different circumstances. First, if there is an omission of a material fact by one with a duty to disclose, the investor to whom the duty was owed need not provide specific proof of reliance. Second, under the fraud-on-the-market doctrine, reliance is presumed when the statements at issue become public. The public information is reflected in the market price of the security. Then it can be assumed that an investor who buys or sells stock at the market price relies upon the statement.

Neither presumption applies here. Respondents had no duty to disclose; and their deceptive acts were not communicated to the public. No member of the investing public had knowledge, either actual or presumed, of respondents' deceptive acts during the relevant times. Petitioner, as a result, cannot show reliance upon any of respondents' actions except in an indirect chain that we find too remote for liability.

Invoking what some courts call "scheme liability," petitioner nonetheless seeks to impose liability on respondents even absent a public statement. In our view this approach does not answer the objection that petitioner did not in fact rely upon respondents' own deceptive conduct.

Liability is appropriate, petitioner contends, because respondents engaged in conduct with the purpose and effect of creating a false appearance of material fact to further a scheme to misrepresent Charter's revenue. The argument is that the financial statement Charter released to the public was a natural and expected consequence of respondents' deceptive acts; had respondents not assisted Charter, Charter's auditor would not have been fooled, and the financial statement would have been a more accurate reflection of Charter's financial condition. . . .

In effect petitioner contends that in an efficient market investors rely not only upon the public statements relating to a security but also upon the transactions those statements reflect. Were this concept of reliance to be adopted, the implied cause of action would reach the whole marketplace in which the issuing company does business; and there is no authority for this rule.

. . . It was Charter, not respondents, that misled its auditor and filed fraudulent financial statements; nothing respondents did made it necessary or inevitable for Charter to record the transactions as it did. . . .

Were we to adopt this construction of § *10(b)*, it would revive in substance the implied cause of action against all aiders and abettors except those who committed no deceptive act in the process of facilitating the fraud; and we would undermine Congress' determination that this class of defendants should be pursued by the SEC and not by private litigants. . . .

The § *10(b)* private cause of action is a judicial construct that Congress did not enact in the text of the relevant statutes. Though the rule once may have been otherwise, it is settled that there is an implied cause of action only if the underlying statute can be interpreted to disclose the intent to create one. . . .

Concerns with the judicial creation of a private cause of action caution against its expansion. The decision to extend the cause of action is for Congress, not for us. Though it remains the law, the § *10(b)* private right should not be extended beyond its present boundaries. . . .

Secondary actors are subject to criminal penalties and civil enforcement by the SEC. The enforcement power is not toothless. Since September 30, 2002, SEC enforcement actions have collected over $10 billion in disgorgement and penalties, much of it for distribution to injured investors. And in this case both parties agree that criminal penalties are a strong deterrent. In addition some state securities laws permit state authorities to seek fines and restitution from aiders and abettors. All secondary actors, furthermore, are not necessarily immune from private suit. The securities statutes provide an express private right of action against accountants and underwriters in certain circumstances, and the implied right of action in § *10(b)* continues to cover secondary actors who commit primary violations.

Here respondents were acting in concert with Charter in the ordinary course as suppliers and, as matters then evolved in the not so ordinary course, as customers. Unconventional as the arrangement was, it took place in the marketplace for goods and services, not in the investment sphere. Charter was free to do as it chose in preparing its books, conferring with its auditor, and preparing and then issuing its financial statements. In these circumstances the investors cannot be said to have relied upon any of respondents' deceptive acts in the decision to purchase or sell securities; and as the requisite reliance cannot be shown, respondents have no liability to petitioner under the implied right of action. This conclusion is consistent with the narrow dimensions we must give to a right of action Congress did not authorize when it first enacted the statute and did not expand when it revisited the law.

Affirmed.

:: CASE QUESTIONS:

1. What is the relationship between Charter, Scientific-Atlanta, and Motorola?
2. How did Scientific-Atlanta and Motorola assist Charter in creating fraudulent financial statements?
3. Why did the Supreme Court agree with the lower courts that Scientific-Atlanta and Motorola are not subject to the claims of shareholders under the 1934 Securities Exchange Act?

This decision appears to restrict plaintiffs' ability to recover against auditors, banks, and other parties associated with major scandals. Prior to this ruling, there have been significant settlements reached with auditors involved in some of the largest corporate scandals in history. Table 15.3 highlights a few of these largest settlements.

Damages   A plaintiff in a suit under Rule 10b-5 must prove damages. The damages of a defrauded purchaser are actual out-of-pocket losses or the excess of what was paid over the value of what was received. Courts in a few

table 15.3 :: Largest Settlements of Securities Cases against Auditors

:: Year	:: Auditing Firm	:: Case	:: Amount
2000	Ernst & Young	Cendant Shareholders	$335 million
2008	Ernst & Young	Cendant Corp.	$300 million
2007	PWC	Tyco	$225 million
2006	Deloitte & Touche	Adelphia	$210 million

Source: David Reilly and Nathan Koppel, "Cendant Case Costs Ernst Almost $300 Million More," *The Wall Street Journal,* February 16–17, 2008.

cases have used the *benefit of the bargain* measure of damages and awarded the buyer the difference between what he or she paid and what the security was represented to be worth. A buyer's damages are measured at the time of purchase.

As Sidebar 15.3 illustrates, a buyer must allege specific damages due to the seller's fraud. An allegation of fraud and a drop in stock price is not enough to prove the case.

:: *sidebar* 15.3

Proof of Loss Due to Fraud

Shareholders of Dura Pharmaceuticals, Inc., sued the company and its directors and officers for violations of the 1934 Securities Exchange Act. These plaintiffs claim they paid an artificially high price for the stock because Dura executives misrepresented that the Food and Drug Administration (FDA) would approve Dura's application to sell a new asthmatic spray. During the time in question, Dura's stock declined in price rapidly when it announced its sales projection would not be met. Later, when Dura announced that the FDA would not approve its new asthmatic spray, the stock declined again. However, within a week, Dura stock had regained much of that lost value.

The shareholder plaintiffs simply alleged they had lost money due to the inflated price of the stock and the misrepresentation by the Dura executives. The Supreme Court held that these simple allegations were not enough to establish the loss of value due to the fraud. More specific proof of the loss caused by the fraud is required.

*Source: Dura Pharmaceuticals, Inc. v. Broudo, 125 S. Ct. 1627 (2005).

Computation of a defrauded seller's damages is more difficult. A defrauding purchaser usually benefits from an increase in the value of the securities, while the plaintiff seller loses this increase. Courts do not allow defrauding buyers to keep these increases in value. Therefore, the measure of the seller's damages is the difference between the fair value of all that the seller received and the fair value of what he or she would have received had there been no fraud. A fraudulent buyer loses all profits flowing from the wrongful conduct.

Plaintiffs under Rule 10b-5 are also entitled to consequential damages. These include lost dividends, brokerage fees, and taxes. In addition, courts may order payment of interest on the funds. Punitive damages are not permitted as they are in cases of common law fraud based on state laws. This distinction results from the language of the 1934 act, which limits recoveries to actual damages.

The issue of whether a defendant who is liable under Section 10(b) can seek contribution from third parties was not resolved until 1993. In Sidebar 15.4, the Supreme Court concludes that a right of contribution does exist in Section 10(b) private actions.

Materiality   Section 10(b) and Rule 10b-5 are usually referred to as the *antifraud provisions* of the act. A plaintiff seeking damages under the provisions must establish the existence of a material misrepresentation or omission made in connection with the purchase or sale of a security and the culpable state of mind of the defendant. Materiality under the 1934 act is the same as materiality under the 1933 act. However, liability under Rule 10b-5 requires

:: *sidebar* 15.4

Right to Contribution from Others

To settle a securities lawsuit by its shareholders, Wausau Insurance agreed to pay $13.5 million. Following this settlement, Wausau filed a lawsuit against the attorneys and accountants involved in the public offering. These defendants sought dismissal of this complaint on the grounds that there is no right of contribution under § 10(b). The

Supreme Court concludes that there is a private right of contribution in § 10(b) of the 1934 act and in Rule 10b-5. Those charged with liability in a § 10b-5 action have a right of contribution against other parties who have joint responsibility for the violation.

*Source: *Musick, Peeler & Garrett v. Wausau Ins.*, 113 S. Ct. 2085 (1993).

proof of the defendant's intent to deceive. Proof of the defendant's simple negligence is not enough to establish liability. The plaintiff also must establish that the defendant's practice is manipulative and not merely corporate mismanagement.

The concept of fraud under Section 10(b) encompasses not only untrue statements of material facts but also the failure to state material facts necessary to prevent statements actually made from being misleading. In other words, a half-truth that misleads is fraudulent. Finally, failure to correct a misleading impression left by statements already made, or silence where there is a duty to speak, gives rise to a violation of Rule 10b-5 because it is a form of aiding and abetting the deception.

One of the most difficult issues concerning materiality arises in preliminary merger negotiations. What should management respond when asked about merger possibilities? Should management reveal information about merger possibilities even when the likelihood of an actual merger is very slight? The Supreme Court uses an objective-person case-by-case analysis to determine whether information about potential mergers is material and thus required to be disclosed. The Court said, "materiality depends on the significance the reasonable investor would place on the withheld or misrepresented information."

In the post-Enron era, a common factual situation litigated under Section 10(b) is the backdating of stock options. Changing the key date to assure a greater value of the options offered to executives can lead to liability. There have been hundreds of articles about this practice, and settlements with the SEC and other plaintiffs involve large dollar amounts. For example, Barcode Communications Systems agreed to pay $160 million to settle a class-action case arising from backdating. Barcode's CEO was previously found guilty of defrauding Barcode shareholders by altering the grant dates of stock options.

13. INSIDER TRANSACTIONS

Section 16, one of the most important provisions of the Securities Exchange Act of 1934, concerns insider transactions. An **insider** is any person who:

- Owns more than 10 percent of any security.
- Is a director or an officer of the issuer of the security.

"As we work together to protect investors and stimulate capital formation, we've got to be sure we don't choke on our own medicine. We understand that regulation that's intended to improve the competitiveness of our markets can—if we're not careful—have the opposite effect."

–Christopher Cox Chairman of SEC

"A stock option gives its holder the right to buy shares at a future date at a fixed price, usually the market price on the date of the grant. If the stock later rises, the recipient can cash in the option for a profit. By backdating a grant to a prior date when the price was lower, the award's value increases."

–Steve Stecklow and Peter Waldman, The Wall Street Journal, August 8, 2007.

The SEC defines an officer for insider trading purposes as the executive officers, accounting officers, chief financial officers, and controllers. The SEC also examines the individual investor's function within the company rather than the title of the position held.

Section 16 and SEC regulations require that insiders file, at the time of the registration or within 10 days after becoming an insider, a statement of the amount of such issues of which they are the owners. The regulations also require filing within 10 days after the close of each calendar month thereafter if there has been any change in such ownership during such month (indicating the change). Sarbanes-Oxley shortens the time period for filing information about insider transactions. Now, these filings with the SEC must be made electronically within two business days of the insider's transaction.

The reason for prohibiting insiders from trading for profit is to prevent the use of information that is available to an insider but not to the general public. Because the SEC cannot determine for certain when nonpublic information is improperly used, Section 16 creates a presumption that any profit made within a six-month time period is illegal. These profits are referred to as **short-swing profits.** Thus, if a director, officer, or principal owner realizes profits on the purchase and sale of a security within a six-month period, the profits legally belong to the company or to the investor who purchased it from or sold it to an insider, resulting in the insider's profit and the investor's loss. The order of the purchase and sale is immaterial. The profit is calculated on the lowest price in and highest price out during any six-month period. Unlike the required proof of intent to deceive under Section 10(b), the short-swing profits rule of Section 16 does not depend on any misuse of information. In other words, short-swing profits by insiders, regardless of the insiders' states of mind, are absolutely prohibited.

While the SEC enforces the requirements of Section 16 that insiders file certain documents, the SEC does not enforce the provision that prohibits insiders from engaging in short-swing profits. This provision of Section 16 is enforced by civil actions filed by the issuer of the security or by a person who owns a security of the issuer.

14. NONPUBLIC INFORMATION

The SEC's concern for trading based on nonpublic information goes beyond the Section 16 ban on short-swing profits. Indeed, a person who is not technically an insider but who trades securities without disclosing nonpublic information may violate Section 10(b) and Rule 10b-5. The SEC takes the position that the profit obtained as the result of a trader's silence concerning information that is not freely available to everyone is a manipulation or deception prohibited by Section 10(b) and Rule 10b-5. In essence, the users of nonpublic information are treated like insiders if they can be classified as tippees.

A **tippee** is a person who learns of nonpublic information from an insider. In essence, a tippee is viewed as a temporary insider. A tippee is liable for the use of nonpublic information because an insider should not be allowed to do indirectly what he or she cannot do directly. In other words, a tippee is liable for trading or passing on information that is nonpublic.

The use of nonpublic information for financial gain has not been prohibited entirely. For example, in one case, a financial printer had been hired to print corporate takeover bids. An employee of the printer was able to deduce the identities of both the acquiring companies and the companies targeted for takeover. Without disclosing the knowledge about the prospective takeover bids, the employee purchased stock in the target companies and then sold it for a profit immediately after the takeover attempts were made public. He was indicted and convicted for having violated Section 10(b) and Rule 10b-5. The Supreme Court reversed, holding that the defendant had no duty to reveal the nonpublic information, since he was not in a fiduciary position with respect to either the acquiring or the acquired company.

In another case the U.S. Supreme Court further narrowed a tippee's liability. The Court ruled that a tippee becomes liable under Section 10(b) only if the tipper breaches a fiduciary duty to the business organization or fellow shareholders. Therefore, if the tipper communicated nonpublic information for reasons other than personal gain, neither the tipper nor the tippee could be liable for a securities violation.

These two Supreme Court cases have made it more difficult for the SEC to control the use of nonpublic information. However, the SEC has successfully argued that a person should be considered to be a temporary insider if that person conveys nonpublic information that was to have been kept confidential. This philosophy has become known as the **misappropriation theory** of insider trading. Case 15.3 approves the misappropriation theory.

case **15.3**

UNITED STATES v. O'HAGAN
117 S. Ct. 2199 (1997)

GINSBURG, J.: . . . Respondent James Herman O'Hagan was a partner in the law firm of Dorsey & Whitney in Minneapolis, Minnesota. In July 1988, Grand Metropolitan PLC (Grand Met), a company based in London, England, retained Dorsey & Whitney as local counsel to represent Grand Met regarding a potential tender offer for the common stock of the Pillsbury Company, headquartered in Minneapolis. Both Grand Met and Dorsey & Whitney took precautions to protect the confidentiality of Grand Met's tender offer plans. O'Hagan did no work on the Grand Met representation. Dorsey & Whitney withdrew from representing Grand Met on September 9, 1988. Less than a month later, on October 4, 1988, Grand Met publicly announced its tender offer for Pillsbury stock.

On August 18, 1988, while Dorsey & Whitney was still representing Grand Met, O'Hagan began purchasing call options for Pillsbury stock. Each option gave him the right to purchase 100 shares of Pillsbury stock by a specified date in September 1988. Later in August and in September, O'Hagan made additional purchases of Pillsbury call options. By the end of September, he owned 2,500 unexpired Pillsbury options. . . . O'Hagan also purchased, in September 1988, some 5,000 shares of Pillsbury common stock, at a price just under $39 per share. When Grand Met announced its tender offer in October, the price of Pillsbury stock rose to nearly $60 per share. O'Hagan then sold his Pillsbury call options and common stock, making a profit of more than $4.3 million.

The Securities and Exchange Commission (SEC or Commission) initiated an investigation into O'Hagan's transactions, culminating in a 57-count indictment. The indictment alleged that O'Hagan defrauded his law firm and its client, Grand Met, by using for his own trading purposes material, nonpublic information regarding Grand Met's planned tender offer. . . .

A divided panel of the Court of Appeals for the Eighth Circuit reversed all of O'Hagan's convictions. Liability under § 10(b) and Rule 10b-5, the Eighth Circuit held, may not be grounded on the "misappropriation theory" of securities fraud on which the prosecution relied. . . .

Decisions of the Courts of Appeals are in conflict on the propriety of the misappropriation theory under § 10(b) and Rule 10b-5. . . . We granted certiorari and now reverse the Eighth Circuit's judgment. . . .

In pertinent part, § 10(b) of the Exchange Act provides:

> It shall be unlawful for any person, directly or indirectly, by the use of any means or instrumentality of interstate commerce or of the mails, or of any facility of any national securities exchange— . . .
>
> (b) To use or employ, in connection with the purchase or sale of any security registered on a national securities exchange or any security not so registered, any manipulative or deceptive device or contrivance in contravention of such rules and regulations as the [Securities and Exchange] Commission may prescribe as necessary or appropriate in the public interest or for the protection of investors.

The statute thus proscribes (1) using any deceptive device (2) in connection with the purchase or sale of securities, in contravention of rules prescribed by the Commission. The provision, as written, does not confine its coverage to deception of a purchaser or seller of securities; rather, the statute reaches any deceptive device used in connection with the purchase or sale of any security.

Pursuant to its § 10(b) rulemaking authority, the Commission has adopted Rule 10b-5, which, as relevant here, provides:

> It shall be unlawful for any person, directly or indirectly, by the use of any means or instrumentality of interstate commerce, or of the mails or of any facility of any national securities exchange,
>
> (a) To employ any device, scheme, or artifice to defraud, [or] . . .
>
> (c) To engage in any act, practice, or course of business which operates or would operate as a fraud or deceit upon any person, in connection with the purchase or sale of any security.

. . . Under the "traditional" or "classical theory" of insider trading liability, § 10(b) and Rule 10b-5 are violated when a corporate insider trades in the securities of his corporation on the basis of material, nonpublic information. . . .

The "misappropriation theory" holds that a person commits fraud "in connection with" a securities transaction, and thereby violates § 10(b) and Rule 10b-5, when he misappropriates confidential information for securities trading purposes, in breach of a duty owed to the source of the information. Under this theory, a fiduciary's undisclosed, self-serving use of a principal's information to purchase or sell securities, in breach of a duty of loyalty and confidentiality, defrauds the principal of the exclusive use of that information. In lieu of premising liability on a fiduciary relationship between company insider and purchaser or seller of the company's stock, the misappropriation theory premises liability on a fiduciary-turned-trader's deception of those who entrusted him with access to confidential information.

The two theories are complementary, each addressing efforts to capitalize on nonpublic information through the purchase or sale of securities. The classical theory targets a corporate insider's breach of duty to shareholders with whom the insider transacts; the misappropriation theory outlaws trading on the basis of non-public information by a corporate "outsider" in breach of a duty owed not to a trading party, but to the source of the information. The misappropriation theory is thus designed to protect the integrity of the securities markets against abuses by outsiders to a corporation who have access to confidential information that will affect the corporation's security price when revealed, but who owe no fiduciary or other duty to that corporation's shareholders.

In this case, the indictment alleged that O'Hagan, in breach of a duty of trust and confidence he owed to his law firm, Dorsey & Whitney, and to its client, Grand Met, traded on the basis of nonpublic information regarding Grand Met's planned tender offer for Pillsbury common stock. This conduct, the Government charged, constituted a fraudulent device in connection with the purchase and sale of securities.

We agree with the Government that misappropriation, as just defined, satisfies § 10(b)'s requirement that chargeable conduct involve a "deceptive device or contrivance" used "in connection with" the purchase or sale of securities. We observe, first, that misappropriators, as the Government describes them, deal in deception. A fiduciary who "[pretends] loyalty to the principal while secretly converting the principal's information for personal gain," "dupes" or defrauds the principal. . . .

Deception through nondisclosure is central to the theory of liability for which the Government seeks recognition. As counsel for the Government stated in explanation of the theory at oral argument: "To satisfy the common law rule that a trustee may not use the property that [has] been entrusted [to] him, there would have to be consent. To satisfy the requirement of the Securities Act that there be no deception, there would only have to be disclosure." . . .

[F]ull disclosure forecloses liability under the misappropriation theory: Because the deception essential to the misappropriation theory involves feigning fidelity to the source of information, if the fiduciary discloses to the source that he plans to trade on the nonpublic information, there is no "deceptive device" and thus no § 10(b) violation—although the fiduciary-turned-trader may remain liable under state law for breach of a duty of loyalty.

We turn next to the § 10(b) requirement that the misappropriator's deceptive use of information be "in connection with the purchase or sale of [a] security." This element is satisfied because the fiduciary's fraud is consummated, not when the fiduciary gains the confidential information, but when, without disclosure to his principal, he uses the information to purchase or sell securities. The securities transaction and the breach of duty thus coincide. This is so even though the person or entity defrauded is not the other party to the trade; but is, instead, the source of the nonpublic information. A misappropriator who trades on the basis of material, nonpublic information, in short, gains his advantageous market position through deception; he deceives the source of the information and simultaneously harms members of the investing public.

The misappropriation theory targets information of a sort that misappropriators ordinarily capitalize upon to gain no-risk profits through the purchase or sale of securities. . . .

The misappropriation theory comports with § 10(b)'s language, which requires deception "in connection with the purchase or sale of any security," not deception of an identifiable purchaser or seller. The theory is also well-turned to an animating purpose of the Exchange Act: to insure honest securities markets and thereby promote investor confidence. Although informational disparity is inevitable in the securities markets, investors likely would hesitate to venture their capital in a market where trading based on misappropriated nonpublic information is unchecked by law. An investor's informational disadvantage vis-à-vis a misappropriator with material, nonpublic information stems from contrivance, not luck; it is a disadvantage that cannot be overcome with research or skill.

In sum, considering the inhibiting impact on market participation of trading on misappropriated information, and the congressional purposes underlying § 10(b), it makes scant sense to hold a lawyer like O'Hagan a § 10(b) violator if he works for a law firm representing the target of a tender offer, but not if he works for a law firm representing the bidder. The text of the statute requires no such result. The misappropriation at issue here was properly made the subject of a § 10(b) charge because it meets the statutory requirement that there be "deceptive" conduct "in connection with" securities transactions. . . .

. . . [T]he misappropriation theory, as we have examined and explained it in this opinion, is both consistent with the statute and with our precedent. Vital to our decision that criminal liability may be sustained under the misappropriation theory, we emphasize, are two sturdy safeguards Congress has provided regarding scienter. To establish a criminal violation of Rule 10b-5, the Government must prove that a person "willfully" violated the provision. Furthermore, a defendant may not be imprisoned for violating Rule 10b-5 if he proves that he had no knowledge of the rule. . . .

The Eighth Circuit erred in holding that the misappropriation theory is inconsistent with § 10(b). The Court of Appeals may address on remand O'Hagan's other challenges to his convictions under § 10(b) and Rule 10b-5. . . .

Reversed and remanded.

:: CASE QUESTIONS

1. What was O'Hagan accused of doing that was illegal?
2. What is the theory that the SEC argues is the basis of O'Hagan's wrongdoing?
3. How did the trial court and the appellate court rule in this case?
4. What reasons did the Supreme Court give for finding that the misappropriation theory is appropriate?
5. According to the Supreme Court, when and against whom did the misappropriation occur?

The SEC continues to focus its enforcement efforts on the misuse of non-public information at all levels of transactions. The SEC's efforts are aided by the fact that the civil penalty for gaining illegal profits with nonpublic information is three times the profits gained. In addition, controlling persons who fail to prevent these violations by employees may be civilly liable for the greater amount of triple damages or $1,000,000.

The penalties were increased to their current levels by the Insider Trading and Securities Fraud Enforcement Act of 1988. This law also provides that suits alleging the illegal use of nonpublic information may be filed within a five-year period after the wrongful transaction. This period, being substantially longer than the one year/three years limitation periods for other federal securities violations, illustrates the emphasis Congress has placed on preventing trading on nonpublic information.

Don't be tempted to take advantage of nonpublic information if you are an insider within your company.

15. ADDITIONAL CIVIL LIABILITY

In 1990, Congress expressed its concern for enforcement of the securities laws. In that year, the Securities Enforcement Remedies Act became law. This legislation provides that civil fines of up to $500,000 per organization and $100,000 per individual may be imposed and collected by the courts. In addition, an individual found to have violated the securities laws may be prohibited by the court from serving as an officer or director of a business organization. These fines and this prohibition from service can be utilized, at the judge's discretion, when a party in a civil case is found to have violated the securities laws. There does not have to be any proof of a criminal violation for these fines to be imposed.

Furthermore, Section 18 of the Securities Exchange Act of 1934 imposes liability on a theory of fraud on any person who shall make or cause to be made any false and misleading statements of material fact in any application, report, or document filed under the act. This liability favors both purchasers and sellers. A plaintiff must prove that the defendant knowingly made a false statement, that plaintiff relied on the false or misleading statement, and that plaintiff suffered damage.

Two distinctions between this section of the 1934 act and Sections 11 and 12 of the 1933 act are noteworthy. First, the requirement that an intent to deceive be proven under Section 18 means that the defendant's good faith is a defense. Good faith exists when a person acts without knowledge that the statement is false and misleading. In other words, freedom from fraud is a defense under an action based on Section 18. There is no liability under this section for simple negligence. Second, the plaintiff in a Section 18 case must prove reliance on the false or misleading filing. The simple fact that the filing is inaccurate is not sufficient. In a Section 11 or 12 case under the 1933 act, the plaintiff does not have to establish reliance.

Take note of the increased statute of limitations provided by the Sarbanes-Oxley Act.

The Sarbanes-Oxley Act extends the statute of limitations for civil actions under the 1934 act. Lawsuits must be filed within two years of the time the wrong was discovered (or should have been) and at least within five years of the wrongful act. The expansion of civil liability under the 1934 act encourages settlement in many cases. Table 15.4 summarizes some of these larger civil settlements.

table 15.4 :: Largest Securities Class-Action Settlements (2005–2007)

:: Dollar Amount of Settlement	:: Company	:: Year
$7.2 billion	Enron	2006
$6.2 billion	WorldCom	2005
$3.2 billion	Tyco	2007
$3 billion	AOL Time Warner	2005

16. CRIMINAL LIABILITY

The 1934 act provides for criminal sanctions for willful violations of its provisions or the rules adopted under it. Liability is imposed for false material statements in applications, reports, documents, and registration statements. In response to the corporate scandals occurring during the beginning of the twenty-first century, Congress in 2002 increased the criminal penalties for violating the Securities Exchange Act of 1934. An individual found guilty of filing false or misleading documents with the SEC may be fined up to $5,000,000 and imprisoned for up to 20 years. A business organization found guilty of filing with the SEC false or misleading documents may be subject to a fine up to $25,000,000. An individual guilty of securities fraud may face a prison sentence of up to 25 years. These increased sanctions emphasize the seriousness with which all businesspeople must treat compliance with securities regulations.

The penalties are not theoretical. Sixteen officials from Enron have pled guilty and face a variety of prison terms. The CEO of WorldCom has been convicted and sentenced to 25 years in prison. The names of other former executives became commonly known because serious prison sentences get the public's attention. Whether these examples serve as deterrents for future fraudulent behavior remains to be seen.

Criminal liability is an important consideration for officers and directors as well as for accountants. Accountants have been found guilty of a crime for failure to disclose important facts to shareholder-investors. Compliance with generally accepted accounting principles is not an absolute defense. The critical issue in such cases is whether the financial statements as a whole fairly present the financial condition of the company and whether they accurately report operations for the covered periods. If they do not, the second issue is whether the accountant acted in good faith. Compliance with generally accepted accounting principles is evidence of good faith, but such evidence is not necessarily conclusive. Lack of criminal intent is the defense usually asserted by accountants charged with a crime. They usually admit mistakes or even negligence but deny any criminal wrongdoing. Proof of motive is not required.

As with issues of civil liability, most cases involving potential criminal liability are litigated under Section 10(b) and Rule 10b-5.

concept :: *summary*

Securities Exchange Act of 1934

:: SECTION 10(B)

Purpose: Creates liability for use of mail or any instrumentality of interstate commerce to defraud any person in connection with the purchase or sale of any security.

Plaintiff's case: Proof of defendant's intent to deceive through use of false information or nondisclosure of truthful information; plaintiff's reliance on fraudulent documents; and damages.

Defendant's defenses: No actual fraud was involved; only aided or abetted fraud; information was not material.

Civil liability: Person in violation of § 10(b) is liable for actual damages, court costs, and reasonable attorney fees.

:: SECTION 16(B)

Purpose: Creates strict liability for any insider making a profit on issuer's securities during any six-month period.

Plaintiff's case: Proof of the short-swing nature of the profitable transaction.

Defendant's defenses: Proof of no short-swing transaction; good faith (lack of intent) is no defense.

Civil fines: Up to three times the illegal profits; ban from service as director or officer.

:: SECTION 18

Purpose: Imposes liability for fraudulently filing false or misleading documents with the SEC or any exchange.

Plaintiff's case: Proof of defendant's intent to make false or misleading documents filed; plaintiff's reliance on documents filed; and damages.

Defendant's defenses: Freedom from fraud; good faith—no intent to defraud; no reliance by plaintiff on documents filed.

:: CRIMINAL LIABILITY

For securities fraud: Up to 25 years in prison.

For false or misleading documents filed: $5,000,000 fine or 20 years in prison or both per individual; $25,000,000 fine per organization.

For trading on nonpublic information: $1 million fine or 10 years in prison or both per individual; $10 million fine per organization.

:: Other Considerations

> "Congress amended the securities laws in 1995 to allow the Securities and Exchange Commission to bring actions against secondary violators that aid and abet securities fraud. Congress wisely declined to extend that right to private parties, out of concern of abusive securities litigation."
>
> **–Paul S. Atkins, "Stoneridge and the Rule of Law," The Wall Street Journal, January 25, 2008.**

In addition to understanding the historical nature of securities laws, every businessperson and investor should be familiar with two additional topics. First, in the next section, we present materials related to private parties suing to enforce the federal securities laws. Second, in the last section of this chapter, you should gain an understanding of how states also regulate the issuance and sale of securities.

17. PRIVATE SECURITIES LITIGATION REFORM ACT OF 1995

In 1994, the Supreme Court held that liability under Section 10(b) and Rule 10b-5 did not extend to parties aiding and abetting the primary violator.[2] The following year, Congress passed and President Clinton signed the **Private Securities Litigation Reform Act (PSLRA).** The law made it clear the Court's decision would not be expanded. Indeed, the PSLRA clarified that only the SEC can pursue claims against third parties not directly responsible for the securities law violation. This part of the law helps form the basis for the decision in Case 15.2.

---

[2]*Central Bank of Denver, N.A. v. First Interstate Bank of Denver, N.A., 114 S.Ct. 1439 (1994).*

table 15.5 :: Number of Federal Securities Fraud Class Actions (filed each year)	
:: Year	**:: Number of Cases**
2000	216
2001	497
2002	267
2003	226
2004	237
2005	182
2006	118
2007	177
2008 (through May)	92

Source: Stanford Law School Securities Class Action Clearinghouse in cooperation with Cornerstone Research
http://securities.stanford.edu

The PSLRA requires any private plaintiff to allege with specificity the scienter, or intent, of a company or its executives when filing a claim under Section 10(b) and Rule 10b-5. A plaintiff "must plead facts rendering an inference of scienter at least as likely as any plausible opposing inference."[3]

Congress, through the PSLRA, limits the amount of damages private plaintiffs can recover and restricts attorney fees. This law also provides requirements for the appointment of lead plaintiffs in securities class-action cases. Even with these restrictions, there are many securities class-actions filed each year. Table 15.5 details the number of these cases during this century. While it appears the amount of securities litigation is declining, new scandals and crises provide opportunities for more cases. Currently, the subprime mortgage crisis creates potential litigation.

18. STATE BLUE SKY LAWS

Throughout their history, state regulations regarding securities laws commonly have been referred to as **blue sky laws**—probably because they were intended to protect the potential investor from buying "a piece of the attractive blue sky" (worthless or risky securities) without financial and other information about what was being purchased. The blue sky laws can apply to securities subject to federal laws as well as to those securities exempt from the federal statutes. It is clearly established that the federal laws do not preempt the existence of state blue sky laws. Due to their broad application, any person associated with issuing or thereafter transferring securities should survey the blue sky laws passed by the various states.

Although the existence of federal securities laws has influenced state legislatures, enactment of blue sky laws has not been uniform. Indeed, states typically have enacted laws that contain provisions similar to the antifraud

[3]*Tellabs, Inc. v. Mabor Issues & Rights, Ltd., 127 S.Ct. 2499 (2007).*

provisions, the registration of securities provisions, the registration of securities brokers and dealers provisions, or a combination of these provisions of the federal laws. To bring some similarity to the various blue sky laws, the Uniform Securities Act was proposed for adoption by all states beginning in 1956. Since that time, the Uniform Securities Act has been the model for blue sky laws. A majority of states have used the uniform proposal as a guideline when enacting or amending their blue sky laws.

Registration Requirements   Despite the trend toward uniformity, state laws still vary a great deal in their methods of regulating both the distribution of securities and the practices of the securities industry within each state. For example, state regulations concerning the requirements of registering securities vary widely. Some states require *registration by notification,* other states require *registration by qualification.* Registration by notification allows issuers to offer securities for sale automatically after a stated time period expires unless the administrative agency takes action to prevent the offering. This is very similar to the registration process under the Securities Act of 1933. Registration by qualification usually requires a more detailed disclosure by the issuer. Under this type of regulation, a security cannot be offered for sale until the administrative agency grants the issuer a license or certificate to sell securities.

In an attempt to resolve some of this conflict over the registration procedure, the drafters of the Uniform Securities Act may have compounded the problem. This act adopts the registration by notification process for an issuer who has demonstrated stability and performance. Registration by qualification is required by those issuers who do not have a proven record and who are not subject to the Securities Act of 1933. In addition, the Uniform Securities Act created a third procedure—*registration by coordination.* For those issuers of securities who must register with the SEC, duplicate documents are filed with the state's administrative agency. Unless a state official objects, the state registration becomes effective automatically when the federal registration statement is deemed effective.

Exemptions   To further compound the confusion about blue sky laws, various exemptions of the securities or transactions have been adopted by the states. Four basic exemptions from blue sky laws have been identified. Every state likely has enacted at least one and perhaps a combination of these exemptions. Among these common four are the exemption:

1. For an isolated transaction.
2. For an offer or sale to a limited number of offerees or purchasers within a stated time period.
3. For a private offering.
4. For a sale if the number of holders after the sale does not exceed a specified number.

The second type of exemption probably is the most common exemption, because it is part of the Uniform Securities Act. Nevertheless, states vary on whether the exemption applies to offerees or to purchasers. There also is great variation on the maximum number of such offerees or purchasers involved. That number likely ranges between 5 and 35, depending on the applicable blue sky law. The time period for the offers or purchases, as the case may be, also may vary; however, 12 months seems to be the most common period.

Usually the applicable time limitation is worded to read, for example, "*any* 12-month time period." In essence, this language means that each day starts a new time period running. For example, assume a security is exempt from blue sky registration requirements if the issuer sells (or offers to sell) securities to no more than 35 investors during any 12-month period. Furthermore, assume the following transactions occur, with each investor being a different person or entity:

- On February 1, 2009, issuer sells to 5 investors.
- On June 1, 2009, issuer sells to 10 investors.
- On September 1, 2009, issuer sells to 10 investors.
- On December 1, 2009, issuer sells to 5 investors.
- On March 1, 2010, issuer sells to 5 investors.
- On May 1, 2010, issuer sells to 10 investors.

Only 30 investors are involved during the 12-month period following February 1, 2009. However, 40 investors are purchasers during the 12 months following June 1, 2009. Therefore, this security and the transactions involved are not exempt from the blue sky law. Civil as well as criminal liability may result for failure to comply with applicable legal regulations.

Although blue sky laws may cause confusion because of their variation, ignorance of the state legal requirements is no defense. This confusion is aggravated when the businessperson considers the further applicability of federal securities laws. To diminish this confusion, any person involved in the issuance or subsequent transfer of securities should consult with lawyers and accountants as well as other experts who have a working knowledge of securities regulations.

:: Key Terms

Blue sky laws 467
Controlling person 448
Due diligence defense 452
Insider 459
Issuer 448
Misappropriation theory 461
Posteffective period 449
Prefiling period 449
Private Securities Litigation Reform Act (PSLRA) 466

Prospectus 449
Registration statement 449
Sarbanes-Oxley Act of 2002 443
Scienter 452
Securities Act of 1933 447
Securities and Exchange Commission (SEC) 443
Securities Exchange Act of 1934 453

Security 441
Seller 448
Short-swing profits 460
Tippee 460
Tombstone ad 449
Underwriter 448
Waiting period 449

:: Review Questions and Problems

1. *What Is a Security?*

W.J. Howey Company and Howey-in-the-Hills Service, Inc., are Florida corporations under common control and management. Howey Company offers to sell to the public its orange grove, tree by tree. Howey-in-the-Hills Service, Inc., offers these buyers a contract wherein the appropriate care, harvesting, and marketing of the oranges would be provided. Most of the buyers who sign the service contracts are nonresidents of Florida who have very little knowledge or skill needed to care for and harvest the oranges. These buyers are attracted by the expectation of profits. Is a sale of orange trees by the Howey Company and a sale of services by Howey-in-the-Hills Service, Inc., a sale of a security? Why or why not?

2. *Securities and Exchange Commission*
   (a) When was this administrative agency created?
   (b) What types of regulatory authorities does the SEC have at its disposal?

Sarbanes-Oxley Act of 2002

3. *Revitalization of SEC*

   What was the primary way the Sarbanes-Oxley Act increased the authority and capabilities of the SEC?

4. *Accounting Reforms*

   List and describe two major developments designed to allow auditors to focus on their review of, and not service to, public companies.

5. *Corporate Governance*

   Some commentators state that the concept of independence is the most important aspect of Sarbanes-Oxley. How is independence required and why is it critical to corporate governance?

6. *Financial Statements and Controls*

   Describe the Sarbanes-Oxley provisions that require certification of financial statements and internal financial controls.

7. *Securities Fraud*

   In what three ways did the Sarbanes-Oxley Act strengthen the enforcement of securities fraud?

The Securities Act of 1933: Going Public

8. *Parties Regulated*

   Who are the four types of parties governed by the 1933 Securities Act?

9. *Documents Involved*
   (a) What are the two important documents required by the Securities Act of 1933?
   (b) Under the provisions of the federal Securities Act of 1933, there are three important time periods concerning when securities may be sold or offered for sale. Name and describe these three time periods.

10. *Liability*

    To secure a loan, Rubin pledges stock that he represents as being marketable and worth approximately $1.7 million. In fact, the stock is nonmarketable and practically worthless. He is charged with violating the Securities Act of 1933. He claims that because no sale occurred, he is not guilty. Is he correct? Why or why not?

11. *Defenses*

    What are three defenses that might be used by a party charged with violating the Securities Act of 1933?

Securities Exchange Act of 1934: Being Public

12. *Section 10(b) and Rule 10b-5*

    (a) Section 10(b) of the Securities Exchange Act of 1934 and Rule 10b-5 are of fundamental importance in the law of securities regulations. What is the main purpose of this section and rule?

    (b) Do you suppose that an oral promise made and not performed can be the basis of arguing a party is guilty of defrauding another under § 10(b) and Rule 10b-5?

13. *Insider Transactions*

    Donna, a corporate director, sold 100 shares of stock in her corporation on June 1, 2007. The selling price was $10.50 a share. Two months later, after the corporation had announced substantial losses for the second quarter of the year, Donna purchased 100 shares of the corporation's stock for $7.25 a share. Are there any problems with Donna's sale and purchase? Explain.

14. *Nonpublic Information*

    Eric Ethan, president of Inside-Outside Sports Equipment Company, has access to information which is not available to the general investor. What standard should Eric Ethan apply in deciding whether this information is so material as to prevent him from investing in his company prior to the information's public release?

15. *Additional Civil Liability*

    What is the purpose of Section 18 of the Securities Exchange Act of 1934?

16. *Criminal Liability*

    What are the dollar amounts related to fines and what are the number of years related to prison terms for those that violate the Securities Act of 1934?

Other Considerations

17. *Private Securities Litigation Reform Act of 1995*

    (a) What is the purpose of the PSLRA?

    (b) List four ways Congress accomplishes this purpose.

18. *State Blue Sky Laws*

    Why is it important for businesspeople to understand the role of state blue sky laws in addition to federal securities regulations?

business :: *discussions*

1. Two former roommates from college contact you about an opportunity to make big money. Their idea is to start a business to market a new video game system (the computer science major developed the software, the engineer created the hardware). They estimate it will take $5 to $10 million to begin production, and they want to raise money by selling shares in the company to investors. They think their product is superior, and they are aware of the time factor. They want to get started as soon as possible. Your field of expertise is securities marketing.

Can the three of you just begin advertising for investors?

What steps must be followed to comply with the law?

How much time is needed before potential investors can be approached legally?

2. You and a former classmate started a computer software company five years ago. Originally, the two of you were the owners and only employees. The foundation of your company was your combined expertise in creating custom-designed applications addressing the human resource needs of your clients. As your company grew, you added programmers that now allow your business to provide a greater array of computer applications. You and your co-owner decide to raise capital by making a public offering of stock. In preparation for going public, you visit with several of your most valuable clients about investing in your company.

What concerns should you have regarding these conversations?

Is there anything about your expectations of the company's future performance you must or must not share?

3. You and two partners operate a graphics design and printing company. The success of this business relates to the high-quality service and products you provide to your clients. To move to the next level requires a considerable financial investment in computer software and hardware. You and your partners are considering forming a corporation and offering to sell stock to the public. You anticipate raising at least $40 million in new capital. As you ponder these moves, you seek answers to the following questions:

What requirements of the Sarbanes-Oxley Act will you have to meet?

What is involved in offering a new company's stock for sale to the public?

Are there aspects of doing business as a publicly traded company that are different from operating as a partnership?

16

Antitrust Laws—Regulatory Competition

Learning Objectives ::

In this chapter you will learn:

1. To gain an understanding of the underlying economic assumptions that create a competitive business environment.

2. Details about antitrust laws developed in response to the perceived needs of society.

3. To appreciate how laws that are nearly 100 years old remain relevant today.

4. To understand why antitrust enforcement is influenced by politics and how this influences business activities.

5. To comprehend international aspects of antitrust laws.

Why is it important to study antitrust laws? First, your failure to understand and comply with antitrust policy could result in the loss of your job. Major fines for you and your company and a prison sentence for you are not beyond the realm of possibility. You need to know that antitrust laws apply equally to small, local businesses and to large, multinational corporations. Even though the dollar figures in the next paragraph are staggering, the details of this chapter should be familiar to businesspeople working for organizations of all sizes.

In 2006 and 2007, the U.S. Department of Justice imposed fines totaling more than $1.1 billion. The Antitrust Office of the European Union fined Microsoft $1.35 billion arising out of a 2004 case. And this record fine does not settle all the antitrust claims the EU has against Microsoft.

These figures are intended to catch your attention and to emphasize the significant impact of the antitrust laws presented in this chapter. Fines and the possibility of imprisonment reflect the seriousness of anticompetitive behavior.

1. HISTORICAL DEVELOPMENT

A legal use of a trust occurs if your grandparents give money to your parents for use in paying your education expenses.

The term *antitrust* is somewhat misleading. Trusts are a legal arrangement used for centuries for such socially desirable purposes as promoting education or caring for spendthrift or incompetent children and for financial and tax planning. A **trust** is a fiduciary relationship concerning property in which one person, known as the **trustee,** holds legal title to property for the benefit of another, known as the **beneficiary.** The trustee's duties are to manage and preserve the property for the use and enjoyment of the beneficiary.

John Rockefeller gained control of the petroleum industry; Cornelius Vanderbilt controlled railroads; and Andrew Carnegie controlled the steel industry.

In the last part of the nineteenth century, businesspeople used the trust device extensively to gain monopolistic control of several industries. Through it, a group of corporations in the same type of business could unite to eliminate competition among themselves. The trust device allowed all or at least a majority of the stock of several companies to be transferred to a trustee. The trustee then was in a position to control the operations and policy-making of all the companies. The trust not only controlled production, but also dominated and divided the market and established price levels. The effect of these concentrations was to destroy the free market—"to restrain trade," as the Sherman Act would put it.

Because the purpose of the laws discussed in this chapter was to "bust" the trusts, these laws became known as the antitrust laws. Today the term is used to describe all laws that intend to promote and regulate competition and make our competitive economic system work. The goal is workable competition and all the benefits that are intended to flow from it.

During its first hundred years, the federal government's role in relation to commerce was that of promoter. The U.S. Constitution itself eliminates trade barriers among the states. In the early and mid-nineteenth century, through its sponsorship of internal improvements such as canals and roads and its support for railroads, the federal government facilitated trade and commerce. But by the end of the nineteenth century business and industrial combinations were so powerful that reformers called on government to break these monopolies and restore healthy competition. The government responded by enacting the **Sherman Act** in 1890.

The goal of the Sherman Act was competition. Competition, these reformers pointed out, tends to keep private markets working in ways that are socially desirable. It encourages an efficient allocation of resources and stimulates efficiency and product innovation. A competitive system that allows easy entry to and withdrawal from the marketplace is consistent with individual freedom and economic opportunity. In 1958, Justice Hugo Black, in *Northern Pacific Ry. Co. v. United States* (356 U.S. 1), reflected on the purpose of the Sherman Act when he stated in part:

> The Sherman Act was designed to be a comprehensive charter of economic liberty aimed at preserving free and unfettered competition as the rule of trade. It rests on the premise that the unrestrained interaction of competitive forces will yield the best allocation of our economic resources, the lowest prices, the highest quality and the greatest material progress, while at the same time providing an environment conducive to the preservation of our democratic, political and social institutions.

The Sherman Act still provides the basic framework for the regulation of business and industry. It seeks to preserve competition by prohibiting two types of anticompetitive business behavior:

- Contracts, combinations, and conspiracies in restraint of trade or commerce (see Section 2 of this chapter).
- Monopolies and attempts to monopolize (see Section 3 of this chapter).

The Sherman Act was general and often ambiguous. It did not define *trust, monopoly,* or *restraint of trade.* It also did not make clear whether it addressed combinations of labor as well as capital.

In 1914 Congress, recognizing that the Sherman Act needed to be more specific, enacted the **Clayton Act** as an amendment to the Sherman Act and later twice amended the Clayton Act (1936, 1950) to clarify its provisions. The Clayton Act declares that certain enumerated practices in interstate commerce are illegal. These are practices that might adversely affect competition but that were not clear violations under the Sherman Act.

In 1914, Congress also passed the **Federal Trade Commission Act.** This act created the Federal Trade Commission (FTC), an independent administrative agency charged with keeping competition free and fair. The FTC enforces the Clayton Act. In addition, it enforces Section 5 of the FTC Act, which prohibits unfair methods of competition and unfair or deceptive acts or practices.

The antitrust laws are enforced by the federal and state governments and by private parties. The federal government's basic enforcement procedures are utilized through the Department of Justice and the Federal Trade Commission (FTC). The Department of Justice alone has the power to bring criminal proceedings, but it shares its civil enforcement powers with the FTC.

State government also plays an important role in the enforcement of antitrust laws. A state attorney general may bring civil suits for damages under the Sherman Act as well as suits for an injunction. In addition, state legislators have enacted antitrust laws that cover both products and services. These laws cover intrastate activities and are designed to prevent loss of competition in local communities.

In addition to these governmental enforcers, private parties may bring civil suits seeking monetary damages or injunction as a means of enforcing the antitrust laws. Section 5 of this chapter discusses the penalties that help protect the competitive nature of the marketplace.

:: The Sherman Act

To fully appreciate the importance that the Sherman Act plays in our legal and regulatory environment of business, you must understand the basic provisions and analysis of the law. The following sections present these basic concepts, as follows:

- Restraint of trade.
- Monopoly.
- Legal analysis.
- Sanctions.
- Exemptions.

Section 1 of Sherman Act states: "Every contract, combination, in the form of trust or otherwise, or conspiracy, in restraint of trade or commerce among the several States, or with foreign nations, is declared to be illegal."

2. RESTRAINT OF TRADE

Section 1 of the Sherman Act prohibits contracts, combinations, and conspiracies in **restraint of trade** or commerce. *Contracts* in restraint of trade usually result from verbal or written agreements; *combinations* usually result from conduct; *conspiracies* are usually established by agreement and followed up by some act carrying out the plan of the conspiracy. An express agreement is not required to create a contract in restraint of trade. Such contracts may be implied. For example, discussion of price with one's competitors together with conscious parallel pricing establishes a violation.

Joint activities by two or more persons may constitute a violation of Section 1. The most common contract in restraint of trade is an agreement among competitors to charge the same price for their products (**price fixing**). Such agreements among producers to set prices in advance rather than allow prices to be set by the operations of a free market are obviously anticompetitive and in restraint of trade. Agreements relating to territories of operation also violate Section 1 of the Sherman Act. So does an attempt to extend the economic power of a patent or copyright to unrelated products or services. These and other examples of Section 1 violations are discussed in Sections 7 to 11 of this chapter.

Sherman Act cases must satisfy an interstate commerce element. The facts must show that an allegedly illegal activity was either in interstate commerce or had a substantial effect on interstate commerce. The facts need not prove a change in the volume of interstate commerce but only that the activity had a substantial and adverse or not insubstantial effect on interstate commerce. As discussed in Chapter 6 , the impact on interstate commerce often is readily apparent.

3. MONOPOLY

Section 2 of the Sherman Act regulates **monopoly** and the attempts to monopolize any part of interstate or foreign commerce. The law establishes the means to break up existing monopolies and to prevent others from developing. It is directed at single firms and does not purport to cover shared monopolies or oligopolies.

Under Section 2 of the Sherman Act, it is a violation for a firm to monopolize, attempt to monopolize, or conspire to monopolize any part of interstate or foreign commerce. Attempts to monopolize cases require proof of intent to destroy competition or achieve monopoly power. This is most difficult to prove, and as a result, there have been few cases concerning attempts to monopolize. A conspiracy to monopolize requires proof of specific intent to monopolize and at least one overt act to accomplish it. Proof of monopoly power or even that it was attainable is not required. This conspiracy theory is usually joined with the allegation of actual monopoly in most cases.

Sidebar 16.1 discusses the factual situation in a monopoly case that the Supreme Court uses to uphold the finding of an illegal monopoly. Note the guilty party becomes responsible for three times the damages caused by the monopoly.

Proof of monopoly power alone is not enough. Some monopolies are lawful. If monopoly power is "thrust upon" a firm or if it exists because of a patent or franchise, there is no violation of Section 2 if the firm does not engage in conduct that has the effect or purpose of protecting, enforcing, or

A utility, such as a power company, usually substitutes regulatory requirements by a public service commission in return for its near-monopoly status.

:: *sidebar* 16.1

Example of Monopoly

The case of *Aspen Skiing Co. v. Aspen Highlands Skiing Corp.*[*] provides an example of the kind of factual situation and legal analysis that leads to a finding of a § 2 violation. In the early years of snow skiing in Aspen, three facilities were operated by three distinct companies. The two parties involved in this case were among these competitors. In addition to offering a daily ski-lift ticket for their own mountain, each competitor sold a multiday, interchangeable, all-Aspen ticket.

Aspen Skiing acquired the third facility and opened a fourth. Eventually, this company sold a multiday ticket that allowed its patrons access to only its facilities. As a result of this action, Aspen Highlands lost a significant share of its business. Ultimately, Aspen Highlands sued Aspen Skiing, alleging that the refusal to sell an all-Aspen ticket was an illegal attempt to monopolize the Aspen Skiing market.

Aspen Skiing argued that it was not in violation of § 2 of the Sherman Act because nothing in this law required it to do business with a competitor. Even though the trial judge agreed with this legal conclusion, the judge instructed

the jury that it could find Aspen Skiing in violation of the Sherman Act unless that company persuaded the jury that its conduct was justified by any normal business purpose.

Apparently the jury was not convinced by Aspen Skiing's presentation. The jury rendered a verdict finding Aspen Skiing in violation of § 2 and awarding Aspen Highlands actual damages of $2.5 million. This award was tripled to $7.5 million, and costs and attorneys' fees were added to this amount.

Aspen Skiing was unable to convince either the court of appeals or the United States Supreme Court to reverse this jury verdict. The Supreme Court was particularly influenced by the market studies that showed skiers wanted to have access to the Highlands facilities but refused to ski there due to the lack of an all-area ticket. The Court concluded that the jury was justified in finding that inappropriate motivations to monopolize were behind Aspen Skiing's decision to stop selling the all-area ticket.

[*] 105 S.Ct. 2847 (1985).

---

extending the monopoly power. The power must have been either acquired or used in ways that go beyond normal, honest industrial business conduct for a violation to exist. To be illegal, the monopoly must have been *deliberatively* acquired or used. A firm is guilty of monopolization when it acquires or maintains monopoly power by a course of deliberate conduct that keeps other firms from entering the market or from expanding their share of it. Deliberativeness is not difficult to prove in most cases.

Conduct that proves deliberativeness may be anything in restraint of trade. For example, predatory conduct would prove deliberativeness. **Predatory conduct** is seeking to advance market share by injuring actual or potential competitors by means other than improved performance. It may be for the purpose of driving out competitors, for keeping them out, or for making them less effective. Pricing policies are frequently examined for proof of predatory conduct. Profit-maximizing pricing; limit pricing, whereby the price is limited to levels that tend to discourage entry; and the practice of price discrimination all may tend to prove monopoly power and predatory conduct.

Recently, in *Weyerhauser Company v. Ross-Simons Hardwood Lumber Company*,[1] the U.S. Supreme Court ruled that alleged predatory conduct associated with low prices charged by a seller or high prices paid by a buyer has to meet the same standards. There must be proof the prices were intended to drive competitors out of business followed by the wrongdoer recouping

---

[1] 127 S.Ct. 1069 (2007).

these initial losses. Sidebar 16.2 describes the proof needed to document the existence of an illegal monopoly.

:: *sidebar* 16.2

Proving an Illegal Monopoly Exists

A firm violates Section 2 if it follows a course of conduct through which it obtained the power to control price or exclude competition. The mere possession of monopoly power is not a violation. There must be proof that the power resulted from a deliberate course of conduct or proof of intent to maintain the power by conduct. Proof of deliberateness is just as essential as is proof of the power to control price to exclude competition.

Section 2 cases require proof of market power—the power to affect the price of the firm's products in the market. Whether such power exists is usually determined by an analysis of the reaction of buyers to price changes by the alleged monopolist seller. Such cases require a definition of the relevant market and a study of the degree of concentration within the market. Barriers to entry are analyzed, and the greater the barriers, the greater the significance of market share. The legal issues in such cases require structural analysis.

In defining the relevant market, the courts examine both product market and geographic market. A relevant market is the smallest one wide enough so that products from outside the geographic area or from other producers in the same area cannot compete with those included in the defined relevant market. In other words, if prices are raised or supply is curtailed within a given area while demand remains constant, will products from other areas or other products from within the area enter the market in enough quantity to force a lower price or increased supply?

Some monopoly cases involve products for which there are few or no substitutes. Other cases involve products for which there are numerous substitutes. For example, aluminum may be considered a product that is generally homogeneous. If a firm has 90 percent of the virgin aluminum market, a violation would be established. However, if a firm had 90 percent of the Danish coffee cake market, the decision is less clear, because numerous products compete with Danish coffee cakes as a breakfast product. The relevant product is often difficult to define because of differences in products, substitute products, product diversification, and even product clusters.

The importance of defining the relevant markets helps explain why the government challenges a proposed merger between Whole Foods Market (of Austin, Texas) and Wild Oats Markets (of Boulder, Colorado) while seeming to have very little concern with the proposed combination of XM and Sirius. In the former situation, these chains are major forces in the organic-food markets. Focusing on this specialized area, the combination of Whole Foods and Wild Oats is significant. The latter merger would have a similar impact if the focus of analysis is on satellite radio. However, the government defines XM and Sirius as being in competition with free AM and FM radio as well as iPods, CDs, and DVDs. When viewing the broad array of listening entertainment options, the XM-Sirius merger appears to have very little impact.

Section 2 cases may involve a variety of proofs and many different forms of economic analysis. The degree of market concentration, barriers to entry, structural features such as market shares of other firms, profit levels, the extent to which prices respond to changes in supply and demand, whether or not a firm discriminates in price between its customers, and the absolute size of the firm are all factors usually considered by courts in monopoly cases. In addition, courts examine the conduct of the firm. How did it achieve its market share? Was it by internal growth or acquisition? Does the firm's current conduct tend to injure competition? These and other issues are important aspects in any finding of the existence of monopoly power.

The monopoly cases that garner the most media attention are those involving Microsoft. Microsoft legally earned its dominant market share through its Windows operating system software. Over a number of years, throughout the 1980s and 1990s, Microsoft proved in the marketplace that its Windows operating system was what customers wanted on their PCs. Microsoft also gained near-monopoly dominance in the application software for word processing, presentations, and spreadsheets. Microsoft's legal problems began in the late 1990s, when competitors and the federal government alleged Microsoft was using its monopoly power to drive out competitors in applications such as browsers, media players, and instant messaging software. Microsoft allegedly uses its Windows monopoly by bundling these other products within Windows. In this way, Microsoft's applications appear on almost all PCs.

In the case accusing Microsoft of illegal monopoly practices in the Internet browser market, Microsoft lost at the trial level. The federal district judge ordered that Microsoft be broken into two companies, one focusing on operating systems and the other focusing on application software. Microsoft appealed, and during the appeal process the Justice Department management team changed from the Clinton to the Bush administration. In 2002, Microsoft and the Justice Department settled this case. Microsoft continues to operate under its unified structure, continues to bundle some applications within its Windows operating software, and continues to face antitrust challenges around the world.

Sidebar 16.3 summarizes some of the cases Microsoft has settled since its monopoly trial and appeal.

:: *sidebar* 16.3

Settlement of Antitrust Lawsuits

As the result of the federal government's successful prosecution of its antitrust suit against Microsoft, a number of corporate rivals sued Microsoft for damages. Following the 2002 settlement with the Justice Department, Microsoft approached settlement talks to resolve the civil lawsuits. The following settlements have occurred:

:: Year	:: Company	:: Payment by Microsoft
2003	America Online	$750 million
2004	Sun Microsystems	$1.6 billion
2004	Novell	$536 million
2005	Gateway Corporation	$150 million
2005	I.B.M.	$775 million
2005	RealNetworks	$761 million

Microsoft continues to enjoy its monopoly in Windows. In several of these settlements, Microsoft achieves not only peace but a business ally. For example, in settling with RealNetworks, Microsoft agrees to join forces to compete against the near monopoly held by Apple through its iTunes software for playing MP3 music files. Microsoft agreed, though MSN, to support RealNetworks' Rhapsody music subscription service.

*Source: John Markoff, "Microsoft to Pay IBM $775 Million in Settlement," *The New York Times*, July 2, 2005.

4. ANALYSIS IN ANTITRUST LAW

As we have seen, the Sherman Act was deliberately vague in expectation that the courts would draw the line between legal and illegal conduct with respect to restraint of trade and monopoly. Courts follow two principles to guide applicability in antitrust law:

- The rule of reason.
- Per se illegality.

The following discussions illuminate these concepts.

The Rule of Reason Section 1 of the Sherman Act provides that "*every* contract, combination . . , or conspiracy in restraint of trade . . is declared to be illegal." However, the United States Supreme Court has held that Congress did not really mean it when it used the word *every*. For example, if you and I enter into a contract whereby I agree to buy your car, this contract restrains trade. You cannot sell your car to another person without becoming liable to me for a breach of our contract. The Court felt that Congress did not intend our contract to be a violation of the Sherman Act.

> The rule of reason is the fundamental principle of analysis under the Sherman Act.

The **rule of reason** was announced in *Standard Oil Co. v. United States* (221 U.S. 1 [1911]). The Supreme Court in that case held that contracts or conspiracies in restraint of trade were illegal only if they constituted *undue* or *unreasonable* restraints of trade and that only *unreasonable* attempts to monopolize were covered by the Sherman Act. As a result, acts that the statute prohibits may be removed from the coverage of the law by a finding that they are *reasonable*.

The *test of reasonableness* asks whether challenged contracts or acts are unreasonably restrictive of competitive conditions. Unreasonableness can be based on:

- The nature or character of the contracts.
- Surrounding circumstances giving rise to the inference or presumption that the contracts were intended to restrain trade and enhance prices.

Under either branch of the test, the inquiry is confined to a consideration of impact on competitive conditions. If an agreement promotes competition, it may be legal. If it suppresses or destroys competition, it is unreasonable and illegal.

For purposes of the rule of reason, Sherman Act violations may be divided into two categories. The first category consists of agreements and practices that are illegal only if they impose an unreasonable restraint upon competitors. The other category consists of agreements or practices that are so plainly anticompetitive and so lacking in any redeeming values that they are conclusively presumed to be illegal without further examination under the rule of reason. These agreements have such a pernicious effect on competition that elaborate inquiry as to the precise harm they may cause or a business excuse for them is unnecessary. They are said to be *illegal per se*. It is not necessary to examine them to see if they are reasonable. They are conclusively presumed to be unreasonable.

Per Se Illegality The concept of **per se illegality** simplifies proof in cases in which it is applied. When an activity is illegal per se, courts are not required to conduct a complicated and prolonged examination of the economic consequences of the activity to determine whether it is unreasonable. If it is illegal per se, proof of the activity is proof of a violation and proof that it is in restraint of trade. It is unreasonable as a matter of law.

> Per se illegality is more likely associated with horizontal agreements among competitors.

Courts develop the distinction between rule of reason and per se illegality on a case-by-case basis. However, history tells us the agreements among competitors are much more likely to satisfy the per se illegality standards. These arrangements among competitors are of a *horizontal nature*. Courts hold that the sharing among competitors of product information, pricing policies, and territorial allocations is not going to increase competition. Indeed, the anticompetitive results of this sharing results in such arrangements being viewed as illegal per se.

Arrangements directed by a supplier to a customer are known as *vertical agreements*. For example, a manufacturer may limit the geographical territory of a wholesaler or direct that a retailer must charge the consumer a minimum price for its products. Whether these arrangements are reasonable or not is less clear than the horizontal agreements. Analysis of vertical agreements usually requires consideration of the rule of reason as opposed to being judged as per se illegal.

5. SANCTIONS

The Sherman Act as amended by the Clayton Act recognizes four separate legal sanctions:

1. Violations may be subject to criminal fines and imprisonment.
2. Violations may be enjoined by the courts.
3. Injured parties may collect **triple damages**.
4. Any property owned in violation of Section 1 of the Sherman Act that is being transported from one state to another is subject to a seizure by and forfeiture to the United States.

The first sanction is criminal punishment. Crimes under the Sherman Act are felonies. An individual found guilty may be fined up to $1 million and imprisoned up to 10 years. A corporation found guilty may be fined up to $100 million for each offense. These sanctions show congressional intent to keep the antitrust laws current. Table 16.1 lists the fines the U.S. Justice Department imposed over the past eight years. The general trend of increasing severity illustrates the serious nature of antitrust violations.

> Review www.usdoj.gov/atr/public/workstats.pdf for statistics on antitrust cases and claims handled by the Antitrust Division of the Justice Department.

> These financial penalties were updated in the Antitrust Criminal Penalty Enhancement and Reform Act of 2004.

table 16.1 :: Criminal Antitrust Fines (2000–2007)

[Fines in millions of dollars by fiscal year]

2000: $152
2001: $280
2002: $75
2003: $107
2004: $350
2005: $338
2006: $473
2007: $630

Source: Antitrust Division, Department of Justice www.usdoj.gov/atr/public/231424/2.htm.

The second sanction of the Sherman Act empowers courts to grant injunctions, at the request of the government or a private party, that will prevent and restrain violations or continued violations of its provisions. An injunction may prevent anticompetitive behavior, or it may even force a breakup of a corporation.

The injunction is frequently used when the success of a criminal prosecution is doubtful. It takes less proof to enjoin an activity (*preponderance of the evidence*) than it does to convict of a crime (*beyond a reasonable doubt*). There have been cases involving this remedy even after an acquittal in a criminal case. In effect, the court ordered the defendant not to do something it had been found innocent of doing.

Do realize that individuals or businesses harmed by an antitrust violation have the incentive of triple damages to act as an enforcer of the law.

The third sanction affords relief to persons, including governments, injured by another's violations of the Sherman Act. Section 4 of the Clayton Act authorizes such victims in a civil action to collect three times the damages they have suffered plus court costs and reasonable attorneys' fees. Normally, the objective of awarding money damages to individuals in a private lawsuit is to place them in the position they would have enjoyed, as nearly as this can be done with money, had their rights not been invaded. The triple-damage provisions of the antitrust laws, however, employ the remedy of damages to punish a defendant for a wrongful act in addition to compensating the plaintiff for actual injury. Today it is perhaps the most important sanction for an antitrust violation, because it allows one's competitors as well as injured members of the general public to enforce the law. Legislation also allows both federal and state governments to file a suit for triple damages.

Successful triple-damage suits may impose financial burdens on violators far in excess of any fine that could be imposed as a result of a criminal prosecution. This significant liability may be far in excess of the damages caused by any one defendant, because the liability of defendants is based on tort law and is said to be *joint and several*. For example, assume that 10 companies in an industry conspire to fix prices and that the total damages caused by the conspiracy equal $100 million. Also, assume that nine of the defendants settle out of court for $25 million. The remaining defendant, if the case is lost, would owe $275 million ($3 \times 100 - 25$). The Supreme Court has held that there is no right of contribution by the losing party against those that settled prior to the final judgment.

A firm that is indicted for violating the Sherman Act often will face civil actions as well. The firm may resolve the criminal case through a *nolo* plea so the civil plaintiffs do not benefit from a criminal conviction.

There is a significant relationship between the criminal antitrust prosecution and the civil suit for triple damages. If the defendant in a criminal antitrust suit is convicted or pleads guilty, the plaintiff in the related triple damages suit is greatly aided. This result arises from the criminal case's prima facie evidence that an antitrust violation occurred. The cost of the investigation and preparation needed to prove the existence of an antitrust violation is usually substantial. Using the defendant's criminal conviction or guilty plea as proof of the wrong allows the civil plaintiff to concentrate on proving damages, which are then tripled by the court. This automatic proof deriving from the criminal case can be avoided if the defendant enters a plea of **nolo contendere** (no contest) in the criminal case. Because this plea technically is interpreted as avoiding a conviction, the civil plaintiff is left with the burden of proving the antitrust violation.

concept :: *summary*

Antitrust Sanctions

1. Four sanctions are recognized by the antitrust laws:
   a. Federal criminal penalties.
   b. Injunctions ordered by the courts.
   c. Triple damages payable to an injured party.
   d. Seizure and forfeiture of property owned in restraint of trade if such property is transported between states.
2. The federal criminal penalties are, for an individual, up to a $1,000,000 fine plus up to ten years in prison, and for a corporation, up to $100 million in fines.

3. An injunction may prevent anticompetitive behavior.
4. Under the triple-damage sanctions, a defendant cannot seek contribution from other wrongdoers.
5. To avoid the impact of a guilty plea or a conviction on a pending civil antitrust suit, the criminally accused defendant often pleads *nolo contendere* (no contest).

6. EXEMPTIONS

Certain businesses may be exempt from the Sherman Act because of a statute or as the result of a judicial decision. Among activities and businesses for which there are statutory exemptions are insurance companies; farmers' cooperatives; shipping, milk marketing, and investment companies. Activities required by state law are exempt. In addition, normal activities of labor unions are exempt.

These exemptions are narrowly construed and do not mean that every activity of a firm is necessarily exempted simply because most activities are exempted. For example, an agreement between an insurance company and a pharmaceutical organization that regulates the price of prescription drugs given to policyholders of the insurance company is not exempt—it was not the business of insurance involved in this transaction. It is the business of insurance that is exempt and not the business of insurance companies. Likewise, a labor union would forfeit its exemption when it agrees with one set of employers to impose a certain wage scale on other employers' bargaining units. It is only the usual and legitimate union activity that is exempt. In Chapter 21, we discuss how a union must deal directly with the company involved in the labor dispute. Therefore, the arrangement in the example above is beyond the normal and proper activities of a union and not protected from antitrust claims.

In a 1943 case known as *Parker v. Brown*, the Supreme Court created a **state action exemption** to the Sherman Act. This state action exemption, referred to as the **Parker v. Brown doctrine**, is based on the reasoning that the Sherman Act does not apply to state government. When a state acts in its sovereign capacity, it is immune from federal antitrust scrutiny. For example, an unsuccessful candidate for admittance to the Arizona bar alleged a conspiracy by the bar examiners in violation of the Sherman Act. He contended that the grading scale was dictated by the number of new attorneys desired rather than by the level of competition and answers on the exam. The courts held that this activity was exempt from the Sherman Act. The grading of bar

Don't rely on an exemption from antitrust laws to justify anticompetitive behavior.

examinations is, in reality, conduct of the Arizona Supreme Court and thus exempt. Action by the courts is just as immune as actions by the legislature.

Another exemption from the Sherman Act extends to concerted efforts to lobby government officials, regardless of the anticompetitive purposes of the lobbying effort. The doctrine, known as the **Noerr-Pennington doctrine** is based on the First Amendment. For example, Budget Rent-A-Car filed suit against Hertz and National Rent-A-Car because the defendants lobbied officials at three state-owned airports to limit the number of car-rental operations.

This lobbying was ruled exempt from the Sherman Act under the First Amendment right to petition government for a redress of grievances and recognition of the value of the free flow of information.

Sidebar 16.4 describes a recent Supreme Court case involving the issue of whether securities laws take priority over antitrust laws in practices related to the sale of securities in public offerings.

:: *sidebar* 16.4

Antitrust vs. Securities Regulation

Buyers of newly issued securities filed an antitrust lawsuit against underwriting firms for allegedly engaging in anticompetitive activities in marketing of the shares. The U.S. Supreme Court reviewed a series of cases that try to balance the role of securities laws and antitrust laws. The implied repeal of antitrust laws should be found only where there is a "plain repugnancy" between the antitrust and securities regulations.

The Court ruled as follows:

We believe it fair to conclude that, where conduct at the core of the marketing of new securities is at issue; where securities regulators proceed with great care to distinguish the encouraged and permissible from the forbidden; where the threat of antitrust lawsuits, through error or disincentive, could seriously alter underwriter conduct in undesirable ways, to allow an antitrust lawsuit would threaten serious harm to the efficient functioning of the securities markets. Thus, the Supreme Court emphasizes that antitrust laws are not to be used to replace other regulations.

*Source: *Credit Suisse Securities LLC v. Billing*, 127 S. Ct. 2383 (2007).

:: Types of Cases

As the courts deal with potential violations of the Sherman Act, the types of cases typically heard can be divided into price fixing, territorial agreements, and concerted activities. Each of these is discussed in the following sections. A further word regarding price fixing is necessary before you start the examination of these types of cases. The philosophy expressed in the Sherman Act believes a competitive marketplace requires that prices be set by the operation of free markets. No competitor should have the economic power to set prices. Since price is an essential element of competition, the legal analysis used in price fixing cases is hotly debated regardless of the form of pricing agreements: horizontal, vertical, or indirect.

7. HORIZONTAL PRICE FIXING

Horizontal price fixing is an agreement between competitors to fix prices. The term *price fixing* means more than setting a price. For example, if partners in a firm set the price of their goods or service, they have engaged in a form of price fixing but not the type envisioned by the Sherman Act. The price fixing covered by the Sherman Act is that which threatens free competition.

Distributors and retailers of CDs agreed to pay $144 million to settle a class-action lawsuit accusing them of fixing the price of CDs.

It is no defense to a charge of price fixing that the prices fixed are fair or reasonable. It also is no defense that price fixing is engaged in by small competitors to allow them to compete with larger competitors. The per se rule makes price fixing illegal whether the parties to it have control of the market or not and whether or not they are trying to raise or lower the market price. It is just as illegal to fix a low price as it is to fix a high price. Maximum-price agreements are just as illegal as minimum-price agreements.

It is a defense to a charge of price fixing if two competitors enter into a joint venture and agree what the combined company will charge for its product. In *Texaco v. Dagher*,[2] the Court found that Texaco and Shell Oil were not fixing prices when they operated a joint venture to refine and sell gasoline.

Historically, the Sherman Act was thought to apply only to the sale of goods. Price fixing in the service sector was commonly engaged in by professional persons such as architects, lawyers, and physicians. Persons performing services argued they were not engaged in trade or commerce and thus they were not covered by the Sherman Act. They also contended there was a "learned profession" exception to the Sherman Act.

In the mid-1970s, the Supreme Court rejected these arguments and held that the Sherman Act covers services, including those performed by the learned professions such as attorneys-at-law. Today, it is just as illegal to fix the price of services as it is to fix the price of goods.

Courts have held lawyers, doctors, real estate agents, engineers, and dentists subject to antitrust laws.

Some professional groups have attempted to avoid restrictions on price fixing through the use of ethical standards. Although such ethical standards are not illegal per se, they are nevertheless anticompetitive and a violation of the Sherman Act. Others have attempted to determine the price of services indirectly by using formulas and relative-value scales. For example, some medical organizations have determined that a given medical procedure would be allocated a relative value on a scale of 1 to 10. Open-heart surgery might be labeled a 9 and an appendectomy a 3. All members of the profession would then use these values in determining professional fees. Such attempts have been uniformly held to be illegal.

Table 16.2 lists examples of horizontal price-fixing cases. The companies and industries listed illustrate the far-reaching nature of the Sherman Act.

In addition to the companies and results listed below, current investigations focus on title insurance companies agreeing on fees and on Hershey, Mars, Nestlé, and Cadbury Schweppes colluding relative to the price of chocolate.

8. VERTICAL PRICE FIXING

Attempts by manufacturers to control the ultimate retail price for their products is known as **vertical price fixing** or **resale price maintenance.** Such efforts result in part from the desire to maintain a high-quality product image,

---

[2]126 S.Ct. 1276 (2006).

table 16.2 :: Examples of Horizontal Price-Fixing Cases

:: Business	:: Type of Case	:: Sherman Act Violation	:: Case Result
Archer Daniels Midland Company and others	Criminal and civil	Fixed prices on citric acid.	$70 million fine and $35 million civil settlement.
Mrs. Baird's Bakery	Criminal and civil	Fixed prices on baked goods.	$10 million fine and $18 million settlement.
President of Pepsi-Cola Bottling Co.	Criminal	Agreed with Coca-Cola bottler to stop discounts to retailers.	4 months in jail, $45,000 fine, 3 years' probation, community service.
Southland Corp. and Borden Inc.	Criminal and civil	Rigged bids for dairy products sold to Florida school-milk programs.	$8 million combined fine and $2.5 million in civil claims.
American Institute of Architects	Civil, injunction	Discouraged competitive bidding, discount fees, and free services.	Consent decree that practices would cease plus $50,000 in costs.
Fireman's Fund Home Insurance Co., Liberty Mutual Insurance, and Travelers Corp.	Civil, class action, triple damages	Boycotted Minnesota law requiring workers' compensation rates to be established by competition.	$34 million settlement.
Kanzaki Specialty Papers Inc. and Mitsubishi Corp.	Criminal	Fixed prices on thermal fax paper.	$6.3 million settlement.
Delta, United, USAir, American, TWA, and Northwest Airlines	Civil	Use of computerized clearinghouse to fix airfares.	$458 million settlement involving the issuance of coupons for future air travel.

For part of its history, Nintendo successfully maintained a uniform resale price for its game players.

the assumption being that a relatively high price suggests a relatively high quality. These efforts are also based on a desire to maintain adequate channels of distribution. If one retailer is selling a product at prices significantly below those of other retailers, there is a strong likelihood that the other retailers will not continue to carry the product.

Although resale price-maintenance schemes can run afoul of the Sherman Act, it is possible for a manufacturer to control the resale price of its products. The primary method of legally controlling the retail price is for a manufacturer simply to announce its prices and refuse to deal with those who fail to comply. Under what is commonly referred to as the **Colgate doctrine,** the Supreme Court recognizes that such independent action by a manufacturer is not a per se violation of the Sherman Act. Resale price maintenance is legal only if there is no coercion or pressure other than the announced policy and its implementation.

Whether or not vertical price fixing should be illegal per se has been a matter of debate among economists and politicians. There is a possibility that a vertical restraint imposed by a single manufacturer or wholesaler may stimulate interbrand competition as it reduces intrabrand competition. This debate produced Case 16.1, in which the Supreme Court announces that the rule of reason is the correct analysis when determining the legality of vertical price-fixing situations.

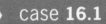

LEEGIN CREATIVE LEATHER PRODUCTS, INC. v. PSKS, INC.
127 S. Ct. 2705 (2007)

Leegin Creative Leather Products, Inc., designs, manufactures, and distributes leather goods and accessories. Leegin sells belts under the brand name "Brighton." To ensure a favorable shopping experience for its retail customers, Leegin sells to independent, small boutiques and specialty stores. Further, Leegin instituted the "Brighton Retail Pricing and Promotion Policy." This policy creates minimum prices for Brighton belts, and Leegin refuses to sell to any retailer who discounts Brighton goods below the suggested prices.

PSKS, Inc., operates Kay's Kloset in Lewisville, Texas. Kay's Kloset originally agreed to the "Brighton Policy" and was successful in selling Brighton products. Later, Kay's Kloset began marking down these products to compete with nearby retailers. When Leegin learned of these excessive discounts, it stopped selling to Kay's Kloset.

Having lost this line of belts and the resulting income, PSKS, Inc., sued Leegin claiming the "Brighton Policy" was in violation of § 1 of the Sherman Act. The District Court refused to allow Leegin's expert to testify on how its resale minimum pricing policy had a procompetitive impact. The trial jury awarded PSKS, Inc., $1.2 million. When the District Judge tripled the damages and awarded attorney fees and other costs, a judgment was entered against Leegin in the amount of $3,975,000.80. The Fifth Circuit Court of Appeals affirmed.

The Supreme Court granted Leegin's petition for certiorari to determine whether vertical minimum resale price maintenance agreements should be treated as per se illegal or analyzed under the rule of reason.

KENNEDY, J.: . . . Section 1 of the Sherman Act prohibits "every contract, combination in the form of trust or otherwise, or conspiracy, in restraint of trade or commerce among the several States." While § 1 could be interpreted to proscribe all contracts, the Court has never taken a literal approach to its language. Rather, the Court has repeated time and again that § 1 outlaws only unreasonable restraints.

The rule of reason is the accepted standard for testing whether a practice restrains trade in violation of § 1. Under this rule, the factfinder weighs all of the circumstances of a case in deciding whether a restrictive practice should be prohibited as imposing an unreasonable restraint on competition. Appropriate factors to take into account include specific information about the relevant business and the restraint's history, nature, and effect. Whether the businesses involved have market power is a further, significant consideration. In its design and function the rule distinguishes between restraints with anticompetitive effect that are harmful to the consumer and restraints stimulating competition that are in the consumer's best interest.

The rule of reason does not govern all restraints. Some types are deemed unlawful per se. The per se rule, treating categories of restraints as necessarily illegal, eliminates the need to study the reasonableness of an individual restraint in light of the real market forces at work . . . Restraints that are per se unlawful include horizontal agreements among competitors to fix prices.

Resort to per se rules is confined to restraints, like those mentioned, that would always or almost always tend to restrict competition and decrease output. To justify a per se prohibition a restraint must have manifestly anticompetitive effects and lack any redeeming virtue.

As a consequence, the per se rule is appropriate only after courts have had considerable experience with the type of restraint at issue, and only if courts can predict with confidence that it would be invalidated in all or almost all instances under the rule of reason. It should come as no surprise, then, that we have expressed reluctance to adopt per se rules with regard to restraints imposed in the context of business relationships where the economic impact of certain practices is not immediately obvious. And, as we have stated, a departure from the rule-of-reason standard must be based upon demonstrable economic effect rather than upon formalistic line drawing.

The Court has interpreted *Dr. Miles Medical Co. v. John D. Park & Sons Co.*, 31 S. Ct. 376 (1911), as establishing a per se rule against a vertical agreement between a manufacturer and its distributor to set minimum resale prices. In *Dr. Miles* the plaintiff, a manufacturer of medicines, sold its products only to distributors who agreed to resell them at set prices. The Court found the manufacturer's control of resale prices to be unlawful. It relied on the common-law rule that a general restraint upon alienation is ordinarily invalid. The Court then explained that the agreements would advantage the distributors, not the manufacturer, and were analogous to a combination among competing distributors, which the law treated as void . . . .

Dr. Miles, furthermore, treated vertical agreements a manufacturer makes with its distributors as analogous to a horizontal combination among competing distributors. In later cases, however, the Court rejected the approach of reliance on rules governing horizontal restraints when defining rules applicable to vertical ones. Our recent cases formulate antitrust principles in accordance with the appreciated differences in economic effect between vertical and horizontal agreements, differences the *Dr. Miles* Court failed to consider.

The reasons upon which *Dr. Miles* relied do not justify a per se rule. As a consequence, it is necessary to examine, in the first instance, the economic effects of vertical agreements to fix minimum resale prices, and to determine whether the per se rule is nonetheless appropriate.

Though each side of the debate can find sources to support its position, it suffices to say here that economics literature is replete with procompetitive justifications for a manufacturer's use of resale price maintenance. Even those more skeptical of resale price maintenance acknowledge it can have procompetitive effects . . . .

The justifications for vertical price restraints are similar to those for other vertical restraints. Minimum resale price maintenance can stimulate interbrand competition—the competition among manufacturers selling different brands of the same type of product—by reducing intrabrand competition—the competition among retailers selling the same brand. The promotion of interbrand competition is important because the primary purpose of the antitrust laws is to protect this type of competition. A single manufacturer's use of vertical price restraints tends to eliminate intrabrand price competition; this in turn encourages retailers to invest in tangible or intangible services or promotional efforts that aid the manufacturer's position as against rival manufacturers. Resale price maintenance also has the potential to give consumers more options so that they can choose among low-price, low-service brands; high-price, high-service brands; and brands that fall in between.

Absent vertical price restraints, the retail services that enhance interbrand competition might be underprovided. This is because discounting retailers can free ride on retailers who furnish services and then capture some of the increased demand those services generate. Consumers might learn, for example, about the benefits of a manufacturer's product from a retailer that invests in fine showrooms, offers product demonstrations, or hires and trains knowledgeable employees. Or consumers might decide to buy the product because they see it in a retail establishment that has a reputation for selling high-quality merchandise. If the consumer can then buy the product from a retailer that discounts because it has not spent capital providing services or developing a quality reputation, the high-service retailer will lose sales to the discounter, forcing it to cut back its services to a level lower than consumers would otherwise prefer. Minimum resale price maintenance alleviates the problem because it prevents the discounter from undercutting the service provider. With price competition decreased, the manufacturer's retailers compete among themselves over services.

Resale price maintenance, in addition, can increase interbrand competition by facilitating market entry for new firms and brands. New manufacturers and manufacturers entering new markets can use the restrictions in order to induce competent and aggressive retailers to make the kind of investment of capital and labor that is often required in the distribution of products unknown to the consumer. New products and new brands are essential to a dynamic economy, and if markets can be penetrated by using resale price maintenance there is a procompetitive effect.

Resale price maintenance can also increase interbrand competition by encouraging retailer services that would not be provided even absent free riding. It may be difficult and inefficient for a manufacturer to make and enforce a contract with a retailer specifying the different services the retailer must perform. Offering the retailer a guaranteed margin and threatening termination if it does not live up to expectations may be the most efficient way to expand the manufacturer's market share by inducing the retailer's performance and allowing it to use its own initiative and experience in providing valuable services . . . .

Respondent contends, nonetheless, that vertical price restraints should be per se unlawful because of the administrative convenience of per se rules. That argument suggests per se illegality is the rule rather than the exception. This misinterprets our antitrust law. Per se rules may decrease administrative costs, but that is only part of the equation. Those rules can be counterproductive. They can increase the total cost of the antitrust system by prohibiting procompetitive conduct the antitrust laws should encourage. They also may increase litigation costs by promoting frivolous suits against legitimate practices. The Court has thus explained that administrative advantages are not sufficient in themselves to justify the creation of per se rules, and has relegated their use to restraints that are manifestly anticompetitive. Were the Court now to conclude that vertical price restraints should be per se illegal based on administrative costs, we would undermine, if not overrule, the traditional demanding standards for adopting per se rules. Any possible reduction in administrative costs cannot alone justify the *Dr. Miles* rule.

Respondent also argues the per se rule is justified because a vertical price restraint can lead to higher prices for the manufacturer's goods. Respondent is mistaken in relying on pricing effects absent a further showing of anticompetitive conduct. For, as has been indicated already, the antitrust laws are designed primarily to protect interbrand competition, from which lower prices can later result. The Court, moreover, has evaluated other vertical restraints under the rule of reason even though prices can be increased in the course of promoting procompetitive effects. And resale price maintenance may reduce prices if manufacturers have resorted to costlier alternatives of controlling resale prices that are not per se unlawful . . . .

Resale price maintenance, it is true, does have economic dangers. If the rule of reason were to apply to vertical price restraints, courts would have to be diligent in eliminating their anticompetitive uses from the market. This is a realistic objective, and certain factors are relevant to the inquiry. For example, the number of manufacturers that make use of the practice in a given industry can provide important instruction. When only a few manufacturers lacking market power adopt the practice, there is little likelihood it is facilitating a manufacturer cartel, for a cartel then can be undercut by rival manufacturers. Likewise, a retailer cartel is unlikely when only a single manufacturer in a competitive market uses resale price maintenance. Interbrand competition would divert consumers to lower priced substitutes and eliminate any gains to retailers from their price-fixing agreement over a single brand. Resale price maintenance should be subject to more careful scrutiny, by contrast, if many competing manufacturers adopt the practice . . . .

The rule of reason is designed and used to eliminate anticompetitive transactions from the market. This standard principle applies to vertical price restraints. A party alleging injury from a vertical agreement setting minimum resale prices will have, as a general matter, the information and resources available to show the existence of the agreement and its scope of operation. As courts gain experience considering the effects of these restraints by applying the rule of reason over the course of decisions, they can establish the litigation structure to ensure the rule operates to eliminate anticompetitive restraints from the market and to provide more guidance to businesses. Courts can, for example, devise rules over time for offering proof, or even presumptions where justified, to make the rule of reason a fair and efficient way to prohibit anticompetitive restraints and to promote procompetitive ones.

For all of the foregoing reasons, we think that were the Court considering the issue as an original matter, the rule of reason, not a per se rule of unlawfulness, would be the appropriate standard to judge vertical price restraints . . . .

The judgment of the Court of Appeals is reversed, and the case is remanded for proceedings consistent with this opinion.

Reversed and remanded.

:: CASE QUESTIONS

1. Why did Leegin establish and maintain a minimum resale pricing policy for its products?
2. How does the Supreme Court describe the procompetitive impact of a resale price maintenance plan?
3. The retailer makes two arguments to justify why a per se illegality analysis is best applied to this resale price maintenance plan. What are these arguments and what is the Supreme Court's response?

In addition to this case holding the maintenance of minimum resale prices are analyzed under the rule of reason, the Court reached a similar conclusion when a manufacturer attempts to fix a maximum price that its distributors can charge.[3] It now appears the Court is comfortable limiting the per se illegality analysis to horizontal agreements among competitors. Vertical agreements involving pricing (high and low) and territorial arrangements within channels of distribution are analyzed under the rule of reason.

9. INDIRECT PRICE FIXING

The ingenuity of businesspersons produces numerous attempts to fix prices by indirect means. Such attempts to control prices take a variety of forms and appear in diverse circumstances. Some arise out of a desire to protect a channel

---

[3]*State Oil Company v. Khan, 118 S.Ct. 275 (1997).*

of distribution or a marketing system. Others result from attempts to keep marginal competitors in business to avoid becoming a monopoly.

In one case, indirect price fixing took the form of an exchange of price information. Economic theory was used to support the assumption that prices would be more unstable and lower if the information had not been exchanged. This case established that conduct directed at price stabilization is per se anticompetitive. The warning to business and industry is clear: Cooperation and cozy relationships between competitors may be illegal.

concept :: *summary*

Price Fixing

1. Horizontal price fixing in the sales of goods or services is illegal per se.
2. It is just as illegal for competitors to fix a low price as it is a high price.
3. Professionals and service providers cannot legally conspire to fix prices.
4. Ethical standards cannot be used to fix prices.
5. Attempts by manufacturers to control the ultimate sale of their product (vertical price fixing) is analyzed under the rule of reason.
6. The mere exchange of price information among competitors may constitute a Sherman Act violation.

10. TERRITORIAL AGREEMENTS

Territorial agreements restrain trade by allocating geographical areas among competitors. They may be either horizontal or vertical. Competing businesses may enter into a **horizontal territorial agreement** for the purpose of giving each an exclusive territory. For example, if all Chevrolet dealers in a state agree to allocate to each an exclusive territory, a horizontal arrangement would exist. This agreement is illegal per se under the Sherman Act. This is true even if the arrangement is made with a third party. For example, an agreement among competing cable television operators to divide the market in Houston, Texas, was found to be a per se violation even though the agreement required city council approval.

A **vertical territorial agreement** is one between a manufacturer and a dealer or distributor. It assigns the dealer or distributor an exclusive territory, and the manufacturer agrees not to sell to other dealers or distributors in that territory in exchange for an agreement by the dealer that it will not operate outside the area assigned. Such agreements are usually part of a franchise or license agreement. These vertical arrangements are not per se violations; they are subject to the rule of reason.

11. CONCERTED ACTIVITIES

Many antitrust cases involve agreements or conduct by competitors that have anticompetitive effects. Competitors sometimes attempt to share some activities or join together in the performance of a function. These are known as **concerted activities**.

Concerted activities are often beneficial to society even though they reduce competition. For example, joint research efforts to find a cure for cancer or to find substitutes for gasoline would seem to provide significant benefits to society. A sharing of technology may be beneficial also. Joint efforts in other areas may reduce costs and improve efficiency, with direct benefit to the public.

Congress has recognized the need to encourage cooperation among competitors. For example, in 1984, the National Cooperative Research Act was enacted. In 1990, Congress created an exception to the Sherman Act so that television industry officials could discuss the development of joint guidelines to limit the depiction of violence on television.

Again, in 1993, Congress made it easier for U.S. companies to engage in joint production ventures. The National Cooperative Production Amendments Act does not protect joint production ventures from all possibilities of antitrust violations. Rather, this law provides protection to activities described in Sidebar 16.5. Despite these exceptions to the Sherman Act that permit specific joint activities, you should always remain aware that concerted activities among competitors can lead to the severe sanctions discussed in Section 5 of this chapter.

:: *sidebar* 16.5

Basic Provisions of National Cooperative Production Amendment Act

- Joint production ventures will be subject to the rule of reason analysis rather than the per se illegality standard.
- A joint production venture must notify the Justice Department and the FTC of its plans to engage in joint activities.

- In a private civil antitrust action brought against the joint production venture, the plaintiff can be awarded only actual damages plus costs. The joint production venture will not be subject to triple damages.

12. INTERNATIONAL CASES

In recent years, the U.S. Justice Department has concentrated much of its antitrust enforcement effort on international cartels. The globalization of business activities means application of antitrust laws to international agreements. Since 1997, over 90 percent of the criminal fines imposed by the U.S. Antitrust Division relate to activities of international cartels. In most cases in which the Antitrust Division obtained a fine of $10 million or more, the corporate defendants have been foreign based. Table 16.3 documents some of these largest cases.

Microsoft also provides an excellent example of the impact of antitrust laws in the international setting. Sidebar 16.6 describes how the European Union's Antitrust Commissioner and similar officials in other countries can have a major impact.

Other areas of interest internationally include how China's new antitrust law will be enforced and whether this will have a major impact on multinational companies. Because they operate in global markets, Microsoft, Intel,

> "The EU Antitrust Commissioner levied fines for price fixing of 2 billion Euros ($2.71 billion) in 2007 compared to 390 million Euros in 2004."
>
> **–Mary Jacoby, The Wall Street Journal, May 4, 2004.**

table 16.3 :: International Antitrust Cartels

:: Amount of Fine (in millions)	:: Company	:: Country	:: Product	:: Violation
$500	F. Hoffman-LaRoche Ltd.	Switzerland	Vitamins	Price fixing and market allocation.
$300	Samsung Electronics	Japan	DRAM chips	Price fixing.
$225	BASF Aktiengesellschaft	Germany	Vitamins	Price fixing and market allocation.
$185	Hynix Semiconductor	South Korea	DRAM chips	Price fixing.
$160	Infineon Technology	Germany	DRAM chips	Price fixing.
$135	SGL Carbon Aktiengesellschaft	Germany	Graphite Electrodes	Price fixing and market allocation.
$110	UCAR International	United States	Graphite Electrodes	Price fixing and market allocation.
$100	Archer Daniels Midland	United States	Lysine and citric acid	Price fixing and market allocation.

:: *sidebar* 16.6

Microsoft and the European Union

Recall the earlier discussion of the United States taking action against Microsoft for bundling its Explorer browser within Windows. In Europe, the focus has been on the bundling of Microsoft's media player with Windows. In 2004, the EU's Antitrust Commissioner ordered Microsoft to pay a $600 million fine and to unbundle its media player from Windows. Microsoft also was to provide technical documentation. The EU Antitrust Office was not satisfied with Microsoft's response and began accessing fines on a daily basis. The dispute continued until October 2007 when Microsoft agreed to license the technical information to rivals. At that time, the maximum fine was 1.5 billion euros. Microsoft has now reached an agreement to pay the EU 899 million euros, which is a record-setting fine of $1.35 billion.

Having resolved this matter with the EU Antitrust Commissioner does not end Microsoft's problems. Two additional investigations are underway in the EU focusing on whether Microsoft's Internet browser, Explorer, is illegally bundled with Windows and whether Microsoft's Office software is compatible with competitors' operating systems.

Microsoft's experience in both the U.S. and EU illustrate that antitrust laws are rigorously enforcement and have significant impact on how business is conducted.

*Source: Ronald Cass, *The Wall Street Journal*, December 16, 2005, and Charles Forelle, *The Wall Street Journal*, February 28, 2008.

Cisco, Coca-Cola, Pepsi, and others will be watching how the Chinese enforce its antitrust law.

:: The Clayton Act

13. INTRODUCTION

By 1914, it was obvious that the Sherman Act of 1890 had not accomplished its intended purpose. Practices that reduced competition were commonplace.

In order to improve the antitrust laws, Congress in 1914 enacted the Clayton Act and the Federal Trade Commission Act. The Clayton Act is more specific than the Sherman Act in declaring certain enumerated practices in commerce illegal. These were practices that might adversely affect competition but were not themselves contracts, combinations, or conspiracies in restraint of trade; such practices did not go far enough to constitute actual monopolization or attempts to monopolize. Further, the enumerated practices did not have to actually injure competition to be wrongful; they were outlawed if their effect **may substantially lessen competition or tends to create a monopoly.** Thus, the burden of proving a violation was eased. The Clayton Act made it possible to attack in their incipiency many practices which, if continued, eventually could destroy competition or create a monopoly. The idea was to remedy these matters before full harm was done.

Note the lesser burden of the Clayton Act test.

Violations of the original Clayton Act were not crimes, and the act contained no sanction for forfeiture of property. However, it did provide that the Justice Department might obtain injunctions to prevent violations. Individuals or organizations injured by a violation could obtain injunctive relief on their own behalf. In addition, they were given the right to collect three times the damages suffered plus court costs and reasonable attorney's fees.

The following three sections of this chapter focus on three important provisions of the Clayton Act. As you study this material, ask yourself what business practices occur today that may violate the Clayton Act.

14. PRICE DISCRIMINATION

Section 2 of the Clayton Act as originally adopted in 1914 made it unlawful for a seller to discriminate in the price that is charged to different purchasers of commodities when the effect may be to lessen competition substantially or to tend to create a monopoly in any line of commerce. Discrimination in price on account of differences in the grade, quality, or quantity of the commodity sold, or that makes only due allowance for differences in the cost of selling or transportation was not illegal.

In the 1920s and early 1930s, various techniques such as large-volume purchases with quantity discounts were used by big retailers, especially chain stores, to obtain more favorable prices than those available to smaller competitors. In addition to obtaining quantity discounts, some large businesses created subsidiary corporations that received brokerage allowances as wholesalers. Another method used by big buyers to obtain price advantages was to demand and obtain larger promotional allowances than were given to smaller buyers. The prevalence of these practices led to the enactment in 1936 of the **Robinson-Patman amendment** to Section 2 of the Clayton Act. This statute attempted to eliminate the advantage that a large buyer could secure over a small buyer solely because of the larger buyer's quantity-purchasing ability.

The Robinson-Patman amendment attempts to ensure equality of price to all customers of a seller of commodities for resale. The law protects a single competitor who is victimized by price discrimination. It is a violation both to knowingly give and to receive the benefits of such discrimination. Therefore, the law applies to both sellers and buyers. It is just as illegal to

Price discrimination originally focused on the seller offering various prices to its customers. The Robinson-Patman amendment addresses the power of large buyers to demand favorable prices.

receive the benefit of price discrimination as it is to give a lower price to one of two buyers.

The Robinson-Patman amendment extends only to transactions in interstate commerce; it does not extend to transactions that affect only intrastate commerce. In addition, the law is applicable only to the sale of goods; it does not cover contracts that involve the sale of services or the sale of advertising such as television time.

The Robinson-Patman amendment gives the Federal Trade Commission (FTC) jurisdiction and authority to regulate quantity discounts. It also prohibits certain hidden or indirect discriminations by sellers in favor of certain buyers. Section 2(c) prohibits an unearned brokerage commission related to a sale of goods. For example, it is unlawful to pay or to receive a commission or discount on sales or purchases except for actual services rendered. Section 2(d) outlaws granting promotional allowances or payments on goods bought for resale unless such allowances are available to all competing customers. For example, a manufacturer who gives a retailer a right to purchase three items for the price of two as part of a special promotion must give the same right to all competitors in the market. Section 2(e) prohibits giving promotional facilities or services on goods bought for resale unless they are made available to all competing customers.

The Robinson-Patman amendment makes it a crime for a seller to sell either at lower prices in one geographic area than elsewhere in the United States to eliminate competition or a competitor, or at unreasonably low prices to drive out a competitor. This statute declared **predatory pricing** to be illegal.

Predatory pricing is pricing below marginal cost by a company willing and able to sustain losses for a prolonged period to drive out competition. (It is assumed that the price will later be increased when the competition or competitor is destroyed.) Predatory pricing also involves charging higher prices on some products to subsidize below-cost sales of other products or cutting prices below cost on a product in just one area to wipe out a small local competitor.

The Robinson-Patman amendment recognizes certain exceptions or defenses:

- Sellers may select their own customers in good-faith transactions and not in restraint of trade.
- Price changes may be made in response to changing conditions, such as actual or imminent deterioration of perishable goods, obsolescence of seasonal goods, distress sales under court process, or sales in good faith in discontinuance of business in the goods concerned (changing conditions defense).
- Price differentials based on differences in the cost of manufacture, sale, or delivery of commodities are permitted (**cost justification defense**).
- A seller in good faith may meet the equally low price of a competitor (**good-faith meeting-of-competition defense**).

Case 16.2 illustrates the complexity and the limited scope of the price discrimination.

VOLVO TRUCKS NORTH AMERICA, INC. v. REEDER-SIMCO GMC, INC.
126 S. Ct. 860 (2006)

Volvo Trucks North America, Inc., sells its heavy-duty trucks through franchised dealers who compete in a competitive bidding process typically with dealers of other manufacturers but occasionally with another Volvo dealer. This bidding process usually begins with a buyer inviting bids on a contract of stated specifications. For example, Big City Paving Company would indicate it is in the market to buy three dump trucks. A Volvo dealer would contact Volvo Trucks for pricing information so it could develop a bid to submit to Big City. At the same time, Big City would be soliciting bids from dealers representing other manufacturers, but it probably would not be dealing with a second Volvo dealer. If the Volvo dealer's bid is accepted by Big City, the dealer submits its order to Volvo Trucks, which then manufactures the trucks. Sometimes, prior to the buyer accepting a bid, Volvo Trucks works with its dealer to provide additional discounts on the trucks in the hope that these discounts could win it the business.

Reeder, a Volvo dealer in Arkansas, sued Volvo Trucks for price discrimination alleging that Volvo Trucks sometimes gave other dealers greater discounts than those given to Reeder. These discounts were not given on competing bids to the same buyer but on bids to various buyers. At trial, Reeder won a $1.3 million judgment on the theory that Volvo Trucks was guilty of violating Section 2 of the Clayton Act as amended by the Robinson-Patman Amendment. The Eighth Circuit Court of Appeals affirmed this judgment and the tripling of the damages. The Supreme Court granted certiorari to determine if price discrimination occurs in a competitive bidding process involving specially ordered trucks sold to a specific customer.

GINSBURG, J.: Section 2, when originally enacted as part of the Clayton Act in 1914, was born of a desire by Congress to curb the use by financially powerful corporations of localized price-cutting tactics which had gravely impaired the competitive position of other sellers. Augmenting that provision in 1936 with the Robinson-Patman Act, Congress sought to target the perceived harm to competition occasioned by powerful buyers, rather than sellers; specifically, Congress responded to the advent of large chain stores, enterprises with the clout to obtain lower prices for goods than smaller buyers could demand. The Act provides, in relevant part:

It shall be unlawful for any person engaged in commerce . . to discriminate in price between different purchasers of commodities of like grade and quality, . . where the effect of such discrimination may be substantially to lessen competition or tend to create a monopoly in any line of commerce, or to injure, destroy, or prevent competition with any person who either grants or knowingly receives the benefit of such discrimination, or with customers of either of them . . . .

Pursuant to § 4 of the Clayton Act, a private plaintiff may recover threefold for actual injury sustained as a result of a violation of the Robinson-Patman Act.

Mindful of the purposes of the Act and of the antitrust laws generally, we have explained that Robinson-Patman does not ban all price differences charged to different purchasers of commodities of like grade and quality; rather, the Act proscribes price discrimination only to the extent that it threatens to injure competition. Our decisions describe three categories of competitive injury that may give rise to a Robinson-Patman Act claim: primary-line, secondary-line, and tertiary-line. Primary-line cases entail conduct most conspicuously, predatory pricing—that injures competition at the level of the discriminating seller and its direct competitors. Secondary-line cases, of which this is one, involve price discrimination that injures competition among the discriminating seller's customers (here, Volvo's dealerships); cases in this category typically refer to "favored" and "disfavored" purchasers. Tertiary-line cases involve injury to competition at the level of the purchaser's customers.

To establish the secondary-line injury of which it complains, Reeder had to show that (1) the relevant Volvo truck sales were made in interstate commerce; (2) the trucks were of "like grade and quality"; (3) Volvo "discriminated in price between" Reeder and another purchaser of Volvo trucks; and (4) "the effect of such discrimination may be . . to injure, destroy, or prevent competition" to the advantage of a favored purchaser, i.e., one who "received the benefit of such discrimination." It is undisputed that Reeder has satisfied the first and second requirements. Volvo and the United States, as amicus curiae, maintain that Reeder cannot satisfy the third and fourth requirements, because Reeder has not identified any differentially-priced transaction in which it was both a "purchaser" under the Act and "in actual competition" with a favored purchaser for the same customer.

A hallmark of the requisite competitive injury, our decisions indicate, is the diversion of sales or profits from a disfavored purchaser to a favored purchaser. We have also recognized that a permissible inference of competitive injury may arise from evidence that a favored competitor received a significant price reduction over a substantial period of time. Absent actual competition with a favored Volvo dealer, however, Reeder cannot establish the competitive injury required under the Act.

The evidence Reeder offered at trial falls into three categories: (1) comparisons of concessions Reeder received for four successful bids against non-Volvo dealers, with larger concessions other successful Volvo dealers received for different sales on which Reeder did not bid (purchase-to-purchase comparisons); (2) comparisons of concessions offered to Reeder in connection with several unsuccessful bids against non-Volvo dealers, with greater concessions accorded other Volvo dealers who competed successfully for different sales on which Reeder did not bid (offer-to-purchase comparisons); and (3) evidence of two occasions on which Reeder bid against another Volvo dealer (head-to-head comparisons). The Court of Appeals concluded that Reeder demonstrated competitive injury under the Act because Reeder competed with favored purchasers at the same functional level and within the same geographic market. As we see it, however, selective comparisons of the kind Reeder presented do not show the injury to competition targeted by the Robinson-Patman Act.

Both the purchase-to-purchase and the offer-to-purchase comparisons fall short, for in none of the discrete instances on which Reeder relied did Reeder compete with beneficiaries of the alleged discrimination for the same customer. Nor did Reeder even attempt to show that the compared dealers were consistently favored vis-à-vis Reeder. Reeder simply paired occasions on which it competed with non-Volvo dealers for a sale to Customer A with instances in which other Volvo dealers competed with non-Volvo dealers for a sale to Customer B. The compared incidents were tied to no systematic study and were separated in time by as many as seven months.

We decline to permit an inference of competitive injury from evidence of such a mix-and-match, manipulable quality. No similar risk of manipulation occurs in cases akin to the chain-store paradigm. Here, there is no discrete "favored" dealer comparable to a chain store or a large independent department store—at least, Reeder's evidence is insufficient to support an inference of such a dealer or set of dealers. For all we know, Reeder, on occasion, might have gotten a better deal vis-à-vis one or more of the dealers in its comparisons . . . .

Reeder did offer evidence of two instances in which it competed head to head with another Volvo dealer. When multiple dealers bid for the business of the same customer, only one dealer will win the business and thereafter purchase the supplier's product to fulfill its contractual commitment. Because Robinson-Patman prohibits only discrimination between different purchasers, Volvo and the United States argue, the Act does not reach markets characterized by competitive bidding and special-order sales, as opposed to sales from inventory. We need not decide that question today. Assuming the Act applies to the head-to-head transactions, Reeder did not establish that it was disfavored vis-à-vis other Volvo dealers in the rare instances in which they competed for the same sale — let alone that the alleged discrimination was substantial.

Reeder's evidence showed loss of only one sale to another Volvo dealer, a sale of 12 trucks that would have generated $30,000 in gross profits for Reeder. Per its policy, Volvo initially offered Reeder and the other dealer the same concession. Volvo ultimately granted a larger concession to the other dealer, but only after it had won the bid. In the only other instance of head-to-head competition Reeder identified, Volvo increased Reeder's initial 17 percent discount to 18.9 percent, to match the discount offered to the other competing Volvo dealer; neither dealer won the bid. In short, if price discrimination between two purchasers existed at all, it was not of such magnitude as to affect substantially competition between Reeder and the "favored" Volvo dealer . . . .

For the reasons stated, the judgment of the Court of Appeals for the Eighth Circuit is reversed, and the case is remanded for further proceedings consistent with this opinion.

Reversed and remanded.

:: CASE QUESTIONS

1. What is the holding of the trial court? The Eighth Circuit Court of Appeals?
2. What does the Supreme Court mean by the levels of price discrimination?
3. What required elements of price discrimination are missing from the sales model used in the heavy-duty truck market?

concept :: *summary*

Robinson-Patman Amendment

1. It is a violation to sell the same goods to competing buyers for resale at different prices.
2. The law also is violated by a buyer that knowingly receives a lower price.
3. The law does not apply to transactions wholly in intrastate commerce or to transactions that do not involve goods.
4. Price discrimination may result from quantity discounts, unearned brokerage allowances, or promotional allowances.

5. Functional discounts must be based on legitimate marketing functions actually performed.
6. It is a crime for a seller to sell at low prices in an attempt to drive out a competitor.
7. Plaintiffs must prove actual injury to collect triple damages for Robinson-Patman violations.
8. The good-faith meeting-of-competition defense is available to both the seller and the buyer.

15. SPECIAL ARRANGEMENTS

Section 3 of the Clayton Act limits the use of certain types of contractual arrangements involving goods when the impact of these contracts may substantially lessen competition or tends to create a monopoly. These special arrangements include sales contracts that tie one product with another, contracts that contain reciprocal arrangements in which each party is a buyer and a seller, and provisions foreclosing buying or selling with others.

A **tying contract** is one in which a product is sold or leased only on the condition that the buyer or lessee purchase a different product or service from the seller or lessor. A common form of tying arrangement is known as **full-line forcing**. In full-line forcing, the seller compels the buyer or lessee to take a complete product line from the seller. Under these arrangements, the buyer cannot purchase only one product of the line. A typical illegal agreement is one in which a clothing manufacturer requires a retailer to carry the manufacturer's full line of articles in order to sell a popular line of shirts. Another common factual situation relates to how a holder of a potential product using the patent protection to market that product and related, but unpatented, products. Sidebar 16.7 summarizes a recent Supreme Court decision discussing tying arrangements involving a patented and unpatented, but related, product.

A **reciprocal dealing** arrangement exists when two parties face each other as both buyer and seller. One party offers to buy the other's goods but only if the second party buys other goods from the first party. For example, suppose that company A is a manufacturer of microprocessor chips for personal computers. Further assume that company B manufactures personal computers. A reciprocal dealing occurs if B agrees to buy processor chips only if A agrees to buy a specified number of B's computers for use in A's offices.

An **exclusive dealing** contract contains a provision that one party or the other (buyer or seller) will deal only with the other party. For example a seller of tomatoes agrees to sell only to Campbell Soup. A buyer of coal may agree to purchase only from a certain coal company. Such agreements tend to foreclose a portion of the market from competitors.

A similar arrangement is known as a **requirements contract.** In a requirements contract, a buyer agrees to purchase all of its needs of a given

:: *sidebar* 16.7

Tying Contracts, Patents, and Standard of Review

Trident, Inc., is owned by Illinois Tool Works, Inc. Trident manufactures and markets printing systems that consist of patented equipment and unpatented ink. In marketing its printing systems, Trident insists its buyers agree to purchase only Trident ink for use in its equipment.

Independent Ink, Inc., produces an ink that is chemically similar to Trident's ink. Independent files an antitrust lawsuit against Trident claiming its tying contracts are per se illegal under Sections 1 and 2 of the Sherman Act and Section 3 of the Clayton Act.

The Supreme Court reviews the history of the patent misuse doctrine and its holdings that tying a patented product to an unpatented one creates a per se antitrust violation. The Court explains that Congress's changes to the patent law removes the patent misuse doctrine and that commentators have been critical of the Court's prior

decisions allowing antitrust claims to limit the benefits of patents. The Court concludes:

> Congress, the antitrust enforcement agencies, and most economists have all reached the conclusion that a patent does not necessarily confer market power upon the patentee. Today, we reach the same conclusion, and therefore hold that, in all cases involving a tying arrangement, the plaintiff must prove that the defendant has market power in the tying product.

In essence, the Court now requires the plaintiff in antitrust claims to prove the defendant acted unreasonably in tying the patented and unpatented product. The anticompetitive nature of the tying arrangement will no longer be presumed.

*Source: *Illinois Tool Works, Inc. v. Independent Ink, Inc.,* 126 S. Ct. 1281 (2006).

Do be wary of the restrictive nature of franchise contracts.

contract from the seller during a certain period of time. The buyer may be a manufacturer who needs the raw materials or parts agreed to be supplied, or it may be a retailer who needs goods for resale. In effect, the buyer is agreeing not to purchase any of the products from competitors of the seller.

Franchise contracts often require that the franchisee purchase all of its equipment and inventory from the franchiser as a condition of the agreement. These provisions are commonly inserted because of the value of the franchiser's trademark and the desire for quality control to protect it. For example, Baskin-Robbins ice cream may require its franchisees to purchase all of their ice cream from Baskin-Robbins. The legitimate purpose is to maintain the image of the franchise and the product. Customers expect the same ice cream from every retail operation. Such agreements, while anticompetitive, are legal because the legitimate purpose outweighs the anticompetitive aspects.

However, a franchiser is not able to license its trademark in such a manner that it can coerce franchisees to give up all alternate supply sources, because such agreements are unreasonable restraints of trade. The quality-control aspect is not present for items such as packaging materials and food items in which special ingredients or secret formulas are not involved; thus, the purpose of the "exclusive source of supply" proviso is only to limit competition. Franchise agreements are not per se violations; they are subject to the rule of reason.

Exclusive contracts and requirements contracts are less likely to harm competition than are tying contracts. Such contracts may add competition by eliminating uncertainties and the expense of repeated contracts. However, the courts tend to give per se violation treatment to exclusive contracts if they substantially affect commerce.

16. MERGERS AND ACQUISITIONS

Section 7 of the Clayton Act makes certain mergers and acquisitions illegal. **Mergers** are usually classified as horizontal, market extension, vertical, or conglomerate. A **horizontal merger** usually combines two businesses in the same field or industry. The acquired and acquiring companies have competed with each other, and the merger reduces the number of competitors and leads to greater concentration in the industry. A **market extension merger** describes an acquisition in which the acquiring company extends its markets. This market extension may be either in new products (**product extension**) or in new areas (**geographic extension**). For example, if a brewery that did not operate in New England acquired a New England brewery, it would have accomplished a geographic market extension merger.

A **vertical merger** brings together one company that is the customer of the other in one of the lines of commerce in which the other is a supplier. Such a combination ordinarily removes or has the potential to remove the merged customer from the market as far as other suppliers are concerned. It also may remove a source of supply if the acquiring company is a customer of the acquired one. A **conglomerate merger** is one in which the businesses involved neither compete nor are related as customer and supplier in any given line of commerce. Some analysts consider product extension and geographic extension mergers to be conglomerate ones with many characteristics of horizontal ones. In any event, there is a great deal of similarity in the legal principles applied to market extension and to conglomerate mergers.

As originally enacted in 1914, the Clayton Act prohibited only horizontal mergers through the acquisition of stock of one competing company by another. A merger between competitors could be accomplished and was permitted through one acquiring the assets of the other. In 1950, Congress passed the **Celler-Kefauver amendment,** which substantially broadened the coverage of Section 7. First, this amendment plugged the stock-versus-assets loophole. After 1950, the acquisition of assets was also covered by Section 7. Second, the Celler-Kefauver amendment prohibited all acquisitions in which the effect lessened competition substantially in any line of commerce in any section of the country. Thus, the amendment added vertical and conglomerate mergers to the coverage of Section 7. In 1980, Congress expanded coverage by including not only businesses engaged in interstate commerce but also businesses engaged in activities that affect commerce. It also substituted the word "person" for "corporation" so as to include partnerships and sole proprietorships.

Table 16.4 presents some details of the 10 largest mergers by the dollar amount paid for the targeted company.

Several thoughts may arise as you study this table. First, the dollar amounts involved are huge. Please note that total amounts are in billions of dollars. Second, almost all of the company names sound familiar. These mergers involve the combinations of very large companies. Why were these combinations allowed? It appears, at least from these mergers, the philosophy of "bigger is better" is acceptable. In truth this philosophy is replacing the desire for many smaller competitors. The fact that each of these combined

table 16.4 :: Ten Largest Mergers (by dollar amount)				
:: Dollar Amount (in millions)	:: Industry	:: Acquiring Company	:: Target Company	:: Year
$95,500	Financial services	Royal Bank of Scotland	ABN Amro Holding NV	2007
$89,167	Pharmaceuticals	Pfizer Inc.	Warner-Lambert	2000
$78,946	Energy	Exxon Corp.	Mobil Corp.	1999
$75,960	Pharmaceuticals	Glaxo Wellcome PLC	SmithKline Beecham PLC	2000
$74,349	Energy	Royal Dutch Petroleum Co.	Shell Transport & Trading Co.	2004
$72,558	Financial services	Travelers Group Inc.	Citigroup	1998
$72,041	Communications	Comcast Corp.	AT&T Broadband & Internet Services	2002
$62,593	Communications	SBC Communications Inc.	Ameritech Corp	1999
$61,633	Financial services	NationsBank Corp	BankAmerica Corp	1999
$60,287	Communications	Vodafone Group PLC	AirTouch Communications	1999

companies operates in a global marketplace and must compete internationally probably has much to do with the government's approval of these mergers.

A third point of emphasis relates to the industries listed above. The ten largest mergers involve only four industries. Again the globalization of these industries likely justifies the combination of large companies to permit the formation of a strong competitor in the international market. Another industry to watch for merger activity involves airlines.

:: The Federal Trade Commission Act—Unfair Competition

As previously noted, the Federal Trade Commission (FTC) enforces the Clayton Act. The FTC also enforces Section 5 of the Federal Trade Commission Act, which made "unfair methods of competition" in commerce unlawful. The **Wheeler-Lea amendment** in 1938 added that "unfair or deceptive acts or practices in commerce" are also unlawful under Section 5.

17. ENFORCEMENT

The FTC has broad, sweeping powers and a mandate to determine what methods, acts, or practices in commerce constitute unfair competition. The original Section 5 of the Federal Trade Commission Act outlawed unfair methods of competition in commerce and directed the FTC to prevent the use of such, but it offered no definition of the specific practices that were unfair. The term *unfair methods of competition* was designed by Congress as a flexible concept, the exact meaning of which could evolve on a case-by-case basis. It can apply to a variety of unrelated activities. It is generally up to the FTC to determine what business conduct is "unfair." Great deference is given to the FTC's opinion as to what constitutes a violation and to the remedies it proposes to correct anticompetitive behavior.

To decide whether challenged business conduct is "unfair" as a method of competition or as a commercial practice, the FTC asks three major questions if there is no deception or antitrust violation involved:

1. Does the conduct injure consumers significantly?
2. Does the conduct offend an established public policy? (Conduct may offend public policy even though not previously unlawful.)
3. Is the conduct oppressive, unscrupulous, immoral, or unethical?

Answering any one of these questions affirmatively could lead to a finding of unfairness. The Supreme Court has declared that the FTC can operate "like a court of equity" in considering "public values" to establish what is unfair under Section 5.

Business conduct in violation of any provision of the antitrust laws may also be ruled illegal under Section 5. However, the purpose of Section 5 was to establish that anticompetitive acts or practices that *fall short* of transgressing the Sherman or Clayton Act may be restrained by the FTC as being "unfair methods of competition." If a business practice is such that it is doubtful that the evidence is sufficient to prove a Sherman or Clayton Act violation, the FTC may nevertheless proceed and find the business practice is unfair.

> Section 5 of the FTC Act gives the FTC power beyond the sections of other antitrust laws.

18. PREVENTION

The primary function of the FTC is to prevent illegal business practices rather than punish violations. It prevents wrongful actions by the use of cease and desist orders. To prevent unfair competition, the FTC issues trade regulation rules that deal with business practices in an industry plus FTC guidelines on particular practices.

The FTC also periodically issues trade practice rules and guides, sometimes referred to as industry guides. These rules are the FTC's informal opinion of legal requirements applicable to a particular industry's practices. Although compliance with the rules is voluntary, they provide the basis for the informal and simultaneous abandonment by industry members of practices thought to be unlawful. For example, the FTC has said the American Medical Association must allow doctors to advertise. FTC guidelines are administrative interpretations of the statutes the commission enforces, and they provide guidance to both FTC staff and businesspeople evaluating the legality of certain practices. Guidelines deal with specific practices and may cut across industry lines.

:: Key Terms

:: Review Questions and Problems

1. *Historical Development*

   (a) The Sherman Act, as amended by the Clayton Act, seeks to preserve competition by declaring two types of anticompetitive behavior to be illegal. Describe these two behaviors.

   (b) Through what agencies does the federal government enforce the antitrust laws?

   (c) What role do state attorneys generally play in antitrust enforcement?

   (d) Can individuals or business organizations enforce antitrust laws?

The Sherman Act

2. *Restraint of Trade*

   All of the orthodontists in your community at their annual holiday party agreed to charge the parents of each child patient a nonrefundable fee of $200 prior to beginning any treatment. They also agreed that the charge for an orthodontia procedure would not be less than $2,000. Are these agreements in violation of the Sherman Act? Explain.

3. *Monopoly*

   The Justice Department filed a civil suit claiming Grinnell Corporation had a monopoly in the operation of central station hazard-detecting devices. These security devices are used to prevent burglary and to detect fires.

   They involve electronic notification of the police and fire departments at a central location. Grinnell, through three separate subsidiaries, controlled 87 percent of that business. It argues that it faces competition from other modes of protection from burglary, and therefore it does not have monopoly power. What argument does the Justice Department have to make to prove its claim that Grinnell is operating an illegal monopoly?

4. *Analysis in Antitrust Law*

   (a) Why is it important for courts to use the rule of reason analysis when considering actions allegedly in violation of the Sherman Act?

   (b) What is the significance of the per se analysis under the rule of reason?

5. *Sanctions*
    (a) Name the four sanctions used to enforce the Sherman Act.
    (b) What is the relationship between the criminal sanction and suits for triple damages?
    (c) What is the impact of the *nolo contendere* plea?

6. *Exemptions*

    The operators of adult bookstores got together and each agreed to contribute $1,000 to a fund for use in lobbying the city council to repeal an ordinance which made the sale of sexually explicit publications a crime. If the operators are charged with violating the antitrust laws, what will be the likely defense? Explain.

Types of Cases

7. *Horizontal Price Fixing*

    The members of a real estate brokers' multiple listing service voted to raise their commission rate from 6 to 7 percent. The bylaws of the association provided for expulsion of any member charging less than the agreed-upon commission. If broker Hillary continues to charge 6 percent, can she be expelled legally? Why or why not?

8. *Vertical Price Fixing*
    (a) Describe the situations when a supplier can legally fix the minimum price that a customer must charge to its buyers.
    (b) What analysis do courts use when judging the legality of a vertical price-fixing plan? Why is this legal analysis the appropriate one to use?

9. *Indirect Price Fixing*

    Assume that all manufacturers of computer chips entered into an agreement whereby each agreed to exchange information as to the most recent price charged or quoted to a consumer. Is this agreement a violation of the Sherman Act? Why or why not?

10. *Territorial Agreements*
    (a) Are franchise agreements which allocate an exclusive territory to the franchisee always illegal? Explain.
    (b) Give an example of a product where intrabrand competition is as important as interbrand competition.

11. *Concerted Activities*

    In response to public pressure, all of the manufacturers of chewing tobacco agree not to advertise on radio or television. The resulting savings are used to reduce the price of the product to consumers. Furthermore, the use of chewing tobacco by teenagers is reduced dramatically. Is the agreement legal? Explain.

12. *International Cases*

    Why has the number of cases against international cartels increased during the past 10 years?

The Clayton Act

13. *Introduction*
    (a) Name the sanctions that can be imposed against a violator of the Clayton Act.
    (b) What is the significance of the word *incipiency* in Clayton Act enforcement?

14. *Price Discrimination*

    You are the sales representative for a manufacturer of insulation. A customer that accounts for approximately one-third of your sales suddenly asks for a discount because of the volume of its purchases. You are politely told that a refusal will cause the customer to take its business to another manufacturer. Your income is solely from commissions on sales, which are calculated on gross profit margins.

(a) If you agree to a discount, have you broken any law?

(b) If you have violated a law, what are the potential consequences?

(c) If you give the same discount to all customers, would your actions be illegal? Explain.

15. *Special Arrangements*

(a) An ice-cream franchiser requires its franchisees to purchase all ice cream, cones, and syrups from the franchiser. Does this contract violate the antitrust laws? Why or why not?

(b) Would your answer be the same if the contract also required the franchisees to purchase all of its paper products and cleaning supplies, such as napkins, from the franchiser? Explain.

16. *Mergers and Acquisitions*

The government challenged the acquisition by Procter & Gamble (P&G) of Clorox. Clorox was the leading manufacturer of liquid bleach at the time of the acquisition, accounting for 48 percent of the national sales. It was the only firm selling nationally, and the top two firms accounted for 65 percent of national sales. P&G is a large, diversified manufacturer of household products, with its primary activity being in the area of soaps, detergents, and cleaners. P&G accounted for 54 percent of all packaged detergent sales, and the top three firms accounted for 50 percent of the market. P&G is among the nation's leading advertisers. What is the basis for the government's challenge to this acquisition? Explain.

The Federal Trade Commission—Unfair Competition

17. *Enforcement*

A group of lawyers in private practices who regularly acted as court-appointed counsel for indigent defendants in District of Columbia criminal cases agreed at a meeting of the Superior Court Trial Lawyers Association (SCTLA) to stop providing such representation until the District increased group members' compensation. The boycott had a severe impact on the District's criminal justice system, and the District government capitulated to the lawyers' demands. After the lawyers returned to work, the FTC filed a complaint against SCTLA and four of its officers, alleging that they had entered into a conspiracy to fix prices and to conduct a boycott that constituted unfair methods of competition in violation of Section 5 of the FTC Act. Does the FTC have the authority to bring a Section 5 case against these lawyers? Explain.

18. *Prevention*

(a) The FTC has responsibility for preventing unfair methods of competition and unfair and deceptive business practices. Describe three examples of business activities that could be declared unlawful by the FTC pursuant to these powers.

(b) Does the FTC have to prove that these examples involve violations of the Sherman or Clayton Acts to be successful in establishing an unfair method of competition or an unfair or deceptive business practice? Explain.

business :: *discussions*

You are feeling very good about your life. This positive feeling is due in large part to your recent promotion to national sales manager of Ever-Present Technologies, Inc. Your company offers full-service consulting and computer sales to manufacturers, especially those in the consumer products areas.

Two weeks into your new responsibilities, you are beginning to lose your good feelings. This change of spirit results from hearing about various activities among your sales personnel. First, you learn one of your new sales representatives has been visiting with a competitor's salesperson about each focusing on particular customers while agreeing not to call on the other's customers. Second, a district manager reports that a large, extremely valuable customer is asking for a pricing structure that is more favorable than prices offered to any other customer. The district manager expressed concern that your company may lose this customer's business.

What legal worries do you have about each of these situations?

What type of information should a training/education program for your sales force include?

What are the ramifications if you decide to ignore these situations as you try to return to your "happy" state of mind?

Consumer Protection

17

Legislatures have passed more consumer protection laws since World War II than in the 175 years of our nation's history preceding the war. To understand what this means requires further analysis of the property-based legal system.

The exclusive legal fence (or boundary) of property protects us in various ways, principally in the possession, use, and transfer of what we own. Yet we cannot use or transfer what we own without limits. We must respect the equal property right of others and not interfere with the exclusive legal fence that protects what belongs to them. For example, the doctrine of nuisance (Chapter 7) prevents us from using our land in a way that interferes unreasonably with the use and enjoyment (really, *possession*) of another's land. We cannot injure what others own. Likewise, in transferring ownership of something we own, we cannot sell it through fraud, sometimes called *intentional misrepresentation* or *deception* (see Chapter 10).

It is a mistake, however, to think that the placement of this fence of law is always clearly understood. In the property system, owners often just assume they can do whatever they want with what they own. Property seems open-ended that way. But what one owner does affects other owners, and property also protects the right of other owners not to have what belongs to them injured or to be defrauded out of what they own by what another owner does. The exact definition of what constitutes "injury" and "fraud" is often uncertain, and this means that it may not always be obvious to owners where the limits are regarding what they can do with what they own and how they can affect other owners.

The settlement of disputes about when legal fences have been wrong-fully crossed or fraud has occurred in transfers of ownership is a major func-tion of courts and alternative dispute resolution. Legislatures also sometimes determine the property fence or boundary between one person and all others. Consumer protection laws arise when legislatures define an ambiguous legal boundary between certain types of sellers and buyers in ways that favor buy-ers. Often this property fence or boundary is being defined precisely for the first time.

In the past, courts mainly used the principles of common law to settle disputes over the property fence and whether it had been crossed or compen-sation was due. Today, however, business sellers are often much larger than the consumers who borrow money and purchase goods and services. Instead of one individual suing another to settle disputes in borrowing and buying, it is often the case now that individuals have to face very large corporations to settle disputes, sometimes about relatively small tort or contract matters. This mismatch and our increasing dependency on large companies to provide credit, goods, and services leads us to put political pressure on legislatures to "do something" about our property relationships with these lenders and sellers, that is, with business. This is a primary reason for the many consumer laws discussed in this chapter.

1. WHO IS A CONSUMER?

The laws discussed in this chapter protect what is proper to consumers. These laws define and protect what is proper to people in their role as consumers. Who is a **consumer?** Consider Case 17.1.

 case **17.1** ::

ANDERSON v. FOOTHILL INDUSTRIAL BANK
674 P.2d 232 (Wyo. 1984)

Appellants Glen and Marlene Anderson contracted with the United States Postal Service to deliver mail on a route. The Andersons borrowed $27,500 from appellee Foothill Industrial Bank for start-up expenses *in establishing the mail delivery route. The Andersons sued the Foothill Industrial Bank while refinancing the loan, claiming that the bank had failed to com-ply with Wyoming's Uniform Consumer Credit Code*

(UCCC) and the federal Truth-in-Lending Act by misrepresenting the annual percentage rate of the loan and other acts.

ROONEY, C.J.: These allegations of appellants are premised on the fact of the loan being a consumer loan and not a commercial loan. The U.C.C.C. applies only to consumer loans and not to commercial loans. A consumer loan is defined in [Wyoming law] as follows:

> (a) Except with respect to a loan primarily secured by an interest in land, 'consumer loan' is a loan made by a person regularly engaged in the business of making loans in which: (i) The debtor is a person other than an organization; (ii) The debt is incurred primarily for a personal, family, household or agricultural purpose; (iii) Either the debt is payable in installments or a loan finance charge is made; and (iv) Either the principal does not exceed twenty-five thousand dollars ($25,000.00) or the debt is secured by an interest in land.

Considering the evidence in this case in accordance with the foregoing, we find that it established the loan to be a commercial loan and not a consumer loan as a matter of fact. Appellant Glen Anderson inquired of three lendors in an attempt to secure the money for his mail route business. He told the loan officer at Person-to-Person that the money was to be used to "buy a mail route." At First Wyoming Bank, he said that it was to be used to operate a truck or otherwise engage in the mail route. He told the representative of appellee Foothill Industrial Bank that it was for a down payment on a truck and for start-up expenses. He did not require a loan until he decided to go into the mail route business. The debt was not "incurred primarily for a personal, family, household . . . purpose" as required by 40-14-304, W.S. 1977, supra. Although part of the proceeds of the loan were used to pay off that due on a second mortgage on appellants' residence, the testimony was that prudent lending practice would require such pay off with transfer of the collateral if the loan were made for the purpose of financing another enterprise. The thrust of all of the evidence was that the debt was "incurred primarily" for the purpose of entering a mail route business and not for a personal family or household purpose. It was not a consumer loan. . . .

Affirmed.

:: CASE QUESTIONS

1. How does the Wyoming Supreme Court define "consumer"?
2. Why do the borrowers not win this case?
3. On what basis do the borrowers argue that they are consumers?
4. Is a farmer protected as a consumer under Wyoming's UCCC?

According to the *Anderson* case, consumers are natural (rather than corporate) persons who incur debt "primarily for personal, family, or household purposes." Most of the statutes in this chapter define "consumer" similarly.

:: The Federal Trade Commission

The Federal Trade Commission (FTC) is the primary federal agency that protects consumers. Although the Federal Trade Commission Act protects businesses as well as consumers, the consumer protection mission of the FTC is promoted by a special bureau called the Bureau of Consumer Protection. This body within the FTC is the regulatory center for federal consumer protection. The next sections examine activities of the FTC and the Bureau of Consumer Protection.

2. THE FTC AND TRADE PRACTICE REGULATION

Created in 1914, the FTC is an "independent" regulatory agency charged with keeping competition free and fair, and with protecting consumers. The FTC obeys its mandate to promote competition through enforcement of the antitrust laws. It achieves its consumer protection goal by trade practice regulation under that section of the FTC Act which prohibits using "unfair or deceptive acts or practices in commerce." It also administers several other consumer protection acts covered in this chapter (see Table 17.1). In the final analysis, promoting competition and protecting consumers overlap considerably. A highly competitive economy produces better goods and services at lower prices, while **trade practice regulation** ensures fair competition by preventing those who would deceive consumers from diverting trade from those who compete honestly.

The FTC furthers consumer protection through trade practice regulation in several ways. For instance, it advises firms that request it as to whether a proposed practice is unfair or deceptive. Although not legally binding, an **advisory opinion** furnishes a good idea about how the FTC views the legality of a given trade practice. Sometimes the FTC also issues **industry guides,** which specify the agency's view of the legality of a particular industry's trade practices. Like advisory opinions, industry guides are informal and not legally binding. The Bureau of Consumer Protection plays the major role in issuing advisory opinions and industry guides on trade regulation issues.

In its function of protecting consumers, however, the FTC goes far beyond merely advising businesses about the legality of trade practices. It also prosecutes them for committing unfair or deceptive trade practices. Such prosecutions arise in one of two related ways. First, the Bureau of Consumer Protection may allege that an individual or company, called a **respondent,** has violated **Section 5** of the FTC Act, which prohibits **unfair or deceptive acts or practices.** Over the years, the FTC's administrative law judges and the commissioners who review decisions of the judges have derived a body of quasi-judicial interpretations as to what constitutes unfair and deceptive acts.

> "Consumer fraud is a serious and pervasive fraud which continues to plague the American marketplace."
>
> **–U.S. Justice Department study**

A deceptive act, or *deception,* usually involves a misrepresentation or omission similar to common-law fraud.

table 17.1 :: Consumer Protection Laws the FTC Administers

:: Laws	:: Duties
FTC Act	To regulate unfair or deceptive acts or practices.
Fair Packaging and Labeling Act	To prohibit deceptive labeling of certain consumer products and require disclosure of certain important information.
Equal Credit Opportunity Act	To prevent discrimination in credit extension based on sex, age, race, religion, national origin, marital status, and receipt of welfare payments.
Truth-in-Lending Act	To require that suppliers of consumer credit fully disclose all credit terms before an account is opened or a loan made.
Fair Credit Reporting Act	To regulate the consumer credit reporting industry.
Magnuson-Moss Warranty Act	To require the FTC to issue rules concerning consumer product warranties.
Fair Debt Collection Practices Act	To prevent debt-collection agencies from using abusive or deceptive collection practices.

Enforcement actions may also arise from allegations under Section 5 that a respondent's actions violate a trade regulation rule of the FTC. At the recommendation of the Bureau of Consumer Protection, the five-member Commission adopts trade regulation rules in exercising its quasi-legislative power. These rules are formal interpretations of what the FTC regards as unfair or deceptive, and they have the force and effect of law. The rules usually deal with a single practice in a single industry, and they cover all firms in the affected industry. Examples of trade regulation rules include required disclosures of the "R" value for siding and installation and the familiar telemarketing sales rule that established the national "Do Not Call" list.

Alleged trade practice violations may come to the attention of the Bureau of Consumer Protection in a variety of ways. A business executive may complain about another's acts that injure competition, or a consumer may direct the attention of the Bureau to unfair or deceptive acts of a business. Such complaints are filed informally, and the identity of the complainant is not disclosed. A letter signed by a complaining party provides a basis for proceedings if it identifies the offending party, contains all the evidence which is the basis for the complaint, and states the relief desired. Of course, other government agencies, Congress, or the FTC itself may discover business conduct alleged to be illegal.

The chief legal tools of the Bureau are the consent order and the cease and desist order. Under the consent-order procedure, a party "consents" to sign an order which restrains the promotional activity deemed offensive and agrees to whatever remedy, if any, the Bureau imposes. Most cases brought by the Bureau are settled by this procedure.

If a party will not accept a consent order, it will be prosecuted before an administrative law judge. If the party is found guilty, the judge issues a cease and desist order prohibiting future violations. Parties may appeal cease and desist orders to the full five-member commission and from there to the court of appeals if legal basis for further appeal is present.

Don't forget that a cease and desist order from an administrative law judge is very similar to an injunction from a trial court.

3. FTC PENALTIES AND REMEDIES

Civil Fines   The basic penalty for trade practice violations under the FTC Act is a civil fine of not more than $10,000 per violation. The punishment function of finding violators is only an incidental one, as the FTC's main purpose is to prevent and deter trade practice violations.

To obtain fines, either the FTC or the Justice Department must ask the federal court to assess them. The exception is when companies agree to fines as part of a consent order. Fines may be assessed in three distinct situations: (1) for a violation of a consent or cease and desist order, (2) for a violation of a trade regulation rule, and (3) for a knowing violation of prior FTC orders against others.

The FTC Act provides that "each separate violation of . . . an order [or rule] shall be a separate offense." It also states that in the case of a violation through continuing failure to obey an order, each day the violation continues is a separate offense. Because of these provisions, the total fine against a violator may be considerably more than $10,000. See Sidebar 17.1.

Other Remedies   In addition to assessing penalty fines, the FTC has broad powers to fashion appropriate remedies to protect consumers in trade regulation cases. One remedy the FTC has used in the past to accompany some of its orders is **corrective advertising.**

:: *sidebar* 17.1

The Scam

Thousands of consumers received similar telemarketing calls. For an advance fee of $319, which was electronically taken from the consumers' bank accounts, the caller promised MasterCard and Visa credit cards, gifts of cell phones, and, sometimes, a free computer. Instead, consumers received only a "member benefits" package with items such as booklets on how to improve their creditworthiness. Some also received a "member merchandise" card in place of cell phones valid only for purchases from a catalog supplied by the caller's company. No one received the promised computers. Instead, they received certificates purportedly redeemable for off-brand computers, but the consumers first had to pay additional fees.

Following complaints to the Federal Trade Commission, the FTC in 2007 sued in federal court several individuals from Canada and over a dozen companies they had set up to hide themselves. The court found that the defendants had violated Section 5 of the Federal Trade Commission Act and assessed damages of $4,997,695.60, based on $10,000 per day per offense for each violation under the Act. These scam artists fared even worse in Canada, where they were prosecuted criminally.

Note that the FTC has not used corrective advertising much when a majority of the five commissioners is politically conservative.

When a company has advertised deceptively, the FTC can require it to run ads that admit the prior errors and correct the erroneous information. The correction applies to a specific dollar volume of future advertising. The theory is that the future advertising, however truthful itself, will continue to be deceptive unless the correction is made because it will remind consumers of the prior deceptive ads. Corrective ads have forced admissions that a mouthwash does not reduce cold symptoms or prevent sore throats, that an oil-treatment product cannot decrease gasoline consumption, and that an aspirin-based drug cannot relieve tension.

Other remedies the FTC may use in its orders, or may seek to impose by court action under certain circumstances, include: (1) recission of contracts (each party must return what has been obtained from the other), (2) refund of money or return of property, (3) payment of damages to consumers, and (4) public notification of trade practice violations. When it is in the public interest, and when harm from an illegal practice is substantial and likely to continue, the FTC may ask the federal court to grant temporary or even permanent injunctions to restrain violators.

4. DETERMINING DECEPTION

The primary law used by the Federal Trade Commission to regulate advertising is Section 5 of the FTC Act prohibiting deceptive trade practices. Here in the FTC's own words is advice to advertisers about how the FTC determines deception.

- The FTC looks at the ad from the point of view of the "reasonable consumer," the typical person looking at the ad. Rather than focusing on certain words, the FTC looks at the ad in context—words, phrases, and pictures—to determine what it conveys to consumers.

Sometimes the FTC will use consumer surveys, and other consumer studies, to collect evidence of what people think and believe about advertising.

- The FTC looks at both "express" and "implied" claims. An express claim is literally made in the ad. For example, "ABC Mouthwash prevents colds" is an express claim that the product will prevent colds. An implied claim is one made indirectly or by inference. "ABC Mouthwash kills the germs that cause colds" contains an implied claim that the product will prevent colds. Although the ad doesn't literally say that the product prevents colds, it would be reasonable for a consumer to conclude from the statement "kills the germs that cause colds" that the product will prevent colds. Under the law, advertisers must have proof to back up express *and* implied claims that consumers take from an ad.

- The FTC looks at what the ad does not say—that is, if the failure to include information leaves consumers with a misimpression about the product. For example, if a company advertised a collection of books, the ad would be deceptive if it did not disclose that consumers actually would receive abridged versions of the books.

- The FTC looks at whether the claim would be "material"—that is, important to a consumer's decision to buy or use the product. Examples of material claims are representations about a product's performance, features, safety, price, or effectiveness.

- The FTC looks at whether the advertiser has sufficient evidence to support the claims in the ad. The law requires that advertisers have proof before the ad runs.

Table 17.2 illustrates some typical FTC deception cases.

table 17.2 :: Typical FTC Deception Cases

.. Company	:: Order
American Home Products	Must not give the impression that pain relievers are something other than aspirin when they are not. Must disclose presence of aspirin when company's product is contrasted with another product containing aspirin. Required to prove claims of product superiority with two controlled clinical studies.
California-Texas Oil Co.	Must not make unsubstantiated claims about gasoline additives improving fuel mileage. Cannot use language that additives improve mileage "up to" 15 percent unless an appreciable number of consumers can achieve that performance under normal conditions.
General Nutrition, Inc.	Must pay $600,000 for health research due to alleged false and unsubstantiated claims that its dietary supplement "Healthy Greens" was effective in reducing cancer risk.
Heatcool	Company must run twelve months of corrective ads stating that its products "do not insulate better than comparable glass storm windows."
Kingsbridge Media & Marketing, Inc.	Must pay $1.1 million into an account to provide consumer refunds. Action based on defendants' claims that diet pills would induce weight loss while sleeping and without exercise or dieting.
Sears	Must cease and desist from making claims that Lady Kenmore dishwashers eliminate the need for scraping and prerinsing dishes. Cannot make claims for *any* major home appliance unless reliable substantiating evidence is available.
Sony BMG Music Entertainment	Must not sell music that installs software on consumers' computers without consent. Must pay for repairs to computers caused by such software.
Zango, Inc.	Must pay $3 million for secretly installing "adware" on consumers computers that caused 6.9 billion uninvited pop-up ads.

5. POLITICS, ECONOMICS, AND THE LAW: THE FTC TODAY

Appreciate that traditional frauds that substantially impact inter-state commerce not only violate the FTC act but also may violate federal and state criminal laws, as well as give consum-ers injured by the fraud a common-law right to sue for actual and punitive damages.

The FTC's consumer protection mission and enforcement of Section 5 varies according to the economic orientation of the president and of Congress. The president appoints the FTC commissioners for four-year terms and Congress annually must approve a budget for the FTC. Although the FTC is an *independent regulatory agency*, it is understandable that the FTC commissioners often reflect the views of the president who appointed them. Additionally, Congress can always cut the FTC's budget if it disapproves of the rules made and the cases brought by the FTC.

According to the majority views of the five commissioners who abso-lutely run the FTC, in some years the FTC is very laissez-faire, meaning that it leaves alone or does not regulate most advertising. The FTC allows the market to regulate advertising under the theory that consumers will not buy again from a seller if they are unhappy with what they bought the first time. In such times, only traditional frauds tend to be regulated. In other years, when politics and the FTC commissioners are more consumer-oriented, the FTC will increase the number of deceptive cases filed and the number of new rules regulating trade practices that are not only deceptive but also "unfair" in the minds of the commissioners. They may allow the Bureau of Consumer Protection to impose new legal remedies like corrective advertising

DO note that the Bureau of Consumer Protection may urge that a case be brought, but a majority of the five commissioners is necessary officially to authorize FTC action by the Bureau of Consumer Protection.

The FTC has great discretion in deciding what is deceptive or unfair and whether or not to make new rules and bring new cases. Politics, economics, and discretion combine to determine the consumer protection mission of the FTC.

:: Federal Credit Regulations

In addition to the FTC Act, the FTC administers several other consumer protection statutes as well. This means that the FTC can bring enforcement actions against those who violate the statutes. Several of these statutes con-cern credit regulation because the extension of credit is such an important economic reality of our consumer society.

$2.5 trillion is a thousand times $2.5 billion.

The large number of credit cards in the average consumer's wallet indi-cates that credit buying has truly become a national pastime. Credit financing of consumer contracts has jumped astronomically in recent years. At the close of World War II, consumer credit outstanding amounted to only $2.5 billion, a figure that had changed little since the 1920s. Today, however, consumer credit debt has soared above $2.5 trillion, or over $8,200 for every person in the United States. And this figure does not include residential mortgage debt.

Considering the importance of credit buying to the consumer and busi-ness, you should not be surprised that a number of laws regulating credit extension have been passed. The laws discussed in the following sections cover nondiscrimination in credit extension, the collection of information for credit reports, and the standardized disclosure of credit charges.

6. THE EQUAL CREDIT OPPORTUNITY ACT

In 1975, Congress passed the Equal Credit Opportunity Act (ECOA). The ECOA's purpose is to prevent discrimination in credit extension. In an economy in which credit availability is so important, the ECOA is a logical extension in a vital consumer area of the antidiscrimination laws found in the employment field.

ECOA Prohibitions This act prohibits discrimination based on sex, marital status, race, color, age, religion, national origin, or receipt of welfare in any aspect of a consumer credit transaction. Although the ECOA forbids discrimination on the basis of all these different categories, it is aimed especially at preventing sex discrimination. As the divorce rate climbs, the age of first marriage grows later, and more women enter the work force, it is expected that sex discrimination in credit extension will increasingly become a subject for litigation.

The law prohibits one to whom the act applies from discouraging a consumer from seeking credit based on sex, marital status, or any other of the enumerated categories. A married woman, for example, cannot be denied the right to open a credit account separate from her husband's or in her maiden name. Unless the husband will be using the account or the consumer is relying on her husband's credit, it is illegal even to ask if the consumer is married. It is also illegal to ask about birth-control practices or childbearing plans or to assign negative values on a credit checklist to the fact that a woman is of childbearing age.

The ECOA applies to all businesses which regularly extend credit, including financial institutions, retail stores, and credit-card issuers. It also affects automobile dealers, real estate brokers, and others who steer consumers to lenders. Many courts are also ruling that ECOA covers consumer leasing situations, which may substitute in place of credit-based sales.

> The point is that a business extending credit should not ask a woman anything that is specific to her gender. If her income does not support the credit she seeks, don't ask "are you married"? Ask, "is there anyone else who could cosign the loan for you"?

Responsibilities of the Credit Extender In basing a credit decision on the applicant's income, the credit extender must consider alimony, child support, and maintenance payments as income, although the likelihood of these payments being actually made may be considered as well. The credit extender must also tell an applicant that she need not disclose income from these sources unless she will be relying on that income to obtain credit. In calculating total income, those subject to the law must include income from regular part-time jobs and public assistance programs.

Information on accounts used by both spouses must be reported to third parties, such as credit reporting agencies, in the names of both spouses. This provision of the law helps women establish a credit history and enables a woman who separates from her husband to obtain credit in her own right.

To date, much of the litigation surrounding the ECOA concerns the requirement that *specific* reasons be given a consumer who is denied credit. Several cases have imposed liability upon credit extenders who have failed to provide any reasons for credit denial or who merely informed the consumer that she had failed to achieve a minimum score on a credit rating system. Other cases have dealt with age and race discrimination. The government filed an action recently against a large consumer finance company which made extension of credit to the elderly conditional upon their obtaining credit life insurance. It has also been established that the practice of **redlining,** that is, refusing to make loans at all in certain areas where property values are low, can discriminate on the basis of race in granting mortgage credit.

> A business that denies a consumer credit must give *specific* reasons for the denial to the consumer.

ECOA Remedies and Penalties Private remedies for violation of the ECOA are recovery of actual damages, punitive damages up to $10,000, and attorney's fees and legal costs. Actual damages can include recovery for embarrassment and mental distress. Punitive damages can be recovered even in the absence of actual damages. In addition to private remedies, the government may bring suit to enjoin violations of the ECOA and to assess civil penalties. In one case, the FTC assessed a $200,000 civil penalty against a major national oil company. The FTC charged that the company practiced race and sex discrimination by using zip codes as a factor in deciding whether to extend credit and by failing to consider women's alimony and child support income.

Note that the ECOA has both private remedies that consumers can pursue as well as public enforcement by the Federal Trade Commission. For this reason, consumers do not depend on the FTC to ensure they have equal opportunities for credit. If there are violations of the ECOA, affected consumers can sue.

7. THE FAIR CREDIT REPORTING ACT

Every year in the United States the credit reporting industry issues twice as many credit reports as there are people in the country. These reports cover not only consumers seeking credit but also persons seeking jobs or insurance. Although most of the information contained in such reports is accurate, the harm caused by occasionally inaccurate information and the potential for undue invasion of privacy led Congress to pass the Fair Credit Reporting Act (FCRA). FCRA applies to anyone who prepares or uses a credit report in connection with (1) extending credit, (2) selling insurance, or (3) hiring or firing an employee. The law regulates credit reports on consumers but not those on businesses.

"The accuracy of credit reports is vital because inaccuracies in credit reports can result in a consumer being denied credit or paying higher rates for credit."

–Sandra F. Braunstein, Director, Division of Consumer and Community Affairs, FTC, 2007

Consumer Rights under FCRA The law gives individual consumers certain rights whenever they are rejected for credit, insurance, or employment because of an adverse credit report. These rights include: (1) the right to be told the name of the agency making the report, (2) the right to require the agency to reveal the information given in the report, and (3) the right to correct the information or at least give the consumer's version of the facts in dispute.

This law does have one important limitation. It provides that a report containing information solely as to transactions or experiences between the consumer and the person making the report is not a "consumer report" covered by the act. To illustrate this limitation, assume that a bank is asked for information about its credit experience with one of its customers. If it reports only as to its own experiences, the report is not covered by the act. The act is designed to cover credit reporting agencies which obtain information from several sources, compile it, and furnish it to potential creditors. If the bank passed along any information it had received from an outside source, then its credit report would be subject to the provision of the act. Also, if the bank gave its opinion as to the creditworthiness of the customer in question, it would come under the act. The limitation is restricted to information relating to transactions or experiences, and the information furnished must be of a factual nature if the exception in the law is to be applicable.

Many businesses can avoid the pitfalls of being a credit reporting agency, but most businesses will be subject to the "user" provisions of this law. The "user" provision requires that consumers who are seeking credit for personal, family, or household purposes be informed if their application is denied because of an adverse credit report. They must also be informed of the source of the report and the fact that they are entitled to make a written request within sixty days as to the nature of the information received. If they request the information in the report, they are entitled to receive it so that they may challenge the accuracy of the negative aspects of its contents.

Investigative Consumer Reports The act also contains a provision on **investigative consumer reports**. These are reports on a consumer's character, general reputation, mode of living, and so on, obtained by personal interviews in the consumer's community. No one may obtain such a report unless at least three days' advance notice is given the consumer that such a report will be sought. The consumer has the right to be informed of the nature and scope of any such personal investigation. Reports which are intended to be covered by this act are those usually conducted for insurance companies and employment agencies.

> **Don't** ignore the difference between a "consumer report" and an "investigative consumer report."

Observing Reasonable Procedures In making investigations and collecting information, credit reporting agencies must observe *reasonable procedures*, or they will be liable to consumers. For example, when a consumer investigative report contained false information about a consumer's character—including rumored drug use, participation in demonstrations, and eviction from prior residences—a court found liability against the credit reporting agency. The agency's investigator had obtained the information from a single source, a person with a strong bias against the consumer, and he failed to double check it. However, if an agency follows reasonable procedures, it is not liable to a consumer, even if it reports false information. Furthermore, several courts have ruled that the FCRA preempts state law. This prevents consumers from filing libel actions against agencies which report false information.

FCRA Penalties and Remedies The Federal Trade Commission can enforce the FCRA. In addition, anyone who violates the provisions of the act is civilly liable to an injured consumer. The consumer may recover actual damages, attorney's fees, and in some instances punitive damages. Consider in Case 17.2 what the court says about punitive damages under the FCRA.

case **17.2** ::

SAFECO INSURANCE CO. v. BURR
127 S. Ct. 2201 (2007)

Safeco Insurance Company and GEICO General Insurance Company issued automobile insurance policies to three applicants without telling them that the companies had obtained credit reports on the *applicants. One applicant filed a lawsuit against Safeco and two applicants sued GEICO under the Fair Credit Reporting Act. The cases reached the Supreme Court and were consolidated for decision.*

SOUTER, J.: ... The Fair Credit Reporting Act requires notice to any consumer subjected to "adverse action . . . based in whole or in part on any information contained in a consumer credit report." Anyone who "willfully fails" to provide notice is civilly liable to the consumer. The questions in these consolidated cases are whether willful failure covers a violation committed in reckless disregard of the notice violation, and, if so, whether petitioners Safeco and GEICO committed reckless violations. We hold that reckless action is covered, that GEICO did not violate the statute, and that while Safeco might have, it did not act recklessly.

Congress enacted the Act in 1970 to ensure fair and accurate credit reporting, promote efficiency in the banking system, and protect consumer privacy. The Act requires among other things, that "any person who takes any adverse action with respect to any consumer that is based in whole or in part on any information contained in a consumer report" must notify the affected consumer. The notice must point out the adverse action, explain how to reach the agency that reported on the consumer's credit, and tell the consumer that he can get a free copy of the report and dispute its accuracy with the agency. As it applies to an insurance company, "adverse action" is "a denial or cancellation of, an increase in any charge for, or a reduction or other adverse or unfavorable change in the terms of coverage or amount of, any insurance, existing or applied for."

In GEICO's case, the initial rate offered to Edo [one of the applicants] was the one he would have received if his credit score had not been taken into account, and GEICO owed him no adverse action notice under the Act.

Safeco did not give Burr and Massey (the other applicants) any notice because it thought the Act did not apply to an initial application, a mistake that left the company in violation of the statute if Burr and Massey received higher rates "based in whole or in part" on their credit reports; if they did, Safeco would be liable to them on a showing of reckless conduct (or worse). The first issue we can forget, however, for although the record does not reliably indicate what rights they would have obtained if their credit reports had not been considered, it is clear enough that if Safeco did violate the statute, the company was not reckless in falling down in its duty.

While "the term recklessness is not self-defining," the common law has generally understood it in this sphere of civil liability as conduct violating an objective standard: action entailing "an unjustifiably high risk of harm that is either known or so obvious that it should be known."

There being no indication that Congress had something different in mind, we have no reason to deviate from the common law understanding in applying the statute. Thus, a company subject to the Act does not act in reckless disregard of it unless the action is not only a violation under a reasonable reading of the statute's terms, but shows that the company ran a risk of violating the law substantially greater than the risk associated with a reading that was merely careless. Here, there is no need to pinpoint the negligence/recklessness line, for Safeco's reading of the statute, albeit erroneous, was not objectively unreasonable.

The Court of Appeals correctly held that reckless disregard of a requirement of the Act would qualify as a willful violation within the meaning of the Act. But there was no need for that court to remand the cases for factual development. Geico's decision to issue no adverse action notice to Edo was not a violation of the Act, and Safeco's misreading of the statute was not reckless. The judgments of the Court of Appeals are therefore reversed in both cases, which are remanded for further proceedings consistent with this opinion.

It is so ordered.

:: CASE QUESTIONS

1. What does it mean to say these cases were "consolidated," and why do you think they were consolidated?
2. Burr and Massey sued Safeco, alleging Safeco was reckless in its reading of the Act. Although not explained in this case excerpt, they could have sued Safeco under the Act for negligence instead. Why do you think they sued for recklessness instead of negligence?
3. Why did the Supreme Court determine that neither insurance company was liable in these cases.

8. THE TRUTH-IN-LENDING ACT

The Truth-in-Lending Act authorized the Federal Reserve Board to adopt regulations "to assure a meaningful disclosure of credit terms so that the consumer will be able to compare more readily the various credit terms available to him and avoid the uninformed use of credit." As previously mentioned, the FTC enforces these regulations.

Truth-in-Lending Coverage The Truth-in-Lending Act covers all transactions in which: (1) the lender is in the business of extending credit in connection with a loan of money, a sale of property, or the furnishing of services; (2) the debtor is a natural person, as distinguished from a corporation or business entity; (3) a finance charge may be imposed; and (4) the credit is obtained primarily for personal, family, household, or agricultural purposes. It covers loans secured by real estate, such as mortgages, as well as unsecured loans and loans secured by personal property. Disclosure is necessary whenever a buyer pays in four installments or more.

Truth-in-Lending imposes a duty on all persons regularly extending credit to private individuals to inform them fully of the cost of the credit. It does not regulate the charges which are imposed.

Finance Charge and Annual Percentage Rate The Truth-in-Lending philosophy of full disclosure is accomplished through two concepts, namely, the **finance charge** and the **annual percentage rate** (APR). The borrower uses these two concepts to determine the amount he or she must pay for credit and what the annual cost of borrowing will be in relation to the amount of credit received. Theoretically, a debtor armed with this information will be better able to bargain for credit and choose one creditor over the other.

> The finance charge is the total cost of the money to the consumer or farmer.

The finance charge is the sum of all charges payable directly or indirectly by the debtor or someone else to the creditor as a condition of the extension of credit. Included in the finance charge are interest, service charges, loan fees, points, finder's fees, fees for appraisals, credit reports or investigations, and life and health insurance required as a condition of the loan.

Among the costs frequently paid by debtors which are not included in the finance charge are recording fees and taxes, such as a sales tax, which are not usually included in the listed selling price. These are items of a fixed nature, the proceeds of which do not go to the creditor. Other items of cost not included are title insurance or abstract fees, notary fees, and attorney's fees for preparing deeds.

The law requires that the lender disclose the finance charge, expressing it as an annual percentage rate, and specifies the methods for making this computation. The purpose is to ensure that all credit extenders calculate their charges in a uniform fashion. This enables consumers to make informed decisions about the cost of credit.

Financing Statement The finance charge and annual percentage rate are made known to borrowers by use of a financing statement. This statement must be given to the borrower before credit is extended and must contain, in

> The financing statement is a disclosure document only. It does not regulate the interest charged.

addition to the finance charge and the annual percentage rate, the following information:

1. Any default or delinquency charges that may result from a late payment.
2. Description of any property used as security.
3. The total amount to be financed, including a separation of the original debt from finance charges.

In 2007, the Federal Trade Commission sent over 200 letters to mortgage brokers and lenders warning them about potential violations of the Truth-in-Lending Act.

Penalties and Remedies under Truth-it-Lending   There are both civil and criminal penalties for violation of Truth-in-Lending. The civil liability provisions make creditors liable to debtors for an amount equal to twice the finance charge, but not less than $100 nor more than $1,000, plus the costs and attorney's fees required to collect it. Creditors may avoid liability in the event they make an error, provided they notify the debtor within sixty days after discovering the error and also correct the error. In this connection, the law allows for corrections in favor of the debtor only. Creditors cannot collect finance charges in excess of those actually disclosed.

The Truth-in-Lending Act gives debtors the right to rescind or cancel certain transactions for a period of three business days from the date of the transactions or from the date they are given the notice of their right to rescind, whichever is later. For example, consumers may generally cancel transactions in which they give a security interest on their principal residence if they do so within the three-day period. If the transaction is rescinded, the borrower has no liability for any finance charge, and the security which he or she has given is void. The act also allows consumer-borrowers to rescind their mortgage agreements altogether if lenders have failed to comply with important disclosure provisions. For an interesting application of this, see Sidebar 17.2.

Small businesses may rely on model forms to avoid violating the Truth-in-Lending Act.

Truth-in-Lending Trends   In 1980, Congress passed the Truth-in-Lending Simplification Act. Two changes from the original act stand out. First, the law eliminates statutory penalties based on purely technical violations of the act. It restricts such penalties to failures to disclose credit terms that are of *material* importance in credit comparisons. Second, the Simplification Act requires the Federal Reserve Board to issue model disclosure forms. These are particularly important to small businesses that cannot afford legal counsel to help prepare such forms. Proper use of the forms proves compliance with the Simplification Act.

Studies conducted by the FTC show that many of those involved in credit extension, such as home builders and realtors, fail to make required Truth-in-Lending disclosures in their advertising. In several instances, the FTC has successfully undertaken programs to educate these businesses about their disclosure obligations under Truth-in-Lending.

:: Debt Collection and Consumer Protection

"The Federal Trade Commission has recently been leveling staggering fines (in the debt collection industry) that were unimaginable a few years ago."

–First Detroit Corporation, financial publishers, 2006

Consumer debt in the United States is staggering. At the end of 2007, American consumers owed $2.46 trillion, not counting their mortgage debt. This averages to $8,200 for every person in the nation. In a consumer-credit-oriented economy, the collection of bad debts is very important. At present, there are more than 5,000 collection agencies in the United States engaged

:: *sidebar* 17.2

Truth in Lending and the Subprime Mortgage Mess

Subprime mortgages refer to mortgages securing loans for consumers who do not qualify for ordinary market rates of interest because of lack of credit worthiness. Generally, this means that their income is not high enough or certain enough to qualify under ordinary circumstances. But during the 1990s and early 2000s house prices nationally kept going up and up, and many banks and other financial institutions—encouraged by the government—became willing to loan money to consumers who ordinarily would not qualify for particular loans, because rising house prices made the mortgage securities quite sound. If consumers became unable to pay monthly loan rates, they found it easy to renegotiate lower rates because of the soundness of the mortgages and the equity provided by rising house values.

When the housing bubble burst and, in many parts of the country, house values stopped rising, disaster struck the subprime market, which by 2007 was estimated to be at least $1.3 trillion. Many consumers became unable to pay back their loans and lenders were unwilling to lower monthly repayments because house prices were no longer rising. Foreclosure filings zoomed. Consumers with adjustable rate mortgages were hardest hit as interest rates

began to rise and their monthly house payments did also. The economic effects began to ripple through the economy, which went into recession. Financial institutions collapsed, credit dried up, joblessness rose, and the government passed emergency legislation to bail out financial institutions to help them extend credit required by businesses. Some homeowners were also assisted to help them repay their mortgages.

Lawyers representing consumers with mortgages in foreclosure sometimes turned to the Truth-in-Lending Act, and sued lenders who had not complied with all of the complicated provisions of the Act, especially with provisions relating to how prominently various disclosures of key terms had to be made. In some instances, class-action lawsuits were filed. In other instances, consumers used the threat of lawsuits to pressure banks into renegotiating loan rates downward. Failure to comply with truth-in-lending requirements could even allow consumers to rescind (take back) their mortgage agreements, and cause lenders to lose their security altogether, making them only general creditors unlikely to be able to recover the debt for the large loans.

in collecting unpaid accounts, judgments, and other bad debts. Thousands of attorneys also collect debts. Annually, creditors turn over bills totaling many billions of dollars for collection. The following sections examine the federal laws of debt collection and consumer protection, which the FTC enforces.

9. THE FAIR DEBT COLLECTION PRACTICES ACT

Due to complaints that some debt-collection agencies used techniques of harassment, deception, and personal abuse to collect debts, Congress in 1978 passed the Fair Debt Collection Practices Act (FDCPA). The act covers only *consumer* debt collections. It applies to agencies and individuals whose primary business is the collection of consumer debts for others. It also applies to the Internal Revenue Service and attorneys who collect consumer debts on behalf of their clients. Creditor collection efforts are exempt from the act. In the following case, the Supreme Court examines whether attorneys who are litigating a case are subject to the FDCPA.

One of the first actions of a debt collector will usually be to locate the debtor. This action, known as "skip-tracing," may require that the collector contact third parties who know of the debtor's whereabouts. The FDCPA permits the collector to contact third parties, such as neighbors or employers,

HEINTZ v. JENKINS
514 U.S. 291 (1995)

Darlene Jenkins borrowed money from a bank in order to buy a car. When she defaulted on her loan, the bank's law firm sued her in state court to recover the balance due. One member of the law firm wrote to Jenkins's attorney listing in the amount she owed an amount that included certain insurance against her failure to repay the loan. Jenkins then sued in federal court under the Fair Debt Collection Practices Act. The case reached the U.S. Supreme Court.

BREYER, J.: . . . The issue before us is whether the term "debt collector" in the Fair Debt Collection Practices Act applies to a lawyer who regularly, *through litigation,* tries to collect consumer debts. The Court of Appeals for the Seventh Circuit held that it does.

The Fair Debt Collection Practices Act prohibits "debt collectors" from making false or misleading representations and from engaging in various abusive and unfair practices. The Act says, for example, that a "debt collector" may not use violence, obscenity, or repeated annoying phone calls; may not falsely represent "the character, amount, or legal status of any debt"; and may not use various "unfair or unconscionable means to collect or attempt to collect" a consumer debt. Among other things, the Act sets out rules that a debt collector must follow for "acquiring location information" about the debtor, communicating about the debtor (and the debt) with third parties, and bringing "legal actions." The Act imposes upon debt collectors who violate its provisions "civil liability" to those whom they harass, mislead, or treat unfairly. The Act's definition of the term "debt collector" includes a person "who regularly collects or attempts to collect, directly or indirectly, debts owed to . . . another." And, it limits "debt" to consumer debt, i.e., debts "arising out of . . . transactions" that "are primarily for personal, family, or household purposes."

The plaintiff in this case, Darlene Jenkins, borrowed money from the Gainer Bank in order to buy a car. She defaulted on her loan. The bank's law firm then sued Jenkins in state court to recover the balance due. As part of an effort to settle the suit, a lawyer with that firm, George Heintz, wrote to Jenkins' lawyer. His letter, in listing the amount she owed under the loan agreement, included $4,173 owed for insurance, bought by the bank because she had not kept the car insured as she had promised to do.

Jenkins then brought this Fair Debt Collection Practices Act suit against Heintz and his firm. She claimed that Heintz's letter violated the Act's prohibitions against trying to collect an amount not "authorized by the agreement creating the debt," and against making a "false representation of . . . the . . . amount . . . of any debt." The loan agreement, she conceded, required her to keep the car insured "against loss or damage" and permitted the bank to buy such insurance to protect the car should she fail to do so. But, she said, the $4,173 substitute policy was not the kind of policy the loan agreement had in mind, for it insured the bank not only against "loss or damage" but also against her failure to repay the bank's car loan. Hence, Heintz's representation about the amount of her debt was false; amounted to an effort to collect an amount not authorized by the loan agreement; and thus violated the Act.

There are two rather strong reasons for believing that the Act applies to the litigating activities of lawyers. First, the Act defines the debt collectors to whom it applies as including those who "regularly collect or attempt to collect, directly or indirectly, [consumer] debts owed or due or asserted to be owed or due another." In ordinary English, a lawyer who regularly tries to obtain payment of consumer debts through legal proceedings is a lawyer who regularly "attempts" to collect those consumer debts.

Second, in 1977, Congress enacted an earlier version of this statute, which contained an express exemption for lawyers. That exemption said that the term "debt collector" did not include "any attorney-at-law collecting a debt as an attorney on the behalf of and in the name of a client." In 1986, however, Congress repealed this exemption in its entirety, without creating a narrower, litigation-related, exemption to fill the void. Without more, then, one would think that Congress intended that lawyers be subject to the act whenever they meet the general "debt collector" definition.

For these reasons, we agree with the Seventh Circuit that the Act applies to attorneys who "regularly" engage in consumer-debt-collection activity, even when that activity consists of litigation. Its judgment is therefore

Affirmed.

:: CASE QUESTIONS

1. Did the debtor have a legal obligation to repay her car loan?
2. Did the debtor have a legal obligation to insure her car?
3. What did the bank do wrong?
4. Why do you think Congress passed the Fair Debt Collection Practices Act?

but it limits the way in which this contact may be carried out. The collector may not state that the consumer owes a debt nor contact any given third party more than once, except in very limited circumstances. When the collector knows that an attorney represents the debtor, the collector may not contact any third parties, except the attorney, unless the attorney fails to respond to the collector's communication.

Having located the debtor, the collector will next seek to get payment on the overdue account. However, the FDCPA restricts methods that can be used in the collection process. Table 17.3 outlines these restrictions.

FDCPA Remedies and Enforcement If the consumer debtor desires to stop the debt collector from repeatedly contacting him or her about payment, the debtor need only notify the collector in writing of this wish. Any further contact by the collector following such notification violates the act. The collector's sole remedy now is to sue the debtor. Violations of the FDCPA entitle the debtor to sue the debt collector for actual damages, including damages for invasion of privacy and infliction of mental distress, plus court costs and attorney's fees. In the absence of actual damages, the court may still order the collector to pay the debtor up to $1,000 for violations. Class-action suits, as well as individual ones, are permitted under the act.

table 17.3 :: FDCPA'S Restrictions on Collection Methods of Collection Agencies

The collector cannot:

1 Physically threaten the debtor.

2 Use obscene language.

3 Represent himself or herself as an attorney unless it is true.

4 Threaten debtor with arrest or garnishment unless the collector can legally take such action and intends to do so.

5 Fail to disclose his or her identity as a collector.

6 Telephone before 8:00 A.M. or after 9:00 P.M. in most instances.

7 Telephone repeatedly with intent to annoy.

8 Place collect calls to the debtor.

9 Use any "unfair or unconscionable means" to collect the debt.

Don't forget that state debt collection laws may be stricter than the FDCPA and may apply to the creditor as well as to the debt collection agency.

Consumers sometimes get credit that they cannot repay, and consequently they end up going bankrupt.

State Laws Regulating Debt Collection   Congress specified that the FDCPA does not preempt state laws regulating debt collections so long as they are more strict than FDCPA standards. Some of these laws apply to debt collections by *creditors* as well as by collection agencies.

10. BANKRUPTCY

The Federal Trade Commission does not administer all consumer protection laws. For instance, the bankruptcy laws are not subject to regulatory enforcement at all. These laws establish a procedure by which the "honest debtor" can get rid of debts by having them "discharged." The bankruptcy laws are not subject to regulatory interpretation and depend upon assertion by private debtors, both in their capacity as consumers and in business. However, as discussed here, the bankruptcy laws help explain one important consumer protection outcome of our consumer credit society: inability to repay debts.

Bankruptcy Proceedings   **Bankruptcy** proceedings begin upon the filing of either a voluntary or involuntary petition to the court. A *voluntary petition* is one filed by the debtor; an *involuntary petition* is filed by one or more creditors of the debtor. The creditors who sign the involuntary petition must be owed at least $10,775. If the court finds in an involuntary proceeding that the debtor is on the table to pay his or her debts as they mature, the court will order relief against the debtor. Relief may be also ordered if someone has been appointed to control the debtor's property for the purpose of satisfying a judgment or other lien.

Two alternatives are possible in a bankruptcy proceeding against an individual. The individual's property either will be **liquidated** under Chapter 7 of the bankruptcy law and the debts discharged, or the debts will be **adjusted** under Chapter 13. Under Chapter 13, individuals who have secured debts (mortgages, security interests against personal property, and so on) of less than $923,000 and unsecured debts of less than $308,000 (these amounts change periodically) can have their debts adjusted by the court for repayment. Time periods for repayment are also adjusted, and the debtor repays the creditors the adjusted debts over a three to five year period.

Do make sure you know the difference between liquidation under Chapter 7 and adjustment of debts under Chapter 13.

Congress amended the bankruptcy law in 2005 to force above median income earners to repay their adjusted debts under Chapter 13 rather than have them liquidated under Chapter 7. When this happened, bankruptcy filings, which had risen to over two million in 2005, dropped to 827,000 in 2006 but were back to over one million in 2007.

Trustee in Bankruptcy   The **trustee** in bankruptcy is an important person in the bankruptcy proceeding. The trustee is someone elected by the creditors to represent the debtor's estate in taking possession of and liquidating (selling off) the debtor's property. Broad powers are granted to the trustee. The trustee can: (1) affirm or disaffirm contracts with the debtor which are yet to be performed; (2) set aside fraudulent conveyances, that is, transfers of the debtor's property for inadequate consideration or for the purpose of defrauding creditors; (3) void certain transfers of property by the debtor to creditors which prefer some creditors over others; (4) sue those who owe the

The trustee may void gifts and other transfers of assets made for inadequate consideration by a bankruptcy that diminishes the assets the creditors can claim against.

table 17.4 :: Priority of Bankruptcy Creditors

1 Creditors with claims that arise from the costs of preserving and administering the debtor's estate (such as the fee of an accountant who performs as audit of the debtor's books for the trustee).

2 Creditors with claims that occur in the ordinary course of the debtor's business after a bankruptcy petition has been filed.

3 Employees who are owed wages earned within ninety days, or employee benefits earned within 180 days of the bankruptcy petition (limited to $10,000 per employee).

4 Consumers who have paid deposits or prepayments for undelivered goods or services (limited to $1800 per consumer).

5 Government (for tax claims).

6 Creditors who have other claims (general creditors).

debtor some obligation; and (5) set aside statutory liens against the debtor's property which take effect upon the beginning of bankruptcy proceedings.

Creditor Priority   Under bankruptcy laws, certain creditors receive priority over others in the distribution of a debtor's assets. The law divides creditors into priority classes, as set forth in Table 17.4. The amounts owing to each creditor class must be satisfied fully before the next lower class of priority can receive anything. Note that secured creditors who hold mortgages or Article 9 security interests in the debtor's property usually have priority over the bankruptcy creditor classes.

Discharge   From the debtor's point of view, the purpose of bankruptcy is to secure a **discharge** of further obligation to the creditor. Certain debts, however, cannot be discharged in bankruptcy. They include those arising from taxes, alimony and child support, intentional torts (including fraud), breach of fiduciary duty, liabilities arising from drunken driving, government fines, and debts not submitted to the trustee because the creditor has lacked knowledge of the proceedings. Education loans which become due within five years of the filing of the bankruptcy petition are also nondischargeable.

In addition to having certain debts denied discharge, the debtor may fail to receive a discharge from *any* of his or her debts if the courts find that the debtor has concealed property, falsified or concealed books of record, refused to obey court orders, failed to explain satisfactorily any losses of assets, or been discharged in bankruptcy within the prior six years. Courts may deny this discharge of debts altogether when relief would amount to a "substantial abuse" of the bankruptcy process, meaning usually that the consumer will have the income in the next several years to repay the debts owed.

> Courts may deny bankruptcy discharge when they believe the debtor will be able to pay off the debt in the next few years, often because the debtor has a good job.

11. ADDITIONAL CONSUMER PROTECTION

Additional statutes protect consumers. This section mentions some of the key laws not otherwise covered by this chapter. Some are enforced by the Federal Trade Commission or other regulatory agency, and many give consumers private remedies and rights of enforcement. What follows are just brief summaries of key consumer protection provisions.

- *Fair Credit Billing Act*—administered by the Federal Trade Commission, this act limits liability on lost, stolen, or misused credit cards to $50. Establishes rules for resolving billing disputes with the credit card issuer. Enables consumers who follow certain procedures to assert any defense against the credit card issuer that could have been asserted against a merchant who has sold shoddy merchandise, given bad service, or failed to perform as promised. Basically, the act allows consumers to require credit card issuers to recredit accounts in such a situation. Applies only to amounts over $50 within the consumer's home state or within 100 mile radius of the consumer's home.

The Fair Credit Billing Act applies to credit cards. The Electronic Fund Transfer Act applies to automatic teller machine transactions and point-of-purchase debit transactions. Note the greater amount that the consumer can be responsible for under the latter act.

- *Electronic Fund Transfer Act*—administered by the Federal Reserve Board, this act limits liability on lost, stolen, or misused automatic teller and check cards (debit cards) to $50 if reported within two business days of consumers' learning of a misuse. After two business days consumers responsibility is up to $500, except that after 60 days without reporting, responsibility becomes unlimited. The act also establishes procedures that banks and other financial institutions must follow when consumers dispute amounts billed by the bank.

- *Consumer Product Safety Act*—administered by the Consumer Product Safety Commission. The act requires the commission to protect consumers against "unreasonable risk" of harm and applies to some 15,000 different consumer products. The commission protects consumers against unreasonable risk of injury by developing mandatory and voluntary standards, banning harmful consumer products, issuing recalls of products, and researching potential product hazards. In recent years, the commission has been widely criticized for inactivity.

- *Magnuson-Moss Warranty Act*—administered by the Federal Trade Commission. Applies to all product warranties on consumer products costing more than $15. These warranties must be identified as "full" or "limited." Under full warranties a warrantor must repair or replace a defective product within a reasonable time and at no charge, including no shipping costs. Implied warranties may not be limited in full warranties, and other limitations must be disclosed fully and conspicuously in readily understood language. All other warranties must be described as "limited warranties," and their limitations must also be described conspicuously and in plain English. Failure to comply with the act enables consumers to sue for damages and reasonable attorney fees.

- *Federal Food, Drug and Cosmetic Act*—administered by the Food and Drug Administration, this act and the rules established under it by the FDA establish that prescription drugs must be proven effective and safe by extensive testing before they can be sold. Medical devices are likewise regulated. The act also empowers the FDA to protect consumers against unsafe and adulterated foods.

- *Various labeling laws*—administered by various federal and state agencies, these laws require informative labels and warnings to be given on various products. Some labels identify the country of clothing manufacture. Other labels specify nutritional amounts for packaged foods. Still other labels, like the surgeon general's warning on cigarette packages, disclose potential dangers of products.

- *State consumer protection*—administered by the states, consumer protection agencies similar to the Federal Trade Commission exist in many states. The states also have other consumer protection laws ranging from the application of warranties under state commercial codes to various antifraud statutes.

Why does this chapter focus primarily on federal rather than state consumer protection laws?

:: Consumer Privacy and Property

As you read about consumer privacy, think of it also in terms of property's exclusive legal fence. The assertion of privacy and laws protecting it is very similar in concept to the assertion of property. Whether you are asserting a legal fence around a piece of land, or around yourself as a person, why should we call one type of legal fence "property" and the other legal fence "privacy"? In fact, both types of legal fences protect objects within their borders from trespass or intrusion by the rest of the world, and to the extent we cannot assert a legal fence, we have neither property nor privacy. This view of property as protecting both land and persons—even if we today call it "privacy" when it applies to persons—is a concept that James Madison, John Locke, and many others of their time accepted.

12. CONSUMER PRIVACY

As society becomes more complex, as population growth creates overcrowding, and as the technology of information gathering becomes more sophisticated, the need for privacy increases. In recent years, the law has come to recognize the invasion of privacy as a tort (see Chapter 10) and even to extend a constitutional right of privacy. For example, a constitutional right of privacy has been asserted by the Supreme Court under the First and Fourth Amendments in cases involving the freedom of association, the possession in the home of pornographic materials, and the use of contraceptive devices. Most of the laws and cases which apply the concepts of privacy protect the individual from being overwhelmed by the intrusive power of the government and other large organizations, including businesses. Many laws directly affect us as "consumers," and almost all apply to protect us in our personal, rather than public, lives. Consumer protection regulation and privacy laws, then, have very much in common.

Several of the consumer protection laws discussed in this chapter contain provisions protecting personal privacy. Under the Fair Credit Reporting Act, for example, a potential employer, insurer, or creditor must inform the consumer that an investigative report is being obtained on him or her. This notice allows the consumer to terminate the contemplated transaction, thus ending the legitimate business reason for the report and preventing the report from being obtained legally.

One of the chief threats to individual privacy comes from the government and governmental agencies which investigate individuals or which collect information from individuals. Several federal statutes are directed specifically at this problem. The Privacy Act of 1974 places constraints on how certain kinds of information collected by the federal government can be used and limits those to whom the information may be released. It also provides a tort cause of action against those who violate the act. A second statute, the Right to Financial Privacy Act of 1978, requires all government agencies seeking depositor records from banks and other financial institutions to notify depositors of this fact. The individual depositor then has fourteen days to challenge an agency's legal basis for seeking the records. Depositors are allowed to sue the government agencies or financial institutions which fail to comply with the statute for actual and punitive damages, plus attorney's fees.

:: Key Terms

Adjusted   526
Advisory opinion   512
Annual percentage rate   521
Bankruptcy   526
Consumer   510
Corrective advertising   513
Discharge   527

Finance charge   521
Industry guide   512
Investigative consumer
   report   519
Liquidated   526
Respondent   512
Redlining   517

Section 5   512
Subprime mortgage   523
Trade practice regulation   512
Trustee   526
Unfair or deceptive acts
   or practices   512

:: Review Questions and Problems

1. *Who is a Consumer?*

   Star Automobile Dealership buys a television set for its waiting room. Is Star a consumer? Explain.

The Federal Trade Commission

2. *The FTC and Trade Practice Regulation*

   (a) Explain the difference between a cease and desist order and a consent order. Which type of order is used most frequently at the FTC for consumer protection? Why do you suppose this type of order is most often used?

   (b) What is a trade regulation rule?

3. *FTC Penalties and Remedies*

   Reader's Digest sent out some 17 million sweepstakes promotions to consumers that featured "travel checks" and "cash convertible bonds" that the FTC claimed were deceptive and violated a previous consent order as well. What potential fine did the *Digest* face?

4. *Determining Deception*

   The Mosquito No Company claims that its electronic mosquito device will "eliminate all mosquito problems within a one-half acre area." Actually, the device will only work if there is no standing water on the half acre. Explain how the FTC will evaluate this advertising for deception.

5. *Politics, Economics, and the Law: The FTC Today*

   Explain what is meant by the text's saying that the FTC's enforcement of its statutory authority is "political."

Federal Credit Regulations

6. *The Equal Credit Opportunity Act*

   Jane Thomas applies for automobile financing at Kenwood Cars, Inc., a used-car dealership. The dealership obtains a credit report on her. On the basis of this report, the dealership denies her credit. The manager informs her that she will have to get her husband to cosign her application if she wants dealership financing. She refuses, and sues Kenwood under the ECOA. What was the result and why?

7. *The Fair Credit Reporting Act*

The ABC department store refuses credit to Mary Jane. Mary Jane has a good job and no debts. She cannot understand the refusal. What would you suggest Mary Jane do? Explain.

8. *The Truth-in-Lending Act*

Under the Truth-in-Lending Act, what is a finance charge? What charges are and are not included as finance charges?

Debt Collection and Consumer Protection

9. *The Fair Debt Collection Practices Act*

The Zenith Credit Bureau telephones Dan and his family almost daily about payment of a $3,500 debt. The phone calls are causing stress for Dan's family. Dan cannot afford to pay the debt at present, and he needs a listed telephone number for his business. Is there anything Dan can do legally to stop the calls from Zenith?

10. *Bankruptcy*

Discuss the concept of "discharge" as used in bankruptcy law. What types of debts are not dischargeable? Explain.

11. *Additional Consumer Protection*

Janet buys a year's membership in a new spa and exercise gym that has just opened. She pays $500 with her credit card. Less than one month later the business closes its doors, leaving 450 members without a place to work out. The owner, who has vanished, also failed to pay his employees, rent on the building, and payments on his leased equipment. Everyone suspects fraud. According to consumer protection laws, what recourse might Janet have under the circumstances?

Consumer Privacy and Property

12. *Consumer Privacy*

Give several examples of how the consumer protection laws you have studied in this chapter protect privacy.

business :: *discussions*

1. Property has been described as the central concept of Western legal systems. Explain how property is related in this broad sense to consumer protection laws. Why might it be important for businesspeople to understand the relationship of property to consumer protection laws?

2. The regulation of deceptive trade practices under Section 5 of the FTC Act, the disclosures required by the Truth-in-Lending Act, and the provisions of many other consumer protection laws aimed at helping consumers by preventing business activities that might violate what common-law and statutory tort found in Chapter 10? Explain.

18

Environmental Laws and Pollution Control

Learning Objectives ::

In this chapter you will learn:

1. To appreciate how environmental law fits into our property-based legal system.

2. To grasp how the government itself regulates its own impact on the environment at both the federal and state levels.

3. To understand the laws regulating private impact on the air, water, and disposal of toxic wastes.

4. To state why environment will be one of the most important challenges and opportunities for business during the twenty-first century.

A 2007 report by the United Nations Framework Convention on Climate Change says that additional investments of $210 billion a year are necessary in the developing world to keep greenhouse gas emissions that cause global warming at their present levels until 2030. The response to environmental change is rapidly becoming big business.

In the United States, environmental regulation remains the single most expensive area of government regulation of the business community. Over the next decade, industry will spend several hundred billion dollars on pollution control. The primary reason for environmental regulation is concern over the effects of human population growth and the impacts of human technology. Almost daily we hear of threats to the environment arising from human behavior. Destruction of the rain forests, extinction of animal and plant species, depletion of the ozone layer, and the greenhouse effect are only some of the current environmental concerns.

Environmental and pollution-control laws govern regulation on three levels:

- Government's regulation of itself
- Government's regulation of business
- Suits by private individuals

Sidebar 18.1 illustrates this breakdown.

:: *sidebar* 18.1

Categories of Environmental and Pollution-Control Laws

:: GOVERNMENT'S REGULATION OF ITSELF

National Environmental Policy Act.
State environmental policy acts.

:: GOVERNMENT'S REGULATION OF BUSINESS

Clean Air Act.
Clean Water Act.
Pesticide Control Acts.
Solid Waste Disposal Act.
Toxic Substances Control Act.

Resource Conservation and Recovery Act.
Other federal, state, and local statutes.

:: SUITS BY PRIVATE INDIVIDUALS

Citizen enforcement provisions of various statutes.
Public and private nuisance.
Trespass.
Negligence.
Strict liability for ultrahazardous activity.

This chapter examines environmental and pollution-control laws by looking first at federal environmental policy and then at specific laws aimed at reducing specific kinds of pollution. The emphasis is on the compliance these laws force on business and industry. The final section of the chapter looks at the rights and liabilities of private individuals under environmental law.

Administering environmental laws at the federal level is the Environmental Protection Agency (EPA). Since many of the laws provide for joint federal-state enforcement, the states also have strong environmental agencies. Policies are set at the federal level, and the states devise plans to implement them. States, and even local governments, also enforce their own laws that affect the environment and control pollution.

:: Government's Regulation of Itself

The modern environmental movement began in the 1960s. As it gained momentum, it generated political pressure that forced government to reassess its role in environmental issues.

1. THE NATIONAL ENVIRONMENTAL POLICY ACT

The way the government considers the environmental impact of its decision making greatly interests the business community. For instance, the federal government pays private enterprise almost $100 billion annually to conduct studies, prepare reports, and carry out projects. In addition, the federal

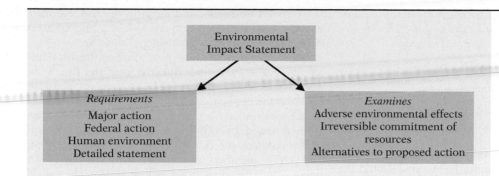

Figure 18.1
Components of the environmental impact statement

government is by far the nation's largest landholder, controlling one-third of the entire area of the United States. Private enterprise must rely on governmental agencies to issue permits and licenses to explore and mine for minerals, graze cattle, cut timber, or conduct other business activities on government property. Thus, any congressional legislation that influences the decision making concerning federal funding or license granting also affects business. Such legislation is the **National Environmental Policy Act (NEPA)**.

NEPA Basics NEPA took effect in 1970. It establishes a "national policy [to] encourage productive and enjoyable harmony" with nature and promotes "the understanding of the ecological systems and natural resources" important to the United States. It imposes specific "action forcing" requirements on federal agencies. The most important requirement demands that all federal agencies prepare an **environmental impact statement (EIS)** prior to taking certain actions. An EIS must be included "in every recommendation or report on proposals for legislation and other major federal actions significantly affecting the quality of the human environment." This EIS is a "detailed statement" that estimates the environmental impact of the proposed action. Any discussion of such action and its impact must contain information on adverse environmental effects that cannot be avoided, any irreversible use of resources necessary, and available alternatives to the action (see Figure 18.1).

There have been hundreds of cases that interpret the EIS requirements. In the following case, the Supreme Court decides whether psychological fear caused by the risk of accident at a nuclear power plant is an "environmental effect."

case **18.1** ::

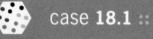

METROPOLITAN EDISON COMPANY v. PEOPLE AGAINST NUCLEAR ENERGY
103 S. Ct. 1556 (1983)

Metropolitan Edison Company decided to reopen its TMI-1 plant at Three Mile Island, Pennsylvania, after it had been shut down when a serious accident *damaged the reactor. People Against Nuclear Energy (PANE), an association of Three Mile Island–area residents, sued, claiming that the Nuclear Regulatory*

Commission failed to consider the psychological harm that reopening the plant and exposing the community to the risk of a nuclear accident might cause.

REHNQUIST, J.: Section 102(C) of NEPA directs all federal agencies to "include in every recommendation or report on proposals for legislation and other major Federal actions significantly affecting the quality of the human environment, a detailed statement by the responsible official on—(i) the environmental impact of the proposed action, [and] (ii) any adverse environmental effects which cannot be avoided should the proposal be implemented. . . ."

To paraphrase the statutory language in light of the facts of this case, where an agency action significantly affects the quality of the human environment, the agency must evaluate the "environmental impact" and any unavoidable adverse environmental effects of its proposal. The theme of section 102 is sounded by the adjective "environmental": NEPA does not require the agency to assess the impact or effect of its proposed action, but only the impact or effect on the environment. If we were to seize the word "environmental" out of its context and give it the broadest possible definition, the words "adverse environmental effects" might embrace virtually any consequence of a governmental action that someone thought "adverse." But we think the context of the statute shows that Congress was talking about the physical environment—the world around us, so to speak. NEPA was designed to promote human welfare by alerting governmental actors to the effect of their proposed actions on the physical environment. . . .

Our understanding of the congressional concerns that led to the enactment of NEPA suggests that the terms "environmental effect" and "environmental impact" in section 102 be read to include a requirement of a reasonably close causal relationship between a change in the physical environment and the effect at issue. The issue before us, then, is how to give content to this requirement. This is a question of first impression in this Court.

The federal action that affects the environment in this case is permitting renewed operation of TMI-1. The direct effects on the environment of this action include release of low-level radiation, increased fog in the Harrisburg area (caused by operation of the plant's cooling towers), and the release of warm water into the Susquehanna River. The NCR has considered each of these effects in its EIS, and again in the EIA. Another effect of renewed operation is a risk of a nuclear accident. The NRC has also considered this effect.

PANE argues that the psychological health damage it alleges "will flow directly from the risk of [a nuclear] accident." But a risk of an accident is not an effect on the physical environment. A risk is, by definition, unrealized in the physical world. In a causal chain from renewed operation of TMI-1 to psychological health damage, the element of risk and its perception by PANE's members are necessary middle links. We believe that the element of risk lengthens the causal chain beyond the reach of NEPA.

Risk is a pervasive element of modern life; to say more would belabor the obvious. Many of the risks we face are generated by modern technology, which brings both the possibility of major accidents and opportunities for tremendous achievements. Medical experts apparently agree that risk can generate stress in human beings, which in turn may rise to the level of serious health damage. For this reason among many others, the question whether the gains from any technological advance are worth its attendant risks may be an important public policy issue. Nonetheless, it is quite different from the question whether the same gains are worth a given level of alteration of our physical environment or depletion of our natural resources. The latter question rather than the former is the central concern of NEPA.

Time and resources are simply too limited for us to believe that Congress intended to extend NEPA as far as the Court of Appeals has taken it. The scope of the agency's inquiries must remain manageable if NEPA's goal of "ensur[ing] a fully informed and well considered decision," is to be accomplished.

If contentions of psychological health damage caused by risk were cognizable under NEPA, agencies would, at the very least, be obliged to expend considerable resources developing psychiatric expertise that is not otherwise relevant to their congressionally assigned functions. The available resources may be spread so thin that agencies are unable adequately to pursue protection of the physical environment and natural resources. As we said in another context "[w]e cannot attribute to Congress the intention to . . . open the door to such obvious incongruities and undesirable possibilities." . . .

Reversed.

:: CASE QUESTIONS

1. Why did PANE members want the Nuclear Regulatory Commission to consider "psychological harm" in the EIS?
2. What did the Supreme Court define the statutory language "adverse environmental effects" to mean?
3. Did the Supreme Court think that the risk of nuclear accident was itself an "adverse environmental effect"? Explain.

Several regulatory guidelines have made the EIS more useful. One guideline directs federal agencies to engage in **scoping.** Scoping requires that even before preparing an EIS, agencies must designate which environmental issues of a contemplated action are most significant. It encourages impact statements to focus on more substantial environmental concerns and reduce the attention devoted to trivial issues. It also allows other agencies and interested parties to participate in the scoping process. Scoping helps ensure that formal impact statements will address matters regarded as most important.

Another guideline directs that EISs be "clear, to the point, and written in plain English." This requirement deters the use of technical jargon and helps those reading impact statements to understand them. The Council on Environmental Quality (CEQ) has also limited the length of impact statements, which once ran to more than 1,000 pages, to 150 pages, except in unusual circumstances.

In Department of Transportation v. Public Citizen, the Supreme Court upheld a CEQ regulation permitting agencies to prepare an environmental assessment (EA) that is less detailed than an EIS when it is not clear that the law requires an EIS.

2. EVALUATION OF ENVIRONMENTAL IMPACT STATEMENTS

Importantly, NEPA does not require that federal agencies follow the conclusions of an EIS. However, as a practical political matter, agencies are not likely to proceed with a project when an EIS concludes that the environmental costs outweigh the benefits. EISs have been responsible for the abandonment or delay of many federal projects.

Some critics point out that the present process fails to consider the economic injury caused by abandoning or delaying projects. They also contend that those preparing EISs are forced to consider far too many alternatives to proposed federal action without regard to their economic reasonableness. Other critics maintain that most impact statements are too descriptive and not sufficiently analytical. They fear that the EIS is "a document of compliance rather than a decision-making tool." A final general criticism of the EIS process notes the limits of its usefulness. As follow-ups on some EISs have shown, environmental factors are often so complex that projections concerning environmental effects amount to little more than guesswork.

Although the NEPA applies only to federal actions, many states have enacted similar legislation to assist their decision making. Many interpretive problems found on the national level are also encountered at the state level. In addition, as the states frequently lack the resources and expertise of the federal government, state EISs are often even less helpful in evaluating complex environmental factors than are those prepared by federal agencies.

Don't forget that many states have laws similar to NEPA which require environmental impact statements.

NEPA Trends   Currently, NEPA is being applied to some of the most significant issues of the day. For instance, those who object to the building of a fence between the United States and Mexico have called for environmental impact statements because of the effect of the fence on wildlife and other environmental aspects. As of this writing, the director of Homeland Security has exercised authority to create an exception to the NEPA requirement for the fence building. However, in another instance federal agencies have begun to include the effect of federal actions on greenhouse gases that cause global warming in environmental impact statement preparation. That evaluation of environmental effects under NEPA should include global impacts of greenhouse gases is suggested by the Supreme Court's decision in a Clean Air Act case (see Case 18.2 later in this chapter).

:: Government's Regulation of Business

In the past 25 years, the federal government has enacted a series of laws regulating the impact of private enterprise on the environment. More and more companies are hiring environmental managers to deal with environmental compliance issues. This trend reflects the continuing importance of government regulation in this area. Congress may fine-tune environmental acts, but the national commitment to a cleaner environment is here to stay. As the CEO of a large chemical company observed about environmental concern, "Sometimes you find that the public has spoken, and you get on with it."

3. THE ENVIRONMENTAL PROTECTION AGENCY

One of the first steps taken at the federal level in response to concerns about the environment was the establishment of the **Environmental Protection Agency (EPA)** in 1970. At the federal level, the EPA coordinates public control of private action as it affects the environment.

Today, the EPA is a large agency with a number of major responsibilities (see Sidebar 18.2). Most important, it administers federal laws that concern pollution of the air and water, solid waste and toxic substance disposal, pesticide regulation, and radiation. The following sections examine these laws.

:: *sidebar* 18.2

Responsibilities of the EPA

- Conducts research on the harmful impact of pollution.
- Gathers information about present pollution problems.
- Assists states and local governments in controlling pollution through grants, technical advice, and other means.

- Advises the CEQ about new policies needed for protection of the environment.
- Administers federal pollution laws.

4. AIR POLLUTION

In 1257, Queen Eleanor of England was driven from Nottingham Castle because of harsh smoke from the numerous coal fires in London. Coal had come into widespread use in England during this time, following the cutting of forests for fuel and agricultural purposes. By 1307, a royal order prohibited coal burning in London's kilns under punishment of "grievous ransoms." This early attempt at controlling air pollution does not appear, however, to have been very effective. As recently as the London smog of 1952, four thousand people died of air pollution-related causes, including coal smoke.

In the United States the key federal legislation for controlling air pollution is the Clean Air Act.

Clean Air Act and Amendments The **Clean Air Act** directs the EPA administrator to establish air quality standards and to see that these standards are achieved according to a definite timetable. The administrator has set primary and secondary air quality standards for particulates, carbon monoxide, sulfur dioxide, nitrogen dioxide, hydrocarbons, and lead. **Primary air quality standards** are those necessary to protect public health. **Secondary air quality standards** guard the public from other adverse air pollution effects such as injury to property, vegetation, and climate and damage to aesthetic values. In most instances, primary and secondary air quality standards are identical.

Government regulation of private action under the Clean Air Act is a joint federal and state effort. The EPA sets national ambient (outside) air quality standards, and the states devise implementation plans, which the EPA must approve, to carry them out. The states thus bear principal responsibility for enforcing the Clean Air Act, with the EPA providing standard-setting, coordinating, and supervisory functions. However, the EPA may also participate in enforcement. The administrator can require the operator of any air pollution source to keep such records and perform such monitoring or sampling as the EPA thinks appropriate. In addition, the EPA has the right to inspect these records and data. Various criminal and civil penalties and fines back up the Clean Air Act. In addition, industries that do not obey cleanup orders face payment to the EPA; payment amounts to the economic savings they realize from their failure to install and operate proper antipollution equipment.

In setting air quality standards, does the EPA have to consider the costs to business? In *Whitman v. American Trucking* (2001), the Supreme Court ruled that the Clean Air Act "unambiguously bars cost considerations" from the air quality standards-setting process.

*The Clean Air Act requires the EPA to set air quality standards without regard to their costs to business.

In 1990, Congress passed significant amendments to the Clean Air Act. These amendments have added billions of dollars annually to the cost of complying with environmental regulations. In cities that did not meet clean air standards, businesses were required to install new pollution control equipment, and tail-pipe emissions for cars and trucks were reduced. A pilot program in California has introduced alternative fuel cars, and cleaner gasoline blends are now sold in specific cities with the worst pollution problems.

Since many cities currently do not meet existing Clean Air Act standards, the amendments force businesses in these areas to install new pollution-control equipment to cut emissions. Tailpipe emissions for cars and trucks must be reduced, and companies must phase in alternative fuel vehicles for their fleets of vehicles. A pilot program for California will introduce up to 300,000 alternative fuel cars. The amendments also required sale of cleaner gasoline blends in cities with the worst pollution problems. The goal of all these requirements is to cut pollution by 3 percent per year until air quality standards are met. The states have prepared blueprints for meeting these goals.

Expressing concern about airborne toxic chemicals, the 1990 amendments require industry to use the "best available technology" on plants to reduce emissions of 189 toxics by 90 percent. Significantly, the plants covered include bakeries and dry cleaning businesses as well as chemical companies. The EPA must also study how to reduce toxic emissions from vehicles and fuels.

"Acid rain" is seldom front-page news anymore because of the Clean Air Act's success in controlling sulfur dioxide emissions.

In 2005, DaimlerChrysler agreed to a $94 million settlement with the EPA to pay a civil fine and improve emissions controls on certain Jeep and Dodge models.

Clean Air Act Enforcement   Civil and criminal penalties enforce the Clean Air Act. Criminal sanctions include fines of individuals up to $250,000 and up to 15 years' imprisonment. Corporations can be fined up to $1 million for knowingly endangering people with emissions and up to $500,000 per incident of negligent emissions. Civil settlements between the EPA and businesses are very common.

Air Pollution Sources   For control purposes, the Clean Air Act amendments divide air pollution sources into two categories: *stationary source* and *mobile source* (transportation). Under the state implementation plans, major stationary polluters, such as steel mills and utilities, must reduce their emissions to a level sufficient to bring down air pollution to meet primary and secondary standards. Polluters must follow timetables and schedules in complying with these requirements. To achieve designated standards, they must install a variety of control devices, including wet collectors (scrubbers), filter collectors, tall stacks, electrostatic precipitators, and afterburners. New stationary pollution sources, or modified ones, must install the best system of emission reduction that has been adequately demonstrated. Under the act's provision, citizens are granted standing to enforce compliance with these standards.

The act requires both stationary and mobile sources to meet a timetable of air pollution standards for which control technology may not exist at the time. This *technology-forcing* aspect of the act is unique to the history of governmental regulation of business, yet it has been upheld by the Supreme Court. In large part due to technology forcing, new automobiles today emit less than 1 percent as much pollution per mile as cars of 25 years ago.

Technology forcing does not always succeed. It is neither always possible nor always feasible to force new technological developments. In recognizing this fact, the Clean Air Act allows the EPA in many instances to grant *compliance waivers* and *variances* from its standards.

5. CLEAN AIR ACT TODAY

As originally implemented, the Clean Air Act did not try to promote efficient pollution. For instance, if an area's air could tolerate a million tons of pollution per year, the authorities made no attempt to identify those who could make the best productive use of air pollution. Likewise, when a business was permitted to pollute a certain annual amount, the act specified the allowable pollution from each smokestack or other polluting source within the business instead of letting the business arrange its total allowable pollution in the most efficient way.

In the past few years, the EPA has moved to make its regulatory practices more economically efficient. All new pollution-control rules are now subjected to cost-benefit analysis. The EPA has also developed specific policies to achieve air pollution control in an economically efficient manner.

Traditionally, the EPA has regulated each individual pollution emission **point source** (such as a smokestack) within an industrial plant or complex. Increasingly, however, the EPA is encouraging the states, through their implementation plans, to adopt an approach called the **bubble concept.** Under the bubble concept, each plant complex is treated as if it were encased in a bubble. Instead of each pollution point source being licensed for a limited amount of pollution emission, the pollution of the plant complex as a whole is the focus of regulation. Businesses may suggest their own plans for cleaning up multiple sources of pollution within the entire complex as long as the total pollution emitted does not exceed certain limits. This approach permits flexibility in curtailing pollution and provides businesses with economic incentives to discover new methods of control. The Supreme Court has upheld the EPA's authority to approve the bubble concept even in states where pollution exceeds air quality standards.

Emissions Reduction Banking A number of states have developed EPA-approved plans for **emissions reduction banking.** Under such plans, businesses can cut pollution beyond what the law requires and "bank" these reductions for their own future use or to sell to other companies as emission offsets. Eventually, we may be headed for a *marketable rights* approach to pollution control, under which the right to discharge a certain pollutant would be auctioned off to the highest bidder. This approach would promote efficiency by offering to those who have the greatest need for pollution rights the opportunity to obtain them by bidding highest for them. Under the 1990 Clean Air Act amendments, Congress specifically allows utility companies to engage in emissions reduction banking and trading. Since 1992 the Chicago Board of Trade has run an auction in pollution credits given by the EPA to the nation's 110 most polluting utility plants.

According to the EPA, emissions trading accounts significantly for the fact that electric utilities today emit a quarter fewer tons of sulfur dioxide than they did in 1980 while producing 41 percent more electricity. The General Accounting Office figures that emissions trading saves the utility industry $3 billion a year over previous pollution-enforcement approaches. The EPA estimates that for every $1 billion of sulfur dioxide reduction there is a $50 billion saving in health costs. As Sidebar 18.3 discusses, emissions reduction banking and trading is rapidly growing and extending beyond the Clean Air Act.

> The bubble concept, emissions reduction, banking, and cap and trade all give incentives to businesses to limit emissions, rather than relying on "command and control," that is, on rules simply requiring attainment of air quality standards.

:: *sidebar* 18.3

Beyond the Clean Air Act

In 2003 the Chicago Climate Exchange began operation. This program for trading marks the first time that major U.S. companies have begun to take voluntary property-based market steps to cut emissions linked to global warming. It is likely that the United States will soon make a market-based approach mandatory to deal with these emissions, called *green house gases* (GHC).

The European Union already takes a market approach to limiting GHC. These markets are based on the principle of **cap and trade.** The government issues a limited number of pollution permits, effectively capping total GHG pollution. Companies then trade the permits. Whoever can reduce emissions can sell the unused amount of a permit. The government may slowly reduce the number of outstanding permits.

Prevention of Significant Deterioration Another important policy of the Clean Air Act is the **prevention of significant deterioration.** Under this policy, pollution emission is controlled, even in areas where the air is cleaner than prevailing primary and secondary air quality standards require. In some of these areas, the EPA permits construction of new pollution emission sources according to a strictly limited scheme. In other areas, it allows no new pollution emission at all. Critics of this policy argue that it prevents industry from moving into southern and western states, where air quality is cleaner than standards require.

The Permitting Process One of the most controversial issues involving the Clean Air Act concerns the delay and red tape caused by the *permitting process.* Before a business can construct new pollution emission sources, it must obtain the necessary environmental permits from the appropriate state agency. Today, the estimated time needed to acquire the necessary permits to build a coal-fired electric-generating plant is 5 to 10 years. This is nearly twice the length of time it took in the early 1970s. The formalities of the permitting process, the lack of flexibility in state implementation plans, the requirement that even minor variations in state implementation plans be approved by the EPA—all these factors contribute to delay. Both the EPA and Congress are considering ways to streamline the permitting process.

The EPA is experimenting with allowing states to issue "smart permits" to air polluters. Under these permits, polluters can engage in "a family of alternative operating scenarios" (i.e., engage in new operations) without the expensive delay of obtaining new permits as the EPA previously required. Some environmental groups oppose smart-permitting as failing to allow communities a time period to determine if new operations really meet clean air standards.

Indoor Pollution The EPA has also grown increasingly concerned about indoor air pollution. Paints, cleaning products, furniture polishes, gas furnaces, and stoves all emit pollutants that can be harmful to human health. Radioactive radon seeping into homes and buildings from the ground has now been recognized as a major health hazard. Some studies have found that indoor levels of certain pollutants far exceed outdoor levels, whether at work or at home. Although the Clean Air Act does not currently apply to indoor pollution, its application may be extended in the future.

Significantly, the EPA does not regulate indoor air pollution under the Clean Air Act although OSHA could regulate it as to the workplace. Numerous major businesses already ban workplace smoking. Many local governments also regulate or prohibit indoor smoking in public buildings.

Conclusion In spite of the controversy generated by the Clean Air Act, evidence indicates that the overall air quality in the United States is steadily improving. The 16,000 quarts of air we each breathe daily are cleaner and healthier in most places than they were a decade ago. Yet an estimated 80 million persons in the United States still breathe air that violates one or more primary air quality standards. Note, also, that air pollution is an international problem and that not all countries of the world have, or can afford, our air quality standards. Air pollution is especially severe in developing nations of the world, which are striving to reach our standard of living. See Table 18.1.

table 18.1 :: World's Worst Air Pollution (Particulate Matter) by City	
:: **Cities Ranked**	:: **Micrograms of Particulate Matter per Cubic Meter***
1. Cairo, Egypt	169
2. Delhi, India	150
3. Kolata, India	128
4. Tianjin, China	125
5. Chongqing, China	123
6. Kanpur, India	109
7. Lucknow, India	109
8. Jakarta, Indonesia	104
9. Shenyang, China	101
10. Zhengzhou, China	97

*The EPA places the danger level to human health for particulate matter at 100. By comparison, Los Angeles measured 34, Chicago 25, and New York 21.

Source: World Bank, 2004.

Air pollution reaches across international borders. Does the Clean Air Act allow regulation of the greenhouse gases, especially carbon dioxide, that causes global warming? Although the act does not mention carbon dioxide or other greenhouse gases, the Supreme Court case that follows (Case 18.2) decides that the EPA has authority to regulate those gases in new automobiles.

case 18.2 ::

MASSACHUSETTS v. ENVIRONMENTAL PROTECTION AGENCY
549 U.S. 497 (2007)

Citing evidence of global warming and asserting contributions to this warming from automobile pollution, various private organizations petitioned the Environmental Protection Agency to regulate motor vehicle emissions under its Clean Air Act authority. When the EPA refused, stating that it had no authority to address the causes of global warming, Massachusetts joined the organizations in suing to force the EPA to exercise its authority, asserting that global warming would affect its coastline through rising sea levels and injure its citizens. The case reached the Supreme Court on the issues of whether the EPA had authority under the Clean Air Act to regulate greenhouse gases, especially carbon dioxide, as they allegedly cause global *warming, and of whether the EPA could refuse to exercise its authority.*

STEVENS, J.: A well-documented rise in global temperatures has coincided with a significant increase in the concentration of carbon dioxide in the atmosphere. Respected scientists believe the two trends are related. For when carbon dioxide is released into the atmosphere, it acts like the ceiling of a greenhouse, trapping solar energy and retarding the escape of reflected heat. It is therefore a species—the most important species— of a "greenhouse gas."

In concluding that it lacked statutory authority over greenhouse gases, EPA observed that Congress "was well aware of the global climate change issue when it last comprehensively amended the [Clean Air Act] in 1990," yet it declined to adopt a proposed amendment establishing binding emissions limitations. Congress instead chose to authorize further investigation into climate change. . . . Having reached that conclusion, EPA believed it followed that greenhouse gases cannot be "air pollutants" within the meaning of the Act.

EPA . . . [also] maintained that its decision not to regulate greenhouse gas emissions from new motor vehicles contributes so insignificantly to petitioners' injuries that the agency cannot be hailed into federal court to answer for them. But EPA overstates its case. [R]educing domestic automobile emissions is hardly a tentative step. Even leaving aside the other greenhouse gases, the United States transportation sector emits an enormous quantity of carbon dioxide into the atmosphere, more than 1.7 billion metric tons in 1999 alone. That accounts for more than 6% of worldwide carbon dioxide emissions. Judged by any standard, U.S. motor-vehicle emissions make a meaningful contribution to greenhouse gas concentrations and, hence, to global warming.

The Clean Air Act's sweeping definition of "air pollutant" includes *any* air pollution agent or combination of such agents, including *any* physical, chemical . . . substance or matter which is emitted into or otherwise enters the ambient air. . . . On its face, the definition embraces all airborne compounds of whatever stripe, and underscores that intent through the repeated use of the word "any." Carbon dioxide, methane, nitrous oxide, and hydrofluorocarbons are without a doubt "physical [and] chemical substance[s]

which [are] emitted into . . . the ambient air." The statute is unambiguous.

The alternative basis for EPA's decision—that even if it does have statutory authority to regulate greenhouse gases, it would be unwise to do so at this time—rests on reasoning divorced from the statutory text. [O]nce EPA has responded to a petition for rulemaking, its reasons for action or in action must conform to the authorizing statute. Under the clear terms of the Clean Air Act, EPA can avoid taking further action only if it determines that greenhouse gases do not contribute to climate change or if it provides some reasonable explanation as to why it cannot or will not exercise its discretion to determine whether they do.

Nor can EPA avoid its statutory obligation by noting the uncertainty surrounding various features of climate change and concluding that it would therefore be better not to regulate at this time. If the scientific uncertainty is so profound that it precludes EPA from making a reasoned judgment as to whether greenhouse gases contribute to global warning, EPA must say so. In short, EPA has offered no reasoned explanation for its refusal to decide whether greenhouse gases cause or contribute to climate change. Its action was therefore "arbitrary, capricious, . . . or otherwise not in accordance with law." We need not and do not reach the question whether EPA must make an endangerment finding, or whether policy concerns can inform EPA's actions in the event that it makes such a finding. We hold only that EPA must ground its reasons for action or in action in the statute.

It is so ordered.

:: CASE QUESTIONS

1. Why did Massachusetts and the organizations want the EPA to regulate new vehicle emissions under the Clean Air Act?
2. What two arguments did the EPA offer in refusing to regulate these emissions?
3. How does the Supreme Court respond to the EPA's two arguments?
4. Does the Supreme Court require the EPA to limit new vehicle emissions of carbon dioxide? Explain.

6. WATER POLLUTION

Business enterprise is a major source of water pollution in the United States. Almost one-half of all water used in this country is for cooling and condensing purposes in connection with industrial activities. The resulting discharge into our rivers and lakes sometimes takes the form of heated water, called *thermal effluents*. In addition to thermal effluents, industry also discharges chemical and other effluents into the nation's waterways.

The principal federal law regulating water pollution is the **Clean Water Act,** passed by Congress in 1972. As with the Clean Air Act, the Clean Water Act is administered primarily by the states in accordance with EPA standards. If the states do not fulfill their responsibilities, however, the federal government, through the EPA, can step in and enforce the law. The Clean Water Act applies to all navigable waterways, intrastate as well as interstate. Although the term *navigable* is much broader than merely meaning being able to get a boat down, in *Solid Waste Agency v. United States Army Corps of Engineers,* 531 U.S. 159 (2001), the Supreme Court ruled that mere small ponds that do not empty into streams or rivers are not "navigable" under the Clean Water Act.

Goals and Enforcement The Clean Water Act sets goals to eliminate water pollution. Principally, these goals are to make the nation's waterways safe for swimming and other recreational use and clean enough for the protection of fish, shellfish, and wildlife. The law sets strict deadlines and strong enforcement provisions, which must be followed by industry, municipalities, and other water polluters. Enforcement of the Clean Water Act revolves around its permit discharge system. Without being subject to criminal penalties, no polluter can discharge pollutants from any *point source* (such as a pipe) without a permit, and municipal as well as industrial dischargers must obtain permits. The EPA has issued guidelines for state permit programs and has approved those programs that meet the guidelines.

The Supreme Court determined in *South Florida Water Management District v. Miccosukee Tribe of Indians* (2004) that a point source did not itself have to generate pollution. It could be merely a pumping station that moved pollution from one site to another.

Since the Clean Water Act applies to "navigable waterways," the criminal penalties of the act cover only the unpermitted point-source pollution of navigable waterways. However, the penalties under the Clean Water Act can still be substantial. Koch Industries agreed to pay a $30 million fine to settle lawsuits involving oil spills from its pipelines and oil facilities in six states.

Under the Clean Water Act, industries adopt a two-step sequence for cleanup of industrial wastes discharged into rivers and streams. The first step requires polluters to install *best practicable technology (BPT).* The second demands installation of *best available technology (BAT).* Various timetables apply in achieving these steps, according to the type of pollutant being discharged. In 1984, the EPA announced application of the bubble concept to water pollution in the steel industry.

In addition to the Clean Water Act, the EPA administers two other acts related to water pollution control. One, the Marine Protection, Research, and Sanctuaries Act of 1972, requires a permit system for the discharge or dumping of various material into the seas. The other is the Safe Drinking Water Act of 1974, which has forced the EPA to set maximum drinking water contaminant levels for certain organic and inorganic chemicals, pesticides, and microbiological pollutants.

The Clean Water Act and other current statutes do not reach one important type of water pollution: *non–point source pollution,* which comes from runoffs into streams and rivers. These runoffs often contain agricultural fertilizers and pesticides as well as oil and lead compounds from streets and highways. Congress has authorized $400 million for the National Non–Point Source Pollution Program to study the problem. Addressing non–point source pollution, the EPA has issued a rule requiring the states to impose antipollution standards for about 20,000 bodies of water. The rule requires states to set standards for the total "maximum daily load" of pollutants in a body of water. This standard would apply to pollutants from non point sources as well as point sources. However, as of this writing Congress was requiring the EPA to conduct further studies of the rule's impact before the rule could be implemented.

7. ENDANGERED SPECIES ACT

Every day entire species of animals and plants die off. As with the dinosaurs, sometimes great catastrophes like comet impacts cause species to become extinct. Gradual climate changes and competition from other species also can kill off animals and plants. However, in modern times, human activity has caused the vast majority of species extinctions. Air and water pollution, the clearing of land for agriculture, the development of water resources, hunting and fishing, and a growing human population all potentially threaten other species.

In 1973 Congress passed the Endangered Species Act (ESA), the world's toughest law protecting animals and plants and, perhaps, the country's most controversial environmental standard. Under the act the Secretary of the Interior can list any species as "endangered," that is, "in danger of extinction throughout all or a significant portion of its range," except for certain insect pests. ("Threatened" species are also protected.) In determining the factors of endangerment, the secretary must consider the destruction of habitat, disease or predation, commercial and recreational activity, and "other natural or manmade factors." Within a year of listing an endangered species, the secretary is required to define the "critical habitat" of the species which is the area with the biological or physical features necessary to species survival. The Fish and Wildlife Services and the National Marine Fisheries Services administer the ESA for the Department of Interior.

As of 2008, approximately 2,000 species of animals and plants are listed as endangered or threatened. The act also requires that recovery plans be drawn up for the listed species, and in 2008 there were such plans for approximately 1,600 of the species. Recovery plans may involve breeding of the species.

*An endangered species is one determined by the Secretary of the Interior to be "in danger of extinction throughout all or a significant portion of its range."

Application of the ESA   Although no federal agency can authorize, fund, or carry out any action that is likely to jeopardize an endangered species, the ESA's application to private business activity has caused the greater debate in recent years. Section 9 of the act prohibits any person from transporting or trading in any endangered species of fish or wildlife (a separate section applies to plants) or from "taking any such species within the United States" or "upon the high seas." *Taking* a species is defined as "harass, harm, pursue, hunt, shoot, wound, kill, trap, capture, or collect, or attempt to engage in any such conduct."

The Secretary of the Interior has further defined the "harm" of taking to mean any act that actually kills or injures wildlife, including harming habitat or essential behavior patterns. Thus, neither private businesses nor individuals can harm the habitats of endangered species. In *Babbit v. Sweet Home Chapter* (1995), the Supreme Court ruled that "the Secretary reasonably constructed the intent of Congress when he defined 'harm' to include 'significant habitat modification or degradation that actually kills or injures wildlife.'"

Note that the ESA does not permit courts or regulators to take economic factors into consideration in applying its provisions. There has been much criticism of the act, and amendments to it have been proposed to Congress. Congress has established a review board that can grant exemptions to the ESA for certain important federal projects. However, the exemptions do not apply to private activities.

The ESA requires recovery plans for the species it protects. Question: If pollution causes or contributes to global warming, and global warming endangers species like polar bears by changing their habitat, does the law require that automobile or plant emissions be regulated to diminish global warming? For now, no courts have addressed this issue.

8. PESTICIDE CONTROL

Pests, especially insects and mice, destroy over 10 percent of all crops grown in the United States, causing several billion dollars of damage annually. In many underdeveloped countries, however, a much greater percentage of total crop production is lost to pests, as high as 40 to 50 percent in countries such as India. Perhaps the principal reason for our lower rate of crop loss is that the United States uses more pesticides per acre than any other country.

The widespread, continual application of pesticides creates environmental problems, however. Not only is it dangerous to wildlife, particularly birds and fish, but it is also harmful to humans and may eventually threaten our agricultural capacity itself. Rapidly breeding pests gradually become immune to the application of pesticides, and researchers may not always be able to invent new poisons to kill them.

Nationwide, nearly half of the farmers responding to one poll expressed increasing concern about their own safety when using pesticides. A National Cancer Institute report concluded that farm families suffer from elevated rates of seven types of cancer, including leukemia, with pesticides suspected as a leading cause.

The Federal Pesticide Acts Federal regulation of pesticides is accomplished primarily through two statutes: the **Federal Insecticide, Fungicide, and Rodenticide Act of 1947,** as amended, and the **Federal Environmental Pesticide Control Act of 1972 (FEPCA).** Both statutes require the registration and labeling of agricultural pesticides, although FEPCA coverage extends to the application of pesticides as well.

> *The EPA must register pesticides for use unless they have unreasonable adverse effects on the environment.

Under the acts, the administrator of the EPA is directed to register those pesticides that are properly labeled, meet the claims made as to their effectiveness, and will not have *unreasonable adverse effects on the environment,* which is defined as "any unreasonable risk to man or the environment, taking into account the economic, social, and environmental costs and benefits of the use of any pesticide." In addition to its authority to request registration of pesticides, the EPA classifies pesticides for either general use or restricted use. In the latter category, the EPA may impose further restrictions that require application only by a trained applicator or with the approval of a trained consultant. Today, the EPA requires that employers train agricultural workers in pesticide safety, post safety information, and place warning signs to keep workers out of freshly sprayed fields.

Enforcement   The EPA has a variety of enforcement powers to ensure that pesticide goals are met, including the power to deny or suspend registration. In the 1980s, the EPA used this power and banned several pesticides suspected of causing cancer. In 2000 the EPA used its authority to halt the manufacture of household products containing the pesticide chlorpyrifos sold under the trade names Dursban and Lorsban. The EPA determined that the pesticide was more harmful to humans, particularly children, than had been thought previously.

The EPA also defines what a pesticide can and cannot be used for and may seek penalties against violators. For example, the EPA sought criminal charges against several quail-hunting clubs in Florida and Georgia that improperly used the pesticide Furadan to kill predators that ate quail eggs.

Pesticide control has been attacked by both affected businesses and the environmental movement itself. Pesticide manufacturers complain that the lengthy, expensive testing procedures required by the FEPCA registration process delay useful pesticides from reaching the market and inhibit new research. On the other hand, many in the environmental movement contend that our country's pesticide control policy is hypocritical in that the FEPCA does not apply to pesticides U.S. manufacturers ship to foreign countries. Companies can sell overseas what they cannot sell in this country.

9. SOLID WASTE

Pollution problems cannot always be neatly categorized. For instance, solid waste disposal processes often create pollution in several environmentally related forms. When solid waste is burned, it can cause air pollution and violate the Clean Air Act. When dumped into rivers, streams, and lakes, solid waste can pollute the water beyond amounts permitted under the Clean Water Act. Machinery used in solid waste disposal can also be subject to the regulation of the Noise Control Act.

Don't forget that total solid waste created in the United States divided by the U.S. population yields some 25 tons of waste for every person.

By all accounts, solid waste pollution problems during the last 25 years have grown as pollution has risen and the country has become more affluent and productive. Currently, total solid wastes produced yearly in the United States exceed 5 billion tons, or almost 25 tons for every individual. Half this amount is agricultural waste, another third is mineral waste, and the remainder is industrial, institutional, and residential waste. Some wastes are toxic and hazardous, while others stink or attract pests. All present disposal problems of significant proportion.

Landfills represent the primary disposal sites for most household and much business solid wastes. Figure 18.2 illustrates the composition of solid wastes in the typical landfill. According to Bill Rathje, professor of anthropology at the University of Arizona, paper is the biggest solid waste category in landfills. And paper, which in 1970 constituted 35 percent of landfill volume, today constitutes 50 percent. By contrast, disposable diapers take up less than 1 percent of landfill volume. Polystyrene foam, such as thermal cups, also takes up less than 1 percent of landfill volume. For additional figures on composition of landfill waste, see Figure 18.2.

The Solid Waste Disposal Act   The **Solid Waste Disposal Act** passed in 1965 represents the primary federal effort in solid waste control. Congress recognized in this act that the main responsibility for nontoxic waste

Figure 18.2 *Composition of a typical landfill by volume*

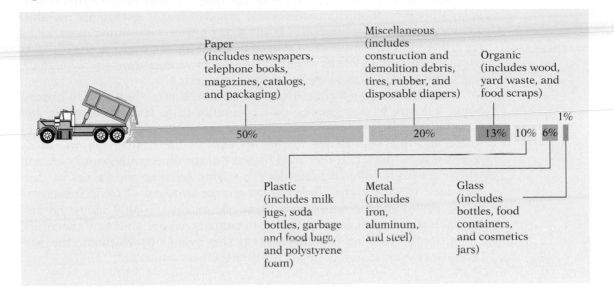

Paper
(includes newspapers,
telephone books,
magazines, catalogs,
and packaging)

Miscellaneous
(includes
construction and
demolition debris,
tires, rubber, and
disposable diapers)

Organic
(includes wood,
yard waste, and
food scraps)

1%

50%   20%   13%   10%   6%

Plastic
(includes milk
jugs, soda
bottles, garbage
and food bags,
and polystyrene
foam)

Metal
(includes
iron,
aluminum,
and steel)

Glass
(includes
bottles, food
containers,
and cosmetics
jars)

management rests with regional, state, and local management and limited the federal role in this area. Under this act, the federal role in nontoxic waste management is limited mainly to promoting research and providing technical and financial assistance to the states.

In responding to solid waste disposal problems, state and local governments have taken a variety of approaches. These include developing sanitary landfills, requiring that solid waste be separated into categories that facilitate disposal and recycling, and granting tax breaks for industries using recycled materials. A report by the Council of State Governments noted that thousands of cities and towns recycle solid wastes, usually in the form of household trash-separation requirements.

One recycling success story involves tires. The Scrap Tire Management Council estimates that two-thirds of the nearly 300 million tires discarded annually end up in dozens of retail and industrial products. Companies use recycled tires in indoor flooring, fuel alternatives, playground surfaces, and automobile parts. General Motors, for example, uses recycled rubber in 35 parts along the production line.

The federal government sets no standards for and enforces no rules about general solid waste disposal.

10. TOXIC AND HAZARDOUS SUBSTANCES

According to the opinion research organization Yankelovich, Skelly, and White, the control of toxic and hazardous chemicals "ranks first" on the public's list of where the government's regulation of industry is needed. In the last several years, regulation of such chemicals has been expanding rapidly. We can divide public control of private action in this area into three categories:

Legislation divides the regulation of toxic and hazardous substances into their (1) use, (2) disposal, and (3) cleanup.

- Regulation of the use of toxic chemicals.
- Regulation of toxic and hazardous waste disposal.
- Regulation of toxic and hazardous waste cleanup.

The Problem   Even as the Clean Air and Clean Water Acts are slowly beginning to diminish many types of air and water pollution, attention is being drawn to another environmental problem that is potentially the most serious of all: toxic substances. Hardly a day passes without the news media reporting some new instance of alleged threat to human health and well-being from one or another of the chemical substances so important to manufacturing, farming, mining, and other aspects of modern life.

Threats to human welfare from toxic substances are not new to history. Some scholars have suggested that poisoning from lead water pipes and drinking vessels may have depleted the ranks of the ruling class of ancient Rome and thus contributed to the downfall of the Roman Empire. More recently, some think that the "mad hatters" of the nineteenth-century fur and felt trades likely suffered brain disorders from inhaling the vapors of mercury used in their crafts. Today, however, the problem of toxic substances in the environment is more widespread. More than 70,000 industrial and agricultural chemical compounds are in commercial use, and new chemicals, a significant percentage of which are toxic, are being introduced into the marketplace at the rate of more than 1,000 substances annually.

Toxic Substances Control Act   To meet the special environmental problems posed by the use of toxic chemicals, Congress in 1976 enacted the **Toxic Substances Control Act (TSCA).** Prior to passage of the TSCA, there was no coordinated effort to evaluate effects of these chemical compounds. Some of these compounds are beneficial to society and present no threat to the environment. Some, however, are both toxic and nondegradable, a fact that in the past has been uncovered only after these compounds were introduced into wide use and became important to manufacturing and farming. The primary purpose of the TSCA is to force an early evaluation of suspect chemicals before they become economically important.

Don't forget that the TSCA requires that businesses report to the EPA any information they possess indicating that a chemical presents a *substantial risk* of injury to human health or the environment.

The EPA collects information under TSCA sections that require manufacturers and distributors to report to the EPA any information they possess that indicates a chemical substance presents a *substantial risk* of injury to health or to the environment. The TSCA further demands that the EPA be given advance notice before the manufacture of new chemical substances or the processing of any substance for a significant new use. Based on the results of its review, the EPA can take action to stop or limit introduction of new chemicals if they threaten human health or the environment with unreasonable risks.

The law also authorizes the EPA to require manufacturers to test their chemicals for possible harmful effects. Since not all the 70,000 chemicals in commerce can be tested all at once, the EPA has developed a priority scheme for selecting substances for testing based on whether or not the chemicals cause cancer, birth defects, or gene mutations. Today, only a small fraction of the total chemicals in production use have been safety tested.

In view of the beneficial role that many chemical substances play in all aspects of production and consumption, Congress directed the EPA through the TSCA to consider the economic and social impact, as well as the environmental one, of its decisions. In this respect the TSCA is unlike the Clean Air Act, which requires that certain pollution standards be met without regard for economic factors.

Resource Conservation and Recovery Act   The congressional Office of Technology Assessment reports that more than a ton of hazardous waste per citizen is dumped annually into the nation's environment. A major environmental problem has been how to ensure that the generators of toxic wastes dispose of them safely. In the past, there have been instances where even some otherwise responsible companies have placed highly toxic wastes in the hands of less-than-reputable disposal contractors.

To help ensure proper handling and disposal of hazardous and toxic wastes, Congress in 1976 amended the Solid Waste Disposal Act by the **Resource Conservation and Recovery Act (RCRA).** Under the RCRA, a generator of wastes has two primary obligations:

* To determine whether its wastes qualify as hazardous under RCRA.
* To see that such wastes are properly transported to a disposal facility that has an EPA permit or license.

The EPA lists a number of hazardous wastes, and a generator can determine if a nonlisted waste is hazardous in terms of several chemical characteristics specified by the EPA. The RCRA accomplishes proper disposal of hazardous wastes through the **manifest system.** This system requires a generator to prepare a manifest document that designates a licensed facility for disposal purposes. The generator then gives copies of the manifest to the transporter of the waste. After receiving hazardous wastes, the disposal facility must return a copy of the manifest to the generator. In this fashion, the generator knows the waste has received proper disposal.

Failure to receive this manifest copy from the disposal facility within certain time limits requires the generator to notify the EPA. Under RCRA, the EPA has various investigatory powers. The act also prescribes various record-keeping requirements and assesses penalties for failure to comply with its provisions. The penalties include criminal fines and imprisonment.

As amended, the RCRA is moving the handling of toxic wastes away from burial on land to treatments that destroy or permanently detoxify wastes. Today, RCRA requirements cost business an estimated $20 billion annually.

Do remember how the RCRA regulates the disposal of hazardous and toxic wastes by the manifest system.

In a recent seven-year-period, the Department of Justice at the request of the EPA brought criminal charges against 253 individuals and corporations under the RCRA.

The Superfund   After passage of the TSCA and RCRA in 1976, regulation of toxic and hazardous substances was still incomplete. These acts did not deal with problems of the cleanup costs of unsafe hazardous waste dumps or spills, which are often substantial. Many abandoned dump sites date back as far as the nineteenth century. Even current owners of unsafe dump sites are frequently financially incapable of cleaning up hazardous wastes. Nor are transporters and others who cause spills or unauthorized discharges of hazardous wastes.

In 1980, Congress created the **Comprehensive Environmental Response, Compensation, and Liability Act (CERCLA)** to address these problems. Known as the **Superfund,** this act has allotted billions of dollars for environmental cleanup of dangerous hazardous wastes.

The act requires anyone who releases unauthorized amounts of hazardous substances into the environment to notify the government. Whether it is notified or not, the government has the power to order those responsible to clean up such releases. Refusal to obey can lead to a suit for reimbursement for any cleanup monies spent from the Superfund plus punitive damages of up to triple the cleanup costs. The government can also recover damages for injury done to natural resources. To date, the biggest Superfund case involved Shell Oil and the U.S. Army. These parties agreed to clean up a site outside Denver. Total costs may exceed $1 billion. In 2007, the EPA received private business commitments of $698 million for superfund site cleanups.

*Under the Superfund, those responsible for unauthorized discharges of hazardous and toxic wastes are strictly liable to the government for cleanup costs and damages. Negligence need not be proved.

Liability under Superfund The Superfund imposes strict liability on those responsible for unauthorized discharges of hazardous wastes. No negligence need be proved. Responsible parties have liability when there is a release or threatened release of a hazardous substance that causes response costs. Responsible parties include (1) those who currently or formerly operate or own waste disposal sites, (2) those who arrange for disposal of wastes, and (3) those who transport wastes. Liability includes the costs of **remediation,** which are basically the costs of restoring land to its previous condition.

In Case 18.3, the Supreme Court grapples with who might be an "operator" of a hazardous waste facility. Note that CERCLA itself gives no help in defining the terms *operator* and *owner.*

case **18.3** ::

COOPER INDUSTRIES, INC. v. AVIALL SERVICES, INC.
543 U.S. 157 (2004)

Aviall Services purchased several pieces of land from Cooper Industries. After operating for several years, Aviall discovered that both it and Cooper had contaminated the land with hazardous substances. Aviall notified the state of Texas, but neither the state nor federal governments sued Aviall or officially ordered it to clean up the land. However, Aviall cleaned up the land voluntarily and then sued Cooper for contribution for the cleanup.

The federal district court ruled that section 113(f) of CERCLA did not authorize Aviall to recover contribution under these circumstances. On appeal the Fifth Circuit Court of Appeals reversed the district court. The Supreme Court agreed to decide the case.

THOMAS, J.: Section 113(f) does not authorize Aviall's suit. The first sentence. . . that establishes the right of contribution provides: "Any person *may* seek contribution. . . *during or following* any civil action. The natural meaning of this sentence is that contribution may only be sought subject to the specified conditions, namely, "during or following" a specified civil action.

Aviall answers that "may" should be read permissively, such that "during or following" a civil action is one, but not the exclusive, instance in which a person may seek contribution. We disagree. First, as just noted, the natural meaning of "may" is that it authorizes certain contribution actions—ones that satisfy the subsequent specified conditions—and no others.

Second, if 113(f) were read to authorize contribution actions at any time, then Congress need not have included the explicit "during or following" condition. . . . There is no reason why Congress would bother to specify conditions under which a person may bring a contribution claim, and at the same time allow contribution actions absent those conditions. . . .

We hold that section 113(f) does not support Aviall's suit. We therefore reverse the judgment of the Fifth Circuit and remand the case for further proceedings consistent with this opinion.

Remanded.

:: CASE QUESTIONS

1. Why was contribution not allowed in this case?
2. What should Aviall have done to make sure it could get contribution from Cooper under CERCLA?
3. Anytime you buy a piece of land which may have been used for industrial or commercial purposes, what should you do to help protect yourself from CERCLA liability?

Superfund provisions also allow a purchaser of land forced by a state or federal agency to clean up hazardous substances to recover contribution from former owners, that is, to make them pay some of the cleanup costs. Case 18.3, however, shows a limit on a purchaser's right to force contribution.

Superfund law has caused land purchasers to be very careful in buying land that may contain hazardous wastes. The law makes current as well as former landowners liable for hazardous wastes. The purchaser may escape liability by proving that it is innocent of knowledge of the wastes and has used *due diligence* in checking the land for toxic hazards. But exercising due diligence can be both costly and difficult to prove. Fortunately, the Superfund permits a land purchaser to sue a land seller if the purchaser incurs response costs due to hazardous wastes left by the seller.

Banks and other lenders who take out a security interest (such as a mortgage) in land that turns out to be contaminated and subject to the Superfund are not liable responsible parties. However, if a lender exerts control over a borrower's contaminated land, or assumes ownership of it, the lender will become a responsible party. Many lenders have become very wary about loaning money to borrowers who wish to put up as security land that may be contaminated.

As responsible parties engage in Superfund-required cleanup, they try to pass on the costs to others, often their insurers. In the future insurers may specifically refuse to cover pollution risks in their policies. Some courts, however, have interpreted existing policies to cover waste-cleanup costs as insured-against *damages* arising from an *occurrence,* which includes an *accidental* discharge of pollutants.

> Before buying land, purchasers may wish to hire consultants to evaluate the land for hazardous and toxic substances in order to show *due diligence.*

Reforms to Superfund

The business community has proposed various reforms to the Superfund law. Possible reforms include:

- Prorating liability for companies in Superfund litigation that agree to pay their share of cleanup costs.
- Exempting companies from liability when they have contributed very small amounts of waste at a dump site.
- Permitting dump site cleanups that meet health and safety standards, rather than requiring that the land be returned to a pristine state.

Finally, take note that both the Clean Air Act and the Clean Water Act also contain provisions related to government suits to recover costs for the cleanup of toxic chemicals. Suits under the Superfund and other acts may be a major area of litigation in coming years. The U.S. Office of Technology Assessment estimates that it will require as much as $500 billion during the next 50 years to clean up the nation's hazardous waste sites. However, since 2000 the pace of cleanups has begun to decline. See Sidebar 18.4.

:: *sidebar* 18.4

Superfund in Decline?

Consider the following statistics:

- 646 U.S. toxic waste sites identified by the EPA remained to be cleaned up as of 2003.
- The total number of completed Superfund cleanups in 2001 and 2002 fell 41 percent compared with the annual average in the preceding eight years.
- The $1.3 billion budgeted by Congress for Superfund cleanup in 2003 represented a 36 percent reduction in real dollars from the 1992 level.

- Penalties assessed under the Superfund against toxic waste polluters were down 41 percent in 2001 and 2002 compared with the annual average in the preceding eight years. Cleanup costs recovered from polluters have declined 13 percent.

---

*Overall control of radioactive materials, their use, disposal, and cleanup, rests with the Nuclear Regulatory Commission.

Radiation   In 1979, the nuclear power plant accident at the Three Mile Island installation in Pennsylvania and subsequent evacuation of thousands of nearby residents focused the nation's attention on the potential hazards of radiation pollution. Although no single piece of legislation comprehensively controls radiation pollution and no one agency is responsible for administering legislation in this technologically complex area, overall responsibility for such control rests with the Nuclear Regulatory Commission. The EPA, however, does have general authority to conduct testing and provide technical assistance in the area of radiation pollution control. In addition, the Clean Air Act and the Clean Water Act also contain sections applicable to radiation discharges into the air and water.

:: Suits by Private Individuals

Achieving environmental goals requires coordinated strategy and implementation. As private citizens, individuals and groups of individuals lack both the power and foresight necessary to control pollution on a broad scale. There is a role, however, for the private control of private action in two principal areas:

- Citizen enforcement provisions.
- Tort law.

The following sections examine suits by private individuals that relate to environmental concerns.

concept :: *summary*

An Environmental Alphabet

Environmental and pollution control legislation seems especially given to acronyms. Here's a key.

BAT: best available technology.

BPT: best practicable technology.

CEQ: Council on Environmental Quality.

CERCLA: Comprehensive Environmental Response, Compensation, and Liability Act.

EIS: environmental impact statement.

EPA: Environmental Protection Agency.

FEPCA: Federal Environmental Pesticide Control Act.

NEPA: National Environmental Policy Act.

RCRA: Resource Conservation and Recovery Act.

TSCA: Toxic Substances Control Act.

11. CITIZEN ENFORCEMENT

Most of the environmental laws, such as the Clean Air and Water Acts, contain *citizen enforcement* provisions, which grant private citizens and groups the standing to sue to challenge failures to comply with the environmental laws. In many instances, private citizens can sue polluters directly to force them to cease violating the law. Private citizens also have standing to sue public agencies (for example, the EPA) to require them to adopt regulations or implement enforcement against private polluters that the environmental laws require.

> Private citizens have standing to sue the government or businesses to enforce rules under environmental statutes like the Clean Air Act and the Clean Water Act.

12. TORT THEORIES

A second area of private control of private action lies in tort law and its state codifications. When pollution directly injures private citizens, they may sue offending polluters under various theories of tort law. Thus, the traditional deterrence of tort law contributes to private control of private action. This section further develops tort law's role in pollution control.

Examination of tort law and pollution control reveals little understanding of the interdependence between ourselves and our environment. Instead, tort theories, as they have been applied to environmental problems, focus on the action of one person (or business) as it injures what legally belongs to another. In other words, tort law attacks the pollution problem by using the established theories of nuisance, trespass, negligence, and strict liability.

Nuisance The principal tort theory used in pollution control has been that of **nuisance.** The law relating to nuisance is somewhat vague, but in most jurisdictions the common law has been put into statutory form. Several common elements exist in the law of nuisance in most states. To begin with, there are two types of nuisances: public and private. (See Chapter 7.)

A *public nuisance* arises from an act that causes inconvenience or damage to the public in the exercise of rights common to everyone. In the environmental area, air, water, and noise pollution can all constitute a public nuisance if they affect common rights. More specifically, industrial waste discharge that kills the fish in a stream may be held a public nuisance, since fishing rights are

> *A public nuisance arises from an act that causes inconvenience or damage to the public in the exercise of rights common to everyone.

commonly possessed by the public. Public nuisance actions may be brought only by a public official, not private individuals, unless the latter have suffered some special damage to their persons or property as a result of the public nuisance.

*Any use of one's land that unreasonably interferes with the use or enjoyment of another's land establishes a common law *private nuisance.* Courts measure the unreasonableness of the interference by balancing the character, extent, and duration of harm to the plaintiff against the social utility of the defendant's activity and its appropriateness to its location. Since society needs industrial activity as well as natural tranquillity, people must put up with a certain amount of smoke, dust, noise, and polluted water if they live in concentrated areas of industry. But what may be an appropriate industrial use of land in a congested urban area may be a private nuisance if it occurs in a rural or residential location.

Note that the proving of nuisance does not demand that a property owner be found negligent. An unreasonable *use* of one's land does not mean that one's *conduct* is unreasonable.

**Any use of one's land that unreasonably interferes with the use of enjoyment of another's land constitutes a *private nuisance.*

Other Tort Doctrines

Private plaintiffs in pollution cases frequently allege the applicability of tort doctrines other than that of nuisance. These doctrines, however, do overlap that of nuisance, which is really a field of tort liability rather than a type of conduct.

One such doctrine is that of *trespass.* A defendant is liable for trespass if, without right, she or he intentionally enters land in possession of another or causes something to do so. The entrance is considered intentional if the defendant knew that it was substantially certain to result from her or his conduct. Thus, airborne particles that fall on a plaintiff's property can constitute a trespass. In recent years, many courts have merged the theories of nuisance and trespass to such an extent that before plaintiffs can recover for a particle trespass, they must prove that the harm done to them exceeds the social utility of the defendant's enterprise.

Negligence doctrine is sometimes used by private plaintiffs in environmental pollution cases. The basis for the negligence tort lies in the defendant's breach of his or her duty to use ordinary and reasonable care toward the plaintiff, which *proximately* (foreseeably) causes the plaintiff injury. A factory's failure to use available pollution-control equipment may be evidence of its failure to employ *reasonable care.*

In suing for damages, private plaintiffs (as opposed to the government) often base their lawsuits on tort doctrines of (1) trespass, (2) negligence, or (3) strict liability for ultrahazardous activity.

Finally, some courts recognize the applicability in pollution cases of *strict liability* tort doctrine. This tort liability arises when the defendant injures the plaintiff's person or property by voluntarily engaging in ultrahazardous activity that necessarily involves a risk of serious harm that cannot be eliminated through the exercise of the utmost care. No finding of *fault,* or *failure of reasonable care,* on the defendant's part is necessary. This doctrine has been employed in situations involving the use of poisons, such as in crop dusting and certain industrial work, the storage and use of explosives, and the storage of water in large quantities in a dangerous place.

Increasing numbers of private plaintiffs are suing companies for pollution-related harm. In one case, residents in northeast Denver, Colorado, sued Asarco, Inc., for environmental property damage caused by its smelter. Asarco settled the suit for $35 million. Not all pollution, however, comes from smokestacks. In agricultural states like Iowa and North Carolina, tort suits arise because of pollution from agricultural production. For example, plaintiffs have sued because of brain damage alleged to be caused by hydrogen sulfide, a by-product of waste from pork production.

:: Trends in Environmental Regulation

A *Wall Street Journal*/NBC News survey suggests strong nationwide support for environment cleanup. A 61 percent majority favored more government regulation of the environment. Only 6 percent thought there should be less environmental regulation.

Public and business awareness of environmental issues has significantly increased. At the World Economic Forum, 650 business and government leaders ranked the environment as the greatest challenge facing business. Yet in a recent poll only 36 percent of Americans responded that business is doing an adequate job of keeping the environment clean.

13. AREAS OF ENVIRONMENTAL CONCERN

Researchers almost daily report new instances of how industry and technology affect life on our planet. For every allegation of pollution-caused environmental harm, however, countertheories maintain that the harm is not as significant as alleged or argue that the harm arises from causes unrelated to industrial pollution. Lack of unanimous scientific opinion on many environmental issues underscores their great complexity. It also reveals a key controversy at the heart of environmental regulation: *How much certainty of harm is required to justify regulatory intervention?*

Don't forget that the environment is extremely complex and our understanding of the impacts of pollution on the environment is only partial.

Loss of Natural Ecosystems A report signed by 1,575 scientists, including 100 Nobel Prize winners, warned of the effects of worldwide destruction to natural ecosystems, the cutting of rainforests being the most widely publicized destruction. The report concluded: "If not checked, many of our current practices put at serious risk the future that we wish for human society and the plant and animal kingdoms, and may so alter the living world that it will be unable to sustain life in the manner that we know." At risk in the next 30 years are up to 20 percent of the planet's species of animals and plants.

Ozone In 1990, 59 countries agreed to stop producing certain chemicals that destroy the Earth's protective *ozone layer* of the atmosphere. The agreement required participating countries to stop production of certain chlorofluorocarbons and halons by the year 2000. Destruction of the ozone layer could lead to hundreds of thousands of cases of cataracts and skin cancer in humans plus unknown serious damage to animals and plants.

As of 2008, these forms of ozone-destroying chemicals are no longer in production. However, a new threat to the ozone has emerged. Air conditioning that uses chemicals that reduce ozone is increasing rapidly in the developing world, especially in India and China, which together have a third of the world's population. New air conditioning installations in India and China are growing at the rate of 25 percent to 30 percent annually.

:: *sidebar* 18.5

Mass Extinction and Its Consequences

Human alterations of the environment are causing a mass extinction of 30–50,000 animal and plant species per year. In the past, most extinctions have occurred after meteorites or comets smashed into the Earth, but the present extinction arises from our own making, mostly from our slashing and burning of tropical rain forests.

Every week we clear an area of the tropical rain forests the size of Rhode Island for lumber, cattle raising, and agricultural uses, including large-scale agriculture that involves companies from the developed economies of Europe and the United States; annually, an area twice the size of Florida vanishes.

Tropical rain forests are an important part of the natural life-support system of the planet, removing carbon dioxide from the atmosphere, and generating a large portion of the oxygen that we breathe. In addition, by destroying entire unique species of animals and plants found in profusion in the rain forests, we lose the genetic information they possess to produce compounds that are useful to people. At least 25 percent of all medicines contain ingredients from the rain forests, and 70 percent of plants known to have anticancer properties (1,430 species) are found in the rain forest. There are likely many more such species. Because a full cataloging of rain forest species is not complete, we do not even know the full amount of patentable genetic information that we are destroying. By the mass extinction of animals and plants through the destruction of rain forests, we lose an irreplaceable library of information with potentially significant benefit to human health and life.

*Source: Contributed by Adam J. Sulkowski, University of Massachusetts Dartmouth.

Rising levels of greenhouse gases might triple the number of Category 5 hurricanes. Source: *Journal of Climate* (2004).

Without ratification of the Kyoto Protocol, global temperature will rise about one degree Celsius by 2050. Even after ratification, the temperature may still rise .94 degrees. Source: United Nations Intergovernmental Panel on Climate Change.

Greenhouse Effect   Overshadowing even ozone destruction as a future pollution concern are increasing atmospheric concentrations of carbon dioxide. The National Academy of Sciences notes that global carbon dioxide levels have increased 6 percent since 1960. The increase is due largely to the burning of fossil fuels such as oil and coal.

Higher carbon dioxide levels will likely lead to warmer global temperatures, the so-called *greenhouse effect*. The last decade has had many of the warmest years on record, and atmospheric scientists believe the rise in global carbon dioxide levels was the cause. Changing climatic patterns and rising sea levels are possible results. The Artic ice cap has shrunk by nearly half in the last 50 years. Carbon dioxide in the atmosphere has reached its highest concentration in the atmosphere in the last 650,000 years.

In 1997 delegates from 150 nations reached a treaty to reduce emission of various greenhouse gases such as carbon dioxide. Under the Kyoto Protocol industrialized nations, including the United States, would lower greenhouse gas emission below 1990 levels. However, the United States had not ratified the Kyoto Protocol as of 2008, and the Bush Administration observed that the developing countries of the world did not have to lower their emissions under the protocol, which would place production in the United States at a disadvantage in global markets by having to compete with nations that did not have to observe emission limitations. The reduction in the burning of fossil fuels—coal and oil—necessary to lower greenhouse gas levels might seriously impact the economy. Business production might also relocate in developing countries like China and India, which the Kyoto Protocol does not require to reduce greenhouse gas emission.

Almost everyone advocates international economic growth as a way of lifting the world's poor from poverty. Yet high-income countries use four to five times as much energy (mostly from polluting fossil fuels like coal and oil) as developing countries. According to the International Energy Agency, in 2005 the United States produced per person nearly two and one-half times the greenhouse gases of the European Union, but five times that of the Chinese, and nearly twenty times that of Indians.

Fifteen percent of the world's population uses more than half of its polluting energy. If all nations in the world consume polluting energy at the same rate as high-income nations, what will be the impact on global warning? One thing seems likely. In the words of Nobel laureate economist Thomas Schelling: "In the 21st century, greenhouse gas emissions, global warming, and climate change is going to be the biggest diplomatic issue there is."

Population Growth The world's population continues to grow. According to a Johns Hopkins University study, if human fertility rates do not drop to roughly two children per woman—merely replacing people who die—the world's population will rise to eight billion by 2025 from its current level of five and a half billion. Concerns about pollution, climate change, and even food production are magnified by population growth, yet birth control raises controversial cultural and religious issues. As a business student, you must be aware of and appreciate the significance of population growth because during your career the social and environmental problems associated with such growth will rise.

> "Without substantial participation by developing economies, greenhouse gas emissions will continue to rise rapidly over the next 50 years even if the U.S. and other developed economies cut emissions to zero."
>
> **–James L. Connaughton, Chair, White House Council on Environmental Quality, 2008**

14. CORPORATE GOVERNANCE AND THE ENVIRONMENT

Concerned about the environment, some investors are turning to corporate governance as a way to make polluting industries more environmentally sensitive. Boards of directors legally control the activities of corporations, but shareholders who own these businesses elect the boards of directors. Increasingly, shareholders are presenting resolutions at the annual meetings of corporations to encourage or require the directors and managers of major polluting industries to analyze and report on certain environmental issues.

In 2008, shareholders filed 54 global warming shareholder resolutions. Pension funds, labor organizations, various foundations, and religious and environmental groups were behind most of the resolutions. Many of the investors belong to the Institutional Network on Climate Risk that controls more than $5 trillion in assets. Each year, a substantial number of these shareholder resolutions are withdrawn when businesses agree to make environmentally friendly changes in their operations.

15. PRIVATE PROPERTY AND THE ENVIRONMENT

Considering the human impact on the natural world, does the existence of exclusive private ownership of resources help or hurt the environment? Theory and practice suggest that improper use of common resources causes more environmental problems than does improper use of private resources. Garrett Hardin called this the "tragedy of the commons." People tend to misuse and waste resources that are common to all, like air, water, and public land. They are more careful with their own private resources. Destruction of the world's rain forests is occurring mainly on public or unowned lands. Overall, then, private ownership contributes to a wiser, less wasteful use of resources than do other ways of using resources.

However, exceptions to the general rule do occur. For instance, species of plants and animals that have little immediate market value suffer even on private land. And some companies dump toxic substances that will be hazardous for generations even on their own land. Some landowners have challenged environmental regulation and zoning as a governmental "taking" of private property without "just compensation," which the Fifth Amendment expressly prohibits. The Supreme Court has ruled that land regulation is not a taking that must be compensated as long as an owner is allowed a "reasonable" use of the land. If a law like the Endangered Species Act is applied to prohibit any building on a piece of land, has there been a "taking"? What do you think?

Remember that "property" includes the concept of the equal right of others. In a strong property system, owners cannot use their land or other resources in ways that harm the resources of others, including the resource that others have in their health. The problem is how does the law define "the equal right of others"? Traditional tort law simply does not deal well with pollution harms that occur over long distances or across many years. It is too difficult to prove that the pollution caused the harm. So the government steps in and sets pollution limits that are themselves controversial.

Note that the emissions trading approach to pollution management is a property approach. Granting private owners an exclusive right to sell a quantity of pollution emission to a buyer is the essence of the exclusionary right of property. The world is heading toward increased emissions trading. Imagine in the future that an international treaty sets acceptable emission levels for greenhouse gases and companies worldwide bid for permits to engage in such pollution. What if everyone on earth were considered to own an equal right to engage in greenhouse pollution and proceeds from the emissions auction were distributed to the countries of the world on a population proportional basis?

:: Key Terms

:: Review Questions and Problems

Government's Regulations of Itself

1. *The National Environmental Policy Act*

    (a) Your firm has been hired to build a large government facility near a residential neighborhood. A committee of residents has been formed to oppose the building. You have been asked to assist in writing the EIS. What factors must your EIS take into consideration?

    (b) The Avila Timber Company has asked for and been granted permission by the Department of the Interior to cut 40 acres of timber from the 10,000-acre Oconee National Forest. Prior to the actual logging, a local environmental group files suit in federal district court, contending that the Department of the Interior has not filed an EIS. Can the group challenge the department's action? Analyze whether an EIS should be filed in light of the facts given.

2. *Evaluation of Environmental Impact Statements*

    Outline criticisms of the EIS process. Why are state EISs often less helpful in evaluating complex environmental factors than are those prepared by federal agencies?

Government's Regulation of Business

3. *The Environmental Protection Agency*

    Explain the function of the EPA.

4. *Air Pollution*

    The Akins Corporation wishes to build a new smelting facility in Owens County, an area where air pollution exceeds primary air quality standards.

    (a) What legal difficulties may Akins face?

    (b) What solutions might you suggest for these difficulties?

5. *Clean Air Act Today*

    (a) What is the difference between an individual point-source approach and a bubble-policy approach to dealing with factory pollution?

    (b) For the factory owner, what are the advantages of employing the bubble concept?

6. *Water Pollution*

    Explain the concept of "navigable waterway" and how it is related to the Clean Water Act.

7. *Endangered Species Act*

    How does the ESA apply to private businesses? Explain.

8. *Pesticide Control*

    Before beginning the manufacture of a new pesticide, what process must a company follow under the pesticide-control acts?

9. *Solid Waste*

    (a) Who has the primary responsibility for nontoxic solid waste disposal?

    (b) Describe the role of the Solid Waste Disposal Act in waste disposal.

10. *Toxic and Hazardous Substances*

  (a) As a manufacturer of paints, you need to dispose of certain production by-products that are highly toxic. Discuss the process the law requires you to follow in disposing of these products.

  (b) An abandoned radioactive waste site is discovered by local authorities. The waste came from a company that manufactured radium watch faces and is now out of business. Who will pay to clean up these radioactive wastes? Discuss.

Suits by Private Individuals

11. *Citizen Enforcement*

  Explain the standing to sue doctrine as it applies to the citizen enforcement of federal pollution laws.

12. *Tort Theories*

  Several years ago, the Spul Chemical Corporation built a new plant near your neighborhood. About once a month clouds of odorous mist have passed across your property, your children have complained of skin rashes, and you have heard that the water table has been contaminated with toxic chemicals. You and your neighbors are fearful of health hazards from the plant, and the neighborhood property values have dropped significantly. Explain possible tort causes of action you may have against the chemical company.

Trends in Environmental Regulation

13. *Areas of Environmental Concern*

  Give examples of why a key controversy at the heart of environmental regulation concerns how much certainty of harm is required to justify regulatory intervention.

14. *Corporate Governance and the Environment*

  How have shareholder groups tried to make environmental concerns relevant to corporate governance?

15. *Private Property and the Environment*

  Explain what it means to say that "emissions trading has propertitized pollution."

1. You are senior project manager for Superior Paper, Inc., a paper processing company with plants in several states. Recently, you have been given responsibility for overseeing the construction of a new plant in High Top, Tennessee, on the edge of the Talladega National Forest. You must also secure a lease from the U.S. Department of the Interior to harvest timber on federal land. Although many residents welcome the new jobs your company will create, others have moved into the area for its natural beauty and are mounting a campaign to keep out new development.

What environmental laws will apply to the new plant construction?

What environmental law will have to be followed as you seek to get the national forest lease?

What steps should you take to maintain good community relations?

2. International Paint Company wants to sell a large tract of land with several facilities on it to U.S. Parts, Inc. As acquisitions manager for U.S. Parts, what do you need to know before buying this land, other than that International Paint has good ownership, that your company needs the site, and that the price is right?

Why might you need to know the environmental condition of the land?

What steps might you want to take before buying the land?

Part FIVE

:: Employment Relationships

This final section of the text discusses the complexity of employment relationships. Consistent with the property theme of this text, the labor and employment laws affect the property interest you have in selling your labor. As you study these chapters, consider the historical development of employment law, as well as how labor and employment law must continually evolve to address technology developments, changing social values, and economic issues affecting the workplace. Labor and employment laws reflect the constant need for balance between the rights and responsibilities of employers and employees.

An important threshold issue is to understand that a business acts through its employees. The first part of Chapter 19 discusses how agency law holds business organizations responsible for the acts of thier agents/employees. The second part of this chapter details major employment laws, including the rules regarding minimum wages and overtime, as well as the limits of employee privacy at work. The scope and limits of the employment-at-will doctrine are also presented, along with ways an employer can protect itself from an unjustified employee lawsuit.

Because the United States enjoys a diverse population, it is important to ensure that there is not discrimination at work, including in the hiring, promoting, and firing of employees. Chapter 20 reviews federal laws prohibiting workplace discrimination, specifically discussing the prohibitions on employment discrimination based on race, sex, national origin, color, pregnancy, age, and disabilities. This chapter focuses on what constitutes illegal discrimination in the workplace, including employment practices—even those that may seem well-intentioned on their face—that may be challenged as discriminatory. In addition to federal protections, you should also consider state laws that may offer additional protection against workplace discrimination. These laws form the framework for fair competition in the workplace free of unlawful discrimination.

The third chapter in this section, Chapter 21, focuses on labor laws that permit employees to organize their labor resources through unions. Unions still play an important role in the U.S. labor market, and the development of labor law in the U.S. illustrates the long history of seeking to protect workers. This chapter presents the major labor laws and helps students to identify unfair labor practices by management and unions. The chapter also discusses current issues important to unions. Many unions maintain active political agendas on behalf of their members, including the role of being high-profile advocates during political elections and on labor-related topics such as international trade. Labor advocates are very vocal about the kinds of provisions that could be incorporated in free trade agreements to allow U.S. workers to compete on a level international playing field. For example, a number of free trade agreements discussed in Chapter 13, in particular NAFTA and DR-CAFTA, faced vocal opposition from labor unions.

19

Agency and Employment Laws

Learning Objectives ::

In this chapter you will learn:

1. To understand how business organizations are held responsible for their agents' acts.

2. To identify major employment laws and their significance for employers and employees.

3. To explain the scope and limits of the employment-at-will doctrine.

4. To discuss ways an employer can protect itself from an unjustified employee lawsuit.

How does a company become liable to customers, shareholders, and other parties? When is a company liable for the acts of its employees? How does a company enter into a contract? The answers are found in agency law. The first part of this chapter discusses the major principles of agency law. The second part of the chapter surveys a number of important employment laws. As you study this chapter, consider the historical development of employment law. Later, as you read Chapter 20 (detailing employment laws addressing discrimination) and Chapter 21 (explaining the labor-management relationship), also consider how these laws contribute to the framework of employment and labor law in the United States. The changes in employment law detailed in these three chapters reflect the complexity of the employer-employee relationship. Labor and employment law is continually evolving to address workplace issues prompted by technology developments, changing social values, and economic issues.

:: Principles of Agency Law

Business organizations cannot accomplish anything without the assistance of individuals. An accounting firm does nothing as an organization. The work of the firm is done through the accountants and other employees. Likewise, as a corporation, Enron did not generate value or destroy fortunes. The corporate directors, officers, and employees did all the positive and destructive acts associated with the name Enron.

The people who get the work done are called *agents,* and the principles presented below are referred to as *agency law.* The concepts presented in the next four sections form the fundamentals of how business is transacted.

1. TERMINOLOGY

The application of agency law involves the interaction among three parties. Although individuals usually are these parties, agency relationship can involve business organizations. Figure 19.1 illustrates a three-step approach to understanding how the law views the purpose of agency relationship.

> Organizations deal with third parties through the actions of agents.

First, a **principal** interacts with someone (or some organization) for the purpose of obtaining that second party's assistance. This second party is the **agent.** Principals hire agents to do tasks and represent them in transactions. All employees are agents of the employer/principal, but not all agents are employees. For example, a principal may hire an **independent contractor** to perform a task. Principals do not directly control independent contractors and independent contractors generally work for more than one principal. Examples of independent contractors include attorneys (other than in-house counsel), outside accountants and subcontractors hired to perform construction projects. The nature of their relationship with the principal determines whether employees or independent contractors have authority to contractually bind the principal.

Next, the agent (on behalf of the principal) interacts with a **third party.** Third, the usual legal purpose of the agent is to create a binding relationship between the principal and third party. Typically, the agent wants Step 3 to involve the understanding that any liability created by Steps 1 and 2 is replaced by the new principal–third party relationship. To accomplish this substitution, the agent must remember to comply with the following duties owed to the principal:

- A duty of loyalty to act for the principal's advantage and not to act to benefit the agent at the principal's expense.
- A duty to keep the principal fully informed.

Figure 19.1
Illustration of the agency relationship

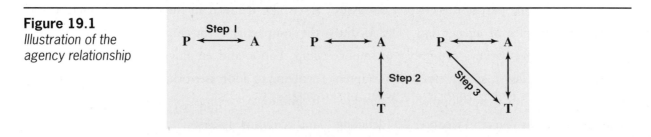

- A duty to obey instructions.
- A duty to account to the principal for monies handled.

In studying the law of agency, keep in mind that the employer/business organization is the principal and the employee is the agent. Whether employee conduct creates liability for the employer is the usual agency issue facing businesses. Such issues may involve either torts or contracts.

2. TORT LIABILITY

The legal elements of a tort are discussed in Chapter 10. For the purpose of this discussion, remember a tort is a breach of a duty that causes injury to a person's property, perhaps the physical body. If you drive your car onto the sidewalk and hit a pedestrian, you are personally liable for the tort of negligence due to your poor driving. Now, suppose the driver was your employee delivering items from your business. Can the injured victim collect damage from you and your business? The answer is found in agency law.

An agent who causes harm to a third party may create legal liability owed by the principal to the third party. The legal test for imposing this "vicarious liability" depends on whether the agent was acting within the scope of employment when the tort occurred. Any time an employee is liable for tortious acts in the *scope of employment*, the employer is also liable. This is because of the tort doctrine of **respondeat superior** ("let the master reply").

Do know when agents are and are not acting within the scope of employment.

The reason for *respondeat superior* is that the employee is advancing the interests of the employer when the tortious act occurs. If the employee is not doing the work, the employer would have to do it. Therefore, the employer is just as liable as the employee when the employee acts tortiously in carrying out the work. In a sense, the employer has set the employee in motion and is responsible for the employee's acts.

Most *respondeat superior* cases involve employee negligence. Note, however, that the employer is strictly liable once the employee's fault is established. And it does not matter that the employer warned the employee against the tortious behavior.

Some *respondeat superior* cases involve an employee's intentional tort. If a store's service representative strikes a customer during an argument over the return of merchandise, the store will be liable under *respondeat superior*. But if the argument concerns football instead of the return of merchandise, the store will not be liable. The difference is that the argument over football is not within the scope of employment.

Usually, the only defense the employer has to the strict liability of *respondeat superior* is that the employee was outside the scope of employment. Sometimes this defense is made using the language **frolic and detour**. An employee who is on a frolic or detour is no longer acting for the employer. If, for example, an employee is driving to see a friend when an accident occurs, the employer is not liable. See Sidebar 19.1 for an example of how this doctrine prompted changes in a company's policy.

An agent on a frolic and detour leaves the scope of employment, and the principal is not liable for the agent's actions.

An employer who must pay for an employee's tort under *respondeat superior* may legally sue the employee for reimbursement. In practice, this seldom happens because the employer carries insurance. Occasionally, an insurer who has paid a *respondeat superior* claim will sue the employee who caused the claim.

The type of business organization in existence determines the extent of responsibility for agents' torts. In essence, partners are liable for all transactions entered into by any partner in the scope of the partnership business and are similarly liable for any partner's torts committed while she or he is acting in the course of the firm's business. Each partner is in effect both an agent of the partnership and a principal, being capable of creating both contract and tort liability for the firm and for copartners and likewise being responsible for acts of copartners. Generally, shareholders of corporations and members of LLCs are protected from tort liability that exceeds the amount of their investment. The details of how organizations attempt to limit liability of its owners are discussed more fully later in this chapter.

:: *sidebar* 19.1

Pizza Delivery: Please Hold the Lawsuits

Years ago, Domino's Pizza promised to deliver a pizza to a customer's door within 30 minutes. If the pizza was not delivered within 30 minutes it was free. (After less-than-scrupulous customers engaged in delay tactics such as shutting off their porch lights to create a delay, Domino's changed the offer to a $3 discount for late pies.) This offer was very popular with customers, but the company ran into trouble after a Domino's delivery person was involved in an auto accident. The injured woman sued the company claiming that its 30-minute pledge led to accidents. Domino's settled the claim for an undisclosed seven-figure sum and scrapped the pledge.

Fourteen years later, Domino's has revived the pledge in a slightly new version: "You Got 30 Minutes." They are not promising delivery in 30 minutes, but trying to tell consumers that they will have 30 minutes of free time if Domino's does the cooking. Will the slogan give Domino's a nostalgic edge in a busy market? The answer is unclear, but executives hope the company can avoid the litigation troubles of the past.

*Source: Janet Adamy, "Will a Twist on an Old Vow Deliver for Domino's Pizza?" *The Wall Street Journal*, December 17, 2007.

---

3. CONTRACTUAL LIABILITY

How is a company bound in a contract? For an employee to bind the employer to a contract negotiated with a third party, the employer must have authorized the employee's actions. Contractual authority can take the following forms:

- Actual authority.
- Expressed, written authority.
- Implied authority.
- Apparent authority.

Only when one of these types of authority is present will the principal and the third party become contractually bound.

> Specific instructions, whether spoken or written, given by an employer to an employee create actual authority.

Actual Authority A simple example helps illustrate the concept of authority. Suppose, as an owner of a restaurant, you hire Alex to be an evening manager. You discover that the restaurant is running low on coffee. You write a note to your friend, Terry, the manager of the local grocery store.

In this note, you ask Terry to allow Alex to charge $100 worth of coffee to your restaurant's account at the grocery store. You give this note to Alex with instructions to purchase the coffee and deliver the note to Terry. If Terry allows Alex to charge $100 worth of coffee, is your restaurant liable to pay $100 to the grocery store? The answer is yes, because Alex had **actual authority**, which was expressed in writing.

Now suppose a week later, you send Alex to the same grocery store to buy pound cake and yogurt. This time you call Terry on the phone and ask that Alex be allowed to charge the cost of the cake and yogurt. Once again, your restaurant is contractually liable to pay for this purchase since Alex was actually authorized to contract through your expressed oral statement to Terry.

Implied Authority What if, sometime later, you and your co-owner are out of town and Alex is in charge of the restaurant for the evening. Alex, realizing that the tuna salad is in short supply, goes to Terry's grocery store and charges to the restaurant $60 worth of tuna fish. Upon your return, you find a bill from Terry for this purchase. Legally, do you have to pay it? Yes. This time Alex's actions contractually bind the restaurant to Terry since Alex had **implied authority** to do what was necessary for the restaurant's benefit. This implied authority arises from the position Alex holds as evening manager and by the history of the express authority situations.

> Implied authority can be inferred from the acts of an agent who holds a position of authority or who had actual authority in previous situations.

Apparent Authority Finally, suppose that you terminate Alex's employment. In retaliation, Alex goes to Terry's grocery store and charges a variety of groceries that are consistent with the food your restaurant serves. When you get the bill from Terry, is the restaurant liable? Answer—yes. Even though Alex lacks any actual (expressed or implied) authority, your failure to notify Terry of Alex's termination left Alex with **apparent authority.** Due to the history of Alex's representing your restaurant, it is reasonable for Terry to assume that this incident is one more in the series of Alex's properly charging items to the restaurant's account. To prevent this unwanted liability from occurring, you should have let Terry know that Alex is no longer employed. This notice destroys the existence of apparent authority.

> Remember to notify third parties if an agent no longer works for you; this notice is essential to cut off apparent authority.

It should be noted that in this last scenario, involving the existence of apparent authority, you would have a claim against Alex for the monies you had to pay Terry. Alex's liability to you arises because Alex breached the duty of loyalty owed to the restaurant.

The basic concepts of agency law apply to the operation of business organizations. Sometimes the law provides technical rules, such as those applicable to how partners can bind their partnership. One such special rule is worthy of mention. A partner in a **trading partnership,** that is, one engaged in the business of buying and selling commodities, has the implied authority to borrow money in the usual course of business and to pledge the credit of the firm. A partner in a **nontrading partnership,** such as an accounting or other service firm, has no implied power to borrow money. In the latter case, such authority must be actual before the firm will be bound.

Ratification What happens when an agent enters into a contract without proper authority? Although the agent does not have the power to bind the principal, the contract may become binding if ratified. **Ratification** occurs when a principal voluntarily decides to honor an agreement, which otherwise would not be binding due to an agent's lack of authority. Returning to the example of the restaurant's evening manager Alex, suppose Alex enters into a contract on behalf of the restaurant to purchase $100,000 worth of kitchen equipment. If Alex had no authority to bind the restaurant, yet you realize that this is a great deal, you could ratify the contract, and follow through with the transaction.

4. CRIMINAL LIABILITY

As with torts and contracts, agents can impose criminal liability on business organizations. Recall from Chapter 12 the variety of ways businesspeople and their organizations can be found criminally responsible. The issue of holding businesses criminally liable has been emphasized by the scandals in the beginning of this century. The repercussions of Enron, WorldCom, HealthSouth, Tyco, and others are still being felt.

:: Employment Laws

A complete review of all laws and regulations that impact how employers and employees interact is beyond our scope. The following sections address some of these laws and examine some current issues arising in many companies. Table 19.1 provides a list of some of the major employment laws and the purpose of each.

Employment laws are among the most emotionally and politically charged topics. The reason tempers flare and even violence happens is that these laws go to the heart of how business makes a profit and how people make a living.

5. MINIMUM WAGES AND MAXIMUM HOURS

The federal government regulates wages and hours through the **Fair Labor Standards Act (FLSA)**. Originally enacted in 1938, the FLSA establishes a minimum wage, overtime pay, record-keeping requirements, and child labor standards. The FLSA has been repeatedly amended to keep it up to date. For example, effective May 25, 2007, the FLSA was amended to increase the federal minimum wage in three steps:

- To $5.85 per hour effective July 24, 2007.
- To $6.55 per hour effective July 24, 2008.
- To $7.25 per hour effective July 24, 2009.

The highest state minimum wages: Washington at $8.02; California and Massachusetts at $8.00 per hour.

Additionally, overtime pay at a rate of not less than one and one-half times the employee's regular rate of pay is required after 40 hours of work in a workweek. For example, if an employee earns $8 an hour, the overtime pay must be at least $12 per hour. Employers of "tipped employees" must pay a cash wage of at least $2.13 per hour if they claim a tip credit against their minimum wage obligation. If the employee's tips combined with the cash *table 19.1* :: Summary of Major Federal Employment Laws

:: Law	:: Purpose
Fair Labor Standards Act (FLSA)	• Provides hourly minimum wage and maximum number of hours before overtime is owed. • Provides restrictions on child labor.
Worker Adjustment and Retraining Notification Act (WARN Act)	• Provides restrictions on plant closings and mass layoffs.
Family Medical Leave Act (FMLA)	• Provides unpaid leave to care for a newborn child, an adopted child, to care for a family member, or for serious health conditions.
Uniformed Services Employment and Reemployment Rights Act (USERRA)	• Provides reemployment rights after performing uniformed service. • Provides those serving in the military the right to be free from discrimination and retaliation based on uniformed service.
Occupational Safety and Health Act (OSHA)	• Provides standards for safe and healthy working environment.
Social Security Act	• Provides unemployment compensation. • Provides disability benefits.
Employment Retirement Income Security Act (ERISA)	• Provides requirements for private pension plans.
Electronic Communications Privacy Act	• Provides standards to protect privacy.
Railway Labor Act, Norris-LaGuardia Act, Wagner Act, Taft-Hartley Act, and Landrum Griffin Act	• Provide national policy for governing the union-management relationship.
Civil Rights Acts, Equal Employment Opportunity Act, Pregnancy Discrimination Act, Americans with Disabilities Act, Age Discrimination in Employment Act, and Genetic Nondiscrimination Act	• Provide national policy governing employment discrimination.

wage do not meet the minimum hourly wage, the employer must make up the difference (with certain conditions). Many states provide for minimum wages higher than the federal rate. Employers are legally required to pay whichever minimum wage is higher. The FLSA does not require breaks or meal periods to be given to workers. Some states, however, may require breaks or meal periods.

Although a minimum wage and a maximum workweek of 40 hours before overtime is owed seems straightforward, there are many exceptions and factual situations complicating the general rules. In Case 19.1, the Supreme Court addresses the legal issue of how an employer is to count work hours. As you read the case, note that the courts count minutes to determine the overall amount in this "donning and doffing" case. In 2008, a Wisconsin federal court certified a similar donning/doffing class-action against Kraft Foods.

IBP, INC. v. ALVAREZ
546 U.S. 21 (2005)

This case actually is the consolidation of two cases. At issue in both cases is the calculation of the workday for the purposes of distinguishing between regular and overtime hours under the Fair Labor Standards Act (FLSA). Both cases involve meat processing companies and whether the employer must count the time workers spend putting on (donning) and taking off (doffing) required protective gear as a part of the workday. Also at issue are the minutes the workers walk from the locker room area to the production area. The Court analyzes the Fair Labor Standards Act and its amendment. Specifically, the Court notes that the Portal-to-Portal Act of 1947 emphasizes that the workday begins when workers engage in their principal activities. This law attempted to make it clear that employers are not liable to pay workers for the time they spend walking on the employers' property from a time clock to the actual workplace or for any time spent in preliminary or postliminary activities to the workers' principal working activities.

STEVENS. J.: . . . IBP, Inc. (IBP), is a large producer of fresh beef, pork, and related products. . . . All production workers must wear outer garments, hardhats, hairnets, earplugs, gloves, sleeves, aprons, leggings, and boots. Many of them, particularly those who use knives, must also wear a variety of protective equipment for their hands, arms, torsos, and legs; this gear includes chain-link metal aprons, vests, Plexiglass armguards, and special gloves. IBP requires its employees to store their equipment and tools in company locker rooms, where most of them don their protective gear.

Production workers' pay is based on the time spent cutting and bagging meat. Pay begins with the first piece of meat and ends with the last piece of meat. Since 1998, however, IBP has also paid for four minutes of clothes-changing time. In 1999, respondents, IBP employees, filed this class action to recover compensation for preproduction and postproduction work, including the time spent donning and doffing protective gear and walking between the locker rooms and the production floor before and after their assigned shifts.

After a lengthy bench trial, the District Court for the Eastern District of Washington held that donning and doffing of protective gear that was unique to the jobs at issue were compensable under the FLSA because they were integral and indispensable to the work of the employees who wore such equipment.

Moreover, consistent with the continuous workday rule, the District Court concluded that, for those employees required to don and doff unique protective gear, the walking time between the locker room and the production floor was also compensable because it occurs during the workday. . . .

The District Court proceeded to apply these legal conclusions in making detailed factual findings with regard to the different groups of employees. For example, the District Court found that, under its view of what was covered by the FLSA, processing division knife users were entitled to compensation for between 12 and 14 minutes of preproduction and postproduction work, including 3.3 to 4.4 minutes of walking time. The Court of Appeals agreed with the District Court's ultimate conclusions on these issues. . . .

IBP does not challenge the holding below that . . . the donning and doffing of unique protective gear are "principal activities" under the Portal-to-Portal Act. . . . Thus, the only question for us to decide is whether the Court of Appeals correctly rejected IBP's contention that the walking between the locker rooms and the production areas is excluded from FLSA coverage by the Portal-to-Portal Act. . . .

IBP emphasizes that our decision in *Anderson v. Mt. Clemens Pottery Co.*, 66 S. Ct. 1187, may well have been the proximate cause of the enactment of the Portal-to-Portal Act. In that case we held that the FLSA mandated compensation for the time that employees spent walking from time clocks located near the plant entrance to their respective places of work prior to the start of their productive labor. In IBP's view, Congress's forceful repudiation of that holding reflects a purpose to exclude what IBP regards as the quite similar walking time spent by respondents before and after their work slaughtering cattle and processing meat. Even if there is ambiguity in the statute, we should construe it to effectuate that important purpose.

This argument is also unpersuasive. There is a critical difference between the walking at issue in *Anderson* and the walking at issue in this case. In *Anderson* the walking preceded the employees' principal activity; it occurred before the workday began. The relevant walking in this case occurs after the workday begins and before it ends. Only if we were to endorse IBP's novel submission that an activity can be sufficiently "principal" to be compensable, but not sufficiently so to start the workday, would this case be comparable to *Anderson*. . . .

For the foregoing reasons, we hold that . . . any walking time that occurs after the beginning of the employee's first principal activity and before the end of the employee's last principal activity . . . is covered by the FLSA.

Barber Foods, Inc. (Barber), operates a poultry processing plant in Portland, Maine, that employs about 300 production workers. These employees operate six production lines and perform a variety of tasks that require different combinations of protective clothing. They are paid by the hour from the time they punch in to computerized time clocks located at the entrances to the production floor.

Petitioners are Barber employees and former employees who brought this action to recover compensation for alleged unrecorded work covered by the FLSA. Specifically, they claimed that Barber's failure to compensate them for (a) donning and doffing required protective gear and (b) the attendant walking and waiting violated the statute.

After extensive discovery, the Magistrate Judge issued a comprehensive opinion analyzing the facts in detail, and recommending the entry of partial summary judgment in favor of Barber. That opinion, which was later adopted by the District Court for Maine, included two critical rulings.

First, the Magistrate held that "the donning and doffing of clothing and equipment required by the defendant or by government regulation, as opposed to clothing and equipment which employees choose to wear or use at their option, is an integral part of the plaintiffs' work [and therefore are] not excluded from compensation under the Portal-to-Portal Act as preliminary or postliminary activities."

Second, the Magistrate rejected petitioners' claims for compensation for the time spent before obtaining their clothing and equipment. Such time, in the Magistrate's view, "could [not] reasonably be construed to be an integral part of employees' work activities any more than walking to the cage from which hairnets and earplugs are dispensed. . . ." Accordingly, Barber was "entitled to summary judgment on any claims based on time spent walking from the plant entrances to an employee's workstation, locker, time clock or site where clothing and equipment required to be worn on the job is to be obtained and any claims based on time spent waiting to punch in or out for such clothing or equipment." . . .

[The Court then reviews the findings of the District Court, which held for Barber, and the 1st Court of Appeals, which affirmed, saying that Barber is not responsible to pay for and count toward the FLSA maximum hours the time the workers spent waiting to put on protective gear, the time these workers spent actually putting on the protective gear, and the time these workers spent walking to the actual work site. Based on the holding in *IBP*, the Court quickly decided the 1st Circuit was wrong with respect to the time workers spent donning and doffing protective gear and walking to and from the locker room and workplace. The Court then concentrates on the issue of how to handle the time workers might spend waiting to get their protective gear.]

Petitioners also argued in the Court of Appeals that the waiting time associated with the donning and doffing of clothes was compensable. The Court of Appeals disagreed, holding that the waiting time qualified as a "preliminary or postliminary activity" and thus was excluded from FLSA coverage by the Portal-to-Portal Act. Our analysis . . . demonstrates that the Court of Appeals was incorrect with regard to the predoffing waiting time. Because doffing gear that is "integral and indispensable" to employees' work is a "principal activity" under the statute, the continuous workday rule mandates that time spent waiting to doff is not affected by the Portal-to-Portal Act and is instead covered by the FLSA.

The time spent waiting to don—time that elapses before the principal activity of donning integral and indispensable gear—presents the quite different question whether it should have the effect of advancing the time when the work-day begins. Barber argues that such predonning waiting time is explicitly covered by the Portal-to-Portal Act, which, as noted above, excludes "activities which are preliminary to or postliminary to [a] principal activity or activities" from the scope of the FLSA.

By contrast, petitioners maintain that the predonning waiting time is "integral and indispensable" to the "principal activity" of donning, and is therefore itself a principal activity. However, unlike the donning of certain types of protective gear, which is always essential if the worker is to do his job, the waiting may or may not be necessary in particular situations or for every employee. It is certainly not "integral and indispensable" in the same sense that the donning is. It does, however, always comfortably qualify as a "preliminary" activity.

We thus do not agree with petitioners that the predonning waiting time at issue in this case is a "principal activity". . . . As Barber points out, the fact that certain preshift activities are necessary for employees to engage in their principal activities does not mean that those preshift activities are "integral and indispensable" to a "principal activity." . . . For example, walking from a time clock near the factory gate to a workstation is certainly necessary for employees to begin their work, but it is indisputable that the

Portal-to-Portal Act evinces Congress's intent to repudiate *Anderson's* holding that such walking time was compensable under the FLSA. We discern no limiting principle that would allow us to conclude that the waiting time in dispute here is a "principal activity," without also leading to the logical (but untenable) conclusion that the walking time at issue in *Anderson* would be a "principal activity" and would thus be unaffected by the Portal-to-Portal Act. . . .

In short, we are not persuaded that such waiting—which in this case is two steps removed from the productive activity on the assembly line—is "integral and indispensable" to a "principal activity" that identifies the time when the continuous workday begins. . . .

For the reasons stated above, we affirm the judgment of the Court of Appeals for the Ninth Circuit. We affirm in part and reverse in part the judgment of the Court of Appeals for the First Circuit, and we remand the case for further proceedings consistent with this opinion.

So ordered.

:: CASE QUESTIONS

1. What is the split between the circuit courts that this case attempts to resolve?
2. Why are companies willing to litigate the issue of what counts and doesn't count as workday activities when so few minutes are likely involved?
3. What three holdings does the Court announce in this case?

The FLSA also sets wage, hours worked, and safety requirements for minors (individuals under age 18). The rules vary depending upon the particular age of the minor and the particular job involved. As a general rule, the FLSA sets 14 years of age as the minimum age for employment, and limits the number of hours worked by minors under the age of 16. In 2008, the FLSA was amended to increase penalties against employers who violate child labor laws. The penalties increased from $11,000 to $50,000 for each FLSA violation leading to the serious injury or death of a child worker. The increased fines are subject to doubling for repeated or willful violations.

6. THE WARN ACT

The WARN notice allows impacted employees and communities some time to prepare for the negative impact of a plant closing or mass layoff.

The Worker Adjustment and Retraining Notification Act (WARN) became law in 1989. Known as the **WARN Act,** this law requires employers to provide notice of plant closings and mass layoffs. This notice must be given in writing and be delivered at least 60 days prior to closing a work site or conducting mass layoffs. The WARN notice must be given to employees or their bargaining representatives (such as a union), the state's dislocated worker unit, and the elected chief officer of the local government impacted.

The WARN notice is required of employers with 100 or more employees. Workers who work less than half-time are not counted to determine this threshold level of 100. Employees entitled to receive the WARN notice include those who are hourly, salaried, supervisory, and managerial. In essence all workers, even part-time, are entitled to receive the notice.

The WARN notice covers plant closings and mass layoffs involving loss of employment. Covered plant closings are defined as the shutting of an employment site resulting in a loss of employment of 50 or more employees during any 30-day period. A mass layoff requires the WARN notice if 500 or more employees lose their jobs in a 30-day period. This notice also must be given if between 50 and 499 employees are laid off if the number terminated make up at least 33 percent of the employer's workforce. Although they are entitled to receive any applicable WARN notice, less than half-time employees are not counted to reach the requirement of 50 for plant closings or the thresholds for mass layoffs. A loss of employment includes (1) termination of employment, (2) layoff exceeding 6 months, or (3) a reduction in an employee's work time of more than 50 percent in each month for six months.

The WARN notice must be provided even if the numbers in the preceding paragraph are not satisfied if there are two or more plant closings or mass layoffs in a 90-day period that when taken together satisfy the threshold numbers. The sale of a business may or may not require the WARN notice. Any required notice prior to the sale being completed is the responsibility of the seller. The buyer of the business assumes this responsibility after the date of the closing.

The penalty for failure to comply with the WARN notice is back pay to employees to cover the required 60-day period. Each day of the 60-day period that an employer fails to provide written notice to the local government can result in a $500 fine.

When an employer is replacing striking employees in large numbers, the WARN notice is not required. Employers may avoid the need to provide 60-day notice if it can show its business is faltering and to give notice of a plant closing would adversely impact its ability to get financing. Also, unforeseen business circumstances may justify a less than 60-day WARN notice for either plant closing or layoffs. Finally, natural disasters, such as storms, floods, and earthquakes, may justify a less than 60-day notice for a plant closing or mass layoff.

> According to the AFL-CIO, "Layoffs continue at a pace of 1.5 million impacted workers every year and almost half a million have been idled by mass layoffs in the first three months" of 2008.

7. THE FAMILY AND MEDICAL LEAVE ACT

On February 5, 1993, Bill Clinton signed his first piece of legislation as president. This was the **Family and Medical Leave Act (FMLA).** While the details of this law have been called burdensome to business, it has provided eligible employees who work for covered employers to take up to 12 weeks of unpaid leave during any 12-month period if one or more of the following events occur:

- Birth and care of a newborn child of the employee.
- Placement with employee of a son or daughter for adoption or foster care.
- Care of an immediate family member with a serious health condition.
- Employee is unable to work due to a serious health condition.

The provisions relating to birth, adoption, and foster care apply to both female and male employees. Increasingly, men are opting to take leave to care for children. See Sidebar 19.2 for FMLA facts and statistics. An immediate family member is a spouse, minor child, or parent of the employee. Under the FMLA, the employee's parents in law do not qualify as an immediate family member. And the employee's children who are over 18 years old do not qualify as an immediate family member, unless that child is incapable of

> "With the Family Medical Leave Act, the United States at last joined more than 150 other countries in guaranteeing workers some time off when a baby is born or a family member is sick."
>
> **—President Bill Clinton in *My Life***

> The parents of a 23-year-old injured so severely in an accident that he is paralyzed are eligible for family medical leave.

self-care due to a mental or physical disability that limits one or more of the major life activities as defined in the Americans with Disabilities Act. For a more thorough discussion of the ADA, see Chapter 20. In 2008, the FMLA was expanded to include leave related to a family member's military service. The law grants employees up to 26 weeks of unpaid leave to care for a family member in the military who has incurred a serious illness or injury, and allows employees to take their current 12-week FMLA leave entitlement "for any qualifying exigency" arising out of the fact that a family member is on or has been notified that he or she is being called to active duty in support of a contingency operation. The Department of Labor has the responsibility of issuing regulations related to these changes, including defining "any qualifying exigency."

:: *sidebar* 19.2

FMLA: Facts and Statistics

:: WHO TAKES FMLA LEAVE?

About 62 percent of workers qualify to take leave under the FMLA.

Over 50 million people have taken FMLA leave.

:: WHY DO PEOPLE TAKE FMLA LEAVE?

To care for their own serious illness: 52 percent.

To care for a seriously ill family member: 31 percent.

To take care of a new child: 26 percent (29 percent women and 23 percent men).

:: HOW HAS FMLA IMPACTED EMPLOYERS?

98 percent of eligible employees return to work for the same employer after returning from FMLA leave.

89 percent of covered businesses report that the FMLA has a neutral or positive effect on employee morale.

90 percent of covered businesses reported that the FMLA had either a neutral or positive effect on business profitability.

*Sources: U.S. Department of Labor's 2000 Report *Balancing the Needs of Families and Employers: Family and Medical Leave Surveys 2000 Update;* Nicole Casta's "Highlights of the 2000 U.S. Department of Labor Report: Balancing the Needs of Families and Employers: Family and Medical Leave Surveys," and the National Partnership for Women & Families' 2005 Report "Facts about the FMLA: What Does It Do, Who Uses It, and How."

> To satisfy the requirement that the employer have 50 employees, all persons who work for the employer within 75 miles can be counted.

Covered employers are those who employ 50 or more employees for each working day of 20 or more calendar weeks during either the current or preceding year. Eligible employees have worked for their employer for at least 12 months and have worked at least 1,250 hours during the preceding 12 months. The 12-month work period does not have to be consecutive months. An employee satisfies this requirement so long as that employee has worked for the employer at least a total of 12 months. Furthermore, eligible employees must work at a location where at least 50 employees are employed.

The FMLA places a number of responsibilities on the employer. These responsibilities include notifying the employees that they are eligible for family medical leave and designating in writing when the employee has requested such leave. The employer may request a medical certification that a qualifying event has occurred in the employee's life, but the employer is not entitled to review the actual medical records of the employee.

Once family medical leave is granted, the employer must keep the employee's job available for when the leave is up and the employee returns to work. In essence, the employee who qualifies for family medical leave is not supposed to be disadvantaged by the fact that the leave was taken. For example, if the employer gives a bonus for perfect attendance, the employee on family medical leave should be awarded this bonus, assuming perfect attendance other than the leave period. If a bonus is based on the amount of sales, the FMLA does not require the employer to award sales that the employee would have made if not on family medical leave.

Employees who believe they have been denied their rights under the FMLA can sue the employer in federal district court for equitable and monetary damages. Such an employee may sue for reinstatement or may seek damages or both.

An international survey of 173 countries revealed that the United States is only one of four countries that does not guarantee any paid leave for new mothers. The other countries are Liberia, Papua New Guinea, and Swaziland. Source: Project on Global Working Families' 2007 Report "Work, Family, and Equity Index."

8. OCCUPATIONAL SAFETY AND HEALTH ADMINISTRATION

Occupational Safety and Health Administration (OSHA) has jurisdiction over complaints about hazardous conditions in the workplace. Employers are required to comply with OSHA standards to furnish a workplace free from recognized hazards. Employees have the right to request an OSHA inspection if they believe that there are unsafe and unhealthful conditions in the workplace. Employees making complaints who are subjected to retaliation or discrimination by their employers may also file a complaint with OSHA. There is no private cause of action under OSHA, which means that an employee cannot sue an employer for damages based on an OSHA violation.

OSHA investigates a wide variety of workplace hazards. For example, following the deaths of 20 workers in 2008 in construction accidents in New York City, OSHA is sending inspectors there in an effort to increase safety and improve working conditions. OSHA inspectors will examine cranes and high-rise construction sites. In addition to the inspections, OSHA sent notices to employers' insurance and workers' compensation carriers. Citations involving training violations at unionized sites will also be sent to the unions representing workers and to their training funds. The U.S. House Education and Labor Committee is reviewing the sufficiency of OSHA's construction enforcement. OSHA is also investigating The Atlanta Ballet following the fall of a 17-year-old dancer wearing a panda costume during a performance of "The Nutcracker" at the Fox Theater in Atlanta. The dancer, who fell about 12 feet into the empty orchestra pit, suffered serious injuries, requiring spinal surgery. OSHA conducted over 38,000 inspections in 2006.

9. PENSION PLANS AND HEALTH CARE

In 1974, Congress passed and President Nixon signed the Employee Retirement Income Security Act (ERISA). This law attempts to protect employees whose employers have voluntary pension plans. These protections include disclosure of information about the management of and fiduciary relationships within the plan. Since ERISA, the federal government has enacted a number of other laws directed at protecting employees' health care. Among these laws are Consolidated Omnibus Budget Reconciliation Act (COBRA), which was passed in 1986, and provides that employees can continue to purchase health insurance even after their employment is terminated. The Health Insurance Portability and Accountability Act (HIPAA) became law in 1996 and protects employees who have preexisting health conditions when they change jobs.

For more details about these laws, visit www. dol.gov/dol/topic/health-plans/erisa.htm#content

During the early part of this century, we have seen a new crisis arising. This involves businesses who are changing their defined-benefit retirement plans to private individual accounts, such as 401(k) plans. A number of companies have gone into bankruptcy and have sought permission to cancel retirement plans. It appears a very real competitive advantage is to be a new company that is not burdened by large pension plans obligations. For example, many of the legacy airlines, such as Delta, United, and Northwest, have gone into and come out of bankruptcy in the hope that they will be competitive with newer airlines, which do not have the large obligation of paying the pensions of thousands of retirees. Sidebar 19.3 provides detail of a major company's changes in pension plans.

:: *sidebar* 19.3

Changes in Pension Plans

IBM announced that beginning in 2008, it would freeze its workers' pension plan and begin offering only 401(k) retirement accounts. This announcement by IBM indicates that even financially healthy companies are moving away from defined-benefit plans, which pay retirement benefits based on the employee's income and years of service. IBM operates the third largest retirement plan with $48 billion in assets. General Electric has the second largest, and General Motors' retirement plan is the largest. This announcement by IBM causes a lot of speculation regarding other companies. Much of the public will watch General Motors with interest since its largest parts supplier, Delphi, already has filed for bankruptcy.

*Source: Mary Williams Walsh, "IBM to Freeze Pension Plans to Trim Costs," *The New York Times*, January 6, 2006.

10. LIMITATIONS ON EMPLOYMENT AT WILL

Historically, unless employees contracted for a definite period of employment (such as for one year), employers were able to discharge them without cause at any time. This is called the **employment-at-will doctrine.**

During the 1930s, employers began to lose this absolute right to discharge employees whenever they desired. The Labor-Management Relations Act prohibited employers from firing employees for union activities. Now, many federal laws limit employers in their right to terminate employees. Table 19.2 provides a listing of some of these laws. Some states also prohibit employers by statute from discharging employees for certain reasons, such as for refusing to take lie detector examinations.

table 19.2 :: Federal Statutes Limiting Employment-at-Will Doctrine	
:: Statute	**:: Limitation on Employee Discharge**
Labor-Management Relations Act	Prohibits discharge for union activity or for filing charges under the act.
Fair Labor Standards Act	Forbids discharge for exercising rights guaranteed by minimum-wage and overtime provisions of the act.
Occupational Safety and Health Act	Prohibits discharge for exercising rights under the act.
Civil Rights Act	Makes illegal discharge based on race, sex, color, religion, or national origin.
Age Discrimination in Employment Act	Forbids age-based discharge of employees over age 40.
Employee Retirement Income Security Act	Prohibits discharge to prevent employees from getting vested pension rights.
Clean Air Act	Prevents discharge of employees who cooperate in proceedings against an employer for violation of the act.
Clean Water Act	Prevents discharge of employees who cooperate in proceedings against an employer for violation of the act.
Consumer Credit Protection Act	Prohibits discharge of employees due to garnishment of wages for any one indebtedness.
Judiciary and Judicial Procedure Act	Forbids discharge of employees for service on federal grand or petit juries.

Courts, too, have begun limiting the at-will doctrine. Under contract theory, several courts have stated that at-will employment contracts (which are not written and are little more than an agreement to pay for work performed) contain an implied promise of good faith and fair dealing by the employer.

Other courts have ruled that the employer's publication of an employee handbook can change the nature of at-will employment. They have held the employer liable for breach of contract for discharging an employee in violation of statements made in the handbook about discharge procedures.

Many contract and tort exceptions to employment at will have involved one of three types of employer behavior:

Do understand that any commitments stated in an employee handbook are viewed by courts as a contractual promise by the employer.

- Discharge of employee for performance of an important public obligation, such as jury duty.
- Discharge of employee for reporting employer's alleged violations of law (whistleblowing). (See Sidebar 19.4 for information about IRS whistleblowers.)
- Discharge of employee for exercising statutory rights.

Most of the cases that limit at-will employment state that the employer has violated *public policy*. What does it mean to say that an employer has violated public policy? Is it a court's way of saying that most people no longer support the employer's right to do what it did?

:: *sidebar* 19.4

IRS Whistleblowers Rewards Program

In 2006, the IRS amended its whistleblower statute to encourage the reporting of tax fraud perpetrated by individuals and corporations. Pursuant to 26 U.S.C. § 7623, whistleblowers have an enforceable right to a reward when they report significant tax violations. A person who provides information regarding tax law violations under the IRS Whistleblower Law is known as a whistleblower. To be eligible to recover compensation from the IRS, a person must bring information to the Internal Revenue Service's attention. The whistleblower may receive compensation only from monies actually collected based on the information provided.

Under the IRS Whistleblower Reform Law, a person can receive a reward of between 15 percent and 30 percent of the total collected proceeds (including penalties, interest, additions to tax, and additional amounts). If the IRS moves forward with an administrative or judicial action based on information brought by a whistleblower, the whistleblower is eligible to receive at least 15 percent and up to a cap of 30 percent of the recovery, depending on the whistleblower's contribution to the prosecution of the action. The IRS may give awards of lesser amounts under certain circumstances (i.e., when the fraud has already been publicly disclosed and the whistleblower is not an original source).

WHAT ARE THE MOST COMMON TAX FRAUD SCHEMES?

- Failing to report income earned in a foreign stock exchange.
- Participating in bogus income tax shelters.
- Hiding or transferring assets or income out of the United States.
- Overstating deductions.
- Making false entries in books and records.
- Claiming personal expenses as business expenses.
- Claiming false deductions.
- Underreporting tip income.
- Paying employees in cash.
- Keeping two sets of books.

Limitations on discrimination and employment at will evidence a growing concern for the rights of employees in their jobs and may suggest a trend that could lead to some type of broad, legally guaranteed job security. In recent years, unions have also increasingly focused on job-security issues in their bargaining with employers.

11. WORKERS' PRIVACY

Don't rely on an expectation of privacy in the workplace; employers may monitor e-mail systems they provide.

Individual privacy is such an important part of individual freedom that both legal and ethical questions regarding privacy are bound to multiply in the computer age. While debate continues concerning the need for further federal privacy legislation, many states have passed their own privacy-related statutes. Several states guarantee workers access to their job personnel files and restrict disclosure of personal information to third parties.

Concerns for individual privacy also contributed to passage of the Electronic Communications Privacy Act of 1986 and the 1988 **Employee Polygraph Protection Act.** Under this latter federal law, private employers generally are forbidden from using lie detector tests while screening job applicants. Current employees may not be tested randomly but may be tested as a result of a specific incident or activity that causes economic injury or loss to an employer's business. The act permits private security companies to test job applicants and allows companies that manufacture or sell controlled substances to test both job applicants and current employees. The Labor Department may seek fines of up to $10,000 against employers who violate the act. Employees are also authorized to sue employers for violating the act.

Another important privacy concern involves drug testing. At present there is no uniform law regarding the drug testing of employees. Many private companies conduct such testing. However, some states have placed some limits on a private company's right to test for drugs.

Public employees are protected from some drug testing by the Fourth Amendment's prohibition against *unreasonable* searches. However, exactly when drug tests are unreasonable is subject to much debate in the courts. In general, public employees may be tested when there is a proper suspicion that employees are using illegal drugs that impair working ability or violate employment rules. Courts have also upheld drug testing as part of required annual medical exams.

> Unlike the U.S., workers in other jurisdictions, such as the European Union, enjoy a much higher expectation of privacy in the workplace.

:: *sidebar* 19.5

Is There Any Reasonable Expectation of Privacy in the Workplace?

There is very little expectation of privacy in the American workplace. For example, of the employers surveyed:

- 73 percent monitored e-mail messages.
- 66 percent monitored Web surfing.
- 48 percent monitored with video surveillance.
- 45 percent monitored keystrokes and keyboard time.
- 43 percent monitored computer files.

Of those employers, a number reported firing employees for violating policies regarding use of the Internet (30 percent), e-mail (28 percent), or phones (6 percent).

*Source: 2007 Electronic Monitoring & Surveillance Survey (released February 2008) by the American Management Association and The ePolicy Institute.

12. EMPLOYEE LAWSUITS

Despite the presence of many examples of the employer's violating an employment law, most employers strive to obey the law. They still risk lawsuits, however, including many brought by unsatisfactory employees who have been disciplined, denied promotion, or discharged. How can employers protect themselves from unjustified employee lawsuits?

One important protection against unjustified employee lawsuits is an established system of adequate documentation. Sometimes called the **paper fortress,** this documentation consists of job descriptions, personnel manuals, and employee personnel files.

Before handing anyone an employment application, the employer should insist that the potential candidate carefully study a job description. A well-written job description will help potential applicants eliminate themselves from job situations for which they lack interest or qualification, thus preventing employers from having to dismiss them later and risking lawsuits.

Once a new employee is hired, the employer should give the employee a personnel manual. This manual should include information about employee benefits and should also outline work rules and job requirements. The employer should go over the manual with the employee and answer any questions. Clear identification of employer expectations and policies helps provide a defense against employee lawsuits if subsequent discipline or discharge of the employee becomes necessary. The employer should ask that the employee sign a form indicating receipt of the manual and an understanding of the employer's explanation of its contents.

The employer should enter this form, with all other documentation relevant to an employee's work history, into the employee's personnel file. Regular written evaluations of employee performance should also be entered into the personnel file. A chronological record of unsatisfactory work performance is a very useful defense against unjustified lawsuits following discipline, denial of promotion, or discharge.

Another piece of documentation that helps justify employer decisions is the written warning. Anytime an employee breaks a work rule or performs unsatisfactorily, the employer should issue the employee a written warning and place a duplicate in the personnel file. The warning should explain specifically what work rule the employee violated. In addition, employers should either have an employee sign that he or she has received a written warning or else note in the personnel file that the employee has received a copy of it. The employer should also give the employee the opportunity to place a letter of explanation in the personnel file.

Laws discussed in this chapter and the next one should not prevent employers from discharging unsatisfactory employees. In an actual termination conversation, however, the employer should provide the employee with specific reasons for discharge, taken from the personnel file. Detailed documentation is vital in successfully responding to unjustified employee lawsuits. Even better is to prevent them in the first place through the development, enforcement, and review of company policies that promote legal compliance.

See Sidebar 19.6 for practical suggestions for employers to prevent employee lawsuits.

> Taking any disciplinary action without documentation fails to build the record for increased sanctions in the future.

:: *sidebar* 19.6

What Can Employers Do to Avoid Employment Litigation?

There are a number of steps that employers can take to avoid employment litigation, including:

- Implementing workplace policies and procedures, and training employees to understand the rules and apply them consistently. The policies should cover how to prevent sexual harassment and other forms of discrimination and how to report the same.

- Conducting regular candid performance evaluations, with clear feedback to employees.

- Investigating all complaints thoroughly, never taking any adverse action against persons making honest complaint.

- Documenting all employee incidents, including disciplinary issues and other problems, in each employee's personnel file.

- Being fair and objective when dealing with employees. Being upfront and honest about action taken in the workplace, including termination, helps employees understand the rationale for the action.

Keep these practical suggestions in mind as you study discrimination in Chapter 20, and realize how many workers could potentially assert one or more discrimination claims against their employer.

:: Key Terms

:: Review Questions and Problems

Principles of Agency Law

1. *Terminology*
   (a) What are the names given to the three parties typically involved in an agency relationship?
   (b) Describe the general purpose of the agency relationship.

2. *Tort Liability*

   Tammy was shopping in Save-a-Lot Grocery Store when Stewart, an employee, brushed Tammy's ankle with a grocery cart. A short time later, while still shopping, Tammy told Stewart that he should say "Excuse me," and then people would get out of his way. Stewart then punched Tammy in the face, knocking her to the floor. If Tammy sues Save-a-Lot, what legal issue must be addressed to determine whether Save-a-Lot is liable?

3. *Contractual Liability*

   For several years, Albert acted as a collection agent for Paulette. Recently, Paulette revoked Albert's authority to collect payments from customers. However, neither Paulette nor Albert told any customers of Albert's termination. Yesterday, Theresa, one of Paulette's customers, paid Albert the money owed to Paulette. Albert never gave this money to Paulette. Is Theresa liable to pay Paulette? Why or why not?

4. *Criminal Liability*

   Describe how business organizations can be found criminally responsible for their actions. What is the way such organizations are punished?

Employment Laws

5. *Minimum Wages and Maximum Hours*
   (a) What federal law establishes the minimum wage and the hours in a work week?
   (b) What is the minimum wage and what is considered the maximum work week?
   (c) What is required regarding overtime compensation or time off?

6. *The WARN Act*
   To show your understanding of the WARN notice, answer these questions:
   (a) Who are the covered employers?
   (b) What format is required for a WARN notice?
   (c) When must the WARN notice be given?
   (d) To whom must the WARN notice be delivered?

7. *The Family and Medical Leave Act*
   In the sixth month of her pregnancy, Suzanne was advised by her doctors to slow down the hectic pace of her consulting career. Upon this advice, Suzanne requested and was granted by

her employer 12 weeks of medical leave. During the tenth week of this leave, Suzanne had a healthy baby. How much family leave is Suzanne entitled to take under the FMLA to care for her newborn?

8. *Occupational Safety and Health Administration*

   Larry, a machine operator, is concerned that the cardboard baler he is working on should have a safety shield to protect his arms from the moving parts. He is also worried that if he reports his concerns, he will be put on the night shift. What should he do? Does he have any protection if he reports the issue?

9. *Pension Plans and Health Care*

   Why has the aging of the "baby boom" generation put so much pressure on the financial stability of historically successful companies?

10. *Limitations on Employment at Will*

    Terry was hired as an assistant manager by the Assurance Manufacturing Company. There was no specific time period related to Terry's employment. During Terry's first day at work, the personnel director of Assurance gave Terry a copy of the employee's handbook. In this handbook, Assurance stated that no employee would be terminated without a justifiable explanation. Five months after beginning work at Assurance, Terry was notified that after an additional two weeks there would be no further job for Terry at Assurance. When Terry asked why this termination was occurring, the personnel director told Terry, "Under state law no reason for termination has to be given. In essence, you are an employee only for as long as Assurance desires." What is the best argument Terry can make that the employment-at-will doctrine is not applicable in this situation? Explain.

11. *Workers' Privacy*

    John Hancock Life Insurance Company instructed its employees to create passwords to protect their e-mail accounts. Employees also were told to create personal folders for messages they send and receive. After a company investigation, Nancy and Joanne were terminated as John Hancock employees for using their e-mail accounts to send sexually explicit messages. These employees sued John Hancock for wrongful discharge on the basis that the company's investigation had violated their rights of privacy. Was John Hancock entitled to examine these employees' e-mail accounts?

12. *Employee Lawsuits*

    (a) What is meant by the phrase "paper fortress"?
    (b) How does maintaining a paper fortress aid the employer when the employee claims unfair treatment?

1. Bob, a sales manager for BuyMore, stopped by The Grill to meet a client for dinner. Bob always enjoyed having an expensive bottle of wine with dinner as a way of impressing his clients. This particular client, Mary, who owns an antique import business, is well traveled and really appreciated the fine French wine that Bob ordered. Because the service was so slow, the wine was gone before they received their entrees. Not wanting to appear cheap, Bob ordered another bottle of wine. During dinner, Bob offered to sell Mary a hundred shipping crates for $500 each. Mary readily agreed, knowing that this was an incredible deal. They both signed the contract Bob had prepared in advance. On his way home, Bob stopped to see his girlfriend. When he was telling her about the evening, Bob suddenly realized that $500 would barely cover the cost of the crates. Distraught at the thought of no commission, Bob immediately left for home. On the way, he ran a stop sign and hit an oncoming car, seriously injuring the driver.

> What kind of liability does BuyMore have for Bob's actions?
>
> Was a valid contract formed, binding BuyMore?
>
> What kind of liability does Bob face personally?

2. You just had one of those days—exciting and overwhelming. As your company's director of human relations, you have dealt with an employee asking how much leave he can take when his wife has their first baby next month. A phone call from the company's CFO involved discussions of potential layoffs in order to "make the budget." A group of employees came to meet with you, and they indicated they were talking with union organizers as a way to combat the company's policy of monitoring phone calls and e-mail messages. Another group of employees expressed their feelings that they were not being paid for all the time they worked.

Before heading home, you take a few minutes to reflect and ask yourself the following questions:

> How is the workday calculated?
>
> What legal requirements have to be met before layoffs can occur?
>
> What is the company's responsibility to educate employees about their rights under the Family and Medical Leave Act?
>
> Can your company properly monitor its employees' phone calls and e-mail messages?

20

Discrimination in Employment

Learning Objectives ::

In this chapter you will learn:

1. To list the federal laws prohibiting workplace discrimination.

2. To discuss the general provisions of Title VII and enforcement procedures.

3. To understand what constitutes illegal discrimination in the workplace, including employment practices that may be challenged as discriminatory.

4. To realize that state laws may also offer additional protection against workplace discrimination.

Laws prohibiting discrimination exist at both the federal and state levels. The opening sections of the chapter focus on antidiscrimination laws at the federal level. The Civil Rights Act of 1964 (including its amendments) is the principal such law. It prohibits certain discrimination based on race, sex, color, religion, and national origin. Other antidiscrimination laws covered are the Equal Pay Act, the Civil Rights Act of 1866 (called *Section 1981*, referring to its federal code designation), the Age Discrimination in Employment Act, Americans with Disabilities Act, and the Uniformed Services Employment and Reemployment Act. The chapter concludes with a discussion of trends in employment discrimination litigation and a section on employment discrimination, corporate governance, and the broad sense of property.

:: THE CIVIL RIGHTS ACT OF 1964

"That all men are created equal" was one of the "self-evident" truths recognized by the Founding Fathers in the Declaration of Independence. However, equality among all our citizens clearly has been an ideal rather than a fact. The Constitution itself recognizes slavery by saying that slaves should count as "three fifths of all other Persons" for determining population in House of Representatives elections. And of course, that all *men* are created equal says nothing about women, who did not even get a constitutionally guaranteed right to vote until 1920.

Historically, common law permitted employers to hire and fire at will. At-will employment still applies today unless modified by legislation.

Nowhere have effects of inequality and discrimination been felt more acutely than in the area of job opportunity. Historically, common law permitted employers to hire and fire virtually at will, unless restrained by contract or statute. Under this system, white males came to dominate the job market in their ability to gain employment and their salaries and wages.

Although the Civil Rights Act of 1866 contains a provision that plaintiffs now widely use in employment discrimination cases, such use is relatively recent. Passage of labor law in the 1920s and 1930s marks the first significant federal limitation on the relatively unrestricted right of employers to hire and fire. Then, in connection with the war effort, President Franklin D. Roosevelt issued executive orders in 1941 and 1943 requiring a clause prohibiting racial discrimination in all federal contracts with private contractors. Subsequent executive orders in the 1950s established committees to investigate complaints of racial discrimination against such contractors. Affirmative action requirements on federal contracts followed from executive orders of the 1960s.

The most important statute eliminating discriminatory employment practices, however, is the federal Civil Rights Act of 1964, as amended by the Equal Employment Opportunity Act of 1972, the Pregnancy Discrimination Act of 1978, and the Civil Rights Act of 1991.

1. GENERAL PROVISIONS

Don't forget that a defense to intentional discrimination is that such discrimination is a BFOQ.

The provisions of Title VII of the Civil Rights Act of 1964 apply to employers with 15 or more employees, labor unions, and certain other employers. The major purpose of these laws is to eliminate job discrimination based on race, color, religion, sex, or national origin. Discrimination for any of these reasons is a violation of the law, except that employers, employment agencies, and labor unions can discriminate on the basis of religion, sex, or national origin where these are **bona fide occupational qualifications (BFOQs)** reasonably necessary to normal business operations. Title VII also permits discrimination if it results unintentionally from a seniority or merit system.

According to the Seventh Circuit Court of Appeals, denial of overtime can constitute an adverse employment action sufficient to trigger Title VII.

The types of employer action in which discrimination is prohibited include:

- Discharge.
- Refusal to hire.
- Compensation.
- Terms, conditions, or privileges of employment.

Employment *agencies* are prohibited from either *failing to refer* or from *actually referring* an individual for employment on the basis of race, color, religion, sex, or national origin. This prohibition differs from the law binding *employers,* where it is unlawful only to fail or refuse to hire on discriminatory grounds—the affirmative act of hiring for a discriminatory reason is apparently not illegal. For example, assume that a contractor with a government contract seeks a qualified African American engineer and requests an employment agency to refer one. The agency complies with the request. Unless a white applicant was discriminated against, the employer likely did not break the law; but the employment agency, by referring on the basis of color, unquestionably *did* violate Title VII.

Employers, unions, and employment agencies are prohibited from discriminating against an employee, applicant, or union member because he or she has made a charge, testified, or participated in an investigation or hearing under the act or otherwise opposed any unlawful practice.

Note that regarding general hiring, referrals, advertising, and admissions to training or apprenticeship programs, Title VII allows discrimination only on the basis of religion, sex, or national origin and only where these considerations are bona fide occupational qualifications. For example, it is legal for a Baptist church to refuse to engage a Lutheran minister. EEOC guidelines on sex discrimination consider sex to be a bona fide occupational qualification, for example, where it is necessary for authenticity or genuineness in hiring an actor or actress. The omission of *race* and *color* from this exception must mean that Congress does not feel these two factors are ever bona fide occupational qualifications.

> Discriminating in employment on the basis of race or color can almost never be a BFOQ.

Additional exemptions exist with respect to laws creating preferential treatment for veterans and hiring based on professionally developed ability tests that are not designed or intended to be used to discriminate. Such tests must bear a relationship to the job for which they are administered, however.

2. ENFORCEMENT PROCEDURES

The Civil Rights Act of 1964 created the Equal Employment Opportunity Commission (EEOC). This agency has the primary responsibility of enforcing the provisions of the act. The EEOC is composed of five members, not more than three of whom may be members of the same political party. They are appointed by the president, with the advice and consent of the Senate, and serve a five-year term. In the course of its investigations, the EEOC has broad authority to hold hearings, obtain evidence, and subpoena and examine witnesses under oath.

Under the Equal Employment Opportunity Act of 1972, the EEOC can file a civil suit in federal district court and represent a person charging a violation of the act. However, it must first exhaust efforts to settle the claim. Remedies that may be obtained in such an action include reinstatement with back pay for the victim of an illegal discrimination and injunctions against future violations of the act by the defendant. See Figure 20.1 for a breakdown of charges received by the EEOC.

> "[M]ajor American businesses have made clear that the skills needed in today's increasingly global marketplace can only be developed through exposure to widely diverse people, cultures, ideas, and viewpoints."
>
> **–Justice Sandra Day O'Connor, *Grutter v. Bollinger,* 539 U.S. 306, 330 (2003)**

The 1991 Amendments In 1991 Congress amended the Civil Rights Act to allow the recovery of compensatory and punitive damages of up to $300,000 per person. These damages are in addition to other remedies such

Figure 20.1 *What Kinds of Claims Are Being Filed with the EEOC?*

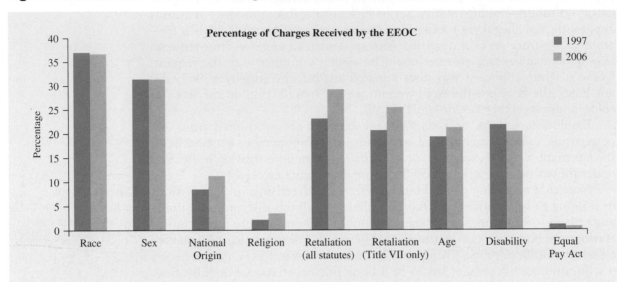

In 1997, the EEOC received 80,680 total charges and in 2006, it received 75,768 charges.

Source: EEOC Charge Statistics FY 1997–2007, www.eeoc.gov/stats/charges.html.

Under Title VII, a plaintiff can recover up to $300,000 in punitive and compensatory damages for *intentional* discrimination. Back pay damages can further add to that amount.

as job reinstatement (depending on the size of the employer) and back pay or front pay. Compensatory damages include damages for the pain and suffering of discrimination. Punitive damages are appropriate whenever discrimination occurs with "malice or with reckless or callous indifference to the federally protected rights of others." The 1991 amendments allow compensatory and punitive damages *only* when employers are guilty of *intentional discrimination.*

In enacting Title VII of the Civil Rights Act of 1964, Congress made it clear that it did not intend to preempt states' fair employment laws. Where state agencies begin discrimination proceedings, the EEOC must wait 60 days before it starts action. Furthermore, if a state law provides relief to a discrimination charge, the EEOC must notify the appropriate state officials and wait 60 days before continuing action.

An employee must file charges of illegal discrimination with the EEOC within 180 days after notice of the unlawful practice. If the employee first filed in a timely fashion with a state fair employment practices commission, the law extends the time for filing with the EEOC to 300 days.

Do remember that the three types of cases permitted under Title VII are for (1) disparate treatment, (2) disparate impact, and (3) retaliation.

Winning a Title VII Civil Action   To win a Title VII civil action, a plaintiff must initially show that steps taken by the employer likely had an illegally discriminatory basis, such as race. Generally, the plaintiff must prove either disparate (unequal) treatment or disparate impact. In proving **disparate treatment,** the plaintiff must convince the court that the employer *intentionally* discriminated against the plaintiff. If discrimination is a substantial or motivating factor, an employer's practice is illegal even though other factors (such as customer preference) also contributed. Even if the plaintiff proves disparate treatment, the defendant can win by showing that all or substantially all members of the plaintiff's class *cannot* perform the duties of the job. This defense is the BFOQ defense mentioned in Section 1 of this chapter.

In a **disparate impact** case the plaintiff must prove that the employer's practices or policies had a discriminatory effect on a group protected by Title VII. The employer can defeat the plaintiff's claim by proving the **business necessity defense.** This defense requires that the employer prove that the practices or policies used are job related and based on business necessity. However, the plaintiff can still establish a violation by showing that other policies would serve the legitimate interests of business necessity without having undesirable discriminatory effects.

A third type of discrimination case concerns **retaliation.** It is illegal for employers to retaliate against employees for making discrimination charges, giving testimony in a discrimination case, or in any way participating in a discrimination investigation. Such retaliation discrimination involves employers taking "adverse employment actions" against employees, such as firing employees or transferring them to less desirable jobs.

What are ways a company can avoid retaliation claims? As illustrated in Figure 20.1, retaliation claims are on the rise. There are a number of steps an employer can take to address allegations of discrimination without triggering a retaliation claim:

- Treat complaints seriously as soon as they are made.
- Investigate the complaint.
- Be sure managers and other employees know and follow the company's policies on discrimination, including harassment.
- Follow-up with the complainant, including explaining how the company will address the problem.
- Create an atmosphere in which the complainant and others with information feel comfortable coming forward with information or other complaints.
- Never take adverse action against a complainant or witnesses, based on information obtained in the investigation.

These straightforward steps go a long way to create an atmosphere of fairness and head off additional claims based on retaliation.

Before the 1991 Civil Rights Act amendments, employees or the EEOC sometimes claimed that proving racial or gender statistical imbalances in a workforce established illegal discrimination. They claimed that such imbalances showed illegal discrimination, much like disparate impact discrimination, even in the absence of proof of an employer's discriminatory intent. However, the 1991 amendments state that the showing of a statistically imbalanced workforce is not enough *in itself* to establish a violation of Title VII.

If an employee who complains about discrimination is transferred to the night shift, even without a loss of pay, he may have a claim for retaliation under Title VII. Burlington Northern and Santa Fe Railroad Co. v. White, 548 U.S. 53 (2007).

3. DISCRIMINATION ON THE BASIS OF RACE OR COLOR

The integration of African Americans into the mainstream of American society is the primary objective of the Civil Rights Act of 1964. Title VII, which deals with employment practices, is the key legal regulation for achieving this goal. Without equal employment opportunities, African Americans can hardly enjoy other guaranteed rights, such as access to public accommodations.

Title VII prohibits discriminatory employment practices based on race or color that involve *recruiting, hiring,* and *promotion* of employees. Of course, intentional discrimination in these matters is illegal, but, as previously stated, policies with disparate impact are also forbidden. Such discrimination arises from an employer's policies or practices that apply equally to everyone but that discriminate in greater proportion against minorities and have no relation to job qualification.

Examples of disparate impact on race include:

- Using personnel tests that have no substantial relation to job qualification, which have the effect of screening out minorities.
- Denying employment to unwed mothers, when minorities have a higher rate of illegitimate births than whites.
- Refusing to hire people because of a poor credit rating, when minorities are disproportionately affected.
- Giving hiring priority to relatives of present employees, when minorities are underrepresented in the workforce.

Often at issue in disparate impact cases is whether a discriminatory policy or practice relates to job qualification. Courts require proof, not mere assertion, of job relatedness before upholding an employer's discriminatory personnel test or other practice.

The law also prohibits discrimination in *employment conditions* and *benefits*. EEOC decisions have found such practices as the following to be violations:

- Permitting racial insults in the work situation.
- Maintaining all-white or all-black crews for no demonstrable reasons.
- Providing better housing for whites than blacks.
- Granting higher average Christmas bonuses to whites than blacks for reasons that were not persuasive to the commission.

> Lockheed Martin settled a race discrimination and retaliation lawsuit for $2.5 million in 2008. The case alleged a racially hostile work environment at several job sites, including threats of lynching and the use of the "N-word."

Researchers revealed racial bias in hiring based on an applicant's name. The study tracked response rates to resumes sent to 1,300 help-wanted ads. The authors found that white-sounding names (such as Anne, Emily, Allison, Neil, Todd, and Matthew) are 50 percent more likely to get called for an initial interview than applicants with African American-sounding names (such as Tamika, Latoya, Latonya, Tyrone, Tremayne, and Rasheed). Additionally, race affects the degree to which applicants benefit from having more experience and credentials. The study showed that white applicants with higher-quality resumes received 30 percent more callbacks than whites with lower-quality resumes. By contract, African-American applicants experienced only 9 percent more callbacks for the same improvement in credentials.

> The State of New York has outlawed the display of a noose as a threat, punishable by up to four years in prison.

It is important to appreciate that Title VII prohibits employment discrimination against members of all races. In one recent case, a federal court jury awarded a white senior air traffic official $500,000 in damages against the Federal Aviation Administration. The official charged the FAA had demoted him and replaced him with an African American following complaints that blacks were underrepresented in senior management levels. Note that this case did not involve affirmative action (see Section 10 of this chapter).

:: *sidebar* 20.1

Abercrombie & Fitch's $40 Million Diversity Lesson

In 2005, Abercrombie & Fitch (A&F) settled a discrimination lawsuit with over 10,000 class members. The suit alleged hiring discrimination against Latino, African American, and Asian American applicants. The checks ranged from several hundred to several thousand dollars each, totaling $40 million. The settlement agreement also requires A&F to:

- Set "benchmarks" (*not* quotas) for hiring and promotion of women, Latinos, African Americans, and Asian Americans.

- Stop targeting fraternities, sororities, or specific colleges for recruitment.

- Hire 25 recruiters who will focus on seeking women and minority employees.
- Implement a new internal complaint procedure.
- Create marketing materials reflecting diversity.

What is A&F saying about diversity now? According to Mike Jeffries, A&F's Chairman and CEO, "Diversity and inclusion are key to our organization's success."

4. DISCRIMINATION ON THE BASIS OF NATIONAL ORIGIN

Title VII's prohibition against national origin discrimination protects various ethnic groups in the workplace. In a recent case, the court ruled that Title VII had been violated when a bakery employee of Iranian descent was called "Ayatollah" in the workplace by the assistant manager and other employees. After he complained, he was fired. In 2005, the EEOC reported that employees of Middle Eastern descent had filed almost a thousand discrimination complaints against employers since the terrorist bombings of in September 11, 2001.

> Approximately 1.2 million Americans are of Middle Eastern or Arab descent, according to the U.S. Census.

Discrimination concerning the speaking of a native language frequently causes national-origin lawsuits under Title VII. For instance, courts have ruled illegal an employer's rule against speaking Spanish during work hours when the employer could not show a business need to understand all conversations between Hispanic employees. On the other hand, some courts have held that if jobs require contact with the public, a requirement that employees speak some English may be a business necessity.

> **Don't** forget that a policy requiring employees to speak English will violate Title VII as disparate impact unless it is justified by *business necessity.*

Direct foreign investment in the United States has doubled and redoubled in recent years. This increasing investment has presented some unusual issues of employment discrimination law. For instance, many commercial treaties with foreign countries give foreign companies operating in the United States the right to hire executive-level employees "of their choice." Does this mean that foreign companies in the United States can discriminate as to their managerial employees on a basis forbidden under Title VII? The Supreme Court has partially resolved this issue by ruling that the civil rights law applied to a Japanese company that did business through a subsidiary incorporated in this country.

5. DISCRIMINATION ON THE BASIS OF RELIGION

Note that religious corporations, associations, or societies can discriminate in all their employment practices on the basis of religion, but not on the basis of race, color, sex, or national origin. Other employers cannot discriminate on the basis of religion in employment practices, and they must make reasonable accommodation to the religious needs of their employees if it does not result in undue hardship to them.

In one case the Supreme Court let stand a lower court ruling that employees cannot be required to pay union dues if they have religious objections to unions. The case determined that a union violated Title VII by forcing a company to fire a Seventh Day Adventist who did not comply with a collective bargaining agreement term that all employees must pay union dues. The union argued unsuccessfully that it had made reasonable accommodation to the worker's religious beliefs by offering to give any dues paid by him to charity. However, in another case the Supreme Court ruled that a company rightfully fired an employee who refused to work on Saturdays due to religious belief. The Court said that the company did not have to burden other employees by making them work Saturdays.

A growing source of religious discrimination lawsuits concerns employees who for religious reasons refuse to perform some task required by the employer. For example, in one case a vegetarian bus driver refused to distribute hamburger coupons on his bus, asserting religious beliefs. When his employer fired him, he sued. The parties settled the case for $50,000. Note that even if an employer wins such a lawsuit, it can be extremely expensive to defend.

In the case of employees of Arab descent, note the close connection between national origin discrimination and religious discrimination.

As mentioned earlier, since the 9/11 bombings religious discrimination against Muslim employees has risen steeply. In 2003 the EEOC settled a complaint by four Muslim machine operators against Stockton Steel of California for $1.1 million. The four operators claimed they were given the worst jobs, ridiculed during their prayers, and called names like "camel jockey" and "raghead."

6. DISCRIMINATION ON THE BASIS OF SEX

Historically, states have enacted many laws designed supposedly to protect women. For example, many states by statute have prohibited the employment of women in certain occupations such as those that require lifting heavy objects. Others have barred women from working during the night or more than a given number of hours per week or day. A federal district court held that a California state law that required rest periods for women only was in violation of Title VII. Some statutes prohibit employing women for a specified time after childbirth. Under EEOC guidelines, such statutes are not a defense to a charge of illegal sex discrimination and do not provide an employer with a bona fide occupational qualification in hiring standards. Other EEOC guidelines forbid employers:

- To classify jobs as male or female.
- To advertise in help-wanted columns that are designated male or female, unless sex is a bona fide job qualification.

Query: Could Victoria's Secret stores legally only hire women for certain positions?

Similarly, employers may not have separate male and female seniority lists.

Whether sex is a bona fide occupational qualification (and discrimination is thus legal) has been raised in several cases. The courts have tended to consider this exception narrowly. In the following instances involving hiring policy, *no bona fide occupational qualification was found to exist:*

- A rule requiring airline stewardesses, but not stewards, to be single.
- A policy of hiring only females as flight cabin attendants.
- A rule against hiring females with preschool-age children, but not against hiring males with such children.
- A telephone company policy against hiring females as switchers because of the alleged heavy lifting involved on the job.

not allowed

In the telephone company case, the court held that for a bona fide occupational qualification to exist, there must be "reasonable cause to believe, that is, a factual basis for believing, that all or substantially all women would be unable to perform safely and efficiently the duties of the job involved." The Supreme Court has indicated that for such a qualification to exist, sex must be provably relevant to job performance.

Other examples of <u>illegal sex discrimination include</u>:

- Refusing to hire a female newscaster because "news coming from a woman sounds like gossip."
- Allowing women to retire at age 50, but requiring men to wait until age 55.
- Failing to promote women to overseas positions because foreign clients were reluctant to do business with women.

The much-talked about Hooters restaurant case involved a lawsuit filed by men in Illinois and Maryland who were denied jobs. Hooters paid $3.75 million to settle the lawsuit. The settlement allows Hooters to continue employing voluptuous and scantily clad female "Hooters Girls," but they must create and fill a few other support jobs, like bartenders and hosts, without regard to gender.

:: *sidebar* 20.2

Sex Discrimination: Wal-Mart's Ongoing Woes

In 2001, six current and former female Wal-Mart and Sam's Club employees filed a class-action against Wal-Mart charging that it discriminates against female employees in making promotions, job assignments, pay decisions, and training, and that it also retaliates against women who complain about these practices. The class consists of over 1.5 million current and former female Wal-Mart employees.

According to the plaintiffs, depositions, hundreds of interviews with women who have worked at Wal-Mart, review of over a million pages of documents, and analysis of Wal-Mart's computerized payroll and PeopleSoft databases reveals a "widespread pattern of discrimination against women in pay and promotions."

The case is currently pending. What is Wal-Mart's best strategy to resolve the lawsuit?

*Source: www.walmartclass.com.

Sexual Harassment A common type of illegal sex discrimination in the workplace is **sexual harassment**. The typical sexual harassment case involves a plaintiff who has been promised benefits or threatened with loss if she or he does not give sexual favors to an employment supervisor. Such a case is also

Think of sexual harassment discrimination in terms of (1) quid pro quo cases and (2) hostile work environment cases.

Well-known talk show hosts Maury Povich and Bill O'Reilly both have been accused of sexual harassment in multimillion-dollar lawsuits. O'Reilly settled the case for an undisclosed amount.

called a *quid pro quo* (this for that) case. Under Title VII and agency law, an employer is liable for this sex discrimination.

Another type of sexual harassment is the **hostile work environment,** one in which co-workers make offensive sexual comments or propositions, engage in suggestive touching, show nude pictures, or draw sexual graffiti. The Supreme Court in *Meritor Savings Bank v. Vinson* ruled that Title VII prohibits "an offensive or hostile working environment," even when no economic loss occurs. By so ruling, the Court acknowledged that the work environment itself is a condition of employment covered by Title VII.

The Supreme Court also addressed the hostile work environment issue in *Harris v. Forklift Systems, Inc.* Specifically, the Court was asked to determine whether, before a person could sue under Title VII, a hostile work environment had "to seriously affect [his or her] psychological well-being" or "cause injury." The Court ruled that illegal sexual harassment goes beyond that which causes "injury." It includes any harassment reasonably perceived as "hostile and abusive."

Is all sexually offensive conduct between employees illegal? The answer is no, although an employee's company may choose to forbid and punish all such conduct. In 2005 the Supreme Court in *Clarke County School District v. Breeden* summarized when offensive sexual conduct becomes illegal:

[S]exual harassment is actionable under Title VII only if it is so severe or pervasive as to alter the conditions of the victim's employment and create an abusive working environment.

The Court continued:

Workplace conduct is not measured in isolation; instead, whether an environment is sufficiently hostile or abusive must be judged by looking at all the circumstances, including the frequency of the discriminatory conduct; its severity; whether it is physically threatening or humiliating, or a mere offensive utterance; and whether it unreasonably interferes with an employee's work performance.

It is not uncommon for a discrimination lawsuit to involve multiple kinds of claims. A good example of this is a recent case against Cracker Barrel, in which the restaurant agreed to pay $2 million to settle a lawsuit alleging sexual harassment, racial harassment, and retaliation by 51 current or former employees. On behalf of the workers, the EEOC alleged that male co-workers and managers subjected female workers to unwelcome and offensive sexual comments and touching. According to the EEOC, "Black employees said that they experienced racially charged language in the workplace, including 'spear chucking porch monkey,' 'you people,' and the 'n-word.'" In addition to the monetary settlement, Cracker Barrel must train all employees in its stores about harassment.

In Case 20.1, the Supreme Court further discusses the difficult issue of what constitutes an illegal hostile environment. Note that this case involves a man harassed by other men.

Employer's Defense to Hostile Environment   Is an employer always liable when fellow employees create a hostile environment based on gender? The answer is that the employer is not always legally responsible for a hostile environment. The employer may have a defense. Courts have ruled that an employer is liable to a plaintiff employee for a hostile working environment

ONCALE v. SUNDOWNER OFFSHORE SERVICES, INC.
523 U.S. 75 (1998)

SCALIA, J.: In late October 1991, Joseph Oncale was working for respondent Sundowner Offshore Services on a Chevron U.S.A., Inc., oil platform in the Gulf of Mexico. He was employed as a roustabout on an eight-man crew which included respondents John Lyons, Danny Pippen, and Brandon Johnson. Lyons, the crane operator, and Pippen, the driller, had supervisory authority. On several occasions, Oncale was forcibly subjected to sex-related, humiliating actions against him by Lyons, Pippen, and Johnson in the presence of the rest of the crew. Pippen and Lyons also physically assaulted Oncale in a sexual manner, and Lyons threatened him with rape.

Oncale's complaints to supervisory personnel produced no remedial action; in fact, the company's Safety Compliance Clerk, Valent Hohen, told Oncale that Lyons and Pippen "picked [on] him all the time too," and called him a name suggesting homosexuality. Oncale eventually quit—asking that his pink slip reflect that he "voluntarily left due to sexual harassment and verbal abuse." When asked at his deposition why he left Sundowner, Oncale stated "I felt that if I didn't leave my job, that I would be raped or forced to have sex."

Title VII of the Civil Rights Act of 1964 provides, in relevant part, that "it shall be an unlawful employment practice for an employer . . . to discriminate against any individual with respect to his compensation, terms, conditions, or privileges of employment, because of such individual's race, color, religion, sex, or national origin." We have held that this not only covers "terms" and "conditions" in the narrow contractual sense, but "evinces a congressional intent to strike at the entire spectrum of disparate treatment of men and women in employment."

Title VII's prohibition of discrimination "because of . . . sex" protects men as well as women, and in the related context of racial discrimination in the workplace we have rejected any conclusive presumption that an employer will not discriminate against members of his own race. If our precedents leave any doubt on the question, we hold today that nothing in Title VII necessarily bars a claim of discrimination "because of . . . sex" merely because the plaintiff and the defendant (or the person charged with acting on behalf of the defendant) are of the same sex.

Courts have had little trouble with that principle in cases where an employee claims to have been passed over for a job or promotion. But when the issue arises in the context of a "hostile environment" sexual harassment claim, the state and federal courts have taken a bewildering variety of stances. Some, like the Fifth Circuit in this case, have held that same-sex sexual harassment claims are never cognizable under Title VII. Other decisions say that such claims are actionable only if the plaintiff can prove that the harasser is homosexual (and thus presumably motivated by sexual desire). Still others suggest that workplace harassment that is sexual in content is always actionable, regardless of the harasser's sex, sexual orientation, or motivation.

Courts and juries have found the inference of discrimination easy to draw in most male–female sexual harassment situations, because the challenged conduct typically involves explicit or implicit proposals of sexual activity; it is reasonable to assume those proposals would not have been made to someone of the same sex. The same chain of inference would be available to a plaintiff alleging same-sex harassment, if there were credible evidence that the harasser was homosexual. But harassing conduct need not be motivated by sexual desire to support an inference of discrimination on the basis of sex. A trier of fact might reasonably find such discrimination, for example, if a female victim is harassed in such sex-specific and derogatory terms by another woman as to make it clear that the harasser is motivated by general hostility to the presence of women in the workplace. A same-sex harassment plaintiff may also, of course, offer direct comparative evidence about how the alleged harasser treated members of both sexes in a mixed-sex workplace. Whatever evidentiary route the plaintiff chooses to follow, he or she must always prove that the conduct at issue was not merely tinged with offensive sexual connotations, but actually constituted "discrimination . . . because of . . . sex."

And there is another requirement that prevents Title VII from expanding into a general civility code: As we emphasized in *Meritor* and *Harris*, the statute does not reach genuine but innocuous differences in the ways men and women routinely interact with members of the same sex and of the opposite sex. The prohibition of harassment on the basis of sex requires neither asexuality nor androgyny in the workplace; it forbids only behavior so objectively offensive as to alter the "conditions" of the victim's employment. "Conduct that is not severe or pervasive enough to create an objectively hostile or abusive work environment—an environment that a reasonable person would find hostile or abusive—is beyond Title VII's purview." We have always regarded that requirement as crucial, and as sufficient to ensure that courts and juries do not mistake ordinary socializing in the workplace—such as male-on-male horseplay or intersexual flirtation—for discriminatory "conditions of employment."

We have emphasized, moreover, that the objective severity of harassment should be judged from the perspective of a reasonable person in the plaintiff's position, considering "all the circumstances." In same-sex (as in all) harassment cases, that inquiry requires careful consideration of the social context in which particular behavior occurs and is experienced by its target. A professional football player's working environment is not severely or pervasively abusive, for example, if the coach smacks him on the buttocks as he heads onto the field—even if the same behavior would reasonably be experienced as abusive by the coach's secretary (male or female) back at the office. The real social impact of workplace behavior often depends on a constellation of surrounding circumstances, expectations, and relationships which are not fully captured by a simple recitation of the words used or the physical acts performed. Common sense, and an appropriate sensitivity to social context, will enable courts and juries to distinguish between simple teasing or rough housing among members of the same sex, and conduct which a reasonable person in the plaintiff's position would find severely hostile or abusive.

Because we conclude that sex discrimination consisting of same-sex sexual harassment is actionable under Title VII, the judgment of the Court of Appeals for the Fifth Circuit is reversed, and the case is remanded for further proceedings consistent with this opinion.

Reversed and remanded.

:: CASE QUESTIONS

1. Before the decision in this case, what had the lower courts decided about whether same-sex harassment could violate Title VII?
2. Did the Court determine that the harassment of Oncale violated Title VII? Explain.
3. Does flirting violate Title VII? Explain.

Don't forget that employers are liable if plaintiffs prove quid pro quo harassment. But employers may have a defense to hostile environment harassment.

created by fellow employees only when the employer knows of the problem and fails to take prompt and reasonable steps to correct it, such as by moving the harassers away from the plaintiff employee. The employer can defend itself by proving the employer exercised reasonable care to prevent and correct promptly any sexually harassing behavior, and the plaintiff employee unreasonably failed to take advantage of any preventive or corrective opportunities provided by the employer.

Recently, the Supreme Court ruled that a hostile, harassing environment was a single employment practice. This decision is important because Title VII says that an employer is liable for discriminatory practices only if an employee files a complaint concerning them with the EEOC within 180 days of their happening (within 300 days if the employee has first filed with a state fair employment practices commission). Employers are liable for acts that occurred before 180 days of EEOC filing if they are part of a single hostile environment that continued within the 180-day period.

Pregnancy Discrimination Act The Pregnancy Discrimination Act amended the Civil Rights Act in 1978. Under it, employers can no longer discriminate against women workers who become pregnant or give birth.

Thus, employers with health or disability plans must cover pregnancy, childbirth, and related medical conditions in the same manner as other conditions are covered. The law covers unmarried as well as married pregnant women. It also states that an employer cannot force a pregnant woman to stop working until her baby is born, provided she is still capable of performing her duties properly. And the employer cannot specify how long a leave of absence must be taken after childbirth. Coverage for abortion is not required by the statute unless an employee carries to term and her life is endangered or she develops medical complications because of an abortion. If a woman undergoes an abortion, though, all other benefits provided for employees, such as sick leave, must be provided to her.

Note that sex discrimination applies to discrimination against men as well as women. For example, under the Pregnancy Discrimination Act the Supreme Court ruled unlawful an employer's health insurance plan that covered the pregnancies of female employees but did not cover the pregnancies of male employees' wives.

Men as well as women may be subject to illegal sex discrimination.

:: *sidebar* 20.3

Pregnancy Discrimination: Claims on the Rise

The EEOC reports that pregnancy-related claims increased 14 percent in 2007 to 5,587, a whopping 40 percent increase from a decade ago.

What does a woman need to bring a successful claim? She must prove that her pregnancy or her status as a mother motivated the employer's adverse action.

In 2007, the EEOC sued Bloomberg LP, the news and financial services company, alleging discrimination against women who became pregnant and took maternity leave. The complaint alleges that Bloomberg engaged in a pattern of demoting and reducing the pay of women after they were pregnant. Other allegations included that some women were subjected to stereotyping about their abilities to do work while they were tending to family and care-giver responsibilities.

For more information, see www.eeoc.gov/types/pregnancy.html.

Equal Pay Act Historically, employers have paid female employees less than males, even when they held the same jobs. In 1964, women earned only 59 cents for every dollar earned by males. By 2004, female employees earned just 77 cents for every dollar earned by males.

Federal legislation prohibits sex discrimination in employment compensation under both Title VII and the Equal Pay Act of 1963. Administered by the EEOC, the Equal Pay Act prohibits an employer from discriminating on the basis of sex in the payment of wages for equal work performed. For jobs to be equal, they must require "equal skill, effort, and responsibility" and must be performed "under similar working conditions." Discrimination is allowed if it arises from a seniority system, a merit system, a piecework production system, or any factor other than sex.

The focus of Equal Pay Act cases is whether the male and female jobs being compared involve "equal" work. Courts have recognized that *equal* does not mean *identical;* it means *substantially* equal. Thus, courts have ruled "equal" the work of male barbers and female beauticians and of male tailors and female seamstresses. Differences in male and female job descriptions will not

According to the Economic Policy Institute, college-educated women between 36 and 45 years old earned 74.7 cents in hourly pay for every dollar that men earned in the same group.

One court ruled that an employer could pay male physician assistants more than female nurses because the physician assistants had administrative duties that nurses did not have to perform.

totally protect employers against charges of equal-pay infractions. The courts have held that "substantially equal" work done on different machines would require the employer to compensate male and female employees equally.

The Supreme Court has ruled that discriminatory male and female pay differences can also be illegal under Title VII. In *County of Washington v. Gunther,* the Court decided that plaintiffs can use evidence of such pay differences to help prove intentional sex discrimination, even when the work performed is not substantially equal. Relying on the *Gunther* case, at least one lower court has held that women must be paid equally with men who perform comparable work. A federal district court ruled that the state of Washington discriminated against secretaries (mostly women) by paying them less than maintenance and other personnel (mostly men). However, the **comparable worth** theory is highly controversial, and other courts have not agreed with the theory.

In a landmark Equal Pay Act decision, *Ledbetter v. Goodyear Tire & Rubber Co., Inc.* (2007), a sharply divided Supreme Court rejected the pro-employee paycheck-accrual theory of pay discrimination previously accepted by many courts. Simply stated, employees must file an EEOC charge within 180 or 300 days (depending on their state) after each discriminatory pay decision or forever lose their claim. For more details about the controversial *Ledbetter* case, see Sidebar 20.4.

:: *sidebar* 20.4

Did the Supreme Court Get It Wrong? Fallout Over the *Ledbetter* Case

Lilly Ledbetter worked for Goodyear for nearly 20 years. During that time, Ledbetter and other salaried employees received or were denied raises based on their supervisors' evaluation of their performance. Near the end of her tenure at Goodyear, Ledbetter discovered that her pay was significantly less—as much as 40 percent less—than her male counterparts. Ledbetter then filed a charge with the EEOC.

PROCEDURAL HISTORY

The district court allowed Ledbetter to present evidence of her entire 19-year career at Goodyear. A jury found in her favor, awarding both compensatory and punitive damages. The Eleventh Circuit reversed and the Supreme Court (5–4) affirmed the decision that a Title VII pay discrimination claim cannot be based on any pay decision that occurred outside of the EEOC charging period.

DISSENTING VIEWS

Justice Ruth Bader Ginsberg wrote a spirited dissent (joined by Justices Stevens, Souter, and Breyer) arguing that "[p]ay disparities often occur . . . in small increments" and "cause to suspect that discrimination is at work develops only over time." She continued, asserting that discriminatory disparities in pay, like hostile work environment claims, rest not on "one particular paycheck, but on 'the cumulative effect of individual acts.'" Incensed about the majority opinion, Justice Ginsberg read her dissent aloud from the bench.

LEGISLATIVE RESPONSE

The House of Representatives approved the Lilly Ledbetter Fair Pay Act by a 225–199 vote, which would allow employees to reclaim lost pay if a claim is filed within 180 days of the issuance of a discriminatory paycheck, regardless of the date of the initial violation. The Senate has a similar bill pending.

Examples of successful Equal Pay Act cases include one against Wal-Mart and another against the New Your Corrections Department. In the first case, a pharmacist who claimed Wal-Mart fired her after asking to be paid the same as her male colleagues won nearly a $2 million award against Wal-Mart. Wal-Mart argued that it fired the pharmacist for leaving the pharmacy unattended and allowing a technician to use her computer security code to issue prescriptions, including a fraudulent prescription for a painkiller. Countering this argument, the pharmacist argued that the prescription incident took place 18 months before her termination and more severe infractions by her male counterparts were unpunished. In the second case, the EEOC settled an Equal Pay Act suit against the New York Department of Corrections for nearly $1 million. The EEOC alleged that female employees were receiving less benefits than their male counterparts.

Sexual Orientation Discrimination   Title VII does not prohibit discrimination against employees based on their sexual orientation, or whether they are gay, lesbian, bisexual, transgendered, or heterosexual. The word *sex* in Title VII refers only to gender, whether someone is female or male. A quarter of the states, however, and numerous cities do forbid discrimination based on sexual orientation, and Congress could amend Title VII to protect employees from such discrimination. Already, thousands of companies ranging from American Express, Coca-Cola, and J. P. Morgan Chase Bank to Ford, General Motors, and Chrysler, offer domestic partner benefits to all employees without regard to sexual orientation.

Although the House of Representatives voted 235–184 to pass the Employment Non-Discrimination Act of 2007, banning employment discrimination on the basis of sexual orientation, it has not yet become federal law. See Sidebar 20.5 for other developments in sexual orientation laws and protections.

:: *sidebar* 20.5

Sexual Orientation Discrimination: State and Local Laws

Although there is no federal protection prohibiting sexual orientation in the workplace based on sexual orientation, many private employers—especially those who operate in many states—have company policies prohibiting sexual orientation discrimination. Consider these facts and legal developments:

- The majority of Fortune 500 companies provide health insurance for domestic partners of their employees.
- According to Human Rights Campaign, a gay political group, more than 7,000 employers offer domestic partner benefits.
- The California Supreme Court (2008) granted same-sex couples the right to marry. Accordingly, employers must provide benefits specified under state law or the employer's policy to same-sex couples.
- *State laws.* Seventeen states and the District of Columbia have laws that currently prohibit sexual orientation

discrimination in private employment: California, Connecticut, Hawaii, Illinois, Maine, Maryland, Massachusetts, Minnesota, Nevada, New Hampshire, New Jersey, New Mexico, New York, Rhode Island, Vermont, Washington, and Wisconsin. Some of these states also specifically prohibit discrimination based on gender identity. (In addition, six states have laws prohibiting sexual orientation discrimination in public workplaces only: Colorado, Delaware, Indiana, Michigan, Montana, and Pennsylvania.)

- *Local laws.* More than 180 cities and counties nationwide prohibit sexual orientation discrimination in at least some workplaces.

For more information and a state-by-state list of antidiscrimination laws, including city and county ordinances, see the Lambda Legal Defense and Education Fund website at www.lambdalegal.org.

:: Employment Practices That May Be Challenged

In studying the Civil Rights Act, we can usefully consider several specific employment practices that employees or job applicants may challenge as discriminatory. These practices include:

- Setting testing and educational requirements.
- Having height and weight requirements for physical labor.
- Maintaining appearance requirements.
- Practicing affirmative action.
- Using seniority systems.

The following sections take a close look at these practices.

7. QUESTIONNAIRES, INTERVIEWS, TESTING, AND EDUCATIONAL REQUIREMENTS

Employers have used a number of tools to help them find the right person for the right job. Among these tools are questionnaires, interviews, references, minimum educational requirements (such as a high school diploma), and personnel tests. However, employers must be extremely careful not to use tools that illegally discriminate. For example, Rent-A-Center, a Dallas-based appliance-rental company, agreed to pay more than $2 million in damages to more than 1,200 job applicants and employees who were asked questions about their sex lives and religious views in a 500-item true-false questionnaire. Plaintiffs claimed the questionnaire discriminated illegally on the basis of gender and religion and that it violated their privacy.

Interviews can also discriminate illegally, and personnel interviewers must be well trained. One study indicated that interviewers can be biased even if they are not aware of it. The study showed that the interviewers tended to select males over females for sales positions because the interviewers *subconsciously* related sales success with height, and males are on the average taller than females. References may not be so reliable, either. A previous employer's letter may reflect personal biases against an applicant that were not related to job performance.

At the other extreme, an employer may give a poor employee a top recommendation because of sympathy or fear of a lawsuit in case the letter is somehow obtained by the employee. Advocates of personnel tests in the selection process feel they are very valuable in weeding out the wrong persons for a job and picking the right ones. They believe reliance on test results eliminates biases that interviewers or former employers who give references may have.

Tests, however, can have a *disparate impact* on job applicants, discriminating on the basis of race, sex, color, religion, or national origin. Setting educational standards such as requiring a high school diploma for employment can also have a disparate impact. To avoid discrimination challenges, employers must make sure that all testing and educational requirements are job related and necessary for the business.

Most employment practices that discriminate illegally do so because of their disparate impact.

In the past, some employers have "race normed" employment tests. *Race norming* is the practice of setting two different cutoff test scores for employment based on race or one of the other Title VII categories. For example, on a race-normed test, the minimum score for employment of white job applicants might be set at 75 out of 100. For minority applicants, the minimum score might be set at 65. *The Civil Rights Act amendments of 1991 specifically prohibit the race norming of employment tests.*

> **Don't** forget that for employers to race-norm employment tests violates Title VII.

8. HEIGHT AND WEIGHT REQUIREMENTS

Minimum or maximum height or weight job requirements apply equally to all job applicants, but if they have the effect of screening out applicants on the basis of race, national origin, or sex, the employer must demonstrate that such requirements are validly related to the ability to perform the work in question. For example, maximum size standards would be permissible, even if they favored women over men, if the available work space were too small to permit large persons to perform the duties of the job properly. Most size requirements have dictated minimum heights or weights, often based on a stereotyped assumption that a certain amount of strength that smaller persons might not have probably was necessary for the work. In one case, a 5-foot, 5-inch, 130-pound Hispanic won a suit against a police department on the basis that the department's 5-foot, 8-inch minimum height requirement discriminated against Hispanics, who often are shorter than that standard. He was later hired when he passed the department's physical agility examination, which included dragging a 150-pound body 75 feet and scaling a 6-foot wall.

9. APPEARANCE REQUIREMENTS

Employers often have set grooming standards for their employees. Those regulating hair length of males or prohibiting beards or mustaches have been among the most common. Undoubtedly, motivation for these rules stems from the feeling of the employer that the image it projects to the public through its employees will be adversely affected if their appearance is not "proper." It is unclear whether appearance requirements are legal or illegal, since there have been rulings both ways. However, in 2000 the EEOC filed a lawsuit in Atlanta against FedEx Corporation for firing a bearded delivery driver who refused to shave in violation of a company policy that permitted beards only when medically necessary. The driver's Islamic beliefs required males to wear beards, and the lawsuit alleged that FedEx's policy constituted religious discrimination.

> Walt Disney World has detailed instructions for employees on "The Disney Look," including eyewear, body piercing, earlobe expansion, facial hair, fingernails, hear length, and sideburns. The goal is to look "friendly, approachable, and knowledgeable."

In another case, a black employee argued that he was wrongfully fired for breaking a company rule prohibiting beards. Dermatologists testified that the plaintiff had a condition called "razor bumps" (which occurs when the tightly curled facial hairs of black men become ingrown from shaving) and that the only known cure was for him not to shave. Although the federal appeals court found that the plaintiff was prejudiced by the employer's regulation, it held in favor of the company, ruling that its *slight racial impact* was justified by the *business necessity* it served. A conflicting opinion in still another case upheld an employee's right to wear a beard because of razor bumps.

> The burden of proof in a disparate impact case requires the employer to prove that appearance is a business necessity.

10. AFFIRMATIVE ACTION PROGRAMS AND REVERSE DISCRIMINATION

Since the 1940s, a series of presidential executive orders have promoted non-discrimination and **affirmative action** by employers who contract with the federal government. The authority for these orders rests with the president's executive power to control the granting of federal contracts. As a condition to obtaining such contracts, employers must agree contractually to take affirmative action to avoid unlawful discrimination in recruitment, employment, promotion, training, rate of compensation, and layoff of workers.

The affirmative action requirement means that federally contracting employers must actively recruit members of minority groups being underused in the workforce. That is, employers must hire members of these groups when there are fewer minority workers in a given job category than one could reasonably expect, considering their availability. In many instances, employers must develop written affirmative action plans and set goals and timetables for bringing minority (or female) workforces up to their percentages in the available labor pool.

The Labor Department administers executive orders through its Office of Federal Contract Compliance Programs (OFCCP). The OFCCP can terminate federal contracts with employers who do not comply with its guidelines and can make them ineligible for any future federal business. For instance, it required Uniroyal, Inc., to give its female employees an estimated $18 million in back pay to compensate for past employment discrimination. The alternative was elimination of $36 million of existing federal contracts and ineligibility for future federal business.

The Labor Department has eased OFCCP regulations on 75 percent of the firms that do business with the federal government. Firms with fewer than 250 employees and federal contracts of under $1 million no longer must prepare written affirmative action plans for hiring women and minorities. The OFCCP has also begun to limit its use of back pay awards to specific individuals who can show an actual loss due to violation of OFCCP guidelines.

Private Employer Affirmative Action   Not all affirmative action programs arise under federal contracting rules. Courts also impose affirmative action on private employers to overcome a history of prior discrimination. Sometimes private employers voluntarily adopt affirmative action or agree to it with unions. These affirmative action programs can give rise to claims of **reverse discrimination** when minorities or women with lower qualifications or less seniority than white males are given preference in employment or training. Even though such programs are intended to remedy the effects of present or past discrimination or other barriers to equal employment opportunity, white males have argued that the law does not permit employers to discriminate against *them* on the basis of race or sex any more than it allows discrimination against minorities or women.

In *United Steelworkers of America v. Weber,* the Supreme Court ruled legal under Title VII a voluntary affirmative action plan between an employer and a union. The plan required that at least 50 percent of certain new work trainees be black. The Court noted that the plan did not require that white

---

It is not unusual for an employment ad to state that the company is an "affirmative action/equal opportunity employer." Some ads also state: "Women and underrepresented minorities are encouraged to apply."

Do remember that the justification for affirmative action is the historic discrimination against protected groups.

employees be fired or excluded altogether from advancement. It was only a temporary measure to eliminate actual racial imbalance in the workforce.

Note the difference between taking affirmative action and setting a "quota." Affirmative action is taken to help correct historic workforce imbalances and usually has target goals that are pursued for a limited time. On the other hand, quotas set rigid standards for various groups, such as that 50 percent of the workforce must be female. The 1991 Civil Rights Act amendments prohibit the setting of quotas in employment.

The EEOC has issued guidelines intended to protect employers who set up affirmative action plans. These guidelines indicate that Title VII is not violated if an employer determines that there is a reasonable basis for concluding that such a plan is appropriate and the employer takes *reasonable* affirmative action. For example, if an employer discovers that it has a job category where one might expect to find more women and minorities employed than are actually in its workforce, the employer has a reasonable basis for affirmative action.

In *Adarand Constructors, Inc. v. Pena,* the Supreme Court emphasized that government-imposed affirmative action plans are subject to *strict judicial scrutiny* under equal protection guaranteed by the Fifth and Fourteenth Amendments. To be constitutional, such plans must now be supported by a *compelling interest.* The *Adarand* decision will make it constitutionally difficult to justify some government-imposed affirmative action plans. Much litigation has followed that tests the constitutionality of various plans.

In California voters approved the controversial Proposition 209. In relevant part it says that "the state shall not discriminate against, or grant preferential treatment to, any individual or group on the basis of race, sex, color, ethnicity, or national origin in the operation of public employment, public education, or public contracting." The Supreme Court refused to hear an appeal from a lower court decision that upheld Proposition 209 against constitutional challenge and the assertion it violated federal civil rights law. Although Proposition 209 *does not* affect private employer affirmative action plans required by federal law, it does illustrate the current opposition that many Americans have to affirmative action. Polls show that almost three-fourths of the general population disapproves of affirmative action. Nearly 50 percent of African Americans also oppose it.

> In 2005, a federal jury found that the New Orleans district attorney discriminated against 43 white employees by firing them and replacing them with African Americans.

> Voluntary affirmative action plans by private employers *may* violate Title VII but do *not* violate constitutional equal protection because they are not "state action."

11. SENIORITY SYSTEMS

Seniority systems give priority to those employees who have worked longer for a particular employer or in a particular line of employment of the employer. Employers may institute seniority systems on their own, but in a union shop they are usually the result of collective bargaining. Their terms are spelled out in the agreement between the company and the union. Seniority systems often determine the calculation of vacation, pension, and other fringe benefits. They also control many employment decisions such as the order in which employees may choose shifts or qualify for promotions or transfers to different jobs. They also are used to select the persons to be laid off when an employer is reducing its labor force. As a result of seniority, the last hired are usually the first fired. Decisions based on seniority have been challenged in recent years as violating the laws relating to equal employment

> *Title VII specifically allows employers to adopt seniority systems even when they may operate to discriminate against protected groups.

opportunity. Challenges often arose when recently hired members of minority groups were laid off during periods of economic downturn. Firms with successful affirmative action programs often lost most of their minority employees.

Section 703(h) of the Civil Rights Act of 1964 provides that, in spite of other provisions in the act, it is not an unlawful employment practice for an employer to apply different employment standards under a bona fide (good-faith) seniority system if the differences are not the result of an *intention* to discriminate. In *Memphis Fire Dept. v. Stotts* the Supreme Court ruled that discrimination resulting from application of a seniority system was lawful even when it affected minorities hired or promoted by affirmative action.

:: Other Statutes and Discrimination in Employment

Although the Civil Rights Act of 1964 is the most widely used antidiscrimination statute, there are other important antidiscrimination laws. They include the Civil Rights Act of 1866, the Age Discrimination in Employment Act, the Americans with Disabilities Act, and various state and local laws. The following sections examine these laws.

12. CIVIL RIGHTS ACT OF 1866

Denny's restaurants have been repeatedly sued for black customers claiming Denny's violated their civil rights. Denny's has paid more than $54 million to settle the lawsuits.

An important federal law that complements Title VII of the 1964 Civil Rights Act is the Civil Rights Act of 1866. One provision of that act, known as **Section 1981** (referring to its U.S. Code designation, 42 U.S.C. § 1981), provides that "all persons . . . shall have the same right to make and enforce contracts . . . as enjoyed by white citizens." Since union memberships and employment relationships involve contracts, Section 1981 bans racial discrimination in these areas.

The courts have interpreted Section 1981 as giving a private plaintiff most of the same protections against racial discrimination that the 1964 Civil Rights Act provides. In addition, there are at least two advantages to the plaintiff who files a suit based on Section 1981. First, there are no procedural requirements for bringing such a suit, whereas there are a number of fairly complex requirements plaintiffs must follow before bringing a private suit under Title VII. For instance, before a plaintiff can file a lawsuit against an employer, the plaintiff must file charges of discrimination with the EEOC and obtain a notice of right to sue from the agency. By using Section 1981, a plaintiff can immediately sue an employer in federal court without first going through the EEOC.

Don't forget that Section 1981 is why racial discrimination is subject to damages far in excess of the $300,000 limit imposed on individuals under Title VII.

Unlimited Damages　A second advantage to Section 1981 is that under it the courts can award unlimited compensatory and punitive damages. There are no capped limits as there are under Title VII. As a practical matter, parties alleging racial discrimination usually sue under both Section 1981 and Title VII.

Note that Section 1981 does not cover discrimination based on sex, religion, national origin, age, or handicap. As interpreted by the courts, this section applies only to *racial* discrimination. However, what is race? The Supreme Court has held that being of Arabic or Jewish ancestry constitutes "race" as protected by Section 1981. The Court stated that when the law was passed in the nineteenth century, the concept of race was much broader than it is today. Race then included the descendants of a particular "family, tribe, people, or nation." Has the Court opened the door for a white job applicant to sue a black employer for discrimination under Section 1981?

In *Patterson v. McLean,* the Supreme Court interpreted Section 1981 to apply only to the actual hiring or firing of employees based on race. Under this interpretation, Section 1981 did not offer protection against discrimination such as a hostile working environment. But the Civil Rights Act amendments of 1991 redefined Section 1981 to include protection against discrimination in "enjoyment of all benefits, privileges, terms and conditions of the contractual relationship." Thus Section 1981 now also protects against hostile environment discrimination. In 2008, the Supreme Court also extended Section 1981 to claims of retaliation for complaining about race discrimination.

Under Section 1981, "race" includes ethnic or national groups.

13. DISCRIMINATION ON THE BASIS OF AGE

The workforce is "graying." The U.S. Census Bureau projects that by 2010 over 51 percent of the workforce will be 40 years of age or older. As percentages of older workers rise in coming years, so will the increase in complaints about age discrimination.

Neither the Civil Rights Act nor the Equal Employment Opportunity Act forbids discrimination based on age. However, the Age Discrimination in Employment Act (ADEA) does. It prohibits employment discrimination against employees ages 40 and older, and it prohibits the mandatory retirement of these employees. Only certain executives and high policymakers of private companies can be forced into early retirement. Specifically, "bona fide" executives and high-level policy makers age 65 and older who are entitled to receive annual retirement benefits of at least $44,000 a year are subject to mandatory retirement policies. The ADEA applies to employers with 20 or more employees. The ADEA also invalidates retirement plans and labor contracts that violate the law.

Types of Age Discrimination The ADEA recognizes both disparate treatment and disparate impact discrimination. The Supreme Court has upheld a jury's finding of disparate treatment in an age discrimination case. The employer had said the employee "was so old [he] must have come over on the Mayflower" and that he "was too damn old to do his job." When the employer later fired the employee, the jury found for the employee in spite of the employer's assertion that it had fired the employee for reasons other than age.

The Supreme Court has also stated that the ADEA recognizes disparate impact in age discrimination cases. The city of Jackson, Mississippi, had awarded pay raises to junior ranks of police officers that were substantially higher than the pay raises given to more senior ranks. These raises had the impact of discriminating on the basis of age. Older officers received lower pay raises becausee they were mostly in senior ranks.

However, the Supreme Court stated that disparate impact alone did not prove illegality under the ADEA. The city of Jackson was merely attempting

"Age bias is still a persistent problem in the 21st century workplace."

–Spencer H. Lewis, EEOC district director

to match the salaries offered to junior officers in nearby cities, which was a "reasonable factor other than age." See Sidebar 20.6 for an example of illegal mandatory retirement policy.

:: *sidebar* 20.6

Did You Read the Law? A Law Firm Runs Afoul of the ADEA

The EEOC filed a lawsuit against Sidley Austin Brown & Wood ("Sidley Austin"), a major Chicago-based international law firm, alleging that it violated the ADEA when it selected 32 "partners" for expulsion from the firm on account of their age or forced them to retire.

After over two years of litigation, Sidley Austin agreed to pay $27.5 million to the former partners. The firm also agreed to refrain from "terminating, expelling, retiring, reducing the compensation of or otherwise adversely changing the partnership status of any partner because of age" or "maintaining any formal or informal policy or practice requiring retirement as a partner or requiring permission to continue as a partner once the partner has reached a certain age."

*Source: EEOC Press Releases.

Employer Defenses in ADEA Cases   The employer defenses to age discrimination, disparate treatment, and disparate impact differ slightly from the defense in Title VII cases.

For instance, under the ADEA age is seldom recognized as the basis for a bona fide occupational qualification. It is recognized that as people grow older, their physical strength, agility, reflexes, hearing, and vision tend to diminish in quality. However, this generally provides no legal reason for discriminating against older persons as a class. Although courts will uphold job-related physical requirements if they apply on a case-by-case basis, they frequently find as illegal those policies that prohibit the hiring of persons beyond a maximum age or that establish a maximum age beyond which employees are forced to retire for physical reasons. Thus, one court ruled that a mandatory retirement age of 65 was illegally discriminatory as applied to the job of district fire chief. In an exception to the general rule, one court has ruled that age can be a BFOQ in a case where the airlines imposed a maximum age for hiring new pilots. The court observed that the Federal Aviation Administration mandated a retirement age for pilots.

| Willful violations of the ADEA allow courts to impose double damage awards against employers. |

The ADEA also does not require the employer to prove a "business necessity" in order to successfully defend an age discrimination case of disparate impact. All the employer need do is establish that a "reasonable factor other than age" accounted for the discriminatory impact. Further, unlike under Title VII, the employer's defense of a reasonable factor other than age cannot be defeated by the employee's showing of a less discriminatory way of achieving the employer's purpose.

Remedies under the ADEA   Courts have disagreed on whether remedies for violation of the ADEA include, in addition to reinstatement and wages lost, damages for the psychological trauma of being fired or forced to resign illegally. One federal district court awarded $200,000 to a victim of age discrimination who was an inventor and scientist, for the psychological and physical effects suffered from being forced into early retirement at age 60. Also awarded were out-of-pocket costs of $60,000 and attorneys' fees of $65,000. Note that *willful* violations of the act permit discrimination victims to be awarded *double damages*.

Note an important exception to this general rule about remedies under the ADEA. In accordance with the Supreme Court case *Kimel v. Florida Board of Regents* (2000), a plaintiff cannot recover money damages against a state entity. State law, however, may offer additional remedies for age discrimination perpetrated by a state.

14. DISCRIMINATION ON THE BASIS OF DISABILITIES

According to a Harris poll, two-thirds of all disabled Americans between the ages of 16 and 64 are not working, even though most of them want to work. To help those with disabilities obtain work, Congress in 1990 passed the Americans with Disabilities Act (ADA). Thereafter, the U.S. Supreme Court rendered a number of employer friendly decisions restricting the scope of the ADA's protection. Responding to criticism that the U.S. Supreme Court unreasonably restricted the ADA's scope, Congress passed the ADA Amendments Act of 2008, effective January 1, 2009. The ADA is now expanded to protect a broader group of individuals.

To prevent disability discrimination, the ADA prohibits employers from requiring a preemployment medical examination or asking questions about the job applicant's medical history. Only after a job offer has been extended can the employer condition employment on the employee's responses to *job related* medical questions.

The ADA prohibits employer discrimination against job applicants or employees based on (1) their having a disability, (2) their having a disability in the past, or (3) their being *regarded as* having a disability. The ADA defines disability as "any physical or mental impairment that substantially limits one or more of an individual's major life activities." "Physical and mental impairment" includes physical disorders and conditions, disease, disfigurement, amputation affecting a vital body system, psychological disorders, mental retardation, mental illness, and learning disabilities. An individual can demonstrate that he or she is "regarded as" having a disability by establishing that he or she has been subjected to an action prohibited by the ADA "because of an actual or perceived physical or mental impairment whether or not the impairment limits or is perceived to limit a major life activity."

The concept of "disability" includes mental disabilities and diseases as well as physical impairment.

"Major life activities" include such activities as "caring for oneself, performing manual tasks, seeing, hearing, eating, sleeping, walking, standing, lifting, bending, speaking, breathing, learning, reading, concentrating, thinking, communicating and working." The definition also includes the operation of any major body function, including functions of the immune system, normal cell growth, and digestive, bowel, bladder, neurological, brain, respiratory, circulatory, endocrine, and reproductive functions. The determination of whether an impairment substantially limits a major life activity must be made without regard to the "ameliorative effects of mitigating measures"—that is, individuals who use medications, artificial limbs, or hearing aids qualify for protection under the ADA, even though those measures may overcome the limiting effects of an impairment. (Ordinary eyeglasses and contact lenses are specifically excluded from this list by the amendments to the ADA.) The ADA also states that an individual with an impairment that is "transitory and minor," defined as having an actual or expected duration of six months or less, does not fall under the ADA. However, individuals with impairments that are episodic or in remission, such as epilepsy, diabetes, or cancer are not barred from coverage under the ADA.

Not included by the ADA as protected disabilities are homosexuality, sexual behavior disorders, compulsive gambling, kleptomania, and disorders resulting from _current_ drug or alcohol use. The emphasis on current drug or alcohol use means that employees who have successfully recovered or are successfully recovering from drug or alcohol disabilities are protected from employment discrimination.

The ADA prohibits employers of 15 or more employees (also unions with 15 or more members and employment agencies) from discriminating against the qualified disabled with respect to hiring, advancement, termination, compensation, training, or other terms, conditions, or privileges of employment. **Qualified disabled** are defined as those with a disability who, with or without reasonable accommodation, can perform the essential functions of a particular job position. Employers must make reasonable accommodation only for the _qualified_ disabled.

Reasonable Accommodation under the ADA The ADA does not require employers to hire the unqualified disabled, but they must make reasonable accommodation so qualified disabled employees can succeed in the workplace. **Reasonable accommodation** is the process of adjusting a job or work environment to fit the needs of disabled employees. It may include:

- Making the work facilities accessible and usable to disabled employees.
- Restructuring jobs or modifying work schedules.
- Purchasing or modifying necessary equipment for use by the disabled.
- Providing appropriate training materials or assistance modified to fit the needs of disabled employees.

In Case 20.2, the Supreme Court decides whether a requested accommodation that conflicts with seniority rules is "reasonable." Note that seniority rules may give employees preference in promotions and in getting or keeping various jobs on the basis of how long they have worked for an employer.

> According to the American Bar Association's *Mental & Physical Disability Law Reporter,* employers prevailed in 94.5 percent of 327 disability discrimination cases decided in federal courts across the United States in 2002.

> Individuals with HIV or AIDS are protected by the ADA. Persons who are discriminated against because they are regarded as being HIV-positive are also protected.

---

case **20.2** ::

U.S. AIRWAYS, INC. v. BARNETT
535 U.S. 391 (2002)

Robert Barnett (respondent), a cargo handler for U.S. Airways (petitioner), injured his back and became disabled. He transferred to a less physically demanding job in the mailroom. When his new job later became open to "employee bidding" under the U.S. Airways' seniority system and other employees _senior to him planned to bid on his job, he requested "accommodation." He wanted to keep his job without allowing senior employees to get it from him by bidding on it. When U.S. Airways refused this accommodation, Barnett sued under the ADA. The district court ruled for U.S. Airways, but the court_ *of appeals reversed. The Supreme Court granted certiorari.*

BREYER, J.: The question in the present case focuses on the relationship between seniority systems and the plaintiff's need to show that an "accommodation" seems reasonable. . . . We must assume that the plaintiff, an employee, is an "individual with a disability." He has requested assignment to a mailroom position as a "reasonable accommodation." We also assume that normally such a request would be reasonable within the meaning of the statute, were it not for one circumstance, namely, that the assignment would violate the rules of a seniority system. Does that circumstance mean that the proposed accommodation is not a "reasonable" one?

In our view, the answer to this question ordinarily is "yes." The statute does not require proof on a case-by-case basis that a seniority system should prevail. That is because it would not be reasonable in the run of cases that the assignment in question trump the rules of a seniority system. To the contrary, it will ordinarily be unreasonable for the assignment to prevail.

For one thing, the typical seniority system provides important employee benefits by creating, and fulfilling, employee expectations of fair, uniform treatment. These benefits include "job security and an opportunity for steady and predictable advancement based on objective standards." They include "an element of due process," limiting "unfairness in personal decisions." And they consequently encourage employees to invest in the employing company, accepting "less than their value to the firm early in their careers" in return for greater benefits in later years.

Most important for present purposes, to require the typical employer to show more than the existence of a seniority system might well undermine the employees' expectations of consistent, uniform treatment—expectations upon which the seniority system's benefits depend. That is because such a rule would substitute a complex case-specific "accommodation" decision made by management for the more uniform, impersonal operation of seniority rules. Such management decisionmaking, with its inevitable discretionary elements, would involve a matter of the greatest importance to employees, namely, layoffs; it would take place outside, as well as inside, the confines of a court case; and it might well take place fairly often. We can find nothing in the statute that suggests Congress intended to undermine seniority systems in this way. And we consequently conclude that the employer's showing of violation of the rules of a seniority system is by itself ordinarily sufficient.

The plaintiff (here the employee) nonetheless remains free to show that special circumstances warrant a finding that, despite the presence of a seniority system (which the ADA may not trump in the run of cases), the requested "accommodation" is "reasonable" on the particular facts. That is because special circumstances might alter the important expectations described above. The plaintiff might show, for example, that the employer, having retained the right to change the seniority system unilaterally, exercises that right fairly frequently, reducing employee expectations that the system will be followed—to the point where one more departure, needed to accommodate an individual with a disability, will not likely make a difference. The plaintiff might show that the system already contains exceptions such that, in the circumstances, one further exception is unlikely to matter. We do not mean these examples to exhaust the kinds of showings that a plaintiff might make. But we do mean to say that the plaintiff must bear the burden of showing special circumstances that make an exception from the seniority system reasonable in the particular case. And to do so, the plaintiff must explain why, in the particular case, an exception to the employer's seniority policy can constitute a "reasonable accommodation" even though in the ordinary case it cannot.

In its question presented, U.S. Airways asked us whether the ADA requires an employer to assign a disabled employee to a particular position even though another employee is entitled to that position under the employer's "established seniority system." We answer that *ordinarily* the ADA does not require that assignment. Hence, a showing that the assignment would violate the rules of a seniority system warrants summary judgment for the employer—unless there is more. The plaintiff must present evidence of that "more," namely, special circumstances surrounding the particular case that demonstrate the assignment is nonetheless reasonable.

We vacate the Court of Appeals' judgment and remand the case for further proceedings consistent with this opinion.

It is so ordered.

:: CASE QUESTIONS

1. What does the employee request the employer to do?
2. Why does the employer deny the accommodation request?
3. Does the Supreme Court decide that a seniority system "trumps" an accommodation request? Explain.

concept :: *summary*

Illegal Employment Practices

Unless bona fide occupational qualifications or business necessity can be proved, federal law prohibits recruiting, hiring, promoting, and other employment practices that involve disparate treatment or produce a disparate impact on the basis of:

- Race or color.
- National origin.
- Religion.

- Sex.
- Test scores and educational requirements.
- Height and weight.
- Appearance.
- Age.
- Disabilities.

Note that an employer need make only reasonable accommodation for disabled employees. The employer can plead *undue hardship,* defined as "an action requiring significant difficulty or expense," as a reason for not accommodating the needs of disabled employees. The ADA specifies that in evaluating undue hardship, the cost of the accommodation, the resources of the employer, the size of the employer, and the nature of the employer's business be considered.

Businesses must reasonably accommodate not only *employees* for their disabilities under the ADA but also customers and others who use public facilities such as hotels, restaurants, theaters, schools (even private ones), most places of entertainment, offices providing services, and other establishments doing business with the public. The Supreme Court ruled that the Professional Golf Association had to accommodate golfer Casey Martin, who suffered a walking disability because of a circulatory disorder, by allowing him to use a golf cart in PGA tournaments. The Court held (1) that PGA tournaments were open to any member of the public who paid a qualifying fee and participated successfully in a qualifying tournament and (2) that accommodating Casey Martin by allowing him to use a golf cart while other golfers walked a tournament course did not "fundamentally alter the nature" of PGA tournament events.

> The remedies under the ADA are basically the same remedies available under Title VII.

Remedies under the ADA   Remedies under the ADA are basically the same remedies available under the Civil Rights Act, including hiring, reinstatement, back pay, injunctive relief, and compensatory and punitive damages. As with the Civil Rights Act, a plaintiff must first seek administration remedies with the EEOC. Compensatory and punitive damages are not available for policies that mere have disparate impact. They are available for intentional discrimination and for other employer actions such as failing to make reasonable accommodation for known job applicant or employee disabilities.

The ADA replaces the Rehabilitation Act of 1973 as the primary federal law protecting the disabled. However, the Rehabilitation Act, which applies only to employers doing business with the government under a federal contract for $2,500 or more, still requires that such employers have a qualified affirmative action program for hiring and promoting the disabled.

15. GENETIC DISCRIMINATION

The **Genetic Information Nondiscrimination Act (GINA),** effective November 2009, prohibits covered employers from firing, refusing to hire, or otherwise discriminating against individuals on the basis of their genetic information, and from discriminating against employees and applicants on the basis of a family member's genetic information. "Covered employers" is defined as all employers subject to Title VII. The act further prohibits the limitation, segregation, or classification of employees in such a way "that would deprive or tend to deprive any employee of employment opportunities or otherwise adversely affect the status of the employee as an employee, because of genetic information with respect to the employee."

Under GINA, it is unlawful for an employer to "request, require, or purchase genetic information with respect to an employee or the family member of an employee," with limited exceptions.

GINA also has ramifications for group health plans and health insurance companies. Although many states have already enacted similar legislation, GINA establishes a federal baseline for protection against employment discrimination based on genetic information.

16. UNIFORMED SERVICES EMPLOYMENT AND REEMPLOYMENT RIGHTS ACT

The **Uniformed Services Employment and Reemployment Rights Act (USERRA)** protects the rights of individuals who voluntarily or involuntarily leave employment positions to undertake military service or certain types of service in the National Disaster Medical System. Specifically, USERRA provides reemployment rights following a period of service if:

- The individual held a civilian job.
- The employee informed the employer that he/she was leaving the job for service in the uniformed services.
- The period of service did not exceed five years (with exceptions).
- The release from service was under "honorable conditions."
- The individual reports back to the civilian employer in a timely manner or submits a timely application for reemployment.

Those eligible to be reemployed must be restored to the job and receive benefits that would have been attained had there not been an absence due to military service. USERRA protects those performing uniformed service from discrimination in:

- Initial employment.
- Reemployment.
- Retention in employment.
- Promotion.
- Any benefit of employment.

Employers may not retaliate against anyone assisting in the enforcement of USERRA rights, even if that person has no service connection.

USERRA also contains health insurance provisions. Covered individuals who leave a job to perform military service have the right to elect to continue existing employer-based health plan coverage for up to 24 months. For those who do not elect to continue coverage, they have the right to be reinstated in the employer's health plan when reemployed, generally without any waiting periods or exclusions (except for service-connected illnesses or injuries). Federal law requires employers to notify employees of their rights under USERRA, including the display of government notices.

17. DISCRIMINATION IN GETTING AND KEEPING HEALTH INSURANCE

A new act prohibits group health plans and health insurance issuers from discriminating against employees based on certain factors. The Health Insurance Portability and Accountability Act (HIPAA) forbids group plans and issuers from excluding an employee from insurance coverage or requiring different premiums based on the employee's health status, medical condition or history, genetic information, or disability.

The act primarily prevents discrimination against individual employees in small businesses. Before the act, individual employees with an illness like cancer or a genetic condition like sickle cell anemia were sometimes denied coverage in a new health plan. The small size of the plan deterred insurers from covering individual employees whose medical condition might produce large claims. The act denies insurers the right to discriminate on this basis. It also guarantees that insured employees who leave their old employer and join a new employer are not denied health insurance. As of this writing, the exact meanings of many HIPAA provisions are still unclear.

Note, however, that the act only applies to prevent discrimination in group health insurance plans. It does not apply to individuals who purchase individual health insurance. Congress is considering legislation to extend HIPAA's antidiscrimination provisions to individual insurance. Behind HIPAA and proposals for new legislation is the concern that new forms of genetic testing will allow insurers and employers to identify and discriminate against individuals who may in the future develop certain medical conditions.

18. OTHER FEDERAL LEGISLATION

Other federal legislation dealing with employment discrimination includes the National Labor Relations Act of 1936. The National Labor Relations Board has ruled that appeals to racial prejudice in a collective bargaining representation election constitute an unfair labor practice. The NLRB has also revoked the certification of unions that practice discriminatory admission or representation policies. Additionally, employers have an obligation to bargain with certified unions over matters of employment discrimination. Such matters are considered "terms and conditions of employment" and are thus mandatory bargaining issues.

Finally, various other federal agencies may prohibit discriminatory employment practices under their authorizing statutes. The Federal Communications Commission, for example, has prohibited employment discrimination by its licensees (radio and TV stations) and has required the submission of affirmative action plans as a condition of license renewal.

19. STATE ANTIDISCRIMINATION LAWS

Federal laws concerning equal employment opportunity specifically permit state laws imposing additional duties and liabilities. In recent years, fair employment practices legislation has been introduced and passed by many state legislatures. When the federal Equal Employment Opportunity Act became effective, 40 states had such laws, but their provisions varied considerably. A typical state act makes it an unfair employment practice for any employer to refuse to hire or otherwise discriminate against any individual because of his or her race, color, religion, national origin, or ancestry. If employment agencies or labor organizations discriminate against an individual in any way because of one of these reasons, they are also guilty of an unfair employment practice. State acts usually set up an administrative body, generally known as the Fair Employment Practices Commission, which has the power to make rules and regulations and hear and decide charges of violations filed by complainants.

State antidiscrimination laws sometimes protect categories of persons not protected by federal law. For example, some protect persons from employment discrimination based on weight.

As discussed earlier, state and local law may prohibit sexual orientation discrimination in the workplace (see Sidebar 20.5). Other state and local laws prohibit employment discrimination based on weight (e.g., Michigan; Santa Cruz and San Francisco, California; and Washington DC). Michigan's antidiscrimination discrimination law also includes height and weight.

State law may also supplement Title VII, offering remedies to victims of sexual harassment. In New York, for example, former Knicks team executive Anucha Browne Sanders sued the owner of the New York Knicks and Madison Square Garden for discrimination using Title VII, as well as New York State Human Rights Law, New York Executive Law §296, and the Administrative Code of the City of New York §8-107, which prohibit unlawful discriminatory practices. After hearing testimony about crude racial and sexual insults and unwanted advances from coach Isiah Thomas, a jury awarded Sanders $11.6 million.

As indicated in Chapter 10 on torts, discrimination plaintiffs can also sue employers under various state common law causes of action, like negligence, assault, battery, intentional infliction of mental distress, invasion of privacy, and defamation. Under common law, plaintiffs may be able to receive unlimited compensatory and punitive damages, and greater numbers of plaintiffs seem to be suing under common law. In Las Vegas a jury awarded over $5 million against the Hilton Hotel and in favor of a plaintiff who had been sexually groped at an aviators' Tailhook convention. The jury determined that the hotel had been negligent in failing to provide adequate security.

20. TRENDS IN EMPLOYMENT DISCRIMINATION AND LITIGATION

Several current trends in employment discrimination and litigation will require close attention from managers in the coming years. These trends highlight the fact that the workforce is increasingly diverse and that new managers must be

> State antidiscrimination laws may permit discrimination lawsuits against employers of fewer than 15 employees, the minimum number for a lawsuit under federal Title VII.

> According to a study by the Rudd Center at Yale University, discrimination against overweight people, particularly women, is as common as racial discrimination.

> **Do** remember that discrimination lawsuits can be based on multiple causes of action, including common law ones.

alert to the full impact of antidiscrimination laws. They also show the effects of new technology.

Surge in Private Lawsuits   Private lawsuits alleging discrimination in employment surged in recent years, more than tripling. Several factors account for the rapid increase. The 1991 revision of the Civil Rights Act to support punitive and compensatory damages has encouraged employees to sue their employers. The passage of the Americans with Disabilities Act has led to a new area of discrimination lawsuits, and some 50 million Americans, according to a conservative estimate, may legally qualify as disabled. Finally, as the large generation of baby boomers ages in the workforce, more lawsuits arise under the Age Discrimination in Employment Act. In the new century, these trends continue, making it ever more important for business managers to understand the law prohibiting discrimination in employment. See Sidebar 20.7 for an interesting study about female CEOs.

:: *sidebar* 20.7

Is It Important to Investors If the CEO Is a Man or a Woman?

The clear answer is, unfortunately, "Yes" according to a study by Lyda Bigelow and Judi McLean Parks at the Olin School of Business, Washington University in St. Louis.

Bigelow and McLean Parks created a prospectus for a fictitious company about to go public, along with a set of qualifications for the company's CEO. To determine if gender played a role in the decision, they gave half of the potential investors information with a female CEO and the other half a male CEO—the qualifications, however, were the same. Only the name and gender were different. They then asked individuals with a background in finance to consider investing in the company.

The researchers found that the CEO's gender clearly affected potential investors. For example, the study showed that the participants were inclined to invest up to three times more with the company with the male CEO.

Executive compensation was also an issue. The participants in the study indicated that they would pay the female CEO 14 percent less than her male counterpart.

Perhaps even more disturbing, female CEOs were evaluated more harshly in other very subjective categories. Although the only difference given in the study was gender, participants deemed female CEOs as less competent leaders in a variety of realms, including handling a crisis and dealing with the company's board of directors.

Overall, the study showed that participants viewed male CEOs as more favorable representatives of the company in the public eye.

Source: U.S. News and World Report, www.usnews.com/usnews/biztech/articles/060508/8investment_bias.htm.

Arbitration in Employment Discrimination Disputes
Arbitration is usually cheaper, quicker, and less public than litigation. Accustomed to using arbitration clauses in contracts with customers and suppliers, many employers also have begun placing arbitration clauses in employment contracts and personnel handbooks. These clauses require arbitration in employment discrimination disputes and with other employment controversies.

The Federal Arbitration Act (see Chapter 5) prefers arbitration over litigation, but that act may not apply to certain employment contracts. The EEOC has issued a policy statement concluding that "agreements that mandate binding arbitration of discrimination claims as a condition of employment are contrary to the fundamental principles" of antidiscrimination laws.

However, without specifically discussing the EEOC's policy statement, the Supreme Court has upheld arbitration clauses in certain employment discrimination cases. In *Circuit City Stores, Inc. v. Adams,* 532 U.S. 105 (2001), the Supreme Court decided that the Federal Arbitration Act did not prohibit enforceability of the following arbitration provision, which an employee had signed in his job application:

> I agree that I will settle any and all previously unasserted claims, disputes or controversies arising out of or relating to my application or candidacy for employment, employment and/or cessation of employment with Circuit City, *exclusively* by final and binding *arbitration* before a neutral arbitrator. By way of example only, such claims include claims under federal, state, and local statutory or common law, such as the Age Discrimination in Employment Act, Title VII of the Civil Rights Act of 1964, as amended, including the amendments of the Civil Rights Act of 1991, the Americans with Disabilities Act, the law of contract and the law of tort.

Congress may ultimately decide whether binding arbitration as a condition of working for an employer is an acceptable part of the employment contract. In the meantime, employers who wish to have employment disputes, including discrimination disputes, arbitrated should consider the following:

- Paying employees separately from the employment contract to sign arbitration agreements.
- Ensuring that arbitration agreements allow for the same range of remedies contained in the antidiscrimination laws.
- Allowing limited discovery in arbitration, which traditionally has no discovery process.
- Permitting employees to participate in selecting neutral, knowledgeable professional arbitrators instead of using an industry arbitration panel.
- Not requiring the employee to pay arbitration fees and costs.

These steps should go far toward eliminating many of the objections to the arbitration of employment discrimination disputes.

Proper arbitration agreements should continue to be considered as a business response to discrimination in employment disputes. Interestingly, at least one study has found that employees alleging discrimination win more often before arbitration panels than before juries and only two-thirds of the time.

Insuring against Employment Discrimination Claims

Employers commonly insure against many potential liabilities. However, the general liability policies carried by many businesses, which cover bodily injury and property damage, often do not insure against intentional torts. Intent is a key element in many employment discrimination claims. In addition, general policies may not cover the back pay or damages for mental anguish that many discrimination plaintiffs seek. As a result, employers are beginning to ask for and get employment practices liability insurance, a type of insurance aimed specifically at discrimination claims.

Even with the availability of the new insurance, not all types of employment discrimination can be insured against in every state. States like New York and California do not permit companies to insure against "intentional acts." Disparate treatment discrimination is an example of such an act. Similarly, some states do not permit companies to insure against punitive damages that can arise in intentional violations of Title VII. Managers should also be aware that what the new policies cover and what they exclude vary widely.

> Insurance policies are more likely to insure against disparate impact claims rather than disparate treatment claims. Do you understand why?

:: Key Terms

Affirmative action 606	Genetic Information	Reverse discrimination 606
Bona fide occupational	Nondiscrimination Act	Section 1981 608
qualifications (BFOQs) 590	(GINA) 615	Seniority system 607
Business necessity defense 593	Hostile work environment 598	Sexual harassment 597
Comparable worth 602	Qualified disabled 612	Uniformed Services
Disability 611	Reasonable accommodation	Employment and
Disparate impact 593	612	Reemployment Rights Act
Disparate treatment 592	Retaliation 593	(USERRA) 615

:: Review Questions and Problems

The Civil Rights Act of 1964

1. *General Provisions*

   Martel, a competent male secretary to the president of ICU, was fired because the new president of the company believed it is more appropriate to have a female secretary.

   (a) Has a violation of the law occurred?

   (b) Assume that a violation of the law has occurred and Martel decided to take an extended vacation after he was fired. Upon his return seven months later, Martel filed suit in federal district court against ICU, charging illegal discrimination under the Civil Rights Act of 1964. What remedies will be available to him under the act?

2. *Enforcement Procedures*

   Muscles-Are-You, Inc., a bodybuilding spa targeted primarily toward male bodybuilders, refused to hire a woman for the position of executive director. The spa's management stated that the executive director must have a "macho" image to relate well with the spa's customers. Discuss whether it is likely that the spa has violated Title VII.

3. *Discrimination on the Basis of Race or Color*

   Does Title VII prohibit employment discrimination against members of all races? Explain.

4. *Discrimination on the Basis of National Origin*

   Ace Tennis Co. hires only employees who speak English. Does this policy illegally discriminate against Hispanic job applicants who speak only Spanish? Discuss.

5. *Discrimination on the Basis of Religion*

Ortega, an employee of ABC, Inc., recently joined a church that forbids working on Saturdays, Sundays, and Mondays. Ortega requested that his employer change his work schedule from eight-hour days, Monday through Friday, to ten-hour days, Tuesday through Friday. Ortega's request was refused because the employer is in operation only eight hours per day, five days a week. After a month during which Ortega failed to work on Mondays, he was fired. The employer stated that "only a full-time employee would be acceptable" for Ortega's position. What are Ortega's legal rights, if any?

6. *Discrimination on the Basis of Sex*

A male supervisor at Star Company made repeated offensive sexual remarks to female employees. The employees complained to higher management, which ignored the complaints. If the company does not discharge or otherwise penalize the employee, has it violated Title VII? Discuss.

Employment Practices That May Be Challenged

7. *Questionnaires, Interviews, Testing, and Educational Requirements*

Jennings Company, which manufactures sophisticated electronic equipment, hires its assembly employees on the basis of applicants' scores on a standardized mathematics aptitude test. It has been shown that those who score higher on the test almost always perform better on the job. However, it has also been demonstrated that the use of the test in hiring employees has the effect of excluding African Americans and other minority groups. Is this practice of the Jennings Company prohibited by the Civil Rights Act of 1964?

8. *Height and Weight Requirements*

(a) An employer hires job applicants to wait tables in the Executive Heights Restaurant only if they are over 6 feet tall. Does this policy likely violate Title VII? Explain.

(b) If a class of job applicants under 6 feet sues the employer, will it likely get compensatory and punitive damages? Explain.

9. *Appearance Requirements*

Silicon Products requires all male employees to wear their hair "off the collar." Does this policy violate Title VII? Discuss.

10. *Affirmative Action Programs and Reverse Discrimination*

Kartel, Inc., found that historically African Americans had been significantly underrepresented in its workforce. It decided to remedy the situation and place African Americans in 50 percent of all new job openings. Discuss the legality of Kartel's action.

11. *Seniority Systems*

Are seniority systems in the workplace legal under Title VII if in fact they discriminate on the basis of gender or race? Explain.

Other Statutes and Discrimination in Employment

12. *Civil Rights Act of 1866*

When is it an advantage for a plaintiff to use Section 1981 as the basis for discrimination litigation as contrasted with using Title VII?

13. *Discrimination on the Basis of Age*

Cantrell, the controller of Xylec's, Inc., was forced to retire at age 58 due to a general company policy. Although Cantrell has a company pension of $50,000 per year, she believes that her lifestyle will soon be hampered due to inflation, since the pension provides for no cost-of-living increases. What are Cantrell's rights, if any?

14. *Discrimination on the Basis of Disabilities*

    Ralph is a systems analyst for the Silicon Corporation, a major defense contractor. When Ralph's co-workers learn that he has AIDS, six of them quit work immediately. Fearing that additional resignations will delay production, the company discharges Ralph. Discuss whether or not the company acted legally.

15. *Discrimination in Getting and Keeping Health Insurance*

    Why does Title VII not apply to preventing discrimination in the getting and keeping of health insurance?

16. *Genetic Discrimination*

    Amy learns that she has the "breast cancer gene." Devastated, she shares the news with her supervisor. A few days later, Amy receives a harsh employment evaluation—the first of her career—criticizing her handling of a client matter. Two weeks later, Amy is fired. Amy cannot understand how she went from being a model employee with strong performance reviews to unemployed in such a short time. Does she have any claim against her employer?

17. *Uniformed Services Employment and Reemployment Rights Act*

    Robert left his position as a commercial airline pilot to undertake his duties in the Marine Reserves for a tour of duty in Iraq. When he returns home a year later, his employer apologetically tells him that they filled his position during his absence and they "will call" when something comes available. They also express concern about his ability to fly commercial jets because he has not flown in the last year. What legal recourse does Robert have, if any?

18. *Other Federal Legislation*

    Do employers have an obligation to negotiate with groups of employees over issues of discrimination? Explain.

19. *State Antidiscrimination Laws*

    Explain how state antidiscrimination laws protect workers in situations where federal laws do not.

20. *Trends in Employment Discrimination and Litigation*

    Can arbitration agreements be used to keep employees from litigating discrimination issues? Discuss.

1. When Maria Suarez got her new job, she was happy. As an oil rigger, she would make enough money to support herself and her two children. But after a week of working with a primarily male crew, her happiness was gone. Her co-workers were the reason. At first the men made unwelcome comments about her body. Then sexual graffiti mentioning her name appeared. When she came to work one morning a nude female picture was pinned to one of the rigs. Her name had been scrawled across the bottom. Maria complained to the crew foreman, who referred her to the site manager. "Let's ignore it for a while," he told Maria. "It's just good fun. The men are testing you. You've got to fit in."

What are Maria's legal rights in this situation?

What would you do if you were the site manager?

Do you think Maria should just try to "fit in"?

2. Delivery Quik, Inc., delivers packages to small retail stores from a central distribution point in a major metropolitan area. Drivers both load and unload their packages, some of which weigh close to 100 pounds. Although equipment helps the drivers in their tasks, there is still considerable lifting necessary. Delivery Quik has a policy that drivers must stand at least 6 feet tall and weigh no less than 180 pounds. All drivers must retire at age 45 and have at least a high school education.

Does the height, weight, age, and education policy discriminate illegally?

How would you change the policy?

If your customers prefer male drivers, does their preference mean that the company can hire only males as drivers?

21

Labor-Management Relationship

Chapters 19 and 20 pertain to "employment law," the area of the law that controls how employers must treat applicants for employment, employees, and former employees. As you know, employment law encompasses a wide variety of employer-employee workplace issues. This chapter focuses on *labor laws*, the area of the law designed to equalize the bargaining power between employers and employees. Specifically, labor law prohibits employers and unions from engaging in specified "unfair labor practices" and establishes an obligation of both parties to engage in good-faith collective bargaining. Labor laws pertain to the relationships between employers and unions, granting employees the right to unionize and allowing employers and employees to engage in certain activities (such as strikes, picketing, seeking injunctions, lockouts). These laws regulating labor-management relations are largely a product of the New Deal era of the 1930s.

Although union membership is not as large as it once was in the United States, unions are alive and well with active agendas on behalf of their members. They are also high-profile advocates during political elections and on labor-related topics such as international trade. A number of free trade agreements discussed in Chapter 13, in particular NAFTA and DR-CAFTA, faced vocal opposition from labor unions. Despite their smaller numbers, labor unions continue to be formidable in the United States.

:: Labor Laws

The National Education Association is the largest union with 2.7 million members.

"The basic principle that brings us here today is that American workers cannot win a better life unless more workers belong to unions."

–Statement of five union presidents announcing the Change to Win Coalition

"Forming this coalition is a step in the wrong direction because it's the first step toward a truly divided labor movement. Splitting the AFL-CIO will mean less power for workers."

–Gerald W. McEntree, president of the American Federation of State, County and Municipal Employees

What is your reaction to the word *union*? Do your thoughts have a mostly positive or negative connotation? Society's reaction and the government's response to the union movement have varied over time. Thus, your reaction is not right or wrong; it is likely formed by where you were raised and what your parents did to support you. Children of business managers probably have a very different perspective of unions, than children of workers whose wages were increased and job security strengthened through the efforts of union bargaining agents.

A union is basically workers organizing their collective voices to increase their ability to communicate with their employer. As a concept, a union is neither good nor bad. How the concept is utilized makes all the difference in one's view of unions.

Does such a viewpoint really matter today? Haven't unions outlived their usefulness? These questions and other similar ones are very much in today's public debate. Interestingly, this debate is occurring among union leaders as well. The statistics tell a varied story. Often cited is the declining percentage of the workforce that is unionized. However, Table 21.1 illustrates that story is more complex due to the decline in private employees being offset by the growth of public employees who are union members.

The largest unions in the United States represent teachers, government employees, and service workers. The focus on how much time and money are dedicated to recruiting new members through intensive organizing campaigns at the work site versus through political efforts caused a split in the AFL-CIO, labor's longtime unified voice. Five of the larger unions formed a group called Change to Win. See Sidebar 21.1 for union statistics.

The goal of labor laws is successful **collective bargaining**, the process by which labor and management negotiate and reach agreements on matters of importance to both. Such matters include wages to be paid workers, hours to be worked, and other terms and conditions of employment. Collective

table 21.1 :: Statistics on Union Membership

:: Year	:: Private		:: Public		:: Total Membership	
1953	35.7%*	15,540,000	11.6%	770,000	32.5%*	16,310,000
1975	26.3	16,397,000	39.6	5,810,000	28.9	22,207,000*
2004	7.9	8,205,000	36.6	8,131,000*	12.5	15,472,000

*Record highs

Source: www.lraonline.org/econ_stats.org.

:: *sidebar* 21.1

Statistics on Union Membership

According to the Department of Labor, the number of workers belonging to a union rose by 311,000 in 2007 to 15.7 million. Other statistics:

- Union members accounted for 12.1 percent of all employed wage and salary workers. (In 1983, the first year data was available, union membership was 20.1 percent.)
- Workers in the public sector had a union membership rate nearly five times (35.9 percent) that of private sector employees (7.5 percent).
- Education, training, and library occupations had the highest unionization rate among all occupations

(37.2 percent), followed by protective service occupations (35.2 percent).

- Among demographic groups, the union membership rate was highest for black men and lowest for Hispanic women.
- Union membership varies substantially by state. For example, union membership is 20 percent or more in Washington and New York, as opposed to 4.9 percent or less in Georgia and Texas.

*Source: Bureau of Labor Statistics (January 25, 2008), www.bls.gov/news.release/pdf/union2.pdf.

---

bargaining can be successful only if the bargaining power of the parties is equal. Most laws regulating labor management relations seek to equalize this bargaining power. As a result, some laws add to the bargaining position of labor and others add to that of management.

These laws have been passed when Congress perceived that one side's bargaining power was excessive. As in any balancing process, it is very difficult to hit the right middle point. Thus, as you read the following sections understand that the labor-management relationship is a delicate one involving many nuances. Table 21.2 lists the major federal labor laws.

1. LAWS BEFORE 1935

Until 1935, Congress viewed management as having greater bargaining power in the labor-management relationship. This view certainly was justified since the union movement historically was met with strong and swift reprisals by employers. It was not uncommon in the 1800s and early 1900s for workers who tried to unionize to be fired or, worse, beaten, even killed. This treatment of workers engaged in unacceptable behavior, from the employers' viewpoint, certainly kept management in a strong bargaining position and prevented unions from growing. In a series of "prolabor" laws, Congress took action to correct the inequalities. It did so by passing the following:

- The Clayton Act.
- The Railway Labor Act.
- The Norris-LaGuardia Act.

The Clayton Act   The first federal statute of any importance to the labor movement is the **Clayton Act** of 1914, which was passed principally to strengthen the antitrust laws. Between 1890 (when the Sherman Antitrust Act was passed) and 1914, labor unions were weak in their ability to represent

> "With all their faults, trade unions have done more for humanity than any other organization of men that ever existed. They have done more for decency, for honesty, for education, for the betterment of the race, for the developing of character in men, than any other association of men."
>
> **–Clarence Darrow,** *The Railroad Trainman* **(1909)**

Do recall that the Clayton Act is considered an antitrust law (see Chapter 16). Congress can use one law to impact various legal areas.

table 21.2 :: Federal Laws Governing Labor-Management Relations

:: Year	:: Statute	:: Major Provisions
1914	Clayton Act	1. Exempted union activity from the antitrust laws.
1926	Railway Labor Act	1. Governs collective bargaining for railroads and airlines.
		2. Created the National Mediation Board to conduct union elections and mediate differences between employers and unions.
1932	Norris-LaGuardia Act	1. Outlawed yellow-dog contracts.
		2. Prohibited federal courts from enjoining lawful union activities, including picketing and strikes.
1935	Wagner Act (National Labor Relations Act)	1. Created the National Labor Relations Board (NLRB).
		2. Authorized the NLRB to conduct union certification elections.
		3. Outlawed certain conduct by management as unfair to labor (five unfair labor practices).
		4. Authorized the NLRB to hold hearings on unfair labor practices and correct wrongs resulting from them.
1947	Taft-Hartley Act (Labor-Management Relations Act)	1. Outlawed certain conduct by unions as six unfair labor practices.
		2. Provided for an 80-day cooling-off period in strikes that imperil national health or safety.
		3. Allowed states to enact right-to-work laws.
		4. Created the Federal Mediation and Conciliation Service to assist in settlement of labor disputes.
1959	Landrum-Griffin Act (Labor-Management Reporting and Disclosure Act, LMRDA)	1. Created a Bill of Rights for union members.
		2. Requires reports to the secretary of labor.
		3. Added to the list of unfair labor practices.

employees. At least one reason for the relative strength enjoyed by management was the fact that it could and did argue that employees acting together were restraining trade illegally under the Sherman Act.

The Clayton Act stated that antitrust laws regulating anticompetitive contracts did not apply to labor unions or their members in lawfully carrying out their legitimate activities. This exemption covered only *legitimate* union practices. Although the Clayton Act exempted employees from the claim that they were restraining trade through unionization, this law did not expressly grant employees the protected right to join a union. Therefore, the Clayton Act did not balance the bargaining power between labor and management. The latter group remained the stronger one.

The Railway Labor Act
Among the first industries to unionize were the railroads. In 1926, Congress enacted the **Railway Labor Act** to encourage collective bargaining in the railroad industry. The goal was to resolve labor disputes that might otherwise disrupt transportation and result in violence. The act was later extended to airlines; today it applies to both air and rail transportation. It established the three-member **National Mediation Board,** which must designate the bargaining representative for any given bargaining unit of employees in the railway or air transport industries. The board generally does this by holding representation elections. Specifically, when the parties

to a dispute over proposed contract terms in the transportation industry cannot reach an agreement concerning rates of pay or working conditions, the National Mediation Board must attempt mediation of their differences. If mediation does not resolve their differences, the board encourages voluntary arbitration. If the parties refuse arbitration and the dispute is likely to disrupt interstate commerce substantially, the board informs the president, who then appoints a special emergency board. This emergency board lacks judicial power, but it encourages the parties to reach an agreement by investigating the dispute and publishing its findings of fact and recommendations for settlement. During the investigation, which lasts 30 days, and for an additional 30 days after the report is issued, business is conducted without interruption. The parties, however, have no duty to comply with the special board's proposals. Thus, if no new collective bargaining agreement is reached after the 60-day period, lockouts by management and strikes by workers become legal.

The Railway Labor Act has played a vitally important role in balancing the labor-management relationship in the transportation industries. However, due to this act's limited application, the management of businesses outside the transportation industry generally continued to have superior bargaining power following 1926.

The Norris-LaGuardia Act Because of management's superior bargaining power, prior to 1932 management often made it a condition of employment that employees agree not to join a labor union. Such agreements became known as **yollow-dog contracts** because any employee who would forsake the right to join fellow employees in unionization was considered a cowardly scoundrel (yellow dog). Passed in 1932, the **Norris-LaGuardia Act** made yellow-dog contracts illegal. In essence, management no longer could explicitly deny an employee the right to unionize.

Seeking injunctions to stop concerted activities had remained an important tool of management in fighting the growth of labor unions. The Norris-LaGuardia Act listed specific acts of persons and organizations participating in labor disputes that were not subject to federal court injunctions. Federal courts cannot enjoin:

- Striking or quitting work.
- Belonging to a labor organization.
- Paying strike or unemployment benefits to participants in a labor dispute.
- Publicizing the existence of a labor dispute or the facts related to it (including picketing).
- Assembling peaceably to promote interests in a labor dispute.
- Agreeing with others or advising or causing them to do any of the above acts without fraud or violence.

Although the Norris-LaGuardia Act greatly restricts the use of injunctions in labor disputes, it does not prohibit them altogether. An injunction may be issued to enjoin illegal strikes, such as ones by public employees. In addition, a party seeking an injunction in a labor dispute must meet the test of a stringent, clean-hands rule. No restraining order will be granted to any person who fails to comply with any obligation imposed by law or who fails to make every reasonable effort to settle the dispute.

"It is one of the characteristics of a free and democratic nation that it has free and independent labor unions."

–Franklin Delano Roosevelt

The timing of the law (1932) likely limited its impact on helping unions. During the Depression, people were more concerned about finding a job than they were about joining a union.

The Norris LaGuardia Act restricts the use of federal court injunctions in labor disputes; it does not limit the jurisdiction of state courts in issuing them. The Supreme Court has upheld the jurisdiction of a state court to enjoin a union's work stoppage and picketing in violation of a no-strike clause in its collective bargaining agreement.

:: The Wagner Act

"Long ago we stated the reason for labor organizations. We said that they were organized out of the necessities of the situation . . . that [a] union was essential to give laborers opportunity to deal on an equality with their employer."

–NLRB v. Jones & Laughlin Steel Corp., 301 U.S. 1 (1937)

The labor movement received its greatest stimulus for growth with the enactment in 1935 of the National Labor Relations Act, known as the **Wagner Act.** Perhaps most significantly, Congress explicitly affirmed labor's right to organize and to bargain collectively. Recognizing that a major cause of industrial strife was the inequality of bargaining power between employees and employers, Section 7 of the act states:

> Employees shall have the right to self-organization, to form, join, or assist labor organizations, to bargain collectively through representatives of their own choosing, and to engage in concerted activities for the purpose of collective bargaining or other mutual aid or protection.

In addition to this Section 7 right to unionize, the Wagner Act contains several other key provisions:

- Creating the National Labor Relations Board (NLRB) to administer the act.
- Providing employees the right to select a union to act as their collective bargaining agent.
- Outlawing certain conduct by employers that generally has the effect of either preventing the organization of employees or emasculating their unions where they do exist; these forbidden acts are called *unfair labor practices.*
- Authorizing the NLRB to conduct hearings on unfair labor practice allegations and, if unfair practices are found to exist, to take corrective action including issuing cease and desist orders and awarding dollar damages to unions and employees.

2. THE NATIONAL LABOR RELATIONS BOARD

"If capitalism is fair then unionism must be. If men have a right to capitalize their ideas and the resources of their country, then that implies the right of men to capitalize their labor."

–Frank Lloyd Wright

Established by the Wagner Act, the **National Labor Relations Board (NLRB)** operates as an independent agency of the U.S. government. This section discusses the organizational structure of the NLRB, its jurisdiction, and its quasi-judicial function. Section 10 examines the NLRB's authority to certify unions as the collective bargaining representative of employees. After this introduction to the NLRB, the remainder of the chapter will illustrate the significant role this agency plays in balancing the labor-management relationship.

NLRB Organization   The NLRB consists of five members, appointed by the president with the advice and consent of the Senate, who serve staggered terms of five years each. In addition, there is a general counsel of the board who supervises board investigations and serves as prosecutor in cases before the board. The general counsel supervises operations of the

NLRB so that the board itself may perform its quasi-judicial function of deciding unfair labor practice cases free of bias. Administrative law judges are responsible for the initial conduct of hearings in unfair labor practice cases.

The general counsel also is responsible for conducting representation elections. In addition, the general counsel is responsible for seeking court orders requiring compliance with the board's orders and represents the board in miscellaneous litigation. The board determines policy questions, such as what types of employers and groups of employees are covered by the labor law.

Jurisdiction   Congress gave the NLRB jurisdiction over any business "affecting commerce." However, the following personnel are exempt from the NLRB's authority:

- Governmental employees.
- Persons covered by the Railway Labor Act.
- Independent contractors.
- Agricultural laborers.
- Household, domestic workers.
- Employees who work for their spouse or parents.

The NLRB cannot exercise its powers over all business because it has a limited budget and time constraints. Sidebar 21.2 describes the guidelines the NLRB uses to decide which businesses to regulate. As a result of these self-imposed restrictions, federal labor laws do not apply to many small businesses. The management of these businesses may still need to know what state labor laws require of them. See Case 21.1 for an example of a recent NLRB decision.

:: *sidebar* 21.2

NLRB Assumes Jurisdiction over the Following

- Nonretail operations with an annual outflow or inflow across state lines of at least $50,000.
- Retail enterprises with a gross volume of $500,000 or more a year.
- Enterprises operating office buildings if the gross revenues are at least $100,000 per year.
- Transportation enterprises furnishing interstate services.
- Local transit systems with an annual gross volume of $250,000.
- Newspapers that subscribe to interstate news services, publish nationally syndicated features, or advertise nationally sold products and have a minimum annual gross volume of $250,000.

- Communication enterprises that operate radio or television stations or telephone or telegraph services with a gross volume of $100,000 or more per year.
- Local public utilities with an annual gross volume of $250,000 per year or an outflow or inflow of goods or services across state lines of $50,000 or more per year.
- Hotel and motel enterprises that serve transient guests and gross at least $500,000 in revenues per year.
- All enterprises whose operations have a substantial impact on national defense.
- Nonprofit hospitals.
- Private universities and colleges.

case 21.1

THE GUARD PUBLISHING COMPANY D/B/A THE REGISTER-GUARD *AND* EUGENE NEWSPAPER GUILD, CWA LOCAL 37194.
Cases 36–CA–8743–1, 36–CA–8849–1, 36–CA–8789–1, and 36–CA–8842–1 (2007)

CHAIRMAN BATTISTA AND MEMBERS LIEBMAN, SCHAUMBER, KIRSANOW, AND WALSH: In this case, we consider several issues relating to employees' use of their employer's e-mail system for Section 7 purposes. First, we consider whether the Respondent violated Section 8(a)(1) by maintaining a policy prohibiting the use of e-mail for all "non-job-related solicitations." Second, we consider whether the Respondent violated Section 8(a)(1) by discriminatorily enforcing that policy against union-related e-mails while allowing some personal e-mails, and Section 8(a)(3) and (1) by disciplining an employee for sending union-related e-mails. Finally, we consider whether the Respondent violated Section 8(a)(5) and (1) by insisting on an allegedly illegal bargaining proposal that would prohibit the use of e-mail for "union business."

After careful consideration, we hold that the Respondent's employees have no statutory right to use the Respondent's e-mail system for Section 7 purposes. We therefore find that the Respondent's policy prohibiting employee use of the system for "non-job-related solicitations" did not violate Section 8(a)(1).

With respect to the Respondent's alleged discriminatory enforcement of the e-mail policy, we have carefully examined Board precedent on this issue. As fully set forth herein, we have decided to modify the Board's approach in discriminatory enforcement cases to clarify that discrimination under the Act means drawing a distinction along Section 7 lines. We then address the specific allegations in this case of discriminatory enforcement in accordance with this approach.

Finally, we find that the Respondent did not insist on its bargaining proposal prohibiting the use of e-mail for "union business." Therefore, we dismiss the allegation that the Respondent insisted on an illegal subject in violation of Section 8(a)(5) and (1).

. . .

FACTS
A. The Respondent's Communications Systems Policy
The Respondent publishes a newspaper. The Union represents a unit of about 150 of the Respondent's employees. The parties' last collective-bargaining agreement was in effect from October 16, 1996 though April 30, 1999. When the record closed, the parties were negotiating, but had not yet reached a successor agreement.

In 1996, the Respondent began installing a new computer system, through which all newsroom employees and many (but not all) other unit employees had e-mail access. In October 1996, the Respondent implemented the "Communications Systems Policy" (CSP) at issue here. The policy governed employees' use of the Respondent's communications systems, including e-mail. The policy stated, in relevant part:

> Company communication systems and the equipment used to operate the communication system are owned and provided by the Company to assist in conducting the business of The Register-Guard. Communications systems are not to be used to solicit or proselytize for commercial ventures, religious or political causes, outside organizations, or other non-job-related solicitations.

The Respondent's employees use e-mail regularly for work-related matters. Throughout the relevant time period, the Respondent was aware that employees also used e-mail to send and receive personal messages. The record contains evidence of e-mails such as baby announcements, party invitations, and the occasional offer of sports tickets or request for services such as dog walking. However, there is no evidence that the employees used e-mail to solicit support for or participation in any outside cause or organization other than the United Way, for which the Respondent conducted a periodic charitable campaign.

B. Prozanski's E-Mails and Resulting Discipline
Suzi Prozanski is a unit employee and the union president. In May and August 2000, Prozanski received two written warnings for sending three e-mails to unit employees at their Register-Guard e-mail addresses. The Respondent contends that the e-mails violated the CSP.

. . .

POSITIONS OF THE PARTIES
The General Counsel
The General Counsel argues that under *Republic Aviation Corp. v. NLRB*, 324 U.S. 793 (1945), rules limiting employee communication in the workplace

632

should be evaluated by balancing employees' Section 7 rights and the employer's interest in maintaining discipline. The General Counsel contends that e-mail cannot neatly be characterized as either "solicitation" or "distribution." Nevertheless, e-mail has become the most common "gathering place" for communications on work and nonwork issues. Because the employees are rightfully on the employer's property, the employer does not have an indefeasible interest in banning personal e-mail just because the employer owns the computer system. The General Counsel distinguishes the Board's decisions that find no Section 7 right to use an employer's bulletin boards, telephones, and other equipment[6] on the basis that those cases did not involve interactive, electronic communications regularly used by employees, nor did they involve equipment used on networks where thousands of communications occur simultaneously. However, the General Counsel concedes that the employer has an interest in limiting employee e-mails to prevent liability for inappropriate content, to protect against system overloads and viruses, to preserve confidentiality, and to maintain productivity.

The General Counsel therefore proposes that broad rules prohibiting nonbusiness use of e-mail should be presumptively unlawful, absent a particularized showing of special circumstances. The General Counsel would evaluate other limitations on employee e-mail use (short of a complete ban) on a case-by-case basis.

With respect to whether an employer may prohibit employees from sending union-related e-mails while allowing other personal e-mails, the General Counsel notes that this conduct would violate Section 8(a)(1) under current Board precedent. The General Counsel disagrees with the Respondent's contention that employees communicating about a union are working on behalf of an "outside organization."

. . .

The Respondent

The Respondent argues that there is no Section 7 right to use the Respondent's e-mail system. E-mail, as part of the computer system, is equipment owned by the Respondent for the purpose of conducting its business. The Respondent notes that under Board precedent, an employer may restrict the nonbusiness use of its equipment. The Respondent argues that *Republic Aviation* and other cases dealing with oral solicitation are inapposite because they do not involve use of the employer's equipment. The Respondent observes that the Union and employees here have many means of communicating in addition to e-mail.

With respect to whether an employer has discriminatorily enforced its e-mail prohibition, the Respondent argues that the correct comparison is not between personal e-mails and union-related e-mails. Rather, the Respondent argues that in order to determine whether discriminatory enforcement has occurred, the Board should examine whether the employer has banned union-related e-mails but has permitted outside organizations to use the employer's equipment to sell products, to distribute "persuader" literature, to promote organizational meetings, or to induce group action. The Respondent argues that under this standard, the enforcement of the CSP against Prozanski was not discriminatory.

ORDER

The National Labor Relations Board orders that the Respondent, The Guard Publishing Company d/b/a The Register-Guard, Eugene, Oregon, its officers, agents, successors, and assigns, shall

1. Cease and desist from

(a) Discriminatorily prohibiting employees from using the Respondent's electronic communications systems to send union-related messages.

(b) Maintaining an overly broad rule that prohibits employees from wearing or displaying union insignia while working with customers.

(c) Issuing written warnings to, or otherwise discriminating against, any employee for supporting the Eugene Newspaper Guild, CWA Local 37194 or any other labor organization.

(d) In any like or related manner interfering with, restraining, or coercing employees in the exercise of the rights guaranteed them by Section 7 of the Act.

2. Take the following affirmative action necessary to effectuate the policies of the Act.

(a) Rescind the rule prohibiting circulation department employees from wearing or displaying union insignia while working with customers.

(b) Within 14 days from the date of this Order, rescind the unlawful warning issued to Suzi Prozanski on May 5, 2000, remove from its files any reference to the unlawful warning, and within 3 days thereafter notify Prozanski in writing that this has been done and that the warning will not be used against her in any way. . . .

:: CASE QUESTIONS

1. What was the employer's policy at issue?
2. Why was the policy challenged?
3. What was the General Counsel's argument?
4. What was the employer-Respondent's argument?
5. What are the implications of the decision?

Quasi-Judicial Authority In Sections 4, 9, and 10 of this chapter, you will study the various unfair labor practices. Congress granted the NLRB the authority to conduct the quasi-judicial hearings that are required to investigate and to enforce sanctions if these unfair labor practices occur.

This authority is extensive in that NLRB has discretion to order whatever action is necessary to correct the unlawful practice. However, as Sidebar 21.3 illustrates, there are limits to the NLRB's authority to order remedial actions.

:: *sidebar* 21.3

Limitation of NLRB's Remedies

After presenting documents that verified his legal status to work in the United States, Jose Castro was hired by Hoffman Plastic Compounds, Inc. Castro participated in a union-organizing campaign at the Hoffman facility where he worked. Hoffman laid off Castro and others engaged in this organizing effort. When it was presented with this factual situation, the National Labor Relations Board (NLRB) ordered Hoffman to reinstate Castro (and the other employees) with back pay. During a compliance hearing before an NLRB administrative law judge (ALJ), Castro acknowledged that he did not have the proper paperwork to be a legal alien eligible to work. In essence, Castro admitted that he has used another person's birth certificate to get a driver's license and social security number. Because of these admissions, the ALJ concluded that the NLRB could not award Castro reinstatement and back pay. Castro appealed to the full board, which reversed the ALJ and awarded back pay. Hoffman sought review by the Court of Appeals for the D.C. Circuit. This court upheld the NLRB's award of back pay.

Upon further review, the U.S. Supreme Court reversed the NLRB's decision. It concluded that back pay awarded to illegal aliens would "encourage the successful evasion of apprehension by immigration authorities, condone prior violations of the immigration laws, and encourage future violations."

*Source: *Hoffman Plastic Compounds, Inc. v. NLRB*, 535 U.S. 137 (2002).

3. CERTIFICATION OF UNIONS

An employer may voluntarily recognize that its workers want to have a certain labor union represent them. The employer is free to agree to bargain with the union as the collective bargaining representative of the employees. In actuality, such voluntary recognition occurs in relatively few situations. More common is the NLRB's certification of a union as the bargaining agent for a group of employees. This certification process is the result of an election or occurs through authorization cards. These certification processes are discussed in the next two subsections.

Certification Elections   Elections are by secret ballot and are supervised by the NLRB. The board decides what unit of employees is appropriate for purposes of collective bargaining and therefore which employees are entitled to vote in the election. It may select the total employer unit, craft unit, plant unit, or any subdivision of the plant.

Obviously, how the board exercises its discretion in this regard may be crucial to the outcome of a given election. If all 100 workers at one plant operated by an employer desire to organize but 400 out of 500 at another of the employer's plants do not, designation of the total employees as the one appropriate bargaining unit would ensure that both plants would remain nonunion.

The NLRB conducts elections upon receipt of a petition signed by at least 30 percent of the employees. In addition, an employer may file a petition for selection of an initial representative. An employer may also file a petition for an election to invalidate certification of an incumbent union. It must show that it doubts, in good faith, the continued support of the union by a majority of the employees. Votes to certify a union or to rescind a union's authority also take place by petition.

After a NLRB election, another is not permitted for one year, regardless of whether the union wins or loses the certification vote. Within the term of a collective bargaining agreement or three years after it has been signed, whichever period is shorter, no elections may take place.

Certification through Cards   A union seeking to represent employees may solicit cards from them indicating their willingness for the union to represent them. An employer may then recognize the union as the bargaining agent for its employees if the cards are signed by a majority of the employees. Employers do not need to recognize the union based on a majority card showing and always have the option to insist on an election. But once an employer recognizes the union—no matter how informally—the employer is bound by the recognition and loses the right to seek an election.

Cards also may substitute for an election if certain conditions are met. The NLRB may issue a bargaining order based on such cards if the cards are unequivocal and clearly indicate that the employee signing the card is authorizing the union to represent him or her. The general counsel of the NLRB does not need to prove that the employees read or understood the cards. If a card states on its face that it authorizes collective bargaining, counts for that purpose, unless there is clear proof that the employee was told that it would not be used for that purpose.

4. UNFAIR LABOR PRACTICES BY MANAGEMENT

Remember that Congress desired to strengthen the bargaining power of labor unions when it passed the Wagner Act in 1935. A principal means of accomplishing this goal was through the creation of five unfair labor practices by management. These practices are summarized as follows:

- Interfering with union activities.
- Dominating a labor organization.
- Discriminating based on union affiliation.

Despite the declining percentage of the workforce that is unionized, unions are winning a greater percentage of the certification elections being held.

- Discriminating as a result of NLRB proceedings.
- Refusing to bargain in good faith.

Conduct may be, and often is, a violation of more than one of the listed unfair labor practices. Indeed, most violations constitute interference with the right to engage in concerted activity (the first category). For example, retaliation against a union leader for filing charges would constitute a violation of both the first and fourth categories.

Interfering with Unionization   The first unfair labor practice has two distinct parts. First, it is unfair for an employer to interfere with the efforts of employees to form, join, or assist labor organizations. The second part covers interfering with "concerted activities for mutual aid or protection." This violation does not have to involve a union; the act protects any group of employees acting for their mutual aid and protection.

The first part of this unfair labor practice by management is a catchall intended to guarantee the right of employees to organize and join unions. It clearly prohibits "scare" tactics such as threats by employers to fire those involved in organizing employees or threats to cut back on employee benefits if employees succeed in unionizing. In addition, less obvious activities are outlawed, such as requiring job applicants to state on a questionnaire whether they would cross a picket line in a strike. An employer cannot engage in any conduct calculated to erode employee support for the union.

Interference with unionization may take the form of a carrot as well as a stick. The conferring of benefits by an employer may be an unfair labor practice. In one case, the employer reminded its employees two weeks before a representation election that the company had just instituted a "floating holiday" that employees could take on their birthdays. The union lost the election, but the NLRB set it aside. It was an unfair labor practice for the employer to engage in conduct immediately favorable to employees. The conduct interfered with the freedom of choice for or against unionization.

Case 21.2 illustrates how an unfair labor practice allegation arises. Note that the issue of a union's status as a certified bargaining agent becomes intertwined with management's duty to refrain from interfering with an employee's right to engage in union activity.

case **21.2** ::

ALLENTOWN MACK SALES AND SERVICE, INC. v. NATIONAL LABOR RELATIONS BOARD
522 U.S. 359 (1998)

SCALIA, J.: Under long-standing precedent of the National Labor Relations Board, an employer who believes that an incumbent union no longer enjoys the support of a majority of its employees has three options: to request a formal, Board-supervised election, to withdraw recognition from the union and refuse to bargain, or to conduct an internal poll of employee support for the union. The Board has held that the latter two are unfair labor practices unless the employer can show that it had a "good faith reasonable doubt" about the union's majority support. We must decide whether the Board's standard for employer polling is rational and consistent with the National Labor Relations Act, and whether the Board's factual determinations in this case are supported by substantial evidence in the record.

Mack Trucks, Inc., had a factory branch in Allentown, Pennsylvania, whose service and parts employees were represented by Local Lodge 724 of the International Association of Machinists and Aerospace Workers, AFL-CIO. Mack notified its Allentown managers in May of 1990 that it intended to sell the branch, and several of those managers formed Allentown Mack Sales, Inc., the petitioner here, which purchased the assets of the business on December 20, 1990, and began to operate it as an independent dealership. From December 21, 1990, to January 1, 1991, Allentown hired 32 of the original 45 Mack employees.

During the period before and immediately after the sale, a number of Mack employees made statements to the prospective owners of Allentown Mack Sales suggesting that the incumbent union had lost support among employees in the bargaining unit. In job interviews, eight employees made statements indicating, or at least arguably indicating, that they personally no longer supported the union. In addition, Ron Mohr, a member of the union's bargaining committee and shop steward for the Mack Trucks service department, told an Allentown manager that it was his feeling that the employees did not want a union, and that "with a new company, if a vote was taken, the Union would lose." And Kermit Bloch, who worked for Mack Trucks as a mechanic on the night shift, told a manager that the entire night shift (then 5 or 6 employees) did not want the union.

On January 2, 1991, Local Lodge 724 asked Allentown Mack Sales to recognize it as the employees' collective-bargaining representative, and to begin negotiations for a contract. The new employer rejected that request by letter dated January 25, claiming a "good faith doubt as to support of the Union among the employees." The letter also announced that Allentown had "arranged for an independent poll by secret ballot of its hourly employees to be conducted under guidelines prescribed by the National Labor Relations Board." The poll, supervised by a Roman Catholic priest, was conducted on February 8, 1991; the union lost 19 to 13. Shortly thereafter, the union filed an unfair-labor-practice charge with the Board.

The Administrative Law Judge (ALJ) concluded that Allentown was a successor employer to Mack Trucks, Inc., and therefore inherited Mack's bargaining obligation and a presumption of continuing majority support for the union. The ALJ held that Allentown's poll . . . violated §§ 8(a)(1) and 8(a)(5) of the National Labor Relations Act (Act) because Allentown did not have an "objective reasonable doubt" about the majority status of the union. The Board adopted the ALJ's findings, . . . agreed with his conclusion, . . . [and] ordered Allentown to recognize and bargain with Local 724.

On review in the Court of Appeals for the District of Columbia Circuit, Allentown challenged both the facial rationality of the Board's test for employer polling and the Board's application of that standard to the facts of this case. The court enforced the Board's bargaining order. . . . We granted certiorari.

Allentown challenges the Board's decision in this case on several grounds. First, it contends that because the Board's "reasonable doubt" standard for employer polls is the same as its standard for unilateral withdrawal of recognition and for employer initiation of a Board-supervised election (a so-called "Representation Management," or "RM" election), the Board irrationally permits employers to poll only when it would be unnecessary and legally pointless to do so. Second, Allentown argues that the record evidence clearly demonstrates that it had a good-faith reasonable doubt about the union's claim to majority support. Finally, it asserts that the Board has abandoned the "reasonable doubt" prong of its polling standard, and recognizes an employer's "reasonable doubt" only if a majority of the unit employees renounce the union. . . . Allentown argues that it is irrational to require the same factual showing to justify a poll as to justify an outright withdrawal of recognition, because that leaves the employer with no legal incentive to poll. Under the Board's framework, the results of a poll can never supply an otherwise lacking "good-faith reasonable doubt" necessary to justify a withdrawal of recognition, since the employer must already have that same reasonable doubt before he is permitted to conduct a poll. . . . While the Board's adoption of a unitary standard for polling, RM elections, and withdrawals of recognition is in some respects a puzzling policy, we do not find it so irrational as to be "arbitrary [or] capricious" within the meaning of the Administrative Procedure Act. The Board believes that employer polling is potentially "disruptive" to established bargaining relationships and "unsettling" to employees, and so has chosen to limit severely the circumstances under which it may be conducted. The unitary standard reflects the Board's apparent conclusion that polling should be tolerated only when the employer might otherwise simply withdraw recognition and refuse to bargain. . . .

If it would be rational for the Board to set the polling standard either higher or lower than the threshold for an RM election, then surely it is not irrational for the Board to split the difference.

[continued]

The Board held Allentown guilty of an unfair labor practice in its conduct of the polling because it had not demonstrated that it held a reasonable doubt, based on objective considerations, that the Union continued to enjoy the support of a majority of the bargaining unit employees. We must decide whether that conclusion is supported by substantial evidence on the record as a whole. Put differently, we must decide whether on this record it would have been possible for a reasonable jury to reach the Board's conclusion. . . .

[The Court reviewed the facts and determined that the evidence supported the petitioner's doubt that the majority of its employees supported the union.] We conclude that the Board's "reasonable doubt" test for employer polls is facially rational and consistent with the Act. But the Board's factual finding that Allentown Mack Sales lacked such a doubt is not supported by substantial evidence on the record as a whole. The judgment of the Court of Appeals for the D.C. Circuit is therefore reversed, and the case is remanded with instructions to deny enforcement.

Reversed and remanded.

:: CASE QUESTIONS

1. What event occurred that allowed the representation of employees by a union to be called into question?
2. What were the findings and order by the NLRB?
3. What issues were presented to the Supreme Court?
4. Why does the Court agree with the NLRB about a unitary standard of "reasonable doubt" for refusing to bargain, polling employees, and requesting a decertification election?
5. How does the Court differ with the NLRB in this case?
6. Do you agree with the Court analyses and conclusions?

Interfering With Concerted Activities The term **concerted activity** is given a liberal interpretation in order to create a climate that encourages unionization, collective bargaining, and all that may flow from such activity. For example, some employees refused to work after a heated grievance meeting. They followed their supervisors onto the workroom floor and continued to argue loudly until they were ordered a second time to resume work. The employer issued letters of reprimand alleging insubordination. This was an unfair labor practice. The protection of employee conduct at grievance meetings is extended to a brief cooling-off period following an employer's termination of such a meeting. Protection of employees' participation in the meetings themselves would be seriously threatened if the employer could at any point call an immediate halt to the operation of the law simply by declaring the meeting ended.

The concerted-activity concept is quite extensive. In one case, an employer was investigating theft by employees. One employee asked that a union representative be present during her interview. She was refused. The Supreme Court held that the employee had a right to representation when there was a perceived threat to her employment security. The presence of a representative assures other employees in the bargaining unit that they, too, can obtain aid and protection if they wish when there appears to be a threat to their job security. Refusing the assistance at the interview was an unfair labor practice.

In addition, the right to engage in concerted activity has been expanded to cover the actions of a sole employee under certain circumstances. If an employee has a grievance that may affect other workers, that employee has rights protected by the concerted-activity language of this unfair labor practice, even though no other worker participates in the activity.

Dominating a Labor Organization

The second unfair labor practice prohibits the domination of a labor organization by employers or their contribution of financial or other support to any union. Under the Wagner Act, any organization of employees must be completely independent of their employers. In the case of a controversy between competing unions, employers must remain strictly neutral. It is an unfair labor practice for the employer to support a union by giving it a meeting place; providing refreshments for union meetings; permitting the union to use the employer's telephone, secretary, or copying machine; or allowing the union to keep cafeteria or vending-machine profits.

Discriminating Based on Union Affiliation

Under the third unfair labor practice, an employer may neither discharge nor refuse to hire an employee to either encourage or discourage membership in any labor organization. Nor may the employer discriminate regarding any term or condition of employment for such purposes. The law does not oblige an employer to favor union members in hiring employees. It also does not restrict him or her in the normal exercise of any employer's right to select or discharge employees. However, the employer may not abuse that right by discriminatory action based on union membership or activities that encourage or discourage membership in a labor organization.

A company may not go partially out of business because some of its employees have organized, nor may it temporarily close that portion of its business that has unionized. If a company closes one plant because a union is voted in, such action discourages union activity at other plants. Partial closings to "chill" unionism are unfair labor practices.

The Supreme Court has held that an employer who reports the possible existence of illegal aliens to the Immigration and Naturalization Service engages in an unfair labor practice when that report is closely associated with the employees' approval of a labor union as their bargaining agent.

Discriminating as a Result of NLRB Proceedings

The fourth unfair labor practice, prohibits discharge or from other reprisals by their employers because they are enforcing their rights under the Wagner Act by filing charges or giving testimony in NLRB proceedings. This protection prevents the NLRB's channels of information from evaporating by employer intimidation of complainants and witnesses. An employer cannot refuse to hire a prospective employee because charges have been filed by him or her.

The main defense of any employer accused of reprisal is that he or she discharged or discriminated against the employee for some reason other than filing charges or giving testimony. Most often such cases boil down to trying to prove what motivated the company in pursuing its course of action. If the company can convince the NLRB that the employee was discharged because of misconduct, low production, personnel cutbacks necessitated by economic conditions, or other legitimate considerations, the company will be exonerated. Otherwise, it will be found guilty of this unfair labor practice.

Take-it-or-leave-it demands in a negotiation are considered bad-faith bargaining.

Refusing to Bargain in Good Faith

The fifth unfair labor practice occurs when management refuses to bargain with the collective bargaining representative of its employees. The Wagner Act did not define the phrase "to bargain collectively." Judicial decisions have added the concept of *good faith* to bargaining. To comply with the requirement that they bargain collectively in good faith, employers must approach the bargaining table with fair and open minds and a sincere intent to find a basis of agreement.

Refusing to meet at reasonable times with representatives of the other party, refusing to reduce agreements to writing, and designating persons with no authority to negotiate as representatives at meetings are examples of this unfair labor practice.

The employer's duty to bargain collectively includes a duty to provide relevant information needed by a union for the proper performance of its duties as the employees' bargaining representative. For example, data about job related safety and health must be furnished so that the union can safeguard its members' health and safety.

A more fundamental issue inherent in the requirement that parties bargain collectively is: "About what?" Must the employer bargain with the union about all subjects and all management decisions in which the union or the employees are interested? Are there subjects and issues upon which management is allowed to act alone? See Sidebar 21.4 for a discussion about the "Writers Strike."

:: *sidebar* 21.4

This Was No Joke: The Writers Guild of America Strike

In November 2007, more than 12,000 film, television, and radio writers joined together in the Writers Guild of America strike against the Alliance of Motion Picture and Television Producers, a trade organization representing nearly 400 American film and television producers.

WHAT WAS AT ISSUE?

The most contentious issues at stake: DVD residuals, union jurisdiction over animation and reality program writers, and compensation for "new media," content written for or distributed through emerging digital technology, including the Internet.

HOW MUCH DID THE STRIKE COST?

According to an NPR report, the strike cost the economy of Los Angeles an estimated $1.5 billion. The "Big Four"

networks (ABC, CBS, FOX, and NBC) suffered ad shortfalls and declines in prime time ratings.

WHAT WAS THE OUTCOME OF THE DISPUTE?

On February 12, 2008, the strike concluded after the parties reached an agreement creating formulas for revenue-based residuals in new media, providing access to deals and financial data to help writers evaluate and enforce the formulas, and establishing the principle for the writers "When they get paid, we get paid." Another outcome was the solidarity that developed throughout the group from the most successful writers to those fighting to get into the business.

For more information about the agreement, see http://unitedhollywood.blogspot.com/

In answering these questions, the law divides issues into two categories—**compulsory bargaining issues** and **voluntary bargaining issues.** Compulsory, or mandatory, bargaining issues are those concerned with wages, hours, and other terms and conditions of employment. Although the parties may voluntarily consider other issues, the refusal by either to bargain in good faith on such other permissive matters is not an unfair labor practice.

Classifying an issue as *compulsory* or *voluntary* is done on a case-by-case basis. For example, questions relating to fringe benefits are compulsory bargaining issues because they are "wages." The NLRB and the courts are called on to decide whether management and labor must bargain with each other on a multitude of issues. A good example of a case in which bargaining was required is *Ford Motor Co. v. NLRB* (441 U.S. 488).

Employees of the Ford Motor Company belong to the United Auto Workers. Ford provides in-plant cafeterias and vending machines as two ways to ensure its employees with food services. An independent caterer managed both the cafeterias and vending machines. This caterer informed Ford that the increased costs associated with these food services required food prices to go up. When Ford notified the union representative of these food cost increases, the union requested bargaining be held over the food prices and services.

Ford refused to bargain, and the union filed a charge with the NLRB alleging Ford's refusal to bargain in good faith, which is an unfair labor practice. The NLRB concluded that in-plant food and related services are "other terms and conditions of employment." Therefore, Ford must negotiate with the union over this compulsory bargaining issue. The Supreme Court's review of these facts results in the NLRB's ruling being affirmed.

A party to labor negotiations may present a demand to bargain about a voluntary issue as long as this issue does not have to be resolved before the parties can resolve compulsory bargaining issues. Tying a voluntary bargaining issue to a compulsory bargaining issue results in a failure to bargain in good faith and is in effect an unfair labor practice.

Courts tend to defer to the special expertise of the NLRB in classifying collective bargaining subjects, especially in the area of "terms or conditions of employment." Examples of board rulings holding that issues such as union dues checkoff; health and accident insurance; safety rules; merit pay increases; incentive pay plans; Christmas and other bonuses; stock purchase plans; pensions; paid vacations and holidays; the privilege of hunting on a reserved portion of a paper company's forest preserve; proposals for effective arbitration and grievance procedures; and no-strike and no-lockout clauses are compulsory bargaining issues.

Remember that neither the employer nor the union must make concessions to the other concerning a mandatory subject of bargaining. The law only demands that each negotiate such matters in good faith with the other before making a decision and taking unilateral action. If the parties fail to reach an agreement after discussing these problems, each may take steps that are against the wishes and best interests of the other party. For example, the employer may refuse to grant a wage increase requested by the union, and the union is free to strike.

:: The Taft-Hartley Act

The Wagner Act opened the door for the rapid growth of the union movement. From 1935 to the end of World War II, the strength and influence of unions grew substantially. Where, prior to the Wagner Act, employers had the greater advantage in bargaining power, by 1946 many persons felt the pendulum had shifted and that unions, with their ability to call nationwide, crippling strikes, had the better bargaining position. To balance the scale, the Labor-Management Relations Act (the **Taft-Hartley Act**) was enacted in 1947 to amend the Wagner Act.

The 73,000 United Automobile Workers went on strike at General Motors in 2007, seeking job security during restructuring of the company. GM is seeking to lower its cost structure and to have a more flexible workforce to compete with other automakers such as Toyota and Honda.

In its attempt to balance the bargaining power between labor unions and management, the Taft-Hartley Act:

- Provides for an *80-day cooling-off period* in strikes that imperil the nation's health or safety.
- Reinforces the employer's freedom of speech in labor-management relations.
- Outlaws the *closed-shop* concept but permits *union shops* in the absence of a state *right-to-know* law.
- Permits suits by union members for breach of contract against unions.
- Creates six unfair labor practices by unions.

The purposes of the Taft-Hartley Act are to ensure the free flow of commerce by eliminating union practices that burden commerce and to provide procedures for avoiding disputes that jeopardize the public health, safety, or interest. It recognizes that both parties to collective bargaining need protection from wrongful interference by the other and that employees sometimes need protection from the union itself. Finally, it sought to protect the public interest in major labor disputes. Congress authorized the creation of the Federal Mediation and Conciliation Service to help achieve the goals of the Taft-Hartley Act. Members of this service are available to assist the parties in settling labor disputes.

5. EIGHTY-DAY COOLING-OFF PERIOD

President George W. Bush used this provision to end the longshoremen's strike on the West Coast in 2002.

Somewhat like the 60-day period provided under the Railway Labor Act, the Taft-Hartley Act provides for an *80-day cooling-off period* following certain procedures. This provision's intent is to limit the adverse impact of the nationwide strikes by steelworkers, mineworkers, autoworkers, and longshoremen that can paralyze the economy. When a threatened or actual strike or lockout affecting an entire industry or substantial part thereof will, if permitted to occur or to continue, imperil the national health or safety, the 80-day period may be enforced. The procedure starts with the president recognizing the emergency and appointing a board of inquiry to obtain facts about the threatened or actual strike or lockout. The board studies the situation and reports back to the president. If the board finds that the national health or safety is indeed affected by the strike, then the president, through the attorney general, goes to the federal court for an injunction ordering the union to suspend the strike (or the company to suspend the lockout) for 80 days.

During the 80-day period, the Federal Mediation and Conciliation Service works with the labor-management parties to try to achieve an agreement. If during this time the reconciliation effort fails, the presidential board holds new hearings and receives the company's final offer. The union members are then allowed to vote on this final proposal by the company. If they vote for the new proposal, the dispute is over and work continues as usual. If they vote against the proposal, the workers may again be called out on strike. At this point, the strike may continue indefinitely until the disagreement causing it is resolved by collective bargaining or unless there is additional legislation by Congress to solve the problem.

Experience has shown that disputes are often settled during the 80-day period. The injunction provided for in the Taft-Hartley Act may not be used for all strikes and lockouts. This injunction is limited to *national emergency* strikes and lockouts, those that involve national defense or key industries or have a substantial effect on the economy.

6. FREE SPEECH

Employers complained that the Wagner Act violated their right of free speech. Statements by management formed the basis of unfair labor practices claims. To meet this objection, Congress, in Taft-Hartley, added the following provision:

> 8(c) The expressing of any views, argument, or opinion, or the dissemination thereof, whether in written, printed, graphic, or visual form, shall not constitute or be evidence of an unfair labor practice under any of the provisions of this Act, if such expression contains no threat of reprisal or force or promise of benefit.

This provision gives employers limited free speech, at best. It is difficult to make statements that cannot be construed as a threat or a promise. For example, if an employer predicts dire economic events as a result of unionization, such may be an illegal threat if the employer has it within his or her power to make the prediction come true. Whether particular language is coercive or not often depends on the analysis of the total background of facts and circumstances in which it was uttered. To be forbidden, the statements of an employer need not be proved to have been coercive in fact but only to have had a reasonable tendency to intimidate employees under the circumstances.

An employer's threats to withdraw existing benefits if employees unionize is not speech protected by Section 8(c). However, mere predictions and prophecies are protected. For example, in one case an employer's speeches and handbills during the union's organizational campaign stated its intention to fight the union in every legal way possible and to "deal hard" with the union at arm's length if it were voted in. The employer also warned that employees could be permanently replaced if the union called an economic strike. This language was held to fall within the protection of Section 8(c). The right of free speech guaranteed by the Taft-Hartley Act applies to labor unions as well as employers. However, there is a rule prohibiting either side from making election speeches on company time to massed assemblies of employees within 24 hours before an election.

:: *sidebar* 21.5

Restricting Workplace Speech: Setting the Parameters

These NLRB cases shed light on the kinds of speech restrictions that are permissible—or not—in the workplace. Section 7 of the National Labor Relations Act (NLRA) guarantees that *all* employees (regardless of union status) have the right to engage in "concerted activities for the purpose of . . . mutual aid or protection."

The Policy: Employees are prohibited from discussing work conditions, wages, benefits, and discipline.

NLRB Decision: This policy is illegally broad and violates the NLRA by promulgating a confidentiality rule prohibiting employees from discussing disciplinary information, grievances and complaints, performance evaluations, or salary information with any persons outside the company or with fellow employees. See *Double Eagle Hotel & Casino,*

341 NLRB No. 17 (January 20, 2004), upheld by the 10th Cir (2005); see also *Longs Drug Stores California, Inc.,* 347 NLRB No 45 (2006).

The Policy: Maintenance of work rules prohibit the use of "abusive and profane language," "verbal, mental, and physical abuse," and "harassment . . . in any way."

NLRB Decision: The rule is lawful and could not reasonably be understood as interfering with employees' Section 7 rights. The rule is lawful because it is based on the employer's legitimate right to establish a "civil and decent" workplace to protect itself from liability for workplace harassment. *Lutheran Heritage Village-Livonia,* 343 NLRB No. 75 (2004).

7. UNION SHOP—MEMBERSHIPS AND FEES

The Wagner Act's strong support of unionization gave unintended bargaining power to unions with respect to an employer's hiring practices. In many bargaining situations, the union became so strong that it successfully insisted on management's hiring only union members. In essence, to apply for a prospective job, a person would have to join the union. These situations became known as **closed shops.**

One of the major changes brought about by the Taft-Hartley Act was outlawing of the closed shop. This act still permitted the **union shop.** In a union shop contract, also known as a **union security clause,** the employer agrees that after an employee is hired that employee must join the union as a condition of continued employment. The Taft-Hartley Act, prohibits such a requirement until the thirtieth day after employment begins.

Through a series of cases, the Supreme Court clarified the limited mandatory relationship created by the inclusion of the union security clause in a contract. This type of relationship requires that the union members pay reasonable membership fees and dues. In turn, the union can use these fees and dues only for collective bargaining, contract administration, and grievance activities. Unions are not allowed to use members' dues to support political activities.

Right-to-work laws are mostly in the South and Southwest, areas that historically have been antiunion.

One of the sections of the Taft-Hartley Act most distasteful to unions is 14(b), which outlaws the union shop in states that have adopted a right-to-work law. **Right-to-work laws** prohibit agreements requiring membership in a labor organization as a condition of continued employment of a person who was not in the union when hired. Approximately 20 states have right-to-work laws today. Workers in these states who do not belong to a union may not be required to pay representation fees to the union that represents the employees. However, such workers are subject to the terms of the collective bargaining agreement, and the union must handle their grievances, if any, with management.

8. SUITS AGAINST UNIONS

Many suits against unions are by members alleging a breach of the duty of fair representation.

Section 301 of the Taft-Hartley Act provides that suits for breach of a contract between an employer and a labor organization can be filed in the federal district courts without regard to the amount in question. A labor organization is responsible for the acts of its agents and may sue or be sued. Any money judgment against it is enforceable only against its assets and not against any individual member. Moreover, individuals cannot be sued for actions such as violating no-strike provisions of a collective bargaining contract.

In addition, members may sue their union and recover the money damages they suffer because of an illegal strike. If a union activity is both an unfair labor practice and a breach of a collective bargaining agreement, the NLRB's authority is not exclusive and does not destroy the jurisdiction of courts under Section 301 of the Taft-Hartley Act.

Since workers cannot bargain individually when represented by a union, the union has an implied duty of fair representation to act reasonably, with honesty of purpose, and in good faith. The union must represent all the employees in the bargaining unit, including those who are nonunion, impartially and without hostile discrimination. Failure to do so may give rise to a lawsuit.

The duty of fair representation applies not only to the *negotiation* of a collective bargaining agreement but also to the *administration* of the agreement. Unions must fairly represent employers in disputes with the employer regarding the *interpretation* and *application* of the terms of an existing contract.

An employee may file suit against the union and its representatives for damages resulting from breach of their duty of fair representation in processing his or her grievance against the employer. A union may not process a grievance in an arbitrary, indifferent, or careless manner.

Finally, a union member may sue a local union for failing to enforce the international union's constitution and bylaws. Thus, Section 301 of the Taft-Hartley Act authorizes an employer to sue a union for breach of contract as well as employees to sue to enforce either the union-management collective bargaining agreement or a union contract with a member.

9. UNFAIR LABOR PRACTICES BY UNIONS

Perhaps more than with any other provision of the Taft-Hartley Act, Congress attempted to balance the bargaining power in the labor-management relationship by enacting six unfair labor practices by unions. These balance the unfair labor practices by management in the Wagner Act, as discussed in Section 4. Six unfair labor practices by unions are:

- Restraining or coercing an employee to join a union or an employer in selecting representatives to bargain with the union.
- Causing or attempting to cause the employer to discriminate against an employee who is not a union member unless there is a legal union shop agreement in effect.
- Refusing to bargain with the employer if it is the NLRB-designated representative of the employees.
- Striking, picketing, or engaging in secondary boycotts for illegal purposes.
- Charging new members excessive or discriminatory initiation fees when there is a union shop agreement.
- Causing an employer to pay for work not performed (featherbedding).

Three of these illegal practices can be presented in a summary fashion due to the preceding discussions in this chapter or because they have very little impact today. The third unfair labor practice by unions is complementary to the fifth unfair labor practice by management. In essence, Congress requires unions to bargain in good faith as is required of management. The fifth unfair labor practice by unions simply means that unions cannot take advantage of the union shop agreement by charging unreasonable dues or fees when members and nonmembers are obligated to pay them. Today, the sixth unfair labor practice, involving *featherbedding,* or payment for work not actually performed, is of less importance than when it was enacted in 1947.

The other unfair labor practices by unions are presented in the following subsections.

Restraining or Coercing an Employee into Joining a Union   This unfair labor practice includes misconduct by unions directed toward employees. The law makes it illegal for a union to restrain or coerce employees in the exercise of their rights to bargain collectively, just as it is an unfair labor practice by employers to interfere with the same rights. Employees also are guaranteed the right to *refrain* from union activities unless they are required to join the union by a legal union shop agreement.

Causing an Employer to Discriminate against a Nonunion Member

If a legal union shop agreement is in effect, a labor organization may insist that the employer observe its terms. But even when a legal union shop contract is in effect, the law prohibits a union from attempting to cause an employer to discriminate against an employee who has been denied membership or had his or her membership terminated for some reason other than failure to pay the dues and initiation fees uniformly required of all members. And even if an employee is a member, the union may not cause the employer to discriminate against him or her for not following union rules. This prohibition prevents the use of the union shop as a means of intimidating employees who were at odds with union officials over their policies.

Striking or Picketing for Illegal Purposes or Engaging in Secondary Boycotts

Jurisdictional strikes are unfair labor practices. A **jurisdictional strike** is used to force an employer to assign work to employees in one craft union rather than another. Since the dispute is between the two unions and not with the employer, the law requires that such disputes be submitted to the NLRB by the unions.

It is also an unfair labor practice for a union to threaten or to coerce by picketing, for example, an employer to recognize or bargain with one union if another one has been certified as the representative of its employees.

It is an unfair labor practice for a union to threaten, coerce, or restrain a third person not party to a labor dispute for the purpose of causing that third person to exert pressure on the company involved in the labor dispute. This law requires that strikes and picketing be directed at the employer with which the union actually has a labor dispute.

An example of illegal secondary activity occurs when a union induces the employees of an employer to strike or engage in a concerted refusal

---

:: *sidebar* 21.6

Change to Win: Securing the American Dream

In 2005, seven unions and six million workers united in *Change to Win* with a mission to "unite the 50 million workers in Change to Win affiliate industries whose jobs cannot be outsourced and who are vital to the global economy."

Their goal: Securing the American Dream for *all* working people.

WHICH UNIONS ARE MEMBERS?

International Brotherhood of Teamsters (IBT)

Laborers' International Union of North America (LIUNA)

Service Employees International Union (SEIU)

United Brotherhood of Carpenters and Joiners of America (UBC)

United Farm Workers of America (UFW)

United Food and Commercial Workers International Union (UFCW)

UNITE HERE

WHAT ARE THE MAIN ISSUES?

- Jobs and wages.
- Health care.
- Retirement security.
- Freedom to join together in unions.
- Employee Free Choice Act (EFCA).
- Immigrant workers' rights.
- Workplace health and safety.
- Trade and globalization.

*Source: www.changetowin.org/

to use, handle, or work on any goods or to perform any service to force the employer to stop doing business with some third person. For example, assume that a supplier (like a bakery) has a workforce that is nonunionized. A customer (i.e., a grocery store) has employees who belong to a union. This union would like to be the bargaining representative for the supplier's employees. It would be an illegal secondary boycott for this union to have its members either strike or picket the grocery store on the basis of it selling nonunionized baked goods from the bakery in the hope that the grocery store would discontinue its buying from this bakery. The union must deal directly with the bakery.

10. AMENDMENTS

Congressional hearings in the 1950s uncovered widespread corruption, violence, and lack of democratic procedures in some labor unions. As a result, Congress passed the **Landrum-Griffin Act,** or Labor-Management Reporting and Disclosure Act (LMRDA), in 1959. Its provisions constitute a "bill of rights" for union members and provide for union reform. Also in this act, Congress included some amendments to the unfair labor practices by management and unions.

In essence, in its continuing attempt to balance the bargaining power in the labor-management relationship, Congress added one unfair labor practice by management and two by unions.

Agreeing to Engage in a Secondary Boycott You should recall from your reading in the preceding section that unions cannot engage in secondary boycotts. Technically, nothing in that unfair labor practice, as enacted in the Taft-Hartley Act, prohibited a union and an employer from agreeing to engage in a secondary boycott. The original restriction applied only to the unilateral acts of the union. The Landrum-Griffin Act clarified the concern over secondary boycotts by prohibiting a union-management agreement that would adversely impact a neutral third party.

It is also an unfair labor practice for both the employer involved and the union to enter into a **hot-cargo contract.** A hot-cargo contract is one in which an employer voluntarily agrees with a union that the employees should not be required by their employer to handle or work on goods or materials going to or coming from an employer designated by the union as "unfair." Such goods are said to be hot cargo. These clauses were common in trucking and construction labor contracts. The law thus forbids an employer and a labor organization to make an agreement under which the employer agrees to stop doing business with any other employer.

Picketing When Not Certified In certain cases it is illegal for unions to force an employer to recognize or bargain with the union if it is not currently certified as the duly authorized collective bargaining representative. The purpose is to reinforce the effectiveness of the election procedures employed by the NLRB by outlawing certain tactics used by unions backed by only a minority of the employees of a particular employer. Thus, picketing to force an employer to recognize an uncertified union is an unfair labor practice in the following cases:

1. When the employer has lawfully recognized another union as the collective bargaining representative of its employees.
2. When a valid representation election has been conducted by the NLRB within the past 12 months.
3. When picketing has been conducted for an unreasonable time, in excess of 30 days, without a petition for a representation election being filed with the NLRB.

Including these amendments by the Landrum-Griffin Act, the law on unfair labor practices is summarized in the following concept summary. Remember, as you review these materials, Congress used three laws to create these lists. The first five items on management's side were enacted in 1935. The first six on the union side came in 1947. The sixth item on the left side and the last two items on the right side were added in 1959.

concept :: *summary*

Unfair Labor Practices

:: BY MANAGEMENT

1. Interfering with unionization and concerted activities by employees.
2. Dominating a union or contributing to it, financially or otherwise.
3. Discriminating in hiring or tenure of employees on the basis of union affiliation.
4. Discriminating against employees who seek to enforce their Wagner Act rights.
5. Refusing to bargain collectively in good faith.
6. Agreeing with a labor organization to engage in a secondary boycott.

:: BY UNIONS

1. Restraining or coercing an employee to join a union.
2. Causing an employer to discriminate against a non-union member.
3. Refusing to bargain collectively in good faith.
4. Striking, picketing, or engaging in secondary boycotts for illegal purposes.
5. Charging excessive or discriminatory fees.
6. Causing an employer to pay for work not performed.
7. Picketing to force an employer to recognize or bargain with an uncertified union.
8. Agreeing with an employer to engage in a secondary boycott.

:: Key Terms

:: Review Questions and Problems

Labor Laws

1. *Law before 1935*
   (a) What is the specific purpose of (1) the Clayton Act, (2) the Railway Labor Act, and (3) the Norris-LaGuardia Act?
   (b) Why did these laws not increase laborers' bargaining power to the degree that is considered equal to management's bargaining power?

The Wagner Act

2. *National Labor Relations Board*

   Describe the nature and limitations of the NLRB's jurisdiction.

3. *Certification of Unions*

   The NLRB conducted a certification election, and the union won by a vote of 22–20. Management refused to bargain with this union.

   The reason for this refusal to recognize the union as the employees' bargaining agent was that the union had used "recognition slips" as a means of indicating the employees' support for the union. Several employees testified that they signed these slips to avoid the payment of the initiation fee. Further, at least a few employees indicated that they thought they had to vote for the union since they had signed a recognition slip. Should the NLRB set aside this election of the union? Explain.

4. *Unfair Labor Practices by Management*
   (a) List the five unfair labor practices created by the Wagner Act.
   (b) Describe a situation for each of these unfair labor practices.

The Taft-Hartley Act

5. *Eighty-Day Cooling-Off Period*
   (a) Under what circumstances is the president authorized to order parties in a labor dispute back to work for 80 days?
   (b) Describe the procedures that must be followed to invoke this cooling-off period.

6. *Free Speech*

   The personnel director of your company has been asked to talk with the employees about the benefits and detriments of voting for or against the union in an upcoming certification election. What should this director keep in mind about the Free Speech Clause in the Taft-Hartley Act? Explain.

7. *Union Shop—Memberships and Fees*

   Pat lives in a state that has enacted a right-to-work law. The company that employs her has recognized the United Clerical Workers (UCW) as the bargaining representative of its workers. The union has sought to collect union dues or their equivalent from Pat. Is she required to pay them? Why or why not?

8. *Suits against Unions*

   Ed is discharged for allegedly stealing property from his employer. He asks his union to have him reinstated because his discharge violates the collective bargaining agreement in force. However, the union does not investigate the incident until it is too late to file a request for arbitration under the collective bargaining agreement. Assuming that Ed is innocent of the charges, does he have any rights against the union? Explain.

9. *Unfair Labor Practices by Unions*
   (a) List the six unfair labor practices created by the Taft-Hartley Act.
   (b) Describe a situation for each of these unfair labor practices.

10. *Amendments*
    (a) What were two basic purposes for Congress's passing the Landrum-Griffin Act?
    (b) What are the additional unfair labor practices added by this law?

1. For years, your small electronics company has given all its employees one week's pay and a turkey each Christmas. But now a recession is eroding profitability and the company is operating at a significant loss, so you consider canceling the Christmas presents for this year. The employees have just voted for union representation, and the extra pay and turkeys are not mentioned in the collective bargaining agreement.

Is a Christmas gift still purely a management decision?

Are you in trouble if you cancel the turkeys?

What is the union's role in the decision?

2. Sarah works at a small accounting firm. The firm's handbook contains the following policy:

Employees are prohibited from discussing their salary, bonuses, or any other forms of compensation, including benefits and vacation time.

Sarah is very careful not to violate the policy but, after she becomes married to her co-worker Bill, Sarah realizes that her salary is 20 percent less than Bill's salary. Bill and Sarah were hired at the same time and at the same position level. Sarah is even more upset when she learns that Bill started at the higher salary on his first day on the job. When Sarah asks her boss about the difference, she is terminated.

What potential claims could Sarah assert against her employer?

What defenses should the employer raise?

appendix 1 ::

:: Case Briefing and Legal Study Tips

To gain the most from this textbook, you should learn how to study written material effectively. You can achieve effective study through use of the SQ3R method, a method widely taught by study-skills psychologists for learning textual material.

SQ3R stands for **survey, question, read, recite,** and **review.** As a study method, it has dramatically improved the grade-point averages of most students who have practiced it. It is based upon the concept that active study of written material improves memory and comprehension of information far better than passive reading. Unfortunately, many students have not recognized the difference between active study and mere passive reading.

Students often read a textbook chapter exactly as they would read a novel or a magazine article. They begin with the first sentence of the chapter and read straight through the material, pausing only to underline occasionally. This way of reading may be suitable for a novel, but it is quite inappropriate for a textbook. Psychologists insist that an active study method must begin with a **survey** of the material to be read. If you plan to spend two hours studying a 30-page chapter, take three to five minutes in the beginning and survey the chapter. First, read the bold-type section headings (each chapter of this book is divided into numbered sections). Second, read a sentence or two from the text of each section. The purpose of this survey is to familiarize you with the topics covered in the chapter. Fight the tendency to stop your surveying process in order to comprehend all of the concepts you are surveying. Comprehension is not the goal of surveying.

Following the survey of all the sections, go back to the beginning of the chapter: Ask yourself a **question** before reading each section. Ask it aloud, if possible, but silently if circumstances demand. The important thing is actually to "talk to yourself." Normally, each section heading can easily be turned into a question. If the section heading reads *Stare Decisis,* ask yourself the question, "What does *stare decisis* mean?"

Only after asking a question are you finally ready to **read** a chapter section. In reading keep your question in mind. By so doing you will be reading for a purpose: To discover the answer to your question.

Upon finishing each section, stop and **recite** the answer to your question. As an example, at the end of the section on *stare decisis* say to yourself, "*Stare*

decisis refers to the legal tradition that a judge in a given case will follow the precedent established in similar cases decided by courts in the jurisdiction." According to psychologists, to recite this way greatly aids memory. Recitation also lets you know whether or not you have understood the material just read.

The last step of the SQ3R method is **review.** When devoting two hours to the study of a chapter, take the final 15 minutes of the time to review the material. Review the questions taken from the headings of each chapter section and recite the answers to them, rereading material if necessary to answer accurately.

A CASE BRIEFING SYSTEM

While the SQ3R method may be used effectively to study any subject, the **case briefing system** is uniquely designed to aid in the study of court decisions. In studying law, students frequently write up case briefs of each decision they read. Whether you are required to write up every decision is up to your individual instructor. However, the case briefing system provides an excellent framework for comprehending complicated judicial reasoning processes, and you should brief cases whether required to do so or not.

To avoid getting lost in a maze of judicial terminology, you should ask yourself a standard set of questions about each case decision and read to discover the answers to these questions. These standard questions lie at the heart of the case briefing system. They are:

1. Who is the plaintiff and who is the defendant?
2. What are the facts of the case? (Who did what to whom? What is the behavior complained of?)
3. Did the plaintiff or the defendant win in the lower court(s), and which party is appealing? (All decisions in this textbook come from appellate courts.)
4. What was the legal issue or issues appealed?
5. Does the plaintiff or the defendant win on the appeal?
6. What rules of law and reasoning does the appellate court use in deciding the issue?

Here is an illustration of a written case brief. It is a brief of the first case in the textbook, which you can find on page 83 in Chapter 3. Before looking at the brief, you should now read that case. An important part of law requires you to learn new vocabulary. To understand the case you read, you need to know several new terms. You can find the terms in the glossary of this textbook, but to make it easier, we will define several new terms for you:

alien A foreign-born person who is not a citizen of the United States.

appeal To ask a higher court to decide whether an inferior court (e.g. trial court) made a legal mistake in its decision; also to ask a higher court to review (decide) the case.

dissent To disagree both with the result and the legal reasoning of the majority opinion.

opinion The court's decision in a case.

petitioner The losing party in the court of appeals who asks (i.e. "petitions") the Supreme Court to decide whether the lower court made a mistake.

respondent The prevailing party in the court of appeals who is responding to the petitioner.

reversed What an appeals court says when it disagrees with the court beneath it. If it agrees with the lower court, it says "affirmed."

ultra vires Acts beyond the scope of the powers of an institution.

writ of habeas corpus Asking a court to release one from unlawful detention.

CASE BRIEF

Boumediene v. Bush, 128 S. Ct. 2229 (2008)
How do I read this citation?

- "Boumediene" refers to the *petitioner* Lakhdar Boumediene.
- "v." means versus or against
- "Bush" refers to the *respondent* President George W. Bush
- 128 is the volume number of the Supreme Court (S. Ct.) reporter, and 2229 indicates the page number where this case begins. 2008 is the year of this decision.

Plaintiff and Defendant The plaintiff/petitioner is Lakhdar Boumediene, as well as certain other aliens designated as "enemy combatants" who are detained at the United States Naval Station at Guantanamo Bay, Cuba. (All detainees at Guantanamo Bay were not parties to this suit.) The defendant/respondent is George W. Bush, President of the United States, but note that there are also other defendants.

Facts The petitioners are *aliens*, or foreign-born individuals who are not citizens of the United States, who are detained at the Guantanamo Bay facility following their capture in Afghanistan or elsewhere. They are designated enemy combatants and being held on that basis. They sought to challenge their detention as unlawful.

Two statutes are relevant to their case:

1. The Detainee Treatment Act of 2005 (DTA), which provides that "no court, justice, or judge shall have jurisdiction to consider an application for habeas corpus filed by or on behalf of an alien detained at Guantanamo" and gave the D.C. Circuit "exclusive" jurisdiction to review any decisions from the Combatant Status Review Tribunal ("CSRT"). CSRTs determine whether Guantanamo detainees are "enemy combatants."

2. The Military Commissions Act of 2006 (MCA), which denies jurisdiction with respect to habeas corpus actions by detained aliens determined to be enemy combatants.

Lower Courts The D.C. Court of Appeals concluded that the MCA must be read to strip from it, and all federal courts, jurisdiction to consider petitioners' habeas applications. In so doing, the D.C. Court of Appeals held that petitioners were not entitled to habeas or the protections of the Suspension Clause.

Issue Appealed Whether petitioners have the constitutional privilege of *habeas corpus*.

Who Wins? The detainees.
The Supreme Court held (5-4) that the petitioners do have the habeas corpus privilege, *reversing* the decision of the Court of Appeals. What does this mean as a practical matter? It means that the detainees may challenge their detention as unlawful; they may or may not ultimately be successful on the merits.

Reasoning

1. The Court held that Article I, § 9, cl. 2, of the Constitution has full effect at Guantanamo Bay and, accordingly, if the privilege of habeas corpus is denied to the detainees, Congress must act in accordance with the requirements of the Suspension Clause.

2. The Court held that the procedures for review of detainees status provided for in the DTA are not an adequate and effective substitute for habeas corpus.

3. Additionally, the Court held that the MCA is an unconstitutional suspension of the writ of habeas corpus.

4. In reaching its decision, the Court emphasized that the Framers "viewed freedom from unlawful restraint as a fundamental precept of liberty" and that the writ of habeas corpus is a "vital instrument to secure that freedom."

5. The four dissenting justices argue that the writ of habeas corpus does not apply to aliens abroad, that the Suspension Clause has no application, and that the Court's "intervention in this military matter is entirely *ultra vires*" or beyond the scope of its power. They also grave expressed about how the decision will affect national security.

:: Sample Complaint

IN THE SUPERIOR COURT OF CLARKE
COUNTY, STATE OF GEORGIA

JOHN DOE,	
Plaintiff,	
v.	CIVIL ACTION FILE NO: 2009
RELIANT MOTOR COMPANY, INC.,	
Defendant.	

COMPLAINT FOR DAMAGES

COMES NOW Plaintiff John Doe, by and through counsel, and hereby files his Complaint, showing as follows:

PARTIES, JURISDICTION, AND VENUE

1.

This Court has subject matter jurisdiction over this matter and venue is proper in this judicial district pursuant to Ga. Const. Art. VI, Sec. II, Para. VI and O.C.G.A. § 14-2-510(b) because the defendant conducts business, its registered agent is located and the cause of action originated in this judicial district.

2.

Plaintiff, John Doe, is a citizen of the State of Georgia and a resident of Athens, Clarke County, Georgia, and submits himself to the jurisdiction of this Court.

3.

Defendant "Reliant" Motor Company is a Georgia Corporation conducting business as an automobile dealer in Athens, Clarke County, Georgia. James Smith is the Registered Agent for Reliant Motor Company on whom service is proper. James Smith may be served at Terry Drive, Athens, Georgia, subjecting Reliant Motor Company to the jurisdiction of this Court.

Statement of Facts

4.

On or about February 1, 2009, John Doe purchased a 2006 Ford Explorer, Serial Number PJSJWMMAP 2006, from Defendant automobile dealership.

5.

The vehicle was identified as having undergone a 50 point inspection, and as having attained a "Platinum Check Quality Assurance." Among the items listed as passed "inspection" were all components of the front-end.

6.

The vehicle was sold with a 90 day/3000 mile warranty that covered all major component parts, including, but not limited to, engine, transmission, drive axle, brakes, steering, and electrical.

7.

While test driving the vehicle, Plaintiff noticed excessive road noise and informed Defendant of the problem. Defendant assured Plaintiff that vehicle had been inspected and was mechanically sound. Defendant said that excessive noise was from worn tires and offered to replace tires.

8.

Relying on Defendant's explanation and offer to replace tires, Plaintiff entered into a sales contract to buy the vehicle from Defendant. After Plaintiff purchased vehicle and had the tires replaced, the excessive road noise continued unabated. While Plaintiff returned the vehicle to Defendant several times to have the problem corrected, Defendant was unable to eliminate the excessive road noise. The vehicle became inoperative when the front-end locked up.

9.

Through an independent mechanic, Plaintiff learned that the entire problem with the vehicle was the "front-end" assembly. Component parts of the front-end were worn and damaged which caused the excessive road noise. Failure to fix the problem resulted in the front-end locking up. The independent mechanic also stated that the front-end had not been properly inspected.

10.

The fraudulent misrepresentations by Defendant that the vehicle had passed a thorough inspection induced Plaintiff to purchase the vehicle.

11.

Defendant refused to honor the warranty on the vehicle, make necessary repairs, or properly diagnose problem with the vehicle.

12.

As a result of these willful and wanton acts by Defendant, Plaintiff has been harmed by purchasing an inoperable vehicle for a sum exceeding $20,000. Plaintiff also has suffered other expenses, including the purchasing of another automobile for transportation and expenses in attempting to repair the vehicle at issue.

COUNT I
Fraud in the Inducement

13.

Plaintiff incorporates by reference the allegations in paragraphs 1 through 12 of his Complaint as if fully restated herein.

14.

Defendant, by its actions, intentionally concealed from the plaintiff the damage to the vehicle.

15.

The intentional concealments, misrepresentations and omissions set out herein were made by defendant in order to deceive plaintiff and induce him to purchase the vehicle.

16.

Plaintiff, in fact, reasonably relied on defendant's misrepresentations, which did, in fact, induce him to purchase the vehicle and to incur damages for repair and replacement of the vehicle as well as other foreseeable and consequential damages.

17.

Defendant's fraudulent concealments, misrepresentations and omissions showed willful misconduct malice, wantonness, and oppression and were conducted with specific intent to cause harm thereby entitling plaintiff to punitive damages.

COUNT II
Breach of Warranty

18.

Plaintiff incorporates by reference the allegations in paragraphs 1 through 17 of his Complaint as if fully restated herein.

19.

Defendant's actions breached the express warranty made to plaintiff in connection with his purchase of the vehicle, thereby entitling plaintiff to compensatory damages.

Prayer for Relief

WHEREFORE, Plaintiff respectfully prays that this Court:

1. Grant to Plaintiff judgment in this action and against Defendant under Counts One and Two of this complaint;

2. Grant to Plaintiff compensatory damages in an amount reasonable and commensurate with the losses imposed upon him by Defendant's unlawful acts, including his pain and emotional distress;

3. Grant to Plaintiff punitive damages in an amount reasonable and commensurate with the harm done and calculated to be sufficient to deter such conduct in the future;

4. Grant to Plaintiff his costs in this action and reasonable attorneys' fees as provided by OCGA § 13-6-11; and

5. Grant to Plaintiff a jury trial on all issues so triable;

6. Grant such additional relief as the Court deems proper and just.

Respectfully submitted this ___ day of _____, 2009,

_____

Joe Lawyer
Ga. State Bar #000000

Attorneys for Plaintiff

:: The Constitution of the United States of America

We, the People of the United States, in Order to form a more perfect Union, establish Justice, insure domestic Tranquility, provide for the common defense, promote the general Welfare, and secure the Blessings of Liberty to ourselves and our Posterity, do ordain and establish this Constitution for the United States of America.

Article I

Section 1. All legislative Powers herein granted shall be vested in a Congress of the United States, which shall consist of a Senate and House of Representatives.

Section 2. The House of Representatives shall be composed of Members chosen every second Year by the People of the several States, and the Electors in each State shall have the Qualifications requisite for Electors of the most numerous Branch of the State Legislature.

No Person shall be a Representative who shall not have attained the Age of twenty five Years, and been seven Years a Citizen of the United States, and who shall not, when elected, be an Inhabitant of that State in which he shall be chosen.

Representatives and direct Taxes shall be apportioned among the several States which may be included within this Union, according to their respective Numbers, which shall be determined by adding the whole Number of free Persons, including those bound to Service for a Term of Years, and excluding Indians not taxed, three-fifths of all other Persons. The actual Enumeration shall be made within three Years after the first Meeting of the Congress of the United States, and within every subsequent Term of ten Years, in such Manner as they shall by Law direct. The Number of Representatives shall not exceed one for every thirty Thousand, but each State shall have at Least one Representative; and until such enumeration shall be made, the State of New Hampshire shall be entitled to chuse three, Massachusetts eight, Rhode Island and Providence Plantations one, Connecticut five, New-York six, New Jersey four, Pennsylvania eight, Delaware one, Maryland six, Virginia ten, North Carolina five, South Carolina five, and Georgia three.

When vacancies happen in the Representation from any State, the Executive Authority thereof shall issue Writs of Election to fill such Vacancies.

The House of Representatives shall chuse their Speaker and other Officers; and shall have the sole Power of Impeachment.

Section 3. The Senate of the United States shall be composed of two Senators from each State, chosen by the Legislature thereof, for six Years; and each Senator shall have one Vote.

Immediately after they shall be assembled in Consequence of the Election, they shall be divided as equally as may be into three Classes. The Seats of the Senators of the first Class shall be vacated at the Expiration of the second Year, of the second Class at the Expiration of the fourth Year, and of the third Class at the Expiration of the sixth Year, so that one third may be chosen every second Year; and if Vacancies happen by Resignation, or otherwise, during the Recess of the Legislature of any State, the Executive thereof may make temporary Appointments until the next Meeting of the Legislature, which shall then fill such Vacancies.

No Person shall be a Senator who shall not have attained to the Age of thirty Years, and been nine Years a Citizen of the United States, and who shall not, when elected, be an Inhabitant of that State for which he shall be chosen.

The Vice President of the United States shall be President of the Senate, but shall have no Vote, unless they be equally divided.

The Senate shall chuse their other Officers, and also a President pro tempore, in the Absence of the Vice President, or when he shall exercise the Office of the President of the United States.

The Senate shall have the sole Power to try all Impeachments. When sitting for that Purpose, they shall be on Oath or Affirmation. When the President of the United States is tried, the Chief Justice shall preside: and no Person shall be convicted without the Concurrence of two-thirds of the Members present.

Judgment in Cases of Impeachment shall not extend further than to removal from Office, and disqualification to hold and enjoy any Office of honor, Trust or Profit under the United States: but the Party convicted shall nevertheless be liable and subject to Indictment, Trial, Judgment and Punishment, according to Law.

Section 4. The Times, Places and Manner of holding Elections for Senators and Representatives, shall be prescribed in each State by the Legislature thereof: but the Congress may at any time by Law make or alter such Regulations, except as to the Places of chusing Senators.

The Congress shall assemble at least once in every Year, and such Meeting shall be on the first Monday in December, unless they shall by Law appoint a different Day.

Section 5.
Each House shall be the Judge of the Elections, Returns and Qualifications of its own Members, and a Majority of each shall constitute a Quorum to do Business; but a smaller Number may adjourn from day to day, and may be authorized to compel the Attendance of absent Members, in such Manner, and under such Penalties as each House may provide.

Each House may determine the Rules of its Proceedings, punish its Members for disorderly Behaviour, and, with the concurrence of two thirds, expel a Member.

Each House shall keep a Journal of its Proceedings, and from time to time publish the same, excepting such Parts as may in their Judgment require Secrecy; and the Yeas and Nays of the Members of either House on any question shall, at the Desire of one-fifth of those Present, be entered on the Journal.

Neither House, during the Session of Congress, shall, without the Consent of the other, adjourn for more than three days, nor to any other Place than that in which the two Houses shall be sitting.

Section 6.
The Senators and Representatives shall receive a Compensation for their Services, to be ascertained by Law, and paid out of the Treasury of the United States. They shall in all Cases, except Treason, Felony and Breach of the Peace, be privileged from Arrest during their Attendance at the Session of their respective Houses, and in going to and returning from the same; and for any Speech or Debate in either House, they shall not be questioned in any other Place.

No Senator or Representative shall, during the Time for which he was elected, be appointed to any civil Office under the Authority of the United States, which shall have been created, or the Emoluments whereof shall have been encreased during such time; and no Person holding any Office under the United States, shall be a Member of either House during his Continuance in Office.

Section 7.
All Bills for raising Revenue shall originate in the House of Representatives; but the Senate may propose or concur with Amendments as on other Bills.

Every Bill which shall have passed the House of Representatives and the Senate, shall, before it become a Law, be presented to the President of the United States; If he approve, he shall sign it, but if not he shall return it, with his Objections to that house in which it shall have originated, who shall enter the Objections at large on their Journal, and proceed to reconsider it. If after such Reconsideration two thirds of that House shall agree to pass the Bill, it shall be sent, together with the Objections, to the other House, by which it shall likewise be reconsidered, and if approved by two thirds of that House, it shall become a Law. But in all such Cases the Votes of both Houses shall be determined by Yeas and Nays, and the Names of the Persons voting for and against the Bill shall be entered on the Journal of each House respectively. If any Bill shall not be returned by the President within ten Days (Sundays excepted) after it shall have been presented to him, the Same shall be a Law, in like Manner as if he had signed it, unless the Congress by their Adjournment prevent its Return, in which Case it shall not be a Law.

Every Order, Resolution, or Vote to which the Concurrence of the Senate and House of Representatives may be necessary (except on a question of Adjournment) shall be presented to the President of the United States; and before the Same shall take Effect, shall be approved by him, or being disapproved by him, shall be repassed by two thirds of the Senate and House of Representatives, according to the Rules and Limitations prescribed in the Case of a Bill.

Section 8.
The Congress shall have the Power to lay and collect Taxes, Duties, Imposts and Excises, to pay the Debts and provide for the common Defence and general Welfare of the United States; but all Duties, Imposts and Excises shall be uniform throughout the United States;

To borrow Money on the credit of the United States;

To regulate Commerce with foreign Nations, and among the several States, and with the Indian Tribes;

To establish an uniform Rule of Naturalization, and uniform Laws on the subject of Bankruptcies throughout the United States;

To coin Money, regulate the Value thereof, and of foreign Coin, and fix the Standard of Weights and Measures;

To provide for the Punishment of counterfeiting the Securities and current Coin of the United States;

To establish Post Offices and post Roads;

To promote the Progress of Science and useful Arts, by securing for limited Times to Authors and Inventors the exclusive Right to their respective Writings and Discoveries;

To constitute Tribunals inferior to the supreme Court;

To define and punish Piracies and Felonies committed on the high Seas, and Offenses against the Law of Nations;

To declare War, grant Letters of Marque and Reprisal, and make rules concerning Captures on Land and Water;

To raise and support Armies, but no Appropriation of Money to that use shall be for a longer Term than two Years;

To provide and maintain a Navy;

To make Rules for the Government and Regulation of the land and naval Forces;

To provide for calling forth the Militia to execute the Laws of the Union, suppress Insurrections and repel Invasions;

To provide for organizing, arming and disciplining, the Militia, and for governing such Part of them as may be employed in the Service of the United States, reserving to the States respectively, the Appointment of the Officers, and the Authority of training the Militia according to the discipline prescribed by Congress;

To exercise exclusive Legislation in all Cases whatsoever, over such District (not exceeding ten Miles square) as may, by Cession of particular States, and the acceptance of Congress, become the Seat of the Government of the United States, and to exercise like Authority over all Places purchased by the Consent of the Legislature of the State in which the Same shall be, for the Erection of Forts, Magazines, Arsenals, dockYards, and other needful buildings;—And

To make all Laws which shall be necessary and proper for carrying into Execution the foregoing Powers, and all other Powers vested by the Constitution in the Government of the United States, or in any Department or Officer thereof.

Section 9.
The Migration or Importation of such Persons as any of the States now existing shall think proper to admit, shall not be prohibited by the Congress prior to the Year one thousand eight hundred and eight, but a Tax or Duty may be imposed on such Importation, not exceeding ten dollars for each Person.

The Privilege of the Writ of Habeas Corpus shall not be suspended, unless when in Cases of Rebellion or Invasion the public Safety may require it.

No Bill of Attainder or ex post facto Law shall be passed.

No Capitation, or other direct, Tax shall be laid, unless in Proportion to the Census or Enumeration herein before directed to be taken.

No Tax or Duty shall be laid on Articles exported from any State.

No Preference shall be given by any Regulation of Commerce or Revenue to the Ports of one State over those of another: nor shall Vessels bound to, or from, one State, be obliged to enter, clear, or pay Duties in another.

No Money shall be drawn from the Treasury, but in Consequence of Appropriations made by Law; and a regular Statement and Account of the Receipts and Expenditures of all public Money shall be published from time to time.

No Title of Nobility shall be granted by the United States: And no Person holding any Office or Profit or Trust under them, shall, without the Consent of the Congress, accept of any present, Emolument, Office, or Title, of any kind whatever, from any King, Prince, or foreign State.

Section 10.
No State shall enter into any Treaty, Alliance, or Confederation; grant Letters of Marque and Reprisal; coin Money; emit Bills of Credit; make any Thing but gold and silver Coin a Tender in Payment of Debts; pass any Bill of Attainder, ex post facto Law, or Law impairing the Obligation of Contracts, or grant any Title of Nobility.

No State shall, without the Consent of the Congress, lay any Imposts or Duties on Imports or Exports, except what may be absolutely necessary for executing its inspection Laws: and the net Produce of all Duties and Imposts, laid by any State on Imports or Exports, shall be for the Use of the Treasury of the United States; and all such Laws shall be subject to the Revision and Control of the Congress.

No State shall, without the Consent of Congress, lay any Duty of Tonnage, keep Troops, or Ships of War in time of Peace, enter into any Agreement or Compact with another State, or with a foreign Power, or engage in War, unless actually invaded, or in such imminent Danger as will not admit of delay.

Article II

Section 1.
The executive Power shall be vested in a President of the United States of America. He shall hold Office during the Term of four Years, and, together with the Vice President, chosen for the same Term, be elected as follows:

Each State shall appoint, in such Manner as the Legislature thereof may direct, a Number of Electors, equal to the whole Number of Senators and Representatives to which the State may be entitled in the Congress: but no Senator or Representative, or Person holding an Office or Trust or Profit under the United States, shall be appointed an Elector.

The Electors shall meet in their respective States, and vote by Ballot for two Persons, of whom one at least shall not be an Inhabitant of the same State with Themselves. And they shall make a List of all the Persons voted for, and of the Number of Votes for each; which List they shall sign and certify, and transmit sealed to the Seat of the Government of the United States, directed to the President of the Senate. The President of the Senate shall, in the Presence of the Senate and House of Representatives, open all the Certificates, and the Votes shall then be counted. The Person having the greatest Number of Votes shall be the President, if such Number be a Majority of the whole Number of Electors appointed; and if there be more than one who have such Majority, and have an equal Number of Votes, then the House of Representatives shall immediately chuse by Ballot one of them for President; and if no Person have a Majority, then from the five highest on the List the said House shall in like Manner chuse the President. But in chusing the President, the Votes shall be taken by States, the Representation from each State having one Vote; a quorum for this Purpose shall consist of a Member or Members from two thirds of the States, and a Majority of all the States shall be necessary to a Choice. In every Case, after the Choice of the President, the Person having the greatest Number of Votes of the Electors shall be the Vice President. But if there should remain two or more who have equal Votes, the Senate shall chuse from them by Ballot the Vice President.

The Congress may determine the Time of chusing the Electors, and the Day on which they shall give their Votes; which Day shall be the same throughout the United States.

No Person except a natural born Citizen, or a Citizen of the United States, at the time of the Adoption of this Constitution, shall be eligible to the Office of President; neither shall any Person be eligible to that Office who shall not have attained to the Age of thirty five Years, and been fourteen Years a Resident within the United States.

In Case of the Removal of the President from Office, or of his Death, Resignation, or Inability to discharge the Powers and Duties of the said Office, the Same shall devolve on the Vice President, and the Congress may by Law provide for the Case of Removal, Death, Resignation, or Inability, both of the President and Vice President, declaring what Officer shall then act as President, and such Officer shall act accordingly, until the Disability be removed, or a President shall be elected.

The President shall, at stated Times, receive for his Services, a Compensation, which shall neither be increased nor diminished during the Period for which he shall have been elected, and he shall not receive within that Period any other Emolument from the United States, or any of them.

Before he enter on the Execution of his Office, he shall take the following Oath or Affirmation:—"I do solemnly swear (or affirm) that I will faithfully execute the Office of President of the United States, and will to the best of my Ability, preserve, protect and defend the Constitution of the United States."

Section 2.   The President shall be Commander in Chief of the Army and Navy of the United States, and of the Militia of the several States, when called into the actual Service of the United States; he may require the Opinion, in writing, of the principal Officer in each of the executive Departments, upon any Subject relating to the Duties of their respective Offices, and he shall have Power to grant Reprieves and Pardons for Offenses against the United States, except in Cases of Impeachment.

He shall have Power, by and with the Advice and Consent of the Senate, to make Treaties, providing two thirds of the Senators present concur; and he shall nominate, and by and with the advice and consent of the Senate, shall appoint Ambassadors, other public Ministers and Consuls, Judges of the supreme Court, and all other Officers of the United States, whose Appointments are not herein otherwise provided for, and which shall be established by Law: but the Congress may by Law vest the Appointment of such inferior Officers, as they think proper, in the President alone, in the Courts of Law, or in the Heads of Departments

The President shall have the Power to fill up all Vacancies that may happen during the Recess of the Senate, by granting Commissions which shall expire at the End of their next Session.

Section 3.   He shall from time to time give to the Congress Information of the State of the Union, and recommend to their Consideration such Measures as he shall judge necessary and expedient; he may, on extraordinary Occasions, convene both Houses, or either of them, and in Case of Disagreement between them, with Respect to the Time of Adjournment, he may adjourn them to such Time as he shall think proper; he shall receive Ambassadors and other public Ministers; he shall take Care that the Laws be faithfully executed, and shall Commission all the Officers of the United States.

Section 4.   The President, Vice President, and all civil Officers of the United States, shall be removed from Office on Impeachment for, and Conviction of, Treason, Bribery, or other high Crimes and Misdemeanors.

Article III

Section 1.   The judicial Power of the United States, shall be vested in one supreme Court, and in such inferior Courts as the Congress may from time to time ordain and establish. The Judges, both of the supreme and inferior Courts, shall hold their Offices during good Behaviour, and shall, at stated Times, receive for their Services, a Compensation, which shall not be diminished during their Continuance in Office.

Section 2. The judicial Power shall extend to all Cases, in Law and Equity, arising under this Constitution, the Laws of the United States, and Treaties made, or which shall be made, under their Authority;—to all Cases affecting Ambassadors, other public Ministers and Consuls;—to all Cases of admiralty and maritime Jurisdiction;—to Controversies to which the United States shall be a Party;—to Controversies between two or more States;—between a State and Citizens of another State;—between Citizens of different States;—between Citizens of the same State claiming Lands under Grants of different States, and between a State, or the Citizens thereof, and foreign States, Citizens or Subjects.

In all Cases affecting Ambassadors, other public Ministers and Consuls, and those in which a State shall be Party, the supreme Court shall have original Jurisdiction. In all the other Cases before mentioned, the supreme Court shall have appellate Jurisdiction, both as to Law and Fact, with such Exceptions, and under such Regulations as the Congress shall make.

The Trial of all Crimes, except in Cases of Impeachment, shall be by Jury; and such Trial shall be held in the State where the said Crimes shall have been committed; but when not committed within any State, the Trial shall be at such Place or Places as the Congress may by Law have directed.

Section 3. Treason against the United States, shall consist only in levying War against them, or in adhering to their Enemies, giving them Aid and Comfort. No Person shall be convicted of Treason unless on the Testimony of two Witnesses to the same overt Act, or on Confession in open Court.

The Congress shall have Power to declare the Punishment of Treason, but no Attainder of Treason shall work Corruption of Blood, or Forfeiture except during the Life of the Person attainted.

Article IV

Section 1. Full Faith and Credit shall be given in each State to the public Acts, Records, and judicial Proceedings of every other State. And the Congress may by general Laws prescribe the Manner in which such Acts, Records and Proceedings shall be proved, and the Effect thereof.

Section 2. The Citizens of each State shall be entitled to all Privileges and Immunities of Citizens in the several states.

A person charged in any State with Treason, Felony, or other Crime, who shall flee Justice, and be found in another State, shall on Demand of the executive Authority of the State from which he fled, be delivered up, to be removed to the state having Jurisdiction of the Crime.

No Person held to Service or Labour in one State, under the Laws thereof, escaping into another, shall, in Consequence of any Law or Regulation therein, be discharged from such Service or Labour, but shall be delivered up on Claim of the Party to whom such Service or Labour may be due.

Section 3. New States may be admitted by the Congress into this Union; but no new State shall be formed or erected within the Jurisdiction of any other State, nor any State be formed by the Junction of two or more States, or Parts of States, without the Consent of the Legislatures of the States concerned, as well as of the Congress.

The Congress shall have Power to dispose of and make all needful Rules and Regulations respecting the Territory or other Property belonging to the United States; and nothing in this Constitution shall be so construed as to Prejudice any Claims of the United States, or of any particular State.

Section 4. The United States shall guarantee to every State in this Union a Republican form of Government, and shall protect each of them against Invasion; and on Application of the Legislature, or of the Executive (when the Legislature cannot be convened) against domestic Violence.

Article V.
The Congress, whenever two thirds of both Houses shall deem it necessary, shall propose Amendments to this Constitution, or, on the Application of the Legislatures of two thirds of the several States, shall call a Convention for proposing Amendments, which, in either Case, shall be valid to all Intents and Purposes, as Part of this Constitution, when ratified by the Legislatures of three fourths of the several States, or by Conventions in three fourths thereof, as the one or the other Mode of Ratification may be proposed by the Congress; Provided that no Amendment which may be made prior to the Year One thousand eight hundred and eight shall in any Manner affect the first and fourth Clauses in the Ninth Section of the first Article; and that no State, without its Consent, shall be deprived of its equal Suffrage in the Senate.

Article VI.
All Debts contracted and Engagements entered into, before the Adoption of this Constitution, shall be as valid against the United States under this Constitution, as under the Confederation.

This Constitution, and the Laws of the United States which shall be made in Pursuance thereof; and all Treaties made, or which shall be made, under the Authority of the United States, shall be the supreme Law of the Land; and the Judges in every State shall be bound thereby, any Thing in the Constitution or Laws of any State to the Contrary notwithstanding.

The Senators and Representatives before mentioned, and the Members of the several State Legislatures, and all executive and judicial Officers, both of the United States and of the several States, shall be bound by Oath or Affirmation, to support this Constitution; but no religious Test shall ever be required as a Qualification to any Office or public Trust under the United States.

Article VII. The Ratification of the Conventions of nine States, shall be sufficient for the Establishment of this Constitution between the States so ratifying the Same.

Amendment I [1791]. Congress shall make no law respecting an establishment of religion, or prohibiting the free exercise thereof; or abridging the freedom of speech, or of the press; or the right of the people peaceably to assemble, and to petition the Government for a redress of grievances.

Amendment II [1791]. A well regulated Militia, being necessary to the security for a free State, the right of the people to keep and bear Arms, shall not be infringed.

Amendment III [1791]. No Soldier shall, in time of peace be quartered in any house, without the consent of the Owner, nor in time of war, but in a manner to be prescribed by law.

Amendment IV [1791]. The right of the people to be secure in their persons, houses, papers, and effects, against unreasonable searches and seizures, shall not be violated, and no Warrants shall issue, but upon probable cause, supported by Oath or affirmation, and particularly describing the place to be searched, and the persons or things to be seized.

Amendment V [1791]. No person shall be held to answer for a capital, or otherwise infamous crime, unless on a presentment or indictment of a Grand Jury, except in cases arising in the land or naval forces, or in the Militia, when in actual service in time of War or public danger; nor shall any person be subject for the same offense to be twice put in jeopardy of life or limb; nor shall be compelled in any criminal case to be a witness against himself, nor be deprived of life, liberty, or property, without due process of law; nor shall private property be taken for public use without just compensation.

Amendment VI [1791]. In all criminal prosecutions, the accused shall enjoy the right to a speedy and public trial, by an impartial jury of the State and district wherein the crime shall have been committed, which district shall have been previously ascertained by law, and to be informed of the nature and cause of the accusation; to be confronted with the Witnesses against him; to have compulsory process for obtaining witnesses in his favor, and to have the Assistance of counsel for his defense.

Amendment VII [1791]. In suits at common law, where the value in controversy shall exceed twenty dollars, the right of trial by jury shall be preserved, and no fact tried by a jury, shall be otherwise re-examined in any Court of the United States, than according to the rules of the common law.

Amendment VIII [1791]. Excessive bail shall not be required, nor excessive fines imposed, nor cruel and unusual punishments inflicted.

Amendment IX [1791]. The enumeration in the Constitution, of certain rights, shall not be construed to deny or disparage others retained by the people.

Amendment X [1791]. The powers not delegated to the United States by the Constitution, nor prohibited by it to the States, are reserved to the States respectively, or to the people.

Amendment XI [1798]. The Judicial power of the United States shall not be construed to extend to any suit in law or equity, commenced or prosecuted against one of the United States by Citizens of another State, or by Citizens or Subjects of any Foreign State.

Amendment XII [1804]. The Electors shall meet in their respective states and vote by ballot for President and Vice-President, one of whom, at least, shall not be an inhabitant of the same state with themselves; they shall name in their ballots the person voted for as President, and in distinct ballots the person voted for as Vice-President, and they shall make distinct lists of all persons voted for as President, and of all persons voted for as Vice-President, and of the number of votes for each, which lists they shall sign and certify, and transmit sealed to the seat of the government of the United States, directed to the President of the Senate;—The President of the Senate shall, in the presence of the Senate and House of Representatives, open all the certificates and the votes shall then be counted;—The person having the greatest number of votes for President, shall be the President, if such number be a majority of the whole number of Electors appointed; and if no person have such majority, then from the persons having the highest numbers not exceeding three on the list of those voted for as President, the House of Representatives shall choose immediately, by ballot, the President. But in choosing the President, the votes shall be taken by states, the representation from each state having one vote; a quorum for this purpose shall consist of a member or members from two-thirds of the states, and a majority of all the states shall be necessary to a choice. And if the House of Representatives shall not choose a President whenever the right of choice shall devolve upon them, before the fourth day of March next following, then the Vice-President shall act as President. The person having the greatest number of votes as Vice-President, shall be the Vice-President, if such number be a majority of the whole number of electors appointed, and if no person have a majority, then from the two highest numbers on the list, the Senate shall choose the Vice-President; a quorum for the purpose shall consist of two-thirds of the whole number of Senators, and a majority of the whole number shall be necessary to a choice. But no person constitutionally ineligible to the office of President shall be eligible to that of the Vice-President of the United States.

Amendment XIII [1865]

Section 1. Neither slavery nor involuntary servitude, except as a punishment for crime whereof the party shall have been duly convicted, shall exist within the United States, or any place subject to their jurisdiction.

Section 2. Congress shall have power to enforce this article by appropriate legislation.

Amendment XIV [1868]

Section 1. All persons born or naturalized in the United States, and subject to the jurisdiction thereof, are citizens of the United States and of the State wherein they reside. No State shall make or enforce any law which shall abridge the privileges or immunities of citizens of the United States; nor shall any State deprive any person of life, liberty, or property, without due process of law; nor deny to any person within its jurisdiction the equal protection of the laws.

Section 2. Representatives shall be appointed among the several States according to their respective numbers, counting the whole number of persons in each State, excluding Indians not taxed. But when the right to vote at any election for the choice of electors for President and Vice President of the United States, Representatives in Congress, the executive and judicial officers of a State, or the members of the Legislature thereof, is denied to any of the male inhabitants of such State, being twenty-one years of age, and citizens of the United States, or in any way abridged, except for participation in rebellion, or other crime, the basis of representation therein shall be reduced in the proportion which the number of such male citizens shall bear to the whole number of male citizens twenty-one years of age in such State.

Section 3. No person shall be a Senator or Representative in Congress, or elector of President and Vice President, or hold any office, civil or military, under the United States, or under any State, who, having previously taken an oath, as a member of Congress, or as an officer of the United States, or as a member of any State legislature, or as an executive or judicial officer of any State, to support the Constitution of the United States, shall have engaged in insurrection or rebellion against the same, or given aid or comfort to the enemies thereof. But Congress may by a vote of two-thirds of each House, remove such disability.

Section 4. The validity of the public debt of the United States, authorized by law, including debts incurred for payment of pensions and bounties for services in suppressing insurrection or rebellion, shall not be questioned. But neither the United States nor any State shall assume or pay any debt or obligation incurred in aid of insurrection or rebellion against the United States, or any claim for the loss or emancipation of any slave; but all such debts, obligations and claims shall be held illegal and void.

Section 5. The Congress shall have the power to enforce, by appropriate legislation, the provisions of this article.

Amendment XV [1870]

Section 1. The right of citizens of the United States to vote shall not be denied or abridged by the United States or by any State on account of race, color, or previous condition of servitude.

Section 2. The Congress shall have power to enforce this article by appropriate legislation.

Amendment XVI [1913].
The Congress shall have power to lay and collect taxes on incomes, from whatever sources derived, without apportionment among the several States, and without regard to any census or enumeration.

Amendment XVII [1913].
The Senate of the United States shall be composed of two Senators from each State, elected by the people thereof, for six years; and each Senator shall have one vote. The electors in each State shall have the qualifications requisite for electors of the most numerous branch of the State legislatures.

When vacancies happen in the representation of any State in the Senate, the executive authority of such State shall issue writs of election to fill such vacancies: *Provided*, That the legislature of any State may empower the executive thereof to make temporary appointments until the people fill the vacancies by election as the legislature may direct.

This amendment shall not be so construed as to affect the election or term of any Senator chosen before it becomes valid as part of the Constitution.

Amendment XVIII [1919]

Section 1. After one year from the ratification of this article the manufacture, sale, or transportation of intoxicating liquors within, the importation thereof into, or the exportation thereof from the United States and all territory subject to the jurisdiction thereof for beverage purposes is hereby prohibited.

Section 2. The Congress and the several States shall have concurrent power to enforce this article by appropriate legislation.

Section 3. This article shall be inoperative unless it shall have been ratified as an amendment to the Constitution by the legislatures of the several States, as provided in the Constitution, within seven years from the date of the submission hereof to the States by the Congress.

Amendment XIX [1920].
The right of citizens of the United States to vote shall not be denied or abridged by the United States or by any State on account of sex.

Congress shall have power to enforce this article by appropriate legislation.

Amendment XX [1933]

Section 1. The terms of the President and the Vice President shall end at noon on the 20th day of January, and the terms of Senators and Representatives at noon on the 3d day of January, of the years in which such terms would have ended if this article had not been ratified; and the terms of their successors shall then begin.

Section 2. The Congress shall assemble at least once in every year, and such meeting shall begin at noon on the 3d day of January, unless they shall by law appoint a different day.

Section 3. If, at the time fixed for the beginning of the term of the President, the President elect shall have died, the Vice President elect shall become President. If a President shall not have been chosen before the time fixed for the beginning of his term, or if the President elect shall have failed to qualify, then the Vice President elect shall act as President until a President shall have qualified; and the Congress may by law provide for the case wherein neither a President elect nor a Vice President shall have qualified, declaring who shall then act as President, or the manner in which one who is to act shall be selected, and such person shall act accordingly until a President or Vice President shall have qualified.

Section 4. The Congress may by law provide for the case of the death of any of the persons from whom the House of Representatives may choose a President whenever the right of choice shall have devolved upon them, and for the case of the death of any of the persons from whom the Senate may choose a Vice President whenever the right of choice shall have devolved upon them.

Section 5. Sections 1 and 2 shall take effect on the 15th day of October following the ratification of this article.

Section 6. This article shall be inoperative unless it shall have been ratified as an amendment to the Constitution by the legislatures of three-fourths of the several States within seven years from the date of its submission.

Amendment XXI [1933]

Section 1. The eighteenth article of amendment to the Constitution of the United States is hereby repealed.

Section 2. The transportation or importation into any State, Territory, or possession of the United States for delivery or use therein of intoxicating liquors, in violation of the laws thereof, is hereby prohibited.

Section 3. This article shall be inoperative unless it shall have been ratified as an amendment to the Constitution by conventions in the several States, as provided in the Constitution, within seven years from the date of the submission hereof to the States by the Congress.

Amendment XXII [1951]

Section 1. No person shall be elected to the office of the President more than twice, and no person who has held the office of President, or acted as President, for more than two years of a term to which some other person was elected President shall be elected to the office of President more than once. But this Article shall not apply to any person holding the office of President when this Article was proposed by the Congress, and shall not prevent any person who may be holding the office of President, or acting as President, during the term within which this Article becomes operative from holding the office of President or acting as President during the remainder of such term.

Section 2. This article shall be inoperative unless it shall have been ratified as an amendment to the Constitution by the legislatures of three-fourths of the several States within seven years from the date of its submission to the States by the Congress.

Amendment XXIII [1961]

Section 1. The District constituting the seat of Government of the United States shall appoint in such manner as the Congress may direct:

A number of electors of President and Vice President equal to the whole number of Senators and Representatives in Congress to which the District would be entitled if it were a State, but in no event more than the least populous State; they shall be in addition to those appointed by the States, but they shall be considered, for the purposes of the election of President and Vice President, to be electors appointed by a State; and they shall meet in the District and perform such duties as provided by the twelfth article of amendment.

Section 2. The Congress shall have power to enforce this article by appropriate legislation.

Amendment XXIV [1964]

Section 1. The right of citizens of the United States to vote in any primary or other election for President or Vice President, for electors for President or Vice President, or for Senator or Representative in Congress, shall not be denied or abridged by the United States or any State by reason of failure to pay poll tax or any other tax.

Section 2. The Congress shall have power to enforce this article by appropriate legislation.

Amendment XXV [1967]

Section 1. In case of the removal of the President from office or of his death or resignation, the Vice President shall become President.

Section 2. Whenever there is a vacancy in the office of the Vice President, the President shall nominate a Vice President who shall take the office upon confirmation by a majority vote of both Houses of Congress.

Section 3. Whenever the President transmits to the President pro tempore of the Senate and the Speaker of the House of Representatives his written declaration that he is unable to discharge the powers and duties of his office, and until he transmits to them a written declaration to the contrary, such powers and duties shall be discharged by the Vice President as Acting President.

Section 4. Whenever the Vice President and a majority of either the principal officers of the executive departments or of such other body as Congress may by law provide, transmit to the President pro tempore of the Senate and the Speaker of the House of Representatives their written declaration that the President is unable to discharge the powers and duties of his office, the Vice President shall immediately assume the powers and duties of the office as Acting President.

Thereafter, when the President transmits to the President pro tempore of the Senate and the Speaker of the House of Representatives his written declaration that no inability exists, he shall resume the powers and duties of his office unless the Vice President and a majority of either the principal officers of the executive departments or of such other body as Congress may by law provide, transmit within four days to the President pro tempore of the Senate and the

Speaker of the House of Representatives their written declaration that the President is unable to discharge the powers and duties of his office. Thereupon Congress shall decide the issue, assembling within forty-eight hours for that purpose if not in session. If the Congress, within twenty-one days after receipt of the latter written declaration, or, if Congress is not in session, within twenty-one days after Congress is required to assemble, determines by two-thirds vote of both houses that the President is unable to discharge the powers and duties of his office, the Vice President shall continue to discharge the same as Acting President; otherwise, the President shall resume the powers and duties of his office.

Amendment XXVI [1971]

Section 1. The right of citizens of the United States, who are eighteen years of age or older, to vote shall not be denied or abridged by the United States or any State on account of age.

Section 2. The Congress shall have power to enforce this article by appropriate legislation.

Amendment XXVII [1992].

No law, varying the compensation for the services of the Senators and Representatives shall take effect, until an election of Representatives shall have intervened.

:: Selected Sections of Article 2 of Uniform Commercial Code

§ 2-104. Definitions: "Merchant"; "Between Merchants"; "Financing Agency."

(1) **"Merchant"** means a person who deals in goods of the kind or otherwise by his occupation holds himself out as having knowledge or skill peculiar to the practices or goods involved in the transaction or to whom such knowledge or skill may be attributed by his employment of an agent or broker or other intermediary who by his occupation holds himself out as having such knowledge or skill.

(3) **"Between Merchants"** means in any transaction with respect to which both parties are chargeable with the knowledge or skill of merchants.

§ 2-201. Formal Requirements; Statute of Frauds.

(1) Except as otherwise provided in this section a contract for the sale of goods for the price of $500 or more is not enforceable by way of action or defense unless there is some writing sufficient to indicate that a contract for sale has been made between the parties and signed by the party against whom enforcement is sought or by his authorized agent or broker. A writing is not insufficient because it omits or incorrectly states a term agreed upon but the contract is not enforceable under this paragraph beyond the quantity of goods shown in such writing.

(2) Between merchants if within a reasonable time a writing in confirmation of the contract and sufficient against the sender is received and the party receiving it has reason to know its contents, it satisfies the requirements of subsection (1) against such party unless written notice of objection to its contents is given within 10 days after it is received.

(3) A contract which does not satisfy the requirements of subsection (1) but which is valid in other respects is enforceable

- (a) if the goods are to be specially manufactured for the buyer and are not suitable for sale to others in the ordinary course of the seller's business and the seller, before notice of repudiation is received and under circumstances which reasonably indicate that the goods are for the buyer, has made either a substantial beginning of their manufacture or commitments for their procurement; or

- (b) if the party against whom enforcement is sought admits in his pleading, testimony or otherwise in court that a contract for sale was made, but the contract is not enforceable under this provision beyond the quantity of goods admitted; or

- (c) with respect to goods for which payment has been made and accepted or which have been received and accepted (Sec. 2-606).

§ 2-205. Firm Offers.

An offer by a merchant to buy or sell goods in a signed writing which by its terms gives assurance that it will be held open is not revocable, for lack of consideration, during the time stated or if no time is stated for a reasonable time, but in no event may such period of irrevocability exceed three months; but any such term of assurance on a form supplied by the offeree must be separately signed by the offeror.

§ 2-206. Offer and Acceptance in Formation of Contract.

(1) Unless otherwise unambiguously indicated by the language or circumstances

- (a) an offer to make a contract shall be construed as inviting acceptance in any manner and by any medium reasonable in the circumstances;

- (b) an order or other offer to buy goods for prompt or current shipment shall be construed as inviting acceptance either by a prompt promise to ship or by the prompt or current shipment of conforming or non-conforming goods, but such a shipment of non-conforming goods does not constitute an acceptance if the seller seasonably notifies the buyer that the shipment is offered only as an accommodation to the buyer.

(2) Where the beginning of a requested performance is a reasonable mode of acceptance an offeror who is not notified of acceptance within a reasonable time may treat the offer as having lapsed before acceptance.

§ 2-207. Additional Terms in Acceptance or Confirmation.

(1) A definite and seasonable expression of acceptance or a written confirmation which is sent within a reasonable time operates as an acceptance even though it states terms additional to or different from those offered or agreed upon, unless acceptance is expressly made conditional on assent to the additional or different terms.

(2) The additional terms are to be construed as proposals for addition to the contract. Between merchants such terms become part of the contract unless:

- (a) the offer expressly limits acceptance to the terms of the offer;
- (b) they materially alter it; or
- (c) notification of objection to them has already been given or is given within a reasonable time after notice of them is received.

(3) Conduct by both parties which recognizes the existence of a contract is sufficient to establish a contract for sale although the writings of the parties do not otherwise establish a contract. In such case the terms of the particular contract consist of those terms on which the writings of the parties agree, together with any supplementary terms incorporated under any other provisions of this Act.

§ 2-209. Modification, Rescission and Waiver.

(1) An agreement modifying a contract within this Article needs no consideration to be binding.

(2) A signed agreement which excludes modification or rescission except by a signed writing cannot be otherwise modified or rescinded, but except as between merchants such a requirement on a form supplied by the merchant must be separately signed by the other party.

(3) The requirements of the statute of frauds section of this Article (Section 2-201) must be satisfied if the contract as modified is within its provisions.

(4) Although an attempt at modification or rescission does not satisfy the requirements of subsection (2) or (3) it can operate as a waiver.

(5) A party who has made a waiver affecting an executory portion of the contract may retract the waiver by reasonable notification received by the other party that strict performance will be required of any term waived, unless the retraction would be unjust in view of a material change of position in reliance on the waiver.

§ 2-210. Delegation of Performance; Assignment of Rights.

(1) A party may perform his duty through a delegate unless otherwise agreed or unless the other party has a substantial interest in having his original promisor perform or control the acts required by the contract. No delegation of performance relieves the party delegating of any duty to perform or any liability for breach.

(2) Unless otherwise agreed all rights of either seller or buyer can be assigned except where the assignment would materially change the duty of the other party, or increase materially the burden or risk imposed on him by his contract, or impair materially his chance of obtaining return performance. A right to damages for breach of the whole contract or a right arising out of the assignor's due performance of his entire obligation can be assigned despite agreement otherwise.

(3) Unless the circumstances indicate the contrary a prohibition of assignment of "the contract" is to be construed as barring only the delegation to the assignee of the assignor's performance.

(4) An assignment of "the contract" or of "all my rights under the contract" or an assignment in similar general terms is an assignment of rights and unless the language or the circumstances (as in an assignment for security) indicate the contrary, it is a delegation of performance of the duties of the assignor and its acceptance by the assignee constitutes a promise by him to perform those duties.

This promise is enforceable by either the assignor or the other party to the original contract.

(5) The other party may treat any assignment which delegates performance as creating reasonable grounds for insecurity and may without prejudice to his rights against the assignor demand assurances from the assignee (Section 2-609).

§ 2-301. General Obligations of Parties.
The obligation of the seller is to transfer and deliver and that of the buyer is to accept and pay in accordance with the contract.

§ 2-302. Unconscionable contract or Clause.

(1) If the court as a matter of law finds the contract or any clause of the contract to have been unconscionable at the time it was made the court may refuse to enforce the contract, or it may enforce the remainder of the contract without the unconscionable

clause, or it may so limit the application of any unconscionable clause as to avoid any unconscionable result.

(2) When it is claimed or appears to the court that the contract or any clause thereof may be unconscionable the parties shall be afforded a reasonable opportunity to present evidence as to its commercial setting, purpose and effect to aid the court in making the determination.

§ 2-305. Open Price Term.

(1) The parties if they so intend can conclude a contract for sale even though the price is not settled. In such a case the price is a reasonable price at the time for delivery if

- (a) nothing is said as to price; or
- (b) the price is left to be agreed by the parties and they fail to agree; or
- (c) the price is to be fixed in terms of some agreed market or other standard as set or recorded by a third person or agency and it is not so set or recorded.

(2) A price to be fixed by the seller or by the buyer means a price for him to fix in good faith.

(3) When a price left to be fixed otherwise than by agreement of the parties fails to be fixed through fault of one party the other may at his option treat the contract as cancelled or himself fix a reasonable price.

(4) Where, however, the parties intend not to be bound unless the price be fixed or agreed and it is not fixed or agreed there is no contract. In such a case the buyer must return any goods already received or if unable so to do must pay their reasonable value at the time of delivery and the seller must return any portion of the price paid on account.

§ 2-306. Output, Requirements and Exclusive Dealings.

(1) A term which measures the quantity by the output of the seller or the requirements of the buyer means such actual output or requirements as may occur in good faith, except that no quantity unreasonably disproportionate to any stated estimate or in the absence of a stated estimate to any normal or otherwise comparable prior output or requirements may be tendered or demanded.

(2) A lawful agreement by either the seller or the buyer for exclusive dealing in the kind of goods concerned imposes unless otherwise agreed an obligation by the seller to use best efforts to supply the goods and by the buyer to use best efforts to promote their sale.

§ 2-307. Delivery in Single Lot or Several Lots.

Unless otherwise agreed all goods called for by a contract for sale must be tendered in a single delivery and payment is due only on such tender but where the circumstances give either party the right to make or demand delivery in lots the price if it can be apportioned may be demanded for each lot.

§ 2-308. Absence of Specified Place for Delivery.

Unless otherwise agreed

- (a) the place for delivery of goods is the seller's place of business or if he has none his residence; but
- (b) in a contract for sale of identified goods which to the knowledge of the parties at the time of contracting are in some other place, that place is the place for their delivery; and
- (c) documents of title may be delivered through customary banking channels.

§ 2-310. Open Time for Payment or Running of Credit; Authority to Ship Under Reservation.

Unless otherwise agreed

- (a) payment is due at the time and place at which the buyer is to receive the goods even though the place of shipment is the place of delivery; and
- (b) if the seller is authorized to send the goods he may ship them under reservation, and may tender the documents of title, but the buyer may inspect the goods after their arrival before payment is due unless such inspection is inconsistent with the terms of the contract (Section 2-513); and
- (c) if delivery is authorized and made by way of documents of title otherwise than by subsection (b) then payment is due at the time and place at which the buyer is to receive the documents regardless of where the goods are to be received; and
- (d) where the seller is required or authorized to ship the goods on credit the credit period runs from the time of shipment but post-dating the invoice or delaying its dispatch will correspondingly delay the starting of the credit period.

§ 2-503. Manner of Seller's Tender of Delivery.

(1) Tender of delivery requires that the seller put and hold conforming goods at the buyer's disposition and

give the buyer any notification reasonably necessary to enable him to take delivery. The manner, time and place for tender are determined by the agreement and this Article, and in particular

- (a) tender must be at a reasonable hour, and if it is of goods they must be kept available for the period reasonably necessary to enable the buyer to take possession; but
- (b) unless otherwise agreed the buyer must furnish facilities reasonably suited to the receipt of the goods.

(2) Where the case is within the next section respecting shipment tender requires that the seller comply with its provisions.

(3) Where the seller is required to deliver at a particular destination tender requires that he comply with subsection (1) and also in any appropriate case tender documents as described in subsections (4) and (5) of this section.

(4) Where goods are in the possession of a bailee and are to be delivered without being moved

- (a) tender requires that the seller either tender a negotiable document of title covering such goods or procure acknowledgment by the bailee of the buyer's right to possession of the goods; but
- (b) tender to the buyer of a non-negotiable document of title or of a written direction to the bailee to deliver is sufficient tender unless the buyer seasonably objects, and receipt by the bailee of notification of the buyer's rights fixes those rights as against the bailee and all third persons; but risk of loss of the goods and of any failure by the bailee to honor the non-negotiable document of title or to obey the direction remains on the seller until the buyer has had a reasonable time to present the document or direction, and a refusal by the bailee to honor the document or to obey the direction defeats the tender.

(5) Where the contract requires the seller to deliver documents

- (a) he must tender all such documents in correct form, except as provided in this Article with respect to bills of lading in a set (subsection (2) of Section 2-323); and
- (b) tender through customary banking channels is sufficient and dishonor of a draft accompanying the documents constitutes non-acceptance or rejection.

§ 2-504. Shipment by Seller. Where the seller is required or authorized to send the goods

to the buyer and the contract does not require him to deliver them at a particular destination, then unless otherwise agreed he must

- (a) put the goods in the possession of such a carrier and make such a contract for their transportation as may be reasonable having regard to the nature of the goods and other circumstances of the case; and
- (b) obtain and promptly deliver or tender in due form any document necessary to enable the buyer to obtain possession of the goods or otherwise required by the agreement or by usage of trade; and
- (c) promptly notify the buyer of the shipment.

Failure to notify the buyer under paragraph (c) or to make a proper contract under paragraph (a) is a ground for rejection only if material delay or loss ensues.

§ 2-507. Effect of Seller's Tender; Delivery on Condition.

(1) Tender of delivery is a condition to the buyer's duty to accept the goods and, unless otherwise agreed, to his duty to pay for them. Tender entitles the seller to acceptance of the goods and to payment according to the contract.

(2) Where payment is due and demanded on the delivery to the buyer of goods or documents of title, his right as against the seller to retain or dispose of them is conditional upon his making the payment due.

§ 2-509. Risk of Loss in the Absence of Breach.

(1) Where the contract requires or authorizes the seller to ship the goods by carrier

- (a) if it does not require him to deliver them at a particular destination, the risk of loss passes to the buyer when the goods are duly delivered to the carrier even though the shipment is under reservation (Section 2-505); but
- (b) if it does require him to deliver them at a particular destination and the goods are there duly tendered while in the possession of the carrier, the risk of loss passes to the buyer when the goods are there duly so tendered as to enable the buyer to take delivery.

(2) Where the goods are held by a bailee to be delivered without being moved, the risk of loss passes to the buyer

- (a) on his receipt of a negotiable document of title covering the goods; or
- (b) on acknowledgment by the bailee of the buyer's right to possession of the goods; or
- (c) after his receipt of a non-negotiable document of title or other written direction to deliver, as provided in subsection (4)(b) of Section 2-503.

(3) In any case not within subsection (1) or (2), the risk of loss passes to the buyer on his receipt of the goods if the seller is a merchant; otherwise the risk passes to the buyer on tender of delivery.

(4) The provisions of this section are subject to contrary agreement of the parties and to the provisions of this Article on sale on approval (Section 2-327) and on effect of breach on risk of loss (Section 2-510).

§ 2-510. Effect of Breach on Risk of Loss.

(1) Where a tender or delivery of goods so fails to conform to the contract as to give a right of rejection the risk of their loss remains on the seller until cure or acceptance.

(2) Where the buyer rightfully revokes acceptance he may to the extent of any deficiency in his effective insurance coverage treat the risk of loss as having rested on the seller from the beginning.

(3) Where the buyer as to conforming goods already identified to the contract for sale repudiates or is otherwise in breach before risk of their loss has passed to him, the seller may to the extent of any deficiency in his effective insurance coverage treat the risk of loss as resting on the buyer for a commercially reasonable time.

§ 2-511. Tender of Payment by Buyer; Payment by Check.

(1) Unless otherwise agreed tender of payment is a condition to the seller's duty to tender and complete any delivery.

(2) Tender of payment is sufficient when made by any means or in any manner current in the ordinary course of business unless the seller demands payment in legal tender and gives any extension of time reasonably necessary to procure it.

(3) Subject to the provisions of this Act on the effect of an instrument on an obligation (Section 3-802), payment by check is conditional and is defeated as between the parties by dishonor of the check on due presentment.

§ 2-615. Excuse by Failure of Presupposed Conditions.

Except so far as a seller may have assumed a greater obligation and subject to the preceding section on substituted performance:

- (a) Delay in delivery or non-delivery in whole or in part by a seller who complies with paragraphs (b) and (c) is not a breach of his duty under a contract for sale if performance as agreed has been made impracticable by the occurrence of a contingency the non-occurrence of which was a basic assumption on which the contract was made or by compliance in good faith with any applicable foreign or domestic governmental regulation or order whether or not it later proves to be invalid.
- (b) Where the causes mentioned in paragraph (a) affect only a part of the seller's capacity to perform, he must allocate production and deliveries among his customers but may at his option include regular customers not then under contract as well as his own requirements for further manufacture. He may so allocate in any manner which is fair and reasonable.
- (c) The seller must notify the buyer seasonably that there will be delay or non-delivery and, when allocation is required under paragraph (b), of the estimated quota thus made available for the buyer.

§ 2-703. Seller's Remedies in General.

Where the buyer wrongfully rejects or revokes acceptance of goods or fails to make a payment due on or before delivery or repudiates with respect to a part or the whole, then with respect to any goods directly affected and; if the breach is of the whole contract (Section 2-612), then also with respect to the whole undelivered balance, the aggrieved seller may

- (a) withhold delivery of such goods;
- (b) stop delivery by any bailee as hereafter provided (Section 2-705);
- (c) proceed under the next section respecting goods still unidentified to the contract;
- (d) resell and recover damages as hereafter provided (Section 2-706);
- (e) recover damages for non-acceptance (Section 2-708) or in a proper case the price (Section 2-709);
- (f) cancel.

§ 2-711. Buyer's Remedies in General; Buyer's Security Interest in Rejected Goods.

(1) Where the seller fails to make delivery or repudiates or the buyer rightfully rejects or justifiably revokes acceptance then with respect to any goods involved, and with respect to the whole if the breach goes to the whole contract (Section 2-612), the buyer may cancel and whether or not he has done so may in addition to recovering so much of the price as has been paid

- (a) "cover" and have damages under the next section as to all the goods affected whether or not they have been identified to the contract; or
- (b) recover damages for non-delivery as provided in this Article (Section 2-713).

(2) Where the seller fails to deliver or repudiates the buyer may also

- (a) if the goods have been identified recover them as provided in this Article (Section 2-502); or
- (b) in a proper case obtain specific performance or replevy the goods as provided in this Article (Section 2-716).

(3) On rightful rejection or justifiable revocation of acceptance a buyer has a security interest in goods in his possession or control for any payments made on their price and any expenses reasonably incurred in their inspection, receipt, transportation, care and custody and may hold such goods and resell them in like manner as an aggrieved seller (Section 2-706).

§ 2-725. Statute of Limitations in Contracts for Sale.

(1) An action for breach of any contract for sale must be commenced within four years after the cause of action has accrued. By the original agreement the parties may reduce the period of limitation to not less than one year but may not extend it.

(2) A cause of action accrues when the breach occurs, regardless of the aggrieved party's lack of knowledge of the breach. A breach of warranty occurs when tender of delivery is made, except that where a warranty explicitly extends to future performance of the goods and discovery of the breach must await the time of such performance the cause of action accrues when the breach is or should have been discovered.

(3) Where an action commenced within the time limited by subsection (1) is so terminated as to leave available a remedy by another action for the same breach such other action may be commenced after the expiration of the time limited and within six months after the termination of the first action unless the termination resulted from voluntary discontinuance or from dismissal for failure or neglect to prosecute.

(4) This section does not alter the law on tolling of the statute of limitations nor does it apply to causes of action which have accrued before this Act becomes effective.

:: Selected Sections of the Sarbanes-Oxley Act of 2002

TITLE I—PUBLIC COMPANY ACCOUNTING OVERSIGHT BOARD

Sec. 101. Establishment; Administrative Provisions.

(a) Establishment of Board.—There is established the Public Company Accounting Oversight Board, to oversee the audit of public companies that are subject to the securities laws, and related matters, in order to protect the interests of investors and further the public interest in the preparation of informative, accurate, and independent audit reports for companies the securities of which are sold to, and held by and for, public investors. The Board shall be a body corporate, operate as a nonprofit corporation, and have succession until dissolved by an Act of Congress.

(c) Duties of the Board.—The Board shall, subject to action by the Commission under section 107, and once a determination is made by the Commission under subsection (d) of this section—

(1) register public accounting firms that prepare audit reports for issuers, in accordance with section 102;

(2) establish or adopt, or both, by rule, auditing, quality control, ethics, independence, and other standards relating to the preparation of audit reports for issuers, in accordance with section 103;

(3) conduct inspections of registered public accounting firms, in accordance with section 104 and the rules of the Board;

(4) conduct investigations and disciplinary proceedings concerning, and impose appropriate sanctions where justified upon, registered public accounting firms and associated persons of such firms, in accordance with section 105;

(5) perform such other duties or functions as the Board (or the Commission, by rule or order) determines are necessary or appropriate to promote high professional standards among, and improve the quality of audit services offered by, registered public accounting firms and associated persons thereof, or otherwise to carry out this Act, in order to protect investors, or to further the public interest;

(6) enforce compliance with this Act, the rules of the Board, professional standards, and the securities laws relating to the preparation and issuance of audit reports and the obligations and liabilities of accountants with respect thereto, by registered public accounting firms and associated persons thereof; and

(7) set the budget and manage the operations of the Board and the staff of the Board.

(h) Annual Report to the Commission.—The Board shall submit an annual report (including its audited financial statements) to the Commission, and the Commission shall transmit a copy of that report to the Committee on Banking, Housing, and Urban Affairs of the Senate, and the Committee on Financial Services of the House of Representatives, not later than 30 days after the date of receipt of that report by the Commission.

Sec. 107. Commission Oversight of The Board.

(a) General Oversight Responsibility.—The Commission shall have oversight and enforcement authority over the Board, as provided in this Act. . . .

TITLE II—AUDITOR INDEPENDENCE

Sec. 203. Audit Partner Rotation.

(j) Audit Partner Rotation.—It shall be unlawful for a registered public accounting firm to provide audit services to an issuer if the lead (or coordinating) audit partner (having primary responsibility for the audit), or the audit partner responsible for reviewing the audit, has performed audit services for that issuer in each of the 5 previous fiscal years of that issuer.

Sec. 204. Auditor Reports to Audit Committees.

(k) Reports to Audit Committees.—Each registered public accounting firm that performs for any issuer any audit required by this title shall timely report to the audit committee of the issuer—

(1) all critical accounting policies and practices to be used;

(2) all alternative treatments of financial information within generally accepted accounting principles that

have been discussed with management officials of the issuer, ramifications of the use of such alternative disclosures and treatments, and the treatment preferred by the registered public accounting firm; and

(3) other material written communications between the registered public accounting firm and the management of the issuer, such as any management letter or schedule of unadjusted differences.

TITLE III—CORPORATE RESPONSIBILITY

Sec. 302. Corporate Responsibility for Financial Reports.

(a) Regulations Required.—The Commission shall, by rule, require, for each company filing periodic reports under section 13(a) or 15(d) of the Securities Exchange Act of 1934, that the principal executive officer or officers and the principal financial officer or officers, or persons performing similar functions, certify in each annual or quarterly report filed or submitted under either such section of such Act that—

(1) the signing officer has reviewed the report;

(2) based on the officer's knowledge, the report does not contain any untrue statement of a material fact or omit to state a material fact necessary in order to make the statements made, in light of the circumstances under which such statements were made, not misleading;

(3) based on such officer's knowledge, the financial statements, and other financial information included in the report, fairly present in all material respects the financial condition and results of operations of the issuer as of, and for, the periods presented in the report;

(4) the signing officers—

(A) are responsible for establishing and maintaining internal controls;

(B) have designed such internal controls to ensure that material information relating to the issuer and its consolidated subsidiaries is made known to such officers by others within those entities, particularly during the period in which the periodic reports are being prepared;

(C) have evaluated the effectiveness of the issuer's internal controls as of a date within 90 days prior to the report; and

(D) have presented in the report their conclusions about the effectiveness of their internal controls based on their evaluation as of that date;

(5) the signing officers have disclosed to the issuer's auditors and the audit committee of the board of directors (or persons fulfilling the equivalent function)—

(A) all significant deficiencies in the design or operation of internal controls which could adversely affect the issuer's ability to record, process, summarize, and report financial data and have identified for the issuer's auditors any material weaknesses in internal controls; and

(B) any fraud, whether or not material, that involves management or other employees who have a significant role in the issuer's internal controls; and

(6) the signing officers have indicated in the report whether or not there were significant changes in internal controls or in other factors that could significantly affect internal controls subsequent to the date of their evaluation, including any corrective actions with regard to significant deficiencies and material weaknesses.

(b) Foreign Reincorporations Have No Effect.—Nothing in this section 302 shall be interpreted or applied in any way to allow any issuer to lessen the legal force of the statement required under this section 302, by an issuer having reincorporated or having engaged in any other transaction that resulted in the transfer of the corporate domicile or offices of the issuer from inside the United States to outside of the United States.

(c) Deadline.—The rules required by subsection (a) shall be effective not later than 30 days after the date of enactment of this Act.

Sec. 303. Improper Influence on Conduct of Audits.

(a) Rules To Prohibit.—It shall be unlawful, in contravention of such rules or regulations as the Commission shall prescribe as necessary and appropriate in the public interest or for the protection of investors, for any officer or director of an issuer, or any other person acting under the direction thereof, to take any action to fraudulently influence, coerce, manipulate, or mislead any independent public or certified accountant engaged in the performance of an audit of the financial statements of that issuer for the purpose of rendering such financial statements materially misleading.

Sec. 304. Forfeiture of Certain Bonuses and Profits.

(a) Additional Compensation Prior to Noncompliance With Commission Financial Reporting Requirements.—If an issuer is required to prepare an accounting restatement due to the material noncompliance of the issuer, as a result of misconduct, with any financial reporting requirement under the securities laws, the chief executive officer and chief financial officer of the issuer shall reimburse the issuer for—

(1) any bonus or other incentive-based or equity-based compensation received by that person from the issuer during the 12-month period following the first public issuance or filing with the Commission (whichever first occurs) of the financial document embodying such financial reporting requirement; and (2) any profits realized from the sale of securities of the issuer during that 12-month period.

Sec. 306. Insider Trades During Pension Fund Blackout Periods.

(a) Prohibition of Insider Trading During Pension Fund Blackout Periods.—

(1) IN GENERAL.—Except to the extent otherwise provided by rule of the Commission pursuant to paragraph (3), it shall be unlawful for any director or executive officer of an issuer of any equity security (other than an exempted security), directly or indirectly, to purchase, sell, or otherwise acquire or transfer any equity security of the issuer (other than an exempted security) during any blackout period with respect to such equity security if such director or officer acquires such equity security in connection with his or her service or employment as a director or executive officer.

(2) REMEDY.—

(A) IN GENERAL.—Any profit realized by a director or executive officer referred to in paragraph (1) from any purchase, sale, or other acquisition or transfer in violation of this subsection shall inure to and be recoverable by the issuer, irrespective of any intention on the part of such director or executive officer in entering into the transaction.

(B) ACTIONS TO RECOVER PROFITS.—An action to recover profits in accordance with this subsection may be instituted at law or in equity in any court of competent jurisdiction by the issuer, or by the owner of any security of the issuer in the name and in behalf of the issuer if the issuer fails or refuses to bring such action within 60 days after the date of request, or fails diligently to prosecute the action thereafter, except that no such suit shall be brought more than 2 years after the date on which such profit was realized.

(3) CIVIL PENALTIES FOR FAILURE TO PROVIDE NOTICE.—(7) The Secretary may assess a civil penalty against a plan administrator of up to $100 a day from the date of the plan administrator's failure or refusal to provide notice to participants and beneficiaries

in accordance with section 101(i). For purposes of this paragraph, each violation with respect to any single participant or beneficiary shall be treated as a separate violation.

TITLE IV—ENHANCED FINANCIAL DISCLOSURES

Sec. 404. Management Assessment of Internal Controls.

(a) Rules Required.—The Commission shall prescribe rules requiring each annual report required by section 13(a) or 15(d) of the Securities Exchange Act of 1934 to contain an internal control report, which shall—

(1) state the responsibility of management for establishing and maintaining an adequate internal control structure and procedures for financial reporting; and

(2) contain an assessment, as of the end of the most recent fiscal year of the issuer, of the effectiveness of the internal control structure and procedures of the issuer for financial reporting.

(b) Internal Control Evaluation and Reporting.—With respect to the internal control assessment required by subsection

(a), each registered public accounting firm that prepares or issues the audit report for the issuer shall attest to, and report on, the assessment made by the management of the issuer. An attestation made under this subsection shall be made in accordance with standards for attestation engagements issued or adopted by the Board. Any such attestation shall not be the subject of a separate engagement.

Sec. 407. Disclosure of Audit Committee Financial Expert.

(a) Rules Defining "Financial Expert".—

The Commission shall issue rules, as necessary or appropriate in the public interest and consistent with the protection of investors, to require each issuer, together with periodic reports required pursuant to sections 13(a) and 15(d) of the Securities Exchange Act of 1934, to disclose whether or not, and if not, the reasons therefor, the audit committee of that issuer is comprised of at least 1 member who is a financial expert, as such term is defined by the Commission.

(b) Considerations.—In defining the term "financial expert" for purposes of subsection (a), the Commission shall consider whether a person has, through education and experience as a public accountant or auditor or a principal financial officer, comptroller, or principal accounting officer of an issuer, or from a position involving the performance of similar functions—

(1) an understanding of generally accepted accounting principles and financial statements;

(2) experience in—

(A) the preparation or auditing of financial statements of generally comparable issuers; and

(B) the application of such principles in connection with the accounting for estimates, accruals, and reserves;

(3) experience with internal accounting controls; and

(4) an understanding of audit committee functions.

TITLE VIII—CORPORATE AND CRIMINAL FRAUD ACCOUNTABILITY

Sec. 801. Short Title. This title may be cited as the "Corporate and Criminal Fraud Accountability Act of 2002".

Sec. 804. Statute of Limitations for Securities Fraud. . . . [A] private right of action that involves a claim of fraud, deceit, manipulation, or contrivance in contravention of a regulatory requirement concerning the securities laws . . . may be brought not later than the earlier of—

(1) 2 years after the discovery of the facts constituting the violation; or

(2) 5 years after such violation.

Sec. 806. Protection for Employees of Publicly Traded Companies Who Provide Evidence of Fraud.

(a) *Whistleblower Protection for Employees of Publicly Traded Companies.*— No company with a class of securities registered under section 12 of the Securities Exchange Act of 1934 or that is required to file reports under . . . the Securities Exchange Act of 1934 or any officer, employee, contractor, sub-contractor, or agent of such company, may discharge, demote, suspend, threaten, harass, or in any other manner discriminate against an employee in the terms and conditions of employment because of any lawful act done by the employee—

(1) to provide information, cause information to be provided, or otherwise assist in an investigation regarding any conduct which the employee reasonably believes constitutes a violation of . . . any rule or regulation of the Securities and Exchange Commission, or any provision of Federal law relating to fraud against shareholders, when the information or assistance is provided to or the investigation is conducted by—

(A) a Federal regulatory or law enforcement agency;

(B) any Member of Congress or any committee of Congress; or

(C) a person with supervisory authority over the employee (or such other person working for the employer who has the authority to investigate, discover, or terminate misconduct); or

(2) to file, cause to be filed, testify, participate in, or otherwise assist in a proceeding filed or about to be filed (with any knowledge of the employer) relating to an alleged violation of . . . any rule or regulation of the Securities and Exchange Commission, or any provision of Federal law relating to fraud against shareholders.

Sec. 807. Criminal Penalties for Defrauding Shareholders of Publicly Traded Companies.

(a) *In General.*—Chapter 63 of title 18, United States Code, is amended by adding at the end the following:

" **§ 1348. Securities fraud**

"Whoever knowingly executes, or attempts to execute. a scheme or artifice—

"(1) to defraud any person in connection with any security of an issuer with a class of securities registered under section 12 of the Securities Exchange Act of 1934 or that is required to file reports under section 15(d) of the Securities Exchange Act of 1934; or

"(2) to obtain, by means of false or fraudulent pretenses, representations, or promises, any money or property in connection with the purchase or sale of any security of an issuer with a class of securities registered under section 12 of the Securities Exchange Act of 1934 or that is required to file reports under section 15(d) of the Securities Exchange Act of 1934 shall be fined under this title, or imprisoned not more than 25 years, or both."

TITLE IX—WHITE-COLLAR CRIME PENALTY ENHANCEMENTS

Sec. 903. Criminal Penalties for Mail and Wire Fraud.

(a) Mail Fraud.—Section 1341 of title 18, United States Code, is amended by striking "five" and inserting "20".

(b) Wire Fraud.—Section 1343 of title 18, United States Code, is amended by striking "five" and inserting "20".

TITLE XI—CORPORATE FRAUD ACCOUNTABILITY

Sec. 1106. Increased Criminal Penalties Under Securities Exchange Act of 1934. Section 32(a) of the Securities Exchange Act of 1934 is amended—

(1) by striking "$1,000,000, or imprisoned not more than 10 years" and inserting "$5,000,000, or imprisoned not more than 20 years"; and

(2) by striking "$2,500,000" and inserting "$25,000,000".

Sec. 1107. Retaliation Against Informants.

(a) In General.—Section 1513 of title 18, United States Code, is amended by adding at the end the following:

"(e) Whoever knowingly, with the intent to retaliate, takes any action harmful to any person, including interference with the lawful employment or livelihood of any person, for providing to a law enforcement officer any truthful information relating to the commission or possible commission of any Federal offense, shall be fined under this title or imprisoned not more than 10 years, or both."

:: Selected Sections of Securities Act of 1933

Section 6—Registration of Securities and Signing of Registration Statement

a. Any security may be registered with the Commission under the terms and conditions hereinafter provided, by filing a registration statement in triplicate, at least one of which shall be signed by each issuer, its principal executive officer or officers, its principal financial officer, its comptroller or principal accounting officer, and the majority of its board of directors or persons performing similar functions (or, if there is no board of directors or persons performing similar functions, by the majority of the persons or board having the power of management of the issuer) . . .

Section 11—Civil Liabilities on Account of False Registration Statement

a. In case any part of the registration statement, when such part became effective, contained an untrue statement of a material fact or omitted to state a material fact required to be stated therein or necessary to make the statements therein not misleading, any person acquiring such security (unless it is proved that at the time of such acquisition he knew of such untruth or omission) may, either at law or in equity, in any court of competent jurisdiction, sue—

1. every person who signed the registration statement;
2. every person who was a director of (or person performing similar functions) or partner in the issuer at the time of the filing of the part of the registration statement with respect to which his liability is asserted;
3. every person who, with his consent, is named in the registration statement as being or about to become a director, person performing similar functions, or partner;
4. every accountant, engineer, or appraiser, or any person whose profession gives authority to a statement made by him, who has with his consent been named as having prepared or certified any part of the registration statement, or as having prepared or certified any report or valuation which is used in connection with the registration statement, with respect to the statement in such registration statement, report, or valuation, which purports to have been prepared or certified by him;
5. every underwriter with respect to such security.

Section 12—Civil Liabilities Arising in Connection with Prospectuses and Communications

a. **In General.** Any person who—

1. offers or sells a security in violation of section 5, or
2. offers or sells a security . . . by the use of any means or instruments of transportation or communication in interstate commerce or of the mails, by means of a prospectus or oral communication, which includes an untrue statement of a material fact or omits to state a material fact necessary in order to make the statements, in the light of the circumstances under which they were made, not misleading (the purchaser not knowing of such untruth or omission), and who shall not sustain the burden of proof that he did not know, and in the exercise of reasonable care could not have known, of such untruth or omission, shall be liable, subject to subsection (b), to the person purchasing such security from him, who may sue either at law or in equity in any court of competent jurisdiction, to recover the consideration paid for such security with interest thereon, less the amount of any income received thereon, upon the tender of such security, or for damages if he no longer owns the security.

b. **Loss Causation.** In an action described in subsection (a)(2), if the person who offered or sold such security proves that any portion or all of the amount recoverable under subsection (a)(2) represents other than the depreciation in value of the subject security resulting from such part of the prospectus or oral communication, with respect to which the liability of that person is asserted, not being true or omitting to state a material fact required to be stated therein or necessary to make the statement not misleading, then such portion or amount, as the case may be, shall not be recoverable.

Section 17—Fraudulent Interstate Transactions

a. It shall be unlawful for any person in the offer or sale of any securities by the use of any means or instruments of transportation or communication in interstate commerce or by the use of the mails, directly or indirectly—

1. to employ any device, scheme, or artifice to defraud, or

2. to obtain money or property by means of any untrue statement of a material fact or any omission to state a material fact necessary in order to make the statements made, in the light of the circumstances under which they were made, not misleading, or

3. to engage in any transaction, practice, or course of business which operates or would operate as a fraud or deceit upon the purchaser.

b. It shall be unlawful for any person, by the use of any means or instruments of transportation or communication in interstate commerce or by the use of the mails, to publish, give publicity to, or circulate any notice, circular, advertisement, newspaper, article, letter, investment service, or communication which, though not purporting to offer a security for sale, describes such security for a consideration received or to be received, directly or indirectly, from an issuer, underwriter, or dealer, without fully disclosing the receipt, whether past or prospective, of such consideration and the amount thereof.

Section 24—Penalties.

Any person who willfully violates any of the provisions of this title, or the rules and regulations promulgated by the Commission under authority thereof, or any person who willfully, in a registration statement filed under this title, makes any untrue statement of a material fact or omits to state any material fact required to be stated therein or necessary to make the statements therein not misleading, shall upon conviction be fined not more than $10,000 or imprisoned not more than five years, or both.

:: Selected Sections of Securities Exchange Act of 1934

Section 4—Securities and Exchange Commission

1. There is hereby established a Securities and Exchange Commission (hereinafter referred to as the "Commission") to be composed of five commissioners to be appointed by the President by and with the advice and consent of the Senate. Not more than three of such commissioners shall be members of the same political party, and in making appointments members of different political parties shall be appointed alternately as nearly as may be practicable. No commissioner shall engage in any other business, vocation, or employment than that of serving as commissioner, nor shall any commissioner participate, directly or indirectly, in any stock-market operations or transactions of a character subject to regulation by the Commission pursuant to this title. Each commissioner shall hold office for a term of five years and until his successor is appointed and has qualified . . .

Section 10—Regulation of the Use of Manipulative and Deceptive Devices.

It shall be unlawful for any person, directly or indirectly, by the use of any means or instrumentality of interstate commerce or of the mails, or of any facility of any national securities exchange—

b. To use or employ, in connection with the purchase or sale of any security registered on a national securities exchange or any security not so registered, any manipulative or deceptive device or any securities-based swap agreement . . . , or contrivance in contravention of such rules and regulations as the Commission may prescribe as necessary or appropriate in the public interest or for the protection of investors.

Section 16—Directors, Officers, and Principal Stockholders

a. DISCLOSURES REQUIRED.—

(1) *Directors, officers, and principal stockholders required to file.*—Every person who is directly or indirectly the beneficial owner of more than 10 percent of any class of any equity security (other than an exempted security) which is registered pursuant to section 12, or who is a director or an officer of the issuer of such security, shall file the statements required by this subsection with the Commission (and, if such security is registered on a national securities exchange, also with the exchange).

(2) TIME OF FILING.—The statements required by this subsection shall be filed—

(A) at the time of the registration of such security on a national securities exchange or by the effective date of a registration statement filed pursuant to section 12(g);

(B) within 10 days after he or she becomes such beneficial owner, director, or officer;

(C) if there has been a change in such ownership, or if such person shall have purchased or sold a security-based swap agreement . . . involving such equity security, before the end of the second business day following the day on which the subject transaction has been executed, or at such other time as the Commission shall establish, by rule, in any case in which the Commission determines that such 2-day period is not feasible.

(3) CONTENTS OF STATEMENTS.—A statement filed—

(A) under subparagraph (A) or (B) of paragraph (2) shall contain a statement of the amount of all equity securities of such issuer of which the filing person is the beneficial owner; and

(B) under subparagraph (C) of such paragraph shall indicate ownership by the filing person at the date of filing, any such changes in such ownership, and such purchases and sales of the security-based swap agreements as have occurred since the most recent such filing under such subparagraph.

(4) ELECTRONIC FILING AND AVAILABILITY.— Beginning not later than 1 year after the date of enactment of the Sarbanes-Oxley Act of 2002—

(A) a statement filed under subparagraph (C) of paragraph (2) shall be filed electronically;

(B) the Commission shall provide each such statement on a publicly accessible Internet site not later than the end of the business day following that filing; and

(C) the issuer (if the issuer maintains a corporate website) shall provide that statement on that corporate website, not later than the end of the business day following that filing.

Section 18—Liability for Misleading Statements

a. Any person who shall make or cause to be made any statement in any application, report, or document filed pursuant to this title or any rule or regulation thereunder or any undertaking contained in a registration statement . . ., which statement was at the time and in the light of the circumstances under which it was made false or misleading with respect to any material fact, shall be liable to any person (not knowing that such statement was false or misleading) who, in reliance upon such statement, shall have purchased or sold a security at a price which was affected by such statement, for damages caused by such reliance, unless the person sued shall prove that he acted in good faith and had no knowledge that such statement was false or misleading. A person seeking to enforce such liability may sue at law or in equity in any court of competent jurisdiction. In any such suit the court may, in its discretion, require an undertaking for the payment of the costs of such suit, and assess reasonable costs, including reasonable attorneys' fees, against either party litigant.

b. Every person who becomes liable to make payment under this section may recover contribution as in cases of contract from any person who, if joined in the original suit, would have been liable to make the same payment.

c. No action shall be maintained to enforce any liability created under this section unless brought within one year after the discovery of the facts constituting the cause of action and within three years after such cause of action accrued.

Section 32—Penalties

a. Any person who willfully violates any provision of this chapter . . . or any rule or regulation thereunder the violation of which is made unlawful or the observance of which is required under the terms of this chapter, or any person who willfully and knowingly makes, or causes to be made, any statement in any application, report, or document required to be filed under this chapter or any rule or regulation thereunder or any undertaking contained in a registration statement . . . or by any self-regulatory organization in connection with an application for membership or participation therein or to become associated with a member thereof, which statement was false or misleading with respect to any material fact, shall upon conviction be fined not more than $5,000,000, or imprisoned not more than 20 years, or both, except that when such person is a person other than a natural person, a fine not exceeding $25,000,000 may be imposed; but no person shall be subject to imprisonment under this section for the violation of any rule or regulation if he proves that he had no knowledge of such rule or regulation.

glossary ::

Abatement   Decrease, reduction, or diminution.

Acceptance   The contractual communication of agreeing to another's offer. The acceptance of an offer creates a *contract*.

Accession   Property acquired by adding something to an owned object.

Accessory   A term used at the state level that is similar to "aiding and abetting." Accessory to a crime generally is either before the criminal act or after it.

Accord and satisfaction   Payment of money, or other thing of value, usually less than the amount demanded, in exchange for cancellation of a debt that is uncertain in amount.

Actual authority   The authority a principal expressly or implicitly gives to an agent in an agency relationship. This authority may be written, spoken, or derived from the circumstances of the relationship.

Ad infinitum   Without limit; endlessly.

Adjudication   The judicial determination of a legal proceeding.

Adjustment   Under the Bankruptcy Act the procedure followed when a debtor's debts are partly reduced and partly rearranged for repayment.

Administrative agency   An organization, usually a part of the executive branch of government, that is created to serve a specific purpose as authorized by the legislative branch. An agency's function usually is characterized as quasi-legislative or quasi-judicial.

Administrative law   The legal principles involved in the workings of administrative agencies within the regulatory process.

Administrative law judge   The individual employed by an administrative agency who is in charge of hearing the initial presentations in a quasi-judicial case.

ADRs   An abbreviation for alternative dispute resolution systems that may be used in lieu of litigation.

Ad substantiation program   A program of the Federal Trade Commission under which the FTC demands that an advertiser substantiate any claims made in advertising. Even if the claims are not provably untrue, they are considered deceptive if they cannot be substantiated.

Ad valorem   According to value.

Adverse possession   Property ownership acquired through open, notorious, actual, exclusive, continuous, and wrongful possession of land for a statutorily prescribed period of time.

Advisory opinion   A formal opinion by a judge, court, regulatory agency, or law officer upon a question of law.

Affidavit   A sworn written statement made before an officer authorized by law to administer oaths.

Affirmative action   Positive steps taken in order to alleviate conditions resulting from past discrimination or from violations of a law.

Affirmative action program   A program designed to promote actively the position of minority workers with regard to hiring and advancement.

Affirmative defenses   Defenses that must be raised and proved by the defendant.

A fortiori   Even more clearly; said of a conclusion that follows with even greater logical necessity from another that is already included in the argument.

Agent   The person who on behalf of a principal deals with a third party.

Agreement on Trade-Related Aspects of Intellectual Property Rights (TRIPS)   The WTO agreement that discusses the applicability of GATT principles and intellectual property agreements in the international sphere.

Aiding and abetting   A criminal action that arises from association with and from assistance rendered to a person guilty of another criminal act.

Alien Tort Claims Act (ATCA)   The federal law that grants jurisdiction to U.S. federal district courts over any civil action by an alien for a tort only, committed in violation of the law of nations or a treaty of the United States.

Alter-ego theory   One method used by courts to pierce the corporate veil when a shareholder fails to treat the corporate organization as a separate legal entity.

Amicus curiae   A friend of the court who participates in litigation though not a party to the lawsuit.

Annual percentage rate   A rate of interest that commercial lenders charge persons who borrow money. This rate is calculated in a standardized fashion required by the Truth-in-Lending Act.

Annuity   A contract by which the insured pays a lump sum to the insurer and later receives fixed annual payments.

Answer   The responsive pleading filed by a defendant.

Apparent authority   The authority that a third party in an agency relationship perceives to exist between the principal and the agent. In fact, no actual authority does exist. Sometimes also called *ostensible authority.*

Appeal   The right of the litigation parties to have the legal decisions of the trial judge reviewed by an appellate court.

Appellant   The party seeking review of a lower court decision.

Appellate court   A court that decides whether a trial judge has made a mistake of law.

Appellee   The party responding to an appeal; the winner in the trial court.

Apportionment   The concept used by states to divide a company's taxable income so that no one state burdens a company with an unfair tax bill.

Arbitration   Submission of a dispute to an extrajudicial authority for decision.

Arbitrator   The individual or panel members authorized by disputing parties to resolve a dispute through the arbitration process.

Arguendo   For the sake of argument.

Articles of incorporation   The legal document that forms the application for a state charter of incorporation.

Articles of organization   The document used to create a limited liability company. Its purpose corresponds to the purpose of the articles of partnership and the articles of incorporation.

Articles of partnership   Another name for a formally drafted partnership agreement.

Artisan's lien   The lien that arises in favor of one who has expended labor upon, or added value to, another person's personal property. The lien allows the person to possess the property as security until reimbursed for the value of labor or materials. If the person is not reimbursed, the property may be sold to satisfy the claim.

Assault   The intentional creation of immediate apprehension of injury or lack of physical safety.

Assignee   A third party, who is not an original contracting party, to whom contractual rights or duties or both are transferred. This party may enforce the original contract.

Assignment   A transfer of contractual rights.

Assignor   An original contracting party who assigns or transfers contractual rights or duties or both to a third party.

Assumed-name statute   A state law that requires partners to make a public filing of their identities if their partnership operates under a name that does not reveal the partners' identities.

Assumption of risk   Negligence doctrine that bars the recovery of damages by an injured party on the ground that such a party acted with actual or constructive knowledge of the hazard causing the injury.

Attachment   The term *attachment* has three meanings. First, attachment is a method of acquiring in rem jurisdiction of a nonresident defendant who is not subject to the service of process to commence a lawsuit. By "attaching" property of the nonresident defendant, the court acquires jurisdiction over the defendant to the extent of the value of the property attached. Second, attachment is a procedure used to collect a judgment. A plaintiff may have the property of a defendant seized, pending the outcome of a lawsuit, if the plaintiff has reason to fear that the defendant will dispose of the property before the court renders its decision. Third, attachment is the event that creates an enforceable security interest under the Uniform Commercial Code (UCC). In order that a security interest attach, there must be a signed, written security agreement, or possession of the collateral by the secured party; the secured party must give value to the debtor; and the debtor must maintain rights in the collateral.

Award   The decision announced by an arbitrator.

Bailee   In a bailment, the person who takes possession of an object owned by another and must return it or otherwise dispose of it.

Bailment   An owner's placement of an object into the intentional possession of another person with the understanding that the other person must return the object at some point or otherwise dispose of it.

Bailor   In a bailment, the person who transfers possession of tangible, personal property to another person with the understanding that the other person must return the object at some point or otherwise dispose of it.

Bait-and-switch promotion   An illegal promotional practice in which a seller attracts consumer interest by promoting one product, the "bait," then once interest has been attracted switches it to a second, higher-priced product by making the "bait" unavailable or unattractive.

Balance of trade   The difference between the amount of exports and imports of goods by a nation. A favorable balance would indicate more exports than imports. The United States has run an unfavorable balance of trade for several years.

Bank Merger Acts   Federal laws passed in 1960 and 1966 that require approval of the appropriate administrative agency prior to the merger of banks.

Bankruptcy   Traditionally, the financial condition where debts exceed assets and one is unable to pay debts as they mature.

Bankruptcy crime   An action involving the falsification of documents filed in a bankruptcy case.

Bargained for   A term used in conjunction with the requirement of contractual consideration to represent the exchange of benefits and burdens between the contracting parties.

Battery   The cause of action for physical contact that is not consented to and is offensive.

Beneficiary   A person entitled to the possession, use, income, or enjoyment of an interest or right to which legal title is held by another; a person to whom an insurance policy is payable.

Best evidence rule   A principle requiring that the original of a document be submitted to the court as proof of the document's contents.

Beyond a reasonable doubt   The burden of proof required in a criminal case. The prosecution in a criminal case has the burden of proving the defendant is guilty, and the jury must have no reasonable doubt about the defendant's guilt. See also *Burden of proof*.

Bilateral contract   An agreement that contains mutual promises, with each party being both a promisor and a promisee.

Bill of lading   A document issued by a carrier indicating that goods to be shipped have been received by the carrier.

Bill of particulars   In legal practice, a written statement furnished by one party to a lawsuit to another, describing in detail the elements upon which the claim of the first party is based.

Battery   An intentional, unpermitted, offensive contact or touching.

Biodegradable   Capable of being decomposed by organic action.

Blue sky laws   Securities law enacted by States.

Bona fide   In good faith; innocently; without fraud or deceit.

Bona fide occupational qualification (BFOQ)   A qualification that permits discriminatory practices in employment if a person's religion, sex, or national origin is reasonably related to the normal operation of a particular business.

Breach of contract   A party's failure to perform some contracted-for or agreed-upon act, or failure to comply with a duty imposed by law.

Brief   A written document produced by a party for a reviewing court that contains the facts, propositions of law, and argument of a party. It is in this document that the party argues the desired application of the law and any contentions as to the rulings of the lower court.

Bubble concept   A procedure by which the Environmental Protection Agency (EPA) allows a business to treat its entire plant complex as though encased in a bubble. The business suggests its own methods of cleanup, provided the total pollution does not exceed certain limits.

Bulk transfer   A transfer made outside the ordinary course of the transferor's business involving a major part of the business's inventory. Bulk transfers are subject to Article 6 of the Uniform Commercial Code (UCC).

Burden of proof   The term *burden of proof* has two meanings. It may describe the party at a trial with the burden of coming forward with evidence to establish a fact. The term also describes the party with the burden of persuasion. This party must convince the judge or jury of the disputed facts in issue or else lose that issue. There are various degrees of proof. See also *Beyond a reasonable* *doubt, Preponderance of evidence,* and *Clear and convincing proof.*

Burglary   Theft by breaking and entering.

Business judgment rule   A legal principle used by the courts to uphold the decisions of corporate directors and officers who have exercised good faith and due care in their business practices.

Business necessity defense   An affirmative defense under Title VII of the Civil Rights Act. It is raised to disparate impact claims and asserts that a facially neutral but discriminatory policy is job related.

Buy and sell agreement   A contract, usually among partners, but perhaps among shareholders, wherein one party agrees to buy the ownership interest held by another party or the first party agrees to sell such an interest to the other party. These contractual provisions help provide for a transition of owners without harming the business of the organization.

Buyer in the ordinary course of business   A buyer who buys from someone who ordinarily sells such goods in his or her business.

Capacity   Mental ability to make a rational decision that includes the ability to perceive and appreciate all relevant facts. A required element of a contract.

Cap and trade   A pollution policy that caps allowable pollution at a certain amount, distributes the rights to engage in that pollution, then allows the owners of the rights to trade them.

Case law   The legal principles that are developed by appellate judges through their written opinions. See *Common law.*

Categorical imperative   A concept by the philosopher Kant that a person should never act in a certain way unless he or she is willing to have everyone else act in the same way.

Caucus   The name used for a private meeting between a mediator and one of the parties involved in a mediation.

Cause in fact   The actual cause of an event; the instrument that is the responsible force for the occurrence of a certain event. A required element of a tort.

Cause of action   This phrase has several meanings, but it is commonly used to describe the existence of facts giving rise to a judicially enforceable claim.

Caveat emptor   Let the buyer beware; rule imposing on a purchaser the duty to inform him- or herself as to defects in the property being sold.

Caveat venditor   Let the seller beware; it is the seller's duty to do what the ordinary person would do in a similar situation.

Cease and desist order   The sanction that may be issued by an administrative agency to prevent a party from violating the law.

Celler-Kefauver amendment   Passed in 1950 to amend the Clayton Act by broadening the scope of Section 7 on mergers and acquisitions.

Central America-Dominican Republic Free Trade Agreement (CAFTA-DR)   An agreement between the United States, Costa Rica, El Salvador, Guatemala, Honduras, Nicaragua, and the Dominican Republic designed to eliminate trade barriers.

Certification mark   A mark used by someone other than its owner to certify the quality, point of origin, or other characteristic of goods or services. The Good Housekeeping "Seal of Approval" is an example.

Certiorari   A Latin word that means "to be informed of." This is the name of a writ that a higher court grants permitting the review of a lower court's ruling.

Changing conditions defense   A defense to a price discrimination (Section 2 of the Clayton Act) case wherein the defendant seeks to justify charging different customers different prices due to a change in the conditions of the product or marketplace.

Charter   The legal document issued by a state when creating a new corporation.

Circuit court   This term frequently is used to describe two distinct courts. First, the appellate courts in the federal court system often are called circuit courts of appeals. Second, the trial courts of general subject matter jurisdiction in some state court systems also are referred to as circuit courts.

Citation   The reference identifying how to find a case.

Civil law   The area of law governing the rights and duties between private parties as compared with the criminal law. This term also describes the system of codifying law in many countries as compared with the judicial orientation of the common law system.

Civil rights   The area of law designed to protect an individual's right to freedom from discrimination. In employment, this area of law prohibits unequal treatment based on race, color, national origin, religion, and sex.

Class-action suit   A method of litigation that allows one or more plaintiffs to file a lawsuit on behalf of a much larger group of persons, all of whom have a common interest in the claims being litigated.

Clayton Act   Legislation passed in 1914 that exempts labor unions from the Sherman Act. This law expanded the national antitrust policy to cover price discrimination, exclusive dealings, tying contracts, mergers, and interlocking directors.

Clean-hands doctrine   An equitable principle that requires a party seeking an equitable remedy to be free from wrongdoing.

Clear and convincing proof   A burden of proof that requires the party with the burden to establish clearly the existence of the alleged facts. This burden requires more proof than merely having a preponderance of evidence on one's side.

Closed shop   A contractual agreement between an employer and a union that all applicants for a job with the employer will have to join the union. This type of agreement was outlawed by the Taft-Hartley Act.

Closely held   An organization that is owned by only a few people.

Code   A compilation of legislation enacted by a federal, state, or local government.

Colgate doctrine   The legal principle that allows a form of vertical price fixing in that manufacturers may maintain the resale price of their products by announcing their pricing policy and refusing to deal with customers who fail to comply with the policy.

Collateral   The valuable thing put up by someone to secure a loan or credit.

Collective bargaining   The process used by an employer and a union representing employees to discuss and resolve differences so that the parties can agree to a binding contract.

Collective mark   A mark representing membership in a certain organization or association. The "union label" is an example.

Commerce clause   A provision in Article I, Section 8, of the U.S. Constitution that grants the federal government the power to regulate business transactions.

Commercial impracticability   A Uniform Commercial Code (UCC) defense to contractual nonperformance based on happenings that greatly increase the difficulty of performance and that violate the parties' reasonable commercial expectations.

Commercial speech   Speech that has a business-oriented purpose. This speech is protected under the First Amendment, but this protection is not as great as that afforded to noncommercial speech.

Common law   That body of law deriving from judicial decisions as opposed to legislatively enacted statutes and administrative regulations.

Comparable worth   Jobs that, although different, produce substantially equal value for the employer.

Comparative negligence   A doctrine that compares the plaintiff's contributory fault with the defendant's fault and allows the jury to reduce the plaintiff's verdict by the percentage of the plaintiff's fault.

Comparative responsibility   A doctrine that compares the plaintiff's contributory fault with the defendant's fault and allows the jury to reduce the plaintiff's verdict by the percentage of the plaintiff's fault. Also called *comparative negligence*.

Compensatory damages   Usually awarded in breach-of-contract cases to pay for a party's losses that are a direct and foreseeable result of the other party's breach. The award of these damages is designed to place the nonbreaching party in the same position as if the contract had been performed.

Complaint   In legal practice, the first written statement of the plaintiff's position and allegations, which initiates the lawsuit.

Complete performance   Degree of performance recognizing that each contracting party has performed every duty required by the contract.

Compulsory bargaining issue   Mandatory bargaining issue regarding wages, hours, or other terms or conditions of employment. Refusal to engage in good-faith bargaining with regard to these issues is an unfair labor practice.

Concealment   An intentional misrepresentation of a material fact occurring through the silence of a party.

Concerted activities   Those activities involving an agreement, contract, or conspiracy to restrain trade that may be illegal under the Sherman Antitrust Act.

Concurrent conditions   Mutual conditions under which each party's contractual performance is triggered by the other party's tendering (offering) performance.

Condition precedent   An event in the law of contracts that must occur before a duty of immediate performance of the promise arises. Contracts often provide that one party must perform before there is a right to performance by the other party. For example, completion of a job is often a condition precedent to payment for that job. One contracting party's failure to perform a condition precedent permits the other party to refuse to perform, cancel the contract, and sue for damages.

Condition subsequent   A fact that will extinguish a duty to make compensation for breach of contract after the breach has occurred.

Conduct   Under the Uniform Commercial Code (UCC) the conduct of contracting parties (i.e., their actions) is important in determining the meaning of a sales contract.

Confiscation   The seizure of property without adequate compensation.

Conflict   The common occurrence in life when two or more points of view exist.

Conflict of law   Rules of law the courts use to determine that substantive law applies when there is an inconsistency between laws of different states or countries.

Confusion   Property ownership that arises when identical masses of objects, such as grain, are mixed together.

Conglomerate merger   The merger resulting when merging companies have neither the relationship of competitors nor that of supplier and customer.

Consent order   Any court or regulatory order to which the opposing party agrees; a contract of the parties entered upon the record with the approval and sanction of a court.

Consequential damages   The amount of money awarded in a breach-of-contract case to the nonbreaching party to pay for the special damages that exceed the normal compensatory damages. Lost opportunities may create consequential damages if the breaching party was aware of the special nature of the contract.

Consequentialism   An ethical system that concerns itself with the moral consequences of actions. Also called *teleology.*

Consideration   An essential element in the creation of a contract obligation that creates a detriment to the promisee or a benefit to the promisor.

Consolidation   The process by which two or more corporations are joined to create a new corporation.

Conspiracy   A combination or agreement between two or more persons for the commission of a criminal act.

Constitutional law   The legal issues that arise from interpreting the U.S. Constitution or a state constitution.

Constitutional relativity   The idea that constitutional interpretation is relative to the time in which the Constitution is being interpreted.

Constructive discharge   The event of an employee resigning because the employer has made working conditions too uncomfortable for continued employment.

Consumer   An individual who buys goods and services for personal use rather than for business use.

Consumer investigative report   A report on a consumer's character, general reputation, mode of living, etc., obtained by personal interviews in the community where the consumer works or lives.

Contempt of court   An order by a judge to punish wrongdoing with respect to the court's authority.

Contingency fee   An arrangement whereby an attorney is compensated for services in a lawsuit according to an agreed percentage of the amount of money recovered.

Contract   A legally enforceable promise.

Contract clause   The constitutional provision that prohibits states from enacting laws that interfere with existing contracts. The Supreme Court has refused to interpret this clause in an absolute manner.

Contract law   The law of legally enforceable promises.

Contribution   The right of one who has discharged a common liability to recover from another also liable the proportionate share of the common liability.

Contributory negligence   A failure to use reasonable care by the plaintiff in a negligence suit.

Controlling person   The person who has the control of, or is controlled by, the issuer of securities in securities laws.

Convention on the International Sale of Goods (CISG)   The agreement that sets forth standard international practices for the sale of goods.

Conversion   An unlawful exercise of dominion and control over another's property that substantially interferes with property rights.

Cooling-off period   A time provided by the Taft-Hartley Act during which labor and management must suspend the work stoppage (strike or lockout) and continue their working relationship while negotiating a resolution of the dispute. This period is for 80 days.

Copyright   A statutorily created property in creative expression that protects authors.

Corporate codes of conduct   Policy statements adopted by companies to define ethical standards for their conduct.

Corporate governance   A term that has at least two meanings. One relates to how business organizations are created and managed. A second concerns how the various levels of government regulate business organizations as they transact business.

Corporation   An artificial, but legal, person created by state law. As a business organization, the corporation's separation of owners and managers gives it a high level of flexibility.

Corrective advertising   A Federal Trade Commission (FTC) remedy that requires companies that have advertised deceptively to run ads that admit the prior errors and correct the erroneous information.

Cost justification defense   A defense to a price discrimination (Section 2 of the Clayton Act) case wherein the defendant seeks to justify charging different customers different prices due to that defendant's costs varying because of the differing quantities purchased by the customers.

Counterclaim   Any claim filed by the defendant in a lawsuit against the plaintiff in the same suit.

Counterdefendant   The party involved in litigation against whom a counterclaim is filed. This party is the original plaintiff.

Counteroffer   An offer made in response to another's offer. Usually made in place of an acceptance. A counteroffer usually terminates an offer.

Counterplaintiff   The party involved in litigation who files a counterclaim. This party is the original defendant who is making a claim against the original plaintiff.

Course of dealing   The way parties to a contract have done business in the past. Important in helping to determine the meaning of a contract for the sale of goods.

Courts of appeal   A court that reviews decisions by lower courts.

Covenant   An agreement or promise in writing by which a party pledges that something has been done or is being done. The term is often used in connection with real estate to describe the promises of the grantor of the property.

Covenant not to compete   An agreement in which one party agrees not to compete directly with the business of the other party; may be limited by geography or length of time.

Criminal law   That area of law dealing with wrongs against the state as representative of the community at large, to be distinguished from civil law, which hears cases of wrongs against persons.

Cross-examination   The process of questioning a witness by the lawyer who did not call the witness to testify on behalf of that lawyer's client.

Cruel and unusual punishment   Protection against such punishment is provided by the Eighth Amendment of the U.S. Constitution. To be cruel and unusual, the punishment must be disproportionately harsh when compared to the offense committed.

Damages   Monetary compensation recoverable in a court of law.

D.B.A.   Doing business as.

Decree   The decision of a court of equity.

Deed   A document representing the title or ownership of land.

Deeds of trust   A type of document to secure an extension of credit through an interest in the land.

Defamation   The publication of anything injurious to the good name or reputation of another.

Default   The failure of a defendant to answer a plaintiff's complaint within the time period allowed by the court. Upon the defendant's default, a judgment is entered in the plaintiff's favor.

Defect   Something that makes a product not reasonably safe for a use that can be reasonably anticipated.

Defendant   The party involved in a lawsuit that is sued; the party required to respond to the plaintiff's complaint.

Deficiency   In a land based security interest, the amount of the loan which remains unpaid after the land has been sold.

Defined benefit plan   A money-purchase plan that guarantees a certain retirement income based on the employee's service and salary under the Employee Retirement Income Security Act. The benefits are fixed, and the contributions vary.

Defined contribution plan   A money-purchase plan that allows employers to budget pension costs in advance under the Employee Retirement Income Security Act. The contribution is fixed, and the benefits vary.

Delivery   The physical transfer of something. In sale-of-goods transactions, delivery is the transfer of goods from the seller to the buyer.

Demurrer   A formal statement by the defendant that the facts alleged by the plaintiff are insufficient to support a claim for legal relief in common law pleading.

De novo judicial review   A proceeding wherein the judge or hearing officer hears the case as if it had not been heard before.

Deontology   An ethical system that affirms an absolute morality. Also called *formalism*.

Deposited acceptance rule   The contractual doctrine that a binding acceptance of an offer occurs when a mailed acceptance is irrevocably placed with the postal service.

Deposition   A discovery process outside the court's supervision that involves the sworn questioning of a potential witness. This oral questioning is reduced to a written form so that a record is established.

Derivative action   A lawsuit filed by a shareholder of a corporation on behalf of the corporation. This action is filed to protect the corporation from the mismanagement of its officers and directors.

Derivative suit   A lawsuit filed by one or more shareholders of a corporation against that organization's management. This suit is brought to benefit the corporation directly and its shareholders indirectly.

Design defect   A defect arising when a product does not meet society's expectation for a safely designed product.

Dicta   Statements made in a judicial opinion that are not essential to the decision of the case.

Directed verdict   A motion for a directed verdict requests that the judge direct the jury to bring in a particular verdict if reasonable minds could not differ on the correct outcome of the lawsuit. In deciding the motion, the judge will view in the light most favorable to the nonmoving party, and if different inferences may be drawn by reasonable people, then the court cannot direct a verdict. In essence, a directed verdict removes the jury's discretion.

Direct examination   The process of questioning a witness conducted by the lawyer who called the witness to testify on behalf of that lawyer's client.

Directors   Those individuals who are elected by the shareholders to decide the goals and objectives for the corporate organization.

Disability   Any physical or mental impairment that substantially limits a major life activity.

Disaffirm   To void. Used to describe a minor's power to get out of a contract because of age.

Discharge   In bankruptcy the forgiving of an honest debtor's debts. In contract law an act that forgives further performance of a contractual obligation.

Discovery   Procedures by which one party to a lawsuit may obtain information relevant to the case from the other party or from third persons.

Discretionary function exception   An exception to the waiver of the doctrine of sovereign immunity. Officials of administrative agencies are exempt from personal liability if their performance or lack thereof is based on a discretionary function.

Discrimination in effect   The discriminatory result of policies that appear to be neutral.

Disparate impact   A term of employment litigation that refers to the disproportionate impact of a policy neutral on its face on some protected class (e.g., race or sex).

Disparate treatment   A term of employment litigation that refers to the illegal discriminatory treatment of an individual in some protected class (e.g., race or sex).

Dispute   The circumstance when a party in conflict claims the right to do or have something and the other party denies, rejects, or ignores the claim.

Dissolution   The cancellation of an agreement, thereby rescinding its binding force. A partnership is dissolved anytime there is a change in partners. A corporation's dissolution occurs when that business entity ceases to exist.

Diversity of citizenship   The plaintiffs filing a lawsuit must be from states different from those of the defendants. This requirement, along with over $75,000 at stake, is one method a federal court gains jurisdiction over the subject matter of a lawsuit.

Divestiture   The antitrust remedy that forces a company to get rid of assets acquired through illegal mergers or monopolistic practices.

Docket   A book containing a brief summary of all acts done in court in the conduct of each case.

Doctrine of abstention   A principle used by federal courts to refuse to hear a case. When used by the federal courts, the lawsuit involved is sent to the state court system.

Domestic corporation   A business organization created by the issuance of a state charter that operates in the state that issued the charter.

Domicile   That place that a person intends as his or her fixed and permanent legal residence; place of permanent abode, as contrasted with a residence, which may be temporary; a person can have a number of residences but only one domicile; the state of incorporation of a corporation.

Donee beneficiary   A noncontracting third party who receives as a gift the benefits of a contract made between two other parties. This third party is empowered to enforce the contract to ensure the receipt of the contract's benefits.

Dormant commerce clause concept   The impact of the commerce clause as a means of limiting state and local governments' powers to regulate business activities.

Double jeopardy   A constitutional doctrine that prohibits an individual from being prosecuted twice by the same governing body based on the same factual situation.

Double tax   A disadvantage of a corporate form of organization in that the corporation must pay a tax on the money earned and the shareholder pays a second tax on the dividends distributed.

Dram shop acts   Statutes adopted in many states that impose strict liability upon tavern owners for injuries to third parties caused by their intoxicated patrons.

Due diligence defense   A defense that experts may assert in a 1933 Securities Act case involving the failure to register securities or the failure to provide accurate documents. The expert utilizing this defense attempts to prove his or her reasonable investigation into all available information.

Due process   Fundamental fairness. As applied to judicial proceedings, adequate notice of a hearing and an opportunity to appear and defend in an orderly tribunal.

Due process clause   A provision found in the Fifth and Fourteenth Amendments of the U.S. Constitution. This clause assures all citizens of fundamental fairness in their relationship with the government.

Dumping   The practice of selling foreign goods in one country at less than the comparable price in the country where the goods originated.

Duress   Action by a person that compels another to do what he or she would not otherwise do. It is a recognized defense to any act that must be voluntary in order to create liability in the actor.

Duty   A legal obligation imposed by the law.

Duty of performance   In contract law the legal obligation of a party to a contract.

Duty of reasonable care   The legal duty owed under negligence doctrine.

Easement   The right of one other than the owner of land to some use of that land.

Economic boycott   Used in three basic forms (primary, secondary, and tertiary), a practice aimed at cutting off trade opportunities for enemy countries.

Eighty-day cooling-off period   A provision in the Taft-Hartley Act that allows the president to require that laborers continue working and that the laborers' representatives and management continue bargaining for at least 80 days during which it is intended that federal mediation will resolve the dispute. This provision can be utilized by the president only when there is a determination that the work stoppage is adversely affecting the national health and safety.

Ejusdem generis   Of the same kind or class; a doctrine of legislative interpretation.

Embezzlement   The fraudulent appropriation by one person, acting in a fiduciary capacity, of the money or property of another.

Eminent domain   The government's constitutional power to take private property for public use upon the payment of just compensation.

Emissions reduction banking   The policy stating that businesses that lower pollution beyond the requirements of the law may use the additional reductions in the future.

Employment at will   A hiring for an indefinite period of time.

En banc   Proceedings by or before the court as a whole rather than any single judge.

Endangerment of workers   A criminal act that involves placing employees at risk with respect to their health and safety in the work environment.

Enforceable contract   A contract that can be enforced in court.

Enjoin   To require performance of, or abstention from, some act through issuance of an injunction.

Environmental impact statement   A filing of documents required by the National Environmental Policy Act that forces governmental agencies to consider the environmental consequences of their actions.

Equal protection clause   A provision in the Fourteenth Amendment of the U.S. Constitution that requires all citizens to be treated in a similar manner by the government unless there is a sufficient justification for the unequal treatment.

Escrow   A deed, bond, or deposit that one party delivers for safekeeping by a second party who is obligated to deliver it to a third party upon the fulfillment of some condition.

Establishment clause   A provision in the First Amendment of the U.S. Constitution that prohibits the federal government from establishing any government-supported religion or church.

Estate   The bundle of rights and powers of real property ownership.

Estoppel   The legal principle that one may not assert facts inconsistent with one's own prior actions.

Ethics   A systematic statement of right and wrong together with a philosophical system that both justifies and necessitates rules of conduct.

European Union (EU)   Created by the Treaty of Rome, an organization that seeks to facilitate the free movement of goods, services, labor, professions, transportation, and capital among European countries.

Exclusive dealing   A buyer agrees to purchase a certain product exclusively from the seller or the seller agrees to sell all of his or her production to the buyer.

Exclusive remedy rule   The rule that limits an injured employee's claim against the employer to workers' compensation.

Exculpatory clause   A provision in a contract whereby one of the parties attempts to relieve itself of liability for breach of a legal duty.

Exculpatory no   The doctrine that merely denying guilt is not a criminal lie in response to a question from an agency of the federal government. This doctrine is no longer valid.

Exculpatory contract   A contract that excuses one from accepting responsibility or blame. For example, a contract that excuses one from having to accept liability for one's negligence or another's injury or loss.

Executed contract   A contract that is fully accomplished or performed, leaving nothing unfulfilled.

Execution   To carry out some action to completion. With respect to enforcing a court's judgment, an execution involves the seizure of the debtor's property, a sale of the property, and the payment of proceeds to the creditor.

Executory contract   An agreement that is not completed. Until the performance required in a contract is completed, it is executory.

Exemplary damages   Punitive damages. Monetary compensation in excess of direct losses suffered by the plaintiff that may be awarded in intentional tort cases where the defendant's conduct deserves punishment.

Exhaustion of remedies   A concept used in administrative law that requires any party to an administrative proceeding to give the administrative agency every opportunity to resolve the dispute before appealing to the court system.

Expectation of privacy   The expectation that one will not be observed by the state.

Experience rating system   A system of sliding taxation under which employers are charged less unemployment compensation tax as they lay off fewer workers due to economic conditions.

Export controls   Action taken on a national and multilateral basis to prevent the exportation of controlled goods and technology to certain destinations.

Express authority   Actual authority that arises from specific statements made by the principal to the agent.

Express conditions   Conditions that are explicitly set out in a contract.

Express contract   A contract in which parties show their agreement in words.

Express warranty   Any statement of fact or promise about the performance of a product made by a seller.

Expropriation   A foreign government's seizure of privately owned property.

Extortionate picketing   Picketing by employees in an attempt to force an employer to pay money to union officials or other individuals when these payments provide personal benefit to the officials or individuals instead of benefiting the union membership generally.

Extradition   The process that one state uses to have another state transfer to the jurisdiction of the first state a person accused of criminal activities.

Failing-company doctrine   A merger between a failing company and a competitor may be allowed, although such a merger would be illegal if both companies were viable competitors.

Fair Labor Standards Act (FLSA)   Originally passed in 1938, this law provides basic protections for employees, including the minimum wage and maximum number of hours before overtime must be paid.

Fair use   A statutorily permitted use of another's copyright for criticism, comment, news reporting, teaching, scholarship, or research.

False advertising   Untrue and fraudulent statements and representations made by way of advertising a product or a service.

False imprisonment   The tort of an intentional, unjustified confinement of a nonconsenting person who knows of the confinement.

Family and Medical Leave Act (FMLA)   This law, which became effective in 1993, allows eligible workers up to 12 weeks of unpaid leave in any 12-month period to care for a newborn baby, to care for a child placed for adoption or foster care, to care for an immediate family member with a serious health condition, or when the employee is unable to work because of a serious health condition.

Family resemblance test   A legal principle used to determine whether or not promissory notes or other similar investment opportunities are securities.

Featherbedding   A term used in the labor laws to describe workers who are paid although they do not perform any work. Under the Taft-Hartley Act, featherbedding is an unfair labor practice by unions.

Federal Employer's Liability Act   The federal act covering transportation workers that establishes an employer's liability to employees for negligence.

Federalism   A term used to describe the vertical aspect of the separation of powers. The coexistence of a federal government and the various state governments, with each having responsibilities and authorities that are distinct but overlap, is called federalism.

Federal question cases   Litigation involving the application or interpretation of the federal Constitution, federal statutes, federal treaties, or federal administrative agencies. The federal court system has subject matter jurisdiction over these issues.

Federal Rules of Civil Procedure   A law passed by Congress that provides the procedural steps to be followed by the federal courts when handling civil litigation.

Federal Trade Commission Act   Passed in 1914, this legislation created the Federal Trade Commission (FTC) and authorized it to protect society against unfair methods of competition. The law was amended in 1938 (by the Wheeler-Lea amendment) to provide the FTC with authority to regulate unfair or deceptive trade practices.

Fee schedule   A plan, usually adopted by an association, that establishes minimum or maximum charges for a service or product.

Fee simple   The maximum bundle of rights, or estate, permitted by law.

Fellow-servant doctrine   The doctrine that precludes an injured employee from recovering damages from his employer when the injury resulted from the negligent act of another employee.

Felony   A criminal offense of a serious nature, generally punishable by death or imprisonment in a penitentiary; to be distinguished from a misdemeanor.

Fiduciary   One having a duty to act for another's benefit in the highest good faith.

Finance charge   Any charge for an extension of credit, which specifically includes interest, service charges, and other charges.

Financing statement   An established form that a secured party files with a public officer, such as a state official or local court clerk, to perfect a security interest under the Uniform Commercial Code (UCC). It is a simple form that contains basic information such as a description of the collateral, names, and addresses. It is designed to give notice that the debtor and the secured party have entered into a security agreement.

Firm offer   An offer in signed writing by a merchant to buy or sell goods; it gives assurances that the offer will be held open for acceptance under the Uniform Commercial Code (UCC).

Fixture   Personal property that has become real property, generally through physical attachment (annexation).

Focus group   A group acting as a mock jury; attorneys present cases to such a group to get the members' feedback on the merits of the various arguments presented.

Foreclosure   If a mortgagor fails to perform his or her obligations as agreed, the mortgagee may declare the whole debt due and payable, and she or he may foreclose on the mortgaged property to pay the debt secured by the mortgage. The usual method of foreclosure authorizes the sale of the mortgaged property at a public auction. The proceeds of the sale are applied to the debt.

Foreign corporation   A business organization, created by the issuance of a state charter, that operates in states other than the one issuing the charter.

Foreign Corrupt Practices Act (FCPA)   A U.S. law that seeks to ban the payment of bribes to foreign officials in order to obtain business.

Foreign Sovereign Immunities Act (FISA)   A federal law passed in 1976 that codifies the restrictive theory of *sovereign immunity* and rejects immunity for commercial acts carried on in the United States or having direct effects in this country.

Foreign subsidiary   A practice common in a multinational corporation that conducts part of its business operations in a foreign country.

Formalism   An ethical system that affirms an absolute morality. Also called *deontology*.

Forum non conveniens   The doctrine under which a court may dismiss a lawsuit in which it appears that for the convenience of the parties and in the interest of justice the action should have been brought in another court.

Franchise A marketing technique whereby one party (the franchisor) grants a second party (the franchisee) the right to manufacture, distribute, or sell a product using the name or trademark of the franchisor.

Fraud A false representation of fact made with the intent to deceive another that is justifiably relied upon to the injury of that person.

Free exercise clause A provision in the First Amendment of the U.S. Constitution that allows all citizens the freedom to follow or believe any religious teaching.

Frolic and detour The activity of an agent or an employee who has departed from the scope of the agency and is not, therefore, a representative of his or her employer.

Full faith and credit clause A provision in the U.S. Constitution that requires a state to recognize the laws and judicial decisions of all other states.

Full-line forcing An arrangement in which a manufacturer refuses to supply any portion of the product line unless the retailer agrees to accept the entire line.

Functional discount A reduction in price as the result of the buyer's performing some service that usually is provided by the seller.

Garnishment A legal proceeding whereby a creditor may collect directly from a third party who is obligated to the debtor.

General Agreement on Tariffs and Trade (GATT) An international treaty that requires member countries to abide by the principles of open and free trade.

General counsel An individual who is responsible for coordinating all law-related issues, such as the quasi-judicial hearings in administrative agencies. This term is also used to describe the principal lawyer of a company.

General partner The owner of a limited partnership that enjoys the control of the partnership's operation. This type of partner is personally liable for the debts of the limited partnership.

General partnership A business organization wherein all owners (partners) share profits and losses and all are jointly and severally liable for the organization's debts.

Generic To lose distinctiveness in reference to the source of goods and thus to lose trademark protection.

Genetic Information Nondiscrimination Act (GINA) Prohibits covered employers from firing, refusing to hire, or otherwise discriminating against individuals on the basis of their genetic information or a family member's genetic information.

Geographic extension merger A combining of companies involved with the same product or service that do not compete in the same geographical regions or markets.

Geographic market The relevant section of the country affected by a merger.

Gift Transfer of ownership by intent and the delivery of the object gifted.

Going bare A professional practicing (in her or his field of expertise) without liability insurance.

Good, the In philosophy the moral goals and objectives that people choose to pursue.

Good faith Honesty in dealing; innocence; without fraud or deceit.

Good-faith meeting-of-competition defense A bona fide business practice that is a defense to a charge of violation of the Robinson-Patman Act. The Robinson-Patman Act is an amendment to the Clayton Act, which outlaws price discrimination that might substantially lessen competition or tends to create a monopoly. This exception allows a seller in good faith to meet the equally low price, service, or facility of a competitor. The good-faith exception cannot be established if the purpose of the price discrimination has been to eliminate competition.

Goods Tangible (touchable), movable personal property.

Greenmail Forcing a corporation to buy back some of its own stock at an inflated price to avoid a takeover.

Guardian One charged with the duty of care and maintenance of another person such as a minor or incompetent under the law.

Guardian *ad litem* A guardian appointed to prosecute or defend a lawsuit on behalf of an incompetent or a minor.

Guidelines A result of an administrative agency's quasi-legislative function that assists parties being regulated to understand the agency's functions and intentions. Guidelines do not have the force of the law, but they can be helpful in anticipating the application of an agency's regulations.

Habeas corpus   The name of a writ that orders one holding custody of another to produce that individual before the court for the purpose of determining whether such custody is proper.

Hearsay evidence   Evidence of statements made or actions performed out of court that is offered to prove the truth thereof.

Hearsay rule   The exclusion, with certain exceptions, of hearsay evidence because of the lack of opportunity to cross-examine the original source of the evidence.

Holding   The precise legal response in an opinion by an appellate court on an issue of law raised on appeal.

Holder in due course   One who has acquired possession of a negotiable instrument through proper negotiation for value, in good faith, and without notice of any defenses to it. Such a holder is not subject to personal defenses that would otherwise defeat the obligation embodied in the instrument.

Horizontal merger   Merger of corporations that were competitors prior to the merger.

Horizontal price fixing   A per se illegal agreement among competitors as to the price all of them will charge for their similar products.

Horizontal territorial agreement   An arrangement between competitors with respect to geographical areas in which each will conduct its business to the exclusion of the others. This type of agreement is illegal per se under the Sherman Act.

Hostile working environment   Under Title VII an environment where co-workers make offensive sexual comments or propositions, engage in suggestive touching, show nude pictures, or draw sexual graffiti.

Hot-cargo contract   An agreement whereby an employer agrees to refrain from handling, using, selling, transporting, or otherwise dealing in the products of another employer or to cease doing business with any other person.

Illegal search and seizure   The area covered by the Fourth Amendment that protects individuals and organizations from unreasonable intrusion without a court-issued warrant.

Immunity   Status of exemption from lawsuits or other legal obligations.

Implied authority   Actual authority that is incidental to express authority.

Implied conditions   Conditions to a contract that are implied by law rather than by contractual agreement.

Implied contract   A legally enforceable agreement inferred from the circumstances and conduct of the parties. Also called an *implied-in-fact contract*.

Implied-in-fact contract   A legally enforceable agreement inferred from the circumstances and conduct of the parties.

Implied-in-law contract   A quasi-contract.

Implied warranty   A warranty implied by law rather than by express agreement of the parties to a contract.

Implied warranty of fitness for a particular purpose   An implied Uniform Commercial Code (UCC) warranty that arises when a buyer specifies a purpose for a product, then relies on the seller's skill and judgment to select the product.

Implied warranty of habitability   A warranty implied by law in a number of states that guarantees the quality of new home construction.

Implied warranty of merchantability   A warranty (implied) that the goods are reasonably fit for the general purpose for which they are sold.

Impossibility of performance   A defense to contractual nonperformance based on special circumstances that render the performance illegal, physically impossible, or so difficult as to violate every reasonable expectation the parties have regarding performance.

Incidental beneficiary   A person who may incidentally benefit from the creation of a contract. Such a person cannot enforce any right to incidental benefit.

Incorporators   Those individuals who are responsible for bringing a corporation into being.

Indefiniteness   When the terms of an agreement are not sufficiently specific, the agreement does not rise to the level of a contract because of the doctrine of indefiniteness.

Indictment   A document issued by a grand jury formally charging a person with a felony.

Individual retirement account   A retirement account for persons who can make either tax deductible contributions, which are taxed on withdrawal, or contributions that are taxed, which produce tax-free withdrawals. This latter type of account is known as a Roth IRA.

Industry guide   An issue of the Federal Trade Commission (FTC) defining the agency's view of the legality of an industry's trade practice.

Infliction of mental distress   An intentional tort of the emotions that causes both mental distress and physical symptoms as a result of the defendant's outrageous behavior.

Information   A written accusation by the prosecutor presented in court charging an accused person with a crime.

Infringement   The tort establishing violation of intellectual property rights.

Injunction   A court order directing a party to do or to refrain from doing some act.

Injurious falsehood   A statement of untruth that causes injury or damage to the party against whom it is made.

In pari materia   Concerning the same subject matter. A rule of statutory construction that two such statutes will be construed together.

In personam   The jurisdiction of a court to affect the rights and duties of a specific individual.

In rem   The jurisdiction of a court to affect property rights with respect to a specific thing.

Insider   A person who owns 10 percent or more of a company or who is a director or officer of the company; a term used in securities law. This term is also used to describe a person possessing nonpublic information.

Intangible property   Something that represents value but has no physical attributes, such as a copyright, patent, or franchise right.

Intellectual property   A type of property in information and its application or expression. Patents and copyrights are examples.

Intent   A legal doctrine indicating that parties meant to do what they did.

Intentional interference with contractual relations   The tort of causing another to break a contract.

Intentional tort   Noncontractual legal wrong caused by one who desires to cause the wrong or where the wrong is substantially likely to occur from the behavior.

Intent to defraud   Applies to an individual who knowingly and willfully makes a misrepresentation of a material fact that is relied on and thereby causes injury or harm.

Interference with contractual relations   A business tort in which persons are induced to breach binding agreements.

International Court of Justice   The judicial branch of the United Nations, which sits at The Hague in the Netherlands and consists of 15 judges representing the world's major legal systems.

International Monetary Fund   An international economic organization.

Interpleader   A legal procedure by which one holding a single fund subject to conflicting claims of two or more persons may require the conflicting claimants to come into court and litigate the matter between themselves.

Interrogatory   A written question submitted by one party to another in a lawsuit; a type of discovery procedure.

Inter se   Between themselves.

Intestate   A person who dies without a will.

Invasion of privacy   A tort based on misappropriation of name or likeness, intrusion upon physical solitude, or public disclosure of objectionable, private information.

Investigative consumer report   A consumer report under the Fair Credit Reporting Act that arises when a credit reporting agency goes beyond reporting financial transactions and also reports the habits and practices of someone seeking credit or a job.

Involuntary petition   The document filed by a creditor to initiate bankruptcy proceedings against a debtor.

Irreconcilable conflicts   When a state or local law requires something different than a federal law or regulation and both laws cannot be satisfied. Under Commerce Clause analysis, the state or local law is declared invalid and void.

Irrevocable letter of credit   Reduces the risk to parties in cases where business is extended across national borders between strangers by providing guarantees of payment and delivery of goods.

Issuer   The term in securities law for an individual or business organization offering a security for sale to the public.

Jointly and severally liable   The legal principle that makes two or more people, usually partners, liable for an entire debt as individuals or in any proportional combination.

Joint tenancy   A property ownership that is undivided (common) and equal between two or more owners. Permits survivorship.

Joint venture   Two or more persons or business organizations agreeing to do business for a specific and limited purpose.

Judgment   Official adjudication of a court of law.

Judgment notwithstanding the verdict   The decision of a court that sets aside the verdict of a jury and reaches the opposite result.

Judgment on the pleadings   A principle of litigation, in the form of a motion, whereby one party tests the validity of the allegations contained in the complaint and answer. Upon this motion a judge might determine that the pleadings contain no issues of fact or law and thus grant a judgment prior to a trial.

Judicial activism   An activist judge tends to abide by the following judicial philosophies: (1) The political process cannot adequately handle society's difficult issues; (2) the courts can correct society's ills through the decision-making process; (3) following precedent is not crucial; and (4) "judge-made law" is often necessary to carry out the legislative intent of the law. See also *Judicial restraint.*

Judicial admission   An exception under the statute of frauds allowing courts to enforce oral contracts when a party acknowledges the oral promise in a formal judicial/court environment.

Judicial restraint   A judge who abides by the judicial restraint philosophy (1) believes that the political process, and not the courts, should correct society's ills; (2) decides an issue on a narrow basis, if possible; (3) follows precedent whenever possible; and (4) does not engage in "judge-made law" but interprets the letter of the law. See also *Judicial activism.*

Judicial review   The power of courts to declare laws enacted by legislative bodies and actions by the executive branch to be unconstitutional.

Jurisdiction   The power and authority of a court or other governmental agency to adjudicate controversies and otherwise deal with matters brought before it.

Jurisdictional strike   A stoppage of work that arises from a dispute between two or more unions as to what work should be assigned to the employees belonging to the disputing unions. This work stoppage is an unfair labor practice. This dispute between the unions should be resolved by the NLRB.

Jurisprudence   The science of the law; the practical science of giving a wise interpretation of the law.

Jury instruction   A statement made by the judge to the jury informing them of the law applicable to the case the jury is bound to accept and apply.

Knowingly   Intentionally.

Laches   Defense to an equitable action based on the plaintiff's unreasonable delay in bringing the action.

Landrum-Griffin Act   The federal law passed in 1959 that provides union members with a "Bill of Rights" and requires union officers to file reports with the Department of Labor. This law, which is known as the Labor-Management Reporting and Disclosure Act, also added unfair labor practices by unions.

Land sales contract   A type of document to secure an extension of credit through an interest in the land purchased.

Lanham Act   A federal law regulating unfair methods of competition regarding trademarks.

Larceny   The unlawful taking of personal property with the intent to deprive the right owner of this property.

Law   The rules of the state backed up by enforcement.

Law of agency   That body of law concerning one's dealing with another on behalf of a principal.

Law of nations   The law embodied in international agreements, treaties, and conventions.

Leading question   A question that indicates the appropriate answer because of the way or manner in which it is asked. Typically, such questions are allowed during the cross-examination of a witness but not during the direct examination.

Leashold estate   The property granted to tenants (lessees) by a landlord (lessor).

Legacy   A gift of money under a will. It is a type of bequest, which is a gift of personal property. The word *devise* is used in connection with real property distributed by will.

Legal capacity   The ability of a business organization to sue and be sued in its own name rather than having to sue or be sued in the name of its owners.

Legal clinic   A term referring to a law firm that specializes in low-cost, generally routine legal procedures.

Legislation   Laws passed by an elected body such as Congress, a state legislation, or local council/commission. Those laws enacted at the federal and state levels are called statutes. At the local level, such laws are often referred to as ordinances.

Legislative history   A technique used by courts in interpreting statutes. Courts often examine the record of the legislators' debate in an attempt to determine what was intended by the legislation.

Letter of credit   A document commonly used in international transactions to ensure payment and delivery of goods.

Libel   A defamatory written statement communicated to a third party.

License   A common method of controlling product or technology transfers across national borders.

Lien   A claim to an interest in property in satisfaction of a debt or claim.

Life estate   A property that grants land ownership for the lifetime of a specified person.

Limited liability   This term is used to describe the exposure of business owners to pay the debts of their businesses when such exposure does not exceed the owner's investment in the business.

Limited liability company (LLC)   A type of business organization that has characteristics of both a partnership and a corporation. The owners of an LLC are called members, and their personal liability is limited to their capital contributions. The LLC, as an organization, is not a taxable entity.

Limited liability partnership   A hybrid business partnership.

Limited partners   Those owners of a limited partnership who forgo control of the organization's operation in return for their liability being limited to the amount of their investment.

Limited partnership   A partnership in which one or more individuals are general partners and one or more individuals are limited partners. The limited partners contribute assets to the partnership without taking part in the conduct of the business. Such individuals are liable for the debts of the partnership only to the extent of their contributions.

Limited personal liability   See *Limited liability*.

Liquidated damages clause   A contractual provision that specifies a predetermined amount of damages or a formula for such a determination to be utilized if a breach of contract occurs.

Liquidation   The process of winding up the affairs of a business for the purpose of paying debts and disposing of assets. May be voluntary or under court order.

Litigation   The process of utilizing the court system to resolve a legal dispute.

Long-arm statute   A state statute that gives extraterritorial effect to process (summon) in specified cases. It allows state courts to obtain jurisdiction in civil actions over defendants who are beyond the border of the state provided the defendants have minimum contact with the state sufficient to satisfy due process.

Mailbox rule   The rule that an acceptance is effective once it is sent. See *Deposited acceptance rule*.

Mail fraud   The use of the United States Postal Service or any interstate carrier to conduct fraudulent activities with the intent to deprive an owner of property.

Malfeasance   Doing of some wrongful act.

Malice   The state of mind that accompanies the intentional doing of a wrongful act without justification or excuse.

Malicious prosecution   An action for recovery of damages that have resulted to person, property, or reputation from previous unsuccessful civil or criminal proceedings that were prosecuted without probable cause and with malice.

Manager   A person designated and charged with day-to-day operations of a Limited Liability Company.

Mandamus   A court order directing the holder of an office to perform his or her legal duty.

Mandatory arbitration   A form of resolving a dispute, as an alternative to litigation, that is required by a statute.

Manifest system   A documentary system required by the Resource Conservation and Recovery Act. Used in the disposal of toxic chemicals.

Market extension merger   An acquisition in which the acquiring company increases its market through product extension or geographical extension.

Master   The term used in an agency relationship to describe the principal (employer) of a servant (employee) who is involved in a tort.

Material breach   A level of performance below what is reasonably acceptable. A substantial failure, without excuse, to perform a promise that constitutes the whole or part of a contract. A party who has materially breached cannot sue the other party for performance and is liable for damages.

Mayhem   Unlawfully depriving a human being of a member of his or her body.

Mechanic's lien   A lien on real estate that is created by statute to assist suppliers and laborers in collecting their accounts and wages. Its purpose is to subject the owner's land to a lien for material and labor expended in the construction of buildings and other improvements.

Med-Arb   An abbreviation for an alternative dispute resolution system that involves parties going through mediation and agreeing to resolve as many issues as possible. These parties agree that any matters not resolved in the mediation process will then be arbitrated.

Mediation   An alternative to litigation whereby a third party attempts to assist the disputing parties in reaching a settlement. The third-party mediator lacks authority to impose on the parties a binding solution to the dispute.

Mediator   An individual who assists disputing parties in their efforts to resolve their differences. Mediators must rely on their persuasive abilities since they have no authority to settle the dispute.

Members   The individuals or business entities that belong to a limited liability company.

Merchant   A term used in the Uniform Commercial Code to describe parties to a contract that regularly do business in the goods being sold and purchased.

Merger   The extinguishment of a corporate entity by the transfer of its assets and liabilities to another corporation that continues in existence.

Minimum rationality   A legal test used by courts to test the validity of governmental action, such as legislation, under the equal protection clause of the U.S. Constitution. To satisfy this test, the government needs to demonstrate that there is a good reason for the government's action.

Minimum wage   Minimum hourly wages, established by Congress under the Fair Labor Standards Act, to maintain the health, efficiency, and general well-being of workers.

Ministerial duty   An example of a definite duty regarding that nothing be left to discretion or judgment.

Minitrial   An alternative dispute resolution system that involves lawyers presenting both sides of a business dispute to the executives of the organizations involved.

Mirror image rule   The common law rule that the terms of an acceptance offer must mirror exactly the terms of the offer. Any variation of terms would make the attempted acceptance a counteroffer.

Misappropriation   A term referring to the wrongful taking of what belongs to an owner. Often used in intellectual property law.

Misappropriation theory   The legal doctrine supported by the Securities and Exchange Commission (SEC) and the courts that any person who shares nonpublic information with another party or who trades on the information violates the securities laws if that information was intended to be kept confidential.

Misdemeanor   A criminal offense of less serious nature than a felony, generally punishable by fine or jail sentence other than in a penitentiary.

Misfeasance   A misdeed or trespass.

Misrepresentation   An untrue manifestation of fact by word or conduct; it may be unintentional.

Mitigate   To lessen the consequences of. Usually used to refer to the contractual duty to lessen damages following breach of contract.

Mock trial   An alternative dispute resolution system that involves lawyers presenting their clients' cases to a group of citizens who render their opinion about the relative merits of the parties' positions.

Monopoly   Exclusive control of a market by a business entity.

Morality   The values of right and wrong.

Mortgage   1. A transfer of an interest in property for the purpose of creating a security for a debt. 2. A type of security interest in land, usually securing an extension of credit.

Mortgagor   The owner of land who places a mortgage on it.

Motion   The process by which the parties make written or oral requests that the judge issue an order or ruling.

Mutual assent   A contractual doctrine requiring that the minds of the contracting parties must meet before there exists a binding contract.

Mutual mistake   A situation in which parties to a contract reach a bargain on the basis of an incorrect assumption common to both parties.

Nationalization   A claim made by a foreign government that it owns expropriated property.

National Labor Relations Board (NLRB)   The federal administrative agency created in 1935 to conduct certification/decertification elections of unions and to conduct quasi-judicial hearings arising from the labor-management relationship.

National Mediation Board   Created by the Railway Labor Act, this federal agency is to help the parties resolve labor-management disputes arising in transportation industries.

Natural law   A philosophy of law that says certain legal rules can be reasoned out from nature itself and always hold true.

Necessaries of life   Food, clothing, shelter, medical care, and, in some states, education. A minor is legally responsible to pay a reasonable value for purchased necessaries of life.

Negligence   A person's failure to exercise reasonable care that foreseeably causes another injury.

Negotiable instrument or document   A special type of written promise to pay money (instrument) or deliver goods (document). Personal defenses do not apply against the holder in due course of a negotiable instrument or document.

Negotiated settlement   A voluntary but binding agreement that settles a legal dispute, such as one involving a contractual breach or a tort lawsuit.

Negotiation   The process used to persuade or coerce someone to do or to stop doing something.

Nexus   A logical connection.

NLRB   National Labor Relations Board.

Noerr-Pennington doctrine   This doctrine exempts from the antitrust laws concerted efforts to lobby government officials regardless of the anticompetitive purposes. It is based on the First Amendment freedom of speech.

No-fault laws   Laws barring tort actions by injured persons against third-party tortfeasors and requiring such persons to obtain recovery from their own insurers.

Nolo contendere   A plea entered by the defendant in a criminal case that neither admits nor denies the crime allegedly committed but, if accepted by the court, permits the judge to treat the defendant as guilty.

Nontrading partnership　A business organization made up of two or more partners engaged in buying and selling goods.

Norris-LaGuardia Act　The federal legislation adopted in 1932 that attempted to increase union membership by prohibiting the use of injunctions issued by federal courts against certain union activities and by outlawing yellow-dog contracts.

North American Free Trade Agreement (NAFTA)　An agreement reached in 1993 among the United States, Mexico, and Canada to increase economic growth through mutual trade.

Noscitur a sociis　The principle that the scope of general words is defined by specific accompanying words; a doctrine of legislative interpretation.

Notary public　A public officer authorized to administer oaths and certify certain documents.

Notice　Communication sufficient to charge a reasonable person with knowledge of some fact.

Novation　The substitution of a new contract in place of an old one.

Nuisance　A physical condition constituting an unreasonable and substantial interference with the rights of individuals or the public at large.

Obligee　One who is entitled to receive a payment or performance under a contract.

Obligor　One who is obligated to pay or perform under a contract.

Obstruction of justice　A criminal act involving the interference of the administration of the laws during the investigations and conduct of trials.

Occupational Safety and Health Administration (OSHA)　The organization that has jurisdiction over complaints about hazardous conditions in the workplace.

Offer　A contractual communication that contains a specific promise and a specific demand. The offer initiates the process of making a contract.

Officers　Those individuals appointed by directors of a corporation to conduct the daily operations of the corporate organization.

Oligopoly　Control of the supply and price of a commodity or service in a given market by a small number of companies or suppliers.

Opinion　The decision of a judge, usually issued in a written form.

Option　A contractual arrangement under which one party has for a specified time the right to buy certain property from or sell certain property to the other party. It is essentially a contract to not revoke an offer.

Oral argument　Attorneys appear in person before the appellate court to explain orally to the court their position in the case and answer the court's questions about the case.

Ordinance　The legislative enactment of a city, county, or other municipal corporation.

Organizers　The parties responsible for bringing a limited liability company into existence. These parties correspond to the functions of incorporators with respect to corporations.

Overbreadth doctrine　A principle used by courts to invalidate legislation that is broader in scope than is necessary to regulate an activity. This doctrine may be utilized to protect constitutional rights, such as freedom of speech, against a wide sweep of some governmental action.

Overt act　An essential element of a crime. Without this action by a party, the intent to engage in criminal activity is not wrongful.

Ownership　The property right that makes something legally exclusive to its owner.

Paper fortress　A term referring to the documentation an employer should keep about an employee's performance.

Parker v. Brown doctrine　The name given to the state action exemption to the Sherman Act. See also *State action exemption*.

Parol evidence　Legal proof based on oral statements; with regard to a document, any evidence extrinsic to the document itself.

Parol evidence rule　Parol evidence is extrinsic evidence. In contracts, the parol evidence rule excludes the introduction of evidence of prior written or oral agreements that may vary, contradict, alter, or supplement the present written agreement. There are several exceptions to this rule. For example, when the parties to an agreement do not intend for that agreement to be final and complete, then parol evidence is admissible.

Partnership A business organization involving two or more persons agreeing to conduct a commercial venture while sharing its profits and losses.

Part performance The contractual doctrine that says when a buyer of land has made valuable improvements in it or has paid part or all of the purchase price, the statute of frauds does not apply to prevent an oral land sales contract from being enforceable.

Patent A statutorily created property in inventions.

Pattern of racketeering Under RICO, two or more similar acts of organized crime in a ten year period.

Pay-for-play A term referencing the need for one to have to pay to get performed a duty that an official, frequently a government official, is already obligated to perform, for example, an appointment by the official. Pay for play usually indicates official corruption.

Per capita By or for each individual.

Per curiam By the court; said of an opinion expressing the view of the court as a whole as opposed to an opinion authored by any single member of the court.

Peremptory challenge The power granted each party to reject a limited number of potential jurors during voir dire examination. No reason for the rejection need be given.

Perfection The status ascribed to security interests after certain events have occurred or certain prescribed steps have been taken, e.g., the filing of a financing statement.

Perjury The giving of false testimony under oath.

Per se In itself.

Per se illegality Under the Sherman Act, agreements and practices are illegal only if they are unreasonable. The practices that are conclusively presumed to be unreasonable are per se illegal. If an activity is per se illegal, only proof of the activity is required, and it is not necessary to prove an anticompetitive effect. For example, price fixing is per se illegal. See also *Rule of reason.*

Personal jurisdiction The power of a court over the parties involved in the litigation process.

Personal property All property that does not involve land and interests in land.

Petitioner The party filing either a case in equity or a petition for a writ of *certiorari* before a supreme court.

Petit jury The fact-finding body during a trial. Also called a trial or traverse jury.

Petty offenses Criminal acts that are viewed as minor and thus are typically punished by a fine only.

Piercing the corporate veil The legal doctrine used by courts to disregard the existence of a corporation, thereby holding the shareholders personally liable for the organization's debts.

Plaintiff The person who initiates a lawsuit.

Plan termination insurance The insurance required by federal law on regulated pension plans. It protects against plan termination that leaves pension benefits underfunded.

Pleadings The system for defining and narrowing the issues by parties who file formal documents stating their respective positions in a lawsuit.

Plenary Entire; complete in all respects.

Point source Any source of air pollution that must be licensed under the Clean Air Act.

Police power The authority a state or local government has to protect the public's health, safety, morals, and general welfare.

Positional bargaining A method of negotiation that focuses on the parties exchanging offers, with concessions being made so that parties find a middle ground. The seller refers to the last offer made as its bottom line, and the buyer refers to the last offer made as its top dollar.

Possession Dominion and control over property; the holding or detention of property in one's own power or command.

Postdispute arbitration clause Can be applicable to arbitration, mediation, or other methods of ADR; such a clause is signed by parties that are already in dispute.

Posteffective period As it relates to an initial public offering of securities, this is the period during which the securities may by sold. This period usually follows a twenty-day waiting period.

Precedent   A prior judicial decision relied upon as an example of a rule of law.

Predatory conduct   An anticompetitive action that is intended to drive competitors out of business. A common example occurs when a business lowers its prices in the hope of gaining such a large market share that it can then raise prices without the fear of competition.

Predatory pricing   A policy of lowering the price charged to customers for the purpose of driving competitors out of business. Typically, this policy involves prices that are below the seller's costs of the products sold with resulting losses to the seller.

Predispute arbitration clause   Applicable to ADR systems agreed to by contracting parties prior to a dispute arising; usually this clause is a part of the original contract between the parties.

Preemption   A condition when a federal statute or administrative rule governs an issue to the extent that a state or local government is prohibited from regulating that area of law.

Preemptive right   A corporation's shareholder's right to maintain the same percentage ownership of the organization whenever newly authorized stock is sold.

Preferred stock   A type of stock issued by a corporation that entitles the owner to receive a dividend before owners of common stock.

Prefiling period   As it relates to an initial public offering of securities, this is that period of time prior to the filing of a registration statement with the SEC.

Prejudicial error   An error in judicial proceedings that may have affected the result in the case.

Preponderance of evidence   In the judgment of the jurors, evidence that has greater weight and overcomes the opposing evidence and presumptions.

Presumption of innocence   The basis of requiring the government to prove a criminal defendant's guilt beyond a reasonable doubt.

Prevention of significant deterioration   A rule implemented under the Clean Air Act that prohibits the degradation of air quality in regions where air quality is better than required by primary air quality standards.

Price discrimination   A seller charging different purchasers different prices for the same goods at the same time.

Price fixing   An agreement or combination by which the conspirators set the market price, whether high or low, of a product or service whether being sold or purchased.

Prima facie   On the face of it; thus, presumed to be true unless proved otherwise.

Primary air quality standards   The standards necessary to protect human health. Secondary air quality standards are stricter standards necessary to protect various environmental amenities.

Primary jurisdiction   A doctrine used by reviewing courts to determine whether a case is properly before the courts or whether it should be heard by an administrative agency first since such an agency might have expertise superior to the courts'.

Principal   The person who gives an agent authority.

Principled, interest-based, negotiations   A method of negotiation that focuses on the parties' interests as opposed to positions. The language used to describe this bargaining includes options, alternatives, objective criteria, and relationships.

Prior consideration   Service or gift from the past that presently induces one to make a promise. Prior consideration does not enable that promise to bind one. It is not legal consideration.

Prior restraint   A principle applicable under the freedom of press and speech clauses of the First Amendment of the U.S. Constitution. The courts have announced decisions that encourage governments to allow the publication or expression of thoughts rather than to restrain such thoughts in advance of their publication or expression.

Private international law   A body of rules that deal with controversies between private persons, such as those created by commercial transactions.

Private law   A classification of legal subject matters that deals most directly with relationships between legal entities. The law of contracts and the law of property are two examples of this classification.

Private nuisance   An unreasonable use of one's land so as to cause substantial interference with the enjoyment or use of another's land.

Private Securities Litigation Reform Act (PSLRA)   A 1995 federal statute that limits the recovery for securities violations against third parties who are not directly responsible for the violation. For example, only the Securities and Exchange Commission can pursue these claims. This law also requires lead plaintiffs in class-action securities suits and restricts recovery of damages and attorneys fees.

Privilege   A special advantage accorded by law to some individual or group; an exemption from a duty or obligation generally imposed by law.

Privileged communication   A rule of evidence that protects conversations that society deems to be confidential. For example, a witness cannot be required to disclose communications between an attorney and a client.

Privileges and immunities clause   A provision found in Article IV and the Fourteenth Amendment of the U.S. Constitution that prevents a state government from discriminating in favor of its citizens and against citizens from another state. This clause, while not interpreted to be absolute, has emphasized national rather than state citizenship.

Privity   Interest derived from successive relationship with another party; a contractual connection.

Probable cause   The reasonable basis on which law enforcement officials convince a judge that criminal activity has occurred. This is the basis that must be satisfied before a judge will issue a criminal search warrant.

Procedural due process   The process or procedure ensuring fundamental fairness that all citizens are entitled to under the U.S. Constitution.

Procedural law   The body of rules governing the manner in which legal claims are enforced.

Product extension merger   A merger that extends the products of the acquiring company into a similar or related product but one that is not directly in competition with existing products.

Production defect   A defect arising when a product does not meet its manufacturer's own standards.

Product liability   The liability that sellers have for the goods they sell.

Prohibiting discrimination   A standard of review under the Commerce Clause that can invalidate state and local laws. When state and local laws discriminate against or negatively impact interstate commerce, such laws are invalid and void.

Promise   A commitment or willingness to be bound to a contract obligation.

Promissory estoppel   Court enforcement of an otherwise unbinding promise if injustice can be avoided only by enforcement of the promise. A substitute for consideration.

Property   A bundle of private, exclusive rights in people to acquire, possess, use, and transfer scarce resources.

Property law   The law of the legal fence that establishes exclusive right in someone called an owner.

Proportionality review   The process that appellate courts use to determine the appropriateness of a criminal sentence.

Prospectus   The legal document required by the 1933 Securities Act to be made available to potential purchasers of securities.

Pro tanto   So far as it goes.

Protestant ethic   A set of beliefs urging that human desire and indulgence be bent to God's will through hard work, self-denial, and rational planning.

Proximate cause   In tort law and legal requirement that an act foreseeably causes an injury.

Proximate causation   The doctrine that limits an actor's liability to consequences that could reasonably be foreseen to have resulted from the act.

Proxy   The legal document whereby a shareholder appoints an agent to vote the stock at a corporation's shareholders' meeting.

Public international law   A body of rules that examines relationships among nations and seeks to bind them to common principles in the international community.

Public law A classification of legal subject matters that regulates the relationship of individuals and organizations to society.

Publicly held A business organization that has hundreds, if not thousands, of owners who can exchange their ownership interests on public exchanges.

Public nuisance An owner's use of land that causes damage or inconvenience to the general public.

Public policy Accepted standards of behavior. For instance, a contract is illegal if it violates public policy.

Punitive damages Monetary damages in excess of a compensatory award, usually granted only in intentional tort cases where defendant's conduct involved some element deserving punishment. Also called *exemplary damages.*

Purchase money security interest (PMSI) A security interest given to the party that loans the debtor the money that enables the debtor to buy the collateral.

Qualified disabled A disabled person who can perform the duties of a job.

Qualified pension plan A private retirement plan that gains favorable income tax treatment from the Internal Revenue Service (IRS). A qualified pension plan allows for the deduction of contributions made to fund the plan. Also, earnings from fund investments are not taxable, and employees defer personal income tax liability until payments are received after retirement. To qualify, the plan must cover a high percentage of workers (usually 70 percent) or cover classifications of employees that do not discriminate in favor of management or shareholders.

Quantity discount The practice of giving a lower per unit price to businesses that buy a product in volume than to their competitors that do not.

Quasi-contract A quasi-contract, often referred to as an implied-in-law contract, is not a true contract. It is a legal fiction that the courts use to prevent unjust enrichment and wrongdoing. Courts permit the person who conferred a benefit to recover the reasonable value of that benefit. Nonetheless, the elements of a true contract are not present.

Quasi-judicial Administrative actions involving factual determinations and the discretionary application of rules and regulations.

Quasi-legislative This term describes the rule-making functions of administrative agencies.

Quasi-strict scrutiny A legal test used by courts to test the validity of governmental action, such as legislation, under the equal protection clause of the U.S. Constitution. To satisfy this test, the government needs to demonstrate that the purpose of the action is substantially related to an important governmental objective.

Quick-look analysis A process of review used by courts in antitrust cases to determine the legality of an anticompetitive act. This analysis is something greater than the per se determination of illegality and less than the full consideration of the rule of reason analysis.

Quid pro quo The exchange of one thing of value for another.

Quitclaim deed The transfer by deed of all the grantor's rights, title, and interest in property.

Quo warranto An action brought about by the government to test the validity of some franchise, such as the privilege of doing business as a corporation.

Racketeering A crime under RICO involving a pattern of actions that are indictable under state or federal laws.

Railway Labor Act The federal law passed in 1926 to encourage collective bargaining in the railroad industry. The law also created the National Mediation Board.

Ratification What occurs when a principal voluntarily decides to honor an agreement.

Ratio decidendi Logical basis of judicial decision.

Real property Property in land and interests in land.

Reasonable accommodation The actions that an employer must take under Title VII of the Civil Rights Act and under the Americans with Disabilities Act to adapt employment conditions to an employee's religious belief or disability.

Reciprocal dealing A contract in which two parties agree to mutual actions so that each party can act as both a buyer and a seller. The agreement violates the Clayton Act if it results in a substantial lessening of competition.

Redlining An act or refusal to act that results in a discriminatory practice. For example, refusing to make loans in low-income areas can discriminate against minorities in granting credit.

Reformation   A contractual remedy exercised by a court to correct a mistake of drafting or some other nonessential mistake. After reformation the parties remain bound to the contract.

Registration statement   The legal document required to be filed with the Securities and Exchange Commission (SEC) prior to securities being offered for sale to the public.

Reimbursement   Restoration; to pay back or repay that expended; the act of making one whole.

Rejection   The refusal of an offer. A rejection terminates an offer.

Release   The relinquishment of a right or claim against another party.

Remand   The return of a case by an appellate court for further action by the lower court.

Remedial statute   Legislation designed to provide a benefit or relief to a victim of a violation of law.

Remedy   The action or procedure that is followed in order to enforce a right or to obtain damages for injury to a right; the means by which a right is enforced or the violation of a right is prevented, redressed, or compensated.

Reorganization   The legal process of forming a new corporation after bankruptcy or foreclosure.

Replevin   An action for the recovery of goods wrongfully taken or kept.

Representational standing   The requirements that must be satisfied for an organization to have the right to file a lawsuit on behalf of its members.

Request for an admission   A method of discovery used to narrow the issues to be litigated by having a party request that the other party admit the facts that are not in dispute.

Request for production of documents   A method of discovery whereby one party asks the other to provide documents for the requesting party's review.

Requirements contract   A contract under which the buyer agrees to buy a certain item only from the seller.

Res   A thing, object, or status.

Resale price maintenance   Manufacturer control of a brand- or trade-name product's minimum resale price.

Rescind   To cancel or annul a contract and return the parties to their original positions.

Rescission   A contractual remedy that cancels the agreement and returns the consideration exchanged to each party.

Res ipsa loquitur   The thing speaks for itself. A rule of evidence whereby negligence of the alleged wrongdoer may be inferred from the mere fact that the injury occurred.

Res judicata   The doctrine that deems a former adjudication conclusive and prevents a retrial of matters decided in the earlier lawsuit.

Respondeat superior   The doctrine imposing liability on one for torts committed by another person who is in his or her employ and subject to his or her control.

Respondent   The party answering a petition for a writ of *certiorari* in the Supreme Court.

Restitution   A contractual remedy involving one party returning to another the value previously received.

Restraint of trade   Monopolies, combinations, and contracts that impede free competition.

Restrictive covenants   Private agreements that restrict land use.

Retaliation   Striking back against someone for what they did to you. Used in labor law, employment discrimination cases, and whistle-blowing as part of a doctrine prohibiting an employer from firing or taking other adverse actions against employees for reporting the employer to federal agencies for violating various laws.

Retaliatory trade practices   Actions by aggrieved nations responding to tariffs and other unfair trade restrictions imposed by foreign governments.

Reverse   Overturn or vacate the judgment of a court.

Reverse discrimination   The advancement and recruitment of minority workers ahead of similarly qualified nonminority workers.

Revocation   The contractual communication of withdrawing an offer.

RICO   The Racketeer Influenced and Corrupt Organizations Act.

Right of redemption   The right to buy back. A debtor may buy back or redeem his or her mortgaged property when he or she pays the debt.

Right-to-work law   A state statute that outlaws a union shop contract—one by which an employer agrees to require membership in the union sometime after an employee has been hired as a condition of continued employment.

Robbery   Illegally taking something by force.

Robinson-Patman Act   The amendment to Section 2 of the Clayton Act covering price discrimination. As originally adopted, the Robinson-Patman Act outlawed price discrimination in interstate commerce that might substantially lessen competition or tends to create a monopoly.

Rule against perpetuities   The rule that prohibits an owner from controlling what he or she owns beyond a life in being at the owner's death, plus 21 years.

Rule of law   The general and equal application of laws, even to lawmakers.

Rule of reason   Under the Sherman Act, contracts or conspiracies are illegal only if they constitute an unreasonable restraint of trade or attempt to monopolize. An activity is unreasonable if it adversely affects competition. An act is reasonable if it promotes competition. The rule of reason requires that an anticompetitive effect be shown. See also *Per se illegality.*

Rules of evidence   The laws governing the admission of evidence, such as testimony and documents, during the trial of a case.

Rule of first possession   The rule that says one becomes an owner by reducing to possession previously unowned objects or abandoned objects.

Sale of business doctrine   The legal principle in securities law that might be used to remove the sale of corporate stock from the securities laws' protection if the purchaser of such stock is to operate the business instead of relying on others to do so.

Sanctions   Penalties imposed for violation of a law.

Sarbanes-Oxley Act of 2002   The law enacted to correct inadequacies in the law that existed and allowed numerous examples of corporate fraud. In essence, through increased criminal sanctions and specific requirements, this law attempts to make corporate CEOs more responsible.

Say-on-pay   A policy of companies that allow the compensation of executives to be reviewed by shareholders.

Scheme to defraud   A plan to misrepresent a material fact in order to obtain something, usually money, from another.

Scienter   With knowledge; particularly, guilty knowledge.

Scoping   A regulatory step required of a federal agency by the Council on Environmental Quality. Before preparing an environmental impact statement, an agency must designate which environmental issues of a proposed action are most significant.

S corporation   A business organization that is formed as a corporation but, by a shareholders' election, is treated as a partnership for taxation purposes.

Search warrant   A court order required by the Fourth Amendment of the U.S. Constitution to be obtained from government officials prior to private property being searched or seized.

Secondary air quality standards   Clean Air Act standards designed to protect environmental quality other than human health.

Secondary boycott   Conspiracy or combination to cause the customers or suppliers of an employer to cease doing business with that employer.

Section 402A   That section of the Second Restatement of Torts that imposes strict liability on product sellers who sell a product in a "defective condition unreasonably dangerous to the user or consumer or his property."

Section 5   Section of the Federal Trade Commission act which authorizes the commission to regulate unfair or deceptive acts or practices in trade.

Section 1981   That provision of the Civil Rights Act of 1866 that forbids racial discrimination in the making of contracts.

Secured transactions   Any credit transaction creating a security interest; an interest in personal property that secures the payment of an obligation.

Securities Act of 1933   The federal law that regulates (through disclosure requirements) the initial sale of securities to the public.

Securities and Exchange Commission (SEC)   The federal administrative agency that regulates the securities industry.

Securities Exchange Act of 1934   The federal law that regulates sales (other than the initial sale) of securities. This law governs the resale of securities whether by individuals or through brokers and exchanges.

Security   Under the securities law, an investment in which the investor does not participate in management.

Security interests   An application of property that gives someone an interest in what belongs to another, usually to secure an extension of credit.

Self-regulation   An entire industry's regulation of itself, as opposed to government regulation of the businesses in the industry.

Seller   In commercial law, a person who sells or contracts to sell goods.

Seniority system   A plan giving priority to employees based on the length of time an employee has worked for an employer. An employer may apply different standards pursuant to a good-faith seniority system if the differences are not the result of an intention to discriminate.

Sentencing guidelines   Adopted by the U.S. Sentencing Commission as a means of standardizing the sentences given to similar criminals committing similar crimes.

Separation of powers   The doctrine that holds that the legislative, executive, and judicial branches of government function independently of one another and that each branch serves as a check on the others.

Servant   The person hired to act on behalf of a principal in an agency relationship.

Service mark   Any mark, word, picture, or design that attaches to a service and indicates its source.

Set-off   A counterclaim by a defendant against a plaintiff that grows from an independent cause of action and diminishes the plaintiff's potential recovery.

Sexual harassment   Under Title VII, for an employer or workplace supervisor to promise benefits or threaten loss if an employee does not give sexual favors.

Shareholders   The owners of corporations. Typically these owners vote on major decisions impacting their corporations, most commonly the election of a board of directors.

Shark repellent   Corporate action to make a threatened acquisition unattractive to the acquiring company.

Shelf registration   The process in securities law under Securities and Exchange Commission (SEC) Rule 415 that allows an issuer to satisfy the registration statement requirements, thereby allowing the issuer immediately to offer securities for sale.

Sherman Act   An 1890 congressional enactment designed to regulate anticompetitive behavior in interstate commerce.

Short-swing profits   The proceeds gained by an insider buying and selling, or vice versa, securities within a six-month time period. Such profits are considered to be illegal.

Simplified employee pension   A type of pension permitted by the Revenue Act of 1978. Under this pension type, employers contribute up to a specified amount to employee individual retirement accounts.

Slander   An oral defamatory statement communicated to a third person.

Small-claims court   A court of limited jurisdiction, usually able to adjudicate claims up to a certain amount, such as $3,000, depending on the state.

Social contract theory   A theory by John Rawls that proposes a way for constructing a just society.

Sole proprietorship   The simplest form of business organization, created and controlled by one owner.

Sovereign immunity   A doctrine of state and international law that permits a foreign government to claim immunity from suit in the courts of other nations.

Sovereignty   The supreme, absolute, and uncontrollable power by which any state is governed.

Specific performance   Equitable remedy that requires defendants in certain circumstances to do what they have contracted to do.

Stakeholder theory   Ethical theory which asserts that in order to be ethical a business must take into consideration not only the making of a profit but the impacts of the business on all interests that are affected by the business.

Standing   The doctrine that requires the plaintiff in a lawsuit to have a sufficient legal interest in the subject matter of the case.

Standing to sue   The requirement that a plaintiff must satisfy by demonstrating a personal interest in the outcome of litigation or an administrative hearing.

Stare decisis   The doctrine that traditionally indicates that a court should follow prior decisions in all cases based on substantially similar facts.

State action exemption   The Sherman Act exemption of the sovereign action of a state that replaces competition with regulation if the state actively supervises the anticompetitive conduct.

State-of-the-art defense   A defense that the defendant's product or practice was compatible with the current state of technology available at the time of the event in question.

States' relations article   Article IV of the U.S. Constitution. Among its purposes, this article prevents a state from favoring its citizens over the citizens of another state, thereby making the United States one nation as opposed to 50 subgroups.

Status quo   The conditions or state of affairs at a given time.

Statute   A legislative enactment.

Statute of frauds   Legislation that states that certain contracts will not be enforced unless there is a signed writing evidencing the agreement.

Statute of limitations   A statute that sets a date after which a lawsuit may not be brought. The statute begins running after the happening of a certain event, such as the occurrence of an injury or the breach of a contract.

Statute of repose   A statute that applies to product liability cases. It prohibits initiation of litigation involving products more than a certain number of years (e.g., 25) following their manufacture.

Statutory construction   The rules courts use in interpreting the meaning of legislation.

Strict liability   The doctrine under which a party may be required to respond in tort damages without regard to such party's use of due care.

Strict products liability   The cause of action under which commercial sellers of defective products are held liable without negligence.

Strict scrutiny   A legal test used by courts to test the validity of governmental action, such as legislation, under the equal protection clause of the U.S. Constitution. To satisfy this test, the government needs to demonstrate that there is a compelling state interest justifying the government's action.

Structured settlement   A periodic payment of damages, usually taking the form of a guaranteed annuity.

Subject matter jurisdiction   The authority of a court to hear cases involving specific issues of law.

Submission   The act or process of referring an issue to arbitration.

Subpoena   A court order directing a witness to appear or to produce documents in his or her possession.

Substantial performance   Degree of performance recognizing that a contracting party has honestly attempted to perform but has fallen short. One who has substantially performed is entitled to the price promised by the other less that party's damages.

Substantive due process   The use of the due process provision of the U.S. Constitution to make certain that the application of a law does not unfairly deprive persons of property rights.

Substantive law   A body of rules defining the nature and extent of legal rights.

Summary judgment   A judicial determination that no genuine factual dispute exists and that one party to the lawsuit is entitled to judgment as a matter of law.

Summons   An official notice to a person that a lawsuit has been commenced against him or her and that he or she must appear in court to answer the charges.

Superfund   The Comprehensive Environmental Response, Compensation, and Liability Act of 1980.

Supremacy clause   Article VI of the U.S. Constitution, which states that the Constitution, laws, and treaties of the United States shall be the "supreme law of the land" and shall take precedence over conflicting state laws.

Supreme Court   The highest appellate court.

Surety   One who incurs a liability for the benefit of another. One who undertakes to pay money in the event that his or her principal is unable to pay.

Symbolic speech   Nonverbal expression.

Taft-Hartley Act   The federal law enacted in 1947 to increase the bargaining power of management by creating unfair labor practices by unions, by outlawing the closed shop, by creating an 80-day cooling-off period, by permitting states to adopt right-to-work laws, and by creating the Federal Mediation and Conciliation Service.

Tangible property   Physical property.

Teleology   An ethical system that concerns itself with the moral consequences of actions. Also called *consequentialism*.

Tenancy in common   A property ownership that is undivided (common) but not necessarily equal between two or more owners.

Tender offer   An invited public offer by a company or organization to buy shares from existing shareholders of another public corporation under specified terms.

Tender performance   The offer by one contracting party to perform a promise; usually associated with the offer to pay for or to ship items under the contract.

Testator   One who has made a will.

Third party   One who enters into a relationship with a principal by way of interacting with the principal's agent.

Third-party beneficiaries   Persons who are recognized as having enforceable rights created for them by a contract to which they are not parties and for which they have given no consideration.

Third-party defendant   A party who is not a party (plaintiff or defendant) to the original litigation. Typically, a defendant might file a claim against a third party stating that if the defendant is liable to the plaintiff, then this third party will be liable to the defendant.

Tippee   A person who learns of nonpublic information about a security from an insider.

Title   A synonym for ownership. Sometimes represented as a document.

Tort   A civil wrong other than a breach of contract.

Tombstone ad   An advertisement announcing the public offering of securities; these usually run during the waiting period.

Trade disparagement   The publication of untrue statements that disparage the plaintiff's ownership of property or its quality.

Trade dress   A legal doctrine giving someone ownership of a distinctive overall appearance or look and feel of a product or service.

Trademark   A statutorily created property in a mark, word, picture, or design that attaches to goods and indicates their source.

Trademark dilution   The impact of something that reduces the distinctiveness of a trademark.

Trade practice regulation   A term generally referring to laws that regulate competitive practices.

Trade secret   Any formula, pattern, machine, or process of manufacturing used in one's business that may give the user an opportunity to obtain an advantage over its competitors. Trade secrets are legally protectable.

Trade usage   Refers to the particular use of a word in business that may differ from its common use.

Trademark dilution   Using someone's trademark in such a way so as to reduce the value of the trademark's significance, reputation, and goodwill even if the public is not confused by the use.

Trading partnership   A business organization made up of two or more partners engaged in providing services.

Treason   Breach of allegiance to one's government, specifically by levying war against such government or by giving aid and comfort to the enemy.

Treaty of Rome   A historic agreement reached by six European countries in 1957 to achieve economic unity in the European Community. The latter is now known as the European Union, and its membership has grown to 15 nations.

Treble damages   See *Triple damages.*

Trespass   An act done in an unlawful manner so as to cause injury to another; an unauthorized entry upon another's land.

Trial court   The level of any court system that initially resolves the dispute of litigants. Frequently, but not always, a jury serves as a fact-finding body while the judge issues rulings on the applicable law.

Triple damages (or treble damages)   An award of damages allowable under some statutes equal to three times the amount found by the jury to be a single recovery.

Trust   A fiduciary relationship whereby one party (trustee) holds legal title for the benefit of another (beneficiary).

Trustee   One who holds legal title to property for the benefit of another.

Truth in lending   A federal law that requires the disclosure of total finance charges and the annual percentage rate for credit in order that borrowers may be able to shop for credit.

Tying contract   A contract that ties the sale of one piece of property (real or personal) to the sale or lease of another item of property.

Ultra vires   Beyond the scope of corporate powers granted in the charter.

Unconscionable   In the law of contracts, provisions that are oppressive, overreaching, or shocking to the conscience.

Underwriter   The party that, in securities law, guarantees the issuer that the securities offered for sale will be sold.

Undue burden   Under the Civil Rights Act of 1964 and the Americans with Disabilities Act an employer need not take action that is excessively costly or creates excessive inefficiency in order to accommodate an employee's religious beliefs or disability. This is the concept of undue burden.

Undue influence   Influence of another destroying the requisite free will of a testator or donor, which creates a ground for nullifying a will or invalidating a gift. A contract will not be binding if one party unduly influences the other since the parties have not dealt on equal terms.

Unenforceable contract   A contract that cannot be enforced in court.

Unfair competition   A group of statutory torts that include misappropriation of trademarks, patent violations, and copyright breaches. One aspect of the Federal Trade Commission's authority. Section 5 of the FTC Act makes unfair methods of competition illegal.

Unfair labor practices   Activities by management or labor unions that have been declared to be inappropriate by the Wagner Act and Taft-Hartley Act, respectively.

Uniform Commercial Code (UCC)   The most successful attempt to have states adopt a uniform law. This code's purpose is to simplify, clarify, and modernize the laws governing commercial transactions.

Uniformed Services Employment and Reemployment Rights Act (USERRA)   The act which protects the rights of individuals who voluntarily or involuntarily leave employment positions to undertake military service.

Unilateral contract   A contract in which the promisor does not receive a promise as consideration; an agreement whereby one makes a promise to do, or refrain from doing, something in return for a performance, not a promise.

Unilateral mistake   Arises when only one of the parties to a contract is wrong about a material fact. It is not usually a basis for rescinding a contract.

Union security clause   The contractual provision that creates a union shop agreement. This clause requires any person hired as an employee to join the union representing the employees.

Union shop   This term applies, in labor law, to an agreement by management and labor that all employees of a business will be or become union members. Union shops are not allowed in states with right-to-work laws.

United Nations   The principal political organization of the world.

Unreasonable search and seizure   A violation of the Fourth Amendment of the U.S. Constitution that occurs when a valid search warrant is not obtained or when the scope of a valid warrant is exceeded.

Usury   A loan of money at interest above the legal rate.

Utilitarianism   A form of consequentialist ethics.

Valid contract   A contract that contains all of the proper elements of a contract.

Venue   The geographical area over which a court presides. Venue designates the court in which the case should be tried. Change of venue means moving to another court.

Verdict   Findings of fact by the jury.

Vertical merger   A merger of corporations where one corporation is the supplier of the other.

Vertical price fixing   An agreement between a seller and a buyer (for example, between a manufacturer and a retailer) to fix the resale price at which the buyer will sell goods.

Vertical territorial agreement   Arrangement between a supplier and its customers with respect to the geographical area in which each customer will be allowed to sell that supplier's products. This type of agreement is analyzed under the rule of reason to determine whether it violates the Sherman Act. Limitations on intrabrand competition may be permitted if there is a corresponding increase in interbrand competition.

Vested rights   Rights that have become so fixed that they are not subject to being taken away without the consent of the owner.

Voidable contract   Capable of being declared a nullity, though otherwise valid.

Void contract   A contract that is empty, having no legal force; ineffectual, unenforceable.

Voir dire   The preliminary examination of prospective jurors for the purpose of ascertaining bias or interest in the lawsuit.

Voluntary arbitration   A method of resolving a dispute, as an alternative to litigation, that the parties agree to utilize. This agreement may be made before or after a dispute arises.

Voluntary bargaining issue   Either party may refuse to bargain in good faith regarding matters other than wages, hours, and other terms and conditions of employment. This refusal does not constitute an unfair labor practice. An issue over which parties may bargain if they choose to do so.

Voluntary petition   The document filed by a debtor to initiate bankruptcy proceedings.

Wagner Act   The federal law passed in 1935 that recognizes employees' rights to organize. This law also created the National Labor Relations Board and defined unfair labor practices by management. It is formally known as the National Labor Relations Act.

Waiting period   As it relates to an initial public offering of securities, this is the period of time that follows the filing of documents with the SEC and that precedes when the securities can be sold. Unless the SEC objects and extends this period of time, the waiting period lasts only 20 days.

Waiver   An express or implied relinquishment of a right.

WARN Act   The Worker Adjustment and Retraining Notification Act of 1989; this law requires employers to give notice of plant closings and mass layoffs.

Warrant   A judicial authorization for the performance of some act.

Warranty of authority   An agent's implied guarantee that he or she has the authority to enter into a contract. The agent is liable for breaching the warranty if he or she lacks proper authority.

Warranty of merchantability   A promise implied in a sale of goods by merchants that the goods are reasonably fit for the general purpose for which they are sold.

Wheeler-Lea amendment   Legislation passed in 1938 that expanded the Federal Trade Commission's authority to protect society against unfair or deceptive practices.

White-collar crime   Violations of the law by business organizations or by individuals in a business-related capacity.

White knight   A slang term that describes the inducement of a voluntary acquisition when an involuntary acquisition is threatened. The voluntary acquisition group is a white knight since it saves the corporation from an unfriendly takeover.

Willful and wanton negligence   Extremely unreasonable behavior that causes injury.

Willfully   With intent to defraud or deceive.

Wire fraud   The use of radio, television, telephone, Internet, or other wired forms of communication to conduct fraudulent activities with the intent to deprive an owner of property.

Workers' compensation   A plan for the compensation for occupational diseases, accidental injuries, and deaths of employees that arise out of employment. Compensation includes medical expenses and burial costs and lost earnings based on the size of the family and the wage rate of the employee.

Work rules   A company's regulations governing the workplace, the application of which often becomes an issue in the ability of employees to organize for their mutual benefit and protection.

World Bank   The world's principal financial institution.

World Trade Organization (WTO)   Mechanism for enforcing the General Agreement on Tariffs and Trade that allows GATT member countries to bring complaints and seek redress.

Wright-Line doctrine   Establishes procedures for determining the burden of proof in cases involving mixed motivation for discharge.

Writ of certiorari   A discretionary proceeding by which an appellate court may review the ruling of an inferior tribunal.

Writ of habeas corpus   A court order to one holding custody of another to produce that individual before the court for the purpose of determining whether such custody is proper.

Yellow-dog contract   An agreement in which a worker agrees not to join a union and that discharge will result from a breach of the contract.

Zoning ordinance   Laws that limit land use based usually on residential, commercial, or industrial designations.

Page 2–3: © Jack Hollingsworth/CORBIS; 26–27: © Ingram Publishing/AGE Fotostock; 62–63: © PhotoLink/Getty Images; 82 top left: © Brooks Kraft/CORBIS; 82 bottom right: © Jason Reed/Reuters/CORBIS; 90–91: Royalty-Free/CORBIS; 94, 108: © Jason Reed/Reuters/CORBIS; 122–123: © Ryan McVay/Getty Images; 156–157: © Artiga Photo/Getty Images; 182: © Jason Reed/Reuters/Corbis; 198–199: © Digital Vision/Getty Images; 234–235: © Royalty-Free/CORBIS; 260–261: © PhotoLink/Getty Images; 280–281: © Digital Vision/Getty Images; 316–317: © Michael N. Paras/AGE Fotostock; 348–349: © Royalty-Free/CORBIS; 351 top left: © James Leynse/CORBIS; 351 bottom left: © Jeff Mitchell/Reuters/CORBIS; 351 right: © Spencer Platt/Getty Images; 353: © James Leynse/CORBIS; 365 top left: © Spencer Platt/Getty Images; 365 bottom left: © Jeff Mitchell/Reuters/CORBIS; 365 bottom right: © Reuters/CORBIS; 378–379: © Royalty-Free/CORBIS; 393 top left & right: © McGraw-Hill Companies/Suzie Ross, Photographer; 393 bottom left: © McGraw-Hill Companies/Jill Braaten, Photographer; 394: © Jorge Silva/Reuters/CORBIS; 398: © McGraw-Hill Companies/Jill Braaten, Photographer; 410–411: © BananaStock/PunchStock; 438–439: © Digital Vision/Getty Images; 474–475: © Jack Hollingsworth/Getty Images; 508–509: © Comstock Images/Alamy; 532–533: © Royalty-Free/CORBIS; 566–567: © Creatas Images/Jupiterimages; 588–589: © Chris Ryan/OJO Images/Getty Images; 624–625: © PhotoLink/Getty Images.

All other individual photos of current members of the United States Supreme Court were provided by Jerry Goldman, Director of the OYEZ project at Northwestern University.

index ::

A

Abandonment, 207
Abercrombie & Fitch, 595
ABN Amro Holding, 502
Abortions, 601
Abuse of discovery process, 103
Accenture, 445
Acceptance of offers, 246–248
Accession, 209–210
Accessories to crime, 373
Accommodating behavior, 125
Accord and satisfaction, 250
Accountant codes of conduct, 42–44
Accounting fraud, 353; *see also* Fraud
Accounting reforms, 444–445
Acts, legislative, 15
Acts of God, 214
Actual authority, 570–571
Actual malice, 163
Acuff-Rose Music, 342
Adams, John, 1, 57, 64
Adams, Samuel, 57
Adamy, Janet, 570n
Adarand Constructors, 169, 170
Adarand Constructors, Inc. v. Pena, 169–171, 607
Adelphia, 22, 351, 420, 439, 457
Adjustment of debts, 526
Adler, Mortimer, 32, 48
Administrative agencies
   false statements to, 368–369
   judicial review of, 191–193
   overview of role, 184–185
   rule-making authority, 186–190
   standing to sue, 185–186
Administrative law
   defined, 13
   as major source of law, 16–17
   sanctions under, 20–21
Admissibility of evidence in arbitration, 139
Admissions, requests for, 102
Advance fee schemes, 360
Advancement, 52
Adverse possession, 208–209
Advertising, 513–514, 516
Advisory opinions, 512
Affidavits, 105

Affirmative action, 606–607
AFLAC, 433
After-acquired property, 218
AGA Medical Corporation, 397
Age Discrimination in Employment Act, 400–402, 581, 609–611
Agency law, 41, 568–572
Agents, 568
Aggrieved parties, 186
Agnew, Spiro, 352
Agreement on Trade-Related Aspects of Intellectual Property Rights, 385
Agreements not to sue, 250
Agricultural pollution, 545, 547, 548, 556
Aiding and abetting, 373
Air conditioning, 557
Air pollution, 538–544
Airport regulation, 175
Airport searches, 355
AirTouch Communications, 502
Aktiengesellschaft, 392
Alcohol consumption, 304
Alien Tort Claims Act, 402–403
Aliens, defined, 652
Alito, Samuel, 80, 82, 94, 108, 182
Allentown Mack Sales, 637, 638
Allentown Mack Sales and Service, Inc. v. National Labor Relations Board, 636–638
Alliance of Motion Picture and Television Producers, 640
Alter-ego theory, 422
Alternative dispute resolution systems
   arbitration basics, 131–137
   focus groups, 130
   judicial review of, 136–137, 141–146, 149
   mandatory arbitration, 132, 139, 142–144
   mediation, 146–150
   overview, 129–130
   policies on arbitration, 137–138
   voluntary arbitration, 132, 140–141
Alternative fuel cars, 539
Alternatives, considering in negotiation, 128
Amazon.com, 332, 334

Ambrose, 56
Amendments to Constitution, 158; *see also* Bill of Rights; Constitution (U.S.)
America Online, 249, 257, 481
American Airlines, 488
American Arbitration Association, 134, 149
American Bar Association, 67
American Express, 603
American Home Products, 303, 515
American Institute of Architects, 488
American Institute of Certified Public Accountants Code of Professional Conduct, 42, 44
American Marketing Association, 42, 43
American Trucking Associations, Inc. v. Michigan Public Service Commission, 177
Ameritech, 502
Anderson, Glen, 511
Anderson, Marlene, 511
Anderson, Pamela, 403
Anderson v. Foothill Industrial Bank, 511
Anderson v. Mt. Clemens Pottery Co., 574
Ann Taylor, 28
Annual incomes, 4
Annual percentage rates, 521
Answers, 100
Antideficiency judgment statutes, 217
Antidiscrimination laws, 9; *see also* Discrimination; Employment laws
Antitrust law
   basic purpose, 9
   Clayton Act, 477, 494–502, 627–628
   exemptions from, 485–486
   Federal Trade Commission Act, 477, 502–503
   international cases, 493–494
   monopoly prohibitions, 478–481
   origins, 194, 476–477
   price fixing prohibitions, 350, 478, 486–492
   principles for applying, 481–483